PORTRAIT OF LISZT

Portrait of Liszt

By Himself and His Contemporaries

ADRIAN WILLIAMS

CLARENDON PRESS · OXFORD
1990

Oxford University Press, Walton Street, Oxford OX2 6DP
Oxford New York Toronto
Delhi Bombay Calcutta Madras Karachi
Petaling Jaya Singapore Hong Kong Tokyo
Nairobi Dar es Salaam Cape Town
Melbourne Auckland
and associated companies in
Berlin Ibadan
Oxford is a trade mark of Oxford University Press

Published in the United States
by Oxford University Press, New York

British Library Cataloguing in Publication Data
Williams, Adrian
Portrait of Liszt: by himself and his contemporaries.
1. Hungarian music, Liszt, Franz, 1811–1886.
Biographies
I. Title
780′. 92′4
ISBN 0–19–816150–6

Library of Congress Cataloguing in Publication Data
Williams, Adrian, 1940–
Portrait of Liszt: by himself and his contemporaries / Adrian Williams
Bibliography: P. Includes index.
1. Liszt, Franz, 1811–1886. 2. Composers--Biography. I. Liszt, Franz, 1811–1886. II. Title.
ML410. L7W55 1989 780'.92--dc20 89–9333
ISBN 1–19–816150–6

Typeset by Pentacor Ltd, High Wycombe, Bucks
Printed in Great Britain by
Courier International Ltd., Tiptree, Essex

My task here below, as a sincere Christian and musician, is to seek and to cultivate the True, the Good, and the Beautiful.

Franz Liszt

PREFACE

'Nobody', declared Samuel Johnson, 'can write the life of a man, but those who have eat and drunk and lived in social intercourse with him.'

Assuming that he does not venture to disagree with the mighty Doctor, how is the hapless would-be biographer to proceed when his subject is not only no longer with us, but, like Liszt, has been in his grave for more than a century? In the pages of the present volume I have tried to get round the difficulty by gathering together numerous contemporary impressions of the great composer-pianist, starting with his father's description of the little boy asking for piano lessons, and ending with reports of people on the scene at the death, some seventy years later, of the titanic musician and personality that little boy had become. Even if not all the writers quoted actually 'ate and drank and lived in social intercourse' with Liszt, they could almost all claim to have done something far more important in respect of an executant musician of transcendent greatness: to have heard him play. Many also associated with him closely enough to be able to pen perceptive and illuminating accounts of his character and conduct; others describe Liszt the teacher and mentor.

My own linking and background passages provide information about his activities, movements, concerts, meetings, etc., so that although adding to and enriching the composite 'portrait' of Liszt that gradually emerges is to some extent given priority over events, the book nevertheless contains a very great deal of biographical information. No other publication offers so much detail about Liszt's visits to the British Isles, for example; in particular about his London concerts of 1840 and 1841, concerts in the English provinces, Ireland, and Scotland during those same years, and last visit to London, as a Grand Old Man, shortly before his death.

A mere three passages out of several hundred relate events not personally witnessed by those describing them. In the first two, Liszt's godson Franz von Milde recounts incidents (in one of which he is himself an infant participant) told him by his parents; in the third, an anecdote of Liszt and Bedřich Smetana is told by someone who had heard it from Smetana himself. Although second-hand, all three reports are, it seems to me, quite unexceptionable.

A far more difficult problem is posed by the *Mémoires d'une cosaque* of the notorious Olga Janina. Were the section — the very long section — relating to Liszt in that curious and controversial publication known to be wholly invention, the matter would be easily resolved, and there would be no question of including any portion of it here. But unfortunately it is impossible to arrive at a definitive conclusion, one way or the other, about Janina. Some commentators have apparently taken it for granted that the details she gives of an affair with Liszt must be fiction because of her behaviour. More than improbable, the thinking seems to be, that the great man had an intimate relationship with someone who was neither completely right in the head nor a 'lady'. She did, after all, threaten him with a revolver, and later, for motives at once malicious and mercenary, publish an account (whether true or false) of their relationship for all the world to read. ('O fie miss, you must not kiss and tell.')

But truth can be revealed, as well as lies told, for money and out of spite; and in any case those reprehensible actions (of the gun and the book) still lay in the future during the weeks and months in which Liszt and Olga were frequently together, as teacher and pupil, at Rome, Tivoli, and elsewhere in 1869 and 1870. At that time he can only have found the clever, pert, vivacious, and witty 'Cossack Countess' both talented (her pianistic gifts were considerable) and amusing company.

To mention these things is not to imply a belief in Olga's outpourings, but only to point out that she cannot be disbelieved *solely* because we now know what Liszt could hardly have been aware of in the early stages of their acquaintance: that she was vindictive and unscrupulous. Whether her memoirs are mainly truth interspersed with sundry flights of imagination, or almost wholly invention, or a mingling of fact and fiction in fairly equal proportions, it is impossible to say, and probably always will be. For this reason I have felt it necessary to include some of the passages describing the affair, real or imagined. Since, however, it seems indisputable that in writing *Mémoires d'une cosaque* Olga Janina's motive was above all to take revenge by humiliating Liszt and harming his reputation, readers are advised to treat with due caution the extracts given here; in particular the concluding, climactic paragraphs, which may from first to last — and not only the comicality of the poisoned dagger and the 'words of love' — be sheer fantasy and wishful thinking.

So far as Liszt's letters are concerned, the only English-language publication containing a large quantity to numerous correspondents appeared as long ago as the end of the last century. But in that collection (Constance Bache's translation of the first two volumes in La Mara's series) can be found virtually nothing to the composer's mother and children, to his closest women friends, or to such friends and associates as Wagner, Bülow, Baron Augusz, and the Grand Duke Carl Alexander. The excerpts given in the present volume have been drawn from Liszt's letters to all these correspondents, as well as from those to many other persons of significance in his life.

A word about footnotes. Whereas some authors pride themselves on the number of these their books contain, I should have been only too happy to be able to boast of none at all. But in what is first and foremost a compilation, it proved impossible to convey certain information other than by their means. Readers for whom they are merely a nuisance may serenely ignore them. Those, on the other hand, who do favour them with a glance, will, I trust, find that the extra knowledge gained makes the effort worth while.

If less emphasis is laid in these pages on what is Liszt's most important and lasting achievement, his great and original series of musical creations, the reason is, of course, that whereas to discover what he was like as man, pianist, and teacher we have no option but to turn to the opinions of his contemporaries, we can listen to and perform his works for ourselves — and, happily, with a more enlightened understanding than many of those contemporaries were able to bring to them. Brief information is given about all his major compositions, however, as well as about many of the minor. They are identified, generally when first mentioned, by the number allotted to them in Humphrey Searle's catalogue in the *New Grove*. Thus, for example: *Christus* (S3), Sonata in B minor (S178), *Glanes de Woronince* (S249).

Authors of the various contemporary extracts are given in italics either at the beginning of the extract or in the previous linking narrative.

It is my hope that with their wealth of first-hand reports and descriptions, including many that are likely to be new even to Liszt devotees and specialists, the pages yet before you will provide a uniquely comprehensive portrait in words of the phenomenally gifted man and musician who has been hailed, by his eminent biographer Peter Raabe, as 'one of the most wonderful human beings that have ever lived, and one of the greatest and most original artists of the nineteenth century'.

For miscellaneous assistance rendered, information imparted, or material supplied, I offer warm thanks to Mario Becchetti (London), Piero Becchetti (Rome), Maria Eckhardt (Budapest), Margaret Eliot (London), Margaret Ellaway (Cheltenham), Erika Fabarius (London), Dezső Legány (Budapest), Eunice Mistarz (Wimbledon), Dudley Newton (London), John O'Shea (Melbourne), Kenneth Souter (Harrow), Charles Suttoni (New York), Frank Warren (Portsmouth), Derek Watson (Edinburgh), Ruth and Robert Wing (London); plus, in a very special category, Hildegard von Zezschwitz-Stumpf (Aachen), now in her ninety-fourth year, pupil of Berthold Kellermann and grandpupil of Liszt.

To those at the Oxford University Press, principally Bruce Phillips and Pippa Thynne, who played a part in preparation and production of this book, I am most grateful; and I owe special thanks to Mary Worthington for the eagle-eyed and conscientious copy-editing which detected and eliminated numerous greater or lesser inconsistencies of presentation.

Adequately to express the enormous debt of gratitude I owe to Geraldine Keeling (San Gabriel, California), Gerald Norris (Reading), and Ria Plum (Eschweiler, North Rhine-Westphalia) is quite beyond my powers. Suffice to say that without the quantity and quality of the help given me so generously and unstintingly by all three, this book would be immeasurably the poorer. Of whatever blemishes or blunders it may contain, I can claim to be sole perpetrator.

ADRIAN WILLIAMS

CONTENTS

LIST OF PLATES

(between pp. 368 and 369)

THE LIFE
1811–1886

1811–1822

On 11 January 1811, Adam Liszt (1776–1827), a native of Edelsthal (Nemesvölgy), a village near the Hungarian city of Pozsony,* married Maria Anna Lager (1788–1866) of Krems in Lower Austria. Adam lived at Raiding (Doborján), a village in western Hungary,† and was employed as *ovium rationista* (superintendent of sheep)‡ by Prince Nicholas Esterházy. His bride had been for some time a chambermaid in Vienna, but had then gone to live with a brother in the village of Mattersdorf (Nagymarton), where there was an Esterházy estate; and it was here, during the previous summer, that the couple had met.

Raiding having no priest of its own at that time, the wedding took place at the Catholic church of the nearby village of Unterfrauenhaid (Alsólók). After the ceremony, however, husband and wife at once repaired to Raiding, to the cottage which was to be their home for the next eleven years. Here, nine and a half months later, on Tuesday, 22 October 1811,§ their son was born, an 'ugly child for the first few days after his birth', his mother later recalled. The baptism took place at Unterfrauenhaid on the 23rd; the godfather, after whom he was named, being one Franciscus Zambothy, the godmother, Julianna Szalay.

A frail, sickly child, Franz was a source of constant concern to his parents; and it is his health—as well as indications of unusual musical gifts—that is mentioned in the earliest-known description of him: *Adam Liszt's diary*, written retrospectively some years later.

After vaccination there began a period of sickness in which the boy had to struggle alternately with nervous disorders and fevers, which several times brought him close to death. Once, during his second or third year, we thought we had lost him and had a coffin prepared. This alarming condition lasted until his sixth year! . . .

When he was six he heard me play Ries's Concerto in C sharp minor, and he leant against the piano listening intently. In the evening, when he

* Known in German as Pressburg, Pozsony is now Bratislava in Czechoslovakia.

† Since the boundary change after the First World War, Raiding has been in the Austrian province of Burgenland.

‡ Adam's own description of his occupation on his son's baptismal certificate.

§ The year of the Great Comet. This spectacular heavenly body was first seen in March. Because of its proximity to the sun, it then ceased to be visible for a time, but after reappearing in August remained a prominent feature of the sky for several months. 'The largest and most splendid that I ever saw,' was William Gardiner's description. 'As it grew bigger every night, in a few weeks it became a most grand and awful sight; it was in the northern hemisphere, with its head towards the sun, and its long expanding tail stretching southwards over a quarter of the heavens.' When Liszt was later told by his mother that the local gypsies had interpreted the dazzling heavenly visitation as a sign of the birth of a great man, the conviction came upon him, and remained lifelong, that he was a man of destiny whose career would be no ordinary one. That he, who was later so often to be compared to a 'comet' or 'meteor', should arrive in the world within hours of the real comet's closest proximity to it, and at the very moment of that proximity should receive the name that was to become so illustrious, is indeed a singular coincidence. 'The Comet was nearest the earth yesterday,' reported *The Times* of 24 Oct.

came back into the house after a stroll in the garden, he was singing the main theme of the work. . . . That was the first sign of his genius, and he entreated me to let him begin learning the piano.[1]

Franz Liszt. My first piano lessons were given me by my father, who desperately wished to ensure that in restricted circumstances his son would not be prevented, as he had been, from devoting himself to music to his heart's content. . . .

My father played not only the spinet [clavichord] but also the guitar, to which my mother enjoyed singing. . . . A piano he bought with difficulty out of his savings; in country districts at that time it was considered an extravagance. . . .

I was soon composing sonatas which have since been lost. With chords which my hands could not span I helped out with my nose. . . .

With childish temerity I went so far as to delve enthusiastically into Beethoven's *Hammerklavier* Sonata, of which my father was very fond. This folly earned me, I remember, a couple of good slaps, which hardly reformed me, however, for secretly, when my father was out on his rounds, I continued to dissect my favourite sonata. What most delighted me was the leap in the bass from B flat to D, and then the one to F. . . .

Not because of disobedience, of which I was never guilty, but because of clumsiness, I often received slaps and thrashings. In those days that was the way of bringing up children—in my opinion a most unjust one.

Hummel often came to our home, where many quartets were played; and with Haydn my father used to take a stroll almost daily.* He was a keen hunter, and I always had to accompany him, although I had no liking for it. . . . Nevertheless, he once praised me because I shot a wild duck. . . .

During my childhood I saw thousands of sheep, a fact to which I probably owe my extremely sheeplike character.[2]

Franz's education was provided at the village school by the local schoolmaster, Johann Rohrer (1783–1868). But it was a very limited education, involving little more than learning to read and write; and even this elementary instruction was broken off when, at the age of ten, he accompanied his parents to Vienna, thereafter to embark upon a life of travel and concert-giving. Adam Liszt was himself an educated man and 'excellent Latinist', who had studied at Pozsony's grammar school, spent two years as a novice in the Franciscan monastery at Malacka, and even undertaken a philosophy course at Pozsony University (before being compelled to abandon it for want of money to pay the fee). But as

* At Eisenstadt (Kismarton) before Franz Liszt's birth. After the accession of Prince Nicholas Esterházy (1794), and his own return from London a year later, Haydn was until 1804 a regular summer visitor to the town. Adam Liszt was a resident only from 1805, but he had also stayed here in earlier years. It was at Eisenstadt, too, that Adam met the renowned pianist and composer J. N. Hummel (1778–1837), Deputy Kapellmeister from 1804 to 1811. (And, from 1819, one of Franz Liszt's predecessors at Weimar, where he died.)

soon as he recognized his son's exceptional talent, he devoted his leisure hours to helping him make progress in music, and Franz's general education was accordingly neglected. Although he became by his own efforts an extremely cultured and well-read man, Liszt always deplored the inadequacy of his early schooling. 'I taught myself how to write down music,' he remarked, 'and far preferred doing that to writing the letters of the alphabet. Before my ninth birthday I had already filled not a few sheets of paper with notes.'

When asked in old age about his childhood reading, and if it was true that he had steeped himself in the philosophy of the mystic and pantheist Jakob Boehme (1575–1624), Liszt replied that he had no recollection of having read Boehme, and that his mystical tendencies had been founded on his reading of the Bible (especially the New Testament), the lives of some of the saints (above all St Francis of Assisi), and *The Imitation of Christ*.

Like Adam and Anna Liszt, Rohrer was German-speaking, and so the boy grew up with little or no Hungarian, another educational deficiency which he strove—but less successfully in this instance—to remedy in later life.

Such progress did Franz make at the piano that he became something of a local celebrity, and in October 1820, the month of his ninth birthday, he was invited by a blind flautist, Baron Sigismund von Braun, to take part in a concert at the Sopron (Oedenburg) casino. Accepting the invitation, he played the Concerto in E flat by Ferdinand Ries (1784–1838) and also, as was the custom of the period, improvised on a theme provided by a member of the audience. He received a considerable ovation.

His next appearance was at the Esterházy Palace in Eisenstadt, where he again earned great applause; and on 26 November he took part in a concert at Pozsony which two days later was reviewed in the *Pressburger Zeitung*.

At noon last Sunday the nine-year-old virtuoso Franz Liszt had the honour of exhibiting his talents on the piano before a large gathering of the local nobility and music-lovers at the residence of Count Michael Esterházy. The young artist's extraordinary skill, and his rapid grasp of the most difficult pieces when playing at sight anything placed before him, excited general admiration and justifies the highest expectations.[3]

Adam Liszt was aware that if his son was to make a name in the wider world, more advanced instruction was needed than he or any local musician could provide. But to study elsewhere entailed travelling and living away from home, a circumstance which would create severe financial problems. Happily, these were now eased by the generosity of a group of Hungarian noblemen, Counts Thadé d'Amadé, Apponyi, Szapáry, Erdödy, Viczay, and Michael Esterházy, who offered to set up a fund to enable Franz to live and study abroad; and, as he himself later confirmed, for six years he received an annual grant of 600 florins.

By the spring of 1822 it was time to make the move, and in April the family journeyed to Vienna. Before this important event, however, the young Liszt received one last pleasure from the intoxicating gypsy music he had already heard frequently. His delight in the Romany rendering of Magyar folk melodies remained with him throughout his life, and it inspired not only the *Magyar Dallok* and Hungarian Rhapsodies but even an original literary achievement, the book *Des Bohémiens et de leur musique en Hongrie*. Now, just before leaving his homeland, to which, apart from a brief visit in 1823, he would not return for many years, he heard the violinist János Bihary (1764–1827), the 'best-known hero and the most highly-praised and popular figure of the whole of gypsy virtuosity', as he later described him.

When, in 1822, I heard this great man among gypsy virtuosi, I was not too young to be struck and impressed by him, or faithfully to cherish the memory of his inspirations. . . . The emotions I then experienced must have resembled the effect produced by one of those mysterious elixirs concocted in their secret laboratories by the bold, almost demoniacal alchemists of the Middle Ages. . . .

With Bihary, gypsy music achieved its greatest renown. It had long been admired and patronized by the Hungarian aristocracy, but it now became an integral part of national representation.[4]

Adam Liszt's first choice of teacher for his son had been Hummel, now Court Kapellmeister at Weimar. His second was the Viennese Carl Czerny (1791–1857), a former child prodigy pianist and pupil of Beethoven, but by this time best known as a composer*—above all of studies and exercises for the piano—and pedagogue. The reason why Hummel had eventually to be left out of consideration was later explained by Liszt himself: 'Before placing me with Czerny, my father wanted to take me to Hummel, who asked for one or several ducats per lesson—which angered my father, who thought it an exorbitant demand on the part of an old friend.'

The lessons with Czerny had been arranged before the Liszts' move to Vienna, father and son having made a brief trip to the capital for the purpose as early as July 1819.

In his memoirs Czerny recalled both that first meeting and the boy's subsequent studies and progress with him.

One morning a man came to ask if I would let his little boy, aged about eight, play to me. He was a pale, delicate-looking child, and while playing he swayed about on the seat as though drunk, so that I often thought he would fall to the floor. His playing, too, was quite irregular, careless and confused, and of the principles of fingering he had such scant understanding that he threw his fingers about on the keys quite arbitrarily. Nevertheless, I was amazed at the talent with which Nature had endowed

* The mingled exasperation and respect with which the prolific Czerny has been regarded, by contemporaries and posterity alike, is well expressed in the *Athenaeum* (London) of 24 Dec. 1842: 'What shall we say of Herr Czerny's Op. 705, No. 3(!), being a rondo on *Rule Britannia*—we presume "for the use of schools"—with *See the Conquering Hero comes* and *The Grenadier's March* interwoven? To see a clever man, of great musical accomplishment, doing the work of a machine, exhausts our patience. But the publishers—and, it may be presumed, the public—encourage the manufacture; and, truth to say, there is little easy music more serviceable to the fingers of the young pianoforte player than these concoctions by Herr Czerny.' Liszt recalled that the only free time Czerny allowed himself was to attend the daily gathering of musicians at the music-publisher Tobias Haslinger's. 'Otherwise he composed incessantly.'

him. Some things that I set before him he played at sight, purely by instinct to be sure, but for that very reason in a manner which made it plain that Nature herself had here formed a pianist. It was just the same when at his father's wish I gave him a theme on which to improvise. Without the slightest formal knowledge of harmony, he yet made something rather special out of it from sheer talent. The father told me his name was Liszt, that he was an employee of Prince Esterházy's, and that up to this time he had been his son's sole teacher—asking me, however, if I would take little Franzi as a pupil when he returned to Vienna a year later. Naturally I agreed with pleasure, and at the same time, by showing him how the scales etc. were to be practised, gave him advice on how best to continue the boy's instruction in the intervening period. About a year [*sic*] later Liszt and his son returned to Vienna, taking lodgings in the same street as ourselves; and, having little time in the day, I gave the boy a lesson almost every evening.

Never had I had so eager, talented, and diligent a pupil. Knowing from long experience that such geniuses, whose spiritual and intellectual attainments outstrip their physical resources, usually neglect to acquire a solid technical foundation, I deemed it essential to use the first few months to regulate and strengthen his mechanical dexterity in such a way that it would not deteriorate in later years. In a short time he could play scales in every key with all the masterly facility that his fingers (extremely well formed for piano playing) allowed; and by serious study of the Clementi sonatas, which will always be the best school for pianists when studied as they should be, he acquired the rhythmical steadiness hitherto lacking, as well as a beautiful touch and tone, the most suitable fingering, and an understanding of correct and appropriate musical declamation; even though, to begin with, this lively and unfailingly cheerful boy found such works rather dry. This method worked so well that some months later, when we took up the works of Hummel, Ries, Moscheles,* and then of Beethoven and Sebastian Bach, I no longer found it necessary to pay too much attention to the technique, but could let him interpret the spirit and character of these different composers. Since he had to study every piece extremely quickly, he eventually acquired such a mastery of sight-reading that he was publicly capable of playing at sight even works of considerable difficulty and importance, just as though he had long studied them. I likewise tried to help him master the art of extempore playing by frequently giving him themes on which to improvise.

The result of little Liszt's unfailing cheerfulness and good spirits,

* The Bohemian pianist and composer Ignaz Moscheles (1794–1870), whom Liszt knew well in later years, was one of the most distinguished musicians of his day. An acquaintance of Beethoven, of whose *Fidelio* he prepared the piano score, he was also a friend of Mendelssohn, to whom he gave piano lessons. For many years he resided in London, and from 1846 was Professor of Pianoforte at the Leipzig Conservatorium.

together with the extraordinary development of his talent, was that my parents loved him like a son, and I like a brother; and I not only taught him entirely gratis but also provided him with all the works he needed from the music literature as it then existed. A year later he was already up to playing in public, and he aroused in Vienna an enthusiasm such as is not shown to every artist.[5]

If an excellent choice had been made with regard to Franz's piano teacher, equally happy was that of a teacher of composition and theory: the veteran Italian composer Antonio Salieri (1750–1825), who, like Czerny, accepted no remuneration from the Liszts for his services. 'When by chance in a private house I heard young Franz Liszt improvising on the piano and playing at sight, I was so amazed that I really thought I was dreaming,' he remarked in a letter of 25 August 1822 to Prince Esterházy. 'Since the middle of last month his father has been bringing him to me thrice a week, and the boy is making astounding progress. . . . Because on warm days he has always arrived hot and bathed in sweat, I have learned that he lives in Mariahilf. I have told his father that in bad weather this journey will be dangerous for his son's delicate health, and that it is necessary to let him live in the inner city.'

'At Vienna in '22 and '23,' Liszt recalled sixty years later, 'Salieri was so graciously kind as to teach me, not the art of composing (which can hardly be taught), but to know and understand the different clefs and procedures used in the scores of his day. I remain profoundly grateful to him.' His first composition under Salieri was a *Tantum ergo* (S702), a sacred choral work now lost.

A former pupil of Salieri's who was also living in Vienna at this time was Franz Schubert; but when, in later life, Liszt talked of his early years, he made it plain that he did not knowingly come into contact with the great composer who became one of his musical idols. 'Weber, Schubert, and Goethe I never knew personally,' he declared.

A famous musician whom the young Liszt did meet in the Austrian capital was Gioacchino Rossini, much fêted and lionized by the Viennese during his sojourn amongst them. 'It was at Vienna in 1822 that I began to love and admire you,' he wrote to Liszt long afterwards. 'The years which have passed since then have served but to increase the affection I feel for you.'

Not long before, the publisher Anton Diabelli (1781–1858) had invited fifty prominent musicians each to write a variation on a waltz theme he had composed. The twenty-fourth in the set (which lost what little significance it possessed when compared with the masterpiece composed on the same theme a little later by Beethoven) was Liszt's contribution (S147), composed in 1822, a lively little study in arpeggios and crossed hands. It was his first published work.

Although he played several times in private circles, Liszt's first public concert in Vienna was not until 1 December 1822, when at the Landständischer Saal he played Hummel's Concerto in A minor and improvised on a given theme. His fellow performers were the violinist Léon de St Lubin and the young singer, and friend of Beethoven, Caroline Unger (1803–77). A notice of his playing appeared in the Leipzig *Allgemeine Musikalische Zeitung* of 22 January following, in a survey of Vienna concerts in December.

The performance of this boy, for his age, borders on the unbelievable, and one is tempted to doubt any physical impossibility when one hears the young giant with unabated force thunder out Hummel's composition, so difficult and fatiguing, especially in the final movement. Feeling, expression, shading, and all the finer nuances are there too; and, further, this musical *Wunderkind* is said to read everything at first sight and already to be without a peer in playing from score! May Polyhymnia protect the tender plant, and preserve it from leaf-robbing storms, so that it may grow and prosper! We should prefer to call the improvisation a *capriccio*, for several themes united by transitional passages do not yet deserve that splendid title, only too often misused nowadays. Nevertheless, it was really delightful to see the manner in which the little Hercules joined together the Andante from Beethoven's Symphony in A and the theme of a cantilena from Rossini's *Zelmira*, kneading them, so to speak, into one paste. *Est deus in nobis!*

On 9 December Liszt appeared with an Italian guitarist, Luigi Legnani, and a Danish cellist, Frederik Christian Funck, in a concert given at the Kärntnerthor-theater as a prelude to a ballet performance. On this occasion he played the Rondo from Ferdinand Ries's Concerto in E flat.

1823

The second of Liszt's Vienna concerts was given in the small hall of the Redoute in the early afternoon of Sunday, 13 April. The second, fourth, and sixth (final) items on the programme were his own contributions: Hummel's Concerto in B minor, the Grand Variations for piano and orchestra by Moscheles, and an improvisation on a given theme.

Two months later *The Harmonicon*, a London music journal, devoted some space to this concert and to Liszt's performance, the first mention of his name in the British press. According to a Vienna correspondent of the journal, Liszt played 'with so much precision, correctness, and execution, united to such taste and elegance, that he is already placed by the side of the greatest pianoforte players of the present day. As to physical powers of hand, he leaves us nothing to wish for; and he indeed seems destined to attain the highest rank in the art.'

The most memorable feature of the occasion, and the reason why half a century later Liszt's jubilee as a public artist was dated from this appearance rather than from that of the previous December, was the presence of Beethoven—who is said to have gone up to the little pianist at the end of the concert, embraced and kissed him. (Whether this took place on the platform or—more probably—behind the scenes, is not known.)

The great composer was almost totally deaf by this time, and such a token of his appreciation will doubtless have been bestowed, not for any musical pleasure given to him by Liszt's playing, but for what he will have been able to judge with his eyes of the youngster's spirit and manner at the keyboard and evident complete mastery of the instrument.

It has been suggested that this *Weihekuss* (kiss of consecration), as it has been called, was actually given at Beethoven's home, and that he did not attend the concert. Against such a hypothesis, however, we have the evidence not only of Liszt's own words, but also, to some extent, that of the Beethoven conversation books. Now that modern scholarship has identified and removed from those books certain remarks added to them *post eventum* by Anton Schindler, there remain only two references to the concert of tolerable significance. The first merely implies an exchange between Beethoven and his nephew about the number of people in the audience, and whether or not the hall had been full; in the second, Johann van Beethoven identifies for his deaf brother the theme (a Hungarian melody) on which the young Liszt had improvised (Beethoven himself having earlier declined to provide one)—the very remark to be expected if Beethoven did indeed attend the concert: the advertised, set programme he would have been able to read for himself, but with eyesight alone would have found it impossible to identify the theme used for the improvisation.

The conversation books do not prove that Beethoven attended the concert, nor do they prove the contrary. Putting them aside, we are left with Liszt's own words.

To numerous contemporaries he maintained both that Beethoven came to the concert and that, having done so, the great composer rewarded him with a kiss on the brow. This is what he told not only his biographer Lina Ramann, but also such other friends and acquaintances as La Mara, Ludwig Nohl (a biographer of Beethoven), the Revd. H. R. Haweis, Carl Lachmund, and August Göllerich. The last-named made an immediate written note of Liszt's words: 'At my second Vienna concert Beethoven turned up, for Czerny's sake, and kissed me on the forehead. I never played at his home, although I visited him twice. There was a piano there with torn-out strings.'

Liszt did not correct such a version when it appeared in the Ramann biography (despite rectifying errors of far lesser significance), just as in 1842, when amending the biography written of him by J. W. Christern, he deleted an erroneous statement about the presence at the concert of 'the entire high and lower nobility', but left untouched—thereby tacitly endorsing its accuracy—an adjoining reference to Beethoven's presence.

Quite out of step with all this is a description furnished by Ilka Horovitz-Barnay, a Hungarian acquaintance of Liszt's who, some years after his death, wrote out for a magazine the version of the meeting with Beethoven which—she claimed—had been related to her by Liszt. This version has Liszt playing to the great composer, and being kissed by him, in the latter's own home. Charmingly though it reads, Horovitz-Barnay's account has too much against it to be credible, and, as two of Liszt's most notable biographers (Julius Kapp and Peter Raabe) have argued, is to be regarded as a fable, either invented by Horovitz-Barnay herself or borrowed by her from some other untrustworthy source.

The *Weihekuss* was *either* bestowed at the public concert of 13 April, as stated so often by Liszt himself; *or* he afterwards genuinely confused Beethoven with some other imposing personage, such as King Maximilian I of Bavaria, who likewise rewarded his playing with a kiss;* *or*—least likely of all—it was a deliberate fabrication to which he stubbornly adhered until the very end of his life.

Two weeks after the concert of 13 April, the Liszts journeyed to Pest, to enable Franz to show his compatriots something of the prowess acquired under Czerny, and as a farewell to them before the more extensive travels now envisaged. On 1 May he played in the salon of the Inn of the Seven Prince Electors (in Váci út), his offerings of Moscheles' Grand Variations and some improvisations being extremely well received. Further concerts followed at the City Theatre on the 10th and 17th. On the 19th he appeared before a smaller gathering, playing the Rákóczy March—out of which several decades later he fashioned his Fifteenth Hungarian Rhapsody—and Weber's *Momento capriccioso*. His farewell concert was given on 24 May.

Before leaving Pest, Adam Liszt went to the city's Franciscan monastery to renew acquaintance with some of the friends he had made during his novitiate many years earlier. With him he took his son, whom he introduced to the friars and asked to play to them. The visit made a powerful impression on the mystically-inclined, deeply religious boy, who was already acquainted with the life of St Francis, would himself one day be a member of the Franciscan order, and would on at least one occasion express the wish—not to be granted—that after his death his remains might repose in this very place.

By September 1823 Franz had progressed enough to be exhibited to a wider audience than that provided by the Austrian capital, and on the 20th of the month the family left Vienna on the first leg of a journey to Paris.

Adam Liszt to Carl Czerny. Augsburg, 2 November. We arrived safely at Munich in the evening of 26 September, and did not leave until 28 October. The reason for our long stay was firstly that Herr Moscheles had already got there before us; secondly, that the very brilliantly celebrated October festival was taking place; and thirdly, because Moscheles delayed in giving his concert. With what applause he was received, the enclosure will tell you.

Our own first concert was on 17 October,† and as we were not well known the audience was not numerous; but we were favoured by having among them the most gracious King‡ and princesses. The applause was immense, and I was at once invited to give a second, which took place on the 24th. Here I must say briefly that it would have been desirable for there to have been as many people at the first as had to be turned away at the

* See Adam Liszt's letter to Carl Czerny of 2 Nov. 1823 *infra*.

† 'A new Mozart has appeared to us, Munich announces to the musical world,' reported the *Augsburger Allgemeine Zeitung* about this concert. 'Young Liszt played Hummel's Concerto in B minor with a facility and purity, with a precision and power, with such deep and true feeling, that even the boldest imagination would not dare to expect anything similar at so tender an age. We have heard Hummel and Moscheles, and do not hesitate to affirm that this child's execution is in no wise inferior to theirs. But what carried admiration to the highest point was an improvisation on given themes. . . . It is not to be wondered at that the numerous and delighted audience could set no bounds to their applause.'

‡ Maximilian Josef I (1756–1825), King of Bavaria from 1806.

second because of lack of room. We had eventually to close the box office. A couple of enclosures will give you a notion of the ovation accorded to Zisy.* At leisure though we were at the beginning, we were extremely busy after the first concert and honoured by the most flattering invitations from all sides. And in response to a pressing request from the directors of the Theatre Royal, I allowed Franzi to appear a third time: at the concert given† by the two Ebner violinists, where among other things he had to repeat by public demand your Variations in E flat with orchestra—although we were given no share in the takings. But we earned immortal glory for ourselves in return, and even the good King told us that we were very kind to support the two of them.

Twice we had the high honour of an audience with this kindliest of kings, and were received with the utmost graciousness. On the first occasion the King said: '*And you, young fellow, had the courage to appear after Moscheles?*' When we were withdrawing, the King said: 'Come here, little one, I must kiss you'—and proceeded to do so. It brought tears to my eyes. Furthermore, at the King's command letters of introduction were at once prepared for Strasbourg and Paris, some of them being handed to us, and so we may look forward to a good reception. On the concert programme I got them to put: 'Pupil of Carl Czerny'. Everyone was delighted and expressed the wish to make the acquaintance of this splendid *Meister*, and I was asked several times if Herr von Czerny had any more such pupils. My reply was that when pupils have talent and are prepared to work hard, then through your wise and thorough instruction they too can reach this level of virtuosity.

We got to Augsburg in the evening of 28 October, and on the 30th were already giving a little concert which had been arranged from Munich. On 1 November he played at the *Harmonie*. Wherever we go the applause is universal, and we are already quite at home in Augsburg. Today Zisy will play gratis at a concert for the poor, and tomorrow we leave for Stuttgart. Despite the cost of carriage and food, wine in particular being very expensive, after deduction of all expenses we are left at present with a net profit of 921 florins. We would have almost as much again, were I not also careful to seek honour and to do kindnesses to others. My wife and child join me in kissing your hands with the utmost gratitude for the good work you have achieved in him. Never will you escape our everlasting gratitude, because it is you alone whom we have to thank for this. Please greet and kiss over and over again on our behalf your dear, good parents; our conversation every day, almost every hour, is of you and of them. They will shortly be receiving a letter from Zisy; he is diligently preparing a travel itinerary for you, which he began on the very first day of our departure

* Nickname for Franz.

† On 27 Oct. The brothers Karl and Anton Ebner were about Liszt's age and likewise from Hungary.

from Vienna and is keeping up with great care. His diary, which he is writing most assiduously and will hand over to you on his return, you should find of particular interest. . . .

The orchestra at Munich is extremely good; I have never heard a better. The people are very likeable too. Hummel's B minor Concerto was done matchlessly, leaving absolutely nothing to be desired. The only pity was that the Theatre is too small. Moscheles has outlived his renown in Munich and people do not speak of him with due respect. I thought he played his concerto unsurpassably; but his improvisation—if it can be called that—was empty. What lost him respect more than anything else was that he charged double prices. . . .[6]

Added to Adam Liszt's letter was a note in his son's hand.

Dearest Herr von Czerny!

I am in good health, and so far everything is going really well for me. I kiss your and Mme Czerny's* hands many times and remain as always your grateful Zisy.

Franz Liszt.

The Augsburg concert of 30 October was reviewed in the *Schwäbische Chronik* (which formed part of the *Schwäbische Merkur*) of 5 November.

Local music-lovers had a great treat: a concert given by Franz Liszt, a young Hungarian. . . . This boy possesses in the highest degree, facility, expression, precision, execution, etc. etc.; in fact all the qualities which reveal a distinguished pianist. To this may be added the profound knowledge of counterpoint and fugue passages which he disclosed when performing a 'free fantasia', for which at the end of the concert a written theme was given him by a local artist. All this justifies the affirmation that this boy already equals the first pianists in Europe, perhaps already surpasses many of them.

On Thursday, 11 December, having continued their journey via Stuttgart (two concerts) and Strasbourg (one private and one public concert), the Liszts arrived in Paris. Taking accommodation at the Hôtel d'Angleterre, rue du Mail, they were very near the Maison Erard, home of the piano and harp manufacturer Sébastien Erard (1752–1831), his brother Jean-Baptiste (1749–1826), and the latter's son Pierre (1794–1855). In a short time they were all on such friendly terms that Franz came to regard the Erards as his 'adoptive family'.

Adam's first priority was to have his son enrolled at the Conservatoire, whose principal was the Italian-born composer Luigi Cherubini (1760–1842).

Franz Liszt. The day after our arrival in Paris, we hurried to see M. Cherubini. An urgent letter of recommendation from M. Metternich was to serve as our introduction to him. . . .

* Czerny's mother.

Scarcely had I passed through the portal (or, rather, the abominable porte-cochère) of the rue du Faubourg-Poissonnière, when a feeling of profound respect came over me. This is a redoubtable place, I thought; here, in this glorious sanctuary, sits the supreme tribunal which condemns or absolves for ever; and I all but knelt down before that bustling crowd of men, whom I took to be the owners of illustrious names and whom I was astonished to see going to and fro like ordinary mortals.

When at last, after we had suffered a very bad quarter of an hour's wait, the office messenger half opened the door of the principal's study and indicated that we were to enter, I, already feeling more dead than alive, and moved by some unknown impulse, rushed forward to kiss M. Cherubini's hand. Then, all of a sudden, it occurred to me for the first time that perhaps this was not the custom in France, and my eyes filled with tears. Confused, humiliated, no longer daring to meet the gaze of the great composer who had stood up to Napoleon,* I tried only not to allow a single one of his words or breathings to escape me. . . .

Happily, my torment did not last long. We had already been warned that my application would meet with some difficulty, but until that moment we had no knowledge of the regulation, allowing of no exceptions, whereby foreigners are refused permission to attend lessons. M. Cherubini apprised us of it at once. What a thunderbolt! I trembled in every limb. Nevertheless, my father insisted, begged. The sound of his voice restored my courage; I, too, tried to articulate a few words. Like the woman of Canaan, I humbly implored that I might at least be allowed to nourish myself on the crumbs falling from the children's table. But the regulation was inexorable—and I wholly inconsolable. Everything was lost, I felt, even honour. . . . My groans and lamentations were unceasing, and it was in vain that my father and my adoptive family sought to comfort me. The wound was too deep and continued to bleed for a long time. It was only eight or ten years later, thanks to assiduous reading of M. Kalkbrenner's† *Méthode de piano* and confidential conversations with a number of the Conservatoire pupils, that it healed completely.[7]

L'Etoile (22 December). Paris possesses at this moment a real phenomenon, in an eleven-year-old Hungarian named Leist [*sic*]. This child already displays pianistic talents of the first order; but his playing is distinguished not only for the rapidity of his fingers, which is what is admired in a number of performers: with perfect lightness and firmness he unites an expression lacking in other artists, even those of high reputation. That,

* The Emperor having complained that Cherubini's music was too noisy, the composer had retorted: 'I understand—you like music which does not stop you thinking of affairs of state.'

† The German pianist and composer Friedrich Kalkbrenner (1785–1849), who lived in Paris for many years. His playing was distinguished by great polish and brilliance on the one hand, but by lack of warmth, feeling, and inspiration on the other. His *Méthode pour apprendre le pianoforte à l'aide du guide-mains* appeared in 1830.

however, is what is least astonishing in the talents of this extraordinary child. He composes in the style of the greatest masters; and on themes given to him he improvises with a facility made all the more marvellous in that the power and grace of his ideas never fail him. Since Mozart, who astonished several European courts at the age of eight, the world of music has certainly witnessed nothing so surprising as young Leist. . . .

Let us not forget to mention a characteristic trait which completes the prodigious talents of this young compatriot of Haydn. It is that, having begun to learn French only a short time ago, he already expresses himself in the language with a clarity, and sometimes with even a finesse, which would do honour to many sixteen- and seventeen-year-olds.

With his son barred from the Conservatoire, Adam Liszt had to find a teacher of merit who would give lessons in a private capacity, and his choice eventually fell on the Italian opera-composer Ferdinando Paër (1771–1839), who in 1812 had succeeded Spontini as Director of the Italian Opera in Paris. It was under Paër's guidance that a year or two later the young Liszt composed his first large-scale work, the opera *Don Sanche* (S1).

1824

Adam Liszt to Carl Czerny. Paris, 17 March. As our arrival here was heralded by the newspapers and by numerous private letters, after a few days of rest we were immediately busy once again and received with the utmost enthusiasm. We have already undertaken three dozen soirées in the leading houses, at which nothing less than 100 francs—often even 150—is paid for a soirée. To give my boy some rest, and so that his studies may not be neglected, I have had to turn down several invitations.

On one occasion he played at Madame la Duchesse de Berry's, where the entire royal family was present, and he improvised four times on themes given to him. Three times at the home of the Duc d'Orléans. The applause was so great that he was invited several more times to each of these princely houses. On 7 March we gave our first public concert—at the Royal Italian Opera.* It was made available to us free of charge (as were the orchestra and lighting) for our own benefit. Having to defray an outlay of only 343 francs, we were accordingly left with a profit of 4,711 francs. A pity the theatre is so small, and I did not want to make a noticeable increase in prices, otherwise the takings would definitely have been doubled. The boxes had already been reserved a week in advance by the subscribers themselves, and so nobody else could obtain one. My boy

* That is, the Théâtre Italien. Liszt played Hummel's Concerto in B minor and Variations for piano and orchestra by Czerny.

received an ovation impossible to describe; and I believe I have told you enough when I say that the general wish at the theatre and in the newspapers, to give a second concert, was expressed repeatedly. You will imagine, and say, that to comply with such a wish is easy, and you will be right; but you must also know that this was a special favour which we owe solely to the high protection of the Duchesse de Berry and the royal minister Lauriston. Such a thing falls to the lot of few artists, least of all in the way in which we had the theatre. At Vienna, I believe, it would be impossible to find an example of the theatre being made available free of charge to a foreign artist for his own benefit, and for an act from an opera to be performed in further support. This one example will suffice to show you how superior the French are to others in generosity and in regard to the arts. I could add much else, but one day my diary will inform you of every last detail. For the moment, note merely this: He who has talent must come to Paris, for artistic understanding is here the norm; here the artist is esteemed, honoured, and rewarded. . . . There are good instruments here too, among which the new invention* of the very clever manufacturer, Erard, stands out in particular. It is my opinion that this man has performed the most essential service for the piano just at present. To describe it would be beyond me, and so I shall mention only one small feature. It has a soft touch and yet one can do with the tone (which is very good) what one will. Without lifting the hand from the keys, one can with a single attack make the chord sound soft or loud as often as desired—it is really astonishing. As yet, only three are ready; the fourth is being prepared for my boy, and in due course we shall send it to Vienna. I am convinced it will meet with your approval. . . .

In society my boy plays your things most of all, and they are heard with great pleasure. My sole regret is that we haven't all of them. On many occasions the keenest desire to make the acquaintance of the teacher of this *enfant prodige* (as they call the lad) has been expressed. 'Won't he be coming to Paris?' they ask. Now this gives me an opportunity to come to your own person, which we treasure and hold dear above all others, to ask: Will you never leave Vienna? If I am to answer this question myself, I say: You *should* do so, and come to Paris with a pile of your works. We shall prepare everything for your reception, and both the welcome given to you and the rewards which will come your way will far exceed what can be hoped for in Vienna. We shall probably not be going to London until next year, as our prospects here are growing ever rosier. And so if you feel like coming to Paris, which would have to be at the beginning of autumn, I beg you to let me know. Your lodging will be with us. You will have a fine room and bedroom on the second floor of a street in the middle of the city,

* The double escapement action, patented by the Erards in January 1822 (and in London in 1825). A device which greatly facilitated rapid repetition of the keys and enhanced the player's control over the instrument, it was used to brilliant effect by the young Liszt.

entirely gratis. Another room and two bedrooms are left for us, and if you will make do with eating with us (we eat at home), it will double our pleasure. If you wish to give lessons, there will be no lack of them. . . .[8]

A review of the concert of 7 March had appeared in the *Drapeau blanc* (9 March), penned by the editor, *Alphonse Martainville* (1776–1830).

I cannot help it: since yesterday I am a believer in metempsychosis. I am convinced that the soul and spirit of Mozart have passed into the body of young Liszt, and never has an identity revealed itself by plainer signs. The same country, the same wonderful talent in childhood, and in the same art! I appeal to all those who have had the good fortune to hear the marvellous little artist. His little arms can scarcely stretch to both ends of the keyboard, his little feet scarcely reach the pedals, and yet this child is beyond compare; he is the first pianist in Europe, Moscheles himself would not feel offended by this affirmation.

Mozart, in taking the name of Liszt, has lost nothing of that interesting countenance which always increases the interest a child inspires in us by his precocious talent. The features of our little prodigy express spirit and cheerfulness. He comes before his audience with exceeding gracefulness, and the pleasure, the admiration, which he awakens in his hearers as soon as his fingers glide along the keys he seems to find extremely amusing and diverting . . .

To give an idea of the impression he can make on those who hear him, I shall mention only the effect his playing had on the orchestra of the Italian Opera, the best in France and Europe. Eyes, ears, and soul were enchained to the magic instrument of the young artist. Meanwhile they forgot that they were coadjutors in the concert, and at the Ritornella every instrument was dumb. The public, by their laughter and clapping, testified their hearty forgiveness of a distraction which was, perhaps, the most favourable acknowledgement the talent of the little prodigy has ever received. . . .

He scarcely looked at the music, and that at long intervals. His eyes wandered continually round the hall, and he greeted the persons he recognized in the boxes with friendly smiles and nods.

At last he threw stand and music aside, and gave himself up to his genius in a free improvisation. Words are wanting to express the admiration he excited. After a harmoniously arranged introduction, he took Mozart's beautiful air from *Le nozze di Figaro*, 'Non più andrai', as his theme, If, as I have said, Liszt, by a happy transmigration, is only a continuation of Mozart, it is he himself who provided the text. . . .

The warmest applause and repeated encores echoed through the hall. The happy child returned his thanks with a smile.

Adam Liszt to his friend Ludwig Hofer at Eisenstadt, 20 March. On one occasion the lad played at Madame la Duchesse de Berry's, where the entire royal family and everyone of distinction were gathered. He improvised four times on given themes. With what acclamation he was received you will understand when I tell you that the talk was of nothing but marvels and miracles. Nothing like it has ever been known in Paris. The honour shown to us it is impossible to describe. . . . They even took my boy into the apartments of the young heir to the throne (the Duc de Bordeaux,* an angel of a prince) and showed him his curios. The boy played in three soirées at the home of the Duc d'Orléans, and we still have invitations to both these noblest houses. On 8 February we gave a private concert, which brought us a net 2,000 francs. . . . Our concert of 7 March was a public triumph for the boy. As soon as he appeared he was greeted by applause that seemed unending; and after every passage enthusiasm was expressed with the liveliest astonishment. After each of his pieces he was recalled and applauded two or three times. The gentlemen of the orchestra beat hard with the backs of their bows on their double-basses, cellos, violas, and violins—and so absolutely everyone was delighted.

The newspapers had already praised my boy's gifts beforehand; but *after* the concert it was quite extraordinary. Think of this: on 9 March fourteen journalists competed with one another to describe his talent, and there is still no end to it. Their usual designation for him is *enfant prodige*, a Mozart reborn. Just a few days after the concert a well-regarded music society ordered a lithograph of his portrait, and also an enlargement for exhibiting at the Louvre. My friend, do you know what I say to all this? I weep, and in all sincerity his improvising at the piano is truly extraordinary, and it is this in particular which arouses the highest degree of amazement and admiration in the Parisian ladies and gentlemen. Just imagine, we go almost every day into one company or another. Everywhere he plays only extempore, improvising or playing on given themes; and yet people are unanimous in declaring that he is new each time. . . .

If fate had not condemned you to be stuck in our dear Eisenstadt, I would advise you (as I know your thirst for knowledge) to travel. That is the true book—all the rest are chimerae; only experience and knowledge of several nations can satisfy the mind eager to learn. . . . During our travels I have seen much, and everywhere inquired about all branches of science and, in particular, culture, and have been pleased to find nothing that is not simple and natural. I have spoken with many men of learning, economists and civil servants, who enjoyed giving me information. . . . The journey from Munich to Paris is like an English garden, eventually leading to Paradise; one doesn't know which to admire most, nature or human industry.

* Posthumous son (1820–83) of the assassinated Duc de Berry, he later took the title Comte de Chambord. As the grandson of Charles X and pretender to the throne of France, he was subsequently known to his followers as Henri V.

If you have a chance to speak or write to my father,* please tell him that we kiss his hand and that I shall shortly be sending a sum of money to Vienna and will arrange its transfer. Tell him that he can be pleased with his grandson. . . .[9]

Allgemeine Musikalische Zeitung (Vienna), 1 May, reviewing the Paris concert of 7 March. Young Liszt is not one of those little phenomena who are taught with sugar-sticks and fasting. He is a true artist, and what an artist! Eleven years old [twelve], they say; but to look at him one would think him only nine. His eyes are bright and vivacious, gleaming with playfulness and joy. They do not lead him to the piano—he flies to it. He is clapped, and appears astonished. The applause is repeated and he rubs his hands; this childish distraction excites loud laughter. One must have heard this child to have any notion of his really wonderful talent. It is impossible to comprehend how ten little fingers, which cannot span an octave, are able to multiply themselves in so varied a manner and bring forth such difficult chords, and so skilfully moderate or accelerate all the masses of harmony. There were some among the audience who cried 'a miracle!'—and several must have thought there was magic in the case, for they requested that the instrument, behind which the young artist was partially concealed, should be placed obliquely; but as soon as this was done the bravos were repeated with redoubled might. . . . The improvisation he seemed to find mere play. . . . The *tours de force* at the conclusion were so strangely wonderful, that one cannot refuse the most honourable recognition to the fire, the spirit, the originality with which they were inspired.

In May, Adam and Franz made their first visit to London. They were accompanied by Pierre Erard, who brought one of the Erard pianos over with him for Franz's use, and on arrival all three lodged at 18 Great Marlborough Street,† headquarters of the firm's London branch.

An entire page of the June issue of *The Harmonicon* was devoted to the young prodigy; above all to a translation of a letter Adam Liszt had sent earlier in the year to a Parisian journal, *La Pandore*, in response to a remark he had noticed in one of its issues: 'The parents of young Liszt are poor, and he supports them by the product of his talents.'

'Fortune, it is true, has not loaded me with her favours, yet I have no reason to complain of her neglect,' Adam had written. 'For the space of twenty-three years I have been in the service of Prince Esterházy, where I filled the situation of steward of part of his sheep farms; the immense income of this prince, and the noble and generous manner in which he acts towards those who have the good

* Georg Adam Liszt (György Ádám List) (1755–1844), thrice-married and the father of twenty-five children, of whom Adam was the second. A village schoolmaster (among other occupations), employee of Prince Esterházy, and a talented amateur musician, he lived long enough to be a happy witness of his grandson's immense fame and, in 1839, triumphal return to his native Hungary.

† The present building on the site bears a plaque commemorating the various occasions when Liszt stayed at No. 18.

fortune to belong to any of his establishments, have long since placed me in that *aurea mediocritas* so happily described by the Latin poet. . . .

'I came to Paris with the permission of the prince, and by the advice of my friends, in order to perfect my son's talents, by affording him an opportunity of hearing the numerous artists whom this capital contains, and of cultivating the French language, of which he has already some general idea; a language which justly lays claim to the title of being that of Europe. At the same time I have not neglected to take advantage of the eagerness testified by the Parisians to hear his performance, in order to indemnify myself for the expenses necessarily attendant upon a long journey, and the removal of my whole family.'

The article in *The Harmonicon* concluded with a general appraisal of the boy's talent and person.

He executes the most difficult of the modern pianoforte music without the smallest apparent effort, and plays at sight things that very few masters would venture upon until they had given to them a little private study. But his extemporaneous performances are the most remarkable. Upon any subject that is proposed to him he improvises, with the fancy and method of a deliberating composer, and the correctness of an experienced contrapuntist. His hand is not unusually large, but is amazingly strong, and his touch has all the vigour of maturity. He has reached the usual growth of boys of his age, and possesses an open, intelligent and agreeable countenance, with a frankness, but at the same time a propriety, of manner, that indicates a good temper and a correct understanding.

During this visit Liszt played on a number of occasions in private houses. His first public appearance was on 5 June, at a dinner given by the Royal Society of Musicians in the Argyll Rooms.

The Morning Post (7 June). Master Liszt (a youth from Hungary) performed on a Grand Pianoforte with an improved action, invented by Sebastian Erard the celebrated Harp-maker, of very great power and brilliancy of tone. To do justice to the performance of Master Liszt is totally out of our power; his execution, taste, expression, genius, and wonderful extemporary playing, defy any written description. He must be heard to be duly appreciated.

Quarterly Musical Magazine and Review (vol. xxii, 1824). We heard this youth first at the dinner of the Royal Society of Musicians, where he extemporized for about twenty minutes before that judgmatical audience of professors and their friends. . . .

There were the marks of acquirement vast at any age, but prodigious at his, and of talent that requires only the assistance of a larger share of acquired knowledge. His genius brightens in his face, and particularly when any thought first rises to his mind. There was an eminent proof of this previous to the commencement of a fugue with his left hand, which he worked with much skill. He feels every note he touches.

Liszt's own concert, likewise at the Argyll Rooms, was given on Monday, 21 June. According to the newspaper announcement: 'Master Liszt . . . respectfully informs the Nobility, Gentry, and the Public in general, that his Benefit Concert will . . . commence at half-past eight precisely, when he will perform on Sebastian Erard's new patent Grand Pianoforte, a Concerto by Hummel, New Variations by Winkhler, and play extempore on a written Theme, which Master Liszt will request any person of the company to give him.'

The Morning Post (23 June). Sir George Smart invited any person in the company to oblige Master Liszt with a Thema, on which he would work (as the phrase is) extemporaneously. Here an interesting pause took place; at length a lady named 'Zitti, zitti'.* The little fellow, though not very well acquainted with the air, sat down and roved about the instrument, occasionally touching a few bars of the melody, then taking it as a subject for a transient fugue, but the best part of this performance was that wherein he introduced the air with his right hand, while the left swept the keys chromatically; then he crossed over his right hand, played the subject with the left, while the right hand descended by semitones to the bottom of the instrument! It is needless to add that his efforts were crowned with the most brilliant success.

On 29 June, at the Theatre Royal, Drury Lane, Liszt made a guest appearance at a benefit concert† given by the famous tenor John Braham (1774–1856), who a few days later wrote to 'my dear Master Liszt' to thank him for his exertions. 'The talent you displayed . . . can never be forgotten by the British Public. The delight they manifested was a tribute paid to your wonderful genius. . . . May you proceed in your career as prosperously as you have commenced,—and that you will emulate the glory of Mozart and the master-spirit of music is not doubted by Yours much obliged John Braham.'

Adam Liszt to Carl Czerny. London, 29 July. When we got to London we had many more difficulties to overcome than in Paris. One reason was that we arrived too late and the season was accordingly far advanced and the soirées arranged. Another was that the artists who are here—Herr Ries, however, was an honourable exception—did nothing at all, Kalkbrenner in particular. Yet, as you know, good material does not remain suppressed for long, and victory is all the more glorious. Our first concert was given on 21 June (we were unable to arrange a second because there were already too many others), to which I invited Messrs Clementi, Cramer, Ries, and Kalkbrenner, who all duly appeared, as well as the leading London artists; and, despite the boy being still little known and there being the same evening another concert plus a benefit performance at the Theatre for one

* From Rossini's *Il barbiere di Siviglia*.

† A fellow performer at the very long concert was the Welsh composer and writer John Parry (1776–1851), who gave several performances on the flageolet. He was the father of the John Orlando Parry with whom Liszt travelled the length and breadth of Britain in 1840 and 1841.

of the leading Italian singers, and not forgetting the immense expenses, we made a net profit of £90, approximately 720 florins. The outcome of the concert was important not only for Franzi's fame, but also in a financial respect, for we had a mass of things to do, and from nothing but soirées (five guineas a soirée, sometimes more, and £20 at the French Ambassador's only) we made in all £172—roughly 1,376 florins. The day before yesterday we were granted the greatest honour of all: we were presented to His Majesty the King* in his summer residence at Windsor. It was a soirée arranged for a handful of ladies and gentlemen only; Franzi played entirely alone and for more than two hours. To begin with, he played your Variations in E flat, which were received uncommonly well. Even during the Introduction it pleased His Majesty to say: *never in my life have I heard anything like this*; and at the close there was a burst of applause from all sides. His Majesty then deigned to give the Minuet from *Don Giovanni* as a theme for an improvisation, the performing of which excited the highest degree of admiration from every quarter, and it pleased His Majesty to say repeatedly in English, French, and German: 'This is quite unlike anything I have ever heard. This boy surpasses Moscheles, Cramer, Kalkbrenner, and all the other great players, not only in the actual playing but in the wealth and development of his ideas too.' (You must know that His Majesty is himself musical and a great music-lover.) On this occasion Prince Paul Esterházy† was present too, and heard Franzi for the first time; you can imagine all the rest. We spent the night at Windsor, and the next morning His Majesty was so good as to convey his great delight once more through a Gentleman of the Chamber, and to send a bill of exchange for £50. Then we visited all the sights of Windsor, which quite exceed any and every expectation, and it would be futile for me even to dare to attempt a description of them—they have to be seen. Yet I cannot pass from Windsor without mentioning briefly that in His Majesty we have found the greatest, kindest and most humane monarch and true connoisseur of music; it is impossible to describe the kind-heartedness with which he deigned to speak to us, and I can assure you sincerely that our entire profit in England is but a trifle to me when compared with this highest favour and distinction, and that my son and I are now quite overjoyed. We had intended to return to Paris tomorrow, but could not refuse an invitation to Manchester, made some time ago. And so we shall be travelling there tomorrow, where Franzi will play at the Theatre‡ on the 2nd and 4th of August, for which we are being paid £100. When we get back from that city

* George IV (1762–1830). Speaking to the Revd Haweis more than fifty years later, Liszt remarked: 'I was very young at the time, but I remember the King very well—a fine pompous-looking gentleman.'

† Ambassador to the Court of St James from 1815 to 1842, Prince Paul Esterházy (1786–1866) was the son of Prince Nicholas, Adam Liszt's former employer.

‡ At the first of the concerts at Manchester's Theatre Royal, Liszt played a Hummel

we are going straight to Paris, where we shall be staying until next year (mid-March, in fact); then we shall be coming to London again, where we have prepared a splendid future for ourselves.

I must tell you a little about the London musicians. The expectations I had formed before knowing them personally were by no means fulfilled, and I found them to some extent like good speakers who preach morality to others. In two words: envy and jealousy! We are looking forward to being back in Paris, just as we are to coming here again next year. For the moment there is nothing to be done in London because everyone is in the country. . . .

People have been badgering me mercilessly to allow my son to give lessons; they wanted to pay me more than all the others, but I declined firmly, saying on each occasion that my son was himself in need of instruction.

A guinea a lesson is the standard fee, and even though the greatest masters have been here, only rarely does one find immaculately trained pupils such as can be found quite often in Paris, and I can assure you that piano-playing here is still almost in its infancy, although the nation, especially the women, are extremely fond of music, and in every home instruments and pieces of music can be found to excess. Incidentally, in London one encounters what can be seen nowhere else: wealth, order, cleanliness, books, paintings, etc. in every home.

A trip on the Thames surpasses everything. One can see from it what an abundance of water England possesses. Whether one sees a village, or a small or large town, everywhere there is wealth, cleanliness, and order. Whoever has not seen England, has not seen the world's greatest treasure. The people are most agreeable, and the countryside is like a real paradise. . . .

Young Aspull,* of whom I had already read extraordinary things in the Paris papers, gave his second concert here of the season. . . . In his playing I found nothing of what I had read about, and even the applause was no more than moderate. Later he paid us a visit and played some little variations to us, from which I concluded that the lad has much talent but is not having the right teaching, and that if he continues with it he will achieve nothing outstanding. I feel very sorry for him, as he is a nice boy and most well behaved, although rather shy. Franz is playing and scribbling

concerto and Moscheles' *Fall of Paris* for piano and orchestra; at the second, Czerny's Theme and Variations for piano and orchestra and an improvisation. The Liszts journeyed to Manchester on 30 July (taking the coach from the White Horse, Fetter Lane), and stayed with the violinist Andrew Ward.

* George Aspull (1813–32), a child prodigy pianist from Manchester who achieved considerable fame, and by Rossini was pronounced one of the most remarkable persons in Europe. He is credited with having given the first British performance of Weber's *Concertstück*.

away diligently. His present playing would be likely to win your approval; he plays cleanly and expressively and his technique is very advanced. I still get him to practise scales and exercises with the metronome, and I adhere to your principles because success shows me that they are the best. His improvising is now on a very high level; indeed, for his age an admirable one. So far as composing is concerned, he has already finished two Rondos di bravura, which people are wanting to buy but which are not yet enough, one Rondo, one Fantasia, Variations on various themes, and one Amusement, or rather Quodlibet, on different themes by Rossini and Spontini, which earned great applause when he played it at His Majesty's. His main work, however, is a French opera: *Don Sanche ou le Château d'Amour*, the libretto of which was written expressly for him.* Apart from the recitatives, he has composed the whole thing here; and because he has sung excerpts from it at several gatherings, it became known to His Majesty too, who invited him to perform something from it, and it received the greatest applause. When it is quite finished I shall be very curious to see what happens. One thing is certain: the opera is to be given at Paris's great Opera House.[10]

To the same. Paris, 3 September. We have been in Paris again these last four weeks, and, as I wrote to you from London, are thinking of staying here until March next year; and, apart from our visit to London in the spring, of not leaving Paris so soon. For music, there is only *one* Paris in the whole world. The French have often been accused of frivolity and instability, but I must affirm the contrary and say that I have never found so great and permanent a liking for what is good as in Paris. The operas of Gluck, for example, are often given here, and the theatre is always packed full and the utmost enthusiasm shown. With what respect the holy names of Mozart, Haydn, Gluck, and the rest are spoken—in short, I can tell you that the French are great and thorough connoisseurs and practitioners of music, and generous in their remuneration of artists. This I can tell you from experience; whoever speaks otherwise either does not know them or has brought bad goods to market, which people don't buy here.

Little Putzi (who, however, is almost as tall as you) is very industrious, and I can assure you that you would be entirely satisfied with how well and nicely he plays sonatas by Dussek, Steibelt, or Beethoven. We often have visits from the highest aristocracy, who get him to play them a Beethoven sonata. We could have something of the sort every day did his education not count for more with me. His imagination is inexhaustible and beyond my comprehension. Of the accuracy of his memory, let me give you an example. When we were in London he played scores for an hour almost every day, mostly operas by Gluck. Now a few days ago we were invited to a soirée at a certain minister's, where the conversation was about Gluck's

* By Théaulon and de Rancé, after a tale by the novelist and fabulist Jean-Pierre Claris de Florian (1755–94).

operas. To everyone's amazement, the lad said he knew them all by heart. The company being very numerous, many people became curious on hearing this and at once several pushed their way to him, one person naming this chorus, another that, one lady this aria etc.—and just imagine, he sang everything exactly as it should be; but what created the most astonishment was that he brought in and named the instruments to which the different parts were allotted.

You will certainly be delighted with his opera, at which he is working hard, and I hope it will be the crowning point of our trip. I must tell you a story in connection with it. When the libretto went to the committee, they asked who would be setting it to music, and, half laughingly, the librettist said: young Liszt. 'What!' replied Cherubini, 'do you think that writing an opera is as easy as playing a piece on the piano! Permission refused.' Some of the others shared his opinion, Paër alone saying it should be given a try. This occurred while we were in London, and when we got back here we naturally knew nothing about it. We went to the Director of the Opéra to tell him that the opera was finished and that he should now begin to set it in score. You will readily understand what a grievous blow this was for us; my lad, who was in imagination already conducting his opera, felt very dejected, but I remained indifferent, playing the philosopher. That same day I sought an opportunity for my boy to have a few pieces played before the Minister of the Royal Opera House. I achieved my goal, and for the moment we are pleased because we have the assurance of his high protection; there will probably yet be a few tricks of one sort or another, but this can only contribute to greater glory. . . .

The perfection of the Erard piano has reached the point that it is a century ahead of its time and impossible to describe—one has to see and hear it for oneself, and play it oneself too.[11]

1825

Quarterly Musical Magazine and Review (vol. xxvii, London, 1825). Whatever vanity the French may betray by styling Paris the Capital of the World and of the Fine Arts, it was at least on the present occasion the Capital of Musicians. Scarcely any distinguished German pianist was at this epoch absent from the French metropolis. There were often seen in the same salon Hummel, Moscheles, Kalkbrenner, Pixis,* Schunke, Felix Mendelssohn Bartholdy,† and little Liszt, without mentioning the brothers Herz . . . and a great number of French and foreign pianists who wanted

* The German pianist and composer J. P. Pixis (1788–1874).

† Mendelssohn was in Paris in March. 'He plays very well; he has many fingers but few brains, and his improvisations are absolutely wretched,' was the 16-year-old's opinion of the 13-year-old Liszt.

little, in respect to facility of execution, to make them rank with these great masters. . . .

When young Liszt came to Paris, about a year and a half ago, he excited unusual notice, and we might even say much enthusiasm. Many were at that time so dazzled by the effects of his premature talents, that they have not even yet properly recovered their sight. The public, in general, however, although they cannot but admire the talents of a lad of 13 or 14 years of age, agree that in his soi-distant extemporaneous performances there is much confusion of ideas, and a continual introduction of passages the intention of which cannot be understood.

In the spring Adam and Franz returned to England. There were again public and private performances in London, another visit to Windsor to play before George IV, and further appearances at Manchester.* One of the London soirées at which Liszt played was at Apsley House, home of the Duke of Wellington, where a fellow artist that same evening was Giovanni Battista Velluti (1781–1861), last of the operatic castrati.†

Adam Liszt to Carl Czerny. Paris, 14 August. Hummel has been in Paris, lodging with Erard the piano manufacturer, his board and all necessities provided—everything gratis, of course. He may have rated himself higher than was the reality, and to begin with overreached himself on the self-interested side, because he knew neither himself nor the French. For a soirée he asked 30 louis d'or—but unfortunately no one wanted to bite. In the end he would have been satisfied with 10, even 5, but there were no takers. To my knowledge he played only once at an evening party, for 10 louis d'or, and for this he had M. Paër to thank. Nor did the four soirées he gave at Erard's come up to his financial expectations. He finished with a concert in the hall of the Conservatoire, which I did not attend as we were already in London; but I have spoken about it with several people, even though my high regard for Hummel keeps me from revealing the outcome. . . . Those who attended his soirées found his improvising dry, and two of the leading connoisseurs told me that Hummel is something between an elegant piano-player and an organist, having something of both but from neither the whole thing. We had expected more.

Mlle Belleville‡ was also here this winter and did very bad business like all the rest, as she deserved—for I can assure you that she more smudges the piano than plays it, and seeks her bravura in nonsensical runs and

* On 16 and 20 June, again at the Theatre Royal. The concert posters proclaimed that 'Master Liszt . . . is allowed by all those who have witnessed his astonishing Talents to be the greatest Performer of the present day on the PIANO FORTE'. At the second concert, a 'Grand Overture' by Liszt was played, that to his opera *Don Sanche*.

† When in later years Liszt recalled this occasion, he placed it in 1824—but Velluti's London début was in 1825.

‡ Anna Caroline Belleville (1808–80), who later married the violinist A. J. Oury, was, like Liszt, a pupil of Czerny.

leaps. We gave our own concert at the Theatre, which is always available for us, and a second at Erard's, where Hummel gave his soirées. But Hummel did not attend; probably so as not to have to see for himself that someone else can have a larger audience than he. But that did not bother me, and at his next soirée I placed my boy at his side to turn the pages for him.

And so we went to England for the second time, and although the leading families were absent because of the coronation* at Reims, we were just as content as last year, despite the fact that the great majority of artists were working against us. When I finally get back to Vienna we shall need several days to discuss it all, and so for the moment I shall dispense with further details; yet I must tell you about one soirée in London, which took place at a very distinguished house where the leading artists were present, including Mr Nicholson† the flautist (the English Drouet), who had brought a Fantasy and Variations of his own composition, with solo passages on the piano. But the piano was unfortunately pitched a semitone lower than the flute, the reason being that Velluti had sung in this company, and on account of his voice he always has the instrument tuned a semitone lower. Mr Potter,‡ who was accompanying the singers at the piano, said to Nicholson: 'Your flute is too high.'—'Then you'll have to transpose the piece,' said the latter, 'as I cannot lower my flute.'—'What? The piece is in C. Do you expect me to transpose it into C sharp? I daren't try it.' The gentlemen argued for a long time, in the end drawing everyone's attention to them, because the interval had already lasted too long—but the refrain was always: 'I daren't risk it.' My boy was standing nearby and could hear these indications of weakness. Mr Potter finally said to Franzi: 'Can you transpose a little?'—'Yes, a little,' rejoined Franzi, 'and I believe that to transpose this will be no great hazard.'—'Good, do try it, because I don't want to risk it in front of such a large audience,' said Mr Potter. Franz hastened to the piano and transposed the piece better than if he had composed it himself. Allow me to tell you what astonishment and enthusiasm this trifle—which is all it was for Franzi—aroused among the artists present as well as the distinguished audience. . . .

Leaving England we went to Boulogne sur Mer, where we bathed in the sea every day and washed away our English exertions. We enjoyed ourselves very much, took early and late strolls along the beach, collected shells, admired the incoming and outgoing ships and the evening fishing from a fine coffee house built near the shore, where many distinguished persons who are here for the sea bathing could always be met; and where in the salon, which had a piano, we always entertained ourselves very well.

* Of Charles X, at Reims Cathedral on 29 May.

† Charles Nicholson (1795–1837).

‡ Cipriani Potter (1792–1871) was at this time a professor of piano at the Royal Academy of Music, of which he became in later years the Principal.

Many people having asked us, we gave a soirée, which met all the expenses of our stay and left a profit of 600 francs.

Arriving in Paris, we wished to stay incognito for a fortnight, to sort ourselves out and to visit our good friends gradually; but our plan was thwarted no later than the fifth day, when we received a letter from the Ministry of Arts saying that within a week we were to arrange for Franzi's opera to be heard by the committee. Just imagine the embarrassment we were in. Nothing was copied out, not a single singer prepared, and so I asked for a postponement of two weeks; but this was not granted, although they allowed a few days. The committee or tribunal (consisting of Cherubini, Berton, Boïeldieu, Lesueur, Catel) sat, and the opera was listened to and accepted with the greatest attestations of approval.

My dear friend, now I regret that you are not a father; it would give me scope to say something about the happy feelings of parents, when all sorrows are forgotten. So the opera is accepted, and, judging by the eagerness the Theatre administration is showing, will be put on during early October at the latest. Curiosity is at fever pitch, and envy running at its highest; the latter has failed in all its endeavours so far, and I hope its wings will later be clipped.

Franz has written two fine concertos, which he will play at Vienna. Do you know that we count on being there by next March? In November we plan to go to the Netherlands, Berlin, and Leipzig, and thence to Vienna; and in the autumn to see our beloved Paris again. Once more I say: there is only one Paris for art, and we should find it difficult to visit Vienna if urgent matters did not call me there.

Franzi has grown so much that he is almost as tall as I am, which astonishes everyone. His sole passion is to compose; it is this alone which gives him joy and delight. A sonata for piano duet, a trio and a quintet should please you greatly. His concertos are too rigorous, and the difficulties for the player immense. I always regarded Hummel's concertos as difficult, but they are very easy in comparison. You will be pleased with his left hand. He still gives two hours a day to practice and an hour to reading; all the rest of his time when we are at home is devoted to composition. We frequently go to the theatre; or, rather, we allow hardly a day to go by without doing so, because we have free passes to several theatres, the leading ones in fact.

Spontini is in Paris, staying with his father-in-law, Monsieur Erard; we often dine together, and if we had more time would do so daily. Whether Spontini will give a new work here, I do not know, but it is presumed he will. He has offered to be useful to Franzi in any way he can, and was absolutely astounded when, without knowing him, he heard him improvising. In this, Franzi has progressed very far, and I greatly look forward to hearing your opinion when we come to Vienna.[12]

At the Paris Opéra (or Académie Royale de Musique, as it was then called) on Monday, 17 October, five days before Liszt's fourteenth birthday, *Don Sanche ou le Château d'Amour*, the one-act opera which he had largely composed as a twelve-year-old in London the previous year, was given its first performance. The title role was sung by the famous tenor Adolphe Nourrit (1802–39) and the conductor was Rodolphe Kreutzer (1766–1831).* The work achieved a *succès d'estime*, but was taken off after a mere four performances. A brief notice which appeared later (1 February 1826) in the Leipzig *Allgemeine Musikalische Zeitung* maintained that it was Kreutzer who had been responsible for the orchestration of the opera. In his old age, however, Liszt remarked that it was Paër who had rendered this necessary assistance, and 'no one else'.

Sometime in late 1825 Anna Liszt returned to Austria to stay with her sister in Graz.†

1826

Accompanied by his father, Liszt in early 1826 undertook a tour through western and southern France, playing in such towns as Bordeaux (where he was presented with the gold medal of the local Philharmonic Society), Toulouse, Montpellier, Nîmes, and Marseilles. It is about his visit to the last-named city that the greatest wealth of details is available. Arriving there in the third week of March, he gave his first concert on 6 April and a second on the 11th.

Journal de la Méditerranée (15 April). All the panegyrics in the world would not suffice to give a notion of his splendid talent; to analyse it one would have to define perfection. . . . The moment preceding his improvisation offered one of the most interesting spectacles imaginable. Music-lovers of all kinds, professors growing white with age and talent, were grouped about him, awaiting impatiently the moment when they could give free vent to their enthusiasm. . . . Surrounded by these most distinguished connoisseurs, Liszt began to improvise on some quite ordinary theme. It was then, when he was entirely given up to his imagination, that the obstacles and difficulties wholly disappeared, to make way for the sublime inspirations of his genius: at one moment could be heard the noise of the storm, above which a graceful melody arose; at another, exquisitely tasteful and skilful modulations in the harmony; and sometimes several themes, despite each being in a different time and of a contrasting character, were made to come together as one, as well as a crowd of innovations of which no idea can be formed except by those who have heard and enjoyed them.[13]

* The dedicatee of Beethoven's Sonata for Violin and Piano Op. 47.

† And not, as stated by many of Liszt's biographers, at the time of his and Adam's visit to London in 1824. See Maria Eckhardt's 'Liszt's Formative Years', *The New Hungarian Quarterly*, ciii (Autumn 1986), 93–107.

At his third concert, on 19 April, Liszt played Hummel's Concerto in A minor and Moscheles' Grand Variations. The Overture to *Don Sanche* was also performed, and a number of arias from the opera sung by local artists.

So well were the concerts received, that he was at once engaged for three more, at the Grand Théâtre on the 21st, 23rd, and 26th of the month. After these had been undertaken with similar success, he departed for Lyons.

To that city, to a Madame Jenny Montgolfier whose acquaintance Liszt wished to make (and who, indeed, became a good friend of his), there wrote from Marseilles a music-lover—a lawyer by profession—named *Joseph Lecourt.*

You have read about young Liszt in the newspapers; perhaps Hummel mentioned him to you. But whatever the notion that you have formed of him, it will be far from the reality. In my opinion it is impossible to achieve playing that is more beautiful or more flawless. I am not enthusiastic about performers, and am prejudiced against big reputations; the first time I heard Liszt I was not satisfied with him. On an ordinary piano in a small salon cluttered with furniture he was playing a polonaise by Czerny. . . . Then it was announced that he was going to improvise and desired a theme. I gave him the Andante in A minor from the Seventh Symphony of Beethoven—but he turned it down and gave us some mediocre variations on Rode's Air in G. You can imagine how vexed I was. Quite beside myself, I cornered him in the salon and voiced my grievance. Quickly seizing my hand, he showed me Beethoven's theme, which he called *airy* and celestial, and said: 'Can one play things like that in front of donkeys! Didn't you see how they applauded the polonaise?' I insisted on the Beethoven theme, and he gave me his promise. But when his first concert came he improvised on some very ordinary melodies and admitted to me afterwards that he had been afraid to tackle the Beethoven.

One has to force the hands of these people, but to do so by warming their heads. At his second concert I got the orchestra to play the Andante. The child was overwhelmed, his chest heaved, his eyes betrayed his admiration—and he rushed to the piano and rendered to Beethoven a homage worthy of him.

It has all been explained to me. He flatters himself that he can play all music as well as anyone. It is only Beethoven's music in which he is never satisfied with himself. He always feels that he is not up to this composer. Nevertheless, he played me several of his works in a superior way. . . .

He is lively and witty, and even makes puns. The day before yesterday he played some variations by Herz . . . and made great fun of those who applauded. 'Oh, how beautiful it is, but difficult too. *Il y a des sauts, des sauts,*' someone remarked. 'Say, rather, *des sottises,*'* replied the child.

You are bound to find it interesting to know Liszt after Hummel. Your opinion of him I shall receive with the greatest gratitude. His very faults please me, because they are inseparable from his youth. I firmly believe

* A pun on *sauts* (skips, leaps) and *sottises* (follies, stupidities).

that he will correct them, and that he will go far. His enthusiasm for Beethoven is a sure guarantee of that.[14]

Held at the Salle de la Bourse in the Palais de Saint-Pierre on 23 and 31 May, and on 13 June, Liszt's three Lyons concerts were enormously successful, particularly the improvisations with which he concluded each appearance. The *Journal du Commerce* (26 May) found that he 'created an impression difficult to describe', and the *Indépendant* (26 May) that he had 'excited a universal enthusiasm'.

It is probable that not long after his arrival in Lyons Liszt also took part in a concert in aid of victims of the Greek War of Independence. Held on 5 May, it was attended by Chateaubriand, whose writings — especially *René* — were later to have a profound effect upon the young musician.

At a soirée in Paris later in the year, Liszt was heard by the *Comte de Montbel* (1787–1861), who not long afterwards heard the nine-year-old violinist Léon Kreutzer (1817–68) give 'a wonderful performance of one of his father's concertos'.

But, so far as this sort of thing is concerned, how could one be astonished after having seen young Liszt a few days earlier? This boy came one evening to M. de Castelbajac's, where we heard from him, on themes provided by the ladies of the house and myself, some admirable improvisations played with a verve and passion well-nigh unbelievable. It gave me extreme pleasure; but my delight in it was disturbed by some ponderous members of the two Chambers, who, shocked that a piano should deprive our circle of the charm of their parliamentary eloquence, continued their talk without restraint. One of them, when reproached, declared himself quite uninterested in child prodigies; and in a loud voice he went on with his tedious monologue on the customs and excise.[15]

Harriet, Countess Gower. * *Paris, November.* No other spectacle is equal to the French Opéra in brilliance. The evening before was Mde. Apponyi's party; not so good as the first. An extraordinary boy of the name of Lizt [*sic*] played on the piano forte with the greatest execution and expression, but the *élégantes* hardly concealed suppressed yawns and whispers.[16]

It was the memory of experiences such as these which a decade later wrung a bitter *cri de cœur* from Liszt.

My father's presentiments tore me away from the plains of Hungary . . . and cast me into the midst of a glittering society which applauded the *tours de force* of him whom it honoured with the glorious and yet stigmatizing name of *petit prodige*. A premature melancholy took possession of me from that time forward, and I submitted with instinctive repugnance to the ill-disguised humiliation of artistic dependency. Later, when death had robbed me of my father, and, having returned alone to Paris, I had begun

* Subsequently the Duchess of Sutherland (1806–68), at whose London mansion, Stafford House, Liszt was to play in 1841.

to have an inkling of what art *might* be, and of what the artist *must* be, I felt all but overwhelmed by the impossibilities which seemed to loom up everywhere along the path on which my thoughts were running. Further, receiving no word of sympathy, not only from society people, but even from artists, who were slumbering in a convenient indifferentism . . . I succumbed to a feeling of disgust for art, which I found thus degraded to being a more or less profitable trade, a mere amusement for the well-bred; and I would sooner have been anything in the world than a musician in the pay of the aristocracy, patronized and remunerated by them like a juggler, or like Munito the performing dog. Peace to his memory.[17]

It seems to have been towards the end of 1826 that Liszt began studies with the Bohemian composer and teacher Anton Reicha (1770–1836). A friend of Beethoven's, Reicha had settled in Paris in 1808, and ten years later become a professor of counterpoint and fugue at the Conservatoire, where his pupils in after years included Hector Berlioz and César Franck. 'My studies in counterpoint and fugue with Reicha . . . took up all my time during '27 and '28,' wrote Liszt in 1842.* The Berlin critic Ludwig Rellstab revealed in his study of Liszt, however, that the latter had 'frankly admitted that he had studied counterpoint with Reicha as far as the last and most complex exercises, but had later lost the resultant expertise therein'.

1827

Little information has come to light about the Swiss tour with which Liszt began the year. Geneva (in late January), Lausanne, and Lucerne were visited, however, as were, probably, Bern and Basle. He also played in the French city of Dijon.

The spring brought father and son to London for the third time. Leaving Paris on Thursday, 5 April, they reached London on the 8th.† Liszt's first public appearance, however, was not until 21 May, when at the seventh Philharmonic Society concert of the season, held at the Argyll Rooms, he played Hummel's Concerto in B minor.‡ Moscheles' opinion was that he performed 'with rare skill, but too restlessly'.

Quarterly Musical Magazine and Review (vol. xxxiii, London, 1827). Liszt, it seems to be universally acknowledged, has more than realized the anticipations that his early progress gave, and in the last two years has made such prodigious advances as to outgo all expectation. Nothing that

* In his copy (now held at the Library of Congress in Washington) of J. W. Christern's *Franz Liszt nach seinem Leben und Wirken* (Hamburg and Leipzig, 1841).

† The dates are given in the diary Liszt kept this year. See *Franz Liszt: Tagebuch 1827*, ed. D. Altenburg and R. Kleinertz (Vienna, 1986).

‡ The conductor was Henry Bishop (1786–1855), the composer of *Home, Sweet Home*.

has been done during the season excited more applause than his playing.

His contribution to a concert given on 25 May by the violinist Nicolas Mori (1796–1839), was a performance of Hummel's A minor Concerto. To the rehearsal came the pianist *Charles Salaman* (1814–1901).

His playing of Hummel's concerto created a profound sensation,* and my enthusiastic admiration made me eager to know the wonderful young pianist, my senior by a couple of years. Very shortly afterwards—just before Liszt's morning concert, for which my father had purchased tickets from his father—we became acquainted. I visited him and his father at their lodgings in Frith Street, Soho, and young Liszt came to early family dinner at my home. He was a very charmingly natural and unaffected boy, and I have never forgotten his joyful exclamation, 'Oh, gooseberry pie!' when his favourite dish was put upon the table. We had a good deal of music together on that memorable afternoon, reading several duets. Liszt played some of his recently published Etudes,† a copy of which he gave me, and in which he wrote specially for me an amended version of the sixth study, *Molto agitato.*[18]

The morning concert referred to by Salaman was held at the Argyll Rooms on Saturday, 9 June. Its most interesting item is likely to have been a Concerto in A minor—now lost, but probably an early version of the so-called *Malédiction* (S121) for piano and string orchestra—of Liszt's own. He also joined three other pianists in an eight-hand arrangement, by Moscheles, of the overture to Cherubini's *Les Deux Journées;* took part in a quartet, by Moscheles and Mayseder, for voice, harp, piano, and violin; ended the first half of the programme with an improvisation, and the entire concert with his own Brilliant Variations (now lost) on *Rule, Britannia*.

In the audience was Moscheles himself, who noted in his diary: 'The Concerto in A minor contains *chaotic* beauties; as to his playing, it surpasses in power and mastery of difficulties everything I have ever heard.'

Returning to France in mid-August, the Liszts stopped at Boulogne once again, to take sea baths and relax after the strenuous weeks in London. Here, however, Adam Liszt went down with typhoid fever. His condition rapidly worsened, and in the morning of the 28th he died.‡ The next day he was buried in the town's eastern cemetery. (During the First World War his remains were disinterred and reburied in a mass grave.)

Writing to his mother many years later (12 September 1862), Liszt paid tribute

* Salaman also reports the presence at the rehearsal of the 75-year-old Clementi. 'The venerable appearance and benevolent expression of the bald-headed veteran, and the deference shown to him by all in that select assembly, attracted my attention, alert with boyish enthusiasm. . . . Keenly did I watch the aged Clementi's face as, with intense interest, and his brilliant dark eyes glistening, he followed [Liszt's] marvellous performance.'

† The twelve Etudes (S136) which Liszt had composed the previous year and dedicated to Lidie Garella, a young woman with whom he had played duets in Marseilles.

‡ To Marie d'Agoult some years later Liszt wrote: 'Did I tell you about the death of my poor father? Crows came and beat their wings against our windows a few days earlier. . . .'

to the father to whose single-minded determination and strength of purpose he owed his entire career. 'I was moved to tears by your affectionate remembrance of my father. . . . His presentiment, that his son was to leave the track beaten by others of his social class and face the hazards of an uncommon destiny, quickly became a real conviction, I could almost say an *article of faith*, with him. . . . He hesitated not for a moment, nor did he yield to all the rational arguments of rational people. He had to sacrifice his secure position, give up comfortable habits, leave his own country, ask his wife to share a doubtful future, meet the costs of our modest standard of living by giving Latin, geography, history, and music lessons; had, in a word, to quit the service of Prince Esterházy, leave Raiding and settle in Vienna, so that I could take lessons from our good, excellent Czerny and thereafter face the risk of a very problematic career. And all this with savings of no more than a few hundred francs! Certainly, dearest Mother, you are entirely right when you say that not one father in a thousand would have been capable of such devotion, or of such persistence in that kind of *intuitive stubbornness* possessed only by persons of exceptional character.'

A few days before his father's death, Liszt had written to warn his mother of the serious nature of the illness and to ask her to return to Paris. She at once did so, and they set up home together, first at 38 rue Coquenard, and later at 7 rue Montholon, near the church of St Vincent de Paul, where Liszt attended mass, prayed, and confessed. To support himself and his mother, and weary of life as a performer with its successes but also its humiliations, he began to give lessons. Among his pupils at this time were Catherine Glynne, later the wife of W. E. Gladstone, and the daughters of the British Ambassador, Lord Granville; he also taught at Madame Alix's school for young ladies in the rue de Clichy.

The sole surviving work of his to date from this year is the attractive and original Scherzo in G minor (S153) for piano solo, composed in London on 27 May.

Equally interesting in its different way is the diary (or, as it might more properly be called, commonplace-book) he kept between April and July. A compilation of quotations from his reading, ranging chronologically from Bias of Priene (*fl. c.*570BC) to the contemporary mystic Prince Alexander von Hohenlohe (1794–1849), and including such writers as St Paul, Tertullian, St Augustine, La Rochefoucauld, Bossuet, and Fénelon, the little book is, as these names imply, filled with religious, moral, and behavioural precepts. Maxims and exhortations such as the following hint at the spiritual crisis the fifteen-year-old was undergoing, and also make it clear that when he later wrote of the 'premature melancholy' to which he succumbed at this time, he was not guilty of overstatement.

> Why do you seek rest, since it was for work that you were born? Dispose yourself to patience rather than to comfort, and to the carrying of the cross rather than to merry-making.
>
> (*The Imitation of Christ*)

> Defects of the soul are like wounds of the body: whatever care may be taken to heal them, they always leave a scar, and they are at any moment in danger of reopening.
>
> (La Rochefoucauld)

The man who by his own exertions became the greatest of all pianists; one of the greatest and most prolific composers of his century; a teacher (who has been compared with Christ and Socrates) of many hundreds of pupils; a writer and correspondent of vast industry; one of the greatest travellers of his time; and an autodidact who rose above his rudimentary schooling to make himself, in the words of his pupil and biographer August Göllerich, 'the most *universally* educated musician who has ever lived'—the man of such achievements evidently chose early in life not to pass his days in idleness, an inference which is reinforced by some of the other quotations copied into his diary in this year of 1827:

> Those who use time badly are the first to complain of its brevity; those who use it well have some to spare.
>
> (La Bruyère)

> At the hour of our death, what would we wish to have done? Let us do now what we would like to have done then. There is no time to lose; any moment may be our last. The more we have lived, the nearer we are to the grave. . . .
>
> (Bouhours)

1828

With one of his pupils, Caroline de Saint-Cricq (1812–72), Liszt formed a friendship which soon ripened into love. But after the death, on 30 June 1828, of Caroline's mother, who had looked favourably upon the attachment of the two young people, her father, the Comte de Saint-Cricq (a minister in the government of Charles X), being apprised of the situation and having loftier aspirations for his daughter than marriage with a musician, terminated the lessons and made it plain to the young artist that he was to return no more. At her father's behest, Caroline became the wife of Bertrand d'Artigaux, owner of an estate at Pau; and there, unhappily married, she lived until the end of her life.

Liszt and Caroline met for the next and last time during his tour of southern France in 1844. In later life her chief preoccupation was the nursing of an incurably sick daughter; and this, together with her loveless marriage, caused her to bear 'death in the soul', as she described it. In the 1850s her plans to visit Liszt at Weimar, and to meet him in Paris, came to nought; and in an effort to provide some distraction through music, he sent copies of Mozart piano concertos and of music and writings of his own to her. 'If the divine mercy would allow me to be able to press your hand, my heart would open again for a few days,' she wrote to him in July 1853. 'I love you with all the power of my soul, and wish for you the happiness that I myself no longer know. I thirst for news of you, for which, however, I dare not ask. Allow me ever to see in you the single shining star of my life. . . .' Princess Marie Wittgenstein, who met Caroline when both were visiting Paris in the early 1850s, later penned a description* of Liszt's youthful love: 'She had at that time a slim, aristocratic figure, delicate, discreet features, dark eyes, and black hair parted unpretentiously. Her simple dress betrayed its

* La Mara, *Liszt und die Frauen* (Leipzig, 1911), 6.

provincial origin. Her manner was not characterized by charm, but rather by the stiffness of restrained passion and deeply-felt misfortune.'

In his will, written in 1860, Liszt bequeathed Caroline d'Artigaux a ring; and when, twelve years later, her melancholy existence came to an end, wrote of her with profound emotion as 'one of the purest earthly manifestations of God's blessing'.

The shock and humiliation of the enforced separation seem to have brought the young Liszt close to collapse. Withdrawing into himself, he went out very little and for a long time made no public appearances.*

That autumn, rumours went around of his death, and on 23 October *Le Corsaire* actually published an obituary.

Death of Young Liszt

Young Liszt has died in Paris. He had captured public attention with his successes at an age in which many children have not yet thought of school; and at nine he was improvising on the piano in such a manner as to astonish masters; that is to say, when other children can barely stammer their own language. He was popularly known at that time as 'le petit Liszt', and thus there was associated with his name something of that graceful childhood from which he never departed. After he had improvised at the Opéra for the first time, he was made to go the round of the boxes and galleries, and was caressed by ladies who, in their naïve admiration, suited to the age of the young virtuoso, could think of no better reward than kisses and burnt almonds, offering sweets with one hand and stroking his silky fair hair with the other.

With this extraordinary child one more name is added to the list of precocious children whose appearance on earth has been all too fleeting; they are like hothouse plants which bear some delicious fruit and then die from the expenditure of effort. Mozart who, like Liszt, astonished by his precocity, died at 31,† but bought a few years of life only by much suffering and sorrow, so that an earlier death would perhaps have been a blessing for him.

When we consider all the misfortunes which fasten on to talent, all the monsters which grow around genius and obstinately pursue and accompany it to the very end; when we think that every success arouses envy, stirs up intrigue and brings a blush to the cheek of mediocrity, perhaps we shall find that this young flower was fortunate to fall before having to endure all the storms which might later have burst upon it. Young Liszt had only admirers; his age was a shield which turned aside all sorrows. 'He is a child,' people remarked at each of his successes, and envy was patient. But had he grown to manhood, had the divine spark which inspired him been

* Geraldine Keeling's 'Liszt's Appearances in Parisian Concerts 1824–1844', Part 1: '1824–1833', *The Liszt Society Journal Centenary Issue* (1986), shows that Liszt took part in no concerts between 30 Apr. 1828 and 22 Mar. 1829.

† At his death in Dec. 1791, Mozart was nearly 36.

allowed to develop, people would then have looked at him with an eye more critical, would have denied his merits, and—who knows?—might perhaps have gone so far as to censure his life. He would have known the caprices of power, the injustices of might, and would have been bruised by the brutal impact of base and hateful passions; whereas now, wrapped in his winding-sheet, he has returned to the sleep of childhood, and, perhaps, has fallen asleep with the desire to dream again the dream of yesterday.

His father, who went before him a year ago, is spared this grief— but not his family, whose name he had begun to render illustrious. We, too, for whom he would doubtless have caused a new spring of musical joy and emotion to flow, count ourselves among the mourners. And thus it is that we express our regret at his demise and join with his family in lamenting his early loss.

In November, *Wilhelm von Lenz* (1809–83), a Russian music-lover and amateur pianist, called to see Liszt.

He was at home. That was something very rare, I was told by his mother, an excellent woman with a German heart whom I liked greatly. *Her* Franz was almost always at church, she said, and *no longer concerned himself with music!* . . .

I found him to be a slim, pale-looking young man with infinitely attractive features. Smoking a long Turkish pipe, and sunk in meditation, he was lying on a broad sofa placed in the midst of three pianos that were standing about. When I entered, he made not the slightest movement; indeed, seemed not to notice me at all. When I explained to him in French (he could at that time be addressed in no other language): 'My family suggested I apply to Kalkbrenner, but I have come to you because you chose to play a Beethoven piano concerto in public,'* he seemed to smile —but it was only the flash of a dagger in the sunlight.

'Play me something,' he said, with indescribable sarcasm; which, however, was not in the least offensive, any more than one is offended when it thunders.

'I'll play Kalkbrenner's Sonata for the left hand (*pour la main gauche principale*),' I said, thinking I had said the right thing.

'*That* I will not hear; I do not know it and do not want to know it!' he replied with increasing sarcasm, scarcely bothering to conceal his contempt.

It seemed to me that I was doing rather badly, having perhaps to pay for the sins of others, of Parisians; but the more I looked at the young man, the more I told myself that *this* Parisian—for so he seemed from his whole appearance—could only be a genius, and without further ado, without

* Lenz had seen a handbill announcing a performance by Liszt of Beethoven's Fifth Piano Concerto. Due to take place on 25 Dec., it was later cancelled (probably because Liszt succumbed to measles at about this time).

attempting a rejoinder, for I did not relish being bested by a Parisian, I strode modestly but firmly to the nearest piano.

'Not that one!' cried Liszt, without in the least changing his semi-recumbent posture on the sofa; 'the other one, over there!'

I approached the second piano.

The music which was wholly absorbing me at that time was the *Invitation to the Dance*. I had embarked upon a love match with it two years previously, and we were still in the honeymoon period. I came from Riga, where, after the matchless success enjoyed by *Der Freischütz*, we had turned to Weber's works for the pianoforte, which would not be known for a long time in Paris, where *Der Freischütz* was known as 'Robin (!) des Bois'. . . .

I had studied with good teachers. When I tried to play the three opening A flats in the *Invitation*, the instrument gave forth not a sound. What was happening? I tried again, with greater pressure, and this time the A flats sounded quite *piano*. Feeling utterly ridiculous, but giving nothing away, I valiantly continued as far as the entry of the chords—when Liszt stood up, stepped over to me, abruptly took my right hand away from the instrument and said: 'What is *that?* It begins well!' 'I should think it does,' I replied with the pride of the sexton to his pastor, 'it's by Weber!'

'Did he compose for the piano too?' he asked in astonishment.* 'Here we know only his *Robin des Bois*.'

'He did indeed write for the piano, and more beautifully than anyone,' was my equally astonished reply. 'In my trunk,' I added, 'are two polonaises, two rondos, four books of variations, and four solo sonatas. One of the sonatas I studied in Geneva with Vehrstaedt. It contains the whole of Switzerland and is *unbelievably beautiful*. It is as though the fairest women on earth were all smiling together within its pages. No one else has written anything like it for the piano, believe you me!'

I spoke from the heart, and so convincingly that I made a visible impression on Liszt. In a winning tone of voice he then said: 'Well, please bring me everything you have in your trunk, and I shall give you a lesson . . . because you have introduced me to Weber at the piano and did not allow this instrument with its stiff action to frighten you. I had it made specially, so that when I have played *one* scale on it I have played ten; it is a thoroughly impossible piano. It was a bad joke on my part, but why on earth did you talk of Kalkbrenner and a sonata by him for the left hand? But now play me that thing of yours which begins so curiously. The piano over there, which I stopped you using just now, is one of the finest in Paris.'

Then I put everything that was in me into playing the *Invitation*, but only the cantilena marked *wiegend*, in two parts. Liszt was delighted with the

* Liszt must have forgotten that he had played Weber's *Momento capriccioso* some years earlier.

piece. '*That* is something you must bring me,' he said; 'we'll interpret it to one another!'

And thus it was that the last letter of the musical alphabet came to the first.

At the lesson Liszt could not tear himself away from the piece. Certain parts of it he went through again and again, tried amplifications, played the second part of the theme in the minor in octaves, and was untiring in his praise of Weber. And what, in those days, did the piano repertoire consist of? That smooth master-joiner, Hummel; the Herzes, Kalkbrenners, and Moscheleses; nothing for the piano that was plastic, dramatic, or eloquent. Beethoven was not yet understood; of his thirty-two sonatas only *three* (!) were played: the Sonata in A flat, Op. 26, the C sharp minor, and the F minor, which a publisher's fancy, not Beethoven, had christened *Appassionata*. The five last sonatas, which in our own day have achieved recognition, were regarded as the monstrous freaks of a German ideologue who knew nothing about writing for the piano. Only Hummel and his consorts were understood; Mozart was too old-fashioned, couldn't write passage-work like Herz, Kalkbrenner, and Moscheles, not to mention the smaller fry.

In this realm of the mediocre dwelt Liszt; and that should be taken into account when measuring the greatness of the man who, at the piano, found alike Weber and himself when he was but twenty years of age!*

With Weber's Sonata in A flat he was utterly delighted. It was a work I had studied lovingly with Vehrstaedt, and I rendered it quite in the spirit of the thing. Liszt showed me that by the way in which he listened, by his animated gestures and movements, and by his exclamations at the beauty of the work. We thus brought two minds to the task. As is well known, this great romantic poem for the piano begins with a bass tremolo on A flat. No earlier sonata had ever begun like that! It is like the sun rising over the enchanted forest in which the action is about to take place! So great grew my teacher's restlessness during the first part of the opening Allegro, that before I had reached the end he shoved me aside with the words: '*Wait! wait! what is that? I must try it for myself!*' Then came a unique experience! Imagine a genius like Liszt, twenty years old, facing for the first time Weber's magnificent work, this apparition of that knight in golden armour!

The first part he tried out again and again in the most different ways. At the passage (in the dominant) in E flat at the end of the first movement, he said: 'It is marked *legato*, but perhaps it would be better to make it *pianissimo* and *staccato*? It is also marked *leggermente*.' He experimented in all possible ways.

And in this manner was it given to me to observe how *one* genius looks at and turns to account *another*!

* Liszt was just 17 at this time.

'Now, what is the next part of the Allegro like?' asked Liszt, looking at it. To me it seemed altogether impossible that this thematic development section, several pages bristling with embattled octaves, could be played at sight!

'It is very difficult,' said Liszt, 'but still more difficult the coda, and how to pull the *whole thing* together, here in the centrifugal figure' (13 bars before the end). 'This passage'—in the second section, naturally in the main key of A flat—'we accordingly shan't make *staccato*, which would be too affected, nor yet *legato*, for which it is too thin; we'll make it *spiccato*, and thus swim between the two waters.'

If in the first part of his performance I had admired Liszt's fire, life, and spiritual passion; then his repose and certainty, confident of victory, and the way in which he knew how to hold himself back, reserving his strength for the closing attack, quite astounded me in the second! So young and so wise, I thought, and felt disorientated and discouraged!

In the Andante of the sonata I learnt more from Liszt in the first four bars than I had learnt in years from my earlier good teachers. 'The exposition must be given in the manner that Baillot* plays in a quartet, the accompanying parts being in the contrasted semiquaver passages. But Baillot's parts are very good—yours should be no less so! I can imagine how the piano hussars will tear it apart! I shall never forget that it was through *you* that I became acquainted with this sonata; well, in return you shall learn something from me: I shall tell you everything I know about our instrument.'

The demisemiquaver passage in the bass of the Andante (bar 35) one only too often hears profaned as left-hand passagework; but it should be played lovingly, should be a cello solo, *amoroso*! That was how Liszt played it—but the octave outburst on the second theme in C (which Henselt calls the 'Ten Commandments', an excellent description) with awesome majesty.

How can I convey what Liszt made of the *Menuetto capriccioso* and Rondo of the sonata, at his *first acquaintance* with those wonderful movements? What was there not in his treatment of the clarinet solo in the Trio of the Minuet, the modulation of that cry of longing, the spiralling ornamentation of the Rondo! . . .

Let all pianists come together and attack the E flat major Piano Concerto of Beethoven (to choose this example), and the moment Liszt touches the keys his hearers will know that it is he and no other! Where Liszt appears, all other pianists disappear in his shadow as though in a magic cloak.[19]

* The French composer and violinist Pierre Baillot (1771–1842).

1829–1832

In the years following the ill-fated idyll with Caroline de Saint-Cricq, Liszt continued to live quietly in Paris with his mother, occasionally leaving the city to travel to the provinces or further afield.* He recovered from the illness which had occasioned the premature obituary notice, but found it more difficult to shake off the state of lethargy and despondency into which he had fallen. Nevertheless, he succeeded in doing some composing, and in 1829 wrote his brilliant Fantasy (S385) on the Tyrolienne from Auber's opera *La Fiancée*. A major commitment was teaching, which took up much of his time and compelled a considerable amount of journeying across Paris. 'I am so full of lessons that between 8.30 a.m. and 10.00 p.m. each day I hardly have time to breathe,' he wrote in December 1829 to an acquaintance, the historian Adrien Jarry de Mancy.

He was eventually aroused by the tumult of the 1830 July Revolution and the 'Three Glorious Days' which led to the abdication of Charles X, the establishment of a constitutional monarchy, and the reign of the *roi citoyen*, Louis-Philippe.† Anna Liszt, who found it difficult to restrain her son from participating in the 'struggle for suffering humanity', later maintained that it was 'the cannon which cured him'. His enthusiasm kindled, he sketched and partly worked out a Revolutionary Symphony (S690), the manuscript of which is headed: '27, 28, 29 July—Paris'. The first movement of this piano sketch (which contains two orchestral indications, 'roll of drums' and 'trumpet') was orchestrated twenty years later, at Liszt's request, by his protégé Joachim Raff; and this version, revised by Liszt himself, became the symphonic poem *Héroïde funèbre* (S102).

At about this time he was attracted by the teachings of the Saint-Simonians, a sect which sought to reorganize society according to the theories of Claude Henri, Comte de Saint-Simon (1760–1825), whose writings advocated social equality, the emancipation of women, the abolition of hereditary rights, and the equitable distribution of wealth throughout a new classless society which would be controlled not, as hitherto, by the property-owning, the priesthood, and the military, but by scientists and industrialists. The touchstone of a person's merit would be the work he contributed. ('A chacun selon sa capacité, à chaque capacité selon ses œuvres.')

Liszt attended meetings of the Saint-Simonians for a time (the sect was disbanded in 1832) and sometimes played to them. Although never a member in the strict and formal sense, he was, and remained, profoundly sympathetic to their demands for a juster society.

Among the poets, writers, and thinkers whose company he began to frequent

* We know, for example, that the first five or six months of 1831 he spent in Switzerland. In January 1832 he played at Rouen; and between late August and early October that year enjoyed a 'long and glorious sojourn of five weeks' at Bourges, which he visited for the wedding of a former pupil, the daughter of General Petit.

† The former Duc d'Orléans at whose home the 12-year-old Liszt had played several times soon after his arrival in Paris.

in these years were some of the greatest in Europe: Honoré de Balzac (who dedicated to Liszt his novel *La Duchesse de Langeais*), Sainte-Beuve, Alfred de Musset,* Théophile Gautier, Heinrich Heine (who hastened to Paris from his native Germany after the July Revolution), Alphonse de Lamartine, Alexandre Dumas *père*, Alfred de Vigny, Edgar Quinet, Pierre Ballanche, Prosper Mérimée, and Victor Hugo.† His correspondence shows that he also knew Chateaubriand (and, apparently, Madame Récamier). Acquaintances among the painting fraternity included Eugène Delacroix, Ary Scheffer, and the two Devéria brothers, Achille and Eugène.

Eager to remedy the deficiencies in his education, and doubtless stimulated by the brilliant minds with which he was coming into contact, he continued to read widely and voraciously, particularly French literature‡ and the Greek and Latin classics (in French translation). One indication of his fervent desire for knowledge was his predilection for dictionaries and encyclopaedias of all kinds; and throughout his life he would keep near at hand as many as circumstances allowed.

The success achieved in this autodidactic quest was attested to by many contemporaries. As early as 1832 the cultivated Caroline Boissier was able to describe Liszt as 'a thinker, who while pursuing his musical studies has found the time to read and study enormously'. Not long afterwards George Sand was reproaching him with being *too* intelligent and well read. ('I remember your profound aversion to my philosophical and ontological knowledge,' he wrote to her a few years later.) In 1838 the music-loving Charles Gay (1815–92), who spent some pleasant days with Liszt in Milan, was impressed by 'the most inexhaustible mind that can be imagined'. 'I find it difficult to understand how, without early studies, and having acquired the most admirable talent in a speciality generally very exclusive, he knows all the things he does and is a stranger to none of the ideas which are current in the world.'

The Comtesse d'Agoult retains a justified reputation as one of the most distinguished of French bluestockings; but as Thérèse Marix-Spire has pointed out, an impartial reading of the Liszt–d'Agoult correspondence, and of the latter's memoirs, shows that 'she knew far less than he'.

All his life Liszt worked assiduously at the broadening and deepening of his knowledge; and if acquaintances could speak of him in the foregoing terms when he was in his early and mid-twenties, small wonder that shortly before his death half a century later others were to describe his erudition as 'unbelievable'.

The insatiable hunger with which the young Liszt attacked the works of great contemporaries was described by his friend *Joseph d'Ortigue* (1802–66), critic and musicologist.

* Whose gifted young sister Herminie was a pupil of Liszt's and the dedicatee of his *La pastorella dell'Alpi e Li marinari* (S423).

† The acquaintance of the two last-named Liszt seems to have made at Hugo's on 5 May 1829. Thus the writer Victor Pavie in a letter of the 9th: 'Last Tuesday I dined at Victor's with Mérimée. During the evening the young Listz [*sic*] (a musician) was introduced to him. . . .'

‡ To the historian François Mignet (or, according to some sources, the lawyer Adolphe Crémieux), he is said to have cried impetuously on one occasion: 'Teach me, Monsieur, I beg of you, the whole of French literature!'—a demand which elicited from Mignet the observation: 'There is a great deal of confusion in the head of that young man!'

He would seize and devour them, reading keenly and exposing the very heart of the writer. A dictionary he would read in the same voracious and restless manner as he did a poet, bringing the same investigative and inquiring mind to bear upon Boiste* as upon Lamartine, and reading both for four hours at a time. Then, when he believed he had entered into the author's thought, he would go and ask him for his own explanation of what he had written.[1]

Another acquaintance was the poet *Pierre-Jean de Béranger* (1780–1857), who penned a memorable tribute.

If there be pretension about Franz Liszt, it is a pretension borne out by far more varied gifts and acquirements than any other artist whom I have known could boast. In his conversation on all subjects, and from the venerable metaphysics of the Middle Ages to the last production of M. Scribe, there was nothing he had not touched and tried; there was a luminous spirit which enchanted me, whether it rose to fervent and mystical eloquence on the highest themes, or sparkled in the pleasantries of social life. There are two people of *genius* in the world, Malibran and Liszt.[2]

Naturally Liszt also had many friends and acquaintances among members of his own profession: not only the Herzes, Kalkbrenners, and other fashionable pianists of the day, but also the mystical Chrétien Urhan (1790–1845), once a protégé of the Empress Joséphine and now a solo violinist at the Opéra, a capable organist (at St Vincent de Paul's, where Liszt worshipped), and a masterly performer on the viola and viola d'amore;† Charles Henri Valentin Morhange (1813–88), better remembered as 'Alkan', virtuoso pianist and original composer; and the German pianist *Ferdinand Hiller* (1811–85). In later life one of Liszt's most relentless opponents, the last-named was a close friend during these Paris years; and it was he who noted Mendelssohn's opinion of Liszt's sight-reading prowess.

Quite soon after Mendelssohn's arrival in Paris,‡ Dr Franck and I were waiting for him in his room, when he came in beaming with delight, saying that he had just seen 'a miracle, a real miracle'. When we questioned him, he continued: 'Well, isn't it a miracle? I was at Erard's with Liszt, and put the manuscript of my concerto in front of him, and though it is barely legible he played it off at sight with the utmost perfection. It simply cannot be played more beautifully than he played it—absolutely marvellously!' I was not surprised, for I had long known that Liszt played most new things best the first time, because they then gave him enough to do. The second

* Pierre-Claude Victoire Boiste (1765–1824), author of the *Dictionnaire universel de la langue française*.

† Urhan was the viola soloist at the première of Berlioz's *Harold en Italie*, and it was with him in mind that Meyerbeer wrote the solo for viola d'amore in Act One of *Les Huguenots*.

‡ Mendelssohn was in Paris again from Dec. 1831 until Apr. 1832. The concerto here referred to is his Piano Concerto No. 1 in G minor.

time he always had to *add* something, if the piece were sufficiently to interest him.[3]

Among the other musicians whose acquaintance Liszt made in the late 1820s and early 1830s were: Auber, Adam, Bellini (who came to Paris in 1834 and died there a year later), Meyerbeer, Halévy, and members of the gifted Garcia family, including Pauline (1821–1910, the subsequent Madame Viardot), to whom he gave piano lessons, and her elder brother and sister, Manuel Garcia *fils* and Maria Malibran.

Far more important than any of these, however, were the friendships Liszt formed in the early 1830s with two of the greatest musical geniuses of the century, both of whom were in different ways to influence his musical development.

He and Hector Berlioz met for the first time on 4 December 1830, the eve of a Paris Conservatoire concert at which the *Symphonie fantastique* was given its first performance. 'Liszt came to see me,' recalled Berlioz in his *Memoirs*. 'I spoke to him of Goethe's *Faust*, which he confessed that he had not read, but about which he was soon as enthusiastic as I. We felt an immediate affinity. . . . He came to the concert and excited general attention by the warmth of his applause and his enthusiastic behaviour.' After the concert, 'Liszt literally dragged me off to have dinner at his house and overwhelmed me with the vigour of his enthusiasm.'

Begun so auspiciously, the friendship would last for many years, but was always rather one-sided. Liszt championed Berlioz's works with complete conviction, transcribed many of them for piano solo, at Weimar in the 1850s held a number of 'Berlioz Weeks' to help disseminate the Frenchman's music in Germany, and in 1855 published a long and appreciative essay, *Berlioz and his Harold Symphony*, whose peroration concludes: 'Everywhere, in church, at the theatre, in the concert hall, his genius appears before us as one of the most stupendous phenomena of the century, a phenomenon to which all of us who are involved with art . . . have to pay homage with admiration and respect.'

On the other hand, although a keen admirer of Liszt's pianistic genius,* Berlioz altogether ignored his friend's creative achievements; and, indeed, when the Gran Mass was performed at Paris in 1866, scathingly denounced it as 'the negation of art!' But by then the friendship had been foundering for some years, chiefly on the rock of Liszt's championship of Richard Wagner, whose creations Berlioz cordially detested.

The playwright Ernest Legouvé (1807–1903). I had invited a few friends around one evening: Liszt, Goubaux, Schoelcher, Sue,† and half a dozen others. Berlioz was one of us. 'Liszt,' he said, 'why not play us a Beethoven sonata.' From my study we passed into the salon. . . . There were no lights, and the fire in the grate had burned very low. Goubaux brought the lamp from my study, while Liszt went to the piano and the rest of us sought

* 'Wherever the conversation is about music,' he wrote on one occasion, 'Liszt is cited as a miracle of verve, audacity, and inspiration. His qualities are so overwhelming, his climaxes so terrifying in their force and precision, his ornamentation so delicate and so novel in style, that truly one is sometimes incapable of applause, he so petrifies one.'

† Respectively the dramatist Prosper-Parfait Goubaux (1795–1859), the politician and Handel enthusiast Victor Schoelcher (1804–93), and the novelist Eugène Sue (1804–57).

seats. 'Turn up the wick,' I told Goubaux; 'we can't see clearly enough.' But instead, he turned it down, plunging us into blackness, or, rather, into full shadow; and this sudden transition from light to dark, coming together with the first notes of the piano, had a moving effect upon every one of us. It was like the *tenebrae* scene in *Moses*. Whether by chance or from some unconscious influence, Liszt began the funereal and heart-rending Adagio of the Sonata in C sharp minor. The rest of us remained rooted to the spot where we happened to be, no one attempting to move. Now and then the expiring embers would pierce through their ashes and fill the room with an eerie glow, making weird and ghostly shapes of us. I had dropped into an armchair, and above my head heard stifled sobs and moans. It was Berlioz. When the music was over we remained silent for a moment, until Goubaux lit a candle. As we were returning from the salon into the study, Liszt stopped me by placing a hand on my arm. Indicating Berlioz, whose cheeks were still streaming with tears, he whispered: 'Look at him—it was as the *heir presumptive* that he listened to that!'[4]

In September 1831 Fryderyk Chopin arrived in Paris, and Liszt, one of the first to recognize the Pole's exceptional gifts, was soon his admiring friend. Attending Chopin's concert at the Salle Pleyel on 26 February 1832, he applauded furiously, as did Mendelssohn. But it was, again, a friendship with more warmth on the one side than the other. Liszt's admiration and liking for Chopin as composer, pianist, and man seem to have been fully reciprocated by Chopin only for Liszt the pianist; and in a joint letter (June 1833) to Ferdinand Hiller he remarked: 'Liszt is at the moment playing my Etudes* . . . I wish I could steal his manner of rendering my own studies.' But of Liszt's compositions he is said to have spoken only slightingly,[†] and, although their personal relations remained tolerably amiable, to have complained about him in letters to others, describing him as a show-off. The discreet and fastidious Chopin was also greatly offended when his apartment was used by Liszt for a tryst with a woman friend, the pianist Marie Pleyel (1811–75). To Wilhelm von Lenz he remarked laconically of Liszt a few years later: 'We are friends; we were comrades.'

Liszt's feelings for Chopin remained unchanged. Deeply shocked in 1849 by news of the latter's death,[‡] he paid tribute in a book which, speaking of the Polish composer as one of 'the two dearest friends we have ever known on earth',[§] concluded with an expression of his 'profound feeling of sorrow' and an avowal of 'the void left in our heart by an irreparable loss'.

For Chopin *qua* composer, his admiration grew only greater with the passing

* Chopin's Etudes, Op. 10, were dedicated to 'my friend Liszt'; those of Op. 25 to the Comtesse d'Agoult.

† Chopin died, it is true, before Liszt's greatest works were written—but he is likely, had he lived longer, to have found them no more to his taste than he did those of other outstanding contemporaries. He was horrified by the music of Berlioz, disliked and ignored that of Schumann, thought Schubert crude, and showed little understanding of the works of Beethoven's last period.

‡ One biographer of Liszt writes that when he came unexpectedly upon a report of Chopin's death in a newspaper he was reading, Liszt 'burst into tears'. No authority is cited for the statement, but even if mere surmise it is likely to be near the mark.

§ The other being Prince Felix Lichnowsky.

years. Until his life's end he took delight in playing and teaching his friend's works; and of the handful of pieces which he had earlier valued below their true worth, he revised his opinion quite unequivocally, writing (January 1876 to Princess Wittgenstein): 'In 1849 I did not yet understand the intimate beauty of the last works of Chopin, the *Polonaise-fantaisie* and the *Barcarolle*. . . . Now I admire them unreservedly. . . . They are not only most remarkable, but also very melodious, nobly inspired and artistically proportioned, in all respects on a level with the enchanting genius of Chopin. No other can be compared with him —he shines alone and unique in the artistic heavens.'

At the beginning of the 1830s Liszt enjoyed a romantic interlude with the Comtesse Adèle Laprunarède (later the Duchesse de Fleury), an attractive and vivacious young woman seeking consolation for the monotony of her marriage with an elderly husband. In early 1831* he was the couple's guest at Marlioz, their *maison de campagne* near Geneva; indeed, in one sense almost their prisoner, for the snow fell during his stay, blocking the roads and making his departure impossible until the thaw. 'But within all was comfortable,' relates Lina Ramann, whose informant was Liszt himself. 'They laughed, jested, read, made music, and only when the approaching spring had kissed away snow and ice from doors and paths did the young artist journey back to Paris. He and the Comtesse kept up a busy correspondence—his first "higher exercises in the French style", as he jocularly described them.'

A newcomer among his pupils at the end of 1831 was a Swiss girl, Valérie Boissier (1813–94), who in later life, under her married name of the Comtesse Agénor de Gasparin, was to achieve distinction as the author of travel books and moralistic writings. Valérie was accompanied to the lessons by her mother, Caroline (*c.*1788–1836), herself an amateur musician and composer; and it is she who provides the most detailed description of Liszt at this period, alike as man, pianist, and teacher.†

Caroline Boissier to her parents. Paris, 21 December. At one o'clock yesterday my drawing-room door opened, and a slim, fair young man of elegant bearing and a most distinguished face entered. It was Liszt. His visit was a very polite and obliging one, and he chatted with us for nearly an hour. He is original and very witty; he says nothing in the way that others would, and his very stimulating ideas are all his own. He possesses

* Elsewhere in the literature this visit is assigned to the winter of 1832–3. However, not only do we know from Liszt's correspondence and concert appearances that he spent most of that winter in Paris, but the Bibliothèque Nationale in Paris actually possesses a letter (Archives Daniel Ollivier No. 25179) dated 9 Jan. *1831* in which Liszt informs his mother of his safe arrival at Marlioz. Other letters confirm that he was at or near Geneva in February and May that year. According to his friend d'Ortigue, Liszt's sojourn in Switzerland ('perhaps the fullest in his life') lasted six months—a statement, from a source close to Liszt, which likewise supports the argument for 1831. (In 1833 his concerts between January and April would have allowed him to be away only in February.) It is also worth noting that a few years later Liszt wrote (to Marie d'Agoult) of 1831 as the time 'in which I shattered, destroyed, and violently annihilated Adèle's love'.

† The extracts reproduced here are from Caroline Boissier's letters. Her diary descriptions of Liszt's lessons were first published, in the original French, in 1927. An English translation by Elyse Mach, with selections from Liszt's technical exercises, was published in 1973 (*The Liszt Studies*, Associated Music Publishers).

the best manner of the nobility, a sustained, concentrated quality, and a modesty that goes as far as humility—almost too far, in my opinion, to be altogether genuine. To begin with he told us that he refused many would-be pupils, that he loved his freedom, and that his time was taken up with urgent matters. He recommended Herz, Bertini, Kalkbrenner, who, he said, were worth more than he! He minimized himself completely before the talents of these gentlemen, but we replied that we wanted his counsel and no one else's. This touched him somewhat. Valérie went to the piano and played him some of my exercises and a solo from the concerto by Hummel. He listened attentively, and several times remarked that she had an innate feeling for music and a great deal of *individuality* in her musical declamation. Finding her playing clear and swift, he was then more disposed to give lessons, and we arranged two hours a week, starting on Saturday. He assigned five or six from among Bertini's finest exercises, so that she might look through them beforehand. 'However,' he said, 'I make my pupils go into the selections in depth, so that often an entire lesson is given up to the study of two pages.'

Caroline Boissier, January 1832. He sheds a flood of light on his art; his explanations, always ingenious and often poetic, are striking in their truth; one feels that this sublime musician could have been a painter, an orator, a poet, for he is all these things in his wonderful playing. When we arrived he was finishing a tedious lesson. You should have seen him when the peevish girl he was teaching had left: his despondency, distress and dejection! He complained most unaffectedly, in the nicest way in the world, like a graceful kitten. Then he began with us. Finding his liking for music once again, he recovered, soared, became electrifying: he was Orpheus. He played a Bertini exercise as no one else has ever played. The others merely play the piano—but *he* is inspired, magnificently inspired. His fingers, by turns light, soft, velvety, then terrifyingly energetic, are familiar with every possible shift and expedient on the keys. Sometimes his expression is impetuous, passionate, troubled; and then melancholy, plaintive and touching; then proud and haughty; then blithe and careless. When listening to him, you find yourself fitting words to his music, composing scenes for it. Forgive me for revealing myself to you in so extravagant and enthusiastic a manner. It is not my fault. On arriving at the lesson I am cool and collected, yet involuntarily this is how I leave it. Poor Valérie is overwhelmed by the power of his talent; she is dazzled and almost discouraged. But no one could be kinder or more indulgent than Liszt, who entirely lacks *amour-propre* and is above all petty vanities. I can assure you that, living alone and shunning society, wrapped up in himself in the lofty and harmonious regions he inhabits, he is like no one else at all.

Caroline Boissier, 7 January. He was so pale, this poor young man, that it saddened me. He is wasting away: he feels too keenly and the blade is wearing out the scabbard. What a shame! His mother watches him lovingly yet anxiously; she is ever concerned about him, and when he brightens up she raises her eyes to heaven. It would be impossible for the two of them to be more dissimilar, the one all emotion, the other all intelligence. This tall, stout woman with her cheerful red face hardly looks the one to have given birth to this pale, slender young man, all soul, all fire. The lesson is, as always, admirable, dramatic. He inspires awe in Valérie. She seems crushed by such musical heights, measures the distance still to be climbed and grows discouraged. But I find a noticeable improvement already in her playing, a much broader and more animated declamation. Oh! had I only her youth, her courage, and, like her, a whole future before me—what good use I should make of Liszt! To speed her progress, he wants to play duets with her; but you can understand how difficult it will be to follow him, he who can play the most difficult works at sight *en virtuose*.

Caroline Boissier, 11 January. After the customary civilities, he told us that he had come to a decision: to give no more lessons. He wished, he said, to be able to study and to develop his talent without hindrance; further, his health was not equal to both teaching and his own endeavours, and he felt the need to gather his thoughts and devote himself to his art without distractions. It was all said with the calm and courteous firmness of a man who will not change his mind. I pleaded my case, and as Valérie is his best pupil, and as we shall be leaving in the spring, I won him over. He was really very kind, gave us a short but perfect lesson, and asked if he could come to take tea with us in the evening.

He arrived at 8.30, bringing us some books. He is a man of letters, has read, pondered and meditated greatly; his opinions are original as well as being *his own*; and this education, the fruit of talent, of genius even, is its most striking result. The same exquisite feeling for the beautiful which, in music, compels him to relish and make a profound study of masterpieces, guides him in literature too, making him truly eloquent when he speaks of the passages that have impressed him. One can see that he retains all of them in his memory. It is astonishing what so young a man has managed to become, aided by nothing but his own splendid and powerful abilities.

He was in a very chatty mood, interesting us with what he said. When one thinks of all the trouble that we poor parents give ourselves with our children, who still remain sullen, gauche, shy, or even rash and irresponsible, one can only marvel when seeing a young man who, outwardly almost an adolescent, has charm, perfect breeding and ease of manner, and yet sincere modesty and an agreeable wit, with all the aplomb of a man of forty. When he discusses politics with Edmond,* his moderation, judgement and close reasoning contrast, it must be admitted, with the democratic tirades of my son. He played a duet with Valérie, then

* Pierre-Edmond Boissier (1810–85), who became a distinguished botanist.

delighted us by letting us sample the finest passages of several pieces. He performed a magnificent sonata by Czerny for us, to combat my prejudice against this composer. And so in future I shall amuse myself by inventing grievances against particular musicians, to get him to try to convert me to them. Nothing could be more admirable than the brilliant, stormy, pathetic manner in which he rendered those pieces; it was like the most inspired improvisation. Poor Valérie is overwhelmed by this gigantic talent, and her progress is above all in humility; she feels annihilated, and despairs of ever arriving at a tolerable level. Liszt awes her, making her feel ill at ease. Nevertheless, all unconsciously she will make progress.

Caroline Boissier, mid-January. Yesterday he first of all went through an overture arranged for duet, which he played with Valérie, who hopped along behind him. Can one run after the hurricane? However, with perfect kindness he broke off several times to give her advice. Then we discussed the merits of Weber, Beethoven, and Rossini, and, growing lively, drawing inspiration from the talk, he went back to the piano and played sublimely. He gave us an idea of twenty masterpieces, playing extracts from operas, symphonies, and all manner of works. He played like the god of music; it was more than eloquence, more than expression: it was admirably beautiful and moving! No one has ever felt music like this man, or ever plumbed so deeply the depths of art and the mysteries of harmony. Under his fingers the piano renders up unaccustomed sounds. He accentuates and declaims like no one else; the least phrase moves one, could make one weep. His hearers are moved to the core of their being; his influence over them is total. But he is overwhelming, and any talent of one's own is so insipid, dull, and ridiculous beside these magnificent fountains of inspiration, this all-embracing memory and this creative imagination, that it could turn one against the piano for ever! . . . We broke up after midnight; such moments are among the brightest that life can offer.

Caroline Boissier, 21 January. It was a delicious morning. He kept us until 1.30 p.m., and but for an intruder foisting his icy face upon us, Liszt would have played from beginning to end the beautiful Concerto by Weber which had such a great success at Geneva last year, even when played by Vehrstaedt. The lesson was admirable. He made Valérie repeat thrice in succession a certain exercise by Moscheles, *agitato* and full of expression. He taught it her with a detail, care, and talent which enchanted me. It is impossible to go further in musical declamation, and Valérie is beginning to make perceptible progress. He got her to sketch another exercise by Moscheles. Wanting to make her grasp his method, he is giving her a notion of his favourite composers and making her play all the masterpieces. Until now Valérie had tried only light music; but under the guidance of such a master it is time to arrive at the classics. Some of these masterworks, incomprehensible to the everyday musician, make a prodigious effect when played by him, and his touch, method, and expression impart such impetus and import to the music, make it so gripping, that it almost hurts me.

He played Weber, Beethoven, Czerny, and Kessler* to us, knowing everything by heart, having a complete repertoire in his memory. This unsociable man, a misanthrope, or, rather, one who shuns the world to devote himself to study, has taken to us and shows us great friendliness. I find that his lessons are of real use to me too: my ideas expand, my prejudices vanish, and I learn a thousand new things.

Caroline Boissier, late January. Our friend Liszt is setting off to Rouen for a few days, to give a concert [28 January] on behalf of the poor. To travel the roads at this time of year to do a good deed, despite being in poor health—that is real charity. . . . Yesterday he was practising in his pleasant little room while his mother was working by the fireside; the one in heaven with the melodious music of his beautiful genius, the other on earth with her carpet slippers; but both united in tender affection, making the best household in the world. . . .

Now that we count as friends of his to some extent, Liszt is extremely kind and obliging; and this mute, inscrutable young man opens his heart to us, displaying the treasures of his talent to give us pleasure. After a few moments' conversation, which he can always enliven by his wit, he went to the piano and gave us Weber's magnificent Concerto from first note to last.

When listening to Liszt, I feel what no other artist has ever made me feel; it is not only admiration, it is ecstasy and fatigue together, which at one and the same time consume and enchant me. To tell you that his fingers have the speed of lightning, and sometimes the vehemence and might of thunder, to tell you that he accelerates certain *agitati* to the point of breathlessness, and that these stormy moments are followed by a soft abandonment, a melancholy full of grace and feeling, and then by magnificent audacity and noble enthusiasm, would be to speak to you in an unknown language, since, not having heard him, you can have no idea of what he is like.

Feeling that he is being listened to with great pleasure, Liszt himself derives pleasure from playing. Once again he let us hear a whole series of masterpieces, going through Beethoven, Weber, Mozart, and Haydn, drawing parallels between them, admiring and loving them with the good faith of a beautiful soul; as it were summoning them, raising them and restoring them to life. Certainly, this young man is destined to push back the frontiers of art very far. There are very bright lights in his head, as well as strong and new ideas. If he does not have genius, and a genius which will become creative, then I know nothing about it, and the prodigious impression made on me both by his music and his conversation would be

* The German pianist and teacher J. C. Kessler (1800–72).

inexplicable without this certainty. . . . I say again: he is a man of genius, and one day he will take his place among his peers.

By turns we discussed politics, political economy, religion, education, and literature, and our contribution was mostly confined to listening, for Liszt is a thinker, and while pursuing his musical studies has found the time to read and study enormously, going into everything very deeply.

When I asked him how he had become such a wonderful sight-reader, he told me that during his childhood he had been made to read music for three or four hours a day before he had succeeded in acquiring such mastery. He claims that anyone can arrive at the same point as himself, and that his ability is not exceptional. But in saying this he is obviously mistaken, and it is enough to know him to be aware that he is not made like other people.

Caroline Boissier, February 1832. When he appears, he will eclipse all others like a sun! Such a talent, or, rather, such powers, would make you believe in miracles! After hearing him one feels weary and overwhelmed; his music hurts one, it acts too powerfully on the soul.

You ask me his method for passage-playing? He recommends many scales, not only the straightforward variety but also in octaves and thirds, plus trills with all fingers. These are his own regular exercises—but there is in addition something very uncommon in his make-up; his intellectual faculties are unrivalled, and his muscles particularly supple and strong. His small hands are at once delicate and tapering, and so flexible that they carry out whatever is demanded of them. With all that, they are powerful enough to break the keys at will. His touch is absolutely his own, and it changes the sound of the instrument, which under his fingers becomes glittering or velvety as required. He coaxes it, possesses it, makes it respond to his heart. One no longer hears the piano—but storms, prayers, songs of triumph, transports of joy, heart-rending despair. It is more than poetry, it is the musical power of a modern Orpheus, and I deplore his obstinacy in not revealing in public a talent which would create a sensation!

Sometimes he reads us a few fragments of his favourite authors, Pascal and Chateaubriand; he links music to literature, leading us to the one by way of the other. Would you believe that, to attain this dramatic expression which animates his playing, he carries out actual research? In quest of every possible emotion, he visits hospitals,* lunatic asylums, and prisons.

Nothing escapes his analysis; he probes, examines, and studies like the philosophical dreamer he is, and I should not be surprised to see him distinguish himself one day by a profound work.[5]

The poet Antoine Fontaney (1803–37), 15 February. Called to see Victor

* Three years later, the *Gazette musicale* (11 Jan. 1835) published an interesting description of the effect Liszt's playing had had on a mentally retarded woman at the La Salpêtrière hospital.

[Hugo]. I stayed a very long time with him; Cazalès and d'Ortigue turned up too. We all went to hear a quintet of Urhan's which is dedicated to Victor. Liszt was there, a fine figure of an enthusiastic and modest young man. His eyes are brilliant and animated, the corners of his mouth turned down.[6]

Caroline Boissier, 23 February. Within this soul there are tempests, and all the chaos of youth, with a total absence of illusions. This highly intelligent face, the pallor and suffering* imprinted on these twenty-year-old features —such things are melancholy, and one would like so splendid a genius, so much spirit and goodness, to lead to happiness. But on the other hand Liszt's sufferings have made him very sensitive: he seeks out the unfortunate, and goes into prisons to bring what comfort he can. To one prisoner he gave a guitar with accompanying self-instruction manual, and visits him from time to time to supervise progress.[7]

Spring 1832. Liszt spends his nights at balls and concerts, his days in the great world. His company is desired at the most brilliant parties; he sees the *savants*, the celebrated men of letters, the artists, the fashionable women, and talks about it all in the most piquant manner, claiming that society offers him a thousand different ways of enriching and developing his art.[8]

Antoine Fontaney, 16 April. Went to Victor Hugo's. Liszt was at the piano in the salon. He played us a Funeral March by Beethoven. It was magnificent! What a beautiful picture that would make! All those dead from the cholera† marching to Notre Dame with their shrouds![9]

The Hungarian diplomat Count Rudolf Apponyi (1812–76), 18 April. The day before yesterday, after dinner, the Ambassador got Liszt to come, and he played us a Weber concerto with the rarest perfection. A few days ago when at home practising for the occasion, he dislocated the thumb of his right hand, and even thought he had broken it. No one would have suspected it on hearing him. He is especially admirable in one passage, written entirely in octaves, which he plays with such speed and strength that his hands seem to multiply. It is impossible to follow them with the eye, such is the inconceivable rapidity with which they move: they fly from one end of the piano to the other.[10]

In March 1832 Niccolò Paganini arrived in Paris. Finding a city in which the cholera was raging, after his first concert on 25 March he gave a second, on 22 April, for the benefit of 'the victims of the cruel scourge which is ravaging the capital'. Thereafter he gave another seven. In Switzerland in the spring of 1831, at the time of Paganini's first visit to Paris, Liszt this time attended one, several,

* Liszt was feeling distressed because of the suicide of two young artists of his acquaintance.

† A cholera epidemic had broken out in Paris early that spring.

or all of the concerts; and, electrified by the fabulous virtuosity revealed to him, determined to achieve on his own instrument a transcendent mastery akin to that displayed on the violin by the legendary Italian. Under this powerful inspiration and example, before another decade had passed he had virtually created modern piano-playing. The stimulus received he made plain in a letter to his friend Pierre Wolff on 2 May, a few days after Paganini's third concert (27 April).

For the past fortnight my mind and fingers have been working away like two lost spirits. Homer, the Bible, Plato, Locke, Byron, Hugo, Lamartine, Chateaubriand, Beethoven, Bach, Hummel, Mozart, Weber, are all around me. I study them, meditate on them, devour them with fury; and in addition I spend four or five hours practising exercises (thirds, sixths, octaves, tremolos, repeated notes, cadenzas, etc. etc.). Ah! provided I don't go mad you will find an artist in me! Yes, an artist such as you desire, such as is required nowadays!

'And I too am a painter!'* cried Michelangelo the first time he beheld a masterpiece. . . . Though poor and unimportant, your friend has not left off repeating those words of the great man ever since Paganini's last performance. . . . What a man, what a violin, what an artist! Heavens! what sufferings, what misery, what tortures in those four strings! . . . As for his expression, his manner of phrasing—they are his very soul![11]

Liszt's new approach to playing, and writing for, the piano can be seen in a work dating from this time: the *Grande Fantaisie de Bravoure sur la Clochette de Paganini* (S420); that is, on the bell theme from Paganini's Violin Concerto No. 2, in B minor, to which Liszt was to return some years later when composing his *La Campanella* (S140/3).

It was in 1832, during a soirée at Hugo's, that Liszt was heard for the first time by the Swiss littérateur Charles Didier (1805–64). 'Before this evening I had no idea what the piano could do,' noted Didier in his diary. 'When he had finished, Liszt seemed exhausted. He looks frail and feminine, which makes him still more interesting. . . . His head fully justifies phrenology.'

Later that year the Irish pianist and composer John Field (1782–1837), inventor of the nocturne, arrived in Paris for a short stay; and on Christmas Day performed his new Seventh Concerto to a capacity audience at the Conservatoire. Although his playing was well received, some of the younger pianists, including Liszt, found it 'sleepy' and 'lacking in vitality', for all its fluency and lucidity. Nevertheless, Liszt admired Field's works, and when editing a selection of the nocturnes long afterwards he accompanied the publication with an interesting and appreciative essay, *John Field and his Nocturnes*.

As for his own appearances in these years, after taking part in numerous concerts in the first four months of 1828, besides giving one of his own (Salle Chantereine, 7 April), Liszt was not heard in public again until 22 March 1829, when at one of Pape's soirées musicales he provided two of the twelve hands required to perform an arrangement of the Overture to *Die Zauberflöte*. In the handful of other concerts in which he took part later that year and during the

* 'Son pittore anch'io,' but said by Correggio (on seeing Raphael's *St Cecilia* at Bologna).

next, he generally restricted himself to a similarly modest or subordinate role, partnering other pianists in multi-piano extravaganzas or accompanying soloists. In 1831, much of which he spent in Switzerland, his sole appearance was as Maria Malibran's accompanist at a semi-private concert in the Salle des Saint-Simoniens;* and the next year he was again heard in Paris, in public, on only one occasion: a concert (given by Scavarda) at the Salle Chantereine on 2 April, in which he took the *secondo* part in a duet with a pupil, Louis Messemaeckers.

The occasions on which he was heard in private were doubtless more frequent. One of them was at the very end of 1832, on 30 December, when he took part in a soirée musicale at the Austrian Embassy. The singers, accompanied by Rossini, were Giulia Grisi, Rubini, and Tamburini; the instrumentalists, besides Liszt himself, Chopin and Kalkbrenner, among others.

The feast of music provided by so illustrious a company, Count Rudolf Apponyi found, not surprisingly, 'delicious'.

1833

Liszt now resumed his career as a professional pianist. Apart from his brief appearance in April 1832, he had not been heard by the Parisian public for nearly three years; but in 1833 he took part in at least sixteen concerts.† Among the most interesting of these were: a charity concert he gave jointly with Garcia *fils*, at the Salle du Wauxhall on 12 March; Hiller's concert at that same venue on the 23rd, in which he, Liszt, and Chopin played a Bach triple concerto; a concert at the Théâtre Italien on 2 April for the benefit of the Irish actress Harriet Smithson; Henri Herz's concert at the Salle du Wauxhall on 3 April, in which Liszt, Chopin, and the Herz brothers performed a 'quartet for two pianos, eight hands'; a *représentation extraordinaire*, again for the benefit of Miss Smithson,‡ on 24 November; Hiller's concert of 15 December; and Berlioz's Conservatoire concert of 22 December, to which Liszt's contribution was a performance of Weber's *Concertstück*. Several Berlioz works, including the *Roi Lear* overture of which a few years later Liszt made a transcription (S474) for piano solo, were premiered at this last event; and in the audience sat a very special listener, described by Berlioz as 'a man with long hair, piercing eyes and a strange, ravaged countenance'—Paganini.

* In reporting this occasion, d'Ortigue writes: 'To return to her dressing-room, Mme Malibran took the arm of her accompanist. As she walked along, the singer was stopped at every row of seats by the numerous congratulations addressed to her. As she was responding to right and left, Liszt suddenly spotted General Lafayette standing in front of him. Abandoning Mme Malibran on the spot, with a single bound he threw himself around the neck of the old general, who responded in his usual kindly way to this spontaneous testimony of admiration and fellow feeling.'

† Full details of which are given by Keeling, 'Liszt's Appearances in Parisian Concerts'.

‡ She was now actually Madame Berlioz, having married her passionate admirer Hector Berlioz at the British Embassy on 3 Oct. Liszt's signature can also be seen in the marriage register, for he was one of the witnesses.

But the event of overriding importance for Liszt at this time was his meeting with the Comtesse Marie d'Agoult, the woman who was to be the central figure in his life for the next eleven years, in a relationship which would experience quite as much turbulence as tenderness, and which, when it came to its inevitable end, would leave the one actively seeking revenge and the other bitter and resentful.

Marie-Catherine-Sophie de Flavigny was born at Frankfurt am Main on 31 December 1805. Through her mother she was descended from the wealthy German banking family of Bethmann; and her childhood had been spent partly in Frankfurt* and partly in Paris. Convent educated and highly intelligent, she had on entering Parisian society been much courted, amongst others by Alfred de Vigny and 'almost the entire young diplomatic corps'. 'She was not exactly pretty, but her elegance, her distinction, her blond hair, her eyes and her charm made a beauty of her,' was the opinion of Comtesse Dash.† 'You forgot her thinness, which she *angelicized* in cascades of muslin and tulle. Involuntarily you looked for her wings.'

When, however, she had eventually married, in May 1827, it had been to a much older man, Comte Charles d'Agoult (1790–1875), a kindly and unpretentious ex-army officer whom she respected but did not love. Even before the end of the honeymoon, spent at Dieppe and in London, d'Agoult had himself become fully aware of their basic incompatibility. 'A few days of my new existence were enough,' he recalled in his memoirs,‡ 'to make me foresee that in my home there would never be that sweet intimacy born of the same duties, the same interests, and the same hearth. Madame d'Agoult had great and charming qualities; but such words as devotion to duty, self-sacrifice, and thought for others were as foreign to her upbringing as to her vocabulary. . . . Her character was cold, her moral and religious principles rather elastic.'

About his wife's educational prowess and intellectual aspirations, he added: 'She spoke and wrote English and German as correctly as she did French. Her memory was a storehouse of all the masterpieces written in these three languages. The nebulous ideology of the Germans was as familiar to her as the bold speculations of English writers. . . . She herself wrote a great deal—both to her friends and for posterity.'

'"Six inches of snow covering twenty feet of lava," has been said of me, and not unjustly,' wrote Marie in her own analysis of her character. 'If to this passionate but reserved temperament is added a horror of the *commonplace* and the impossibility of borrowing the wit of others, it will be understood that my

* Where, one September Sunday, occurred an encounter with Goethe: 'As he talked with my parents I gradually grew bold enough to lift up my eyes to him. Straightaway, as though he felt my gaze, he returned it. The effect upon me of his two enormous, glowing pupils, his beautiful, open—as it were luminous—forehead, was nothing less than dazzling. When he took his leave, Goethe put his hand on my head and kept it there for a moment, caressing my golden locks. I dared not breathe; indeed, almost went down on my knees. Did it mean that I had sensed in that magnetic hand a blessing, a tutelary promise for me? I do not know. All I can say is that more than once in my long life I have bowed in spirit under that benedictory hand, and that on rising I have always felt better and stronger.'

† Pseudonym of the Vicomtesse de Poilloüe de Saint-Mars (1804–72).

‡ Unpublished, but quoted at some length in J. Vier's *La Comtesse d'Agoult et son temps*, i (Paris, 1955).

conversation is by no means what would be required to contribute liveliness to a gathering or amusement to a salon.'

In addition to her literary and other acquirements, she also possessed some knowledge of music. She had a good voice and was a respectable amateur pianist. At the time of his visit to Paris in 1825 she had been given lessons by Hummel, and 'played his celebrated Septet with a certain relative virtuosity, the virtuosity of an amateur and well-bred young lady; but, nevertheless, with my youth, my curly blond hair, my figure and my Loreley manner, it did not fail to please my well-disposed audiences.'

With their two little daughters, Louise and Claire (born respectively in 1828 and 1830), and Marie's mother, the Comtesse de Flavigny, the d'Agoults lived in an apartment at the Hôtel Mailly, rue de Beaune. They also spent much of each year at Croissy, the country château situated some six leagues (fifteen miles) from Paris which Marie had acquired a year or two earlier.

At the time of their first meeting, Liszt was twenty-one and Marie twenty-seven.

Marie d'Agoult. It was towards the end of the third year following the revolution of 1830.* A great movement had taken place in literature and the arts. Numerous talents had arisen, gathered together, formed a procession, illuminated one another with a radiant light. Among these diverse talents, poets, writers, artists, there shone in the musical sphere a prodigious genius who when still a child was said to have equalled the young Mozart. . . .

At the period of which I am speaking, Franz, although little more than twenty years of age, had just quitted that world in which unheard-of successes had welcomed him on his entry into it and then continued for a decade. An incomparable virtuoso, he was no longer anywhere to be heard. To support his aged mother† he still gave a few lessons, but, this duty done, kept himself in strict confinement, living in the most complete seclusion. Of his reasons for this solitude nothing was known. The salons in which he had been acclaimed, and especially the women, were astonished at such a sudden resolve, and, as it seemed, one so unwarranted. There was a rumour of an unhappy love-affair, and some people even maintained that he was going to become a priest.

Among the persons really interested in this Romantic mystery was an elderly lady with whom I was friendly.

A pretty niece [Charlotte Talleyrand] whom she was bringing up was one of the small number of privileged pupils retained by Franz. Now and then he came to the home of that lady, the Marquise L. V.,‡ for music-making, on the express condition that it would be *en famille* and that no invitations

* It is impossible to pin-point the exact date. Marie's 'towards the end of the third year' can be interpreted in several different ways. However, it is clear from the dates of her published correspondence with Liszt that the meeting can be assigned to late 1832 or early 1833.

† At the beginning of 1833 Anna Liszt was 44.

‡ Le Vayer.

would be issued. But the Marquise had been unable to keep faith. Imperceptibly her doors, to begin with kept firmly closed when Franz was playing, had first been left ajar and then opened fully; and now she was inviting the whole of society. Weary as I was of going out into the world, I had on several occasions refused the Marquise's invitations, being by no means anxious to hear yet another virtuoso, having heard nearly all of them already; but I feared that my refusals might eventually offend my kind friend, and, at her request, I betook myself to her home one evening—the last in which Franz was to be heard.

When I entered Mme L. V.'s salon at about ten o'clock, where everyone was already gathered, and where, the Marquise came to tell me, I was impatiently awaited, Franz was not to be seen. The mistress of the house apologized for the fact. Anticipating a question which I would not have asked, she told me that they were preparing to sing a chorus by Weber, and that the artist had gone into the next room to write out a missing part. . . . Mme L. V. was still speaking when the door opened and my eyes fell upon a strange apparition. I say 'apparition' for want of any other word to describe the extraordinary sensation that came over me at this sudden sight of the most remarkable person I had ever seen.

A tall figure, excessively thin, a pale face with great sea-green eyes in which glistened swift flashes of light like waves catching the sunlight, features at once suffering and powerful, a hesitant step which seemed less to tread the floor than glide over it, an absent-minded and uneasy look, like that of a ghostly visitant for whom the hour of returning to the shades is about to sound—that was how I saw before me this young genius whose hidden life was at that moment arousing a curiosity as keen as his triumphs had formerly excited envy.

When he had been introduced to me and, sitting beside me with the bold grace of an acquaintance of long standing, Franz began to chat in an easy, unconstrained way, I felt, under the strange exterior which I had at first found so astonishing, the power and freedom of a mind which attracted me; and long before our conversation was over I had come to regard as very simple a manner of being and of speaking quite foreign to the society in which I had spent my life. He spoke impetuously and abruptly. With some vehemence he delivered himself of ideas and opinions that seemed bizarre to ears accustomed, as were mine, to the banality of received opinions. His flashing glances, his gestures, his smile, which was at one moment profound and infinitely sweet, at another caustic, seemed to wish to provoke me simultaneously to contradiction and to agreement. And I, who remained hesitating between the one and the other, surprised at the speed of this unexpected relationship, barely responded. The mistress of the house saved me from embarrassment. The piano was open, the candles lit on both sides of the music rack. Mme L. V. murmured a few words which Franz did not allow her to finish. Abruptly he quitted his seat next to me (with resentment, or so I believed); and as it were involuntarily, unthinkingly, and without his having requested me, I followed him to the piano where the chorus of young ladies awaited him; and, taking a mezzo-soprano part from one of them, I added my own agitated voice to those fresh and calm ones around me. When the piece was finished, Franz, who had not seen me until that moment as I was hidden behind him among the singers, caught sight of me as he turned round. A gleam of light passed over his brow, which at once darkened again; and for the rest of the evening he made no move to come near me.

After he had played, like everyone else I expressed in my turn and out of courtesy a few words of admiration, to which he responded by bowing in silence. I returned home rather late; I had difficulty in falling asleep, and during my sleep was visited by strange dreams.

The very next day, with kind assiduity and in the company of a relative of hers, Mme L. V. came to see me, to inquire about my health; she had thought me rather pale when I took my leave of her the previous day, and she wished to reassure herself that I was not unwell. Then, without giving me time to reply, and with a look of delight, she cried: 'Isn't Franz incomparable? What fire! What soul! What genius! . . . But it must be said that he surpassed himself yesterday. Even his pupils say he has never played like that before. You inspired him. It was you his eyes were constantly seeking. When you applauded, his face became radiant.'

Mme L. V. could have continued in this fashion for a long time, and I did not dream of interrupting her. Her relative, a discreet and sober-minded man, ventured a few remarks on the eccentricities of artists and the inconvenience of admitting them to one's home on an equal footing. These observations displeased me, and I was grateful to the Marquise for ignoring them. As though nothing had been said she continued her praise of Franz: his character was as beautiful as his genius, his soul as noble as his talent. As for his piety, it was evangelical, and, despite the daily cares of circumstances that were far from well-to-do, he helped the poor with limitless charity. In short, it was impossible to know him without loving him. Then, changing her tone and with an air of reproach: 'You did not grant him permission to pay you his respects. But he deserved the honour. I am sure that by doing so you would have made him very proud and happy.'

The relative made a gesture as though to say: 'How unfitting!' It was this gesture which determined my reply. I asked the Marquise for Franz's address, and as soon as she had left I took up my pen to invite him to my at-home day. Three times I began a note of three lines. I could not word it to my satisfaction. Either it sounded as though I were insisting too much on the pleasure it would give me to have Franz in my home, or I was too formally polite. In my conversation with him the previous evening I had discerned a kind of touchiness, almost a haste to remember the difference in our ranks, as though he feared that he would be made to feel it. The remarks made by the Marquise's relative had brought before my eyes something on which I had never before had occasion to reflect: the difference in name, in blood, and in fortune which we owed to the accident of birth, and which placed us in a position of superiority over the rest of mankind. At that moment I felt troubled by this apparent superiority in my relations with someone whose immense talent, and what I felt I already knew of his character, put him in my own opinion so far above me. When writing that note I feared that by using the set phrases of society to address an artist who did not belong to it, I might appear haughty when I wished simply to be correct; but I also feared that if I neglected those phrases I should be revealing more interest than was seemly in such new relations with a man so young and so much a stranger to my own people.

Without replying, Franz accepted the invitation. The welcome extended to him in my intimate circle showed him that he could come again; and indeed I asked him to do so. My well-known liking for music made his presence in my home perfectly natural. Furthermore, the consideration by which I was surrounded gave me, after six years of marriage, complete independence. There was therefore no obstacle of any kind to the frequency of the meetings between Franz and me which were soon taking place. They were from the beginning of a very serious nature and, as though tacitly agreed, devoid of all banality. Without hesitation or effort, but simply by natural inclination, we at once came to the elevated topics which alone held attraction for us. We spoke about human destiny, its uncertainties and its sorrows, about the soul and about God. We exchanged serious thoughts on the present time as well as on the life to come and the promises attaching thereto given by religion. We said nothing personal or too intimate to one another, but it was obvious from the tone of our exchanges that we were both of us very unhappy, and that, although young, each of us had already known more than one bitter experience.

To those things hinted at but left unsaid, to those veiled confidences, to those outpourings which were at once very free and very discreet and which proved more attractive to us with every day that passed, Franz brought an impulse, a wealth and originality of impressions which awakened an entire world lying dormant within me, and which, after his departure, would leave me in endless reveries. Although his education had been scanty, since from childhood he had been obliged to apply himself without respite to the practice of his art, having been at grips with the difficulties of life, having seen things from very different points of view, at one moment in the dazzling brilliance of a theatrical celebrity, at another in the privations of a precarious existence tied to the crowd and its caprices, one day like the little Mozart in the laps of queens and princesses and the next in isolation and bitter poverty, Franz, much more than I, had felt the inconsistency, the injustice and the folly, the cruel shallowness and tyranny of public opinion. More adventurous both by nature and situation, he had also probed much further than I into good and evil. Although he was still, in imagination at least, very Catholic, and although the rumour according to which he had taken holy orders was not without some foundation, his intellectual misgivings were impelling him towards heresy. In the last few years he had been diligently following the preachings of certain schools and sects which proclaimed new revelations, and frequenting the meetings of the disciples of Saint-Simon. . . .

In politics as in religion Franz detested moderation and boldly embraced extreme opinions. He despised bourgeois royalty and middle-of-the-road government, and prayed for the reign of justice; which, he explained to me, meant the Republic. With the same restiveness he turned to innovations in the arts and letters which threatened the old disciplines: *Childe Harold, Manfred, Werther, Obermann*,* all the proud or desperate revolutionaries of romantic poetry were the companions of his sleepless nights. With them he enthused in proud disdain of the conventions; like them he shuddered under the hated yoke of those aristocracies which had no foundation in genius or virtue; he wanted an end of submission and resignation, and in their place a holy hatred, implacable and avenging of all iniquities.

So many names, so many ideas, feelings, and rebellions, which had until then been almost unknown to me in the narrowly exclusive circle of the antiquated, tradition-dominated society into which I had been born, fell on my languid thoughts like sparks. . . . At the voice of this young enchanter, at his vibrant words, there opened up before me a boundless universe. Sometimes filled with light, sometimes with darkness, it was ever changing, and my thoughts plunged into it in bewilderment. In my close friendship with Franz there was no suggestion of coquetry or *galanterie*, as occurs between persons of a different sex, between men and women of the world. Between us there was something at once very young and very solemn, very profound and very naïve. Content with seeing one another daily, taking our leave of one another with the assurance of meeting again the next day at the same hour and with the same freedom, we both surrendered to that security, to that plenitude of spontaneous and shared feeling which does not examine or analyse itself, and which does not even need to declare itself, so much does it feel that it is understood, shared, necessary, and beyond words. . . .[1]

In the spring, at Marie's invitation, Liszt paid his first visit to Croissy.

* The celebrated pre-Romantic epistolary novel (of 1804) by Etienne Pivert de Senancour (1770–1846), which with its atmosphere of gloom, melancholy, and ennui eloquently evokes the desolating 'mal du siècle'. It was of considerable influence on Liszt; and the remote Alpine valley described in its pages inspired his *Vallée d'Obermann* (sixth piece of the *Années de pèlerinage, Suisse*), which he dedicated to Senancour and prefaced with a long quotation from the novel.

When he was shown into the salon, my children were there with me. He had never seen them before, as in Paris he had come to my home only in the evening after the time when they were taken away. What passed suddenly through his mind at that moment? What thought went through it like an arrow? I do not know, but his beautiful face changed expression and his features contracted. For a moment neither of us was able to speak. Franz had stopped on the threshold; I took a few steps towards him, abashed and trembling. In the same lightning flash of conscience we had felt our guilt; or apparently so, for neither of us dared mention it. From that day forward there came a change in my relations with Franz. I saw him only at long intervals, and rarely tête-à-tête; and at times I no longer knew if I really desired those meetings or if I feared them more, so agitated did they leave me. In our briefest and most often interrupted conversations, something had supervened which was no longer entirely us. If our talks remained the same in substance, their tone was quite different. Franz brought a whimsical humour to them; and I, constraint and embarrassment. Sometimes long silences fell between us; sometimes, on the contrary, Franz talked with feverish animation, affecting gaiety—but it was a mocking gaiety which hurt me. He whom I had seen so full of enthusiasm, so eloquent in speaking of the good and the beautiful, so ambitious to elevate his life and dedicate it to great art, so religious in all his thoughts—he never now expressed himself on anything except in a tone of irony. He made a parade of incredulity; the things he respected and the things he scorned, his admirations and his sympathies, he mingled them on purpose, with equal indifference.

He extolled the wisdom of the common people and the easy life; he took pleasure in defending the freethinkers. All of a sudden, without anything having occasioned them, he made bizarre remarks to me, utterly unheard of on his lips. He praised what he called my splendid life, congratulated me on my great situation in the world, and admired, he said, my royal dwelling-place, the opulence and elegance of everything surrounding me. Was this said in all seriousness? Was it mere banter? From his impassive air and gloomy voice I could no longer tell.

Strangely, Franz's talent seemed no less changed than his mind. When he improvised at the piano, it was no longer to entice from it sweet harmonies which opened heaven to me, but to make his brazen fingers produce sounds which were at once discordant and strident. Although he did not actually reproach me with anything, Franz, to whom my presence no longer brought either peace or joy, appeared to be harbouring some secret resentment against me. On one occasion I even caught his eyes resting on me with what was not unlike hatred . . . What was it? I dared not ask. When our eyes met, I believed that I could still read sudden, involuntary emotions in his, but as soon as he saw my own emotion his lips resumed their sardonic curl. The coolness of his manner, if I attempted to bring back the intimacy of the outpourings of earlier times, disconcerted me. Worried and withdrawn, I lost myself in suppositions and was filled with anguish.

One day, under the blow of some stinging words whose keen wound I could not endure, a lament escaped me. Tears, long restrained, now flowed in streams. Franz stared at me in consternation. He remained silent, appearing to be struggling with himself, torn by conflicting emotions which made his lips quiver. Suddenly, falling at my feet, embracing my knees, with a profound and sorrowful look and in a voice I can still hear, he implored me to grant him my forgiveness. This forgiveness, shown in the burning grasp of our hands, was an explosion of love, a vow, a mutual oath to love one another—to love one another without sharing, without limit, and without end, both in this world and throughout the duration of the next!

The hours, the days, the weeks and months that followed were pure enchantment. Forming no plans, premeditating nothing, arranging nothing, we found that matters always went of themselves and brought us the one to the other. Franz, as he had promised, no longer seemed the same person. At all our meetings he was invariably tender and sweet. . . . He related his past life to me, telling me that his childhood had been joyless and his adolescence devoid of counsel or support; he confessed his temptations, his faults, his feelings of remorse, and his desire to escape them by taking refuge in the cloister.

In strokes of fire he painted for me the conflicting passions which well before their time tore at one another within his breast, his worldly ambitions and ascetic fervours, his pride and cupidity, his keen curiosity about forbidden things, all the stimuli of flesh and spirit, excited by the intoxication of a frivolous celebrity for which he felt only contempt.

Franz also referred, but with infinite tact, to the tumultuous emotions of the passion I had inspired in him, to his blind, guilty, insane hopes, and, with each return of clear-sightedness, the lure of suicide. But how far from his thoughts was such a thing from this time forward! . . .

In our long walks at Croissy, through the meadows and cornfields, Franz breathed in with delight the peace of the countryside which his childhood, exposed to all the bustle of cities, had not known. He listened with an artist's ear to the slow cadence of rural activities; he could distinguish under the grass the stealthiest noises, could catch in the air the least buzzing of insects. In gathering up all these murmurings and breathings he was following, in his heart, the rhythm of his thoughts.[2]

An interesting original work which dates from this time is the *Harmonies poétiques et religieuses* (S154). A single piece, and not to be confused with the great set of pieces under this title composed many years later, it derives its name from a collection of poems by Lamartine, to whom it was dedicated.

The year 1833 also saw two of Liszt's Berlioz transcriptions come into being:

that of the *Francs-juges* overture (S471) and, most memorably, the tremendous recasting for the piano keyboard of the *Symphonie fantastique* (S470). The publication expenses of this latter transcription were borne by Liszt himself, who wished to help his friend by bringing the work to as wide a public as possible.

1834

On 5 January appeared the first issue of the *Gazette musicale*, a weekly publication to which Liszt, one of its founders, contributed articles regularly throughout the decade. The editor of this new periodical was the music-publisher Maurice Schlesinger (1798–1871),* and among the other prominent musicians whose writings appeared in its pages were Berlioz, Schumann, and Wagner.

The occasions in which Liszt was heard in public during the early months of the year included a concert at the Salle Pleyel on 19 January, in which he and Hiller played a two-piano work of the latter's; a soirée at Erard's on the 26th; and a concert on 25 February in which Chopin was a fellow performer.

The relationship with Madame d'Agoult was meanwhile developing, and there were clandestine meetings at a little apartment rented by Liszt which they jocularly called the *Ratzenloch* (rat hole). 'Not an angel's, not God's, but thine alone,' was the motto which recurred frequently in the epistolary outpourings she received from him. 'With Caroline I was merely a child, almost an imbecile; with Adèle only a wretched, faint-hearted milksop. With you alone do I feel young and manly,' he told her.

In the third week of May he travelled to Bernay (Normandy) to stay at the Château de Carentonne† with the d'Haineville family. 'I am being allowed much freedom,' he wrote to his mother, 'and hope to put it to good use, for I shall work. I must go forward and not look back. *The Imitation of Christ* teaches: "What is undertaken must be brought to a conclusion." '

Liszt to Marie d'Agoult. Carentonne, late May or early June. I have an immense need (immense is very ambitious) to know, to learn, to study—and am going through everything again from the beginning. I am reading Bayle,‡ the Bible, the history of philosophical systems, and that good classic La Harpe,§ whom I have never had the courage to read from one end to another. . . . I am also practising many cadenzas, octaves, and tremolos—enough to split one's head. I have the studies of Hiller, Chopin, and Kessler with me. . . .

* For whom Liszt on one occasion acted as second in a duel.

† In editing Liszt's letters to his mother, La Mara inadvertently misdated those from Carentonne, giving the uninitiated reader the erroneous impression that the visit took place a year or two earlier.

‡ The philosopher and critic Pierre Bayle (1647–1706) was author of *Nouvelles de la république des lettres* (a literary review) and of the *Dictionnaire historique et critique*, which consists for the most part of biographies of historical personages.

§ Jean François de la Harpe (1739–1803), whose best-known works are his critical lectures, *Lycée, ou Cours de littérature.*

If you wish, I shall speak to you one last time about my life from 1830 to 1833. It is very simple and very sad, very little like that of a Don Juan—but, all your penetration of mind notwithstanding, it is impossible for you not to form a wrong opinion of it. . . . In the isolation in which I am living, *love* is tormenting and destroying me—but I shall find some relief in the grave.[1]

To the same. I do not retract *one iota* from my past life, however shameful, however bitter it may have been! . . . not one iota. I accept absolutely everything, and were I a hundred times more criminal I would still accept everything, for I want the woman I love to be *happy* to forgive me. It is from her alone that I shall *receive* forgiveness.[2]

Two days after playing numerous pieces at a charity concert (19 June) in Bernay, Liszt took his seat in the diligence for the journey back to Paris, which he reached in the evening of the 22nd.

Some months earlier (probably during the first half of April), he had been introduced by d'Ortigue to the Abbé Félicité de Lamennais (1782–1854), who was to have a considerable influence upon his social and religious outlook. Ordained in 1816, Lamennais had first attracted attention by his apology for Roman Catholicism, the *Essai sur l'indifférence en matière de religion,* and after declining a cardinal's hat in 1824 had begun to preach the separation of church and state, believing that he could deliver the former only by freeing it from the yoke of the latter. The July days of 1830 had made him a convert to the sovereignty of the people, and in September of that year he published the first issue of his *L'Avenir,* to which he gave the motto 'God and Freedom'. This journal, which advocated religious and political reforms, had in 1832 been condemned by the Pope and suppressed. And shortly after Liszt made his acquaintance, Lamennais brought out his *Paroles d'un croyant*, the book in which he had finally rebelled against Rome. Creating an almost unexampled sensation, it had swiftly been condemned by the Encyclical *Singulari nos*.

'I have made the acquaintance of Liszt, whom I liked greatly, a young man full of soul,' Lamennais wrote (18 April) to Montalembert. To another, later correspondent he described Liszt as 'one of the finest and noblest souls I have met on this earth, where they are not excessively common'. He was equally enthusiastic about his new friend's talent, remarking to Ferdinand Denis a year or two later that Liszt was 'the greatest pianist he had ever heard or who had ever existed'.

The affection and admiration were warmly reciprocated. 'I *love* that man,' Liszt told Marie. And it was to Lamennais that he dedicated *Lyon*,* one of the most original and remarkable of his early piano works, as well as the unfinished *De profundis* (S691) for piano and orchestra. A literary fruit of the friendship was an essay that Liszt wrote this year to demonstrate the 'necessity of setting up a contest for the composition, both words and music, of the airs, hymns, and

* In the spring of 1835, Lamennais was one of the most eloquent and courageous supporters of certain rebellious Lyons workmen who were detained and brought to trial. To the subscription which he opened on their behalf, Liszt donated a generous 50 francs. *Lyon*, composed, probably, in late 1837, was published as the opening piece of the *Album d'un voyageur* (S156), the earliest form of the *Années de pèlerinage, Suisse.*

songs, and the national, moral, political, and religious anthems, which will have to be taught in schools'. Although the essay remained unpublished, part of it was included in *De la musique religieuse,* the penultimate section of Liszt's long and important essay *De la situation des artistes et de leur condition dans la société,* published in 1835.

In the late summer he was finally able to accept a longstanding invitation from Lamennais to visit La Chênaie, the Abbé's home near Dinan in Brittany. After a week at Croissy with Marie, and taking Ballanche's *Orphée* to read on the journey, he set out on 13 September, arriving three days later.

Liszt to his mother. La Chênaie, September. The Abbé is altogether charming and quite extraordinarily kind; after Longinus* he is my greatest passion. I have a very attractive room, good food, very many *agréments spirituels*—in short, things have never gone so well for me.[3]

To Marie d'Agoult. Truly, he [Lamennais] is a wonderful, prodigious, and quite exceptional man. So much genius and so much heart. High-mindedness, piety, passionate ardour, perspicacity of mind, a wide and profound judgement, the simplicity of a child, sublimity of thought, and power of soul—in him can be found everything which makes man in the image of God. Never yet have I heard him say the word *I*.[4]

The work which occupied Liszt during this visit was the composition of his *Grande fantaisie symphonique* (S120) for piano and orchestra on themes from Berlioz's *Lélio* (a 'new fantastic enormity', as he described it to Marie), of which he gave the first performance the following April.

Liszt to Marie d'Agoult, early October. Believe it or not, I can already no longer endure the admirable life I am leading here. . . . My stupid and hateful existence in Paris, with all its wretched fatigues, its tortures, and its empty and profound tedium, but where I can find from time to time my poor M, I still prefer a hundred times to this unceasing celebration of intelligence and soul, to these active, serious, varied, and singularly fortifying days at La Chênaie, where she has never been, where she will not come. . . . *Ah! mon Dieu, que je souffre pauvrement!!!* Tomorrow I leave for Dinan; from there to Saint Malo is not more than two hours. The steamboat will take me on Friday morning. For the whole of that day and the next I shall not leave the beach. I feel an inexpressible thirst for the music of the ocean.[5]

By mid-October, after a three-week sojourn at La Chênaie, Liszt was back in Paris. He had promised his services at a charity concert (in which he played *La Clochette*) on 5 November and a Berlioz concert at the Conservatoire on the 23rd.†

* Liszt's nickname for Marie d'Agoult, presumably because he thought her 'sublime'. (The title of the most important work generally attributed to the 3rd-century Neoplatonic philosopher Longinus is *On the Sublime.*)

† At which *Harold en Italie* received its première, the solo viola being played by Urhan. However, according to a review in *L'Artiste,* Liszt's contribution was omitted.

Liszt to Lamennais, 4 November. Dear father, don't accuse me of laziness, I beg you. All this past fortnight I have been moiling and toiling away like a slave. Just imagine, even before my arrival I had already been announced, my name stuck up and placarded in big letters on every street corner. To face up to all these wretched concerts I have been obliged to spend whole days and nights writing, correcting, and working at my miserable demisemiquavers. What a change from, what a contrast to, what a sad compensation for, my beautiful life at La Chênaie! . . . How kind, how immensely kind, you were to me! Allow me to hope that you will not forget me entirely and that you will always keep for me a little of that holy affection, memory of which makes me so happy and so proud.[6]

Soon after his return from Brittany Liszt made the acquaintance of another celebrity: Madame Aurore Dudevant, better remembered as George Sand (1804–76), the pen-name she had adopted for the publication of her novel *Indiana*, in 1832, and then retained after the book's brilliant success. The two were introduced by Alfred de Musset, the lover with whom she was enjoying a reconciliation after a period of estrangement. Numerous other liaisons lay ahead of her, most notably the decade-long relationship with Chopin. Greatly though he admired her works, however, Liszt seems to have remained impervious to the spell cast by the mannish, cigar-smoking novelist over so many others. Nor, apparently, did she succumb to his own charms. 'If I could have loved Monsieur Liszt, I should have done so out of pure spite, but I could not. . . .' Nevertheless, they met fairly frequently and enjoyed long conversations late into the night, until signs of jealousy on de Musset's part compelled a short break in relations.

George Sand, 28 November. Liszt told me this evening that it was only God who deserved to be loved. Possibly, but when one has loved a man it is very difficult to love God. It's so different. Liszt added, it is true, that in his whole life he has felt keen affection only for M. de Lamennais, and that an earthly love would never take possession of him.

He is very fortunate, that little Christian.[7]

On 24 November, Liszt celebrated St Cecilia's Day by joining Urhan in a performance (postponed from the 22nd) of Beethoven's Kreutzer Sonata during low mass at St Vincent de Paul. His last appearances of the year were at a matinée in Stoepel's Institution Musicale on Christmas Day and at a Berlioz concert on the 28th.

Gazette musicale (28 December, referring to the Stoepel matinée). Messieurs Liszt and Chopin opened it brilliantly in the Grand Duo for four hands by Moscheles. We need hardly say that this work, one of the composer's masterpieces, was performed with a rare perfection of talent by the two greatest pianoforte virtuosi of the age. . . .

The storm of applause told MM Liszt and Chopin better than our words could do of the delight they had given their audience, whom they electrified a second time when playing M. Liszt's duo for two pianos.* . . . The performance of the two artists was greeted with unanimous applause. M. Ernst† furnished new proofs of his talent by playing, on the violin, a solo which M. Liszt, called upon at a moment's notice, accompanied with his habitual dexterity.

Earlier in the month tragedy had come to the d'Agoult household: after an illness lasting two months, six-year-old Louise had died.

Marie d'Agoult. What happened next I have never been able to remember, but I have been told that I was at once taken away. When I returned to my senses I was at Croissy surrounded by my family. I was given a mass of letters which had arrived since the calamity, and which they had thought it best to keep from me until then. Opening one at random (since I was unable to make out the different handwritings), I found that it was from Franz. He did not hope to see me, he said, at such a moment. He did not think that his presence could bring me any consolation. He was leaving for La Chênaie.‡ He did not say for how long, nor did he ask me to write to him. In the tone of his letter, and in the determination it showed, there was a coldness which should have hurt me. But on the contrary I felt a kind of bitter relief. Suffering brings its own grim selfishness. Mine I wished neither to share nor to ease. In withdrawing, Franz seemed to divine this, and I was grateful to him for leaving me thus wholly given up to myself and my despair.[8]

In addition to those works already mentioned, there came into being this year one of the most remarkable of Liszt's early piano compositions: *Apparitions* (S155), three pieces of which the last is based on a Schubert waltz to which Liszt was to return in his *Soirées de Vienne*.

1835

In a letter to Lamennais of 14 January, Liszt mentions that from the next day he will be away for two months. No information is available about his destination, but since the Abbé's reply of the 26th (sent to Anna Liszt's address to await Liszt's return) begins 'Je vous croyais en Suisse depuis longtemps', it may be inferred that Liszt spent this period in Switzerland; a private visit, apparently, for no concert reports have been traced.

After his return to Paris in March he played in public on several occasions, and

* This can only be the *Grosses Konzertstück* (S257) on themes from Mendelssohn's *Lieder ohne Worte*. It, too, was composed this year.

† The Austrian violinist and composer H. W. Ernst (1814–65).

‡ It is true that Liszt shortly afterwards left Paris for some considerable time (mid-January until March); but either he misled Marie about his destination or her memory is at fault, for his September visit to La Chênaie remained the first and last.

at the Hôtel de Ville on Thursday, 9 April gave a concert (for charity) of his own, the first for seven years. (Apart from that given jointly with Garcia *fils* in March 1833, he had given no concert in Paris since April 1828.) For this important event he chose the *Lélio* fantasy (its première) and the two-piano fantasy on themes of Mendelssohn, in which he was partnered by his pupil Mme Vial. Probably because of the emotional stresses he was suffering at this time, he fainted at the keyboard, in a scene described by *Henry Reeve* (1813–95), the later editor of the *Edinburgh Review*.

Yesterday after dinner, Ballanche and I sallied on to our friend Liszt's great concert. . . . It was very full, and I stood the greater part of the evening. . . . Liszt's person is slight and tall, a delicate frame, not worn or wasted by weakness and malady, but perpetually strained by the flow of animated thoughts, by the violence of a musical soul, for which no sound affords an adequate expression. He had already played a great Fantasia of his own, and Beethoven's 27th Sonata,* in the former part of the concert. After this latter piece he gasped with emotion as I took his hand and thanked him for the divine energy he had shed forth. At last I had managed to pierce the crowd, and I sat in the orchestra before the Duchesse de Rauzan's† box, talking to her Grace and Mme de Circourt;‡ my chair was on the same board as Liszt's piano when the final piece began. It was a duet for two instruments, beginning with Mendelssohn's 'Chants sans Paroles' and proceeding to a work of Liszt's. . . . As the closing strains began, I saw Liszt's countenance assume that agony of expression, mingled with radiant smiles of joy, which I never saw in any other human face, except in the paintings of our Saviour by some of the early masters; his hands rushed over the keys, the floor on which I sat shook like a wire, and the whole audience were wrapped in sound, when the hand and frame of the artist gave way; he fainted in the arms of the friend who was turning over for him, and we bore him out in a strong fit of hysterics. The effect of this scene was really dreadful. The whole room sat breathless with fear, till Hiller came forward and announced that Liszt was already restored to consciousness, and was comparatively well again. As I handed Mme de Circourt to her carriage, we both trembled like poplar leaves, and I tremble scarcely less as I write.[1]

* It was actually the Sonata in C sharp minor, Op. 27, No. 2. The first movement was played in an orchestral arrangement, the second and third by Liszt.

† In one of the earliest of his letters to Marie d'Agoult, Liszt mentions his 'mad and hopeless passion' for Clara, Duchesse de Rauzan (1799–1863), one of the leading *salonnières* of the Faubourg Saint-Germain, whose name recurs often in their correspondence. It was to her that he dedicated the first of the *Apparitions*.

‡ The former Anastasia de Klustine (1808–63), an 'incomparable Russian' who later presided over another remarkable Parisian salon. She had married Comte Adolphe de Circourt (1801–79), prolific correspondent, tireless seeker after knowledge, and, like his wife, exceptionally gifted linguist. She was said to know seventeen languages and he eighteen. Circourt's stupendous erudition, incidentally, included knowing the *Divina Commedia* by heart, 'from first line to last'.

On 3 May the *Gazette musicale* published the first of six instalments of Liszt's essay *De la situation des artistes et de leur condition dans la société*. Written, as were most or all of his literary publications of the next six years, in collaboration with Marie d'Agoult, it is first and foremost an impassioned protest against the *subalternité*, as he termed it, of the artist's position in society; and it called on all musicians, all those who possessed a profound feeling for art, to come together to found a 'universal society' whose aim would be: 'To bring about, encourage and hasten the upward movement, the propagation and the indefinite development of music; and to elevate and ennoble the status of artists, by remedying the abuses and injustices they are having to suffer. . . .'

An emotional reunion in March had brought to an end Liszt and Marie d'Agoult's long separation following the death of Louise; and when Marie found that she was pregnant, the lovers agreed to elope to Switzerland. The first to leave was Marie, who at the end of May set out for Basle, accompanied by her mother and brother-in-law (husband of her half-sister), neither of whom was aware of the real reason for the journey. Before departing she had left a letter of explanation for her husband, and also found the strength to withstand the eloquent pleas of Lamennais, who, having learnt of the planned elopement from Liszt, and fearful that the latter might be taking a step which would ruin his life and career, had requested an interview in an attempt to dissuade her from so irrevocable a course.

On 1 June, having proved equally obdurate when faced by the Abbé's arguments, Liszt left Paris by himself, and, via Troyes, Belfort, and Mulhouse, arrived at Basle in the morning of the 4th. Apprised of the real situation, the Comtesse de Flavigny and the brother-in-law at once returned to Paris; whereupon, left at liberty to enjoy themselves and with no immediate cares or concerns to trouble them, the lovers set out on a tour* of some of the most picturesque regions of Switzerland.

Marie d'Agoult. To live alone together, to put a considerable distance between ourselves and our past, to change horizons just as we were going to change our lives—these were our only goals. We wanted solitude, self-communion, work. Wearied and in a way humiliated by the brilliance of a celebrity of which nothing would remain after him, and tormented by loftier ambitions, Franz wished there to be a silence around his name and his life so that he could devote himself undisturbed to the serious study of the Masters and to the creation of a great work of art.

It was religious art which preoccupied him above all. Biblical subjects and the Christian legends absorbed his thoughts; and even, at certain moments when his genius spoke more loudly than his doubts, the Passion of Our Lord. To return to the temple the sacred music banished from it by the profane tastes of our century; to offer to God a purified form of

* The diary kept by Liszt during this tour is now the possession of the Bibliothèque Nationale in Paris. Its contents were made known by Maria Párkai-Eckhardt in 'Diary of a Wayfarer: The Wanderings of Franz Liszt and Marie d'Agoult in Switzerland, June-July 1835', *Journal of the American Liszt Society,* June 1982, 10–17, source of the itinerary provided here.

worship, in the most ideal of all the arts; to lead and uplift the masses, filling them with adoration and divine love: such was the secret hope cherished by Franz, one which he allowed me to glimpse during those all too rare moments when, confiding and happy beside me, he abandoned himself to his dreams. Nor did Franz believe me incapable of giving lasting shape to my own thoughts and feelings; and he urged me to apply myself to my work [of writing]. . . .

No letters reached us during our fantastic excursions through the mountains. No one knew our names in the isolated houses and hamlets in which we stopped by preference. Almost everywhere, seeing us so similar in height, in colour of eyes and hair, in complexion and voice, people took us for brother and sister*—which delighted both of us. Did not such an error reveal better than all else the secret affinities which had so powerfully attracted us to one another? Was it not the certain proof that we were born for one another, and that, even had it been our wish, it would have been impossible for us not to love one another?[2]

Leaving Basle on 14 June,† the couple the next day visited the celebrated Rhine Falls near Schaffhausen, and on the 16th the town of Constance. By the 18th they had arrived at Heinrichsbad (at Herisau), where a 'miraculous bath' alleviated the discomfort caused to Marie by an attack of colic. They also visited nearby St Gallen and its Baroque cathedral. On the 19th they came to Weesen on the westernmost tip of Lake Walenstadt (the Walensee)—'whose shores held us for a long time,' remembered Marie long afterwards. 'It was there that Franz composed for me a melancholy piece,‡ imitative of the sighing of the waves and the rhythm of the oars, that I have never been able to hear without weeping.' On the 20th they crossed Lake Walenstadt by boat to the town of that name in the eastern corner of the lake, and then returned to Weesen.

A pilgrimage was made on the 21st to Einsiedeln and its great Benedictine Abbey ('Black Virgin—cemetery, exhibition of skulls—pagan sculptures at the main altar' noted Liszt); and on the 22nd their goal was the 'island mountain' of the Rigi. Reaching Goldau, a village on the northern slope, they continued to ascend, and spent the night in a mountain shelter.§ Descending the south-western flank of the mountain in the morning, they breakfasted at the beautiful resort of Weggis on Lake Lucerne, and then took the steamer to Brunnen at the eastern end of the lake.

On 24 June they proceeded along the eastern shore of the lake to Flüelen,

* When Hans von Bülow first met Marie d'Agoult (1858), he found the resemblance between her profile and Liszt's striking enough to remind him of Siegmund and his twin sister Sieglinde in Wagner's *Die Walküre*.

† It was on this same day that, back in Paris, the first 'official' biography of Liszt was published, in the *Gazette musicale*. Although it appeared above the name of his friend Joseph d'Ortigue, there is a possibility that the real author was Marie d'Agoult.

‡ *Le lac de Wallenstadt* (the spelling used by Liszt), the second piece in the *Album d'un voyageur*. Revised, and entitled *Au lac de Wallenstadt*, it later formed part of the *Années de pèlerinage, Suisse*.

§ Cf. *Un soir dans les montagnes* in the *Album d'un voyageur*.

visiting *en route* the chapel* linked with William Tell. Lunch was taken at Amsteg. 'Magnificent scene,' noted Liszt in his diary, 'nothing but mountains and rocks.' Crossing the Devil's Bridge and passing through Andermatt, they found accommodation at Hospenthal; and here the weary Marie spent the next day in bed. In the afternoon of the 26th they visited the nearby St Gotthard Hospice.

Entering the Rhône valley through the Furka Pass on the 27th, they spent the night at Gletsch, at the foot of the Rhône Glacier. The next evening they reached Lax, near the Aletsch Glacier, and, via Brig and Turtmann, on the 30th arrived at Martigny. Here, Liszt also saw the Pissevache Falls.

Leaving the Rhône on 1 July, Liszt and Marie then went along the Drance valley towards the Great St Bernhard Pass, taking lodging that night at the St Bernhard Hospice. Retracing their route the next day, in the morning of 3 July they returned by mule-cart to Martigny; and later in the day arrived at the little spa of Bex.

Liszt's diary entries cease at this point—but the couple seem to have spent the next fortnight in or near Bex. Marie would later write: 'We stayed in the Rhône valley, near Bex, where we read *Obermann* and [Lamartine's] *Jocelyn*; and it was there that, abruptly, our first dream came to an end.'

On 19 July they reached Geneva, in which they had chosen to settle. After spending a week at the home of Liszt's former pupil Pierre Wolff, on 28 July they rented a handsome apartment in a house on the corner of the rue Tabazan.

Among the residents of Geneva already known to Liszt were Caroline and Valérie Boissier, with whom he had kept in touch since the lessons in Paris. Calling at their lakeside home, he was heedless of the risk he ran, by his open liaison with another man's wife, of receiving a cooler welcome than that which might have been given him in more decorous circumstances. The prevailing rigid morality of Calvinist Geneva naturally quite precluded any possibility of Madame d'Agoult being received in the homes of respectable members of her own sex, just as there was no question of any lady setting foot inside the apartment in the rue Tabazan.

From the diary of Caroline Boissier. Liszt entered. His appearance is somewhat improved; no one could deny that he looks both refined and distinguished. He is excessively thin . . . but has charm and an interesting face. His clothes no longer have the bad taste which marked him out in Paris; it is easy to see that he has received some good feminine advice. He was friendly, and is *au fond* a very nice boy. But he is an unfortunate young man, badly spoilt by the world and by success.

His conversation is more wearisome than agreeable. I don't mean that he lacks ideas or wit; he is even capable of tackling profound and serious matters; but he loses his way in them. It has been his misfortune to live among present-day men of letters who have beguiled him with their dangerous doctrines, their erroneous opinions, and their disbelief. He

* The inspiration for *La chapelle de Guillaume Tell* (of the *Album d'un voyageur* and, later, the *Années de pèlerinage, Suisse*).

rejects accepted beliefs and principles, but I'm not too sure what he puts in their place. He is enmeshed in a highly immoral system which is connected with the Saint-Simonians on the one hand and Madame Dudevant [George Sand] on the other. The consecration of marriage and other such trifles make him shrug his shoulders. He abandons himself to his passions with perfect coolness and candour. If it came to it, he would introduce his countess to me quite unblushingly. He once had, perhaps still has, a noble soul—but he is crazy.

(After their third meeting.) He had dinner here with us. A nicer young man couldn't be found; and in certain respects he has improved since Paris. . . . After dinner we chatted. Then a little fellow of thirteen arrived in search of him, the pupil* of whom he is so fond. How kind and fatherly he is towards this child; it is touching to see how he behaves with him. The child idolizes him, hardly taking his eyes off him. We got to talking about serious matters; but this unfortunate Liszt's mind has been turned by today's extravagant doctrines.

Caroline Boissier. Edmond spent yesterday evening at Liszt's. Madame la Comtesse d'Agoult received!! Like a queen on her throne! Not the slightest embarrassment, not a trace of bashfulness, a dignified, noble, and easy manner. A clever and witty woman, good at repartee; very French, very *bon ton*. No longer young, nor pretty, but with countenance and character.

Besides the *master* and *mistress* of the house, there were Wolff, who played the *grand seigneur*; an Italian, a good pianist,† wearing spectacles and a toupet; and lastly a Prince Belgiojoso,‡ an extremely handsome Milanese Alcibiades who is an excellent musician and possessor of one of the biggest and finest voices in Italy. Then poor little Puzzi, who is receiving his education in this atmosphere of seduction, talent, wit, and perversity.

They talked. The countess was very amiable, and it was she who introduced the various topics of conversation, holding forth on Paris, on literature, the sciences, the passions. She talked about Parisian society as

* The very talented Hermann Cohen (b. 1821), nicknamed 'Puzzi', had been studying with Liszt since shortly after coming to Paris from his native Hamburg the previous summer. To resume lessons, and with mother and brother in tow, he had arrived in Geneva on 14 August. 'The ascendancy Liszt achieved over others amounted almost to fascination,' he recalled. In 1847, following years of dissipation, Hermann was 'like another Saul, struck by Divine Grace', writes his biographer. 'He forthwith renounced Judaism, demanded baptism, and launched into a career of penitence and sacrifice.' Becoming a barefoot Carmelite, he died (Jan. 1871) at Spandau near Berlin, whither he had gone to minister to French prisoners of war, from whom he caught smallpox.

† Probably the composer and pianist Francesco Bonoldi, who also made a brief appearance in the concert of 1 Oct. (see *infra*).

‡ Prince Emilio Barbiano di Belgiojoso d'Este (1800–58), husband of Liszt's much-admired friend Princess Cristina Belgiojoso.

though she were still a member of it. She behaved in such a manner, says Edmond, that after a quarter of an hour one felt as though one were with a married woman and gave no more thought to the matter.

Liszt was dignified, serious, a trifle over-formal, receiving the guests jointly with the countess, with ceremonial politeness. He and the Italian pianist played some admirable overtures together *à quatre mains*. M. Belgiojoso sang. Edmond enjoyed himself greatly, coming home at 10.30.

Caroline Boissier. Today, Valérie and I are still under the spell cast over us yesterday. Liszt was sublime, and I wept while listening to him. He played us a work of his own. Full of pathos, well composed, terribly difficult, and making the greatest effect. Liszt is a musical demon, a Talma* in moments of declamation. . . .

He asked Valérie's permission to dedicate to her a beautiful piece† that he is having engraved at this moment, one which he composed here. No one could have been politer or more modest in making this request. He spoke of it as though it were a kindness that was being done to him, while really it was he who was granting the favour. Valérie was touched and flattered.

A singular young man, this Liszt! Outstanding abilities, full of verve, fire, mind, and genius. Then he has, too, a noble soul, greatness, unselfishness, much generosity. And with that, total confusion about good and evil, committing enormous sins without the least remorse, happy in the midst of vice. Sometimes he behaves like a boy of fifteen—then puts on the airs of a man! In short, black and white, and yet an attractive person, of whom one grows fond![3]

Marie d'Agoult. My passion for Franz, which had become still more ardent in the solitude of these last months, had something of the fanatical about it. In him I saw a being apart, superior to everything I had ever known. Inclined as I was to superstitions of the heart, in a kind of mystical delirium I sometimes felt that I had been summoned by God, somehow offered to the greatness and the salvation of this heavenly genius who had nothing in common with other men and was above the common law! In those ecstasies of love, which doubtless came to me from my German blood, I felt that nothing had to remain within me any more of desires, whims, affections, duties, or even conscience, but what was to be sacrificed for him. . . .

We took up once again, Franz and I, regular reading, study, and conversation. He began to compose. My presence, when he was writing, was not unwelcome to him: on the contrary, when I wished to retire discreetly he kept me back, saying that he had more difficulty in collecting his thoughts and that his ideas arranged themselves less well when he no

* The great French tragedian François Joseph Talma (1763–1826).

† The *Fantaisie romantique sur deux mélodies suisses* (S157).

longer felt me near him. For me, who then pretended to read but in reality missed no movement either of his pen or his lips, it was profoundly moving to see him thus entirely given to his art and to the splendid genius radiating from his eyes which I silently worshipped.[4]

As a person of intellectual interests and ambitions, Marie was soon richly compensated for the lack of female society by having that of Geneva's most prominent men of science and letters, some of whom enjoyed a European as well as a local celebrity. Among the most frequent visitors to the apartment in the rue Tabazan were the historian and economist Simonde de Sismondi (1773–1842); the orientalist Alphonse Denis; the botanist Pyrame de Candolle (1778–1841); and the philologist Major Adolphe Pictet (1799–1875). The politician James Fazy (1794–1878), the Genevan head of state between 1848 and 1861, was another good friend.

Ever desirous of adding to his own store of knowledge, Liszt likewise welcomed the company and conversation of such distinguished *savants*. He also enrolled in several courses at the Academy.*

Invited to take part in a grand charity concert given on 1 October and organized by Prince Belgiojoso, he chose as his principal contributions Weber's *Concertstück* and the Fantasy on *La Fiancée*.

Le Fédéral (6 October). In the opinion of some connoisseurs, Liszt is the first pianist in the world; and in truth that would not astonish us; we should be much more surprised were he only the second. Unbelievable speed and perfect precision are the least of his qualities; but the lightness of his touch, the easy and natural grace of his playing, his attack and energy, are such that they are not to be conceived of by those who have not heard this young artist. . . .[5]

As Liszt remarked in his *Lettre à M. George Sand*, dated 23 November and published in the *Revue et gazette musicale*† of 6 December, the concert was attended by the ex-King of Westphalia, Jérôme Bonaparte, and his 'ravishing fair-haired daughter', the young Princess Mathilde. Also present was *Marie d'Agoult*.

I sat behind a tall screen which hid me almost completely. The hall was splendidly illuminated and filled to its limits. My eyes peered vaguely down into it, and then closed, quite dazzled. It had been a very long time since I had seen such a large gathering of people. The brilliant lights, the undulating colours, the surging movement, the whispers, gestures, and eyes of an expectant crowd, made me feel strangely dizzy. An open abyss

* One learns with a certain amusement of the rebuke administered to him at the first philosophy class, to which he turned up late. 'Gentlemen, you will kindly be here punctually at the start of each lesson,' the lecturer, Professor Choisy, remarked reprovingly, as he bestowed a severe look upon the errant and unknown newcomer. Sheepishly, Liszt bowed his apologies.

† In November the *Gazette musicale* had merged with the *Revue musicale*. The new, combined title remained unchanged until publication ceased in 1880.

beneath my feet could not have frightened me more. All at once, silencing this confused hum, there came an immense, deafening, and prolonged clapping of hands; repeated twenty times over, it seemed that it would never end. It was Franz, who had entered and was bowing to his public. I could no longer draw breath. For a few moments I remained breathless, almost stifled. . . . The applause came to an end. Amidst a profound silence, the first chords rang out. Suddenly restored, I lowered slightly the screen which was obstructing my view. By either a strange chance or some secret magnetism, my eyes met those of Franz who was looking for me. How can I describe what I felt at that moment? It was Franz I saw, and yet it was not Franz. It was as though someone were portraying him on the stage with much skill and verisimilitude, but who for all that had nothing in common with him exept mere physical appearance. His playing disturbed me too. To be sure, his virtuosity was prodigious, shattering, incomparable, but I felt, nevertheless, as though it were foreign to him. Where was I? Where were we? Was I dreaming? Was I delirious? Who had brought me here? For what purpose? . . . My anguish was inexpressible. . . .

From the day following the concert, congratulations and invitations, expressions of admiration and of enthusiasm, of recognition and of fellow feeling, and every possible token of goodwill, rained upon Franz from all quarters, so that the better part of his days was spent in replying to them. The city's most eminent personages solicited the honour of being introduced to him. Everyone courted him: the young for his wit, the old for his talent; the women for his beauty, his ardent appearance, his mysterious and Romantic existence.[6]

Liszt's arrival in Geneva had coincided with an important event in its musical life: the founding of a Conservatoire de Musique; and, wishing to make his own contribution to the new institution, he indicated that he was willing to give lessons, gratis, to some of the advanced piano students. The offer was eagerly accepted, ten of the thirty-three pupils being assigned to him. Hermann Cohen, for whose 'talents and morality' Liszt made himself responsible, was entrusted with another ten, and Pierre Wolff with the remaining thirteen. In recognition of his work,* Liszt was at the end of the academic year made an 'honorary professor' of the Conservatoire, and by its founder and president, François Bartholoni, given a repeater watch with gold chain.

Liszt to his mother. Geneva, November. From 9 o'clock in the morning—I get up no earlier than that—until 11 at night, my entire day is filled. The mornings belong to the Conservatoire, to the Method,† and to my

* His *livre de classe,* containing perceptive and amusing comments on the pianistic—and occasionally the personal—endowments of his pupils, is preserved at the Conservatoire.

† A *Méthode de Piano* which Liszt had offered to write for the Conservatoire. Nearly forty years later he told his biographer Lina Ramann that he never had written and never would think of writing such a work. (*Lisztiana*, Mainz, 1983, 39.) Nevertheless, there are indications in several of his letters to his mother that the Method had at least been well started. Further, in October 1836, after conferring with Liszt, Bartholoni reported to his committee that the

compositions. The afternoons I devote to reading, piano-playing, visiting, or writing articles. In the evenings I copy or do nothing at all.

Day after day I intend to write to one person or another. In this manner I salve my conscience, which, as you know, is very tender. ('My son, you are a hypocrite!!!') But as yet I have required neither pen nor ink. Perhaps, instead, I shall devote the whole of December to letter-writing.[7]

At the end of the year Liszt wrote to inform his mother of the happy outcome to the event which had occasioned the flight to Switzerland seven months earlier: 'On 18 December Mme d'A. was safely delivered of a sweet and extraordinarily beautiful baby girl. All necessary precautions had been taken in good time, and up to now I can only congratulate myself on this addition to the family. I should very much like you to come to us in the spring to see the little creature. . . .'

It was for this daughter of his, named Blandine-Rachel, that Liszt wrote the poetic piano piece *Les cloches de G . . .*, one of the *Impressions et poésies* of his *Album d'un voyageur*. Revised and given its full title, *Les cloches de Genève*, it eventually formed the concluding item of the *Années de pèlerinage, Suisse*.

1836

Early in the year Liszt was intrigued by reports of the success being enjoyed in Paris by the Viennese pianist Sigismond Thalberg (1812–71), a masterly and finished performer who rendered operatic fantasies and display pieces of his own composition with great brilliance, a speciality being passages in which a melody played in the middle of the keyboard by the thumbs rang out clearly through swirling arpeggios in treble and bass, producing an effect as of three hands. 'Totally unlike in style to either Chopin or Liszt, Thalberg was admirable and unimpeachable in his own way,' remembered Charles Hallé. 'He created a great sensation in Paris and became the idol of the public, principally, perhaps, because it was felt that he could be imitated, even successfully, which with Chopin and Liszt was out of the question.'

Liszt to his mother. Geneva, March. If you see Berlioz, thank him for his letter, which I shall be answering as soon as possible. Tell him about your journey* in May, and ask him to entrust you for two months with the score of his Harold symphony. I should like to arrange it for piano,† if that suits him. . . .

composer had decided to have the work engraved at his own expense and was seeking permission to dedicate it to the Conservatoire. According to the late Robert Bory, the printer entrusted with the finished work first lost Liszt's manuscript and was then obliged to pawn the engraving plates, which were subsequently destroyed.

* It had been arranged that Anna Liszt would travel to Geneva in May; but when Liszt subsequently decided to visit Paris his mother's trip was cancelled.

† The transcription (S472) of *Harold en Italie* was done within the next year.

If you see Chopin, tell him that I am as fond of him as ever, and that I would give much, very much, if he would spend a month or two with us in the most beautiful season of the year. Madame d'Agoult is extremely keen to see and hear him again. Try to persuade him; we would do our utmost to make his stay with us a pleasant one. . . .

Thalberg I should like to know. Those works of his which I have seen I find *so so*. The newspaper eulogies impress me very little. Let me know if it is true, as I have been told, that without knowing you he sent you a ticket for his concert.[1]

On 6 April, at the Salle du Casino, Liszt gave a soirée musicale at which he played Hummel's Septet (with six local musicians), his own recently completed 'Divertissement sur la cavatine "I tuoi frequenti palpiti" ' (S419) from Pacini's *Niobe*, and, with Hermann Cohen and Joseph Schad (a professor at the Conservatoire), Czerny's *Potpourri brillant, pour six mains et deux pianos, sur des thèmes de Mozart et de Beethoven.* On the 13th, at a Société de Musique concert, he and his colleagues gave a further performance of the Septet. 'Liszt is one of those artists predestined to allow us a glimpse of certain affinities between universal life and our individual existence,' ran the review in *L'Europe centrale*. 'He elevates music to the destination dreamt of by those who believe that eternal bliss consists in listening everlastingly to music.'

Countess Marie Potocka to Honoré de Balzac. Geneva, 11 April. I often see the prodigious Liszt, whom I enjoy greatly. There is more to him than his fingertips. Nature has bestowed rich gifts upon him, made him one of her finest creations. This astonishing man has just given us a soirée musicale in which he was sublime. The Geneva audience thrilled to this powerful inspiration. Never could the spells cast over the wild animals by the music of Orpheus have been greater.[2]

In the second half of April Liszt left for Paris, first stopping at Lyons, where he gave three concerts (2, 5, and 7 May) and worked on his *La Serenata e l'Orgia* (S422), a Grand Fantasy on themes from Rossini's *Soirées musicales*. The purpose of the journey was to explain his and Marie's situation to her brother, Maurice de Flavigny. He would also gladly have seized the opportunity to hear Thalberg; but at Lyons he heard that the acclaimed Austrian pianist had left Paris on a concert tour.

Although his initial plan had been to spend no more than 'six or seven days' in Paris, Liszt eventually extended his visit by several weeks, in order to see Lamennais, who did not arrive until the beginning of June. Among other friends and acquaintances he saw Ballanche, de Vigny, Montalembert, de Musset, Lamartine, Meyerbeer, Delacroix, and Princess Cristina Belgiojoso.

The last-named (1808–71) was on terms of affectionate friendship with Liszt throughout the 1830s and early 1840s. A member of the ancient Milanese family of Trivulzio, she was described in her early twenties as 'slim, *distinguée*, pale, eyes as big as saucers, very slender hands, grand and gracious manners, extremely intelligent, *de l'esprit comme un démon*'. More than a decade later her haunting beauty inspired a celebrated portrait by Henri Lehmann, the sensation of the 1844 *Salon*. But it had been her misfortune, when only sixteen, to marry Prince Emilio Belgiojoso (of the magnificent voice), a profligate and voluptuary who soon infected his young bride with syphilis, a disease which, in the words of her biographer, 'was to lead her on a *via crucis* for the next forty years'. As if this were not enough she was also afflicted with epilepsy.

Having settled in Paris, whither she had fled from her husband on the one hand and the agents of Metternich on the other (her political convictions having incurred the displeasure of Lombardy's Austrian overlords), Cristina soon became one of the most brilliant of the salon hostesses; and her fascinating and elusive personality, combined with her unusual beauty and high intelligence, inspired so many of the leading creative artists of the period (including Balzac, de Musset, and Heine) that she became known, then and afterwards, as the Romantic Muse.

An ardent Italian patriot, she was also a committed feminist and social reformer. Her days were spent in study and the writing of numerous learned articles; and it was she who made the first complete translation into French of Vico's *Scienza Nova*.*

Count Rudolf Apponyi, May. Princess Belgiojoso, in addition to her pretension of being a second Sappho or Corinne, likes to assume the aspect of a spectre: she is pale and wan, wears unusual head-dresses and turbans, and excessively low-necked dresses which are so extremely diaphanous, and her draperies so bizarre, that you constantly believe you are going to espy a dagger hidden in their folds. Her black, protruding eyes, which she turns sinisterly in all directions; her features, immobile moreover; her mouth whose thin, pale lips seem made only for heaving sighs of sorrow; her whole bearing, gait, and every movement she makes are in harmony with the role she is playing: thus the sad and bizarre condition of a woman whose mind has gone wrong.

I recently waited upon her at her home. She was sitting on a Renaissance-style sofa, in a small room furnished in the same manner. It was morning; she was wearing a white dressing-gown under which I could see a kind of red velvet bodice. On her head she had an immense turban which reminded me of the one given by Michelangelo to his Sybil. M. Mignet[†] was standing behind the sofa, leaning nonchalently against its back of sculpted oak; M. Liszt, the pianist, in a black velvet blouse, long smooth hair falling down on to his shoulders, tieless and wearing a beret, was seated on a stool in front of the Princess. His clothes, and the fact that I believed him to be in Switzerland, prevented my recognizing him at first;

* The more bizarre legends about Cristina Belgiojoso (that, for example, according to which she kept an embalmed corpse in a hidden wardrobe in her bedroom) have now been shown to be mere fiction. See Beth Archer Brombert's *Cristina: Portraits of a Princess* (London, 1978).

† The historian François-Auguste Mignet (1796–1884), who in 1838 became the father of Princess Belgiojoso's only child, a daughter.

he made himself known to me and said that he had come to Paris for a few days only and was expecting to return to Switzerland.

I was so astonished and dumbfounded by all these extravagances surrounding me that I could scarcely start a conversation. The Princess, who on the one hand loves to surround herself by all the most extravagant young people, and on the other by the most distinguished scholars, presents a bizarre mixture of absurdities and rhapsodic learning, which inspires, turn and turn about, admiration and pity; but in the end one pities her.[3]

Another friend seen by Liszt soon after his arrival was Chopin—who 'loves me tenderly and exclusively,' he reported to Marie on the 14th. 'The manner in which he spoke to me today gave me extreme pleasure. He professes a certain measure of criticism for Thalberg,* and above all cannot admit that the least comparison can be established between us.' By 18 May he had already played twice at the Salle Erard and was able to tell Marie: 'My works and my playing have made a very great sensation.'

Hector Berlioz, writing in the Revue et gazette musicale *(12 June)*. Never, perhaps, has this great artist excited the Parisian musical world to such a degree as during these last weeks. . . . Liszt did not give a concert, but it seems to me that no Conservatoire audience could have been more impressive than the gathering of music-lovers and distinguished artists who dogged his footsteps in all those places where there was a hope of hearing him. M. Erard's salons were invaded more than once in a way that seldom occurs even when a full concert is trumpeted in all the newspapers and advertised on huge placards at all the street corners. And yet nothing more was in question than to hear Liszt play his latest works *entirely alone*. . . .

No more than ten or a dozen invitations had been sent out, but news of the event had spread so rapidly, and the curiosity it aroused was so great, that four to five hundred persons turned up, and instead of finding himself, as he expected, amidst a small group of friends, Liszt had to face a real public, among whom were not only the indifferent but also the hostilely-inclined curious. His immense success, and the *electrifying* impression he made on all, can be compared only with the surprise he excited even in those whom he has the right to count among his most enthusiastic supporters. For his audience became aware of a fact as unexpected as it was strange: Liszt's *reappearance* was actually more of a *new appearance*: by which I mean that the Liszt we all know, the Liszt of last year, has been left far behind by the Liszt of today. . . .

This is the great modern school of piano-playing. If everything may now be expected of Liszt as a composer, it is equally true to say that no bounds

* After hearing Thalberg a few years earlier, in Vienna, Chopin had written: 'He plays splendidly, but he's not my man. He's younger than I and pleases the ladies—makes *potpourris* on *La Muette*—produces his *piano* and *forte* with the pedal, not the hand—takes tenths as I do octaves and wears diamond shirt-studs.'

can be set upon his progress as a performer. . . . In support of my opinion I appeal to the judgement of all those who have heard him play the great Beethoven sonata [Op. 106], that sublime poem which until now has been the riddle of the Sphinx for almost every pianist. Liszt, a new Oedipus, has solved it in a manner which would have made the composer, had he heard it in his grave, thrill with pride and joy. Not a note was omitted, not one added (I followed, score in hand), not a single alteration made to what was indicated in the text, not an inflexion or an idea weakened or changed from its true meaning. In the Adagio above all . . . he remained constantly at the level of the composer's inspiration. No higher praise can be given, I know, but since it is true I cannot say less. . . . By such a rendition of a work totally misunderstood until now, Liszt has proved that he is the pianist of the future.

In early June Liszt rejoined Marie, and with young Hermann Cohen the couple then spent a few weeks at Veyrier, a village at the foot of Mont Salève; after which they ascended to a chalet in the resort of Monnetier, where they remained throughout July and from which Liszt departed only to give concerts at Lausanne and Dijon.

On 9 August he was a guest of the Turettini-Necker family at Cologny, a lakeside village near Geneva.

From the diary of Albertine de la Rive-Necker. Today is the great day. . . . We get ready, dress, tidy the salon. All of us feel a certain excitement and a quickening of the pulse. Three o'clock strikes. We are all expectant. The door opens and Liszt appears, as does Hermann. Colladon* follows them in, walking slowly, with an air of ceremony. He makes a deep bow to each of the ladies. Liszt, however, with a much more natural manner merely makes some pleasant small talk.

While we are waiting for the meal, all eyes are fixed on him. He seems not to notice, being used to it. His appearance, his manners, the first words he speaks, show him to be a man *comme il faut.* He talks in an easy, pleasant manner, with no trace of an accent. His conversation is witty, and to everything he says his mobile, animated face lends added expression.

We go to table, and Liszt is placed between my aunt and Albertine.† Conversation languishes for a while; or, rather, no one succeeds in starting any lasting topic. Eventually Albertine manages to get it going, and soon it is flowing along very cheerfully. We are no longer compelled to fill the silences by desperately offering dishes and wines. The talk passes from literature to music, and then to politics. This last topic leads to a passionate discussion between my uncle and Liszt. The whole family hasten to take Liszt's side, and my uncle has to struggle on alone. . . .

* A Geneva lawyer and politician.
† Albertine Turettini, a pupil of Liszt's at the Geneva Conservatoire.

Throughout the meal Liszt puts on and takes off his glasses. He eats little and drinks still less; what he seems to like best are potatoes.

He is nicely dressed. He has very attractive hands. On his index finger he wears a ring showing a silver skull on a gold background. His beautiful fair hair streams down on to his shoulders, curling only slightly. He often pushes it back behind his ears, in a way that makes the gesture seem almost an affectation. . . .

After we have eaten, coffee is served on the balcony. Hermann looks at the view through the telescope. Liszt sits on the bench facing my aunt. When he is shown our white cat his delight knows no bounds. 'Oh! what an enchanting little creature!' he cries out several times in his joy. He picks the cat up, turns it in all directions, strokes it, blows in its ears, and gives it two little kisses on the end of its pink nose. He mentions that M. de Chateaubriand is very fond of cats. 'Ah! if only I dared steal it from you!'—and then he gets up and, with some difficulty, puts it in his pocket, head first. Poor pussy struggles free and runs away.

Gradually we come to talk about pianos. 'There's one that isn't very good,' remarks my aunt, pointing to the one in the salon. 'I'll try it out,' says Liszt, on a sudden kindly impulse. He at once gets up and goes to the piano. This decision surprises and delights us in equal measure, and we hurry into the salon. Liszt preludes deliciously. He has hardly set the keys in motion and yet it already seems a different instrument.

But the weather had grown darker and darker. Everything points to a storm, and it bursts at the very moment when Liszt begins to play. All of a sudden the wind rises furiously, and we hasten to bring in the chairs and to raise the balcony sunshade which has been violently tossed about. The bustle makes me impatient and uneasy. Happily, Liszt is not at all put out by it; on the contrary, his inspiration seems redoubled. It is as though it is no longer him that one sees but the spirit of music itself. His features have changed; all his thoughts and impressions are reflected in his face. His listeners are altogether enchanted, as though they have been touched by a wizard's wand. There are no words to describe what one feels. One's very senses are enchained. One no longer hears or sees anything but him. No one notices that the storm has grown more violent; the sounds that he draws from the piano muffle those of the thunder, and, frail though they look, his fingers possess a strength capable of stifling the noise of the tempest. He 'plays a storm'. On hearing a roll of thunder, he murmurs to Albertine: 'I shall hold my own.' And indeed he confounds and enraptures us, putting us into a state of ecstasy such as we have never known before. 'I win, I am the master,' he seems to say. And yet while playing he takes no notice of his hands, which he never looks at. His eyes wander upwards; he seems to be reading invisible pages, or rather to be composing and playing according to the inspiration of the moment. The piano was not strong enough: two or three strings have been unable to withstand him—but the missing notes have not proved a hindrance. He continues without anyone being aware of their lack. One no longer breathes when listening to him; one trembles lest he finish, and when he finally comes to an end one would like to say: 'Play on, play on, for ever and ever.'

After those magnificent pieces, Liszt accompanies Albertine in a song. He shows her all the nuances of expression and urges her to sing with as much abandon as though there were no one in the room (and not to sing like an archduchess).

At last he rises from the piano, leaving everyone in a state of extraordinary emotion and profound admiration. Our feelings of delight persist, as though we had for a moment been admitted into another world, into a heavenly concert. For how to believe that it was only two hands which produced such an effect! A piece becomes quite different when played by him. He combines strength with lightness and feeling. He seems to find notes between those which actually exist. And then the thoughts, the abandon, mirrored in his features as he plays, are utterly devoid of affectation. He does not make those sudden grimaces of which he has been accused. Everything is felt, graduated, right, and compatible with what he is playing. The play of his features follows the playing of his fingers. His musical soul is revealed in his whole being. . . .[4]

In early September Liszt, Marie, and young Hermann were at Chamonix, a holiday resort at the foot of Mont Blanc, where they had arranged a rendezvous with friends. The first of these to arrive, accompanied by her children Maurice and Solange, and her maid Ursule Josse, was *George Sand*.

And so there we were at Chamonix; the rain was falling and the darkness deepening. By chance I went to the Union Hotel. . . . Taking care not to ask for the European artist by name, but complying with the notions of the enlightened people whom I had the honour of visiting, I gave a concise description of his person: tight blouse, long, dishevelled hair, battered leather hat, tie rolled into a string, temporarily lame, and usually humming the *Dies Irae* quite agreeably.

'Certainly, Monsieur,'* the hotelier replied; 'they have just arrived. The lady is very tired and the young lady in excellent humour. If you go up the stairs you will find them in No. 13.'

I hurried to No. 13. . . . The first object to get entangled in my legs was what the innkeeper called the *young lady*. It was Puzzi astride the travelling-bag, and so changed, so grown, his head covered with such long brown hair, and his figure encased in so feminine a blouse, that, dear me, I got quite confused. . . .

From beneath an English bonnet there emerged, when I spoke, the blonde head of Arabella.† As I hastened towards her, Franz flung his arms

* In her *Lettres d'un Voyageur*, and in accordance with her pen-name, George Sand referred to herself in the masculine.

† Nickname for Marie d'Agoult.

around my neck and Puzzi gave a cry of surprise. On seeing the tangled group we made as we embraced one another, and amazed to see so mud-bespattered a boy, whom until that moment she had taken for a groom, embrace so beautiful a lady as Arabella, the chambermaid dropped her candle and rushed downstairs to report that No. 13 had been invaded by a troupe of mysterious people difficult to categorize, but that they were as long-haired as savages, and which of them were men, which women, which masters and which servants, it was quite impossible to say. . . .[5]

The party was now complete, save for *Major Adolphe Pictet*, who on arrival at the hotel at once asked to see the visitors' book.

The first thing he* recognized was the large and impulsive scrawl of his friend Franz, *musician-philosopher*, born on *Parnassus*, coming from *Doubt*, and journeying towards *Truth*. Then, further on, he . . . read:

Travellers' names:	Piffoël† family.
Residence:	Nature.
Coming from:	God.
Journeying towards:	Heaven.
Place of birth:	Europe.
Occupation:	Loafers.
Date of passports:	Everlasting.
Issued by:	Public opinion.

'A lot of good that's done me!' said the major.

'Has the gentleman come to arrest them?' asked the hotelier, coming forward respectfully.—'Arrest whom?'—'Why, that gypsy family in long hair and blouses who are making such a frightful racket up there. . . . All my guests are moving out.'

'How many of them are there?'—'Four or five, as far as I know. Men, women, coming, going, changing from one sex into the other. . . . There are two children as well.'. . .

'Where are they lodged?'—'In No. 13.'

The major hastened upstairs and straight into the room in question. 'Ah! Here is our dear travelling companion,' cried Franz, bounding forward to meet him. 'Welcome! Here is a man of his word!'. . .

At that moment there came a lot of shouting from the street, interspersed with cries of 'devil' and 'goddam', while simultaneously a burst of stifled laughter could be heard in the adjoining room being used by George.

'That's her getting up to her tricks!' said Franz, running to the door.

The major hurriedly opened the window, and saw three Englishmen

* Throughout his account of the holiday, Pictet refers to himself in the third person.

† The nickname chosen for her family by George Sand because of the large noses with which she and Maurice were endowed (*pif* in French slang being more or less equivalent to 'conk' in English). Shortly afterwards, amused to hear himself referred to by an Englishman as 'that fellow', Liszt bestowed the name of 'the Fellows' upon himself and Marie.

angrily shaking their fists and complaining that water had been sprinkled on them from a certain window (which they pointed at) while they were quietly sitting taking the evening air. They were insisting on obtaining satisfaction from the rascal who had taken them for flower-pots. When Franz got downstairs, he tried to explain that the said rascal was merely a pretty lady who had inadvertently thrown into the street some flowers whose scent was bothering her. Nevertheless, he had a job to calm them down. George had to appear at the window, vase in hand, and offer a word or two of apology before they would be appeased.

'D'you think she did it on purpose?' the major asked Franz when the latter returned.

'Hm, shouldn't be surprised—she hates the English.'

Franz went to scold George for her carelessness, and the major retired to bed.[6]

The week (7–15 September) spent together, partly at Chamonix and partly on an excursion by mule through the mountains to Fribourg, by this well-assorted quartet (not forgetting maid and children), made an impression vivid enough for two of them afterwards to recapture the most colourful moments in writing. Humour and playfulness were much in evidence. Of the four, it was Marie who was least disposed to cast aside, or who most successfully retained, a sense of decorum. 'I really thought you had all lost your senses,' she told Liszt after an evening in which generous libations of punch, and cigars specially prepared with the hallucinogenic leaf of the *datura fastuosa*, had played havoc with rationality. 'You, Franz, were singing at the top of your voice, and, armed with a pair of snuffers, were going around the room striking the chairs which, you said, were singing out of time and tune; the major was talking Sanscrit with invisible persons he thought he could see on the ceiling; and George was dancing about with astonishing agility, bursting into shrieks of laughter, and uttering remarks that were quite unintelligible. In the end I fled, to escape being sucked into the vortex with the rest of you.'

Along with the skylarking there was much cerebration. One by one, philosophy, music, the stars, Creation, and God were brought on to the carpet for discussion. Schelling's 'the Absolute is identical with Itself' was exercising the mind of the major at this time; and, having little relish for metaphysical speculation, Sand put her artistic talent to use at one point by producing a caricature of her three companions as, seated together on a sofa, they sought to dissect that same proposition. 'What exactly does it mean?' a dishevelled-looking Liszt is asking. 'It's a bit vague,' the major concedes, while Marie confesses: 'I've been lost for ages.'

Via Martigny, Bex, Vevey, and Bulle, they reached Fribourg, where an awesome improvisation by Liszt (on the *Dies Irae* from Mozart's *Requiem*) on the great Mooser organ of St Nicholas' Cathedral, in the presence of the organ-builder* himself, provided an unforgettable climax and conclusion to these

* Aloys Mooser (1770–1839), the most eminent Swiss organ-builder of the first half of the 19th century. This Fribourg organ, with its 67 stops and 7,800 pipes, remains his best-known achievement.

carefree days spent together by a musician, a novelist, a scholar-soldier, and an aristocrat.

The remainder of September Liszt and Marie spent at Geneva extending hospitality to the Sand family. On the 26th Liszt participated in a concert given by Hermann Cohen, at which, according to *Le Fédéral*, 'the presence of Madame Dudevant provided the artists with redoubtable competition'. A week later, on 3 October, he lent his services at a soirée musicale given by Aloys Mooser in the salon of the Cour de Saint-Pierre. This occasion, in which he took part in a performance of Beethoven's Archduke Trio besides playing two solos, marks the end of Liszt's public appearances in Geneva, a city in which after his departure from it a few days later he never set foot again.

On 16 October he and Marie arrived in Paris. It was his second and her first return since the elopement to Switzerland a year and a half earlier. Taking an apartment at the Hôtel de France, 23 rue Laffitte, and sharing the salon with George Sand who arrived a week later, they were soon receiving many old friends and acquaintances, including Berlioz, Ballanche, Lamennais, Meyerbeer, and Nourrit. A particularly welcome visitor was Chopin, who on several occasions reciprocated the hospitality. This was the time of his fateful first meeting with George Sand, to whom he was introduced by Liszt.

From the diary of the writer and traveller Ferdinand Denis (1798–1890). 5 November. 2.30 a.m. I spent the evening at Chopin's. Liszt was magnificent. 'It was *the Apocalypse*,' someone aptly said of his playing. George Sand's feeling for that powerful music was admirable. Some splendid mimicry by Chopin*—but the prayer from *Les Huguenots*† was so beautiful that I no longer had the heart to laugh.[7]

Chopin was again the host on 10 November, as on 13 December, on which occasion he and Liszt played Moscheles' Sonata in E flat for piano duet and Liszt accompanied Nourrit in some Schubert *Lieder*. 'Chopin and Liszt played a duet, and Liszt's genius astonished me greatly,' reported another guest, the Polish composer Jósef Brzowski (1803–88). Madame Sand was once more of the company.

On Sunday, 18 December, Liszt contributed several items to a Conservatoire concert given by Berlioz: the *Lélio* and *Niobe* fantasies, plus the 'Bal' and 'Marche au supplice' from the *Symphonie fantastique*. Writing in the *Revue et gazette musicale* (25 December), Berlioz remarked that, despite being greeted with icy reserve by the audience, Liszt had scored a dazzling success with his first piece and completed the victory with the *Niobe*.

Brzowski's opinion after this concert was that in comparison with Liszt all other pianists were merely 'flies'.

Also in the audience was the young German pianist Carl Halle (1819–95), later, as *Charles Hallé*, to be the founder of the Manchester concerts bearing his name. His impressions of Liszt, whom he had waited upon at the Hôtel de France

* Who was an extremely gifted mimic and impersonator.

† Liszt's Fantasy (S412) on Meyerbeer's *Les Huguenots* had been composed earlier in the year. It was dedicated to the Comtesse d'Agoult.

a week earlier armed with a letter of introduction from Meyerbeer, he set down in a letter of the 19th to his parents.

How curious I was to see this man, who has so remarkable a fame, you can easily imagine, especially as he has the reputation, even in his outward appearance, of being a most original creature; and so I found him. Liszt is the most original being in existence. When I entered I found an assembly of thirty or forty persons, among them many of the first artists of Paris, and even several ladies, who had come to pay him homage. . . . He, the fêted Liszt, came to me at once, and I gave him my letter. When he opened it he glanced at once at the signature, and seeing the name of Meyerbeer he shook me again by the hand and kindly bade me sit down. I did not accept the invitation, as there were forty persons in the room and only ten chairs, all of which were occupied. He did not notice it, spoke to me a little while, and then sprang off to someone else. I then had time to look at him carefully, and saw that I had not been told too much about the originality of his outward appearance. His aspect is truly remarkable. He is tall and very thin, his face very small and pale, his forehead remarkably high and beautiful; he wears his perfectly lank hair so long that it spreads over his shoulders, which looks very odd, for when he gets a bit excited and gesticulates, it falls right over his face and one sees nothing but his nose. He is very negligent in his attire, his coat looks as if it had just been thrown on, he wears no cravat, only a narrow white collar. This curious figure is in perpetual motion: now he stamps with his feet, now waves his arms in the air, now he does this, now that. My hope of hearing him play in his own house was deceived. He has *no instrument*! I remained a few hours with him. . . .

I have now heard him twice: at the rehearsal, where he played only once, and at the concert three times, for I invested five francs in a ticket. When I heard him first I sat speechless for a quarter of an hour afterwards, in such a stupor of amazement had the man put me. Such execution, such limitless —truly limitless—execution no one else can possess. He plays sometimes so as to make your hair stand on end! He who has not heard Liszt can have no conception—literally no conception—of what his playing is.[8]

In his autobiography, written long afterwards, Hallé went into further detail.

A few days after having made the acquaintance of Chopin, I heard Liszt for the first time at one of his concerts, and went home with a feeling of thorough dejection. Such marvels of executive skill and power I could never have imagined. He was a giant, and Rubinstein* spoke the truth when, at the time when his own triumphs were greatest, he said that, in comparison with Liszt, all other pianists were children. Chopin carried you with him into a dreamland, in which you would have liked to dwell for

* The great Russian pianist Anton Grigorevich Rubinstein (1829–94).

ever; Liszt was all sunshine and dazzling splendour, subjugating his hearers with a power that none could withstand. For him there were no difficulties of execution, the most incredible seeming child's play under his fingers. One of the transcendent merits of his playing was the crystal-like clearness which never failed for a moment even in the most complicated and, to anybody else, impossible passages; it was as if he had photographed them in their minutest detail upon the ear of his listener. The power he drew from his instrument was such as I have never heard since, but never harsh, never suggesting 'thumping'. His daring was as extraordinary as his talent. At an orchestral concert given by him and conducted by Berlioz, the 'Marche au supplice', from the latter's *Symphonie fantastique*, that most gorgeously instrumented piece, was performed, at the conclusion of which Liszt sat down and played his own arrangement, for the piano alone, of the same movement, with an effect even surpassing that of the full orchestra, and creating an indescribable *furore*. The feat had been duly announced in the programme beforehand, a proof of his indomitable courage.*

If, before his marvellous execution, one had only to bow in admiration, there were some peculiarities of style, or rather of musicianship, which could not be approved. I was very young and most impressionable, but still his tacking on the finale of the C sharp minor Sonata of Beethoven to the variations of the one in A flat, Op. 26, gave me a shock, in spite of the perfection with which both movements were played.[9]

1837

In early February Marie left Paris to spend a few weeks as the guest of George Sand at Nohant, the latter's estate near La Châtre in Berry. With his friend Urhan and the Belgian cellist Alexandre Batta (1816–1902), Liszt was meanwhile devoting four consecutive Saturday evenings (28 January; 4, 11, and 18 February) to chamber concerts at the Salle Erard. The main item on each occasion was a work by Beethoven, and in addition Liszt contributed various solo pieces, by himself, Chopin and Moscheles.

* Although this reminiscence has been much quoted, no one has pin-pointed the occasion to which Hallé is referring. At the concert of 18 Dec. 1836, Liszt played both the 'Bal' and 'Marche au supplice' from his transcription of the *Symphonie fantastique*—but there was no orchestral performance of those movements. He had also played the transcription two years earlier (concert of 28 Dec. 1834)—but the conductor had not been Berlioz. On 4 May 1844, at the Théâtre Italien, Liszt again played a movement from the *Symphonie fantastique*. His performance was preceded by one of the original orchestral version; the feat had been announced beforehand; and Berlioz was the conductor. However, the movement performed was the 'Bal' and not the 'Marche au supplice'. Not one of these concerts fits Hallé's report. To take his remarks to be a description of the 1836 concert would be a grievous error; nor is the 1834 concert really plausible, when Hallé was in any case not in Paris. Most probably the passage is a reminiscence of the concert of 4 May 1844—and Hallé simply failed to remember correctly which movement was performed.

The first of these soirées musicales was reviewed in *Le Monde* (5 February) by the Spanish poet and writer *Juan Florán*.

When MM Liszt, Batta, and Urhan made their appearance before the assembly which was impatiently awaiting them, they were greeted with clamorous applause. M. Liszt's presence excited real rapture; his pallor revealed the poor state of his health. . . .

The most profound silence followed this explosion, and the great Trio in B flat [Op. 97] began. It was then that a sudden transformation came over the great pianist's features; one would have said that he could see before him the spirit of the sublime Beethoven himself. The expressive power of his playing . . . did not take long to produce an electric effect upon his audience. What has been said of translators can equally well be said of musicians: an author's thought can be rendered only in so far as it can be understood; to translate Pindar, Byron's wings are needed; to render Beethoven's inspirations, one must be Liszt. . . .

Mozart alone excepted, what man has ever possessed the magic art of depicting every shade of thought to the same degree as the composer of the Symphony in C minor, known by the name of Beethoven? How well he prepares one, in the majestic Andante of his Trio, for the finest dramatic movement that can be interpreted on the piano! What poetry of feeling, what wealth of colour, in this work! And yet none of it surpasses M. Liszt's talent as a performer. The solo which follows the second ensemble passage he rendered with admirable precision; thanks to him, those listeners who were hearing it for the first time understood it as easily as did those who have, perhaps, made a special study of it. To be just, it must be said that M. Liszt was worthily supported by MM Batta and Urhan; the violin of the one and the cello of the other kept up to the level of the piano, and to say this is to give no mean praise.

But M. Liszt did not content himself with astonishing us by the performing power and the intelligence which have already put him among the musical glories of the age; he showed us his talent for composition, or, rather, gave us new proofs of it, in the harmonic treasures of his delicious *Yo que soy contrabandista**. . .

Placed between criticism and art, we shall frankly acknowledge that the first of the soirées given by MM Liszt, Batta and Urhan has set our minds at rest about the fate of music. . . .[1]

Writing to Marie after the concert of 4 February,† Liszt described Thalberg's reaction on hearing him for the first time: 'He was stupefied with amazement. In

* *Rondeau fantastique sur un thème espagnol (El Contrabandista)* (S252). Based on a song by Manuel Garcia *père*, and composed in 1836, it was dedicated to George Sand, whose story 'Le Contrebandier' it inspired.

† At which, in addition to two Beethoven chamber works (Trio in D, Op. 70, and Sonata in A for cello and piano) with Urhan and Batta, he had played his Fantasy on Halévy's *La Juive* (S409a) and Chopin's 11th and 12th Etudes.

front of several people he said aloud that he had never heard anything like it. He even added that he would be "incapable of playing four lines" of my piece.'

Another week or more was to pass before Liszt heard Thalberg. 'It's utter humbug,' he told Marie. 'Of all the things declared superior, it is assuredly the most mediocre I know. His latest piece, on *God save the King*, is even below mediocre. "He is a *grand seigneur manqué* who as an artist is still more *manqué*," I remarked to Chopin.'

Later in the month, and as a brief respite from his round of professional appearances in the capital, he was able to spend a week (27 February to *c*.6 March) with Marie at Nohant, his first visit to Madame Sand's home. After his return to Paris, Marie stayed on at Nohant for a further fortnight.

On 12 March Thalberg gave a concert at the Conservatoire before a small audience; on the 19th Liszt appeared at the Opéra before an audience three times the size.

Ernest Legouvé writing in the Revue et gazette musicale *(26 March).* As an artist, M. Liszt has always reminded us of those heroes of Ariosto, the Knights of the Round Table,* who, armed at all points, mounted their great warhorses and rode off to conquer or defend a country. Like them, M. Liszt has in his talent, and in his progress through the realm of art, something adventurous and chivalrous which we find infinitely attractive. . . . Like Madame Malibran, he is one of those artists who cause art to advance, because they are always seeking; those who love an obstacle, need it, and create it when it does not already exist. Liszt's whole career has been a challenge hurled at the word impossible. . . . Finally, he announced last week that he would play the piano at the Opéra! Play the piano at the Opéra! Transport the thin and puny sounds of a single instrument into that vast space, into the hall still resounding with the overwhelming effects of the *Huguenots* and accustomed to the whole gamut of dramatic emotions, and which even the most powerful tones of the human voice can barely manage to fill . . . and on a Sunday . . . before an inexpert and mixed audience! A bold undertaking indeed! And so when the curtain rose, and this tall young man, so thin and so pale, and made yet thinner and paler by the distance and the lighting, appeared all alone with his piano on that immense stage, a kind of fear came over us; and all our sympathy went out to this noble folly, for it is only madmen who do great things. The entire audience seemed to share our unease and, ears strained, everyone anxiously awaited the first sounds. By the fifth bar the battle was already half won; under Liszt's fingers the piano vibrated like the voice of Lablache.

Liszt played two pieces in this concert:† a caprice on a theme by Pacini, a work full of invention, brilliance, and verve, which obtained such an

* Ariosto's *Orlando Furioso* actually relates the adventures, not of the Arthurian knights, but of the paladins of Charlemagne, above all those of 'mad Roland'.

† Which took place between an opera and a ballet.

immense success at the Berlioz concert, a triumph ratified by the universal applause it received here at the Opéra; then Weber's great Concerto.* This was the chief piece of the evening, and it was in this that we were awaiting Liszt. He has always had great liking for Weber, whose warm, passionate, and fantastic music well suits his imagination. . . . On Sunday, Liszt performed marvels of power, of precision, of lightness, and of soul! The translation was as beautiful as the poem! At the admirable concluding return of the theme, and after having soared up the whole length of the keyboard in dazzling double octaves, with his piano alone he victoriously dominated the entire orchestra armed with its horns and basses. We have heard nothing greater. . . .

On Friday, 31 March, Liszt and Thalberg appeared at the same event: a matinée, to a paying audience of nearly 200, held at the home of Princess Belgiojoso for the benefit of impoverished Italian refugees.

Revue et gazette musicale (9 April). Three factors combined to make this a concert outside the common run: it was given at the home of a princess; the admission tickets cost 40 francs each; both Liszt and Thalberg were to be heard, the two artists whose rivalry, or if you prefer, comparison, was the great business of the day. . . .

Thalberg appeared first and played his Fantasy on themes from *Moses*; Liszt followed with his Fantasy on the theme from *Niobe*. Each of the two artists displayed in his performance the qualities which are his own; and these qualities have been so much discussed, in speech and writing . . . have recently been analysed so shrewdly and conscientiously, that we consider the matter exhausted, and have scruples about returning to it. Here it behoves us to record that applause was equally divided† between the two artists. Had one of them obtained more of it than the other, we should say so, and without hesitation, for it would prove absolutely nothing, either way. From the outcome of just one trial, what conclusion could reasonably be drawn about the worth of an artist in general? . . .

As pianists, as performers, Liszt and Thalberg have little progress to make. Liszt, who has already rid himself of numerous faults, still has one bad habit to lose, that of stamping with his foot when using the pedal, and marking the time by the same means; he should also moderate the strength of his fingers when striking the keys, and sacrifice some of his impetuous energy for the quality of the sound. Thalberg, who in this respect can serve him as a model, should vary his procedure, seek combinations other than the arpeggios from which he draws such powerful effects; but this belongs rather to the work of the mind than to that of mechanism. . . .

* Probably the *Concertstück*.

† An opinion shared by Jules Janin in the *Journal des Débats* (3 Apr.): 'Liszt and Thalberg were both proclaimed victors by this brilliant and intelligent assembly. . . . Thus two victors and no vanquished.'

Some distinguished artists, MM Massart,* Urhan, Lee, Dorus, Brod, Pierret, Mathieu and Géraldy, and Mmes Taccani and Loïsa Puget, were associated with the two celebrated pianists. We also heard with keen pleasure M. le chevalier de Candia.†. . . In sum, everyone must have been satisfied with his morning, artists and auditors alike. The receipts came to more than 7,000 francs.

Ernest Legouvé. Liszt's attitude at the piano, like that of a pythoness, has been remarked again and again. Constantly tossing back his long hair, his lips quivering, his nostrils palpitating, he swept the auditorium with the glance of a smiling master. . . .

Thalberg was the gentleman artist, a perfect union of talent and propriety. He seemed to have taken it for his rule to be the exact opposite of his rival. He entered noiselessly; I might almost say without displacing the air. After a dignified greeting that seemed a trifle cold in manner, he seated himself at the piano as though upon an ordinary chair. The piece began, not a gesture, not a change of countenance! not a glance towards the audience! If the applause was enthusiastic, a respectful inclination of the head was his only response. His emotion, which was very profound, as I have had more than one proof, betrayed itself only by a violent rush of blood to the head, colouring his ears, his face and his neck. Liszt seemed seized with inspiration from the beginning; with the first note he gave himself up to his talent without reserve, as prodigals throw their money from the window without counting it, and however long was the piece his inspired fervour never flagged.

Thalberg began slowly, quietly, calmly, but with a calm that thrilled. Under those notes so seemingly tranquil one felt the coming storm. Little by little the movement quickened, the expression became more accentuated, and by a series of gradual crescendos he held one breathless until a final explosion swept the audience with an emotion indescribable.

I had the rare good fortune to hear these two great artists on the same day, in the same salon, at an interval of a quarter of an hour, at a concert given by the Princess Belgiojoso. There was then revealed to me palpably, clearly, the characteristic difference in their talent. Liszt was incontestably the more artistic, the more vibrant, the more electric. He had tones of a delicacy that made one think of the almost inaudible tinkling of tiny spangles or the faint explosion of sparks of fire. Never have fingers bounded so lightly over the piano. But at the same time his nervosity caused him to produce sometimes effects a trifle hard, a trifle harsh. . . .

At this concert, in hearing Liszt I felt myself in an atmosphere charged

* The Belgian violinist Lambert Massart (1811–92) was a close friend of Liszt's. As a foreigner, he too had been refused admission to the Paris Conservatoire, but in 1843 was appointed Professor of Violin there.

† The famous Italian tenor (Giuseppe) Mario (1810–83).

with electricity and quivering with lightning. In hearing Thalberg I seemed to be floating in a sea of purest light. The contrast between their characters was not less than between their talent.[2]

Heinrich Heine. It was at the concert in aid of the most deserving of the unfortunate Italians that . . . I last heard Liszt play. I no longer know what he played, but I could swear that it was variations on a theme out of the Apocalypse. At first I could not see them distinctly, those four mystic animals, I could hear their voices only, especially the roaring of the lion and the screeching of the eagle. The ox with the book in his hand I saw distinctly enough. What Liszt played best of all was his rendering of the Valley of Jehoshaphat. There were lists as at a tournament, and around the immense enclosure the people pressed as spectators, deathly white and trembling. First, Satan galloped into the lists, in black armour, mounted on a milk-white horse. Slowly behind him, Death caracolled on his pale horse. Last of all rode Christ in armour of gold on a black horse. With his sacred spear he straightaway thrust Satan to earth, and thereafter Death, and the onlookers shouted with joy. . . . A storm of applause was awarded to this performance of the valiant Liszt, who rose from the piano exhausted, and bowed to the ladies. On the lips of the most beautiful among them [Princess Belgiojoso] there dawned the sweet mournful smile at once reminiscent of Italy and a presage of heaven.

This same concert had another interest for the public. You doubtless know to satiety, from the newspapers, of the unfortunate estrangement which exists between Liszt and the Viennese pianist Thalberg, and of the commotion which an article* by Liszt against Thalberg created in the musical world, also of the role which lurking enmities and gossipings have played alike to the detriment of the critic and the criticised. At the very height of this scandalous strife, the two heroes of the day determined to play at the same concert, one after the other. They both set aside their wounded private feelings in the furtherance of a scheme of benevolence; and the public, to whom they thus gave the opportunity of contemporan-

* Published in the *Revue et gazette musicale* of 8 Jan. this year. Not unjustly but certainly unwisely—for it gave the impression that he was motivated by envy—Liszt had described Thalberg's music as mediocre, monotonous, and pretentious. This had antagonized Thalberg's admirers; and the Belgian musicologist F. J. Fétis (1784–1871), author of the monumental *Biographie universelle des musiciens*, had come out with an essay (*Revue et gazette musicale*, 23 Apr.) whose culminating charge against Liszt was: 'You are the product of a school which is ending and has nothing further to say; you are not the man of a new school. *That* man is Thalberg. This is the whole difference between you.' (About this judgement, the erroneousness of which became all too apparent even in Fétis's lifetime, the late Bernard Gavoty remarked: 'Scarcely would it be possible to poke one's finger more effectively into one's own eye!') Liszt then responded with an open letter to Fétis (op. cit., 14 May) in which he rebuked that scholar for meddling in matters about which his information was inadequate, wrote of the whole debate as 'resembling the title of Shakespeare's *Much Ado About Nothing*', and concluded with the words 'Truth will not fail those who have believed in and suffered defeat for her'.

eously recognising and appreciating their particular diversities, accorded to them a generous and merited approbation.

It is, indeed, sufficient to make a single comparison between the musical temperament of each composer, to be convinced that there is as much of hidden malice as of narrowness of mind in the endeavour to praise one at the expense of the other. Their technical proficiencies counterbalance one another; and as regards their spiritual character, no more striking contrast could be imagined than the noble, soulful, intelligent, good-natured German, or rather Austrian, Thalberg, face to face with the wild, lightning-flashing, volcanic, heaven-storming Liszt![3]

'There is only one Thalberg in Paris, but there is only one Liszt in the world,'* ran Cristina Belgiojoso's verdict—a judgement which was modified thus by Marie d'Agoult: 'Thalberg is the first pianist in the world, Liszt the only one!'

Thalberg enjoyed a successful career. His path crossed Liszt's on several occasions, and their relations were always cordial. After retirement he settled in Italy, and died, at Posilipo, some fifteen years before Liszt, who subscribed 100 francs towards a proposed statue of his one-time rival. Perhaps the essential difference between the two is found in an observation made by Liszt still later, at a time when the trial of strength in Cristina's salon and all other competitiveness were but distant memories: 'Thalberg was one of the most fortunate of artists: the passion for the ideal tormented him not at all; successes were enough.'

Composed this year, but not finished in time to be performed, as originally intended, at Cristina's charity concert, was a set of bravura variations by Liszt himself, Thalberg, Pixis, Herz, Czerny (then visiting Paris), and Chopin on the march *Suoni la tromba* from Bellini's *I Puritani*. Entitled *Hexameron* (S392) and dedicated to Cristina, the work was to form a staple element of Liszt's repertoire during his virtuoso years.

At the Salle Erard on 9 April he gave a concert—announced as 'the last before his departure'—in which a participant was Chopin; they concluded the programme with a *Grande valse* for piano duet.† A handful of guest appearances remained, however: at two concerts (afternoon and evening) on the 13th; another on the15th; and a last on the 23rd, when fellow performers were Alkan, Pixis, and the fourteen-year-old César Franck (who played a Fantasy by Hummel). About 9 May, with Italy as their ultimate goal, he and Marie once again took the road to Nohant.

Liszt to Adolphe Pictet. I found shelter in the remotest corner of Berry, that prosaic province so divinely poeticized by George Sand. There, under the roof of our illustrious friend, I lived for three months a life that was full and keenly felt, the memory of whose hours I reverently cherish. Our days

* Different versions of this utterance haunt the literature. The one cited here is that given by Brombert, *Cristina*.

† According to *Le Moniteur universel* (12 Apr.) , Chopin was warmly applauded; but *Le Monde* (11 Apr.) reported that he had been too unwell to play the duet with Liszt and that, yielding to the audience's wishes, the latter had performed alone. He also played some of Chopin's unpublished Etudes (Op. 25) at this concert.

were simple, easy to fill. We had no need to beguile the time, nor to go hunting in royal forests, nor of amateur theatricals, nor of those *fêtes*, so-called *champêtres*, in which society people each bring their own particular tedium to contribute to the general amusement. Our pursuits and pleasures were these: the reading of some ingenuous philosopher or some profound poet, Montaigne or Dante, Hoffmann or Shakespeare; a letter from an absent friend; long walks on the secret shores of the Indre; then, on returning, a melody which summed up the emotions of the walk; the joyous cries of children who had just come upon a beautiful hawk-moth with diaphanous wings, or some poor warbler which, impelled by curiosity, had fallen from its nest to the lawn. Is that all? Yes, truly all. But, as you know, it is not by the surface but by the depths that the joys of the soul are measured. . . .

George wrote a fine book [*Les Maîtres Mosaïstes*], and I delved into my old scores once again, to seek out some of the sundry secrets of our masters.*. . .

You, too, are astonished to see me so exclusively occupied with the piano, so little inclined to tackle the wider field of symphonic and dramatic works. . . . You are unaware that to speak to me of quitting the piano is to make me anticipate a day of sadness. . . . My piano, you see, is to me what his frigate is to the sailor, his charger to the Arab; even more, perhaps, for my piano has been until now my very self, my words, my life; it is the intimate repository of everything that stirred and tossed within my mind during the most ardent days of my youth; all my desires, dreams, joys, and sorrows were found in it. Its strings have shuddered under all my passions, its submissive keys obeyed my every whim—and you, my friend, would like me to hasten to desert it and to run after the more brilliant reverberations of theatrical and orchestral successes. Oh, no! Even if I allow what you doubtless allow too easily, that I am already ripe for chords of that kind, my firm wish is not to abandon study and development of the piano until I have done everything possible, or at least everything that it is possible for me to do today.

Perhaps I am deceived by this kind of mysterious feeling which attaches me to the piano, yet I consider its importance very great. It has, it seems to me, the leading place in the hierarchy of instruments. It is the most generally cultivated, the most popular of all; and this importance and this popularity it owes in part to the harmonic power which it alone possesses; and, as a consequence of this power, to the faculty of summarizing and concentrating within itself the whole of the art of music. In the span of its seven octaves it embraces the range of an orchestra; and the ten fingers of

* Liszt's musical labours at Nohant are revealed by his letter of 29 July to Massart. This announces that he will be sending to Paris shortly the MSS of: transcriptions for piano solo of Beethoven's symphonies 5, 6, and 7 (S464); of seven Schubert *Lieder* (probably from S558); of Berlioz's *Francs-juges* and *Roi Lear* overtures; and the *Hexameron*.

one man suffice to render the harmonies produced by the concourse of more than a hundred instruments playing together.[4]

George Sand, 3 June. Arabella's room is on the ground floor, below mine. There stands Franz's splendid piano, under the window with its screen of lime leaves. And from that window issue forth those sounds which the whole world would like to hear. . . . Mighty artist, sublime in great matters, ever superior in little ones. But sad, tormented by a secret wound. Fortunate man, loved by a woman who is as generous, intelligent, and chaste as she is beautiful. Ungrateful wretch! What, then, do you crave! Ah, if only *I* were loved! . . .

When Franz plays the piano, I feel uplifted. All my sorrows are transformed into poetry, my instincts into enthusiasm. . . .

I love those broken phrases which he tosses on to the piano, and which seem to remain suspended, with one foot in the air, dancing in space like limping will-o'-the-wisps. The leaves on the lime trees undertake to finish the melody, doing so in a hushed, mysterious whisper as though confiding nature's secrets to one another. . . .[5]

Marie d'Agoult, 25 June. George said to Franz: 'Meyerbeer's music creates only images. Beethoven's gives rise to feelings and ideas. Meyerbeer makes a magnificent spectacle pass before one's eyes; he places his characters in front of one. Beethoven makes us return to our innermost depths; everything we have felt and experienced, our loves, sufferings and dreams—it is all brought back to life by the breath of his genius, and plunges us into an infinite reverie.

'The one creates objective, the other subjective, music. You unite the two.'[6]

Taking their leave of Madame Sand and Nohant* on 24 July, the lovers journeyed to Lyons, where on 3 August Liszt and Adolphe Nourrit gave a concert for the benefit of the city's indigent silk weavers, for whom a considerable sum was obtained. Accompanied to Chambéry by another friend, the poet and writer Louis de Ronchaud (1816–87), they also called upon Lamartine at Saint Point and visited the Grande Chartreuse near Grenoble.

Marie d'Agoult, 7 August. Sometimes, when he is very excited, or deeply moved by one of nature's grand scenes, by beautiful music, or, above all, by some holy word of love, the *spirit* awakens within him, and whatever is most mysteriously buried in his heart gushes forth like a bubbling stream. I compared him one day to the statue of Memnon. Like it, his soul gives out divine sounds when touched by the rays of enthusiasm; but, like it, in the shadow of earthly things he remains mute and inscrutable in his strength.

* Chopin often came here in later years, but Liszt's second visit was also his last, and the two great composer-pianists were never fellow guests at Nohant.

When stirred like this, he seems to suffer greatly; he speaks under the compulsion of an unknown power which puts into his mouth words of fire that neither he nor I can later remember. It is then that he makes me aware of what in ancient times the sibyls and pythonesses could be.* I no longer feel his equal, for he has attained a far higher degree of initiation than I. But at the same time I feel that in the immensity of his love he is drawing me to him, raising me to his own level.[7]

At Etrambière they saw two-year-old Blandine, in the care of her wet-nurse. Marie found her 'very beautiful'. 'The prodigious development of her forehead, her serious, intelligent air, show her to be a quite exceptional child.' Via the Simplon Pass they then entered Italy.

Marie d'Agoult, 17 August. We arrive at Baveno, on the shore of Lake Maggiore, and find a charming little inn, full of flowers. A boat takes us to Isola Madre, one of the Borromean islands. It was once an arid rock, but nowadays the most luxuriant vegetation grows on it. Orange and lemon trees cover the walls with a perfumed tapestry; a trumpet creeper with flame-coloured corollae, and a caper bush with long stamens of soft lilac, hang down lazily from them. The aloe with its thick leaves, so motionless that one could take it for a bronze plant piercing the rock; sassafras, camphor trees and magnolias are astonished to find themselves blossoming beside the Scotch fir, and like the latter they admire their reflections in the blue waters of the lake, bordered on the horizon by the Rhaetian Alps. One could easily imagine oneself transported to the magical retreat of a Peri, or in that first garden created by the imagination of biblical poets for the love of two sinless beings.

Isola Bella, on which the Borromean Palace stands, is a *tour de force* in rather bad taste. Yet there are vastness and grandeur in the inner rooms; a picture gallery and statues of Monti give them an artistic interest. Further, Napoleon slept here on the eve of Marengo, and on one of the two gigantic oleanders (unequalled in all Europe) they show you where he cut the word *Battaglia*. On the way there in the boat, I was filled with admiration at the sight of a large flowering aloe stretching its burning stamens to the sun. For a long time I gazed at this flower of the poets, symbol of those divine loves, those which likewise blossom only once in a lifetime.[8]

From Lake Maggiore Liszt and Marie continued through Varese to Lake Como, along whose shores they proceeded as far as Colico. They then made the short journey to Milan, whose cathedral, churches, museums, and galleries they explored thoroughly, extending their sight-seeing even as far as the famous Certosa di Pavia in the south.

* Arthur Friedheim: 'All through life Liszt sensed the spiritual, could see and hear things and sounds beyond ordinary ken. He had the intuition, the mystic power to penetrate beyond the empyrean. . . . Surely some occult factor is the only real key to Liszt's character, his art, and the manner in which he affected his audiences.'

Marie d'Agoult. The Brera Gallery has no great wealth of good paintings. *The Wedding of the Virgin* is of interest because it dates from Raphael's youth, for he was barely twenty-one when he painted it; but its composition is monotonous, the painting dry, and the men's faces much too effeminate. All these Virgins, repeated to satiety by the Italian school, are not at all to Franz's taste. He finds their faces commonplace and totally devoid of intelligence. Veronese's luxury and Salvator Rosa's cult of the horrible are more to his liking. But he spared a Virgin by Sassoferrato, whose sleeping Child is rendered admirably.[9]

Liszt to Louis de Ronchaud, September. There I was strolling through the streets of Milan, just as I would along the boulevards of Paris. Soon, without knowing how, I found myself facing La Scala, at the entrance to Ricordi's shop. You know—or perhaps you don't know, for, thank God, you have never written or sold semiquavers—that Ricordi* is Italy's leading publisher, and one of the most notable in Europe. . . . And so I went in and, without preamble, seated myself at the open piano. I began to improvise, my way of presenting my credentials. Ricordi was there. I did not know him; he did not know me; he listened and grew enthusiastic. . . . He did not speak to me, but I heard him say to his assistant: *Questo è Liszt o il Diavolo.* Finding myself suspected so vehemently, I introduced myself. Five minutes later, without my now being able to remember what we said, Ricordi had placed at my disposal his country house in the Brianza, his box at La Scala, his carriage, his horses, the fifteen hundred scores he owns. . . . That very evening we went together to La Scala. . . . They were doing [Donizetti's] *Marino Faliero.* . . .

I am not remaining in Milan: the heat here is too overpowering; we intend to seek a cooler refuge.[10]

They chose Bellagio, which they had already visited briefly. The eight or nine weeks they spent here were devoted to composing and writing, to the reading of Molière, Bossuet, Corneille, and others, to games of draughts, and to excursions into the surrounding countryside.

Liszt to Louis de Ronchaud. Bellagio, 20 September. When you write the story of two happy lovers, place them on the shores of Lake Como. . . .

Towards the middle of the lake, at the point where it splits into two branches, of which one reaches as far as Lecco and the other ends at Como, the pretty village of Bellagio rises up like an amphitheatre. . . .

Often, in the most extreme heat of the day, we go and rest under the plane-trees of the Villa Melzi, and read the *Divina Commedia*† while

* Giovanni Ricordi (1785–1853).

† Liszt's admiration of Dante's masterpiece, which he read over and over again, for the spiritual solace it afforded him as well as for its supreme poetry, was lifelong. According to

seated under Comolli's* marble monument showing *Dante led by Beatrice.* What a subject! And what a pity that it was so misunderstood by the sculptor!—who made a thickset, material woman of Beatrice; and of Dante a shabby, sheepish sort of fellow, and not that *signor de l'altissimo canto,* the words with which he describes Homer! But to understand Dante, a Michelangelo was needed! And yet shall I confess something to you? In this immense, incomparable poem, there is one thing I have always found strangely shocking: that the poet conceived of Beatrice as the ideal, not of love, but of learning.[11]

To Lambert Massart. Bellagio, October. If it amuses you to know that I made *furore, furorissimo* in an *accademia* (the word they use here for concerts) at Ricordi's in Milan six weeks ago,† I shall mention it. Newspapers large and small are already much occupied with me. Generally, they find me very handsome, and after their own fashion the little Piedmontese ladies are making of me the hero of a novel. It all moves me very deeply. Since the beginning of September I have been living withdrawn and absolutely alone in a delicious little inn at Bellagio. . . .

Schlesinger must by now have received two articles‡ of mine: the first being on Schumann, and the second on Alkan, to whom I beg you to give my regards.[12]

Marie d'Agoult, 5 October. I sometimes feel astonished to see him so constantly lively, so happy in this absolute solitude in which we are living. At an age in which everything impels one towards outer activity, in which movement and diversity are virtually a necessary condition of existence, he, whose mind is so communicative, whose profession has caused him always to mix with people—in a word, an artist (that is to say, a man of fellow-feeling, imagination and emotions)—is concentrating all his faculties in the narrow framework of a tête-à-tête life. A bad piano, a few books, and the conversation of a serious-minded woman suffice him. Not only does he forgo all the pleasures of *amour-propre,* the excitement of competition and the amusements of social life, but even the joy of being useful and of doing good; gives them up without seeming even to realize that he is doing so![13]

23 October. Yesterday Franz was twenty-six. We had reserved the day—lit

Göllerich, hearing some passages from the *Divina Commedia* gave Liszt 'one last joy' a week before his death. 'This book has accompanied me on all my travels,' he remarked; 'it counts among the profoundest achievements of the human mind.'

* The Piedmontese sculptor G. B. Comolli (1775–1830). His *Dante e Beatrice* at the Villa Melzi dates from 1810.

† On 3 Sept. Liszt played his *Niobe* fantasy and *Grande valse di bravura* (S209).

‡ Respectively, *R. Schumann's piano compostions, Op 5, 11, 14*; and *Alkan's Trois Morceaux dans le genre pathétique.* The Alkan article was published in the *Gazette musicale* of 22 Oct., the Schumann in the issue of 12 Nov.

by dazzling sunshine—for an especially joyous celebration. At 9 o'clock we set off towards the mountain, escorted by Buscone, our ideal ferryman; and, mounted on a *somarello* (the delicate name they here give to the *asino*), I traversed sweet solitudes bearing scattered chestnut and olive trees. From time to time we encountered a few isolated houses rather like Swiss chalets, where in the open sheds we could see maize hanging down ready for the winter. In front of them were grazing, indolently, some of the small local breed of cows. Then, suddenly, turning a path, we came upon a view of Lake Lecco; on the way back, Bellagio and the surrounding villages standing out in white against a sea of foliage of a thousand different purple, orange, and violet tints. . . .

Today has been utterly serene. Franz has just finished his twelve preludes;* it is a beautiful work, a worthy start to his series of original compositions. And so he was mentally relaxed; and as for me, I had succeeded in shutting away within myself this impious voice which is forever doubting and denying. He asks me to *believe* despite everything; to await, in religious confidence, the solution of mankind's great problems, the extinction of evil in the world, in fact the reign of God. He is right.[14]

Early in November they moved to Como. Liszt journeyed frequently to Milan, however, where on Sunday, 10 December, he took part in a concert at La Scala.†

Liszt to Lambert Massart. In all conscience, I must have cut a peculiar figure, I so thin, so *scrawny,* all alone with my faithful Erard, facing an audience used to the pomp of a great spectacle and to musical effects of a highly pronounced nature. If to these local circumstances you add the fact that instrumental music is generally regarded by Italians as something secondary, inferior to vocal music, you will have an idea of the temerity of my undertaking.

Very few great pianists are known in Italy. Field, I believe, was the last (if not the only one) to be heard here. Neither Hummel, nor Moscheles, nor Kalkbrenner, nor Chopin, has appeared on this side of the Alps. . . .

And so it was before an audience very little prepared for certain old ideas on composition and performance, ideas which have sometimes caused learned critics to grimace, but to which I nevertheless stubbornly cling despite the infallibility of these gentlemen . . . that I risked two or three of my own kind of *fantaisies,* ones that were neither very severe nor very learned, but which nevertheless did not fall into the usual framework. They were applauded, thanks, perhaps, to some octave passages rendered with a fairly laudable dexterity and to a few cadenzas prolonged beyond

* The *Grandes Etudes* (S137), based on the juvenile studies of 1826 and dedicated to Carl Czerny.

† The programme published in the *Gazzetta privilegiata di Milano* (9 Dec.) shows that Liszt's contributions to the many items were: his *Niobe* fantasy and an Etude in Part One, and *La Serenata e l'Orgia* in Part Two.

those which are sung, and capable of tiring the throat of the most stubborn nightingale of hereabouts. Encouraged by this flattering approval, and believing myself sure of my ground, I became still more reckless and all but cruelly compromised my poor little success by presenting to the public one of my favourites from among my last-born, a prelude-study (*studio*) which, in my opinion, is a very beautiful thing. But this word *studio* immediately created terror. 'Vengo al teatro per divertirmi e non per studiare' [I come to the theatre to enjoy myself and not to study] shouted a gentleman in the pit, who in so doing expressed the feelings of a very great majority. And indeed I entirely failed to make the audience appreciate the quaint idea that had come to me—that of playing anywhere but in my own room a *study* whose aim was apparently that of loosening my joints and making my ten fingers more supple. And so I regarded the assembly's forbearance in hearing me to the end as proof of a quite special goodwill. . . .[15]

At Como on Sunday, 24 December, Marie gave birth to their second child, another girl, who was christened (in the Cathedral on the 26th) Francesca Gaetana Cosima.*

The professional part of Liszt's year ended with his participation in a charity concert (Accademia Musicale per Pubblica Beneficenza) at Como on the 29th. He chose *La Serenata e l'Orgia* for the occasion, and also took part in a two-piano duet with the French pianist Henri Mortier de Fontaine (whose wife contributed some of the vocal items) before bringing the concert to an end with an improvisation on themes submitted.

Glissons, No. 2 (6 January 1838). This last was Liszt's real triumph, and, excited by these melodies, the solid people of Como did not leave off honouring the player with their cheering and clapping. He took all the themes, played every single one, and then, noting the special welcome given to some, concentrated wholly on these. The vote went to a hunting chorus by Weber and a theme from *La Sonnambula*, which the player varied in a thousand different ways. The *Sonnambula* theme being graceful, and the other one of a German character, they are difficult to combine harmoniously. But for Liszt nothing is difficult. It would be impossible to describe how he brought them together. . . . At Como he played even better than in Milan; and if our readers ask why, the reply is that Liszt himself does not know. The genius has certain moments of inspiration which he is unable to foresee, and in which he is not absolutely master of his movements: a secret divinity guides him. . . . And so Hungary has given us an artist of the highest quality, who, seated at his pianoforte, is Rossini, Paganini, Rubini, la Malibran, Talberg [*sic*]; in short, is all and everything.

* The name by which she was known, its choice was explained by Liszt long afterwards to Adelheid von Schorn: 'He took me to the church of SS Cosmas and Damian [in Rome], and told me that the two saints were Arab physicians who had done much good, and that it was after the first-named that he had had his daughter christened Cosima.'

1838

Liszt to Marie d'Agoult (at Como). Milan, early 1838. Oh! how wrong you are, dear good Marie, to torment yourself with things that you suspect to be hidden inside me and of which you never hear me speak. Dear, beautiful child, if you but knew of the profound tenderness, the ineffable affection for you—like those of a brother and friend—which lie buried within the depths of my heart! Oh! fret no more, suffer no more. That would be cruel and unjust. Be aware that all the sincere and loving things I have been able to tell you are only the cold, dull shadow of what you have made me feel and understand. Oh! how I wish you could open up my chest, and with your beautiful hands take hold of, and keep, my soul and my entire life! Sometimes in those hours of enchantment and delight in which through you everything seems so beautiful, so pure, so divine, when I believe I can touch and feel all around me a world more entrancing than the one it is given men to dream of, in those hours which I sometimes rashly seek to recall, when I loved and possessed you entirely, the illusion took hold of me that my life was no longer my own. I had ceased to exist for myself, was wholly merged in you, and we spoke to one another soul to soul. . . . A presentiment of our future destiny? Allow me to believe so.[1]

To Lambert Massart. Milan, February. I have left my delightful Lake Como to return to Milan for good. After those two months of work and solitude, I am now leading a completely worldly life: going to balls and making three dozen visits to La Scala. . . . Further, I go horse-riding, and am even learning a little Italian without giving too much thought to it. . . . Rossini is still here. We see each other very often, and *very gladly*. . . .

Send me the proofs of the monster piece (which I have decided to call *Hexameron*) as soon as possible.[2]

On 18 February Liszt gave a morning concert in La Scala's Sala del Ridotto. Taking the piano part in Hummel's Septet, he also played the *Hexameron* and, joined by Hiller, Pixis, Schoberlechner, Origgi, and Pedroni, an arrangement, for twelve hands at three pianos, of the overture to *Die Zauberflöte*. In the audience was Rossini, who 'paid tribute to the celebrated pianist with the liveliest applause', according to *La Moda* (12 March). The 'wonderful' performance of the overture was encored.

Liszt to Lambert Massart. At my final musical session,* a charming little silver chalice, of exquisite workmanship, attributed to one of Cellini's best pupils, was placed at the entrance to the hall, to receive the themes on which I was to improvise. On going through them, I found, as expected, a quantity of themes by Bellini and Donizetti; and then, to the audience's

* Liszt's last two Milan concerts were on 12 and 15 Mar.

great amusement, on a piece of paper carefully folded by some anonymous person who had felt not a moment's doubt about the immense superiority of his choice: *Il duomo di Milano* [Milan Cathedral]. 'Oh! oh!' said I, 'here is someone who derives profit from his reading; this gentleman has remembered Madame de Staël's definition: *Music is architecture in sound*; he is curious to establish its accuracy and to compare the two architectures: the pseudo-Gothic of the Cathedral's façade with the Ostrogothic of my musical construction.' I would gladly have procured him this satisfaction, thus enabling him to confirm or refute the illustrious writer's assertion; but since the audience displayed no eagerness to see my bell-turrets of demisemiquavers, my cornices of scales, and my spires of tenths, I proceeded further. . . . A gentleman preoccupied with the progress being made by industrialism, and struck by the advantage there would be in having oneself transported from Milan to Venice in six hours, gave me for a theme: *La strada di ferro* [the railway]. A theme like this I saw no way of dealing with other than by an uninterrupted series of glissandi from the top of the piano to the bottom; and, fearing to break my wrists in this contest of speed with a locomotive, I hastened to open the final note. What do you think I found this time? One of the most important questions of human life to be decided by arpeggios, a question which, dealt with on a certain scale, can be applied to anything, religion as well as physiology, philosophy as well as political economy: *Is it better to marry or remain a bachelor?* Feeling incapable of answering this question other than by a never-ending sigh, I preferred to remind my audience of the words of a sage: 'Whatever the decision that you reach, whether to marry or remain single, it is certain that you will always regret it.'

I should be ungrateful were I not to mention that the kindness shown me by the Milanese public has gone far beyond what I expected.[3]

Leaving Milan on 16 March, and sight-seeing *en route* at Brescia, Verona, Vicenza, and Padua, Liszt and Marie travelled to Venice, where he took part in concerts on 28 March (Concert Apollinaire) and 1 April (Teatro San Benedetto). 'His person pleases as much as his talent,' noted Marie. They also enjoyed the social life of the Serenissima and took full advantage of the opportunity to inspect her treasures of art and architecture.

Marie d'Agoult, 29 March. In the evening, a visit to Countess Polcastro. Am in a bad humour because Franz kept me waiting. He is always patient, equable, in fact perfect. When shall I be a little more like him?[4]

31 March. Read in the *Journal des Débats* a letter from Beethoven to Wegeler, and was struck by the affinity I found between him and Franz. The same fortitude and the same feeling for the miseries of life, the same aversion to correspondence. I read it while he, this other Beethoven, was correcting [transcribing] at the piano the melodies of Schubert.

We visited the church of San Zaccaria with a very intelligent young painter. Franz greatly admires a painting by J. Bellini (a Virgin with St Paul, St Jerome, etc.)[5]

Liszt to Lambert Massart. At Venice one morning I read in a German newspaper a detailed account of the disastrous floods at Pest. It caused me real emotion. I felt an unwonted compassion, a keen and irresistible need to help so many unfortunate people. What, I wondered, could I do for them? What assistance offer them? I have none of the things that make one mighty among men. I possess neither the influence bestowed upon the owner of great wealth, nor the power of a great position. No matter; I shall go there all the same, for I feel that I shall enjoy no rest, and that my eyes will not close in sleep, so long as I have not contributed my mite towards alleviating this great suffering. Besides, who can say that Heaven will not bless my puny offering?

It was through these emotions, this outburst of feelings, that there came to me the meaning of the words *native land*. Before my eyes arose a magnificent landscape: it was the familiar forest, ringing with the cries of hunters; it was the Danube on its hurried course through the rocks; it was the vast plains in which the peaceful herds were grazing; it was Hungary, that robust and fertile soil which bears such noble children; it was, in a word, my country. For I too, I cried to myself in a fit of patriotism which will make you smile, I too am a member of that ancient and hardy race.[6]

On 7 April, Liszt left for Vienna, his route taking him past Lake Wörth, a sight which, he told Marie, he found 'melancholy and bewitching'.

The main road which runs alongside it is bordered by admirably picturesque forests of pine trees. As I gazed upon those sad but beautiful woods, my eyes filled with tears and I thought intensely of you, my fair archangel. . . . I felt that divine anguish which your image always arouses within my breast when we are far apart.[7]

Liszt arrived in the Austrian capital on the 10th. During the next two or three days he played several times in private for fellow musicians, and was able to report to Marie 'an enthusiasm of which you can have no idea'. Among those who heard him was the eighteen-year-old Clara Wieck (1819–96), at this time still in the early stages of a notable pianistic career. 'She is a very simple person,' he told Marie, 'entirely preoccupied with her art, but nobly and without childishness. She was flabbergasted when she heard me. Her compositions are truly most remarkable, especially for a woman. They have a hundred times more invention and real feeling than all the past and present fantasies of Thalberg.'

With Clara was her father, the piano pedagogue *Friedrich Wieck* (1785–1873), whose diary for 12 April records his first impressions of Liszt.

He can be compared to no other player—he stands alone. He arouses terror and amazement, and is a very engaging artist. His appearance at the piano is indescribable—he is an original—is absorbed by the piano. . . . His passion knows no limits, and not infrequently he jars on one's sense of beauty by tearing melodies to pieces. He uses the pedal too much, and so is bound to make his works still more incomprehensible, to laymen if not to experts. He has a great intellect; one can say of him that 'his art is his life'.[8]

14 April. He plays Clara's *Soirées* at sight—and *how*! If he could keep his strength and fire in check, who could play after him? That is what Thalberg has written too. And where are the pianos which will respond to even half of what he can do and wishes to do?[9]

The diplomat Philipp von Neumann (1781–1851), 16 April. The pianist Liszt paid a visit to Princess Metternich.* He astonished us by the self-sufficiency of his manners. He is a product of 'la jeune France' beyond anything one can imagine.[10]

Friedrich Wieck to his wife, 17 April. The powers of musical perception of this Liszt truly verge on the unbelievable. If he had been given the right training . . . no one could play after him.[11]

Liszt's first concert was for the benefit of the Pest flood victims,† and was given at the Musikverein on the 18th. 'Tremendous success,' he told Marie. 'Recalled fifteen to eighteen times. A packed house. Universal amazement. Thalberg hardly exists at the moment in the memory of the Viennese. Never have I had such a success.' In the opinion of Heinrich Adami (1807–65), Liszt's technical mastery went 'beyond that of any pianist alive, not excepting even Thalberg'. Liszt's works, he declared, 'have the merit of originality, and if they sometimes seem far-fetched and bizarre, and to go beyond the bounds of what we are used to, yet one could say with Polonius: "There is method in't." '

Wieck's diary, 18 April. Liszt's concert: *Concertstück* by Weber on Thalberg's English piano, *Réminiscences des Puritains* [S390] on the Konrad Graf; *Valse di bravura* and Etude‡ (twice) on a second Graf—all three smashed to pieces. But it was all full of genius—immense applause—the artist engaging and informal—it was all completely new and unprecedented; in fact: Liszt. In the evening Clara played him Schumann's *Carnaval*, as well as his own Pacini Fantasy [*Niobe*]. He writhed his whole body about as she played, just as though he were playing too.[12]

* Princess Melanie Metternich (1805–54), third wife of the Chancellor.

† For whom he was able to send the considerable sum of 25,000 gulden. Elsewhere in the literature it has been stated that the proceeds of *all* Liszt's concerts during these weeks in Vienna went to the flood victims. However, his remaining concerts were for his own benefit. But he also took part in two charity concerts (6 and 24 May) and in a concert given by Angelica Lacy (15 May).

‡ During 1838 Liszt completed his six *Etudes d'exécution transcendante d'après Paganini* (S140), which he dedicated to Clara Wieck. The Etude played at this first Vienna concert was in G minor, and could have been either the sixth of the *Grandes Etudes* or the first of the Paganini group.

Philipp von Neumann. Heard Liszt, whose execution is the most massive and incoherent that can be conceived. He astounded more than he pleased an audience composed of the first professors and connoisseurs of the capital.[13]

Friedrich Wieck to his wife, 19 April. It was the most remarkable concert of our lives, and he will not be without his influence on Clara. And that Clara will not follow his many tricks and eccentricities—of *that*, an old schoolmaster will take care.[14]

Clara Wieck to Robert Schumann. Graz, 23 April. He is an artist whom one must hear and see for oneself. I am sorry that you have not met him, for you would get along very well together, as he likes you very much. He rates your works extraordinarily highly, far above Henselt, above everything he has come across recently. I played your *Carnaval*, which quite enchanted him.* 'What a mind!' he said; 'that is one of the greatest works I know.' You can imagine my joy.[15]

To the same, 28 April. My own playing I find so dull now, and, I really don't know why, I have almost lost the desire to travel any further. Since hearing and seeing Liszt's bravura I feel like a schoolgirl.[16]

At Nohant the previous summer Liszt had begun his transcriptions† of Schubert *Lieder*, of which he eventually completed more than fifty. His second Vienna concert, on 23 April, included two of them: *Serenade* ('Horch, horch') (S558/9) and *Lob der Tränen* (S557). To Marie he reported: 'A furore, a mania of which you can form no idea. . . . The Thalbergites (for these comparisons will never end), who prided themselves on their impartiality to begin with, are beginning to be seriously vexed. In living memory no one has had such a success in Vienna, not even Paganini.'

Philipp von Neumann. Went to a concert given by Liszt, who played in an electrifying manner. He is a meteor. Under his touch the piano becomes an altogether different instrument.[17]

Thalberg arrived in Vienna at this time, and the two great pianists dined together on the 28th with Thalberg's father, Prince Moritz Dietrichstein,‡ who told Liszt that he was delighted to have 'Castor and Pollux' together in his home. During the evening, Thalberg remarked to Liszt with admirable candour: 'In comparison with you, I have never enjoyed more than a *succès d'estime* in Vienna.'

Liszt's third concert (which included Etudes by Chopin and Moscheles) was on

* 'Your *Carnaval* and *Fantasiestücke* I find exceptionally interesting,' Liszt wrote a few days later to Schumann. 'I play them with real delight, and God knows that I cannot say as much of many things. To speak plainly and candidly, it is in general only Chopin's and your works which have a powerful interest for me. *The rest do not deserve the honour of being mentioned* . . . at least, with a few exceptions.'

† Apart from that of *Die Rose* (S556), which dates from 1833.

‡ A legitimate son of Joseph Thalberg and Fortunée Stein, as is confirmed by his birth certificate at Geneva, Thalberg was adopted later by Prince Dietrichstein.

29 April; after it, he and Thalberg were both dinner guests of Metternich. At his fourth, on 2 May, he played amongst other things a Sonata in A flat (probably Op. 26) by Beethoven, and, for the first time in public, his *Grand galop chromatique* (S219), composed earlier this year. He also joined the clarinettist Josef Friedlowsky and the tenor Benedict Gross in a performance of Schubert's *Der Hirt auf dem Felsen.*

Heinrich Adami in the Allgemeine Theaterzeitung *(5 May).* Liszt's advantage over many virtuosi in his field is that *he never imitates himself.* . . . In all honesty it must be said that what he plays is not to show off his virtuosity, but—this becomes clear from the whole manner of his performance—because the work stimulates him; and *of all his listeners he is himself perhaps the most carried away.* Just as Lessing declared that Raphael would have had to become the greatest painter even if he had come into the world without hands, so with equal justice could the same be said of Liszt as pianist.[18]

The music publisher Pietro Mechetti (1777–1850) in the Wiener Zeitschrift für Kunst *(5 May).* About his *technical* perfection there is in my opinion nothing to be said but that it is the *highest* which human hands have yet achieved on the keyboard. Aristotle said 'the finger is the most artistic instrument'—which can be believed by anyone who has seen and heard what Liszt can do with *ten* such instruments. . . . Many passages in his works suggest that one of his immediate objects seems to be to turn the piano as much as possible into an orchestra. Shall we also mention his remarkable memory, which enables him to play several hundred pieces by heart?[19]

In Venice, meanwhile, Marie had fallen ill and was longing for Liszt's return. Kept at Vienna by demands for more concerts, however, he was unable to rejoin her as soon as she wished.

Liszt to Marie d'Agoult. Vienna, May. And I, too, my poor angel, am mortally sad. The torment of great thoughts, the thirst for the impossible, the wild and passionate aspiration towards what cannot be—are not these the heaviest of all our tribulations? No, never have I suffered from all my lonely follies as during this past week. To have to endure the din and bustle of Fame (as it is called), constantly to be the cynosure of a thousand eyes—it all makes me feel still more bitterly the absolute isolation of my heart. Why did I not leave during the first few days? Or, rather, what made me decide to come here at all? I swear to you, my good, my only Marie, I do not believe I am in the wrong. I am suffering just as you are; less nobly but just as profoundly. I still feel worthy of your love, of your compassion. . . .

The other evening I heard some of Schubert's *Lieder*, sung by a friend of his. I listened to only three or four, then I came home and dissolved into tears. Surprised by my abrupt departure, one or two acquaintances came in search of me and then spread it about from one end of the city to the other that you were making me extremely unhappy, etc. etc. I do not know why this publicity given to my most sacred emotions so angered me.[20]

Liszt's fifth concert (8 May) introduced the *Hexameron* to Vienna. So extraordinary was its success that he had to repeat it at the sixth (14 May), in which he also played the C sharp minor Sonata of Beethoven, pieces by Handel and Kessler, Scarlatti's Cat's Fugue Sonata, and accompanied songs by Schubert and Randhartinger.* His seventh concert followed on the 18th; his 'farewell concert' on the 25th. About this last, given as a soirée musicale, Adami reported: 'Never was there, nor will there ever be again, such a concert. It almost seemed as though this time he wished to exhibit the most dazzling riches of his art, to make the parting doubly hard for us.' As on previous occasions, several members of the royal family attended; and the programme included two movements from the transcription of the *Symphonie fantastique* as well as certain new transcriptions: the Overture to Rossini's *William Tell* (S552) and Schubert's *Erlkönig* (S558/4), two pieces which with the *Hexameron* and the *Grand galop chromatique* were to be the great warhorses of Liszt's virtuoso years.

The Czech pianist and composer Wilhelm Kuhe (1823–1912). Liszt! What memories cluster round the name! What a vista of recollections it conjures up—especially in the mind of one who, like myself, entertained the most profound admiration and sincere regard for the pianist and composer! He had come to Vienna for the purpose of giving a concert in aid of the unfortunate people who were suffering from the disastrous inundations in Pest. Would that I could adequately describe the effect produced by that phenomenal artist! Suffice it that Vienna—artistic, music-loving and enthusiastic Vienna—was in a state of excitement such as I have rarely or never seen. Such playing had never been heard before. It was almost more than human. This was the universal expression of opinion, and everyone appeared electrified. That first and memorable concert was followed by many others, at which the same rapturous enthusiasm and indescribable excitement prevailed. . . .

His personality was an extraordinary one. On all subjects an excellent conversationalist, he was extremely witty, possessing a keen sense of humour; his manners were, as all who knew him can testify, most fascinating; while his literary ability was indeed remarkable. And when I come to speak of his generosity, words altogether fail me to indicate that striking phase of his genial and kindly nature. Not only did Liszt give concerts and recitals promiscuously in the cause of suffering and distress, benefiting institutions in whatever town he found himself, but out of his pocket he assisted all who appealed to him to the fullest extent of the means at his disposal.[21]

* A friend of Schubert's, Benedikt Randhartinger (1802–93) was a composer, conductor, and singer. He and Liszt had first met many years earlier, as fellow pupils of Salieri.

No musician of the century contributed more than Liszt to demolishing the old class barriers whereby an artist was regarded as a mere tradesman, his talents to be enjoyed by, but his person to be kept at a suitable distance from, his social superiors. Liszt's impact on the rigid caste system of Vienna was observed by the young pianist and composer *Heinrich Ehrlich* (1822–99), a pupil of Thalberg.

In those days, when the railways were under construction and the press concerned itself almost solely with artistic tittle-tattle, the position of the artist was . . . a subordinate one; and only he who could make himself popular enjoyed the favour of the aristocracy, especially in Vienna. Even Thalberg, who lived in the house of his [adoptive] father, Prince Dietrichstein, displayed a certain deference towards families of the higher nobility. . . . But Liszt at once broke through all social barriers. At his first concert . . . people heard piano-playing such as they had never dreamt of; it was received with thunderous applause and the enthusiasm knew no bounds. That was the reward given to the *artist*—but the concert was followed by a phenomenon hitherto unknown, news of which flew round the city like lightning. With easy vivacity, Liszt had jumped down from the platform into the hall, and with the higher nobility seated on the benches had started a conversation in French, 'as though he were one of the family'. The next concert . . . offered another sight never previously seen: on the platform, grouped closely around the artist, sat ladies of the highest aristocracy, with whom he chatted during the intervals. And the conversations were still continuing when there came to our ears a still more significant piece of news. Invited to dinner by Princess Metternich, the proudest of the proud, Liszt had been talking rather more animatedly with a beautiful neighbour than was approved of by his hostess, who suddenly interrupted with a question about Venice and if he had done good business there. 'I made music, Princess, not business,' his reply had run.

The impression made on the public by all these incidents can nowadays* hardly be imagined. The young artists thought of Liszt as a god. And how he behaved towards them, in what contrast to Thalberg! Whereas the latter could be seen only by appointment in writing . . . and always received his guests in an orderly salon and in formal attire, Liszt's sitting-room at the Stadt Frankfurt Hotel was like an army camp in which all sorts and conditions mingled indiscriminately. . . . He was equally kind to all, but kindest and most bewitching to any young artist in whom he had discovered talent. Was it any wonder that wherever he went he was followed by a swarm of admirers, that he was adored, idolized?[22]

A month after Liszt's departure, the *Allgemeiner Musikalischer Anzeiger* (21 June) took a retrospective look at him.

He who appears before the multitude must be capable of impressing his

* Ehrlich was writing more than fifty years later.

personality upon it. In this, too, Liszt can serve as a model and example to all concert-givers. Towards you there steps a young man of sophisticated appearance, almost too slenderly built, his smile of greeting at once revealing his social graces. With the hall filled almost to excess, a few ladies find it difficult to make their way to their places. Hurrying forward, the virtuoso offers them his arm. Taken by surprise, they hesitate, and he points to chairs by his side, with which they appear not discontent. A hush descends, and the artist seats himself at the piano. The opening passages ring out. People are amazed at the novelty and boldness of it, at such playing as has never before been heard. The Adagio begins; the young man's delicate features grow almost transparent, his eyes become transfigured, and his lightly constructed frame seems to hover over the ethereal music. In the Scherzo he philanders; in the Finale he thunders with full chords. Ending with the same power, and the same grace, as he began, he first turns to express his thanks to the orchestra which had accompanied him, while the audience gives vent to its wild enthusiasm with loud clapping and cheering.

The good Viennese are quite changed. The second and third concerts follow; people intrigue for tickets, and on a hot summer's day sit in the hall for a full hour before the start of the concert. The orchestra is removed so that the élite of the ladies of fashionable society may have seats near the virtuoso. Liszt remains the same, but new merits are daily discovered in him. People exchange anecdotes about his life, wait for him in the street, try to catch a word or two from him, order his portrait, buy his handwriting —in short, he becomes the vogue. Any pretext is used to make his acquaintance; he is regularly besieged with dinners, suppers, and parties. The honour of inviting him and receiving him graciously is coveted by even the great and mighty. And this was where his Parisian upbringing stood him in excellent stead. With amiable ease of manner, cheerful, chatty, and courteous, he moved in the world to which he had long been accustomed. If, to begin with, people sometimes expected a different kind of behaviour from him, the young artist's sophisticated manner soon cleared up any slight misapprehension, and they began to take pleasure in his company; all the more so since French, the language spoken everywhere here, he knows perfectly. In return, he gave dinners and suppers at his hotel.[23]

On Sunday, 27 May, Liszt left Vienna to return to a jealous and impatient Marie in Venice, his impressions of this unique city and former republic being eventually set down in an article serialized a year later in the Parisian journal *L'Artiste*. Recounting conversations with friends on sundry aspects of the history and daily life of Venice, it also describes the couple's sight-seeing (with special emphasis on St Mark's Basilica) and visits to the Lido and the island of San Lazzaro (whose Armenian monastery was of great interest to Liszt for its Byron associations), considers the respective merits of the three giants of Venetian Renaissance painting, Titian, Veronese, and Tintoretto, and concludes with an admiring appreciation of the 'sovereignly intelligent' Caroline Unger ('one of the greatest actresses, one of the most perfect singers, ever to have appeared in the theatre'), whom the evening before their midnight departure they heard at La Fenice in Donizetti's *Lucrezia Borgia*.

The summer was spent mainly at Genoa and Lugano. By late August they were once again in Como, whence Liszt made several trips to Milan, where he was frequently a guest in the celebrated salons* of the Countesses Clara Maffei and Giulia Samoyloff. In May, an article of his containing adverse criticism of La Scala had appeared in the *Revue et gazette musicale,* creating anger among the Milanese; but he received powerful support from Rossini, also in Milan at this time. In his leisure hours he read Byron; and on 6 September attended the coronation of the Emperor Ferdinand I at Milan Cathedral. 'Although very well placed, I saw nothing,' he told Marie. 'It was probably my own fault. At a given moment I heard the cry "He is crowned", followed by applause—and there was an Emperor.'

During the autumn they visited various parts of northern Italy. In early October Liszt was invited to play at Cattaio, the Duke of Modena's residence near Padua, where the guests included the ex-Empress Marie Louise, widow of Napoleon and now ruler of the Duchy of Parma, as well as the Austrian Emperor and Empress. To Pierre Erard he was able to report: 'Your piano, which I had the inspired idea of transporting here, created an immense effect. The Vicereine and Marie Louise in particular were enchanted with it.'

Later in October Liszt and Marie arrived in Florence, where he appeared in at least seven concerts, including two (17 November and 11 December) at court, during their three-month sojourn in the city. Admiring Cellini's *Perseus*, he contributed an article to the *Revue et gazette musicale* (13 January 1839) on that bronze masterpiece. For *L'Artiste* he wrote some lively impressions of Genoa and Florence which also describe his meeting with a renowned contemporary Italian artist: the sculptor Lorenzo Bartolini (1777–1850), a former protégé of Napoleon.

I had already been living in Florence for two months, and, I confess to my shame, had grown almost tired of masterpieces. I was beginning to find the *Medici Venus* devoid of charm and the *Madonna del Cardellino*† rather insipid; I felt infinitely grateful to Masaccio for having left only two frescoes, and had begun to pass the Loggia dei Lanzi without slowing my steps. . . . Enthusiasm is a violent state of the mind; it agitates and wearies it, and causes it to require complete rest—a kind of numbing of the poetic faculty that few people dare admit, although all have experienced it. And so I was in that mortifying condition when one would not walk a single step

* Which he already knew from earlier visits. On 2 Mar. he and Marie had been invited to leave a souvenir of themselves in Clara Maffei's album. Liszt's contribution ran: 'There are people who with a few words can give one much food for thought: others who, despite a great flow of words, arouse few ideas; like the two hands of a clock, one of which moves rapidly but marks only the minutes, while the other, proceeding more slowly, indicates the hours.'

† Raphael's *Madonna of the Goldfinch*. In the original publication of the article in *L'Artiste,* an unfortunate misprint caused 'Cardellino' to appear as 'Lardellino'—a word meaning, if anything at all, 'little piece of bacon'.

to see the sublimest works of God and man, so incapable does one feel of remaining at their level, when a friend called one morning to suggest that I visit Bartolini's studio with him. . . .[24]

After he and his companions had been virtually ignored by Bartolini in a brief encounter at the studio, Liszt sent the sculptor a ticket for the concert he was giving two days later.

I had no idea if he liked music,* but on the off chance that he did I was glad to do him a courtesy. The concert came to an end without my having noticed him in the hall, and so, just when I was about to withdraw, I was not a little surprised to see him coming eagerly towards me. Holding out his hand, he said: 'Sir, how long will you be staying in Florence?'

'A fortnight at most,' I replied.

'That should be enough. Would it be a nuisance if I were to do a bust of you?'

Quite taken aback by this sudden apostrophe, I stammered a few words of thanks. . . . 'Well then, if you can give me a dozen sittings, we'll begin tomorrow. There is something in your head . . . something I like! . . I'll try not to make a mess of it.'

As you can imagine, I was punctual for the appointment the next day, curious to see at close quarters a man whose manners were as unusual as his talent was prodigious. He received me with charming cordiality on this occasion. We chatted a lot, for he works with wonderful facility and without ever *posing* his model. He put trust in some bump or other that he discovered on my forehead, and took a liking to the angle of my face. We were soon talking freely to one another; he told me the story of his life, and I got to know one of the grandest and finest artistic temperaments which have yet presented themselves to my admiration.[25]

Leaving Marie at Florence, Liszt spent Christmas in Bologna, where he played at the Casino—'with a success unheard of since Malibran, and still more complete than hers'—and once again enjoyed the company of Rossini. He also saw and admired Raphael's *St Cecilia*, another masterpiece of art on which an article above his name later appeared in the *Revue et gazette musicale* (14 April 1839).

1839

On New Year's Day Liszt returned to Marie at Florence; and in mid-January they were joined by Blandine, brought by her nurse. Via Pisa, the family then moved on to Rome. Here, in a private concert given at the Palazzo Poli in March, Liszt for the first time provided the entire musical fare by himself,

* Bartolini was in fact not only a keen music-lover but also an excellent practising musician.

without the participation of other artists. To this inauguration of the modern solo recital he later made light-hearted reference in a letter (Albano, 4 June) to Princess Belgiojoso. Congratulating her on the musical evenings she had been holding at her Paris home, he continues:

What a contrast to the tiresome *musical soliloquies* (I know not what other name to give to this invention of mine) which I have devised specially for the Romans, and which I am quite capable of importing to Paris, so boundlessly impudent do I become! Imagine that, failing to concoct a programme which would have any kind of sense, I dared, for the sake of peace and quiet, to give a series of concerts entirely alone, affecting the style of Louis XIV and saying cavalierly to the public, 'Le Concert—c'est moi.' For the curiosity of the thing, here is the programme of one of these soliloquies.

1. Overture to *William Tell,* performed by M. L.
2. *Réminiscences des Puritains.* Fantasy composed and performed by the above-mentioned!
3. Etudes and fragments, by the same to the same!
4. Improvisation on given themes—still by the same.

And that's all; neither more nor less, except for lively conversation during the intervals, and enthusiasm, if appropriate![1]

In addition to these solo appearances, Liszt also took part in orchestral concerts, on one occasion playing Weber's *Concertstück* at the Teatro Argentina.

At their Rome apartment (80, Via della Purificazione) on Thursday, 9 May, Marie gave birth to their third and last child, a boy to whom they gave the name Daniel.*

It was while he was in Rome, or at nearby Albano to which they repaired to enjoy the lake, that Liszt received from Robert Schumann copies of the latter's *Kinderscenen*, Op. 15, and of a work dedicated to him, the Fantasy in C, Op. 17.

Liszt to Schumann. Albano, 5 June. The latest pieces you have been so kind to send to Rome for me, I find admirable both in inspiration and craftmanship. The Fantasy dedicated to me is a work of the highest class, and I am really proud of the honour you do me in linking my name with so imposing a composition. . . .

As to your *Kinderscenen,* I owe them one of the keenest pleasures of my life. You know, or you don't know, that I have a little three-year-old daughter whom everyone agrees in finding *angelic* (what a commonplace!). Her name is Blandine-Rachel, and her nickname *Moucheron* ['gnat' or 'midge']. It goes without saying that she has a peaches-and-cream complexion, and that her fair golden hair† reaches to her feet just like a savage. . . .

* A few years later Liszt arranged for all three children to be legitimized.

† It was during this year, 1839, that, under the inspiration of the 'little angel' and her 'golden hair', Liszt composed his first song, to words by the Marchese Cesare Bocella: *Angiolin dal biondo crin* (S269).

Well, my dear Monsieur Schumann, two or three times a week (on fine and good days!) I play your *Kinderscenen* to her during the course of the evening; this enchants her, and me still more, as you can imagine, so that often I play the first repeat over for her twenty times without going any further. I really believe you would be content with this success if you could be a witness of it![2]

To Rome in early June came Sainte-Beuve, whose travel notes for the 11th record: 'Accompanied Liszt and Mme d'A to Tivoli, to see Hadrian's Villa; great impression made by the evening sunset between the tall cypresses, near those reddened ruins. Describe it, recount it to Liszt in an extended piece which will be my Poussin landscape.' And the renowned critic did indeed set down his memories of the visit, in the poem 'La Villa Adriana', dedicated to Liszt.

Marie's health remaining poor following the birth of Daniel, a few days after the excursion to Tivoli she, Liszt, and Blandine set out for Lucca, from whose celebrated *bagni* she wished to profit. Daniel was given into the charge of a peasant family at Palestrina, their friend Lehmann* undertaking to keep a watchful eye on him.†

Journeying via Terni, and stopping to explore Assisi, they first spent a week in Florence (where they were all made 'extremely dejected' by the disappearance of their black greyhound, Othello), and it was not until the last week of the month that they arrived at Lucca. Here they took up residence in the Villa Massimiliana, situated on the slope of a hill overlooking the valley. Before long they were joined by Lehmann, who put his sojourn with them to good use by painting their portraits.‡

Marie d'Agoult. One evening, alone on the terrace with Lehmann and me, Franz is sad. 'I see with sorrow,' he said, 'a period of my life coming to an end. Nothing will ever bring back these three years; I have nothing further to learn or to wish for; plans are taking the place of a free, spontaneous life. I am at the age in which one feels that nothing is good enough. I realize, bitterly, that I am not what I would have wished to be. When one has shattered everything around one, one has shattered something in oneself too.'

It is my impression that he is grieving at not being able to give me more happiness. He is not aware of what *I* sense only too well: the atrophy of my brain, the presentiment of old age, the death of the will.[3]

In September, Liszt, Marie, and Blandine moved to San Rossore, a fishing village on the coast near Pisa. Here they took accommodation in a wooden house

* The painter Henri Lehmann (1814–82), for whom Liszt and Marie's nickname was 'Clear placid', or simply 'Clear'—from Byron's apostrophe, in *Childe Harold,* to Lake Geneva: 'Clear, placid Léman!'

† A task he carried out conscientiously, making regular trips on horseback to Palestrina and sending detailed reports to the parents. 'Prince Daniel is in perfect health,' he wrote to Marie on one occasion. 'I got there before sunrise, taking those good people by surprise, but found their house and themselves as clean as they were when you saw them. They called Liszt *il nostro principe* [our prince].'

‡ It was his outstanding portrait of Liszt which, when exhibited with two other paintings of his at the Paris *Salon* of 1840, helped earn Lehmann a Gold Medal.

near the beach and made good use of the opportunity to go bathing and to dine under the pine trees. 'We've just spent a fortnight at San Rossore,' wrote Marie to Lehmann on the 26th, 'days of great beauty, purity, and harmony; but one can't describe things like that, one can only indicate to certain fine, poetic beings, of whom you are one, where to look in their own memories to find similar emotions, parallel joys. . . . The *bravo suonatore* is this morning beginning a Dantesque fragment,* which is driving him to the very devil. He is delighted to miss going to Naples† if it will enable him to finish this piece.'

Liszt to Hector Berlioz. San Rossore, 2 October. Having nothing to seek in present-day Italy, I began to scour her past; having but little to ask of the living, I questioned the dead. A vast field opened before me. The music of the Sistine Chapel, that music which is gradually deteriorating, wearing away from day to day with the frescoes of Raphael and Michelangelo, induced me to undertake research of the highest interest. Once embarked upon it, I found it impossible to limit myself, to come to a standstill; I had no wish to send you a few fragmentary judgements on the whole of this great school of sacred music which is still too little known to us, and so I waited. Too many matters were making demands on me; the hours were too short, the field of study too wide. I felt that before writing I ought to see, hear, ponder. In this privileged country I came upon the beautiful in the purest and sublimest forms. Art showed itself to me in the full range of its splendour; revealed itself in all its unity and universality. With every day that passed, feeling and reflection brought me to a still greater awareness of the secret link between works of genius. Raphael and Michelangelo enabled me better to understand Mozart and Beethoven. In the works of Giovanni Pisano, Fra Angelico, and Francia I found an explanation of Allegri, Marcello, and Palestrina; Titian and Rossini I thought of as two stars with similar rays. The Colosseum and the Campo Santo seem more familiar when one thinks of the Eroica Symphony and [Mozart's] *Requiem*. It was in Orcagna‡ and Michelangelo that Dante found his expression in painting; and will perhaps one day find his musical expression in the Beethoven of the future.

* The first sketch of Liszt's so-called Dante Sonata, the *Après une lecture du Dante, fantasia quasi sonata,* seventh and last piece of his *Années de pèlerinage, Italie*.

† Contrary to what some of his biographers would have us believe, Liszt *never* visited Naples. In 1842, when correcting and annotating Christern's biography of him, he wrote in the margin at one point: 'I have never been to Naples.' In 1868 he wrote to Agnes Street-Klindworth: 'I have now been living in Rome for seven years without visiting Naples, which I know only from descriptions, pictures, photographs.' And in January 1886, just before he left Rome and Italy for the last time, he remarked to August Göllerich: 'I have thrice been to the station to go to Naples, but something always prevented my going.' (See *infra*, 1886.)

‡ Liszt's allusion here to the 14th-century painter and sculptor Andrea Orcagna reminds one that just as the great fresco *Il Trionfo della Morte* (The Triumph of Death) in Pisa's Campo Santo was once thought to be the work of Orcagna but is now attributed to Francesco Traini, so Liszt's *Totentanz* (S126) for piano and orchestra was long believed to have been inspired by that fresco, despite the compelling evidence linking it to Holbein's woodcut series *Der Todtentanz* (The Dance of Death). See Sharon Winklhofer's 'Liszt, Marie d'Agoult and the "Dante" Sonata', *19th Century Music,* 1/1 (July 1977), 15–32.

A circumstance which I count among the most fortunate of my life, has contributed not a little to strengthening both my inner feeling for these things and my keen desire to make still further progress in understanding and comprehending art. M. Ingres,* a man whose genius, supported by exquisite taste and virile enthusiasm, has produced the finest achievements of modern painting, admitted me at Rome into the most intimate friendship, the recollection of which still makes my heart swell with pride. . . . This great artist, who knows all the secrets of antiquity, and whom Apelles himself would have hailed as a brother, is not only an incomparable painter but also an excellent musician. Mozart, Haydn and Beethoven speak the same language to him as Phidias and Raphael. Wherever he encounters the beautiful he takes possession of it, and his passionate devotion seems to render still greater the genius to which it addresses itself. I shall never forget the day when we visited the rooms of the Vatican, and walked together through those long galleries filled with countless monuments representing Etruria, Greece, Ancient Rome, and Christian Italy. As we went respectfully past those yellowing marbles and those paintings that time has half-effaced, he discoursed, and we, his eager disciples, hung on to his every utterance. His glowing words seemed to re-create all those masterpieces; his eloquence transported us back to centuries long gone; line and colour took on new life before our very eyes; the forms obliterated by time and by the hands of vandals were reborn in pristine purity, revealing themselves to us in all their youthful beauty. A poetic mystery was taking place: the genius of our own age was evoking that of ancient times.[4]

In this same letter, Liszt refers to a subscription got up by a committee at Bonn for the erection in that city of a monument to Beethoven.

Is what I read possible? In France, the subscription for a monument to the greatest musician of our century has produced 424 fr. 90. What a disgrace for all! What an affliction for us! Such a state of affairs must not be allowed to continue. It is not with such a slow and niggardly almsgiving that Beethoven is to be assured a monument. It must not be—and will not be.[5]

From Pisa, where he and Marie took lodgings when driven from San Rossore by rain, Liszt addressed a letter (3 October) to the Bonn committee in which he offered to make up from his own pocket the sum still wanting, asking in return only the privilege of choosing the artist who would execute the work; and he put forward the name of Lorenzo Bartolini. Initially accepting the offer, the committee later found it more fitting to commission a bronze statue from a German sculptor. Liszt fulfilled his financial promise, however, and made an eventual contribution of no less than 10,000 francs. It was principally to obtain

* Jean Auguste Dominique Ingres (1780–1867), the leading 19th-century exponent of the classical tradition in French painting, was from 1834–41 Director of the French Academy of Art at the Villa Medici in Rome. His well-known drawing of Liszt, who later dedicated to Ingres the transcriptions of Beethoven's 5th and 6th symphonies, was done in May 1839.

such a sum that he now embarked on a career as a touring pianist; and later in October he set out for Vienna. Collecting Cosima *en route* at Genoa, Marie returned to Paris with their two daughters.

By way of Venice, where, hiring by chance a gondolier who had once ferried Byron, he was inspired to visit the Palazzo Mocenigo, in which the poet had once stayed, Liszt arrived on 26 October at Trieste—his reading matter during the crossing of the Gulf being the Book of Job.

Much of his time at Trieste was spent in the company of the attractive Caroline Unger, conversations with whom he felt obliged to report to Marie; and his concert of 5 November (in which he played the *Niobe* and *Lucia** fantasies, the *Grand galop chromatique*, and the *Hexameron*, and was recalled more than twenty times) was so great a success that on the 11th he gave a second.

On 15 November he reached Vienna, and was soon in the company of Czerny, Tobias Haslinger, Dessauer, Saphir, and other friends and acquaintances. Attending a concert, he found himself the cynosure of all eyes. 'The entire hall turned towards the place where I was sitting with Saphir. . . . I feel profoundly moved by this welcome, and am practising like a madman every day, so that if possible I may keep myself up to the level of this tide of enthusiasm, of which moreover a good part relates to my personality.' His first concert, given on 19 November in the hall of the Musikverein and attended by the Dowager Empress and the Archduchess Sophie, included his transcription of the last three movements of Beethoven's Pastoral Symphony; the *Hexameron;* the fourth of the *Grandes Etudes;* Schubert's *Ave Maria* (S558/12); and, as an encore and by public demand, Schubert's 'Horch, horch'. His success was immense. 'The Pastoral Symphony was understood by only half the audience,' he told Marie, 'but, as always, I maintain and uphold the right of the artist to impose on the masses the best and most beautiful.'

The day after his arrival he had fallen ill. Rising from his sickbed to give the first concert, he felt too unwell for the second, which was postponed until the 27th.

Heinrich Adami in the Allgemeine Theaterzeitung *(30 November).* The enthusiasm which this great virtuoso is exciting in Vienna cannot be described. . . . No sooner is one of his concerts over than everyone is already longing for the next. . . . Not since Paganini has an artist made such a magical impression on the Viennese public . . . and years will pass before we shall find a third name worthy of being placed beside these two great masters. But we are convinced that this unknown third, even if we do not await him in vain, will surpass the triumphs of his two predecessors neither on the violin nor the piano, because for these two instruments the account can be considered a closed one.[6]

Liszt was meanwhile writing to Marie: 'How, you will ask, could I give a concert without being fully recovered? But how do otherwise? I am horribly bored and irritated. A concert is at least a kind of distraction.'

* The Fantasy on Donizetti's *Lucia di Lammermoor* is divided into two parts. The first (S397) is a transcription of the celebrated sextet; the second (S398), far more rarely played, of the March and Cavatina.

The third concert was on 2 December.

Adami in the Allgemeine Theaterzeitung *(4 December).* Liszt began with the F minor Sonata [*Appassionata*] of Beethoven, the one which when played by Clara Wieck had given rise to such vehement debate in our newspapers. The argument, it is hoped, is now decided, and the earlier so small crowd of opponents now looks around with triumphal pride, for Liszt's magic tones brought the entire well-armed host of his adversaries, perhaps not a single person excepted, into the enemy ranks. For younger listeners in particular, who never had the opportunity of hearing Beethoven himself in his piano sonatas and concertos, Liszt's renderings are of exceptional interest, and from them they are best able to study these works, often capable of so multifarious an interpretation, and to form a correct view for themselves.[7]

Liszt's fourth concert was at the Musikverein on 5 December. On that same day, at a *concert spirituel* in the Redoute, he played the C minor Concerto of Beethoven, a work not known to him until then which he was obliged to learn in one day (improvising the cadenza*).

Adami in the Allgemeine Theaterzeitung *(7 December).* By his performance of the Beethoven Concerto, everything we have thus far heard from Liszt seems to have been surpassed. The Concerto has been played here by a number of great artists, but in so wonderful a fashion by none.[8]

The fifth concert (8 December) included Beethoven's Sonata in D minor, *Le lac de Wallenstadt,* and *Erlkönig.* According to Adami (*Allgemeine Theaterzeitung*, 10 December): 'The word "enthusiasm" will soon no longer suffice to describe the interest, intensified to its utmost limits, felt by our public for the concerts of this virtuoso. They are concerts which we in Vienna shall only with difficulty ever experience again!'

Liszt's sixth and last concert, on 14 December at the Musikverein, included a performance, with Joseph Mayseder and Josef Merk, of the Archduke Trio, and his own Fantasy (S393) on Bellini's *La Sonnambula.* Just before his departure from Vienna, on 17 December, he took part in a concert given by Marie Pleyel, whom he joined in a four-hand Fantasy by Herz on themes from *William Tell.*

On the 18th he arrived at Pozsony. The next day, at his first concert, he was given an overwhelming reception by his compatriots and it was proposed that the Hungarian Diet raise him to the nobility. 'As it is a national matter, which I have in no wise sought, requested or coveted,' he told Marie, 'I admit that it will give me pleasure.'

On the 20th he gave a concert for charity. A further concert followed on the 22nd, after which, accompanied by Counts Casimir Esterházy and Leó Festetics, he set out for Pest, where on his arrival next day he was greeted by a vocal quartet with choral accompaniment, an immense military band, and a performance by the best local amateurs of Beethoven's Septet. His first concert was on 27

* Of which perhaps something survived in the magnificent cadenza he wrote for the Concerto forty years later.

December. When, on the 28th, he entered the Hungarian Theatre to attend a performance of *Fidelio,* the audience unanimously began to applaud and to cry 'Éljen! éljen!' [Hail! Long live!] His second concert, on the 29th, was followed by a banquet given in his honour by the flower of the aristocracy then in Pest. To the half-dozen toasts offered to him, Liszt responded with one in French to 'the well-being, progress, and liberty of our motherland'. After the dinner, subscriptions for a bust of him were solicited, and in the space of a few minutes 1,500 francs were donated.

1840

Liszt gave several more concerts at Pest in early January (on the 2nd, 4th, 6th, 11th, and a farewell concert on the 12th). He also played on the 8th at a concert given by the violinist János Táborszky, and on the 9th at a soirée held in the Buda home of Count Gábor Keglevich.

Visiting Pest at this time was the English historian, novelist, and travel-writer *Julia Pardoe* (1806–62), who in her ensuing book on Hungary described the reception given to Liszt by his compatriots, and the historic event which followed his concert of Saturday, 4 January.

This talented *artiste* is tall, and slight even to attenuation—the sword has worn away the scabbard—his appearance is extremely peculiar, and very distinguished; and his general attainments of a high caste. . . . He plays with the piano as with a toy; and frequently brings out sounds so wild and startling, and so unlike any to which the ear is accustomed, that I christened him the 'Paganini of the Piano', and really he merits the name. . . .

My readers will readily picture to themselves the enthusiasm with which he was expected and received. An enthusiasm in no wise diminished by the fact that his political principles were well known; for his admirers had not suffered it to escape their memory that George Sand in one of her works had said: 'Je ne connais qu'un seul homme qui vivra et qui mourra démocrate, et cet homme est François Liszt.'. . .

When his concerts were announced, the great saloon of the Redoute did not suffice to contain the crowd, although the admission-tickets were distributed at a price considered very high for the country. The hotels overflowed with guests from distant provinces, some of them at three and four days' journey from the capital, who hastened to Pest to swell the triumph of the Artist-Liberal. Barons were in his train; and the fairest countesses, in a land where almost all are fair, contended for his smiles; and here I must permit myself to remark that I never yet met an individual who so gracefully repaid the honours that were heaped upon him, and a homage as universal as it was unmeasured; and thus, strange and enviable destiny! when he departed he left not one enemy behind him. There was no plausible pretext for dislike, for he had 'borne his honours meekly', and disarmed even envy, the most subtle and consequently the most dangerous of foes.

I was particularly struck by his manner at a ball given to him by the ladies of the *haute-volée*, where he was little less than deified. In the course of the evening he was presented to me; and I have seldom spent a pleasanter half hour than in conversing with this talented and amiable man, who will create, if I mistake not, a great sensation in London.

He performed during his stay for the benefit of the Hungarian Theatre, on which occasion the house was brilliantly lighted up, and so densely filled that there was not even standing-room to be procured by a disappointed crowd which besieged the doors several hours before the commencement of the concert. Even the back and wings of the stage were converted into boxes; and when Liszt appeared in a Magyar costume the acclamations were deafening, and almost interminable. At the close of the advertised performances, when the public enthusiasm was once more reluctantly subsiding, the *artiste* again seated himself at the piano, and struck up Rákóczy's March, the liberal air of Hungary—the magnificent and melancholy melody which was composed after the defeat of that celebrated Transylvanian Prince, and which ever acts like magic on the feelings of the Hungarians.

To attempt a description of its effect at this particular moment, when previous excitement had quickened the pulses and swelled the hearts of the audience, would be about as rational as to undertake to put into words the spirit-sound of the mighty Niagara; nor could sober English fancies enable them even to trench upon the reality—it was almost enough to have awakened the dead.

During the outburst several magnates and gentlemen* appeared upon the stage, and by degrees silence was restored; when drawing from its case a costly sword enriched with jewels, which had formerly belonged to Stephen Báthory,† one of the party presented it to Liszt, whom he addressed at once as a patriot and an *artiste*. It was probably the most perfect drama ever enacted on that stage; and the silence was so dense that every word was distinctly audible.

Liszt was painfully overcome; and during several moments could not

* Describing the event to Marie d'Agoult, Liszt wrote: 'Just when I was about to return to the wings, Count Leó Festetics, Baron Bánffy, and Count Teleki (all magnates), Eckstein and Augusz, and a sixth whose name I forget, came on, all in Hungarian gala costume.' It was the first-named who presented the sword to Liszt. The sixth was Pál Nyáry, Director of the Hungarian National Theatre.

† 1533–86. King of Poland from 1576, his plans to liberate Hungary from Turkish rule were frustrated by his early death. He was the uncle of the notorious Elisabeth Báthory, the 'Bloody Countess'. Julia Pardoe was in error, however: far from having once belonged to Báthory, the sword was a new one, made in 1839 and never used in battle.

utter a syllable, while large tears rained through his long and slender fingers; but at length he rallied; and buckling the weapon about his waist with a sudden gesture of mingled pride and gratitude, he looked round the house with a long earnest look, and then, by a violent effort, compelled himself to speak.

But I cannot, I think, do better than transcribe his reply, for it will at once enable the reader to comprehend the excited state of feeling both of the *artiste* and of the Hungarian public. . . .

'My dear countrymen! For here indeed I cannot feel as though it were a mere public that I address—this sword which has been presented to me by the representatives of a nation whose valour and chivalry are so universally admitted, I shall preserve throughout my life, as the treasure which is the dearest and the most precious to my heart.

'To express to you in words at such a moment, when my breast labours with emotion, how deeply I am touched and gratified by this demonstration of your esteem and sympathy, as well as of your warm affection, I feel to be impossible. May I be permitted, nevertheless, to say a few sentences on our present position?

'This sword, which was once gloriously borne in defence of our dear country, is consigned today to weak and pacific hands. Is not this a symbol? Does it not declare, gentlemen, that Hungary, after having covered herself with glory on every battlefield, now asks new honour from the arts, sciences, and literature of peace? Does it not say, gentlemen, that men of application and intelligence have also a noble duty and a high mission to fulfil among you?

'Hungary, gentlemen, must not remain a stranger to any kind of glory. She is destined to move at the head of nations no less by her heroism than by her pacific genius. For us *artistes,* this sword is also a noble image and a striking symbol. Its hilt is enriched with diamonds and rubies, but they are mere accessories—brilliant futilities—the blade makes the weapon! and thus may we ever hold in our hearts, under the thousand fitful forms in which our fancy clothes them, the love of our kind, and of the country which is our life itself!

'Yes, gentlemen; let us follow up, by every legitimate and peaceful mean, the work in which we must all assist, each according to his strength and power.

'And if ever any should dare unjustly or violently to impede us in the accomplishment of this work, then, gentlemen, should it be requisite, let our swords quit their scabbards—they are untarnished, and their blows will fall as heavily as heretofore—and let our blood flow even to the last drop for our rights, our king, and our country!'*

I am not going to follow up the transcription of this speech by defending

* When Liszt had finished, his friend Baron Antal Augusz (1807–78) stepped forward and gave a Hungarian translation of the speech.

either the consistency or the judiciousness of the gift which produced it; and still less shall I permit myself to analyse the good taste of the whole exhibition. There is probably not another country in the world where it could have occurred without provoking laughter, but the Hungarians are far too earnest in their excitement to induce ridicule.

In Paris such a scene would have dwindled from bombast into twaddle; in London it would have commenced with an uproar and ended with a dinner; and in both it would have afforded food for pasquinades and party-spirit during the month ensuing; but here all was real, unadulterated, genuine enthusiasm. . . .

When he left the theatre on the occasion which I have described, he was attended to his residence* by upwards of five thousand persons. Not a mob of the idle and the vagabond, but all the young men of family and fortune in the city, the tradesmen, and the students; half the number carried torches; and a band of ninety persons, all amateurs, headed the procession. In short, during the fortnight of his residence in Pest, the existence of Liszt was one continual triumph; and his departure created universal regret, in which I, stranger though I was, sincerely participated.[1]

Prolonging his stay by several days, Liszt gave on the 11th a concert on behalf of the Pest Conservatoire, funds for which had been voted by Parliament. For the first time in his career he conducted an orchestra, and was also the soloist in Beethoven's Choral Fantasy and Weber's *Concertstück*. The next day saw his farewell concert at the Redoute.†

Not the least significant event during this visit to Pest was Liszt's meeting with the great epic and romantic poet Mihály Vörösmarty (1800–55), who in his glorious ode *Liszt Ferenchez* (To Franz Liszt) later gave memorable poetic expression to the patriotic feelings aroused in the Magyars by their world-renowned fellow countryman.

Liszt to Marie d'Agoult. Pest, 13 January. You ask me for permission to be unfaithful! Dear Marie, you name no names, but I assume it is Bulwer.‡ It matters little. You know my way of looking at these things. You know that for me deeds, gestures, and acts are nothing; feelings, ideas, nuances (above all nuances), everything. I want and wish you always to have your freedom, for I am convinced that you will always use it nobly and

* Liszt stayed at the home of his friend Count Leó Festetics (1800–84).

† This concert hall was later destroyed by fire during the Hungarian War of Independence.

‡ The diplomat and writer Henry Lytton Bulwer (1801–72), elder brother of the celebrated novelist Edward Bulwer-Lytton. He had been paying assiduous court to Marie, who found him, 'minus the grimace, and also the grace', as like Chopin 'as one fly is like another'. Although she was flattered by his attentions, it is evident from her letters that she was not seriously interested in taking Bulwer as a lover; and her request for permission to be unfaithful was a rather obvious attempt to arouse Liszt's jealousy, doubtless springing from her fears about his behaviour with some of the more attractive women with whom his travels were bringing him into contact. His sage reply effectively called the bluff, and although she later complained that he had not actually answered the question, she also admitted that his response had 'filled her with respect' for him.

delicately, until the day when you say to me: 'What I am, and what I can be, such and such a man has felt more energetically, understood more intimately, than you have done.' Until that day there will be no infidelity, and nothing, absolutely nothing, will change between us. That day, allow me to say, will not arrive and cannot arrive; such is my profound inner conviction.[2]

Leaving Pest in mid-January (having sent the sword of honour to his mother in Paris for safekeeping), Liszt went, via Győr (one concert), to Pozsony, where he stayed with Count Casimir Esterházy. Among his appearances here was a concert at the City Theatre on 26 January at which he conducted the *William Tell* and *Oberon* overtures.

Ida von Kiss de Nemeskér. Liszt's arrival caused a great stir in society. . . . I took part in all the matinées and soirées at which he played. He is a great artist, a musical wizard, the justified pride of his homeland! The old Countess Esterházy gave a *conversazione* in his honour to which only ladies were invited. Archduchess Hermine, who avoids public occasions because of her health, delighted us all by coming too. From there we went to Count Széchenyi's,* to present the golden goblet† to Liszt. István Széchenyi invited me with a note in his own hand: 'This evening, at about 9 o'clock, my wife will present Liszt with the goblet; please be sure to come.' The goblet, on which the names of the twelve donors are engraved, Liszt accepted with emotion, saying that from this cup only nectar should be drunk, and that he would accordingly never profane this precious treasure with any other drink. After a ball given in his honour by Lajos Batthyány, this radiant star left our city.[3]

In late January Liszt arrived in Vienna. A new acquaintance here was the writer, traveller, and *grand seigneur* Prince Hermann von Pückler-Muskau (1785–1871), who 'got me to smoke four or five of the most admirable Turkish, Egyptian, and Chinese pipes. Then he took me to see his Arab horses. They filled me with delight! the joy of a child!'

His first concert was in the hall of the Musikverein on 2 February; it included two of his transcriptions (S561) of songs from Schubert's *Winterreise* and a Fantasy on themes from Mercadante's *Giuramento*. At the Hofburgtheater on the 6th he gave a concert for the benefit of the Sisters of Charity, playing further Schubert transcriptions as well as the fantasies on *La Sonnambula* and *La Fiancée*. On 9 February, again at the Musikverein, came a concert which included the *Huguenots* fantasy, Weber's *Invitation to the Dance*, two of the Paganini Etudes, and, as an encore, according to Heinrich Adami, 'a glorious Etude by Chopin, from which he passed into a Hungarian theme, of truly electrifying effect'.

After a brief visit to Brünn (now Brno in Czechoslovakia) for concerts on 10

* The eminent statesman Count István Széchenyi (1791–1860), ever remembered, in the words of Kossuth, as 'the greatest Hungarian'.

† Now on display at the National Museum, Budapest.

and 11 February, Liszt concluded his Vienna appearances with a charity soirée at the Musikverein on the 14th (taking the piano part in Hummel's Septet), and a farewell concert on the 16th, playing *inter alia* Weber's *Concertstück* and Beethoven's Choral Fantasy. 'Liszt is truly every inch a virtuoso, in the word's noblest meaning,' wrote Adami. 'He practises art not for mercenary reasons, but because of an inner necessity.'

On 17 February he moved on to Sopron, where he gave a charity concert on the 18th. The next day, accompanied by his friend Franz von Schober (1796–1882), the poet and writer who had been a member of Schubert's circle, and by Count Alberti, he made a pilgrimage to his native Raiding.

Liszt to Marie d'Agoult. Vienna, 22 February. As we went along I recognized all the villages, the bell-towers, the crossroads, and even some of the houses. I fail to understand the persistence of childhood memories, which for me, as you know, have so little attraction. Two leagues from Raiding, a score of mounted peasants, very attractively rigged out, came to meet me, and escorted me as far as the judge's house. The entire population (about a thousand people) was assembled. The children, boys and girls alike, bent the knee as I passed them. I had all the trouble in the world to persuade them to get up.

A few peasants came to kiss my hands, the greater number staying at a respectful distance. The priest who had come to meet and welcome me took me to my birthplace, which is in more or less the same condition as when I left it. I saw everything without emotion—you were not with me. . . .

The priest said low mass, the crowd filling the church the while. Then we returned to the judge's house, where an omelette and coffee had been prepared for us. I had wine served to the peasants outside, and urged the musicians who had preceded us to play waltzes. It was a complete open-air ball in the snow.

The peasants brought me their most attractive daughters, asking me to dance with them. I don't know why I began to think of a note you wrote me from Croissy in which you told me about a *bal champêtre*. The memory of it cast an indefinable melancholy over the whole scene.[4]

On 3 March he arrived in Prague, where he lodged at the Black Horse Hotel. Pleased with the rapturous reception* accorded to his three concerts (5, 6, and 7 March) at the Platýz Hall, he gave three more (9th, 11th, and 12th). 'Music, where are thy boundaries? Music, how mighty is thy magic!' sighed a reviewer in the newspaper *Květy*.

During his stay he paid a courtesy call on the veteran Bohemian composer V. J. Tomášek (1774–1850), and was also invited to the home of Countess Elsa Šlik, whose salon was a meeting-place for the whole of musical Prague. It was she who placed on the piano rack before him the manuscript of a melody—dating from

* 'Everyone says my success surpasses even that of Paganini, which here as everywhere is the ultimate yardstick,' he told Marie.

the 1820s, but thought by most people at the time to be a traditional Hussite song — which became the basis for his *Hussitenlied* (S234) for piano solo. Completed that August, it was dedicated to the premier count of Bohemia, Count Karel Chotek, and published by Hoffmann of Prague in December.

Marie d'Agoult to Liszt, March. I am still astonished that for the six months in which I have been bowed down under a suffering which has nearly proved fatal, you have said not a word to me about my health. . . .

What opinion, then, do you wish me to have of myself, I who die of anxiety when thinking of the coffee you drink and the cigars you smoke, I who have never been able to imagine you in the arms of another woman without a complete overthrowing of all reason, I who even today would give my place in Paradise for six months of unalloyed happiness with you? You are too preoccupied with being great, are too much the philosopher. You are so strong that you take no account of the weakness of others. For you, everything is very simple. Forgive me, I really don't know what I am saying. . . . I feel myself the equal of other people. I feel that they have my weaknesses, my fears, my jealousies. I sense their uncertain will carried away by passion; I see them preoccupied like myself with the miseries of life. You, no. What afflicts me does not afflict you. What I dream of makes you smile. What I desire, you take no account of. You subsist arrogantly on the consciousness of your greatness and fail to appreciate the little sorrows of weaker souls.[5]

On 14 March Liszt arrived in Dresden, where he made the acquaintance of Schumann, who had journeyed from Leipzig to meet him. His three concerts here (16, 27, and 29 March) alternated to some extent with those at Leipzig and caused him much travelling back and forth between the two cities.

Robert Schumann writing in the Neue Zeitschrift für Musik.* Still fatigued by a series of six concerts which he gave in Prague, Herr Liszt arrived in Dresden last Saturday. . . . On Monday he gave a concert; the hall was brilliant with an assemblage of our aristocratic society, including several members of the royal family. All eyes were fixed on the door at which the artist was to enter. Many portraits of him were in circulation, and that by Kriehuber,† who has most correctly seized his Jupiter profile, is excellent; but the youthful Jupiter himself, of course, interests us to quite a different degree. There is a great deal said about the prose of our day, the air of courts, the spirit of the railway, etc.; but let the right man only appear, and we piously watch his every movement. So it was with this artist, whose phenomenal accomplishments were talked of twenty years ago, whose name we have been accustomed to hear mentioned among the very first — before whom, as before Paganini, every head has bowed in apparently

* The Leipzig newspaper which Schumann, its editor, had founded in 1834.

† The German painter and graphic artist Joseph Kriehuber (1800–76), who over the years did a number of excellent portraits of Liszt.

instantaneous recognition. The whole audience greeted his appearance with an enthusiastic storm of applause, and then he began to play. I had heard him before; but an artist is a different person in the presence of the public compared with what he appears in the presence of a few. The fine open space, the glitter of light, the elegantly-dressed audience—all this elevates the frame of mind in giver and receiver. And now the demon's power began to awake; he first played with the public as if to try it, then gave it something more profound, until every single member was enveloped in his art; and then the whole mass began to rise and fall precisely as he willed it. I have never found any artist, except Paganini, to possess in so high a degree as Liszt this power of subjugating, elevating, and leading the public. . . . We are overwhelmed by a flood of tones and feelings. It is an instantaneous variety of wildness, tenderness, boldness, and airy grace; the instrument glows under the hands of its master. All this has been described a hundred times already, and the Viennese, especially, have tried to catch the eagle in every way: with pitchforks, poems, by pursuit, and with snares. But he must be heard—and also seen; for if Liszt played behind the scenes, a great deal of the poetry of his playing would be lost.

He played and accompanied at this concert from beginning to end. . . . Only Madame Schröder-Devrient*—almost the only artist capable of maintaining a position in such company—took part, singing Schubert's *Erlkönig* and some of his smaller songs.[6]

On the 17th, accompanied by Schumann, Liszt took the train to Leipzig, where his first concert was given that same evening. 'Don't be worried,' he wrote to Marie a day or two later, when a sudden fever obliged him to postpone his second concert, 'you know that towards the spring I am always compelled to take to my bed for a day or two. I have been completely free of fever since yesterday. The tedious part of it is that I am forced to spend a further three days here. Mendelssohn, Hiller, and Schumann hardly leave my room. Mendelssohn brings me syrups, jams, etc. I am very content with him; he is much simpler than I had imagined. Further, he is a man of remarkable talent and a highly cultivated mind. He draws marvellously, plays the violin and viola, reads Homer fluently in Greek, speaks four or five languages easily. . . . Schumann came to Dresden to look me up. He is an excessively reserved man, who speaks hardly at all, except with me now and again. I believe he will be extremely devoted to me. People here have quoted your remark about Thalberg and me: he being the first and I the only pianist. This does not please Schumann, who maintains that I am at once the first *and* the only one.'

Robert Schumann to Clara Wieck. Leipzig, 18 March. Liszt and I are together almost the whole day. 'I feel as though I had known you for twenty years' he said yesterday—and I feel exactly the same. We are already quite rude to one another, and I often have cause to be, for Vienna

* The celebrated dramatic soprano Wilhelmine Schröder-Devrient (1804–60).

has made him really spoilt and capricious. But . . . how extraordinarily he plays, how boldly and breath-takingly, and then again how softly and tenderly—I've now heard it all. But, little Clara, *this* world—*his*, I mean —is no longer mine. Art such as you practise it, and often I too when composing at the piano, that beautiful cosy intimacy, I would not give for all his splendour—and there is even some tinsel mixed with it, too much.[7]

Clara Wieck to Robert Schumann. Berlin, 20 March. How fortunate Liszt is, to be able to play at sight what the likes of us toil over and in the end get nowhere with. I fully agree with your judgement on him! Have you heard him play any of his Etudes yet? I am now practising the ninth, which is beautiful and magnificent, but simply frightfully difficult. . . . I laughed a lot at what you wrote about being rude to him: you say he is spoilt, but doesn't that apply to you too, a little?[8]

Robert Schumann to Clara Wieck. Leipzig, 20 March. I could have wished you with us at Liszt's this morning. He really is too extraordinary. The way he played from the *Novelettes,* the Fantasy, and the Sonata moved me greatly. Many things he rendered differently from how I had imagined them, but always with genius, and with a tenderness and boldness of feeling such as probably even he can't match every day. Only Becker was there, and the tears came to his eyes, I believe. The second *Novelette,* the one in D, gave me especially great pleasure. You will hardly believe what an effect it makes. . . .[9]

Schumann in the Neue Zeitschrift für Musik. Would that I could, ye distant ones and foreigners, who can scarcely hope ever to see this surpassing artist, and who therefore search out every word that is spoken or written concerning him—would that I could give you a correct idea of him! But the task is a difficult one. It is most easy to speak of his outward appearance. People have often tried to picture this by comparing Liszt's head to Schiller's or Napoleon's; and the comparison so far holds good, in that extraordinary men possess certain traits in common, such as an expression of energy and strength of will in the eyes and mouth. He has some resemblance to the portraits of Napoleon as a young general—pale, thin, with a remarkable profile, the whole significance of his appearance culminating in the head. But his resemblance to the deceased Ludwig Schunke* is remarkable, and this resemblance extends to their art. While listening to Liszt's playing, I have often almost imagined myself listening again to one I heard long before. But this art is scarcely to be described. It is not this or that style of pianoforte-playing; it is rather the outward expression of a daring character, to whom Fate has given, as instruments of victory and command, not the dangerous weapons of war, but the peaceful ones of art. No matter how many and great artists we may possess, or have

* German pianist and composer (1810–34), a close friend of Schumann.

seen pass before us during recent years, though some of them equal him in single points, all must yield to him in energy and boldness. People have been very fond of placing Thalberg in the lists beside him, and then drawing comparisons. But it is only necessary to look at both heads to come to a conclusion. I remember the remark of a Viennese designer, who said, not inaptly, of his countryman's head, that it resembled 'that of a handsome countess with a man's nose'; while of Liszt he observed, that 'he might sit to every painter for a Grecian god'. There is a similar difference in their art. Chopin stands nearer to Liszt as a player, for at least he loses nothing beside him in fairylike grace and tenderness; next to him, Paganini, and, among women, Madame Malibran;—from these Liszt himself acknowledges that he has learned the most. . . .

Since the establishment of our paper, we have followed Liszt's career, concealing nothing that has been publicly said for or against his art, though by far the greater number of voices, especially those of all great artists, have sounded his praise. Thus he appeared among us of late, already honoured with the highest honours that can be bestowed on an artist, and his fame firmly established. It would be difficult to raise this, or to say anything new about him, though it would be easy enough to try to unsettle and injure it, as pedants and rascals are fond of doing at all times. This was lately tried here. Not from any fault of Liszt, the public had been made restless with previous announcements and rendered ill-humoured* by mistakes in the concert arrangements. A writer, notorious here for his lampoons, made use of this to attack Liszt anonymously, on account of his visit to us—'made with no object except to satisfy his insatiable avarice'. Such vileness is unworthy of further thought. . . .[10]

Robert Schumann to Clara Wieck. Leipzig, 22 March. How I wish you were with me! We are leading a pretty hectic life here at the moment, and I think you might sometimes find it a bit frightening. You see, Liszt arrived here so spoilt by the aristocracy, and continually complained so much about our lack of fine dresses, countesses and princesses, that I got annoyed and told him that 'we too had our aristocracy, namely, 150 bookshops, 50 printing-presses, and 30 newspapers, and that he had better take care'. But he only laughed, and paid so little heed to our local customs etc. that he is now having a very hard time of it in the newspapers. It must have dawned on him what I meant by aristocracy, for he has never been so charming as in these last two days when people have been pulling him to pieces.

But with every day that passes he grows mightier and mightier. This morning he played again at R. Härtel's in a way that made us all tremble and jubilate; Etudes by Chopin, a piece from Rossini's *Soirées,* and several other things. In his honour, and to show the public the kind of artist it is

* Because Liszt had been received coolly at his first Leipzig concert, it was thought by some that his brief illness was a mere taking to bed out of pique.

dealing with, Mendelssohn has had a splendid idea. Tomorrow evening he is giving an orchestral concert for him at the Gewandhaus, to which only a few people have been invited, and at which some of Mendelssohn's overtures, Schubert's symphony, and Bach's Triple Concerto (with Mendelssohn, Liszt, and Hiller) will be performed. Isn't that decent of Mendelssohn?*[11]

Clara Wieck to Robert Schumann. Berlin, 22 March. When I heard Liszt for the first time, at Graf's in Vienna, I was overwhelmed and sobbed aloud, it so shook me. Don't you feel the same, that it is as though he wanted to be absorbed by the piano? And then again, how heavenly it is when he plays tenderly. . . . In comparison with Liszt other virtuosi seem so small, even Thalberg.[12]

In the *Neue Zeitschrift für Musik* Schumann also recorded his impressions of the musical evening (23 March) organized by Mendelssohn, and of Liszt's second and third Leipzig concerts (24th and 30th).

The musical festival which was prepared for him will never be forgotten by Liszt himself or by the other persons present. . . . Those were three such happy musical hours as years do not always bring. At the end, Liszt played alone,† and wonderfully. The assembly broke up amid the most joyous excitement, and the gaiety and happiness that sparkled in all eyes must have sufficiently attested the guests' gratitude towards the giver of a festival offered by him in homage to the artistic talents of another.

Liszt's most dazzling performance was yet to come: Weber's *Concertstück,* which he played at his second concert. Virtuoso and public seemed to be in the freshest possible mood on that evening, and the enthusiasm during and after his playing almost exceeded anything hitherto known here. Although Liszt attacked the piece from the beginning with such force and grandeur of expression that a charge on a battlefield seemed to be in question, yet he carried this on with continually increasing power, until the passage where the player seems to stand at the summit of the orchestra, leading it forward in triumph. Here indeed he resembled that great commander to whom he has been compared, and the tempestuous applause that greeted him was not unlike an adoring 'Vive l'Empereur!' He then played a Fantasy on themes from *Les Huguenots,* the *Ave Maria* and *Serenade*,‡ and, at the request of the public, Schubert's *Erlkönig*. But the *Concertstück* was the crown of his performances on this occasion. . . .

With visible delight in the enthusiastic reception he had received at his

* Asking Marie to have an item about the concert inserted in the French press, Liszt stressed that he particularly wished it to give praise to Mendelssohn, 'who is certainly the most eminent composer in Germany at the moment'.

† The Fantasy on *Lucia di Lammermoor* and *Erlkönig*.

‡ As elsewhere, this may be either the transcription of Schubert's 'Horch, horch' or that of the still more famous 'Leise flehen' (S560/7) from the *Schwanengesang*.

second concert, he declared himself at once ready to give one for the benefit of any charitable institution, the selection of which he left to the decision of experienced persons. So, for the third time, he played again last Monday, for the benefit of the pension fund for aged or invalid musicians, though he had given a concert for the poor in Dresden the day before. The hall was completely crowded; the object of the concert, the programme, the assistance of our most famous songstress, and, above all, Liszt himself had created the highest interest in the concert. Still fatigued from his journey and his frequent playing in recent concerts, Liszt arrived in the morning and went at once to the rehearsal, so that he had little time to himself before the concert hour. It was impossible for him to take any rest. I would not leave this unmentioned: a man is not a god; and the visible effort with which Liszt played on that evening was but a natural consequence of what had preceded the concert. With the most friendly intentions, he had selected three pieces by composers residing here: Mendelssohn, Hiller, and myself; Mendelssohn's latest concerto,* études by Hiller, and several numbers from an early work of mine, entitled *Carnaval.* To the astonishment of many timid virtuosos, I must state that Liszt played these compositions almost at sight. He had had a slight former acquaintance with the études and *Carnaval*, but he had never seen Mendelssohn's concerto until a few days before the concert. . . He displayed his virtuosity in its fullest force, however, in the closing piece, the *Hexameron*. . . . Everybody wondered where he found the strength to repeat half of the *Hexameron,* and then his own galop, to the delight of the enraptured public. How much I hoped that he would give us some of Chopin's compositions, which he plays incomparably, with the deepest sympathy! But in his own room he amiably plays anything that is asked of him. How often have I thus listened to him in admiration and astonishment![13]

Felix Mendelssohn to his mother. Leipzig, 30 March. There has been too great a hither and thither in the last few weeks. Liszt has been here for a fortnight and been the cause of a tremendous uproar in both a good and a bad sense. I consider him to be fundamentally a good, warm-hearted man and an admirable artist. There is no doubt that he plays most of all of them, yet Thalberg, with his composure, and within his more restricted sphere, is more nearly perfect as a real virtuoso; and after all this is the standard by which Liszt too must be judged, for his compositions are inferior to his playing, and, in fact, are calculated solely for virtuosi. A fantasia by Thalberg (especially that on *La Donna del Lago*) is an accumulation of the finest and most exquisite effects, and a crescendo of difficulties and embellishments that is astonishing. Everything is so calculated and so polished and shows such assurance, skill and superlative taste. At the same

* Mendelssohn's Piano Concerto No. 2 in D minor, composed in 1837.

time the man has incredibly powerful hands and such practised, light fingers that he is unique.

Liszt, on the other hand, possesses a certain suppleness and differentiation in his fingering, as well as a thoroughly musical feeling that cannot be equalled. In a word, I have heard no performer whose musical perceptions extend to the very tips of his fingers and emanate directly from them as Liszt's do. With his directness, his stupendous technique and experience, he would have far surpassed all the rest, were not a man's thoughts in connection with all this the main thing. And these, so far at least, seem to have been denied him by nature, so that in this respect most of the great virtuosi equal or even excel him. But that he, together with Thalberg, alone represents the highest class of pianists of the present day, seems to me indisputable. Unhappily, Liszt's behaviour here towards the public has not made a favourable impression. The whole wrangle gives one the feeling of listening to the perorations of two people, both of whom are wrong, and whom one would like to interrupt at every word. The Philistines, who are mostly concerned with the high prices, and who never wish to see a clever fellow get on too well, and grumble accordingly—they can go to the devil. But the newspaper articles, on the other hand, there you had explanations, and counter-explanations, criticisms and complaints, and all kinds of stuff dragged in that was totally unconnected with music; so that his stay here caused us almost as much annoyance as pleasure; though the latter was often great beyond words.

Then it occurred to me that this unpleasantness might be most effectually allayed if people could see and hear Liszt at close quarters. So I suddenly determined to give a *soirée* for him in the Gewandhaus (for 350 people), with orchestra, chorus, bishop, cakes, *Calm Sea and Prosperous Voyage,* Bach's Triple Concerto (Liszt, Hiller and I), choruses from *St Paul,* a fantasia on *Lucia di Lammermoor, Erlkönig,* the devil and his grandmother; and everyone was so delighted and played and sang with such enthusiasm, that they swore they had never had a jollier evening.[14]

Leaving Leipzig on 31 March, Liszt returned via Metz to Paris, where he spent April with Marie. In a recital (for which no admission fee was charged) at the Salle Erard on the 20th he was heard by *Friederike Mueller* (1816–95),* a pupil of Chopin.

Liszt played, as always, very brilliantly, and the next morning I had to give Chopin a minute account of what and how he had played. He himself was too unwell to be present. When I spoke of Liszt's artistic self-control and repose in overcoming the greatest technical difficulties, he exclaimed: 'So it seems that I am right. The final thing is simplicity. After having exhausted all the difficulties, after having played an immense quantity of notes, it is simplicity in all its charm which emerges as the ultimate secret of art.

* Later the wife of the Viennese pianoforte manufacturer J. B. Streicher.

Whoever wishes to achieve it at the beginning will never find it; you cannot begin at the end. One must have studied a great deal, even immensely, to attain this goal, which is not easy.'

'It was impossible for me,' he continued, 'to attend his matinée. With my health one can do nothing.'[15]

Lamennais and the Princess Belgiojoso were also in the audience; as was the *Comtesse Agénor de Gasparin,* the former Valérie Boissier. 'He has grown once again,' wrote the last-named to her father.

There is the same distance between the Liszt of today and the Liszt of Geneva as between the Liszt of Geneva and mediocrity. He was then, as you know, the last word in energy and power. Now, he is the last word in elegance, delicacy, and shading. His *jeu perlé,* his *piani* and *staccati,* are so admirable, subtle, light, and piercing, that one has to strain one's ears to hear them—and they never fail to come with crystal clarity and purity. It is impossible to create, even with the imagination, anything more completely above and beyond everything one knows. He gave the concert entirely alone. The first item was the finale of the Pastoral Symphony, arranged for piano solo; in precision and power it surpassed anything that can be conceived. Then came a fantasy on *Lucia di Lammermoor,* which was delicious. I must tell you that he has made giant strides in composition too, for his earlier works had something abortive and laboured about them which was painful. The fantasy was followed by two Schubert *Lieder* (one of them being the *Ave Maria*, which he played sublimely), an *étude,* and finally a *galop,* utterly capricious, pleasing and incredible. It was a real triumph; every piece brought the house down. I regret only one thing: that such a talent has devoted itself to so imperfect an instrument as the piano.

We ran into him in the courtyard as we were leaving; he was very friendly and seemed most eager to visit me. What a pity that such elevated faculties and so kind a heart should be joined in him to an immoral existence, which he seeks to mitigate by a religiosity far more dangerous than frank scepticism.[16]

On 6 May Liszt crossed the Channel on his first visit to London since his childhood. Between Paris and the French coast, as he told Marie in a letter written aboard the steamer, he had witnessed a dreadful spectacle. 'So far as events *en route* are concerned, we were present at a terrible fire (half a league from Beauvais), which burnt down an entire village in less than an hour. Very few people were awake, and it is to be feared that a number perished, caught unawares by the flames as they were sleeping. (It was about half an hour after midnight.) You cannot imagine the silent stupor of the men trying to save their cattle and horses. It was an awful sight. "Oh! how beautiful!" cried my neighbour in the coach. But I, for my part, was far from considering it from its picturesque viewpoint!'

His first public appearance was in a concert given by Mrs A. Toulmin and John Orlando Parry at the Queen's Concert Room, Hanover Square, on the 8th. To

Marie he was able to report an immense success. 'There is already no parallel possible, unless with Paganini. . . . I have been given an admirable welcome. Many people still remember Master Liszt.'

The Musical Journal (12 May). The securing the services of M. Liszt, the great *pianist*, who had just arrived in England . . . and whose fame had been echoed and re-echoed throughout Christendom as the unrivalled master of his instrument, caused a sensation and excitement among both professors and amateurs scarcely ever witnessed. . . .

When last in England he was an infant prodigy; he is now one of the wonders of the world. His performance was perfectly astounding, incomprehensible! At one moment in arpeggio, in octave, or in full chords, a hurricane of rich and varied harmonies fell upon the ear with all the effect of a full orchestra, while at the next the most delicious flow of pure, beautiful, and expressive melody stole upon the senses, leaving the soul in a delirium of wonder and delight. The hands and fingers of this artist are but the machines, the slaves of his superior will. . . .

The Morning Post (12 May). Moscheles gave a *soirée musicale* to a select number of professional amateurs on Saturday evening, at his house in Regent's Park, for the purpose of introducing Liszt to them.

On Monday the 11th Liszt played Weber's *Concertstück* in a Philharmonic Society concert (the 5th of the season) at the Hanover Square Rooms. 'My success here is unheard of,' he was able to report to Marie two days later.

In the *Athenaeum* of 16 May, the critic *Henry Fothergill Chorley (*1808–72), hailing Liszt as 'the Poet of the Pianoforte' and describing his return to London as 'the musical event of the week, of the year', reviewed the impression made so far by the pianist.

In the mere chapter of difficulty vanquished, language breaks down. All former most elaborate combinations of melody with accompaniment—all manifestations of independence, not merely of the two hands, but of the separate fingers—all difficulties of execution, whether as accomplishing the grasp of wide intervals, or the close, dazzling and delicate texture of semitonic sequences, principal or accidental, in single notes or triple chords—all former displays of rapidity—the lightning velocity in his case never distinct from expression—have been already surpassed by him, and yet not exhausted, since a treasury of countless new effects must be at the disposal of one so prodigiously gifted. Every variety of tone, too, of which his instrument is capable. . . . His whole performance meanwhile is animated by a spirit so bright, so all-pervading, as to be no less incommunicable in words than it is irresistible. . . . The peerless feature is the bright, eager, elevated poetical genius to be heard in every tone and touch—the utterance of a high-soaring enthusiasm, if at times near to, never wholly coincident with extravagance.

On Sunday the 17th Liszt threw a little musical party of his own. 'Moscheles, Batta, Lord Burghersh,* d'Orsay, Polez, and a dozen others. Ole Bull played a Mozart quartet admirably, Batta an *étude* and the *Romanesca*. I, the *Tarentelles*.† Everyone delighted.'

The d'Orsay named by Liszt was Count Alfred d'Orsay (1801–52), 'the last of the dandies', who in defiance of conventional morality was established at Gore House‡ with the notorious Lady Blessington (1789–1849), once a friend of Byron. Their circle included many of the most distinguished men of the time. Introduced to Lady Blessington on 15 May,§ Liszt the next day waited upon her at Gore House, and thereafter saw the couple frequently. To d'Orsay he sat for his portrait; and for Lady Blessington—who, as he told Marie, 'maintains that I resemble Bonaparte and Lord Byron!!!'—he selected a new piano, an Erard of powerful tone encased in stout Spanish mahogany. It was at Gore House, on 31 May, that he was heard by Macready the actor, who wrote of the occasion in his diary: 'Went to Lady Blessington's, where I saw . . . and Liszt, the most marvellous pianist I ever heard. I do not know when I have been so excited.' Another of the *habitués* of her salon to whom Lady Blessington introduced Liszt was Louis Napoleon,¶ then an exile in London.

Of the musicians he met in London, Liszt seems to have been most impressed by Ole Bull (1810–80), the Norwegian violinist. 'He is a great artist; or, at least, has all the stuff of a great artist in him. And you know that I count barely four such in Europe. . . . He is a kind of savage, very ignorant of counterpoint and fugue, but a savage of genius who is brimming over with charming and original ideas.'

It was arranged that Marie would join Liszt in London in early June, and on 24 May he went to Hampstead to seek a suitable residence for her. 'The countryside is charming, and I believe you will like it there. The air is very healthy. . . . Send me word, and I shall rent you a cottage with which you will, I hope, be content. We shall be able to spend virtually all our days together. . . . Once or twice a week we shall be able to go on delightful excursions to Richmond, Greenwich, etc.'

On Monday the 25th he was one of several prominent musicians commanded to perform at Buckingham Palace as part of Queen Victoria's twenty-first birthday celebrations. 'Everyone regards it as a great progress, since she never asks for instrumentalists,' he told Marie. 'D'Orsay arranged it, by saying everywhere that the Queen was foolish always to allow herself to be bored by Italian singers while artists like Bull and myself were in London.'

Liszt to Marie d'Agoult, 27 May. The Queen was more or less alone with

* John Fane, 11th Earl of Westmorland (1784–1859), known as Lord Burghersh until he succeeded to the earldom in 1841. A soldier and diplomatist who devoted all his spare time to music, his most lasting achievement was the foundation (1822) of the Royal Academy of Music, of which he was the first president.

† *Tarentelles napolitaines,* the fourth section of the original version of *Venezia e Napoli* (S159).

‡ A mansion in Kensington which stood on the site now filled by the Royal Albert Hall.

§ By Henry Reeve, to whom Lady Blessington then remarked about Liszt: 'What a pity to put such a man to the piano.'

¶ In later years, as the Emperor Napoleon III, he would have few keener admirers than Liszt.

Prince Albert the other evening. I believe I amused her. She laughed a lot (which she likes doing) when I told her that 'my vanity was not at all wounded by her not remembering me' (her mother had just asked me if I had not played at her home fourteen years ago).[17]

On 8 June he appeared, for the second and last time this season, at a Philharmonic Society concert,* playing the Kreutzer Sonata (with Ole Bull), some studies† by Moscheles, and his own *Marche hongroise* (S231). Of the performance of the sonata, the *Musical World* (11 June) remarked:

Certain portions were admirably played by both parties, but the system of amplification and embellishment pursued in general was quite sufficient to obscure the composer's intentions, and once, indeed, provoked unequivocal expressions of displeasure, which M. Liszt noticed by very coolly rising from his seat and scrutinizing the room with his glass as if in search of malcontents.

Another witness of this interesting scene was the composer *John Barnett* (1802–90).

At the commencement of [the] sonata Liszt was disturbed by an audibly whispered conversation between two ladies in the audience. Whereupon he suddenly stopped playing, and rising abruptly from the piano, came deliberately forward to the front of the platform. Adjusting his monocle and fixing his gaze on the delinquents, he said in the suavest tones, 'Pray do not let me disturb your conversation by my playing.' There was a dead silence—during which the unfortunate ladies shrivelled and would gladly have hidden under their seats, for all eyes were turned in their direction—after which Liszt calmly resumed his seat at the piano.[18]

Related by Barnett to his children, the foregoing was recorded in the reminiscences of his daughter Clara Kathleen Rogers; and it certainly provides a more credible explanation of the incident with the 'glass' than that given by the *Musical World* critic. But probably nearest of all to the truth, so far as the audience's opinion of the performance is concerned, comes the account of the occasion given by Barnett to *Frederick Buffen,* who set it down in writing shortly

* Later in the month the Society made a presentation to him, about which the *Musical Journal* (14 July) then commented: 'Liszt has been presented by the Philharmonic Society with an elegant breakfast service, for doing that which would cause every young student to receive a severe reprimand, *viz.* thumping and partially destroying two very fine pianofortes. The society has given this to M. Liszt as a *compliment* for performing at two of its concerts *gratuitously*! Whenever did they present an Englishman with a *silver breakfast service* for gratuitous performances?' The service is now on display at the Liszt Museum, Weimar.

† About Liszt's performance of which, the *Morning Post* remarked: 'The composer, who sat near us, seemed mentally perplexed between pleasure and surprise.' Moscheles' own opinion was: 'Faultless in the way of execution, by his talent he has completely transformed these pieces. They have become more his studies than mine. With all that, they please me, and I shouldn't like to hear them played in any other way by him. . . . He does anything he chooses, and does it admirably; and those hands raised aloft in the air come down seldom, wonderfully seldom, upon a wrong note.'

afterwards 'almost in Mr. Barnett's words'. The 'delinquents', we now find, were far less harmless than the ladies referred to by Mrs Rogers.

The performance had scarcely commenced, and while the great movement which opens this fine work was being delivered, several English professors, conspicuous among whom were an eminent critic and a no less well-known teacher, whose names I suppress, began hissing violently, the sound of which caused Liszt immediately to cease playing, and regard the authors of this disturbance with amazement. The audience, however, well able to judge the merit of the performance, loudly expressed their indignation at this treatment of the artists at the hands of a few, and soon silenced the disapprobation, while Liszt and Bull finished the performance, the perfection of which, Mr. Barnett says, seemed to cause no admiration on the part of the malcontents, whose animosity was roused by the evident superiority of Liszt. Mr. Barnett a few days afterwards met Liszt at dinner at Ole Bull's house when the subject was referred to, but Liszt only laughed, and treated it with good-natured contempt.[19]

'It is sad to reflect now,' adds Buffen, 'that one who had taught the world to be generous to artists and liberal to the poor, and whose munificence was equalled only by his transcendent gifts, should have been insulted in the face of the British public through the jealousy of inferior men.'

Liszt's own first concert was given on the 9th, at the Hanover Square Rooms. It contained his transcription of the Scherzo and Finale of the Pastoral Symphony; those of Schubert's *Serenade* and *Ave Maria*; the *Hexameron*; the *Tarentelles*; and the *Grand galop chromatique*. In the audience, escorted by Henry Reeve, was Marie d'Agoult, who had arrived in London a day or two earlier and taken accommodation, not at Hampstead, but at the Star and Garter Hotel, Richmond.

The word 'recital' to describe a musical performance was used for the first time in connection with this appearance of Liszt's at the Hanover Square Rooms. 'This now commonly accepted term had never previously been used,' recalled Charles Salaman, 'and people asked, "What does he mean? How can anyone *recite* upon the pianoforte?" '

The Musical World (11 June). Viewed as a display of pianoforte playing, and putting *music* out of the question, it was little short of a miracle. No system of words can accurately describe the power which Liszt possesses of *dividing* himself, as it were, into two, or sometimes, even, three performers; the feathery delicacy of his touch at one moment, and its enormous forte at another; and the exquisite neatness of the artifices by means of which he, almost every moment, appears to achieve physical impossibilities. . . . In that sleight-of-hand which addresses itself to the ear, we think he even transcends Thalberg. He seems to occupy *more space* on the instrument than even his great rival; reflection constantly reminds us that the human conformation does not permit the simultaneous execution of three groups of passages, lying respectively at the extreme ends, and in the middle of the keyboard, and yet we are scarcely less constantly required to take the evidence of our ears that Liszt does all this in seeming defiance of the restrictions of nature. His most wonderful performance throughout the morning was the scherzo, storm and finale of Beethoven's Sinfonia Pastorale. . . . On the whole Liszt has never vouchsafed a display of his wonderful powers, since his arrival in the metropolis, at all comparable to any of these, his 'recitals' on Tuesday morning.* The force of pianoforte playing could go no further—he fairly met Thalberg on his own ground, and in mechanical acquirement, we think, surpassed him.

The Athenaeum (13 June). Without entering on comparison, which is an insufficient aid as well as an ungracious measure, when Genius of the highest order is to be approached, we must insist on the unprecedented variety of range taken by M. Liszt in his intercourse with the public. . . . Artists of European reputation could be named whose repertory for many seasons' success in England was more restricted than this, gone through without the slightest faltering or fatigue in the course of four-and-twenty hours. Nor is this universality a show got up to dazzle the public. With all the prodigal generosity of unbounded resources at his command, there is not a private circle entered by M. Liszt which will not long keep its own tradition of some display of his consummate musical skill, and his self-sacrificing familiarity with everyone's music beside his own. And it is necessary to insist upon this; because such an extent of acquaintance with every style and school, aided by a prodigious memory, must by itself establish M. Liszt's reputation as a first-rate musician, did not his performance, in addition, place him higher than any contemporary or predecessor as a mechanist— and did not, above all, his *reading* of every work he takes in hand prove him to be yet more of a poet than a musician or a mechanist! . . .

We have but to add to this notice that the success of M. Liszt's unassisted Concert on Tuesday was brilliant beyond all expectation.

Meanwhile, the 'delightful excursions' seem not to have been turning out quite as Liszt had hoped.

Liszt to Marie d'Agoult (at Richmond), [20] June. 'I can do nothing else at this moment, and probably for ever, than live utterly alone.'

That is what you had to say to me! Six years of the most absolute devotion have brought you only to this. . . .

And that is how it is with so many words of yours! Yesterday (to recall but one day) for the entire journey from Ascot to Richmond you spoke not a single word which was not calculated either to hurt or offend. But what is the good of coming back to such sad things, of counting all our wounds one

* The recital began at 2.00 p.m., but according to the custom of the day was described as a 'morning' concert.

by one in this manner? Is it not better to suffer and be silent? You will perhaps add these words to the number of those that you will no longer acknowledge! My language is so changed! At least, that is what you say.[20]

Liszt's second recital was given on Monday, 29 June at Willis's Rooms*—'before an audience extremely fashionable and as extremely crowded', reported the *Musical World.* 'Their Royal Highnesses the Duke and Duchess of Cambridge, with the Princess Augusta and Prince George, were present.' The programme contained Handel's Fugue in E minor; the Overture to *William Tell*; the Kreutzer Sonata (again with Bull); Schubert's *Serenade* and *Erlkönig*; Etudes and Mazurkas by Chopin;† and the *Marche hongroise.*

The Times (2 July). Nothing could have been better than the music selected on this occasion for displaying the extraordinary versatility of Liszt's talent. The programme contained the names of Handel, Rossini, and Beethoven, as if to refute the often-repeated but unjust opinion that the great pianist excels only in the performance of his own compositions or of those in which mechanical dexterity of execution is the chief characteristic. His performance commenced with Handel's Fugue in E minor, which was played by Liszt with an avoidance of everything approaching to meretricious ornament, and indeed scarcely any additions, except a multitude of ingeniously contrived and appropriate harmonies, casting a glow of colour over the beauties of the composition, and infusing into it a spirit which from no other hand it ever before received. The next piece was the overture to *William Tell,* which brought all the performer's power at once into action. In this overture, as in the fugue, Liszt with exquisite taste and tact confined his additions to the harmonies; and though this composition is probably one of the fullest scores that Rossini ever wrote, yet the most complete orchestra by which we have ever heard it performed never produced a more powerful effect, and certainly was very far behind Liszt in spirit and unity of execution. How all this is accomplished with ten fingers we confess ourselves unable to guess; and even could description convey any idea of Liszt's performance, its possibility would still appear incredible, except to those who heard it. The overture to *William Tell* was succeeded by one of Beethoven's sonatas (violin obligato) [*sic*], the violin part being performed by Ole Bull and the pianoforte by Liszt. During the performance of this sonata we were forcibly struck with the truth of an observation made by Schindler, in his memoirs of Beethoven, recently published in Germany. Schindler, who is a most enthusiastic worshipper of

* The former Almack's, in King Street, St James.

† Chopin's publisher, C. R. Wessel, had asked Liszt to play some of the Polish composer's works in London, in order to make them known. 'No one has dared risk it yet,' Liszt told Marie. 'I shall do so on the first good occasion. . . . You can tell him that when you see him. I am delighted to be able to do him this small service. I shall play his Etudes, his Mazurkas, and his Nocturnes, all things virtually unknown in London. That will encourage Wessel to buy other manuscripts from him.' Liszt was thus the first pianist to play works by Chopin at a public recital in London.

his departed friend, and who condemns with inflexible severity all erroneous and imperfect interpretations of the great master's ideas, emphatically says, that 'Franz Liszt has contributed more than almost any instrumentalist of the present day to the just comprehension of Beethoven's music.' Liszt gave decided proof of the accuracy of this observation by his performance of the sonata yesterday. There was not a note to which he did not give meaning, and passages which in the hands of other performers would have fallen, as it were, dead on the ear, were prominently brought out by Lizst [*sic*], and the hearers sensibly felt their connexion with, and importance to, the beautiful whole. This sonata of Beethoven, and Schubert's songs, appeared to us to be the masterpieces of Monday's performance. In Schubert's songs it is no exaggeration to say that he made the instrument sing. The soft whisperings of his piano passages seemed to compete with the tones of Rubini's voice, and the showers of light notes which he scattered through some of the variations realized every idea that can be formed of fairy music. In fine, we have no hesitation in saying that Liszt leaves every other performer, whether on the pianoforte or any other instrument, at an immeasurable distance behind him.

The Athenaeum (4 July). We cannot call to mind any other artist, vocal or instrumental, who could thus by his own unassisted power attract and engage an audience for a couple of hours. The critics may not understand M. Liszt, but the musicians crowd to listen to him; and every hearing must rivet the conviction that as a brilliant, versatile and fantastic genius, surpassing all his predecessors, he cannot be too enthusiastically admired —or too little followed as a model. . . . Among the most fascinating things of the morning were Schubert's *Serenade,* which was encored, and repeated with deliciously fanciful amplifications, and his *Erl King*—the latter hardly felt, as it deserved to be, by the audience. Two Mazurkas by Chopin, also, were exquisitely played, with an embroidery on their quaint and national framework, of fancies, the wildest, the newest, the most delicate, ever thrown off by mortal fingers—positive faëry-work upon the piano. The last piece—for M. Liszt gives place to every composer before himself—was his own *Marche hongroise.* It left the audience in a state not common among concert-goers—namely, eager for more.

Among the other occasions on which Liszt played during his two-month sojourn in London were: at a soirée musicale given by the cellist Lidel at the Hanover Square Rooms on 14 May; a concert on the 15th, again at those Rooms, in which he played Weber's *Concertstück* and the *Grand galop chromatique*; Mrs Anderson's* concert of 20 May at Her Majesty's Theatre (where, reported *The Times*, 'Liszt's extraordinary power over the instrument, combined with a very

* According to Brown's *Dictionary of Musicians,* Lucy Anderson (1789–1878) was 'acknowledged in her day to be the best pianist in England'.

delicate execution, took the audience completely by surprise'); the matinée musicale given at the Perkins residence, 26 Queen Anne Street, on 27 May by Mme Belleville Oury, with whom he played a duet by Bertini; the annual concert given by Eliason, with whom he played the Kreutzer Sonata; a concert given by Miss Masson and the Misses Broadhurst on 2 June; and Theodor Döhler's concert of 22 June, in which he joined Döhler in a performance of Thalberg's two-piano Fantasy on *Norma*.

Most of July and part of August he devoted to concerts in or near the Rhineland, playing in such towns as Bonn, Wiesbaden, Frankfurt, Mainz, and Baden. Marie was with him for most of this time, and their periods of separation were few.

At Ems, in which he spent three days, he played before the Tsarina Alexandra Feódorovna (consort of Nicholas I). After a chilly reception because he, an artist of world fame, had not yet been to St Petersburg, Liszt won the Tsarina over with his rendering of Schubert's *Ave Maria*. He then accepted her 'gracious invitation' to travel to Russia (which he eventually reached in 1842).

Paganini had died that May, and on 23 August Liszt's tribute to the great violinist appeared in the *Revue et gazette musicale.* It concluded: 'May the artist of the future set his goal within, and not without, himself; may virtuosity be a means and not an end for him; and may he never forget that, though the saying is *Noblesse oblige,* still more than nobility—*Génie oblige*!'

A week before publication of that tribute, Liszt had already crossed the Channel once again, for a tour of southern England. Marie meanwhile returned to Paris.

The organizer of the tour, which lasted six weeks, was a young musician named Louis Lavenu (1818–59); and the other members of the party were: the pianist and composer Frank Mori (1820–73), two female vocalists, Mlle de Varny and Miss Louisa Bassano, and the popular *buffo* singer John Orlando Parry (1810–79), renowned for his renderings of such comic songs as 'Wanted, a Governess'. Already known to Liszt from London, Parry was an amazingly versatile musician, who, had he not chosen to specialize in the comic song, could easily have made his way in any of several other musical fields. 'A skilled harpist, a superb organist, and a magnificent pianist', was George Augustus Sala's description of him, one endorsed by many of their contemporaries. (He was also a talented painter and draughtsman.) As a provider of musical merriment, he seems to have been without peer; indeed, 'genius' was the word perhaps most frequently used of him. According to the *Athenaeum,* there was something besides, and far beyond, the buffoon in his performances—'a spirit of quaint humour told in and aided by music, nothing short of artistic, the like of which we have never met. . . . We have seen Mendelssohn sit and listen by the hour with the eager face of an enjoying child, and we have heard Chopin laugh till he was almost "ready to die" (so frail in his case was the machine) at the travesties, parodies, etc. of the racy humorist.' A classic example of the mirth-maker who is himself far from happy, the super-sensitive Parry was an extremely nervous performer. 'As time passed by, he became painfully hysterical,' remembered Willert Beale. 'I have seen him in floods of tears before going on the platform, being impressed with the conviction, which no argument could remove, that he would break down.'

It is the diaries kept by Parry on this and a second tour with Liszt which are the best source of information about their concerts; Liszt's own indications, in his correspondence with Marie d'Agoult and others, being extremely sparse.

Liszt's stock pieces on the tour were the Overture to *William Tell, Marche hongroise* and *Grand galop chromatique,* with from time to time an operatic fantasy or an improvisation. He also occasionally performed a duet with Mori. When an orchestra was available, he played Weber's *Concertstück.* Accompanying the party throughout was an Erard grand pianoforte.

Delayed after experiencing a 'frightful' Channel crossing on Sunday, 16 August, he was just in time to join his colleagues for the opening concert: at Chichester's Assembly Rooms on the 17th. In its review (22 August), the *Hampshire Advertiser* remarked on the 'highly fashionable and numerous assemblage' and reported that 'the miracles which Liszt performed on the instrument drew forth rapturous applause'. It also printed a tribute in verse, 'The Piano of Liszt', penned by 'The Blind Bard of Cicestria', Francis Champion. The evening concert that day, at which both Liszt and Parry were encored, was at Portsmouth's Green Row Rooms.

The 18th was spent on the Isle of Wight, its most unpleasant aspect for most of the party being the crossing of the Solent. It was a rough day, and Parry records that all but he were sick. Nor could the Erard be taken over, and the instruments used by Liszt at Ryde (in the Town Hall) and Newport (the Assembly Rooms attached to the Green Dragon Hotel) were respectively a square and cottage piano.

Back on the mainland on the 19th, the party gave their first concert of the day at the Royal Victoria Assembly Rooms, Southampton, and the evening one at Winchester's St John's House.

Hampshire Advertiser (22 August). M. Liszt made his bow to a Southampton audience, and electrified and delighted them with a skill that seems superhuman. At one moment the most delicate and silvery tones sweep over the senses, and at another, a torrent of magnificent sound which has never been heard from the instrument before—even thunder seems to roll across the keys, and then subsides into the breathing tones of an Aeolian harp. No description can give even a faint idea of the wonders achieved.[21]

The morning concert on the 20th was at Salisbury's Assembly Rooms, the audience according to Parry being 'stupid' and 'dreadful! Laughed in *Soave sia il vento*'. After Salisbury* came Blandford Forum in Dorset, where they gave a concert at the Assembly Rooms that same evening and stayed at the Crown

* A letter from Liszt to Franz von Schober is headed: 'Stonehenge, Salisbury, 29 August 1840.' The date and place are incompatible, since on the 29th Liszt and his colleagues were far away at Exeter. But in any case one takes leave to doubt the possibility of a visit to Stonehenge. The only chance would have been on the 20th. But Stonehenge was far to the north of their route, and would have added many miles (and cost them several more hours in their slow-moving carriage) to the journey from Winchester in time for the morning concert at Salisbury. Still less likely are they to have made an excursion to Stonehenge *after* that concert, when, to arrive in good time at Blandford, they had some 30 miles to cover in a south-westerly direction. Parry's diary shows that their carriage trundled along at not much more than six miles an hour, and also reveals that they all heartily disliked the long hours spent cooped up

Hotel. Then followed Weymouth (morning concert on the 21st); Lyme Regis (morning concert on the 22nd); Sidmouth (evening concert at the London Hotel on the 22nd); Exmouth (morning concert at Ewen's Beacon Hotel on the 24th); Teignmouth (evening concert at the Assembly Rooms on the 24th); Plymouth (evening concert at the Royal Hotel Assembly Room on the 26th); and Exeter (evening concert at the Royal Clarence Hotel on the 28th, and a morning one at the same venue on the 29th). The concert arranged for Torquay on the 25th was cancelled, apparently because of Liszt's poor health that day.

Liszt to Marie d'Agoult. Exmouth, 24 August. Our concerts are mediocre, and Lavenu is losing quite a lot of money at the moment. The expenses are enormous. For two days we have had four horses and two postilions. Everywhere we are putting up at the best hotels. In this respect, nothing could be more convenient—but I am sorry he is not doing better business. To tell the truth, we have so far been in small places only (except for Southampton), and he is counting on Bath, Exeter, Plymouth, etc. to make up.

The countryside we have just come through is delightful. Sidmouth and Exmouth, from where I am writing to you, I find particularly attractive. Everywhere there are admirable parks. The cathedrals of Chichester, Winchester, and Salisbury are remarkable. At Salisbury I went among the tombs surrounding the cathedral to warm myself in the sun.[22]

To the same. Exeter, 28 August. Yesterday we had rather an amusing adventure. We were at Plymouth, where we had given a very fair concert the previous day. Lavenu had announced a second for one o'clock in the afternoon; but at 1.15 there were not four people in the hall. A crowd of more than 10,000 was making its way to the port, where a huge 120-gun ship was to be launched. Just think what an attraction for all classes of society!

Lavenu doesn't lose heart and immediately runs in search of seven men, whom he decks out in enormous posters announcing the postponement of the concert until the evening. These seven men spent the whole day walking around the town and the port. At 8 o'clock the hall was lit up, half a dozen people arrived, whose money to their great discontent was returned to them at the door, and the concert was called off for a second time. Actually, as a slight consolation they told us that at *his* concert Thalberg had fewer than twenty people.

At Plymouth I visited a splendid park belonging to Lord Edgecombe [Edgcumbe]. Imagine the Villa Serbelloni, or rather the entire coast at Bellagio, laid out as a park, with fine groups of trees and numerous lawns such as can be seen only in England, exotic plants and flowerbeds

inside it, deeply deploring and resenting a moment more than necessary. The diary makes no mention of Stonehenge, nor does Liszt do so in the letter to Schober or in his letters to Marie d'Agoult; and in writing the name of the famous monument he perhaps meant merely to indicate that he was in its general vicinity.

interspersed artistically here and there, the whole thing by the sea with a view of the port and of the city of Plymouth in the background. It really was most beautiful, and I dreamt sadly of how much I should have enjoyed it had you been there.

I also visited some very beautiful cathedrals at Chichester, Salisbury, and Exeter. They are all surrounded by magnificent widely-spaced trees. In France, when we have a beautiful monument, we can hardly wait to suffocate it under a pile of stalls, poky little houses and filthy buildings. Look at Notre Dame, the cathedrals of Lyons, Metz, etc. Here in England they respect the majesty of the edifice. Its splendour preserves it from vulgar contact. I have sometimes compared those beautiful buildings of France and Italy, surrounded by the wretched little shops leaning against them, to the great men of all times and all countries, forever bothered, badgered, and exploited by the lowest rabble motivated by the vilest self-interest.[23]

The first of the concerts in Somerset was given at the Assembly Rooms, Taunton, in the morning of 31 August.

Somerset County Gazette (5 September). The chief attraction of the concert was that wonderful pianist, Liszt. It would be only making ourselves appear ridiculous to attempt to convey in words a notion of the extraordinary performance of this great master of his art. He makes the instrument speak; he produces a volume of sound which we should previously have deemed the pianoforte incapable of yielding. His fingers wander wildly over the notes, and seemingly without plan, and a stream of music bursts upon the ear, not one tune only, but many; not as if one instrument were discoursing eloquent music, but as if a full band were flooding the air with harmony. He is more wonderful than Thalberg, but we do not think him so pleasing. He has more intellect, but less feeling. His music more recommends itself to the mind, but it does not so touch the heart. And the personal appearance of these two men of genius differs as do their characters. Thalberg's countenance is mild, pensive, and sensitive. Liszt's is the very *beau idéal* of those German students who figure in the old German tales of *diablerie*, contemplative, stern, abstract, mysterious, his frame tall and gaunt, his face thin and sharp, his eyes deep set and keen, his hair hanging long and straight over his face and shoulders. But genius in every shape is always delightful: in every walk, whether of *art,* science, literature, politics, whatever its country, its creed, its party, its sect, its social station, we love and honour it, we look at it with a feeling of reverence almost approaching to worship, for men of genius are nature's nobility, holding their patent from the divinity. Therefore we should never weary of seeing or hearing such men as Liszt and Thalberg.

The evening concert that day was at Bridgwater (where Liszt had to play with a bandaged hand).

At Bath they made three appearances: two at the Theatre Royal, in the evenings of 1 and 2 September, and one at the Assembly Rooms in the morning of the 2nd. It was here that Liszt and his colleagues were joined by the flautist Joseph Richardson (1814–62), who remained with them until 19 September.

Bath Herald (5 September). M. Liszt was beyond all question *la crème de la crème* of these concerts, though associated with other talent of a very high order. His *physique* is rather remarkable: a tall spare figure, apparently about 25, though said to be a few years older—a pale face, distinguished by calmness and repose of feature, placid but not inanimate eyes, and a prodigious length of forearm and finger complete his *personnel,* while his disposition and character are obviously marked by great modesty, and a total absence of affectation or pretension. It is no exaggeration to say that, in point of execution, this pianist was never equalled in the world. . . .

At the close of each separate triumph of his performance, a burst of astonished acclamation rang from every part of the house, and repeated encores were demanded—and most kindly and smilingly complied with.

The sole concert on Thursday, 3 September, was given in the Bristol suburb of Clifton. At Cheltenham (where they lodged at the George Hotel in the High Street), the party gave an evening concert on Friday at the Assembly Rooms, and another on Saturday at the Montpellier Rotunda.

Cheltenham Looker-On (5 September). We have on several occasions noticed Liszt's marvellous performance on the pianoforte, which, however, is of that extraordinary character that cannot be described; it must be heard and witnessed to be truly appreciated. . . . The Overture to *Guillaume Tell*, the 'recital' selected by him last night, afforded a fine opportunity for the display of his astonishing powers, nor was that opportunity thrown away, for a performance more truly wonderful we certainly never heard. . . . The second concert takes place this morning, at the Rotunda, and we recommend all who are fond of, or themselves aspire to, pianoforte performances, to avail themselves of one of the richest treats they ever have [enjoyed] or ever can hope to enjoy.

Concerts followed at Royal Leamington Spa (where they spent the night of the 6th at the Crown Hotel and appeared the next day in the Music Hall); Coventry (7th); Northampton (8th); and Market Harborough (9th). In several of these towns the audiences were disappointingly small. At Leicester on 9 September, however, they were more fortunate. It was a race week, the hotels were full of visitors eager for an evening's entertainment, and in the New Hall* of the Mechanics' Institute Liszt and his colleagues performed to a relatively large and distinguished audience (including the Duke of Rutland), some 400 or 500 in all.

* Viewing sundry curios exhibited here, the members of the concert party seem to have been most astonished by the breeches once worn by Daniel Lambert (1770–1809), the heaviest man ever known in England. A native of Leicester, Lambert had been only 5′ tall, but his bodily circumference had been 9′4″, his legs each 3′1″, and he had weighed 53 stone.

Hailing Liszt as 'the Paganini of the pianoforte', the *Leicester Journal* (11 September) found him 'beyond all question, without a rival'. 'What excites the most wonder on listening to this genius is the perfection he has attained in *every* mode of expression of which his instrument is capable. . . .'

'He has developed the hitherto unknown capabilities of the pianoforte much in the same way that Paganini did of the violin,' declared the *Leicester Mercury* (12 September). 'In general terms he may be spoken of as beyond a question the first pianist ever heard.'

Then came Derby (morning concert at the Lecture Hall on the 10th) and Nottingham (evening concert, also on the 10th, at the Assembly Rooms, Low Pavement).

Liszt to Marie d'Agoult, 10 September. We are giving two concerts almost every day, and the rest of the time are travelling the highroads. Often we hardly have time left for a meal. So don't be surprised or worried not to hear from me more frequently. I am well; my sole, sweet, fortifying and unbounded thought is always you, my delightful and angelic Marie.

As we shall be passing Newstead Abbey* tomorrow, I have asked them to stop there. My feeling for—I could almost say affinity with—Lord Byron remains the same. After you (a long way after), it is him alone towards whom I feel closely drawn. I know not what burning, whimsical desire comes over me from time to time to meet him in a world in which we shall at last be strong and free, and living a real life—where Cain will no longer ask: 'And wherefore should I pray? Wherefore should I offer sacrifices?'[24]

Continuing their journey, the Lavenu party gave the first concert of the day (11 September) at Mansfield Town Hall, to just 30 people; and then, after a further stretch in the coach, the evening concert at Newark Town Hall, this time to an audience of 130, described by Parry as 'stupid' and 'horrid'. Parry also writes that on this day Liszt was 'very ill indeed'.

After a concert at Lincoln's County Assembly Rooms on the 12th, the party spent the night of Sunday the 13th at the little market town of Horncastle, where the first of the next day's concerts was given at the Assembly Rooms. 'Funny people—Encores,' recorded Parry. The evening concert was at Boston (where they lodged that night at the Peacock and Royal Hotel), in the Assembly Rooms. Parry: 'Fine Hall. Stupid (asses) the people in the room!!! No encores—no laughter—no nuffin!!'

Concerts followed at: Grantham Town Hall (15th); Stamford Assembly Rooms (16th); Peterborough (evening of the 16th†); Huntingdon Town Hall

* The ancestral home of the Byron family. The poet, who had died at Missolonghi in 1824, had sold the property in 1818, to pay his debts; but the new owners provided facilities for its inspection by visitors.

† Parry reports that before leaving Peterborough the next morning, the whole party visited the Cathedral. As an enthusiast of the history, language and culture of France, Liszt may have taken special note of the marble slab marking the site of the former tomb of a queen of that country, Mary, Queen of Scots, whose remains had been interred here before their removal to Westminster Abbey.

(17th); Cambridge (18th); and Bury St Edmunds (a morning and evening concert, in the Concert Room, Market Hill, on the 19th).

Liszt to Marie d'Agoult, 16 September. At Newstead Abbey I lay on the grass in the bright sunshine. Swarms of crows were cawing above my head, and for a long while I listened to their funereal music. Then I entered the rooms. I was shown a cup which Lord Byron had had carved for himself from the skull of a monk, and the grave of his dog. As I was leaving, the moaning of the pine trees awakened corresponding harmonies within me, and, hollow-voiced, I sang and mused out loud. I shall write all that down one day. . . .

I have been giving myself to Roman history again. Incidentally, I should like you to ask [Ferdinand] Denis if a fairly inexpensive edition of Bayle's Dictionary is available. I very much wish to read it. . . .

I shan't give you any description of the countryside I am travelling through, and so on this point am emulating the classical writers of the century of Louis XIV, and for two very good reasons: firstly, because I hardly know how to describe; secondly, because all this nature (if nature is what it is) says nothing whatever to me. Yet I find it very beautiful. We passed Warwick Castle and Kenilworth. The one place which has made an impression on me is Newstead Abbey—and that was because of the man associated with it.[25]

Sunday, 20 September, was spent travelling. Leaving Bury after breakfast ('Great mob to see us start. Fight on the road with sheep driver. Great brute, bloody noses!!' writes Parry), they arrived that evening at Norwich. Here, the next day, two concerts were given: in the morning at the Assembly House, and in the evening at the Theatre.

In its review, the *Norfolk Chronicle* (26 September) acknowledged 'the perfection of Liszt's execution' and 'the almost superhuman control he possesses over his instrument', but expressed disappointment in his choice of programme, for which it blamed 'the system, not the *artiste*'.

Notwithstanding our disappointment we believe Liszt to be a man of real genius, and to have merited all that his most ardent admirers have uttered in his praise. His countenance, his conversation, his manners, nay even the eccentricities of his costume, all conspire to proclaim him a man of no ordinary mind. . . .

In these *vagabondizing* concerts, money is the sole moving power, so the scheme is to be let down to what the *entrepreneur* modestly assumes to be the level of his audience, and consequently the performer, be he the finest that ever visited the shores of this country, is fettered to airs with variations from *I Puritani* and *Lucia di Lammermoor*.

The *Norwich Mercury* (26 September) wrote of Liszt's 'transcendent talents' and 'execution defying all description', declaring that it was 'impossible not to adjudge to him the palm above all his competitors. . . . What he can do by mere mechanical power and dexterity surpasses all credence—it must be heard to be believed.' It too, however, regretted to see him 'following the beaten track marked out by lesser minds, and composing and playing music which must depreciate both general taste and the art itself, because amateurs, when they attempt it, can only bewilder themselves and stun their auditors'.

We know *what* Mr. Liszt can do—we know that he possesses an extraordinary memory, stored with the works of the finest masters—we know that he can give those works a character which would add to their immortality—we know by every note that drops from his inspired hand, as well as by positive experiment, that he possesses resources which by a little less love for common admiration would enable him to rise to far truer greatness—and we look forward to the time when a more mature judgment shall ensure a consummation so devoutly to be wished. . . .

Mr. Liszt was most enthusiastically applauded, and the audience appeared intensely interested throughout each of his performances.

Via Scole, the party proceeded on the 22nd to Ipswich, where the one concert of the day—to a large audience—was at the Theatre.

Liszt to Marie d'Agoult, 22 September. I am well. These last few days I have been correcting some passages in the Dantesque fragment and preparing the *Tarentelles* for printing.

Have also been rereading, with keen interest, the two volumes of Michelet's *Histoire romaine* which we read together at Nohant. Our concerts are going better.[26]

Marie d'Agoult to Liszt, 22 September. You are very near to being happy! May God hear you! Sometimes I too feel that it would be quite simple, yet I fear that Genius and Happiness are two irreconcilable enemies.[27]

The final concerts of the tour were at Colchester (morning of the 23rd at the Assembly Rooms); Chelmsford (24th); and, last of all, at Brighton, with a concert at the Newburgh Rooms on the Friday evening (25th) and a morning one at the same venue on the Saturday. The *Brighton Gazette* (1 October) found it difficult to single out a particular piece of Liszt's, 'for he displayed alike in each the perfect taste, feeling and sound knowledge that distinguish the thorough musician.'

If we named any, it would be the *Marche hongroise* and the accompaniment to Mr. Parry's song of the *Inchcape Bell*—an example, by the way, which we cannot help pointing out to the notice of 'artistes' who, with infinitely less talent than Liszt, have at the same time infinitely more assumption.

After a few pleasant weeks with Marie at Fontainebleau,* Liszt left for Hamburg, spending the first night of travel at the postmaster's in 'a hole called

* Where apparently, and fittingly (the Forest of Fontainebleau plays a part in Senancour's

Solre-le-Château'. 'As I write to you I am surrounded by three old women sitting around the stove, and Ferco,* smoking a cigar I have given him,' he told Marie. On the journey he read Fourier, the autobiography of Alfieri, and George Sand's *Spiridion.* Arriving at Hamburg in the evening of 25 October, he gave his first concert on the 28th, another on the 31st ('with an unheard-of success'), and a third on 6 November; he also took part in concerts on the 2nd and 10th.

To the concert of Saturday, 31 October came the young pianist *Carl Reinecke* (1824–1910), later also a composer, teacher, writer, and conductor of the Leipzig Gewandhaus concerts.

With a pounding heart I tramped from the neighbouring town of Altona to the Alte Stadt London Hotel in Hamburg's Jungfernstieg. It was in the days before the terrible Hamburg fire [1842], when the small, cosy concert halls still existed. The most fashionable one, which held about four or five hundred people, was in the aforesaid hotel. As far as I am aware, Liszt was the first pianist to give concerts entirely alone, without assistance from other artists. Such was the case at this concert too, except for the celebrated Septet in D minor by Hummel, in which he was accompanied by some local musicians. Uncommonly slim and elegant, he began with Beethoven's Sonata in C sharp minor, *quasi una fantasia;* and I very well remember being as delighted with his matchless rendering of the first two movements as I was astonished at the rhythmic liberties he took in the last. My impressions were equally mixed during the other pieces. When he played like the real Liszt, he played in a way that no other pianist has ever played, before or since. His marvellous, unsurpassed bravura and virtuosity were always blended with poetic feeling and the keenest musical intelligence. Boldness, passion, grace, elegance, humour, simplicity of expression—all were there when appropriate, compelling a boundless admiration. If, however, it came into his head to dazzle the ignorant throng a little, he would allow himself to be carried away by all manner of fantastic tricks, at which even I, a mere boy, had to shake my head. I remember, for instance, my astonishment when in his otherwise wonderful rendering of the Overture to *William Tell* he hammered out the *ranz-des-vaches* with the side of his right index finger! Incomparable, absolutely flawless performances, which I can still hear clearly after nearly sixty years, were those of Hummel's Septet, the Chromatic Study in G by Moscheles, Schubert's *Serenade,* and the two above-mentioned movements from Beethoven's so-called Moonlight Sonata. That between the different pieces Liszt did not withdraw, but came down from the platform to chat like an accomplished courtier with the beautiful ladies present, was something that impressed me greatly.[28]

novel), he composed *Vallée d'Obermann.* See S. Gut, 'Nouvelle approche des premières œuvres de Franz Liszt d'après la correspondance Liszt-d'Agoult', *Studia Musicologica,* xxviii (Budapest, 1986), 237-48.

* Liszt's general factotum for about a year from early 1840.

Passing through Hamburg on his way south, and present at the concert of 6 November (likewise at the Alte Stadt London Hotel), was *Hans Christian Andersen* (1805–75), Danish story-teller extraordinary.

The Orpheus of mythology could set stones and trees in motion with his music. The modern Orpheus, Liszt, had electrified them already ere he played. Fame, with her many tongues, had opened the eyes and ears of the multitude, so that all seemed to recognize and hear what was to follow. I myself felt in the beams of those many sparkling eyes an expectant palpitation of the heart, on the approach of this great genius, who with magic fingers defines the boundaries of his art in our age! . . .

When Liszt entered the saloon, it was as if an electric shock passed through it. Most of the ladies rose; it was as if a ray of sunlight passed over every face, as if all eyes received a dear, beloved friend.

I stood quite near to the artist: he is a slim young man, his long, dark hair hung around his pale face; he bowed to the audience and sat down to the piano. The whole of Liszt's exterior and movements reveal one of those persons we remark for their peculiarities alone; the Divine hand has placed a mark on them which makes them observable amongst thousands. As he sat before the piano, the first impression of his personality was derived from the appearance of strong passions in his wan face, so that he seemed to me a demon who was nailed fast to the instrument whence the tones streamed forth—they came from his blood, from his thoughts; he was a demon who would liberate his soul from thraldom; he was on the rack, the blood flowed, and the nerves trembled; but as he continued to play, the demon disappeared. I saw that pale face assume a nobler and brighter expression: the divine soul shone from his eyes, from every feature; he became beauteous as spirit and enthusiasm can make their worshippers. . . .

When Liszt had ceased playing, flowers showered around him: beautiful young girls, and old ladies who had once been young and beautiful, cast each her bouquet. He had cast a thousand bouquets of tones into their hearts and heads.[29]

At one of the concerts Liszt played his transcription of *Erlkönig*. Present was Heine's niece, Maria Embden Heine. 'When played by him, it was sheer poetry in music. In the closing bars a shudder came over the entire audience; my mother saw women weeping. . . .'

While at Hamburg, he noticed in the *Revue des Deux Mondes,* the French literary periodical long edited by François Buloz, an article which concluded: 'We would allow Beethoven and Weber to die of hunger to present a sword of honour to M. Lizt [*sic*].' His reply, drawn up by Marie according to certain points he sent her, appeared in the 15 November issue of the *Revue.* It stressed in particular the patriotic significance of the sword.

It is the sign of manhood *par excellence;* it is the weapon of every man who has the right to carry a weapon. When six of the leading men of my country presented it to me amidst the cheers of my compatriots, while at the same moment the authorities of Pest asked His Majesty to grant me letters of nobility, it was to acknowledge me afresh as a Hungarian after an absence of fifteen years; it was to reward me for some slight services rendered to art in my country; it was above all, and this is how I interpreted it, to bind me gloriously to her once again by imposing serious duties on me, lifelong obligations as both man and artist.

I agree with you, Sir, that it was without doubt going far beyond my merits up to the present moment. In that moving and solemn act I therefore saw more the expression of a hope than of a satisfaction. Hungary hailed in me the man *of whom she expects* notable achievements in art. . . .[30]

In late November Liszt returned to Britain for a second provincial tour, again with a party got together and led by Louis Lavenu. Their colleagues were Louisa Bassano, John Orlando Parry, Joseph Richardson (from 11 December), and, chaperoned by her mother, the singer Mary Sarah Steele (1815–81); and the itinerary this time took them not only into the Midlands and North of England, but also to Scotland and through virtually the entire length of Ireland.

Arriving too late for the opening concert, at Reading Town Hall on 23 November,* Liszt joined the rest of the party in time to appear with them at the Star Hotel, Oxford, on Tuesday the 24th. His performances, according to *Jackson's Oxford Journal* (28 November), were 'perfectly astounding' and 'distinguished not only by great power and rapidity of execution, but by correct taste and judgment'.

After an evening concert at Leamington the next day,† the party proceeded on the 26th, passing Warwick Castle ('Liszt very excited!!' noted Parry), to Birmingham, where they performed that evening.

'The playing of M. Liszt is not extraordinary, it is miraculous,' averred the *Birmingham Journal* (28 November).

In the very tempest, torrent and whirlwind of his discourse, there is no scrambling, no confusion—the wildest passages are most exquisitely arranged, each under each, and all of them duly subordinate to the general effect. . . . M. Liszt has been represented, by some of the London journals, as a mere mechanical player, as possessing a wonderful dexterity of manipulation, but without the higher spirit which alone can give charm to a musical performance. This appears to us to be a very great and decided mistake. . . . We should say no pianist can possess in a more eminent degree the art of pleasing as well as of surprising. Long pieces, on the piano, are as proverbially dull as long sermons. M. Liszt's recitals are all long, and yet they appeared remarkably short; and the applause bestowed upon the last was more marked and loud than that bestowed upon the first.

* 'When they heard Liszt was not come, great many left!' wrote Parry. 'We were obliged to go on with the concert, tho' to only a few persons. Everything went flat.' The evening concert at Newbury was cancelled.

† Of the journey, Parry recorded: 'Most lovely morning. Liszt brought his great Hungarian coat with him, composed of skins and ornamented with different coloured leathers—it is a most enormous concern and weighs at least as heavy as three greatcoats.'

He is a very good-looking young man, pale, thin, and intellectual; with a fine forehead, good nose, and well cut mouth; not a little resembling the portraits of Bonaparte, when a captain of artillery. He is plainly, in his department, a man of great genius and originality.

John Orlando Parry, 27 November. At 2 started for Wolverhampton. . . . At 3 we found ourselves in a dense fog, and what with the smoke and *desolate* appearance of the villages and whole country covered with the shafts which lead to the mines, we were one and all perfectly miserable. . . . Went to the Swan Hotel. Dinner at 5—everything underdone! I dined off bread, cheese and salary [*sic*]. Some wine and *smoke* and then dressed for the concert—130. All went as usual.[31]

Wolverhampton Chronicle (2 December). Liszt's appearance was hailed with great applause, and a most extraordinary being he is—tall and slim, his hair hanging in masses behind his ears, his eyes lighted up with the fire of imagination. . . . At the conclusion he was rapturously encored, so that after keeping the audience in suspense for some minutes he returned to the instrument and gave an impromptu on *God Save the Queen* [S235]. . . . Although we went to the concert with our expectation raised to an unusual pitch, the reality exceeded as much as it is possible what the imagination had anticipated.

Then came a concert at Newcastle under Lyme (where they stayed at The Roebuck, with, according to Parry, 'horrible dirty bedrooms') on the 28th, and one at Chester's Royal Hotel ('capital bedrooms') on the 30th.*

Parry, 1 December. Left at 11—arrived at Birkenhead at ¼ to 1. Had oysters, pickles, bread and cheese in *the open air*!! We enjoyed it very much—Liszt treated us all. Boat arrived—crossed to Liverpool—Liszt all alive on board—put on his Hungarian *great* bearskin cloak! Everybody thinking he was a little touched—great fun tho'. Went to the Rainbow Hotel, but being full went to 'The Feathers', Clayton Square—most extraordinary people! The niece (!) the daughter (!) the chambermaids (!) etc. etc., all a little touched I think! . . . Dressed and went to the Theatre Royal, where the concert was held. . . . Liszt was tremendously received. . . . The house was so full, many left directly Liszt had played his last piece, to get to their carriages.

The writer of the review which appeared in the *Liverpool Mercury* (4 December) confessed himself 'at a loss to express how the performance of this Paganini of the piano exceeded our expectations'.

The next day, 2 December, having been to the dentist to have a tooth extracted ('I was quite terrified, but hardly suffered at all,' he told Marie), bought a pair of spectacles and visited an exhibition of paintings, Liszt

* Walking with Liszt to visit Chester Cathedral, Parry noted: 'Liszt's coat and cap astonished the Welshmen.'

(accompanied by Parry) left for Preston, rejoining the others in time for the evening concert at the Theatre.

Concerts followed at Rochdale (3 December); Manchester (at the Athenaeum on the 4th, Liszt being encored three times);* Huddersfield (at the Philosophical Hall on the 5th); and Doncaster (at the Mansion House on the 7th).

Doncaster Gazette (11 December). However highly our expectations were raised by the flattering encomiums we had heard of M. Liszt, the lion of the evening, those expectations fell far short of the reality. We have had the gratification on former occasions of hearing the most celebrated pianists of our day, such as Cramer, Moscheles, Herz, Döhler, and lastly Thalberg, whose exquisite performances left us nothing more to wish for; and in short, we had conceived it utterly impossible that any subsequent performer would ever be found to rival that *artiste*. What, then, was our wonder on hearing M. Liszt, whose brilliancy and rapidity of touch and tone, combined with exquisite delicacy and feeling, proved him to be at least the equal of any of his talented predecessors?. . .

He is in appearance prepossessing, tall and graceful, and his countenance, when under excitement, is lighted up with enthusiasm; his fingers we have heard likened to talons on account of their thinness and length, pouncing upon the keys of the pianoforte with the eagerness and velocity of an eagle. . . .

He is on the pianoforte what Paganini was on the violin —a wonder.

On Tuesday, 8 December the party were at Sheffield, where the concert was held at the Music Hall. Liszt was obliged to give an encore of his *Grand galop chromatique* as well as of the *William Tell* overture and the *Réminiscences des Puritains*. He also played Weber's *Invitation to the Dance* and his own paraphrase of *God Save the Queen*.

Sheffield Iris (15 December). It is enough for us, though, perhaps, but little for this celebrated *artiste,* that we pass the highest eulogium we have to offer, viz. that his like we never before heard, and perhaps never shall again.

At Wakefield, on the 9th, Liszt was again encored three times. 'Liszt has been denominated the Paganini of his instrument,' observed the *Wakefield Journal & West Riding Herald* (11 December). 'The fame of the latter, however, was drawn in part from his unrivalled excellence upon a single string. Liszt would seem to have fingers enough for a thousand strings.'

At Leeds, on the 10th, the concert party stayed at the Scarborough Hotel and performed at the Music Hall. Parry: 'All went well! Took *me* for Liszt—great fun.'

Leeds Mercury (12 December). The concert . . . was beyond all doubt one

* Where they stayed at the Mosley Arms, the hotel in which Maria Malibran had died four years earlier.

of the most remarkable and interesting that we ever attended in this town. We have rarely witnessed a similar enthusiasm amongst our music-loving public. . . . We have been urged by various parties to institute a comparison between Thalberg and Liszt. But this is a matter of no slight difficulty, for in each we acknowledge the great master. As a composer, Thalberg undoubtedly stands higher: his compositions are truly classical: but, as a performer, we prefer Liszt, and he is, in our opinion, the greatest pianoforte player we ever had the happiness to hear.

Leeds Intelligencer (12 December). To judge of his greatness, he must be heard; language would fail in the description. He is, indeed, 'greater on his instrument than was Paganini on the violin'.

On the 11th they went by rail to Hull, staying at the Kingston Hotel and performing in the Public Rooms.

At York, where they stayed at the White Swan, they performed, on the 14th, at the Great Rooms in Blackwall Street. Parry: 'The concert was brilliantly attended! 650 at least!!! The ladies were mostly in *ball* dresses, as there was a dance after the concert.'

Yorkshire Gazette (19 December). The performance of Thalberg so fresh in our minds had scarcely cooled before the announcement of M. Liszt summoned us to hear one of the greatest musical declaimers in the world.

When we heard Thalberg, we then thought all possibilities were exhausted, and that no other performer could ever achieve or surmount greater difficulties; but the performances of this evening have opened a new avenue of hearing to us, and prove how wonderfully the art has advanced of late years, and with it mechanical power to an astonishing rapidity, and sometimes more so than is intellectual, as the greater the facility the more liable to abuse, and the performer may himself be deceived by the force of his own imagination, and attempt too much; but M. Liszt possesses qualities peculiar to himself, and to compare him with any other performer now living would be as unjust as to compare a moderate violin player to Paganini; but if comparison may be allowed, he is, both in physical appearance and mental power, the nearest to the great, the lamented Paganini. . . .

M. Liszt's condescension in playing a duet with Mr. Lockwood is another mark of his great and liberal mind, and it would be well if all provincial professors would act with the same liberality towards each other; then indeed would music flourish and one kind feeling beget another.

From York the party turned westward, to cross to Ireland. The concert at Manchester on the 4th, however, had pleased so much that a second had been arranged in that city. Leaving York early in the morning of the 15th, and breakfasting at Hebden Bridge, by mid-afternoon they were in Manchester, where the concert was held once again at the Athenaeum. The Erard having been left at York, Liszt played on a Broadwood.

At Liverpool the next day, the steamer was boarded for the crossing of the Irish Sea.

Parry, 16 December. Off went *The Prince* and her cargo. The view of Liverpool, with its thousands of gas lights, the fires from some neighbouring mines etc., formed a most beautiful 'tableau'. The wind was 'getting up' *still*! Liszt went into our carriage, which was on deck, covered over with tarpoline [*sic*], and read by the light of a wax taper he had brought with him. It looked so odd, the light shining thro' the yellow tarpoline. We walked up and down for some time, then Joey and I went down in the cabin, where we found a capital supper or tea spread out. We two, fell to —and demolished some fowl, beef, and beautiful broiled *haddock*, tea, etc. The fish was lovely. . . . Finding the vessel began to pitch about very much, I shut up my book and *tried* to walk to my bed—but this was a matter of the greatest difficulty. . . . I hadn't been in my cabin two minutes, before—Oh! my! Oh Lor!—I was dreadfully ill. . . . The vessel rolled dreadfully, and what with hearing the surrounding neighbourhood 'casting up their accounts' etc. etc. I never passed so miserable a time for nearly six hours. . . .

During this first visit to Dublin (where they stayed at Morrison's Leinster Hotel), the party gave three concerts: on the 18th, 21st, and 23rd.

Parry, 17 December. Liszt went to the Theatre Royal, and saw Charles Kean in *Macbeth* until 9 o'clock. Then he went to the Rotunda (where the concert is tomorrow night). We met him there. He played over his Concert Stück (Weber) with a very fair band chiefly composed of amateurs and men from the regiments quartered here. The Duke of Leinster played principal double bass, and there were in the band 'Sir Frederick' this and 'Sir John' the other, with 'Lord' so and so, colonels and captains, etc. etc.!! They were so pleased with Liszt that they *encored* his March in the Concert Stück. There were a few people in the room, which is very large indeed—holds 1200!!

18 December. The concert was most splendid sight I ever saw—1200 persons at least, all elegantly dressed, numbers of officers etc. Also the *Lord Lieutenant of Ireland* attended with a guard of honour! 'Twas magnificent! There was a fine band of 60 or 70 performers, the Duke of Leinster playing the principal double bass, Sir Gore Booth violoncello etc., and several lords, colonels and captains in the band as amateurs, besides the military brass instruments. 'Twas superb effect—so brilliant—all gas! They began to the minute. . . . I stood my ground very well. *Liszt* was not so rapturously applauded as I expected from last night, but still it was a very good reception. He had a *new Grand* from Erard's expressly, but it was the worst Erard for *public* I ever played on. Things went rather flat till Joey touched them up with *Nel cor*—I think he had much more applause than the great gun. . . . *Liszt* only played twice. *Guillaume Tell* was tremendously encored. They seemed to like it much better than the Concert Stück which was his first piece.

Saunder's Newsletter (19 December). The great lion of the evening was M. Liszt, and his performance did not disappoint the expectations which his name had raised. . . . He appears to be absorbed, when at the piano, in tracing the progress of his subject through all its windings; and his countenance lights up with an air of evident superiority as he proceeds to fling himself into the midst of those involved combinations which would confuse and alarm one less confident in his own resources in the endeavour to solve them. M. Liszt's style is more eccentric than that of Thalberg; but you observe at once that any eccentricities are those of genius. . . . In place of repeating the overture to *William Tell*, when encored, he played *God save the Queen* with extempore variations, and the harmonies introduced were bold and finely worked up.

'Liszt is decidedly a great master of his instrument,' opined *Freeman's Journal*, 'but his school of playing can have but few admirers amongst musicians.'

On the 19th the concert party went to see the famous animal trainer van Amburgh. 'His lions and tigers seemed too nice,' Liszt remarked to Marie. 'They are tired and stupefied. I was expecting something more impressive.'

'There was but a poor room this evening,' wrote Parry after the second concert. 'Kean's benefit and the O'Connell dinner completely spoilt it.* The concert went off very gaily indeed—Liszt encored in *Lucia* and *Galop*.'

Parry, 23 December. The room was better attended than on Monday, but still not half enough to pay—only £34 rec'd. But the audience were a great deal more enthusiastic. They applauded *Liszt* to the skies. His *Hexameron* was encored—he played the two last variations. . . . Tonight he played for the first time here *extemporaneously*, and a most wonderful performance it was. When Lewis asked the audience if they had any themes ready written, one was handed in only, but Mr. Pigott[†] gave him 'The Russian Hymn' in addition. This was not enough, so after *talking to the audience in the most familiar manner, and making them laugh* very much because he had got no *lively* air to work on, he turned round suddenly and said—'I play *de Wanted Governess!*' And off he started, with the Irish Air and then the Russian Hymn and last my Song, which he played most wonderfully, not all the way thro', but the waltz part in the first symphony. He played it at least 12 different ways and then wound up with the 3 together in a manner truly extraordinary! 'Twas rec'd as it deserved with tumultuous applause.

* That is, a benefit performance for the actor Charles Kean and a dinner at which the Irish political leader Daniel O'Connell was presiding.

† A Dublin cellist, with whom Liszt also played a duet at the concert.

This concert caused *Freeman's Journal* (24 December) to revise its opinion.

Liszt is decidedly among the greatest of the almost innumerable masters who have appeared of late years on the pianoforte; and his wild and enthusiastic style, and almost unequalled execution—while they can have but few imitators—cannot fail to excite universal admiration.

Since the next concert of the tour was not to be until Monday the 28th, at Cork, Christmas was spent in Dublin, Liszt being invited to Lord Morpeth's for dinner on Christmas Eve. For entertainment on Christmas Day, amateur dramatics were arranged.

Parry. Rehearsed for nearly two hours. . . . After dinner we drank healths etc. Joey up in the moon!—Liszt versus Richardson! Grand flare up! Speeches both sides hot and instantaneous! At last Liszt very friendly gave his hand to Joey. 'Tears such as tender' etc. All right now! Ladies all in tears one minute; all smiles the next!! Much *merrier* than before. . . . The tragedy passed off very well, and the 3 performers *crawled* off the stage (there being no curtain) amidst the loudest applause!

At midday on the 26th began the long journey to Cork, via Naas and Kilcullen (where they lunched and were importuned by beggars). Lodging that night at the Hibernian Hotel, Kilkenny, they resumed the journey in the morning. 'Beggars dreadful!' recorded Parry. 'Women with children almost knocking each other down to try and get near the carriage.' Lunching at Clonmel, they arranged to give a concert there on the return journey. Parry: 'It was past 4 before we started again—almost dark. The crowd of lookers on and *beggars* must have amounted to 150 I'm certain. The scene baffled description just as we left! Little babies under the wheels of the carriage almost screeching out for money—the lame, the halt and the blind! I never was so glad to get away.'

Via Clogheen, Fermoy, and Rathcormac, they arrived at Cork's Imperial Clarence Hotel in the early morning of the 28th. 'It was a consolation to find they had been expecting us,' wrote Parry. 'Our rooms were all ready etc., and in less than half an hour we were snug in bed, tired out of our lives. . . . Thus ended one of the longest journeys I ever undertook on a tour.'

A concert was given later that day, at the hotel.

Cork Constitution (29 December). The long-expected, and much-talked-of, visit from the great phenomenon, M. Liszt, took place yesterday. . . . His performance commenced with the Overture to *William Tell*, which brought all his powers at once into action . . . and the most complete orchestra never produced a more wonderful effect both in spirit and unity of execution. The finale from *Lucia di Lammermoor*, followed by the *Galop chromatique*, exquisite delicacies of their kind, were played with admirable effect, and were received with vehement applause. The force of pianoforte playing could go no further.

Parry, 29 December. Breakfasted on the most beautiful *white* butter and brown bread, grilled fowl etc. At ½12 we all (save Mrs. Steele who was queer in bed) started in our own carriage for the Cove of Cork*—'tis about 9½ miles off. A most lovely sunshiny morning, everything gay and bright. We arrived at Monkstown Ferry in an hour (7 miles), crossed in small boat to the opposite side, and then walked by the side of the water for 2 miles and upwards to Cove, a small fort situated in a most beautiful part of Cork Harbour. Liszt, Mary and I walked ahead of the others and admired 'the beauties of nature!' We arrived at the Navy Hotel, a small house but snug, facing the most beautiful harbour . . . and the open sea in the distance. 'Twas a beautiful sight and well worth the visit. We lunched here. Had cold turkey, oysters (splendid), more beautiful butter etc. Liszt stood treat! We enjoyed ourselves very much. There was a *concert upstairs—Mr. Jacobowitch*! He had about 40 people, and I heard singing thro' the door of a most wonderful nature. . . . We returned to the ferry in an open jaunting car—capital things; I liked the ride very much—crossed in a small boat, getting very cold now and beginning to sleet. Found our carriage waiting and arrived home at 6, but could not eat a thing, so dinner was sent to the right about—we had tea instead. After tea it was proposed that we four gentlemen should go to the *small* theatre to see 'The Lady of Lyons!'. . . But when we were out it seems that the 'Eminent Pianist' was bent upon fun. He took us to his 'logement' he had found out in Cork. I was quite surprised to see him take his 'patent copying' machine with him. He introduced us to *Miss* Burke, and the 'Turk' was quite at home—the only fear was that he 'eat mice'! *Bagpipes* for upwards of an hour—dancing, reels, *German* gavottes, porter, whisky etc. etc. *Eliza*—Ellen—'Triste'—Mary, The Captain—'The Clergyman'! The dramatical gentleman and 'the Turk' that lives on mice! No end of fun—'bagpipes' *second* edition! Coffee, riddles, and Grand Finale. Home by ½11. Had some bread and cheese and pickles—and at ½12 Liszt, Joey, and I were in bed. A more unexpected event never happened to me, and it was truly *national* and *rational*. The dancing of Joey was beyond all praise. The bagpipe player was superb—Joey and Louis had a *try* but could not get up the wind! 'Twas the *merriest* party I ever was at!

The next day came the second Cork concert. 'The people were very enthusiastic indeed,' thought Parry. 'Liszt extemporized wonderfully on *Rory O'More*, March in *Norma* and *The Last Rose of Summer*.' Describing Liszt as 'the greatest pianoforte player now in existence', the *Cork Constitution* (31 December) reported that 'nothing could exceed the ecstasy of the audience at the manner in which this wonderful performer acquitted himself'.

Parry. Cork, 31 December. At 1 Mr. and Mrs. Roche got permission for us to go over the LUNATIC ASYLUM. We went accompanied by an officer and one of the Governors.

I never yet have beheld a sight which so fully impressed with melancholy

* The present-day Cobh.

feelings. There are 460 inmates at present. It is immensely large—kept beautifully clean—and the wards all full of poor wretched beings, who stared at us, laughed, howled, grinned, screamed, and some made every possible distortion of the body etc. The women's wards were by far the most frightful. . . . We (the gentlemen of the party) went into the female Idiots' room, and where the *unclean* patients are kept. So dreadful a sight I never beheld. The place was more offensive than any menagerie. . . . It was altogether quite frightful! Liszt was obliged to go away. . . .

We left this place after seeing the kitchen, tasting their oatbread cakes etc.—all so nice and clean—and went (by way of being lively) to the *Cemetery*. . . .

In the evening I went to Collins Theatre, Nelson Square. . . . I returned home by 11. Found *Liszt* amusing Mr. Roche and the party by his delightful talents on the piano. (We had an old square here pro tem.) We had some oysters for supper, and saw the old year out and the new one in over some Whiskey. Drank health and happiness to all absent friends—and thus faded away old 1840 and thus we welcomed in the year 1841.

Great excitement prevailed on our going to bed—Whiskey triumphant! Fine fun with Nos. 27, 26, 25 and 24! All quiet by half past two! and high time *too*!

1841

On New Year's Day the third and last of the Cork concerts was given. Leaving the city that evening, the party travelled through the night, arriving in Clonmel at dawn.

Parry, Saturday, 2 January. It was a lovely moonlight night last night. I went to bed the moment we got in (7 o'clock). Got up at ½11, dressed for the *Grand* (!) Concert. No tickets sold. The Court House filthy dirty, and not a *decent* piano for love or money!!! Liszt suggested asking two or three ladies, who had come in their carriages, to the hotel, and to come in *our sitting room,* where there was a little Square of Tomkinson. This being done, we began and went thro' the *whole programme* to 25 ladies and gentlemen. 'Twas like a private *matinée.* So funny to see Liszt firing away at *Guillaume Tell* on this little instrument, but it stood his powerful hand capitally. . . . After this funny sort of concert we dined, and at ½6 left for Kilkenny, where we arrived at 11 o'clock.

Spending the night at Kilkenny, they continued the next day (Parry's 31st birthday) to Dublin. Parry: 'It was an awful morning. We could hardly see the houses opposite for hail! The hurricane was terrific. Liszt *would* go outside in spite of it all. . . . Could hardly see to read, the windows were so blocked up with snow and frost.' Reaching Dublin just after midnight, they were met by unwelcome news.

Parry. They had been expecting us since two or three in the afternoon. Found Wade* up, but what was our astonishment to find there was not any concert *tomorrow* (Monday), after all our posting up and *losing* the morning concert at Cork. Thro' some misunderstanding, bills were only out announcing that we would give a concert on our return from the provinces! This will be a dreadful loss to Lewis—he and Liszt were very angry with Wade, as he had been left here expressly to arrange matters. We shall now have *nothing to do till Thursday,* as there will be no time to advertise etc. before!!—'All in the *downs* the *crew* were moored!'—Had tea, but everybody silent, so I was off to bed, and thus passed the most *desolate* birthday I have ever had.

The three days of enforced rest were given to sight-seeing and theatre-going. On the 4th, Liszt, Parry, and Miss Steele went to see *Fra Diavolo* at the Theatre Royal; on the 5th, Parry and Richardson went to a pantomime.

Parry, Wednesday, 6 January. Played a little on Liszt's piano. He came up and to my great delight played to me *his* arrangement [S575] of *Der Freischütz* overture—'twas gigantic! Quite wonderful and yet beautiful. He also played to me his arrangement [S418] from *Don Giovanni,* in which *Là ci darem* has been preserved by him as a *duet*, the left hand playing the bass part and the right the soprano. It has a very beautiful and novel effect. N. B. He has bought two waistcoats of *gold cloth*!! They are called poplins, but all gold thread. They are magnificent. Went out at one to *Library* and *Museum* of the College opposite. I saw it on 24 Dec. Liszt much pleased. . . . I left Liszt and Miss Steele and went to a bookseller's and bought a French and English Dictionary for Liszt—made him a *present* of it.

Parry, 7 January. While Joey and I were at tea last night, we little thought *who* was next door—'Follow, follow over mountain!'—*Miss* Burke† and friend. 'The eminent' and 'the unknown'! (Doors locked! Liszt and . . . his love—great affection. 126 miles long! 2 for 1, small beds—single and 'family'!)

The morning concert here took place at Rotunda as usual. Bad attendance. . . . Everything flat as dish water—no applause, no nothing. . . . The people half frozen—a more miserable set were never seen. We left out two pieces, and Liszt *would* not play *extemporaneously* as announced — played his *Galop chromatique*. . . .

* J. A. Wade (1801–45), who had joined the company at Manchester for the visit to his native Dublin, was an odd character but a gifted musician, and several of his works were performed in the Dublin concerts, although he took no active part himself. One of his works was a *Handbook to the Pianoforte*. It was dedicated to Liszt, whose portrait appeared in the frontispiece.

† The woman Liszt had picked up at Cork.

The evening concert was the Anacreontic Society 2nd concert, but given in the small room of the Rotunda. . . . It was not quite so full as I had anticipated (400). There was a large band, as usual. . . . Liszt and Rudersdorff played a piece, 'Sonata of Beethoven'—20 minutes long! 'Twas dreadful!

On the 8th the travelling troupe left for Limerick. Via Kildare, Monasterevin and Roscrea, they journeyed through the night, arriving at Limerick's Royal Mail Hotel in the morning of the 9th and giving a concert later in the day at Swinburne's Room. Parry: 'They were uncommonly lively for a morning concert and gave everything applause.'

After a second Limerick concert on the 11th, they returned for the last time to Dublin, arriving in the evening of the 12th in time for their sixth concert in the capital. 'The concert went off very well indeed,' opined Parry, 'and we all sang and played wonderfully well considering the fatigue we had undergone.'

The seventh and last of the Dublin concerts was held on the 13th, and the next day, via Drogheda, Newry (where they spent the night) and Lisburn, they journeyed to Belfast, arriving at the Donegal Arms in the afternoon of the 15th and performing that evening at the Music Hall. 'There were seven encores!' recorded Parry. 'I never sang to an audience fonder of fun, 'twas capital.'

The night of Saturday the 16th they spent at Donaghadee (Liszt and Parry sharing a room), and on the 17th took the packet across the North Channel to Port Patrick, whence they made their way to Stranraer to await the departure of the *Sir William Wallace* steam packet to Ayr.

Parry, 18 January. At ½2 we called for some sandwiches, and after a glass of whisky and water the carriage was brought to the door—with Liszt asleep in it—and having got all our things we prepared for a start. 'Twas now ½3 and a fine starlight morning!—freezing very hard. As the quay was very near (that is, a quarter of a mile), the ostlers and boots etc. put a rope to the carriage and proceeded without horses to the quay. But as our carriage was very heavy we lent a hand, and a funny procession it was — Miss Steele carrying a lantern and we all tugging the carriage and the 'great pianist', who was fast asleep all the while and knew nought of the honour being conferred on him. . . . Had some difficulty in getting the carriage on board over two planks. At last she was shipped and all right. (We had to *wake* the 'Eminent Pianist', being still fast asleep.) Liszt and I took our seats in our own carriage, while the rest lay down on sofas. We were by far the best off. At ½5 'Sir William' slipped his moorings (!) —and away faded the gas lamps on the pier and away faded Liszt and I into a sound sleep! I woke at ½8, and found myself opposite some fine mountains covered with snow and the glorious sun rising behind them! Everything was tinged with gold colour! So fresh, so gay, and the sea blue as possible. . . .

We glided into Ayr harbour, and to our dismay saw the railway train — just leaving!! Impossible to catch or stop it, so there we were left in the lurch. No train till 2!! (The concert begins at 1!!—40 miles off!) However, on inquiry we found there was a *third class train* (where they carried pigs and cattle etc. and luggage!) starting at 11—and it was proposed we should go in this! So after taking porter etc. at the King's Arms . . . we set off in the *open* train, this bitter cold day, and went the 43 miles in three hours, which appeared an age owing to the intense cold and the long stoppages on the road.

On our arrival at the city of Glasgow, we went to the *George*, in George Square. Found we were too late for the concert! People all gone away! So Mr. Mitchenson advised our not giving any until Wednesday next, as before proposed, but have another on Friday evening. This advice was followed—and very glad I was, for we were all perished in the horrible *open train* on the railway. . . . At ½ to 10 we were again seated in 'our moveable house' (as we have christened the old carriage) and slept and woke and woke and slept etc. until 5 the next morning when we found ourselves in the great and wonderful city of Edinburgh!

Because of the arrangements whereby concerts were to be given in Edinburgh on the 19th, 21st, and 23rd, and in Glasgow on the 20th and 22nd, the party were compelled to travel daily between the two cities. At Edinburgh, where they stayed at the Royal Hotel in Princes Street, the first concert was given at the Assembly Rooms, to an audience of about 300. Parry: 'The audience applauded Liszt immensely—he was encored *twice*.'

At Glasgow the next day they again had a substantial audience. Commending all the performers, the *Glasgow Argus* (21 January) declared that 'a more splendid exhibition of musical talent, taken as a whole, has not been heard in Glasgow for many years. Liszt alone has the power to delight and electrify an audience, even were he not attended by the galaxy of talent which shines around him.'

Glasgow Courier (23 January). Passing over several pieces in which the Misses Steele, Bassano, and Mr. J. Parry performed in their respective departments, not from want of will or inclination to notice in the most favourable manner their fascinating appearance as concert singers, we for the present come at once to the exquisite productions of M. Liszt. In the first part of the concert given on Wednesday night in the Assembly Rooms, attended by a fashionable audience, the overture of *Guillaume Tell* was given with that force and magnificence which was calculated, as it well deserved, to bring down unqualified approbation. M. Liszt was cheered to the echo, and encored with raptures. . . .

In the second part, he volunteered to 'perform' on any theme which might be written, and, accordingly, the music of 'Logie o' Buchan', 'Woo'd and married and a'', and 'Jingling Johnny', were handed up to him, and from these he, with apparently no effort whatever, produced a splendid and most amusing fantasia.

Parry, 21 January. At 12 we left for our 43 miles *back* again to Edinburgh. Nothing happened of any consequence on the road, save having two horses down once! We arrrived at about 5. . . . At 8 we went to the concert. Good room—people very close. Liszt was encored in *every* piece. After the concert the whole party went to Mr. Paterson's (the music seller) to supper. Beautiful rooms: gas etc. Separate room for the good things — ham, celery, etc. Enjoyed my supper very much. Boucher the great flute player was there. . . . 'Master Paterson' favoured the company with a *grand* solo on the top of the flute. Mr. Lewis Lavenu burst out in aria patetica on the violoncello. Liszt frightened the 7 and ½ octave grand with a Waltz à la Diable.* Miss Steele looked on rather 'disgusted'.

The Scotsman (23 January). The audience was highly fashionable, but not so crowded as the genius of the musician deserved, or as his fame led us to expect. What, however, it wanted in numbers it made up in enthusiasm. M. Liszt is considered the greatest master of the pianoforte who has ever visited this city, and is, we believe, unequalled by any performer now living. His style is different from that of his great rival Thalberg, but few will deny that it is superior. What Paganini was on the violin, Liszt is on the pianoforte—possessing perfect execution, directed by the highest genius. He seems to tear the very soul out of his instrument. . . . M. Liszt gives one more concert this morning, when we advise all who wish to know of what the pianoforte is capable to attend. . . . We have often seen the Assembly Rooms filled to an inferior concert company, leaving Liszt out of the question.

Parry, 22 January. The wind blew a hurricane this morning. At ½12 we started for our '43 miles' as usual. But I never remember seeing such hail and terrific sort of sleet—which was impelled by the wind so that it almost broke the glass of the carriage windows. . . . The postboys were drenched thro' and thro'. We arrived at ½5 after a most miserable ride. . . .

The second concert was not half so good as we expected. Very badly attended indeed. Liszt brought in some very dashing Scotch girls with him (where he had been dining). *He* sat in the room with them—to the great dismay of the poor 'artistes'. For a wonder I was *not encored* in a single thing. Everything rather flat. I sang my 'Trio' shamefully—but this was entirely owing to Liszt sitting right under me—made me dreadfully nervous. I will not suffer it again. I hardly got any applause, what the previous Wednesday was rec'd with shouts!! And tonight too, '*by desire*'!

Shortly after this second Glasgow concert, Liszt and the others left the city for the last time, travelling through the night and arriving in Edinburgh for breakfast. Their final concert in Scotland was given that evening at the Hopetoun Rooms, to an audience of about 400.

Parry, Sunday, 24 January. Packed, breakfasted, and at 1 we left with 4

* Probably the Fantasy (S413) on Meyerbeer's *Robert le Diable*, published later in the year.

white horses and the jockeys in velvet caps! An immense crowd to see us start. Took a last farewell of Holyrood, Arthur's Seat, Calton Hill etc. in our way, and thus we left the great city of Edinburgh. . . . Arrived at Dunbar about ¼ to 5 where we stopt to dine. While dinner was preparing, the landlord took us to see Dunbar Castle, a celebrated ruin on the rocks, just at the end of the town. It is a very grand sight—the waves always roaring and dashing around it and sometimes *over* it!—howling thro' caverns and subterranean passages. In a storm it must be frightful. Was very well worth seeing indeed.

Via Berwick on Tweed, Bedford, Alnwick (where Liszt got out of the crowded carriage, spent the night at an inn, and rejoined his companions the next day by taking the mail coach) and Morpeth, they arrived at Newcastle upon Tyne in the morning of the 25th, stopping at the Queen's Head and giving a concert that evening. ('Everything went pretty,' wrote Parry.)

The first of the two concerts arranged for the 26th was at Sunderland.

Parry, 26 January. Passed over the beautiful Iron Bridge; arrived very late. Went in the *only* fly in the town to the beautiful! (?) Assembly Rooms. About 70 people (!). Found we had left the whole of the music *somewhere* —but no one could tell *where*. We went thro' the *whole concert* without a note of music!!!

The audience were very kind indeed, considering we had kept them waiting at least 3 quarters of an hour. . . . Liszt extemporized.

We returned home to dinner rather queer. Had a battle with post boy and the landlord of the house, whose horses ought to take us to Durham (13 miles). Locked up the carriage! Wouldn't take *his* horses out! A mob of people (100) round the door—quite a scene!

At last it was arranged—by threat'ning to call the police! Mrs. Steele had sent a man to Newcastle after the music, but when I was putting the things into the carriage, to my great astonishment there was all the music in its proper place in the sword case. *I* and two boots had seen everything *out* of the carriage when we *arrived* and there was certainly not a bit there then! 'Twas very mysterious, and no one could account for it. At length we got off amidst the groans of the landlord and shouts of the mob! I never saw such a scene. It was shocking. We left this beautiful '*coal hole*' and arrived about ¼ past 8 at Durham.

After a concert in that city later in the day, one in the morning of the 27th at Richmond, and another in the evening at Darlington ('A drunken man offered Liszt a sovereign to play Rule Britannia,' noted Parry), the party proceeded via Boroughbridge and Leeds to Halifax, where the last concert of the tour was given at the Oddfellows Hall on 29 January. Here they were warmly received by a large house (about 400).

Halifax Guardian (30 January). The Overture to *Guillaume Tell* was rapturously encored; upon which M. Liszt substituted some splendid variations upon the National Anthem. The company were electrified with their majestic grandeur, and with the most vociferous shouts testified their applause; in fact they were completely overcome with the sublimity of his effects, and ere the close of the last variation broke out into cheers which completely drowned the finale. . . .

We never remember a concert which was marked by so much enthusiasm, or so many rapturous encores, as that of last night.

Travelling through the night to Leeds, Liszt and his companions there took the train, via Derby and Rugby, to London, arriving at Euston Square Grand Birmingham Station in the early morning of the 30th.

His only remaining public engagement before crossing the Channel once again was at the Hanover Square Rooms on 3 February, at a concert given by Dulcken and Benedict.

The Athenaeum (6 February). Siberian as was the temperature of Wednesday evening, this concert was a pleasant one. . . . The best thing was the casual apparition of M. Liszt, and M. Liszt in all his glory, playing the *Hexameron* as none save himself could play it; and when tumultuously encored by the audience, giving a fragment of a new fantasia, in which *God Save the Queen* was arranged in a more dazzling magnificence than it has ever hitherto worn.

Writing to Marie about the tour just ended, Liszt remarked: 'I have taken my English bankruptcy* very well, and have gained ground enormously. . . . In sum, it is an immense and fitting success.'

Via Ostend he proceeded to Brussels, where on the 12th he played at the home of F.J.Fétis (the champion of Thalberg), who exclaimed after the very first piece: 'This is the creation of the piano; until now we had no idea what it was.' On the 15th he played in Liège. 'I am playing much less than in England and yet feel ten times more tired,' he wrote that day to Marie. 'I cannot read, write, or even sleep. The constant dinners and suppers are bad for me too; I have grown somewhat thinner.' On the 16th, and again on the 26th, he played in Brussels; on the 20th at Ghent. On 2 and 7 March he gave concerts in Antwerp.

Later that month he returned to Paris, where on 27 March and 13 April he gave matinées musicales at Erard's, and on 25 April, at the Conservatoire, a 'grand concert whose proceeds will be sent to the subscription opened in Germany for the Beethoven monument . . . and in which only Beethoven's music will be heard'. The conductor was Berlioz. After the second item, the E flat Concerto played by Liszt, M. Geffroy of the Théâtre Français read some verses by Antony Deschamps in honour of Beethoven. Liszt then played his transcription (S466) of Beethoven's *Adelaide.* The Kreutzer Sonata, with Liszt and Massart, should have followed, but in the event could be given only after

* Although, as the reviews indicate, the tour was an immense *artistic* success, the small audiences in many of the provincial centres had created a financial deficit. Calling Lavenu 'un pauvre diable', Liszt generously waived his entire fee (500 guineas a month) for the ten-week engagement.

Liszt had unwillingly acquiesced with the audience's vociferous demand and played the Fantasy on *Robert le Diable*.

On Monday the 26th he attended Chopin's concert at Pleyel's, about which he wrote a critique for the *Revue et gazette musicale* (2 May). When told by Legouvé that Liszt would create a 'magnificent kingdom' for him, the suspicious Chopin had retorted: 'Yes, within his own empire.' But the review was totally eulogistic.

Arriving in London on 7 May,* he took part that same evening in a concert given by John Orlando Parry, playing the Overture to *William Tell* and, as an encore, his paraphrase of *God Save the Queen*.

During this time he was 'working like a madman' at certain operatic fantasies, including those on *Norma* (S394), *Der Freischütz* (S451), and *Don Giovanni*. 'It is a new vein I have found and want to exploit,' he told Marie. 'When I am with you I shall work at more serious things, not to be entirely unworthy of my poor dear Marie.'

On 14 May he took part in a concert given by another of his colleagues of the previous winter: Mary Sarah Steele, who in gratitude presented him with an inscribed silver cigar-box.†

The Athenaeum (22 May). Anything more colossal, not merely as regards splendour of execution, but also volume of sound, we cannot recall or imagine. He is, if we mistake not, better appreciated than formerly by his audiences, and they may appreciate him without misgiving—for the variety of resources to please them which he possesses is next to inexhaustible.

On the 17th he took part in Benedict's concert at Her Majesty's Theatre. His performance of the *Hexameron*, declared Chorley, 'roused up the most crowded and coldest audience of the season to something nearer a *furore* than English men and women often indulge in'. Among fellow artists on this occasion were Pauline Viardot-Garcia and Henri Vieuxtemps.

On 31 May Liszt appeared at the annual London concert given by Marie Louise Dulcken (1811–50), which was duly reviewed by Chorley in the *Athenaeum* (5 June).

We have to speak in the highest terms of Madame Dulcken: not merely for her performance of Thalberg's fantasia and Benedict's duet, but for the force and fervour with which she kept pace with Liszt in a grand duet for two pianofortes [S654] arranged from his stupendous *Hexameron*. To keep pace with Liszt on Monday was no child's play. It was a race not only with mechanical omnipotence, but with fancy in its most excursive mood: he has never played so brilliantly in London. *Apropos* of this artist, we have to call attention to the thoroughly munificent sacrifice, made by him, of the day fixed for his concert and his own prodigious talent, to the Polish

* The night of the 6th he spent at Boulogne. Whether that evening or the next morning he tried to find his father's grave is not known; but its importance to him is shown by a letter to his mother five years later (29 May 1846): 'Should the children need sea-bathes, take them to Le Havre, Ostend, or Boulogne. In the last-named town, look for Father's grave.'

† Now on display at the Liszt Ferenc Memorial Museum in Budapest.

matinée. We hope that this will not be forgotten on the morning to which he has postponed his performances.

Later on the 31st Liszt played in private for the Duke and Duchess of Cambridge—but in the evening was involved in an accident.

Philipp von Neumann, 1 June. I dined yesterday at Norwood with the two Loewe sisters and Liszt. On returning our coachman overturned us and only by a miracle did we escape being hurt. The horses got out of hand and ran away, and we were thrown out by the shock. Liszt received a contusion on the head, the two sisters were luckily unhurt, and I was equally fortunate.[1]

Having sprained his left wrist, Liszt had to cancel his intended appearance at Giulia Grisi's concert on 2 June;* and his own concert, announced for the 5th, he had (as the *Athenaeum* pointed out) postponed for a week so that he could participate in the 'Polish *matinée*' at Stafford House,† home of the Duchess of Sutherland. Among fellow performers at this prestigious event—'one of the gayest and grandest shows you can imagine', in the words of the actress Fanny Kemble—were the great French *tragédienne* Rachel, and the singer Adelaide Kemble (1814–79), the subsequent Mrs Sartoris. 'She has a truly magnificent voice,' remarked Liszt of the last-named, to whom he later gave 'a beautiful old black German bible'.

His wrist having had eight leeches applied to it and being in a sling, he was limited to playing a duet with Benedict in which he used his right hand only. After the concert the Duchess showed him around her private apartments.

The Athenaeum (12 June). The Polish *matinée* will be long spoken of as the most brilliant entertainment of its kind within our memory. There were Mlle Rachel's recitations; and there was M. Liszt placing another feather in his cap, as a man and an artist, by playing, in his disabled state, a duet, *with one hand,* with M. Benedict; and doing more, it may be added, than many a well-versed pianist with all his ten fingers. After the sacrifice of a very lucrative week's engagements, the steadfast resolution to keep his faith with Charity, seems to us even more worthy of honourable notice than the wonderful skill which made the performance so surprising.

On 7 June Liszt took part in Eliason's concert; on the 11th he dined at Chiswick with the Duke of Devonshire. His own matinée, postponed from the previous Saturday, was given at Willis's Rooms on the 12th. It was attended by many of the social élite, including the Duke and Duchess of Cambridge, the Duchess of

* The announcement of Liszt's inability to appear, reported *The Times*, was 'little calculated to induce the audience to support with patience the delay caused by the tardy arrival of some of the principal performers. Accordingly, Signor Costa, the conductor, was greeted with one or two hisses on his appearance, at which he pettishly remarked that it was "no fault of his".'

† Seven years later Chopin came to Stafford House, to play before Queen Victoria, Prince Albert, and the Duke of Wellington. In Stable Yard and still standing, it has been renamed Lancaster House.

Gloucester, the Duchess of Sutherland, and Prince Paul Esterházy. His left hand being still rather swollen, he played only three solos and a two-piano duo with Benedict. 'I never heard anything so beautiful as Liszt's touch,' was the opinion of young Elisabeth Knox.

The Times (14 June). There has perhaps been no instrumentalist since Paganini who is so happily organized for his art as M. Liszt, and accordingly, his talent comprises, though perhaps not all in the highest degree, every quality which is required to form a perfect pianist. He possesses a fire and nervous energy which is peculiarly adapted to the style of music which he in general selects—brilliant, rapid, and emphatic; but let him have to execute an adagio, or any passage which requires sostenuto, and we immediately detect what may be called the great fault of modern pianists—the substitution for the natural vibration of the notes of a repeated *doigté au marteau.* It is in the want of this medium quality alone that M. Liszt is in any way liable to criticism, for in the other extreme, delicate, smooth, and light-fingering, he is unsurpassable. Among the pieces which M. Liszt executed was a fantasia on the *Sonnambula,* of his own composition, the chief, and we might almost say only, merit of which consisted in the occasion which it purposely afforded him to display his marvellous *tours de force.* The most extraordinary of these was a variation, in which the theme and an accompaniment were distinctly heard in the middle octaves of the instrument, while a brilliant trill in the treble and a powerful bass were kept up, thus producing all the effects of four hands. In another piece, which introduced the Tarantella, *La Danza* [S424/9], he kept his audience in a thrill of breathless delight and amazement at the interminable and playful accentuation which he gave to his theme, in the execution of which his hands danced over the keys with graceful lightness and rapidity, producing a continued ripple of fairy-like melody. The entertainment was closed by an unlooked-for treat: Thalberg's piece on *Norma*, played on two pianofortes by MM. Benedict and Liszt. This fine composition gathered additional power and brilliancy from the execution of M. Liszt, who had no feeble second in M. Benedict, for between the two performers there almost appeared to be a kind of galvanic circle which electrified the audience. . . . The Duke of Cambridge honoured M. Liszt with his presence, and appeared highly delighted with his performance. Indeed, no laurelled conqueror could desire a more complete triumph than M. Liszt was greeted with on this occasion.

On Monday, 14 June, Liszt made his sole Philharmonic Society appearance of the season.

Ignaz Moscheles. When he came forward to play in Hummel's Septet,* one

* In which the double-bass part was taken by the celebrated veteran virtuoso on that instrument, Domenico Dragonetti (1763–1846).

was prepared for enormities, but heard only the well-known piece, which he plays with the most perfect technique, storming heavenwards now and then, but basically free from extravagance, and splendidly interpreted; for a particular characteristic of Liszt's mind and genius is that he knows perfectly what he is playing, where he is playing, and to whom he is playing, and his all-embracing powers he uses merely as a means of bringing out the most varied kinds of effects.[2]

The Athenaeum (19 June). The classicists, again, must have had a convincing proof of the soundness of his attainments by his amazing performance of Hummel's Septet at the Philharmonic Concert. This was played from memory—an effort prodigious enough with anyone else to have absorbed all that animation and force and brilliancy which must belong to the moment's enthusiasm, or they become formal and fatiguing. Yet so far from this being the case, the artist was never more at his ease in the most whimsical drollery thrown off on the spur of the moment than when infusing a new vigour of life and vividness of character into Hummel's fine solid composition, and enough cannot be said of his performance without praise entrenching upon the boundaries of extravagance. The reception given to it by the audience will, we hope, open a way to our hearing other master works of the classical composers for the pianoforte, rendered with a like splendour by the same matchless interpreter.

H. F. Chorley also told Liszt at this time: 'A year ago we wanted to hear you because you were the latest; this year we want to hear you because you are the best!'

On 25 June, Liszt and Vieuxtemps—'the two great guns of the season', according to *The Times*—lent their services at a concert given by Mlle Dubray. Liszt's offering was his *Réminiscences des Puritains,* to which, reported that same newspaper, 'he gave that grace and fire, that endless variety of meaning, which so peculiarly characterize his style'. Later that day he played at Prince Esterházy's, 'before the cream of London (about sixty people)'. On the 28th he took part in a concert given at Her Majesty's Theatre for the widow of Willman the clarinettist. *The Times:* 'Messrs. Liszt and Vieuxtemps lent the weight of their valuable talents to this work of charity, each performing a fantasia, which was crowned with the most stunning signs of admiration.'

In a concert given by Adelaide Kemble at No. 4 Eccleston Street, the home of Harriet and George Grote (author of the famous *History of Greece*), in the afternoon of 29 June, Liszt made his last London appearance as a professional pianist. Fellow performers on this occasion were Balfe, Rubini,* and Pauline Viardot-Garcia.

At midnight on Friday, 2 July, he embarked at the Tower of London on the boat to Hamburg. Before he next set foot on English soil, forty-five years were to pass.

* Giovanni Battista Rubini (1794–1854), the renowned Italian *bel canto* tenor.

His purpose in visiting Hamburg was to attend and play at the 3rd festival of the North German Music Society, held from 4 to 8 July, the first such event he had witnessed. Arriving on the 5th, he took part in a festival concert on the 7th (with Beethoven's Choral Fantasy for piano and orchestra plus a solo), and on the 9th gave one of his own, offering Beethoven's Piano Quintet Op. 16 as well as several solos.

On 11 July, accompanied by the Danish composer J. P. E. Hartmann (1805–1900), he left for Copenhagen (*en route* playing at Kiel), where he stayed from the 15th to the 26th. Not the least appreciative of his listeners here was King Christian VIII, for whom he performed on the evening of his arrival. 'A musical court! A king who loves and understands music!' he wrote in delight to Léon Kreutzer (in an open letter published in the *Revue et gazette musicale*), to whom he also penned some more solemn thoughts which came to him during his sojourn in the Danish capital.

Let me talk to you about an art which is not my own and which I envy for the power of its duration; and about a man who, in bequeathing to Copenhagen a glorious realization of his ideas, has erected on the soil of his native city an everlasting monument to love and gratitude. When I entered the Church of Our Lady, a feeling of profound admiration and quite involuntary awe came over me. As you know, it was Thorvaldsen* who alone and unaided adorned this church. Above the altar is a Christ in white marble, while the statues of the twelve apostles standing with their backs against the pillars of the nave seem to guide the faithful along the path leading to the Man-God; and the round arch of the chancel is formed by a magnificent bas-relief representing the road to Calvary. Everything is simple and great. The unity between the conception and its execution strikes the beholder immediately, leaving a lasting impression. One God, one art, one man. It could be considered a solemn and profound meeting between Jesus and the artist, a glorification of those mystical dialogues, those sublime outpourings whose secret has likewise been revealed to us by a book of wonderful simplicity!

Oh, how could one gaze without envy upon this permanence, this enduring quality of the plastic arts, this human immortality gained by the work of the painter and the sculptor? How not feel sorrow at the impotence of our own art to create and found lasting monuments? Thorvaldsen, Rubens, Michelangelo—great artists, happy men! With your conceptions you fill a whole church, a whole city, a whole country! Your inspirations, clothed in imperishable forms, survive throughout the ages, casting immortal rays on the lands of your birth! Identified with those lands, you are their representatives before posterity! Copenhagen is synonymous with Thorvaldsen, Antwerp with Rubens, Rome with Michelangelo!

* After Hans Christian Andersen and Søren Kierkegaard, the sculptor Bertel Thorvaldsen (*c.*1770–1844) is probably the best-remembered and most notable Dane of the 19th century. His *Christ and the Twelve Apostles* (with St Paul replacing Judas) was completed in 1827.

But, alas, even if there came a musician as mighty as Michelangelo, as chaste as Raphael, as dazzling as Rubens—he could bring forth nothing that time would not efface! With every day that passed he would see sympathy for his work grow a little cooler, and soon find it scarcely known other than to those gloomy scholars who ransack the past to parade their empty learning, seeing in a masterpiece only something with which to confirm their pedantry, and resembling—in this if in nothing else — Cleopatra in that they would gladly dissolve the pearl of genius in the vinegar of their criticism. Palestrina, Gluck, and even thou, divine Mozart, whose ashes are still warm—what are all of you today for the crowd removed so far from you by the music of Rossini? And Rossini, he too! Will not his eagle eye already be perceiving that the latest waves of his harmony are gradually drawing near that fateful shore where the dry sand of indifference awaits them, to absorb genius and renown into its nothingness.

I was still lost in these thoughts—when of a sudden a long and mighty roaring made the very walls of the church shake. It was the organ, vibrating under the hands of its master. To me it seemed a solemn and moving reproach for my doubt and despondency, and I long listened in silence. . . .[3]

Liszt's Copenhagen concerts 'succeeded admirably' and the court was 'more than charming'. In gratitude for King Christian's kindness, and as an expression of thanks for the Order of the Dannebrog which was bestowed upon him, he two years later dedicated to that monarch his Fantasy on *Don Giovanni*.

Returning to Hamburg, he gave another concert there on 29 July. In the audience was *Emma Siegmund* (1817–1901), future wife of the revolutionary poet Georg Herwegh (1817–75), whom Liszt would know well in after years.

Like a resplendent highway in which the sun loves to admire itself and to be reflected in a thousand different colours—that was his playing. With him, the notes, sparks of his genius, tend, like little stars, to descend from the firmament to penetrate our innermost being.

No less interesting is his appearance. Pale and fragile like an adolescent, features stamped with great nobility, he gives the impression of a spirit whose wings have already knocked often at death's doors, but one that is destined to go on vibrating for some time before its swansong. There is nothing terrestrial in the playing of this artist; I thought I saw open up before me the whole of infinite space.

It was not Liszt who was playing, but only his mortal frame, being used by God.[4]

In early August Liszt and Madame d'Agoult were reunited on Nonnenwerth, an island in the Rhine magnificently situated near Rolandseck and the Drachenfels, where they rented accommodation in an old convent used as a guest house. Barring a few occasions when Liszt was away briefly for professional reasons, and Marie once to visit Frankfurt, they stayed here for the next three months.

Marie von Czettritz (wife of General von Czettritz) to her step-daughter Isidore von Kitzing. Nonnenwerth, 15 August. Nine days ago a French lady dressed in black, and accompanied by her maid and a mass of elegant luggage, arrived here in the rain on the boat from Mainz. Taking the three rooms above ours, she asked for all of them to be filled with flowers. She also ordered a bath, dissolved a quarter of a pound of starch in it, and then poured in a quantity of perfume too. She passed our window once, and I could see that there was something rather refined about her; indeed, that she must once have been a great beauty, although just beginning to fade a little. The rain drove her back to her room. She entered her name in the guest-book as Mad. Mortier Defontaine. In the night a lot of noise was caused by the arrival of someone else, who went straight up to her. . . . The next morning your father came in from the garden saying that the lady was sitting in the grove and that the gentleman with her looked like Franz Liszt. I ran out, looked for them and, sure enough, it *was* Liszt—when you have seen him once you know him for ever. It was evident that they did not wish to be disturbed, and so naturally we kept out of their way. He seemed to be showing her the greatest consideration. The next day they were alone, and the day after that there was a trip to Bonn for a few hours, during which time Prince Felix Lichnowsky* and Emile Girardin† arrived. . . . Liszt returned on the next boat. With him was Thiers,‡ whom I at once recognized, both because I had seen his portrait and because he was talking to Liszt. . . . After dinner they all came down and drank coffee in front of our window, and shot at the target with some finger-length pistols that Liszt had brought from London. You can imagine what a lively, witty conversation it was. He played on the bad piano in the hall. We listened, and I prevailed upon Frau von Cordier to offer him her grand piano, but he declined as he had already ordered one. Eventually the grand piano was put in the hall; and in the evening he played to all who wished to hear him. Your father considered it indiscreet to go in just like that; but I did, and then sent for him. When he came in, Liszt said: 'Je jouerai une marche pour le général,'—and there and then improvised a heavenly march. . . .

On Wednesday [11 August] he gave a concert in Bonn, and at midday a lunch for the Beethoven Society, to which he invited your father too, but he didn't accept. We went into town for the concert, at which he was the sole performer. It is something I shall never forget; nor shall I ever hear a pianist again: this memory will remain with me for ever. Even *he* does not

* The grandson of Beethoven's patron Prince Carl von Lichnowsky, Felix Lichnowsky (b. 1814) had become a close friend of Liszt's after their meeting earlier in the year. He often accompanied Liszt on his travels, and was also his host on several occasions. During the Frankfurt uprising of 1848 he was killed by a mob.

† One of Marie's most ardent admirers, the publicist and journalist Emile de Girardin (1806–81).

‡ Adolphe Thiers (1797–1877), statesman and historian.

always play thus, and that evening he gave his very best, reaching an unsurpassable peak of achievement. During the concert he twice came over to me, and you can imagine the stir it caused. Everyone in the place turned to look at me, according to your father. Liszt is the best and kindest man imaginable: generous, liberal, and, for all his brilliance, just like a child.

Referring to his playing in the hall that evening, Augustchen said: 'I would not have had the courage to speak to him; had I done so, I should have had to say "Your Majesty".' At the concert I said nothing to him about his playing, except: 'What can one say to him who *reaches* the stars!?'—and this is true. People from Cologne were here, to ask him to play for the Cathedral. He agreed at once. On Monday he will be playing at Ems. . . .

There was another delightful surprise on Friday. Mad. Tormann arrived with about thirty young ladies, teachers, and Professor Breidenstein. They adorned the doors of Liszt's room, his mirror and piano very attractively with laurel wreaths, keeping one wreath back in readiness for him. And that is how they welcomed him. He was very pleasantly surprised, invited them and all the rest of us, including the strangers, into his room, and played three pieces in a way that astonished everyone. . . . We admired the tender, affectionate way in which she [Marie d'Agoult] spoke to the children. When she sat down her beautiful features were quite altered, the tears rolling down her cheeks. No doubt she was thinking of her own children. . . . Liszt then invited the entire gathering into the hall, played blind man's buff with the youngsters and was as merry as a child. After that, for an hour and a half he played waltzes and galops for them to dance to, not stopping until it was time to leave.

Nonnenwerth, 26 August. Liszt was expected back. We were looking forward to seeing him again and hoping he would have a lot to tell us about what he had been doing. He got here at 1.00 p.m. and soon came round cheerfully to report to us about Ems and the baths. He had heard the little Russian boy, [Anton] Rubinstein, play, and described him as truly remarkable and the greatest of all the child prodigies he had heard. . . .

Passion on both sides is so great, it is as though they were on their honeymoon, although it is not expressed in the usual way and always makes one inclined to consider it a Platonic relationship, because until midday both of them read and write; and then again they spend the evening until late in the night with lively conversation, reading and writing. She has few books. The ones I have seen are these: de luxe editions in one volume, with the most beautiful copperplate engravings, of Byron, Shakespeare, Delavigne, the Bible, and the Abbé de Genonde's Philosophy of Religion, Mysticism of Religion, Letters to the Past, as well as J. B. Wolff's Grammar of Grammars, and, in German, Heine's *Salon* of 1840. This last she gave me because it contains something about Liszt. He, Liszt, is said to have made a rejoinder to it. . . .

Liszt is winning our hearts more and more by the hour, and through nothing other than his exuberant kind-heartedness and truly childlike nature. As for his playing, I am convinced the culminating point has been reached; more is not possible.

So far as the Comtesse is concerned, on the other hand, I am frightened by so much intellect and erudition in a woman, and am becoming more and more reserved with her. I find it uncanny, and have no fear of being thought modest for saying so. What can my company give her? I am not knowledgeable enough to give her information about present-day German literature; a woman like that sees everything from a different side, has investigated, explored and exhausted everything, and falls from one theory, perhaps from one error, into another. Sometimes I wonder what sort of an end she will come to. Perhaps in a convent, either as a recluse or extravagantly. I should not like to enjoy her more than I have done already. When the talk is of paintings her judgement is great, just as it is in architecture, landscapes, books, and persons; everything small and petty is banished. Do you know how I should still like to enjoy her? Sitting quietly in a corner when she talks with Liszt about music, with Thorvaldsen about sculpture, with Cornelius about painting; in short, when she talks with great men about great things.[5]

In late August and September Liszt gave several concerts at Frankfurt, including one on 25 September whose entire proceeds he presented to the Mozart Foundation.

On Saturday the 18th he had been admitted into the Union Lodge of the Frankfurt Freemasons. Like all other candidates he was obliged first to enter a preparation room, where the curtains were drawn and illumination provided by a single lamp. On a table, among a Bible and various other items, lay a sheet of paper containing the three questions posed to candidates:

1. What is man's vocation?
2. What do you expect from Freemasonry for your mind, your heart and your temporal happiness?
3. What may Freemasonry expect from you?

Liszt's answers to these questions were:

1. Man's vocation is to strive as far as possible for perfection in Truth, Goodness and Beauty, and thus—so far as his feeble limitations allow—to draw near his Creator by growing to resemble Him.
2. I believe and hope I shall be joining a society of good and upright men who are united in working for wise and long-range goals; I believe and hope that my mind will find nourishment therein, and that in time of need or peril fraternal hands will be held out to me.
3. Your order will always find me ready in word and deed to take part in all its worthy aims and to be associated with all its venerable works.

   In all those matters which do not run counter to my religious and political views, my honour and my conscience, your order, in whose profound wisdom I respectfully believe, will find in me a docile neophyte and an obedient member.

Liszt seems, however, never to have taken further part in the proceedings of the Frankfurt Freemasons—and his name was erased from their register in May 1874 after he had failed to respond to communications. He also became an honorary member of lodges in Berlin, Solingen, Iserlohn, and Zurich, took part in the works of three other ateliers (one at Reims and two at Cologne) and met members of the clandestine Russian freemasonry.*

Marie von Czettritz. Nonnenwerth, 21 September. Many have liked Thalberg better than Liszt. This I can understand: the difference between them is that between genius and talent, and it is talent which is the more easily understood, especially on the Rhine.

30 September. Talking about the little Rubinstein, Liszt said: 'De tous les enfants il est le plus grand.' In Bonn they told us he was just as good as Liszt and Thalberg, and played all their pieces; but Simrock told us it was true that when Rubinstein heard Liszt he wept and said sadly: '*I can't do that!*'

Marie von Czettritz, 24 October. Their relationship has now lasted nine years, hallowed by an inexpressible mutual love and respect, indestructible in either this world or the next. She is his *first* and only love. Earlier, he said, *only* God was in his heart (for he was and is very devout). She came after God. . . . He can write and compose only when she is there. He sits beside her and sings or plays to her what he has just written. When he is away on his travels and asks her to work hard, she sits writing until about one o'clock in the morning. She has written a novel here and also a description of Nonnenwerth and the Rhine; of this latter work she read us several pages: glorious and sublime!

Marie von Czettritz, 1 November. We spoke to a lady who had heard Thalberg at the Court of Dresden. When the Queen told him he was the greatest, he replied: 'Your Majesty has not yet heard Liszt.' Fräulein Haak, too, said that Thalberg had told her that he could not be compared with Liszt.[6]

In early November Liszt and Marie took their leave of one another, she to return to Paris, he to resume his life as a touring virtuoso. His first concerts were at Düsseldorf, Elberfeld, Krefeld, Wesel (7 November, on behalf of the poor), Münster (9th and 11th—'an unheard-of crowd, to the point that the entire stage and wings were used for the audience'), Osnabrück (12th), and Bielefeld (13th). During this time he transcribed for piano solo the Funeral March from the Eroica Symphony,† for a publication in aid of the Beethoven Monument.

Then followed Detmold, Gotha, and Kassel (two 'superb' concerts and a first

* The most informative publication on Liszt and Freemasonry is Philippe A. Autexier's *Mozart & Liszt sub Rosa* (Poitiers, 1984), source of the information presented here.

† As has been noted, Liszt transcribed Beethoven's 5th, 6th, and 7th symphonies in 1837. This single movement now followed, and the remaining symphonies were completed, and the earlier transcriptions revised, in 1863–4. The full series was first published in 1865, with a dedication to Hans von Bülow. The 9th was also transcribed (S657) for two pianos, *c.*1850.

meeting with Spohr, who at the second concert, on 21 November, encircled Liszt's head and shoulders with a laurel wreath amidst the cheers of the audience).

On the 24th he played at Göttingen,* where he was joined by Lichnowsky, who then accompanied him to Weimar, Jena, Leipzig, and Dresden.

To the Göttingen concert came young *Kurd von Schlözer* (1822–94).

On Wednesday Liszt played here. I can imagine nothing more perfect! Several things left me cold; several delighted me to an extreme. His Fantasy on *Don Giovanni* was ravishingly beautiful. 'Là ci darem la mano' he rendered in a way that I shall never forget, and then came the stone guest's trombone solo, the heavenly finale and, at the end, the champagne aria! He played it with such bravura, and at so hurtling a tempo, that one could hardly breathe. And with it all you had to *see* him at the piano! Everything he did on the keys was mirrored in his features, flashed in his eyes and electrified all his movements—especially in the duet between the Don and Zerlina, in which at one moment he looked timid and the next leapt from his very seat into the air for joy. It was divine! Afterwards I was sitting with fellow students in the Stadt London Hotel where he was staying, when the landlord came and told us that this great artist, who had just bewitched a huge throng of people, was eating his dinner completely alone in his room. On hearing this, all fifteen of us, carrying burning candles and full champagne glasses, went upstairs to the *Meister* and drank a toast to him. He was quite moved. 'Ah! c'est bien aimable, je suis enchanté!' he exclaimed over and over again, shaking each of us by the hand, clinking glasses, and apologizing only for being unable to come down to us: his carriage was already loaded and waiting to bear the lonely man away to further triumphs.[7]

Thursday, 25 November was the day on which Liszt first set foot in Weimar. Capital of the Grand Duchy of Saxe-Weimar-Eisenach, its golden age had been in the late eighteenth and early nineteenth centuries, when such giants as Goethe, Schiller, Wieland, and Herder had lived and worked in the little town. The reigning Grand Duke was Carl Friedrich (1783–1853). Son of the Grand Duke Carl August who had been the friend and patron of the illustrious men of letters, he was a simple man of slow intelligence, outshone by his gifted art-loving Russian wife Maria Pavlovna (1786–1859), granddaughter of Catherine the Great, daughter of the assassinated Tsar Paul, and sister of Tsar Alexander I and of the reigning Tsar Nicholas I.

One of the first in Weimar to make Liszt's acquaintance was the actor and stage manager *Eduard Genast* (1797–1866), then working at the Court Theatre.

One dark evening . . . I was sitting cosily in the dining-room of the Russischer Hof Hotel with that artistic couple Clara and Robert Schu-

* One wonders if Liszt was aware that an appreciative member of his audience here was one of the world's supreme geniuses, the virtual peer of Archimedes and Newton: Carl Friedrich Gauss.

mann,* when a tall slim man with expressive features and long smoothed-back, light-brown hair entered and walked over to my companions, calling out 'Bon soir, Ihr Lieben' as he did so. 'Liszt!' they cried with one voice. So there in person before me was the man whose acquaintance I had so long desired, about whom rumour had for years been spreading abroad the most extraordinary and astonishing things, extolling his enormous virtuosity, his modesty and kindness, and also his magnificent generosity. After Frau Schumann had introduced me to him, he sat next to her and, without taking special notice of my presence, eagerly engaged her in conversation. As they chatted together, my attention was riveted more and more by the sheer genius of the man, so that in the end I had eyes and ears for him alone. Of his generosity, too, I was to be a witness that very evening. Frau Schumann had but to express admiration of the tasteful and expensive tie-pin he was wearing, a globe of blue enamel spangled with stars and attached by a gold eagle's claw, for Liszt with elegant courtesy to present it to her there and then as a keepsake. . . .

Before we took our leave of one another that evening we had become rather better acquainted, and the next morning I went round to see him. During our fairly long talk, the friendly courtesy with which he had received me gradually changed to warmth, doubtless because he recognized in me someone who shared his own glowing enthusiasm for art, and who in everything connected with it expressed his feelings as uninhibitedly as he did himself. That brought us closer together, and later in the day he returned my visit, which gave me the opportunity to introduce my family to him. That was the beginning of our later friendship. . . .

It was to Maria Pavlovna, who as a pupil of Hummel was herself an excellent pianist, able not only to compose but also to read and transpose a score like a Kapellmeister, that the public owed the great treat of a Liszt concert. It took place at the Theatre on the 26th.† Every seat was taken and the artist was rewarded by a tremendous ovation. Here, too, his princely generosity was shown: the next day he sent the substantial proceeds of 600 thalers to the Frauenverein, a charitable institution founded by Maria Pavlovna. In recognition of his outstanding musical achievements, he was presented by the Grand Duke with the Order of the Falcon. I was present when he received this distinction, the first of a long series, and witnessed the keen joy it gave him, which he made no attempt to conceal—unlike many others in a similar situation who have feigned

* Since their last meeting with Liszt, Robert Schumann and Clara Wieck had married. They had come to Weimar for a charity concert at which Clara had played some solos and Schumann's 1st Symphony had been performed.

† Genast is here in error. It was to Maria Pavlovna's private circle at court that Liszt played on the 26th. On the 28th he performed at a court concert. The public concert, with vocal and orchestral items, was on the 29th. At this last event Liszt played the Fantasy on *Don Giovanni,* the *Hexameron,* Weber's *Invitation to the Dance, Erlkönig,* and the *Grand galop chromatique.*

indifference. Once when I congratulated a man who had been honoured by his prince with the 'Golden Bird', he replied: 'I prefer them roasted!'—which was not merely a cheap joke but also an untruth. . . .

During Liszt's stay I gave a big evening party in his honour, at which Frau von Heygendorf (formerly Jagemann*) was a guest. Liszt had heard a great deal about this brilliant woman and wished to meet her. Charming though he was to all the other ladies, he made a point of singling out Frau von Heygendorf and spending almost the entire evening in the place beside her. Finally he asked her to sing something to him. 'Provided you don't just want to laugh at an old sexagenarian!' she replied good-humouredly. Actually, her great blue eyes and noble features still retained much beauty! To Liszt's accompaniment she sang an Italian aria; and although the youthful freshness of her voice had gone, her singing showed the excellence of the school in which she had been trained. After the song had ended to loud applause, Liszt was about to leave the piano, but this she would not allow him, saying: 'No, dear Sir! You shan't escape so easily! I have granted your request; now you grant mine and give us *Erlkönig* at your best!' To immense applause he took his seat at the instrument again and complied with her request, one which was seconded by all present.[8]

From the diary of Robert Schumann. Thursday, 25 November. Liszt arrived —great joy. We bumped into him in our hotel; the champagne flowed in streams. He was very kind and cordial. For his sake we stayed in Weimar on Friday as well.

Liszt played a few things too. He can be recognized through closed doors. Judgement on him remains unshaken. We took lunch together.

The evening was one of the most ridiculous and boring. Liszt was invited to court, but also wanted to come to Lobe's, who had invited a considerable number of people. Awaiting Liszt they now agonized for four long hours. Finally he turned up—at half past eleven. It was still night-time when we returned to Leipzig. Liszt had promised to play at our concert, and he kept his word, having always proved himself in every way a good friend to us.[9]

From the diary of Clara Schumann. Leipzig, 1 December. Liszt came from Weimar, and in the afternoon we rehearsed the *Hexameron*† together. It is an extremely brilliant piece—probably nothing exceeds it. We were delighted to see Liszt within our walls once again, and to be able to enjoy his presence here as a married couple (last time we were still only engaged).

2 December. We gave a dinner in his honour—my first great début as a housewife. Among others the Freges, the Härtels, and the Davids came.

* An actress at the Weimar Theatre, Caroline Jagemann had borne a son to the Grand Duke Carl August, who had then elevated her to the name and title of von Heygendorf.

† The 2-piano arrangement.

Liszt brought everything to life by his clever conversation and charm. He also played—only a trifle, but enough to reveal the master on the piano, his command of it being quite without equal.

Sunday, 5 December. Liszt came back from Dresden,* to play the duo with me on the 6th. How the audience reacted to his kindness to us can be imagined. It caused a *furore*, and we had to repeat part of it. I was not content, even very unhappy this evening and the following days, because Robert was not satisfied with my playing; and I also felt vexed that Robert's symphonies were not particularly well played. This evening there were several little incidents—the carriage, the music left behind, a wobbly chair when playing, nervousness in front of Liszt, and so on. There was too much that was good—Liszt, an immensely large audience (900)—for something unpleasant not to have disturbed my enjoyment.

In the interval Liszt was so attentive as to bring me a bouquet, which the audience received very warmly.

We showed Liszt our pleasure at his kindness towards us with a present, a beautiful silver cup inscribed with both our names which he found on returning from Dresden again for his own concert, into giving which he finally let himself be persuaded.

After the concert Liszt gave an exquisite and delicious supper, starting with oysters and trout. But we were both tired and soon left. The others may well have continued for a long time—the next morning we found Liszt in bed, where he stayed the whole day until Wednesday the 8th, when he returned to Dresden again.

Clara Schumann, Sunday, 12 December. David gave a dinner for Liszt, to which we too were invited. After we had eaten he tried out Hummel's Septet, which he plays extraordinarily, although here and there one could perhaps have wished a passage played differently. Yet what artist in the world could do everything right! . . . He utterly amazed me in his concert on the 13th, especially in the Fantasy on *Don Giovanni*, which he played captivatingly. His performance of the champagne aria I shall never forget: the boisterousness and desire with which he played were unique! You could see the Don in front of the popping champagne corks in all his exuberance, just as Mozart must have imagined him.

Clara Schumann, 16 December. Liszt played for the last time: Beethoven's E flat Concerto in masterly fashion, but then Robert's Fantasy dreadfully crudely, and after it the *Galop*. He seemed tired, which with his way of life . . . is not to be wondered at.

N.B. We played the *Hexameron* at the Liszt concert once again, with the same *furore* as the first time.[10]

* Liszt's Dresden concerts were on 4, 9, and 11 Dec.; those in Leipzig on the 13th and 16th, plus an appearance at Clara's concert on the 6th.

Liszt to Marie d'Agoult. Leipzig, 17 December. I am living very quietly, resigned to my arduous labour and without outer ambition. You may perhaps remember that I said one day to Felix (and have since repeated on other occasions): 'Put the Golden Fleece on one side of a table and the Pastoral Symphony on the other, and allow me the choice between carrying off the former or writing the latter—and I shall not hesitate for a single moment.'[11]

Clara Schumann. On the 17th we gave a small soirée. Liszt came—as always, very late! He seems to love making people wait for him, which displeases me. I find him just like a spoilt child, good-natured, masterful, kind, arrogant, noble, and generous, often severe towards others—a strange mixture. We have become very fond of him, however, and towards us he has never behaved in any but the friendliest way.[12]

On 18 December Liszt gave a concert at Halle. A few days later he arrived in Berlin, where his ten-week sojourn constituted one of the most spectacular triumphs of his career. Among the first calls he paid were those to Mendelssohn, Meyerbeer, and Spontini; and on the 23rd he was gratified to receive a visit from the world-famous Alexander von Humboldt.*

His first concert was on Monday, 27 December. 'Unprecedented success,' he reported to Marie. 'More than 800 people; that is, a full house. I played entirely alone. The King† did me the honour of coming, and applauded greatly. In doing so, he made a great exception for me, as court mourning is very strict. I am probably indebted for it to Humboldt.'

From the diary of the writer and diplomat K. A. Varnhagen von Ense (1785–1858), 27 December. In the evening, in the hall of the Singakademie, Liszt's concert, without orchestra. He played quite alone, marvellously, matchlessly, magically, earning himself universal and tempestuous applause. Not since Paganini have I heard such a master. The best things were the Overture to *William Tell*, a Fantasy on themes from *Robert le Diable,* and Schubert's *Erlkönig*. Our places were quite near the front, and we had a very good view of this brilliant, clever, handsome man. His last piece was a *Grand galop chromatique,* which I couldn't take: he had control of my pulse, and his playing accelerated it so much that I became giddy. The King was in his box; present too were the Count of Nassau,

* The younger of the two brilliant Humboldt brothers, and perhaps the last of the universal minds of history, Alexander von Humboldt (1769–1859) contributed, often very much, to a small galaxy of scientific fields, including geology, geography, vulcanology, seismology, meteorology, mineralogy, oceanography, climatology, mining, magnetism, botany, bryology, physiology, and zoology. In June 1802, during a scientific exploration of South America, he had climbed, almost to the top, Mount Chimborazo, which was then, at well over 20,000 feet, believed to be the world's highest mountain—an outstanding physical act which took him to the greatest altitude ever achieved by a human being up to that time. Among his literary achievements, pre-eminent is *Cosmos,* a vast and comprehensive survey of natural phenomena.

† Frederick William IV (1795–1861), King of Prussia from 1840.

Prince and Princess Karl, Prince August, and the Crown Prince of Württemberg. As well as Meyerbeer, Felix Mendelssohn, Spontini, Rellstab, and a whole crowd of other acquaintances.[13]

The last of the persons named by Varnhagen was Ludwig Rellstab (1799–1860). A poet whose verses were set to music by both Schubert and Liszt,* amongst others, and a writer of short stories, novels, opera libretti, and miscellaneous articles whose complete works fill twenty-four volumes, his talents as a reviewer have also caused him to be dubbed 'the first great music critic'. At Dresden he had made friends with Weber, at Weimar been the guest of Goethe (on the very day that the twelve-year-old Mendelssohn played to the venerable Olympian), and in Vienna thrice visited Beethoven, upon whose Piano Sonata in C sharp minor he had bestowed the nickname *Moonlight.* Less happily, he had also long been a savage critic of the works of Chopin (whom, nevertheless, he waited upon in Paris in 1843 furnished with a tactfully phrased letter of introduction from Liszt—history does not relate how he was received).

Rellstab writing in the Vossische Zeitung. People have exhausted themselves in witty, partly poetic, comparisons between Liszt and Thalberg; the latter has been called *l'ange du piano,* the former *le diable du piano*, and thus they have been classified and opposed. Yet in our opinion these comparisons are not formulated from the right point of view. Liszt contains Thalberg fully within himself. If he does not give what the latter gives, he could do so. *Any* task that Thalberg can solve, he could at once solve too—but the reverse is not the case. Thalberg's art lies in a harmoniously cultivated and very beautiful *material* skill; never does it fail to display regularity, composure, repose, grace, and strength. Yet that charm which passes to the physical state from a higher, psychic one he possesses in such small measure, or Liszt so much *more*, that in comparison with the former's we could call the latter's an inspired art. Nor does he lack *repose.* Thalberg's consists in being undisturbed by any inner drive or turmoil; it is a more negative thing. Liszt's repose is that of the most complete *mastery* of all stirring forces of passion, the *positive* aspect of superior power. Thalberg is master of a tranquil steed, Liszt of a fiery one; indeed, a winged one, whose wild frenzy he can either compel to the most docile obedience or let go at full rein. His art is a poetic one, belonging to higher, spiritual elements, and accordingly we too consider ourselves justified in attempting to *describe* it poetically rather than analyse it critically. . . .

Liszt is the first virtuoso to give concerts without assistance; he played *seven* pieces on the piano entirely *alone*. Yet the hall was filled to the last place. The capital's most cultured and most brilliant society was present, grouped around the two instruments placed at the foot of the amphitheatrical orchestral pit: an English piano (owned by a famous composer†

* The songs *Es rauschen die Winde* (S294), *Wo weilt er?* (S295), and *Ihr Auge* ('Nimm einen Strahl der Sonne') (S310), were all inspired by poems of Rellstab's.

† Mendelssohn.

resident in Berlin, himself a great pianist) and one made, as we hear, in Cologne. This latter instrument, however, struck me as too sharp in tone and little suited to cantabile playing.

The writer of this review had no very favourable place: he sat too close to the piano, in the danger zone as it were, so that for him the actual tonal impression, which appreciably increases in beauty at a certain distance, was for the most part lost. He therefore candidly confesses that in the first three pieces he had to comprehend the artist more through the intellect than through direct sensation. These works, too, were the least attractive; not the player's spiritual power but only his astonishing dexterity, relentless and unfaltering strength, combined with spring-like, elastic touch and the gentle murmuring of the music, were in evidence. The fourth piece, Beethoven's *Adelaide,* was in our opinion the weakest; indeed, the effect it created was to some extent an unpleasant one. This lay as much in the transcription itself, which has not always turned out happily, as in the melodic interpretation. The player was here making a sacrifice to the times in which we live, in which appreciation of a thing of simple beauty is more and more lost in over-excitement and over-abundance; blame should therefore be attached more to *them* than to *him*, although we believe that in this connection *he* is the man to *dominate* rather than obey the times. From Bach's Chromatic Fantasy onwards, the effect, the spiritually captivating element, increased at every moment. For the performance of this work the second instrument was more favourable. In the fanciful Introduction, the most fiery inspiration, a truly tempestuous rapidity in the passage-work, was combined with the most perfect lucidity, and in the Fugue the afore-mentioned all-governing repose played its part in the shaping of the most magnificent *style.* Each voice came out with the utmost independence, the theme always being dominant, however, even in the middle register.

To a quite different sphere, increasing the *sensual* excitement still further, belonged his playing of Schubert's *Erlkönig,* a work widely known and heard, and yet now heard *for the first time*, truly electrifying the audience, which caused it to be encored more by their ever-renewed applause than by express demand. This was a request which we, despite the marvels of elastic energy the artist had already shown us, would scarcely have dared believe his strength equal to; but to which he responded as though effortlessly, since he even slightly increased the tempo. In this piece his playing also revealed romantic charms of the most characteristic and irresistibly enchanting kind. . . .

With these seven pieces the artist has confirmed *seven times over* that, with Paganini's magic lying spellbound in his Merlin's grave, he is the greatest virtuoso of our time. He has indeed performed before us not twelve labours of Hercules but *seven*, and given us the certainty that seven times seven would be easy for him. Let us hope then that he will perform them for us![14]

'Rellstab was to have been my adversary,' Liszt wrote to Marie. 'He is the critic *par excellence* in Berlin. I refused to pay him the first visit. After my first concert he came to see me, and, although of differing opinions on several points, we can understand one another.'

1842

Liszt's second Berlin concert was given on New Year's Day, and thereafter he gave another nineteen, making twenty-one in all (apart from numerous performances in private residences). His first ten appearances were at the Singakademie, after which, for its greater audience capacity, he transferred to the Royal Opera House. He also played at the Potsdam Casino, twice at the University Hall, and several times at the Hôtel de Russie (in which he stayed).

By assiduous analysis of press reports and reviews, Lina Ramann calculated that Liszt played eighty different works at these concerts, some fifty of them from memory. Her catalogue includes works by Bach (Chromatic Fantasy and Fugue, C sharp minor Prelude and Fugue from *The Well-Tempered Clavier,* two organ Preludes and Fugues); Beethoven (five sonatas, including the *Appassionata* and *Hammerklavier,* as well as the C minor and E flat concertos); Chopin (études, mazurkas, waltzes); Handel (Fugue in E minor, Theme and Variations from the Suite in D minor); Hummel; Mendelssohn (Capriccio in F sharp minor); Moscheles; Scarlatti (various sonatas, including the Cat's Fugue); and Weber (*Momento capriccioso, Concertstück,* Sonata in A flat, *Invitation to the Dance*); plus numerous operatic fantasies, transcriptions of works by Beethoven, Paganini, Rossini, and Schubert, the *Hexameron*, and sundry original works of Liszt's own.

The writer and actor-manager Eduard Devrient (1801–77), 3 January. Went at eight to Rellstab's. . . . We had already been sitting a long time at table when Liszt appeared. A slender, rather narrow-chested figure, tightly buttoned into his black dress-coat; a pale, oval face with large features but a fine ever-changing expression; and long, smooth hair, which gives his head atop his slim figure a rather gnome-like lack of proportion. A tinny, rather blaring voice, which often leaps into falsetto when he is talking loudly, but which is soft and delicate in conversation. He spoke a great deal, in a lively, friendly, courteous manner; and when German was insufficient for him he helped himself out with French phrases. He does not express himself quite fluently, stopping and mumbling when talking; but in the end he conveyed his meaning very precisely, and his thoughts are worth hearing. He is interested in philosophy, clearly revealing himself to be a man of culture, but one which has taken its own special direction. After we had eaten he offered to play, but it didn't come off on the bad piano—which he wrecked in his second piece. This playing rounded off my view of the whole man. He is by no means the charlatan he is reputed to be, although a certain charlatanry has become his truest nature. His strangely volatile quality, the engagingly attractive going hand in hand with the demoniacally dreadful, the power exercised over one by this fully formed individuality, despite all that one knows and feels to the contrary, his unquestioned supremacy on his instrument—it all adds up to a unique phenomenon. . . . His playing entirely surpasses everything we have yet known.[1]

Liszt to Marie d'Agoult. Berlin, 6 January. Impossible to write, especially to you. You can have no idea of my life. . . . At certain moments I feel as though my head and heart were bursting. . . . I am ill from concerts and successes. Berlin outdoes even Vienna. Meyerbeer doesn't cease telling me that my triumphs in Paris and Vienna are nothing in comparison.[2]

The fourth concert, on 9 January at the Potsdam Casino, contained a surprise item: a piano quartet by the much-loved and highly musical Prince Louis Ferdinand of Prussia (b. 1772), who had fallen at Saalfeld in 1806. The royal family, and indeed the entire audience, were moved by the work and greatly appreciative of Liszt's gesture in performing it.

Liszt to Marie d'Agoult, 11 January. People want to hear me as much as possible, and to hear no one but me. At my third concert there were two vocal items on the programme. People complained, and many had their tickets retained for the next concert, at which I was to play alone.

As a success, and a satisfaction to one's *amour-propre,* it is splendid — but horribly tiring. My friends say I have become embittered, and I have a fever almost every day. I am longing to finish with this trade.

The King has come to three of my concerts, something very rare. I was presented to him at a soirée at Count Redern's. . . . So far as artists were concerned, the King spoke to me alone that evening. Hauman,* who also played, was furious. And that is the case with several of the artists here, my old friend Felix Mendelssohn not excepted, although our relations are still on a very good footing.† What to do? There are many people who will never understand me, and who will spend their lives envying me for what I would gladly make them a present of.[3]

To the same, 25 January. You have guessed correctly: I am horribly nervy, sick, exhausted. Four days ago I fell backwards, was delirious for more

* The Belgian violinist Théodore Hauman.

† They were not to remain so. Mendelssohn had removed to Berlin from Leipzig the previous year, having been appointed Kapellmeister to the King. But he was not happy in Berlin, where he felt that his plans for the musical life of the city were being hampered by intrigue and ignorance. In such circumstances he may have allowed the overwhelming enthusiasm for Liszt to embitter him. Be the reason what it may, when the two musicians happened to run into one another in the street, Mendelssohn returned Liszt's friendly greeting with a remark intended to offend—whereupon Liszt turned and walked away. When, years later, Lina Ramann asked him if he had seen Mendelssohn again, Liszt replied: 'Oh yes—several times! But I no longer spoke to him.'

than two hours and, at the present moment, have retired to another room in the hotel, leaving my apartment to Belloni* and Lefèvre and requesting my friends not to visit me for at least four days. I feel an overwhelming need for rest.

Eight consecutive concerts, four matinées at the home of the Princess of Prussia, at which I alone, absolutely and exclusively alone, did the honours, playing seven or eight pieces each time.

Dinners, soirées, balls, smoking-parties, non-stop conversations, proof-correcting, writing, and scoring; it all provides a physical explanation of my physical state. . . .

Every day I get up at about nine. Between then and two o'clock, about fifty people come and go in my room. The other day, Schober told me that when he happened to take a stroll along the Unter den Linden just after leaving me, it seemed almost deserted in comparison. What do all these people want of me? Most of them—money. A few (especially the young ones) come merely to see me seated or standing; others to be able to say that they have seen me and that they visit me; yet others (above all the scoundrels) to write about it in the newspapers. While chatting and smoking, I dictate (for writing tires me dreadfully) to Lefèvre, Schober, and Villers the indispensable replies to the hundreds of letters I am receiving, arrange my programmes, put my manuscripts in order and, now and then when an idea comes to me, jot down some music. In this past fortnight I have written two new songs,† one for myself and the other for you, dear Marie.[4]

'I see two women here fairly often, Bettina von Arnim and Charlotte [von] Hagn,' Liszt remarked in a long continuation of the foregoing letter, written a day later. 'The former became the exalted servant of genius: she is a sprite of magnetic intelligence. The latter has been the favourite odalisque of two kings; in talent she seems to be the Mlle Mars of Germany. I shall send you Bettina's two books, *Briefwechsel mit Goethe* and *Günderode,* which are most remarkable. They will interest you all the more because of the lines, or rather the pages, she has added to them for me.'

On meeting, he and the celebrated Bettina (1785–1859), widow of Ludwig Achim von Arnim and sister of Clemens Brentano, but best remembered for her friendships with Goethe and Beethoven, had at once enchanted one another. But if Marie felt no pangs when reading her lover's reference to a woman who, though fascinating, was now approaching sixty, she was, with reason, far less understanding so far as the beautiful Charlotte von Hagn (1809–91), one of the most admired actresses in Germany, was concerned; and even a year later Liszt was having to write defensively about a relationship in which he was perhaps more quarry than hunter.

* From Feb. 1841 until his career as a professional pianist came to an end in 1847, Liszt employed Gaetano Belloni as his secretary and concert manager.

† *Titan* (S79), for baritone solo, male chorus, and piano, to words by Schober; and *Oh! quand je dors* (S282), a setting of words by Victor Hugo.

Although, after this brief fling in Berlin, he and la Hagn met only rarely, they from time to time exchanged letters. Writing banteringly in April 1849, when recommending a young singer who sought his protection ('Poor girl! She doesn't know what danger she is running!'), Charlotte made ample amends a few weeks later: 'Years have passed since I found and lost you, but I must admit that because of you I have been spoilt for all other men; for none, *not a single one,* can bear the least comparison. You are and remain *unique.*'

Varnhagen von Ense, 27 January. Liszt continues to be the delight of the city. He is the glory of the winter here, and its brightest splendour. His unselfishness, his cheerful good-breeding, his benevolent, charming personality earn him applause no less than does his all-conquering mastery. His concert in the great hall of the University,* for the students alone and at an admission fee of only ten silver groschen, the proceeds going to his native village in Hungary, won him the hearts of more than just the youngsters.[5]

Liszt to Marie d'Agoult. Berlin, 15 February.† The eagerness, I could almost say the mania, of the public continues to increase. For tomorrow, my twelfth or thirteenth concert (including those I have given for charity), there have been no tickets left since midday yesterday. . . .

At the last of my concerts at the Singakademie, on going to the piano I found a laurel wreath. As it happened, on the music rack there was a volume of Beethoven sonatas. Taking the wreath, I placed it around the volume. . . .

The Princess of Prussia has sent me the works of Prince Louis Ferdinand of Prussia and the autograph score of a flute concerto by Frederick the Great, the whole thing magnificently bound and enclosed in a very beautiful box in velvet with his arms.‡

The Prince of Prussia sent me a beautiful walking-stick studded with diamonds.

Forgive me these details. You know that they interest me only as much (and all the more) as they can interest you.

I am so happy that you finally believe in my profound love.[6]

In review after review of these concerts, *Rellstab's* enthusiasm remained undiminished. Conversing with Liszt in private he also made a point of ascertaining his musical and literary tastes.

* On 25 Jan. Present was the great Swiss historian Jacob Burckhardt (1818–97), then a student in Berlin. 'I generally regard *virtuosi* as the corrupters of art,' he wrote home. 'But for once it really was something quite out of the ordinary, and it would be impossible to form any idea of it without hearing him. The Parisians are, in fact, not far wrong in picturing Liszt with twenty fingers.'

† In his edition of Liszt's correspondence with Marie d'Agoult, Daniel Ollivier erroneously assigned this letter to Feb. 1843.

‡ Liszt expressed his gratitude for these gifts with his dedication to the Princess of his Elegy (S168) on themes of Prince Louis Ferdinand.

We do not wish to speak here of the immortal geniuses placed by the world's recognition at the summit of Art—although it is significant that he seems to accord Beethoven the highest place among them—but rather to turn to those with whom he has lived, striven, and developed. In piano virtuosity he reveres Chopin, esteems Moscheles, and gives all the rest their due, despite the aversion he feels towards mechanical perfection unaccompanied by spiritual and intellectual insight. His love of Schubert we have already noted; but it is Berlioz in Paris with whom he feels the closest affinity. The lighter, newer French music of Auber, Adam, and Halévy attracts him very little; and it is his opinion that with Boïeldieu the comic opera has played itself out.

It is not difficult to understand how the artist's feelings must react similarly to and against painting, literature (especially of the religio-philosophical kind), and creative writing. Few can be acquainted with French *belles-lettres* so comprehensively as he; the new Romantic movement, Victor Hugo in particular, has profoundly stimulated him. German literature he knows less well: only a few things by Lessing, Goethe's *Faust,* and some of the newer things which have caused a stir among us too; but these could more easily mislead than instruct him about what is true and genuine in German culture. The closest affinity, however, he feels with Lord Byron, who, according to his own admission, is both the poet of his choice and the one to whom he has most devoted himself. So far as his intellectual development is concerned, the choice is crucial.[7]

On 18 February Liszt was elected a member of the Royal Prussian Academy of Arts.

On 2 March, the day before his departure, he gave his farewell concert at the Opera House, playing Beethoven's C minor Concerto and several solos.

Marie von Czettritz. But something happened which was bound to distress his friends profoundly. In the interval the Court Marshal, Herr von Meyerinck, brought him a diamond ring from the King to which by an oversight (although no one will now admit it) the jeweller's ticket showing the price, 620 thalers, was still attached. Liszt had hardly set eyes on it when he flew into such a fury that in full view of all the theatre people and of Meyerinck he threw the ring to the ground and trod on it, raging and storming. Whether the cause was the ticket or the ring itself—he is said to have been expecting a medal—we don't know.* In this fit of rage he ran to Meyerbeer in one of the boxes, railing in several languages at once in a manner that nothing could appease. The next morning his hand was cut and swollen, because back at his hotel he had smashed a windowpane in his fury!!! With all our love for him, can we justify this behaviour? Whether the King learnt what had happened, I do not know; but the Prince and

* Referring to this incident in a letter to Marie, Liszt wrote of 'the way in which HM sent me *une petite cochonnerie de bague*' (a beastly little ring).

Princess of Prussia heard about it the next day and were both extremely angry.[8]

Eduard Devrient. It was rather unsubtle, but it is good that it happened. In Liszt is seen the complete mastery of an artist over all relationships.[9]

Before leaving the city on Thursday, 3 March, Liszt gave a charity concert at the Hôtel de Russie, after which the students and people of Berlin gave him a memorable farewell. 'More than 50,000 people were on the move to say or shout a final godspeed,' he told Marie.

Ludwig Rellstab. From eleven o'clock onwards spectators began to gather in front of the hotel. . . . The moment of departure came. A carriage drawn by six white horses rolled to the front of the hotel; and amidst the cheers of the crowd Liszt was all but carried down the steps and lifted to his seat among the seniors of the University. Thirty four-horse carriages with students, and a number of riders in academic festival dress, formed his retinue, which was joined by countless other carriages, all of them surrounded by a multitude of many thousands. The procession first made its way to the Unter den Linden, turned into the square for which the monument to Frederick the Great is designated, and then headed for the new Schlossbrücke . . . and along the Königstrasse to the Frankfurt Gate. Not only the streets and squares, but the windows of all the houses too, were filled with onlookers of both sexes; among them many of the uncommonly great number of the artist's personal friends and acquaintances, who exchanged waves and farewell salutations with him. . . .

The Schloss had been made available with the most commendable promptitude by its hospitable owner, Herr von Treskow, and it was he who most kindly and courteously welcomed this great influx of visitors. Together with the students, Liszt at once went to the spacious room on the upper floor, where in the background musicians had taken their places. As soon as the assembly was complete, the Hungarian National March rang out. . . . His emotion long preventing him from speaking, Liszt at last managed to express in the simplest words his gratitude for '*a joy, an honour, such as had never previously befallen him*'—except in his own country, during an evening in Pest which he would remember everlastingly. Whereupon he shook hands heartily with all who could reach him. . . .

Surrounded by the jubilating throng, he left us not *like* a king but *as* a king, *a king in the imperishable kingdom of the intellect.*[10]

Eduard Devrient. His triumphal procession through the streets reduces to naught a multitude of conventional triumphs, and shows that the time is ripening for a recognition of the significance of mental and intellectual abilities.[11]

Via Marienburg (Prussia, now Malbork in Poland), where he visited the mighty castle of the Teutonic Knights, and Elbing (now Elblag), Liszt arrived at Königsberg (now Kaliningrad, USSR), the ancient coronation city of the kings of Prussia. Here he gave two concerts, of which the second, for the students, was held in the hall of the University. And that same institution awarded him, on 14 March, the degree of Doctor of Music *honoris causa*. 'A slap in the face for the Berlin faculty, who in their wretched pride denied it him,' observed Varnhagen.

The presentation speech was made by the Professor of Mathematics, *K. G. J. Jacobi* (1804–51).

The philosophical faculty of the Albertus University has entrusted us with awarding to you the degree of a Doctor of Music. The immortal Haydn* once enjoyed this distinction, and for that reason perhaps you too will not disdain it. By the universities of Germany and England it has been conferred only rarely; but everything which can justify it comes together in your genius in the utmost perfection. Marvels of technique are for you but an element, merely an organ and medium for the expression of higher states of the soul. The true master gives us a new artistic revelation, and with it he enters the circle and community of those free spirits whose calling is to represent the age in which they live.

And so we too greet you as a true child of our time, called to express your thoughts and feelings through the tonal art. In the rows made to vibrate by your music, we shall for long believe we can hear the breathing of your spirit, just as the charming legend relates that the stone against which Amphion leant his lyre when building the walls of Thebes was still resounding centuries later.

It is for your consummate musical science, and for the admirable execution which has earned the ovations of an entire world, that the philosophical faculty has created you a doctor. But it has not forgotten your beautiful human qualities, and the generosity with which you granted this truly ennobling joy to the youngsters of our university.

Accept our gratitude for it, and for having enriched our lives. Accept in friendliness the expression of our admiration and love—and this token thereof.[12]

'With the honourable name of a *Teacher* of Music (and I refer to music in its grand, complete, and ancient signification), I am well aware that I have undertaken the duty of unceasing *learning* and untiring labour,' wrote Liszt in his formal reply (Mitau, 18 March) to the award.

The writer Fanny Lewald (1811–89). When he played in Königsberg, my native city, there could be no question, with the increased prices, of a numerous family like ours attending. And yet I did see him at that time — at a party given by a family with whom we were friendly, at which he was so good as to go uninvited to the piano to play two of his song transcriptions.

Everyone pressed about him. The ladies assailed him with both their

* On hearing this name, Liszt made a profound reverence.

admiration and all manner of questions; and to one of them, who was inquiring in undue detail about George Sand, her looks and her age, I heard him reply: 'She is young! We are all young, so long as we can please!'[13]

Mitau (present-day Jelgava) and Riga followed, and by 11 April Liszt was in the Estonian city of Dorpat (Tartu), where he gave 'two beautiful concerts in three days'.

In the evening of Saturday, 16 April (NS), he arrived in St Petersburg, taking accommodation at the Grand Hotel in Michael Square. Commanded by the Tsarina, the next day he presented himself at the Winter Palace. A court soirée was in progress—presided over by one of the most feared and formidable of human beings: Tsar Nicholas I (1796–1855), disciplinarian and despot, who ruled his huge empire (and his own family) with harsh rigidity and ruthlessness, who cared for his army and its prowess above all else, and whose awesome presence and baleful glare* had been known literally to paralyse with terror. On seeing Liszt, the autocrat accosted him: 'We are almost compatriots, Monsieur Liszt.' —'Sire?'—'You are Hungarian, are you not?'—'Yes, Your Majesty.'—'I have a regiment in Hungary.' Apostrophized thus fatuously by the military-minded Nicholas, even Liszt seems to have found no suitable rejoinder, or not one that could very well be addressed to the Ruler of All the Russias himself. When asking during the course of the evening if he might play his *Marche hongroise* for the Tsar, however, he remarked quietly to Wielhorsky:† 'Before His Majesty comes to experience the rhythm of Hungarian sabres, it may perhaps be a distraction for him to listen to their musical rhythm.'

On Wednesday, 20 April, in the great Hall of the Nobility, Liszt gave his first concert, appearing alone and playing seven pieces. The Tsarina and the entire court were present, excepting only the Tsar. Among the musical notabilities in the audience was Mikhail Glinka (1804–57).

Another person who had determined not to miss this first public performance of Liszt's in Russia was the young *Vladimir Stasov* (1824–1906), later a celebrated critic and champion of Russian national art.

Suddenly there was a kind of commotion in the crowded Hall of the Nobility. Turning to one side, we all beheld Liszt strolling through the gallery behind the columns arm in arm with Count Wielhorsky. Moving very slowly, and rolling his huge goggle-eyes as he did so, the Count was wearing a wig curled *à l'Apollo Belvedere* and an enormous white cravat. Liszt also had on a white cravat, above which he was showing off the Order

* Queen Victoria, who received Nicholas at Windsor during his state visit in 1844, afterwards wrote: 'The expression of his eyes is terrible. I have never seen anything like them.' Alexander Herzen used the same word: 'I know nothing so terrible, nothing which could so banish hope, as those colourless, cold, pewter eyes.' It was to Nicholas, rather surprisingly, that Berlioz dedicated his great *Symphonie fantastique*.

† Count Mikhail Wielhorsky (1788–1856), whom Liszt had first met in Italy, was a patron of the arts whose home was a meeting-place for many of the most eminent musicians of the time. He was himself a composer, and his song *Autrefois* was transcribed (S577) by Liszt for piano solo.

of the Golden Spur,* given him not long before by the Pope. Various other decorations hung from the lapel of his frock-coat. He was very thin and had to stoop; and though I had read a lot about his famous 'Florentine profile', which apparently made him resemble Dante, I did not find his face handsome at all.

I at once greatly disliked this mania for decorations, and later had equally little liking for the sugary, affected manner Liszt adopted towards everyone he met. Most astonishing of all, however, was his enormous mane of fair hair. No one in Russia would have dared wear his hair like that in those days; it was strictly forbidden.

The hall was immediately filled with the murmur of people making remarks and comments about Liszt. . . . Mme Palibina asked Glinka if he had heard Liszt already. Yes, came the reply, the previous evening, at Count Wielhorsky's. 'Well, then, what did you think of him?' inquired his importunate friend. To my utter astonishment and indignation, Glinka replied, without the slightest hesitation, that Liszt sometimes played superlatively, like no one else in the world, but at other times intolerably, falsifying the expression, stretching the tempi, and adding to the works of others, even those of Chopin, Beethoven, Weber, and Bach, a multitude of embellishments of his own that were often quite unsuitable, tasteless, and frivolous. I was absolutely scandalized. What! How dare some 'second-rate' Russian musician, who had as yet achieved nothing in particular himself, talk like this about the great genius Liszt, over whom all Europe had gone mad. It vexed me beyond words. Mme Palibina, too, seemed not entirely to share Glinka's opinion, for she laughed and said, 'Allons donc, allons donc, tout cela ce n'est que rivalité de métier!' Glinka laughed likewise, and said with a shrug, 'As you please!'

But at that moment Liszt, noting the time, descended from the gallery, squeezed through the crowd, and walked quickly towards the stage. Instead of climbing the steps, however, he gave a sideways leap straight on to the platform. Then, after tearing off his white kidskin gloves and tossing them on to the floor beneath the piano, and bowing low in all directions to such a thunder of applause as had surely not been heard in Petersburg since 1703,† he took his seat at the instrument. Throughout the hall there instantly reigned a silence as of death. Without any preluding on the keys, Liszt began the opening cello phrase of the *William Tell* overture. As soon as the piece was finished, and while the tumultuous applause was making the very hall shake, he quickly walked over to a second piano which had been placed the other way about. For each different piece he changed pianos in this same fashion, now facing one half of the hall, now the other.

* Stasov is here in error. Unlike Orlandus Lassus, Gluck, Dittersdorf, and Mozart, amongst others, Liszt was never made a Knight of the Golden Spur. (In 1859 Pope Pius IX conferred on him the Order of St Gregory the Great.)

† The year of the founding of the city by Peter the Great.

Still to come were the Andante from *Lucia,* his Fantasy on *Don Giovanni,* transcriptions of Schubert's *Serenade* and *Erlkönig*, and of Beethoven's *Adelaide,* plus, to conclude, his own *Galop chromatique*. . . .

After the concert we were like madmen, Serov* and I . . . as delirious as lovers. . . . And no wonder. Never had we heard anything like it; never had we been face to face with such genius, with such a brilliant, demoniacal temperament, that at one moment rushed like a whirlwind, at another poured forth streams of tender beauty and grace. . . . Liszt's playing was absolutely overwhelming. . . .[14]

By the critic of the *St Petersburger Zeitung,* Liszt was hailed as 'unique, peerless, unapproachable'; and the writer Bulgarin remarked: 'One must see Liszt's face and eyes when he is playing! Passions chase like clouds through a clear sky. . . . If you have never seen a genius in action, even if you do not like music, watch Liszt when he plays!'

On the 21st the Tsarina and the Grand Duchess Elena Pavlovna† invited themselves to Wielhorsky's to hear Liszt play, with orchestra, Weber's *Concertstück,* as well as several solos. On the 23rd came his second concert, this time attended by the Tsar. Three more followed, all immensely successful. Apart from works by Beethoven, Weber, Chopin, and others, the pieces Liszt offered were his own operatic paraphrases and song transcriptions. Long afterwards the composer and theorist Yuri Arnold (1811–98) remembered the 'thrilling' effect of *Erlkönig*: 'I say *thrilled*, for indeed I returned home *more than merely moved;* by such a music-hurricane, of which I had never before had the least presentiment, my whole being was *dissolved.* No sooner had I pulled off my coat than I flung myself on to the sofa and for a long time wept the *bitterest* and *sweetest* tears!'

Osip Senkovsky (1800–59). Liszt's presence eclipses all other news of this kind. Conversations and discussions of a musical nature all inevitably make their way to one topic only—Liszt. . . .[15]

The sole jarring note to be struck during these weeks of triumph did little to detract from the general enthusiasm. Asked if he would play for the benefit of needy veterans of the battle of Borodino, Liszt, usually so ready to assist all charitable causes, declined, saying: 'To France I owe both my education and my celebrity; it is impossible for me to join in chorus with her conquerors.' The suggestion for the recital had emanated from the Tsar himself, however, and his displeasure at the refusal was expressed in the words: 'I like neither his long hair nor his political opinions.' This utterance being reported to Liszt, his response

* Alexander Serov (1820–71), later the composer of several operas. To Stasov, after this first of Liszt's Petersburg concerts, he ecstasized in a note: 'Oh, how happy I am, what a day of celebration! It is as though the whole of God's world looked quite different! And all this was done by the playing of one man!' And later: 'Who will dare treat us to his playing after these supernatural sounds? No one, because such a wondrous phenomenon has never before been known, and are not many centuries likely to pass before anything like it appears again?'

† Born, like the Tsarina, a German princess, the highly educated Elena Pavlovna (1807–73) was a passionate music-lover; and it was she who, in 1861, founded the St Petersburg Conservatoire.

was to say: 'I grew my hair in Paris, and nowhere but in Paris will I have it cut. As for my political opinions, I have none, and shall have none until I have 300,000 bayonets to back them up!'

On several occasions he played at receptions given by the Tsarina, the Grand Duchess Elena Pavlovna, Prince Peter of Oldenburg, and other members of the highest nobility. Most of his time, however, was spent with Wielhorsky and with Prince Odoyevsky, the reformer of Russian church music. He also struck up friendship with the great German pianist Adolf Henselt (1814–89),* who had been living at Petersburg since 1838. Henselt was renowned for his beautiful touch, and on hearing him Liszt is said to have exclaimed in astonishment: 'I, too, could play with velvet paws if I wished.'

What he got to know at this time of the music of Glinka, made Liszt a keen admirer of the creative talent of the man he long afterwards designated 'the patriarch-prophet of music in Russia'. His first acquaintance with *Ruslan and Lyudmila,* then an entirely unknown work which was not premiered until later in the year, was made when, in the composer's presence, he played at sight several sections from the autograph score, astonishing everyone by not missing a single note. (Attending a performance of the opera during his next visit he showed, conceded Glinka, a 'true understanding of its key passages'.†) At his fourth concert he improvised on themes from *A Life for the Tsar,* filling the audience with indescribable enthusiasm.

A musical souvenir of this first visit to Russia was a *Petite valse favorite* (S212) which Liszt jotted down in one of the Tsarina's albums. A decade later it was published in a revised and amplified form under the title *Valse impromptu* (S213).

When he left St Petersburg, the aristocracy escorted him on a special steamer with a chorus of musicians to Kronstadt in the Gulf of Finland, whence he voyaged down the Baltic to the North German town of Travemünde.

By mid-June he was back in Paris, having arrived, as the *Journal des Débats* noted, with an Austrian passport bearing the words *Celebritate sua sat notus* (Sufficiently known by his celebrity).

On the 30th he gave a concert on behalf of a German opera group that he planned to conduct in London (but in the event nothing came of the plan). Another appearance was at Neuilly in aid of the poor. He also seized the opportunity to visit his friend Cristina Belgiojoso at her home in Port Marly near Versailles.

In mid-July he crossed into Belgium, having accepted an invitation to attend the celebrations in Liège commemorating the centenary of the birth of Grétry. At his concert here on the 20th he played the first movement of Beethoven's Concerto in E flat as well as several solos. At Brussels (concert on the 24th) he was decorated by King Leopold I with the Order of Leopold.

* As a performer Henselt was very highly regarded. Clara Schumann, who made his acquaintance during her visit to Petersburg in 1844, said that so glorious and 'fragrant' a touch as his she had never heard, nor would ever herself achieve. Comparing six of the greatest pianists of the century, Wilhelm von Lenz observed: 'Liszt, Chopin, and Henselt are continents; Tausig, Rubinstein, and Bülow are countries.' Wielhorsky's opinion was: 'If you have heard Henselt once, you have heard him at all times—but Liszt you have never heard, because he is always different.'

† In 1843 he also made a delicious piano transcription (S406) of Chernomor's Circassian March from the opera.

'After having made two or three tours through Belgium which were nothing less than triumphal processions, and on each of which he was accompanied by our local celebrities (even women who, to follow him, disguised themselves as men), this fabulous artist, this glorious man, this shining meteor, departed from our midst,' recalled Charles Dubois.

Liszt and Marie again spent the summer on Nonnenwerth. In early September she returned to Paris and he resumed his life as an itinerant virtuoso.

Liszt to Marie d'Agoult. Quiévrain, 7 September. You have made me suffer, have wounded me with blow upon blow. But I feel that from these wounds there will one day spurt beautiful harmonies; and the sufferings you have caused me have compelled me to accept religiously the sorrows that Providence inflicts on mankind (whether as a test, or as expiation, or as something that we shall never understand), and to bless God, against whom, but for you, my thoughts would have rebelled.[16]

Arriving in Cologne on 9 September, Liszt at once received a royal command to nearby Castle Brühl, where he was given an 'extremely gracious' welcome by King Frederick William IV and his family. On the 13th he played at Cologne, giving the proceeds towards completion of the great Cathedral. He also made a brief excursion to Koblenz for an audience with Metternich.

After returning to Paris, he made his way via Liège and Aachen to Weimar, where he spent his thirty-first birthday, 22 October. The Grand Duchess Maria Pavlovna was eager to attach him to the town, and overtures were made. 'I shall accept for two months in the year as a study and transition,' he told Marie; 'it will be an honourable base for my premature old age.' On 2 November the official announcement was made: 'Monsieur Liszt has been appointed Kapellmeister Extraordinary* by HRH the Grand Duke of Saxe-Weimar. His duties oblige him to spend three months of the year in Weimar and to conduct the court concert.'

As part of the festivities celebrating the marriage of the young Hereditary Grand Duke of Saxe-Weimar, Carl Alexander (1818–1901), with Princess Sophie of Holland (1824–97), which had taken place at The Hague on 8 October, Liszt organized a concert at court to which he brought Rubini as a fellow performer. On behalf of the poor of nearby Jena, which afterwards made him a freeman of the town, and to give the general public a chance to hear Rubini, he also arranged a second concert at the theatre.

After a week at Coburg (plus concert) with Felix Lichnowsky, Liszt proceeded to Frankfurt am Main, where on 15 November he and Rubini gave a concert at the Weidenbusch Hall.

Present was *Malwida von Meysenbug* (1816–1903), known in later life for her best-selling memoirs and her friendships with such figures as Herzen, Mazzini, Garibaldi, Wagner, Nietzsche, and the young Romain Rolland. Her impressions of the concert she set down in a letter to her sister-in-law Sophie von Meysenbug.

I have had the delight of hearing this son of the gods. When he came towards us we spoke to him, and he was most kind and amiable. Bettina,†

* The official Court Kapellmeister at this time was Hippolyte Chélard (1789–1861).

† With Bettina von Arnim in Frankfurt were her three daughters, Maxe, Armgart, and Gisela.

one of his closest lady friends, sat right up against his grand piano. The first piece was his Fantasy on *Don Giovanni*, which he had played at Detmold. I was very happy to hear it again, for Mozart could not have thought and felt his work more deeply in creating than Liszt in rendering it. Then came Rubini with an Italian arietta. Oh, my dear Sophie, how can I describe the river of enchantment which flooded my soul! I am writing of it to you so that you can share my joy. A new world opened for me, that of perfection. Yes, never had I heard anything so beautiful; and I could have wept from the happiness of knowing that man can conquer matter in this way, that terrestrial forces submit to him, enabling him to fill life with a foretaste of perfect beauty. What is, in comparison, the brief imperfection of our existence, when we can participate in a world of the spirit in which development is limitless? Next, Liszt played a *Marche hongroise,* a work at once very original and very difficult, but brilliantly performed. Then a duet by Rubini and a lady [Mlle Ostergard] who accompanies him on his tours. Finally, what I found most beautiful of all, a Prelude and Fugue by Bach.*. . .

At the exit, by the door, I was stopped by the crowd, which was unable to move. I was waiting patiently, when Liszt came by with Bettina on his arm and made a hurried departure. On seeing me, he cheered me by throwing a friendly 'bonsoir, bonsoir' to me over the people between us. He is now on his way to Holland, and will then go on to St Petersburg. Such a flame is sure to burn itself out all too soon; and, besides, my wish for him is that he may die in the midst of his successes. The harmonies of this evening are still resounding within me like a persistant echo, and the happiness with which they have filled my soul will not quickly fade.[17]

Travelling to Mainz, Liszt then took a steamer down the Rhine to Holland, where, in a short tour, he gave four concerts at Amsterdam, two at The Hague, and one in each of Rotterdam, Leyden, and Utrecht. At The Hague he also appeared in several court soirées.

Liszt to Marie d'Agoult. Utrecht, 8 December. The day is cold and dark. The only ray which comes to me, the sole source of life and warmth, is my memory of you, dear Marie. I think back to our awakenings in Como and Florence. . . . It is the month in which our two daughters were born. I feel as though I have forgotten how to live. . . .

I do not conceal from myself the fact that for three years my life has been only a series of feverish and often wilful excitements, ending in disgust and remorse. I have to spend, and go on spending, life, strength, money, and time without present enjoyment or future hope. I have compared myself to a gambler. Minus the ceaseless excitement, the unfailing thirst, I could

* According to the concert announcement, two more vocal items followed before, to conclude, Liszt's performance of the *Norma* fantasy.

compare myself to a man wandering through the fields, uprooting and throwing to the winds flowers, trees, fruit, and seed, without sowing, ploughing, or grafting.

My health has remained of iron. My moral strength has not diminished, my character has grown more vigorously firm. Are these the conditions of happiness? Is the ideal still possible? These are questions I could not answer. It is for you to decide.[18]

In late December he reached Berlin, arriving two days later than planned because of a lawsuit in Halle. A music teacher had claimed the right to an indemnity of four louis d'or for having advertised Liszt's concert in the town. Liszt had to appear in court, 'to the great confusion of the litigant; and after it had been verified that the aforesaid litigant was a knavish imbecile, and that his complaint could in no way be upheld, I sent eight louis d'or to his poor wife who was in childbed. In the evening, more than 300 students gave me a serenade with my *Rheinweinlied*,* after which they went and made an almighty din in front of the house belonging to the litigant's lawyer.'

The most important feature of Liszt's sojourn in Berlin on this occasion was his meeting, in the last days of December, with Richard Wagner, whom he had already met fleetingly in Paris in April 1840 and the early spring of 1841. Still several months short of his thirtieth birthday, Wagner, who some weeks later was to be appointed Royal Kapellmeister at Dresden, was not yet the dominating figure of German music that he would become; indeed, of his maturer works only *Der fliegende Holländer* had yet been written. He had, however, recently scored a notable success with *Rienzi*.

In the years that lay ahead, the lives of these two remarkable men were to grow ever more entwined; and from 1870, when Wagner married Liszt's daughter Cosima, were even to encompass a familial relationship. Never blind to what he called 'certain asperities of Wagner's character', Liszt remained unfaltering in his admiration† and championship of his friend's creative achievements; and for many years it was to him above all that Wagner looked for moral and financial support.

Wagner's enthusiasm for Liszt's works (in particular the symphonic poems and symphonies), which he showed in the clearest possible way by helping himself liberally to their harmonic innovations, and even their themes, lasted until his overweeningly egotistical old age, when he condemned the music of Liszt just as he did that of all other important contemporaries. Of Liszt himself his appreciation remained more constant. 'Your father was the first man to give me the impression of nobility,' he remarked to Cosima many years later. And from such a view, notwithstanding the vicissitudes their friendship was to undergo, and despite his own frequent outbursts of jealousy and ill humour in respect of Liszt, he never fundamentally deviated.

In his *Mein Leben* Wagner recalled both this meeting in the Prussian capital and one of the earlier encounters in Paris.

* S72/1, a setting for 4-part male chorus of Georg Herwegh's *Wo solch ein Feuer*.

† Culminating in what was from Liszt the *ne plus ultra* of praise, when, in a letter (22 Aug. 1879) to Olga von Meyendorff, he wrote in all sincerity: 'To me he is the equal of Dante.' Wagner for his part hailed Liszt as 'the most musical of all musicians'.

My brief trip to Berlin was memorable for a meeting with Franz Liszt, which afterwards proved of great importance. It took place under singular circumstances, which placed both him and me in a situation of peculiar embarrassment, brought about in the most wanton fashion by [Wilhelmine] Schröder-Devrient's exasperating caprice.

I had already told my patroness the story of my earlier meeting with Liszt. During that fateful second winter of my stay in Paris, when I had at last been driven to be grateful for Schlesinger's hack-work, I one day received word from Laube* . . . that Liszt was coming to Paris. He had mentioned and recommended me to him when he was in Germany, and advised me to lose no time in looking him up, as he was 'generous' and would certainly find means of helping me. As soon as I heard that he had really arrived, I presented myself at the hotel to see him. It was early in the morning. On my entrance I found several gentlemen unknown to me waiting in the salon, where, after some time, we were joined by Liszt himself, pleasant and affable, and wearing his indoor coat. The conversation was carried on in French, and turned upon his experiences during his last professional journey in Hungary. As I was unable to take part, on account of the language, I listened for some time, feeling heartily bored, until at last he asked me pleasantly what he could do for me. He seemed unable to recall Laube's recommendation, and all the answer I could give was that I desired to make his acquaintance. To this he had evidently no objection, and he told me he would take care to have a ticket sent me for his great matinée, which was to take place shortly. My sole attempt to introduce an artistic topic was a question as to whether he knew Loewe's *Erlkönig* as well as Schubert's. His reply in the negative frustrated this somewhat awkward attempt, and I ended my visit by giving him my address. Thither his secretary, Belloni, presently sent me, with a few polite words, a card of admission to a concert to be given entirely by the master himself at the Salle Erard. I duly wended my way to the over-crowded hall, and beheld the platform on which the grand piano stood, closely beleaguered by the cream of Parisian female society, and witnessed the enthusiastic ovations they gave to this virtuoso, who was at that time the wonder of the world. Moreover, I heard several of his most brilliant pieces, such as the Fantasy on *Robert le Diable,* but carried away with me no real impression beyond that of being stunned. This took place just at the time when I was abandoning a path which had been so contrary to my truer nature, and had led me astray, and on which I now emphatically turned my back in silent bitterness. I was therefore in no fitting mood for a just appreciation of this prodigy, who at that time was shining in the blazing light of day, but from whom I had turned my face to the night. I went to see Liszt no more.

* A Leipzig friend (and, in later years, implacable enemy) of Wagner's, Heinrich Laube (1806–84) was a writer, dramatist, and theatre director.

I had given Schröder-Devrient only a bare outline of this story, but she had noted it with particular attention, for I happened to have touched her weak point of professional jealousy. As Liszt had also been commanded by the King of Prussia to appear at the grand state concert in Berlin, it so happened that the first time they met Liszt questioned her with great interest about the success of *Rienzi.* She thereupon observed that the composer of that opera was an altogether unknown man, and proceeded with curious malice to taunt him with his apparent lack of penetration, as proved by the fact that the said composer, who now so keenly excited his interest, was the very same poor musician whom he had lately 'turned away so contemptuously' in Paris. All this she told me with an air of triumph, which distressed me very much, and I at once set to work to correct the false impression conveyed by my former account. As we were still debating this point in her room, we were startled to hear from the next the famous bass part in the 'Revenge' air from *Donna Anna,* rapidly executed in octaves on the piano. 'That's Liszt himself,' she cried. Liszt then entered the room to fetch her for the rehearsal. To my great embarrassment she introduced me to him with malicious delight as the composer of *Rienzi,* the man whose acquaintance he now wished to make after having previously shown him the door in his glorious Paris. My solemn asseverations that my patroness—no doubt only in fun—was deliberately distorting my account of my former visit to him, apparently pacified him so far as I was concerned, and, on the other hand, he had no doubt already formed his own opinion of the impulsive singer. He admitted that he could not remember my visit in Paris, but it nevertheless shocked and alarmed him to learn that anyone should have had reason to complain of such treatment at his hands. The hearty sincerity of Liszt's simple words to me about this misunderstanding, as contrasted with the strangely passionate raillery of the incorrigible lady, made a most pleasing and captivating impression upon me. The whole bearing of the man, and the way in which he tried to ward off the pitiless scorn of her attacks, was something new to me, and gave me a deep insight into his character, so firm in its amiability and boundless good-nature. Finally, she teased him about the Doctor's degree which had just been conferred on him by the University of Königsberg, and pretended to mistake him for a chemist. At last he stretched himself out flat on the floor, and implored her mercy, declaring himself quite defenceless against the storm of her invective. Then turning to me with a hearty assurance that he would make it his business to hear *Rienzi,* and would in any case endeavour to give me a better opinion of himself than his evil star had hitherto permitted, we parted for that occasion.

The almost naïve simplicity and naturalness of his every phrase and word, and particularly his emphatic manner, left a most profound impression upon me. No one could fail to be equally affected by these qualities, and I now realised for the first time the almost magic power exerted by Liszt over all who came in close contact with him, and saw how erroneous had been my former opinion as to its cause.[19]

1843

The first Berlin concert (8 January) was to a packed house which included the King and Queen. Liszt's success was considerable—but, nevertheless, this second visit to the Prussian capital could not compare with the triumphs of the previous year, when he had been all but deified. As though ashamed of their former near-hysterical enthusiasm, people now showed him a cooler, more reserved face. From Breslau (now Wroclaw in Poland) where he then spent several weeks, he wrote to Marie: 'I am entirely of the opinion that I should soon bring my virtuoso career to an end. Hungary is the natural and necessary conclusion.'

At Breslau he was offered the huge sum (which he did not accept) of 1,000 louis for ten concerts; the students gave him a torchlight procession, with a crowd of several thousand assembled in front of his windows; and the theatre, selling no tickets for those days in which Liszt was not to appear, asked him if he would conduct an opera. Accepting the invitation, on 1 February he conducted *Die Zauberflöte*.

After a brief return to Berlin (concert on 16 February) and Potsdam (concert on the 18th), Liszt played at Fürstenwalde (19th) before making further appearances at Breslau (21st, 22nd, and 24th). In late February he played at Posen (now Poznán), and then, via Glogau (now Glogów) (concert on 1 March), Liegnitz (now Legnica),* and again Breslau (concert on 7 March), arrived on 10 March at Krzyzanowitz, the home near Ratibor (now Racibórz, Poland) of his friend Felix Lichnowsky. Here he enjoyed such amusements as eagle and gerfalcon hunting; excursions to Grätz (or Hradec), another Lichnowsky palace; visits to farms and sheepfolds; ballooning, fireworks, routs, banquets, balls, and whist. On the 20th he left for Warsaw, *en route* giving three concerts (28, 29, 30 March) at Cracow, where his hotel was illuminated for his arrival and the proprietor refused all payment for board and lodging.

It was at Warsaw, where he arrived at the beginning of April and enjoyed an overwhelming success, particularly with his playing of Chopin, in his four concerts (6, 9, 10, 12 April), that Liszt made the acquaintance of Marie Kalergis (1822–74), the subsequent Madame von Mouchanoff, a niece of Count Nesselrode, the Russian Chancellor. Beautiful, intelligent, and fascinating, she was still only in her twenty-first year, but already married and separated. A gifted pianist (admired by both Liszt and Chopin†) and indefatigable seeker after

* Where he had already played on 6 Feb.

† The latter gave her lessons a year or two before his death, and found that she played 'truly admirably'. Liszt, who dedicated to her both the *Petite valse favorite* and his transcription (S431) of 'Salve Maria de Jérusalem' from Verdi's *I Lombardi*, was equally enthusiastic: 'She plays as does no one else, and those who have heard her will never forget her unique interpretation.'

culture, she was in the years to come to achieve prominence for her social and political activities (especially her efforts to heal the rifts between Russia and her native Poland), her brilliant salon at Baden-Baden, and her championship of the music of Liszt and Wagner. She also became notorious for her affairs with celebrities, which caused Heine to write of her mockingly as 'a Pantheon in which so many great men lie buried'.

Two other residents of Warsaw whom Liszt visited during his stay were Nicolas Chopin (1771–1844) and Józef Elsner (1769–1854), respectively the father and mentor of his friend Chopin.

After ten or twelve days in the Polish capital, three of which he was constrained by illness to spend in bed, he left for St Petersburg, where shortly after his arrival he waited upon the Polish-born Countess Eveline (Eva) de Hanska, *née* Rzewuska (1801–82), a wealthy and attractive widow living in the city with her fifteen-year-old daughter Anna. At Neuchâtel in Switzerland ten years previously, and almost under the nose of her elderly husband, she had become the mistress of Honoré de Balzac, whom she eventually married a few months before his death in 1850.

From the diary of Eva Hanska, April. I have made Liszt's acquaintance. He had been here for two days. I had a few lines* from M. de Balzac which I sent him, and he wrote me a very nice note saying that he would come at two the next day, 'unless his visit was positively disagreeable to me'. . . .

The servant announced 'Monsieur Liszt' with no more ado than if M. Liszt had simply been the owner of the coat he was wearing, and if his rights and privileges did not extend to those vast domains of intelligence and genius whose possession does away with the 'Monsieur' for present and future alike. . . . I rose and went towards him, stammering a few polite words of welcome.

He is of average height, thin, pale, and drawn, with the bilious complexion seen in persons of great talent and personality. His features are fairly regular. His forehead is less high than it is depicted in his portraits; it is lined with wrinkles and lacks loftiness. His eyes are glassy, but the sparks of his wit make them light up and then they flash like the facets of a cut diamond. His hair, which is long and well groomed (whatever people say), is light brown. His nose is straight and well-chiselled, but the best thing about him is the curve of his mouth. There is something particularly sweet, I would even say seraphic, about that mouth, which, when it smiles, makes heaven dream. In general, the great artist's eyes, above all his brow, belong to the fallen angel, to the evil spirit of sensual pleasures and worldly

* Dated 14 Nov. 1842, and written on the back of a note Balzac had received *from* Liszt, they ran: 'If you care to do me a personal service, you will spend an evening at the home of the person who sends you this note, and you will play something for Mademoiselle Anna de Hanska, a little angel whom you will doubtless fascinate.' Shortly before Liszt's arrival in St Petersburg, Balzac had written to Madame Hanska: 'I hear that you will be seeing Liszt—ridiculous man, sublime talent. He is the Paganini of the piano, but Chopin is far superior to him.' A few weeks later, on the other hand: 'I love him dearly, and consider his talent to be as sublime as those of Chopin, Paganini, and Batta.'

woes; and the lower part of his face, particularly his ineffable smile, to the angel of harmony, to the instinct of noble and beautiful feelings. One's impression is that there must have been more than one inner struggle in the life of this man, and that often—too often, alas!—the spirit of evil has gained the upper hand. . . .

He was dressed entirely in dark colours, but with nothing that was showy or in bad taste; his clothes were as impeccable in this as his conversation. We sat down. He told me what pleasure M. de Balzac's note had given him, that my name was not new to him, however, that he had come to Geneva after my departure and been told a lot about me, that he had everywhere sought me in vain, including at Warsaw recently, believing that as a Pole I was sure to be living there. In short, a thousand pleasing things. We also talked about M. de Balzac. 'People have tried to set us at loggerheads,' he said, 'by attempting to insinuate that he had portrayed me rather unflatteringly under the name of Conti in his novel *Béatrix*;* but, not recognizing myself in it, I didn't accept the portrait.'

I asked him to play, which he very kindly did; but I admit that, beautiful though it seemed, his performance did not astonish me; and as I listened to it I felt grievously disappointed. While continuing to chat, he played me a passage from Weber's Concerto in a jerky and occasionally casual manner; he frequently broke off and in the gaps interspersed improvised modulations.

The next day, 14 April [OS], Anna and I went to his concert at the Engelhardt Hall. There were still very few people when we arrived; we had hurried so as to have good seats. On a platform in the middle of the hall two pianos were placed, facing one another, so that turn and turn about the great artist could show his profile to a different part of the audience. The hall gradually filled up, and finally the Genius with the long hair and pale,

* A *roman à clef* inspired by the story of Liszt (model for a minor character, the Italian singer Gennaro Conti) and Madame d'Agoult (the eponymous antiheroine), material for which had been supplied to Balzac by George Sand, angered to learn of Marie's spiteful remarks about her in letters to a common friend. The first two parts of the novel had been published in 1839; the third and final part (in which Conti makes no appearance and is barely even mentioned) came out in 1845. Apparently the only reason why Sand (original of another important character, the likeable, good-natured writer and bluestocking Camille Maupin) had not herself written it was for fear of offending Liszt. The latter, however, is on the whole let off lightly. Not so Marie, who had every reason to resent being presented in the guise of the selfish, heartless Béatrix, Marquise de Rochefide, humiliation of whom forms the book's culminating point. Balzac on several occasions denied any similarity between his fictional personages and their apparent real-life counterparts. To Madame Sand he wrote in January 1840: 'I adore in Listz [*sic*] both the man and the talent, and to claim that Gennaro can resemble him is a double injury both for him and for me.' To Eva Hanska in a letter of 15 May 1843 he remarked: 'You have seen Liszt, and I am happy to have obtained this pleasure for you. Alas! I have never been able to tell him that Conti is Sandeau [Jules Sandeau, a former literary collaborator of both Sand's and Balzac's] made musician.' And it was 'very conceited' of Madame d'Agoult, he declared, to recognize herself in the novel. Naturally the characters do owe much to Balzac's limitless imagination; but, this and his disclaimers notwithstanding, there can be little doubt that it was the Liszt/d'Agoult relationship which provided him with, at the least, the *point de départ* of his novel.

expressive face appeared before us, preceded and followed by a hurricane of *bravos*, stamping feet and frenzied cheering. I was uneasy. I had little confidence in either myself or in this man so applauded or in this fanatical mass of people. I wondered if my ability to admire was dead, if this crowd was stupid, or this man nothing but a clever impostor. For I too had heard him—and yet!

Liszt greeted his idolatrous audience with a somewhat coy grace, tossing his long hair back with a sudden movement of the head and sitting down. He began with the overture to *Freischütz*, and no sooner did I hear the muffled sounds of the distant storm rumbling under his left hand, than the electric spark of admiration suddenly kindled my sluggish feelings; they understood, felt, admired! What shall I say? To hear him is to contemplate nature, for his playing is the whole of nature felt and revealed by the inspiration of genius. . . .

Inspiration is the special and distinguishing hallmark of this great talent. I believe that in general he owes less to study than is thought; perhaps in the long run purely mechanical practice would even cause him to deteriorate, would gradually destroy the verve and impulse of his inspiration. I have heard Thalberg play the same thing several times in succession, and it was always the same despair-inducing perfection of touch, exactly the same nuances and gradations; at the third repeat one could have prompted him oneself if necessary. In him, can be recognized the triumph of labour and patience; he is art's favourite, most accomplished adept. But Liszt!—Liszt is the master, the sovereign, the conqueror of art for the benefit of nature. He is in performance what Beethoven is in composition, alone and unique. . . .[1]

Osip Senkovsky. Only an unusual intellect makes someone a great writer, a great artist, a great virtuoso. Here we have the secret of the incredible impression Liszt has made all over Europe, intrigues, jealousy, rivalry, and ill-will notwithstanding. . . . Everyone thinks he is playing even better now than last year. But Liszt has not practised during the past year! Why, in that case, does his playing seem even better, even more wonderful? Only because he has thought over many passages again and made them expressive in a new and different way. . . .[2]

Although Liszt's playing was once again received with tremendous enthusiasm, this second visit of his to St Petersburg was in another respect less successful, as he explained long afterwards: 'The favour which Tsar Nicholas showed me in '42, I entirely lost during my second sojourn in the city . . . chiefly because of the peevish and partly *false* reports of the then Chief of Police in Warsaw about my Polish sympathies, which it was a matter of honour with me not to deny. However, what some newspapers wrote about my "expulsion" from Petersburg is wholly erroneous.'*

* Lina Ramann, *Lisztiana* (Mainz, 1983), 401.

Loss of the Tsar's goodwill notwithstanding, the great pianist's reception in the homes of the aristocracy seems to have been no less cordial than during his previous visit, and he played several times before the Tsarina and the Grand Duchess Elena Pavlovna. On one occasion he earned immense applause for an improvisation on themes from Glinka's *A Life for the Tsar,* his auditors declaring that they had never before heard such a 'master improvisation'. But Liszt apparently felt that he had not come up to his own standards, and on the way home was extremely taciturn with his companions, Henselt and Yuri Arnold. Once at his lodgings he tore off his coat and ran excitedly up and down, exclaiming: 'I improvised like a pig! But I can do better, a hundred times better! I can, I can!' It was only with difficulty that his two friends could calm him.

His playing of Beethoven's Fifth Piano Concerto at Count Wielhorsky's was recalled by Leonid von Lwow more than forty years later with the words: 'I can still hear him playing that concerto. I must have heard it a hundred times by different pianists—but *like that*, never, never again!'

Eva Hanska. Liszt visits me regularly. He is an extraordinary mixture which I enjoy studying. There are sublime things in him, but also deplorable ones; he is the human reflection of what is grandiose in nature —but also, alas, of what is abhorrent. There are sublime heights, the mountains with dazzling peaks, but also bottomless gulfs and abysses. . . .

He has left for Moscow. When he came to say farewell it was with an earnest air which touched me. I do not believe in *friendship* on his part; I understand too well the ancient value of this noble word to profane it; but I believe that he is fond of me. . . .[3]

Liszt's reception in Moscow, which he reached in the evening of 22 April (OS), was brilliant. His first recital, beginning with the *William Tell* overture and concluding with the *Grand galop chromatique,* was given on Sunday the 25th at the Bolshoi Theatre. Seven others followed (27 and 29 April; 2, 4, 9, 12, 16 May), all to packed houses. 'The Moscow public are extremely kind to me,' he was able to tell Marie.

The writer and revolutionary *Alexander Herzen* (1812–70), who found Liszt 'charming and intelligent' and was 'moved to tears' by his 'amazing talent', noted with mild scorn the attention shown to the famous musician by Moscow society.

Enough silly things were done in Liszt's honour in Germany, but here his reception was of quite a different quality. In Germany it was all old-maidenish exaltation, sentimentality, all *Blumenstreuen* [strewing of flowers], while with us it was all servility, homage paid to power, rigid standing at attention; with us it was all 'I have the honour to present myself to your Excellency'. And here, unfortunately, there was also Liszt's fame as a celebrated Lovelace to add to it all. The ladies flocked round him, as peasant-boys on country roads flock round a traveller while his horses are being harnessed, inquisitively examining him, his carriage, his cap. . . . No one listened to anybody but Liszt, no one spoke to anybody else, nor answered anybody else. I remember that at one evening party Khomyakov, blushing for the honourable company, said to me: 'Please let us argue about something, that Liszt may see that there are people in the room not exclusively occupied with him.'[4]

With two bear cubs which had been presented to him, Liszt returned from Moscow to St Petersburg.

Eva Hanska. Liszt spent a few hours with me today (24 May); he spoke to me of a thousand things, and especially of himself, with a lack of restraint such as he had not hitherto shown, saying that he was in love, or believes himself to be, with a young woman of Moscow society who is committing a thousand follies for him. . . . At one moment he made me laugh—when I reminded him of the lessons of the past and of Mme d'Agoult and his children. 'Set your mind at rest about that,' he said; 'I have become more reasonable: this time, if I abduct the woman, I shall take the husband too.' (Behold the reasonable man!) And, indeed, they say that the husband is almost as taken with him as is the wife. . . .

Eva Hanska, 1 June. I do not know if it is because of the influence of some evil genius, or of some particular failing in our reciprocal personalities, but my intimacy with the great artist has imperceptibly taken on a stormy and fatiguing character. . . . This misunderstanding dates from a dinner in the country to which I had been invited by M. Senkovsky, the editor of a literary magazine, a great orientalist and very witty man. Liszt was to be of the company, as well as Glinka the composer and several other artistic notables. I was expecting to enjoy myself greatly, but someone (I do not know if out of concern for me, or out of spite at not himself being invited) hinted to me that these gentlemen were heavy drinkers and that this might cause me some bother, especially since we were to travel together on the train—and after giving it a lot of thought, I decided not to go and to make my excuses. Having learnt of this, Liszt wrote me one note after another, and even came running here in person, but on the pretext that I was unwell I did not have him admitted. For several days in succession he did not come. . . . But finally he turned up one morning, and said that he had been furious with me, that once already I had given him a proof of my prudery by not wishing to go to his concert with him—but that this beat everything. 'Don't think I was taken in by your illness,' he said, running about the room like the most headstrong of spoilt children. 'I *know you*! And I also know those who told you that you should not associate with artists. Tell me what they called *me*, for example!' He stopped and looked hard at me, stamping his foot the while. ' "*A gypsy*", wasn't it? Well, just get them to say it to my face and I'll show you how the gypsy avenges an insult. . . .' He carried on speaking with the same vehemence, and I listened in silence. He stopped again. 'Well, Madame, you say nothing?'—'What do you expect me to say, Monsieur? I am astonished and pity you, that's all.' He gradually calmed down, continuing to walk to and fro, but in silence, and now and then looking at me furtively. I asked him to play something; he played Schubert's *Serenade,* but wearily and despondently, after which we chatted quietly and he asked my forgiveness, even going so far as to admit his faults. . . . He has been back several times since, sometimes being brusque and violent and sometimes agreeable. He is charming on the latter occasions, but when he flies into a rage he frightens me. He is vehement and passionate by nature, and the dissolute environment in which his character is developing is having a really pernicious influence on him.

Eva Hanska, 3 June. Yesterday I saw Liszt for the last time . . . which saddens me to think of it. He is so changed, so destroyed, that I who saw him frequently could see almost from one day to the next the traces of the ravages produced perhaps not so much by his disorderly life as by a restless soul, by an agitated mind which has upon his body the effect that a sharp two-edged sword has upon a too narrow scabbard. This last visit went well and was spoilt by no transports of rage. He asked me to forgive him, begged me not to forget him, to write to him sometimes and to see him once more before his departure. 'I have nothing to forgive you,' I said, 'for I could not be angry with you. As for forgetting, if it is difficult when one knows you, it becomes impossible when one loves you and is loved by you. So far as writing is concerned, I shall do so once a year.' At this, he looked sulky and protested. 'Listen,' I said; 'I am making you only a promise I am sure I can keep—once a year will be my duty, more than once will be a favour for you.' He took my hand, kissed it and held it between his own. Withdrawing it gently, I said: 'Monsieur Liszt, believe me, do not come again; let this be our last meeting.' He tried to insist, but I repeated most earnestly, from the heart: 'I beg you not to come again—it would be bad for me and perhaps for you too—so let me say farewell to you under the influence of today's pleasant visit; tomorrow you would perhaps be less good, or I myself would be naughtier—and so, farewell.' He kissed the hand I held out, squeezed it tightly, and left rapidly. I followed him to the door, but he did not even turn around. I went to the window and saw him climb into the calèche. He raised his head and I saw him gazing towards me until the horses had carried him out of sight.

Eva Hanska, 5 June. This morning a note came from Liszt, who wrote: 'I didn't force my way in, I didn't disobey you—and yet I should have liked to see you once again, Madame! Forgive me; I was brusque, violent, and unjust, but for the moment please do not judge, condemn, or absolve me —perhaps we shall meet again two years from now. Perhaps you will then be less displeased with me. . . .'

Liszt's departure has left, I admit, a certain emptiness in my heart. I feel that I shall miss him for a long time yet. I had grown accustomed to expecting and awaiting his two o'clock visit; I would try to guess in advance the kind of mood he was in. . . . I was very fond of him; he had won my trust, as it were. I spoke to him of myself with the enthusiasm of the pen and of a written diary. It is a long time since I encountered a more pronounced individuality, one more strongly self-assertive and standing out so vividly from this crowd of mediocrities living all around me. His very faults often seemed likeable. In short, his company would be one of the most dangerous for a young and inexperienced person, and so I kept my Anna at a discreet distance from this will-o'-the-wisp whose glowing and seductive light can lure to the abyss.[5]

Liszt gave Madame Hanska a portrait of himself on which he had penned these words of Dante's (*Inferno,* Canto IX, lines 101–3):

> ma fè sembiante
> d'uomo cui altra cura stringa e morda
> che quella di colui che gli è davante.

Many years later she presented it to his disciple Marie Jaëll; and after the latter's death (1925) it was given to the Musée Balzac in Paris.

From St Petersburg Liszt took a boat to Hamburg, giving a concert there as well as at Lübeck. Via Aachen he then joined Marie and the children for their third, and last, summer together on Nonnenwerth.

In early October they parted, he to move through Germany, she to return to Paris. By way of Frankfurt, Würzburg (whose magnificent Palace of the Bishops, with its hall of mirrors and chinoiserie, impressed him), and Nuremberg ('a marvel'), where he gave concerts on the 11th and 13th, Liszt arrived at Munich, where he renewed acquaintance with Bettina von Arnim and her daughters. The first of his four concerts was given on Wednesday, 18 October.

Maxe von Arnim (1818–94). Liszt's playing aroused an enthusiasm similar to that of Berlin. During the interval the King* came up to us, to greet my mother. We were presented to him . . . and also to the Queen. . . .

After the concert there was a small party for Liszt . . . who then gave a few small soirées of his own, at which he played and Armgart sang some of his songs. I felt sorry for poor Bethlen,† who suffered the torments of hell when having to witness the open homage continually paid to Armgart by Liszt, who is very taken with her.[6]

Liszt's remaining Munich concerts took place on the 21st, 25th and 30th, the last two containing Weber's *Concertstück* and Beethoven's Fifth Piano Concerto respectively as well as solo pieces. On the 27th the city's 'literary society' gave a banquet for him. Among the guests were the painter Wilhelm von Kaulbach (1805–74), with whom Liszt struck up friendship, and Count Franz von Pocci (1807–76), who in Liszt's honour organized an outing, with the Arnims and others, to Schloss Ammerland, his residence on Lake Starnberg.

* Ludwig I (1786–1868), King of Bavaria 1825–48.

† Liszt's friend Count Sándor Bethlen (1823–84), a native of Transylvania. Having been introduced to the Arnims by Liszt, he had soon become enamoured of Armgart.

After two concerts (1 and 4 November) at Augsburg, Liszt moved on to Stuttgart, where he was received, according to the *Athenaeum,* by 'an illumination from the people, and a cordiality little short of an embrace from the King'. Here he gave concerts on the 7th, 12th, 14th, 16th, and 21st. He also played at Heilbronn on the 15th, Ludwigsburg on the 17th, and Hechingen on the 18th; and, on a date that has not been ascertained, at Tübingen.

In late November he spent a weekend at Donau-Eschingen. 'Here I am,' he wrote to Marie, 'at the source of my native river. . . . Two paces from the palace, near the entrance to the residence of Prince Fürstenberg, with whom I am staying, there is a small spring . . . with a stone framework and a short flight of steps. A few small and rare grey fish are swimming in it, doubtless content with their lot. That is the source of the Danube.'

In the Karlsruhe and Frankfurt region from 27 November onwards, he also made visits to Heidelberg, Mannheim, and Baden-Baden, choosing for his reading *en route* Custine's *La Russie en 1839*, with its description of the fate of Princess Troubetskoy, 'which moved me to tears'.

On Christmas Eve he arrived at Weimar.

1844

Several times a week Liszt was invited to court, for tea or dinner, and sometimes to take part in a musical or literary soirée. In a concert on 7 January he conducted for the first time in Weimar, and also contributed a virtuoso performance of Hummel's B minor Concerto.* On the 14th he directed his first court concert. Although it took a little time for the players to grow accustomed to his unconventional approach, since he regarded the conductor's task as being above all to inspire, and to convey the meaning and content of a work rather than merely act as a 'time-beater', he eventually established a mutually satisfactory rapport with them and gained their loyalty. These first concerts were a great success.

Allgemeine Musikalische Zeitung. He possesses the chief gift of the genuine conductor, that of being able to cause the *spirit* of a work to be illuminated in its full splendour. By his movements he knows how to impress every subtlest nuance on each and every one of the performers without degenerating into a hand-thrashing caricature. The joys and sorrows of the music are shown by his mobile features, which reflect everything he is feeling; and his eyes, which flash with great energy, would inspire any orchestra to unaccustomed activity. Liszt is the soul of music personified. He radiates as brightly as the sun, and whoever comes into proximity with him feels warmed and illumined.[1]

* Delighting the composer's widow who was present. 'So haots halt do' mei Alder nit g'spielt' (My old man played it well, but not as well as this) she enthused in her Viennese dialect.

In a letter to Marie d'Agoult of 23 January, Liszt outlined his plans for the artistic and intellectual regeneration of Weimar, which since the great days of Goethe had fallen into decline, despite the presence of the art- and music-loving Maria Pavlovna. His hopes for the future were encouraged by the friendship he was forming with the Hereditary Grand Duke Carl Alexander. 'The young prince is extremely kind to me, and with every day that passes I am growing fonder of him,' he added on 16 February.

Directing several other concerts at Weimar in January and February, he also gave charity concerts in the nearby towns of Jena,* Rudolstadt, Erfurt, and Gotha. On 9 February he was in Dresden to attend a performance of Wagner's *Rienzi,* and to the gratification of the composer, whom he met between the acts, expressed great enthusiasm for the work, which he saw and heard on this occasion for the first time. There, too, on 21 February he played on behalf of the city's Naumann monument, towards the completion of which he was able to hand over 1,350 thalers. On the 24th he played at Dessau; on the 26th, again at Dresden; and in March he made appearances in the North-German towns of Bautzen, Bernburg, Stettin (now Szczecin in Poland), Brunswick, Magdeburg, and Hanover.

By early April he was back in Paris, where on the 16th and 25th, and again on 4 May, he played with enormous success at the Théâtre Italien. 'Let's admit it calmly,' remarked a reviewer in *Le Corsaire* (28 April), 'this man has something in him that the others haven't.' He also organized a concert given on 11 May on behalf of 'orphelines recueillies par les sœurs du Gros-Caillou'.

Awaiting Liszt in Paris, however, was an event of far greater moment than any concert: the final break with Madame d'Agoult. It was in fact she who took the initiative in the matter. Domineering, proud, jealous, and ill-tempered though she may have been, Marie had been Liszt's wife in all but name, borne his three children, and made considerable sacrifices for him; and it is he who deserves the major portion of blame, less perhaps for his lack of fidelity† towards a censorious, nagging woman of whom he had probably tired, than for his well-nigh total disregard of discretion and moderation. His long absences were hard enough for Marie to bear, but the burden was made all the heavier by the reports and gossip which reached her of Liszt's womanizing with a succession of attractive and talented creatures of the type of Charlotte von Hagn and Caroline Unger; and she was left free to assume, correctly, that there were yet others which had not come to public notice.‡ 'I am willing to be your mistress, but not

* Here, on 5 Feb., he took part in one of the town's Academic Concerts—organization of which was largely in the hands of Carl Gille (1813–99), a Councillor of Justice who became a close friend of Liszt's and, after his death, first Curator of Weimar's Liszt Museum.

† Marie was herself not without guilt. During her stay with Liszt at Nohant in the summer of 1837, a fellow guest for several weeks had been Charles Didier (one of the many ill-fated lovers of Madame Sand), whom from the time of her return to Paris in late 1839 she had determinedly sought to seduce. Her efforts had brought their reward, for the rather reluctant Didier's diary eventually records, referring to a ball to which he escorted Marie on 29 Jan. 1842 (when Liszt was in Berlin): 'Nous restons peu et revenons souper chez elle. La nuit. Le mystère. . .' Didier had soon broken with Marie, who, ever unforgiving, had taken revenge in a short story, *Hervé,* published in *La Presse,* Dec. 1842.

‡ The diary of John Orlando Parry, for example, reveals Liszt successfully contriving trysts with local wenches even amidst the hectic travelling and concert-giving of his British tours of 1840–1.

one of your mistresses,' she had written to him. There had been discord between the two after the Fantasy on *Norma* had been published together with a flattering letter which addressed the work's dedicatee, the enchanting Marie Pleyel (with whom, as Madame d'Agoult well knew, Liszt had enjoyed an *affaire* some years previously), as 'dear and ravishing colleague'. The newspapers then reported his encounter (how close, is a matter of conjecture), at Dresden in February, with the Irish adventuress Lola Montez.* Having already asked Liszt earlier in the month to 'spare me vulgar publicity', Marie seems to have regarded this latest episode as the final straw.

'It is obvious that . . . our two points of view are diametrical opposites,' Liszt had written (Berlin, 11 March) in reply to her protests. 'However, after having reflected profoundly and painfully, I felt that it was impossible to justify myself and to reply, in any manner, to your letter sealed five times over. And so I do no more than enclose with these lines the broken sphinx you gave me in Rome.' 'I am very sad and deeply distressed,' he added on 11 April. 'One by one I am counting all the sorrows I have given you, and no one nor anything will ever be able to save me from myself.'

All this notwithstanding, Liszt vehemently opposed and resisted the break; and yet, after his initial shock and resentment had passed, it was he who proved the stronger and more resolute in accepting it. Marie, on the other hand, who felt herself wronged and sought revenge by writing and publishing a *roman à clef* (see *infra*) which foolishly attempted to belittle Liszt's creative gifts and aspirations, was to regret the severing of relations until her life's end.

The biggest problem facing the former lovers pertained to custody of Blandine, Cosima, and Daniel, now in their ninth, seventh, and fifth years respectively. As the father, Liszt had total rights under the law, a prerogative which he exercised fully, assuming thereby complete responsibility for the children's upbringing and education; and, despite her protests, Marie was to see very little of them during the remainder of their childhood and youth. 'One day,' she wrote to Liszt, 'your daughters will perhaps ask you, "where is our mother?" You will reply: "It was not my wish that you should have one." '

Nevertheless, given that only one parent was to be the arbiter of their youthful destinies, the children were fortunate that it was their father who now took control, for he took care to see that they remained in the charge of his own surviving parent—simple, uneducated, but warm-hearted Anna Liszt, who loved her grandchildren and lavished upon them much devotion and tenderness. A contrast, indeed, with the attitude of their maternal grandmother, the Comtesse de Flavigny, as is made clear in a note of about this time from Madame d'Agoult to Georg Herwegh: 'When my mother is here, don't speak of Blandine. She *protests* by her constant silence against the very existence of these children, and grows terribly embarrassed whenever they are mentioned.'

* The name assumed by Eliza Gilbert (1818–61) of Limerick, remembered now, above all, for the ascendancy she gained at Munich in 1846 over the elderly art-loving Ludwig I of Bavaria (who created her Countess of Landsfeld), and the political influence she was enabled to exercise thereby—until the 1848 revolution swept away king and courtesan alike. (The story strangely parallels that of Liszt's later son-in-law, Richard Wagner, who formed a similarly close—but in this case not sexual—relationship with Ludwig's grandson, Ludwig II, and was likewise compelled to leave Munich after meddling in local politics.)

For some years a sporadic correspondence was to be maintained between Liszt and Marie, but before their next meeting a full seventeen years were to pass.

After the parting of the ways Liszt was free to indulge in female company still more openly than before; and most of the month of June he spent at Princess Belgiojoso's home at Port Marly near Versailles. 'Liszt is absolutely like the master in Cristina's house . . . ordering the carriage harnessed in front of her to take me to the train,' noted Balzac sourly (since, like Heine and de Musset, he too was an admirer of the Princess) after a visit to Port Marly on the 10th. And a fortnight later, after meeting Liszt in Paris, he complained: 'Liszt is at the Princess Belgiojoso's, and *so openly*, that he goes back there at 11.30 p.m.! Cristina is no longer worthy of respect!'

On the 15th Liszt played several pieces at a concert given by the baritone Ciabatta at the Grand Théâtre, Versailles.

At the Conservatoire on Sunday, 23 June, in a concert on behalf of the widow of the composer Henri-Montan Berton, he made his last ever public appearance in Paris as a pianist, playing his transcription of the Scherzo, Storm, and Finale of the Pastoral Symphony; Fantasy on *Don Giovanni*; and *Mélodies hongroises* (S425), based on Schubert's *Divertissement à la hongroise*.

The literary and dramatic critic Jules Janin (1804–74) to his brother Sébastien at Saint-Etienne. Paris, 29 June. Liszt is coming to your part of the world. Give him a good welcome, for he is a great artist; not only an inspired genius but also a good man. Last Sunday he played—admirably—at the benefit concert for Mme Berton. He and Kontski* performed a duet together too. Kontski was covered with bouquets; Liszt received only a white rose—but the rose carried a kiss![2]

On the 29th Liszt arrived at Lyons. His reception at the six concerts he gave here was ultra-enthusiastic; a banquet was given in his honour, speeches delivered, poems composed. 'More than a great pianist,' declared *La Revue du Lyonnais*, 'he is a great artist, a great soul.'

Leaving Lyons on 17 July, visiting Lamartine at St Point on the 18th, spending a day or two at Avignon, and making a brief digression to visit the village of Vaucluse (for its association with Petrarch), Liszt proceeded to Marseilles, which he reached on 23 July.

On the 24th a 'family dinner' was given for him, with many of the most distinguished residents of Marseilles among the guests. In proposing a toast, the poet and critic *Gustave Benedit* singled out for special mention Liszt's generosity and wish to serve others.

Talent, which for so many others is but a means of arriving at riches, you use to alleviate misery and to help the afflicted. Since you entered upon this career which you have rendered so illustrious, not a single person in distress has sought your help in vain. Numberless are the good deeds you have sown along your path, so that there is none who would venture to claim to have followed better than you in this world the precept of charity,

* The Polish pianist Antoine de Kontski (1817–89), a composer of salon and virtuoso pieces for his instrument.

the greatest and most sublime of all. Towns and cities welcome you with the enthusiasm they show to their favourite princes. . . . You, too, are a prince, in heart and mind. Your titles to nobility are inscribed in all those places wherein you have scattered the treasures of your inexhaustible generosity.[3]

After dinner, inspired by the beauty of the panorama that met his gaze when he took a stroll on the heights of the Reserve, Liszt composed on the spot a choral setting of words by the Marseilles poet and dramatist Joseph Autran (1813–77) that he had received that morning. The work thus rapidly brought into being was *Les Aquilons* (The North Winds), the second part of *Les Quatre Elémens* (S80).

The first of the Marseilles concerts was on 25 July. Liszt's own contributions to the programme, which also contained orchestral and vocal items, were the Overture to *William Tell*, the *Robert le Diable* and *Lucia* fantasies, a Chopin mazurka, the Polonaise from *I Puritani* (S391), and the *Grand galop chromatique.* The instrument he used came from the workshop of his friends the Boisselots.*

Another concert followed on 29 July, and a third, attended by Lamartine, on 2 August. The next day a *fête champêtre* was given for Liszt at the Château Colomb. Autran toasted him in verse, and there were musical fanfares, illuminations, and fireworks.

Between 4 and 6 August he visited Toulon, where he played at the Town Hall. The 6th was also the date of the last Marseilles concert, given on behalf of the city's welfare board.

On the 9th he arrived at Nîmes, and the next day gave his one concert in the town.

Courrier du Gard (13 August). Sparkling in conversation as much as in the practice of his art, he draws portraits for which he seems to have stolen the pen of Timon, more willingly discusses a point of whist than a musical question, and above all forbids money to be mentioned in his presence, unless however it is a matter of helping someone in distress or paying homage to some great unrecognized genius.

At Montpellier Liszt gave three concerts, on the 13th, 16th, and 19th. Between the second and third he also gave two concerts at Sète. On the 20th came a concert at Béziers Town Hall. 'We could not describe the enthusiasm of the audience,' reported the *Indicateur de l'Hérault,* 'as the hands of this inimitable artist flew over the piano, creating unknown harmonies. . . .'

From Albi, where he gave no concert but was the guest at the Château de Saliès of the d'Aragon† family, Liszt turned towards Toulouse, Agen, Bordeaux, and Pau.

* The founder of the Boisselot piano-manufacturing firm at Marseilles was Jean-Louis (1785–1847), whose acquaintance Liszt had made during his visit to the city in 1826. Louis (1809–50), the elder son of Jean-Louis, accompanied the great pianist during his visit to Spain later in 1844. The younger son, Dominique François Xavier (1811–93), who also made a name for himself as a composer, took charge of the firm after Louis's death until the latter's son Franz (named after Liszt, his godfather) attained his majority.

† Thérèse Visconti, Comtesse d'Aragon, half-sister of Princess Cristina Belgiojoso, had been a pupil of Liszt's in Paris.

At Toulouse, where he arrived on 25 August and stayed until 5 September (apart from a brief excursion to Montauban for a concert on 2 September), he gave four concerts (27 and 30 August; 1 and 4 September), as well as a free matinée for local workmen.* His success was overwhelming.

Bordeaux detained him for a month, during which time he also visited Agen (recitals on 20 and 22 September) and Angoulême (concert on 29 September). In addition to several concerts he also gave a short organ recital (at the church of Saint-Dominique on 2 October), playing two pieces 'with a power of talent which transported his audience'.

On 5 October Liszt played in Libourne, and on Monday the 7th he reached Pau, where his advent had been feverishly awaited for several weeks, a sense of anticipation heightened still further by such newspaper descriptions of him as that which alluded to his 'occult, magnetic and indefinable power'. His sojourn here lasted a fortnight, during which time he also made two brief trips to Bayonne (concerts on the 14th and 18th). His first appearance, at the Theatre on 8 October, he turned into a benefit concert for a former pupil, Madame Molina, who was finding it difficult to earn a livelihood from teaching. The doors were opened two hours earlier than usual, and in poured an eager and expectant multitude, residents not only of Pau itself, but of Nay, Tarbes, Bagnères, Oloron, and other neighbouring towns and villages. Liszt's success was enormous. A second concert took place on the 11th; on the 17th he gave a charity matinée at the home of Lady Fitzgerald.

The Erard piano awaiting him at the Theatre may have seemed familiar. It had been at this same instrument† that in Paris sixteen years earlier he had given lessons to the person who had lent it for the occasion: Caroline d'Artigaux, *née* Saint-Cricq. Their meeting, when she went to him at the end of the first concert to offer her congratulations, was for both of them a profoundly moving experience; and during his stay in the town Liszt paid several visits to Caroline's home in the rue du Collège. The sad memories and melancholy emotions aroused in him by this brief reunion later inspired the composition of his song *Ich möchte hingehen wie das Abendroth* (S296), a setting of a poem by Georg Herwegh.

On 21 October, the day after a banquet given for him at the Prefecture, Liszt took the road for Spain. In his company were Louis Boisselot and Ciabatta.

At Madrid, which he reached several days later, he gave four public concerts‡

* Reporting this event in its issue of 14 Sept., *The Athenaeum* (London) passed by chance to a brief mention of the latest turn in the tumultuous career of another extraordinary man and musician, whose life had at this time barely impinged upon Liszt's, but whose name was so often to be linked with his in the years and decades to come: 'M. Liszt has been exciting the enthusiasm of the Toulousians, as much by the popularity of his proceedings as by his art. The workmen's chorus having serenaded him at his hotel, the great performer came forward to thank them; and some of these expressing their regrets that they had never heard him, M. Liszt offered to give a concert specially for them, and distributed six hundred tickets gratuitously amongst them.—From Dresden, we learn that Herr Wagner, the author of "Cola Rienzi", a five-act opera which has had great success at the German theatres, has been appointed Kapellmeister to the King, a post which has remained unfilled since the death of the great Weber.'

† Having become rather dilapidated, it is now the possession of a religious college at Bétharram near Lourdes.

‡ At the Teatro del Circo, on 31 Oct., 2, 5, and 9 Nov. He also gave a semi-private recital

and also played at court. Of the first, 'in the presence of the entire fashionable and aristocratic world', *Iberia musical* reported: 'It is impossible really to describe his manner of playing, because his Heaven-sent genius constantly inspires him to change it. . . . The audience cheered, shouted *evvivas,* and went home quite beside themselves. Never have we witnessed so great a frenzy. Greetings to thee, thou artist, darling of gods and men alike!'

'No one could believe that it was a mere mortal who sat at the piano,' declared *El Globo*. And *El Heraldo*: 'His sublime playing will admit of no analysis: it is more inspiration than art. . . . What delirium!'

The great banquet given in Liszt's honour on 4 November later rated a mention in the columns of the *Allgemeine Musikalische Zeitung* of far-away Leipzig: 'The elegant Salon de Genyeis, furnished with gilt candelabras, was strewn with flowers; at the far end Liszt's portrait glittered amidst a profusion of myrtles and laurels. The first toast, received with enthusiastic applause, was proposed by the Spanish opera composer Eslava:* "Al gran pianista Liszt, al genio del arte, los artistas españoles, como tributo de admiración y respeto." '

At court on 7 November, Liszt played before the Queen,† who made him a gift of a diamond brooch worth 20,000 reales and bestowed upon him the title of Knight of the Order of Charles III.

Having been 'fêted in Madrid as perhaps nowhere else' (*AMZ*), Liszt on 4 December left the capital for Cordoba, where he arrived on the 8th, was received with a 'marvellous sample of hospitality *à l'espagnole*', and was the guest of Don Domingo Pérez de Guzmán. His first public concert was on 11 December.

On Tuesday the 17th he reached Seville, where he spent Christmas. Overcome by the size and splendour of the Cathedral, he wrote to an acquaintance: 'During the ten days I have just spent at Seville, I did not allow a single one to pass without going to pay my very humble court to the Cathedral, that epic of granite, that architectural Symphony whose eternal harmonies vibrate in infinity!' So completely was he captivated by the vast edifice, that it was not until the evening before his departure that he found time to visit the Alcázar.

Liszt to his mother, late 1844. I must admit that I find it rather entertaining when, sitting comfortably at their firesides, certain people complain about my concert plans and calculate the sums I am earning and spending. What have *they* achieved, and where has their infallible wisdom brought *them*? What have *they* earned by their talent and their labours so that in the precise workings of their double-entry bookkeeping they can compare their profits with mine? Were one to compare small things with great, I should say that they were playing the role of the Committee of Public

at the Liceo Artistico y Literario on 28 Oct.; took part in a benefit concert at the Teatro del Principe on 13 Nov.; appeared at a private concert in the Instituto Español on the 14th, and at a charity concert in the Teatro del Circo on the 21st; and played at a farewell party on the 22nd.

* Hilarion Eslava (1807–78).

† Isabella II (1830–1904), who had succeeded to the throne at the age of three. A bad monarch—she has been described as 'the queen who danced away her throne'—she was in 1868 expelled to France, where she abdicated in favour of her son, Alfonso XII.

Safety in Paris, which used to draw up the plan of campaign of its military commanders and issue orders stipulating that a general was 'within three days to bombard and take a specified city and to put to the sword those of its occupying forces which did not surrender'. All such prattle . . . is ridiculous and reminds me of the Italian proverb: 'Protect me, O Lord, from my friends—from my enemies I can protect myself!'

But if only you, at least, do not lose heart or your trust in me amidst all this jeering, I shall not complain. Here on earth, those who are conscious of their worth are pursuing a goal. I feel that I am drawing near to mine, and that suffices me. Amen![4]

1845

Liszt to Princess Belgiojoso. Cádiz, 6 January. So far as music is concerned, Spanish folk songs and the guitar are both giving me enormous enjoyment, especially when the songs are sung by some blind man; a very frequent occurrence in Spain, where in general much greater use is made of the blind than elsewhere. At the Escorial it is an old blind man who acts as your guide—and what a guide! There is no cattle-shed, no painting, no historic spot which he does not point out to you with the most scrupulous accuracy! . . . At Seville it is a blind man who tunes the instruments, and the same at Jerez. I have no doubt that somewhere or other there is a blind professor of painting or teacher of ballet.

As regards painting, the museums of Madrid and Seville contain some dazzling marvels; and with such a painter as Velasquez, Philip IV was well able to console himself for his lack of success in war. Talking of the Seville museum, I found myself the hero of a party which deserved a more brilliant one. All the rooms were illuminated, the great gallery had been chosen as the gathering place, and dinner was given in the room reserved exclusively for works by Murillo. Here can be seen, among others, the celebrated *Piété à la serviette,* painted after dinner with the Franciscans, who outdid the graciousness of our present-day *maîtres de maison*—since the latter are generally satisfied with an album sketch or some little flight of fancy of no special importance—by demanding of him as a digestion piece nothing less than a great painting.

Poor great Murillo! M. de Vigny forgot him in his *Stello*!*[1]

From Cádiz Liszt proceeded eastwards to Granada, where he visited the Alhambra, finding it an 'enchanting marvel'. He then journeyed down to Gibraltar, where on 12 January he embarked on the *Montrose,* a British steam

* A volume of tales inspired by the tragic destinies of the young poets Thomas Chatterton, Laurent Gilbert, and André Chénier.

packet, for the short voyage to Lisbon, arriving here on Wednesday the 15th and taking accommodation at the Hôtel de France. Apart from a visit to the São Carlos Opera House to hear Donizetti's *Lucrezia Borgia,* he seems to have made no public appearance until his first concert, on the 23rd. At this and the concerts which followed (25 and 30 January, 6 and 17 February), his success was enormous; above all the improvisations, which were received with a frenzy of enthusiasm. He also played on 8 February at a charity concert in which he invited the composer and pianist João Guilherme Daddi (1813–87) to join him in the two-piano *Réminiscences de Norma* (S655), at another charity concert on the 12th, and on the 15th at a benefit concert for the Italian tenor Enrico Tamberlik. His final appearance had initially been planned for the concert of 17 February, but on the 22nd he played again at a benefit for the soprano Rossi Caccia.

He also played at the homes of Costa Cabral (the chief minister) and the Visconde de Cartaxo, and at the Ajuda Palace before Queen Maria II 'da Gloria',* who made him a Knight of the Order of Christ and purchased his Boisselot piano, which she afterwards presented to the composer Manuel Inocencio. Liszt reciprocated by later dedicating to the Queen his transcription (S402) of the Funeral March from Donizetti's *Dom Sébastien*,† and to her consort, Dom Ferdinando (a Prince of Saxe-Coburg-Gotha), the *Heroischer Marsch im ungarischen Styl* (or *Marche hongroise*).

An interesting work composed during Liszt's stay in the Portuguese capital was *Le Forgeron* (The Blacksmith) (S81) for male chorus and piano (subsequently orchestrated by August Conradi). A setting of a poem by Lamennais, it bears a thematic resemblance to Siegfried's Forging Song—which perhaps it inspired—in Richard Wagner's much later music drama *Siegfried.*

Leaving Lisbon on 25 February, Liszt returned to Gibraltar and then proceeded up the east coast of Spain, his principal stopping-places being Málaga, Granada (a second visit), Valencia, and Barcelona.

Arriving in Valencia on 24 March, he stopped at the Cid Hotel, opposite the Archbishop's Palace and near the Cathedral. On the 27th, at the Teatro Principal, he took part in a concert at which he played the *William Tell* overture, the *Norma* fantasy, *Réminiscences des Puritains, Mélodies hongroises,* and the *Grand galop chromatique.* His performance created a sensation, and on the 29th he appeared at the Teatro again, this time playing Weber's *Invitation to the Dance,* the *Lucia* fantasy, and improvisations on themes provided by the audience.

On 31 March he was visited at the Cid Hotel by Pérez Gascon, a celebrated organist, and Escorihuela the cathedral choirmaster. With them came their young pupil *Benito Busó.*

We felt very moved. Liszt was dressed in a long black gown, sewn up to the neck. I could not stop looking at him, and the warts on his so expressive face I found quite extraordinary. His eyes shone so brilliantly that one's own hardly dared meet them. His hair fell down to his shoulders. . . .

* Born in 1819, queen from 1834 until her death in childbirth in 1853.

† The dedication was an appropriate one, for the opera had itself been dedicated to the Queen. In a letter of 15 Mar. that year to his brother-in-law Antonio Vasselli, Donizetti remarked: 'Buy Liszt's arrangement of the March; it will make your hair stand on end.'

Music at once became the topic of conversation. Showing himself to be both kind and amiable, Liszt went to the piano. What he played, I no longer remember; but what I have not forgotten is the effect produced on me by that music, in which tenderness alternated with power. Having finished, he asked Pérez Gascon to give him a fugal subject together with its countersubject; and after a few moments' reflection he went to the piano and improvised an admirable fugue. Very moved, Gascon embraced the master; my companion and I remained seated, unable to utter a word, so great was our ecstasy. . . . When we took our leave of the master, he promised to visit us at the cathedral the next day. In the evening there was a concert at the Theatre. Variations and improvisations on a given theme were greatly to the public's taste at that time; and the ease with which Liszt was able to treat a popular tune (a dance air, the so-called Dwarfs' Air, from the sixteenth century) earned him a new triumph.

As he had promised, Liszt came to the cathedral the next day, after vespers. We had hoped to be alone; but the canons, who had learnt of the meeting, had stayed on in their choirstalls, without making a sound however. The windowpanes, flooded by the sunlight, cast down their multi-coloured rays of light on to the gilt woodwork of the altar. To show off all the richness of his instrument, the organist improvised a fugue. Liszt stood next to me, for a long time listening calmly. But he gradually grew more animated, and, when the fugue was over, ran to the organ, seized the organist's hands and covered them with kisses. Hands so small, and yet capable of playing so wonderfully! When Liszt played in his turn, the canons came very near to betraying their enthusiasm by applause.[2]

On Wednesday, 2 April Liszt visited *Antonio Ayala,* the Procurator of Tribunals of Valencia, who was lying ill in bed.

A common friend brought him to our home on . . . the feast-day of his patron saint, Francis of Paola. Beside my bed, where I lay prostrate, stood the sweetest-toned grand piano. What did he play? Schubert's heavenly *Serenade.* I cannot describe my emotion. His playing revived me, brought me back to myself, restored my health. Before leaving, he embraced me like an angel of the resurrection.[3]

On 4 April Liszt arrived in Barcelona. Here, between the 7th and the 19th, he gave a total of six concerts, being received with rapture by his audiences and ecstasy by the critics. On the 21st, on board the vessel *Fenicio* (bound for Marseilles), he took his leave of both the Catalonian capital and Spain. His peregrinations through and around the Iberian peninsula had lasted almost exactly six months.*

* Detailed information, plus a generous selection of press reviews and comments, about Liszt's travels and concerts in Spain and Portugal can be found in various articles by Robert Stevenson: 'Liszt at Madrid and Lisbon: 1844–45', *The Musical Quarterly,* lxv (Oct. 1979), 493–512; 'Liszt on the East Coast of Spain', *Journal of the American Liszt Society,* iv (Dec.

On French soil once again, he remained for several weeks in the south-east, visiting and playing in such cities as Avignon,* Lyons, and Grenoble.†

For some five years his children had been in the care of his mother, and in a letter of 2 May (from Marseilles) to Marie d'Agoult he firmly rejected the latter's request to have Blandine in her own home.

About a year ago, Madame, I was able to think that the unbelievable opinion of me which you had invented for yourself, and had expressed to me in several letters, remained your and my secret. From your past, so full of ardent devotion for me, I had even concluded that to everyone else you would be as discreet about me as I had imposed on myself to be about you. But I have now had to abandon this illusion, for it is impossible for me to remain unaware any longer that you are telling all and sundry the silliest and most foolish things about me. If you would only reflect for a moment, you would realize without difficulty that it is quite impossible for anyone to find the least substance in any of the accusations that you are hurling at me. But it no longer behoves me to get into this argument again, and that was not my intention in addressing these lines to you. Their sole purpose is to ask if you seriously believe that I can consider it suitable for Blandine to be brought up in your home so long as you are keeping up hostilities towards me.[4]

If his correspondence with the mother of his children caused Liszt some melancholy moments, tolerably pleasing was the news that on 27 April he had been made a Chevalier of the Legion of Honour‡—'in a manner that was very flattering for me', he told his mother.

On 24 May he gave a recital at Mâcon. It was attended by Lamartine, who had

1978), 11–17; and 'Liszt at Barcelona', Ibid. xii (Dec. 1982), 6–13. See also Gerald S. Bedbrook's 'Liszt in Lisbon', *The Liszt Society Journal,* vi (1981), 29–30. The most comprehensive source on Liszt's sojourn in Lisbon is *Liszt na sua passagem por Lisboa em 1845* (Lisbon, 1945) by Pedro Batalha Reis.

* Liszt's two Avignon concerts took place on 8 and 11 May. After the first, a reviewer in the *Gazette de Vaucluse* (11 May) posed the rhetorical question: 'To describe a talent which is so far removed from everything we are accustomed to, which is akin to poetry on the one hand and to fantasy on the other, Hoffmann's pen would be needed; and which of us would dare take it, even for an hour?' Liszt's host at Avignon, the music-loving *littérateur* Comte Armand de Pontmartin, may not have aspired to write like Hoffmann, but he did offer a modest little 'conte fantastique' of his own, which appeared (above the initials Z. Z. Z.) in the *Gazette* of 15 May and was reprinted on 1 June in the Parisian *Le Ménestrel.* Still under the spell of Liszt's magic playing, two young men stroll along the bank of the Rhône; and one of them recalls a 'belle et sainte histoire'—of which Liszt had been the hero—related to him in Bohemia the previous year.

† In Liszt's audience at Grenoble, and 'bowled over' by his playing, was Nanci Pal (1806–50), elder of the two surviving sisters of Hector Berlioz.

‡ Instituted by Napoleon in 1802, this non-hereditary order contains five classes: Chevalier, Officier, Commandeur, Grand-Officier, and Grand-Croix. In 1834, Liszt had forfeited his first nomination to the Legion after snubbing King Louis-Philippe when the two chanced to meet (30 Apr.) at the Erard piano exhibition on the eve of the opening of a national Exposition of which it formed part. 'L. Ph. found that I had changed a lot,' he had written the next day to Marie d'Agoult; 'I permitted myself to reply that many other things

already sent Liszt a note inviting him* back to the Château de Monceau, a half-hour carriage ride away. During this visit the musician met, probably not for the first time, the poet-statesman's niece Valentine de Cessiat (1820–94).

It is difficult to imagine what joy Liszt hoped to find in union with a woman who seems to have been as little prepossessing physically as she was mentally; and he may have felt a surge of relief when his hasty, unpremeditated—as one surmises—proposal of marriage was refused. Valentine has been described† as a thin young girl with a 'remarkably large nose and mouth' who lacked the wit, sparkle, and gaiety of her sisters. She was also a 'confirmed dyspeptic'. Nor would music have been a bond between the two, since she had not the least feeling for it, her interests being confined to agriculture and literature. Perhaps she possessed, more important than all these things, a kind heart. That same year she rejected the offer of a friend and political associate of her uncle; and then in 1847, still unwedded, and after being jilted by the young man who had at last won her favour, sank into a state of depression. In 1849 she suffered further distress when another engagement was broken off on the very eve of the ceremony. No later suitors are known of, and involuntary spinsterhood‡ remained the destiny of the woman who had rejected one of the most brilliant and sought-after men in Europe.

The failure of Liszt's suit was no secret either to other members of the Lamartine family or to his own. Years later his daughter Blandine wrote to him, after making the acquaintance of Valentine: 'She tries to please, but she lacks charm. She's a horsy type: not very intelligent and possessing the merest smattering of knowledge—and certainly not worth the tip of your little finger nail.'

After further concerts in French towns (including Mulhouse and Colmar), and at Basle and Zurich, Liszt journeyed through the Rhineland in the direction of Bonn, where the Beethoven monument was at last in position and waiting to be unveiled.

Karl Schorn (1818–?). A welcome break in my law studies was provided by the great Beethoven Festival. . . . Soon after the death of the celebrated master, people had expressed a desire to honour his native city by erecting a monument to its greatest son; and so in 1835 a committee had been formed of professors (Breidenstein§ and others), civil servants, and

had changed too.' The errors with which the Liszt literature abounds on this topic have been rectified in Geraldine Keeling's 'Liszt and the Legion of Honour', *The Liszt Society Journal,* x (1985), 29.

* 'There is no *piano*—but it is you we want and not your hands,' Lamartine had written.

† Laura M. Ragg, *The Lamartine Ladies* (London, 1954), 256.

‡ As Lamartine's adopted daughter and (after his wife's death) heiress, Valentine was styled 'Madame' in legal documents, a title which, coupled with the real devotion and love with which she at all times tended her aged uncle, gave rise years later to a rumour that Lamartine had obtained papal dispensation for marriage with his niece—a rumour stamped, as his biographer has observed, with inherent improbability. The republican statesman whose poetic works had been placed on the Vatican's *Index librorum prohibitorum* was unlikely either to seek, or receive, such dispensation.

§ Heinrich Carl Breidenstein (1796–1876), musicologist, university professor, and composer, had planned a Beethoven statue in Bonn as early as 1828; and it was he who formed and presided over the committee.

leading citizens. But donations towards costs came in only scantily, and by 1839 the committee had still not progressed beyond the stage of preliminary discussions. Then Franz Liszt took a hand in the matter, writing to offer to have, at his own expense, a statue of Carrara marble prepared by the Italian sculptor Bartolini and erected in Bonn. This generous offer had to be declined, as it had already been decided that bronze was suitable material for a northern climate; and, further, that the task should be entrusted to none but a German artist. Not allowing himself to be discouraged by this refusal, Liszt abandoned his own suggestion, made a donation to the fund of 10,000 francs, and, by his presence on the Rhine . . . put new life into the matter. Eventually entrusted to the Dresden sculptor Ernst Hähnel, the statue was ready by 1845. August was chosen for the unveiling, and at Liszt's suggestion it was decided to combine the ceremony with a large-scale music festival (to be held on the 10th, 11th, and 12th of the month), to which musicians and admirers of Beethoven would be invited from all civilized countries. Liszt was the moving spirit of the whole thing, and at Cologne, where he had taken up residence, he enthusiastically held rehearsals. It was decided that only major works by Beethoven were to be performed, above all the Ninth Symphony. Breidenstein had composed a chorus for the inauguration ceremony, and Liszt a Festival Cantata* based on a theme of Beethoven. As venue for the concerts the committee had chosen a riding-school, and work had already begun on the décor when Liszt arrived just in time to give his decisive veto to the proposal. For the place had poor acoustics, was far too small, and in every way quite inadequate for such a festival. While the committee were still recovering from this sudden setback to their arrangements, the great magician put an end to their financial problems by offering to have a special festival hall erected, for the costs of which he would himself take responsibility. Ever accustomed to thinking big, and with the outlook of the creative artist, he straightaway turned to just the right man: Zwirner, the architect in charge of work on Cologne Cathedral. The two met in Bonn the next day, chose a suitable site near the Koblenz Gate . . . and within twenty-four hours Zwirner, with the assistance of a number of Bonn architects, had produced not only skilled carpenters but also scaffolding, for which the Rhine timber works supplied the requisite material. The décor and furnishings were prepared at Cologne, and within ten days an imposing building had sprung out of the earth as though by magic. Two hundred feet long, 75 wide, it was 1,800 square feet larger than the Cologne Gürzenich. The pillars were entwined with ivy and oak leaves, the walls covered with paper the colour of pink marble, the ceiling painted blue, and the interior fused into a harmonious whole. And, what was most wonderful of all, when on 8 August that venerable master Ludwig Spohr,

* A setting (S67) for soloists, chorus, and orchestra of a text by Liszt's friend Professor O. L. B. Wolff (1799-1851). The Beethoven theme used in the 2nd section of the work is the *Andante cantabile* from the Archduke Trio, Op. 97.

who had undertaken to conduct the Ninth Symphony and the *Missa Solemnis*, held the first rehearsal, to everyone's amazement the hall was found to have glorious acoustics. The Cologne Choral Society, which had combined with its Bonn counterpart to provide singers for the chorus, came over to the rehearsals on the new Cologne–Bonn railway in cheap special trains, refreshing themselves before their cheerful return journey in the newly-built rooms of Bonn's well-known Golden Star Hotel. . . .

Also in Bonn was the adventuress Lola Montez, apparently lying in wait for the great Franz Liszt. Although nothing else was known about her, her strange appearance and provocative manner made her particularly striking. She was small in stature, endowed with a graceful figure, and wore an extremely simple, almost shabby, black dress. But with her tumbling dark hair, her fiery eyes, and glowing southern glances, she could not fail to catch attention. All the more so since she was quite alone. To inquisitive questioners she had given herself out to be a *seconde soubrette au grand Opéra à Paris,* and even as *invitée par M. Liszt*; but she was soon recognized, and her identity revealed, by the Berlin opera singer Mantius. As was only to be expected, during the days of the festival at least, she was by her alleged friend Liszt entirely disowned and ignored. . . .[5]

Ignaz Moscheles, 10 August. I am at the Golden Star, abode of all the crowned heads of music*—brown, grey, or bald—all bewigged or lacquered pates; meeting-place of all ladies, young or old, who are fanatical about music; of all connoisseurs of art, German and French reviewers and English reporters; and, lastly, the headquarters of Liszt, who by virtue of his princely gifts outshines absolutely everyone. . . . I have already seen and spoken to colleagues from all four corners of the earth, and have also been with Liszt, who had his hands full dealing with secretaries and masters of ceremonies, whereas Chorley was sitting quietly in the corner of a sofa. Liszt kissed me, spoke a few hurried and confused words, and then I did not see him again until we were in the concert hall, when he was doing the honours to la Pleyel and other ladies. About 400 of us ate at the *table d'hôte*; and in the new Beethoven Hall shortly after 6.00 the first concert take place, conducted by Spohr. The great *Missa Solemnis* gave me much pleasure, except that it diverges from the genuine ecclesiastical style and so lacks that unity of colour which I value so highly in other works of the Master. The Ninth Symphony, which followed afterwards, was given almost faultlessly. . . . Liszt is particularly kind to me whenever we meet.[6]

Karl Schorn. The 11th had been set aside for the unveiling ceremony and the second concert. But, to the disappointment of many, they had at the

* Berlioz, Meyerbeer, and Jenny Lind were among the celebrities who attended the festival. The most notable absentees among German musicians were Schumann, Mendelssohn, and Wagner.

wish of King Frederick William IV to be postponed for a day. The King had been in the Rhineland since 28 July, awaiting a visit from Queen Victoria of England and Prince Albert. . . . As he had expressed a desire to be able to attend at least part of the festival with his distinguished guests, and they did not arrive until 11 August, it went without saying that each of the following two days had to be postponed by one day. Arriving in Cologne towards the evening of the day in question, Queen Victoria was received at the city's Aachen station by the King and a large retinue, and then drove with him to Castle Brühl, where a suite of rooms fitted out with the most costly furniture had been prepared for her. . . .

The 12th was accordingly fixed for the unveiling ceremony, at which the presence of Their Majesties could safely be counted on. The festival committee had gradually lost whatever wits they had possessed to begin with; only at the last moment was it realized that they had completely forgotten to provide suitable places in the Cathedral Square for the distinguished guests and their entourage. Great was the embarrassment, and any possibility of being able to make good the omission was precluded by the lack of time. Luckily, Count Fürstenberg owned a palace equipped with a balcony in the Cathedral Square, which he obligingly placed at the disposal of the distinguished guests, while making speedy arrangements for their fitting reception.

The ceremony began with a splendid procession from the Royal Hotel in the Coblenzerstrasse to the Cathedral Square and the Cathedral, where under Breidenstein a highly successful and uplifting performance of the C major Mass was given, in which the Cologne concert chorus took part as well as many outsiders. Because of the great throng of Bonn citizens, the Cathedral was so tightly packed that many notabilities from elsewhere were unable to gain admittance, a further act of negligence on the part of the committee, which had forgotten to provide reserved seats and unhindered access to the Cathedral for their invited guests.

After the glorious *Benedictus* with the *Agnus Dei* had been sung, and the Mass brought to an end, everyone streamed out to the richly decorated Cathedral Square for the unveiling. The statue still wore its shroud, surrounded by garlands, flags, and banners. The royal visitors had made their appearance in the mean time, and the ceremony began with the performance of a festival cantata composed by Professor Breidenstein, which entirely failed in its effect however, just as do all mixed choruses given out of doors; and just as did the speech then made from the raised speaker's desk by the same gentleman. What with the noise and bustle of the waiting crowd, and the strong wind which suddenly got up, words and music alike were completely drowned—perhaps without much loss for posterity.

Then, at a given sign, the shroud fell away—and when the image of the fêted hero of music gleamed golden in the sunlight, the loud shout of joy given by the thousand-headed throng, to the accompaniment of a fanfare of trumpets and the roar of cannon, made the very air shake.

A mood very little in keeping with the solemnity of the occasion came over Count Fürstenberg's illustrious guests. When the shroud had fallen and Beethoven was seen to present to them not his face but the rear of the human body, some of the ladies-in-waiting laughed out loud, Queen Victoria looked indignant, and King Frederick William exclaimed in amazement: 'He's turning his back on us!'. . . While Their Majesties were withdrawing, to leave for Cologne, there followed the signing of the foundation charter;* and one of the first to step proudly forward to the monument was Liszt, his face radiant with joy.† A piece which the choir then sang found few listeners, and for hours on end thousands approached the bronze hero, whose features were an exact likeness, as was testified by a number of surviving acquaintances‡ of his who were present.[7]

Ignaz Moscheles. The unveiling of the statue moved me deeply. . . . Another crush at the *table d'hôte* in the Golden Star. I sat near Bacher, Fischhof, and Vesque; a commanding presence was Liszt with his suite of ladies and gentlemen, Lola Montez among the former. . . .[8]

Karl Schorn. In the evening of the same day, the second concert took place, conducted for the most part by Liszt. His interpretation of the C minor Symphony showed great insight and understanding, and, to the astonishment of many envious and jealous artists who had been expecting a fiasco, came off very well. Even the Frenchmen present were filled with admiration by the fact that he performed it strictly according to the original score, with the use of twelve double-basses§ in the well-known quaver passages in the Scherzo, something which until then not even the Paris Conservatoire had dared. . . .¶

To conclude the festival, a third concert was arranged for nine o'clock in the morning of 13 August. Liszt's Festival Cantata was to be performed, and there were to be numerous solo contributions by other artists. For this, too, Their Majesties had promised their presence. The King, to be sure, who had by this time doubtless grown well used to the whims and changing

* The charter, bearing the signatures of Liszt and Queen Victoria among others, is now on display at the Beethovenhaus in Bonn.

† Henry Chorley (*Modern German Music,* London, 1854): 'Some will not forget the expression on Liszt's countenance as he went up to the monument—the first, as was fitting, after one or two town authorities. . . . I think that an expression so nobly and serenely radiant I have never seen on any face.'

‡ Wegeler, Schindler, and Moscheles among others.

§ Led by the great Dragonetti, now in his 83rd year.

¶ Liszt also played Beethoven's Concerto in E flat at this concert. 'The performance almost entirely satisfied me,' remarked Moscheles. 'I cannot imagine a better rendering of the energetic and spirited part of the work. In other parts I could have wished for a slightly more leisurely approach.' 'He adhered scrupulously to the text, and a finer and grander reading of the work could not be imagined,' recalled Hallé, the Beethoven specialist. 'The finest piece of pianoforte playing I ever listened to,' was Chorley's verdict.

moods of his royal guest, considerately asked the committee not to wait for him before beginning the concert; but naturally this could not be taken literally. And so rather an awkward situation arose: with people sitting tightly packed together in the festival hall, several hours of uneasy waiting passed without a single crowned head putting in an appearance. To fill up the time, the celebrated pianist Marie Pleyel played Weber's *Concertstück,* and was granted a noisy ovation. I can still see her mastering her Erard with her bare arms and powerful hands. But after she had finished, once again a tremendous tedium overcame everyone, for Liszt was keeping his Cantata until the royal visitors arrived, and by so doing he increased still further the prevailing mood of restless ill humour which was beginning to be voiced—and which was not confined to the waiting audience but had also taken hold of orchestra and choir. An unlucky star hovered over this last concert, and it began under gloomy auspices. The cause was the clashing of the currents running among musicians, artists, and music-lovers for and against Liszt. His opponents were annoyed with the committee for awarding him—a non-German who as a composer stood far behind Spohr and other German celebrities who were present—the sole honour of a festival composition, and people were hoping his work would fail. . . .

When the audience's impatience began to be expressed more and more vociferously, Liszt could no longer postpone the start of his Cantata; but unfortunately neither in the choir nor in the orchestra did he find the warmth and dedication necessary for a festival performance. Wolff's sublimely beautiful poem, of which the Cantata was a setting, and Liszt's very successful composition, with its opening chorus 'Was versammelt hier die Menge', dragged on unheeded, as did, too, the closing chorus, 'Heil Beethoven', in celebration of the hero of the festival and set to the wonderful theme of the Adagio from the great Trio in B flat, Op. 97. The disparaging comments of envious critics were already being prepared when, suddenly, the final bars were interrupted by a great commotion in the hall, and, to a great ovation, King Frederick William and Queen Victoria, with their respective retinues, entered the royal box. . . .

Ever quick to grasp a situation, the clever conductor and composer struck the desk with his baton, called *Da capo* to his performers, and the Cantata began once more. The brilliance of the court, with its splendid pomp and pageantry, had such a stimulating effect on all the musicians, that this second performance was an extremely successful one, which earned for work and composer a distinct success with both audience and critics. Local and foreign music periodicals were as one in describing this Festival Cantata as 'a product of genius', as a substantial and beautifully orchestrated work, and so forth. And with that the musical part of the festival, for all its anxious moments, came to a splendidly harmonious conclusion, after a good part of the excessively long programme had been omitted.

At the great international banquet which followed the third concert, naturally all the celebrities and festival guests staying in Bonn turned up with prepaid admission tickets, and, as is always the case on such occasions, crowds of unexpected guests poured in too, and neither in the banqueting hall itself, which was already completely full, nor in the adjoining rooms was it possible to gain admittance and find a seat. And so at the rear entrance a crowd of jostling people formed, through which the ticket-holders could scarcely make their way, and, after coming safely through this ordeal, they had to endure inside the hall that of trying to keep their own legitimate places at table from being stolen by gate-crashers. Among the latter was Lola Montez, who, having for a long time vainly begged to be allowed in free of charge, had finally found a broad-minded and well-known local gentleman, who, to the general amazement, brought her in with him, the only woman present. . . .

The first formal toasts over, the dinner talk, carried on in every European tongue, and the waving, beckoning, and greeting from one table to another, soon livened up the company, who were still in the exalted mood created by the concert; and the popping of champagne corks accompanied the aforesaid toasts with an incessant salvo. When Liszt then got to his feet, to express his thanks and to propose a toast to the non-German guests, the champagne had already taken its effect, and the hero of the day, otherwise so fluent and nimble-witted, became rather confused in his remarks, in both their form and content. He was observed to be not particularly conversant with the set phrases of the German language, in which he had had very little practice. So far as dinner speeches are concerned, it is strange how people who are witty and skilled debaters often come to an alarming standstill when having to propose a simple toast, and, conversely, how people of far slighter significance manage best. And so Liszt got somewhat entangled, failed to observe more than one propriety of form, and ended with the words: 'To all who have made the pilgrimage here: the English, the Dutch, the Austrians!' Whereupon there was a great outburst from the French, and one of them shouted angrily at Liszt: 'Vous avez oublié les Français!' This in its turn caused much shouting and commotion, which riled the French still more. One of them—I believe it was the clever Janin—complained angrily that Queen Victoria had been toasted but not Louis-Philippe, at which a sarcastic son of Albion shouted mockingly at the Parisian in a stentorian voice: 'Why not also toast the Emperor of China or the Shah of Persia, since they, too, failed to come to the festival and therefore had the same right *to be forgotten* as "le roi citoyen"?' Liszt tried in vain to make himself heard, to offer his apologies and to show his regard for the French, but in his excitement could not strike the right note, and his keenest admirer, Professor Wolff, the skilled panegyrist from Jena, gave him support and tried to defend what he had said; but the hubbub was so deafening that even his clear, high-pitched voice was drowned and reduced to silence. Then the unbelievable happened: suddenly, and with the audacious agility of a dancer, Lola Montez sprang on to the table amidst the bottles and glasses, and, gesticulating violently, shouted at Professor Wolff: 'Parlez donc, Monsieur Wolff, parlez donc, je vous en prie' etc. 'Hurrahs' and 'bravos' greeted the bold demimondaine's saucily comic performance, which eclipsed everything that had preceded it. . . .[9]

In honour of Queen Victoria and the other distinguished visitors, a concert was given that evening (13 August) in nearby Castle Brühl, at which Liszt, Pauline Viardot-Garcia, Jenny Lind, and other artists were commanded to appear. Liszt opened the proceedings with his Fantasy on *Norma*. Hardly had he begun, however, when there was a disturbance: Victoria was too hot, and an attendant was being dispatched to open a window. A moment later there was a further bustle: Her Majesty could feel a draught, and the window was being closed once again. Upset by the commotion, Liszt, who had played little more than the beginning of his piece, now improvised an ending to it. Becoming fainter and fainter, the music died away to a whisper and with a few broken chords was brought to a conclusion just as the company were at last about to give it their attention.

'Your Fantasy seemed very short,' King Frederick William remarked to him later. 'I was afraid of disturbing Her Majesty, Queen Victoria, while giving orders,' was Liszt's reply, which amused the King greatly.

Shortly afterwards Liszt went down with jaundice and 'utter exhaustion'. Confined to bed at Cologne, he was nursed by Marie Kalergis, another visitor to the Beethoven Festival.

On Friday, 24 October he arrived in Paris, where he wished to spend a quiet holiday with his mother, his children, and a few good friends. Among the latter was Jules Janin, who at once set to work to translate the text of the Beethoven Cantata into French verse for a private hearing in January.

It seems to have been Janin who, in November, introduced Liszt to one of the most celebrated of French courtesans: Marie Duplessis (1824–47), immortalized in literature and the theatre as *La Dame aux camélias,* and in the opera-house as *La Traviata.* Falling heavily for the wandering pianist, she begged to be allowed to go away with him. 'Anywhere you like. I shan't bother you. I sleep all day; in the evening you can let me go to the theatre; and at night you can do with me what you will!'

To soothe the ravishing creature, to whom he felt powerfully attracted, Liszt promised to take her to Constantinople. But she was already in the grip of consumption, and by the time he did finally reach that great city, two years later, the tragic young woman was lying in her grave at the Montmartre cemetery. 'I would have tried to save her at any price,' he told Madame d'Agoult, 'for hers was a truly delightful nature in which practices commonly held to be corrupting (and rightly so, perhaps) never touched her soul.'

Of Liszt's remaining concerts this year, best documented is the one given at Luxembourg on 24 November, a review of which filled most of the front page of the *Courrier du Grand-Duché de Luxembourg* of the 26th. On 6 December the newspaper made an unexpected return to the subject of the celebrated pianist, to correct certain errors of fact which had appeared elsewhere about Liszt's behaviour in Luxembourg—an indication of the ease with which figments of misinformation were, and have since been, disseminated about his life and conduct.

A Brussels newspaper, the *Politique,* very badly served by its Luxembourg correspondent . . . is hardly fortunate in the information it has received about the Liszt concert, and about the banquet given the next evening. Liszt came amongst us quite voluntarily; his concert was announced and advertised long before his arrival; we had no need to make *repeated entreaties* to him; the hall was filled well enough, but was not *packed to overflowing.* The proceeds came to only *nine hundred francs,* of which the artist sent *one hundred* to the welfare board. As for the eulogies bestowed upon Liszt's great talent, nothing was exaggerated. But the article which occasions our remarks concludes thus:

'The evening was marked by a small incident. Either by accident or design, Liszt dropped a pair of gloves; and these were at once seized by a few enthusiastic ladies, cut literally into fragments and shared among those members of the sex who were present—who vied with one other for possession of the remains of the material which had covered the hands of the *great man,* precious relics to be kept among their sweetest treasures. Is that idolatry, yes or no! The free-thinkers will find it quite natural, whereas . . . but let us hold our peace, not mingle sacred and profane. The day after that concert, which Luxembourg will long remember, a great banquet was given in Liszt's honour. It is said that during this meal the celebrated musician performed other feats of valour which excited no less admiration. Already beloved of Apollo, the god of music, it seems that he is also a votary of Bacchus, god of wine.'

About the little comedy of the kidskin relics, we have nothing to say. We laughed at it, and perhaps that was what it was worth. Moreover, it is rather curious that Liszt has thrown down his gloves before every piano in Europe, and that it was at Luxembourg alone that someone had the temerity to pick them up: a sure proof that art is making progress amongst us!

As for Liszt's behaviour during the banquet, opinion is unanimous that the illustrious artist displayed much wit, an easy and elegant manner of speaking, and a most expansive cordiality, as well as the perfect breeding of the man of the world accustomed to observing the strictest proprieties.[10]

1846

In early January Liszt returned to Paris to supervise and take part in the private performance of his Beethoven Cantata, given on Tuesday the 13th at Janin's home, rue de Vaugirard, before an audience of 'literary, artistic and even political notabilities', according to *Le monde musical* (15 January). 'An orchestra was lacking, but Liszt being there with his piano, who would have noticed it? The work produced the liveliest impression on this élite audience. . . . People wished to hear it twice, and a repeat was called for at the end of the evening.'

Shortly afterwards he gave concerts at various towns in northern France: Lille on the 17th and 24th, Douai on the 22nd, Valenciennes on the 23rd.

*Liszt to Marie d'Agoult. Valenciennes, 23 January.** A singular correspondence, ours! But since we no longer have anything but words for one another, why not say them? They will not close our wounds, it is true, but they will not reopen them either. To what are we condemned? Do we know? We used both of us to be noble natures, and you have cursed me, and I have banished myself from your heart because you misunderstood mine. Is it a test or a calamity that we are undergoing? The future will teach us.[1]

After a visit to Belgium, he arrived in the second week of February at Frankfurt, having stayed briefly at Sedan *en route*. Later that month he reached Weimar. Here he played at court, and in a charity concert on the 22nd performed the Fifth Piano Concerto of Beethoven as well as conducting, *inter alia,* the *Oberon* and *Waverley* overtures.

From Weimar he wrote again to Marie, from whom he had received a letter taunting him with 'failure' at the Beethoven Festival in Bonn.

Failure? What failure?

Was it a failure to have brought to a good end so enormous an undertaking, especially one so enormously mismanaged, of which not only my friends but the great majority of the musicians and public of Bonn and Cologne were utterly despairing at the time of my arrival?

Was it a failure to have made a majority, indeed even the unanimity of a small minority of one against seven, and among other things to have brought about in ten days, and to the great astonishment of residents and visitors alike, the construction of a hall large enough to seat 3,000 people?

Was it a failure to have understood that at my début as a conductor it was in good taste to share the honours of this form of musical leadership with Spohr, veteran of the German classics, and to have shown him, contrary to his expectation, all possible deference and respect?

Was it a failure so to have arranged matters that, instead of a deficit of several thousand thalers, which they were all anticipating with terror, there was eventually a surplus of a thousand thalers?

Was it a failure to have modestly postponed the torchlight procession that the students and people of Bonn were wanting to give me, and for which everything was prepared, and to have accepted no other honour

* Incorrectly dated 27 Jan. in Daniel Ollivier's edition of the Liszt–d'Agoult correspondence.

than that of allowing my name to be given to a new street close to the Beethovenstrasse?

Was it, finally, a failure to be addressed in this manner by the King at Brühl: 'I am aware, Monsieur Liszt, of everything that the city of Bonn owes you; allow me to compliment and thank you, etc. . . .'?

The same letter rebuts a further accusation.

If you will merely take the trouble to run through the lists of my concerts and my works, such as they are, not to mention my travels and my appalling correspondence, you will see that I have hardly had time to amuse myself very much, and to lead this alleged life of debauchery and immorality which make it the duty of every honest woman to shun and repudiate me!!

Let us candidly and unhesitatingly separate . . . what *is* from what *is said*. . . .[2]

At Gotha that February, Liszt attended the first performance of *Zaire,* an opera by Duke Ernst of Saxe-Coburg-Gotha. On the 23rd he left Weimar for Vienna, where between 1 March and 17 May, travelling and playing elsewhere between whiles, he gave ten concerts of his own besides making a number of charity appearances.

Prince Friedrich Schwarzenberg (1800–70). Vienna 1846. I am no particular lover of artists, but I cannot deny that I find Liszt's presence and manner most appealing. He is a true prince of music, a genuine *grand seigneur,* as far from artistic arrogance as he is from servility, thoroughly gentlemanlike; a noble—I should like to say an aristocratic—nature, shown in word, manner and behaviour. *Il y a de la véritable chevalerie en lui.* He is a priest of art, and I allow him—and this is saying not a little—even his Hungarian sword.[3]

Anton Rubinstein. I had often heard Liszt in Paris, when he was at the zenith of his glory, and been deeply impressed by his playing. . . . In 1846 I went to Vienna, because that city was one of the principal musical centres in Europe, and there too lived Liszt, the king of musicians, on whose help and protection I relied. These hopes, however, were at first dashed by the cold and distant manner with which he received me, bidding me remember that a talented man must win the goal of his ambition by his own unassisted efforts. This estranged me from him. . . .

In Vienna I gave lessons, mostly at cheap rates; I lived in the attic of a large house, and often for two or three days in succession I had not money enough to pay for a dinner at the nearest restaurant, and so I went without. . . .

It was now two months since I had called on Liszt. My prolonged absence had at last reminded him of my existence. He took it into his head to pay me a visit; and one day he made his way up to my attic accompanied by his usual retinue, his so-called courtiers, who followed him wherever he went—a certain prince, a count, a doctor, an artist; all ardent admirers and servants of the master. The first sight of my quarters seemed to shock the whole party, more especially Liszt himself, who during his sojourn in Moscow had visited my family and knew our style of living. He showed however much tact and delicacy, and in the most friendly manner asked me to dine with him on the same day—a most welcome invitation, since the pangs of hunger had been gnawing me for several days. After this I was always on good terms with Liszt.[4]

During Liszt's previous visit to Vienna, in 1840, young *János Nepomuk Dunkl* (1832–1910), later a music-publisher and editor, had played to him. 'Of the audition I no longer remember much,' recalled Dunkl, 'but it was likely to have been to Liszt's satisfaction, for had this not been the case he would have shown me to the door then and there, as later he was to do so often with, in addition, an accompaniment of solid cuffs and slaps.'

When Liszt returned to Vienna in early 1846 he took over my instruction. How and what he taught me I can now hardly say; only a few pieces which I studied by preference do I recall: Hummel's Concerto in A minor, Field's Nocturnes, Doehler's Ballade, and Chopin's Impromptu in A flat. Whether or not I played studies, I no longer remember. On the other hand I have never forgotten Liszt making me play all scales with the usual C major fingering. All in all the lessons were anything but systematic; nor were they given at set times: I simply had to go to the piano whenever time and inclination permitted.

Frequently, partly through my own fault, but also to some extent for reasons beyond my control, it happened that I came to lessons unprepared. On such occasions I had to endure severe punishment, mostly consisting of my being thrown out after a few sharp slaps. More than once after such executions, howling and lamenting I bumped on the staircase of the Stadt London Hotel (where Liszt was staying) into [Carl] Haslinger the music-seller, who always showed me great sympathy and took me back to Liszt—who had usually forgotten that a few minutes earlier he had been breathing fire and fury at me.

Among Liszt's friends there was one who really terrified me. It was Simon Löwy, to whom the *Soirées de Vienne** are dedicated. The very name given him by his friends, 'Corpse Conveyor', was sufficient to fill me with fear and horror. In addition, there were his stern manner and harsh way of speaking. It is still a puzzle to me today how this man came into the company of such constant companions of Liszt's as Baron Lannoy, Dr Gros, H. Ehrlich, Mortier de Fontaine, Otto Nicolai, Haslinger, Spina, Prince Richard Metternich (later the Ambassador to the French Court),

* Nine *Valses caprices d'après Schubert* (S427), dating from *c.*1852. Simon Löwy was a Viennese banker whose acquaintance Liszt had made in 1838.

Dr Becher, the witty writer and composer (afterwards shot under martial law), Count Laurencin, and Dr Bacher (who died in a lunatic asylum).

I went to Liszt every day, usually spending the mornings with him. Sometimes he allowed me to attend the evening entertainments he gave, and one of them remained vividly in my memory because of a little eccentricity of Czerny's, which gave rise to a delicious bit of fun as he was leaving. Taking Czerny's coat off the peg to help him on with it, Liszt all at once gave a shriek when two pet cats of Czerny's, who always carried them around with him in his pockets, snarled at him because he dared disturb their quiet musings.[5]

While based at Vienna, Liszt gave three concerts (12, 14, and 24 March) in nearby Brünn, the last being in aid of the town's St Elisabeth Convent, for which it brought 561 gulden. 'Not like a good and gracious ruler but like an angry despot does he command his instrument, but the next instant he fondles and caresses it like a young and yearning lover his beloved,' wrote the critic of the journal *Moravia*.

On 9 April Liszt arrived in Prague, where he gave three concerts (13th, 16th, and 19th) at the Platýz Hall. 'We did not experience such stormy excitement [as in 1840],' reported the *Bohemia* critic, 'but perhaps, for that very reason, the enjoyment was purer and more deeply felt.'

Referring to his recent labours (some twenty concerts in six weeks, at which he had played about fifty different works), Liszt wrote (14 April) to Marie d'Agoult from Prague: 'My patience and courage are being fully tested. Thanks to God and my mother, my health is of iron. . . . Within the next year or two my travels will be coming to an end.'

Also visiting Prague at this time was *Hector Berlioz*.

I gave six concerts there, either in the theatre or in the Sophia Hall. I remember the great joy it gave me that at the last of them Liszt was able to hear my *Roméo et Juliette* symphony for the first time. . . .

Afterwards there was a supper at which Prague's musicians and music-lovers presented me with a silver goblet. Most of the city's virtuosos, critics, and amateurs were there; and I even had the pleasure of seeing among the latter a fellow countryman, the kindly, witty Prince de Rohan. Liszt was unanimously called upon as speaker in place of the president, whose French was not equal to the task. When the first toast was called, he addressed me for at least a quarter of an hour, and in the name of the entire gathering, with a warmth of feeling, a wealth of ideas, and a turn of phrase that many an orator might have envied. I was deeply touched. Unhappily, if he spoke well, he imbibed likewise. From that treacherous goblet (passed from guest to guest) flowed such an ocean of champagne that all Liszt's eloquence was shipwrecked in it. In the streets of Prague at two in the morning, Belloni and I were still trying to get him to see that it would be better to wait until daybreak before duelling (as he insisted on doing) with pistols at two yards' range with a Bohemian who had drunk *better* than he. With the coming of daylight we felt somewhat uneasy, for

Liszt's concert was due to begin at noon. At eleven thirty he was still sleeping. They finally woke him, he climbed into a carriage, arrived at the hall, entered to a triple-barrelled round of applause, and played as I do not believe he has ever played in his life.

Truly there is a God . . . for pianists.[6]

From Prague Liszt proceeded to Olmütz (Moravia, now Olomouc in Czechoslovakia), where he gave a concert on 26 April. Not long before, the Bohemian pianist Alexander Dreyschock (1818–69) had played in the town, and the *Moravia* critic seized the opportunity to compare the two.

Liszt, this shining meteor in the artistic heaven, and he alone, could cause such an upturn, interest, and excited expectation among a public enthusiastic about Dreyschock. Liszt's début with his *Norma* was so breathtaking that his playing was repeatedly interrupted by storms of applause, which reached still greater intensity after his *Don Giovanni.* As a parting tribute, this artistic genius played the delightful *Magyar Dallok* [S242, A],* which were received with enthusiasm. So at last we have heard Liszt, whom we have so long looked forward to hearing, and if we have not forgotten Dreyschock, but are able only now to judge him fairly, here too, in the long run, Liszt must be awarded the palm, as the everywhere acknowledged victor.[7]

From Pest, where between 3 and 13 May he gave five concerts (the proceeds of one going to the Conservatoire, and of three others to various institutions) and sat to Miklós Barabás for his portrait, Liszt returned to Vienna. On 17 May he gave the last of his series of concerts in this city.

Between 20 May and 12 June he was Felix Lichnowsky's guest at Grätz. Undertaking the role of organist at a performance of Beethoven's Mass in C on the 24th, he also improvised on a theme from the *Sonate pathétique*, a work Beethoven had dedicated to Felix's grandfather. 'Liszt's musical poem and its incomparable rendering made the deepest impression on all present,' reported the *Schlesische Kirchenblatt*. Proposing a toast at the subsequent banquet, he concluded with the words of Beethoven: 'There is nothing higher than to draw nearer to the Godhead than other men, and to pour out its divine rays over the human race.'

Liszt to Marie d'Agoult. Castle Grätz, 26 May. You are right in saying that I exercise by my presence a kind of fascination for certain people, which obliges them, willy-nilly, to be my friends, a fascination for which they avenge themselves as soon as my back is turned. . . .[8]

During his sojourn at Grätz, he gave recitals at Troppau (in Austrian Silesia, now Opava in Czechoslovakia), Ratibor, and Teschen,† several of them being for charities. 'His incomparable playing is poesy itself; beside

* Eleven pieces composed between 1839 and 1847. With the *Magyar Rapszódiák* (S242, B) and the *Ungarische Nationalmelodien* (S243), they were the precursors of the better-known Hungarian Rhapsodies.

† Then in Austrian Silesia, its eastern side is now Cieszyn (Poland), its western side Český Těšin (Czechoslovakia).

him that of all others is only dull prose,' declared Eduard Simon, conductor at the Troppau Theatre. In mid-June Liszt returned to Vienna.

J. N. Dunkl. Liszt spent the summer in Vienna, and almost every day we were invited somewhere or other into the country. Most often it was to Dr Bacher's at Hietzing, to Countess Jeanette Esterházy's, and to Haslinger's in Rodaun, where Liszt enjoyed playing skittles and running races with his much-loved friend. Once when we were invited to dinner at Countess Esterházy's, my later generous patroness, I had to go to the piano and play. As it was known that I was Liszt's pet, I was overwhelmed with all manner of coddlings and kindnesses by those present, in the belief that, should they wish to obtain something from Liszt, I was the best lightning-conductor. As we were leaving, the Countess handed me an envelope. Opening it in the carriage, Liszt found that it contained a 100-gulden note, which for those days must have been a particularly generous gift, since he exclaimed in surprise: '*I* have been given, at most, a worthless tie-pin, but such a large banknote—never.'

Liszt enjoyed going with Balfe and Wallace to the Volksgarten, as, like Wagner, he was especially fond of the Strauss dance tunes.

An incident occurred at about this time which bears witness to Liszt's highly excitable temperament, which at any contradiction, even the most justified, discharged a thunderstorm. A charity concert was being given in the Brühl,* and it was arranged that on the day of the concert we should meet Liszt's uncle, Eduard Liszt,† the present Solicitor-General, at Mechetti's. On the drive out to the Brühl, Liszt told his uncle that I had surprised him with the gift of a pretty China-ink drawing. Quite innocently I remarked that the picture in question was actually a water-colour and not a China-ink. That was enough. A violent storm suddenly burst about my poor unsuspecting little head. Liszt's features darkened and I felt some heavy blows, so that Uncle Eduard had a job to divert the storm away from me. But, as always, the heavens very soon smiled upon me again. Liszt became his usual kindly self, and tried to put everything right by delving into his pockets and, without so much as counting it, giving me handfuls of money. . . .

Practising is something I never heard Liszt do. There were times when we were alone for days on end, but it never occurred to him to go to the piano. When people expressed astonishment at this, he would say that

* On 20 July, at Wolfsberger's Sans-Souci (in the Brühl), the proceeds going towards the cost of a church clock for the village of Rodaun. The musical fare was provided by Liszt on the one hand, and Johann Strauss the elder (with his orchestra) on the other. Both were received with great enthusiasm.

† Liszt's step-uncle (1817–79), youngest of the 25 children of Georg Adam Liszt's three marriages. Being actually several years his senior, Liszt generally referred to Eduard, of whom he was very fond, as 'cousin' or 'uncle-cousin'. A gifted musical amateur, Eduard spent most of his life in Vienna, where he enjoyed a distinguished career as lawyer and jurist. From the 1850s onwards he was Liszt's financial and legal adviser.

there had been times when he had 'done enough practice'. Practising three hours a day for ten years was quite sufficient, he said.[9]

Eduard von Bauernfeld (1802–90). Vienna, 28 June.* Yesterday, after the Italian opera (*Don Pasquale*), I went to Frau von Prokesch's. Liszt, who behaves theatrically enough at concerts, and tastelessly in the salon, played in his violent manner. A wonderful virtuoso to be sure, for all his striking at random and occasional wrong notes. He told me recently that he intended to retire soon, to gather his forces and compose—even to write an opera: the first Act in Italian, the second in French, the third in German! He is and remains a brilliant buffoon.[†10]

Liszt's excursions from Vienna this summer included visits to Graz (concerts on 14 and 19 June); Marburg (Austria, now Maribor in Yugoslavia) (concert on 16 June); Rohitsch-Sauerbrunn (Austria, now Rogaška Slatina in Yugoslavia) (concert on 25 July); Agram (Zagreb) (concert on 27 July); Sopron (charity concert on 3 August and a brief visit to Raiding); and Kőszeg (Güns) (concert on 27 September) in north-western Hungary, where on the eve of his arrival the general assembly elected him a freeman of the town.

In early October he set out for Pest and southern Hungary, the first part of the journey being by ship to Győr.

J. N. Dunkl. He told my mother that he was thinking of taking me with him; and with a beating heart my mother packed my goods and chattels and handed both them and me over to Liszt. . . . The signal was given and away we went to the accompaniment of Liszt's cheerful humming. Placing his fez on my head and my own little cap on his, he then to my mother's terror held me over the ship's railing and waved goodbye with me like that.

We spent a whole day at Győr. Liszt used it to pay a visit to the bishop with whom he was friendly. But in the evening he sent for gypsies, who had to play for him with all the skill they could muster.

It occurs to me that in the afternoon of that same day, when we went for a stroll, we came to a tiny chapel in front of which some peasants were praying. To my no small astonishment, the elegant Liszt went down on his knees among them in the open, dirty street, not rising until he had offered up a fervent prayer. I repeatedly experienced this sort of thing with him, which to me makes his much-discussed piety all the more understandable, as it is really at all times deeply rooted in him and definitely forms an important part of his most admirable individuality.

Here I can recall another instance which supports this assertion of mine, and which Dr A. Schmidt and I experienced at the ceremony inside St

* Poet, playwright, civil servant, and in earlier years a member of Schubert's circle.

† Bauernfeld evidently realized that he was the victim of a gentle leg pull. Liszt was indeed planning to compose an opera, *Sardanapalus* (S687), for which, thanks to the good offices of the Princess Belgiojoso, the libretto was prepared by the Italian poet Rotondi (after Byron), and there was no question but that the text was to be in either Italian or French (the language of the surviving prose sketch)—from start to finish.

Paul's for the unveiling of the statue of Gluck. It was a dreadfully rainy day and the floor of the church had become extremely wet and dirty from the mud that had been brought in. None the less, when we entered Liszt immediately sank to his knees, thinking neither of his smart clothes nor of anything else.

To return to Győr, it occurs to me that Liszt could not refrain from laughing at my horror over his demand that I should eat up a portion of snipe droppings he had ordered for me.

How great his popularity was already in those days is shown by the fact that in little Győr hundreds of people crowded all the time around the hotel in which he was staying, merely to be able to see him. When we left Győr at noon the next day, thousands of people were gathered to shout 'Éljen Liszt' after us.

During the journey in the carriage I had to recite my geography lessons. At Castle Dáka we spent several days [6 to 10 October] as guests of Count Leó Festetics. I now remember only that we shared a room and that every evening Liszt sat on my bed and played all sorts of jokes and pranks on me. How he laughed when on unpacking my trunk he noticed right at the bottom a pistol I had brought with me as a protection against possible attacks by robbers. . . .

The reception given to Liszt in Pest was something I shall never forget. At Waitzen two ships with magnates, dignitaries, and their ladies were awaiting us. Literally pelted with flowers we proceeded to Pest. There, the entire body of university students in Hungarian gala dress and with drawn swords, was waiting for him. On our arrival, István Széchenyi, the great Hungarian, came on to the ship at the head of a deputation and greeted Liszt with an address. Endless 'éljens' rang out along the banks of the Danube, and, accompanied by the constant cheering of a vast crowd, Liszt was brought like a triumphant victor to his hotel.[11]

Staying in Pest from 10 to 12 October, Liszt gave a concert on the 11th on behalf of the Joseph Orphanage. He then travelled to Szekszárd, a wine-producing town in southern Hungary, where he was the guest of his friend Baron Antal Augusz. On the 15th he visited Count György Apponyi at nearby Högyész; on the 18th gave a concert at Szekszárd; and on Thursday the 22nd celebrated his thirty-fifth birthday.

Liszt to his mother. Szekszárd, 22 October. Thirty-five years! In the middle of my life, amidst my plans and strivings, it is to you, dear Mother, to you who have always been so kind and good to me, that I turn with profound emotion and the most heartfelt yearning. . . .

Spare me henceforth advice about my health and my career. Certainly, were I to listen to anyone on this topic, it would be *you*. But, as things are at present, any anxiety or admonishment I find quite superfluous. I can adopt no other course, cannot change my habits and convictions. The mistakes I make are not serious ones; they are more easily made good than those into which suggestions from another person would cast me. Up to now, no one can seriously accuse me of having steered my life's ship badly. Among my colleagues I see none who has managed it better. To be sure, I realize that if I want to avoid becoming a half-wit or an idiot, I must exchange this ship for a better, roomier, and more comfortable one. Well, a lot of ballast will then have to be thrown overboard—but I shall land where and when it pleases me. . . .

Write to me in detail about everything. . . . What is Berlioz doing? How is Chopin?[12]

For the night of 24 October Liszt was the guest of János Scitovszky (1785–1866) the Bishop of Pécs,* at the latter's summer home of Nádasd; and from the 25th to the 27th, at his Pécs residence. Scitovszky was 'captivated by the wonderful playing, the extensive culture and the outstanding human qualities of the great musician';† and the meeting was to result ten years later in the composition of Liszt's Gran Mass. During dinner at Nádasd he set to music János Garay's poem 'A patakhoz' (To the brook) (S81a) for male-voice quartet, and the piece was sung to the guests before the meal was over. At Pécs he gave a recital at the Hattyú (Swan) inn and also played the cathedral organ.

On 27 October Liszt began to move in a south-easterly direction, passing through Mohács (which he will have looked upon with particular interest, for it was here that was fought the disastrous battle of 29 August 1526 that brought Hungary under Turkish domination), Eszék (Hungary, now Osijek in Yugoslavia), Zimony (Hungary, now Zemun in Yugoslavia) and Bánlak, where he was the guest, for the night of the 29th, of Count Guido Karácsonyi. On 1 November he arrived at Temesvár (Hungary, now Timişoara in Romania), where the streets were thronged with people intent on giving him an enthusiastic welcome. His two recitals here, on the 2nd and 4th, achieved a resounding success. Next came Arad (Hungary, now in Romania), where he gave two concerts (on 8 and 10 November at the White Cross restaurant) and was made a freeman of the town.

'Guido Karácsonyi . . . is with princely munificence doing me the honours not only of Bánlak, but even of all the relays and the most splendid draught-horses, not to mention the amazing illuminations and fireworks at Bánlak, Temesvár, and Arad,' he wrote on 10 November to Baron Augusz. 'In a word, it is the most fantastically glorious journey that ever an artist could have dreamt of, and without my having had the least inkling of it beforehand—rather like the "Bourgeois Gentilhomme", who did not realize that he was writing prose without knowing it!'

After a recital on 15 November at Lugos (Hungary, now Lugoj in Romania), a brief return to Temesvár for a charity concert on the 17th, and a recital at Nagyszeben (Hungary, now Sibiu in Romania) on the 20th, Liszt proceeded to the Transylvanian city of Kolozsvár (Hungary, now Cluj-Napoca in Romania). Received with great enthusiasm and affection, he spent a fortnight here, from 24

* And from 1849 the Cardinal Prince Primate of Hungary.

† The words of Margit Prahács, *Franz Liszt: Briefe aus ungarischen Sammlungen 1835–1886* (Budapest, 1966), 315.

November to 8 December, and gave no fewer than four recitals, of which the last was for charity. At Nagyenyed (Hungary, now Aiud in Romania), which he reached on the 8th, he gave a recital at the Town Hall that same evening, raising 500 forints for the local kindergarten.

On Wednesday, 16 December, accompanied by Counts Sándor Teleki, Gábor Bethlen, and Guido Karácsonyi, Liszt arrived at Bucharest, again receiving a most enthusiastic welcome. 'Our caravan could not have been more picturesque,' he told Georg von Seydlitz. 'Four carriages each drawn by eight horses . . . a profusion of chibouks and cigars . . . and, to cap it all, three hours of taroc [tarot] a day. Do you know this marvellous game and the charming finesses of the *Pagat ultimo*!? Assuredly, this week of travel with such excellent companions is one of my best memories. At Bucharest, Prince Michel Ghika has had the kindness to put his entire palace, one of the finest in the city, at my disposal.'

Three Bucharest recitals, on the 21st at the Ieronim Momolo Theatre, on the 23rd and on New Year's Eve at the palace of Prince Gheorghe Bibescu, were enormously successful. 'When you see Liszt, you see inspiration personified,' was the impression of the poet Catina. 'His brow is broad and lofty, his face long and pale, with chestnut curls falling carelessly all about it. He is slim, and his eyes lack lustre—but yet contain some indefinable quality of poetry.'

1847

Liszt to Marie d'Agoult. Bucharest, 3 January. I reply, first and foremost, to your questions about *Nélida*.*

No, a hundred times no, reading this book offended me not for a single moment. This is what I have said and repeated a score of times to a hundred people, who maintain, just the same, that it has filled me with bitterness. In general, in Paris as in Vienna, in Berlin as in Milan, this novel has been taken as a definite attack on my poor self. Madame de Sagan, the Princess of Prussia, my mother, and the Princess Belgiojoso have judged it from the same viewpoint as M. de Girardin. Why!? I really

* After the break with Liszt, and perhaps prompted by Balzac's *Béatrix* and George Sand's *Horace*, in both of which she had herself been a victim, Marie d'Agoult had worked assiduously at this *roman à clef* of her own, which she began in late 1843 (before the break) and brought out in 1846 under her pen-name Daniel Stern. The eponymous heroine, beautiful, high-born, and noble-souled, was intended to be a portrait of Marie herself (Nélida is an anagram of Daniel), and Guermann Régnier, a painter of plebeian origin who becomes Nélida's unworthy lover, a representation of Liszt—denigration of whom was the real intention of the book, much of the setting and many of the incidents of which come with a sense of *déja vu* to the reader familiar with the Liszt–d'Agoult adventures of a decade earlier. The depiction of Guermann, an artist 'endowed with rare abilities' and 'every indication of genius; a keen perception, an infectious enthusiasm, a marvellous facility. . .' but who possessed 'only the power of expansion, and not that of concentration, the one which forms philosophers, great personalities and true artists'—contained enough in common with Liszt (great generosity, rudimentary early education, haphazard and voracious reading, Saint-Simonian sympathies, etc.) to seem convincing to contemporary readers, few of whom in the mid-1840s could have had any inkling that the celebrated virtuoso possessed real and unique

don't know, unless it is that in our works we all carry a little of our destiny; and yours and mine alike, although in different degrees, is to be somewhat tossed about. In Germany, the stupid, pedantic critics hostile to me have seized upon *Nélida* to draw all sorts of conclusions against the sincerity of my feelings and the relative morality of my life. . . . To conclude this topic, I shall merely add that in response to the hail of questions, insinuations, condolences and malignities of every kind which have fallen on me *en masse* in regard to *Nélida*, I have always imperturbably replied that never in my life have I had any intention of doing painting, still less of dining in the servants' hall of any Highness, and, finally, that so long as my full baptismal name be not spelled out, nor my present address given . . . I shall always flatly and absolutely refuse to recognize myself in the articles and books in which people are so kind as to concern themselves indirectly with my humble self.

If you have a good memory, you will recall that I already established this principle when *Béatrix* was published.[1]

From Bucharest, and accompanied by Karácsonyi, Liszt proceeded in a north-easterly direction to Jassy (Iasi), the capital of Moldavia, which he reached on 13 January. His first concert took place on the 17th, in the salon of the *vistiernic* (Minister of Finance) Alecu Balş, one of the greatest of Moldavian boyars. At the second, a matinée on the 20th, likewise given in the Balş salon, his programme included the *William Tell* overture. 'On one poor piano,'* wrote a reviewer in *Albina Românesca,* 'the great poet Liszt rendered Rossini's whole vast conception, replacing an entire orchestra and imitating to perfection the special character of every instrument entrusted with a solo in the score. From which we see that Liszt has not restricted himself to mastering the piano, but that he has extended his studies to all the other instruments too.'

The third and last of the Jassy concerts was on 23 January. Because of the numbers who had arrived from the provinces to hear Liszt, the hall of the city's New Theatre had to be opened specially. On his appearance he was greeted by thunderous applause and a rain of flowers. After the first piece, his bust, the work of a local sculptor, appeared at the back of the platform, and, amidst a frenzied ovation, a society lady went forward to crown it with a laurel wreath. The programme also included a Moldavian Overture and Romanian *hora*

creative gifts. This being so, it was his fictional counterpart's inability and failure when faced with a great artistic challenge that, for all the emphatic denials of the letter to Marie, may have been most wounding to Liszt: 'At sight of that immense gallery, Guermann felt a painful constriction of the heart; a cold sweat broke out upon his brow. . . . He was seized by doubt; a feeling of inadequacy took possession of him; he became aware of the dreadful discrepancy between his abilities and his ambition. . . .' If Madame d'Agoult's desire for vengeance can be understood, if not condoned, no excuse can be found for her decision to republish the novel twenty years later, at a time designed to cause Liszt maximum harm. To do so was in any case pure folly, since it could only underline the fact that *Nélida* had itself ultimately failed. For, unlike the wretched Guermann, Liszt proved anything but inadequate when faced with the numerous challenges of his Weimar period; indeed, used those years to bring many of his greatest and most original works into existence.

* An Erard sent specially from Paris.

(national dance) conducted by their composer, Alexandru Flechtenmacher, later to be known, because of the popular airs which he was the first to collect, as the creator of Romanian opera. As a compliment to the young musician, Liszt then combined the themes of the Overture and the *hora* in a brilliant improvisation, bringing the audience's enthusiasm to a peak.

On this same occasion, a sonnet in French and Romanian was addressed to Liszt by one of the most cultivated Romanians of the time, the poet, painter, mathematician, and minister, Gheorghe Asachi.

Leaving Jassy on 25 January* and entering Russia, Liszt made his way to the ancient city of Kiev, the Ukrainian capital, picturesquely situated on the banks of the Dnieper. He had particularly wished to be here during the first three weeks of February, the time when local and provincial landowners were in the city making their 'contracts' for the supply of sugar, beet, grain, and other produce, and for the sale of property.

One of these landowners was the young and immensely rich Princess Carolyne von Sayn-Wittgenstein (1819–87).

Born at Monasterzyska, near Kiev, to richly-landed Polish parents, Peter and Pauline von Ivanovski, she had as a seventeen-year-old—but only at her father's behest—given her hand in marriage to Prince Nicholas von Sayn-Wittgenstein (1812–64), an amiable but superficial man wholly concerned with the more trivial pursuits and pleasures of existence; which made him, if spiritual and intellectual affinities were the criteria, an altogether unsuitable husband for the serious-minded Carolyne, who had been trained by her father and a succession of governesses to love knowledge and to develop her mind. During the eleven years of the marriage she had steeped herself in the writings of such thinkers as Fichte, Schelling, and Hegel, acquired a profound knowledge of the Talmud and of Dante, and written a commentary on Goethe's *Faust*. From the union of this ill-matched couple, the one fruit pleasing to both partners was an enchanting little daughter (their only child), Princess Marie (1837–1920).

The circumstances of the fateful meeting which took place at Kiev between Franz Liszt and Princess Carolyne von Sayn-Wittgenstein have been described by their acquaintance Marie Lipsius (La Mara), from information provided by Princess Marie:

> For a charity concert he was arranging, and without yet knowing him, she sent Liszt a 100-rouble note. So generous a gift surprised and delighted this most open-handed of all artists, and, his interest aroused from the outset in the donor, who had been described to him as miserly and eccentric, he waited upon her to express his gratitude.
>
> A flame was ignited at this very first meeting. Even if the Princess could not be called beautiful, her eyes and countenance proclaimed special qualities of mind and soul, qualities which were as considerable as they were attractive. In addition she possessed wonderful eloquence and a well-nigh unbelievable wealth of knowledge. . . . She, who had travelled

* It was on this day that Eisenbach, the Austrian consul at Jassy, sent a report to Metternich about Liszt's sojourn in the city. Referring also to Karácsonyi, it concluded: 'Many people travelling abroad could be recommended to take as a model the decent and tactful behaviour shown by both gentlemen during their stay here. . . .'

> greatly, and the artist who was at home in every country in Europe, found that they had numerous connections in common. The recital he gave on 2 February* in the hall of the University she made sure not to miss . . . and for the rest of her life preserved the programme of that memorable evening like a holy relic. . . .
>
> To see him, hear him and fall in love with him were one and the same for the Princess. The ardent, art-thirsting soul of the lonely woman succumbed to the magic which held the whole of educated Europe in thrall. . . .
>
> By chance, a few days later she heard a *Pater noster*† of Liszt's sung at church, and the profoundly moving impression it made convinced her of the creative vocation of the unparalleled master of the piano.

Almost at once the Princess invited Liszt to be her guest at Woronince, the vast estate lying between Kiev and Odessa in the province of Podolia which, together with its 30,000 serfs, had formed her marriage dowry. Short though the visit was, he could not resist mentioning his interesting new acquaintance in a letter of 10 February (OS) to Marie d'Agoult: 'I have just met at Kiev, by chance, a very unusual woman, a truly exceptional and distinguished one—to the point that I decided, joyfully, to make a detour of twenty leagues to spend a few hours chatting with her. . . . It is from [her] home that I am writing to you.'

Via Czarny-Ostrov (where he spent Easter with Count Przezdziecki, whose orchestra entertained him with works by Rossini, Donizetti, and others) and Kremenets (two concerts), Liszt arrived on 13 April at Lemberg (Austria, now Lvov in the USSR), where in a stay of several weeks he gave four concerts of his own and took part in others given by the pianist Sophie Bohrer and the violinist Karl Lipinski. On 19 May he reached Cernovcy (Austria, now in the USSR), and here gave two concerts (24 and 25 May) at the Hotel Mikuli.

From Jassy, which he reached again on 27 May, he journeyed to Galatz, an inland port whence, after an obligatory spell in quarantine, he embarked for Constantinople, arriving in early June and being warmly received by Sultan Abdul-Medjid (1823–61). The piano he used here had been sent from Paris by Erard.

Liszt to Pierre Erard.‡ Before I embarked at Galatz, the Constantinople newspaper informed me of this kindness in such good taste on your part; but I was none the less agreeably surprised when, at the Palace of Tcheragan, I let my fingers wander over an instrument 'of such power and perfection', as you expressed it so felicitously in your letter to M. Donizetti,§ which the Constantinople paper publishes in its entirety. After having figured brilliantly twice at His Imperial Majesty's and twice at my

* OS (14 Feb. NS). Liszt played the *Hexameron*, a concerto (probably the *Concertstück*) by Weber, his own transcription (S564) of Schubert's *Die Forelle*, an Etude by Chopin, Weber's *Invitation to the Dance*, and an improvisation on themes submitted by the audience.

† S21/1, for male voices. This Kiev performance was its first.

‡ In an undated letter received by Erard on 5 Aug.

§ Eldest brother of the celebrated composer, Giuseppe Donizetti (1788–1856) had come to Constantinople in 1828. Becoming Chief of Music to the Ottoman Armies, he was instrumental in introducing Western scales, harmony, and notation to Turkey, for which, as a reward, he was from 1840 onwards allowed to enter the harem as a singing master.

concerts (the last of which was held in the splendid salons of the Russian Embassy, where the view extends from the Bosphorus to the Sea of Marmara, from Pera to Constantinople, from the Seraglio promontory to Mount Olympus, from Europe to Asia!), the piano was sold for 16,000 piastres to a young man, M. Baldagi, who has offered it to his beautiful fiancée. . . .

This instrument's fate is quite a romantic one; and it must be conceded that, for the classic qualities it possesses, it well deserves it.[2]

To Madame d'Agoult he reported (letter of 17 July): 'His Majesty was extremely gracious to me, and after having recompensed me both in money . . . and with a gift (a delightful enamel box with brilliants), he conferred on me the Order of Nichan-Iftikar in diamonds. I admit that I was greatly surprised to find him so well informed about my bit of celebrity.'

Leaving Constantinople on 13 July on board the *Peter the Great*, he returned to Galatz. After a second spell of quarantine here, followed by a further journey of four or five days, he arrived in early August at the Black Sea port of Odessa, where he had arranged a rendezvous with Princess Carolyne, with whom he was looking forward to 'taking up once again the long thread of our labyrinth of ideas and dreams'. Here, too, he met her estranged husband and her mother.

During the several weeks he and the Princess spent together at Odessa, Liszt gave ten concerts. In September, having arranged to meet again at Woronince a month later, they took their leave of one another, and Liszt set off, via Nikolayev (concert on 17 September NS), for Elisavetgrad (now Kirovograd), where, still a month short of his thirty-sixth birthday, he gave the last concert of his career as a professional pianist. It was a decision he had been meditating for some time,* and one which was warmly supported and encouraged by the Princess, whose ambition to see him devoting himself wholly, or principally, to creative work was at least as powerful as Liszt's own. In the years and decades to come he occasionally played the piano in public, but never again to earn money for himself. 'Elisavetgrad marks the last stage of the concert life I have been practising throughout this year,' he wrote shortly afterwards to Carl Alexander. 'Henceforth I count on being able to make better use of my time, and I am meanwhile holding myself in repose so that I may advance more rapidly.'

Abandoning a plan to visit Poltava (to see the site of Peter the Great's historic victory over the Swedes), Liszt then made his way for the second time to Woronince, where, apart from a brief absence in November to make gratis appearances in some of the nearby towns and to accept invitations from neighbouring landowners, he remained until the following January.

In a letter to Marie d'Agoult at the end of May, he had referred to Carolyne Wittgenstein as 'my new discovery in princesses. . . . [but] we have not the least intention of falling in love. . . .' Writing (22 December NS) to the same correspondent during the weeks he and the Princess were able to relax and really get to know one another at Woronince, however, he emphasized the profound and increasing attraction he felt for his hostess, whose 'great character' was

* 'The moment is coming for me to break out of my chrysalis of virtuosity and to allow my thoughts to take free flight,' he had written a year earlier to Carl Alexander.

'joined to a great intellect'. And if it was the qualities of Carolyne's mind and character which attracted him first and foremost, that did not exclude physical appeal, as he argued chivalrously when writing to his mother a year or two later:* 'I do not know in what connection Princess G[agarina] told you that Princess Wittgenstein is not beautiful. When the opportunity presents itself, tell your friends and acquaintances from me that I believe myself to be as good a connoisseur of beauty as anyone, and that Princess W. *is* beautiful, very beautiful even, for she possesses that rare and imperishable beauty which can be imparted to the countenance only by a radiant soul. . . .'

Before Liszt left Woronince it had been agreed that so soon as was practicable Carolyne would join him in Germany.

A delicious musical fruit of these months was his *Glanes de Woronince* (S249), three short piano pieces, *Ballade d'Ukraine, Mélodies polonaises,* and *Complainte,* inspired by gypsy themes heard at Woronince. Published two years later, the work was dedicated to the young Marie von Sayn-Wittgenstein.

1848

Leaving Woronince in mid-January, and travelling via Radziwilow, Lemberg, Cracow, Ratibor, Krzyzanowitz (home of Felix Lichnowsky), Löbau, and Dresden, Liszt arrived in early February at Weimar, where on the 16th he conducted Flotow's *Martha* in celebration of the birthday of the Grand Duchess Maria Pavlovna. Two evenings later he played to a small private audience at the Grand Duchess's.

In the weeks that followed he conducted performances of Gustav Schmidt's *Prince Eugene* and of *Fidelio,* and at a court concert played Henselt's Piano Concerto. He also gave singing lessons to Princess Sophie, wife of Carl Alexander. Most important of all, he maintained an animated correspondence with Princess Carolyne, his letters expressing love and devotion on the one hand and dealing with the practicalities of their planned reunion on the other.

Liszt to Princess Carolyne. Weimar, 24 March. I understand only two things: work, and Chapter V of *The Imitation of Christ.* Oh! what sublime and beautiful things there are in your letter† to me. They have seared my very soul. Yes, I shall wait for you, for I have nothing else to think of or do if it be not to wait for you. It is only necessary for this *waiting* to be worthy of you. I shall try![1]

In late March he set out for Lichnowsky's Castle Grätz, where the reunion with Carolyne was to take place; and she shortly afterwards, accompanied only by her daughter and one or two members of her household, left Russia on the pretext of

* His undated letter was a reply to his mother's of 13 Feb. 1849 (unpublished, Richard Wagner Archiv, Bayreuth, II Cg 21.).

† Very few of Carolyne's letters to Liszt have been published. The remainder—a vast quantity—are held at the Goethe- und Schiller-Archiv in Weimar.

travelling to Carlsbad (in Bohemia)* to take the waters. Before setting out she had by selling an estate provided herself with a million roubles from the fortune that came with her dowry. To the church authorities she had sent a petition for divorce; and for her husband and mother-in-law had left letters explaining her desire to link her destiny with that of Liszt.

Arriving safely at Ratibor in Silesia, she was there welcomed by Lichnowsky, who escorted her to Grätz. Here, on 18 April, took place the reunion with Liszt. 'May the Lord's angel guide you, O my radiant morning star!' he had written shortly before her departure.

Liszt to Franz von Schober (in Weimar). Castle Grätz, 22 April. I should be so pleased if you had an opportunity of getting to know Princess Wittgenstein. She is beyond any question a most extraordinary and quite brilliant example of soul, mind, and intellect (plus, of course, immense *esprit*). . . . Serfdom of the political kind may come to an end, but the bondage of the soul in the realm of the spirit, is not that said to be indestructible?[2]

Taking leave of Lichnowsky[†] at the end of April, Liszt and Carolyne went via Prague to Vienna.

J. N. Dunkl. When Liszt reappeared in Vienna, it was once again all up with my studies, for he laid total claim to me and took me everywhere.

It gave me special pleasure during this time to be able to admire Thalberg's playing while in the company of Liszt. I vividly remember how badly attended the concert [3 May] was, as a great part of the educated public had already left the city on account of the approaching disturbances. To this day I can see Liszt as he sat on the platform listening and loudly applauding.

There was also a concert in which Liszt conducted a performance of the overture to Erkel's[‡] opera *Hunyady*. The work displeased, being received with a storm of booing. Shaking his head like an enraged lion, Liszt gave a sign to the orchestra, and the overture was played through again. Taken aback by Liszt's action, the entire audience this time listened in silence, and at the end broke into a tempestuous roar of applause. Erkel's overture gained a victory which may have been forced but was none the less brilliant.[§]

* The carriage used for the journey is now on display at a museum in Rothenburg ob der Tauber.

† For the last time. Lichnowsky's death, at the hands of the Frankfurt mob, occurred on 18 Sept.

‡ After Liszt, Ferenc Erkel (1810–93) was the foremost Hungarian composer of the 19th century, and with his *Hunyady László* of 1844 the creator of Hungarian national opera. He was also a gifted pianist, the founder and conductor of Budapest's Philharmonic Concerts, and Director of the Academy of Music founded, with Liszt as President, in 1875. It is his statue which, with that of Liszt (both being the work in 1882 of the sculptor Alajos Strobl), can be seen in the façade of the Budapest Opera House.

§ Dunkl's memory seems to be at fault: Liszt had conducted the overture at his Vienna

In those turbulent days of 1848 I accompanied Liszt on a visit to the barricade commanded by the well-known bass Karl Formes. To the workers posted there Liszt gave cigars and money; and in place of all his decorations he wore in his buttonhole the Hungarian national cockade.*

Shortly before, in circumstances which turned out none too well for me, I had also had the pleasure of making the acquaintance of Liszt's friend Princess W., subsequently so celebrated. Having been told by Liszt to betake myself to the second-floor apartment where the Princess was staying and to pay her my respects, I was more than a little surprised to find, lying on an ottoman, a small, unattractive woman already past her first youth. Beside her was a long chibouk. That she had been smoking it, I cannot guarantee; but so much is certain: the chibouk was there. After the usual greeting, the first thing she did was ask me if I was a Catholic. When I replied in the affirmative she went on to ask if I attended church regularly and if I confessed.

It was only from Liszt that I learnt that apparently instead of replying properly I laughed. How Liszt told me about this, readers will easily imagine when I remind them of the journey to the concert in the Brühl.†[3]

After an excursion to Eisenstadt and to Liszt's native Raiding, he and the Princess, whom he had persuaded to seek the protection of the Grand Duchess Maria Pavlovna (sister of the Tsar), made their way via Prague and Dresden to Weimar. At Dresden Liszt sought out Richard Wagner, whom he had not seen since their brief encounter in 1844. Together they spent an evening (9 June) of music and conversation with Schumann—but this highly interesting meeting between three of the greatest musicians of the century unfortunately ended on a discordant note when Liszt and Schumann fell out over the respective merits of Mendelssohn and Meyerbeer. Receiving from Wagner soon afterwards a note asking for a loan of 5,000 thalers (a sum equivalent to three and a half years of Wagner's salary as Dresden Kapellmeister), Liszt, whose own financial circumstances were now much reduced, was unable to help, but in the years to come was to do so often. He had yet to learn that friendship with Wagner had to be paid for, literally; that giving money to the latter was tantamount to dropping it into a bottomless well; and that the ingenuity displayed by the ever-resourceful Saxon in extracting money from others was surpassed only by the talent with

concert of 17 May 1846, and there is no record that he did so again during this 1848 visit. In his review of the 1846 concert, Heinrich Adami reported that the overture was received with 'a tremendous ovation, so that Liszt could hardly help repeating it'.

* Linked to the revolutionary movement throughout Europe that year, the uprising in Vienna was largely a reaction against the autocratic rule of Metternich and the despotism of his police forces. After the rioting which occurred in the city early in the year, Ferdinand I consented to the dismissal of Metternich (who fled to England) and to the drafting of a constitution, but shortly after the October insurrection abdicated in favour of his nephew Franz Joseph. Hungary's revolt against Austrian rule was suppressed in August 1849 when Tsar Nicholas of Russia sent an army to intervene on Austria's side.

† On 20 July 1846. See *supra*.

which he could dispose of the vast sums thus obtained and still remain in a state of dire financial embarrassment and insolvency.

At Weimar, Carolyne rented the Altenburg, a thirty-room mansion standing in the outskirts of the town. Liszt returned to the Erbprinz Hotel, until moving a year or so later into a wing of the Altenburg.* The house was bought in 1851 by the Grand Duchess, who charged the couple no rent.

There now began the dozen most fruitful years of his career. No longer chained to the fitful itinerant life of a touring virtuoso, reinvigorated by the stimulating companionship and conversation of the Princess, with whom he could discuss all manner of literary and cultural topics, as well as the religious and philosophical problems which troubled him, and provided with the domestic stability and environment that best allowed him to concentrate on creative work, he was able to bring all his energy to bear upon composition, teaching, and the carrying out of his demanding duties as Court Kapellmeister Extraordinary.

Among the numerous works which came into being during these years were: the Faust and Dante symphonies; the first twelve symphonic poems (a musical form of his own invention); two piano concertos; two of the three great works for organ; the *Missa Solennis* (Gran Mass); parts of the oratorios *Christus* and *The Legend of St Elisabeth;* and many magnificent works for piano solo, including two volumes of *Années de pèlerinage,* the *Harmonies poétiques et religieuses,* two Polonaises, two Ballades, three *Etudes de concert,* the *Grosses Konzertsolo* (and the two-piano *Concerto pathétique* derived from it), the Scherzo and March, the final versions of the *Etudes d'exécution transcendante* and *Grandes Etudes de Paganini,* and his greatest masterpiece for the instrument, the Sonata in B minor. Plus many songs, transcriptions, smaller-scale piano pieces, and miscellaneous choral, chamber, and orchestral compositions.

Not long after his arrival at Weimar he was joined by the capable if routine conductor and operetta composer August Conradi (1821–73), and early in 1850 by the versatile, self-taught Swiss composer Joachim Raff (1822–82), who had made Liszt's acquaintance at Basle in 1845. From both Conradi (who stayed in Weimar only until 1849) and Raff, who had at this time considerably more experience than he in writing for orchestra, Liszt was to receive valuable assistance during the time he was acquiring his own mastery of the medium.

Among the many operas whose Weimar premières took place under his direction were Berlioz's *Benvenuto Cellini,* Cornelius's *The Barber of Bagdad,* Donizetti's *La Favorita,* Gluck's *Orfeo ed Euridice,* Lortzing's *Zar und Zimmermann,* Meyerbeer's *Les Huguenots,* Nicolai's *The Merry Wives of Windsor,* Rossini's *Le Comte Ory,* Anton Rubinstein's *The Siberian Hunters,* Schubert's *Alfonso und Estrella,* Schumann's *Genoveva* and *Manfred,* Sobolewski's *Comala,* Verdi's *Ernani* and *I Due Foscari,* and Wagner's *Der fliegende Holländer, Tannhäuser,* and *Lohengrin.* Of these, the Cornelius, Rubinstein, Schubert, and Sobolewski works, and, most notably, *Lohengrin,* were world premières. Naturally Liszt also brought to performance great operas (by Mozart, Beethoven, Weber, and others) which had already been given in Weimar by his predecessors, as well as premières and repeats of other works (by such

* For the sake of appearances, however, the Weimar court continued to address communications to him at the hotel.

composers as Dorn, Hoven, and Duke Ernst of Saxe-Coburg) which have since fallen into oblivion.

With but few exceptions, such as Hermann Cohen, and the Hungarian prodigy Carl Filtsch (1830–45), to whom he (and Chopin) had given lessons in Paris, his pupils until this time had been at best moderately gifted. But during his years at the Altenburg some of the finest pianistic talents of the second half of the century were to come into his hands, foremost among them Carl Tausig and Hans von Bülow.

Nor was literary activity forgotten. With the Princess as his collaborator and co-author, Liszt brought out during their life together in Weimar two full-length books in addition to a large quantity of essays and articles.*

Rich in achievement though they were, however, the Weimar years were also a period of frustration for Liszt and the Princess in so far as they hoped to exchange their illicit relationship for the more spiritually satisfying and socially acceptable state of matrimony. Carolyne's divorce from Prince Wittgenstein was the immediate desideratum, but it was one for which she intended to sacrifice neither custody of her child nor the much-needed revenues from her Russian estates. And since she was subject to the authority of the Tsar, to whom Prince Wittgenstein was close, it was inevitable that sooner or later there would be a clash of wills with that redoubtable ruler. This eventually occurred when she ignored his order to return to Russia—the immediate consequence of which was that her presence in Weimar became an embarrassment to the court, whose dominating figure was Tsar Nicholas's sister, the Grand Duchess Maria Pavlovna.

The diary of Frédéric Soret (1795–1865), a Swiss intellectual who had in earlier years been tutor to Carl Alexander and in the 1850s was on several occasions the latter's guest at Weimar, reveals, as late as 1858, not only the difficulties facing the Grand-Ducal family in regard to the ménage at the Altenburg, but also the reason why for so many years they hesitated to take decisive action:

> This scandal is doing the greatest harm to the reigning house, and Her Imperial Highness, loved and respected though she is, cannot escape being blamed by a public opinion which fails to understand how she can carry tolerance so far as to suffer the Princess in a house belonging to her; a tolerance which is all the greater seeing that, from what people say, the last thing the Princess bothers about is paying the rent. Alas! they would be severer did they not fear that in sending away his lady friend they might lose Liszt too.

Not a few people believed that Liszt was fundamentally insincere in the relationship with Carolyne, and that, had it been possible, he would gladly have extricated himself from it. And since he was also caused much disappointment and vexation by the savage attacks to which his works were subjected as they made their appearance, it is evident that, whatever his true feelings for the Princess, he had during these years as much to bear as in any other period of what was *au fond,* and for all its glittering outer aspects, an unhappy life. Many

* Five of the six volumes (a seventh was planned but never published) of Liszt's literary works, edited by Lina Ramann and published between 1880 and 1883, contain writings dating from the Altenburg years.

acquaintances would have endorsed the words written later* by his perceptive younger daughter, in reference both to the 1840s and to the time, from 1853 onwards, when she saw him more frequently: 'Even as a child I *knew* that my father suffered—the father whom I was accustomed to seeing only in the splendour and the intoxication of triumph; I *knew* it, and I suffered with him, secretly and silently. . . .'

One of the first visitors to the Altenburg after the Princess had taken up residence there was *Fanny Lewald,* who arrived at Weimar on Sunday, 22 October 1848 in the company of her friend Therese von Bacheracht (1804–52), wife of the Russian Consul General in Hamburg.

Therese had made Liszt's acquaintance in Hamburg. . . . He was among those she had welcomed into her home on various social occasions, and they had become good honest friends.

She had written to tell him that we were coming to Weimar and of the time of our arrival, asking him to order two connecting rooms for us; and this he had done. When we reached the Erbprinz—still a thoroughly bad hotel at that time—whose first floor had been taken over for the most part by Liszt himself, Therese found only a greeting in writing from him, as he had been invited to court. We took our meal, and it must have been about nine when Liszt was announced. He entered the room with a quick lively movement, and it gave me great pleasure to witness the delight with which the two of them, the beautiful Therese and he, greeted one another.

I, of course, was a complete stranger to him . . . but eager as always to give pleasure to others, he mentioned that the Grand Duchess had spoken appreciatively of me when he told her that Therese and I had arrived and were staying at the Erbprinz. To Therese, who was known at the Weimar court, he reported that the Grand Duchess hoped to see her again, and that the Russian Ambassador, Baron von Maltitz,† who was then residing at the Goethe House, would wait upon her to arrange the audience. . . .

I had heard much of the pomp with which he made his entrance into society and the concert hall, of the artificial manner in which he would proudly throw back his mighty head, and of how, when taking his seat at the piano, he would deliberately toss his gloves to the floor, for them to be seized and kept as precious souvenirs by his enthusiastic lady admirers. It pleased people to represent him as a man who wished to excite attention through empty externals.

In my own acquaintance with him I always found Liszt very unpretentious; and that a man who from his earliest childhood onwards knows the eyes of others to be turned upon him with curiosity and admiration gradually arrives at presenting himself to them in a particular way, I find most natural; indeed, necessary. While he was young he will have enjoyed such

* In a letter (1866) to King Ludwig II of Bavaria.

† The popular Apollonius von Maltitz (1795–1870) was his country's representative at Weimar for many years.

homage, just as anyone else would have enjoyed it in his place; nor could he very well have rejected it without disappointing those who found satisfaction in offering it to him. . . .

When I met Liszt in Weimar we were both thirty-seven, and it so happened that it was both his birthday and Stahr's.*. . . He was still as slim and easy in all his movements as he had been when I saw him at Königsberg. I was surprised once again, just as I had been in my native city, by his cheerfully sparkling eyes, by the power of their gaze, and by a strange nobility illuminating his entire countenance. The long, undulating, brownish hair springing up from the middle of his forehead, his complexion and facial structure, were quite un-German; and yet they could not be called Slav or Sarmatian either, for in profile, until he became stouter in old age, they were strikingly reminiscent of Dante. When he gazed about him he looked like a man to whom the world belonged; one who had been born to such a possession so that he took it as a matter of course. There was such nobility in his head that in the 1830s, when he lived mostly in Paris, it influenced the portraitists as much as did the classical beauty of the Comtesse d'Agoult. Both heads can still easily be recognized in many pictures dating from that time. Foyatier's statue of Spartacus, in particular, which stood in the Tuileries garden opposite the palace, was regarded —rightly or wrongly— as a definite portrait of Liszt. . . .

In 1848 Liszt generally spoke French when appropriate; but he used it in a way that struck me as rather special, and which was most charming, as was likewise the manner in which he would offer you his hand and 'cordialement' shake it. That is not something I could explain or describe, and yet you felt that it was something free and beautiful, something which for the moment brought him closer to you, something which showed trust and inspired confidence. . . .

These memories of mine have induced me to seek out the letters I wrote from Weimar in 1848 to Stahr and to my brothers and sisters, in which I described that meeting with Liszt in all its details. . . . All our conversations were in French. In those days Liszt's German was really bad, an ugly Viennese variety with a strong Hungarian flavour. With the passing years it became essentially clearer and more refined; but his French was certainly always better than his German.

According to my letter of 23 October 1848, Therese and he spent the first moments exchanging questions about common acquaintances; and Liszt did not tire of assuring Therese over and over again how delighted he was to see her once more.

'You really cannot know', he said, turning to me, 'how devoted I am to Therese; and would you like to know why?—Because she has always shown me an honest friendship, and never love! *Il y a en apparence de la*

* The writer Adolf Stahr (1805–76), who in 1855, after the death of his first wife, became Fanny Lewald's husband.

fatuité dans cette confidence, but I don't hesitate to affirm it since it is the most sincere truth. Let Therese put me to the test when she will, and she will find that she can count on me!'

'That is true, Heaven knows!' cried Therese. 'And you have never proved it more kindly than in Kassel,' she added. 'Fanny knows about it too, and it delighted her as much as it did me.'

And indeed the incident to which she referred was a beautiful testimony to the goodness of heart they had in common. This is what it was about:

When Liszt had once given concerts in Kassel, and, as everywhere else, been most eagerly lionized by court and society, Therese had written to tell him that living in Kassel was Wilhelm von Humboldt's friend Charlotte Diede, with whom Therese—I no longer remember exactly how—had long been in contact, and whom after Humboldt's death she had looked after with great kindness.

Frau Diede, who was old, poor, ailing, and lonely, had told Therese how sorry she was not to be able to hear Liszt, whereupon Therese had written to him: 'You can do a kindness to an old, unhappy woman. Go to Frau Charlotte Diede and play something to her.' And in the midst of all his triumphs Liszt had gone to the lonely and forgotten woman, and on her 'miserable piano' had played her 'whatever was possible on such a thing!'

He laughed at the recollection, and Therese went on to refer to the truly regal gift that Liszt had sent from Petersburg to Hamburg after the great fire in that city. I believe it was 10,000 silver roubles, if not more. . . .

He then came to speak of our stay in Frankfurt and of the murder of Prince Lichnowsky, who had been a close friend of his, and at whose home, he told us, Princess Wittgenstein had stopped off for a while on her journey to Germany and Weimar. He spoke of the Prince with great emotion. . . .

From the Frankfurt Parliament and our experiences there it was but a short step to our stay in Paris and to French affairs. Therese told him about the great changes she had found in the appearance of the city as well as in the feelings of her acquaintances; and I mentioned the moving impression made on me by Rachel when, on the stage and in French classical costume, she had sung the *Marseillaise.*

'How is that possible!' exclaimed Liszt all at once in a passionate tone of voice. 'How could that have moved you? How could you admire it? *Now* to sing the *Marseillaise* is a folly, a crime, a sin. What has the present revolution in common with that of the last century? What is the good of so bloodthirsty a hymn in a social upheaval whose basic principle is love, whose sole solution is only possible through love? Where are the *féroces soldats* now? Where is *le sang impur*? That in this revolution the words *qu'un sang impur abreuve nos sillons* were sung should never have been tolerated! I know and appreciate what I am saying. I would be one of the first to call to arms, to give my blood and not tremble before the blade of the guillotine, if it were the guillotine that could bring peace to the world and happiness to mankind. But who believes that to be the case? Peace must be brought into the world and justice accorded to each of the individuals who together comprise the whole! . . . It is as much a matter of economics, and of the profound studies which have to be undertaken, as of seeing that Christianity's teaching of love is finally taken seriously. And in such a non-violent task, to call to arms, to excite the wild passions of the people, to invite *gaieté de cœur* in shedding blood, and, to cap it all, to dedicate even the stage—art—to the same dreadful end, that is an atrocity, a crime, and nothing else.'

This outburst of feeling, and the sequence of his thoughts, took us completely by surprise. Other sides of his character were suddenly revealed by this quick change in the conversation: his belief in a better future for mankind by the transformation of existing conditions, his roots in Christianity, and that striving for knowledge and truth which had once turned him towards Saint-Simonism.

A silence had fallen over our conversation, and I observed to him that what had attracted me in his career quite as much as, if not still more than, his artistic glory, had been his connection with the Saint-Simonians, which I had interpreted as a sign of his search for the union of the seemingly irreconcilable, his striving after the ideal.

He understood that. 'Look,' he said, 'Christianity has been propounding these noblest and most profound teachings of the brotherhood and equality of all men for well-nigh two thousand years—but who has understood them, and what has been made of them?'

We continued the conversation, and it took us far. Here, however, I am giving only what I have taken word for word from that old letter. We agreed with one another on almost every point; and when Liszt took his leave after midnight, he shook my hand with the words: 'If I have understood you aright, you likewise are one of those who have but two options: to love the human race or to despise it!'

With that he departed; and the two of us, Therese and I, were aware that we had experienced something unforgettable. . . .

The next morning he came to see us again. He brought me a new volume of the Comtesse d'Agoult's *Lettres républicaines* which had been sent to him, and in which she again addressed a letter on 'les orateurs modernes' to me. Therese was still dressing, and so Liszt and I were alone. He asked after the Comtesse d'Agoult—it was no trivial conversation but one which required deliberation, and it ended with the remark: 'She found it necessary to reproach me, but also gave me much occasion to do so to her.' After asking whether I had seen George Sand (I had not), he turned the conversation to her *Lettres au peuple,* which had left him almost as cold as they had me; and he described la Sand—as did later almost everyone who spoke to me about her—as selfish and cold-hearted to the point of forgetfulness of any consideration for others. That was how she had shown herself towards Jules Sandeau and Pierre Leroux, and indeed towards all her friends, Liszt remarked. 'She has warmth solely in the works of her imagination, and an utterly cold heart.'. . .

As arranged with Liszt, we went to the Altenburg that evening, to visit the Princess. The mansion as it stood there that dark autumn night seemed to have something rather eerie about it; nor was the impression we received on entering by any means a pleasant one. Despite the poor lighting we could see that it had long been uninhabited; and although it was quite unlike the Italian palazzi, I was reminded of the way in which in Italy in certain circumstances people would conceal themselves in a corner or wing of such a building.

Upstairs, in the room into which we were shown, the furniture likewise bore the unmistakable stamp of the casual, of the temporary, although certain individual items and pieces were impressive. As the doors were opened for us we saw the Princess, whom two gentlemen were keeping company, sitting by the fireside. At a little table at the other end of the room Liszt was playing draughts with the Princess's daughter, a beautiful child on the threshold of youth. Watching the game, which was broken off as we came in, was an English governess,* as stiff as though carved out of wood.

The Princess, a slender-boned woman of medium height, could from her outer appearance have been about our own age. Her black hair, dark eyes, and unusually sharp profile smacked somewhat of the Oriental, of the Semitic; and yet again there was a certain resemblance to Bettina von Arnim's eldest daughter, the later Countess Oriolla—who, however, was easily the better-looking of the two. She was wearing a coat made of some white woollen material and a little bonnet with pale blue ribbons: she really looked rather peculiar. On our entry she put aside the large cigar she was smoking, which in any case went rather strangely with the delicate colours of her dress. . . .

The conversation was lively. Liszt led it with the abandon which became him so well, while the Princess constantly brought up important subjects —political, scientific, religious, artistic—and in all of them gave evidence of a fine intellect and great knowledge. To both of us women, Therese and me, she was quite unquestionably superior in philosophical culture on those lines, apart from the fact that she possessed acute and incisive dialectic powers. But as Liszt always brought her back when she plunged in earnest into one of her political or philosophical topics, the constantly changing conversation became rather unsettling, and I could not help thinking that we would all have felt better if the two gentlemen had not

* Miss Anderson, who had accompanied Carolyne and Marie to Weimar from Woronince. She was, however, Scottish not English, and Liszt in his letters often made friendly reference to her as 'Scotland', 'Scotch', or 'Scotchy'. Her real forename was Janet.

been present and we had been able to talk about ourselves, and not about the lofty matters which just then could interest neither Liszt and the Princess, nor Therese and me, so keenly as the still unresolved and unclarified circumstances in which the two of them were managing as best they could, and whose gravity was revealed, too, in the way they behaved with one another. We felt sorry for both of them. The evening failed to become a really cosy one, and I am sure that the mistress of the house was aware of this still more than we were, and that she was upset about it. . . .

As we had kept our carriage waiting at the Altenburg, and as it had begun to pour with rain, out of compassion for the driver we left after about an hour. Liszt followed us. At that time Weimar was still insufficiently provided with carriages, and the small two-seater we had been given had only just enough room for the two of us and for Therese's train. (She had stayed in court dress.) After we had seated ourselves, Liszt made to get in as well.

'But that's impossible!' we cried, 'there's no room.'

'What do you mean by your *pas moyen de se fourrer là dedans*!' he retorted with his merriest laugh. 'If you had a large poodle, there would be room for him!'—and quickly jumping in he placed himself on the floor, feet tucked under him like a Turk, and said: 'à présent mettez vos quatre jolies pattes sans gêne sur moi; vous serez à merveille et je serai à l'abri de cette grosse pluie!'

Amidst much laughter we arrived at our hotel, and were soon taking tea together in Therese's room. One of her first questions was about his forthcoming marriage (as people then supposed) to the Princess, and, having no claims to Liszt's confidence, I was about to remove myself with a suitable excuse, when he stopped me.

'Do stay! I am not one of those people who stick their heads in the sand like ostriches, so as not to be seen. I know nothing so stupid as making a secret of things which can be seen by the whole world. Our circumstances are complex; we shall have to see how they turn out. The Princess is tied to Russia on all sides, and here in Weimar they always forget that we are not Protestants—that not for anything in the world could either I or the Princess think of changing our religion.'

'Oh,' exclaimed Therese, 'don't speak of marriage. You are not constant—and you don't know what an unhappy marriage can be!' she added with a sigh. 'In any marriage you would only make the other person unhappy and become unhappy yourself.'

'Very possibly!' he interrupted. 'Basically, I believe that myself. An oath is a serious thing. What one *has done*, one knows and can take an oath on. What one *will* feel, *will* do, *will not* do, can't be known; to take an oath on it is much more hazardous. Who can swear that he will always remain the same! I am certain that I am best dealt with if I am left my freedom, and that it is risky to tie me, whether to a person or to a place.' He spoke half in jest half in earnest, but the earnest prevailed when he added: 'You must get to know the Princess. There is something great about her, and she has just as much intelligence as strength of character. It was sheer determination which made her follow me here; I had not expected her.'

The topic was quickly broken off. Liszt related a few anecdotes about Metternich and his wife, about the Emperor of Austria, and about the Viennese in general. From Austria he turned to Bavaria, and on account of Lola Montez jocularly praised King Ludwig as the happiest of mortals.

'She is the most perfect, most enchanting creature I have ever known!' he cried with enthusiasm. He asked me whether I had seen her—but such had not been the case.

'Oh! one must have seen her! She is always new! always plastic! Creative at every moment! She is truly a poet! The genius of charm and love! All other women pale beside her! One can understand everything that King Ludwig has done and sacrificed for her! Everything!'

On he went in this manner for a while, himself becoming creative and poetic in his retrospective admiration of her beauty. We listened to him as to an extempore speaker—and it was again midnight before we parted.[4]

In a Court Theatre concert on Sunday, 12 November, Liszt for the first time conducted music by Wagner: the overture to *Tannhäuser*. He also appeared at the piano, playing the Andante from Henselt's Piano Concerto as well as a solo, his bravura paraphrase (S386) of the Tarantella from Auber's *La Muette de Portici*. In the second half he conducted Act IV of *Les Huguenots*.

Among his fellow artists on this occasion were the baritone Feodor von Milde (1821–99) and the soprano Rosa Agthe (1827–1906). Both outstandingly gifted, and from 1851 husband and wife, they became loyal friends of Liszt's, and of all his Weimar colleagues were probably those he most esteemed. In August 1850, when he conducted the historic première of Wagner's *Lohengrin*, it was Milde who sang the part of Telramund, and Fräulein Agthe that of Elsa. 'Whoever saw Feodor and Rosa von Milde in their starring roles, received an impression rarely to be approached,' was Adelheid von Schorn's opinion. 'In addition to their magnificent voices, there was their wonderful artistry, their inspired acting, and not least their striking good looks. As human beings, too, the Mildes could not have been more highly regarded by the people of Weimar.'

A fellow guest of Liszt's at the Erbprinz in late 1848 was the Austrian political writer and playwright *Hermann Rollett* (1819–1904).

I heard some excellent chamber-music performances there, for which on pre-arranged evenings various members of the Court Theatre orchestra would come along.

On one such occasion I had an opportunity to admire Liszt's quite extraordinary musical ability. One of the players had brought with him a quartet which Liszt had never seen or heard before. After he had taken a fleeting look through it and found it interesting, they began to play. It went quite excellently, just as though they had already rehearsed the piece. Then the door opened quietly and a latecomer entered. Wishing to say something to him, Liszt beckoned him over. I was leaning on the other end of the piano and could see very clearly how, every time he turned a page of his piano part, Liszt would give one swift glance at the whole page and then softly converse with the newcomer, with only an occasional look at the music. The entire page would be played in this manner, and no one else had the least notion that he was playing most of it from the memory of that rapid initial glance.

His cleverness and presence of mind were also once displayed in quite another fashion. When, in those troubled times, I was once returning to the hotel from a people's assembly at which I had been speaking, a Grand-Ducal carriage was standing in front of it, and Liszt, who as Court Kapellmeister was about to leave for a festive banquet, passed me in the middle of the staircase as I was going up. He was quite laden with decorations, of which he possessed a rich variety. Between someone returning from a democratic people's assembly and someone hung all over with decorations on his way to court, a greater difference could hardly be imagined. Liszt, who knew where I was coming from, perceived this of course at the same moment. Clever man of the world that he was—and, be it said in passing, anything but a 'Hungarian'—he offered me his hand and said with a smile as he went down the steps: 'How lucky you democrats are! You can go through life so easily and unceremoniously, and not, like others, in chains and ribbons!'

But during my stay in Weimar I also witnessed a really crazy incident with Liszt, one which sounds almost unbelievable—yet, as said, I *did* witness it. A Pole with whom he was friendly was moving away from Weimar, where he had been living for a year or two, and on the eve of his departure gave a farewell lunch. Liszt and I were both among the guests, as were two professors from Jena: O.L.B. Wolff, also renowned as an extempore speaker, and Siebert the pathologist. The champagne-filled Polish boot from which the guests had to drink set off on its rounds right at the start, and it did not take long for the atmosphere to become a really merry one; by the end of the meal everyone present was to a greater or lesser degree a bit tiddly. All of a sudden it occurred to Liszt, who had taken off his jacket and tie and was in a very jolly mood, that Professor Siebert, who was sitting beside him, had promised to sound his chest when the opportunity arose, and—such a good one having presented itself—he now invited him to do so, tearing open his shirt as he spoke. Equally far gone, Siebert agreed laughingly, took a piece of paper out of his coat pocket, formed it into a stethoscope and placed it shakily on Liszt's bared chest. This was the moment that Professor Wolff, who was due to give an English lesson to Princess Wittgenstein's daughter, decided to use to slip away unseen by Liszt, who a short while before had not wanted to let him go. He now succeeded in getting down the stairs before Liszt noticed his departure. Still half undressed, the latter leapt out of his seat and chased after the fleeing Wolff, to hold him back. Reaching the door of the house without catching his quarry, Liszt in his wine-induced excitement rushed outside and as far as the corner of the next street—but could see nothing of Wolff, who had taken another route. Bare-chested and in his shirt-sleeves, his hair flying in all directions, Liszt then ran half-way down the street, but during this strange outing spotted a pretty girl standing knitting at one of the front doors. Stopping in front of her, he addressed her in the most passionate language, wanting to kiss and embrace her. Taking fright, the girl fled into the courtyard of the house, through the cellar door and down the steps, with Liszt in hot pursuit. But it so happened that just at that moment one of the servants was drawing a pail of water out of the well, and, seeing what was going on, he carried it over to the cellar steps and emptied the entire contents over Liszt—who, naturally somewhat sobered up by this, dashed back up the steps and out into the street, dripping with water. And it was like this that the rest of us, who had hurried along behind, found him and in rather an odd little procession took him back to our host's.

The sensation caused in quiet little Weimar by an incident such as this in broad daylight can be imagined. The Grand Duchess was very vexed at the public scandal it created; and it was only her great affection for Liszt, and, in particular, the girl's declaration that he had not harmed her and that she had only been frightened and taken him for a madman, which allowed the whole crazy story to be covered with a dense veil.[5]

It was at about this time that *Carl Reinecke* first came into personal contact with Liszt.

In 1848 I was living in Leipzig. One day Ernst, who on the violin was not unlike Liszt on the piano, and who had been staying in Leipzig for some time, invited me to accompany him to Weimar, to pay a visit to Liszt. That I was overjoyed to be able to make the Master's acquaintance goes without saying. We got to Weimar at about midday and hastened to the Altenburg. . . . Liszt welcomed Ernst most warmly, and me, the latter's protégé, with the heartwarming kindness so characteristic of him. The meal to which he invited us was not Lucullan, but it was a very good one, and Bavarian beer was served with the food, as was champagne. This latter drink Liszt refused utterly, and in doing so said how strange it was that he had the reputation of drinking a good deal of champagne and of often breaking strings, whereas in reality he did neither the one nor the other. (Indeed, I never knew him break a string; his touch was always elastic even during the most titanic eruptions.) At that time he preferred a glass of liqueur brandy to the best champagne, and during the meal he drank several glasses of it. When he offered it to us too, and Ernst declined on my behalf with the words, 'Reinecke is a Puritan who drinks nothing strong,' Liszt said: '*Enfin*, my dear Reinecke, you are quite right; I intend to give it up too.' All the same, he then took his coffee with a dash of cognac in it. After the meal he invited me to accompany him to Alexander Winterberger* to whom he was giving a lesson. No greater treat could have come my way than to witness a piano lesson given by Liszt! He stood for the whole time behind his pupil's chair, accompanying the playing with remarks that were both subtle and often tinged with humour. Now and then he would play passages himself, absolutely inimitably, and —from time to time take a sip of cognac from a little travelling flask he had in his breast pocket. In the evening, as I could take no active part in the rubber of whist which had been arranged, he invited me to play to him; and the interest he took in it was all the kinder. But as, during the whist, he helped himself to several stiff doses of cognac, I could in my astonishment not refrain from asking whether on that day he had abandoned his resolve to 'give it up'. He laughed and said that such was not the case, adding that a thing like that could be given up only gradually, and regaling me at the same time with an account of many heroic feats of the kind in his earlier years.

When, a few years before his death, Liszt visited me in my third-floor flat, I was compelled to remember that first personal meeting with him. It was a dreadfully hot summer's day, and the venerable master was visibly exhausted. My wife naturally offered him every refreshment generally considered appropriate on such days—but without tempting him. Then suddenly I remembered our first meeting, and I offered him a glass of liqueur brandy. '*Enfin, that* would be the thing!' he said. So this inclination of his had still not quite left him; but it never proved his undoing, for, as is well known, in his old age he was constantly active, mentally alert, and even creative.

Soon after that first visit of mine to Weimar under Ernst's wing, Liszt invited me to stay with him for a few days, and even now it is with a grateful heart that I recall them and all the pleasure and instruction they gave me. On one occasion, when we were dining quite alone one evening, the name of Hummel cropped up in our conversation, and I called the D minor Septet his masterpiece, telling Liszt at the same time that I had heard him play it years earlier in Hamburg. But his own opinion was that the Septet had Hummel's F sharp minor Sonata to contend with for pride of place; and when I was obliged to admit that the latter work was not known to me, he sat down at the piano and played the entire Sonata from memory! And another time, when I said how much I regretted that he had never transcribed Beethoven's Coriolan Overture for piano, he went straight to the instrument, gave an ideal rendering of it and said at the end:

* Composer (1834–1914), pianist, and organist, and for a long time a teacher at the St Petersburg Conservatoire. He was particularly esteemed by Liszt for his virtuoso organ-playing.

'That's roughly how I would have done it.' He also played me Chopin's Etude in E major from the Op. 10 set dedicated to him, and on finishing said, rather sadly: 'I would give four years of my life to have written those four pages.' After I had heard this Etude played by Liszt no one else could ever play it to my satisfaction. It was exactly at such moments, in private, that Liszt played most beautifully. When in front of a large audience, he was all too often seized by a demon and, as I have said, seduced into all sorts of whims and fancies.[6]

1849

Two of Liszt's outstanding collections of piano works were coming into existence at this time: the *Années de pèlerinage, première année, Suisse* (S160) and *Années de pèlerinage, deuxième année, Italie* (S161). The Swiss volume would not receive its final form until 1854, but the Italian set, inspired by some of the treasures of art and literature whose acquaintance Liszt had made during his travels of a decade earlier with Marie d'Agoult, was completed this year, 1849.

Its seven items are entitled:

1. *Sposalizio* (1838–9), inspired by Raphael's *The Marriage of the Virgin* at the Brera Gallery, Milan.
2. *Il Penseroso* (1838–9), after the celebrated statue by Michelangelo in the chapel of San Lorenzo, Florence.
3. *Canzonetta del Salvator Rosa* (1849), the only one of the set not inspired by a masterpiece of art or literature, is based on a song once attributed to the Italian painter and improvisatore Salvator Rosa.
4. *Sonetto 47 del Petrarca. 5. Sonetto 104 del Petrarca. 6. Sonetto 123 del Petrarca.* Revised versions (1846–9) of three earlier pieces (1844–5) which in their turn were arrangements for piano solo (S158) of Liszt's *Tre Sonetti di Petrarca* (S270). These were settings for voice and piano (originally dating from 1838–9, and existing also in later versions) of three of the best-known sonnets in Petrarch's *Canzoniere*: 'Benedetto sia 'l giorno' (No. 47); 'Pace non trovo' (No. 104); and 'I' vidi in terra angelici costumi' (No. 123).
7. *Après une lecture du Dante, fantasia quasi sonata*, known as the Dante Sonata. Sketched in 1839 (see *supra*), and revised in 1849, its title is derived, imperfectly, from that of a poem in Victor Hugo's *Les voix intérieures.*

Ten years later Liszt revised his *Venezia e Napoli* of *c.*1840 and reissued it as a Supplement (S162) to the Italian volume of the *Années de pèlerinage.* In this final form it consists of three pieces, *Gondoliera, Canzone,* and *Tarantella*, of which the first and third are based respectively on the third and fourth sections of the original version.

On 16 February, the birthday of the Grand Duchess, he conducted a performance of Wagner's *Tannhäuser,* its first production since the Dresden première of October 1845. Liszt, who considered the work 'the most remarkable opera, the most harmonic, the most complete, the most original and independent as regards both substance and form, that Germany has produced since Weber', had been forced to fight hard for it, against the general opinion. None the less, a considerable success was achieved.

On 13 May, during one of the most calamitous episodes of his turbulent life, Wagner himself arrived in Weimar; not, as had earlier been planned, as a welcome guest at the third performance in the town of *Tannhäuser*, but as a hard-pressed refugee after his part in the ill-fated Dresden uprising. Liszt proved not only a loyal friend and protector but also a source of funds for the penniless fugitive, who a few days later was compelled to take to his heels once again.*

Details of this rather fraught meeting between the two composers were recalled by Wagner when preparing his autobiography many years later.

When we met at the home of Princess Wittgenstein, whose acquaintance I had made the year before when she paid her fleeting visit to Dresden, we were able to hold stimulating conversations on all manner of artistic topics. One afternoon, for instance, a lively discussion sprang up from an outline I had given of a tragedy to be entitled *Jesus of Nazareth*. Liszt maintained a sceptical silence after I had finished, whereas the Princess protested vigorously against my proposal to bring such a subject on to the stage. . . .

An orchestral rehearsal of *Tannhäuser* took place,† which in various ways stimulated the artist in me afresh. Liszt's conducting, though mainly concerned with the musical rather than the dramatic side, filled me for the first time with the flattering warmth of emotion aroused by the consciousness of being understood by another mind in full sympathy with my own. . . . After the rehearsal I accepted Liszt's invitation to a simple dinner, at a different hotel from the one where he lived. I thus had occasion to take alarm at a trait in his character which was entirely new to me. After being stirred up to a certain pitch of excitement his mood became positively alarming, and he almost gnashed his teeth in a passion of fury directed against a certain section of society which had aroused my own deepest indignation too. I was strongly affected by so wonderful a contact with this extraordinary man, but was unable to see the association of ideas which had led to his terrible outburst. I was therefore left in a state of amazement, while Liszt had to recover during the night from a violent attack of nerves which his excitement had produced. Another surprise was in store for me the next morning, when I found my friend fully equipped for a journey to Karlsruhe—the circumstances which made it necessary being absolutely incomprehensible to me. . . .[1]

Another visitor from Dresden, at the end of the month, was the young Hans von

* A note from Liszt to the Princess runs: 'Can you give the bearer 60 thalers. Wagner is obliged to flee, and I cannot come to his assistance at the moment.' Ten days later Wagner safely crossed the frontier into Switzerland, and shortly thereafter made his way to Paris. Eleven years of exile lay ahead of him.

† At which Wagner of necessity remained hidden in a box.

Bülow (1830–94), a former piano pupil of Friedrich Wieck. Studying with Liszt from 1851 to 1853, he thereafter earned for himself equal renown as pianist, conductor, and acerbic wit, and, eight years after this brief initial stay in Weimar, became Liszt's son-in-law. The first meeting between the two seems to have been at Dresden in December 1841, shortly after Liszt had made the acquaintance of Franziska von Bülow (1800–88), Hans' mother.

Hans von Bülow to his mother. Weimar, 2 June. I met Liszt at one o'clock on Wednesday. . . . He appointed me to meet him at half-past four at the Altenburg, the abode of the Princess Wittgenstein, where he is accustomed to spend the whole day. There I met a pupil of his, young Winterberger, a very talented fellow. Liszt was with us both till nine o'clock. I played the Schumann song to him, and he was pleased with my manner of playing, although I had not got his own conception of the piece. It was also very interesting to me to see how he let his pupil play Beethoven's E flat Concerto; and his splendid hints with regard to the conception of it, even in the apparently most trifling matters, are of great use to me. On Thursday he dined with me at the Russischer Hof Hotel, where I am stopping. He came with the most notable artists and singers, who all adore him, and whom he treats with unspeakable kindness. He is a quite perfect man. . . . Liszt's playing, and his whole personality, have completely enchanted and inspired me; all the brilliant gifts of former days he still possesses in the fullest measure, but a more manly repose, an all-round solidity, complete his truly exalted character.

Early yesterday I was with him at the rehearsal of *Fidelio*. I was perfectly carried away by his conducting—admirable, astounding! In the evening he played trios at the Altenburg. We were again with him from seven to eleven. Tomorrow he is going to have my quartet played. He has placed his room, piano, and library of music at my disposal every morning. . . .[2]

To the same. Leipzig, 21 June. Liszt sent me a short time ago . . . his newest work, three great Etudes* . . . His performance of the *Tannhäuser* overture, which he has transcribed† in a most wonderful manner and with the greatest assiduity (he made three different arrangements of it), gave us immense pleasure; he has managed to give the effects in such a wonderful manner on the piano, as no other pianist, I am sure, will ever be able to do. In all probability he will publish this arrangement, as well as the transcription of Wolfram's song.‡ The latter is not particularly difficult; and the former does not look so very awful on paper, yet the playing of it was such a strain upon him that he was obliged to stop for a moment once near the end, and he very seldom plays it because it exhausts him too

* The *Trois Etudes de Concert* (S144), in A flat, F minor, and D flat, composed *c.*1848 and dedicated to Eduard Liszt. In one early edition they were given the names *Il lamento, La leggierezza,* and *Un sospiro*.

† S442, dating from 1848. The first public performance seems to have been that (creating a sensation) given by Bülow at a Wagner concert in Zurich on 25 Feb. 1851.

‡ *O du mein holder Abendstern* (S444), dedicated to Carl Alexander.

much, so that he said to me afterwards: 'You can write down today in your diary that I have played the *Tannhäuser* overture to you.'. . .

After frequently hearing Liszt, I have now made a special study of what was particularly defective in my playing, namely, a certain amateurish uncertainty, a certain angular want of freedom in conception, of which I must completely cure myself; in modern pieces especially I must cultivate more *abandon*, and, when I have conquered the technical difficulties of a piece, I must *let myself go* more, according to how I feel at the moment; and, if one is not devoid of talent, of course anything absurd or unsuitable does not come into one's mind. . . .

According to what Liszt tells me, there is really a foundation for the report that he has begun some big works, and that several piano concertos with orchestral accompaniment are lying completed in his desk, with which he means to 'pay off some of his debts'; and an Italian opera, *Sardanapalus* (after Byron), is far on towards completion.* These are secrets at present, which he does not want all the world to know.

He usually worked at the Altenburg in the mornings, so that I seldom saw him at that time, but in the afternoons and evenings I was almost always with him. His talk was always intensely interesting, and he hardly ever said an insignificant thing. He spoke French by preference, and even when he talked in German he constantly interpolated not merely words but whole phrases in French.[3]

Liszt to the Hereditary Grand Duke Carl Alexander, 24 June. Next Thursday, at Ettersburg, I shall take the liberty of offering Your Royal Highness the volume of Dante that you reminded me about yesterday. These last few years he has become for my mind and spirit what the column of clouds was for the Israelites when it guided them through the desert. At this very moment I am quitting the Poet just as he quitted Virgil.†[4]

On Tuesday, 28 August, the 100th anniversary of the birth of Goethe, Liszt conducted the first performance of his symphonic poem *Tasso, Lamento e Trionfo* (S96), a work which the Grand Duchess had charged him to write as a prelude to Goethe's *Tasso*, a presentation of which then followed. As he explained in a preface to the score, he wished with his music to express the 'antithesis of the genius misunderstood in life but in death surrounded by dazzling glory'.

In early September, he, Carolyne, and Marie took a holiday on Heligoland, at that time a British possession. Among other visitors to the island were Adolf Stahr and *Fanny Lewald*.

The afternoon following their arrival Liszt came to see us, accompanied by Dingelstedt.‡ It was the first time Liszt and Stahr had met, and they took to

* But which in the end remained uncompleted.

† That is, with great sorrow.

‡ Franz Dingelstedt (1814–81), a gifted poet and dramatist whose *Schwebe, schwebe, blaues Auge* inspired Liszt's song of that title (S305). Royal librarian at Württemberg at this time, he

one another at once, both being lively by nature and both inclined to recognize what was fine and good in others and to speak up with enthusiasm on behalf of those in whom they found praiseworthy qualities. True to themselves were both the one and the other.

By chance a work of Lamartine's about the 1848 revolution lay open on the table at which we were sitting. It was, if I remember correctly, his *Trois mois au pouvoir*, and it followed as a matter of course that Liszt, as we spoke about the book and the portrayal and characterization of the persons it dealt with, was able to call upon his personal knowledge of them and to relate experiences he had had with them at different times. His manner of doing so revealed the impartial and creative aspects of his own character admirably. He was like a clear mirror in which men and events were reflected truthfully, because he took them *into* himself without consideration *of* himself—being in this the antithesis of Dingelstedt, whose judgement of people and circumstances was always influenced by whatever importance they held for him and his own ends. We noticed that whenever Liszt was warming up to his subject he was regularly interrupted by Dingelstedt, mostly with a sarcastic contrary opinion. Liszt paid no attention however, and eventually took his leave, saying to Stahr: 'I believe we understand one another, although I regret the failure neither of the French nor, like you, of the German revolution! For to tell the truth, I don't believe in the blessings of political revolutions. But I speak only for myself and don't wish to disturb the belief of anyone else, such as I did last year with Fräulein Lewald in her admiration of 'Rachel chantant la Marseillaise!'

He laughed as he said that, and Stahr remarked that I had written to him about it in detail. 'In that case,' Liszt interrupted him, 'I hope she also told you that it didn't prevent us parting as friends.' He shook hands with us and we parted cheerfully. . . .

Without having planned it particularly, we were together almost every day: crossing over to the Dune, at the restaurant there, and when sitting and lazing about on the soft sandy hillocks, refreshing ourselves in the sun and sea air which played about them; and it was one of Liszt's pleasures, when no outsiders were there, to roll himself down the warm sand slopes like a little boy, a game he repeated over and over again.

Everyone tried to see, be introduced to, and speak to him; but he spent most of his time with the Princess and in our little circle. Nor was he entirely without a following on Heligoland, as two young musicians had accompanied him. He was in excellent spirits. . . .

Even in those days it was his eager wish for a society to be founded at

was eight years later, on Liszt's recommendation, appointed Intendant of the Court Theatre at Weimar—where, however, his efforts to raise up the drama at the expense of music, and above all his intriguing and high-handedness, soon brought the two men into conflict. In 1876 he was ennobled.

Weimar in memory of Goethe. He and his princely patron and friend, the then Hereditary Grand Duke, had probably conceived the idea between them; and as the Germans gathered on Heligoland had just come together to celebrate the centenary of Goethe's birth, as had been done throughout Germany, we often came back to the subject, of the realization of which Liszt had frankly only a vague general notion. He thought of the *Fondation Goethe** as a *Concours* which would be held, as were once the Olympic Games, at regular intervals, and at which all the arts would compete together, each within its own field. Even if the practicability of such a project had to be doubted, one could not but admire the way in which a non-German, out of sheer enthusiasm for the greatest genius of the German people, had conceived and held fast to it.

Stahr often applied to Liszt the words which, I believe, Wieland used of Goethe: 'Who can resist the selflessness of this man!'

As Stahr had never heard him play, Liszt climbed with us one day to the upper hall of the Konversationshaus to play something to him—which, unpretentious as ever, he did, even though the piano at his disposal was one that had been hammered to death by young and old alike. But as soon as people noticed that Liszt had gone upstairs, and the first notes were heard, all those who were in the vicinity or passing by poured in too, for the hall was open to everyone; and soon, unobserved by Liszt, a crowd of listeners had quietly gathered who, the moment he stopped playing, broke into loud and prolonged applause. The quiet pleasure we had hoped for was thus quickly at an end. It was delightful to see how people tried to express their gratitude, however, and likewise to witness the friendly courtesy he showed in accepting it, just as though he had not received similar and greater homage from the potentates of this world. Only when a Bremen merchant would not stop repeating over and over again that it was the finger dexterity which was the most astonishing of all, did Liszt turn to us with a smile and shake of the head to say: 'On a tant de fois fait l'éloge de mes doigts au détriment de ma tête, que je commence à prendre mes dix doigts en grippe! Allons nous en!'. . .

And thus our quiet, pleasant way of life continued, and the day drew near in which the greater number of our acquaintances, Liszt among them, were to leave the island, whereas Stahr and I intended to stay on for another three or four days. The morning of 15 September we spent very enjoyably with Liszt and the Princess on the Dune sandhills, returning to the island by the last boat. It had been arranged that in the evening we would all have supper together at the Konversationshaus in one big party; and the landlord had had the hall decorated in a special festive way for the occasion. About thirty to forty people must have been present altogether.

Dingelstedt, Stahr, and others had made speeches, and we were all in

* See *infra*.

excellent spirits. Only one very beautiful and aristocratic lady had tears in her lovely eyes. She it was to whom one of the departing guests had most conspicuously and passionately paid court the whole time, but whom that evening he had rebuffed with icy coldness, because showing gallantry and affection to a lady was for him merely part of the entertainment of the spa. She had my full sympathy, for the conceited man had treated her abominably. Liszt thought so too. 'That is brutal!' he remarked quietly. 'Only someone heartless could treat a woman like that! But it's all we can expect! I have known him for a long time—he's all sham!' In the mean time it had become Liszt's turn to speak, and rising to his feet he began: 'Our party is composed almost entirely of Germans! We are on British soil and territory! *Donc, parlons français*!' And he went on to speak in praise of all the happy hours we had spent, toasted Britain, Germany, Art, Science, Women, Friends, and had captivated everybody anew, when someone asked him to be wholly Liszt and to end by letting us hear him again!

He did not wait to be begged but went to the piano and played the great Chopin Polonaise—played it with the energy he alone possessed when he put everything that was in him into the music. When he had finished, some of the people who had heard him earlier called out: 'The Fantasy on *Don Giovanni*! The Fantasy on *Don Giovanni*!'

And once again Liszt turned to the keyboard. My knowledge of music and the works of Liszt is so slight that I do not know whether such a piece exists among the latter, or whether it was a free improvisation on themes from *Don Giovanni* into which he plunged. The only thing I remember is that the motif from 'Finch'han dal vino calda la testa' returned again and again, that the music became ever wilder, ever more bacchanal, ever more daemonic, that the men, glasses in hands, finally all sprang up from the table and surrounded the player, and that in the end Liszt, as excited as everyone else, rose from the piano and, half laughing, half angry, burst out: 'Il ne faut pas me faire jouer ces sortes de choses là! Je ne devrais pas me faire entraîner! Mais enfin—c'est fait!'

He broke off, took his seat beside me again, and, finding the drink insipid, called over a waiter and asked for a further two bottles of cognac to be poured into the great champagne punch which had just been refilled—and the hearty drinking continued.

We women left immediately afterwards. The men, or some of them, stayed together until getting on for dawn. . . .

In Stahr's notebook I find the words: 'Evening. Supper. Liszt played magically. Crazy night. General madness!'[5]

The Hereditary Grand Duke Carl Alexander to Fanny Lewald, 4 October. What you say about my friend Liszt truly pleases me, for you have expressed my very own thoughts. The world's judgement of what it does not understand is generally distorted. . . . How many have listened to the revelations of his playing; how few to those of his mind. You call him great —how I agree! He is one of the rarest phenomena there are or have ever been. This, I am proud to say, is something I feel within my innermost being. He possesses the gift of inspiring, and of stimulating, such as I have found in no other person with whom I have associated. Never before in a man's personality have I been so struck by the meaning of the word *mind*. I love him with all the power of admiration and gratitude.[6]

On their return journey, Liszt and the two princesses stopped at the spa of Bad Eilsen, near Bückeburg, to take the waters. Planning to spend October here, they were then detained for several weeks when Princess Marie was taken ill, and it was not until the New Year that they arrived back in Weimar.

1850

Reaching Weimar on 5 January, Liszt, Carolyne, and Marie were welcomed at the station by Joachim Raff, who had begun his duties with Liszt at Eilsen in December and got to Weimar a day or two earlier.

Escorted by Belloni, Anna Liszt soon afterwards arrived for a fairly lengthy stay. Raff found her 'a well-preserved lady from Lower Austria of about fifty-eight or sixty, good for another twenty years at least'. 'The manner in which mother and son behaved with one another was often really moving. All the same, the good woman was yearning to be back in Paris with her grandchildren, her little dog, and her dozen canaries.'

Writing (25 March) to his mother after her departure, Liszt brought up the subject of the children, in the matter of whose education he was to take decisive steps later in the year.

You need do nothing else for the moment but purely and simply keep the children with you. . . . It matters little that their piano studies have been temporarily broken off; but, in return, I want them to read a lot and to remain actively occupied. And so give them about ten of M. de Chateaubriand's volumes: the *Génie du Christianisme*, the *Martyrs*, and the *Itinéraire de Paris à Jérusalem*. They are also to have M. de Ségur's universal history, which is in my library, and to continue their historical studies as best they can.[1]

Sometime in the early part of the year the young composer *Ludwig Meinardus* (1827–96) presented himself at the Altenburg.

'Since I know you *à peu près* from your C major Sonata,' said Liszt jocularly, 'you must smoke—for every good musician is a smoker.' The cigar gave a flavour of free and easy familiarity to the conversation, which Liszt's exuberant flow of words made very stimulating. He spoke of the afore-mentioned sonata, to which I owed such an extremely kind letter. 'You wanted a recommendation from me at that time,' he said; 'but it is a responsible matter to recommend someone we do not know, and in days gone by I did it often—too often! I have been dreadfully let down. *Enfin*: I no longer recommend anyone unknown to me. When we are young we indulge in illusions; but we become more cautious later on, although unfortunately it is then often too late. Yes, indeed—too late!' The memories which wrung such confessions from this fount of rich experience could not have been happy ones.

He asked if I had any acquaintances in Weimar. My name was not unknown to Herr von B. M.* I replied; years ago he had been a friend of my parents.

'Ah! very good!' said Liszt. 'Herr von B. protects my own humble self—yes, I may say he is my friend—*j'ai l'honneur*. Herr von B. is a first-rate *personnage* for Weimar. I'll let him know you are here. Generally speaking, dispose of me as you will. To be sure, I can do little enough, but make use of me even if I can be only of slight assistance.'. . .

The day before yesterday I had the honour of accepting Liszt's invitation to lunch. He still takes meals at the Erbprinz Hotel, where he used to live. Unfortunately I arrived only after the soup; but, even so, Liszt had kept me a seat next to him. A large company was gathered around the focal point, formed as an absolute necessity by the imposing personality of Liszt.

Coming so late to table greatly embarrassed me. Liszt noticed. 'Where, then, do you live?' he asked. 'At the Horn?! That explains everything: the long journey excuses your tardiness. At the Horn! For those who wish to call upon you, there is no help for it but to race there on a mule. Preferably, you come to me at the Altenburg. Whoever lives at the Horn must put up with the penalty of coming daily to the Altenburg. *Comprenez-vous?*'

As a host, too, this rare man displayed his dazzling charm in a gracious solicitude that could hardly be surpassed. . . .

I was told that the members of Liszt's circle have agreed to take turns at keeping a salon in readiness, which between lunchtime and evening they can use for social gatherings. Periodically, the change from one house to another takes place, it being at present the turn of Winterberger, the court actor. After coffee the whole crowd of us, with few exceptions, went there. The musical atmosphere of the spacious salon was apparent at once: a harmonium, grand piano, music stands, as well as violins and cellos in their cases—it all looked very cosy. Under the window had been erected a platform, on which stood a table and chairs. Cigars and jugs of brandy and water had been placed on the table for refreshment. The room adjoining

* When Liszt settled at Weimar in 1848, the Intendant of the Court Theatre was Baron Ferdinand von Ziegesar (1812–55). His successor was Baron Carl Olivier von Beaulieu-Marconnay (1811–89), Court Marshal from 1848 and Intendant 1850–2 and 1854–7.

was a smaller one in which card tables had been set up. Into this room some of the men withdrew at once. Liszt invited me for a game of whist, which put me in rather a predicament. 'You must know the clever game?' he asked when he saw my hesitation. No argument was acceptable—I had to play. Fortune at least smiled upon me enough to make me Liszt's partner. How many years must have passed since I last touched a card! My fellow players kept in practice every day. At each of my blunders Liszt remarked excusingly: 'Whist is a difficult game—yes, indeed, a difficult game!' This oft-repeated phrase now circulates like small change on every occasion when someone behaves clumsily. . . . When it was my turn to deal the cards, as ill luck would have it I bungled it. For the practised players that was a crime which quite spoilt the fun for them. Liszt was kind enough to spare me further embarrassment by rising after the first rubber with the excuse that he had business to attend to at court. Before leaving, to my no small fright he invited me to play my sonata or something; but fortunately did not insist on this rather unreasonable request to perform before him and so critical a company.

Liszt actually went to court in a heavy downpour, in grey under-clothing, black velvet jacket, and—without an umbrella. 'I shall be back in about half an hour,' he said. When he had gone, Herr Winterberger invited me to fetch the sonata, assuring me that Liszt would play it.

You can understand how such a prospect lent me wings. It is a long way, but I was back in good time and laid the manuscripts on the piano. Liszt had just returned too. His attention was drawn to the music, and at once he placed the Leipzig sonata on the music rack, lit a fresh cigar, and seated himself at the piano as comfortably as he could—like Walther von der Vogelweide,* 'leg upon leg'; that is, right foot resting on left knee. Never before had I heard him, and this first time he was to play my own stuff to me! And how he read the scribbled handwriting, which looks no better than a much-revised draft generally does! At the piano this wonderful man knows nothing of what ordinary mortals call difficulties. You are mistaken if you think he played only the notes I had written. On the contrary he gave it as his opinion that the sonata was a sketch for a symphony, and he played it as though he had a full orchestral score in front of him, not only enriching it in sonority but also broadening its form in a manner to suit a large-scale symphony. Nor, long after my own cigar had gone cold, did he allow his to go out: without interrupting his playing, he knocked the ash off by making now his left, now his right hand, free; and he took his right foot from his left knee only to reverse the positions of his feet in the same comfortable way. Into the bargain he chatted to me almost uninterruptedly about the work's structure and other relevant matters, including the eventual orchestration; turning now and again for a change to 'Sasha'

* Most celebrated of the German minnesingers (*c*.1170-1230).

Winterberger—who was also sitting at the piano—to point out details, even though sometimes these did not occur until the right-hand page of the manuscript, while the magic figers were still occupied with what was on the left-hand page. In this fashion he played the entire C major Sonata, and then at once passed to the one in D. This was completely new to him, and he first of all leafed through it, declaring it 'gratefully written for the piano'. While playing the work, however, he introduced so many instructive alterations that I perceived how much could still be done to it to obtain the 'gratitude' of pianists. The theme of the last movement, which winds through it uninterruptedly from beginning to end, he also played, even in uncomfortable hand positions, with a fullness of harmony in which only now for the first time were my intentions realized. Until then I had been content with a thin, dry mode of expression, which could be considered as no more than an outline of what I really wanted to say. In vain had I sought to find something better. But before Liszt played a note of that movement he recognized the defect, grasped how it should be done and said impishly: 'Why are you playing hide-and-seek with your own children? We must fetch you out of the bush— yes, indeed, whist is a difficult game!' And so the main theme came out fully and satisfactorily, in the fashion in which I immediately rewrote the entire movement.

When Liszt had come to an end, I felt an irresistible compulsion to embrace him warmly—which seemed to surprise no one, neither him nor anyone else. . . .

He procured me a *passe-partout* for all opera performances; on occasion let me take part in the piano lessons he gave; invited me to accompany him to Leipzig as his guest at the first performance of Schumann's *Genoveva* [25 June]; and extended his hospitality so far as not even to allow me to smoke my own cigars. 'Whoever travels with me,' he said jestingly, 'must also put up with smoking my bad cigars.'. . .

I became familiar with the magic of this wonderful man chiefly in sporadic moments when I found him in melancholy mood! 'Don't believe,' he said on one such occasion, 'that the sun always shines on my life; sometimes dew falls at twilight too. And as a souvenir of such moments, take this little volume of mine and let it remind you of me.' And after writing a dedication thereon, he handed me a copy of his recently published *Consolations*.*

Liszt is not the man to encourage and draw up to him someone faint-hearted and in need of comfort like myself. One has to love him—just as the beggar loves the rich alms-giver. Nor does he trouble to emphasize or even to make felt the ascendancy of his powerful personality; and so he has nothing to do with that *mutual* love which is just as willing to *receive* as to

* Six short piano pieces (S172), of which the fourth employs a melody composed by the Grand Duchess Maria Pavlovna. The group's title was inspired by Sainte-Beuve's collection of poems *Les Consolations*, dating from 1830.

give. For him, the basis and prerequisite of love is admiration. Whoever fails to comprehend his giant greatness is scarcely likely to see in him anything other than a daemonic vision with long hair, piercing grey eyes, warts on brow and cheek, and triumphantly rapid fingers, each of which seems to rule a whole world by itself. Whoever, on the other hand, is affected by the magic of his personality, and can recognize and appreciate his true merit, sees realized in him the embodied ideal of a great and striking artistic temperament, in which a soul filled with noble humanity carries on its work, generously radiating its wonderful gifts in all directions, here giving warmth, there refreshing coolness; with tender perspicacity reading in one's eyes one's secret wishes, and seeming to know no higher satisfaction than that of moving as the mood takes it within the circle of those grateful persons upon whom it has bestowed devotion and delight. Yet I should not wish to be in constant close contact with him: without deliverance my own personality would sink into his and disappear like a raindrop in the ocean; all my own thoughts would more and more bear the stamp of his mode of expression; and eventually I should be nothing but his slave, his mute servant who, parrotlike, would be capable of uttering nothing but: *Liszt—Franz Liszt*![2]

Ludwig Meinardus. Erfurt, Summer 1850. Visiting Wettig and me, Liszt came quite alone and unaccompanied. I happened to be at my friend's remote lodgings, and so it was difficult to find us. But happily, and despite the hot time of day, the long dusty trek on the wrong road had not caused him to lose his good humour. On the contrary, he was more engaging than ever, and put up with our company until the evening. We had to show him our unedifying workplace, which, empty of people in the dazzling sunlight, was so desolate, shabby, and humdrum that I felt deeply ashamed of it. Liszt must have noticed my feelings. He made a witty comparison and kindly jest about this caricature of an art arena, and the chaotic and inferior work we did therein, until we too saw only the comical side of the thing, and all three of us burst into side-splitting laughter. At present he is busy rehearsing Richard Wagner's latest opera, *Lohengrin*,* which is to be given its première at Weimar during the celebrations marking Goethe's birthday. To satisfy the exorbitant demands Wagner is said to make on singers, orchestra, conductor, machinists, and even on the audience, in this giant opera, calls for enormous exertions. Raff had already made me acquainted with some incredible details. A bass clarinet for example—a brand-new instrument—Liszt has had to order from Paris, and to induce a first-rate violinist to familiarize himself with it. The baritone, Herr von Milde, he has sent to Manuel Garcia, to study the part of Telramund, or

* Earlier in the year, Wagner had written to Liszt: 'I have an intense longing for this work to be performed. I hereby beseech you: perform my *Lohengrin*! You are the only man to whom I would make such a request. . . . to you I submit it with full confidence.'

whatever it's called, with that master. It was against the background of this mighty artistic activity that Liszt now judged our Tivoli exercises. We really had to laugh about it. Incidentally, he is inviting to the performance all the hard-working musicians he can. And so he insisted that I too was to go over to Weimar. . . . It seems that we younger musicians are to lend a helping hand at the birth of this strange Wagnerian offspring, to make it legitimate for the general public. . . .

At all events, I am glad that on 28 August I shall be in personal contact with Liszt once more. If you could just once be in his company! It is wonderful how he attracts each and all of us to his magnetic heart, whirling us up to the height of the sun, in whose heat one could fear to scorch one's wings.[3]

At Weimar's Court Theatre on Saturday, 24 August, the eve of the unveiling of the town's Herder monument, Liszt's *Prometheus* music—overture* and choruses (S69) to Herder's *Prometheus Unbound*—was given its first performance. In the evening of the 25th came a performance of Handel's *Messiah*, and on the 28th Liszt conducted the successful première of *Lohengrin*.

Among the visitors was the gifted, versatile, and eccentric Gérard de Nerval (1808–55), a longstanding acquaintance of Liszt's. When they made a pilgrimage together to Schiller's house, Liszt sat down at the clavichord and played his transcription (S563/2) of Schubert's *Des Mädchen's Klage*, a setting of words by Schiller. 'And as I listened,' wrote Nerval, 'I was thinking that the shade of Schiller must have rejoiced to hear the words his heart and genius had uttered find such a beautiful echo in two other geniuses who lent them a double radiance.'

That autumn the singer *Mathilde Marchesi*† (1821–1913) spent a week in Weimar.

My first visit was to Liszt, to whom I had been given a letter of introduction by a relative of mine in Paris, M. [Ferdinand] Denis, an old friend of his.

Liszt received me very warmly, and I dined at the Altenburg every day with him and the Princess Wittgenstein. . . .

How can I adequately describe her idolatrous worship of Liszt at that time? She generally sat at his feet, kissed his hands, and hung, as it were, on his very lips. Seeming quite accustomed to receiving her homage, he submitted to it with lordly indifference. In his absence I often spent hours chatting with this extremely intelligent and amiable lady, whose habit it was to lie full length on her *chaise longue*, incessantly smoking strong cigars, and usually taking off her silk stockings and black satin soleless shoes to display her elegant snow-white little feet, in whose beauty she seemed to take great pride. Once, after the midday meal, when I wished to leave a little earlier than usual because of a rehearsal, Liszt called me back with the words: 'Wait a moment! I'll fetch my hat and cloak and accompany you.'

* Which in 1855, after revision, became the symphonic poem *Prometheus* (S99).
† Later also a celebrated teacher, of Melba among others.

Frowning ominously, the Princess said in a commanding tone: 'You will remain here with me!'

A violent argument then broke out, to my unspeakable embarrassment; the storm soon abated, however, and peace was restored, but Liszt had his way and accompanied me to the rehearsal.

On his recommendation I was invited to take part in a court concert, at which he himself played my accompaniments. I sang several of his own songs, as well as arias by Rossini and Handel. He also asked me to undertake the contralto part in Handel's *Messiah* at church, and to sing in a concert he was conducting at the Theatre. . . .

At his request I sang to his pupils on several occasions, always to his own accompaniment; and once, when I had finished Desdemona's *romanza* in Rossini's *Otello*, he sprang up from his seat exclaiming: 'Only make the piano sing like that, my children, and I shall be satisfied!'

I must have been looking rather delicate at that time, for the Master took quite an unusual interest in my diet. When he fetched me in the mornings for the rehearsals, his first question would be: 'What have you had for breakfast?' If my answer failed to satisfy him, he would give a violent tug at the bell and call to the waiter: 'Quick, a good steak, and some of your best Bordeaux'—and would not be content until I had eaten up every morsel. . . .

The week in Weimar was so delightfully interesting and instructive that I would gladly have prolonged my stay, but time pressed, for engagements called me to Leipzig. . . .[4]

Liszt was at this time preoccupied with the matter of his children's education, in particular that of Blandine and Cosima, whom earlier in the year, after learning of a clandestine visit they had made to their mother (something strictly forbidden them), he had rebuked severely and removed from the school run by a Mme Bernard which they had been attending. He now put them into the charge of Mme Patersi de Fossombroni (*c.*1778–1862), a most respectable if somewhat austere old lady whose former pupils had included the young Princess Carolyne. The girls' grandmother, who had been looking after them since the termination of their studies at Mme Bernard's, was required to hand them over to the newcomer, who arrived in Paris in mid-October and, with her sister Mme Saint-Mars, took up residence at No. 6 rue Casimir-Périer. 'I have asked Mme Patersi to bring my daughters to see you frequently,' Liszt wrote to his mother. 'She alone has to decide what is or is not allowed them. She knows the views I hold on their education and on their future, which accord fully with her own. It is my hope that under her influence the bad and worrying results of the education given them by Mme Bernard will soon disappear.'

To Blandine he wrote (5 October) in more detail.

I have had the good fortune to meet someone who, in the course of a life of sorrows and frustrations, has given proof of a character so rare, and of a mind so sound, that she will know how to show you the better path you will have to follow to become a respectable and distinguished woman. . . .

You will be going to live with Mme Patersi, and I presume that in her company you will soon forget those sadnesses which you try to alleviate, you say, by strumming on your piano. Study it seriously; take the trouble to acquire some talents and you will soon see how ill suited are work and study to idle musings. Apply yourself in particular to acquiring a good knowledge of geography and history, which Mme Patersi promises me to make you study a good deal, and of the languages in which she will supervise your progress. Your letters in English and German are not bad at all, assuming that your teachers have not corrected them. In those which in future you will write to me regularly on the first of each month (without expecting equally regular replies, for I have other tasks to attend to), while your chief concern must be to satisfy me, you will tell me what you have been reading, of the impressions you have gained from it, and of the persons you meet and of the things you see, so that I may better than hitherto be able to judge your moral and intellectual understanding.[5]

Daniel Liszt, probably the most brilliant, academically, of the three children, meanwhile entered the Lycée Bonaparte, where, to his father's satisfaction, he acquitted himself with distinction.

In mid-October the violinist Joseph Joachim (1831–1907) came to Weimar as leader of Liszt's orchestra. The two had met at Vienna in 1846, when, in a private performance at Liszt's hotel, the talented youngster had played the Mendelssohn Concerto, Liszt accompanying at the piano. 'To this day,' remarked Joachim's biographer half a century later,* 'Joachim cherishes the memory of Liszt's wonderful playing, particularly of the manner in which he accompanied the finale of the concerto, all the time holding a lighted cigar between the first and middle fingers of his right hand.'

In the latter part of the month a rheumatic illness compelled Princess Carolyne to return to Bad Eilsen, whither she was accompanied by her daughter and Liszt. During her sojourn at the spa, Carolyne first suffered the shock of the news of her mother's death and then succumbed to typhoid fever; and for one reason or another remained at Eilsen until the following summer.

Liszt to Blandine. Eilsen, 5 November. You tell me you have played Weber's Sonata in D minor, which you regard as one of the most beautiful pieces you know. Not knowing what works of the kind you have studied hitherto, I am not aware of the comparisons you are establishing, and of what in particular you like and find more striking about this sonata. I should be glad if you would enter into more detail on this subject, as on others, in your next letters, for to utter generalities is to say almost nothing; and as I am anxious for your taste to become more refined and for your judgement to spring more and more from genuine understanding, I shall give myself the pleasure of talking over with you the causes and reasons which must necessarily have a part in it. I, too, have a great fondness for this sonata, notwithstanding its rather obvious defects, such as

* A. Moser, *Joseph Joachim* (London, 1901).

the abrupt and shortened ending of the first and second part of the opening movement, and a certain lack of proportion between the Allegro, the Andante, and the Finale; a proportion which, it seems to me, is handled much more successfully in the same composer's Sonata in A flat, and even in the one in C (dedicated to the Grand Duchess of Weimar), which both form a more harmonious and complete ensemble.

What Etudes are you working at? Have you learnt the 24 Preludes and Fugues in Bach's *Well-Tempered Clavier*, of which at Grandmama's you will find an old edition that I once used? What do you know by Beethoven? Have you a good memory and do you play easily and correctly by heart? Give full replies to these questions so that I may be able to give both of you some profitable advice. . . .

I shall keep for another time a discussion of your Roman enthusiasms and your appreciation of what you refer to as Montesquieu's 'little work', *De la grandeur des Romains et de leur décadence*. This little book is full of grand things, great ideas, and firm judgement. No cultivated mind can afford not to read and reread it, and to ponder its contents carefully. . . . Since you are fond of the Romans, you will do well to make the acquaintance successively of their principal historians: Livy, Sallust, and lastly Tacitus. In the excellent Rollin* you will find substantial extracts, well within your grasp, of these authors. When you have sufficiently read and digested them, you will better be able to understand and enjoy Montesquieu, and you will no longer base your preference for the first part over the second on impressions which, very valuable in other matters, are irrelevant for the philosophy of history, an expression used almost to excess since Montesquieu, which does not prevent his book remaining one of the most accomplished models of its kind.

Your observation about the absence of great female characters in Greek history does not lack a certain justness. Tell me sincerely if it comes from your own thinking, or if you have heard it argued by someone else, and if so, by whom.[6]

Carl Reinecke. When I was living at Bremen, I received a most charming letter from Liszt [from Eilsen in late 1850] announcing a visit and at the same time making the suggestion that I arrange a concert at Bremen in which he too would take part. He said that he had never played in Bremen, and perhaps it would be of benefit to my concert. That I was grateful to accept this generous offer need hardly be said. I met him at the station and we went straight to the concert hall, to run through the Mendelssohn-Moscheles variations for two pianos on the March from *Preciosa* which had just been published. After the Introduction he suddenly broke off and said: 'We'll make a pause here this evening and I'll improvise a cadenza.' And that evening—how he did so! It was as though he gave the audience a

* Charles Rollin (1661–1741), author of an *Histoire romaine*.

visiting-card on which was inscribed in golden letters 'Franz Liszt'. In the third variation, unmistakably the work of Moscheles, he gave so comical and quaint an imitation (for me alone of course) of Moscheles' rather mannered way of playing in later life, that I found it difficult to keep a straight face. To conclude, he played his Fantasy on *Don Giovanni*. Every great singer, both male and female, might have learned from him how the parts of the Don and Zerlina should be sung. When he played the most difficult bravura passages, the longest cadenzas, which sooner or later in the performances of all other virtuosi seemed to me but superfluous virtuoso glitter, gave with him the impression that he was open-handedly scattering pearls and blossoms abroad. The enthusiasm of the audience was indescribable. But when, because of the unending applause, I ventured to ask him if he would give a little encore, he shook his head and pressed my hand against his heart—and I was horrified to feel how violently, almost audibly, it was beating.

As I intended to travel from Bremen to Paris, he furnished me with several letters of introduction: to Berlioz, Erard, the Escudier brothers, Prince [Eugène] Wittgenstein, the Marquise de Foudras, and Madame Patersi (his daughters' governess), and furthermore wrote an article about me for *France musicale*, to introduce me to the Parisian public. He also asked me if while I was in Paris I would give piano lessons to his daughters Blandine and Cosima, a request with which I complied faithfully and conscientiously.[7]

Among the songs Liszt composed in the mid and late 1840s were three, *Hohe Liebe* (S307, a setting of a poem by Uhland), *Gestorben war ich* (S308, Uhland), and *O lieb, so lang du lieben kannst* (S298, Freiligrath), of which in 1850 he published versions for piano solo. Entitled *Liebesträume* (S541), these transcriptions (which count as original works) are among the most attractive of his shorter pieces for the instrument; and it is only to be regretted that the popular appeal of the third of the set should have cast into comparative obscurity the equal charms and beauties of its two companions.

1851

Remaining at Eilsen until January, Liszt then had to return to Weimar to resume his duties. *En route* he finished reading Plato's *Phaedo* and the first volume of the *Meditations* of Marcus Aurelius; and at Brunswick station ran into an old acquaintance, the celebrated Prussian general Joseph von Radowitz (1797–1853), about whom he wrote to Carolyne: 'I envy him neither his diplomatic post nor his intimacy with the King—but very much the happiness of going to see his wife!'

Arriving in Weimar on the 22nd, he at once repaired to a rehearsal of Raff's opera *King Alfred*, shortly to receive its première. Later that day he wrote to Carolyne.

With what emotion I saw once again my little books in their green bindings —your gift—and my Histories, which I shall probably never read but which are likewise one of your beautiful presents; and the Bible in 18 volumes, and Proudhon, and so many other presents of yours! Truly, when I ponder and reflect now and then, I wonder if it wasn't you who once gave me my eyes and my hands, and if each evening it isn't you who *wind up* the movements of my heart—so much have you done, and are still constantly doing, for me! In any case, this poor heart hasn't a single beat which isn't for you![1]

On 1 February he conducted Lortzing's opera *Zar und Zimmermann*, a performance given on behalf of the family of that composer, whose death, in straitened circumstances, had occurred ten days earlier. He was also busy at this time with the proofs of his memoir of Chopin, who had died in October 1849. Written in collaboration with Carolyne, it was serialized from 9 February onwards in the periodical *La France musicale*, and only later appeared in book form.

February also saw the publication of Liszt's essay *De la fondation Goethe à Weimar*, in which he proposed that a foundation, named after Goethe, should be set up which would promote the arts by means of annual competitions, whereat in one year poets, in the next painters, in the third sculptors, and in the fourth musicians would compete for prizes, the judges to be invited from all parts of Germany. Every year the winning work would be 'crowned' and performed, printed, or exhibited under the aegis of the foundation; in addition, there would every fourth year be a music festival at the Wartburg.

Nothing came of this idealistic proposal. According to Liszt's biographer Peter Raabe, 'To put such a plan into action, and to maintain the foundation permanently, would have been possible only if men such as Liszt himself—in whom selflessness and humanity were combined with a noble mind—were the rule and not rare exceptions.'

The revision and reshaping of the *Etudes d'exécution transcendante d'après Paganini* and of the *Grandes Etudes* was another task which occupied Liszt during the early part of the year. The new, simplified versions of the former were published later in 1851 under the title *Grandes Etudes de Paganini* (S141); and those of the latter, renamed *Etudes d'exécution transcendante* (S139), in 1852, with ten of the twelve pieces now bearing titles:

1. *Preludio* (C); 2. (A minor); 3. *Paysage* (F); 4. *Mazeppa* (D minor); 5. *Feux follets* (B flat); 6. *Vision* (G minor); 7. *Eroica* (E flat); 8. *Wilde Jagd* (C minor); 9. *Ricordanza* (A flat); 10. (F minor); 11. *Harmonies du soir* (D flat); 12. *Chasse-neige* (B flat minor).

On 18 February Liszt set out once again for Eilsen, where he spent several weeks with Carolyne and Marie. Back at Weimar on 4 April, he at once plunged into rehearsals of *Lohengrin* and *Don Giovanni*. On the 12th his essay on *Lohengrin* came out in the Leipzig *Illustrirte Zeitung*.

At a concert on 13 April he conducted Berlioz's *Harold en Italie*, and his pupil Salomon Jadassohn (1831–1902) gave the first performance of the arrangement (S367) for piano and orchestra of Weber's *Polonaise brillante*, Op. 72.

Richard Wagner to Liszt. Enge, Zurich, 18 April. I have just read your printed essay once again, from beginning to end, and find it difficult to describe to you the impression your work of friendship has made on me again, particularly at the present time. . . .

And how remarkably things always happen with you! Would that I could describe my love affair with you! There is no torture and no bliss which does not vibrate in this love! Today I am tormented by jealousy, fear of what is foreign to me in your special nature; then I feel anxiety, worry, even doubt; and then again things flare up inside me like a forest fire, causing a conflagration in which everything is consumed, and which can ultimately be quenched only by a stream of the most blissful tears. You are a wonderful man, and wonderful is our love! Had we not so loved, we could only have terribly hated, one another.[2]

Liszt to Princess Carolyne, Easter Tuesday, 22 April. The music of our Catholic church, and in particular the organist, jangled my nerves so much on Palm Sunday that I wondered whether to go to church at Easter—feeling quite incapable of turning my thoughts to God during an hour of such discordance. When you are there, that is quite different. My eyes turn to you, and that serves me for prayer; but without you this music assails my ears so severely that I can no longer pray. . . .

On Easter Sunday . . . I went to Joachim's. By chance they were playing one of Beethoven's last quartets, the one whose Adagio is headed *Canzone di ringraziamento offerta alla Divinità da un guarito*. That was my real Easter.[3]

Fanny Lewald. On 30 April 1851 Stahr and I met in Weimar and took rooms at the Erbprinz Hotel, where Liszt too still retained the quarters he had had three years earlier, even though a music room and apartment had been prepared for him at the Altenburg, which, in accordance with her requirements, was now fully furnished and fitted out as the Princess's permanent residence. . . . Nevertheless, there was no more comfort at the Altenburg than there would later be in her apartment in Rome. Somehow it always gave the impression of the temporary—it was just like being in a caravanserai. Impressive though she was in other respects, the Princess lacked feminine charm and tact, and only too often this caused her to behave over-familiarly with strangers; while people who had a high regard for her she could often quite shock with her indiscretions, even if her fervour fascinated them.

Liszt's devotion to the court, his friendship with the Hereditary Grand Duke, his continuing association with the Princess Wittgenstein, his official duties, and, in addition, his idea (which he linked in his mind with the

Goethe Foundation) of turning Weimar into an ideal centre for music, both its study and its practice, had drawn him away still more from his wandering life and been of considerable advantage to him. . . .

He had with him at that time a number of pupils and young musicians, all of whom have since become masters. . . . Quite apart from the great musical enjoyment afforded by the performances of these young men who had gathered around Liszt with such enthusiasm, it was a joy to witness the love and devotion with which he watched over and guided them, the delight he took in their abilities, and, when they pleased him, the warmth with which he expressed it. I can still hear him calling out to them: 'Bravo, Joachim! Bravo, Hans! *je ne pourrais pas faire mieux*!'—and how, turning to the listeners, he asked: 'You won't find that everywhere, will you?' . . .

Although very busy, he appointed himself our guide to Weimar. With him we viewed the frescoes at the *Schloss* and the many beauty spots with their wealth of historical associations in the surrounding countryside. And we were indebted to him and the Princess for the music we heard in their home—music that was incomparable, but of which I am not qualified to write. In Stahr's notebook, however, I find frequent references to it, such as: 'I have never heard Beethoven played like that before!' or: 'How great everything becomes when interpreted by Liszt!' . . .

Busy though Liszt always was with things and people in general, he was never too busy to have time for the problems of individuals. That he was at all times ready to help and be of service, in matters small as well as great, his pupils could confirm too.

Joachim Raff, for example, loved to tell how, when young and unknown, he had screwed up courage to go to Liszt when the latter once gave some concerts in [Switzerland], to ask him for an admission ticket, since he lacked the wherewithal to buy one. 'And not only did he give me the ticket, but, seeing that it would not be wasted on me, came to my assistance with word and deed in a manner that I can never hope to repay, but which will ensure my lifelong gratitude!'. . .

Giving, helping, serving came so naturally to him, were so much part of him, that no one ever wondered at this in itself, but only at the charming way in which he did it. . . .

There was something indestructibly simple in him; and there was no trace of that surfeit which cloys and then insatiably seeks ever-stronger stimulants. The slightest attention, the least consideration, shown to his own habits and inclinations pleased him quite unmistakably; and I often felt even then that, surrounded though he had been from youth onwards by the love of women and by every kind of homage, the blessing of a calm, stable domestic life was good for him, and that in later life he would find it difficult to do without it. My foreboding unfortunately did not deceive me. He was very susceptible to quiet, loving care, and he died, as he almost always lived, amidst the confusion of the most casual surroundings.

We often sat with him in my room until long past midnight, when he would become lost in his quest for an ideal reshaping of the human condition, in brooding over the beginning and end of things. . . .

At the end of [one] conversation he explained to us at some length how his view of the dreadful inequality of the human condition, and the conflict between the Christian moral law and man's nature, had first made him aware of, and led him to, the teaching of the Saint-Simonians. He spoke about Bazard's state banks, in which all income was to be deposited and from which it would then be distributed to individuals; about Père Enfantin's* teaching of the sanctity of the flesh; and about conjointly responsible communities, united by brotherly love and equality before the law (in which, however, the freedom of the individual would be preserved and the widest latitude given to the ennobling, priestly influence of the arts), which were to be held together by the wisdom of a lawgiving leader freely elected by the communities as a whole. He considered all this outdated; and yet while reminiscing, and when speaking of his desire to believe in a better and happier future, he spoke very warmly, until he suddenly broke off with the exclamation: 'You are listening to me, my friend, but yourself say nothing. Do you, then, regard the conditions in which mankind lives as the right ones? Do you regard as impossible a condition which would be a compromise between misery on the one hand and the most senseless extravagance on the other, a condition in which mankind could peaceably aspire to its greatest possible perfection?'

Stahr did not give him an outright answer, not wanting to disturb him in such exalted mood. 'Was willst Du?' he said. 'Everyone sees and looks into the future with his mind's eye; everyone hopes and wishes with every fibre of his being. I see the world differently from you. I do not share your hopes —for the motive force in nature is not love! But one must love *you*! You are much better than many others who fancy themselves to be very good indeed. You are much younger than your forty years, and, for all your Saint-Simonian memories, much more Catholic than you know and believe!'

Stahr and I often thought back to that evening when we saw Liszt some fifteen years later. It was in Rome and he was in priestly garb.[4]

During May Liszt worked on his two Polonaises (S223) for piano solo, some of the pieces in the collection of *Harmonies poétiques et religieuses*, and his arrangement (S366) for piano and orchestra of Schubert's Wanderer Fantasy. Prompted by study of the opera *Alfonso und Estrella*, which he planned to bring to performance, he was also giving thought to a biography of Schubert, and to

* Barthélemy Prosper Enfantin (1796–1864) and Armand Bazard (1791–1832) both became in 1825 followers of Saint-Simon, and after the last-named's death that same year the leading lights—the *pères suprêmes*—of Saint-Simonism. When, in 1829, dissension arose between the two, Bazard and others seceded, and the remnants followed Père Enfantin to Menilmontant, then a suburb of Paris.

this end sent questionnaires to friends of the composer. The project unfortunately never came to fruition.

On 20 May he left Weimar to rejoin Carolyne at Eilsen.

In June, *Hans von Bülow* arrived in Weimar, whence he wrote to his father on the 17th.

I have taken up my quarters in Liszt's house, the Altenburg. There, in the second storey of the adjoining building, I have four beautiful rooms at my disposal. . . . When I got here, Liszt was expected back at the beginning of July; but the latest tidings are different, and he has had all his clothes sent on to Eilsen, a proof that we must not expect him back yet awhile. His plan is that I should first of all prepare myself for the career of a virtuoso. . . . I have already begun, and practise eight to ten hours a day. Thus I have in these few days drummed into myself a tremendously difficult Trio of Raff's, one with which even Liszt had to take no end of trouble, and tomorrow evening I shall play it before a small audience on Liszt's good piano with Joachim and Cossmann*—I have never yet had two such capital players to play with. . . . After I have thoroughly studied the pieces I now have in hand, I shall begin Liszt's First Piano Concerto (still in manuscript), and when there is an opportunity of an orchestral rehearsal I shall try it with them. Liszt has not yet played it here himself.[5]

At Bad Eilsen, meanwhile, Meinardus's sister *Hermine* was writing to tell him that she and their parents were close neighbours of another visitor to the spa, the 'great and celebrated Liszt'.

Just think—he is staying right opposite, so that whenever he plays the music comes floating over to us. Yesterday morning, too, as I was writing, I heard the bewitching sounds once more. They made Mother and me abandon all thought and desire of doing our toilet; we just dropped everything, grabbed our hats and mantillas and hurried towards the enticing music.

When we got there, a young gentleman was already standing beneath the open first-floor window where Liszt was playing. We followed his example. Very soon the little audience had increased in number, even Father joining it. Everyone listened with breathless attention. Liszt seemed to be practising or composing something very difficult. Every now and then he would come to a stop and repeat a passage—and occasionally sing a few notes in between. Oh, it is altogether too interesting to listen to this famous master; especially for us, who have heard such splendid things about him from you! At this very moment he is playing again, and while I write my ears are glued to his window. In the end I shall leave the letter and run over there. It really is too tempting!

If you were here we should probably be lucky enough to make his

* The distinguished cellist Bernhard Cossmann (1822–1910), later Professor of Violoncello at the Moscow Conservatoire.

acquaintance at close quarters. So far he has emerged into the daylight only very seldom. He is said to be terribly bored here, and his stay to be a sacrifice he is making for certain reasons. He probably has little inkling what a topic of conversation he has been for the spa society here. They have already long been talking about the presents he is said to have given the Princess, and for days on end have with eager expectation been discussing his *probable* appearance at table in the Konversationshaus the next day!

Just imagine: the first time he passed our windows I had the greatest difficulty in holding Mother back. She was set on running after him, to pour out her grateful heart to him![6]

Hans von Bülow to his father. Weimar, 6 July. I have been corresponding with Liszt for some time. . . . His plan is as follows: he wishes me to remain a year in Weimar, and to drum into my brains, principally, the *newer* works of his own, the bigger sonatas of Beethoven, the best of Chopin, Schumann—in short, to make such a repertoire for myself as not every pianist, or indeed no pianist, can show; besides this, I am to study instrumentation and that kind of thing, and am specially to learn to write for the piano myself. He thinks it is necessary for me to have a Härtel grand piano (a new one) from Leipzig, as the instrument I now have is worth nothing. . . .[7]

Ludwig Meinardus joins his family at Bad Eilsen. In his account of his meetings there with Liszt, he refers to himself in the third person and under the name of Sigfrid.

Liszt, who in actual fact had sometimes felt forsaken, not having set eyes on a musical colleague for months, welcomed him with unfeigned delight. Constant solitude was by no means to the Master's taste: it contrasted too sharply with his usual way of life, making him feel sorely the want of greater social intercourse and external artistic stimulation. Sigfrid to be sure was unable to remedy these shortcomings of the spa, but the Master found in him at least a fellow artist, whom he could credit with understanding of higher artistic questions and subjects of common interest.

Favoured by solitude and Liszt's feeling of long privation, relations between master and disciple grew during a happy fortnight into an ever more exclusive mutual devotion. In the early morning Sigfrid had often hardly left the sulphurated bath when Liszt's servant Heinrich appeared, to say that new music had arrived from Leipzig which the Herr Doktor wished to look through in the young gentleman's company.

Sigfrid no longer allowed himself to be kept in the house, and sometimes returned only in the evening; and, indeed, in the company of Liszt himself, who obligingly put up with a few hours in the family's sitting-room. Sigfrid's mother soon got to know her undemanding guest's little preferences and wishes, and how to prepare a cosy place and congenial drink for him. And when he felt himself installed as comfortably as the given means allowed, he would repeatedly indulge in memories of his past, of the time of his hectic childhood and first appearances in Paris; and with the most modest reserve he revealed features of a youthful character of a kind that were so great-minded, so noble, so worthy of sympathy, that his little circle of listeners could hardly control their excitement, and the alderman, a stouthearted, imperturbable man, said one evening after Liszt had left, that he felt as though he were intoxicated, and that he had never before found anyone who by his personality could exercise a similar magic on him.

To give particular details of how Liszt gained such a magical influence over this calm and collected manly soul would not only be impossible in writing, but would also betray the implicit confidence in which they were communicated in the intimacy of that quiet, secluded little group. But it is to be regretted that, for reasons of delicacy, such an insight into this rare, noble, and magnificent person must remain undisclosed to a wider circle; as likewise some of the remarks he uttered, which allowed one to gaze deeply into the severe self-appraisal, clear self-knowledge, and the artistic and moral goals towards which this man, ever striving after the highest, was aiming at that time, and which with the most unaffected candour he confided to his astonished disciple on solitary evening walks. In a word, those days in Eilsen offered abundant material which would be of immeasurable value to any future biographer of Liszt wishing to throw light upon his human and artistic qualities alike. . . .[8]

After leaving Eilsen and before their return to Weimar, Liszt and the two princesses travelled in the Rhineland. On 31 August they were in Düsseldorf, where that day Liszt, and the next day all three, called on the Schumanns.

Clara Schumann. We were surprised to find the Princess quite a matronly lady. It can only be her charm, her intelligence and her wide culture—all of which she possesses in the true sense of the word—that fascinate him. She loves and admires him passionately, and he himself told Robert that the devotion she shows him is quite indescribable. Only the daughter, a sweet child, makes one feel a little sad; there is something dejected and melancholy in her look. . . . We had a good deal of music . . . and to conclude Liszt played a new concert piece and some of his *Harmonies*. He played, as always, with truly diabolical bravura—he masters the piano like a demon (I can't put it any other way. . .)—but, oh, his compositions, they were simply too dreadful!* When a youngster writes that sort of stuff he can be forgiven because of his youth, but what can one say when a grown

* For obtuse, almost wilful, incomprehension of music which lay outside a strictly limited range, the narrow, carping Madame Schumann can have been surpassed by very few. This opinion of the great series of *Harmonies poétiques et religieuses* is of a piece with such judgements of hers as those on Berlioz's *Roméo et Juliette* symphony ('infernal, devilish music') and Wagner's *Tristan und Isolde* ('the most repulsive thing I ever saw or heard').

man is still so blind. . . It is really depressing and made us both feel quite sad. Liszt himself seemed taken aback when we said nothing, but one cannot say anything when one feels so profoundly indignant.[9]

Hans von Bülow to his mother. Weimar, 15 October. Today I have to announce to you the long-delayed joyful tidings that my protector and master, Liszt, finally arrived here in good health last Sunday evening [12 October]. I was at the station both morning and noon to await his arrival; but the servants, who were sent on in advance, said he would not come till the last train, at ten o'clock. So I went quite unconcernedly to hear *Cortez**—music so full of power and nobility, like a steel bath to be-Flotowed ears. There he appeared suddenly and unexpectedly a few yards before me in the stalls, as though he had sprung from the earth by magic; a whisper ran through the whole house and reached the orchestra, which during his absence had run wild and gone to sleep—in their terror they played twice as badly, and Liszt got in a rage, and would have liked to seize the sceptre from his humdrum deputy, and to have made an end to the easy-going Philistine-anarchy by the despotism of his own conducting-genius, had his scruples allowed it; and as they did not allow it someone else got in a rage too, and that was myself.

Liszt silently greeted me, and eased his mind by pouring out some of his ill-humour in my ear. After the theatre I had supper with him, together with Joachim. The Princess looked very ill, but strange to say has already got wonderfully better in these few days. She still possesses her admirable eloquence and art of disputation; I doubt if there ever was a woman of such astonishing knowledge and such quick and penetrating intelligence. I shall probably now be promoted to the office of house-disputator, as I am more accustomed to French than Raff. . . .

Yesterday evening I was again alone at the supper, and went on with a discussion with the Princess right into the night; I could not break off, but the wearied Liszt at length spared me the misery of deciding between the twofold dictates of courtesy. I played a couple of pieces to him, in which the principal things he found fault with were a want of the necessary precision and decision in rhythm, and of a certain *aplomb*, in which, owing to my anxiety at the moment, I was more than usually deficient. The first pieces I am to study with him next week are a Scherzo by Chopin, a Liszt–Schubert paraphrase, and Liszt's transcription [S410] of the Wedding March from Mendelssohn's music to *A Midsummer Night's Dream*. . . .

Farewell for today, dear Mother, with the exclamation 'Long live Liszt!'[10]

At the end of October the Prussian historian *Theodor von Bernhardi* (1803–87) and his wife came to Weimar for a few months. Bernhardi's diary records not

* Spontini's opera *Fernando Cortez*.

only his impressions of the more prominent of the town's personalities, but also much of the local tittle-tattle, to which he seems to have been an avid listener.

The Princess Wittgenstein . . . sent an extremely friendly note to Charlotte, and I called on her with the reply. I found a small, dark, ugly, sickly—but very clever and adroit—Polish woman, with something rather Jewish about her; and was received with effusive *empressement*. (The house an awful mess—an untidy pile of books in one corner of the entrance hall, music and papers on the floor—everywhere very simple, old, rather dirty furniture.) She talked very frankly about the situation she is in, the 'douloureux provisoire', but things are now going somewhat better for her —for a time they looked very bad and her entire existence became very precarious. 'Nous étions réduits aux dix doigts de Liszt.' (Clever woman: I happen to know that she brought away with her, and arrived here safely with, two million roubles; *c'est une poire pour la soif*, but she certainly doesn't let on! She makes herself as small and poor as she can—her sacrifice as great and unconditional as possible. Thus the all but shabby furnishings, and the more than simple clothing!) . . . Once or twice she thought she could hear Liszt in the next room, and ran to each of the two doors of the room in turn: 'Is that you, my angel?' Liszt does finally appear, a very ugly man, *manières décousues*, but who on the whole makes an agreeable impression.* He is not a man of surpassing intelligence, but his good nature makes him likeable. I came away from the visit with rather an uncanny impression.

Theodor von Bernhardi, 10 November. In the evening went to a concert at court with my sister-in-law Julia, in honour of Princess Carl of Prussia, who is here with two utterly charming daughters. The poets' rooms were used, the music being in the Goethe Room. Liszt carried out his duties as Kapellmeister—and I admire his tact! He stayed entirely with the musicians, who remained in the Wieland Room during the intervals, and did not mingle with the company, coming to Princess Carl only when summoned; in short, was *wholly* the Kapellmeister, without the least claim to be taken for a *man of fashion*. The ladies sat in the Goethe Room, the rest of us remaining for the most part in the unnamed red salon next to it. Liszt played a trio with violin and cello accompaniment—marvellously beautifully. There is something ethereal about his touch; I can describe it in no other way! He, a truly ugly man, becomes handsome at the piano; a peculiar light comes over his features. . . .

* This was translated by the late Ernest Newman, in his disparaging and inaccurate *The Man Liszt*, as 'a disagreeable impression'—but the German is definitely *einen angenehmen Eindruck*. This particular blunder Newman perhaps perpetrated inadvertently, but there is in that case some irony in the fact that it was he who, to score off Fritz Kreisler, once wrote: 'The truth is that most people, in any department of life or of thought, are psychologically prone to believe what they want to believe, or see what they want to see.'

Theodor von Bernhardi, 11 November. With Julia called on Carolyne Wittgenstein, who made an embarrasing impression on us. She is very indiscreet. She asks a great many questions, *pour avoir le secret de tout le monde,* and to use the knowledge thus gained to achieve an ascendancy that will deter anyone from venturing anything to her detriment. It follows necessarily that for her own part she is very secretive, and so of her views on politics, religion, art, and literature absolutely nothing whatsoever was revealed. If I had not already known that she is a fanatical Catholic, and a rabid Polish patriot, I should have learnt little about it in Weimar or from her. She now wants to know my views on religion, presses on with her tactless questions, and entangles me in a conversation which is altogether disagreeable to me. Liszt joined us, and took over the defence of strict Catholic ecclesiasticism, which prohibits opinions and convictions of one's own. He *must*, it seems, take on this defence; at least, he tries, while speaking, to read in Carolyne's eyes how far he may, or should, go. His arguments, however, are again solely external, concerning as it were the law. He was formerly a freethinker, associating with Lamennais and others, but has recently seen the light, as such a thoroughly negative view, he says, has to lead to the most extreme revolutionary action—*que la guillotine serait introduite partout comme un instrument permanent de l'orchestre politique,* and that had determined him *de se rejetter fortement dans le système catholique.* Of Truth in its own right, and of a real conviction of its existence, there was therefore no mention! Many people in France are in a similar situation, he assured us. This religiosity, springing from fear, is therefore nothing more than the wish that others (the lower classes above all) may be true believers, so that they will leave *us* alone!

Theodor von Bernhardi, 14 November. Visit to Frau von Plötz. To begin with, talked about the Hereditary Grand Duke, whose principal defect and misfortune is lack of belief in himself. She would be glad to inspire him with more self-confidence. Then we came to Liszt, of whom she has really only a poor opinion. He has, she said, no very outstanding intelligence and is childishly conceited; but she thinks Carolyne Wittgenstein on the other hand a most excellent woman, 'elle lui donne l'esprit et les qualités qu'il n'a pas'.

(It is striking that in conversation Carolyne always seeks to depict herself as someone utterly insignificant—but Liszt as an overwhelming and quite tremendous genius.) They also say that Liszt actually behaved badly towards her. In Poland she led rather an odd, isolated life, never going out into society etc. Having gone to Kiev on business connected with the so-called 'contracts', she there encountered Liszt; and he, being attracted by the Princess's originality and intelligence, her millions and her title, *lui fit la cour tout bonnement*, but assumed it would be a liaison of the usual kind, with lovers' oaths in which each knows from the start what he is going to get out of it. But she took the matter very seriously, something he at first seems not to have noticed. He had probably forgotten the whole thing, and was living here in a Weimar hotel with another woman, a typical Parisian *femme entretenue*—they shut their eyes to it so as to keep him here—when to his dismay he received quite out of the blue a letter from Carolyne, *que le sacrifice était fait, qu'il n'y avait qu'à venir la prendre à la frontière.* He had to fetch her, conventional honour not permitting of a refusal, but what he really wished was to be rid of her. He did his utmost to induce her to break off the affair, since without her millions—as it then seemed—Carolyne was not at all to his liking. She has never complained, according to Frau von Plötz, 'mais je l'ai vue éternellement en larmes'. She has also been treated badly by so-called society. If she had quite simply had an illicit love-affair with Liszt, nobody would have had anything against it at all, *mais on lui jette la pierre, parcequ'elle a voulu être vraie dans ses relations avec Liszt. . . .*

Theodor von Bernhardi, 15 November. Frau von Plötz is right. Liszt has certain ambitious designs in mind. Since I am now alert to it, I see the entire plan on which he will found his greatness. Literary activity will be the first step. Carolyne is talking of a plan—prefacing her words with a few deprecatory remarks about the great and dazzling ideas of genius naturally losing a great deal when expressed through the mouth of a weak woman, etc. The Grand Duchess and the Hereditary Grand Duke both to a certain extent wish to maintain the renown enjoyed by Weimar in former days. How to do it? Liszt tells the Hereditary Grand Duke that a periodical must be founded here in Weimar, making out that as they now have a printing-press here it is a power which must be taken over, and also a means to win over and fetter a crowd of people who could otherwise become dangerous (Strauss,* Adolf Stahr, and Fanny Lewald, for example, who are already in the vicinity). In order to avoid danger, unrest, recriminations with other courts, and bad relations with anyone, this periodical must keep its distance from all contemporary political questions—and move with childlike innocence in the realms of the Ideal! (If Liszt is going to be in charge, then naturally there is going to be no question of scientific and critical seriousness.) This harmless magazine can become very important even politically—so Liszt tells the Grand Duke—and can spread such an Arcadian light around Weimar that even in the tempest of worldshaking revolutions people would think and say: Let us leave this little Temple of the Muses in peace! They want to win me for this journal too. *I*, contribute to Liszt's greatness![11]

Hans von Bülow to his mother. Weimar, 21 November. As to my relations with Liszt, I have every reason to be satisfied. I have the most sincere attachment for him, and I endeavour to prove it to him. It is not merely

* The theologian and Hegelian philosopher D. F. Strauss (1808–74). His controversial *Leben Jesu* was translated into English by George Eliot.

based upon gratitude, but also comes from a sympathy which is quite involuntary, for the mere sight of his noble and expressive features rejoices and expands my soul. I need not describe to you in detail the healthy and encouraging influence which his presence exercises in so many ways on all those around him, and especially on a pupil who enjoys his more intimate friendship and protection. Enough that, although beset by work of all kinds, he regularly devotes two consecutive hours a week to my development as a pianist, and I find every time new matter for admiration of his genius; and as my intelligence, thanks to Nature (which has been less stingy to me in this respect than to many others), is not very slow in divining his hints, I flatter myself that my musical education does not go much against the grain with him. Apart from the lessons I see him almost every day, either in the afternoon in company with other artists or with strangers, or else at the family supper in the evening. In a word, Liszt does far more for me than just fulfil his promises. I am happy to be able to do some small services for him, such as copying his manuscripts, or doing some of his commissions by correspondence. . . . The other day Ziegesar invited me to a small party at his home; Liszt played a Trio by Beethoven, and enchanted even the musicians themselves, which means a great deal.[12]

Theodor von Bernhardi, 24 November. Liszt called. He is no great intellect, but has a certain cleverness at living; and the tact which goes with it he possesses in a high degree. Further, it is a definite system with him never to express an opinion on anything, even the most trifling matters, so as not to compromise himself or give offence. . . .

He and Carolyne belong to those people for whom there is no question of having any personal convictions in life, but only personal interests. Life has no principal as a basis, but only a personal interest as goal, towards which it moves without any consequent moral behaviour. For them there are therefore no noble and ignoble people, estimable or contemptible persons, but only those who are either useful or dangerous. Accordingly their gaze lingers with goodwill on the rascal who can be won, while candid serious-mindedness they regard as something quite abominable! Since Liszt considers me a passionate reactionary, he believes he can annoy me by holding forth on how lamentably the princes behaved in 1848.

26 November. Evening at Frau von Schwendler's.* She talks a good deal about Liszt, of whom she thinks very highly: about his charity and generosity, the way in which quite free of envy he concerns himself with young artists and strives to further their careers—these are indeed fine qualities of his.[13]

* Henriette von Schwendler (1773–1853).

Princess Carolyne to Richard Wagner. Weimar, 4 January. How moved I was by the manner in which you speak of him whose glorious name I am soon to bear. Who could not speak of his spirit, his genius, his intelligence? But to understand the *infinite tenderness* of his soul, which so few are capable of feeling or divining, one must oneself have a soul that is at once elevated and perceptive.[1]

Hans von Bülow to his father, 21 January. I don't go into society at all. Privy Councillor X, whose wife and daughters adore me, occasionally invites me, but I decline to go there any more, because he is a violent antagonist of Liszt's. If I went over to the anti-Liszt side I should soon be immensely popular. Liszt's enemies here are like refuse by the sea: for he interests himself in other things besides piano-playing—the *Fondation Goethe* etc.—and that is a thorn in people's side. They allow him, in fact, only the right to entertain them as a pianist, which he has given up once and for all.[2]

To Weimar, and to a first meeting with Liszt, there came in March the idealistic and multi-talented Peter Cornelius (1824–74), nephew of the famous painter of the same name. Already a composer of choral works, chamber music, and sonatas, Cornelius had gained practical orchestral experience when playing among the violins with the touring Mainz orchestra. He had studied acting, was a gifted linguist and translator, and had written good poetry and several opera libretti, as well as a number of excellent articles on music.

On 20 March Liszt conducted the first Weimar performance of Berlioz's opera *Benvenuto Cellini*. The roles of Fieramosca and Teresa were sung by Feodor and Rosa von Milde.

Hans von Bülow to his mother, 23 May. The Princess gave me to understand that I might write a few words on Liszt's *Chopin*. I have been accustomed to be a *bon entendeur*, and had therefore first set myself to read it, for which I had not previously found time. As I have now finished with it, I send you the book, which will perhaps excite and interest you more than it did me. Although I doubt whether anyone could have handled the subject more suitably, or even more poetically, than Liszt has done, yet there are many things in it which are not quite sympathetic to me, especially because they make me think that the Princess has had a hand in it. That does not prevent me from having found much beauty in it, such as Liszt alone could give to it. . . .

He has allowed me and his other pupil (from Munich)—the third is studying musical theory at Eisenach—to play a great deal under his direction; he has made me study the great B flat Sonata of Beethoven, which I play not at all badly (in the Adagio he praised me tremendously), also Weber's *Concertstück* with some added effects, and Beethoven's [Choral] Fantasy. Next time I shall play him the first movement of the E flat major Concerto. My playing has lately very much changed for the better; my fingers are gradually gaining that elasticity in which a good touch really consists, because it makes one capable of giving every possible *nuance*, and I find Liszt's method more and more to be the only truly artistic and practical one. . . .

My unpopularity here is unbounded; I rejoice in it to the utmost, because it is a sort of filial unpopularity to that of Liszt, and the saying 'qu'ils me haïssent, pourvu qu'ils me craignent' is applicable. A caricature has even circulated here: Liszt as Don Quixote and I as Sancho Panza.[3]

To his father, 25 May. My piano-playing has latterly made substantial progress; I have gained in elasticity and a certain virtuoso *chic*, which was formerly entirely wanting. The great mastery of Liszt—apart from his individual appearance and personality—rests principally on his remarkably expansive and manifold power of expressing outwardly what he feels inwardly; not merely in the perception and grasp of a musical work, but in the way he can reproduce it outwardly, the extraordinarily faithful embodiment of the spiritual. Nothing is further from him than calculated effects; his genius as an artist consists chiefly in his certainty of the effect he gives so brilliantly at every performance. This point in Liszt seems to me the most worthy because the most possible of imitation, and I have tried for some time, and not without result, to copy him somewhat in this.[4]

A frequent visitor to Weimar in the 1840s and 50s, thanks to his friendship with the Hereditary Grand Duke Carl Alexander, was Hans Christian Andersen, who in 1852 spent three weeks (19 May to 10 June) in the town.

Andersen's diary, 25 May. Went up to Liszt's place, outside the town; the heat was deadly. He received me cheerfully and invited me to lunch, but I had to decline and accepted an invitation for Thursday. He said he was wanting to mount a performance of [J. P. E.] Hartmann's *The Raven*,* gave me a copy of his French book, *Lohengrin and Tannhäuser*, and was extremely agreeable. . . .

27 May. Lunch at Liszt's. Princess Wittgenstein resembles him somewhat, is not young, but very lively. . . . She took me to table. I later read *The Nightingale* and *The Ugly Duckling*; she applauded and was alert to every merry idea. Over coffee she smoked a cigar and asked me if I did not find it surprising to see a lady doing such a thing. . . . They asked me to regard their house as my own home. . . .

* An opera to a text by Andersen (after Gozzi). It was at Weimar a few years later (Jan. 1856) that Hartmann's *Little Kirsten* (libretto by Andersen), the most frequently performed Danish opera, was given its first German production, Andersen helping with the translation during his visit in 1855.

29 May. Lunch at 3 o'clock at Princess Wittgenstein's. (Liszt had visited me this morning.) The French Ambassador, Talleyrand,* was there, a relative of the famous one. . . . In Holland the Princess had bought a beautiful picture of Scheffer's, the *Three Holy Kings*; one of them is a portrait of Liszt. . . . I had to read again; she wanted *The Nightingale*, but I read *The Swineherd* and had a feeling that she cared less for the choice.

31 May. Visit from Liszt.—He and the Princess seem to me like salamanders, blazing and flaming; they can give one instant warmth, but one cannot draw near without getting burnt. . . .

2 June. To Princess Wittgenstein's in the morning. Liszt gave me a beautiful sheet of paper in Schiller's hand, with his name below. Talleyrand and Bryancourt were there. I read a lot of tales. *The Nightingale* was the most popular, and the Princess interpreted it as meaning that Liszt was the nightingale and Thalberg the artificial bird. She said that I was very clever and resembled Liszt. They were both extremely complimentary to me. . . .

4 June. At 4 o'clock to Frau von Schwendler's, where there was a crowd to hear me. Liszt wanted, and got, *The Shadow*. Princess Wittgenstein quite aglow with delight. . . .

9 June. Went to Liszt, who was exceptionally forthcoming and friendly. He entrusted me with writing to Hartmann about *The Raven*. . . . asked about a couple of my poems to set to music. . . . Princess Wittgenstein extremely kind. . . .[5]

Later in June, accompanied by his pupil Dionys Pruckner (1834–96), Raff, and Bülow, Liszt went to Ballenstedt, to direct the music festival held there on the 22nd and 23rd. The main items were Beethoven's Ninth Symphony and Choral Fantasy (with Bülow as soloist); Liszt's own *Die Macht der Musik* (S302) for soprano and orchestra (with Rosa von Milde); Wagner's *Das Liebesmahl der Apostel* (male chorus); Berlioz's *Harold en Italie*; and Mendelssohn's *Walpurgisnacht*.

Bülow to his father. Weimar, 28 June. Liszt really worked wonders; in three days' rehearsals everything was in trim, and the orchestra, which was brought together from all parts, and the members of which were quite unknown to one another (chorus and orchestra numbered some 300 persons), so well co-ordinated that it seemed as though they all belonged to *one* society: Liszt's personality in conducting had inspired and carried them away.[6]

During Liszt's absence, his mother, who had been staying at the Altenburg, set out on her journey back to Paris, but, breaking a leg at Erfurt, was brought back

* C. A. Talleyrand-Périgord (1821–?), French Ambassador to Weimar 1852–4, was for a short time engaged to marry the young Princess Marie Wittgenstein.

to Weimar to recuperate. Altogether she was away from Paris for a year and a half.

Bülow to his father, late July. I am at present writing a dozen songs, eight of which are already done. Liszt is very much interested in them. His criticism is of the greatest advantage to me; he at once perceives all my intentions, and then knows not only how to discover any chance contradiction between thought and form, but how to suggest the simplest and best means of putting it right. Hence he is, by his own experience, the best and most impressive adviser as to the observance of simplicity and clearness in the piano accompaniment—he who formerly did the most important things in exactly the contrary direction.[7]

Liszt to his son Daniel, 22 August. The news of your *first prize in history* has given me the most agreeable satisfaction, and I am grateful to you, my dear Daniel, for having responded in such a manner to the trouble I am taking, and to the expectation I have of you. Once seriously entered upon a life of application and study, it is to be presumed that you will not feebly stop half way, and that you will have the ambition to aspire to successes and satisfactions ever more difficult to obtain. You would not be my son, and I should have to disown you as such, if you were not animated by a sincere love of work, by a passionate zeal for the task it is given you to accomplish.

Realize once and for all, and remind yourself unceasingly, that it is only by dint of constant work and sustained efforts that, by the gradual ennoblement of his faculties and his character, man is permitted to acquire his freedom, his morality, his value, and his greatness. And so the best aspect of whatever success we obtain is that it spurs on in us the need we have to extend the limits of our intellectual ability and enlarge our horizons. . . . 'Idleness is the mother of all vices' is the simple proverb which can serve you as a text. It will lead you straight to the corollary maxim, which I recommend you alike to ponder and to practise: 'Work is the father of all virtues.' By virtue we mean strength, superiority, nobility, greatness. . . .[8]

*Adelheid von Schorn.** In November there was a Berlioz Week† in Weimar. Liszt put on *Benvenuto Cellini*, in a translation by Peter

* In later life the author of a history of Weimar in the 19th century, and during Liszt's final years a sharp-eyed observer of his activities, about which she sent detailed reports to the Princess (then living in Rome), Adelheid von Schorn (1841–1916) was at this time a child living with her widowed mother Henriette (1807–69). The latter, a former lady-in-waiting to Maria Pavlovna, was Carolyne's closest woman friend in her Weimar years.

† On 20 Nov., at the Court Theatre, Berlioz conducted his *Roméo et Juliette* and Parts One and Two of *La Damnation de Faust*. Ignaz Moscheles, who came to Weimar to make the acquaintance of this music, noted in his diary: 'Berlioz's conducting imparted to the performance a vitality which impelled everything along with it. I was glad to have got to know him as both composer and conductor.' *Cellini*, conducted by Liszt, was given twice.

Cornelius. . . . It had already been performed in March that year, and in doing it Liszt had once again proved his courage, for neither in France nor Germany did anyone want anything to do with the works of Berlioz. . . .

We ran into the two of them in the street, and when Liszt introduced his friend to my mother I had time to have a good look at the Frenchman's remarkable head. His sharp, handsome, but rather birdlike features, with bright, piercingly penetrating eyes and bushy grey hair, could have been called attractive had their expression been softer. Particularly striking was the contrast they formed with the indescribably engaging manner of Liszt, which often made his face seem nothing short of transfigured.[9]

Franziska von Bülow to her daughter Isidora, Christmas Eve. Friday evening we spent with Liszt—glorious music—two quartets; then he and Joachim played a duo by Schubert, and again he struck me with the wonderful power of his genius—or daemon.[10]

For the *Méthode des Méthodes de piano* of Fétis and Moscheles, Liszt had in 1840 composed a piano solo entitled *Morceau de salon, étude de perfectionnement* (S142). This short, violent but attractive piece (one of whose melodies foreshadows a theme used in the symphonic poem *Les Préludes*) was in 1852 revised and published with the title *Ab irato* (S143).

1853

In 1848 the first version of No. 9 (*Pester Karneval*), and in 1851 Nos. 1,2, and the first version of No. 15 (Rákóczy March), of the Hungarian Rhapsodies (S244) for piano solo had been published. The year 1853 saw the appearance in print of another eleven of these colourful, nationalistic works, of which with only a few exceptions the various dedicatees were, appropriately, compatriots of the composer. No. 15 was for long the last of the set, but it was followed in the final years of Liszt's life by another four.

The *Harmonies poétiques et religieuses* (S173), a collection of piano pieces composed between 1845 and 1852 and dedicated to Princess Carolyne, were also published this year. Their titles are: *Invocation*; *Ave Maria* (from S20/2); *Bénédiction de Dieu dans la solitude*; *Pensée des morts* (from S154 andS691); *Pater noster* (from S21/2); *Hymne de l'enfant à son réveil* (from S19); *Funérailles*; *Miserere, d'après Palestrina*; *Andante lagrimoso*; and *Cantique d'amour*.

Of these, the beautiful, melodious *Cantique d'amour*; still more, the moving, powerful *Funérailles*, an elegy for Lajos Batthyány and other Hungarians executed after the failed insurrection of 1848–9; and, above all, the incomparable, mystical *Bénédiction de Dieu dans la solitude,* are among the very finest of Liszt's creations for the piano.

Early in January came the departure from Weimar of Joseph Joachim, who a few weeks earlier had resigned from leadership of the Weimar orchestra after finding a more lucrative position at Hanover. It was Liszt, an affectionate admirer of Joachim, who had recommended him for the new post. To Heinrich Ehrlich he had written (12 September 1852): 'I shall see his departure with *great regret*, but I have his interests too much at heart to prevent him advancing his career.' Not prescient, however, as events were to prove, was Liszt's opinion (letter of 24 November to Julius Stern) that Joachim possessed a 'thoroughly loyal nature'.

The latter's replacement at Weimar was the violinist Ferdinand Laub (1832–75).

On Wednesday, 2 February, Liszt completed his Sonata in B minor (S178), greatest of all his works for the piano. He dedicated it to Robert Schumann, who many years earlier had dedicated to Liszt his own finest work for the instrument, the Fantasy in C.

On 16 February, the birthday of Maria Pavlovna, he conducted the first Weimar performance of *Der fliegende Holländer*, the third Wagner opera to be given by him.

Peter Cornelius to his mother. The Altenburg, 12 March. I have been thinking, Mother dear, that if you want to perform a stroke of genius, you could knit or sew some trifle or other for *Liszt*, and send it him with a friendly note. Even if only a pair of socks. He'll be as pleased as a child, you'll see—and it will bring you a letter from him![1]

In April, Liszt's little band of pupils was joined by *William Mason* (1829–1908), one of the nineteenth century's most prominent American pianists, teachers and composers. He had already spent several years in Europe, studying with Moscheles in Leipzig and with Dreyschock in Prague.

I had no idea then, neither have I now, what Liszt's means were, but I learned soon after my arrival in Weimar that he never took pay from his pupils, neither would he bind himself to give regular lessons at stated periods. He wished to avoid obligations as far as possible, and to feel free to leave Weimar for short periods when so inclined—in other words, to go and come as he liked. His idea was that the pupils whom he accepted should all be far enough advanced to practise and prepare themselves without routine instruction, and he expected them to be ready whenever he gave them an opportunity to play. The musical opportunities of Weimar were such as to afford ample encouragement to any serious-minded young student. Many distinguished musicians, poets, and literary men were constantly coming to visit Liszt. He was fond of entertaining, and liked to have his pupils at hand so that they might join him in entertaining and paying attention to his guests. He had only three pupils at the time of which I write, namely, Karl Klindworth* from Hanover, Dionys Pruckner from Munich, and myself. . . . Joachim Raff, however, we regarded as one of

* The pianist, conductor, and composer Karl Klindworth (1830–1916) is now best remembered for his work as editor (e.g. of Chopin) and arranger. He was on friendly terms with Wagner as well as Liszt, and it was his adopted daughter, Winifred Williams, who married Wagner's son Siegfried.

us, for although not at the time a pupil of Liszt, he had been in former years, and was now constantly in association with the master, acting frequently in the capacity of private secretary. Hans von Bülow had left Weimar not long before my arrival, and was then on his first regular concert-tour. Later he returned occasionally for short visits, and I became well acquainted with him. We constituted, as it were, a family, for while we had our own apartments in the city, we all enjoyed the freedom of the two lower rooms in Liszt's home, and were at liberty to come and go as we liked. Regularly on every Sunday at eleven o'clock, with rare exceptions, the famous Weimar String Quartet played for an hour and a half or so in these rooms, and Liszt frequently joined them in concerted music, old and new. Occasionally one of the boys would take the pianoforte part. . . . Henri Wieniawski, who spent some months in Weimar, would occasionally take the first violin. My favourite as a quartet-player was Ferdinand Laub, with whom I was intimately acquainted, and I find that the greatest violinists of the present time hold him in high estimation, many of them regarding him as the greatest of all quartet-players. On ceremonial occasions we were invited upstairs to the drawing-room, where Liszt had his favourite Erard. We were thus enjoying the best music, played by the best artists. In addition, there were the symphonic concerts and the opera, with occasional attendance at rehearsal. Liszt took it for granted that his pupils would appreciate these remarkable advantages and opportunities and their usefulness, and I think we did. . . .

Liszt never taught in the ordinary sense of the word. During the entire time that I was with him I did not see him give a regular lesson in the pedagogical sense. He would notify us to come up to the Altenburg. For instance he would say to me, 'Tell the boys to come up tonight at half-past six or seven.' We would go there, and he would call on us to play. I remember very well the first time I played to him after I had been accepted as a pupil. I began with the Ballade of Chopin in A flat; then I played a fugue by Handel in E minor.

After I was well started he began to get excited. He made audible suggestions, inciting me to put more enthusiasm into my playing, and occasionally he would push me gently off the chair and sit down at the piano and play a phrase or two himself by way of illustration. He gradually got me worked up to such a pitch of enthusiasm that I put all the grit that was in me into my playing.

I found at this first lesson that he was very fond of strong accents in order to mark off periods and phrases, and he talked so much about strong accentuation that one might have supposed that he would abuse it, but he never did. When he wrote to me later about my own piano method, he expressed the strongest approval of the exercises on accentuation.

While I was playing to him for the first time, he said on one of the occasions when he pushed me from the chair: 'Don't play it that way. Play it like this.' Evidently I had been playing ahead in a steady, uniform way. He sat down, and gave the same phrases with an accentuated, elastic movement, which let in a flood of light upon me. From that one experience I learned to bring out the same effect, where it was appropriate, in almost every piece that I played. It eradicated much that was mechanical, stilted, and unmusical in my playing, and developed an elasticity of touch which has lasted all my life, and which I have always tried to impart to my pupils.

At this first lesson I must have played for two or three hours. For some reason or other Raff was not present, but Klindworth and Pruckner were there. They lounged on a sofa and smoked, and I remember wondering if they appreciated the nice time they were having at my ordeal. However, not many days afterwards came my opportunity to light a cigar and lounge about the room while Liszt put them through their paces. . . .

The best impression of Liszt's appearance at that time is conveyed by the picture which shows him approaching the Altenburg. His back is turned; nevertheless, there is a certain something which shows the man as he was better even than those portraits in which his features are clearly reproduced. The picture gives his gait, his figure, and his general appearance. There is his tall, lank form, his high hat set a little to one side, and his arm a trifle akimbo. He had piercing eyes. His hair was very dark, but not black. He wore it long, just as he did in his older days. It came almost down to his shoulders, and was cut off square at the bottom. He had it cut frequently, so as to keep it at about the same length. That was a point about which he was very particular.

As I remember his hands, his fingers were lean and thin, but they did not impress me as being very long, and he did not have such a remarkable stretch on the keyboard as one might imagine. He was always neatly dressed, generally appearing in a long frock-coat. . . . His general manner and his face were most expressive of his feelings, and his features lighted up when he spoke. His smile was simply charming. His face was peculiar. One could hardly call it handsome, yet there was in it a subtle something that was most attractive, and his whole manner had a fascination which it is impossible to describe.

I remember little incidents which are in themselves trivial, but which illustrate some character trait. One day Liszt was reading a letter in which a musician was referred to as a certain Mr. So-and-so. He read that phrase over two or three times, and then substituted his own name for that of the musician mentioned, and repeated several times, 'A *certain* Mr. Liszt, a *certain* Mr. Liszt, a *certain* Mr. Liszt,' adding: 'I don't know that that would offend me. I don't know that I should object to being called "a *certain* Mr. Liszt".' As he said this, his face had an expression of curiosity, as though he were wondering whether he really would be offended or not. But at the same time there was in his face that look of kindness I saw there so often, and I really believe he would not have felt injured by such a reference to himself. There was nothing petty in his feelings.

On one occasion, however, I saw Liszt grow very much excited over what he considered an imposition. One evening he said to us: 'Boys, there is a young man coming here tomorrow who says he can play Beethoven's Sonata in B flat, Op. 106. I want you all three to be here.'

We were there at the appointed hour. The pianist proved to be a Hungarian, whose name I have forgotten. He sat down and began to play in a conveniently slow tempo the bold chords with which the sonata opens. He had not progressed more than half a page when Liszt stopped him, and seating himself at the piano, played in the correct tempo, which was much faster, to show him how the work should be interpreted. 'It's nonsense for you to go through this sonata in that fashion,' said Liszt, as he rose from the piano and left the room. The pianist, of course, was very much disconcerted. Finally he said, as if to console himself: 'Well, he can't play it through like that, and that's why he stopped after half a page.'. . .

When the young man left I went out with him, partly because I felt sorry for him, he had made such a fiasco, and partly because I wished to impress upon him the fact that Liszt could play the whole movement in the tempo in which he began it. As I was walking along with him, he said, 'I'm out of money; won't you lend me three louis d'or?'

A day or two later I told Liszt by the merest chance that the hero of the Op. 106 fiasco had tried to borrow money of me. 'B-r-r-r! What?' exclaimed Liszt. Then he jumped up, walked across the room, seized a long pipe that hung from a nail on the wall, and brandishing it as if it were a stick, stamped up and down the room in almost childish indignation, exclaiming, 'Drei louis d'or! Drei louis d'or!' The point is, however, that Liszt regarded the man as an artistic impostor. He had sent word to Liszt that he could play the great Beethoven sonata, not an inconsiderable feat in those days. He had been received on that basis. He had failed miserably. To this artistic imposition he had added the effrontery of endeavouring to borrow money from someone whom he had met under Liszt's roof. . . .

Before I went to Weimar I had not been of a very sociable disposition. At Weimar I had to be. Liszt liked to have us about him. He wished us to meet great men. He would send us word when he expected visitors, and sometimes he would bring them down to our lodgings to see us. In every way he tried to make our surroundings as pleasant as possible. It would have been strange if, in such circumstances, we had not derived some benefit from our intercourse with our great master and his visitors.

I shall always recall with amusement a breakfast which, at Liszt's request, Klindworth and I gave to Joachim and Wieniawski, the violinists, then, of course, very young men, and to several other distinguished visitors. Liszt had been entertaining them for several days. We knew that it was about time for him to bring them down to see one of us. So I was not surprised when he turned to me one evening and said, 'Mason, I want you and Klindworth to give us a breakfast tomorrow.' I asked him what we should have. 'Oh,' he replied, 'some *Semmel*, caviare, herring,' etc.

The next morning Liszt and his visitors came. I remember looking out of my window and watching them cross the ducal park, over the long footpath which ended directly opposite the house where Klindworth and I lived. It had been raining, and the path was slippery, so that their footsteps were somewhat uncertain.

The breakfast passed off all right. When he had finished, Liszt said, 'Now let us take a stroll in the garden.' This garden was about four times as large as the back yard of a New York house, and it was unpaved and, of course, muddy from the rain of the previous night. Never shall I forget the sight of Liszt, Joachim, Wieniawski, and our other distinguished guests 'strolling' through this garden, wading in mud two inches deep.

Time and again at Weimar I heard Liszt play. There is absolutely no doubt in my mind that he was the greatest pianist of the nineteenth century. He was what the Germans call an *Erscheinung*—an epoch-making genius. . . . There have been other great pianists, some of whom are now living,* but I must dissent from those writers who affirm that any of these can be placed upon a level with Liszt. Those who make this assertion are too young to have heard Liszt other than in his declining years, and it is unjust to compare the playing of one who has long since passed his prime with that of one who is still in it. . . .

In March, 1895, Stavenhagen† and Reményi‡ were dining at my house one evening, and the former began to speak in enthusiastic terms of Liszt's playing. Reményi interrupted with emphasis: 'You have never heard Liszt play—that is, as Liszt used to play in his prime;' and he appealed to me for corroboration, but, unhappily, I never met Liszt again after leaving Weimar in July, 1854.

The difference between Liszt's playing and that of others was the difference between creative genius and interpretation. His genius flashed through every pianistic phrase, it illuminated a composition to its innermost recesses, and yet his wonderful effects, strange as it must seem, were produced without the advantage of a genuinely musical touch.

I remember on one occasion Schulhoff§ came to Weimar and played in the drawing-room of the Altenburg. His playing and Liszt's were in marked contrast. He was a parlour pianist of high excellence. His compositions, exclusively in the smaller forms, were in great favour and universally played by the ladies.

* Mason's reminiscences were written *c.* 1900.

† Bernhard Stavenhagen (1862–1914) became a pupil of Liszt's in 1885.

‡ The brilliant Hungarian violinist Ede Reményi (1828–98), who in 1854 became solo violinist to Queen Victoria, had a special flair for performing gypsy music.

§ The Bohemian pianist and composer Julius Schulhoff (1825–98).

Liszt played his own *Bénédiction de Dieu dans la solitude*, as pathetic a piece, perhaps, as he ever composed, and of which he was very fond. Afterwards Schulhoff, with his exquisitely beautiful touch, produced a quality of tone more beautiful than Liszt's; but about the latter's performance there was intellectuality and the indescribable impressiveness of genius, which made Schulhoff's playing, with all its beauty, seem tame by contrast. . . .

It seemed to me that there were certain indications in his playing which warranted the belief that his mechanical powers would begin to wane at a comparatively early period in his career. There was too little pliancy, flexion, and relaxation in his muscles; hence a lack of economy in the expenditure of his energies.

He was aware of this, and said in effect on one occasion, as I learned indirectly through either Klindworth or Pruckner: 'You are to learn all you can from my playing, relating to conception, style, phrasing, etc., but do not imitate my touch, which, I am well aware, is not a good model to follow. In early years I was not patient enough to "make haste slowly"—thoroughly to develop in an orderly, logical, and progressive way. I was impatient for immediate results, and took short cuts, so to speak, and jumped through sheer force of will to the goal of my ambition. I wish now that I had progressed by logical steps instead of by leaps. It is true that I have been successful, but I do not advise you to follow my way, for you lack my personality.'

In saying this, Liszt had no idea of magnifying himself; but it was nevertheless genius which enabled him to accomplish certain results which were out of the ordinary course, and in a way which others, being differently constituted, could not follow. His advice to his pupils was to be deliberate, and through care and close attention to important, although seemingly insignificant, details to progress in an orderly way towards a perfect style.

Notwithstanding this caution, and falling into the usual tendency of pupils to imitate the idiosyncrasies and mannerisms, even faults or weak points, of the teacher, some of the boys, in their effort to attain Lisztian effects, acquired a hard and unsympathetic touch, and thus produced mere noise in the place of full and resonant tones.

Before going to Weimar I had heard in various places in Germany that Liszt spoiled all of those pupils who went to him without a previously acquired knowledge of method and a habit of the correct use of the muscles in producing musical effects. It was necessary for the pupil to have an absolutely sure foundation to benefit by Liszt's instruction. If he had that preparation, Liszt could develop the best there was in him.

There is danger of unduly magnifying the importance of a mere mechanical technique. In Liszt's earlier days he inclined in this direction, and wrote the *Etudes d'exécution transcendante*. I remember his saying to his pupils one day, when these were the subject of our conversation, that having completed them, his interest in that direction had ceased and he wrote no more. Moreover, he added, 'I expected that some day a pianist would appear who would make this subject his speciality, and would accomplish difficulties that were seemingly impossible to perform.'. . .

One evening early in June, 1853, Liszt sent word to us to come up to the Altenburg next morning, as he expected a visit from a young man who was said to have great talent as a pianist and composer, and whose name was Johannes Brahms. He was to come accompanied by Reményi. The next morning, on going to the Altenburg with Klindworth, we found Brahms and Reményi already in the reception room with Raff and Pruckner. After greeting the newcomers, of whom Reményi was known to us by reputation, I strolled over to a table on which were lying some music manuscripts. They were several of Brahms's yet unpublished compositions, and I began turning over the leaves of the uppermost in the pile. It was the piano solo 'Op. 4, Scherzo in E flat minor', and, as I remember, the writing was so illegible that I thought to myself that if I had occasion to study it I should be obliged first to make a copy of it. Finally Liszt came down, and after some general conversation he turned to Brahms and said: 'We are interested to hear some of your compositions whenever you are ready and feel inclined to play them.'

Brahms, who was evidently very nervous, protested that it was quite impossible for him to play while in such a disconcerted state, and, notwithstanding the earnest solicitations of both Liszt and Reményi, could not be persuaded to approach the piano. Liszt, seeing that no progress was being made, went over to the table, and taking up the first piece at hand, the illegible scherzo, and saying, 'Well, I shall have to play,' placed the manuscript on the music rack.

We had often witnessed his wonderful feats in sight-reading, and regarded him as infallible in that particular, but, notwithstanding our confidence in his ability, both Raff and I had a lurking dread of the possibility that something might happen which would be disastrous to our unquestioning faith. So, when he put the scherzo on the rack, I trembled for the result. But he read it off in such a marvellous way—at the same time carrying on a running accompaniment of audible criticism of the music—that Brahms was amazed and delighted. . . . Liszt also played a part of Brahms's C major Sonata, Op.1.

A little later someone asked Liszt to play his own Sonata, a work which was quite recent at that time, and of which he was very fond. Without hesitation he sat down and began playing. As he progressed, he came to a very expressive part of the Sonata, which he always imbued with extreme pathos, and in which he looked for the especial interest and sympathy of his listeners. Casting a glance at Brahms, he found that the latter was dozing in his chair. Liszt continued playing to the end of the Sonata, then rose and left the room. I was in such a position that Brahms was hidden from my view, but I was aware that something unusual had taken place, and I think it was Reményi who afterwards told me what it was. It is very strange that among the various accounts of this Liszt–Brahms first interview—and there are several—there is not one which gives an accurate description of what took place on that occasion; indeed, they are all far out. The events as here related are perfectly clear in my own mind, but not wishing to trust implicitly to my memory alone, I wrote to my friend Klindworth—the only living witness of the incident except myself, as I suppose—and requested him to give an account of it as he remembered it. He corroborated my description in every particular, except that he made no specific reference to the drowsiness of Brahms, and except, also, that, according to my recollection, Brahms left Weimar on the afternoon of the day on which the meeting took place; Klindworth writes that it was on the morning of the following day—a discrepancy of very little moment. . . .

Liszt's playing of the Brahms scherzo was a remarkable feat, but he was constantly doing almost incredible things in the way of reading at sight. Another instance of his skill in this direction occurs to me and is well worthy of mention. Raff had composed a sonata for violin and pianoforte in which there were ever-varying changes in the rhythm; bars of 7/8, 7/4, 5/4, alternated with common and triple time, and seemed to mix together promiscuously and without regard to order. Notwithstanding this apparent disorder, there was an undercurrent, so to speak, of the ordinary 3/4 or 4/4 time, and to the player who could penetrate the rhythmic mask the difficulty of performance quickly vanished. Raff had arranged with Laub and Pruckner that they should practise the sonata together, and then, on a favourable occasion, play it in Liszt's presence. So on one of the musical mornings at the Altenburg these gentlemen began to play the sonata. Pruckner, of sensitive and nervous organisation, found the changes of rhythm too confusing, especially when played before company, and broke down at the first page. Another and yet a third attempt was made, but with like results. Liszt, whose interest was aroused, exclaimed: 'I wonder if I can play that!' Then, taking his place at the instrument, he played it through at sight in rapid tempo and without the slightest hesitation. He had intuitively divined the regularity of movement which lay beneath the surface.[2]

In late June Liszt went to Karlsruhe, to make preparations for the music festival he was to direct there in the autumn; and thence proceeded to Zurich, where he had arranged to visit the exiled Wagner. 'We almost stifled one another with our embracing,' he wrote to Carolyne. 'On seeing me again he wept, laughed and stormed with joy for at least a quarter of an hour. We went to his place straightaway and spent the whole day together. . . . He loves me with heart and soul and doesn't leave off saying: "Look what you have made of me!" Yesterday we sang together the duet between Elsa and Lohengrin. *Ma foi, c'était superbe*! as our poor friend Chopin used to say. . . . His manners are decidedly overbearing . . . . For me, however, there is complete and absolute exception. Yesterday he remarked once again: "For me, thou art the whole of Germany." If, as I believe, his importance continues to increase, and to become altogether predominant in Germany and Switzerland, there is no doubt that the 100,000 francs needed to enable him to realize his idea of a *Bühnenfestspiel* [stage festival drama] will be found. . . . If Monseigneur* follows my advice, he will offer him Weimar and Eisenach to carry out this colossal project—but it is to be feared that our local parsimony and niggardliness may be an obstacle.'

Richard Wagner. My flat was so charmingly furnished with carpets and decorative furniture that Liszt himself was surprised into admiration as he entered my *petite élégance*, as he called it. Now for the first time I enjoyed the delight of getting to know my friend better as a fellow composer. In addition to many of his celebrated pianoforte pieces, which he had only recently written, we went through several new orchestral works with great ardour, and especially his Faust Symphony.†. . . My delight in everything I heard by Liszt was as great as it was sincere; above all, it had a stimulating effect upon me that was very significant. I even thought of beginning to compose again after the long interval that had elapsed.‡ What could be more promising and more important for me than this long-desired contact with the friend who had been engaged all his life in his masterly practice of music, that same friend who had devoted himself so exclusively to my own works and to making them properly understood. Those almost bewilderingly delightful days, with the inevitable rush of friends and acquaintances, were interrupted by an excursion to the Lake of Lucerne, accompanied only by Herwegh, to whom Liszt had the charming idea of offering a 'draught of fellowship' with himself and me from the three springs of the Grütli. . . .

After Liszt's departure I felt quite disconsolate.[3]

Before leaving Zurich Liszt received a telegram informing him of the death, on 8 July, of the Grand Duke Carl Friedrich. (Whose son, Liszt's friend Carl Alexander, was installed as ruler of the Grand Duchy at a ceremony on 28 August.)

On his way home, Liszt stopped at Frankfurt (from which he also made an excursion to nearby Wiesbaden to attend a performance of *Fidelio*). It was here that *Ludwig Meinardus* witnessed 'one of the most unbelievable feats of this rare master musician'.

* Carl Alexander, who a few days later became Grand Duke of Saxe-Weimar. Liszt's fears about 'parsimony and niggardliness' proved well founded: Carl Alexander showed indifference to the plans for Wagner's festival theatre, and it eventually came into being not in Weimar but at Bayreuth.

† Liszt did not write down the Faust Symphony until the next year. What he is likely to have shown and played to Wagner at this time were his sketches for the work, its principal themes, etc.

‡ Wagner composed no music between *Lohengrin* (completed in 1848) and the commencement (Nov. 1853) of *Das Rheingold*.

He invited us to André's piano shop in Mozart's house in the Zeil, where one of the best-known of piano virtuosi—whom we shall here name Rolf (he is Danish)*—wanted to perform a new concerto he had written. A considerable crowd of musicians had accordingly assembled at the appointed place. Rolf had brought his wife with him, a quiet, graceful person, it appeared. After greetings had been exchanged, Liszt asked in his courteous way if they could begin soon, as Kapellmeister Schmidt had been so considerate as to put *Fidelio* down for that evening, and it would be a shame to miss the overture.

'Unfortunately I have no piano version of the orchestral accompaniment,' said Rolf doubtingly. 'That is very bad,' rejoined Liszt roguishly. 'Is your score then of such mighty difficulty?'—'Thirty staves in small writing,' said Rolf rather smugly. 'I myself have difficulty in playing it, and as yet know no pianist who has managed to read it without trouble.'—'Oh,' replied Liszt, 'I am only a tolerable musician, to be sure—but let me have a try at least. You must be patient with me, of course.'

After this preliminary, Liszt asked Rolf's wife for permission to light a cigar. Then he put on his spectacles and sat at the piano; Rolf was already preluding rather woodenly at the other. At Liszt's request I turned the pages for him, and so it did not escape me how truly Rolf had described the astounding difficulties of this overcrowded score. In the entire thirty staves I found it hard to find a single rest: every instrument in the orchestra was bowing, blowing, blaring, or rattling away almost uninterruptedly from the beginning of the work to the end; and Liszt took pleasure in reproducing the literally stunning orchestral effect so accurately on the piano that soon nothing more could be heard of the solo player—who in fact hardly ever played solo—even though his mighty exertions were making the sweat run down him in streams. Added to this, during the most intense reading and playing Liszt often made witty remarks to me *sotto voce* when I came near him to turn over; indeed, at times he played with one hand alone so that with the other he could turn down the corner of a page, or give attention to his cigar. His circle of listeners sat as though turned to stone. None of them had thought such a fantastic achievement possible.

When the piece was at an end, Rolf deigned to offer some trite compliment, but Liszt waved it aside, saying that in respect of the solo part the orchestration would 'very well bear' a reduction in sonority, and added: 'Your handwriting is quite excellent, my friend, but a few small slips have crept in. I have taken the liberty of turning down the relevant pages. On one page the second bassoon part lacks a sharp before the C. On the other you have forgotten to write the B flat clarinets transposed. And there are a few other trifles of the sort!'

Herr Rolf remarked—he had become rather more subdued—that such

* Probably the Danish pianist and composer *Rudolf* Willmers (1821–78), a pupil of Hummel.

an overall grasp and rapidity of reading he had never before believed possible. The *lady's* presence shielded her husband, otherwise Liszt would probably not have spared him a witty lesson in modesty.[4]

Reaching Weimar on 16 July, Liszt wrote that same day to Carolyne, who a fortnight earlier had left with Marie for the Bohemian spa of Carlsbad (now Karlovy Vary).

I found it absolutely impossible to write anything during the fortnight's travelling—and I really need to write music to keep my equilibrium. When I spend several days without music paper, I feel as though I were dried up. My brain becomes congested and I feel incapable of taking pleasure in things external. This is something I have often noticed; it is a kind of sickness which has increased with the years. Music is the breathing of my soul; it becomes at once my work and my prayer.[5]

Leaving again on 27 July, Liszt joined Carolyne at Carlsbad, where he stayed at the White Lion. Among his acquaintances at the spa was the German poet and playwright *Emanuel Geibel* (1815–84).*

From Aldrige's Othello, which all of us had seen, we came to talk about Shakespeare in general, first *A Midsummer Night's Dream* and Mendelssohn's music, and then *The Tempest*. Here, too, I said, was rich material for a musical setting. Liszt agreed. We went through the principal moments of the enchanting play, and the more we immersed ourselves in the magic world of the great poet the warmer grew our enthusiasm. In the end Liszt sprang up and took his seat at the piano. I have always enjoyed hearing him improvise, but yesterday he played more captivatingly than ever. Everything we had been discussing we now heard once more in fantastic musical form: a storm at sea and a shipwreck; fear and love; Caliban's bestial cursing and Stephano's laughing drunkenness; and then again, as though whispering towards us from on high, the silvery notes of Ariel's ivory bell; and at the last, over and above all else, the dominion of Prospero as he puts all to rights again, as with his golden wand he subdues the roaring elements and their spirits, and with mellow wisdom smooths and unravels the entanglements of human passion. I really cannot give you any conception of it: you would have had to hear it with us. Even Liszt felt that he had surpassed himself.[6]

From Carlsbad, Liszt went on 16 August to another popular watering-place, Teplitz (Teplice).

Antonin Mayer, an organist at Teplitz. One day Prince Edmund Clary's servant brought me a confidential note telling me to be at the Castle punctually at 8 p.m. Supposing it would be for some chamber music, I took

* Whose *Die stille Wasserrose* Liszt later (*c*.1860) set for tenor or mezzo-soprano and piano (S321).

my fiddle with me and some piano music. At the Castle, the Prince introduced me to three gentlemen with the words: 'One of your colleagues—our teacher and organist.' I don't know what I managed to stutter—before me stood Franz Liszt. With him were Alexander Dreyschock and the Danish pianist Willmers. They shook hands with me heartily. First I listened entranced to Liszt's virtuoso playing.* With equal interest I then heard the other two pianists. I was only afraid that I, too, might be asked to play. Liszt noticed and said: 'And you, Herr Lehrer, if not today, then in church tomorrow, at High Mass.' I did not shut an eye the whole night. Liszt wanted to hear me play the organ! The next day, the church was full of people. . . . But Liszt was nowhere to be seen. I had just breathed a sigh of relief, when at the Sanctus Liszt was at my side. He pushed me gently from the bench and himself sat down to play. A storm of harmonies flowed through the church. Long after the Mass was over, groups of townspeople stood in the Market Place and, still amazed, said they had never heard such playing in their lives.[7]

Returning to Weimar on 17 September, Liszt first visited Raff, in prison for an unpaid debt. 'Although it's only a matter of 80 écus,' he told Carolyne, 'I shan't pay them on principle! I have advised him to stay in his new lodgings as long as it suits his creditor to keep him there.'

The next day he went on to Karlsruhe, where Carolyne and Marie later joined him for the music festival, held from 3 to 5 October. It passed off successfully, save for a player's wrong entry which nearly wrecked one of the performances. According to William Mason, who was present: 'Because of his strong advocacy of Wagner and modern music generally, Liszt had many enemies, as was to be expected of a man of his prominence. If perchance a mishap occurred during his conducting, there were always petty critics on hand to take advantage of the opportunity and to magnify the fault. One of these occasions happened at Karlsruhe. . . . In a passage where the trombone† enters on an off beat, the player made a mistake and came in on the even beat. This error, not the conductor's fault, occasioned such confusion that Liszt had to stop the orchestra and begin again, and the little fellows made the most of this opportunity to pitch into him.'

Accompanied by Bülow, Cornelius, Joachim, Pruckner, Reményi, and Richard Pohl,‡ Liszt then crossed the Swiss border and entered Basle, where a further meeting with *Richard Wagner* had been arranged.

* Years earlier, Chopin had played on this 'light cherrywood piano'. A tablet bearing the names of both great composer-pianists is now attached to the instrument, which stands in the music room of the Castle (now a museum) to this day.

† Actually a bassoon, in Beethoven's 9th Symphony. Incidentally, it was at this festival that Liszt's *An die Künstler* (S70), for soloists, chorus and orchestra, was premiered.

‡ A writer (1826–96) who under the pen-name 'Hoplit' contributed many articles to the *Neue Zeitschrift für Musik* in support of the music of Liszt, Wagner, and the New German school. From 1854 he lived for several years in Weimar, and his wife Jeanne, a gifted harpist, became a member of the orchestra.

I was the first to arrive, and in the evening, while sitting alone in the dining-room of the hotel 'Zu den drei Königen', I heard from the adjacent vestibule a small but powerful male-voice choir intone the trumpet fanfare from *Lohengrin* which announces the King's arrival. The door opened and Liszt entered at the head of his joyful little band. . . .

The bright and merry spirit which prevailed at that gathering (which, like everything that Liszt promoted, in spite of its intimate nature, was characterised by magnificent unconventionality) grew to a pitch of almost eccentric hilarity as the night wore on. . . . On the following day our celebrations were completed by the arrival of the ladies, who for the next few days formed the centre of our little party. In those days it was impossible for anyone coming into contact with Princess Carolyne to resist her uncommon vivacity and the charming way in which she listened to what others were saying.

She was as much interested in the more important questions that concerned us as in the most casual details of our life in relation to society, and she had the magnetic power of extracting the very best out of those with whom she associated. Her daughter gave one quite a different impression. She was only fifteen [sixteen] and had rather a rapturous look on her young face, being at the stage 'in which womanhood and childhood meet', thus allowing me to pay her the compliment of calling her 'the child'. . . .

When Liszt was obliged to leave for Paris on a visit to his children, we all accompanied him as far as Strasbourg, and I decided to follow him to Paris. . . .

We were very sorry to part from our younger friends. Bülow told me that Joachim, who had been holding himself rather aloof, could not forget my tremendous article on 'Judaism', and that he consequently felt shy and awkward in my presence. He also said that when Joachim had asked him (Bülow) to read one of his compositions, he had inquired with a certain gentle diffidence, whether I should be able to trace 'anything Jewish' in it.

This touching trait in Joachim's character induced me to say a few particularly friendly words to him at parting and to embrace him warmly. I never saw him again, and heard to my astonishment that he had taken up a hostile attitude to both Liszt and myself almost immediately after we had left. . . .

Our journey to Paris and our stay there were full of important incidents, and left indelible traces of our exceptionally devoted friendship. . . .

One day Liszt invited me to spend an evening with him and his children,* who were living very quietly in the care of a governess in Paris.

* Whose upbringing and education Liszt had been directing with some severity (amounting occasionally even to harshness) from afar, but whom he had not actually seen for more than seven years. His younger daughter, Cosima, now in her 16th year, was to become 17 years later Wagner's second wife and he her second husband. This Paris meeting, of 10 Oct. 1853, was their first.

It was quite a novelty to me to see Liszt with these young girls on the threshold of adulthood, and to observe him with his son, still a growing lad. Liszt himself seemed to feel strange in the role of a father, which for several years had brought him only cares, without any of the attendant joys. . . .

A dinner, followed by a musical evening at the home of the celebrated piano manufacturer, Erard, gave us much entertainment. At this house, as well as at a dinner party given by Liszt at the Palais Royal, I again met his children. Daniel, the youngest, made a particularly moving impression on me because of his vivacity and his resemblance to his father; but as far as the girls were concerned, I noticed only their shyness.[8]

Jules Janin to his wife. Paris, 14 October.* Franz Liszt, the great Liszt, dropped in on me yesterday, just like a bomb—talking at the top of his voice, smoking, singing, and striking the piano in so tremendous a fashion that, awakened for a moment by that all-powerful hand, the unfortunate instrument must have believed its last hour had come. He was accompanied by his spouse, the Princess, and the prince his brother-in-law,† as well as his entire household including the children—and you would hardly believe the universal disappointment when they learnt that Madame Janin, the beautiful and elegant Madame Janin, was absent from home and far, far away! What moans, groans and lamentations there were! For my part, if Liszt had been alone I would have been very sorry that my dear wife was not here to give him a good welcome—but the Princess is too much! She is not honest wife enough to associate with mine, and I am like Antonio in *The Marriage of Figaro*:‡ 'Tout beau! le mariage des parents va devant!' But Liszt is as good a fellow as ever, boisterous and rowdy, well content with his glory, and pretty ignorant of all that has happened in Paris since he was last here! He is staying for only five or six days. . . . The Princess's admiration for him is such that yesterday, at a point in the conversation when nothing of particular moment was being said, she fell *on her knees* at Liszt's feet, crying: '*Let me worship thee*!' To which he replied: '*Get up, Princess*'—in the tone of an Ajax or an Agamemnon! You can imagine my bewilderment at this pointblank adoration! 'Don't be astonished,' she said to me as she got to her feet; 'the more I see him, the greater my admiration. Behind that brow are the treasures of genius, and the world will one day think as I do!' She is a kindly woman, fairly well built, rather ugly, and with a pointed nose; smokes cigars like a grenadier and has teeth as black as the bottom of the frying-pan. She is evidently a little mad, and I fear will make the poor fellow very unhappy with her follies![9]

* Adèle Janin, *née* Huet (1820–76).

† Probably Carolyne's nephew (by marriage), Prince Eugène Wittgenstein (1825–86), son of Nicholas Wittgenstein's elder brother Alexandre.

‡ The play by Beaumarchais.

A guest of the Grand Duke Carl Alexander at Weimar this autumn was *Frédéric Soret*.

The extreme limit of Princess Wittgenstein's absence from Russia has expired. If she does not return, she is laying herself open to having all her property confiscated; if she *does* return, Liszt will not be able to follow her, since he would probably not be allowed into Russia. I believe that deep down he would not be averse to such an outcome; but his lady friend has quite different ideas, and he will find it more difficult to get rid of than he did to win her. . . .

The Grand Duke fears that she may cause him to lose this eminent artist, for marriage seems to be becoming less and less possible; and in any case neither he nor his wife can accept the responsibility of tolerating so public a scandal in Weimar. His parents could do so, he said, while there was yet hope of arriving at a solution, but after five years of fruitless efforts this could no longer be the case. . . .

Beulwitz told me of the pronounced opposition of one section of society to entering into relations with the Princess, and of the embarrassment felt by another section which would prefer not to receive her, but which is constrained by obligations towards those on high to accept these relations.[10]

Liszt to Richard Pohl. Weimar, 5 November. The letter killeth the spirit, a thing to which I shall never subscribe, however specious in their hypocritical impartiality be the attacks to which I am exposed.

For the works of Beethoven, Berlioz, Wagner, *et al.*, I see less than elsewhere what advantage there can be . . . in a conductor setting about his task like a *windmill*, getting into a lather of sweat in order to impart a little warmth to his players. Above all, when understanding, feeling, the ability to convey one's meaning intelligently and to kindle hearts are called for in a kind of communion of the beautiful, great, and true in art and poetry, the mere *adequacy* and old routinism of the general run of conductors are no longer *adequate*, and are even inimical to the dignity and the sublime liberty of art. . . .

The real work of the conductor consists, in my opinion, in making himself *publicly* quasi-useless. We are helmsmen, not oarsmen.[11]

In early December Berlioz was in Leipzig for performances of his works at the Gewandhaus on 1 and 11 December (his fiftieth birthday). Liszt was present on both occasions, and during his brief stay renewed acquaintance with Brahms, 'who behaved towards me with tact and good taste,' he told Bülow. 'And so I invited him to dinner several times, and like to think that his "new paths" will later bring him closer to Weimar. You will be pleased with his Sonata in C, which he had already shown me here in Weimar, and the proofs of which I went through at Leipzig. It was precisely this work which had given me the best idea of his talent as a composer.'

Peter Cornelius to his sister Susanne. The Altenburg, 5 December. About ten days ago Frau Bettina von Arnim was here with Giesel [Gisela]. I was with them daily. But I was sorry that her friendship with Liszt was soured, bringing several embarrassing evenings in which it was quite obvious. To describe the cause of this mutual ill-feeling would require too long an explanation; suffice to say that Bettina is infatuated with, and relates everything to, Goethe, in whom she finds her alpha and omega, whereas Liszt prefers the idealistic Schiller, as does the Princess. I find both views one-sided, and further examples of the foibles of brilliant people. Bettina calls the preference for Schiller Jesuitical; and Liszt in his eagerness to contradict goes so far as to say that he prefers the very worst Jesuit to the whole of her Goethe.*[12]

To his brother-in-law Franz Schily. 12 December. For the time being I am staying at Liszt's. From the moment I met him he has not ceased to be the kindest and most active friend, giving me every day further opportunities of becoming still better acquainted with the noblest heart ever to beat in an artist's breast. Carried by the overwhelming might of his genius, and by it alone, to a position in the world far above the misery which is generally the lot of artists, it is one of the chief objects of his life, so far as it lies within his power, to give everywhere a helping hand to unrecognized genius or talent. He presents what is in our day the rare spectacle of a great personality who possesses and develops the inner strength to make himself the focal point of the artistic aspirations of the century. Even as I write, the successes of such composers as Wagner and Berlioz, who together with him are the chief representatives of modern art, are already evident. They are due solely to the perseverance and consistent activity of Liszt, and it can be foreseen that in the next few years this unprecedented practice of an artist making the endeavours of other outstanding masters his own, shunning no sacrifice for them and gathering together within himself all the different trends of the age, making them radiate forth with renewed strength, will have a similar unheard-of success. Whoever, like Liszt, unites the will to achieve great things with the requisite ability, will triumph—were the whole world against him.[13]

As companion and contrast to an attractive Ballade in D flat (S170) for piano which Liszt had composed in 1845 (and revised three years later), there came in 1853 the magnificent Ballade in B minor (S171). Whereas the Sonata, whose key it shares, has been viewed as one of several Lisztian representations of the Faust legend, the Second Ballade has by some been associated with the story of Hero and Leander. Sacheverell Sitwell, on the other hand, found in it 'great happenings on the epical scale, barbarian invasions, cities in flames—tragedies of public, more than private, import'.

* Nevertheless, many of Liszt's works were inspired by Goethe, among them not only the Faust Symphony and several choral pieces, but also some of the very finest songs: *Mignons*

It was in 1854 that Liszt put the final touches to his *Années de pèlerinage, première année, Suisse*, a collection of piano pieces evocative of the Switzerland through which he had wandered long before in the company of Marie d'Agoult. With but two exceptions, the various items are reworkings (and generally also simplifications) of pieces found in the *Album d'un voyageur*, that earlier, spontaneous response of the youthful composer to the haunting sounds and scenes of the Swiss landscape.

The titles of the nine pieces are:

1. *La chapelle de Guillaume Tell.*
2. *Au lac de Wallenstadt.*
3. *Pastorale.*
4. *Au bord d'une source.*
5. *Orage* (a new piece, not based on material in the *Album d'un voyageur*).
6. *Vallée d'Obermann.*
7. *Eglogue* (composed and first published in 1836).
8. *Le mal du pays.*
9. *Les cloches de Genève.*

Princess Carolyne to Eduard Liszt. 20 January. What you say about Liszt I find most touching. Heavens, what would I not give to obtain the *impossible*—Justice for him. But the brilliant aspects of his destiny have heaped up such envy, such relentless envy, in places *both high and low*, that we must almost despair of seeing him judged impartially during his lifetime. The manifest nobility of his character inspires a personal esteem inside which people barricade themselves to launch their opposition to his genius, to his creative work. And this ill-will is so *general*, so systematic, that it is making me feel more and more apprehensive, for I am intimately persuaded that a moment will come when, discouraged by this inexorable censure, Liszt will begin to doubt himself, will abandon *his* way of doing things, *his* originality, *his* individuality, *his* innovations in music, renouncing his true greatness and descending to the ranks of the mediocre and vulgar artists whom posterity holds in little account. Oh, who can say that, attacked ever and anon, an artist will not eventually grow weary and descend to the level of banality which people would like to impose on him. Liszt will soon be publishing a series of *nine overtures* [symphonic poems], large-scale orchestral pieces. I tremble, I assure you, when I think of all the stupid abuse which will be inflicted on these works, and what would I not give for them to receive just enough Justice to keep their value intact and

Lied (S275), *Es war ein König in Thule* (S278), *Der du von dem Himmel bist* (S279), *Freudvoll und leidvoll* (S280), *Wer nie sein Brot mit Tränen ass* (S297), and *Ueber allen Gipfeln ist Ruh* (S306).

to prevent him from quitting the right path. . . . If you hear Liszt's works censured and criticized, tell yourself that the real misfortune would be for them to be praised and extolled *immediately*.[1]

On 16 February, the birthday of the Dowager Grand Duchess, Liszt conducted a performance of Gluck's *Orfeo* (its first hearing at Weimar), and as an introduction to that opera the première of his own symphonic poem *Orpheus* (S98). A week later (23 February), at the Court Theatre, he conducted the first performance of another symphonic poem, *Les Préludes* (S97).*

In late March he spent two weeks at Gotha, having been invited to conduct the première of Duke Ernst's opera *Santa Chiara*. (To Carolyne he wrote in some astonishment: 'A superb *negro* received me, on behalf of His Grace, and took me to the palace in a pretty little brougham. . . . He is attached to my person, and permanently installed at my door. His name is Philippe. . . .') His free time here he used to finish the orchestration of the final version of the symphonic poem *Ce qu'on entend sur la montagne* (S95), after Hugo, the earliest version of which had been composed in 1848–9.

At Weimar on Sunday, 16 April, he conducted the première of *Mazeppa* (S100), a symphonic poem inspired by Victor Hugo's poem and evolved from the fourth of the *Etudes d'exécution transcendante*; and on the 19th the first performance of the final version of *Tasso, Lamento e Trionfo*.

Liszt to his son Daniel. Weimar, 20 April. That's a beautiful Easter egg you have cooked for yourself with your diligence, and I congratulate you on it with all my heart. Try to increase your library of prizes, of which the Sallust you have won in this competition will be such a splendid adornment. I always remember with pleasure a library of this kind which was at my disposal about twenty years ago; it had been gained as a college and examination prize by M. de Ferrières, the present French Ambassador at Weimar. Until now I have always envied its owner; but if you acquire a similar one for yourself I shall be consoled for not having been able to put my own youthful years to greater profit. However much one applies oneself later on, those who have not gone through the progressive steps of a college education always lack a certain fund of knowledge that may easily be called upon and put to good use; and to this day I regret having neglected the lecture courses I should have attended after the death of my father. But on the one hand I knew no one who possessed the higher outlook which would have enabled them to give me more judicious advice; and on the other, from the age of twelve I was obliged to earn my living and to support my parents. This necessitated specifically musical studies, which absorbed all my time up to the age of sixteen, when I began to teach the piano (and even harmony and counterpoint), and, as well as I could, to make my way as a virtuoso both in the salons and in public. In fact, I

* Composed in 1848 (as a prelude to *Les Quatre Elémens*), but revised for this première. The score is prefaced by the words: 'What is our life but a series of preludes to that unknown song of which the first solemn note is sounded by death?'

managed to acquire a fairly lucrative position quite quickly, and to make a reputation as a kind of artistic personality. Nevertheless, I should have done better to apply myself more, and regularly, to cultivating my mind and thus to putting myself more on a level in real learning with the outstanding men with whom I had the advantage of associating when I was still very young. A number of them honoured me with their friendship, and this led me to reflect on different subjects and to compensate as much as possible, by attentive reading, for my lack of regular studies; and to distinguish myself in this too, perhaps, from other members of my profession who aspire to nothing very much beyond their semiquavers and the humdrum round of ordinary bourgeois life.[2]

In mid-May Liszt made a brief visit to Leipzig, reading on the journey the recently published *Memoirs* of Berlioz ('His mother's curse on his artistic career wrings one's heart. . . .'); and at the end of the month visited Joachim at Hanover and Litolff at Brunswick.

To close the Weimar opera season, on 24 June, the birthday of the Grand Duke Carl Alexander, he conducted the world première of Schubert's opera *Alfonso und Estrella*.

In early July he attended a music festival at Rotterdam. Journeying from Weimar to Mainz (where he wished to call upon the Schott publishing-house), he there embarked on a Rhine steamer, the *Agrippine*.

Liszt to Princess Carolyne. The Agrippine, 9 July. The first time I crossed the Rhine was on the bridge at Mainz, at the end of March 1840. It was about one o'clock in the morning. . . . I was returning to Paris for the first time after three or four years of absence—during which I had become a kind of phantom of celebrity at Vienna and Pest, and to some extent elsewhere too. I remember that in a hushed silence I long listened to the noise of the river, which was rather majestic that night. My own destiny has never filled me with either fear or anxiety. With a kind of presentiment of the unknown, which secretly urged me on in all moments of solitary reflection, I was then going to meet things which I already knew only too well. This elasticity did not break within me until a day rather close to us, that in which I felt that I was loved still more than I was forgiven and understood—that in which you revealed to me the limitless love which is my soul's thirst. May you be everlastingly blessed for it![3]

Joined on board the *Agrippine* at Cologne by Anton Rubinstein, Liszt arrived at Rotterdam on the 10th. His night on board had not, however, been a restful one, as he told Carolyne: 'The engine made a terrible row, and the reverberation in my cabin was altogether diabolical—so much so, that I was even seized by fear, and leapt up with a somersault to see if there had been some accident.'

The festival over, on the 16th Liszt visited Ary Scheffer at Scheveningen. Later in the day he dined with Prince and Princess Henry at The Hague, returning to Rotterdam just in time to contribute one or two pieces to a soirée musicale given in his honour.

At Brussels on Tuesday the 18th he had a rendezvous with Blandine and Cosima, escorted from Paris by Mme Patersi and Belloni. On the 20th they all made an excursion to Antwerp, to see the Rubens paintings in the Cathedral and to visit the zoo. In Brussels Liszt also called upon Marie Pleyel, now teaching at the Conservatoire, and Baron Miklós Jósika (1794–1865), the Hungarian novelist. Dining on the 19th at the home of the German pianist H. F. Kufferath, he played his *Grosses Konzertsolo*,* an Etude, and *Les Patineurs* (The Skaters' Waltz);† and the next evening he and Rubinstein played the two-piano arrangement of the Ninth Symphony.

Parting from his daughters on 22 July, Liszt went to Cologne with Rubinstein. The next morning, after visiting the Cathedral,‡ towards the completion of which he had in earlier years donated so large a sum, he left for Bonn on the first stage of his journey back to Weimar.

In early August *George Eliot* (1819–80) and her life companion, the writer George Henry Lewes (1817–78), came to Weimar to do research for Lewes's *Life and Works of Goethe*. Although no stranger to the pen, having already done much work as editor and translator, she had not at this time begun the series of novels that would bring her fame; nor had the illustrious pen-name yet come into being. To Liszt and his circle, with whom she and Lewes were soon on friendly terms, she was known by her real name: Miss Marian (or Mary Ann) Evans.

Liszt's conversation is charming. I never met with a person whose manner of telling a story was so piquant. The last evening but one that he called on us, wishing to express his pleasure in George's article about him, he very ingeniously conveyed that expression in a story about Spontini and Berlioz. Spontini visited Paris while Liszt was living there, and haunted the opera —a stiff, self-important personage, with high shirt collars, the least attractive individual imaginable: Liszt turned up his own collars, and swelled out his person, so as to give us a vivid idea of the man. Everyone would have been glad to get out of Spontini's way—indeed, elsewhere 'on feignait de le croire mort,' but at Paris, as he was a member of the Institute, it was necessary to recognise his existence. Liszt met him at Erard's more than once. On one of these occasions Liszt observed to him that Berlioz was a great admirer of his (Spontini's), whereupon Spontini burst into a terrible invective against Berlioz as a man who, with the like of him, was ruining art, etc. Shortly after, the *Vestale* was performed, and

* Composed *c.*1849 for a piano competition at the Paris Conservatoire in 1850, and dedicated to Adolf Henselt, the *Grosses Konzertsolo* (S176) also exists in a version for two pianos, under the title *Concerto pathétique* (S258), and another for piano and orchestra (S365).

† The second of Liszt's *Illustrations* (S414) from Meyerbeer's *Le Prophète*, dating from 1849–50.

‡ William Mason reports being told by Rubinstein of a characteristic incident during this visit. 'They were walking together in the cathedral, and quite suddenly Rubinstein missed Liszt, who had disappeared in a mysterious way. He searched for quite a while through the many secluded nooks and corners of the immense building, and finally found Liszt kneeling before a *prie-dieu*, so deeply engrossed that Rubinstein had not the heart to disturb him, and so left the building alone.'

forthwith appeared an enthusiastic article by Berlioz on Spontini's music. The next time Liszt met him of the high collars, he said: 'You see I was not wrong in what I said about Berlioz' admiration of you.' Spontini swelled in his collars and replied: 'Monsieur, Berlioz a du talent comme critique!'

Liszt's replies were always felicitous and characteristic. Talking of Mme d'Agoult, he told us that when her novel, *Nélida,* appeared, in which Liszt himself is pilloried as a delinquent, he asked her: 'Mais pourquoi avez-vous tellement maltraité ce pauvre Lehmann?'

The first time [10 August] we were asked to breakfast at his house, the Altenburg, we were shown into the garden, where, in a saloon formed by overarching trees, the *déjeuner* was set out. We found Hoffmann von Fallersleben,* the lyric poet, Dr. Schade, a *Gelehrter* who has distinguished himself by a critical work on the 11,000 virgins (!), and a Herr Cornelius, an agreeable-looking artist. Presently came a Herr or Doctor Raff, a musician who has recently published a volume called *Wagnerfrage*. Soon after we were joined by Liszt and the Princess Marie, an elegant, gentle-looking girl of seventeen, and last, by the Princess Wittgenstein with her nephew Prince Eugène and a young French (or Swiss?) artist, a pupil of Scheffer.

The appearance of the Princess rather startled me at first. I had expected to see a tall distinguished-looking woman, if not a beautiful one. But she is short and unbecomingly endowed with embonpoint; at the first glance the face is not pleasing, and the profile especially is harsh and barbarian, but the dark, bright hair and eyes give the idea of vivacity and strength. Her teeth, unhappily, are blackish too. She was tastefully dressed in a morning robe of some semi-transparent white material, lined with orange colour, which formed the bordering, and ornamented the sleeves, a black lace jacket, and a piquant cap set on the summit of her comb, and trimmed with violet colour. The breakfast was not sumptuous either as to the food or the appointments. When the cigars came, Hoffmann was requested to read some of his poetry, and he gave us a bacchanalian poem with great spirit. I sat between Liszt and Miss Anderson, the Princess Marie's governess, an amiable but insignificant person. George sat next to the Princess and talked with her about Goethe, whom she pronounced to have been an egotist. My great delight was to watch Liszt and observe the sweetness of his expression. Genius, benevolence and tenderness beam from his whole countenance, and his manners are in perfect harmony with it. A little rain sent us into the house, and when we were seated in an elegant little drawing room, opening into a large music-salon, we had more reading

* A. H. Hoffmann von Fallersleben (1798–1874) lived in Weimar from 1854–60. His diaries record many convivial occasions with Liszt, Carolyne, and their circle, to which he, his verses and improvisations, made no small contribution. Saying farewell when Hoffmann eventually left Weimar (having obtained the post of Librarian to the Duke of Ratibor at Corvey), Liszt remarked: 'The most delightful hours I have spent here, I owe to you.' Poems by Hoffmann inspired Liszt's songs *Wie singt die Lerche schön* (S312), *Lasst mich ruhen* (S317), *In Liebeslust* (S318), and *Ich scheide* (S319).

from Hoffmann, and from the French artist who with a tremulous voice pitched in a minor key read us some rather pretty sentimentalities of his own.

Then came the thing I had longed for—Liszt's playing. I sat near him so that I could see both his hands and face. For the first time in my life I beheld real inspiration—for the first time I heard the true tones of the piano. He played one of his own compositions—one of a series of religious *fantaisies*. There was nothing strange or excessive about his manner. His manipulation of the instrument was quiet and easy, and his face was simply grand —the lips compressed and the head thrown a little backward. When the music expressed quiet rapture or devotion, a sweet smile flitted over his features: when it was triumphant, the nostrils dilated. There was nothing petty or egoistic to mar the picture. Why did not Scheffer paint him thus instead of representing him as one of the three Magi? But it just occurs to me that Scheffer's idea was a sublime one. There are the two aged men who have spent their lives in trying to unravel the destinies of the world, and who are looking for the Deliverer—for the light from on high. Their young fellow-seeker, having the fresh inspiration of early life, is the first to discern the herald star, and his ecstasy reveals it to his companions. In this young Magus, Scheffer has given a portrait of Liszt; but even here, where he might be expected to idealise unrestrainedly, he falls short of the original. It is curious that Liszt's face is the type that one sees in all Scheffer's pictures—at least, in all I have seen.

In a little room which terminates the suite at the Altenburg, there is a portrait of Liszt also by Scheffer—the same of which the engraving is familiar to everyone. This little room is filled with memorials of Liszt's triumphs and the worship his divine talent has won. It was arranged for him by the Princess, in conjunction with the Arnims, in honour of his birthday. There is a medallion of him by Schwanthaler, a bust by an Italian artist, also a medallion by Rietschl—very fine—and cabinets full of jewels and precious things—the gifts of the great. In the music salon stand Beethoven's and Mozart's pianos. Beethoven's was a present from Broadwood, and has a Latin inscription intimating that it was presented as a tribute to his illustrious genius. One evening Liszt came to dine with us at the Erbprinz, and introduced M. [Anton] Rubinstein, a young Russian, who is about to have an opera of his performed in Weimar. Our expenses at Weimar, including wine and washing, were £2. 6s per week. . . .[4]

Dear Weimar! We were sorry to say goodbye to it, with its pleasant group of friends—the grand, fascinating Liszt, the bright, kind Princess. . . . We breakfasted with them twice, by way of farewell—the first time without any other visitors. The Princess Marie showed me a remarkable series of sketches from Dante, while Liszt went to rest and George talked with the Princess. After this, we all sat down together in the Princess Marie's rooms, Liszt, the Princess and her daughter on the sofa, George and I opposite to them, and Miss Anderson a little in the rear. I like to recall this moment, and Liszt's face with its serious expression, as we talked about his coming to London, and I asked the Princess if she should come too. The next time we breakfasted with them the Marquis de Ferrières and young Cornelius were there, and I had a long theological séance with the Princess on the sofa. She parted from us very prettily, with earnest wishes for my happiness in particular. George was so grateful for this that he couldn't help saying 'God bless you' to her, and she repeated it, calling after me too, 'God bless you'. The evening before I left, Liszt called . . . and brought me a paper of bon-bons which the Princess had sent to refresh us on our journey.

On the 4th of November, after a stay of just three months, we turned our backs on Weimar to seek 'fresh streets and faces new' at Berlin.[5]

In a letter of 16 August to Charles Bray, Marian Evans had written: 'Above all, Liszt is here. He is a Grand Seigneur in this place . . . and is the first really inspired man I ever saw. His face might serve as a model for a St John in its sweetness when he is in repose; but seated at the piano he is as grand as one of Michelangelo's prophets. When I read George Sand's letter to Franz Liszt in her *Lettres d'un voyageur*, I little thought that I should ever be seated tête-à-tête with him for an hour, as I was yesterday, and telling him my ideas and feelings.'

Writing to Bessie Rayner Parkes on 10 September, she described Liszt as 'a bright genius, with a tender, loving nature, and a face in which this combination is perfectly expressed. He has that *laideur divinisée* by the soul that gleams through it, which is my favourite kind of physique . . .'

And the next July, *Fraser's Magazine* published an article ('Liszt, Wagner, and Weimar') which contained her more considered view of Liszt.

Most London concert-goers, for whom Liszt has 'blazed the comet of a season', think of him as certainly the archimagus of pianists, but as otherwise a man of no particular significance; as merely an erratic, flighty, artistic genius, who has swept through Europe, the Napoleon of the *salon*, carrying devastation into the hearts of countesses. A single morning's interview with him is enough to show the falsity of this conception. In him Nature has not sacrificed the man to the artist; rather, as the blossom of the acacia is a glorious ornament to the tree, but we see it fall without regret because the tree itself is grand and beautiful, so if Liszt the pianist were unknown to you, or even did not exist, Liszt the man would win your admiration and love. See him for a few hours and you will be charmed by the originality of his conversation and the brilliancy of his wit; know him for weeks or months, and you will discern in him a man of various thought, of serious purpose, and of a moral nature which, in its mingled strength and gentleness, has the benignest influence on those about him.[6]

Daniel Liszt stayed at the Altenburg during the summer. Meanwhile, in Paris, Blandine and Cosima were making progress in their studies and their piano-playing. 'Cosima is immersed in a translation of *Lohengrin* into French, which is absorbing her entirely,' wrote Blandine on 18 September. 'We practise constantly. . . . At the moment I am playing the Scherzo and March [S177] that you sent us, and the delicious *Berceuse* [S174/1] with its tender, melancholy reverie.'

Liszt to Blandine and Cosima, 25 September. Daniel is returning to you with a supply of descriptions and narrations, pictures, parallel definitions, etc., just as in literary courses. I hope that as Weimar's historiographer he acquits himself well, and that what he tells you will give you some pleasant hours. . . .

How is it with your piano-strumming? Are you working hard? Is M. Seghers* giving you regular lessons? Try to make good use of the coming winter, in which you will not be bothered by other teachers, since you are already accomplished and model examples of an excellent education and have finished learning how to express in several languages the ideas which will come to you later.

Music being the universal language, and even to a certain extent able to dispense with ideas, it is not my intention to end your studies with M. Seghers. But try to learn by yourselves what even the best teachers cannot convey. . . .[7]

On Thursday, 19 October, Liszt completed his Faust Symphony (S108), three character pictures after Goethe, the writing down of which, after long years of meditation and gestation, had taken only two months. To the last of its three movements, entitled respectively 'Faust', 'Gretchen', and 'Mephistopheles', he added three years later, as a solemn conclusion to the whole, a choral setting, with tenor solo, of the *Chorus mysticus* ('Alles Vergängliche ist nur ein Gleichnis') from Part II of *Faust*.

This, his greatest work for orchestra, he dedicated, appropriately, to Hector Berlioz, who had first introduced him to Goethe's masterpiece.

A visitor to the Altenburg at about this time was *Richard Pohl*.

Tugging the bell and entering the house, I gave my name and was at once led through a spacious, tastefully-decorated passageway into an elegant ground-floor reception room, with latticed windows giving on to the quiet garden. Here already I found myself standing at the centre of today's art. Around the walls were portraits of all the best-known composers of the eighteenth and nineteenth centuries, grouped around Beethoven's original death mask and medallions of Wagner, Berlioz, and Schumann. Over the door a charming drawing showed amoretti playing with crotchets and quavers above the words *Éljen Liszt*—the handiwork, as I learnt later, of Bettina von Arnim. Three much larger drawings hung resplendent on the main wall, immediately recognizable as the work of their brilliant creator:

* The Belgian musician François Seghers (1801–81) was Blandine and Cosima's piano teacher for several years.

two scenes from Genelli's* *Oedipus* saga and a sketch by the same artist for a large theatre curtain, one richly and profoundly allegorical. At the window, between music-stands for quartet players, a Viennese grand piano stood open. The room was evidently used for performances of chamber music. Leafing through the music lying in piles on the shelves, I found, apart from an extensive library of earlier chamber music, almost nothing but works dedicated to Liszt and sent to him by composers both young and old: works by proven masters cheek by jowl with the bashful first productions of young beginners with unknown names, all in strange variegated array. Then again, trios and quartets by Brahms, Rubinstein, Volkmann, and Schumann; Liszt's Sonata 'To Robert Schumann'; works by Joachim, Bülow, Raff—pure 'Music of the Future',† which bade me friendly welcome to its home and headquarters. Also lying in abundant quantity on the shelves were the scores of symphonies, overtures, quartets, sonatas, and even of operas.

The double doors to the adjoining room stood open; access was therefore allowed. Inquisitive like all tourists, I availed myself of this tacit permission and entered a comfortable and appropriately decorated gentleman's salon. On the walls a splendid display was made by elegant groups of weapons of every kind: Hungarian, Turkish, Asiatic, Italian, and Spanish. In the window recesses, in elegant glass cabinets, a valuable collection of artistically carved meerschaum heads, splendidly inlaid amber cigar-holders and Turkish pipes; and in addition, a large collection of walking sticks, pipe-tubes and other male gadgets, whose rich abundance the connoisseur and amateur collector would explore with as much joyful surprise as I had burrowed among the stacks of music. In one of the window alcoves a complete Turkish coffee service with table in silver and mother-of-pearl were to be seen, together with costly Turkish chibouks. This large and rich collection consists, as I learnt later, entirely of gifts presented to Liszt by Russian and Turkish aristocrats and Spanish grandees, among others, as well as by the magnates of his native land. To his salon they give the comfort and splendour of which a true-born nobleman may for ever only dream. So far as works of art are concerned, the room is adorned by no more than the model of a statue of Carl August and a fine portrait of the ill-fated Prince Lichnowsky, who, as is generally known, was one of Liszt's closest friends.

I had just taken hold of a splendid copy of Marx's *Nineteenth–Century Music* and seated myself comfortably in a chair of saffian

* The painter Bonaventura Genelli (1798–1868), remembered for his illustrations of scenes from Dante and from classical mythology (his preoccupation with which earned him from friends the nickname 'the last of the Centaurs').

† 'Music of the Future' (*Zukunftsmusik*) was the name bestowed on the music of Wagner, Liszt, and their associates by one Professor Bischoff of Cologne in mocking allusion to Wagner's *Art-Work of the Future* (1849) and its advocacy of a powerful new alliance between music and the drama.

leather, when I was informed by a manservant that Liszt was ready to see me . . . and I climbed the elegant carpeted staircase to the first floor. Here I was escorted through a large, magnificently appointed library (in which as I passed by I caught a fleeting glimpse of two grand pianos, each richly laden with salon treasures) and into a royally furnished corner salon, into which, a moment later, through the door facing me, stepped Liszt.

I shall say no more than that the power of Liszt's personality, his enchanting amiability, the gentle indulgence of his comments on others, his unfettered understanding of all aspects of life and art, the brilliance of his conversation, replete as it is with trenchant, witty, and subtle turns of phrase—everything captivated and delighted me to the utmost degree, just as it does all those (unless blinded by envy or partisanship, or downright stupid) who come into his company. . . .

Liszt most kindly invited me to be his guest for lunch and then to stay on at the Altenburg for the afternoon. Other guests now began to arrive. Liszt, it seems, keeps open house daily and is accustomed to seeing at his table an almost unbroken succession of artists and writers—alike those living locally and those who, travelling through Weimar, seize the opportunity to call upon him. . . .

After we had risen from the table, the company dispersed into various rooms over its coffee and cigars, giving me leisure to continue undisturbed my inquisitive inspection of the rooms in which Liszt lives and creates. In the corner salon, the one furnished in Moorish taste in which Liszt had received me, my attention was caught by a deeply-pondered and artistically perfect oil-painting by Ary Scheffer (depicting the Wise Men from the East eagerly following their star); and also by Rietschel's delightful marble bust of the Princess Marie Wittgenstein, with its wonderfully poetic charm. Drawings by Genelli and water-colours by Preller lay spread out on a folder.

Noticing my interest in these works of art, Liszt took me into a little closet to the left of the dining-room. It was so rich in costly rarities and art treasures that I glanced around this small-scale 'green vault' in wondering amazement. On the walls was a series of works of art of the first rank, forming a complete portrait-gallery of Liszt: busts and medallions in bronze and marble by Rietschel, Schwanthaler, Bartolini, and others; a glorious oil-painting by Ary Scheffer (a portrait of Liszt in the 1830s) and other items. In the corner cupboards, however, was a collection of precious objects of which it would be hard to find the equal. Gold medallions showing Liszt's profile; gold chains of honour; the famous Hungarian sword of honour; a large artistically engraved platinum writing-set with high reliefs; a series of gold boxes adorned with brilliants and enamel; a collection of rings, each more costly than the next; a music-stand of solid silver; a collection of gold and silver conducting batons; and so it continued —all these items were assembled to form a treasure chamber that can claim something further still of special value: that everything it contains was designated solely for Liszt, and was presented to him by the rulers and the great of every country in Europe. Furthermore, a precious collection of autograph scores of the great masters, Bach, Haydn, Mozart, Beethoven, and others, is here given worthy display, the collection's sublime keystone being the original scores of Wagner's complete operas. His *Rheingold*,* too, the first evening of his great *Ring des Nibelungen*, lies here, already magnificently bound: a treasure hoard which will not be excavated for the world until many years have passed! . . .

Liszt's playing is of a kind so unique that one must hear it for oneself: it is not something that can be described. . . .

He played one of his original Hungarian Rhapsodies (which no one can play after him) and his magnificently conceived Sonata; one must have heard it played by him fully to understand it. In the silence which followed —no one being able to give adequate expression to the feelings which possessed him—Liszt took me to the other grand piano, which stood opposite the Erard. It was an English concert grand dating from the 1820s, and so at this time about thirty-five years old. The lid was raised, and there was the name: Beethoven! The manufacturer, Broadwood, had made him a present of it, and it was the last on which the immortal master had played! A shiver of awe seizes the beholder when he lets his fingers wander over the keys once set in motion by the great genius of our music. 'This is a relic no less holy to the musician than Schiller's desk must be to the poet!' I exclaimed. 'That being so, I'll show you a relic equally holy but still older, which you will find no less interesting,' replied Liszt; and he invited us to accompany him to the music salon on the second floor.

The salon, which lies over the library, was opened, and we found ourselves facing the Giant Pianoforte,† the mysterious construction with which the newspapers had been busying themselves for three years without so far being able to give their readers any accurate notion of it. While I in my amazement wanted to linger by the giant, Liszt moved towards a small piano‡ grown dark brown with age, one made of simple oak with black keys and metal tangents, and said: 'This is the relic I wanted to show you —Mozart's instrument!'

Only one generation lies between Mozart's piano and Liszt's giant pianoforte, but from the earlier to the later, what infinite progress! The two of them, standing there side by side, represent the first beginnings and

* Which Wagner had sent to Liszt that October.

† The 3-keyboard instrument made to Liszt's specifications by the French harmonium-makers Alexandre & Fils. Sent from Paris, it had arrived at the Altenburg on 11 Aug. 1854. Now on display at the Kunsthistorisches Museum, Vienna.

‡ Purchased by Princess Wittgenstein *c.*1852 as a gift for Liszt, this instrument, made by C. E. Friederici at Gera in 1772, would more appropriately be designated a clavichord. Eventually making its way to the Historisches Museum der Stadt Wien, it was a casualty of the 2nd World War.

the highest peak of our modern piano technique. They form the two boundary lines of eighteenth- and nineteenth-century music culture!

I had no time to indulge in further reflections, for Liszt was already sitting at his giant pianoforte to show us its immense capabilities. A Bach organ fugue, Beethoven's Funeral March (from the Sonata in A flat), the Dance of the Sylphs* from Berlioz's *Damnation de Faust*, and his own *Ave Maria* from the *Harmonies poétiques et religieuses*, succeeded one another; at one moment with sounds ghostly, soft, celestial and far-off, at the next with mighty, convulsing, swelling masses of tone, revealing to us the full greatness and range of sonority of the instrument, whose effects are truly surprising in the highest degree. It is an example of the real progress of our time. Nothing quite like it existed before, and it contains within itself the seeds of important improvements to the pianoforte. I surrendered myself wholly to my impressions, without just then pondering the reasons. A further dimension was added to our enjoyment when Dionys Pruckner, one of Liszt's best pupils, took his place at a second grand piano standing next to the giant (and which in size as in sonority is related to the latter roughly as was Mozart's piano to Tomášek's), and a duo began between the two instruments, of the kind that can be heard only at the Altenburg: Liszt at the giant pianoforte he had created, and one of his most outstanding pupils beside him at a second piano, in a performance of one of Liszt's symphonic poems (*Orpheus*) in the Master's own arrangement [S638]. Seek where you will to hear such a performance elsewhere![8]

From the diary of Peter Cornelius. Weimar, 22 October. For his birthday, Liszt received a letter from Reményi—from *Jersey*! Added to it (after a greeting from Teleki) were the following words from Victor Hugo: 'The exile of Jersey† shakes hands with the Orpheus of Weimar.' Since this was the first sign of life from Hugo for twelve years, Liszt was delighted.[9]

23 October. At Liszt's there were of course several people for lunch once again. He was still quite excited from yesterday, and at table talked about many things. His whole extraordinary life, his concert career from early youth onwards, make him a walking encyclopaedia of modern times, in which it is his destiny to play such a leading role. We discussed recognition of artists in their lifetimes, and Liszt said that Mendelssohn's concertos, for example, were played very little when he was alive, but nowadays to excess. Likewise, at the start of Liszt's Paris period Beethoven was still appreciated very little . . . and when Liszt played the great Trio in B flat at one of his concerts, people who took a friendly interest in him advised him not to choose such strange, tedious music. At the same concert he joined Herz in a performance of the latter's Variations for piano duet on themes

* Liszt's transcription (S475) for piano solo.

† Rather than remain in the France of Napoleon III, whom he abominated, Hugo had gone into self-imposed exile on Jersey (and, in 1855, Guernsey).

from *Tell*, earning an ovation in some of the technically brilliant passages. On this topic, another fine anecdote belongs here; it is quite excellent. In 1834* Liszt, Urhan, and Batta gave so-called *séances musicales*, at which there gathered not only celebrities in the arts but also a brilliant aristocratic public. Pixis asked him to perform a new trio of his, and so on the next occasion Liszt put it down as the *last* item. But the first was to be a trio by Beethoven, and Pixis, fearful of being overshadowed by such competition, asked for the order to be changed. Liszt, who dislikes making alterations to a programme, was not at all keen to do so, but on being requested by Urhan, who was a kind of spiritual uncle to him at that time, finally decided to play the Pixis trio first—but without announcing the change. In short, the large audience, including the artists, listened to the supposed Beethoven with delight. Berlioz, who was there too, was put wise by Liszt, and found the whole thing highly amusing. And when Beethoven was played later, under the name of Pixis, the greater part of the audience left. How can one listen to such stuff after a work by Beethoven!

But if Liszt related excellent anecdotes at table, what he played for us afterwards was still better. For this, his pupils Pruckner, Bronsart,† and Schreiber came, plus the Paris organist Lefébure-Wély accompanied by rather a clever Parisian bookseller. Just as Lefébure's views on art were mercenary, so the shopkeeper seemed to have a considerable knowledge of painting, and they accordingly complemented one another perfectly: *l'artiste-marchand et le marchand-artiste*. Liszt played us his Etude in D flat [*Un sospiro*], to which he improvised a bravura ending. Then, as a special treat for Pohl and Ritter‡ to whom he had promised it, he played his Sonata. We were all moved by this double masterpiece, and I balked at having to hear something else after it. Yet it was not without pleasure that we listened to Lefébure improvise a few things. His modulations in particular were entirely modern and attractive.[10]

Peter Cornelius, November. Liszt told me about his visit to Bettina [von Arnim] yesterday. On his arrival she had greeted him with the words: 'Well, you are still the *old Jesuit*!' And on she went in this fashion. Among other things she said: 'You call yourself my friend, but are not!' Liszt replied: 'And vice-versa!' When he left she said to him: 'I shall see you no more! I shall see you no more today, no more tomorrow, no more ever!'[11]

At the Court Theatre on 9 November Liszt conducted the first performance of his symphonic poem *Festklänge* (S101), as an introduction to Schiller's 'Huldigung

* Actually, the early part of 1837. See *supra*. The concert in which the unannounced change took place was on 11 Feb. that year.

† The pianist and composer Hans von Bronsart (1830–1913), for whom Liszt's nickname was 'Hans II', to distinguish him from Bülow. He married another Liszt pupil, Ingeborg Stark, and from 1867 was Intendant of the Court Theatre at Hanover.

‡ The composer and conductor Alexander Ritter (1833–96), who was a member of Liszt's orchestra at this time.

der Künste'; the next day, at the Town Hall, the first concert performance of *Orpheus*; and on the 11th the première of Anton Rubinstein's opera *The Siberian Hunters*.

That same month, at Hoffmann von Fallersleben's suggestion, the New Weimar Club was founded, its purpose being to provide Liszt and his circle with a meeting-place at which, by forgathering at specified times, they could obtain a 'centralization of common endeavours'. The first meeting took place on the 20th: Liszt was elected president, and Hoffmann (who drew up the Club's 'Twelve Commandments') vice-president.

Franz von Milde (1855–1929), son of Rosa and Feodor. When so many fiery artists were gathered together, it was natural that there was often friction. About one particular incident I was later told by my father. Liszt had grown very angry with one of the members, and into the bargain done more than ample justice to the wine. He and Father left the Club together, and in the open air Liszt's condition steadily worsened. In his anger he made more and more of a racket, and when they reached the market-place he rushed up to a horse which was standing there attached to some countryman's cart, grabbed the reins and shouted at it: 'Scoundrel, you shall dance!' Father had great difficulty in getting the madman away, back to the Altenburg and to bed. The Princess came running up and, sobbing loudly, threw herself down at the bedside. No later than 7.00 the next morning, Liszt came to see my father, saying: 'A silly business yesterday evening. Forgive me, and my thanks for looking after me so loyally.'[12]

Whereas the foregoing anecdote was related to the young Milde by his father, his impressions of Princess Carolyne were formed (somewhat later) from personal experience. 'At the Princess's special request, my mother often took me with her to the Altenburg. . . . The Princess was very fond of me, and her eccentric partiality for children's feet allowed my mother no rest until she had taken off my shoes and stockings so that the Princess could kiss my little feet. These curious caresses I would probably have found very repugnant, had she not each time given me the most costly toys to take home with me.'

1855

On Thursday, 8 February, her thirty-sixth birthday, Princess Carolyne was presented by Liszt with the revised score of his *Ce qu'on entend sur la montagne*, as well as that of another symphonic poem, *Hungaria* (S103), likewise completed during the previous year. The dedication concluded: 'To her who remains the companion of my life, the firmament of my thought, the living prayer and Heaven of my soul—Jeanne Elisabeth Carolyne.'

At a court concert on 17 February he was the soloist in the première of his Piano Concerto No. 1 in E flat (S124). Hector Berlioz, who found Liszt's playing 'dazzling with verve and power, as always', was the conductor, having come to Weimar for a second 'Berlioz Week'. In addition to the *Symphonie fantastique*, his *Lélio* was given a successful performance on the 21st, with Liszt undertaking both the piano part and that of the Chinese gong.

The Concerto was performed again a few weeks later, at an Academic Concert in Jena on 12 March. Dionys Pruckner was the soloist on this occasion and Liszt the conductor. 'We would say,' ran the review in the *Neue Zeitschrift für Musik*, 'that Pruckner played incomparably, had Liszt's presence not reminded us that there is only this one incomparable but also peerless *Meister*.'

Franz von Milde (born on 4 March). No less a person than Liszt was my godfather, and it was after him that I was named Franz. He is said to have behaved very clumsily at the christening ceremony; and my wise mother, realizing that his hands were better suited to dealing with difficult chords than to holding a baby, came to the rescue by quickly freeing me from his awkward clasp just before the fall. . . .[1]

Richard Wagner to Liszt. London, 5 April. Klindworth has just played me your great Sonata!

We spent the day alone together; he dined here with me, and after we had risen from table I made him play. Dearest Franz! Now you were with me. The Sonata is beautiful beyond all conception; great, lovely, deep and noble, sublime even as thyself. I feel most profoundly moved. . . . More than this I cannot say, immediately after hearing it; but of what I *do* say, I am as full as man can be. Once more: you were with me—oh, could you only soon be with me wholly and bodily, then might we endure life beautifully!!

Klindworth astonished me with his playing: no one less than he could have ventured to play your work to me for the first time. He is worthy of you. Surely, surely, it was beautiful![2]

It was on 17 May (Ascension Day), at a concert in Leipzig's Catholic church at which he conducted his *Ave Maria* (S20/2) for four voices and organ, that Liszt was seen for the first time by Marie Lipsius (1837–1927), a native of Leipzig who was to become one of his most devoted admirers. Under her pen-name *La Mara*, after his death she edited and published numerous volumes of his correspondence, as well as other Lisztian books and articles; and in her memoirs, the section describing her first meeting with him she entitled, not inappropriately, 'Liszt, my Destiny'.

I had never seen a picture of him, but even before the music began I knew that the wonderfully formed and carried head, with its features of such outstanding nobility and spirituality, could belong to him alone. Head held high, majestic repose emanating from his every pore, his face suffused with an unearthly radiance, that was how he stood before me, the sublime sounds brought into being by his baton filling me with reverent devotion.[3]

While journeying in late May to the thirty-third Lower Rhine Music Festival at Düsseldorf (stopping at Halle to visit the gifted *Lieder* composer Robert Franz and spending a night at Brunswick with the Litolffs), Liszt reread Adolph Marx's *Nineteenth-Century Music*, which contained, he thought, 'the best substance of the ideas which must predominate today . . . even the metaphysical part does not displease me.' His review of the book came out at this time.

The principal attraction for him at Düsseldorf was the presence of Agnes Street-Klindworth (1825–1906), an intelligent and good-looking young woman, briefly married to an Englishman, who had come to Weimar in 1853,* studied with Liszt, and, as can be deduced from his letters to her, become his mistress. In April 1855 she had left Weimar to go to Brussels, where she supported herself and her children by giving piano lessons.

He also renewed acquaintance with Brahms, among others, and saw his friend Marie Kalergis. About the festival itself, he wrote to Carolyne: 'All in all it teaches me nothing and satisfies me little.' Haydn's *Creation* he did not care for, nor was Schumann's *Paradise and the Peri* entirely to his taste—'but it contains some fine moments. Schumann's great merit lies in the distinction of his style. He has certain ways of saying certain things such as others haven't said before.' On Ferdinand Hiller his verdict ran: 'Hiller's conducting is like his personality: easy-going, all right, very seemly, even distinguished—but without energy and elasticity, and so without authority or communicative electricity.'

On the 30th there was music at the home of Clara Schumann, 'who received me in the most friendly manner—but without saying a single word about the article in the *Neue Zeitschrift*.'† After Clara and Joachim had performed Schumann's Violin Sonata in D minor, she and Liszt played the Overture to *Genoveva*.

Clara Schumann. But it was so horrible, that my feelings could find an outlet only in tears. How he banged the piano, and what a tempo he took! I was beside myself that His work should be so desecrated in these rooms which have been hallowed by Him, the dear composer. Liszt afterwards played Bach's Chromatic Fantasy equally dreadfully.‡. . .[4]

Liszt returned to Weimar on 1 June, having stopped briefly at Kassel to pay his respects to Spohr. 'Of all the musicians of his period, I regard him as by far the best and most valuable,' he wrote to Agnes. 'His double career as virtuoso and composer is equally honourable; but both the one and the other have lacked that element of the extraordinary which, quite simply, is what we mean by genius.'

* Apparently as a secret political agent. See A. Walker, 'Liszt and Agnes Street-Klindworth: A Spy in the Court of Weimar?', *Studia Musicologica*, xxviii (Budapest, 1986), 47–63.

† After Schumann's attempted suicide and subsequent confinement, Clara had resumed her career as a pianist, and the previous October had begun a tour with a concert at Weimar. To assist her in this difficult period of her life, Liszt had written a long article in praise of her playing and musicianship; it had been published in the *Neue Zeitschrift für Musik* of 1 Dec. 1854.

‡ Mentioning the musical matinée when writing to Agnes the next day, Liszt remarked that he had had little desire to play, and after repeated entreaties had done so 'only so as not to offend Frau Schumann'.

Later in June, *Frédéric Soret* was again in Weimar.

Liszt, the poor fellow, has aged greatly. His hair is turning grey, and, like many another, he has evidently discovered that in the joys of a romantic existence not all is roses and sunshine. . . .

An audience this morning [20 June] of Her Imperial Highness [Maria Pavlovna]. Much of our conversation was about the difficulties that Princess Wittgenstein continues to cause. . . . Approaches made to the Archbishop [of St Petersburg] to obtain his consent to the divorce have been absolutely fruitless,* so that, since she continues to wish to live far away from her husband, the Princess has been accused of adultery by the Russian authorities and her property confiscated; and since she has now lost any hope of a settlement, it has been decided that she should no longer be received at court, just as she is already no longer received by Weimar society. . . . Apparently Liszt has no fault in all this other than in having out of vanity allowed her to follow him, and in now continuing to live with her; but at the point which things have reached he can hardly abandon her.[5]

Liszt to Princess Carolyne (in Berlin), 14 July. I fetched Bach's [St Matthew] Passion, and went through the whole of the first part, 100 pages of score. . . . This work is still one of my own passions, unhackneyed for me, and every time I immerse myself in it its attractions redouble. If we were less poorly off at Weimar, it would give me great pleasure to mount a performance, such as I know how, of this colossal marvel. The one you heard at Leipzig can give you no more than a very feeble idea of it, despite the considerable number of players and singers they assembled for the occasion.[6]

To Agnes Street-Klindworth, 15 July. Yes, you are right, 'life is only a long and bitter suicide,' and faith alone—but an ardent, positive faith, that which moves mountains—can transform this *suicide* into *sacrifice* and thus luminously resolve any and every enigma and lapse. By it alone does each of our smallest actions, the most secret of our thoughts, acquire an eternal value, an infinite reward, and who knows what perfume and sonority entirely unknown to the *world*.[7]

On 21 July Liszt accepted Carl Tausig (1841–71), a thirteen-year-old boy from Warsaw, as a pupil. 'He has an *astonishing* talent,' he told Carolyne, 'and although of the tribe of Jacob will not displease you, I believe. He will probably spend eighteen months or two years here, after which he will be perfectly able to make a fine career as pianist and composer, for he is already very advanced on both counts.'

* Actually, Prince Nicholas Wittgenstein, a Calvinist, obtained a divorce (from the general Protestant consistory) this very year, and remarried in Jan. 1856. But for the Princess, a Catholic, matters pertaining to divorce and remarriage were naturally far more difficult and complex.

Liszt to Princess Carolyne, 24 July. In everything I do I believe I have something quite new to say. And so it is essential that *my* thought and *my* feeling are assimilated, so that they are not betrayed by a ruinous performance. . . . Albeit to a lesser degree than Wagner, I need *men* and artists—and cannot be satisfied with manœuvres and a mechanically regular performance. The Spirit must breathe on these sonorous waves* as on the great waters of the Creation.[8]

To Agnes Street-Klindworth, 15 August. The Princess has returned very satisfied with her artistic explorations of Berlin. Among other things she has brought back a beautiful sketch of Kaulbach's *Hunnenschlacht* [Battle of the Huns]—and I feel greatly tempted to base a musical work† on this sketch. That it won't be a guitar solo goes without saying, and I shall have to set a good portion of the brass in motion. But for the moment I first have to finish my Psalm.‡. . .[9]

During the weekend of 18/19 August, a fellow guest at Wilhelmsthal, the Grand Duke's summer residence, was the sixteen-year-old *Walburga Hohenthal* (1839–1929), the later Lady Paget.

Liszt used to read out to the Grand Duchess by the hour, galloping on at a most frantic pace. It was generally out of Sainte-Beuve's *Causeries du Lundi* that he selected passages. These hours in the Grand Duchess's boudoir 'à nous trois' enchanted me, for she and Liszt discussed the questions mooted by the readings, and they both of them spoke exquisite French. Liszt always wore lemon-coloured kid gloves, a frock coat and top hat; and one day when we had got out of the carriage and were walking on the brink of a precipice, I spied a rare flower growing on the rocks half-way down. No sooner had the exclamation of delight passed my lips, than to my horror I saw frock coat and top hat clambering nimbly down a place which was like the side of a quarry and victoriously flourish the little flower in the lemon-coloured hands. I thought of the odium which would attach to me had anything happened to this great genius, who was then at the culminating point of his celebrity.[10]

Carolyne and Marie's visit to Berlin was followed shortly afterwards by one to Paris; and on 21 August, accompanied from that same city by Frau von Bülow, Liszt's three children arrived for a fortnight's holiday with him, Blandine and Cosima then going on to Berlin, where they were to live with the Bülows. 'For the first months of your stay there, I am keen for you to work seriously at your piano-playing,' he told them. 'I want M. Hans to make you study like Conservatoire pupils and not to treat you as *princesses enchantées*.'

* Of the *Missa Solennis* or Gran Mass, composed this year for the consecration of the Cathedral at Gran (Esztergom) in 1856.

† The symphonic poem *Hunnenschlacht* (S105) was completed in 1857 and first performed in December that year.

‡ The setting (S13) of Psalm 13 ('How long wilt thou forget me, O Lord?') for tenor solo, chorus, and orchestra.

Shortly after the girls' departure, Liszt received from Madame Patersi in Paris a copy of three letters sent to them by their mother after she had learnt of the planned visit to Weimar. Madame d'Agoult's fury seemed to have been aroused, above all, by the fact that by staying at the Altenburg they would, in her opinion, be 'eating the bread of a STRANGER, a stranger who is not and never will be the wife of your father!'

Liszt to Blandine and Cosima. Weimar, 14 September. From your birth to this day your mother has not concerned herself in the least about the *bread* you eat, about the *place* in which you dwell, etc. Although she has always tranquilly enjoyed a fairly considerable income, she has seen fit to spend it on her personal pleasure, and to leave me, for nineteen years, the *entire* and *exclusive* burden of providing for your needs as well as for all the expenses of your education. Were a stranger to provide you with your bread (which is not the case), then I confess that I for my part would consider her to be less of a *stranger* to you than your mother has been until now. . . .

Since she wishes me harm, at all costs and on all occasions, and yet can strike at me neither in my outer position nor in the entrenchment of my conscience, she takes pleasure in attacking me in your affection, and in the respect and profound love I retain, as the purest passion of my life, for a woman who should be *holy* to you too in view of the devotion she has so nobly shown me for nine years, through incessantly renewed trials, sacrifices and sorrows. . . .[11]

Daniel Liszt, who in his examinations at the Lycée Bonaparte had again distinguished himself and carried off several prizes, stayed on at Weimar and did not return to Paris to resume his studies until early October. 'He is a really good, hardworking and dear boy,' wrote Liszt to his (own) mother. 'He is straightforward but not lacking in flexibility, and I am delighted at his cheerful disposition. I want to do everything possible for the children. May God protect and watch over them everlastingly!'

Liszt was working during this time at his Prelude and Fugue on the name BACH (S260), which was to be played by Alexander Winterberger at the inauguration of the organ of Merseburg Cathedral on 26 September. The piece was not completed soon enough, however, and Winterberger instead performed another great work for the instrument, composed five years earlier, the Fantasy and Fugue (S259) on the chorale 'Ad nos, ad salutarem undam' from Meyerbeer's *Le Prophète*—and played '*astonishingly*' in the opinion of Liszt, who spent two days at Merseburg. (Winterberger had given the première of the work at Weimar's town church on Friday, 29 October 1852.)

A visitor in late September was the German poet *Otto Roquette* (1824–96).

The Princess told me that the Grand Duke wanted an artistic representation of the life of his ancestress, St Elisabeth,* and that Liszt, who hoped I

* The daughter of Andreas II of Hungary, Elisabeth (1207–31) had at the age of fourteen married Ludwig IV of Thuringia, with whom she then lived at the Wartburg Castle near

would undertake the libretto, was willing to compose a cantata. Despite my objections to the saint, who was by no means to my liking, no refusal was allowed.

Then the Princess's daughter, knowing full well what we were discussing, came in to unloose her own weapons against me; and shortly afterwards we were joined by Liszt, who was of course in league with the two women. How was I to withstand the Princess's eloquence and Liszt's charm, particularly when supported by the delightful blandishments of young Princess Marie? It can be counted my good fortune that they wanted no more than a cantata.[12]

In Berlin, meanwhile, *Hans von Bülow* was making the acquaintance of Blandine and Cosima, as he wrote to Liszt on 30 September.

You ask me, *très cher maître*, to give you news of Mesdemoiselles Liszt. Until now that would have been impossible, seeing the state of stupefaction, admiration, and even exaltation to which they have reduced me, especially the younger. So far as their musical gifts are concerned, it is not so much talent they possess as genius. In this, they are indeed the daughters of my benefactor—beings altogether exceptional. . . .

Yesterday evening Mlle Blandine played Bach's Sonata in A, and Mlle Cosima the E flat Sonata of Beethoven, with Laub,* who will often make music with them. . . . I shall never forget the delightful evening when I played and replayed them your Psalm. Wholly given up to adoration of their father, the two angels were almost kneeling. Had you been present, incognito, it would have been a very happy moment for you. They understand your masterpieces better than anyone, and truly you have in them 'a public provided by nature'.

How moved and touched I was to recognize 'ipsissimum Lisztum' in the playing of Mlle Cosima when I heard her for the first time! She, it seems to me, resembles the Scheffer and Mlle Blandine the Bartolini.[†13]

In October Liszt spent several days at Brunswick (with Litolff among others), where *Orpheus* and *Prometheus* were performed at a concert on the 18th. In late November he went to Berlin, where he stayed at the Brandenburg Hotel with Agnes Street-Klindworth, and on 6 December, at the Singakademie, conducted the première of Psalm 13. As well as his daughters and Bülow (who was moved to tears of rage when Liszt's music was attacked by the critics), he saw numerous friends and acquaintances during the visit, including the aged Alexander von

Eisenach. Known for her prayerful life and ceaseless almsgiving, she had after her husband's death (1227) undergone great privations; but, having provided for her children, she renounced the world, entered the third order of St Francis, and at Marburg, where she died and was buried, devoted herself to caring for the poor and sick. She was canonized in 1235. Liszt's setting of Roquette's text became the oratorio *The Legend of St Elisabeth* (S2).

* Ferdinand Laub had moved from Weimar to Berlin in late 1854.
† That is, the portrait of Liszt by Ary Scheffer and his bust by Lorenzo Bartolini.

Humboldt. The outcome of a stroll along the Unter den Linden with Bülow one evening was that 'I shall probably give him my daughter in marriage. . . .' On 14 December he returned to Weimar.

1856

In early January Liszt returned to Berlin for the first performance in that city of *Tannhäuser*, given at the Court Theatre on the 7th; and on the 9th, at the King's invitation, he was a guest at a court concert. A week later, to conduct the Mozart centenary concerts of 27 and 28 January, he arrived in Vienna, where he stayed until 2 February. To Agnes he reported: 'The two concerts had the *most complete* success, and the official eulogies made to me sum up the general impression perfectly. . . . The great hall of the Redoute, freshly decorated and brilliantly illuminated, looked very beautiful. Several days beforehand it was impossible to obtain tickets. The Emperor and Empress were present, and the overall musical performance, with more than 500 participants, was very satisfying.' To Carolyne: 'I have rarely spent "greyer" days within myself than this last week. . . . No one here has troubled to understand that I no longer play the piano—but gradually it will become clear.' Among the old acquaintances he saw were Metternich, with whom he dined, and Grillparzer; and he is likely also to have spoken with a figure of general interest who attended the centenary celebrations: Carl Thomas Mozart (1784–1858), second son of Wolfgang Amadeus.

On hearing that the concerts were to be directed by Liszt, Clara Schumann, to whom he had always behaved with gallantry and generosity, and on whom a year earlier, to accompany the resumption of her concert career, he had written and published a highly laudatory article, had declined to take part—the first adumbrations of the pathological hatred she came to feel for him, indications of which can be seen in her correspondence, her recorded remarks, and her behaviour.*

Liszt to Hans von Bülow. Weimar, 14 March. Berlioz spent three weeks here. The performance of his *Cellini*† was very satisfying. . . . At the request of the Princess of Prussia, a week later we gave *Lohengrin*, which Berlioz found little to his taste. We said not a great deal to one another about it, but to others he expressed himself in no uncertain terms, which vexed me.[1]

On Tuesday, 13 May, a concert was given in Merseburg Cathedral, whose organ had been inaugurated the previous year with the Fantasy and Fugue on 'Ad nos, ad salutarem undam'.

* One instance being the deletion, in her edition of Schumann's Fantasy in C, of the dedication to Liszt.

† Conducted by Liszt on 16 Feb. On the 17th Berlioz conducted a concert at court, and on the 28th his *Damnation de Faust*.

Adelheid von Schorn. Liszt was asked to draw up the programme, and among other things he invited Edmund Singer* to play a violin solo with organ accompaniment. Singer was in something of a quandary about choice of work, as he preferred to play something other than the much-played Adagios from the Bach violin sonatas; and in the end he asked Bronsart to compose something new for the occasion. As time was pressing, Bronsart took only a day or two to write an Adagio for violin and organ, and it found such favour with Liszt that he expressed a wish to play the organ part himself. Even at the rehearsal those present were delighted at the Master's brilliant registration, at his rich range of nuances in creating only soft tone colours, and at how he was able to find his bearings and select the most beautiful of everything in what was to him rather an unfamiliar musical field. After the concert it was evident to participants (among whom was Feodor von Milde) and audience alike, that in his *accompaniment* of a violin solo the Master had beaten the famous organists in their solo performances of the mightiest organ works.[2]

It was at this concert that Alexander Winterberger gave the première of the Prelude and Fugue for organ on BACH.

In June, *La Mara* was one of a small group who accompanied Liszt from Weimar to St Augustine's Church, Erfurt, where Mozart's *Requiem* was being performed.

What a jolly excursion it was in the Master's company! My collection of rarities still contains a yellowed bunch of lily of the valley which he presented to me that evening. There was time, too, for us to visit the Cathedral, as well as the Augustinian monastery in whose quiet cells Luther's early years of struggle were passed.

After the performance we went to take tea with the Princess Wittgenstein, who that day held court in an Erfurt hotel instead of at the Altenburg in Weimar. For the first time I found myself facing the extraordinary woman who was admiringly regarded as one of the outstanding figures of the nineteenth century, and whose romantic bond of love with Liszt had captured the world's attention. There was nothing imposing about her outer appearance. Next to the slim, aristocratic figure of her beautiful, enchanting, and intelligent daughter, Princess Marie, her own figure seemed rather short and stocky. Her facial features lacked a clear contour; instead, the fascination she exercised was of an eminently intellectual and spiritual quality, that of the blazing fire and power of expression of a wonderful pair of eyes which, although frequently half-closed as is the case with the shortsighted, seemed to penetrate into the heart of persons and things alike. A marvel of genius and knowledge, of sparkling intellect and eloquence, she, at whose feet Liszt's soul lay as at those of none other, held

* A gifted Hungarian violinist (1830–1912) who had succeeded Laub as leader of Liszt's Weimar orchestra.

me captive from the first moment that her eagle eyes fell upon me. . . .

Taking tea with us we found all the distinguished and friendly elements that Erfurt could offer. Conversation was lively and informal. Princess Marie . . . whose wonderful dark eyes seemed to wish more to veil than to reveal her depths of soul, prepared the tea, and the rest of us sat cheerfully gathered around her. Princess Carolyne plunged into an erudite discussion of the Talmud with Dr Paul Selig-Kassel, who from a Jewish Saul had become a Protestant Paul. . . .

At noon the next day we were once again in Liszt's company. There was a party at my friends' home [in Weimar]: artists were invited and Liszt had indicated that he might come too. Accordingly, everything was done to prepare a fitting reception. . . . When the hour arrived which brought him to us among the other guests, I bashfully kept at a distance—the foregoing days had not given me more courage. I hardly dared raise my eyes to him when I was his vis-à-vis at table; and the place at his side, enviable though I thought it, I had firmly refused to accept. And yet I saw and heard only Him! What did I care about the other artists in my immediate proximity? With our gaze fixed on the sun, do we seek the stars, whose pale light must fade before its dazzling splendour? And on this day the sun shone brightly. Liszt was in the most cheerful of moods, the conversation extremely animated. At the end of the meal he beckoned his pupil Ratzenberger* to the piano and placed Chopin's Polonaise in A flat on the music rack. But we heard scarcely a page. 'I can't play today,' said the youth. It was a well-calculated trick. He knew his master, and knew that nothing was more likely to make him play than music left unfinished. And, indeed, without a word he pushed his pupil from the stool and himself took his place upon it—and then began that unique playing, whose transporting power no one who did not hear it for himself, experience it resounding within his soul, can even guess at. To describe Liszt's playing, or the impression it evoked, would be a futile undertaking. It was something incomparable, a phenomenon of the kind the world sees but *once*. Other great pianists we admire; Liszt we had to *love*; he won the hearts of all. And where do we find, as with him, the union of subjectivity and objectivity, the wonderful fusion of the demoniacal and the divine, which made us at one moment shudder and shake in the depths of our souls, and the next quietly fold our hands and in pious enthusiasm be borne heavenwards? Therein have I sought the key to the spell-binding effect of Liszt's playing. And yet, why seek to explain the inexplicable when it appears before our minds and souls in the guise of a beauteous marvel?

Chopin's most magnificent Polonaise had died away, but only for a moment did the artist's hands lie still. The Hungarian Storm March [S232] lay on the piano, one of the early works of his virtuoso period. 'That's

* Theodor Ratzenberger (1840–79), pianist and conductor.

something I haven't played for a long time,' he said, reaching for it. Then the music flowed over us like stormy waves. Fire, passion, and hot Hungarian blood pulse through this youthful work, which is genuine martial music. . . .[3]

In late June, *Hans Christian Andersen* again spent a few days in Weimar.

27 June. Went to Liszt's; he had gone out for a walk. Talked with Frau Beaulieu [-Marconnay] about him. The affair with Princess Wittgenstein is a scandal; she has not obtained a renewal of her Russian passport and so is reduced to nothing in Russia. The daughter, who is apparently under the Dowager Grand Duchess's protection, has everything, and the mother is now living on that; and so she does not want her daughter to get away and was to blame for the engagement with Talleyrand being broken off. The Dowager Grand Duchess gave the daughter a room in Countess Fritsch's* apartment at the palace, and said that she could go to her mother as often as she wished, but that, unlike her, the mother could not go into society. 'Where my mother cannot go, I do not wish to go either!' said the girl. And when lightning struck that part of the old palace in which Countess Fritsch was living, she ran back to her mother and remained there. That was nice of the daughter. Liszt says: 'I do indeed want to marry the Princess, and she likewise, but we are not allowed to. And so what shall I do. Now that she has nothing I cannot abandon her!'

When Johanna Wagner† was recently in Weimar, Liszt was delighted; the Princess became jealous and, spiteful tongues say, wanted to hang herself. —It is her custom to send Princess Marie to Liszt, to kneel before him and say: 'Do not make my mother unhappy, do not abandon her!'[4]

Richard Wagner to Liszt. Mornex, near Geneva, 12 July. When I consider your artistic career, which is so different from any other, I clearly perceive the instinct which led you on to the path you are now treading. You are by nature the genuine, fortunate artist who both creates and re-creates. May you formerly, as a pianist, have played whatever took your fancy, it was always the personal communication of your beautiful individuality which revealed things entirely new and unknown to us; and the only person able and competent to judge you was the one to whom you had played in a happy mood. This new and indescribably individual element was still wholly dependent on your personality, and without your actual presence it did not exist, properly speaking. On hearing you one lamented that these marvels were to disappear and be irretrievably lost with your person, for it is absurd to think that your art could be passed on through your pupils (as someone at Berlin boasted recently). But nature, by some unfailing means, always provides for the continued existence of that which she

* Constance von Fritsch (1786–1858).
† Dramatic soprano (1826–94), the adopted daughter of Richard Wagner's brother Albert.

produces so seldom; and she showed you the right way. You were led to seek to preserve the miracles of your personal communication in a manner which made it independent of your individual existence. What you earlier played on the piano would not have served for the purpose, for only through your personal interpretation did it become what it appeared to us to be; for which reason (I say it again!) it was often unimportant *what and whose* work you played. Without any effort, therefore, you hit upon the idea of replacing your personal art by the orchestra; that is, by compositions which, through the orchestra's inexhaustible means of expression, were able to reflect your individuality without the need, in future times, of your actual presence. And so, for me, your orchestral works are, so to speak, your personal art put into a monumental form; and in this respect they are so new, so incomparable with anything else, that criticism will take a long time to find out what to make of them. . . .

How tremendously beautiful your *Mazeppa* is. Merely reading it through for the first time made me quite out of breath! I am sorry for the poor horse too; truly, nature and the world are atrocious.[5]

In July, Blandine and Cosima spent a fortnight at the Altenburg *en route* to Paris, whence, in September, Cosima returned alone to Berlin.

In early August, Liszt travelled to Hungary, where at the consecration of Gran (Esztergom) Cathedral on Sunday, 31 August, his specially commissioned *Missa Solennis* (S9)—thereafter to be known as his Gran Mass—was to be performed. ('I may say that I have *prayed* it rather than *composed* it,' he had written to Wagner in May 1855 after completing the work.) Making a fleeting visit to Gran on the 10th, he then proceeded to Pest, his first visit to the city for ten years.

Liszt to Princess Carolyne. Pest, 13 August. This evening I shall be going to the German theatre. . . . Afterwards I shall hasten to the gypsies, as I did yesterday evening. You know what an attraction this music has for me —and so I plan to steep myself in it. I could well be defined in German: 'Zu einer Hälfte Zigeuner, zur andern Franziskaner!'* There is, however, something else which holds sway over these two contrary elements, isn't there my adorable darling? It is this something else which is writing to you, thinking of you and blessing you unceasingly![6]

After a rehearsal on the 27th, Liszt was able to report to Carolyne: 'The singers and players had already grown passionately fond of my Mass at the previous partial rehearsals—and in town it is generally being said: "This is entirely new music, but music for kneeling to." There was much applause after each section, and at the end I was recalled three times. It went very well, even though still lacking several half-tints which will increase the impression greatly. I don't think my thought and feeling are precisely understood by the public here—but they have a keen realization that it is something out of the ordinary.'

At noon on the 29th, he and the other musicians embarked on the steamboat *Marianna* to travel up the Danube to Gran.

* 'Half gypsy, half Franciscan friar!'

Liszt to Princess Carolyne. Gran, 31 August. It is a quarter to three. The last Amen of the Mass has just been pronounced. HM the Emperor, who is staying opposite, is returning to the sounds of the melody of Haydn's *Gott erhalte*—and I am coming to kiss your hands . . . and to tell you that it all went according to your wishes, and that God blessed me. My Mass began at one thirty. As I had anticipated, the whole work lasts only 45 to 50 minutes at most, watch in hand. The performance was perfect, even admirable in several places—without the least hitch, without the shadow of a Karlsruhe bassoon.* In all, we were more than 130 singers and performers. Unless I am greatly mistaken, the general impression produced by the work is beyond what I could have flattered myself I would obtain. . . . I thank and bless you for having inspired me with good thoughts and for having helped me to work for God! Be blessed 1,000 and 1,000 times![7]

Vilmos von Csapó (1840–1933), landowner and editor. I saw Liszt several times in the streets of Pest, as, always with a large entourage, he hurried along with swift, elastic steps, head held high and a constant smile on his lips, from time to time shaking his long brown shoulder-length hair under his high silk hat and making disconnected remarks in his deep baritone voice. He was a phenomenon whom, despite themselves, people simply could not take their eyes off. When he conducted his Mass at Gran, his chest was covered with the numerous orders which had been presented to him over the years; they shone brilliantly against the red silk garment he was wearing.

But those who arranged the gala dinner omitted to give him a seat at the Emperor's table, assigning him instead a place with the retinue and the other guests; and so, offended, the great artist chose to go aboard the steamer hired for the orchestra, where he played host to the musicians who had taken part in the performance of his Mass.[8]

On 1 September Liszt made the acquaintance of Lajos Haynald (1816–91) the Bishop of Transylvania, who eleven years later was appointed Archbishop of Kalocsa and in 1879 a cardinal. Becoming a great friend and admirer of Liszt's, he was in after years Honorary President of the Liszt Society founded at Pest in 1870.

On 4 September another performance of the Gran Mass was given, this time at Pest's Inner City Church. 'It could scarcely hold the enormous crowd of people curious to hear it,' Liszt told Carolyne. 'The sonority was much better than at Gran, and the performers in still better form and still more imbued with a feeling for my work. And so it was enormously moving. I am told that many persons wept.' On the 8th, at a concert in the Hungarian National Theatre which included *Les Préludes* and the world première of *Hungaria* (received with tremendous enthusiasm), a thousand copies were distributed of a poem to Liszt by the poet Kálmán Lisznyai, then seriously ill. Liszt visited Lisznyai to thank

* See footnote to Oct. 1853 *supra*.

him, and the report of the visit which appeared in the periodical *Hölgyfutár* (Ladies' Messenger) stated that the composer had told the poet of his deep sympathy for Hungarian poetry and singled out for special mention Lisznyai's *Magyar vendégszeret* ('Hungarian hospitality'). On the 11th he dined with the Franciscans, just as he had done in 1823, 1840, and 1846. 'My old attachment to this monastery has not diminished with the years, and the Franciscans welcomed me as one of their own.'

Arriving in Vienna on the 14th, the next evening he attended a concert given by Johann Strauss the younger, whose performance of the finale of *Mazeppa*—'in honour of the presence of Dr Liszt'—was encored.

Liszt to Agnes Street-Klindworth. Vienna, 16 September. On the one hand I have become fully conscious of the fact that the task it is given me to carry out in this world forms an integral part of the national glory. (It was in this sense that the Archbisop of Udine addressed me as the 'gloria dell'Ungheria'*—which gives me much scope for being *ad libitum* modestly proud or proudly modest.) And on the other I have adopted a serious position as a religious and *Catholic* composer. Now that is an unlimited field for art, which I feel the *vocation* to cultivate vigorously. . . .

The fact is, I believe I can say with a clear conscience and full modesty that among composers known to me not one has so intense and profound a feeling for religious music as your very humble servant. Moreover, both my former and my more recent studies of Palestrina and Lassus to Bach and Beethoven, who are the summits of Catholic† art, give me a great foundation on which to build, and I am altogether confident that in three or four years I shall have taken full possession of the spiritual domain of church music, which for about twenty years has been occupied only by mediocrities by the dozen, who will indeed not fail to reproach me with not composing *religious music*—which would be true, if their own trumpery stuff counted as such.[9]

Leaving Vienna during the evening of 20 September, Liszt arrived the next morning at Prague, where he stopped at the Black Horse Hotel in which he and Carolyne had stayed in June 1848. Among acquaintances seen by him were Dreyschock, to whom he played the Sonata in B minor, and the eminent music historian A. W. Ambros (1816–76). On the 28th the Gran Mass was performed here—the first time outside Hungary.

During his stay in Prague he wrote two letters to the twenty-three-year-old Lilla Bulyovszky (1833–1909), a celebrated Hungarian actress whom he had met at Pest. In the first, of 22 September, he thanked her for searching for a lost pair of spectacles of his and offered to be her guide when she visited Weimar. Her immediate reply elicited another letter from him on the 28th.

Your dream is the dream of a child: I am too old to love a young girl—and even in my youth I do not recall a similar enamourment. How to define

* At a banquet in Gran on 1 Sept.

† Liszt must momentarily have forgotten that Bach was a Protestant.

what I *understand* by this word love? If in your capacity as a novelist you have some psychological interest in this topic, then read the chapter in the *third* book of *The Imitation of Christ* (on 'the effects of divine love'). You will find therein the familiar nourishment of my thought, the heavenly manna on which my soul has subsisted during long years in the desert of this earthly existence—and when you come to Weimar I shall be able to continue this chapter for you orally; if, that is, your interest and your novelist's patience are not at an end!

In any case, I promise you a *compatriot's* welcome, without nonsense or pedantry of any kind whatever. You have accused me of coquetry of the spirit, and I have permitted myself to remark that you are mistaken. If you retain for me a little of the goodwill that I dare lay claim to, you will, I am convinced, perceive your error and understand me better. 'You live as though you were immortal!' a very intelligent woman [Cristina Belgiojoso] once said to me. 'Why not?' I replied. My task in this world is an arduous and resigned one. I am like one of those age-old mountain peaks, on which the roses do not grow but from which the gaze of my thought embraces a vast horizon and is brightened by the appearance of some friendly star.[10]

Leaving Prague on 29 September, and spending the day at the home of Count Chotek at Grosspriesen, Liszt returned via Dresden to Weimar. A few days later, Carolyne and Marie set out for Lake Constance; and shortly afterwards Liszt made his way, via Stuttgart, Baden-Baden, and Mainau,* to Zurich, where he had arranged to visit the exiled Wagner. The two women were to join them later.

Richard Wagner. Liszt arrived on 13 October, and my house at once became a musical centre. He had finished his Faust and Dante symphonies† since I had last seen him, and it was nothing short of marvellous to hear him play them to me on the piano from the score. As I felt sure that he must be convinced of the great impression his works made on me, I felt no scruples in persuading him to alter the mistaken ending of the Dante Symphony. If anything had convinced me of the man's masterly and poetical powers of conception, it was the original ending of the Faust Symphony, in which the delicate fragrance of a last reminiscence of Gretchen overpowers everything,

* An island in Lake Constance containing the Grand Duke of Baden's holiday villa, celebrated for its beautiful gardens and flora.

† The Dante Symphony (S109) was completed on 8 July this year. Liszt's original intention had been to compose three movements, 'Inferno', 'Purgatorio' and 'Paradiso', corresponding with the three divisions of the *Divina Commedia*; but, allowing himself to be persuaded by Wagner, to whom he dedicated the work, that no human being could portray the joys of Paradise, he concluded the symphony instead with a Magnificat. He had also planned to have the entire work performed to the accompaniment of a diorama showing Bonaventura Genelli's illustrations to the *Divina Commedia*, but nothing came of this. Slides were prepared from them in modern times, however, and the first illustrated performance of the Dante Symphony was given at Brussels in September 1984.

without arresting the attention by a violent disturbance. The ending of the Dante Symphony seemed to me to be quite on the same lines, for the delicately introduced Magnificat in the same way gives only a hint of a soft, shimmering Paradise. I was the more startled to hear this beautiful suggestion suddenly interrupted in an alarming way by a pompous plagal cadence which, as I was told, was supposed to represent Domenico. 'No!' I exclaimed loudly, 'not that! Away with it! No majestic Deity! Leave us the fine soft shimmer.'

'You are right,' remarked Liszt. 'I said so too; it was the Princess who persuaded me differently. But it shall be as you wish.'

All well and good—but all the greater was my distress to learn later that not only had this ending of the Dante Symphony been preserved, but even the delicate ending of the Faust Symphony, which had appealed to me so particularly, had been changed, in a manner better calculated to produce an effect, by the introduction of a chorus. And this was exactly typical of my relations to Liszt and to his friend Carolyne Wittgenstein!

Before the latter and her daughter arrived, a most irritating incident occurred in my flat between Liszt and Karl Ritter.* Ritter's looks alone, and still more, a certain abrupt contradictoriness in his way of speaking, seemed to put Liszt into a state in which he was easily riled. One evening he was speaking in an impressive tone of the merits of the Jesuits, and Ritter's inopportune smiles appeared to annoy him. At table the conversation turned on the Emperor of the French, Louis Napoleon, whose merits Liszt rather summarily insisted that we should acknowledge; whereas we, on the whole, were anything but enthusiastic about the general state of affairs in France. When Liszt, in an attempt to make clear the important influence of France on European culture, mentioned as an instance the *Académie française*, Karl again indulged in his fatal smile. This exasperated Liszt beyond all bounds, and in his reply he included some such phrase as this: 'If we are not prepared to admit this, what do we prove ourselves to be? *Baboons*!' I laughed, but again Karl only smiled—this time, with deadly embarrassment. Bülow told me afterwards that in some youthful squabble Karl had had the word 'Baboon-face' hurled at him. It soon became impossible to hide the fact that Ritter felt grossly insulted by 'the Doctor', as he called him, and he left my house foaming with rage, not to set foot in it again for years. After a few days I received a letter in which he demanded, first, a complete apology from Liszt, as soon as he came to see me again, and if this were unobtainable, Liszt's exclusion from my home. . . . For a long time my relations with this family, intimate as they had been, were painfully strained, as I found it impossible to make them see the incident in the right light. When Liszt, after a time, heard of it, he

* Homosexual and would-be composer (1830–91) whom Liszt had seen at Zurich three years earlier and found 'absurd'. His mother, Julie Ritter, provided Wagner with an annual allowance.

regretted the disturbance, and with praiseworthy magnanimity made the first advance towards a reconciliation by paying Ritter a friendly visit. There was nothing said about the incident, and Ritter's return visit was made, not to Liszt, but to the Princess, who had arrived in the meantime. After this, Liszt decided that he could do nothing further. . . .

Not only my own modest residence, but the whole of Zurich seemed full of life when Princess Carolyne and her daughter took up their abode at the Hôtel Baur for a time. The curious spell of excitement which this lady immediately threw over everyone she succeeded in drawing into her circle amounted, in the case of my good sister Clara who was staying with me, almost to intoxication. It was as though Zurich had suddenly become a metropolis. Carriages drove hither and thither, footmen announced one or brought excuses, dinners and suppers poured in upon us, and we found ourselves suddenly surrounded by an increasing number of interesting people whose existence at Zurich we had never even suspected. . . . It was principally the University professors whom Princess Carolyne coaxed out of their hole-and-corner Zurich habits. She would enjoy each one of them for herself, and then again serve them up *en masse* for us. If I looked in for a moment from my regular midday walk, the lady would be dining alone, now with Semper,* now with Professor Köchly, then with Moleschott, and so on. Even my very peculiar friend Sulzer was drawn in, and, as he could not deny, in a manner intoxicated. But a really refreshing sense of freedom and spontaneity pervaded everything, and the unceremonious evenings at my house in particular were really remarkably free and easy. On these occasions the Princess, with Polish patriarchal friendliness, would help the mistress of the house in serving. . . .

The crown of our little festivities was, however, Liszt's birthday, on 22 October, which the Princess celebrated with full pomp at her rooms in the hotel. Everyone who was anyone at Zurich was there. A poem by Hoffmann von Fallersleben was telegraphed from Weimar, and at the Princess's request was solemnly read aloud by Herwegh in a wondrously altered voice. . . .

Unfortunately, our circle was soon to suffer a great loss by Liszt's illness—a skin eruption—which confined him to bed for a considerable period. As soon as he was a little better, we quickly went to the piano again to try over by ourselves my two finished scores of *Rheingold* and *Die Walküre*. Princess Marie listened carefully, and was even able to make intelligent suggestions in connection with a few difficult passages in the poem. . . .

Princess Carolyne's high spirits were as marked as the curious amiability of her nature; for when I one day explained to her, in illustration of the

* The German architect Gottfried Semper (1803–79), designer of, in addition to many other notable buildings, the Victoria and Albert Museum in London.

first of these two qualities, that four weeks of uninterrupted companionship with her would have been the death of me, she laughed heartily. . . .

I remember one fine evening at Herwegh's, when Liszt was moved to the same state of enthusiasm by a grand piano abominably out of tune, as by the disgusting cigars to which at that time he was more passionately devoted than to the finer brands. We were all compelled to exchange our belief in magic for a belief in actual witchcraft as we listened to his wonderful fantasies on this instrument. To my great horror, Liszt still gave evidence on more than one occasion of an irritability which was thoroughly bad-tempered and even quarrelsome, such as had already manifested itself in the unfortunate scene with young Ritter. For instance, it was dangerous, especially in the presence of Princess Carolyne, to praise Goethe. Even Liszt and I had nearly quarrelled (for which he seemed to be very eager) over the character of Egmont, which he thought it his duty to depreciate because the man allows himself to be taken in by Alba. I had been warned, and had the presence of mind to confine myself to observing the peculiar physiology of my friend on this occasion, and turning my attention to his condition, much more than to the subject of our dispute. We never actually came to blows; but from that time forward I retained throughout my life a vague feeling that we might one day come to such an encounter, in which case it could not fail to be terrific. . . .

We had agreed to spend a week at St Gallen, where we had an invitation from Sczadrowsky, a young conductor, to give our support to a society concert in that district.

We stayed together at the Hecht Inn, and the Princess entertained us as if she had been in her own home. She gave my wife and me a room next to her own apartment. Unfortunately, a most trying night was in store for us. Princess Carolyne had one of her severe nervous attacks, and in order to preclude the approach of the painful hallucination by which she was tormented at such times, her daughter Marie was obliged to read to her all through the night in a voice deliberately raised a good deal above its natural pitch. I got fearfully excited, especially at what appeared to be an inexplicable disregard for the peace of one's neighbour. At two o'clock in the morning I leapt out of bed, rang the bell continuously until the waiter awoke, and asked him to take me to a bedroom in one of the remotest parts of the inn. . . . The next morning I was much astonished to see Marie appear as usual, quite unembarrassed, and without showing the least traces of anything unusual having occurred in the night. I now learned that everyone connected with the Princess was thoroughly accustomed to such excesses. . . .

At the rehearsal, to my genuine delight, Liszt impressed two of his works, *Orpheus* and *Les Préludes*, upon the orchestra with complete success, in spite of the limited resources at his command. The performance turned out to be a really fine one, and full of spirit. I was especially delighted with *Orpheus* and with the finely proportioned orchestral writing, to which I had always assigned a high place of honour among Liszt's works. On the other hand, the special favour of the public was awarded to *Les Préludes*, of which the greater part had to be encored. I conducted Beethoven's Eroica Symphony. . . . My conception and rendering of the work made a powerful impression upon Liszt, whose opinion was the only one which had any real weight with me. We watched each other over our work with a closeness and sympathy that were genuinely instructive. . . .

The next day, 24 November, we all met, for various festivities, in the house of an ardent music-lover, Herr Bourit, a rich merchant of St Gallen. Here we had some pianoforte music, and Liszt played to us, among other things, the great Sonata in B flat [*Hammerklavier*, Op. 106], by Beethoven, at the close of which Kirchner* dryly and candidly remarked: 'Now we can truly say that we have witnessed the impossible, for I shall always regard what I have just heard as an impossibility.'[11]

On 27 November, accompanied by Wagner as far as Rorschach on Lake Constance, Liszt and the two princesses left St Gallen for Germany, where they spent some time in Munich before returning to Weimar.

In the winter *Adelheid von Schorn* and her mother went to a party at the Altenburg.

We were invited in honour of Marie Seebach, who was then making her first guest appearance in Weimar. As Gretchen she won all hearts and was much lionized. Looking very graceful, with beautifully chiselled features and a mass of fair, curly hair, she declaimed Hebbel's *Heideknaben* that evening with great enthusiasm, Liszt accompanying her at the piano. It was the first time I had heard a melodrama, and my impression then was that music and the spoken word rather hinder than help one another, even though Marie Seebach was one of the few who can speak musically.

Liszt made his appearance wearing a short black velvet jacket; he looked pale and poorly, having been ill, but so handsome that I could not keep my eyes off him. So radiant was his expression as he sat at the piano that we hardly noticed that he was playing with one hand only: the other was causing him such pain that he could not use it. Of those present that evening, I remember Friedrich Preller,† Herr and Frau von Milde, and Hoffmann von Fallersleben. About the last-named, Princess Marie told me that no one could bind bouquets of flowers more attractively than he. We had already been gathered for some time when a tall, very slim young man with long fair hair appeared, whom I probably regarded with undisguised

* Theodor Kirchner (1823–1903), organist and composer.

† Friedrich Preller (1804–78), a distinguished painter of the period, remembered for his landscapes and for his scenes from the *Odyssey*, was on very friendly terms with Liszt and the Princess during their Weimar years.

amazement—for he looked just like a younger version of Liszt—until Princess Marie introduced him to me as 'Daniel, Liszt's son'. He had arrived that very day from Paris, where he had passed his school-leaving exams brilliantly; now he was to spend a few relaxing weeks at the Altenburg as the hard work had been bad for his health. . . .

Supper, as always at the Altenburg, was set out on little tables for four. I can still see my mother sitting next to Princess Carolyne, whom that evening I beheld for the first and only time in evening dress. She was still fairly slim in those days, and very active, small and bubbling over with vivacity. Dark hair and eyes as well as a yellowish complexion gave her rather a foreign appearance, and indeed she was of pure Polish extraction. A fairly large nose gave her face a peculiar significance, while the expression around her mouth was one of indescribable friendliness. She loved to wear bright colours, a habit she retained into old age. 'In old age women must have beautiful colours in their dress, but its form must suit their years,' she remarked to me much later in Rome.

Princess Marie, who with her youthful aristocratic grace brought a quite special magic to the artistic circle at the Altenburg, and was adored to a greater or lesser degree by Liszt's pupils, was a charming creature. . . .

The next day Daniel visited us, and then came more and more often, for he too felt very much at ease with my mother, in her simple, comfortable home. Perhaps my sixteen-year-old youthfulness was also an attraction for the eighteen-year-old. We danced and skated together, and I had to teach him how to do both. This made me regard him as someone not older but younger than myself. The best things that the gifted youngster was able to do I did not at that time understand.[12]

It was in 1856 that Liszt and *Alexander Wilhelm Gottschalg* (1827–1908), the cantor and organist at Tiefurt near Weimar, made one another's acquaintance. Gottschalg became one of the most devoted of the local adherents of the composer, who generally referred to him as 'my legendary cantor'—'for,' he explained, 'should I ever myself become a legend, Gottschalg will live on with me.'

I have often been asked if the Princess was a beauty. No—a physically attractive personality she was not! Of medium height, she was rather thickset, had irregular features, a somewhat yellowish complexion, and dark hair. But the qualities of her mind, her lofty and indulgent philosophy of life, her acute intelligence, her lively imagination, her generous heart, and her great strength of will, impressed all who came in contact with her.

With Liszt it was otherwise. When I first met him, he was a handsome man in his prime. A strong, rather lean and slim figure, with an elastic step, a kind of Schiller head with long blackish locks which remained abundant even in his advanced old age, piercing blue eyes, an uncommonly friendly manner and approach, a rapid mental grasp, a tremendous power of imagination, a generous heart, an outlook of great charity and nobility, and a profound religious feeling—made Liszt the most wonderful human being I have known in a long life.[13]

1857

At the Court Theatre on Wednesday, 7 January, came the première of Liszt's Piano Concerto No. 2 in A (S125). First sketched in 1839, it had been revised extensively. Liszt conducted, and the soloist, to whom the work was dedicated, was Bronsart. On the same occasion the first public performance of the final version of *Ce qu'on entend sur la montagne* was given.

At Berlin on 22 January, in a concert which inaugurated the first Bechstein grand piano,* the B minor Sonata was played in public for the first time. The pianist was Bülow, who was able to write to Liszt of 'an unexpected, almost unanimous success'. 'After a trio by Volkmann which preceded it, some hisses could be heard through the applause, whereas the Sonata completely dumbfounded the cretinous scoundrels.'

Liszt to Dionys Pruckner. Weimar, 11 February. At home, our whole life through, we have to study and to devise how to mature our work and to attain as near as possible the ideal of Art. But when we enter the concert hall the feeling ought not to leave us that, by very reason of our conscientious and persevering striving, we stand somewhat higher than the public, and that we have to represent our portion of 'mankind's dignity', as Schiller says. Let us not err through *false* modesty, and let us hold fast to the *true*, which is much more difficult to practise and much rarer to find. The artist—as we understand it—should be neither the servant nor the master of the public. He remains the bearer of the *Beautiful* in the inexhaustible variety which is appointed to human thought and perception—and it is his steadfast awareness of this which alone ensures his authority.[1]

Liszt had been invited to have some of his recent works performed at Leipzig, in a concert of 26 February for the benefit of the Gewandhaus Orchestra's pension fund. The second half of the programme was placed at his disposal, the first having been given to Julius Rietz.†

La Mara. 'Great was the public's curiosity to get to know Liszt's works, which had been much discussed in the periodicals, sometimes with

* Carl Bechstein (1826–1900) had founded the Berlin piano firm in 1853.

† Kapellmeister at Leipzig, and from 1860 Court Kapellmeister at Dresden, Julius Rietz (1812–77) was a musical reactionary of the Clara Schumann type, and an inexorable opponent of Liszt, Wagner, and their followers.

extraordinary praise, sometimes with adverse criticism,' writes Grenser the flautist, historiographer of the Gewandhaus concerts, 'and so we could not help taking good receipts.' Liszt chose the symphonic poems *Les Préludes* and *Mazeppa*, the E flat Concerto, played by Bülow, and the duet from Wagner's *Der fliegende Holländer*, sung by Feodor and Rosa von Milde.

Naturally my friend and I made sure not to miss even the rehearsals. Hardly had Liszt noticed us in the hall when he greeted us in his overwhelming way and invited us to visit him at the Hôtel de Bavière, where we found a swarm of his pupils and friends, among them his youthful image, his son Daniel, as well as Richard and Johanna Pohl, the latter having undertaken the harp part in the Liszt works. The concert was sold out, the performance magnificent. Never have I seen a more ideal figure as a conductor than Liszt. Animated though he could be at rehearsals, such a transfigured peace—not an artificial one, not the kind of pose adopted by certain great names in conducting of the present day—came over him at the performance. But as well as applause there was also, in *Mazeppa*, some hissing. It was the opening chord with its shrill shriek that frightened the Leipzigers right at the start. The choice of this particular work was too daring, smacked too much of the unusual: Liszt presented his contemporaries with innovations all at once. Only decades later was it able to gain acceptance.

At the entry of the triangle in the Piano Concerto, Rietz was seen to leave the hall.* In those days they were more sensitive than now,† when Mahler's introduction into the orchestra of cowbells, hammers, and the like has hardened us.[2]

Liszt stayed on in Leipzig for a few days, to conduct a performance of *Tannhäuser* at the City Theatre.

Liszt to Wilhelm von Lenz. Weimar, 24 March. I am still nailed to my bed by a lot of boils which are flourishing on my legs, and which I take to be the exit doors for the illness which has been troubling me rather violently since the end of October.[3]

To Eduard Liszt, 26 March. Your last letter again gave me great joy, because of your loving understanding of my works. That in composing them I do not adopt a hit-or-miss attitude and grope about in the dark, as my opponents in so many quarters reproach me with doing, will be gradually acknowledged by those of them who may be honest enough not to wish entirely to obstruct a right *insight* into the matter through *prejudice*. Having now for several years been fully conscious of my artistic task, I shall lack neither the consistent perseverance nor the quiet deliberation needed

* Liszt mentioned this in a letter to the Princess, adding that Rietz had 'listened without shuddering to the much more frequently employed triangle in Vieuxtemps' concerto which had been given shortly before'.

† La Mara was writing some sixty years later.

to fulfil it. May God's blessing, without which nothing can prosper and bear fruit, rest on my work![4]

In April, *Georg von Schultz* (1808–75), an Estonian doctor and writer of German origin who lived at St Petersburg and was a friend (and biographer) of Henselt, visited Weimar, whence he wrote to his wife on the 27th.

I have just spent a couple of hours with Liszt—a man of genius! He is a strict Catholic and has just composed a beautiful Psalm. On Saturday he will be conducting *Lohengrin*. Should I hear this Wagneriad again? I think it's my duty; but it lasts from 6 until 10.30, and Liszt himself—so they say—dozes off during the performance. He nothing short of tyrannizes the Weimarians. When a mistake is made in an opera, he springs up as though it were a rehearsal and shouts: 'From such and such a place again!'—and in the presence of the court too! But the audience claps its approval and is proud to have so energetic a conductor.[5]

Liszt to his mother, 27 April. I am glad that Rubinstein's success* has so pleasantly reminded you of the applause bestowed upon me before my journey to Italy. My own memory of that time, and even of the period following it, which surrounded me with still more pomp and hullabaloo, is somewhat dim and nebulous. Whatever people may say, I feel conclusively that the foundations of my true fame and of the real purpose of my life as an artist have been laid only by my works of the last four to five years. Through them alone will my name go honourably down to posterity, which will base its judgement on what I achieve and not on the hostility shown to me and the attacks committed upon me, to which I shall probably be subjected lifelong thanks to the envy and jealousy clinging to me. Instead of regretting that I turned my back on an activity now over and done with, I am more inclined to reproach myself for not having finished with it ten years earlier. And indeed I would have done so, had I not, because of obligations undertaken, had to be preoccupied with earning money.

If, dearest Mother, we are not of the same opinion in this matter, I know all the same that you are not angry with me because I am incapable of subordinating my higher convictions to the vacillating goodwill of the public. I believe I can promise you with certainty that my works will have greater justice done to them when they are better understood and judged more impartially than at present, when I have a very hard battle to fight—which nevertheless neither worries nor disheartens me.[6]

On 20 May Liszt arrived in Aachen, having agreed to direct the thirty-fifth Lower Rhine Music Festival, held in that city between 31 May and 2 June. Among the works to be given was Berlioz's *L'Enfance du Christ*, of which the first and last sections had to be dropped because of a singer's illness. 'Berlioz's not very kindly

* Anton Rubinstein had made a sensational appearance in Paris earlier that month.

attitude towards my activities and inclinations has become known here, and is not helping to put him in a better light, for the majority explain it simply by envy, and are perhaps not entirely mistaken,' Liszt wrote to Carolyne.

Despite a determined and vociferous opposition, led by his former friend Ferdinand Hiller, both to his conducting (above all of Handel's *Messiah*) and to his works (the First Piano Concerto, played by Bülow, and *Festklänge*), everything went very well. Bülow 'played like a lion', and *Festklänge* was a sensational success. After the final item on the last night of the festival, the burgomaster's young and pretty daughter presented Liszt with a laurel wreath, to the accompaniment of a fanfare, a shower of bouquets, and cheering from the entire audience.

In mid-July he journeyed to Berlin, to give Cosima the necessary papers for her marriage to Bülow. 'It seems to me,' he told Carolyne, 'that there is every likelihood of a happy union.'

Several boils having remained on his legs after his illness, he then returned to Aachen, where he took the waters for a few weeks. On the journey he read Chateaubriand's recently published *Mémoires d'outre-tombe*; and during his stay perused the correspondence of Goethe and Schiller, Cardinal Wiseman's *Fabiola*, and Chamfort's *Maximes, caractères et anecdotes*.* He also added the final touches to the symphonic poem *Die Ideale* (S106), orchestrated his Goethe Festival March (S115), *Huldigungsmarsch* (S357) and *Festvorspiel* (S356), and composed his *Weimars Volkslied* (S87). It may be wondered if all this left him much time to enjoy the company and person of Agnes Street-Klindworth, with whom he had arranged a clandestine meeting here.

Having gone to Berlin for Cosima's wedding on Tuesday, 18 August, Liszt returned that same evening to Weimar, accompanied by the young couple, who did not stop in the town but continued to Switzerland, where—the worst possible omen—part of their honeymoon was spent under Richard Wagner's roof.

In early September a three-day festival was held at Weimar to commemorate the centenary of the birth of the Grand Duke Carl August. The foundation stone of his monument was laid, the Goethe-Schiller monument unveiled, as also the Wieland monument, and at a Court Theatre concert on the 5th Liszt conducted the first performances of his Faust Symphony and *Die Ideale*.

It was with this festival that Franz Dingelstedt began his duties as Intendant at the Court Theatre.

On 19 August Liszt had written a friendly letter to Joseph Joachim, inviting him to attend the Carl August celebrations. 'The new musical Weimar is still so much yours by reason of many delightful memories, that it would give us all, and me especially, real pleasure to see you again at our festival.' Joachim, however, whose musical sympathies were restricted to Bach, the Viennese classics, Schumann, and Brahms, and who had never shown genuine understanding of the music of Liszt, Wagner, and their followers, replied (Göttingen, 27 August) by telling Liszt, frankly and bluntly, of the hostility he felt towards his music. Having virtually announced the severance of all relations, he concluded: 'Forgive me if I have given you a moment of sadness during your preparations for the

* Which became a favourite of his. He was particularly fond of quoting the epigram: 'Celebrity is the punishment of talent and the chastisement of merit.'

festival; I had to do it. Your awe-inspiring industry, the number of your followers, will soon console you; but when you think of this letter believe one thing of me: that I shall never cease to carry in my heart a grateful pupil's profound and faithful memory of all that you were to me, of the often undeserved praise you bestowed upon me at Weimar, of all your divine gifts by which I strove to profit.' If Joachim's courage and candour were praiseworthy, less so were the 'grateful pupil's' constant belittlement from this time forward of Liszt's music and his pronounced hostility towards a man who had shown him much kindess and whose sole 'fault' was that he had chosen to strike out on a new musical path. 'We must oust the name of Liszt' became Joachim's watchword. The two did not meet again for more than twenty years, until, impelled by regret and shame, Joachim sought a reconciliation, being then very warmly received by the greater man and musician, who had never shown rancour and never ceased to praise Joachim's musical talents.

Adelheid von Schorn. It was at the unveiling of the double statue of Goethe and Schiller that I saw for the first time how my mother stood up publicly for her friend Princess Wittgenstein. A friend whose house overlooked the square had placed it at the disposal of his acquaintances so that they might view the ceremony; and Mama had asked him for places for the Princess and her daughter. We got there early and I welcomed the ladies and Liszt at the front door. Upstairs, my mother took them to the window reserved for them. In the rooms there was a crowd of people known to us, mostly women. When they saw the Princess they all conspicuously withdrew, so that we suddenly found ourselves alone. That did not escape Liszt, and he kissed Mama's hand, thanking her with special warmth for having taken care of the Princess and her daughter. He then went to one of the stands erected for the invited guests, and we stayed at the corner window from which we had a very good view over the whole festival area. The unveiling was performed reverentially, and a great emotional feeling of mingled joy and solemnity came over the assembled throng when the covering fell and the two beloved figures were seen standing out in their bright golden splendour against the dark blue sky.[7]

A visitor to both the festival and the Altenburg was Bedřich Smetana (1824–84), whom Liszt had captivated and inspired with his Prague concerts of 1840, given much help and encouragement to in 1848 and thereafter (particularly in the matter of finding a publisher for the Six Characteristic Pieces, Op. 1, which Smetana dedicated to him), and seen frequently during his visit to Prague in 1856. An incident involving both great composers, and also the Viennese conductor Johann von Herbeck (1831–77), is told by *Václav Novotný* (1849–1922), as related to him by Smetana himself.

The question arose in conversation as to what had been achieved by individual nations in the field of music, and Herbeck seized the opportunity to launch a scathing attack upon the honour of the Czechs. Scornfully he turned to Smetana: 'What have you Czechs produced as yet? Nothing but itinerant fiddlers who like good artisans have mastered merely the technical side of the art of music! To the creative development of the art you have contributed nothing, not a single work animated by anything that could be called a Czech spirit, or which by its originality could be considered in any way to have enriched European music!'

These words pierced Smetana's very soul. He could not but be aware that they contained a serious accusation which at the beginning of the nineteenth century was not without justification. It was generally known that the Czechs consistently provided all military bands and theatre orchestras with instrumentalists, who as mere 'players' were always dependent on the creative artists whose works they performed. And in view of the vast number of these 'players', the little group of creatively gifted musicians who had been born in Bohemia, but who roamed the world becoming estranged from the Czech spirit and mere epigoni of celebrated foreign masters, dwindled into insignificance.

Smetana was very conscious of all this, and he felt that in much of what he said his antagonist was only too right. To find a fitting reply was not easy. He began by mentioning the names of earlier musicians of Czech origin, Mysliveček in particular.

'You call him Czech?' laughed Herbeck. 'Under the name of Venatorini he wrote Italian operas to Italian texts in an Italian style!'

'And Tomášek?' persisted Smetana.

'Well,' retorted Herbeck, 'we all know how in everything he did he timidly followed Mozart, the German master!'

Smetana had to content himself with referring to the outstanding musical gifts of the Czech people, who among the nations of Europe had been the very first to understand the epoch-making works of this great master and pay him due tribute. 'Yes! Smetana is right! It was for his beloved Prague that Mozart wrote his *Don Giovanni*!' cried the other musicians in the circle.

But this agreement so provoked the hot-tempered Herbeck that he could not refrain from exclaiming: 'Hah, this Prague has been gnawing long enough at that old bone of Mozart's!'

Smetana sprang up as though bitten by a serpent, his eyes flashing in justified anger. It was at this point that Liszt, who had been following the exchange with a quiet smile, held up his hand soothingly, took some sheets of music from the table and seated himself at the piano with the words: 'Allow me, gentlemen, to give you a sample of the latest authentic Czech music!'

Whereupon he played the first three of Smetana's Six Characteristic Pieces—played them with the unsurpassable enchantment of genius.

Having come to an end, he shook hands with Smetana, who had been moved to tears, and took his leave of the company with the words: 'Here you have the composer with the genuine Czech spirit, the God-inspired artist!'

Herbeck had got over his fit of rage. Stretching out his hand to Smetana, he apologized for his ill humour.[8]

In mid-September Blandine Liszt became engaged to a rising young French lawyer, Emile Ollivier (1825–1913).* Having first met at Madame d'Agoult's salon in Paris, they had drawn closer together as members of a group (which included Mme d'Agoult herself) visiting Italy; and it was from Florence (where Ollivier's father was living in exile) that Blandine wrote to Liszt with the news. 'I was not your daughter for nothing,' she told him. 'It was in its love for you that my heart grew and developed, and I did not believe I could ever meet anyone else to love. . . . Now I have met what I did not hope to find, and it only remains for you to bless our union.'

In the evening of Thursday, 22 October, Liszt's forty-sixth birthday, the date specially chosen by Blandine, the marriage took place at Florence Cathedral. Liszt found it impossible to be present, but sent his blessing and expressed full approval of the match. 'Thought of you will be alive in my heart,' Blandine told him, 'and you will be more present than the witnesses.'

In early November, he, the Bülows, and the Princesses were all in Dresden for the world première, at the Theatre Royal on the 7th, of the Dante Symphony. New and difficult, and badly handicapped by lack of rehearsals, it was a total failure.

Cosima von Bülow to Emma Herwegh, November. At Dresden I heard my father's Dante Symphony and *Prometheus*. And, to tell you the truth, the two poems seem to me to be no more than libretti prepared for my father's music: they were created and bound, and then had for long centuries to wait amidst mankind's ignorance and incomprehension until HE came to release, illumine, and glorify them. I firmly believe that the *Divina Commedia* and *Prometheus* awaited my father just as, in Hell, Adam and Eve awaited the Messiah.[9]

At Breslau on 10 November, Moritz Schön conducted the first performance of *Héroïde funèbre*, a symphonic poem fashioned, as has been noted, from the early Revolutionary Symphony. And on 29 December Weimar's Court Theatre saw yet another Liszt première, that of *Hunnenschlacht*, conducted by the composer.

1858

On New Year's Day Blandine and her husband arrived in Weimar to spend a few days with Liszt, his first meeting with his new son-in-law. 'I am very pleased with both of them,' he wrote to a friend.

* Also a politician, whom in Jan. 1870 Napoleon III asked to form a government. He is generally remembered, and censured, for the 'light heart' with which later that year he took his country into the disastrous Franco-Prussian War. The words were unfortunate, but, as he explained at the time, they meant merely 'with a heart not weighed down by self-reproach, with a heart that is confident we shall come through the war we are waging, for our cause is just and entrusted to the French army'.

During the early part of the year the composer *Wendelin Weissheimer* (1838–1910), at this time still a student, came to Weimar to attend a performance of *Lohengrin*. It had been cancelled, however, and Weissheimer and his friends instead received an invitation to visit Liszt.

Up we went through the fir copse with its 'three times thirty steps' (to quote Schiller), and to the Altenburg, dwelling-place of the Mighty One. From the upper floor piano passages rolling like thunder boomed out towards us, and, our expectations pitched at their highest, we entered. Liszt was seated at a grand pianoforte, a group of delighted ladies and gentlemen all around him. When he heard of our ill-fated *Lohengrin* trip he at once came over to us and asked, most charmingly, if there were something he could play for us as a small consolation. Remembering Wagner's enthusiastic description of Liszt's playing of the *Hammerklavier* Sonata, I gave my reply without hesitation: if Dr Liszt would give us the treat of hearing him in Beethoven's Op. 106, it would be a favour that we could not treasure too highly. With a beaming smile he consented at once. Seating himself at the piano and placing us around him, he began to prelude; as the fancy took him, to begin with, and then more and more in the manner of Beethoven—until at last the principal theme of the opening movement boomed forth in all its splendour, and the colossal work was under way. In such glory might this majestic, overwhelming theme have sprung from the mind of its divine creator himself some forty years earlier, just as it was now brought to life again before his astonished audience by the wonder-working hands of Franz Liszt. How the *piano* murmured after the fermata, and how expressive the return *poco a poco crescendo* to the *forte*, until the instrument trembled as for a second time the gigantic theme rose up before us like some towering rock. What sparkle there was in the soft but so eloquent quaver passage for both hands; and how lucidly it was all brought out, not the least detail being overlooked. Who could pen even an approximate description of it all! We had heard the unbelievable— and *seen* it too, for Liszt's features played their part with the rest! He had opened the music only *pro forma*. Standing beside him, and allotted the task of turning the pages, in my emotion I sometimes forgot to—but without incommoding him in the least: he knew the whole work by heart.

The profound Adagio, one of Beethoven's longest and most soul-stirring, became a true revelation as rendered by Liszt. The opening sounded as solemn as though performed by wind instruments. As is well known, when he had already reached the stage of correcting the engraving, Beethoven decided to make a new introductory bar precede this wonderfully solemn theme; and so important did he deem this addition, that at his wish a new plate had to be engraved, it being impossible to fit the bar to the old one. It provides a kind of intimation of what is to come. The new bar, if arranged for orchestral instruments, would be given to a string quartet; the second bar, to wind instruments. Perhaps this was Liszt's view too, for at the beginning of the second bar he quickly touched the lower octave of Beethoven's keynote, as if the inserted introductory bar (in the double-basses) had only here come to an end. A whole orchestra could be heard in Liszt's performance of this Adagio, such as for example the deepest notes of the tuba at the entry of the second theme in the major, and expressive violin passages in the demisemiquaver figures at the return of the first. The expression with which he rendered this important figuration it is quite impossible to describe, as also the frisky playfulness with which he performed the Scherzo. The leaping triplets in the left hand were played in the most eminent sense of the word 'virtuosic'; and in the Prestissimo the F major scale swept in a *split second* up the entire length of the keyboard from bottom to top—like raging storm and flashing lightning!

Of the Largo which forms a kind of prelude to the great fugue of the last movement, Liszt made a poem of infinite melancholy, sweet dreaminess, and sudden exultation. It was as though the two of them, Beethoven and Liszt, had mobilized all their powers to accomplish the gigantic fugal feat—the former in its creation, the latter in the conquest of its immense difficulties. Just as Beethoven in the inexorable flow of his thoughts almost entirely forgot that he was writing the work for the piano, whose scope it had unquestionably gone far beyond, so Liszt likewise soon seemed to forget that he was dealing with a limited keyboard instrument: he again played an *orchestra* on it, with all possible and quite unbelievable doublings. Thus, shortly before the end of the twelve-page fugue, where the hands of ordinary mortals threaten to drop from the keyboard from sheer exhaustion, he was still able to set before his astounded listeners six *octave trills, with turn*, one after another *in both hands*, instead of the usual simple trills; and yet with such mighty power that it was as though he had only just begun and was about to reward the piano, now quivering in all its joints, by dealing it its death blow. Into my mind unbidden there came Heine's sally—that every Erard piano in Paris 'trembled' when Liszt so much as arrived in the city to *announce* a concert. And yet with even the most demoniacal display of strength, he at no time harmed the instrument: he knew exactly how far he could go; and when a *piano* passage came, it whispered under his hands with a sweet and tender magic that only Liszt could conjure up. We had involuntarily to hold our breath when the wonderful *cantabile* passage in D, which briefly interrupts the fugal figuration, he caused to sound like a quiet and infinitely heartfelt prayer—a passage among the most sublime that Beethoven created, and to which the entire music literature has but *one* companion piece to offer: bars 10–25 of the E flat major Prelude in the first book of Bach's *Well-Tempered Clavier*.

All aglow from the memorable treat we had enjoyed, and filled with gratitude for such princely generosity, we took our leave of the great master; and still aglow we arrived back in Leipzig, where naturally we did not fail to tell our colleagues of the joyous event, for which we were envied not a little.[1]

On 5 March Liszt arrived in Prague, where at a concert on the 11th he conducted performances of the Dante Symphony and *Die Ideale*, and Tausig was soloist in the Concerto in A. During a rehearsal on the 10th he was given an agreeable intimation of how the symphony would be received on this occasion. 'Here's a phenomenon for you!' he wrote to Carolyne. 'Somewhere in the middle of Francesca's melody about a hundred people began to applaud enthusiastically, in such a manner as almost to bring the rehearsal to a halt. My arms fell to my sides. In this respect, as you know, I am not used to being spoilt, except by my very dear domestic critic, to whom I owe all that is sweet and good in my poor life.'

The concert was a great success, and after the final chords of the symphony the composer was recalled half a dozen times.

On the 14th there was another successful concert, this time at the Prague Conservatoire.

Liszt then moved on to Vienna, where Daniel was living (temporarily sharing Tausig's hotel room) and doing well in his law studies. On 22 March (and again on the 23rd) a successful performance of the Gran Mass was given. Earlier that day the composer was granted an audience with the Emperor.

On the 30th he took a steamer down the Danube to Pest, where he stayed at the home of his friend Count Guido Karácsonyi.

Liszt to Princess Carolyne. Pest, 1 April. Oh, why do I not know how to paint, were it only water-colours for Magne's [Princess Marie's] portfolios, and why cannot I stay peacefully at home without having to take part in all the discordant hullabaloo of the world! The necessity of dragging my person about in public, and of needing the co-operation of so many other individuals before my work can be produced, I am finding more and more unbearable. Truly, after the dancer the musician is the most badly placed of all artists when, as I do, he finds the hubbub of the human anthill a distressing spectacle. The advantage possessed by painters, sculptors, and writers, of being able to put forth their ideas with no intermediary other than colour, marble, and typography, and to lead quiet, withdrawn lives independently of other human beings, strikes me as a boon beyond compare. And so I should greatly envy them, did I not know that each of us must bear his cross in this world and trust only in the Good Lord![2]

On 10 April the Gran Mass was 'perfectly performed' in the festival hall of the National Museum, the takings of 1,000 forints being set aside for the Pest Conservatoire. The next day it was repeated, this time at the Inner City Church. After receiving a deputation from the Conservatoire, who had come to thank him for the previous day's gift, Liszt then went to the Franciscan Church, where in a solemn ceremony he was made a *confrater*. On the 12th he returned, via Pozsony, to Vienna.

Here, on the 14th, he was presented with a solid-silver music-rack adorned with busts of Beethoven, Weber, and Schubert. Later that day he played at a soirée given by Countess Bánffy.

On 23 April he arrived at the town of Löwenberg (in Silesia), where with Bülow and Tausig he was the guest of Prince Constantin von Hohenzollern-Hechingen (1801–69), a keen music-lover whose private orchestra greeted Liszt on his arrival with performances of *Tasso* and *Les Préludes*. 'The Prince is most affectionately cordial towards me, and indignant about the attacks to which I am subjected,' he told Carolyne.

Via Berlin, where he spent a day or two with Cosima, Liszt returned to Weimar on 2 May.

Peter Cornelius to his sister Susanne. Weimar, 6 May. Liszt has now gone through two thirds of my opera* with me. His ability to grasp things instantaneously is altogether remarkable. The overture, for example, he understood immediately, exactly as I had meant it, and he considered it pretty well concocted. The further we went into the work, the more it interested him, and after our second session he expressed himself very favourably about it to various people (the Princess, Dingelstedt, Lassen,† and so on). The Princess, Princess Marie, and Miss Anderson congratulated me. Liszt told the Princess that Berlioz (with whose style in *Cellini* there is a certain similarity) might well envy me the work. What pleases me is that Liszt finds my *forms* very sound and *creative*, so that when he makes suggestions for improvement of the orchestration, he leaves the forms quite untouched, and regards the melody and harmonization as for the most part extremely interesting and piquant.

His dislike of the subject-matter remains (unexpressed for the present!) the same! That is quite natural, as comedy is far from being his own line. But if *he* finds the music excellent, and Schöll and others the text, then eventually there will be some kindly souls who will enjoy both the one and the other when presented entertainingly. Lassen and Tausig, for example, enter *very* much into the humour of the thing. Just imagine, the razor minuet was a marvellous hit with Liszt; he was only astonished, and annoyed, that he could not at once play it at sight, although this greatly amused him afterwards. But sometimes in other places too he involuntarily burst into such laughter that I could hardly go on singing.[3]

A visitor in June was the great German dramatist Friedrich Hebbel (1813–63), author of the *Nibelungen* trilogy. 'I spent some lovely days in Weimar,' he told a friend, 'especially at the Altenburg. As a layman, I can pass no opinion on Liszt's music—but he has gathered about him a circle the like of which I have never yet seen in this world. I felt as though I were "on an island in the heavenly heights".'

Hebbel to his wife. Weimar, 26 June. In the evening a great gathering at the Altenburg. Liszt played—which he is said to do very seldom now—his

* *The Barber of Bagdad*, Cornelius's comic masterpiece to his own libretto, received its first performance at the end of the year.

† The Danish composer and conductor Eduard Lassen (1830–1904) succeeded Liszt as Court Kapellmeister. Among his best works are his songs, two of which Liszt transcribed for piano solo: *Löse, Himmel, meine Seele* (S494) and *Ich weil' in tiefer Einsamkeit* (S495).

gypsy-rhapsodies, and utterly electrified me. At the piano he is a demigod; and behind him, in Russo-Polish national costume with a tiara and golden tassels, stood the young Princess turning the pages, a task which compelled her at times to pass her hand right through his long hair, sent fluttering all around him in the heat of his playing. It was as fantastical as a dream![4]

Liszt to Agnes Street-Klindworth, 26 June. One number still lacking to make my symphonic poems a round dozen (for the Faust and Dante symphonies are separate), I have just brought forth a *Hamlet.** We tried it out yesterday with the orchestra. I am not displeased with it—he will remain just as he is: pale, fevered, suspended between heaven and earth, the prisoner of his doubt and irresolution![5]

A visitor to the Altenburg in July was *Otto Roquette.*

The house was not empty of guests, some of whom had been staying there for months. All residents went their own ways quite independently of one another, coming together only for the two meals, which took place at midday and at seven. These apart, and if no special arrangements had been made, all were free to come and go as they wished. One of my fellow-guests was the painter Wilhelm von Kaulbach, then at the height of his powers and ever a stimulating companion. Varnhagen von Ense,† whom I had not seen for a long time and only now got to know, came too, with his niece Ludmilla Assing. Acquaintances of longer standing—Preller, Herr von Beaulieu, and Genast among others—were also visited again, and then themselves put in an appearance at the Altenburg. There was much to be seen and heard, especially the music-making which took place every Sunday morning.

My own relationship to the music which the house stood for, was, frankly, rather a strange one. For the so-called 'Music of the Future' I could acquire no real taste at all; and since I never kept my opinions to myself, and always expressed my views readily and uninhibitedly, they called me the 'enfant terrible', as someone of whose judgements they were terrified, but which they also challenged good-humouredly, laughing and making merry at such heresies. Liszt said he would punish me for my 'bad jokes' by giving me a better musical education, and soon I really did receive a punishment for each of my musical impertinences; indeed, I increased these so as to be punished still more, since it was a punishment that anyone would envy me. For Liszt played to me—mostly in private—all his symphonic poems, but also sonatas by Beethoven, and ultimately

* S104, composed as a prelude to Shakespeare's tragedy. The short central section depicting Ophelia was added later.

† Varnhagen and his niece stayed in Weimar from 26 July to 3 August. Having, on their arrival at the station, run unexpectedly into Liszt and the Princess (who greeted them with 'cries of joy'), they visited the Altenburg on several occasions, and were also accompanied by the Princess on excursions to local beauty spots and places of interest.

anything that I fished out and wished to hear. And thus it was that pleasures came my way which can be properly appreciated only by those who heard this true genius among artists and had come under the spell of his personality. To deny him a request was anything but easy. And indeed he then came out with one: would I write the text of a gypsy opera for him? That was something I could have done without. *The Legend of St Elisabeth* was not yet composed, and an opera libretto would take me into a genre to which I was inwardly opposed and make of me an ally of the 'Music of the Future', something I was far from being. I hesitated to give my consent, and was allowed some time to think it over. But not very much, for that same day I had to withstand an attack from the Princess, against which all I could do was insist that I would not commit myself immediately. But let no one believe he is immune from womanly wiles! They already knew how to get at me. After breakfast, Princess Marie called me into the garden to teach me badminton. The eyes of this captivating young woman had already proved more dangerous than was good for me. After we had played for a while she suddenly brought up the gypsy opera, spoke of it as though it were already agreed on, and then invited me into their private salon, which I had never previously entered, to show me pictures of gypsies and all manner of miscellaneous bits and pieces that she had collected on the Romany folk. She also gave me the book written by Liszt in French on gypsy music, which I was to read beforehand. This last was something I really did want to do, but—she was only laughing! Despite my objections, to which she vouchsafed no reply whatsoever, she would not drop the subject, put herself out to be as engaging as possible, and—what shall I say?—such charm I found impossible to resist. Princess Carolyne came after a while, learnt that I had agreed, and at once sent word to Liszt. And now I found that in consultation with the ladies the latter had already completed the entire outline of the opera's plot, which, though cleverly enough thought out, left me no freedom at all in the way I was to put it together. For this I now had to fight one step at a time, as I could not concede everything and had no desire to be tied down completely. Finally we were agreed, and I repeated my promise, albeit without either a clear conscience or a happy heart.

If I expressed my heresies against the Music of the Future more often than was necessary. . . the moment was to come in which my conversion was proclaimed amidst loud laughter. My bedroom adjoined an upper music room in which Liszt taught his pupils. Being unable to sleep one night, and deciding that perhaps my head was not high enough, I fetched from the music room a pile of scores which I put under my pillow; but neglected in the morning to take this musical base back to where it belonged. The manservant found this odd makeshift and was mischievous enough to tell my hostess. That he had done so, I was to learn only in the evening. As we sat at table, and the talk turned to music, the Princess, pointing at me, began to recount a moving example of a hitherto inveterate heretic who was now seeking the path of conversion—for every night he placed under his pillow entire bundles of pieces belonging to the new school, in the hope that by so doing he might hasten his transformation. The story made a fine joke and was told and retold, an early variant being that I refused to sleep on anything but Music of the Future. It bore no fruit however. For even now, more than thirty years later, I have become, if no firm opponent, no unconditional supporter of this school either. I put together the libretto shortly afterwards, but have never heard that it was set to music.*[6]

Another guest was *Alexander Serov*.

Yesterday [Wednesday, 28 July] Princess Wittgenstein received some twenty-five guests—a company of artists, *literati* (of whom there are plenty in Weimar), with their wives and other female relatives; the Russian priest Sabinin, whose daughter [Martha], although meagrely gifted, is a pupil of Liszt; that veteran of men of learning, Varnhagen von Ense,† et al, all in full dress. . . .

When all were assembled, Liszt went up to the magnificent grand piano and obstinately insisted on opening the musical *soirée* with—now, what do you suppose?—the duet by Vollweiler‡ on themes from *Ruslan and Lyudmila*, assisted by Fröhlich! I warned Liszt that this leather-lunged clarinettist is a horribly poor player, but, as a matter of courtesy, he did not wish to deprive Fröhlich of the flattering gratification of tooting something with Liszt! Well, they started—perhaps you remember how Fröhlich plays!! It was simply frightful! We all (one being Bärmann, the son of the finest clarinettist in the world) listened and were horrified. Liszt did his best to cover up the 'hissing' of the clarinet with the most wonderful arpeggios—but it was of no avail! While he played on and on with a smile of pitying resignation, he signalled me with his eyes to approach, and whispered in my ear: 'You are right, Serov, he's atrocious!' At last—it was really too much for him—he said: 'Well, let's have a brief pause. The gentleman needs a little rest.' Liszt having thus arranged matters after a fashion, our tortures were at an end and speedily forgotten in the joys of the ensuing rich compensation. Liszt soon sat down at the piano again (he had promised the Princess to make *much* music that evening) and played

* The manuscript of the libretto, *Kahma the Gypsy Girl*, is held at the Liszt Museum in Weimar, together with several other texts (by various authors) considered by Liszt, whose abandonment of the project of a Hungarian opera was possibly due to the unfavourable reception accorded in Hungary to his book on the Hungarian gypsies and their music.

† Whose diary shows that among the other guests that evening was Liszt's pupil Hilda Thegerström, a protégée of the Swedish composer Franz Berwald.

‡ Carl Vollweiler (1813–48), a German pianist and composer who had lived at St Petersburg. To Olga von Meyendorff, in a letter of 5 Nov. 1884, Liszt remarked: 'I used to play at the St Petersburg theatre another transcription of *Ruslan*, very brilliantly arranged by Vollweiler—an artist who died too young.'

one of his Hungarian Rhapsodies. How I felt! It seemed as if I were again in the Engelhardt Hall, or the Great Hall of the Nobility, in St Petersburg, as I was in 1842—the same beatifically transfigured countenance of that 'artist of all artists', the same electrical, magnetical, magical ascendancy over his listeners, the same virtuosity to which nothing on earth is comparable, that knows no difficulties, and yet is but the *servant* of the thought. To me it is a matter for wonderment how the concert-giving pianists (not excepting even Clara Schumann) can ever venture to present themselves to the public so long as such a *daemon* of pianistic art exists in the world! If there be a disparity between the Liszt of today and the earlier Liszt, it is, outwardly, *only* that he has grown gray, and, inwardly, *only* that he plays even more enchantingly and composes incomparably better. (Yesterday, before the *soirée*, he played—entre nous—some fragments from his *Legend of St Elisabeth*; the music is truly marvellous in its simplicity, the melody—*genuine*—to say nothing at all about the rest, for this 'rest' is a matter of course in the works of *such* a brain.) When he had displayed the wonders of his Rhapsody—sometimes replete with trills and figurations, while in other passages the piano was transformed into a 'steel-ribbed Leviathan', and with the piano vibrated Liszt, and all of us, and the entire room—after all these wonders he arose, radiant with the aureole of his renown (you remember how his face is *transfigured* when he is *playing*), and was instantly surrounded by his guests, especially the ladies, who always and everywhere overwhelm him with compliments. People of our sort find it rather difficult to say anything whatever to him. Liszt is so *frightfully* clever, so surfeited with adulation, that any expression of enthusiasm must seem to him like a platitude. Still, I felt unable to renounce the pleasure of saying a word or two to him; he was really pleased, and pressed my hand heartily, remarking: 'No more of your compliments, my *new old* friend!'. . . Following the Rhapsody, Miss Genast* sang very charmingly two songs by Liszt: *Ueber allen Gipfeln ist Ruh* (Goethe) and *Die Loreley* (Heine) [S273]. He *himself* accompanied her. The *Loreley* is supremely beautiful. . . . Then he played again, this time his Fantasy on *Don Giovanni* (with a good many cuts—he omitted all the variations on *Là ci darem la mano*). Therewith ended the concert, for which many people would have been glad to pay no end of money! And now, what can one say to people who assert that Liszt has *forgotten* how to play the piano, or to others who deny him a talent for composition!!

We supped at small tables in two rooms (champagne, truffles, ices). Liszt seated me in the place of honour, that is, next to himself (on his right sat

* Genast's daughter, Emilie or 'Mitzi' (1833–1905), from 1863 Frau Merian, was the possessor of a mezzo-soprano voice whose great quality inspired not a few of Liszt's *Lieder*. 'You bear most blame for my song-stuttering,' he told her jocularly. The Princess was later to believe, with or without justification, that after her own departure from Weimar (May 1860) Emilie became Liszt's mistress.

the very pretty Miss Genast). Tell me, may I not rightly say of myself that I am dwelling somewhere on *Olympus*? I can't imagine how I ever got up there.[7]

Elsewhere, Serov described Liszt as being 'still the same, a giant compared with whom all other pianists are pygmies'. 'At one of his matinées he played Beethoven's Op. 106. The performance was a veritable act of creation. He himself was deeply moved, and he reduced all of us to tears. For such moments it would be worth journeying from Petersburg to Weimar on foot!'

Varnhagen's diary, 2 August. To lunch at the Altenburg. The French Ambassador introduced the new Secretary of his Legation, a Count von Mulinen. . . . At the meal were Roquette, Serov, Fräulein Soest from Erfurt, and Music Director Montag from Weimar. Liszt has gathered about him here a great number of pupils of both sexes, to whom he diligently gives lessons. He works hard, and most hours of the day are employed.

After the meal, two Fräulein Stark from St Petersburg arrived with their mother. Unexpectedly, Liszt said that he wished to play to us. General rejoicing! First of all he played Hungarian gypsy-rhapsodies, then a sonata by Henselt. No words can describe the power of this magic, and the great master was greeted with a tempest of delighted applause. As he was not satisfied with the piano, we went to an upper room, where others were standing about—fourteen in all, among them a curious one containing three strata of keyboards. Once again he played with captivating mastery; one felt blessed, uplifted, and refreshed by his virtuosity.

The rainy weather notwithstanding, the Princess drove with us to Osmannstedt, where we made a careful inspection of Wieland's house, garden, and grave. . . . On the way we had much lively conversation, and once again I had to talk a good deal about Rahel,* the Princess being most eager to form a clear picture of her.[8]

Enjoying a 'Russian anecdote' told by Liszt after a court dinner on 11 August, Frédéric Soret recorded it in his diary. With his great hunting-dog bringing up the rear, Tsar Nicholas got into a droshky to go for a ride. The dog stopped by a boundary post, and the carriage remained stationary. 'Well, what's happening?' cried the Tsar brusquely; 'are we leaving or not?'—'Forgive me, Sire,' replied the driver; 'it's His Excellency, who hasn't finished yet!'

On the 27th, Liszt and the two Princesses set out for a holiday in the Austrian Tyrol, where a 'profound impression' was made upon him by Lake Achen and the Oetz valley. They also stayed at Innsbruck. Then came three weeks in Munich, for the festivities celebrating its 700th anniversary, after which he spent a few days in Salzburg, returning to Weimar on 20 October.

* Perhaps the most distinguished woman in German history, Rahel Varnhagen (1771–1833), a Jewess turned Christian who married Varnhagen in 1814, is remembered above all for the encouragement she gave to philosophers, poets, and artists, and for her keen support of the patriotic struggle against Napoleon.

Josephine von Kaulbach to Princess Carolyne. Munich, 22 November. King Max* visited my husband's studio today. . . and was astonished to see the portrait of the great master, Liszt. His amazement grew still greater when he heard that Liszt had been here recently. 'Why didn't he visit me? I know him well, am a friend of his. Tell him that if he comes to Munich again he is not to fail to come and see me.'[9]

Liszt to the poet Ludwig Eckardt (1827–71). Weimar, 24 November. Art is for us none other than the mystic ladder from earth to Heaven—from the finite to the Infinite—from mankind to God: an everlasting aspiration and impulse towards redemption through love![10]

In early December Liszt went to Coburg (reading on the journey A. B. Marx's book on the life and works of Beethoven), having received from Duke Ernst an invitation to attend the première of the latter's opera *Diana von Solange*.

A December visitor to Weimar, where she sang the title role in *Norma*, was *Pauline Viardot-Garcia*, who described her meetings with Liszt in letters to her friend Julius Rietz.

Weimar, Sunday, 12 December. Liszt has taken supper with me. He has only just gone away, and I shall not go to bed until I have told you that *Norma* went off quite well, that your friend was very well received and appreciated, and that I felt *present* tears welling in many *future*† eyes. Liszt assured me that he was deeply moved and enthusiastic—if I were sure that he was telling the truth I should be very glad. Yesterday he played for me—no one can play as he does—and altogether enchanted me. I heard the Rhapsodies and the *Funérailles* from his *Harmonies*. Do you know the latter? It is really very interesting, and in my opinion very easy to understand. Today I was at the Altenburg again to give my voice some practice, and heard something that pleased me less: *Orpheus*, arranged for two pianos. Too inchoate for my taste—and yet it has form, and there is a desire of melody in it. But one must admit that he is a most attractive person. It is quite impossible for anyone to be kinder than he is to me. He is very unaffected with me, which makes him doubly charming; he is even childlike, and I believe it comes naturally, for he has known me since my childhood . . . perhaps he knows that he would be wasting his efforts, and so welcomes the opportunity to find rest and relaxation with someone from his constant mental tension.

Wednesday, 4 o'clock. Here I am, back from the Altenburg once again. They are beginning to like me a little there—I go in and out without the least ceremony, as much as I please, and their faces look really delighted when I enter the Princess's rooms. Liszt is charming to me, but all our ideas

* King of Bavaria from 1848 until his death in 1864, Maximilian II was the father of Ludwig II (1845–86), Wagner's patron.

† A reference to the 'Music of the Future'—of which Rietz was a diehard opponent.

are too different for there ever to be complete sympathy between us. He has not a *friend's nature*. . . . he cannot assimilate his own life with someone else's, or blend his heart with another heart. His personal vanity is far too great for that. He would think it a comedown from his rank as an exceptional man, towering above everyone! I don't wish to speak badly of him, for despite all that I am very fond of him, and, I repeat, he treats me with much affection—only I believe that the flame in his heart is nothing but a straw fire. Moreover, I find a dreadful lot of ashes in that heart of his—poor devil; I believe he is thoroughly *unhappy*. There is a bitter sadness in him deep down, which arouses my pity and increases my affection for him. Now and then he comes to spend an hour or two quietly with me. It does him a lot of good, he says, and rejuvenates him. The life he has led has aged him within—and the one he is leading now is totally lacking in tranquillity and refreshment. If I were in his place, I should greatly fear the Tsar of Russia giving his consent to his marriage with the Princess, and I believe that in his own mind this idea does not seem particularly attractive.

Thursday, 1 o'clock. He is a man of honour and, should *the fatal day* arrive, will do his duty *decently*. More probably, the Princess will not consent to risk losing the power she now has over him as his mistress, by becoming his wife. . . .

Now I must break off again; I have to go to the Altenburg—I am invited there every day. But I find the atmosphere artificial. The P. acts so very affectedly all the time! Don't think I am too prudish—no, not that—I understand that a woman can and must sacrifice everything to the man she loves—I can even admire a liaison of that sort, and prefer it a hundred times to the hypocritical virtue of an unfaithful wife; but, my God, I can feel no *sincerity* between L and the P., for sincerity cannot be other than simple.[11]

On Wednesday, 15 December, Cornelius's *The Barber of Bagdad* was given its première. Liszt conducted the performance, which adversaries covertly organized by Dingelstedt endeavoured to wreck by booing and hissing. The real target was not Cornelius's sparkling music but Liszt himself. So appalled was the latter at this reception accorded to an outstanding work by a protégé, and at such a culmination to his own long years of toil at Weimar, that he resigned his official duties in the musical life of the town.

Cornelius to his sister Susanne. Weimar, 17 December. My opera was given before a full house. The performance took the entire evening, and, considering the difficulty of the work, was an excellent, first-rate one. A hostile faction, such as has not been known in the annals of Weimar, opposed the applause right from the start with determined hissing; its members were hired, well organized, and suitably scattered. They inhibited the artists' humour but could exert no harmful effect on the excellence of the performance. At the end, a battle ten minutes long broke out. The Grand Duke applauded incessantly, but the boos continued none the less. Finally, Liszt and the orchestra applauded, and Frau von Milde dragged me out on to the stage.

Dear Susanne! From now on I am an artist whose name will also be known in more distant circles. With one strong jerk my whole being has been lifted up. Until my last breath I shall go my way more zealously than ever.

My gain in experience is rich and splendid after this one evening. Soon I shall be busy on a second work—this time a highly serious and pathetic one [*The Cid*]. The artists are *all* enthusiastically on my side. Liszt's behaviour to me is incomparable. May all those who wish me well stand up body and soul for this man, who is the standard-bearer of a new age.

The Grand Duke received me yesterday; he was extremely gracious and encouraging, and predicted glory for me. In the course of conversation Liszt said: 'Your Royal Highness! Cornelius is a noble-minded man.'[12]

To the same, 18 December. I am glad to be able to tell you briefly something about the celebrations of yesterday evening, when, not too sure what to expect after recent events, I went to the theatre. In my prologue I had made a clear reference to Liszt; but, whatever the outcome was to be (for the opposition is aimed not at me but at him), this time I had no intention of making myself invisible.

Going to the stalls as usual, I sat in the very front row. The opening bars of the Overture *The Consecration of the House* rang out—and then broke off. The curtain rose and, with fine, manly composure and infectious enthusiasm, Milde read my prologue to the Beethoven birthday celebrations. But he was no more than half-way through when applause broke out and acquaintances were clapping me on the back and wanting to shake my hand. At the end there was long applause, and with quiet satisfaction I was waiting for Milde to reappear, when, instead, they hurried to the stalls to fetch—me! I hastened to go up, cast aside hat and gloves—fortunately I was wearing evening dress—and with Milde stepped out before a large, enthusiastically applauding audience. . . .

The concert then continued with exemplary solemnity. After the Symphony in A there was a storm of applause, whose waves subsided only when, amidst the loudest and most enthusiastic acclaim, Liszt returned to the podium. When he had stood on it today, so overpowering had been his daemon that I had often not dared look at him. This concert was also his last public appearance for the present. As they have ventured to maltreat a protégé of his, he is handing over stage and pit to the General Intendant, Dingelstedt.[13]

Cornelius to his brother Carl, 19 December. There is to the beginning of my career a strange significance: that my humble self should spark the final break between Liszt and Dingelstedt. Liszt wants—Art; Dingelstedt—himself. Hence the conflict.[14]

Pauline Viardot-Garcia to Julius Rietz. Paris, 27 December. I assure you that Liszt is infinitely better than his reputation, and his music too. He should not be made responsible for the absurdities that fanatics write and perpetrate. I had a long chat with him on the subject, and he is *almost* right when he says: 'I deplore their stupidities; I am the victim of them, and find it outrageous that they should be laid at my door—yet I cannot disown these young people, whatever harm they do me.' We parted very good friends. He has been charming to me; I have again found my dear Liszt of times gone by. After him, I shall not for a long time be able to listen to anyone else playing the piano. He is still *the colossus*.[15]

1859

Pauline Viardot-Garcia to Princess Carolyne. Paris, 10 January. If you but knew, Princess, the questions I am overwhelmed with here about the *maître*—and the astonishment caused by my replies! For sheer credulity and absurdity even the Yankees are no match for these Parisians! They find it difficult to believe that Liszt walks only with his feet, that he sees only with his eyes, and that he talks just like a normal human being! His hair is longer than the comet's tail, and he can no longer bear the sound of the piano! In fact, the *Thousand and One Nights* have nothing to offer in comparison with the fantastic nonsense spouted about the Altenburg. Liszt should put an end to it by showing that fine, noble head of his here. His simple, eloquent manner of speaking would very quickly convince all these unbelievers that he is just the same Liszt as of old—only simpler and greater.[1]

At a concert in Berlin on 14 January, Hans von Bülow experienced a failure with Liszt's symphonic poem *Die Ideale*. Princess Carolyne then offered to defray the costs of a second concert, at which Liszt himself would conduct the work; and on 24 February he travelled to Berlin, where he stayed until 3 March. Held at the Singakademie on the 27th, and including among other items two Schubert *Lieder* and Liszt's *Mignons Lied* (Goethe's 'Kennst Du das Land'), all sung by Emilie Genast, the concert was a great success.

Invited to the Bülows' home to meet Liszt were the Stahrs, Ernst Dohm, editor of the satirical magazine *Kladderadatsch*, Lilla Bulyovszky, Roquette, and Ferdinand Lassalle the socialist. He also took the opportunity to pay his respects to Alexander von Humboldt, now in his ninetieth year and soon to die. Among the concerts he attended was one given by the pianist Leopold de Meyer; on another evening he was a dinner guest of the Prince Regent and his wife (the subsequent Emperor and Empress).

On 10 April the Austrian Emperor awarded Liszt the decoration of the Iron Crown; and in consequence of this a hereditary knighthood* was later bestowed upon him. In 1867, however, having by then no male heir of his own, he was granted permission to transfer the knighthood to Eduard Liszt.

On Good Friday, 22 April, Liszt was able to write to Carolyne (visiting Munich) to say that the previous day, 'Between 9.00 and 1.00 the *Beatitudes* were composed almost in their entirety. . . . The whole thing will last only some 5 to 8 minutes; it will be finished on Monday morning.' First performed on 2 October that year (in Weimar's Stadtkirche), the *Beatitudes* (S25) were later incorporated into the oratorio *Christus*.

Accompanied by Bronsart, and by Franz Brendel (1811–68), editor from 1845 until his death of Schumann's *Neue Zeitschrift für Musik*, and a keen champion of the new German music, Liszt was in the first week of May again a guest at Löwenberg. His regime here was to remain alone in his room in the mornings, dealing with correspondence, and after lunch to take a short siesta. At 3.30 each day a programme of music was performed to the Prince, who, a gout sufferer, would be making his first appearance of the day. The evenings were passed with whist.

Leaving Löwenberg on 7 May, Liszt returned to Weimar via Breslau, where on the 12th he and his companions attended a concert given by the composer-conductor Leopold Damrosch (1832–85). *Tasso* and *An die Künstler* were both warmly applauded.

On 22 May he went to Leipzig for the Tonkünstler-Versammlung (Musicians' Gathering), held at the beginning of June. Among those present was the young Arthur Sullivan (1842–1900), then studying at Leipzig. 'Liszt, David, Bronsart and I had a quiet game of whist together, and I walked home with Liszt in the evening,' he wrote to his father. 'The next evening a grand concert in the theatre, Liszt conducting. . . . He is a very amiable man, despite his eccentricities, which are many. What a wonderful player he is! Such power and at the same time such delicacy and lightness.'

Wendelin Weissheimer. A considerable number of musicians arrived in Leipzig. There was much activity and, with so many heterogeneous elements, a lively exchange of ideas too. We were witnessing the dawn of a new era. A so-called Allgemeine Deutsche Musikverein was founded, whose object was to do everything within its power to support needy musicians, to have works by members printed and publicly performed (if deemed worthwhile by the society's committee), and above all to heal damaging rifts between various partisans. This motion was proposed by the astute Louis Köhler† of Königsberg and supported with the utmost vigour by Franz Liszt, so that it was adopted unanimously. Liszt spoke really inspiringly off the cuff, carrying the entire assembly with him. During the banquet held in the riflemen's club-house, Dr Ambros of Prague hailed Liszt as the 'protector and preserver of Art', toast followed toast, and the hundreds of table companions got into the merriest of moods. . . .

* A higher degree of nobility than a mere 'von', it would have enabled him, had he chosen, to call himself Franz Ritter von Liszt.

† Composer, writer, teacher, and pianist (1820–86).

The *artistic* highlights of this first Tonkünstler-Versammlung were: the Riedel Society's* rendering of Liszt's Gran Mass in the packed St Thomas Church; the first-ever performance of the Prelude to Wagner's *Tristan und Isolde*,† at a concert given on the stage of the old City Theatre; the recitation of Liszt's melodrama on Bürger's *Lenore* [S346]; and the first public performance of his glorious *Loreley*, in the hall of the riflemen's club-house. It will be difficult for any of those present ever to forget that performance: Liszt at the piano, and in front of him, interpreting the Loreley, Emilie Genast, one of the finest *Lieder* singers of the time!

The success of the festival was considerable and found a loud echo in the German press. . . . The musicians dispersed to the four winds, and on the first Sunday in June Liszt and I journeyed together to Weimar in his coupé, as he had told me the previous evening that I was to visit him soon, adding with a broad smile: 'You already have your *pass*, as you know.' Naturally I went there with him at once.

Already the next day I had to go to the Altenburg for dinner. Hans von Bronsart and Count Laurencin (a well-known writer on music from Vienna) had also been invited. Princess Wittgenstein did the honours of the table in the friendliest way, and Liszt, her idol, was in high good humour. The meal over, and after champagne had been served by Otto the butler, we rose from the table and repaired to the upper rooms—to the smoking room and music salon, which were actually one and the same, for smoking and music-making were inseparable for Liszt on such occasions. He always kept in readiness excellent, and unusually long, Havana cigars, which were likewise served by Otto, together with the mocha. The Princess came up with us, and when Liszt took his place at one of the two pianos she pushed an armchair up to it and sank back expectantly; she too had one of the long cigars in her mouth and was puffing away contentedly. We others drew around Liszt, who . . . sitting at his Bösendorfer once again, had the manuscript of his Faust Symphony open in front of him. I had already admired this work . . . when I had heard it performed by an orchestra under his direction two years earlier, and was delighted this time to hear it conjured up by his magic hands on the piano. Naturally he again played the *whole* orchestra; naturally, once again, his *way* of doing so went beyond anything we could have imagined; and naturally it raised us hearers to the highest pitch of exaltation. After the glorious 'Gretchen', the Princess sprang from her armchair, seized Liszt and kissed him so fervently as to move us all. (Her cigar had gone out beforehand.) There followed 'Mephistopheles', a movement as brilliant as it was daredevil, the *most perfect* rendition of which we listened to in amazement. At the entry of the *Chorus mysticus*, Liszt at first sang the theme alone, but then soon looked

* Founded at Leipzig in 1854 by the organist and composer Karl Riedel (1827–88), the Society became famous for its promotion of new works.

† Actually, the first performance had been in March that year.

around for support, which Bronsart and I at once gave him. He was thus able to devote himself entirely to the tenor solo, which he gave with full voice, while we did the chorus; but when it came to the *forte*:

> Alles Vergängliche ist nur ein Gleichnis;
> Das Unzulängliche, hier wird's Ereignis;
> Das Unbeschreibliche, hier ist's gethan.

we abandoned the chorus and in unison with Liszt sang the ravishing passage with *all the power of our lungs*. The performance of the Faust Symphony was over, and 'the indescribable, had here been done'!

Liszt now very generously gave up his precious hours to me thrice a week. Any compositions that I had ready were gone through meticulously and most painstakingly polished. One of the pianists, Bendel* or Pflughaupt,† was usually present too, or the fair-haired, red-cheeked Jungmann,‡ who like me was chiefly concerned with composition. Once our creative efforts were out of the way it was the turn of the pianists. Liszt would take his place at the second piano, and any phrase or passage not played to his satisfaction on the first would be answered, absolutely perfectly, on the second. The pupil then did his best to imitate what he had heard. If he succeeded, the second piano remained silent; if he did not, then once more the passage would ring out under Liszt's hands. Often a passage would go to and fro in this manner as much as twenty or thirty times. With Pflughaupt, Liszt's patience would occasionally run out, and allowing him no further say in the matter he would then play to the end of the particular piece himself. This of course was what was enjoyed best by all of us, Pflughaupt included. In this way we heard many of the greatest piano works, including Weber's *Concertstück* and the Beethoven concertos and sonatas, played by Liszt himself, and *one* hour usually turned into three or four. On the table there would be a lighted candle, and around it a princely selection of cigars, to which full justice had to be done. It need hardly be said that there was no question of a 'fee'—the mere mention of such a thing Liszt would have considered an insult.

During the summer Carl Tausig and the Bohemian Smetana also stayed with Liszt for a short time. Both brought works of their own with them: Tausig, among other things, the *Gespensterschiff*, a piece, not then published, containing an incredible passage which put even Liszt in difficulties. It was an ascending *chromatic* glissando ending shrilly on a top black note! After a few vain attempts, Liszt eventually said to Tausig: 'Junge, wie machst du das?' Tausig sat down, performed a glissando on the white keys with the middle finger of his right hand, while *simultaneously* making the fingers of his left hand fly so skilfully over the black

* Franz Bendel (1833–74).
† Robert Pflughaupt (1833–71).
‡ Louis Jungmann.

keys that a chromatic scale could clearly be heard streaking like lightning up the entire length of the keyboard, ending on high with a shrill 'bip'. Then Liszt had a go again, and after some half a dozen practice-runs he too finally achieved the desired high 'bip' without accident.

In contrast to Tausig, who was reserved and somewhat prone to sarcasm, Smetana was outgoing and good-humoured. The one thing he could not bear was to hear his name mispronounced. I too once thoughtlessly addressed him—he was at that time still almost completely unknown—as Smetàna. Whereupon, and without a moment's hesitation, he sang me the opening theme of the *Fidelio* overture, to the words: 'Smètana, Smètana, Smètana pro-nounce!'. . .

A big attraction were the Sunday matinées at the Altenburg, at which young Eduard Lassen, recently appointed Court Kapellmeister, the violin virtuoso and leader of the Court orchestra, Edmund Singer, and the outstanding violinist J. M. Grün seldom failed to appear. Emilie Genast and Elvira Berghaus usually sang songs by Liszt and Lassen, while Liszt and Ingeborg Stark from St Petersburg, a young and extremely pretty blonde girl who was studying with him, played piano works. For duet-playing, Liszt sometimes roped me in too. Princess Wittgenstein and her daughter were always present at these matinées, at which among other things Liszt would play his Italian opera transcriptions. When on one occasion Tausig played Chopin's *Berceuse*, he transported the entire gathering, and Liszt called out to him: 'Boy, no one else in Europe can play it like *that*!' (He was only eighteen and very short, and so was almost always called 'little Tausig'.)[2]

Ignaz Moscheles, who had also been at the Leipzig music festival, was another visitor to the Altenburg shortly afterwards.

Liszt went to the piano, and to my no small astonishment I heard my old Op. 42 Variations, which I have completely disregarded for the last forty years. He played them from memory, introducing sensational effects, and then gave us his own organ fantasy on the name BACH,* a piece full of dazzling combinations and stupendously played.[3]

On 23 June the seventy-three-year-old Maria Pavlovna passed away. How Liszt would remember his kindly music-loving patroness and employer is seen in words penned by him long afterwards: 'The late Grand Duchess Maria Pavlovna. . . whose name I shall never mention without blessings and gratitude.'

Cosima von Bülow to Emma Herwegh. In Paris, the volume *Des Bohémiens et de leur musique en Hongrie*,† by Franz Liszt, has just come

* The transcription for piano solo (S529).

† Finished in 1854 but not published until the summer of 1859. The German and Hungarian translations, by Peter Cornelius and József Székely respectively, appeared in 1861. In writing (in collaboration with Princess Carolyne) a book on the Hungarian gypsies and their music,

out. I have not yet finished it, but am delighted with it so far, although as a stupid purist I would have preferred fewer neologisms and even a less mannered archaism.

My father's *Ce qu'on entend sur la montagne* is an admirable work, simple, moving, and as profound as the eternal words which for eighteen centuries have been making our unhappy world think, weep, and hope. . . . You know his ever-productive, ever-astonishing genius, in which on one day we admire his serenity, on the next are struck by his boundless compassion and understanding of sorrow. A veritable trismegistus,* he is poet, musician, and man in the loftiest meaning of those words; and I would be quite ready to make a god of him, were it not too consoling for our poor humanity to have produced so perfect a paradigm.[4]

Liszt to Princess Carolyne, 3 September. I have been reflecting with bitter sadness on my fit of bad temper yesterday on the subject of my [*Legend of St*] *Elisabeth*. How can I possibly have caused you the least shadow of distress once again? I really cannot forgive myself! But I promise you that the *Elisabeth* will be finished sooner than you think.[5]

To Louis Köhler. Weimar, 3 September. For the very reason that people cannot (as you so wittily remark) straightaway 'index and catalogue me properly and place me in an already existing drawer', I can hope that my working and striving will eventually prove to be in accordance with the spirit of the time and bear fruit. . . . As I have often said to my friends, even if all my compositions were failures (which I neither affirm nor deny), they would not on that account be quite without their use, because of the stimulus and impetus they can give to the further development of the art. Consciousness of this so completely satisfies me that I continue to compose and persevere as I do.[6]

It was at this time that honorary membership of the Philharmonic Society of

Liszt's principal intention had been to expound and elucidate the genesis and background of his Hungarian Rhapsodies; and *Des Bohémiens et de leur musique en Hongrie* treats not only of the music and playing of the Hungarian gypsies, but also of such matters as the first appearance of the gypsy race in Europe, its character, customs, and manner of living, and its role in European art and literature. Additional interest is provided by sundry personal reminiscences of Liszt's own. These include descriptions of the great gypsy musicians he had heard in Hungary during his childhood and later, and when visiting Russia, Romania, and Spain; an account of an unforgettable impression received at a synagogue in Vienna from the singing of the celebrated Jewish precentor Salomon Sulzer; and an amusing report of the futile attempts he had made to educate a little violin-playing gypsy boy entrusted to his care in 1844. The book aroused great displeasure in Liszt's native country, owing to his well-meant but ill-conceived endeavours to show that Hungary possessed no music but that of the gypsies—the very reverse of the true situation, for what he had heard performed by the gypsies, albeit in their own manner, was actually genuine Hungarian folk-music, which was not to be studied scientifically until the advent, several decades later, of such musicians as Béla Bartók and Zoltán Kodály.

* Thrice-greatest.

London was conferred upon Liszt. In his letter of acceptance (3 September) he remarked that 'the numerous services which this renowned Society has rendered to art . . . make me attach a special value to the kindness that later on I shall be happy to deserve still more'.

At Weimar on Saturday, 15 October, Princess Marie Wittgenstein was married to Prince Constantin von Hohenlohe-Schillingsfürst (1828–96), younger brother of the Prince Chlodwig Hohenlohe who later became German Chancellor, and of the Prince Gustav Hohenlohe (1823–96) who, first as Papal Grand Almoner and then as Cardinal, was to prove a good friend to Liszt during the latter's years in Rome. Prince Constantin was himself an aide-de-camp to the Emperor Franz Joseph of Austria, and, later, Chief Comptroller of the Imperial Household. After a honeymoon visit to Russia, the young couple settled in Vienna.

Liszt to Princess Carolyne. Weimar, 20 October.* Hans [von Bülow] has communicated Wagner's letter to me, and its sense corresponds well enough with what you predicted. Although he does not explain himself clearly, and even retains a certain delicacy of language which he has not used in other circumstances, it is apparent from this letter that he wishes to put asunder those whom God hath joined; that is, you and me. He complains about my reserve, about the unbound copy of my Dante [Symphony] that I sent him (six weeks after publication!), about the unreceived copies of my Mass and the *Bohémiens*, and about Pohl's few lines† on the subject of the introduction to *Tristan*. . . . In sum, he seems to wish to insinuate to Hans that you exert a regrettable influence on me, one which is contrary to my true nature. If Wagner does not have the merit of having invented this foolish idea, I for my part shall take care not to share its absurdity. Every time people have tried to lampoon me in this way I have put a quick end to it—regarding such a falsehood as a triple injury. Wagner is now living at 16, rue Newton, avenue des Champs Elysées. Perhaps you will see him. I almost urge you to. But treat him very gently, for he is sick and incurable. That is why we must simply love him and try to serve him as best we can.[7]

Writing to Carolyne again on the 24th, Liszt referred to another great contemporary musician.

I received your sweet letter of the 21st yesterday evening, and envy you for having heard the duet from *Les Troyens*, but think it was charming of Berlioz to offer you this beautiful surprise. Poor great friend. He is making a sad departure from this world of woe, 'bleeding from every pore', as you tell me! If one could at least alleviate his troubles a little—but it is difficult

* Who after her daughter's wedding was paying a brief visit to Paris.

† In his letter of 7 Oct. to Bülow, Wagner had written: 'There are many matters which we are quite frank about among ourselves (for instance, that since my acquaintance with Liszt's works my treatment of harmony has become very different from what it was formerly), but it is indiscreet, to say the least, of friend Pohl to babble this secret to the whole world.' When, many years later, Ferruccio Busoni read those words, he commented that they suggested 'the morality of a fraudulent bank'.

to imagine how. Tell him again how profoundly devoted I have remained to him, and how happy I should be if I could be of use to him in anything.[8]

Liszt's chief activity in November was a trip to Zwickau, where at a concert on the 15th he conducted the *Prometheus choruses*.

Publication of his *Gesammelte Lieder* (Collected Songs) was being planned at this time; and on 6 December he was delighted to be able to write to his friend Franz Brendel: 'A couple of them made a *furore* in certain salons which are very much set against me, as *posthumous songs of Schubert*—and were encored! Of course I have begged the singer to carry the joke on further.'

A few days later, disquieting news arrived: Daniel Liszt, now in his twenty-first year, had fallen gravely ill while holidaying with his sister in Berlin. Liszt arrived in the city during the evening of 11 December.

Liszt to Princess Carolyne. Berlin, 15/17 December. I did not stop at the Anhaltstrasse when I got here at 10 o'clock on Sunday evening. When I went there the next day at 8.30, the only person up was the housemaid, who told me that Cosima had been watching over Daniel until six in the morning. A few minutes later he arrived in the dining-room, pushed along on his couch; he seemed very happy to see me again. My first impression was that he was near to death, his weakness extreme; but he was hardly conscious of it. Neither Hans nor Cosima . . . had the least inkling of what was to occur so soon! We breakfasted quietly, Daniel remaining as usual and gently complaining that for several days he had quite lost his appetite. He was given some milk. His breathing was extremely laboured, and his words painfully broken, although there was no sign of his reason being affected; and indeed his intelligence remained unclouded to the very last moment, save that he already lacked the strength to exercise it. Although he appeared to take a certain interest in the conversation which got going quite animatedly between Hans, Cosette, and me, I felt that he was not in a condition to follow it, and urged him to be patient. . . . At ten, Bücking* arrived. Cosima told him that the night had been a very bad one and that Daniel had not managed to get to sleep until past five in the morning. To sustain and revive him a little he was prescribed a few sips of Tokay. After the medical consultation I took Bücking aside and told him that I was prepared for the worst. Despite his caution and his wish not to fear too much, he was unable to reassure me. He said little more than that the illness was not in the nature of an ordinary pulmonary or consumptive malady, that there was absolutely nothing contagious about it, that in fact no organ was seriously threatened, and that if he should succumb it would simply be from depletion of his vitality. 'If it should come to the worst, he will simply pass away, very quietly, without death agony and probably without pain.' This prediction came to pass with well-nigh unbelievable accuracy. . . .

The rest of Monday was spent around his couch. Two letters arrived for

* A Berlin doctor.

him, one being from Mlle Seraphine* of Pozsony. Cosima read it out to him, and I tried to engage him a little in conversation about this young person, in whom I presume he was taking some interest. But he no longer had understanding of things external to himself, and his strength was so reduced that it scarcely sufficed to keep him alive. We gave him a few more drops of Tokay, and at two, while we were lunching, he took a cup of broth. His sister's nursing had become indispensable to him. When she moved the least distance away from his couch he asked for her again. He dozed off repeatedly, but whether he was awake or asleep the only outward sign of suffering was his laboured breathing. To stay alive was not within his power! . . .

The next morning, Tuesday, at 9.00, Hans came in tears to tell me that there was no more hope, and I went to Daniel. His face was not drawn, just extremely pale. Up to the very moment in which the coffin was closed his features retained their expression of gentle composure. His beard and hair had a slight reddish tinge, causing Cosima to remark that he resembled a Christ by Correggio. In one of his attacks of sleepiness he pronounced, quite clearly, these words: 'Je vais préparer vos places!' Bücking, however, still thought he would survive the night. Cosima and I knelt by the bed and asked God that His holy will might be done—and, especially, that He might associate us with that Holy will by granting us the grace steadfastly to do it.

This dear and noble child and I opened our hearts to one another—and I shall tell you orally of the fine thought which came to her, which she will carry out. Daniel reminisced to me once more about his law studies, which he was counting on taking up again in the spring! Hans, Cosette, and I stayed by his bed in turn. God was in our hearts—but His name was pronounced only between my daughter and myself. Daniel was nearer to Him and to the Kingdom of Heaven which the Lord has promised to those who have become as little children! At ten in the evening I lay down on the bed which had been put in the piano room. Without anyone having alerted me, at 11.15 something made me get up and go into Daniel's room. Cosette was kneeling. There was only silence—silence and mystery. A few minutes went by, grains of sand on the shore of eternity. 'I can't hear his breathing any more,' I said. She placed her hand on his heart—it was no longer beating. A moment before we had heard the merest sigh. He had gone to his rest in Our Lord. . . .

The same letter reports Daniel's funeral on Thursday, 15 December.

At 11.00 the chaplain arrived at the mortuary. He recited the service for the dead, and at 11.30 the procession set off, the hearse in front, twelve men accompanying it, and three carriages following. In the first were the

* Seraphine Vrábelyi, who in 1864 married Carl Tausig.

chaplain and Hans; in the second, Cosima and myself. The third I had ordered for the return journey from the cemetery with Hans and Cosette. The Catholic cemetery is outside the Oranienburg gate, a long way from the Anhaltstrasse. We went through the Oranienburgerstrasse, where Humboldt lived. A magnificent sun shone down on us, and we felt a little of its warmth even at the cemetery.

At the graveside the coffin was lifted up, three sacristans in white surplices shook their censers, while for several minutes a flock of pigeons circled high up in the air, almost vertically above the grave. The chaplain said some prayers, and the coffin, a beautiful oaken one, was then finally lowered into the ground. We threw the last spadefuls of earth on to the mortal remains of him who has gone, as he said, to prepare our places! May God have mercy upon him—upon him and upon us![9]

1860

Liszt to Baron Antal Augusz. Weimar, 14 January. I have spoken little to you about my son. He had a dreamy, tender, deep nature. His soul's yearnings elevated him above the earth, as it were, and he had inherited from me a powerful propensity towards that region of ideas and aspirations which brings us ever closer to the divine mercy. And so the thought of entering the priesthood had been taking firmer and firmer root in his mind. My sole desire was that before carrying out this holy resolve he should undertake solid and serious studies, in order to fit himself for the task of giving good service to the causes of religion. You know how much he applied himself to responding fully to my expectations of him, and to what he rightly considered an obligation imposed by his name. After he had carried off the *prix d'honneur* at the *concours général* in Paris, he was preparing to sit his law examination in Vienna, and would, I doubt not, have acquitted himself with honour. On the eve of his death he . . . strove to explain to me the chapter from the *Code* dealing with the different kinds of obligations. A little earlier he had taken pleasure in reciting by heart a few lines of Hungarian, to prove that he was keeping the promise he had given me to acquire a good knowledge of this language even before the completion of his legal studies!

May the God of goodness and mercy keep his soul in the everlasting peace of our heavenly homeland!

Our earthly homeland, alas, is in a state of much agitation. . . . Patriotism is a great and admirable sentiment, to be sure; but when in its exaltation it reaches the point of disregarding necessary limits, and takes for counsel solely the inspirations of fever, it too will end by 'sowing the wind to reap the whirlwind'. . . .

I firmly hope not to fail in my own task, and shall apply myself ceaselessly to bringing honour to *my country* (as I told HM the Emperor) by my work and by my character as an artist. Even if not precisely in the way understood by certain patriots, for whom the Rákóczy March is more or less what the Koran was for Omar and who would gladly destroy—just as the latter destroyed the Library of Alexandria—the whole of Germanic music with this fine argument: 'Either it can be found in the Rákóczy or it is worthless.'. . . The fuss made about my volume on the gypsies has made me feel much more truly Hungarian than my antagonists, the Magyaromanes, for loyalty is one of the distinctive features of our national character. . . . Why not render unto the gypsies the things that are the gypsies', while retaining for the Hungarians their own rights and possessions?—and have I done anything other than this?[1]

At a concert in Vienna on 26 February, Herbeck conducted Liszt's symphonic poem *Prometheus* and the *Prometheus choruses*. 'The symphonic poem pleased fairly,' he recorded in his diary. 'Chorus of Tritons pleased extremely. The Vintagers' and Reapers' choruses and concluding chorus pleased, but of course there was hissing from a formally organized opposition. They had sworn the downfall of this music, without knowing even a note of it.' The previous month, Liszt had written: 'Time levels all things, and I can quietly wait until people are more occupied in learning to know and to hear my scores than in condemning and hissing them. Mean-spirited, blackguard tricks, even when played in concert rooms and newspaper reviews, are no arguments worthy of a lasting import.'

Wendelin Weissheimer. Relaxation was provided in those days by the New Weimar Club, which met at the Town Hall in the Market Place. Liszt would spend the occasional evening there, usually with only a few other gentlemen, playing cards or chatting; and he was so good as to introduce me into the circle. . . . He would generally bring an excellent cognac with him, which would be drunk either neat or as a punch. It was a splendid stimulant, but for Liszt, who was highly strung in those days, an eminently unsuitable favourite drink, particularly when a heated discussion took place, such as happened for example one evening with Dingelstedt, with whom peace had still not been fully restored after Liszt's resignation from the conductor's podium. One *word* followed another, and likewise one *glass* another. It could not be denied—Liszt was 'tipsy'. He seemed to realize it himself, for all at once he made off. I followed him, to see him home, an offer he was pleased to accept. After we had slowly climbed the steps through the fir copse and arrived in front of the Altenburg, I made to take my leave. It was then that with great emphasis Liszt said: 'No! You have brought me this far; now I shall take *you* home!' My protestations that to the Wieland monument where I lived was half an hour's walk, and that it was a dark night, were of no avail. He insisted on taking me home. There being no help for it, I set out with him on the long walk. When we arrived at my lodgings it was only too clear that I could not think of letting Liszt return alone, and I said: 'Well, Herr Doktor, here we are—and now I shall take *you* home again!' Laughing, we turned back, past Goethe's house again, across the town, past the mill, up the steps through the fir copse—and once more we stood in front of the Altenburg. Then Liszt took a deep breath and said: 'How good the fresh air is for me! All good things come in threes. Now I'm taking *you* home again!' I: 'For God's sake, Herr Doktor, it's past midnight—you need rest!' He: 'I need air. All good things come in threes. Come along!' This time, to be on the safe side, instead of going down the treacherous steps we went along the lane curving round the fir copse, and then again past the mill and through the town. As we were passing Goethe's house, Liszt stopped for a moment and said: 'What would the old gentleman say if he could see us now?'—'Ihr naht euch wieder, schwankende Gestalten!'* was my immediate reply, and laughing we arrived at my lodgings. Although Liszt now felt significantly better, I insisted on taking him home for the third and last time. His door key was at last allowed to perform its function, and a hearty goodnight kiss brought our well-nigh three-hour nocturnal ramble to an end. . . .

On Palm Sunday I accompanied Liszt to Leipzig, where the Riedel Society were giving Beethoven's great Mass in the St Thomas Church. During this interesting performance we followed the grandiose work with the score, Liszt several times giving way to great emotion and excitement. The eyes of the entire gathering were fixed upon him.[2]

On 21 March, Liszt's erstwhile friend and colleague Joseph Joachim wrote to Robert Franz to ask him to sign a protest against the music of Liszt, Wagner, and their followers of the 'New German' school. In his reply Franz declined to do so: 'I hear that for some time past, in consequence of many bitter experiences, L. is as though crushed—surely a fresh blow would render his condition yet more unhappy. But sentimental considerations of that kind would bear no weight if I could convince myself that the "New Germans" were a serious and lasting menace to art. . . . If I did not owe L. so much—he has always treated me in a generous and disinterested manner—it would be another matter.'

In the event, a mere four names were appended to the protest when it was published in the *Berliner Echo*: Joachim's own, and those of Brahms, Julius Otto Grimm, and Bernhard Scholz. Some three years earlier, Liszt had written to Wagner: 'Several of my intimate friends—Joachim, for example, and formerly Schumann and others—have shown a strange, doubtful, and unfavourable attitude towards my musical creations. I owe them no grudge on that account, and cannot retaliate, because I continue to take a sincere and comprehensive interest in their works.'

Blandine Ollivier to Liszt. Paris, 30 March. You are my first thought and my last. As yet, I have no experience of loving as a mother, but think it impossible that I could ever love more fondly than I love you—you with

* 'Once more you approach, you hovering forms'—the opening line of *Faust* (the Dedication).

whom, however, I have hardly had the happiness of living other than in my thoughts and memories, in my dreams and the yearning of my heart.[3]

On Thursday, 17 May, Princess Carolyne left Weimar for Rome, to seek the Pope's permission to marry Liszt. The invalidity of her marriage with Prince Wittgenstein (from whom she had been divorced in 1855) had been pronounced formally that March by the Catholic consistories of Russia and countersigned by the Archbishop Metropolitan of St Petersburg, but the annulment had then been suspended by the Bishop of Fulda. Although she and Liszt had no inkling of it at this time, Carolyne would never return to Weimar, and would still be living in Rome at the time of her death twenty-seven years later.

Peter Cornelius to Marie Gärtner. Weimar, 31 May. Yesterday we had a rare musical coffee, to which Liszt had invited his Sunday staff. The quartet played Beethoven's Op. 127 and Op. 131. That was a really great treat, which was then crowned when Liszt was moved to play the great Sonata in B flat. But *how* he set about it, after those excellent musicians had played. My God, it's not a question of a *difference*—one simply believes that music doesn't exist except when he is playing. How he shapes the phrases, puts them together, softly unfolds them; how he stands *above* everything, having to give not the least thought to technical matters, but only to letting the spiritual concept emerge, as though unconsciously, from beneath his fingers. In each movement, another world![4]

To his mother. Vienna, mid-June. You ask about Liszt. Just a day after your letter I received one from him too! Our relationship remains unchanged—Liszt is such an extremely good person! The only thing he perhaps holds against me deep down is that I love freedom still more than I do him. But he never shows it and leaves me free to do as I wish, yet always remaining the same true friend. Our friendship is founded on identical convictions in art and religion, none of the rest of his friends being so much in agreement with him on the latter point as I. He shows me every consideration, and in all manner of ways demonstrates the warmth of his friendship for me.[5]

Liszt to Princess Carolyne. Weimar, 11 July. On Sunday I went to Leipzig to hear Allegri's *Miserere* and Lotti's magnificent *Crucifixus* at a concert given by the Riedel Society. . . . Hearing these works has in a way brought me nearer to you in Rome, and put me back, if I may express it thus, on to the 'ascending' slope of my fervent desire to compose religious music. I must soon write the *Stabat mater dolorosa* and the *Stabat mater speciosa*,* the text for which has been supplied to me by Emile [Ollivier]. All this music is moaning, singing and praying within my soul. For the moment I am entirely absorbed by the work† mentioned in my last letter. Do not

* Both eventually included in the oratorio *Christus*.

† *Les Morts*, composed in memory of Daniel and dedicated to Cosima. A setting of a text by Lamennais, it is an oration for full orchestra with male chorus ad lib, and forms the first of the *Trois Odes funèbres* (S112).

scold me for not having yet finished the *Elisabeth*—for tasks awaiting me, I haven't always as much free time as I should like. However, I shall keep my word. The *Elisabeth* will be ready in time and as she must be.[6]

Returning to Weimar in late August after a brief visit to Berlin, Liszt learnt that Napoleon III had raised his rank in the Legion of Honour from Chevalier to Officier.

Richard Wagner to Liszt. Paris, 13 September. There is something about you which causes you to appear ever surrounded by light and splendour, and makes it difficult for us to understand what could actually make you sad. Least of all do I feel inclined to attribute the reason for this to your vexation at the stupid reception given to your works now and then; for it seems to me that no one can know better than you that the reason for this animosity is not your works, but the false light in which you appear to the multitude. This light, which shows you to be so exceptional a phenomenon, that a misconception of it can occur only too easily, is sometimes too powerful, particularly for German eyes.[7]

It was in September that Liszt wrote his Will.

I am writing it on 14 September, the day on which the church celebrates the Exaltation of the Holy Cross. The name of this festival also describes the ardent and mysterious feeling which like a sacred wound has pierced my entire life.

Yes, 'Jesus Christ crucified', a yearning after the Cross and the exaltation of the Cross—this was my true calling. . . .

I have felt it in my innermost heart since the age of seventeen, when with tears and entreaties I asked to be allowed to enter the Paris Seminary, hoping that it would be granted to me to live the life of the Saints and perhaps to die the death of the Martyrs. Alas, it did not turn out thus! But nevertheless, and despite my many errors and transgressions, for which I feel sincere repentance and contrition, the divine light of the Cross has never been wholly withdrawn from me. At times it has even flooded my entire soul with its glory! I render thanks to God for it, and shall die with my soul fixed upon the Cross, our redemption and supreme beatitude; and to bear testimony to my faith, I wish to receive before my death the holy sacraments of the Roman, Catholic, and Apostolic Church, and thereby to obtain the remission and absolution of all my sins. Amen!

What I have thought and achieved for the last twelve years or more, I owe to Her whom I have so ardently desired to call by the sweet name of wife—a desire which until now human malignity and the most deplorable wrangling and quibbling have stubbornly opposed.

To Jeanne-Elisabeth-Carolyne, Princess Wittgenstein, *née* d'Ivanovska.

I cannot write her name without indescribable emotion. She is the source of all my joys, and it is ever to her that my sufferings go to seek alleviation. Not only has she associated and identified herself utterly and unwearingly with my life, work, cares, and career—helping me with her counsel, lifting me up with her encouragement, restoring me by her enthusiasm, with an unimaginable prodigality of attentions, of expectations, of sweet and wise words, of ingenious and persevering efforts; more than that, she has often entirely disregarded herself, laying aside the legitimately imperious in her character better to be able to bear the whole of my burden, whose richness and sole luxury she herself has made!!!

After further words of devotion and gratitude to the Princess, the Will asks her to watch over his legacy and to ensure its equal division between his two daughters, Blandine and Cosima. The 'modest pension' which his mother, Anna Liszt, had been receiving from the interest on his savings, she was of course to retain.

With reverence and devotion I thank my mother for her constant proofs of goodness and love. In my youth people called me a good son—but that was certainly no special merit of mine, for how would it have been possible not to be a good son with so loyally self-sacrificing a mother? Should I die before her, her blessing will follow me into the grave.

Recommending his daughters to honour his name above all by their feelings of affection, respect, gratitude, and filial devotion towards Princess Carolyne, the Will then refers to the monument to be erected over Daniel Liszt's grave in Berlin, offers thanks to the loyal and steadfast Eduard Liszt, who 'by his merits, ability and character does honour to the name I bear', and passes to Liszt's friendship with Richard Wagner, 'a name that is already glorious and will become ever more so'.

There was a time (about ten years ago) when I envisaged for Weimar a new epoch comparable to that which flourished under Carl August, and of which Wagner and I would have been the leading spirits just as were Goethe and Schiller in days gone by. The niggardly, not to say mean, conditions we faced locally, as well as all sorts of jealousy and nonsense both here and elsewhere, prevented the realization of this dream, the honour of which would have redounded to Monseigneur, the present Grand Duke. . . .

The Will asks Carolyne to keep in Liszt's memory for her lifetime his few personal possessions at the Altenburg. (Most of the furniture, books, paintings and *objets d'art* in the house were hers.) Among them were the Hungarian sword of honour; the ivory-bound prayer book given to Liszt by Cardinal Scitovszky at the time of the first performance of the Gran Mass; the golden goblet presented to him at Pozsony in 1840; the solid-silver music-rack adorned with busts of Beethoven, Weber, and Schubert; the gold, silver and bronze Mozart medals, presented to Liszt by the Burgomaster of Vienna for his direction of the Mozart Festival in 1856; the autograph MS of a flute concerto by Frederick the Great; a portfolio in red velvet bearing Goethe's signature; Beethoven's original death mask (given to Liszt by the painter Joseph Danhauser); Beethoven's Broadwood piano (presented to Liszt in 1846 by C. A. Spina, a publisher in Vienna); the MS

1. Adam Liszt, an anonymous gouache, Raiding, 1819.

2. Liszt in 1832, a drawing by Achille Devéria.

3. Marie d'Agoult, *c.*1833, a bronze relief by David d'Angers.

4. Liszt at the piano, a pencil drawing by J. G. Scheffer, Geneva, 1836.

5. Liszt, Marie d'Agoult, Major Adolphe Pictet, a caricature by George Sand, September 1836.

6. Franz Liszt, an oil painting by Ary Scheffer, 1837.

7. Liszt in his travelling coat, after a drawing by J. Kriehuber, May 1838.

8. Life mask of Liszt, 1838.

9. Liszt in his Hungarian greatcoat, a lithograph, 1840, by J. Kriehuber. Beneath it, in Liszt's hand, a verse from Byron's *To Thomas Moore*.

10. John Orlando Parry, aged thirty-five, a drawing by Baugniet.

GRAND INSTRUMENTAL & VOCAL CONCERTS.

The greatest Novelty ever produced in Bath!

MONS. LISZT,

The Extraordinary Pianiste, (First performance in Bath.)

Theatre-Royal Bath.

(By Permission of G. B. DAVIDGE, Esq.)

On TUESDAY EVENING, SEPTEMBER 1st, 1840.

THE Public is respectfully acquainted that a

GRAND CONCERT

Of VOCAL and INSTRUMENTAL MUSIC, will take place, Consisting of ENTIRE NOVELTIES!

VOCAL PERFORMERS:

MADLLE. DE VARNY,

Who will Sing some of the most popular AIRS and DUOS;

SIGNORA L. BASSANO,

Who will Sing some admired AIRS and BALLADS;

AND

MR. J. PARRY,

Who will introduce his celebrated Terzetto, in Imitation of Madame GRISI, Signor RUBINI, and Signor LABLACHE; also the universally admired Song, "WANTED A GOVERNESS;" the success of which elicited an encore at all the Public and Private Concerts in London.

INSTRUMENTAL PERFORMERS:

MONS. LISZT

(The greatest Pianist in Europe) will, on this occasion, perform his Grand Marche Hongroise, Morceaux Choisis (from his celebrated Recitals), and a Grand Duet on Two Piano-Fortes, with

MR. MORI.

MR. RICHARDSON,

The eminent Flautist, will perform Two of his most popular Fantasias.

Conductor .... MR. LAVENU.

The Performance at the Theatre Royal, on Tuesday Evening will commence precisely at Half-past Seven. Dress Circle Boxes, *Six Shillings*; Second Tier, *Four Shillings*; Pit, *Three Shillings*; Gallery, *Two Shillings*. Box and Pit Tickets to be obtained at all the MUSIC WAREHOUSES, and at the THEATRE-ROYAL, where places may be secured, as usual, of Mr. BROWNELL, between the hours of One and Four o'clock, from Wednesday, August 27th, to the day of Performance.

A Grand Morning Concert

Of VOCAL and INSTRUMENTAL MUSIC, will take place on WEDNESDAY, SEPT. 2d, at the *Assembly Rooms*. The Concert will comprise some of the choicest *Morceaux and Classical Compositions*, by the most eminent Masters, which will be performed by

MONS. LISZT, MR. MORI, MR. RICHARDSON,
MADLLE. DE VARNY, SIGNORA L. BASSANO,
And MR. JOHN PARRY.

First Violin... Mr. LODER. | Conductor... Mr. LAVENU.

The Concert at the Assembly Rooms to commence at Half-past One. Programmes of the Concerts will be speedily published. Single Tickets, 7s. each; Family Tickets (to admit four,) £1 4s. each; may be had at all the MUSIC WAREHOUSES, and at the Rooms. Stall Tickets, to be reserved Seats near the Orchestra, 10s. 6d. each; and Gallery Tickets, 3s. 6d. each; to be had only at the Rooms.

11. From *The Bath Herald*, 29 August 1840.

12. Princess Carolyne von Sayn-Wittgenstein, a daguerreotype, St Petersburg, 1847

13. Daniel, Cosima (*at rear*), and Blandine Liszt, with Liszt's mother (*left*) and Mme Patersi de Fossombroni, a photograph, *c.*1852.

14. Cosima, Blandine, and Daniel Liszt, a drawing by Friedrich Preller, Weimar, 1855

15. Franz Liszt, photograph by F. Hanfstaengl, Munich, 1858

16. Liszt approaching the Altenburg, a water-colour by Carl Hoffmann, 1859

17. Liszt, Reményi, and Plotényi (*right*), photograph by 'Photo Américaine', Rome, 1864

18. Anna Liszt photographed in later life

19. The Abbé Liszt, Paris, 1866, photograph by P. Petit

20. Opening of the March of the Three Holy Kings, from the autograph score of *Christus*
(By permission of the British Library)

21. The Villa d'Este, Tivoli

22. Weimar, a panorama

23. The Hofgärtnerei, Weimar

24. Liszt's music room and study at the Hofgärtnerei

25. Liszt at the piano, photograph by Hanfstaengl, Munich, 1869

26. Carl Tausig.

27. Liszt plays at the Vigadó, Pest, 18 March 1872, an oil-painting by Schams and Lafitte. Seated to the right of the piano, the Emperor Franz Joseph and other members of the imperial family

28. Liszt in 1873, photograph by Kozmata, Budapest

29. Berthold Kellermann, aged twenty-nine

30. Liszt Jubilee Committee, Budapest, 1873. From the left (*front*): Archbishop Haynald (Chairman of the Committee), Liszt, Count Albert Apponyi, Count Guido Karácsonyi; (*rear*): Imre von Huszár, Count Imre Széchényi, Ödön von Mihalovich, Baron Antal Augusz, Hans Richter, J. N. Dunkl

31. Cosima Wagner, *née* Liszt, photograph, *c.*1878

32. Liszt and Count Géza Zichy, photograph by E. Kozics, Pozsony, April 1881

33. The relationship between Liszt and Wagner, a caricature by Georges Villa

34. Liszt, Weimar, January 1884, photograph by Louis Held

35. The Abbé Liszt, photograph by Nadar, Paris, March 1886

36. Liszt on his deathbed

scores of *Lohengrin* and *Der fliegende Holländer*; and a number of other articles of value, including gifts from Carolyne and her daughter.

Asking that his colleagues of the 'New German School' (Bronsart, Cornelius, Tausig, and others) be given certain mementoes of him, Liszt also stipulated that Caroline d'Artigaux, the former Caroline de Saint-Cricq, was to be sent one of his talismans mounted in a ring.

The Will concludes:

I wish to be buried simply, without pomp, and if possible at night. May the Eternal Light shine upon my soul!

My last sigh will be a blessing for Carolyne.

F. Liszt.[8]

In mid-October Liszt went to Vienna to talk to Monsignor Gustav Hohenlohe and the Papal Nuncio about his hoped-for marriage with the Princess. Carolyne had broken off relations with her daughter and son-in-law at this time because of Prince Constantin's refusal—despite an obligation—to remunerate Okraszewski, a Pole whom the Princess had employed to bring her marriage annulment petition to a successful conclusion. 'Monsignor Gustav spoke to me a great deal about the chagrin felt by Magne no longer to be receiving your news,' wrote Liszt on the 17th. 'My heart is so swollen with all your mortifications and set-backs that I know not how to speak to you—but my soul remains steadfastly united with yours, for eternity!'

From the diary of Peter Cornelius. Vienna, 25 October. On the 16th my dear Liszt arrived; we visited him that evening. On Wednesday he came to my room quite early—with tears in his eyes! He had been hearing mass, held by Bishop Hohenlohe in the Papal Nuncio's chapel. We drove together to Eduard [Liszt]. On the way there in the fiacre he fell on my neck, weeping like a child about——'s* behaviour to Princess Carolyne; said it was quite the continuation of the W's.†

But what fresh air Liszt brought into our lives. What days they were![9]

4 November. Carolyne's name-day! Yes, I have thought of you today, you lofty woman, struggling soul! And prayed for you—that one day, and for all eternity, you may possess your Liszt![10]

Liszt to Agnes Street-Klindworth. Weimar, 16 November. You speak to me of Weimar, where on 22 October there was a torchlight procession in my honour which set the whole town in commotion, and after which the municipal council unanimously named me a freeman of the town. . . .

If I have remained a dozen years at Weimar, I have been sustained here on the one hand by a sentiment not lacking in nobility, and on the other by a great idea. By the first, I mean protecting a woman's honour, dignity, and lofty character against infamous persecution. By the second, renewing

* Presumably, Prince Constantin's.

† The Wittgensteins'.

Music through its most intimate alliance with Poetry. . . . Despite the opposition it has encountered and the obstacles raised up against it on all sides, this idea has not failed to make a little progress. Let people do what they may, it will triumph invincibly, because it forms an integral part of the sum of the just and true ideas of our age; and the knowledge that I have served it conscientiously, loyally and disinterestedly is a great consolation to me. If, when I settled here in '48, I had wished to attach myself to the *posthumous* party in music, associate myself with its hypocrisy, cherish its prejudices, etc., then because of my previous relationships with the principal bigwigs in that same party, nothing would have been easier. I would certainly have gained outwardly in consideration and acceptance; and those very newspapers which now find fit to heap insults and abuse upon me would have vied with one another in singing my praises. . . . They would readily have declared me *not guilty* of a few youthful peccadilloes, in order to extol and call attention in every way to the *enthusiastic upholder* of the fine, wholesome traditions from Palestrina to Mendelssohn. But such was not to be my lot; my conviction was too sincere, my belief in the present and future of art at once too ardent and too positive to allow me to put up with the empty objurgatory formulae of our pseudo-classicists who do their utmost to cry out that art is going astray, that art is lost.

The waves of the spirit are not like those of the sea. They have not been told 'thus far and no further'. On the contrary: the spirit 'bloweth where it listeth', and the art of the present century has something to say just as had that of previous centuries—and it *will* say it, without fail.[11]

On 12 October a daughter, Daniela Senta, had been born to Cosima and Hans von Bülow. She was Liszt's first grandchild, and on 24 November he attended the christening ceremony in Berlin.

Henriette von Schorn to Princess Carolyne. Weimar, 8 December. We have just come from the Altenburg, where the good Miss Anderson received us most kindly. Liszt was—as cannot be expressed in words. He played as no one else can play, or has ever played, or ever will play. I had continually to struggle against tears. But while he was playing the Skaters' Waltz from *Le Prophète* he was very comical, and wouldn't stop interjecting: 'Rope dancing! Not domestic music! The newspapers call it finger dexterity!' Finally he did the stunt piece of his younger days, and performed it not only with fingers but elbows too. He played on the Hungarian piano in Miss Anderson's room and showed us the huge instrument from Paris with three keyboards, telling us that it had not turned out as he had imagined it. . . .[12]

Adelheid von Schorn. Liszt often came to see us that winter. . . . Christmas evening he spent with us too. I cannot find words to describe how good and kind he was to me; he had a way of speaking to me like a loving, fatherly friend. But I was also deeply devoted to him and felt profoundly distressed if he was spoken of disparagingly by anyone. It happened, alas, not infrequently, for the Philistines were ever hostile to him. . . .[13]

1861

Liszt to Princess Carolyne. Weimar, 8 February. At our miserable little church this morning I abundantly prayed and wept where I have so often seen you pray and weep! . . .

Yesterday morning I confessed at the same confessional where I have seen Magne kneeling. An examination of my conscience has brought me to feel all the monotony of my numerous faults. My entire life is only a long odyssey, if you will excuse me this comparison, of the feeling of love. I was fit only for love—and so far, alas, I have managed to love only *badly*! But, thank God, I have never loved what is bad—and on every occasion when I have felt that I was doing wrong, my heart has felt profoundly 'contrite and humbled'. Many vices are, if I do not deceive myself, completely alien to me. In remembering those long years during which I did not confess at all, I have not found in them a single feeling of pride or envy, still less of avarice or hatred. For me, the dangerous hidden rock is this need of I know not what intensity of emotion, which easily leads me to paradox in matters of intelligence and to intemperance in the use of spirituous liquor. I have promised you that I shall reform on this last point—but am not likely to do so without difficulty. Even music herself—the minx—drives me dreadfully to this excess (not counting the frequent opportunities to fall that come my way). Continue to be merciful and indulgent to me, my dear, sweet angel. I firmly hope that God will grant me the grace of not being too unworthy of you. May He reunite us soon—and for ever![1]

In mid-February Liszt visited Löwenberg again, where at a concert on the 15th *Die Ideale* and *Mazeppa* were 'perfectly performed'. He then went to Leipzig for an 'Euterpe' concert on the 19th.

Wendelin Weissheimer. Liszt's *Prometheus* was received very well indeed. The splendid choruses and brilliant orchestra did not fail to arouse an enthusiastic storm of applause. The audience was determined to see Liszt, whose presence had become known. The ovation long continued, but in vain—Liszt did not appear. No one had anticipated the success in the slightest, and so the Master had preferred to stay at the hotel rather than perhaps expose himself to unpleasant demonstrations! In some of the newspapers a number of the local Philistines had in fact already tried to influence the public against this work in advance, calling *Prometheus* a 'caterwauling' and comparing it with 'cow's tripe'. Not unnaturally, the audience came to the concert prepared for the worst; but already after the Reapers' Chorus their opinion was quite the opposite, and the inspiring conclusion 'Heil der Menschheit' brought a decisive victory.[2]

Cosima von Bülow to Emma Herwegh. Weimar, 27 February. How right you are, dearest Emma, and how justly you speak when you apply the word *grandiose* to this personality, who seems to have been made of love and inspiration!

Whenever I am here I feel that I am renewed. . . . I wear myself away in incessant wishes for him. But exactly *what* I wish for him is hard to define; it is so vague, great, and boundless. What can one desire for him that is positive? The riches of this world? His great soul would scorn them. The kingdom of Heaven? It is his already. The most I can ask is for this world to be made better in his eyes, so that he may not remain too much a stranger on this bizarre and confused planet of ours. . . .[3]

To see his mother before he joined Carolyne in Rome, Liszt journeyed in late April to Paris, where he stayed with Blandine and her husband, at whose home Anna Liszt was living. During the visit he also saw, among others, Lamartine, Berlioz, Rossini, Pauline Viardot, and Gounod.* At Fromental Halévy's on 24 May he witnessed the masterly piano-playing and brilliant sight-reading of Halévy's pupil Georges Bizet (1838–75), upon whom he bestowed warm praise.

He also dined at the Tuileries with Napoleon III and the Empress Eugénie. Already an Officier of the Legion of Honour, he was elevated by the Emperor to the rank of Commandeur.

Liszt to Princess Carolyne. Paris, 16 May. My task from now on will consist in writing things which have some value—and not in personally pushing them forward in the markets of Germany or France. The bit of celebrity attached to my name will prevent their passing entirely unnoticed. To cite only one small detail in support of this opinion, I know that Verdi had several of my scores on his table at Genoa. I am even assured that he speaks of them with particular consideration.[4]

On 26 May, accompanied by Tausig (who while living in Vienna had launched a series of orchestral concerts to win that city over to Liszt's music), *Richard Wagner* arrived in Paris.

Liszt had already fallen back into his old current of life, and even his own daughter, Blandine, could only manage to get a word with him in his carriage, as he drove from one visit to another.† Nevertheless, impelled by

* Of whose *Faust* waltz he made a superb transcription (S407) at about this time, lifting it, in Sacheverell Sitwell's words, 'on to a higher spiritual plane than it could ever aspire to upon its own merits'. Among his later Gounod transcriptions is the exquisite rendering of *Les Sabéennes, berceuse de l'opéra La Reine de Saba* (S408).

† This is to some extent Wagnerian hyperbole. Liszt certainly paid many visits during his

his goodness of heart, he found time once to accept an invitation to 'beef-steaks' at my house. He even managed to spare me a whole evening, for which he kindly placed himself at my disposal for the settlement of my small obligations. In the presence of a few friends, who had remained true after the recent days of trouble,* he played the piano to us on this occasion, during which a curious coincidence occurred. The day before, poor Tausig had filled up a spare hour by playing Liszt's Fantasy on BACH, and now when Liszt chanced to play us the same piece, he literally collapsed with amazement before this wonderful prodigy of a man.

Another day we met for lunch at Gounod's, when we had a very dull time, which was only enlivened by poor Baudelaire, who indulged in the most outrageous witticisms. This man, *criblé de dettes*, as he told me, and daily compelled to adopt the most extravagant methods for a bare subsistence, had repeatedly approached me with adventurous schemes for the exploitation of my notorious fiasco. I could not on any account consent to adopt any of these, and was glad to find this really capable man safe under the eagle-wing of Liszt's 'ascendancy'. Liszt took him everywhere where there was a possibility of a fortune being found. Whether this helped him to anything or not, I never knew. I only heard that he died a short time afterwards, certainly not from an excess of good fortune.†. . . .[5]

Before he left Paris, Liszt received a note from Madame d'Agoult asking to see him. They had not met for seventeen years.

From the diary of Marie d'Agoult, 27 May. I went into the salon and, turning the door, found myself in the presence of Liszt! I offered him my hand. He remained silent, visibly moved. 'It's a long time since you last came to Paris,'—and our conversation went on in this fashion for an hour. He has aged greatly, but has not lost his looks. His face has bronzed and his eyes no longer have their fire; but he is still young in demeanour. His beautiful hair tumbles down in long flat locks on both sides of his noble, saddened face.

He spoke animatedly but quite without naturalness, in a manner that sought to be trenchant and sententious. Not a word about either Blandine or Cosima, although I mentioned Herr von Bülow. He was astonished at

month in Paris, but as his daughter's guest he was constantly in her company too. A number of his meetings with friends took place at her home and in her presence, and on several other occasions they and Ollivier were guests together at the homes of others. Ollivier's diary laments that Liszt was 'gradually carried off', but it also records that 'he frequently took us out with him'.

* The fiasco (because of a cabal organized against it) of *Tannhäuser* at the Paris Opéra earlier in the year.

† The reference is of course to Charles Baudelaire (1821–67), author of *Les Fleurs du mal*. Two years later there appeared in the *Revue nationale* (10 Dec. 1863) his prose poem *Le Thyrse*, which concludes: 'Dear Liszt, through the mist, beyond the rivers, above the cities where pianos sing your glory, where the printing-press translates your wisdom, wherever you may be, in the splendours of the Eternal City or in the haze of dreamy countries consoled by

my feelings for Italy and Hungary. In Italy he admires solely Antonelli.*. . .

When he left I offered him my hand again with emphasis; he will be coming to lunch on Friday.

Marie d'Agoult, 30 May. After seeing him I have not left off thinking about him. The first night I had difficulty in sleeping. Identifying him with what he was is still proving difficult. Although he has aged as we all must age, with nothing violent or contrary to nature, the picture of his young, lively self was so deeply impressed on me that I am unable to make it accord with this new image, grave and quiet.

I still feel a force there; but I too have become a force, equal if not superior. What was—still is—the mysterious bond of sympathy between us, despite the contradictions that burst out so obviously in our opinions and our pride!?

Marie d'Agoult, 31 May. Lunch with Edmond Texier. . . . Liszt strikes me as being still, like the first time, slightly on the defensive, uneasy about what one thinks of him, ever engaged in repelling any innuendo. He thinks highly of me for the delicious meal, and we exchange a few friendly words, gracious or courtly memories. I went to table alone; returning from it, I passed my arm through his. He squeezed my hand effusively!

He is certainly very pleased, or rather very proud, about our reconciliation. As for me, I find him still very handsome, very remarkable, very engaging. I feel more pleasure in his presence than in that of anyone else; but the great ideal he personified has vanished.

Who would ever have said that we would meet again like this! That is at once sad and sweet. Above all, it cuts things human down to size: the great passions, the great sorrows, the great ambitions which rend and tear—they all come to a *poulet à la portugaise* eaten together in the company of people who are complete strangers to the whole of a long life that has passed.

Marie d'Agoult, 8 June. He entered without being announced. After general topics our conversation comes to personal ones. When talking about Cosima he said: 'I have a passion for her. She takes after you.' I: 'In my opinion it is *you* she takes after.'

Gambrinus, improvising songs of delectation or of ineffable sorrow, or confiding to paper your abstruse meditations, singer of everlasting Delight and Anguish, philosopher, poet and artist, I greet you in immortality!'

* Cardinal Giacomo Antonelli (1806–76), the very able Secretary of State and Foreign Minister of Pope Pius IX. Having 'control of all formal and official transactions, besides influencing in a great degree all matters relating to the diplomatic intercourse of the Vatican with the outside world', he wielded a power and enjoyed a prestige second only to those of the Pope himself. During their long sojourn in Rome both Liszt and Carolyne came frequently into contact with Antonelli, who used generally to refer to Liszt as 'lo stregone ungherese' (the Hungarian sorcerer).

When saying farewell, I rose spontaneously and, very moved, embraced him; he too was moved, extremely so, and as he left me uttered a kind of vow or blessing. The exact words I do not remember, but they reminded me of certain moments in the past.

Ineffable charm! It is still he, and he alone, who makes me feel the divine mystery of life. With his departure I feel the emptiness around me and I shed tears.[6]

In the evening of 8 June Liszt left Paris to return via Brussels to Weimar.

Emile Ollivier, 11 June. For the first few days he was with us a great deal; but gradually he was hemmed in and carried off, so that our own enjoyment of him was at an end. During the last week he hardly came to see his mother at all, and his last dinner, instead of being taken at her bedside, was at Mme d'Obreskoff's. His is a weak character, spoiled by admiration—but upright, loyal, and charming. I have come to feel a most warm and genuine affection for him; and how transported, moved and filled with wonder I have been by his truly supernatural playing, it is impossible to describe. I allude not to the technical marvels, but to poetry, inspiration, nobility, pathos, and grace. While listening to him I have often experienced the same feelings that have come to me when listening to Berryer, or when reading Mirabeau or Bossuet.

Unfortunately, nowadays he finds playing tedious, and has wholly given himself up to the pursuit of glory as a composer. Nevertheless, he played very often; but the two occasions on which he surpassed himself were in our own home the day after his arrival, and at Lamartine's.

Chez nous there were few people. . . . Blandine began by playing *Le lac*,* and then Liszt went to the piano and improvised. It was sublime. Ortolan wept and wept. 'I enjoy playing this evening,' Liszt said to Blandine when he went back to her. At Lamartine's he gave us the first two movements of the A major Sonata of Beethoven in a way that I shall never forget.

He often took us out with him, more especially to Lamartine, whom I was pleased to see again and who was most affable. . . . Liszt went to the Emperor twice, was very well received and made a Commandeur. The Empress asked him for Chopin's Funeral March; after hearing it she withdrew into an adjoining room to hide her tears. To the Emperor he played from *Alceste*, of which apparently he is particularly fond. In the course of conversation the Emperor came out with these characteristic words: 'Il est des questions insolubles. Par moments, il me semble que j'aie un siècle.' To which Liszt replied, courtier-like: 'C'est que vous êtes le siècle.'. . .

* Probably an arrangement for piano solo of the very popular song of that title by the Swiss composer Louis Niedermeyer (1802–61).

Liszt was astonished at Blandine's talent. At Mme d'Obreskoff's he made her play after him. One day as he was dressing in his room he came out on hearing her play *Mazeppa*, and embraced her, saying: 'C'est bien ma fille.'[7]

Liszt to Blandine, 14 June. Buy for me, also, a copy of the *Dictionnaire ou Encyclopédie des Pensées et Maximes* (I don't know the exact title), published recently by Hachette. It costs from 20 to 25 francs and, in view of my longstanding craze for dictionaries of all kinds, is becoming absolutely indispensable to me![8]

Blandine to Liszt. Paris, 19 June. I live only through you. You are my living ideal, you alone have made me understand this passage in the Bible: God created man in His own image. Exceptionally, I, who am always a member of minorities, share the opinion of the whole world so far as you are concerned.[9]

Peter Cornelius to his brother Carl. Vienna, 22 June. The Princess W. is said to be living very sadly in Rome, and in extremely straitened circumstances. I feel the deepest sympathy for this poor woman. The whole world is against her, and she has to bear her distress silently and alone. But God in His mercy will take her to Him, because her love is true. My friendship and veneration for her will last lifelong, and I should make any sacrifice to be able to prove it to her. Weimar will certainly not see me again if *she* is not living at the Altenburg. Least of all at the Tonkünstler-Versammlung in August!* Liszt, I fear, has been dashed to pieces in the very act of soaring, for in abandoning the Princess† he is abandoning his motive force. She was responsible for every good thing he achieved.[10]

In July Liszt received the proofs of his Faust Symphony, which was published later in the year; and on 1 August *Hamlet* and *Hunnenschlacht* were published by Breitkopf & Härtel. To Carolyne, who was already broaching the topic of a Liszt Museum, he wrote at this time: 'I do not go along very enthusiastically with the idea of a Liszt Museum—and even feel a certain antipathy towards a display of personal objects. Nevertheless, as the idea is yours I shall make no objection to it at the moment. . . .'

Feodor von Milde to his wife, 29 July. There were a great many people at the Altenburg yesterday afternoon, and by chance four of Liszt's flames were there together: Madame Street, Frau Palleske, Emilie Genast, and Frau Marr. The looks of mutual jealousy exchanged between them are said to have been quite remarkable.[11]

* Cornelius did, however, attend the music festival at Weimar.

† During the months before he joined Carolyne in Rome, Liszt had, as agreed with her, been deliberately evasive about his plans, and responded to inquiries by talking vaguely about spending the winter at St Tropez or Athens. Some persons, including Cornelius, had therefore begun to believe that he was abandoning Carolyne.

Between 4 and 8 August a Tonkünstler-Versammlung was held at Weimar to inaugurate the Allgemeine Deutsche Musikverein.

Wendelin Weissheimer. When I got back to Weimar in August, I found Draeseke,* Leopold Damrosch, Peter Cornelius, Carl Tausig, and many others already present; above all Hans von Bülow, who was busy with the rehearsals of Liszt's Faust Symphony. . . . Liszt was putting the whole lot of us up at the Altenburg. When more and more musicians marched in, the number of available beds finally ran out, and so in a large room in the side wing a great heap of straw was spread out and covered with large cloths; and it was on this that, in a state of semi-undress, our merry company slept in the few hours given to sleep—if it can be so called. Liszt insisted on lying there in the midst of us. Only towards dawn did enough peace and quiet descend to allow one to close one's eyes. Liszt was the first up, and he at once imitated that soft *pizzicato* passage played by the double-basses in the first movement of the Faust Symphony, which impresses itself on the minds of all who hear it, and which at the last rehearsal had been repeated several times. The rest of us immediately cupped our hands over our mouths and in chorus blew the horns in F which follow the *pizzicato*. This amused Liszt so much that he cried 'Once more!' And again he began the *pizzicato* with his 'bim, bim, bam, boom, bam, bim', and again our chorus came in with a long-held 'ber-ber'. Amidst such jollities as this we got dressed and sat down to breakfast at the long table in the main building. More and more people joined us. Among the new arrivals were the celebrated Paris lawyer Emile Ollivier and his wife, Liszt's elder daughter. Madame Ollivier was shorter than her sister, dark-haired, and rather chubby. Her husband was moderately thickset, of pale complexion, with dark hair and expressive black eyes which were assisted by a gold lorgnon. Next to Liszt he was the centre of general interest. Had we only known that nine years later this same man would be at the head of the French government, and that 'with a light heart' he would so recklessly approach the terrible war that threatened!—with what different eyes would we have looked upon him!

After breakfast we all set off for the different rehearsals. . . . The much-enlarged court orchestra diligently rehearsed Liszt's Faust Symphony. On this occasion the score had been forgotten and left at the Altenburg. Liszt nevertheless rehearsed 'Gretchen' from memory. When he came to the rhythmically rather complex passage to which the words 'He loves me—loves me not' etc. can be set, the orchestra simply could not get this flower language right. When the flutes and clarinets put the question, the four solo violins would not give the right response; and when the questions became livelier, at the *accelerando* enough confusion arose to turn the pretty flower play into anything but graceful instrumental play. When it

* The composer Felix Draeseke (1835–1913), an ardent champion of the music of Wagner and Liszt. In support of his own music a Draeseke Society was founded in Germany in 1931.

continued to go wrong after further practice, Liszt said to Bülow: 'Hans, how do *you* conduct this passage?' Bülow came over, took the bâton, rested his left arm against his back, stretched himself up as far as he could so that he could be seen by everyone, and with his right arm raised high drew the complex figuration of the passage so clearly and distinctly in the air that the players at once repeated it correctly.

When Bülow then made to hand the bâton back to Liszt, the latter said: 'You go on wielding the sceptre—it's in good hands with you!' And so Bülow continued the conducting, from memory. He had not only all the notes of the score in his head, but even the *letters* added here and there for easier orientation. . . .

Unfortunately I could not be present for the whole rehearsal, because Liszt came to ask me if, as a precaution, I would fetch the forgotten score. He said it would be lying somewhere upstairs in the music room. Hurrying to the Altenburg, I found it on the spinet [clavichord] which had belonged to Mozart. . . . On this closed instrument now lay—*les extrêmes se touchent*—Liszt's Faust Symphony. Setting out with it, I had not gone twenty paces before I received a quite extraordinary surprise. As I approached the steps going down through the fir copse, I saw come into view first the head and then the rest of a man who was climbing the steps and had almost arrived at the top. Looking at his face I was most agreeably surprised to find that the man in front of me was none other than Richard Wagner.*. . .[12]

Richard Wagner. I reached Weimar at two in the morning and was conducted later in the day to the rooms which Liszt had arranged for my use at the Altenburg. They were, as he took good care to inform me, Princess Marie's rooms. This time, however, there were no women to entertain us. . . . There was only Miss Anderson, Princess Marie's governess, left to help Liszt entertain his guests. The Altenburg was about to be closed; Liszt's youthful uncle Eduard had come from Vienna for this purpose, and also to make an inventory of all its contents. But at the same time there reigned an unusual stir of conviviality in connection with the Allgemeine Deutsche Musikverein, as Liszt was putting up numerous musicians himself, first and foremost Bülow and Cornelius. Everyone, including Liszt, was wearing a travelling cap; and this strange choice of head-dress seemed to me typical of the lack of ceremony attending this rural festival at Weimar. On the top floor of the house Franz Brendel and his wife were installed with some splendour, and a swarm of musicians soon filled the place. . . . Tausig put in an appearance too,† but excluded himself from most of our free and easy gatherings to carry on a love affair

* Wagner's exile from Germany in general had ended in 1860. (Permission to re-enter Saxony without fear of prosecution was granted in 1862.)

† And played Liszt's 2nd Piano Concerto at the festival.

with a young lady. Liszt gave me Emilie Genast as a companion on one or two short excursions, an arrangement with which I found no fault, as she was witty and very intelligent. . . . Bülow's activity was extraordinary. He had learned the entire score of Liszt's Faust Symphony by heart, and gave us an unusually precise, intelligent and spirited performance with an orchestra composed of anything but the pick of German players. After this the *Prometheus* music had the greatest success. . . .[13]

Emile Ollivier's diary, 6 August. Performance at the Theatre of Liszt's Faust Symphony and *Prometheus*. The latter work, flabbily conducted* moreover, struck me as rambling and empty, except for an entrancing chorus—the Reapers—which was encored.

But the Faust Symphony is a true masterpiece. During the Andante I cried and cried. What a bewitching idea it was in the third movement to make Mephisto parody the themes of the first. What nobility, strength, lucidity, and pathos there is in the work. '*Faust* can't be done again after this,' Wagner said. In the face of such a work only the most inveterate ill-wishers could deny Liszt's powers. My sole criticism—one shared by Wagner—would be that the final chorus seems out of place. After Marguerite's singing has vanquished Mephisto's irony, the ultimate limit of emotion has been reached; the drama is over. Anything super-added only diminishes the effect. I made this observation to Liszt, who received it well. Bülow conducted the orchestra in masterly fashion and played a large part in a success which was undeniable.[14]

Richard Wagner. There was little else that was enjoyable at the festival concert with the exception of a cantata, *Das Grab im Busento*, by Weissheimer, and a regular scandal arose in connection with Draeseke's Germania March. For some obscure reason, Liszt adopted a challenging and protective attitude towards this strange composition, written apparently in mockery by a man of great talent in other directions. Liszt insisted on Bülow conducting the March, and ultimately Hans made a success of it, even doing it by heart; but the whole thing ended in the following incredible scene. The jubilant reception of Liszt's own works had not once induced him to show himself to the audience, but when Draeseke's March, which concluded the programme, was at last rejected by the audience in an irresistible wave of ill humour, Liszt came into the stage box and, stretching out his hands, clapped vigorously and shouted 'Bravos'. A real battle set in between Liszt, whose face was red with anger, and the audience. Blandine, who was sitting next to me, was, like me, beside herself at this outrageously provocative behaviour on the part of her father, and it was a long time before we could compose ourselves after the incident. There was little in the way of explanation to be got out of Liszt;

* By Karl Stör. Liszt himself took no active part in the festival, attending solely as a listener.

we only heard him refer a few times, in terms of furious contempt, to the audience, 'for whom the March was far and away too good'. I heard from another quarter that this was a form of revenge on the regular Weimar public, but it was a strange way of wreaking it, as they were not represented on this occasion. . . . I could of course see that Liszt had much to bear in other directions. . . .

Very pleasant were the select gatherings which on several occasions met round Liszt's dinner-table. . . .[15]

A. W. Gottschalg. In contrast to Liszt, whose charm of manner could at once win over people of all ages and conditions, Wagner was rather unfriendly and uncouth. . . . He was given the place of honour at table, where there were about nineteen of us altogether. Not far from him sat Felix Draeseke, to whom all of a sudden Wagner remarked: 'Your March is a signal for running away, and your "Germania" gives an excellent description of the disrupted state of affairs now existing in Germany!' Other guests, too, such as Gille, Tausig, and Hans von Bülow, were on the receiving end of similar caustic remarks, until one by one they left the table and took refuge from this malice, and the unpleasant atmosphere it created, by withdrawing into the adjacent music room; so that Wagner, who sat nervously rolling himself cigarettes, was eventually left quite alone. Liszt, who had been called away during this time, to honour a bill of exchange for Wagner, came back and found his beloved Richard sitting in solitary state. Coming to the rest of us in great excitement, he asked why we were neglecting his friend. 'To have dealings with Wagner is quite impossible!' was the reply he received from Bülow. Whereupon Liszt went back into the dining-room and said rather sharply: 'Now listen, my dear Richard, if you continue haranguing my people like this, in a week we shall be left quite alone at the Altenburg. There is no help for it—you must apologize!' For Wagner this was no easy matter. I can still see him standing rather embarrassedly in the doorway as he explained to us that his mood of embitterment was only the result of the hard blows his destiny had inflicted upon him. At a sign from Liszt we all trooped back into the dining-room, and Wagner this time kept his tongue under greater control.[16]

Richard Wagner. The day for parting was drawing near for us all, after a week of very varied and exciting experiences. A happy chance enabled me to make the greater part of my prearranged journey to Vienna in the company of Blandine and Ollivier, who had decided to visit Cosima at Reichenhall, where she was staying for a 'cure'. As we were all saying goodbye to Liszt on the railway platform, we thought of Bülow, who had distinguished himself so remarkably in the past few days. He had started a day in advance, and we exhausted ourselves in singing his praises, though I added with jesting familiarity, 'There was no necessity for him to marry Cosima.' And Liszt added, bowing slightly, 'That was a luxury.'[17]

Wagner summed up his visit to Weimar a few weeks later when writing to Malwida von Meysenbug: 'Liszt was very agreeable, and his hospitality, which I shared with half the musicians of Germany, delightful. But rather too many people. I found that I was having to relate my life history to some new person virtually every half hour. All of them absurd for the most part! Everywhere little talent, much folly. The music often very bad. But Liszt's Faust Symphony was altogether excellent. Thus, as ever, the only achievements those of the few; the general mass merely a nuisance.'

Meanwhile in Rome the documents relating to Carolyne's marriage and divorce had been examined once again, and papal consent had at last been given for her marriage with Liszt. The latter had been notified and was now preparing to leave Weimar before his own journey to Rome and reunion with his bride-to-be. The date chosen for the wedding was the auspicious one of 22 October, Liszt's fiftieth birthday.

Writing to Carolyne from the Erbprinz Hotel (12 August), he found it 'impossible to assemble and bring together in concentrated form the emotions of my final hours at the Altenburg'. 'Every room, every piece of furniture, to the very steps of the staircase and the garden lawn—everything was illumined by your love. . . . When I went through the rooms in the morning I could not restrain my tears. . . . I carried away with me your daguerreotype portrait from Petersburg, and the box for your letters, delivered to me by Bauer three days ago, in which I had your Rome photograph framed. These are my lares and penates—or, to put it more like a Christian, my sweet guardian angels!'

Leaving Weimar on 17 August, and after visiting the Duke of Saxe-Coburg at Reinhardsbrunn, Liszt proceeded via Wilhelmsthal (where Carl Alexander appointed him a Chamberlain) to Löwenberg, where from the 22nd until 19 September he was the guest of Prince Hohenzollern-Hechingen. Here he was joined for a few days by Cosima; and when Adolf Henselt called, father and daughter then accompanied the German pianist on a brief trip to his home at nearby Gersdorf.

In the evening of 19 September he arrived in Berlin, where he wished to say a final farewell to the Bülows. Among acquaintances seen during his fortnight's stay were Meyerbeer and Anton Rubinstein. His time, however, was chiefly given to awaiting Carolyne's instructions as to the date he was to set out for Rome.

Leaving Berlin on 6 October, he journeyed to Marseilles, whence he was to take the boat to Civita-Vecchia. On the 17th he embarked on the *Quirinal*; on the 20th he reached Rome, where he was reunited with his Princess, their first sight of one another for a year and a half. Later in the day they signed a joint declaration that they were free to marry.

At six o'clock the next evening, Monday the 21st, they took communion together at San Carlo al Corso, the church, dedicated to Carolyne's name saint, in which they were on the morrow to be joined in holy matrimony. To spend the rest of the day quietly and alone, they then repaired to the Princess's rooms at 93, Piazza di Spagna. Only hours now remained before the joyous outcome to the fourteen years of waiting and hoping; and when authenticating her will, postdated the 23rd, the Princess, in eager anticipation of the long-desired change of name, had signed 'Carolyne Liszt'.

And yet—the wedding never took place.

Adelheid von Schorn. The church was decorated and everything ready. But it was precisely because of these decorations that certain of the Princess's relatives who were staying in Rome were by chance alerted; and that same day they took steps to get the Pope to prevent the wedding. In the evening of the 21st an emissary from Cardinal Antonelli appeared at the Princess's with a message saying that the ceremony was to be postponed because the Pope wished to have the documents examined yet again. The principal argument of the relatives was that the Princess had not been forced* into her marriage with Prince Wittgenstein, and, as she would have to confirm this by oath, she would be committing perjury. . . .

But this would not in itself have been enough to make the Princess renounce the long-desired union with Liszt. For that, there were emotions yet more profound and reasons yet more cogent. What she told me and others, leaving us in no doubt that she was speaking with the utmost veracity and the deepest sorrow, [was that] during the period of their separation Liszt had grown more indifferent, and the idea of a legal tie with her was no longer a necessity for him. She observed this change in him when he arrived in Rome, and he confirmed it himself by never again asking whether the marriage was to be made possible or not. He would, of course, have been prepared to go to the altar with her on any day that was appointed, but her feminine fine-feeling recognized that it would have been merely in fulfilment of his duty. And so she, too, never spoke of it again—and thus sacrificed the principal object of her life.

During this year in Rome the Princess had devoted herself more to the church, had associated much with Antonelli and other prelates, and her enthusiasm for the Catholic faith probably made her renunciation appear easier to her. She had given herself up to writing, delving into any and every subject that she found of interest. Her freedom, and her ability to develop as fully as possible, she began to regard as a blessing, and she urged Liszt on to the path he was to tread from that time. She wished him to create solely for the glory of God, to become director and regenerator of the Papal Chapel. . . .

When, in March 1864, Prince Wittgenstein died, and nothing could any longer have stood in the way of their union, both had already projected themselves so much into the thought of renunciation that the subject of marriage did not arise. . . . This is the true course of events, as related to me by the Princess herself.[18]

In so far as it described a change of feeling on Liszt's part, Schorn's account was challenged by both Carolyne's daughter, Princess Marie Hohenlohe, and La

* Carolyne's own argument for annulment had been based above all on the box on the ears given her (in accordance with Polish custom) by her father before the marriage, specifically so that she would later have, if necessary, a ground for maintaining that she had married under compulsion.

Mara. The last-named referred to letters of later years from Liszt to Carolyne which seem to show that marriage with her was still his sole desire. But those letters were written when there was no longer the least question of marriage, and Liszt's words remain mere words. Nevertheless, the inference is that he never admitted to Carolyne a change (if any) in his feelings. Further, Schorn is to a considerable extent supported by the note made by Liszt's biographer Lina Ramann of a conversation with the Princess at Rome in 1876.

After referring to the evening messenger, Ramann continues:
'The Princess told me that she and Liszt had sat together that fateful evening as though utterly shattered. Finally he rose, to go to his hotel. In a dull and yet laughing tone, he said: "Tomorrow I shall sleep until 11.00."—"And *I* until 12.00," replied the Princess coolly. The irony he was evidently aiming at this stroke of fate she had erroneously taken to be *indifference* to *her*—something which must have inflicted a more fatal wound than any prohibition of the Pope. Hurt pride was her response. . . .'

Ramann later raised the topic with Liszt himself. 'He had felt "stunned, crushed," he said. "And the Princess?" I asked; "how did she take the news?"—"Astonishingly," he replied, his voice still betraying the amazement he had felt. "She was *calm*, *controlled*—remarkable woman!" '

Such details ring too true for it to be credible that the protagonists of the drama were simply adhering to a story they had concocted to hide a more painful or embarrassing reality (such as that Liszt had himself called off the wedding). Although documentation concerning the eleventh-hour objections lodged at the Vatican by Carolyne's relatives or in-laws either does not exist—perhaps because no written memorandum was made of what was apparently an oral petition—or has not yet come to light, Emile Haraszti seems to be justified in calling the appearance of the nocturnal messenger an 'historical fact'.*

Whatever the validity of the Princess's interpretation of Liszt's feelings, the couple seem never again seriously to have discussed the possibility of marriage, even after the death two and a half years later of Prince Wittgenstein, when no spiritual or temporal power on earth could have prevented their union, had this still been their desire.

Carolyne's life now became more and more that of a blue-stocking. Her writings during the quarter-century remaining to her were to deal mainly with religious and ecclesiastical topics, their culmination being *Des causes intérieures de la faiblesse extérieure de l'Eglise*, a twenty-four-volume treatise which aimed at nothing less than reform of the Roman Catholic Church.

Liszt meanwhile immersed himself in composition, his ambitions from this time forward being above all in the field of sacred music. The Princess continued to do her best to superintend his life, even when, from 1869 onwards, she had perforce for long periods to do so from afar. But the gratitude owed her by posterity for her unceasing concern for his creative work, must be tempered by the fact that it was her failure to provide a stable domestic existence for him during these years which was more than all else the reason why by the end of his life Liszt had become a melancholy, homeless wanderer.

* Roman archival material, providing further information, has recently been discovered and made available by Alan Walker. See his 'Liszt, Carolyne, and the Vatican: The Story of a Thwarted Marriage', *JALS*, xxiv, 33–43.

Princess Carolyne to Eduard Liszt. Rome, 22 November. You probably know . . . that I have not attained my goal. If we say to God each day, *Thy will be done*, it is in circumstances such as these, above all, that one should be able to repeat those words. The world with its thousand resources is stronger than I. The most dignified course we can take, which is at the same time the simplest and most Christian, is to remain silent, without giving our adversaries the unnecessary spectacle of our futile complaints. The persecution of which I am the object may very well continue for a whole lifetime, wishing to poison my entire existence. . . . But God is making resignation easier for me by the joy I have had, not only in seeing Liszt again, and seeing him in good and magnificent health, but still more, and above all, by finding in him again in every circumstance, however unforeseen, that same noble-mindedness, tact, and loftiness of view which make me admire, cherish, and esteem him more than ever.[19]

Liszt to Blandine. Rome, 25 December. My life here is more peaceful, more harmonious and better ordered than in Germany. I am hoping that it will be to the advantage of my work. . . . I am living at 113 Via Felice, very near the Pincio, in a very attractive first-floor flat in which Léopold Robert lived for seven or eight years. Tenerani's and Overbeck's* studios, the Quirinal, Santa Maria degli Angeli and Santa Maria Maggiore are nearby, and I intend to go to them often, to take possession of them, for beautiful things belong to those who know how to feel and become imbued with them. On Sundays I go regularly to the Sistine Chapel to bathe and reinvigorate my spirit in the sonorous waves of Palestrina's *Jordan*; and every morning I am awakened by a concert from the bell-towers of the surrounding churches . . . which charm me far more than all the concerts of the Paris Conservatoire could do. Our friend d'Ortigue is keeping me agreeable company with his recently published volume, *La Musique à l'Eglise*, and his *Dictionnaire de Plain-Chant*. . . .

Let me know what Wagner is up to this winter. He replied so sourly to my last lines from Berlin that I don't quite know how to set about resuming correspondence with him. . . .[20]

1862

It was in 1862 that Liszt's path crossed that of the young Giovanni Sgambati (1841–1914), who was to become a distinguished figure in the history of Italian

* Respectively the Swiss painter Léopold Robert (1794–1835), the Italian sculptor Pietro Tenerani (1789–1869), and the German painter Johann Friedrich Overbeck (1789–1869).

instrumental music. Their first meeting took place in circumstances described* by Maria Tibaldi Chiesa, an acquaintance of Sgambati's son, Oreste Sgambati.

'Liszt began to frequent the musical matinées organized by the violinist Tullio Ramacciotti, firstly in Via dei Pontefici and then in Via del Vantaggio. One day he was struck by the rare pianistic gifts of a young man he heard taking part in a performance of Hummel's Septet. Inviting the youngster to his home, Liszt offered to give him lessons. . . .

'Sgambati was happy to have such a teacher, and the two musicians soon enjoyed the most cordial friendship. The Italian's admiration for the great Hungarian was profound; and for his part Liszt at once discerned Sgambati's merits, both as pianist and composer. Putting all his experience at the younger man's disposal, and revealing to him the beauties of the classics, he realized that he had found someone who would be a valuable collaborator in making German instrumental music known in Italy, and also in helping with, and continuing, the task of reforming music in Rome.'

In April, the German historian Ferdinand Gregorovius (1821–91), then working on his *History of Rome in the Middle Ages*, met Liszt for the first time. 'A striking, uncanny figure—tall, thin, and with long grey hair,' he noted. 'Frau von S maintains that he is burnt out and that only the outer walls remain, from which a little ghost-like flame hisses forth.'

Blandine Ollivier to Liszt. Gémenos [a village near Marseilles], 16 May. We went to hear Thalberg in his first session at the Salle Erard. . . . What a bourgeois amazement our arrival caused! When people caught sight of me, they leant forward, gossiped with their neighbours, and used their lorgnettes the better to establish whether it was I. Last of all they greeted me. We sat beside Mme d'Ortigue; her husband had not cared to waste his afternoon. She seemed not to want to allow the player anything—but I drew her attention to some beautiful, effortlessly-produced organ-like sounds. His programme, moreover, was virtually the same as twenty years ago: a Thalberg fantasy preceding a piece by Thalberg and following a ballade by Thalberg. He was received well enough, but I thought the audience cold, almost as cold as the virtuoso.

Mme d'Ortigue recalled how extraordinarily excited she used to feel after hearing you. 'This man,' replied Emile, 'is a little Jura hill beside Mont Blanc.'[1]

In early June, Liszt was visited by *Walter Bache* (1842–88), a young English pianist who later devoted his energies to making the composer's works known and appreciated in Britain—the chief aim of the annual recitals and orchestral concerts he gave in London from the mid-1860s onwards.

Bache had written to his father on 21 May.

Liszt is living at Rome, and Mme Laussot† most strongly advises me to go

* *Nuova Antologia*, July 1936.

† The English-born Jessie Laussot (1827–1905), a keen supporter and admirer of Liszt and his music, lived at Florence, where she founded a choral society, the Società Cherubini. From 1879 she was the wife of the German historian Karl Hillebrand (1829–84).

to him, ask him to hear me play and give me his opinion and advice, and then trust to the chance of his offering to give me lessons. Liszt is without doubt the *greatest pianist*, and the kindness with which he treats all young artists who are really in earnest is proverbial. . . . I can't tell you how it would grieve me to leave Florence; but still I should do it without a moment's hesitation, for Liszt is without doubt the greatest pianist and piano teacher living, and in every respect a most wonderfully educated musician and man, and the advantage of being with him would be incomparable. . . . Mme Laussot (though knowing Liszt well) will not give me any introduction to him; she says it is much better to go without one, to say who I am and what I want, and she says that she has never known him disappoint anyone, although he has been applied to by people of very inferior ability.[2]

'Liszt has been very kind indeed to me,' Bache was able to report to his father on 6 June. According to Constance Bache (1846–1903), Walter's sister: 'When Walter called upon Liszt, he was dreadfully hurt because Liszt thought he had come to borrow money! What an insight it gives into Liszt's life that this should be his first thought when a young stranger came to him.'

Walter to Constance Bache. Livorno, 25 July. I hope I have not exaggerated in talking about Liszt; he won't make me anything wonderful, so that I can come home and set the Thames on fire—not at all, so don't expect it; *but*—his readings or interpretations are greater and higher than anyone else's; if I can spend some time with him and go through a good deal of music with him, I shall pick up at least a great deal of his ideas. . . . The two or three lessons I had of him this summer showed me what an immensity I might learn.[3]

On Tuesday, 9 September,* Blandine Ollivier died at St Tropez two months after giving birth (at Gémenos on 3 July) to a son.† The loss, for the second time, of a highly promising child of his in early adulthood was almost more than Liszt could bear; and an acquaintance described him as 'shattered' by the news. In writing to his mother he found words of comfort: 'Michelangelo said that it was wrong to rejoice at the birth of a child, and that, on the contrary, we ought to weep to see one more being about to participate in mankind's sufferings, and to reserve our cries of joy exclusively for those who, after a noble life, die in the Lord.'

Among those who set down their impressions of Blandine was Malwida von Meysenbug: 'Of all the women I met in Paris, this lovely creature attracted me the most. She combined the grace of a Frenchwoman's fine, witty, almost sarcastic mind, with a deep, soulful, feminine charm which, with her handsome physique, made her irresistibly attractive.'

Blandine was buried at St Tropez. Shortly afterwards, Emile Ollivier sought distraction from his grief by visiting Rome, where he stayed for several weeks.

* The 11th is the date given elsewhere in the literature, but Emile Ollivier's letter to Liszt of the 9th clearly states: 'Blandine died this morning.'

† Daniel Ollivier (d.1941) became a distinguished lawyer, and in later life the editor of several volumes of his grandfather's correspondence.

Ollivier to his father, 3 October. I am staying with Liszt, who is most charming to me. He is doing all he can to distract me: playing to me, singing to me, taking me out to visit the artistic community, the monsignori, even the cardinals. Unfortunately, it is all indifferent to me and only wearies me.

To the same, 11 October. Liszt is unfailingly kind. He compels me to go out, to see; and so I am travelling a little through this ecclesiastical world, one quite unknown to me. On the other hand he has introduced me to some liberals, among others a Duke of Sermoneta,* a highly intelligent Roman prince with whom I am reading Dante's *Paradiso*. The Princess is excellent too.[4]

Under the immediate inspiration of his profound grief, Liszt composed his great Variations (S180) for piano solo on the bass line from the first movement of Bach's cantata *Weinen, Klagen, Sorgen, Zagen* and the Crucifixus of the B minor Mass. He dedicated the work to Anton Rubinstein.

Three fine piano works also came into being at about this time: two concert studies (S145), *Waldesrauschen* and *Gnomenreigen*, and the beautiful *Ave Maria* (*The Bells of Rome*) (S182).

Liszt to the Grand Duke Carl Alexander. Rome, 1 November. The Legend of St Elisabeth is finished. May this work contribute to the glorification of the 'dear Saint', and may it disseminate the celestial perfume of her piety, of her grace, of her sufferings, of her resignation to life, and of her meekness towards death!

I have in addition written some other works connected with the same order of emotion. One of them is called *Vision at the Sistine Chapel.*† Its great figures are Allegri and Mozart. I have not only brought them together, but as it were *bound* them to one another. Man's anguish and wretchedness cry out in distress in the *Miserere*, to which God's infinite mercy and forgiveness respond and sing in the *Ave verum corpus*. This comes close to the sublimest of mysteries; to Him who shows us Love triumphant over Evil and Death.

If this outline were to seem too mystical, then to explain the musical idea I have indicated I could fall back on an incident in Mozart's biography. It is known that when he visited Rome he wrote down Allegri's *Miserere* during its performance in the Sistine Chapel, both to retain it better in his memory, and, perhaps, to breach the prohibitive system which, in the good old days, extended even to music manuscripts. How not to remember this fact, in that same enclosed space where it occurred? And so I have often

* The distinguished Dante scholar Michelangelo Caetani, Duke of Sermoneta (1804–82), whose acquaintance Liszt had made shortly after arriving in Rome. 'From Scott to Gregorovius, from Peel to Liszt, from Chateaubriand to Taine,' declares the Duke's entry in the *Enciclopedia Italiana*, 'there was no foreigner of note who was not received at the Caetani palace. Stendhal was a friend of his, and Balzac dedicated a novel to him.'

† *A la Chapelle Sixtine* (S461).

sought the place where Mozart must have been. I even imagined that I saw him, and that he looked on me with gentle condescension. Allegri, too, was standing nearby, almost as though he were committing an act of penitence for the celebrity that pilgrims, generally little given to musical impressions, have taken care to bestow exclusively upon his *Miserere*.

Then, slowly, there appeared in the background, beside Michelangelo's *Last Judgement*, another shade, of unutterable greatness. I recognized him instantly and with joy, for while still an exile here upon earth He had consecrated my brow with a kiss. Once, He too sang his *Miserere*, and until that time no sobs and lamentations of so profound and sublime an intensity had ever been heard. Strange encounter! It was on Allegri's mode, and on the same interval—a stubborn dominant—that Beethoven's genius thrice alighted, to leave thereon, and everlastingly, its immortal imprint. Listen to the Funeral March on the Death of a Hero, the Adagio of the *Sonata quasi Fantasia*, and the mysterious banquet of phantoms and angels in the Andante of the Seventh Symphony. Is there not a striking analogy between these three motifs and Allegri's *Miserere*?[5]

To Eduard Liszt. Rome, 19 November. Blandine has her place in my heart beside Daniel. They remain with me as atonement and purification—intercessors crying 'Sursum corda!' On the day when Death approaches, he shall not find me unprepared or faint-hearted. *Our* faith hopes for and awaits the salvation to which it leads us.

Yet as long as we are here on earth, we must perform our daily task. Mine shall not be shirked. Though others may have no great opinion of it, for me it is essential. For the tears of my soul I must prepare, as it were, lacrymatoria; for those of my dear ones who still live I must ignite flames; and my dear dead I must preserve in *spiritual-corporeal* urns. That is how I see my *Art task*. . . .

I am now about to undertake the great task of an oratorio on Christ. By 22 October '63* I hope to have brought it, as best I can, to completion.[6]

To his mother, 2 December. You know, dearest Mother, how for several years on end during my youth I ceaselessly dreamt myself, so to speak, into the realm of the saints. Nothing seemed to me so self-evident as Heaven, nothing so true or so great a source of happiness as the goodness and mercy of God. Despite all the errors and aberrations of my life, nothing and no one have been able to shake the belief in immortality and the salvation of the soul which came to me during my prayers in the churches of Raiding and Frauendorf, at the Mariahilf church in Vienna, and at Notre Dame de Lorette and St Vincent de Paul in Paris. All the storms notwithstanding, the good seed in me has germinated, and is more deeply filled than ever before with all the truths of religion. When I now read the Lives of the

* That is, by his next birthday. However, the oratorio *Christus* was ultimately not completed until 1866.

Saints, I feel as though after a long journey I am meeting old and venerable friends from whom I shall part no more.

An extraordinary coincidence led me lovingly to St Elisabeth. Born, like her, in Hungary, I spent twelve years—of decisive importance for my destiny—in Thuringia, not far from the Wartburg in which she dwelt. How eagerly I followed the restoration of the Wartburg Castle, which *my* Grand Duke of Weimar undertook; and the Elisabeth passage-way leading to the chapel of the newly-risen castle was painted under my eyes by [Moritz von] Schwind. It was his depiction of scenes and events from the legend of St Elisabeth that I adopted for my work.[7]

1863

Liszt to Franz Brendel. Rome, 18 June. The day after tomorrow I shall be quitting my rooms in Via Felice and moving to Monte Mario (an hour's distance from the city). Father Theiner* is so kind as to let me use his apartment in the almost uninhabited house of the oratorians. The view is magnificent beyond words. I wish now at last to be able to live more *naturally*, and hope that I shall manage to approach more closely to my monastico-artistic ideal.[1]

Liszt's new residence was the monastery of the Madonna del Rosario, situated close to the spot on Monte Mario where, according to legend, Constantine the Great was converted to Christianity in 312 after seeing a vision of the Cross of Christ superimposed upon the sun, accompanied by the words, 'In this sign conquer'.

In a letter to Brendel of 18 July, Liszt reported 'an extraordinary, nay, incomparable honour which came my way last Saturday, 11 July'.

His Holiness Pope Pius IX† visited the church of the Madonna del Rosario and hallowed my dwelling-place with his presence. After I had given the Pope a small proof of my skill on a harmonium and on my workaday upright piano, he most graciously addressed some very significant words to me, urging me to strive after heavenly things in things earthly, and through my ephemeral harmonies to prepare myself for those that will be everlasting. His Holiness stayed for about half an hour. . . .[2]

The pieces Liszt chose to play to his august visitor, in addition to some Beethoven, were the recently composed Legends (S175), *St François d'Assise: la prédication aux oiseaux* and *St François de Paule marchant sur les flots*. Pius IX,

* Father Augustin Theiner (1804–74) was Prefect of the Vatican Archives.

† Giovanni Maria Mastai Ferretti (1792–1878), elected pope in 1846 after the death of Gregory XVI.

whose visit to Liszt is said to be the only one ever paid by a pope to a musician, was thus among the very first to hear two of Liszt's finest piano works.

Five days later Liszt was granted an audience in the Vatican, at which the Pope presented him with 'a beautiful cameo of the Madonna'.

Liszt to Karl Klauser (1823–1905) in Farmington, New Mexico, 2 September. It is the persistent search for the *best possible* which characterizes the true artist.[3]

1864

Ferdinand Gregorovius, Easter Sunday. A few days ago [21 March] Liszt gave his great concert (Accademia Sacra) for Peter's Pence in the new barracks on the Praetorian Camp. Several Legitimists and inquisitive foreigners gathered there. Four cardinals spoke, Liszt played, the Papal Choir sang; and finally Monsignor Nardi* returned thanks for the lavish sympathy on behalf *del più generoso e del più povero monarca dell'Europa.* Tremendous applause. Liszt shows himself fanatically Catholic.[1]

Heinrich Ehrlich. A concert of Bülow's at Berlin in March 1864 which contained Liszt's symphonic poem and choruses to Herder's *Prometheus* . . . gave rise to an exchange of letters between Bülow and me which caused a long rift between us. I would not mention this, had it not occasioned a letter of Liszt's that is connected with one of the strangest events in my career: *my very strong claim to the universally known Hungarian Rhapsody No. 2.* To give an exact account of this matter, I have to go back rather a long way.

In 1846 Liszt spent a long time in Vienna. I had recently returned from my wanderings and was just managing to scrape a living. On an estate in Hungary I had composed a sonata which I sent to him anonymously. Through Belloni he sent me much praise and also an invitation to visit him. . . . Showing great interest in me, he inquired about my circumstances and asked if I had composed anything shorter and more convenient for the publishers than the sonata and symphony on which I was working. And so I played him some of my Hungarian Fantasies. He liked them, and, seeing that he was about to undertake a concert tour in Hungary, I asked him to play one or two in Pest, to increase my chances of obtaining a decent payment for them. He promised to do so. . . .

In 1852, on my way to Paris, I visited Liszt in Weimar . . . and he played me his latest Rhapsody. 'But that is the Hungarian Fantasy I gave you in 1846 for you to play in Pest!' I exclaimed. 'What?' he replied, 'I thought

* Francesco Nardi (1808–77), a Venetian prelate and canonist.

they were themes you had arranged!'—'Yes, but the themes were my own.'—'Well, in that case I shall write on the title-page *d'après des motifs de M. Ehrlich*.' Princess Wittgenstein then joined in the conversation and the subject was dropped. The next day Liszt called to see me, took me around Weimar, showed me all the interesting sights, gave me letters of recommendation to Countess Kalergis, Berlioz, and others in Paris, and was as irresistibly charming as only he could be. I forgot all about my Fantasy. Only in later years, when it was this very Rhapsody which had become the most popular, being played everywhere, even in orchestral arrangements, did it occasionally occur to me to lay claim to my very considerable share in its success. I raised the matter with Bülow . . . and in 1864, when we exchanged angry letters after the concert to which I have referred, I declared *inter alia* that people had no right to consider me an enemy of Liszt's, seeing that I had behaved with such resignation after his use of the manuscript with which he had been entrusted. This remark. . . may have prompted Bülow to invite Liszt to express his own opinion, for shortly afterwards I received the following letter:

I am very happy, Monsieur, to accede to your desire to give you (without any fight) full satisfaction on the field of the Hungarian Rhapsodies. In publishing under this title a kind of patriotic Anthology whose character I sought to define in my volume on the Hungarian gypsies and their music, I was not in any way laying claim to rights of ownership as far as the melodies themselves, or even certain details inseparable from their manner of expression, are concerned. The use and fruit, but not the property, were enough for me, and my task as Rhapsode was limited to a simple *mise en œuvre* as congeneric as possible. And so, in all good faith, I was justified in taking my material everywhere I could find it, firstly in my childhood memories of Bihary and other gypsy celebrities, and later in my excursions across country amidst bands of gypsy musicians from Sopron, Pozsony, Pest, etc. Lastly, I retained and reproduced in my own manner many themes, traits, and characteristic features which over a couple of decades were communicated to me in generous profusion, both at the piano and in musical notation, by Counts Amadé, Apponyi, [Imre] Széchényi, Barons Augusz and Fáy,* Messrs Egressy,† Erkel, Doppler,‡ Reményi—and by you, dear Monsieur Ehrlich. An embarrassment of riches, is it not? And yet I hope that I have managed to extricate myself tolerably well from it by means of the fifteen Rhapsodies that you know. They protest resolutely, and in all the keys, that I have wronged none of my numerous creditors in the domain of the *csárdás*, among whom it gives me pleasure to count yourself, while assuring you of my affectionate acknowledgements as well as of my sincere esteem for your rare talents.

30 March 1864. Rome. F. Liszt.

* István Fáy (1809–62), a gifted amateur pianist and enthusiastic collector of Hungarian music.
† Béni Egressy (1814–51).
‡ The Austrian musician Franz Doppler (1821–83).

To this letter I replied . . . by remarking that there was a vast difference between the use made of national themes already known and that made of wholly original ones entrusted to an artist by a youthful composer; that I left it to him to judge the feelings which came over me when I had to hear this most popular Rhapsody and recall its genesis, and the time when, in very straitened circumstances, I gave him the manuscript and asked him to play something from it in Pest; and that, this said, I considered the whole incident closed. . . .

But I must at once go on to say that in relating these matters I am not in the least intending to belittle Liszt's memory, and that to this day I cherish feelings of the keenest admiration for him. With all his weaknesses, he was one of the kindest and most lovable of men, possessing a character such as can be found only too rarely. In intellect, culture, and personal charm he was the first among all contemporary artists, none of whom could even begin to equal him in his power of winning people's affection.[2]

Kurd von Schlözer (now Secretary of the Prussian Legation in Rome). After an intimate dinner at Cavriani's* recently, Liszt seemed in a strikingly cheerful and excited frame of mind there. As is generally known, he is a close friend of Richard Wagner's, and he was now overjoyed at the flattering invitation Wagner has received from the young King Ludwig of Bavaria to go to Munich, where he is guaranteed a life free from cares. Liszt read out the King's letter (in transcript) to us. In it the King tells the composer how enthusiastic about his music he has been from early youth onwards, and of the joy it has given him; and so if he now offers him Munich as a place of residence, it is merely an expression of the sincere gratitude he owes him.†

The day before yesterday I visited Liszt at his monastery of Santa Maria del Rosario, situated on Monte Mario and blessed with a magnificent view over Rome and the mountains. It must have housed a good many people in days gone by, for the number of cells is considerable. Its present residents are just one Dominican monk, a monastery servant, and Liszt. In the little church, which lies open towards the main road, the Dominican reads mass every morning. Liszt never fails to attend, sitting like a prince in a box provided with a window partition which is only a few paces from his cell—like Charles V at the monastery of Yuste. . . .

The monastery is approached from the main road by a lofty and magnificent double flight of steps. The gate is always closed; you have to tug on a bell, whose melancholy tone penetrates every passage-way in the monastery. For my ears, a monastery bell and the church clock of an old

* Count Philipp Cavriani, a diplomatist at the Austrian Embassy.

† 'What a royal and marvellous act is Ludwig of Bavaria's letter to Wagner!' wrote Liszt to Brendel. 'It ought verily to be engraved in the Valhalla in letters of gold. Oh that some other Princes would adopt a similar style!'

castle have always had their own special magic. The servant who announces Liszt's visitors to him then appears.

This lodging-place of his Liszt owes to the well-known ultramontane, Father Theiner, a friend of his whom he told of his desire for a quiet, peaceful cell. . . .

In the middle of the rather large room there is a long desk; on the walls a few bookshelves; and in addition I counted on them and in the window recesses about a dozen pictures—both large and small—of the saints. On a corner table lies a marble cast of Chopin's hand, and next to it a case containing a ring presented to Liszt by Pius IX when he visited him here last year. Beside the desk stands rather an antiquated upright piano, out of tune into the bargain and—the best of the joke—with a D in the bass that doesn't sound. This is the instrument now used by that same Franz Liszt before whom the most massive pianos in Europe once trembled, and who for half a generation ruled the entire world of art like a *Jupiter tonans*. He hardly ever plays nowadays—at his lodgings he touches the piano only when composing. At present he is working on a piano arrangement of Beethoven's Ninth Symphony.

It always gives me immense pleasure to see him. Everything he says bears the stamp of originality and great genius, and it is easy to see that he once occupied a colossal position in the world. He still has the historic long hair—now grey—of earlier days; and when seated at the piano he does not forbear, at least once while playing, suddenly to fix his listeners sharply and penetratingly, to see whether they are being duly attentive. This trait, a relic of his great past, I have noticed here each time I have heard him. It is really priceless when he is in company and is invited to play when he has no desire to. He then becomes overpoweringly polite to his hosts, talks wittily about music, goes to the piano, plays some chord or other, his daemonic-sardonic eyes blitzing around the room as he does so, mutters to himself 'you oxen', takes his hat and departs. . . .

The day before yesterday . . . there arrived a compatriot of his, the brilliant violinist Reményi, who brought along not only the British Vice-Consul in Naples, Mr Douglas, and the latter's wife and daughter, but his violin too; and as Liszt had a short time ago set Lenau's *Zigeunerlied** to music, Reményi played it to us in his own arrangement for fiddle. Liszt accompanied on the upright piano with the missing D. But the piece is highly original, and Reményi's Hungarian blood became so excited that during the performance he was virtually dancing about, just as his fellow Magyars do in the puszta.

To end, a truly British scene was enacted. Douglas suddenly went over to Liszt with the words: 'May I ask a favour?'—'With pleasure.'—'May I

* *Die drei Zigeuner* (S320), for tenor or mezzo-soprano and piano. Liszt also made an arrangement of the song for violin and piano (S383)—perhaps the one attributed here to Reményi, to whom it was dedicated.

play *one* chord on your piano?'—'As many as you like.'—Whereupon Douglas strode majestically to the piano, played a chord, took out his notebook and wrote therein that at four o'clock in the afternoon of Monday, 30 May 1864, he had been in Franz Liszt's room at the monastery and played a chord on his piano.[3]

Kurd von Schlözer, 1 July. Returning from Genzano today, I bumped into Liszt and the impressive Transylvanian Bishop Haynald in the coupé. They had been on a visit to the Carthusians in the Trisulti monastery. The day before yesterday, in the evening, I accompanied them and Castano to the observatory of the Jesuit College here, where the learned astronomer Padre Angelo Secchi* allowed us to admire not only Jupiter but also Saturn and its moons through a magnificent telescope.[4]

In late July Liszt accompanied his friend the Grand Almoner Hohenlohe to the Pope's summer residence at Castel Gandolfo. 'The Holy Father is most graciously kind to me,' he told Carolyne. 'Yesterday, Saturday, at about noon, he deigned to receive me and to remark that it gave him pleasure to see me, speak with me and listen to me here. Shortly afterwards, between one and two o'clock, I played him several pieces on an upright piano that Monsignor Hohenlohe had managed to find. Today, at the same hour, I continued to exhibit my little repertoire to him. . . .'

In the second week of August, in order to attend the Tonkünstler-Versammlung at Karlsruhe, held from the 21st to 26th, Liszt returned to Germany for the first time since coming to live in Rome. Those works of his which were performed at the festival—including Psalm 13, the Sonata in B minor, the First Mephisto Waltz (both the orchestral and piano solo versions†), the two-piano *Concerto pathétique* (played by Bendel and Pflughaupt), and *Festklänge*—obtained a 'complete success'. Soloist in the Sonata and the Mephisto Waltz was a pupil of Bülow's, Fräulein Alide Topp, whom Liszt found 'quite simply a marvel'. Her performances were received with warm applause, and she was recalled several times.

At Karlsruhe Liszt was pleased to see his daughter Cosima. Among other visitors to the festival with whom he associated were Reményi (who contributed several performances), Pauline Viardot, Ivan Turgenev, Brahms, Lassen, Chorley, and Agnes Street-Klindworth.

Also present was Alexander Serov, who wished to hear Liszt's opinion of his opera *Judith*, which had been given at St Petersburg with great success. Finding the piano transcription (done in part by the unpractised pen of Valentina Serova, the composer's wife) very badly written, Liszt took up the full orchestral score.

Valentina Serova (1846–1924). Now the problem was, to play from the score. Masterly though the titanic musician's command of the orchestra

* The astronomer (1818–78) who originated classification of the stars by spectrum analysis, and was also one of the first to put photography to astronomical use, by photographing the sun during various phases of an eclipse, taking a complete set of photographs of the moon, etc.

† The Two Episodes from Lenau's Faust for orchestra (S110) date from *c.*1860 and consist

was, he did not succeed in reading Serov's complex orchestration quite smoothly. Besides, the Russian text stood in the way of a complete understanding of the work. When he had finished the first act, Liszt exclaimed: 'What? A whole act with Jews holding their jugs in the air and asking for water? Not very amusing, *parbleu*!'

So, when he began the second act, the whole spirit of the occasion was spoiled; a 'wrong note' persisted in sounding; both player and composer were malcontent and groaning, so to speak, under a heavy burden. Serov, without the least zeal or animation, explained the scenario; Liszt merely played 'correctly'; evidently Judith and Avra were for him fully as uninteresting as the weeping Hebrews. For the time being, however, the two friends remained outwardly calm. Suddenly Liszt stopped, and said: 'Here the harps cannot make themselves heard.'—'I have heard them precisely thirty-two times,' replied Serov, dissembling his irritation. 'I tell you, they cannot be heard—harps in the middle register always sound weak.'—'I have heard them thirty-two times!' repeated Serov in an irascible tone.

After this incident it was of course impossible to go on playing. Liszt rose, and frankly acknowledged that the opera did not please him. Noticing the expression of embarrassment on our faces he continued with decision and, so it appeared to me, with the utmost sincerity: 'This opera does not please me, it is not sufficiently interesting. It is only to my friends that I say just what I think; that is their privilege, to them I do not pretend.'[5]

To Carolyne, Liszt wrote: 'Serov is most displeased with me, because of my sincerity about his opera *Judith*—to which I advised him to do what Judith did to Holofernes!'

From Karlsruhe he went to Munich to see Bülow, who was suffering from nervous trouble and paralysis of the legs; and from that city accompanied Richard Wagner to Lake Starnberg, where the former fugitive was living in a villa placed at his disposal by King Ludwig. 'Solomon was wrong,' Liszt remarked to Carolyne, 'there *is* something new under the sun. I am fully convinced of it since yesterday evening, after Wagner acquainted me with some of the King's letters. . . . At bottom nothing can have changed between us. The great good fortune that has at last come his way will sweeten as much as possible certain asperities of his character. . . . He introduced me to his *Meistersinger*, and in exchange I produced my *Beatitudes*, with which he seemed more than content! His *Meistersinger* is a masterpiece of humour, spirit, and lively grace. It is animated and beautiful, like Shakespeare!'

Via Stuttgart (where the proprietor of his hotel refused all payment), Liszt proceeded to Weimar, which he reached in the early morning of 5 September. 'At the station there was no room in the only fiacre. When I was about to get in, I

of *Der nächtliche Zug* and *Der Tanz in der Dorfschenke* (1st Mephisto Waltz). The transcription (S514) of the second of these is the famous virtuoso work for piano solo. Like the two orchestral pieces it was dedicated to Carl Tausig.

found three gentlemen inside already. In preference to them, I joined Fortunato* to profit by the dark night to make *my midnight walk*—from the railway to the Altenburg. How many ghosts did I not meet! Schubert's *Doppelgänger* would be the nearest cousin to this spectral family!' With Cosima he then journeyed to Löwenberg, where they were the guests of Prince Hohenzollern-Hechingen. 'The Prince's orchestra being on holiday, it is I who have to provide the music. . . . Yesterday I played our Shepherds and Three Kings† to the Prince, as also the two St Francises.'

In early October, accompanied by Cosima, Liszt arrived in Paris. 'My mother is in perfect health,' he reported to Carolyne, 'and on many things retains a perfectly sound judgement, which she seasons with a charming good humour that does not lack a certain sweet and honest malice.' Among the friends and acquaintances he saw during this visit were Berlioz and Rossini.

Fanny Lewald. From our visit to Paris in the autumn of 1864 an event that took place on 12 October has remained vividly in my memory. As always, we were staying at the *pension* run by General Chamorin's wife in the rue Castiglione, where we had two rooms and a small ante-chamber. Liszt, who was very much sought after, had come to us once or twice at eleven in the morning; and did so likewise on 12 October. . . .

I felt rather uneasy, however, because the Comtesse d'Agoult had written to me a few days earlier: 'I shall call on you one of these days, and at an early hour to be sure of finding you in!' The thought that she might come that very morning, causing her an unexpected encounter with Liszt, I could not get out of my mind. I knew that since their separation they had not seen one another—or not for a very long time at least‡—and that any meeting could be agreeable to neither of them.

At first everything went very tranquilly. We chatted about all sorts of things, and then—suddenly there was a ring at the door of the ante-room. Because of my premonition, I went to answer it myself, and there, standing before me in all her proud beauty, was the Comtesse d'Agoult.

I felt it incumbent upon me to tell her that Liszt was with us. 'Qu'est-ce que ça me fait!' she said, and stepped into the room. Both men got to their feet and, head held high, she offered her hand to Stahr with a 'bonjour mon ami!'—and then turning to Liszt said: 'Mais imaginez vous, Madame Stahr, qui ne veut pas me faire entrer à cause de vous!' However, the smiling lips with which she pronounced those words had become pale; Liszt too, well though he maintained his composure, was bewildered and dismayed. His greeting sounded forced. We sat down, the superficial questions about each other's health were put by Liszt and the Comtesse in the customary way with artificial ease, and we strove as well as we could to

* Fortunato Salvagni, Liszt's Italian manservant.

† Respectively the *Shepherds' song at the manger* and *March of the Three Holy Kings* from *Christus*.

‡ Liszt's letter to Carolyne of 8 Oct., however, shows that he had seen Marie d'Agoult at dinner on the 6th.

introduce another topic. With no success however. Being together was embarrassing for all of us; and yet neither Liszt nor the Comtesse seemed to be agreed about which of them should be the first to leave; how they should most fittingly part from one another. The minutes weighed heavily on both of them. Finally the Comtesse took out her watch and rose to her feet. We followed her example. Going over to Liszt, she gave him her hand. He shook it in his hearty way and, accompanying her to the door with me, called after her an 'Adieu, Marie! adieu!' before the door closed behind her.[6]

Liszt and Cosima left Paris in the evening of Wednesday, 12 October, travelling initially to St Tropez where they wished to pray at Blandine's grave. Spending the night of the 14th here with Emile Ollivier and little Daniel, they went the next morning their separate ways, she to Germany, he to Rome.

Kurd von Schlözer, 26 November. On the 15th there was a most delightful dinner at the Meyendorffs'* with Liszt. As soon as the meal was over he sat at the piano and let fly with some of his showpieces again, which are nearly all so difficult and brilliant that no one else can play them. First there was a march, *Vom Fels zum Meer* [S229], composed for the Prussian army. A majestic piece. Then his Mephisto Waltz, not very well known, but demonic, mysterious. When animated, Liszt is most captivatingly likeable, and when he sees that his works are being enjoyed he is as pleased as the youngest novice.

[A few evenings later] I was at the Meyendorffs' again, where I heard Liszt once more. According to the legend, St Francis is said to have gone on one occasion into a wood and begun preaching to the birds, and with such eloquence that the singers of the skies fell silent and listened to him. This incident has been dealt with by Liszt, who played us the marvellous piece he has made out of it.[7]

1865

Kurd von Schlözer. Rome, 27 January. Liszt has been here. I am pleased every time I see him; someone original to the very core of his being. So, too, his wonderful works, the quintessence of the Music of the Future. . . . All in all, a deep vein of melancholy runs through him; but he can also be most cheerful, sarcastic, and rude. This last especially in circles where they have the impudence to ask him to play in front of strangers. A recent example was at Monsignor Nardi's, whose Thursday salon was overflowing

* Baron Felix von Meyendorff (1834–71) was First Secretary at the Russian Embassy in Rome. After his death his widow Olga became a close friend of Liszt's. See *infra*.

with monsignori, prelates, and English ladies, all of whom had been invited for Liszt, who is very friendly with Nardi and puts up at his place for the day when he comes in from his hermitage on Monte Mario. His beautiful Bechstein, too, is kept not at the monastery but at Nardi's.*

Liszt arrives, having been tricked by Nardi into thinking that only a few individuals have been invited—but instead finds the place packed with people. He recoils, Nardi implores, but Liszt is as hard as iron, and catching sight of me he addresses me loudly, half in German half in French, on the impossibility of playing anything—he cannot throw himself away: he values Art too highly for that, and himself as well. The bystanders were able to hear and take in every word.[1]

Herbert Oakeley (1830–1903), composer, organist, and scholar, writing to George Grove. Rome, 19 February. It [a recital by Liszt] was at the house of a lady [Mrs Isabel Cholmeley] whose clever bust of him was in our 1862 Exhibition.† The audience was limited—only nine. The piano was in the middle of the room. The great artist, who has the manners of royalty, came round and spoke to each of us, and then sat down to play. Although I have heard, and written about, all the great pianists of our time, I seemed to myself never before that afternoon to have realized the possibilities of the pianoforte! Difficulties so mastered as to have become mere child's play; the most ethereal touch; fire, poetry, tenderness; the marvels, ten times multiplied, of Thalberg; the cantabile of Henselt, the science of Moscheles, the grace of Chopin, the classical perfection of Clara Schumann, the chastened refinement of Hallé, the thundering onset of Rubinstein; imagine all these combined, with still something else beyond them—something that is Liszt, and Liszt alone. No wonder that whatever difference of opinion exists in Germany as to other eminent players, the great Hungarian is acknowledged always to be enthroned above them all. Among his selections were Chopin's A major Polonaise, his own exquisite D flat Etude, and, in a totally different style, his stupendous fantasia on *Ernani* [S432]. Then he persuaded our hostess to sing *The Last* (but ever-recurring) *Rose of Summer*, during each verse of which he improvised a gradually developed accompaniment. In the last verse there occurred a passage of sixths, *pianissimo e prestissimo*, where the wonderful hands went together up and down the keyboard with the most astonishing equality and rapidity, suggesting Briareus with his hundred hands; the player meanwhile looking anywhere but at his fingers, and smiling at the astonishment of his audience at the alteration of harmony and improvement to the melody in its new and gorgeous attire, and at the surprise of the singer, who pluckily maintained her *canto fermo*, notwithstanding the total change of accompaniment and colour of her tune at every recurrence

* Who lived at the Palazzo Torlonia, Via Bocca di Leone.
† The International Exhibition held at South Kensington that year.

of the first phrase, which by the way comes no less than six times in each verse. The memory of that recital will never perish![2]

Liszt to Jessie Laussot. Rome, 6 March. Knowing from experience with what little favour my works meet, I have been obliged to impose on myself a kind of systematic negligence and resigned passivity towards them. And so during the years of my exterior activity in Germany, I constantly observed the rule of never asking anyone to have any of my works performed; indeed, I went so far as positively to dissuade from doing so various persons who had shown me some intention of the kind—and that is what I shall do elsewhere too. There is neither modesty nor pride in this, it seems to me: I am simply taking into account the fact that M. Litz* is welcome virtually everywhere when he appears *at the piano* (especially since he has made a profession of the contrary), but that he has not been forgiven for taking it into his head to think and write according to his own fancy. Indeed, for some fifteen years this unfortunate M. Litz, who is at the end of his tether, has had people (and not only the indifferent or ill-disposed, but even so-called friends) yelling at him from all sides: 'Be a pianist, and nothing but a pianist. *How can you not be a pianist*, when etc. etc.'[3]

On 23 March, a charity concert organized by Liszt was held. 'The Senate had allowed it to be given in their palace on the Capitol,' noted Schlözer; 'and the Papal Choir was supplemented by the Vatican and Santa Maria Maggiore singers, so that hundreds of the most beautiful voices were joined together.' Liszt's *Beatitudes* were among the works performed, as was also Bach's Concerto in D minor for three keyboards, played by Liszt, Filippo Capocci, and Andrea Meluzzi. In addition, Liszt contributed a piano solo.

On Tuesday, 25 April, feast day of St Mark the Evangelist, Liszt, in his own words, 'entered the priesthood on receiving the minor orders in the chapel of His Serene Highness, Monsignor Hohenlohe, at the Vatican'.

It was a decision taken entirely by himself, and even Princess Carolyne had been informed only when preparations were well in hand. To Olga von Meyendorff many years later he wrote (of the Princess): 'People almost blamed her for my having entered the Vatican, of which she had no suspicion and which I simply announced to her, a month earlier, as settled.'

The last of all his preparations was to spend 'three or four days of transition' at the Lazarist Mission. 'They have been very sweet,' he wrote to Carolyne on the 24th. 'I shall retain a profounder and more serene memory of them than of my alleged successes of former times! Man is really only what he is in the eyes of God!'

Early in the morning of the 25th, Liszt, accompanied by Hohenlohe, made his way from the Lazarist Mission to the Vatican, where mass was preceded by the ceremony of his admission into the priesthood. 'The constitutive words of the ceremony are taken from Psalm 16. I uttered them with heart and tongue as the

* Liszt is deliberately quoting the misspelling of his name which was frequently encountered from the time in Paris when he was known as 'le petit Litz'.

Bishop was applying the marks of the tonsure to me. "The Lord is the portion of mine inheritance and of my cup: Thou maintainest my lot.". . . As you know, the tonsure must be in the form of a crown. This is so that on the cleric's head may be impressed the image of the crown of thorns of Our Saviour, Jesus Christ. It also signifies the "royal dignity" of him who is admitted into the ranks of the clergy. The word "cleric" comes from the Greek *kleros*: heritage, lot.'

Liszt was indeed now a cleric, a member of the clergy, but not—nor ever became—a full-blown priest. His admission into four of the seven degrees of priesthood—confirmed by the successful sitting of his minor orders examination three months later (30 July)—made him doorkeeper, reader, exorcist, and acolyte. He could not celebrate mass or hear confession; nor was celibacy enjoined upon him.

That same day he moved into the Vatican, where he lived in Hohenlohe's apartments until the latter was appointed a cardinal the following year. 'My rooms are very comfortable, well distributed and furnished, and suit me extremely well,' he told Carolyne. 'The view is *ad libitum*. If I go to the window, which I shall do only rarely, I can enjoy the whole of the façade of St Peter's. Otherwise I can see only a *buon pezzo* of the dome, which overlooks my writing-table. Apart from the bells, I can hear almost no noise. Do you remember the words of Felix Lichnowsky's father? "If Liszt had been an architect, he would have built the dome of St Peter's." '

His private audience with the Pope that evening he described to Carolyne in a letter of the 26th.

His Holiness . . . received me with great kindness and sweetness. At my second genuflexion, your recent prayer for the workman and his work came into my mind, and I said more or less this: 'The gospel for this day teaches us that the harvest is great. I, alas, am only a small and feeble workman—but I feel very happy now that I belong to you a little more. . . .' The Pope then said: 'You will now have some theological studies to undertake.'—'I have not remained a complete stranger to them, and shall resume them with all the more joy and zeal. It is also indispensable for me to work at my Latin.' Pius IX: 'The Germans have great facility.' Ego: 'In particular my compatriots, the Hungarians—my father was an excellent Latinist.'. . . My audience lasted about ten minutes. At the end the Holy Father gave me his blessing *in extenso*.*[4]

Kurd von Schlözer, 25 April. The move had long been prepared. Rumours had been going around for months—but now that the bomb has gone off people are rubbing their eyes in amazement. . . . Of his reasons for this step, different versions are circulating, in all of which, however, Princess

* One of the wilder bits of nonsense put about by some of the more unthinking of Liszt's biographers, is that according to which he confessed to the Pope, at this meeting, for a full five hours—before being dismissed with the words 'Tell the rest of your sins to the piano!' See, e.g., William Wallace, *Liszt, Wagner and the Princess* (London, 1927), 104. As this extract from Liszt's own immediate résumé makes plain, confessions formed no part of an interview which was entirely devoted to conversation and lasted a mere ten minutes. Furthermore, 19th-century Popes did not receive confessions.

Wittgenstein plays the chief role. Some maintain that fear that the unpredictable Franz might yet marry some young woman agitated her so much that she set the whole Vatican in motion to see that influential clerics gently propelled the good Franz into the clergy. Others turn the page and say that the Princess's family had got wind of a misalliance and persuaded Monsignor Hohenlohe, whose brother is the Princess's son-in-law, to influence Liszt.

I am now uncommonly keen to see the good Liszt again, in his new costume. At that Thursday concert [20 April at the Palazzo Barberini, for charity] he looked poorly and preoccupied, so that when I greeted him he did not let fly those piquant little jokes of his as usual.[5]

Ferdinand Gregorovius, 30 April. Liszt gave his farewell concert in the Palazzo Barberini. . . . Amateurs played and sang: he played the *Invitation to the Dance* and *Erlkönig*—a curious farewell to the world. No one suspected that he had the abbé's stockings already in his pocket. . . . He now wears the abbé's frock, lives in the Vatican, and, as Schlözer told me yesterday, looks well and contented. This is the end of the gifted virtuoso, a truly sovereign personality. Am glad that I heard him play again; he and the instrument seem to be one, as it were, a piano-centaur.[6]

Emile Ollivier's diary. (Paris) 3 May. This morning Madame Liszt sent to say that she wished to speak to me. Going up, I found her in floods of tears, and she showed me a letter from her son telling her that he has received the tonsure and will henceforth be the Abbé Liszt. The letter contains some very kind words about me. I consoled this poor woman as best I could; and indeed she told me that it was not the first time he had entertained the idea. Twice already he had wished to become a priest: first, at the age of fourteen, and then after the death of his father, before his meeting with Madame d'Agoult. I passed the news on to the latter, telling her that it was a spiritual suicide.[7]

Liszt's mother to her son. Paris, 4 May. My dear child! One often speaks about a thing for so long, until it actually comes to pass—and thus it is with the present change in your status. It has on several occasions been reported here in the newspapers that you had entered the Church. When people mentioned such a thing to me, I was very opposed to it! Your letter of 27 April, which I received yesterday, affected me deeply—and I burst into tears. Forgive me, I was really not expecting such news from you! After reflection—they say *la nuit porte conseil*—I resigned myself to your will, as also to the Will of God. I became calmer—for all good inspirations come from God! This decision to which you have come is not an *ordinary* one. May God give you the grace to accomplish it to His satisfaction. It is a great thing—but you have already prepared for it for a long time on Monte Mario. I have noticed it for some time in your letters to me. They were worded so beautifully, so religiously, that I was often very moved—and devoted some tears to you. And now in this last one, my child, *tu me demandes pardon*! Oh, I have nothing to forgive you! Your good qualities outweighed many, many of your youthful errors. You have always strictly and in all respects done your duty—giving me joy and tranquillity thereby. My life is peaceful and untroubled, something for which I have only you to thank.

Now live happily, my dear child. If the blessing of a weak, mortal mother can have effect with God—then by me be blessed a thousand times. I commend you to God and remain your devoted mother, Anna Liszt.[8]

Kurd von Schlözer. Rome, 5 May. Last week Princess Wittgenstein asked me to visit her. The Liszt business is leaving her no peace. All the explanations going around were false, she told me. 'He has taken this step neither to escape a marriage nor to obtain a cardinal's hat.' Had they wished to marry, this—she said—would have been possible to them at any time. Four years ago it had been their intention. They had already rented a house here, fixed the day of the wedding—and then the Holy Father's wish had been made known to them, that they were not to marry in Rome; family influences of all kinds had been brought to bear at the Vatican, and as good Catholics they had obeyed. Fear of marriage had therefore had nothing at all to do with Liszt's decision. 'If he is now devoting himself to the Church,' said the Princess, 'he took the step partly from religious impulse, partly from lofty artistic reasons—to kings and princes one must offer only flowers gathered in their own gardens.' She added: 'Liszt wishes to immerse himself in religion so that he may dedicate his Art to the Church.'

As Liszt had sent a message to say that he wished to visit me, I went from the Princess's straight to the Vatican, where, at the Pope's behest, rooms have been set aside for him (in the apartments used formerly by Hohenlohe). He seemed very content. I did not notice the small tonsure. The shortening of his world-historic hair suited him very well. He wore a long black cassock, shoes and stockings. The black three-cornered hat lay on the table. He is an indescribably good fellow. With all this it is by no means his intention—as he put it—to give up music: 'I shall show them what music in a cassock is!'[9]

Ferdinand Gregorovius, 7 May. Yesterday I saw Liszt, clad as an abbé. He was getting out of a hackney carriage, his black silk cassock fluttering ironically behind him—Mephistopheles disguised as an abbé. Such is the end of Lovelace![10]

Liszt to Prince Constantin von Hohenzollern-Hechingen. The Vatican, 11 May. Convinced that by this act I would be confirming to myself that I was on the right path, I accomplished it without effort, in total simplicity and uprightness of intention. Moreover, it accords with the antecedents of my youth, just as it does with the development undergone by my work of musical composition during these last four years—work which I intend to pursue with renewed vigour, since I consider it to be the least defective part of my nature.

To speak familiarly: if 'the habit does not make the monk', neither does it prevent him being one; and in certain cases, when the monk is fully formed within, why not assume the outer garb as well?

But I am forgetting that I do not in the least intend to become a monk in the strict sense of the word. I lack the necessary vocation, and it is enough for me to belong to the hierarchy of the Church to the degree that the minor orders allow me. And so it is not the frock but the cassock that I have donned. And on this subject, Your Highness will forgive me the slight vanity of mentioning that people pay me the compliment of saying that I wear my cassock as though I had worn it all my life.[11]

To an unidentified correspondent. The Vatican, 20 May. Yes, Sir, it is true that I have embraced the priesthood—not in any way out of dislike of the world, and still less out of weariness with my art. I know that in remaining in the world the artist can serve the cause of the Beautiful, which in certain elevated regions is identified with that of the Good and of the True; but I also believe that among those called to one expression of art or another, there are more pronounced vocations which wholly determine one's thought. Whoever feels the blessing, the grace, the bliss of Faith, naturally regards religious music as pre-eminent. It is joined and incorporated with the sublimest acts—those which, in worship, establish mankind's most direct relations with Divinity, the created and their Creator. This supreme virtuality exercises so powerful an ascendancy even over artists denied the Christian religion, that I have seen some of them, including several of the greatest, bitterly regret that they are outcasts from the field of action which is the pinnacle of our art.[12]

Kurd von Schlözer, 26 May. Last Tuesday we gave a small dinner party, the guests being the Chimays, Baroness Meyendorff, Russell,* and Liszt. Arnim† brought an excellent Amontillado back with him from Portugal, which Liszt sipped with great appreciation during the winter. Nor did his abbé's dress prevent him from doing all honour on Tuesday to this offspring of the West European coast. After we had dined, he played entrancingly on Arnim's beautiful Bechstein for about two hours. One of his Polonaises was incomparable. At the piano he looked like a Mephisto as he sat there triumphantly hurling those demoniacal glances of his to left and right.[13]

During the spring and summer Liszt also spent some time at the Villa d'Este at Tivoli, the property of his friend Monsignor Hohenlohe. Famed for its

* Odo Russell (1829–84), the later Baron Ampthill, was a younger brother of the 9th Duke of Bedford and a second cousin of the mathematician and philosopher Bertrand Russell.

† The Prussian Ambassador, Count Harry von Arnim (1824–81).

magnificent gardens with their immense fountains, the Villa had been built *c.*1550 for Cardinal Ippolito d'Este, son of Lucrezia Borgia. 'Everything here is perfect,' he told the Princess, 'beginning with my "patron". He has arranged three rooms very attractively for me—with piano, harmonium, and furniture which could not be better assorted. . . . I began my sacristan studies this morning, by serving mass to Hohenlohe. I hope to be able to perform this office properly before long.'

While at the Villa d'Este he finished his *Missa choralis* (S10) for mixed chorus and organ, and also worked on the *Stabat mater dolorosa*, the antepenultimate section of *Christus*.

In early August, shortly after passing the minor orders examination for which he had been studying, he left for Pest, to attend the first Hungarian Music Festival. It was to include the première of his *Legend of St Elisabeth*, given in Hungarian ('Szent Erzsébet Legendája') in the translation prepared by his friend Kornél von Ábrányi (1822–1903).

Liszt reached Pest in the evening of 8 August, having journeyed by sea to Genoa and then overland. Some free time at Milan he had used to visit the church of San Carlo al Corso and the great Cathedral.*

St Elisabeth, performed (under Liszt himself) on 15 August at the Vigadó concert hall, was received with acclamation. 'The newspapers are filled with my name—I have become a kind of public event!' he reported to Carolyne. Present among many other friends and supporters were Cosima and Hans von Bülow, and Liszt's uncle-cousin Eduard.

At a concert on the 17th, Liszt conducted the first movement of the Dante Symphony ('which created such a sensation that I had the whole of the first part, from Francesca's episode to the end, repeated') and his arrangement for orchestra (S117) of the Rákóczy March. On the 22nd *St Elisabeth* was given again. 'The performance was remarkable. The 500 singers and the orchestra performed their task with a kind of passionate piety—and at certain moments with transports of enthusiasm.'

The last of these immensely successful concerts was at the Vigadó on 29 August, when as a kind of 'thank you' to the public Liszt played his two St Francis Legends (their first public performance), *Ave Maria*, and *Cantique d'amour*. Bülow and Reményi also took part. The 26th and 27th, together with the Bülows, Reményi, and Baron Augusz, he had spent at Gran as guest of the Prince Primate of Hungary.

On Saturday, 2 September, having taken the steamer down the Danube, the same party arrived at Augusz's home in Szekszárd, where they stayed for a week. Liszt had not been here since 1846.

Anna Augusz (1848–89), eldest of the five children of Liszt's host, took care to record in her diary each day details of this visit 'from the greatest and noblest man of the century'.

2 September. If only I could tell the whole world of the joy that our entire family, and the town of Szekszárd with us, felt when we heard these words:

* Carolyne was eager to know his impressions of both sacred buildings (which he had not seen since the 1830s), since the church is dedicated to her name saint, San Carlo Borromeo, whose remains are housed in the Cathedral.

'The Abbé Liszt is arriving!'. . . It would be impossible to describe the ineffable goodness emanating from his noble features, the angelic smile he gives his daughter from time to time, or when he addresses a remark to her. At every moment his noble soul seems to be listening to sublime and incomparable melodies. . . .

At dinner I had the pleasure of being placed beside the charming Cosima. Ilona* was to propose a toast to the Abbé, to express to him in the name of the whole family the joy and happiness we felt at seeing him amongst us—but when the great moment arrived and she began her toast, she could not continue; but the tears which ran down her cheeks must have shown her joy and gratitude still better than her words. With his great kindness, the Abbé—he who so well understands the language of the heart and the soul—accepted it in this manner too.

Anna Augusz, Sunday, 3 September. After lunch we went to Decs, a little village an hour from here, to see the countryfolk in their Sunday best. . . . On the way home M. l'Abbé shelled nuts for Cosima and Toni, then took Cosima's hand in his own and caressed it. Cosi was charming. She read out some poems to her father, and then hummed and talked. It was really interesting to see the tableau of this excellent father and his dear and good daughter chatting together so delightfully and animatedly in the carriage. In the evening . . . the large square in front of our home was filled by an immense crowd of people, standing tightly together. Then, winding about as they approached through the trees in the square, lighted torches could be seen. The procession lined up in front of our windows. M. Halász, at the head of the Dalárda [philharmonic society], made a speech on behalf of the people of Szekszárd, greeting the great Liszt and informing him that the town of Szekszárd wished to add its modest flower of esteem and devotion to the crown of glory of the great master whom the whole world had honoured. M. l'Abbé meanwhile appeared at the salon window and was greeted with loud cheering. The entire scene was illuminated by magnificent moonlight and by a Bengal fire which had been lit in the square. . . . The Dalárda then sang three melodies in honour of Him who has created so many magnificent ones. M. Reményi spoke to the assembled crowd of the joy that each of us had to feel in being able to welcome the great master, the king of music, to the town of Szekszárd. . . .

Interpreting for M. l'Abbé, Papa then told the audience that, in response to their kind reception, M. Liszt wished to reply to them in the intimate language of the heart, that of music. And so he went to the piano and played some Hungarian Rhapsodies with Reményi, and then, very grandiosely, the Rákóczy March as a duet [S608] with Herr von Bülow, his noble features expressing extreme goodness and lively joy at every moment. . . .

* The second of the Augusz children.

Anna Augusz, 6 September. M. l'Abbé gave both Ilona and me great pleasure by inscribing his name in our albums. In one of my diaries everyone writes his name on the anniversary of his birth. M. l'Abbé, whose birthday is the 22nd of October, wrote there for me: *Wolle stets, was du sollst.** They are words of Leonardo da Vinci's. . . .

Anna Augusz, 7 September. During lunch M. l'Abbé drank the health of M. Plotényi,† who was celebrating the anniversary of the day when M. Reményi adopted him as his son, three years ago. After the meal we went in two carriages to the Csörgető, a pond situated in the puszta. When we got there we found some fishermen who had cast their nets; they caught some fish and crabs, and at once cooked them on a big fire lit on the bank. While this was going on, M. l'Abbé climbed into the boat with M. Rosty,‡ Baron von Bülow, and Plotényi. . . . After that we went to a little wooden pavilion on the bank, where we ate fish and cakes. . . . On the way home the good Abbé said: it was not a miraculous draught of fishes, but a delicious one!

In the evening the excellent Abbé played his beautiful piece *La Notte*§ to us again. Then M. Rosty showed Cosima and the Abbé the book of his 'travels in America', while M. Plotényi played the piano.¶ Then M. l'Abbé took Toni on his back and carried her around the salon while the rest of us cheered; Herr von Bülow played the piano and M. Reményi sang. . . .

Anna Augusz, 8 September. The good Abbé, alas, decided on his departure for tomorrow morning, which gave us great sorrow. Before lunch he again very kindly played us his *Ave Maria* and the chorus of angels from *St Elisabeth*. . . .

Herr von Bülow presented us with his photograph, and after lunch came into the garden with us, where he took his coffee and smoked. M. Rosty came out too, as did, a little later, M. l'Abbé, who had been resting in his room; he looked at M. Rosty's book, and M. Rosty told him how he had spent a night on America's great mountain, Popocatepetl (meaning: Mountain which smokes a lot). . . . M. l'Abbé remarked that the name of Popocatepetl was 'a name for popularity'. 'One has only to get used to it,' he said.[14]

Via Pest, Venice and Florence, Liszt reached Rome on 15 September, having enjoyed his brief stops *en route*. 'What an imposing and irresistible architectural symphony, the Grand Canal from the Doges' Palace to the Rialto, St Mark and

* This seems to be a German equivalent of the Italian *Volere è potere*. (Where there's a will there's a way.)

† The Hungarian pianist and violinist Nándor Plotényi (1844–1933).

‡ Pál Rosty (1830–74), a world traveller.

§ The (unfinished) piano-solo version (S699) of the second of the *Trois Odes funèbres*.

¶ The former Augusz home in Szekszárd now houses a Liszt museum, one of whose exhibits is this instrument, an 1865 Beregszászy. Its soundboard bears the signatures of Liszt, Bülow, Reményi, Plotényi, Rosty, and Augusz.

his lion! . . . At Florence, where I was obliged to stop from midnight until 4.00 a.m., I prowled around the statue of Dante* in the Piazza Santa Croce, and at the Loggia found an old friend, the *Perseus* of Benvenuto Cellini, of glorious and swaggering memory.'

Princess Carolyne to Henriette von Schorn. Rome, 12 November. You will have heard of the tremendous success of Liszt's *St Elisabeth* at Pest. It was written more or less with the Wartburg in mind, but things have turned out better thus. The Catholic legend would have proved difficult for many non-Catholic ears. In the Saint's homeland no one thought of her but as a fellow countrywoman, and Otto Roquette's poetry worked wonders. At present, thank God, all goes splendidly with Liszt, who is rejuvenated both in health and appearance. He is living in *the Vatican*, and this great musical genius of the century there finds himself in company worthy of him. His door is just opposite *Raphael's Loggie* and two paces from *Michelangelo's Sistine*. So everything is in harmony. . . .[15]

1866

Ferdinand Gregorovius, 7 January. Last Wednesday [3 January] Liszt conducted a cantata in [the church of] Ara Coeli, the *Stabat mater speciosa* of Fra Jacopone [da Todi], set to a composition of his own. It was rather tame; leaning over towards me, he whispered: 'Church music! Church music!'[1]

In early February Liszt received news from Paris of the death of his mother, who had died at Ollivier's home in the rue St Guillaume on Tuesday the 6th. After the funeral service at the church of St Thomas Aquinas, she was buried in the cemetery of Montparnasse.

Ferdinand Gregorovius, 15 February. Liszt . . . has aged greatly, his face is quite shrunken; but his vivacity is always most attractive. Countess Tolstoy† told me yesterday that an American lady living here had caused the covering of a chair, on which Liszt had sat, to be framed and hung on the wall. She had told the story to Liszt, who at first feigned annoyance and then asked whether it was true. If a man such as he does not hold mankind in contempt, the fact must be reckoned to his honour.[2]

Invited by King Ludwig II of Bavaria to attend a performance (the first in the original German) of *The Legend of St Elisabeth* at Munich on 24 February, Liszt

* Which Liszt would not have known from previous visits to Florence, for it had been inaugurated only four months earlier, during the Dante sexcentenary celebrations.

† Wife of the Russian writer Count Alexei Tolstoy (1817–75) whom Liszt saw frequently in Rome and whose ballad *The Blind Singer* he set (S350) as a recitation for voice and piano.

declined with regret. Two months later the King, to whom the oratorio was subsequently dedicated, bestowed upon him the Order of St Michael.

On Monday, 26 February, Sgambati conducted the Dante Symphony at the inauguration of the new Sala Dante. Liszt, noted Gregorovius, 'reaped an Indian summer of homage. The ladies of the gallery overwhelmed him with flowers from above—Frau L. almost slaying him with a laurel wreath.'

Shortly afterwards he left for Paris, which he reached on Sunday, 4 March. The musical reason for the journey was the performance of the Gran Mass to be given at St Eustache on the 15th; the personal reason, to attend to his mother's effects and visit her grave.* 'We have just opened my mother's desk and cupboards,' he wrote later to Carolyne. 'She left very few objects of value—a bracelet, two watches, some rings, a shawl, some false teeth—that is virtually everything!'

Emile Ollivier. Deep down [Liszt] is sad and unhappy, and his soul is certainly not joyful; but he is very kind and affectionate to me, and I feel a sincere pleasure in seeing him. He is using his mother's rooms, and we see one another often.[3]

On 8 March Liszt accepted an invitation to the salon of the ugly, but vivacious and popular, Princess Pauline Metternich (1836–1921), wife of the Austrian Ambassador. 'About fifteen people were there,' he reported to Carolyne. 'I played the two St Francis Legends, the "fried chicken",† as a reminiscence, and by order—the Sanctus and Credo from the [Gran] Mass, four hands with Saint-Saëns,‡ a first-class musician.' Princess Metternich: 'It was a memorable experience to hear such a pair. "There's no doubt about it, we two play remarkably well together," said Liszt, laughing heartily over this self-praise. Then he turned to Saint-Saëns, and exclaimed: "It is possible to be as much of a musician as Saint-Saëns; it is impossible to be more of one!"'

Camille Saint-Saëns. I already considered him to be a genius and had formed in advance an almost impossible conception of his pianism. Judge of my astonishment when I realized that he far exceeded even this expectation. The dreams of my youthful fancy were but prose beside the Dionysiac poetry evoked by his supernatural fingers. It would be impossible to give any idea of what he was like to those who never heard him in full possession of his talent. . . . As I write I see again that long pale face casting seductive glances at his audience while from beneath his

* Which was not omitted, for before his next visit to Paris (June 1878) he wrote in a letter of condolence: 'I, too, have wept at the grave of my mother.'

† Liszt's nickname for his *Soirées de Vienne* after Schubert.

‡ Camille Saint-Saëns (1835–1921) himself recalled this occasion many years later: 'Liszt was not only a very great musician, but also a very wonderful man. He knew how to put one at ease with just a few kind words. I myself experienced this trait the first time he asked me to play. He wanted me to sight-read at the piano an orchestral score with him. As I stood shaking, he said quietly, "You will see, everything will be fine. You have nothing to worry about. I know you sight-read very well. This is how we shall do it: I shall take the lower parts and work the pedal while you will take the upper parts and turn the pages. In this way you will have only *some* of the instrumental parts. I shall take the others. Things will go together, you will see!"'

fingers, almost unconsciously and with an amazing range of nuances, there murmured, surged, boomed and stormed the waves of the *Légende de St François de Paule marchant sur les flots.* Never again shall we see or hear anything like it.[4]

At St Eustache on Thursday, 15 March, the Gran Mass was received very coolly, and several of Liszt's oldest friends, including Berlioz and d'Ortigue, showed open hostility to it. Emile Ollivier, on the other hand, noted in his diary: 'Although the performance was by no means flawless, I found it very beautiful.' The Comtesse d'Agoult sent word to Liszt that she found his absence from her salon inexplicable, while at the same time she was arranging for an unfavourable review of the Mass to be printed. She also republished her disparaging novel *Nélida.*

Walter Bache to Jessie Laussot, 17 March. The execution was tolerable: unfortunately there were no women's voices in the chorus, so that the accents, etc. were not given with much vigour: the orchestra and chorus were unfortunately not raised, which of course lessened the effect in so vast a church. . . . Just fancy, there was a detachment of soldiers in the church, and occasionally during the music the officer gave the word of command at the top of his voice! During the Sanctus the drummer performed an obbligato! Can you believe me? Before the Mass we had several polkas played by the military band, and the Mendelssohn Wedding March badly played on the organ!! (One of the papers said that Liszt did it.) Directly after the last notes of the *Agnus Dei,* orchestra and chorus began some other piece belonging to the service in a Donizetti style, all the people believing that it was by Liszt! During the music, lady patronesses came round rattling money boxes, and upsetting chairs with their crinolines! The audience was just like the one at the Palazzo Barberini.

In spite of all this, the whole affair was a great event and immense pleasure to several people; and nobody talks of anyone but Liszt at present. . . . I saw him twice yesterday. *I can't tell* you how kind and delightful he was—I shall never forget it as long as I live. . . . Today he came to breakfast here; I can't find adjectives enough to tell you how divine he was: he played so splendidly. . . . It seemed to me today as if I had never heard him before — it was something entirely new for me.[5]

Liszt to Princess Carolyne. Paris, 18 March. I am trying to find the right word. Success, yes; sensation even—but a difficult situation.* St Gregory will help us! One gets an idea of certain things only by doing them! I was hoping to be able to inform you by this evening of the second performance

* Many years later, Liszt wrote of 'the Gran Mass—which was so unhappily performed at Paris in 1866, and more unhappily criticized then. . . . The mistake I made was not to have forbidden a performance given under such deplorable conditions. A philanthropic reason, which is valueless in matters of Art, kept me from doing so. I did not wish to deprive the fund for the poor of the assured receipts of more than 40,000 francs.'

of the Mass. Three or four proposals have been made to me on the subject —but no conclusion yet. . . .

The day before yesterday I asked Prince Metternich to express to the Emperor my desire to be allowed to thank His Majesty for his kindnesses towards me. Princess Julie, whom I saw yesterday for the first time, called me the most sought-after man in Paris! That is much too much for the little that I am! The newspapers are concerning themselves with me daily, I am told. . . . Rossini is being very kind, and proposed a toast to me at yesterday's dinner. . . . In the evening more than a hundred people turned up, the young Rothschilds among others. Rossini had the tact not to ask me to play, although everyone was counting on hearing me. I deliberately refrained from offering—for newspapers large and small would have torn to pieces this unfortunate pianist, the Abbé Liszt![6]

The American singer Lillie Moulton. The famous pianist Liszt, the new Abbé, is pervading Paris just now, and is, I think, very pleased to be a priestly lion, taking his success as a matter of course. There are a succession of dinners in his honour, where he does ample justice to the food, and is in no way bashful about his appetite.

He does a great deal of beaming; he has (as someone said) 'so much countenance'.

He dined with us the other night, the Metternichs, and twenty-five other people, among whom were Auber and Massenet.*

In the boudoir before dinner, he spied a manuscript which Auber had brought that afternoon. He took it up, looked at it, and said, *'C'est très joli!'* and laid it down again. When we went in to dinner, and after his cigar in the conservatory (he is a great smoker), he went to the piano and played the *'joli'* little thing of Auber's. Was not that wonderful, that he could remember it all the time during dinner? He seemed only to have glanced at it, and yet he could play it off like that from memory. He is so kind and good, especially to struggling artists, trying to help them in every way. He seemed extraordinarily amiable that evening, for he sat down at the piano without being asked and played a great many of his compositions—quite an unusual thing for him to do! One has generally to tease and beg him, and then he refuses. But I think, when he heard Massenet improvising at one of the pianos he was inspired, and he put himself at the other (we have two grand pianos), and they played divinely, both of them improvising. He is by far the finest pianist I have ever heard, and has a very seductive way of looking at you while playing, as if he were playing for you alone, and when he smiles you simply go to pieces. I don't wonder he is such a lady-killer, and that no woman can resist him; even my father-in-law stayed in the

* Liszt and Jules Massenet (1842–1912) had first met in Rome two years previously, and it was Liszt who had introduced the French musician to Constance de Sainte-Marie, the young woman who became Madame Massenet.

salon, being completely hypnotized by Liszt, who ought to consider this as one of his greatest triumphs, if he only knew.

I sang some of Massenet's songs, accompanied, of course, by Massenet. Liszt was most attentive and most enthusiastic. He said Massenet had a great future, and he complimented me on my singing, especially my phrasing and expression. . . .

He has the most wonderful magnetism. His appearance is certainly original as you see him in his soutane, his long hair, and his numerous moles, that stand out in profile whichever way he turns his broad face. . . .

I invited him to go to the Conservatoire with me in the box which Auber had given to me for last Sunday's concert. . . . The orchestra played Wagner's overture to *Tannhäuser.* The applause was not as enthusiastic as Liszt thought it ought to be, so he stood up in the box, and with his great hands clapped so violently that the whole audience turned towards him, and, recognizing him (indeed, it would have been difficult not to recognize him, such a striking figure as he is), began clapping their hands for him. He cried *'Bis!'* And the audience in chorus shouted *'Bis!'* And the orchestra repeated the whole overture. Then the audience turned again to Liszt and screamed *'Vive Liszt!'*

Auber said such a thing had never been seen or heard before in the annals of these severe and classical concerts. People quite lost their heads, and Auber, being afraid that there would be a demonstration at the *sortie,* advised us to leave before the end.

I think Liszt was very pleased with his afternoon.[7]

In 1842 Liszt had renewed acquaintance with César Franck, in whose three Piano Trios, Op. 1, he had shown great interest (and which he afterwards played at Weimar); and in gratitude for his advice and encouragement Franck had later dedicated to him the Piano Trio, Op. 2. Now, during this visit to Paris, Liszt took the opportunity, on Tuesday, 3 April, to go to Sainte-Clotilde to hear Franck's masterly playing of several of his own works on that church's great Cavaillé-Coll instrument; afterwards coming down from the organ-loft and leaving the church, in the words of Franck's pupil Vincent d'Indy, 'lost in amazement and evoking the name of J. S. Bach in an inevitable comparison'.

Liszt to Princess Carolyne. Paris, 13 April. I have put off speaking to you about Nélida until now—although I have twice seen and spoken to her *tête-à-tête.* Ollivier and others urged me to make this visit, a few days after the Mass at St Eustache. She told me that it was her intention to publish her memoirs. I retorted that I did not believe it possible for her to write them, for what she would entitle memoirs would be reduced to lies and postures. In saying that, I put plainly to her for the first time the distinction between the True and the False. Those are big words—but it was necessary to use them, to do my duty. Since the continuation of a communion of minds between the two of us is now becoming an immorality, nothing was left to me when seeing her again but to lean on duty. Besides, the role of Guermann is a very silly invention; it is time to finish once and for all with such a doctrinal sentimentalism. Madame d'Agoult does not have to be indulgent towards me. Hand on heart, I believe Right is on my side—and shall be able to reproach myself only with having used a little violence in the form. Unfortunately it is impossible to say certain things in a way that is agreeable to those they hurt! Surgical operations are not carried out with strokes of a fan![8]

To the same, 21 April. My session at Léon Kreutzer's with d'Ortigue, Damcke* and Berlioz has had one good outcome: that I am quite at ease with two of my old friends, d'Ortigue and Léon. . . . Using the piano-duet version of the Gran Mass, in less than an hour I explained to them how I proceeded in my works, and made a special point of vindicating myself against the unjust charge that I am overturning accepted notions of harmony, rhythm, and melody. Far from overturning, I believe I have developed and enriched them. Damcke agreed that in my Mass there is not a single bar which infringes the rules of harmony. He is a teacher of harmony with a big reputation—but has been opposed to the new school until now, Berlioz excepted. Well, he assured me that he could undertake to teach at any conservatoire in accordance with the examples contained in my work. He was not present at the St Eustache performance, of which only false reports had reached him. As for Berlioz, I treated him with all the respectful consideration I owe him. I imagine that this hour of friendly chat has not lessened the good opinion he may have of my bit of musical *savoir-faire.* Naturally we spoke of you—and on this topic we shall always be in agreement![9]

On Saturday, 21 April, Liszt was granted an audience at the Tuileries with Napoleon III. 'The Emperor received me with a Napoleonic grace, and I stayed with him for about half an hour.'

On the 24th he arrived in Amsterdam, where he was met by Cosima and Hans. At a concert the next day his Psalm 13 was performed, and Bülow played the arrangement for piano and orchestra of Schubert's Wanderer Fantasy as well as several solos. Mounting the platform to acknowledge the applause, Liszt was presented with an inscribed silver laurel wreath. A second concert followed on the 27th, at which, in addition to Beethoven's Fourth Piano Concerto, Bülow played Liszt's *Rapsodie espagnole (Folies d'Espagne et Jota aragonesa)* (S254), dating from *c.*1863, a brilliant virtuoso piece for piano solo. On the 29th the Gran Mass was performed at the church of Moses and Aaron. In response to an invitation from Queen Sophie of Holland, Liszt then proceeded to the Hague, where the Queen gave him a 'wonderful' reception. Via Brussels on the 30th, he returned to Paris on 1 May.

Liszt to Baron Antal Augusz. Paris, early May. People being as they are, it seems to me very simple that they should . . . envy me and seek all possible

* Berthold Damcke (1812–75), German composer, teacher, and admirer of Berlioz.

means of giving me a hard life. Far better, loftier, and worthier souls than I have been subjected to worse treatment, both now and in days gone by. This, it must be said, is no consolation; but these examples can help to bolster our courage. A man endowed with some superiority will accomplish his task only at the cost of many sufferings. But so long as we have clear consciences; there is nothing to fear. 'If God is with us, who will be against us?'

Once again, my very dear friend, please do not be distressed by attacks upon myself, whether spoken or in print. *I* am not complaining, for I have been nobly loved, far beyond what I could ever deserve.[10]

Emile Ollivier, 4 May. Liszt played the C minor Symphony to me yesterday. How uplifting it was! What a genius, and at bottom what a good and affectionate heart! When I told him of my cemetery plan, he said with emotion: 'You will put me there, won't you?'[11]

Liszt's activities in Paris before his return to Rome included a matinée at Rossini's at which he and the pianist Francis Planté (1839–1934) played, on two pianos, *Les Préludes* (S637) and *Tasso* (S636)—which 'succeeded beyond my expectation. People seem gradually to be forming a certain opinion of my talent as a composer, but as yet we are only at the preliminaries'; a soirée at Gustave Doré's; and a long meeting and talk with Gounod. On 10 May he was commanded to the Tuileries by the Empress Eugénie. 'I had not requested this audience, of which I retain a most gracious memory. Her Majesty did not ask me to play, but the conversation having taken a musical turn I proposed to her that I should make my Saint walk on the waters, and we went into the salon. The Empress had received me alone at first; but she summoned her two ladies-in-waiting and her chamberlain to the salon—so as not to mortify them!'

Emile Ollivier, 22 May. Today Liszt left for Rome. I was really sorry to see him go. During his stay we had grown closer together, and he had had an opportunity to convince himself that he could trust me.

Before leaving his mother's sitting-room he cast a melancholy glance at the open piano, Blandine's piano, played a few chords on it as though to bid it farewell, and then went out.

Before going downstairs we embraced one another tenderly, and he said: 'Have me buried at St Tropez. . . .'

On the train he could not hold back his tears. I, too, was very moved. . . . I have become fully aware of his genius as a composer, which is no longer a matter of doubt to me. When everyone is as enthusiastic as certain of those I see around me, they will no longer hesitate to give him his rightful due.[12]

Shortly after Liszt's return to Rome, his friend and host, Monsignor Gustav Hohenlohe, was appointed a cardinal and had to vacate the Grand Almoner's rooms at the Vatican. Liszt accordingly returned in mid-June to his former quarters in the Madonna del Rosario on Monte Mario.

Here on Saturday, 29 September, he completed (subject to later revisions) his oratorio *Christus* (S3), whose text he had put together himself, using passages from the Bible and the Catholic liturgy, plus some Latin hymns, and into which he incorporated the *Beatitudes* and *Pater noster* composed at Weimar.

The greatest and most sublime of all his sacred choral works, it consists of three sections:

1. Christmas Oratorio (*Introduction, Pastorale and Annunciation, Stabat mater speciosa, Shepherds' song at the manger, March of the Three Holy Kings*);
2. After Epiphany (*Beatitudes, Pater noster, The Foundation of the Church, The Miracle, The Entry into Jerusalem*);
3. Passion and Resurrection (*Tristis est anima mea, Stabat mater dolorosa, O filii et filiae, Resurrexit*).

Two of the movements— *The Foundation of the Church* and *O filii et filiae*—were added later.

Liszt to Agnes Street-Klindworth. Rome, 24 November. The news given by some newspapers about my oratorio *Christus* is only half correct. I have indeed finished this work . . . but I know neither *when* nor *where* it will be performed. . . . Besides, in several respects my circumstances are at once exceptional and very unfavourable. I can push myself neither to the *fore* nor to the *rear*. What is perfectly becoming and profitable for other composers is no longer suited to my position. To organize concerts, for example, to search for ways of having my works performed, to accept the half-kindnesses of certain proposals, are things entirely forbidden me. And so, standing away from the beaten track, I am unlikely to make my way. . . . It therefore pleases me to profess complete disinterest in the fate of my works. If they are worth anything, it will be noticed in time, without my needing to bother about anything other than writing them as best I can. . . .

Despite the bad weather now looming up on Rome's political horizon, I shall remain here. So as not to vex a few people who are fond of me, I have quit my favourite dwelling-place at the Madonna del Rosario for the winter, and since 22 November, St Cecilia's Day, have been living in a splendid apartment still more splendidly situated: right in the middle of the Forum, opposite the palace of the Caesars and facing the full light of the sun, at the monastery of Santa Francesca Romana. . . . My new apartment was formerly occupied by Cardinal Piccolomini. I have left one of my pianos and some furniture at the Madonna del Rosario, where I shall return in the spring.

At the Dante Gallery Beethoven's Eroica Symphony is being rehearsed; it will be a novelty for Rome. Sgambati, who will conduct the performance, is a true and rare artist, with something of both Bronsart and Tausig in him. What a singular mixture, don't you think, for a pure-blooded* Italian, who in addition has eyes as beautiful as those of the King of Bavaria. After

* Sgambati's mother, however, was an Englishwoman.

the Eroica, my Dante Symphony will be performed once again (for the third or fourth time). It actually enjoys a kind of popularity here! I would have been the last to believe in the possibility of so bizarre a thing—but it's a fact![13]

Fanny Lewald, late 1866. Although he lived at a distance from the centre of the city, and from those parts frequented by visitors, we saw Liszt often; and wherever he appeared, the *Signor Commendatore,* as he was called on account of the many decorations which had been conferred upon him, was the cynosure of all eyes. We met him at the Prussian Embassy in the Palazzo Caffarelli, and repeatedly at the Palazzo Lovatti in the Piazza del Popolo where Marie Espérance von Schwartz*—a keen supporter of Garibaldi—was then living.

At Liszt's wish we met there for 'early and substantial teas', and the company which moved through the rooms bespoke the international outlook of the mistress of the house. . . .

I do not recall ever having heard a fanatical utterance from Liszt. He was peace-loving by nature, although he knew how to resist attack firmly and fiercely, and to stand up for his friends resolutely; indeed, to allow nothing to deter him when it was a matter of his and their artistic convictions. To no one more than Wagner did he prove that. . . .

His surroundings at Santa Francesca Romana wonderfully suited the Romantic in him. From the tall windows of the hall in which his grand piano stood, there was a view over the Arch of Titus to the Farnesina gardens rising above the ruins of the palaces of the Roman emperors; and just as in his hectic virtuoso days he had moved rapidly through the world, so now he could look out upon the remains of the Ancient World and of the Middle Ages, while the daily and ever-changing stream of foreigners from all corners of the earth swept past his windows, those who knew of his residence at the monastery looking upwards in the hope that by some lucky chance Liszt might appear at them or be seen stepping through the doors into the open air.[14]

1867

Adolf Stahr, 14 January. Liszt has some splendid accommodation at Santa Francesca Romana, with a view scarcely to be equalled anywhere on earth: to the right the Forum and its monuments, to the left the Colosseum, and

* Philanthropist and anti-vivisectionist (1821–99) who wrote under the pseudonym of Elpis Melena, the Graecized form of her name. Writing to her in 1876, Liszt praised her stand against 'the atrocities perpetrated against animals in almost every country, which are, alas, only a sad corollary of the countless cruelties and abominations committed by the human—so inhuman—race!'

directly in front the marble Arch of Titus and the Palatine with its ruins of the imperial palaces. We found him—Fanny being allowed to come in too, as the monastery's period of seclusion has been lifted for a time—in the company of a young cleric, a professor of philosophy and mathematics, with whom he was engaged in all manner of learned studies. As always, we were given a warm and affectionate welcome.[1]

Liszt to Agnes Street-Klindworth, 14 February. At the risk of appearing insufferably arrogant, I believe that the *understanding* of certain music requires a more elevated, educated, and refined intelligence and moral sense among artists and their audiences than are generally found. The prevalence of coarse habits, of prejudices, of spite and ineptitude of every kind and in the most varied forms (pedantic or trivial, turgid or scatter-brained), is still excessive in the world of music. Perhaps it will gradually diminish, and perhaps, too, I shall then find *my* public. I am not seeking it, and have little enough time left to wait for it.[2]

Kurd von Schlözer. Rome, 10 June. On Saturday of last week Liszt called to take his leave of me, as he was leaving for Pest that same evening [1 June]. For the coronation there he had composed a Mass which he was himself supposed to conduct—but he was still uncertain whether it would come to a performance. For the right to provide a Coronation Mass belongs of old to the Imperial Chapel at Vienna. But this time Liszt's invitation to compose the Mass came from the Primate, and in Hungary the press and deputations had whipped up such a storm of protest against the right of the Imperial Chapel that at the Vienna Hofburg they had to yield to Magyar national feeling even in this musical respect. Liszt telegraphed yesterday to Princess Wittgenstein to say that his Mass was given a splendid performance on Saturday.[3]

The coronation, which took place at the Matthias Church in Buda on 8 June, was that of the Austrian Emperor and Empress (Franz Joseph and Elisabeth) as King and Queen of Hungary, a necessary consequence of the *Ausgleich* (compromise) earlier in the year which had established the Austro-Hungarian Dual Monarchy under Habsburg rule. After Hungarian arguments had prevailed in the debate about composition of a Mass, Liszt had not received word that he was to compose the work until 30 April, less than six weeks before the date set for the ceremony. Fortunately, his Hungarian Coronation Mass (S11) had already been completed.

Arriving in Pest on 4 June, Liszt attended the main rehearsal the next day. Having received no official invitation to the coronation itself, however, he was able to hear his work only by going up into the organ loft. The conductor was Gottfried von Preyer (1807–91), Kapellmeister at St Stephen's Cathedral, Vienna.

'The musical success of my Mass is complete,' Liszt wrote later that day, 8 June, to Princess Carolyne. 'It surprised everyone by its brevity, its simplicity, and —dare I say it—its character. . . . The decision whereby the performance was entrusted exclusively to the Imperial Chapel of Vienna was favourable rather than detrimental to the effect of the work. During the preliminary rehearsals in Vienna, it seems that the majority of the Chapel musicians expressed themselves in my favour. This good initial impression increased still more at the final rehearsal, and at the performance.'

Leaving the church, he was given one of the most astonishing, and unexpected, ovations of his life. It was witnessed by the writer *Janka Wohl* (1846–1901), who had known the composer since her childhood.

I have many times seen Liszt being acclaimed by fanatical audiences, who covered him with flowers and laurels; but everything pales beside the ovation, without precedent in the annals of the fetishism of art, which was accorded to him at the coronation of our present sovereign. . . .

To understand that never-to-be-forgotten scene, you should try to visualize the surroundings. You must have before your eyes the majestic river—the blue waters of the Danube; and the suspension bridge, that striking link between Buda and Pest. You must picture the fortress of Buda and the royal palace with its encircling hillside gardens; you must see the whole of the smiling and picturesque landscape stretching along the right bank of the river and facing the long rows of palaces on the other side. Above all you must see them adorned with countless garlands and flowers, looking festive, and bathed in the spring sunshine.

This was where an immense multitude was waiting in eager expectation—on stands, at windows, on the roofs, and in flag-bedecked boats—to see the royal procession which was soon to cross the bridge. The Emperor of Austria, after being crowned King of Hungary at the church of St Matthias, was to go from the fortress to take the traditional oath on a hillock, consisting of a mound of earth, brought from all the different counties of Hungary, which had been built up opposite the bridge on the left bank of the river.

It was during these moments of feverish expectancy that the tall figure of a priest suddenly appeared on the broad white road leading from the fort to the Danube which had been kept clear for the royal procession. He was dressed in a long black cassock studded with numerous decorations, and as he advanced hat in hand his snow-white hair stirred gently in the breeze and his features seemed cast in brass. At sight of him a murmur arose, which grew in volume as he drew nearer and was recognized. Swift as lightning, the name of Liszt flew from mouth to mouth, from row to row; and soon he was being given frenzied greeting by a hundred thousand men and women intoxicating themselves with the enthusiasm expressed in this thunderous vocal hurricane. The crowd gathered on the other side of the river naturally thought it must be the king who was approaching and being acclaimed with the spontaneous emotion of a reconciled people. It was not *the* king, but it was *a* king, to whom were addressed the sympathies of a grateful nation proud of the possession of such a son.[4]

In mid-June Liszt returned to Rome. Here, at the Dante Gallery in the evening of Saturday, 6 July, before a large gathering, Sgambati conducted the première of a considerable part of *Christus*—'an erudite and profound work', according to *L'Osservatore romano* (18 July), whose 'majestic harmonies and inexhaustible resources . . . produced a magical effect upon the assembled throng.'

Kurd von Schlözer, 22 July. A few weeks ago I accompanied Liszt to the Villa Farnesina to see the magnificent Sodoma* frescoes, which, be it said in passing, made no impression on him at all.

As we found ourselves in the Lungara and he knows a doctor, Sofanelli, at the lunatic asylum there, he suggested that we visit this establishment. The doctor escorted us through the rooms with the greatest kindness; their furnishings made a pitiable impression, however, because they revealed that treatment of the sick is still at the most primitive level. We arrived at the women's quarters, and Liszt remembered having heard of a young woman barely twenty years of age, Anna Bona da Fiorentino, said to be the possessor of a wondrously beautiful voice and to have become mentally ill as the result of a recent and unfortunate love-affair. The doctor sent for this poor Anna Bona. Slow, timid steps approached—a dark-haired Gretchen. The whole sadness of her soul could be seen in her glance; her nameless misfortune in every movement of her features. With magnificent *disinvoltura*, her melancholy eyes raised to the ceiling, she stopped in the doorway. When the doctor asked her courteously to sing something, she shook her head. 'Ma, cantate un poco,' Sofanelli persisted, 'ecco il Commendatore Liszt.' At this name some memory seemed to come to her almost involuntarily; she looked about her for a moment, then her apathy returned. Suddenly Liszt moved closer, fixed her with his eagle eye, said gently, 'Perché non volete cantare? Cantate: "Casta diva",' and softly began to intone that wonderful melody of Bellini's. This electrified the unfortunate girl, and she began to move her lips, taking up at the point where Liszt left off. Singing the aria with touching tenderness and purity, she remained in a state of gentle excitement up to the very last note. But when that note had died away, her eyes lost their soulful expression and apathetically she fell once more under the spell of her misfortune—from which for those few minutes Liszt had been able to release her. It was a scene I shall remember as long as I live. The sad thing is that this poor girl is housed cheek by jowl with really deranged women, instead of being kept apart and an attempt made to alleviate her affliction, perhaps by musical treatment.[5]

In late July Liszt travelled to Germany, to take part in the celebrations at Eisenach marking the 800th anniversary of the building of the Wartburg. A high point of the festivities was to be performances of his *Legend of St Elisabeth*.

Awaiting him at Weimar was a letter of 25 July from *Princess Carolyne*.

* Il Sodoma was the sobriquet of the religious and historical painter Antonio Bazzi (1477–1549). His *Alexander and Roxana* frescoes at the Villa Farnesina date from 1512.

Blessed are those whose sufferings here below expiate their least faults! God has forgiven us the irregularity of our position, in as much as it was atoned for by maternal struggles! Besides, He has loved us long enough not to wish us to be a subject of scandal, even the smallest! He has tested us as gold is tested in fire—and when our souls have regained their original splendour, God will give us all that is requisite for our welfare!

You have been valiant and admirable, loyal and gentle during this test of adversity—and I admire you infinitely more, and love you infinitely more, than before! Only God knows what it has cost me not to return to Woronince, to return no more to Weimar! But the same feeling has sustained me in the one crisis as in the other—the feeling that we are not in this world to attach ourselves to a place, but to an idea, to a work! . . .

Weimar in its circumstances was a greater idea than Woronince—and Rome is a greater idea than Weimar!

And so I sacrificed Woronince to Weimar, and Weimar to Rome—for you are and will be greater at Rome than you could be at Weimar. What a difference in horizon and pedestal! And then— the day will come in which all that will be formulated in tangible deeds and events.[6]

Adelheid von Schorn. At Weimar, Jena, Eisenach, and Leipzig, choir rehearsals had already been held for a long time; and these choirs were to be united for the performance. Professor Müller-Hartung was rehearsing in Weimar, and Liszt was to come at the end of July. His rooms at the Altenburg* were reopened and made ready for him, and one day as I was on my way to a rehearsal in the theatre, I saw him in the street with some other gentlemen. It gave me a pang to see him wearing the long gown of an abbé, for although the Princess had written with such contentment about the step he had taken, deep down we had not reconciled ourselves to it. I saw how expectantly, almost questioningly, he looked towards me. Probably he did not feel quite sure what reception to expect from the Princess's best friends. But when he saw me going straight up to him, he came to meet me, and as he stretched out both hands towards me his face shone with such friendliness that he would have won any heart. He at once asked after Mama, and whether he might visit her. That I wished to sing in his work pleased him greatly; and at all the rehearsals I stood close to him, to be sure of hearing the least word he uttered. Never have I sung with such enthusiasm. To my mind, Liszt at that time was at his best. From Rome he had come back softened and mellowed, pleased to be musically active again, mentally and physically fresh and enterprising. The struggles of his earlier Weimar period lay behind him; by putting on the cassock he had transported himself to another sphere. Though he had received only the

* This was the last time that Liszt stayed at the Altenburg. The Grand Duke now needed it for an army officer and his family; and, after part of the furnishings and household objects had been sold at auction, the remainder were stored away. When, eighteen months later, Liszt returned to Weimar, it was to a new home prepared for him elsewhere in the town.

minor orders, had not become a priest, and could therefore not say mass, as a secular priest he had put himself on ground in which his life could have glided along tranquilly, had he not himself later brought unrest and disquiet into it again.

After this first rehearsal under Liszt, I had hardly reached home when he too arrived. For a long time he sat at my mother's bedside, and when he left I could see that he was very moved. My mother then said to me: 'Now I understand why he took this step—it was the right one!'[7]

The performance of *St Elisabeth* at the Wartburg was to be on Wednesday, 28 August, and rehearsals continued throughout the month. For one week, however, they were broken off to enable Liszt and some of the Weimar musicians to attend the Tonkünstler-Versammlung at Meiningen (23 to 25 August).

Peter Cornelius. Meiningen, 24 August. I lunched with Liszt. . . . What a lofty, noble spirit! Yesterday evening before going to bed I made him a declaration of love. 'Doctor!' I said, 'I wept during Gille's eulogy of you! Please know that I do not see in you mere details—but the *totality* that you are I love and revere.' That pleased him, and he sat at the piano and breathed *Löse, Himmel, meine Seele* into the strings, his transcription of Lassen's song—played it for me! That was a moment never to be forgotten![8]

Another visitor to Meiningen was the young *Friedrich Nietzsche* (1844–1900).

The Abbé Liszt presided. They played Hans von Bülow's symphonic poem *Nirvana* . . . which was awful. Liszt, on the contrary, succeeded remarkably in finding the character of the Indian *nirvana* in some of his religious works, for example in his *Beatitudes.*[9]

Adelheid von Schorn. Liszt came to Eisenach direct from Meiningen, and almost all the artists gathered there followed him to the performance of his work. The rehearsal was a long one: it was a terrible task for Liszt to get the different choirs and the orchestra to come together in harmony. Although such excellent performers were taking part, a single rehearsal is very little. Frau Dietz from Munich sang Elisabeth; Milde, the Landgrave. The two singers Liszt had had in mind for Elisabeth were Frau von Milde and Frau Merian-Genast; but the former was unwell and the latter now a married woman living in Basle, and so Frau Dietz was entrusted with the role. At the violin stands were David from Leipzig, Singer from Stuttgart, Damrosch from Breslau, Fleischhauer from Meiningen, Reményi from Pest, and Kömpel from Weimar. Most of the people in the chorus and many in the orchestra did not know Liszt, and were unaware of his singularities. He was no *time beater* but a *spiritual leader,* who did not merely conduct with a baton but made his wishes known with every expression of his face; indeed, with every movement of his fingers. We

Weimarians already knew his manner well enough from the rehearsals, and the tradition had been maintained in the orchestra too, by those who had played under him. But the outsiders could not make him out at all, and by the end they were giving more attention to their own conductors, who had placed themselves amongst the choirs. Once or twice Liszt was quite beside himself, only immediately afterwards to be doubly kind again. The next day the old experience was proved once more: that after a bad rehearsal comes a good performance. From sheer anxiety everyone gave a maximum of effort and attention. I stood in the middle and had Liszt directly in front of me. He stood there like a demigod (at such moments he seemed as tall as a giant), his beautiful face reflecting every emotion: at any given moment one had only to look at him to know what was appropriate. To hear this moving work ringing out in the glorious hall, and to allow the memories always awakened by the Wartburg to well up within one—it was an unforgettable experience![10]

Emile Ollivier. I attended three performances of Liszt's *St Elisabeth*. . . . It is an admirable work, containing pathos, simplicity, and a moving serenity; and it went marvellously.[11]

Otto Roquette, the oratorio's librettist, attended one of the two performances at the Wartburg (the third being at the town church). 'The audience was enchanted by Liszt's music, but unfortunately I have to confess that it made me "sick in my ears"—as once happened to Walther von der Vogelweide in a like situation.'

Roquette also witnessed some of the auditions given by Liszt to the many young pianists who desired to play to him. 'Only rarely did he let one of them play to an end. . . . The unconditional Lord of the Piano at times even lost his patience—and with this rush of piano-players who could have kept it!'

Wendelin Weissheimer. I shall never forget the visit paid by Liszt and his entourage to a private house in Eisenach—whose, I no longer remember for certain. . . . Once again I had to go to the piano, and, this time, play the last act of my opera *Theodor Körner*. When I came to the place where Körner draws his sword and rushes into the battle in which he falls, the words he sings made the listeners so enthusiastic that I had to repeat them several times, even though the melody does not close in the tonic at this point but comes to a standstill in the subdominant; for only at the approaching conclusion of the opera, in the thunderous chorus, does it find its truly satisfying ending in the tonic. Liszt guessed this at once, and when, at the final repeat, I had sung the words to Queen Louisa and Prince Ferdinand, he pushed me quickly from the piano, sat down, and played *me* the ending—*with which he was not yet acquainted*, but well knowing that it could arrive at the tonic in such a way and in no other. It was astounding: he had foreseen and rendered the conclusion exactly as I had actually written it! At this remarkable feat everyone was dumbfounded, only one of us finding words to remark: 'One can say nothing to that, only *kneel*!'[12]

At Leipzig on 12 September Liszt attended the musical celebration held at St Thomas's to commemorate the twenty-five years in office of that church's cantor, Moritz Hauptmann (1792–1868).

La Mara. When we arrived at the church it was already filled to overflowing, but there was just room for us near the altar. Laura [La Mara's sister-in-law] and I framed the Master, who had at once become the cynosure of all eyes. Bach's cantata, *Herr, deine Augen sehen nach dem Glauben,* began, and was accompanied, especially in the fugue, by Liszt's active interest. . . . Hauptmann's works then followed: a Salve Regina, the psalm *Sei mir gnädig, Gott!* and a Mass. It was the Salve Regina that obtained the profoundest effect. 'Beautiful, very beautiful,' Liszt remarked several times. Occasionally he closed his eyes, as though to listen with less distraction. At the concluding words of the psalm, 'For I acknowledge my transgressions,' he said with a smile that it was an unfortunate confession at a composer's jubilee. The Mass seemed rather outmoded and in places thin. 'Nowhere does he bring it to excess,' joked Liszt. Yet the fugal movements fascinated him. 'Now comes the inevitable fugue,' he said at the Sanctus. 'A fugue is like cheese after a meal: it helps digest and is itself indigestible. The Holy Ghost is always set to a fugue—but He can take it.' In the Agnus, at the *Dona nobis pacem,* which was based on scales, he remarked: 'A scaled peace!'

Before the end of the concert he asked us if we would like to accompany him to Zschocher's, the director of a music institute where he was to be fêted with a performance by pupils. We had not far to go, for the institute was situated at the former Thomas Gate, opposite the old Thomas School. 'Here lived the great Bach,' he said, pointing to the cantor's residence; and he stopped in front of the Bach monument given by Mendelssohn: 'This is something we must take a good look at!—but ideal this monument is not!'

At Zschocher's a presidential chair stood ready for the eminent guest. He beckoned me to his right side, and the other place was taken by Professor Götze the singing teacher, a Weimar friend of his. The first item was *Orpheus.* 'Here comes Frau Pohl!' he whispered to us at the introductory chords on the harp, and a 'Very accurate!' encouraged the nervous young players. When a brother and sister performed Raff's pieces for children, *The Miller's Boy* and *The Echo,* his kindness was overwhelming; and as though he were their teacher he sat down beside them. 'You are a real miller's boy, and that's why you have made yourself white,' he joked, slapping the valiant, white-costumed young pianist on the back. 'That's right, don't allow yourself to lose your place; just look at the nasty bit once again!' he said encouragingly when the boy stopped at a difficult passage but at once collected himself and continued. His slightly older sister followed with *The Echo.* 'Aha, now we are in the wood,' said Liszt during the introduction—'and now comes the echo. Just go at it bravely!' he called out at a difficult passage, playing it to her himself. Now and again he played a note in between or struck a few in the bass. 'And now we come back into the wood—and here comes the echo again—and now we are going home! Bravo, my child!' And with that he patted the little girl on the back.

When after a short interval a teacher was about to sit at the piano to accompany the institute's prima donna in Liszt's song *Es muss ein Wunderbares sein*,* he pushed her gently away with the words, 'I'll have a try; it's only a few chords, which I should still be able to manage.' Then he preluded wonderfully over the concluding phrase, and as tenderly as a breath of air began his sweetest love song.

To conclude, his *Les Préludes* was served up for him. He conducted, helping out now at the first piano, now at the second, giving life and movement to the whole. 'I'll see to the drums,' he said, reaching across from one piano to the other. 'Faster, ever faster!' he urged at the great climax, and in the bass energetically set the changed tempo. 'But I can't go any faster,' gasped his neighbour. 'Well, just play as quickly as you can!' he soothed her, and they brought it to a safe conclusion. 'But you made it very difficult,' sighed one of them as hot and excited they left their places. 'Do you think so?' replied the Master with a smile, adding quickly to us: 'It wasn't written for such people as this either.'

With Liszt as our escort, we then made our way home, Laura on his arm. She had already asked him earlier if she would have the good fortune of seeing him in her home again, and he had given her a friendly promise for the next evening. In reply to her bashful remark, 'Frankly, my circle lacks the elements worthy of you,' he said: 'You are element enough for me. But you should not be troubled on my account. After all, I am an old family friend!'

The next evening he came to the Nicholas School, finding only a small circle there: Stern,† Wenzel,‡ Riedel, and a few *savants*. To talk about his enchanting kindness would be superfluous. It was as much a part of his nature as eyes are part of the human face. I borrow a few lines from a letter sent to my brother Adalbert by my mother, who was not given to effusiveness. 'Marie was so immensely lucky as to be invited by Liszt to play something with him. They chose his symphonic poem *Orpheus* and a Fantasy by Schubert, during which he said many nice things to her about her playing. "Excellent! quite splendid! capital! superb!" he exclaimed repeatedly during the performance. At the end he kissed Marie's hand and escorted Laura and her to the table. He also played a sonata by Beethoven. His playing was ethereal. I was delighted to have the good fortune to hear him. His great unpretentiousness, kindness, and goodness of heart pleased me immeasurably.'

* A setting (S314), dating from 1857, of a poem by Oskar von Redwitz.

† Adolf Stern (1835–1907), poet and literary historian.

‡ The pianist and teacher E. F. Wenzel (1808–80), a friend of Mendelssohn and Schumann.

The Fantasy chosen by Liszt was the one in F minor. He asked about the *Divertissement à la hongroise,* in which he wished to introduce all kinds of gypsy effects which would entertain me. But unfortunately there was no copy of it at hand. When, full of fear, I took my place beside him at the beginning of *Orpheus,* he whispered: 'Not academically; for me no one can play freely enough.' . . . After we had finished he picked up his own edition of the Beethoven sonatas, published by Holle and now long out of print. 'If you would like to hear something from it, you have only to say!' We shyly indicated Op. 106! 'That would take too long,' he said; 'but how about Op. 110?' And he played it. I was later to hear the sonata performed by Bülow, Rubinstein, and others—but as rendered by Liszt, *never* again! We were all enraptured. Wenzel stood there as though turned to stone. 'This playing is a miracle,' he said. 'We know every note, but under these hands it is something never before heard, a revelation. An unparalleled inspiration makes something newly created arise before us, as though formed out of the universal abyss.'

Liszt then spoke for a long time about Beethoven . . . whose greatest creations, still virtually unknown almost twenty years after his death, and decried as impossible, had made their way only very gradually. 'What Beethoven gave the world in them,' said Liszt, 'was too much, and too great, for his contemporaries to be capable of understanding what they had received. It is as though we asked a rich man for a hundred thalers and he gave us a thousand. Yes, compared with Beethoven we are all poor people. He has preceded us in everything; and in no field have we been able to keep up with him except in the opera, in which Wagner has attained the heights. At his centenary in 1870 we must do something, if I am still living.'. . .

I admitted to Liszt . . . that a biographical sketch of him from my own modest pen was on the way, and asked him to be so good as to correct any errors I might have made. Although there was constant mention of him in the musical press, nothing detailed had yet been written about him for the general public. He expressed his pleasure at what I had to say, and I also acquainted him with my future plans, albeit somewhat timorously. 'Let not the highest be high enough for you!' he encouraged me. 'To those only is it given who aspire and believe.'[13]

After visits to Wilhelmsthal and Meiningen, a longish stay at Munich with the Bülows, where he sat to the sculptor Kaspar von Zumbusch (1830–1915), and a visit to Stuttgart, Liszt journeyed to Basle to see Frau Merian-Genast. In his company was *Richard Pohl.*

After two days he surprised me with the news that he had to be back in Munich on the next day but one, and that he would be returning there by way of Triebschen* . . .

* The villa, overlooking Lake Lucerne, in which Richard Wagner was living.

The next morning [9 October] we travelled there by the first train. Liszt had sent a telegram to Wagner to announce his arrival, but made no mention of me. He wished to speak to Wagner alone. . . .

Such an itinerary I found somewhat mysterious. To begin with I could not understand why Liszt showed no desire, after their six-year* separation, to spend more time with Wagner—until I realized that he wanted no one to know that he was going to Triebschen. The world, which always and everywhere followed his movements with interest, was to believe that he was merely returning from Basle to Munich; the detour was his secret. . . .

Eventually it occurred to me that the visit to Basle was merely a pretext, and that Triebschen had been his goal from the start. What had induced him to make this incognito visit? What did he have to say to Wagner that was so special? He offered not the least hint about it, just as it was a general rule with him to keep a diplomatic silence about his personal plans. . . .

When we arrived at Lucerne, Liszt and his valet were met at the station by Stocker, Wagner's servant, and driven off to Triebschen in a one-horse carriage.

At his hotel some hours later, Pohl himself receives an invitation to Wagner's home.

When I arrived at Triebschen it was already quite dark. . . . Liszt had been alone with Wagner for about six hours, quite sufficient to enable them to have a heart-to-heart talk together. When I entered, Liszt was sitting at the Bechstein grand piano, the recently completed score of Wagner's *Meistersinger* open on the music rack in front of him. The First Act had been played through and he had begun the Second. How Liszt played at sight this extremely difficult score, then entirely unknown to him, was altogether astonishing, something unique of its kind. To the accompaniment he was providing, Wagner was singing. I have never heard a finer performance of *Die Meistersinger*. The sincerity of expression, the beauty of the phrasing, the clarity of detail—it was all enchanting. Only in the finale of the Second Act did Liszt break off. 'This must be heard on the stage,' he said; 'it is too polyphonic to bring out on the piano.'

We had music until midnight, but Liszt then brought it to an end, as he wished to depart at five the next morning. Wagner saw him to his room on the upper floor; I was given a room opposite. . . .

Liszt, ever an early riser, was the first awake the next morning. Just as we were about to leave, Wagner came out on to the landing, despite the early hour, to wish us a hearty farewell. . . . On that quiet October

* Pohl was evidently unaware that Liszt and Wagner had been together in Munich and at Lake Starnberg three years earlier.

morning I accompanied Liszt into Lucerne. Via Lake Constance, he was travelling to Munich, where he wished to arrive that evening. . . .

At Lucerne station he expressed great satisfaction with his visit to Wagner, but when I asked him why he did not in that case prolong it he cut me short with the words: 'It wouldn't be right. One must behave correctly and scrupulously in all circumstances.' I raised the matter no more.[14]

'I spent only half a day with Wagner,' Liszt wrote to Carolyne. 'He has changed somewhat in appearance—has grown thin and wrinkled. But there is no weakening of his genius. His *Meistersinger* astonished me with its incomparable vigour, boldness, vitality, richness, verve, and mastery.'

In a letter to his patron King Ludwig, Wagner for his part described Liszt warmly as 'a dear, great, unique creature'.

The purpose of the visit had been to discuss the relationship, which had already produced two children (Isolde and Eva), between Wagner and Liszt's daughter Cosima. Aware of the distress felt by Bülow, whom he loved like a son, Liszt had determined to thrash the matter out with Wagner and, if possible, to find a solution acceptable to all. The meeting had been planned for some time. 'Liszt's visit,' wrote Wagner afterwards; 'dreaded, yet agreeable.' When, however, a year later, Cosima left Bülow and joined Wagner on a permanent basis, Liszt, obliged to stand by his wronged son-in-law, sorrowfully broke off relations with his daughter and her lover. Several years were to pass before a meeting and reconciliation.

Describing Liszt's reaction to this turn of events, Princess Carolyne later remarked to Lina Ramann: 'I went through the death of his son with him, as well as those of his daughter Blandine and of his mother—but nothing that can be compared with this despair.'

On 2 November Liszt arrived in Rome. He did not leave Italy again for more than a year.

1868

Kurd von Schlözer. Rome, 14 January. When I visited Liszt one morning recently, he was amusing himself by sitting at a little dummy piano without strings and practising a trill from a Beethoven sonata (Op. 109), which until then he had played his whole life long with second and third fingers. Now, in later life, he has taken it into his head to do it with the third and fourth.

At the Paris Exhibition the prize was won by a concert piano made by an American, Chickering, who for publicity purposes then presented it to Liszt.* It is the most sonorous I have ever heard—only when *he* is at the

* Chickering and Steinway pianos were both awarded Gold Medals at the Exhibition. It was Frank Chickering (1827–91), his firm's representative in Paris, who then took the Chickering piano to Italy to present to Liszt.

keyboard of course! Last week he played the *Tannhäuser* overture on it, in his arrangement of twenty years ago. It contains so many difficult passages that the good man is—he says—no longer quite master of it. During his performance he stopped several times with the despairing cry: 'Sapristi, je suis trop vieux!'—which I don't believe for a moment: it sounded magnificent.[1]

28 February. The day before yesterday Liszt gave a small matinée at his place, to play the *Erlkönig* to Lady Emily Villiers, Lord Clarendon's daughter. He plays it only rarely because—in his opinion—he can no longer play it well enough without practising octaves for half an hour beforehand. He had to do so this time too. It was a magnificent treat.[2]

George Grove (1820–1900), English musicologist and editor, to Olga von Glehn. Rome, 20 April. I forgot all about Liszt's being here till Saturday, when the thought suddenly flashed into my head. So I discovered his address and wrote a note, humble, but fragrant with incense asking him to deign to receive his slave. Then I went to the convent at which he lives, yesterday morning, and got an answer, saying he should be glad to see me today between three and four. Guess if I were punctual! . . . He was capitally lodged—a jolly drawing-room with a grand piano—a library beyond, and a bedroom beyond that. He was awfully kind and nice. I stopped with him for nearly two hours and never enjoyed myself more. We talked of all kinds of things, music, religion, Germany, England, the people we mutually knew, etc., and it pleased me, as you will understand, to find him quite simple and good-hearted, a thorough, accomplished man of the world, without spite or conceit, no forcing forward of his own music, or abuse of other musicians, etc. . . . Then some people were announced—a blind man with his daughter whom Liszt had kindly asked to come and let him hear her play. . . . The girl played her two feeble little pieces, and you can't think how kind he was —without a morsel of humbug. And then he said he would play to her and she would sit by '*pour me corriger, vous savez*', so down we all sat, he in the middle and she and I on the two sides, and he played away most charmingly for a quarter of an hour. Of course it was modern style, but not the least extravagant, and lovely to hear: loud, then soft, and then loud again, and so easy and graceful, no *tours de force.* Then he said in German that we should have something '*lustiges*', and, turning to me, as I had been asking about his transcriptions of Schubert's songs, said he would play the *Soirées de Vienne*—Schubert's waltzes, and he played two, most lovely. I never was so delighted and he saw I was pleased and liked it. I had a capital opportunity of looking at his face, for he kept turning round to me, as he played, to see how I liked it. Three things occurred to me—which I will tell you as I thought them at the time. 1. A great general likeness to Napoleon when young. The instant I shook hands with him, the words came to the tip of my tongue, 'the young lieutenant of Engineers' (Carlyle, somewhere about Napoleon). 2. The mouth just like Kingsley's. 3. He was not tall, but in that limited space was concentrated the pluck of thirty battalions. He was in an Abbé's dress, long black coat and knee breeches, with buckles in his shoes; which became him well. His hair is grey, his face very refined and *luminous,* and his hands the perfection of delicacy. It was quite different from Rubinstein or any of the great players, and I could have listened for ever.[3]

It was at Rome this year that Liszt's playing was first heard by *Marie Jaëll* (1846–1925), *née* Trautmann, Alsatian wife of the Austrian pianist Alfred Jaëll (1832–82). A pupil of Moscheles and Herz who had at the age of sixteen carried off first prize for piano-playing at the Paris Conservatoire, she had also studied composition with Franck and Saint-Saëns (who later dedicated to her his First Piano Concerto and *Etude en forme de valse*).

Her gifts were altogether exceptional. 'She has the brain of a philosopher and the fingers of an artist,' declared Liszt admiringly; and after the latter's death Saint-Saëns remarked: 'There is only one person in the world who can play Liszt —Marie Jaëll.'

In later life she achieved eminence as a teacher (of among others Albert Schweitzer*) and as a writer of books on the psycho-physiological aspects of piano-playing, in particular the problem of touch.

When I heard Liszt for the first time, all my auditory faculties seemed to be transformed from the moment he began to play. This transformation, which was so unexpected, struck me still more than his playing itself. . . .

While I listened to this music, so different from any I had heard until that moment, I perceived my thoughts circulating as though they had acquired, independently of my will, the faculty of proceeding to and fro along paths unknown to me. . . .[4]

Liszt was at once a musician of genius and a virtuoso of genius. Accumulations of notes were as easy for him to conceive as to perform. To the physical problem of movements carried out on the keyboard there corresponded a cerebral problem that no one has been able to work out after him. . . .

In studying the works of Liszt one has to face not only the necessity of moving ten fingers with exceptional combinational dexterity, but also that of getting the mind to acquire a combinational dexterity far superior to that of the fingers. Without this fusing of the functional and intellectual mechanisms, the work interpreted is bound to be disfigured, bearing not the least resemblance to what Liszt imagined and worked out on the keyboard. No one will really play a work of Liszt's until he can make it expressive. . . .

* 'How much I owe this gifted woman!' he exclaimed in his autobiography.

Certain pieces, rendered very accurately, seem to signify nothing and to have no appreciable musical worth; but—with the notes played just as accurately—they can also be made to express a transcendent, moving beauty. More than others, these works need a twofold creation: on the one hand that of the composer, and on the other that of the interpreter, who must have some affinity with the genius of the composer if he is to penetrate the sphere of his creations.

The spiritual content of Liszt's works will be revealed only with the advent of interpreters who can re-create them. With his works for orchestra it is the same as with those for piano: with an inspired interpretation, both rise to radiant heights; if the imagination of the interpreter be not fertilized by them, they are ineffective.

It is thus that Liszt *wished his art to be.* His highest aim was to suggest another creation through his own; his ambition was an ultra-intense communion with his interpreters. . . . The interpreter was to feel as free as though he were conveying his own thought. Therein lies the principal innovation contained in the works of Liszt. It was thus in the supreme self-sacrifice of his conception of art that his lofty nature revealed itself.[5]

From the diary of Emile Ollivier, 30 May. Yesterday I lunched at Girardin's with George Sand. . . . She has an air of indifference, of being no part of anything that is happening. But she misses not a word of what is said, openly taking and adapting it for the story she is working on. I told her that Liszt had wanted to call. 'He did well not to. For someone like myself, who knows everything he thinks about such matters, it was forbidden him to make himself a priest. Either he believes, in which case he is an imbecile, or he does not believe, in which case he is a scoundrel.' In all this, as in everything she says, no tenderness, no femininity—a masculine being.[6]

Sunday the 21st of June was the 22nd anniversary* of the coronation of Pius IX. The bouquet Liszt offered the Pontiff was a musical one, as he told Carolyne: 'At about six o'clock Hohenlohe took me to the Holy Father. My Bechstein had been placed in the beautiful hall of the [Vatican] library, where I played five or six pieces, including the *di tanti palpiti*. . . . To reward me, His Holiness offered me a box of cigars, identical to the one he gave Hohenlohe. Tomorrow evening I'll come round to give you various little details.'

A close friend of Liszt's in Rome was Don Antonio Solfanelli, who taught at the St Peter's Seminary, 'a priest of a rare distinction of heart and intelligence', as Liszt described him. When, convalescing after illness and planning to spend part of the summer at Grotta Mare on the Adriatic coast, Solfanelli asked Liszt to accompany him, the composer could not refuse; besides, the trip would provide a fine opportunity to study the breviary with his friend. Taking the pilgrims' route of Spoleto, Cascia (where they gazed upon the incorrupt body of St Rita), Assisi, Fabriano, and Loreto, they set out early in July.

* Not the 20th, as Liszt wrote, erroneously, at the head of his note to Carolyne.

Liszt to Princess Carolyne. Grotta Mare, 19 July. I get up at about six. As soon as I am dressed I go to church, just a hundred paces away. Between seven and eight Fortunato brings me coffee in my room, or rather my salon, for I have a separate bedroom as well as two salons and a gallery at my disposal. . . . At about 11.00 we read part of the breviary, either in the garden—rather restricted in size and not very luxurious, but containing a good many orange trees, fig trees, and vines—or in the gallery. At one o'clock, lunch, on the floor below my rooms. There are about twelve of us at table. Every imaginable attention is shown me, being translated into cutlets, beefsteaks, beetroot, figs, and so forth. After lunch, siesta. At 5.00 we continue our breviary with Solfanelli, and do some reading in Italian or Latin. Then we take a walk on the beach; sometimes we say vespers and compline in a boat resting quietly on the sandy shore. At 9.00 Fortunato brings me my snack supper, which I prefer to eat alone. It suits me best to retire to bed before 11.00, except for reading a few more pages before going to sleep.

The rest of the time I read or write—but no music yet. I shall see about that next week perhaps. The sole and great event of the establishment is the arrival of the post at noon. Don't fear for one moment that boredom is taking hold of me, however. Given that I am not in Rome, there is nowhere I would rather be (or could better employ my time) than at Grotta Mare. Solfanelli assures me I am bothering no one. It is equally certain that no one is bothering me in any way whatever.

1 August. Frankly, I desire nothing, for the very simple reason that I possess well beyond my needs—and have no taste for collecting and accumulating. . . . I make an exception only for books, which I confess I sometimes buy for the pleasure of possessing them—without succeeding in reading them, as I intend. Alas! I have very little time left in which to instruct myself. By going out only rarely, and keeping my relations with others to what is strictly necessary, I manage with great difficulty to read one volume a week.

18 August. I do not know what you will think of my annotations.* If you find them utterly stupid, I shall not mind at all—and will only beg you to forgive the presumptuousness of my literary and other blunders. Alas! my elementary education was more than neglected, and unfortunately I have never since been able to make up for this cardinal deficiency whose consequences are so distressing to me. Want of study and sufficient knowledge reduces me intellectually to the sad condition of a shamefaced pauper! And I feel it all the more as my bit of celebrity brings me into frequent contact with the 'rich'! Some imagination and a certain integrity

* On Carolyne's book *Simplicité des colombes, prudence des serpents: quelques réflexions suggérées par les femmes et les temps actuels*, a copy of which had reached Liszt a week earlier.

of character pulled me through well enough when I was young—but I should now like to do better, and learn more. I find this need so imperative that my only thought is to satisfy it; and I am accordingly resolved to withdraw from the world and to live in the country, so that I may read, educate myself, and work peacefully and consistently until my dying day. Believe me, nothing better and more reasonable is left for me to seek in this world!

29 August. I thank God and yourself for these two months of tranquillity and simple contentment. The principal object of my journey was to become acquainted with the breviary.* Solfanelli has rendered me excellent service in this, and I am beginning to read the offices quite tolerably. Such an occupation is enough to live and die well![7]

Returning to Rome on 1 September, Liszt spent the remainder of the year there or with Cardinal Hohenlohe at the Villa d'Este, much of his time being given to preparation of an edition of the piano works of Schubert, which he finished by early December. 'Our pianists are scarcely aware of what a glorious treasure they have in the piano works of Schubert. . . . O tender, ever-welling genius! O beloved hero of the heaven of my youth! From your soul's depths and heights pour forth melody, freshness, power, grace, reverie, passion, soothings, tears, and flames; and such is the enchantment of your world of emotions that we almost forget the greatness of your craftsmanship!'

A frequent visitor to the Villa was *Nadine Helbig* (1847–*c*.1923), a Russian pupil. Born the Princess Shahavskaya, she had come to Rome in 1865 and a year later married the German archaeologist Wolfgang Helbig. 'A woman of remarkably colossal figure, but also of remarkable intelligence,' was Gregorovius' description of her.

Cardinal Hohenlohe lived on the ground floor, which consisted of a series of enormous, sparsely-furnished state rooms. Ice-cold in winter, they totally lacked any modern comfort. For Liszt he had had some rooms prepared on the upper floor. The Master's study had been built into the highest landing of the deserted circular staircase and was just large enough for his piano. With much love but little taste the Cardinal had chosen the wallpaper himself. I can see it still: light blue with huge roses—in memory of St Elisabeth's miracle of the roses. I recall them because this wallpaper gave rise to an interesting talk with Liszt. I asked the Master whether the landgravine had really acted quite honestly when, on being asked by her husband what she was carrying in her lap, she had answered 'roses'. Liszt's reply was that, in his opinion, the saint had already sensed intuitively the miraculous transformation of the food into roses which had just taken place! During my first visit Liszt lamented that his eyes had become so weak that from the one small window of his study he could no longer enjoy

* Another task which Liszt began at Grotta Mare was the writing of Technical Exercises for the piano, eventually published in twelve volumes (S146).

the view of which he had grown so fond. I at once went into the adjoining bedroom and came back armed with a bowl of water and a cloth. After a few minutes the window, which had been darkened by tobacco smoke, was clean again, and our dear Master could once more enjoy the delightful view of his beloved cypresses with the clear background of the Roman Campagna, and from afar could greet the dome of St Peter's. From sheer gratitude he kissed my hands, wet though they still were! His own hands were quite thick, red, swollen, and sore from chilblains! He showed me the little tin lantern by whose light he went at three o'clock every morning to early mass in the nearby church.

Chilblains notwithstanding, he played to me with quite extraordinary rapture his *Bénédiction de Dieu dans la solitude.* He felt calm and happy in his solitude near the Cardinal, who could be immensely witty, humorous and amusing. Despite his piety, Liszt too could be exuberant, and I enjoy thinking back to an afternoon when he played, and even sang, to the Cardinal and me the whole of Peter Cornelius's *The Barber of Bagdad.*[8]

In response to repeated invitations and entreaties from the Grand Duke Carl Alexander, Liszt now agreed to return to Weimar for some months; and, having made this start, would do so regularly for the rest of his life. It was his hope that he would be able to spend a more peaceful winter there than he had been able to do at Santa Francesca Romana, which, he told Agnes Street-Klindworth, was made 'almost unbearable by the excessive number of visitors from all countries who congested my rooms'.

Princess Carolyne to Henriette von Schorn, 12 November. He will have a new servant, as his present one is too delicate to stand up to a winter in Germany. They won't know how to manage for themselves, *impractical* as is Liszt, and that worries me a little. But I am sure that you will be good enough to take some interest and see that his health does not suffer from the *cold*, after so many winters in Italy, and that he is well nourished. As his hair is already quite white, I am sure that you will allow Adelheid to look after him; that you will allow her to go to see him and to find out whether everything is being attended to as it should be! I am sure, my dear friend, that you won't object to my asking this little favour of you. Out of kindness you would do it, I am sure, for any distinguished man; and all the more so since in this you will be replacing *me.* Above all I wish to know if he is well and faithfully looked after by his servant, whom I hardly know. Thank you in advance! Please also give me more details about him than he himself gives me, as he never bothers about material things and never mentions them in his letters. . . . You ask me what he is doing. Things more and more beautiful, but in a more and more *elevated* sense, far above the commonplace. This summer he composed a *Requiem** for the Emperor Maximilian, which I find one of his greatest works. Now he is going to

* For tenor and bass soloists, male chorus, organ, and brass (S12). The Emperor

spend a fortnight with Cardinal Hohenlohe at the Villa d'Este at Tivoli—a fairyland, which is so beautiful it is like a dream, an Italian vision! And I am sure that he will bring back some masterpieces once again![9]

On New Year's Eve Liszt made the acquaintance of the American poet Henry Wadsworth Longfellow (1807–82), then visiting Rome with members of his family. The meeting, at Santa Francesca Romana, was arranged by a fellow countryman of Longfellow's, the portrait painter *G. P. A. Healy* (1813–94).

In my studio the picture Longfellow looked at most often was a large portrait of Liszt seated at the piano. I had recently painted it, and I told the poet how, during the sittings, Liszt had played, for hours at a time. I showed him casts I had taken of the musician's hands; and these greatly interested him, for they were extraordinary—thin, nervous, and well-shaped; revealing much of the man's passionate, unquiet, earnest nature. . . .

Longfellow expressed a desire to see the great musician; and as I had remained on good terms with my sitter, I asked permission to present the American poet to him.

One day, towards sunset, we drove together to the old monastery, and rang at Liszt's private entrance. It was already quite dark in the vestibule, the door of which was opened by means of an interior cord. No servant was visible. But the Abbé himself came forward to greet us, holding a Roman lamp high up, so as to see his way. The characteristic head, with the long iron-gray hair, the sharp-cut features and piercing dark eves, the tall, lank body draped in the priestly garb, formed so striki , a picture that Longfellow exclaimed under his breath: 'Mr. Healy, you must paint that for me!'

Our visit was most agreeable, for, when he chose, no man was more fascinating than Liszt. He played for us on his fine American piano, with which he was delighted; then he showed us over his bachelor establishment, which was by no means the cell of an austere monk; and evidently wished to make a good impression on his illustrious visitor.

Taking advantage of this amiable disposition, I told him how much we had both been struck by his appearance as he came towards us, light in hand. He willingly consented to sit, and I made a small picture,* as exact a reproduction as possible of what we had seen, and which gave great pleasure to Longfellow.[10]

Maximilian of Mexico, younger brother of the Emperor Franz Joseph of Austria, had been executed in June 1867. It was this *Requiem* which was performed at Princess Carolyne's funeral in March 1887.

* The painting hangs in Craigie House, the Longfellow home at Cambridge, Massachusetts. Healy's portrait of Liszt at the piano is now the possession of the Newberry Library, Chicago.

With Longfellow and one or two others, Liszt was on 4 January a dinner guest of the Healy family; and the next afternoon he welcomed them and the Longfellows to his own abode. 'He is a tall, thin man with gray hair brushed straight back and dressed in a long coat, black stockings, and shoes with buckles,' noted Alice Longfellow, one of the poet's daughters. 'I never imagined such playing before. His hands were all over the piano; I don't believe he left a note untouched. Some of it was very soft and sweet, and some loud and decidedly showing off. It was enough to make any ordinary mortal despair of ever playing at all.' Longfellow's sister, Mrs Anne Pierce, observed the musician's 'mouth of unusual firmness', the contrast between his sombre costume and his 'merry nature', and thought that his hands 'seemed no longer human, but like phantom hands sweeping and doubling over the keys—the fine face pale but aglow with feeling, the body in perfect repose but every inch alive.'

In the late evening of 12 January, Liszt returned to Weimar, where a home had been prepared for him on the upper floor of the Hofgärtnerei (Court Gardener's House). A small villa which had earlier housed Friedrich Preller's studio, it stood in an attractive situation at the end of the Marienstrasse and on the edge of the park. The decoration and furnishing had been personally supervised by the Grand Duchess Sophie. 'Nothing has been neglected to make my dwelling-place agreeable and even elegant,' he told Carolyne. 'It consists of four rooms: a four-window salon, divided into two by red and green Algerian curtains, which can be drawn when desired; a dining-room, bedroom, and Fortunato's room. There are fine carpets everywhere, four Berlin stoves, double windows, curtains and portières all of a rich material, matching furniture, three bronze clocks, several triple candlesticks in bronze, half a dozen or more carcel lamps, two gilt-framed mirrors, silver plate, glass, and chinaware for six. . . . The fact is, my new lodging is of a "Wagnerian" luxury—to which they have hardly been accustomed in this good town of Weimar.'

With the gift of a magnificent grand piano, Carl Bechstein had added the crowning touch to the furnishings. 'Accept a seven-octaved chromatic scale of thanks for your kindness,' Liszt wrote to him.

Adelheid von Schorn. So Liszt was back in Weimar! Had moved into the rooms in which from then on—until his death—he was to spend a few months every year. . . .

For musical Weimar those rooms became a meeting-place such as there has probably never been the like. . . . Pupils gathered as soon as he arrived, going to him twice a week from 4.00 until 6.00 p.m. . . . Whenever he pushed one of them off the piano stool and sat down himself —to show how it should and should not be done—the whole crowd would press round the piano as closely as possible. . . . But to see *how* this teacher behaved with the youngsters! There are no words for such kindness. Not only did he give them lessons entirely free of charge, but even dipped into his pocket to help anyone who appealed to him for money—and that may not have been so rarely! He supported them with both word and deed; sometimes, alas, without taking account of the type of person he was dealing with. And so experiences both good and bad came his way, but to the time of his death he did not leave off caring and helping.[1]

Henriette von Schorn to Princess Carolyne. Weimar, 27 January. On the 20th there was a concert at court for which Reményi and Wachtel made *faux bond.* What to do? Help came from your friend, who, the day before, offered to contribute a solo. Surprise—joy—jubilation! You cannot imagine the enthusiasm; everyone who told me about it struggled to hold back tears: 'He played like an angel and looked like a saint.' . . .

Everything is in best order in Liszt's rooms. Fortunato and Pauline* came to see me. I told them that they were to let me know if anything were needed. Pauline is very well intentioned; she is a good girl and a tireless worker. Fortunato seems to watch over the finances very properly.[2]

Reményi turned up shortly afterwards.

Adelheid von Schorn. Reményi was a most original character. When he played, the whole man danced. I never heard him play in public—perhaps on those occasions he was more restrained—but at Liszt's he gave free rein to his temperament. Of the manner in which *he* played Hungarian dances, we Germans have no conception. One day at the Hofgärtnerei he played gypsy melodies with Liszt, making on me an impression I shall never forget! The two Hungarians not only *played* music, *they themselves were* music—in every nerve—to their very fingertips; I simply cannot put it any other way. When they came to an end, Reményi fell at Liszt's feet and clasped his knees—whether he was laughing or weeping for joy I do not know—and Liszt's features glowed as only his could.[3]

For two months Liszt stayed quietly in Weimar, among the tasks which occupied him being revision of the 300 pages of *St Elisabeth* and correction of the proofs of his *Requiem*. All work had to be done in the free moments snatched from a stream of visitors. 'Weimar has become a place of pilgrimage,' remarked Marie von Mouchanoff (the former Madame Kalergis); 'all the musicians of Germany have been to pay homage at the feet of the great man.' Among the arrivals was Anton Rubinstein, who gave a recital in Weimar on 8 February. 'Rubinstein is tormented by an ideal that is not only insufficient but even somewhat incoherent!' Liszt told Carolyne. 'His great project now is to set the Bible to music, in the form of dramatic oratorios for which he would require, as with Wagner's *Ring*, a separate theatre, a Prince or a company of shareholders, who would see to the costs, and an impresario—whose choice would present no

* Pauline Apel, who had in earlier years been a servant girl of the Princess's, now became Liszt's housekeeper at the Hofgärtnerei. She would be showing visitors around the Liszt Museum, as the house became, until shortly before her death more than fifty years later.

difficulty, for Rubinstein himself would be this impresario. Wagner's theatre will be built—but Rubinstein's will be postponed to the Greek calends!'

On 25 March Liszt arrived in Vienna, for the first performance there of *St Elisabeth,* which took place on 4 April under Johann von Herbeck.

Present at a rehearsal was the writer and journalist *William Beatty-Kingston* (1837–?).

Just as we had settled down in our places, and Herbeck had taken his seat at the conductor's desk, a tall, spare, elderly man, with strongly-marked features and long, flowing grey hair, clad in a closely-fitting black cassock, suddenly made his appearance among us, threading his way through the maze of occupied chairs and benches towards the orchestra. . . .

Hellmesberger* recognised him as he was advancing up the room, and, touching Herbeck on the shoulder, whispered something to him, whereupon the Hofkapellmeister rose, sprang down the steps leading from the orchestra to the auditorium, and loudly ejaculating '*Der Meister, der Meister*!' seized Liszt's hands, bent over them, and devoutly kissed them.

All present—audience and performers alike—were on their feet in an instant, greeting the reverend maestro with enthusiastic and prolonged acclamation, which he repeatedly acknowledged with manifest gratification.

When the cheering had subsided, Liszt took his seat in a chair placed for him a little to the left of Herbeck, and below the orchestral platform, on a level with the places occupied by the audience. Immediately afterwards the rehearsal began. Though it lasted considerably over three hours, not a soul quitted the room until its conclusion, when the musicians present who had any personal acquaintance with Liszt gathered round him, eager to exchange a few words or a hand-grasp with the worshipped hero of the hour. . . .

In private houses, Beatty-Kingston on several occasions heard Liszt play and improvise.

At that time all his capabilities of invention, memory, and technique, were still entirely at his disposal; and, as a pianist, he was not only unrivalled, but unapproachable. . . .

To any conscientious pianist thitherto inclined to 'fancy himself' as a performer, it was at once inimitable joy and bottomless despair to hear Liszt extemporise when strongly moved by some more than usually sympathetic theme or happy fancy. After listening, awe-stricken and breathless, to one of those unequalled musical utterances, marvels alike of invention and execution, the revulsion of feeling experienced by a pianist of the class above alluded to was little short of crushing, suggesting grim

* The violinist, conductor, and teacher Josef Hellmesberger (1828–93) was leader of both the Vienna Philharmonic Orchestra and a notable string quartet.

vows of never again laying finger on key, of advertising one's favourite 'grand' for sale at an unprecedented sacrifice, and of foregoing throughout life all musical enjoyments save that derivable from a Liszt improvisation. Perhaps the most wonderful feature of his playing was his touch, or rather, plurality of touches—one as light as a falling snowflake or the flutter of a butterfly's wing, another as rich as Genoa velvet of triple pile, a third as clinging as a young lover's first kiss, a fourth as hard and bright as the blow of a diamond-headed hammer. He could make the instrument, to others a machine of readily exhaustible tone-resources, do anything—sing, talk, laugh, weep, and mimic orchestral effects without number. There never was and probably never will be another such genius. . . .

Practice and will had so disciplined his fingers and accustomed them to fulfil infallibly the orders transmitted to them from his brain, that, in all probability, the word 'difficulty' (in connection with *technique*) had ceased to possess any exact significance, as far as Liszt the executant was concerned. Nobody who has heard him improvise can doubt that, absolutely free from any kind of preoccupation as to the ability of his hands to execute whatever he may call upon them to do, he gives play to the creative and constructive faculties of his intellect without troubling himself in the least about the mere mechanical instruments attached to his wrists. However unexampled the sequences or complicated the groups of notes suggested by his imagination, he unhesitatingly gives them expression, being certain that his executant machinery can and will carry them out faultlessly in obedience to an unconscious exercise of volition on his part. This has always seemed to me one of the most extraordinary powers ever acquired and wielded by a human being. Within my remembrance only three pianists have possessed it— Liszt, Mendelssohn, and Rubinstein, the first-named in a far higher degree of development than the other two. . . .

There is, I think, abundant justification for the belief I have entertained ever since I first heard him perform—namely, that he is in all respects the greatest pianist who ever lived. This, moreover, was Richard Wagner's opinion of him. Wagner, who was not given to hero-worship, and whose capacity for enthusiasm was always kept under control by his critical faculty, frequently confessed that words failed him to express his wondering admiration of the gift that enabled Liszt to invest himself with the personality of whatsoever composer whose work he might be engaged in rendering. On one occasion he wrote:

'He who has enjoyed frequent opportunities, particularly in a small intimate circle, of hearing Liszt play—Beethoven's music, for example—must have realised the fact that the playing in question was not mere reproduction, but actual *re-creation*. . . . It would be impossible to make this comprehensible to those who have heard nothing but ordinary performances and professional renderings of Beethoven's pianoforte works. In the course of time I have gained so melancholy an insight into the evolution and essence of such renderings that I had rather not wound anybody's feelings by expressing myself more clearly with regard to them. On the other hand I would ask all musicians who have, for instance, heard Beethoven's Op. 106 or 111 played by Liszt to friends in private, what they previously knew about those works, and what they learned of them on these occasions?'[4]

So great was the success of *St Elisabeth,* that on 11 April it was repeated, and received with even greater enthusiasm. After a fleeting visit to Regensburg, to study the *Magnum opus musicum* of Orlandus Lassus, of which a publication was being planned, Liszt went to Pest for a fortnight. Stopping again at Vienna *en route*, he spent a day (20 April) with Eduard and Henriette von Liszt at their home in the Schottenhof. They persuaded him to sleep there that night; and the overnight stay brought so much joy to all, that from this time forward during his visits to Vienna Liszt stayed at the Schottenhof as a matter of course.

In his company at Pest were a young German pupil, Georg Leitert (1852-1901), and Sophie Menter (1846-1918), one of the greatest of women pianists. The latter had made Liszt's acquaintance a year or two before when at the very start of her career; and had later scored a triumph at Vienna with his First Piano Concerto, which she had insisted on playing despite warnings that it would be ill received. 'My only legitimate piano daughter,' was Liszt's admiring description of her.*

At Pest, Liszt conducted two successful performances of his Hungarian Coronation Mass: at a concert on 26 April in which Ferenc Erkel conducted the Dante Symphony, and again on the 30th after Erkel had conducted *Hungaria* and the first performance in Hungary of Liszt's Psalm 137 ('By the waters of Babylon') (S17). He was also received by the Queen-Empress, to whom he played; and on 3 May he attended a recital of Leitert's which included the first public performances in Hungary of two outstanding peaks of the piano literature: Beethoven's *Hammerklavier* Sonata and Liszt's own Sonata in B minor.

Accompanied by Leitert, he left on 4 May for Italy, on a train which carried him along the shore of Lake Balaton. Complying with the wishes of Princess Carolyne, who feared that so long a journey without a break would prove exhausting, he spent the nights of the 5th and 6th at Sagrado,† the home in northern Italy of Princess Therese Hohenlohe. Also present was his hostess's young daughter *Marie* (1855–1934).‡

* A Concerto in the Hungarian Style, published long ago in Sophie Menter's name, is now thought by one or two scholars to be the work of Liszt in his last years. There is, however, no real evidence (internal or external) for Liszt's authorship of this piece, which is in a style abandoned by him decades earlier; and his part (if any) in its creation may have been limited to correcting Sophie's efforts and helping her work her themes into a coherent whole.

† During his brief stay Liszt also visited another of Princess Therese's residences: the famous clifftop castle of Duino, a two-hour carriage ride from Sagrado. Some fifty years later, a guest at Duino was the pianist Magda von Hattingberg, a pupil of Busoni. Of its White Room, she wrote: 'There were no carpets, but under chairs and table were fine white skins on the beautifully inlaid parquet. The only dark object was a great Bösendorfer grand piano on which Liszt had once played. His hands had raised the lid; his fingers had touched the keys! I hardly dared to begin.'

‡ Who, as Princess Marie von Thurn und Taxis, became many years later the friend and patroness of Rainer Maria Rilke.

The great man arrived with a young pianist from Saxony whom he was taking with him to Italy. He spent a few days in Sagrado, which he seemed to like very much; he was extremely agreeable and good-natured and once, to please Mamma, he forced me to play piano duets with him. I was in despair. I was always miserable when I had to perform my tricks, playing *Valses mélancholiques, Moments musicaux, Pluies de perles* or similar inanities for our visitors, but this time I nearly died of fright.

Liszt amused himself by introducing variations while we were playing, and this threw me into terrible confusion. Then he terminated the final cadenza by flicking the tip of my nose with his long, nimble fingers—which I considered an unforgivable insult to the dignity of my thirteen years, and I began to detest Liszt notwithstanding his surprising good-naturedness.

One evening he actually sat down at the piano and played dance-music for us! Another time Madame da Mosto, his pretty compatriot, came to supper and afterwards he played one of his Hungarian Rhapsodies for her, which made an unforgettable impression on me. Then he played on our poor little Pleyel piano the improvisation on Viennese themes he had played for Napoleon III: the piano never quite recovered from having been subjected to the lion's claw for several days.

One afternoon the young man from Saxony was practising a sonata by Beethoven in the little white boudoir; I was listening devoutly in the drawing-room. Suddenly the door next to the piano opened and Liszt appeared on the threshold—his tall, black-garbed figure very erect, his silver-white hair flowing, his long arms raised. He remained motionless in this hieratical attitude, indicating the mood of a majestic passage—how I regret that I no longer remember which it was! He appeared to me like the high priest of his august art, and from that day I began, though still vaguely, to realize what the essence of music could be. I can still see the great magician with his magnificent head, his fine, grave features, his upraised arms, and the passionately intense expression of the young virtuoso whose playing seemed to flow from this mute invocation.

It is sad that I was still too young to enjoy the wonderful music he made for us and that he wasted his time by playing an overture by Mercadante with me. And that I had even felt cross with him.[5]

Liszt to Adelheid von Schorn. Rome, 14 May. You ask me to send news, at the earliest, about my health. Now that is a subject with which for long years I have professed never to bother myself, either in writing or in conversation, finding that I am always well enough not to have to think about it. This method of silent exclusion I would gladly extend to many other topics. Those, for example, concerned with temperature, money, vague and general opinions, etc. That would make me still less sociable, it is true, but no one would lose from it, while I should gain a lot by following literally the evangelical precept of avoiding superfluous words.[6]

In the second half of August, for the planned première of Wagner's *Rheingold*, and not allowing the break in relations to prejudice his support for Wagner's music, Liszt made a trip to Munich. The performance had been commanded by King Ludwig against the wishes of the composer, who protested and stayed away. Liszt attended the final full rehearsal on 27 August, but in the event the première itself did not take place until 22 September, by which time he had returned to Rome.

Among those who came into contact with him during his stay in the Bavarian capital was *Judith Gautier* (1845–1917), daughter of Théophile and wife of the French writer Catulle Mendès.

The appearance of Franz Liszt stupefied me. I was quite uninformed, knew absolutely nothing. Why that long black cassock? Was he, then, a priest? Was there, behind that clean-shaven face, a tonsure in those locks falling so straight and smooth to his shoulders? What leonine eyes, what glowing pupils under those shaggy brows! What sovereign irony in the curves of the wide, thin-lipped mouth! In his whole bearing, what majesty tempered with benevolence. . . .

Liszt's entrance caused extreme excitement in the gathering, and my surprise grew ever greater. Was he a saint? They showed him such extraordinary veneration—the women above all! Hurrying towards him, they virtually knelt down, kissed his hands and raised looks of ecstasy to his face.

But my attention was suddenly distracted by a woman who had arrived at the same moment. It was she, the mysterious beauty who had come from the north in a whirlwind of snow, herself whiter than the snow; the lady with eyes like Parma violets, of whom the poets have sung with such desire, the Countess Kalergis, now Countess Mouchanoff—in fact the *Symphonie en blanc majeur** herself! As yet, she was standing with her back to me, on the other side of the grand piano, taking the outstretched hands of all those crowding about her. . . .

I really dreaded the moment when she would turn, and, as she made a movement to do so, I closed my eyes, to keep for a moment longer the illusion of the past.

Almost at once I heard the rustle of silk beside me, and a clear musical voice addressed me, sweetly modulated and with a slight Russian accent. Countess Mouchanoff has seated herself next to me, and, pressing my hand, she assures me that no introduction is needed, for she has recognized me without hearing my name. Since we share the same admirations and the same passions, she continues, we belong to the same ideal family and loved one another even before we met.

She seems a very great lady, self-assured, intelligent, and filled with a passionate love of art. I look for the white camelias near the snow of her breast—very marble-like, in truth, but perhaps assisted by pearl white and

* The title of the poem by Théophile Gautier (in the collection *Emaux et Camées*) which had been inspired by Marie Kalergis.

a touch of rice powder. Her features are regular, pale under the so cleverly arranged fair hair. And yet she is held to be above any lingering over the artifices of coquetry. She undoubtedly seeks to retain, and to prolong, her celebrated beauty, but depends still more on the graces of her mind, unimpaired by the passing years, on her intellectual culture and musical talent. . . .

Liszt has in his turn approached me. He speaks of my father, whom he knows; he saw me when I was a child and remembers me, who had retained no memory of him. I find that he has the very suave manners well suited to a priest— but how can he be one, and why are all these women so taken with him? At that very moment they are greatly perturbed at seeing him occupied with one who has made no advances, and so they cluster about him again, begging him to play something, pestering him to go to the piano. This he refuses to do, and drives them back rather brusquely, saying that it is Madame Mouchanoff who ought to play, and that he himself takes too much pleasure in listening to her to seat himself at the piano when she is present.

The Countess rises, nonchalant and disdainful; she draws off her gloves, slowly, her smile saying plainly enough that she is sacrificing herself solely to spare Liszt a drudgery, and that she is amused, to the point of derision, at the jealous rage of all those women who will be forced to applaud her. . . .

Liszt offers me his arm to take me to the refreshment table, notwithstanding the looks of envy and disappointment on the faces of most of the women. He allows everyone to pass before us, with the idea, doubtless, of withdrawing a little to one side with me. In fact, as soon as we are alone, he says in a low voice: 'You have seen Cosima?'

I had no knowledge of Liszt's lofty personality; was utterly ignorant of the beauty of his works, which later I was to admire so much, and of the incomparable nobility of his character. I regarded him only as a very celebrated pianist. Accordingly, I was not in the least intimidated, and, believing him to be hostile to the decisions of his daughter, I replied with decided vehemence: 'I beg you to say nothing to me against your daughter. I am on her side to the point that I can blame her for nothing. When it is a question of such a superior being as Richard Wagner, the prejudices and even the laws of men count for nothing. Who would not submit, and with joy, to the fascination and prestige of genius? In Cosima's place you would have done likewise, and it is your duty as a father to put no obstacle in the way of the realization of the great event to which she has the right to look forward.'

Liszt gripped me warmly by the arm. 'I am entirely of your opinion, but I may not express it,' he said in a still lower voice. 'The habit I wear imposes certain conditions which I cannot openly deny. I know the temptations of the heart too well to judge them with severity. Conventions force me to be silent, but within myself I desire more than anyone the legal solution of this painful matter. I can do nothing to hasten it; as to delaying it in any way at all, I have never had such a thought.'*. . .

We very quickly formed a close relationship with Franz Servais,† and it was to him that I turned in an attempt to penetrate some of the mysteries by which, it seemed to me, Liszt's life was surrounded. First of all I asked how, and why, he was a priest. 'It was only four years ago that he took holy orders and became the Abbé Liszt,' said Servais. 'How and why, no one knows. Perhaps by this step he wished to explain to the world, which had been so preoccupied about his plans to marry the Princess Wittgenstein, that they were abandoned for good. I believe, also, that he was glad to be able to take away from all the women who adore him, the hope of obtaining his hand.'

'But in fact all the women seem, even now, to be quarrelling over him quite openly. Does his cassock make no difference to them?'—'On the contrary, it excites them all the more, having the attraction of the forbidden fruit! Moreover, on those who understand and admire him Liszt exerts an extraordinary fascination. I can speak of this from personal experience, because I confess to submitting to it myself, and I am proud to be a pupil of his. But some of the women really go too far. It is a kind of idolatry or fetishism. They dispute over a flower he has touched, and collect the ends of his cigars; and those who are independent enough to do so follow him from city to city throughout the year.'

'And doesn't that exasperate him?'

'On the contrary, he would be very unhappy without the atmosphere of adoration surrounding him. He loves the incense and the excessive flatteries. He feels the need of this mystical kingdom, and to keep it he distributes his favours, according either to merit or to his own preferences.'

'But how is he able to maintain harmony in his harem, and to banish jealousy and rivalry?'

'That is the most difficult thing to understand,' said Servais. 'He succeeds in keeping the peace among his votaries, and even makes them accept and respect a favourite. When astonishment is expressed at a self-denial so unusual among women, his unexpected reply is: "In me, they love themselves." '[7]

* Cosima's diary (28 Aug): 'A letter from Judith; she tells me that my father wishes to settle my affairs for me, that he loves me. . . . The letter did me infinite good.'

† Belgian composer, conductor and pianist (*c.*1847–1901). Because he bore a certain resemblance to Liszt, it was long rumoured that he was an illegitimate son of the latter and Princess Wittgenstein. When, however, someone finally asked Liszt himself whether this was the case, he replied unequivocally: 'I know his mother only through correspondence, and such a thing can't be done by correspondence.' For bogus claims made on behalf of other persons, see Alan Walker's *Franz Liszt. The Virtuoso Years: 1811–1847* (New York, 1983), 23–5. An openly fictional variation on the same theme is provided by J. G. Huneker's short story 'A Son of Liszt' (*Melomaniacs*, New York, 1910).

During these days in Munich, *Vladimir Stasov* met Liszt again.

As soon as he gets caught up in conversation, his clerical posture vanishes. His movements lose their restraint and pious humility; he raises his head and, shedding, as it were, his monkish pose, once again becomes forceful, dynamic. You see before you the old Liszt, the genius, the eagle.[8]

Of the extraordinary individual who had entered Liszt's life some months before his trip to Munich, a graphic description was penned by the German sculptor Josef von Kopf (1827-1903).

> An interesting personality came to Rome: Madame Janina from Lemberg, a woman of about thirty. Both a pupil and one of the most ardent admirers of Liszt, her love often made life very difficult for him. Small, vivacious in her speech, quick in her movements, passionate, excitable and quick-tempered —she was a great piano-player. With her wide mouth, turned-up nose, close-cropped hair, she made an impression of no great beauty. But that soon faded away when she spoke, or when she sat at the piano and gave a virtuoso performance of her sonatas. She had a man's suit made for her, of the kind that I used to wear in my studio. Garbed thus, in the evenings and at night she would prowl the streets, 'a dagger in her dress'. She had, as she said, 'no end of fun'. Wearing this same outfit she would visit Liszt at Santa Francesca Romana in the Forum. She was terribly jealous of the Master; and for her rivals, of whom there were dozens, she felt a violent hatred.

As Kopf intimates, the pianistic talents of *Olga Janina* (1845–?), the so-called Cossack Countess,* were considerable. Liszt held her abilities in very high esteem; and Laura Kahrer, herself a brilliant pianist who had no reason to be indulgent in her judgement, described her as 'extremely gifted'.

Olga not only saw Liszt frequently in Rome and at Tivoli over the next few months, but in due course followed him to Weimar, Pest and Szekszárd. When, however, her unseemly behaviour forced him to sever relations, she sought revenge, first by threatening him with a revolver (see November 1871 *infra*), and then by writing the book *Souvenirs d'une Cosaque*. Published in 1874 under the pseudonym 'Robert Franz', its intention, identical with that of *Nélida* three decades earlier, was to belittle Liszt, who is shown as her lover, 'X'.

Although the passages setting out details of the *affaire* cannot positively be disproved, it is the opinion of many writers on Liszt—in view of Olga's neurotic and eccentric character, as well as of certain obvious inventions and exaggerations in the book—that they are mere fantasy and wishful thinking. It is interesting to note, however, that an acquaintance of Liszt's who *did* consider him guilty of an illicit relationship with la Janina, was the Princess Wittgenstein, no less. (See her letter of 30 May ?1875 to Eduard von Liszt *infra*.)

The paragraphs reporting Olga's initial impressions of Liszt, his and his pupils' demeanour at the classes etc., are likely to be fundamentally accurate, albeit written with the intention of depicting the great man in none too flattering a light.

* *Née* Olga Zielinska, she had in 1863 married Karol Janina Piasecki. Adopting his middle name, she then gave herself out to be the 'Countess Janina'.

He was tall, with grand manners and a dignified bearing; ugly, with a profusion of long and extremely beautiful grey-white hair combed backwards. His eyes were deep-set and pensive, and could on occasion be hard. There was, too, his smile—a smile which flashed like a ray of sunlight. This combination of charm and ugliness made him of the race of those who from the beginning inspire either profound aversion or passionate worship.

His very first words put me at my ease: 'Well! So we are not a young man. That's rather a mishap. Who the devil could have guessed a woman from your letter?'

'That is not the only extraordinary thing you will find, *maître*, if you keep me. You will find a devoted disciple in me. Take me!'

'Take you, take you . . . ' and he looked at me attentively. This sustained gaze troubled me. There was something other than curiosity in it; it was as though he were applying memories to me, confused memories that he was trying to disentangle. 'Take you, *Eccellenza*,' he repeated with a laugh. 'It's done.'

He was speaking in all seriousness. 'What? But as yet you know neither my position, nor my person, nor my talent!' (I was quoting words from his letter.) 'Your position and your person, what do they matter? Your talent'—and here his eyes took on an expression of vague curiosity—'I know already. You must have more or less the manner of Chopin. He was my best friend.'

He sat down at the piano and played Chopin's Polonaise in C sharp minor. I do not know what passed within me; I remained nailed to my seat; never had I heard or dreamt anything like it. The instrument was not a piano; the man playing did not have human fingers. I shivered at those heart-rending chords, interspersed with silence, and after the last note I wept. X pretended not to notice. The fact is, he had put me in a cruel embarrassment. I could have feared that he would take me for an elegiac provincial. Terrible timidity and fear of ridicule thus put mutes on all feelings.

He played a few more things, all by Chopin, and then he said: 'In what part of Rome will you be staying?'—'I don't know. I do not yet know Rome. I need space, air. I must see the sky and some greenery.'—'The part to the north of the Via del Babuino will suit you. You will have a view of Mount Pincio, if you are not afraid of going high up.'

I said farewell, but he reminded me why I was there. 'Perhaps you would play me something?' I began one of his paraphrases, but he stopped me. 'No, not that, something else. A Chopin scherzo.' I played the Scherzo in B flat minor. It was terrible. I was paralysed by an idiotic fear; and then, in addition, I had been aware for several minutes that, beside his, my own playing did not exist; nor did any in the world.

He spoke again: 'You know nothing. Your playing is soft and feminine, but you have great qualities of sound, and then, as I said, you are of the family of Chopin; you have his accent. Go, *Eccellenza,* and come back on Friday an hour before the Ave Maria. You will find here a few youngsters who study with me on Fridays.'

How odd, I thought. He had written to me: 'You foresee my objections. I do not give lessons, and I am by profession neither a teacher nor a player of the piano.' So what difference was there between giving lessons and allowing others to study with you? I took my leave both charmed and discontent. I felt disappointed. . . .

In his salon on the Friday I found about ten or twelve young people of both sexes, accompanied by their families. I was surprised to see a girl arrive escorted not only by father and mother but by an aunt and two cousins as well. . . . I sat in a window recess and looked out. In front of me, on the other side of the Forum, there was a long, high wall, full of cracks and covered with climbing plants; on the left, fallen columns and the Arch of Constantine; on the right, the ruins of the palace of the Caesars; on the horizon, a row of cypresses. Beneath the windows there were some old women and ragged children among the stones, warming themselves in the sunshine. By leaning out slightly it was possible to see the upper part of the Colosseum's highest wall.

X came in. Then I received one of the greatest surprises of my life. There was a frantic rush towards him. The mothers, the daughters, the men took possession of his hands in turn, planting long and unctuous kisses on them. Smilingly he allowed it. I stood where I was, isolated from the group pressing about him. He came towards me. 'Ah! c'est vous. Bonjour.' His voice sounded cold and dry; it was not that in which he had welcomed me.

'He is irritated because I didn't kiss his hand. Well, the irritation will last long,' I said to myself. I thought too: 'What a strange great man! And these Italians, how they humiliate themselves! All right for the women perhaps—but the *men*!'

X called on me to play. What a strange lesson! He admonished me, pointed out my faults, sometimes showed me a better fingering; but when I ventured the least observation, when I asked him how I was to do such and such, or why a certain movement, a certain position of the hand, were preferable to others, he looked at me in great astonishment, anger even. It was obvious that he did not allow people to question him. Towards the end he became almost rude. I left the piano and took my place silently in a corner, hurt above all to feel myself dominated in spite of myself by his haughtiness. Then I took my leave with the others, who had all gone through their pieces without so much as opening their mouths.

I went into the Colosseum. It was deserted. I lit a cigar and whistled to myself while walking, to avoid coming face to face with my thoughts. One in particular twisted within me like a serpent: 'What a joke, these lessons! He is bolted and padlocked, will say nothing!' I threw away my cigar in a rage: 'What of it? He will say nothing, but he will play—and then I shall open eyes and ears. Fancy finding nothing more interesting in this man! And I had come to him from afar with so much faith, enthusiasm and—I forced myself to say it—so much liking for him!'

Sadly I went home. I spent part of the evening arranging my hours of study and drawing up a kind of programme, which included a great deal of practice, Italian lessons, and a visit every day to an art gallery or museum. At about nine o'clock my landlady came in and gave me a card: 'A gentleman wishes to see the signorina.' I read the name of X. I was utterly taken aback, could not move, felt completely paralysed. . . . X entered. He was no longer the same man. He took my head in his two hands and kissed it. 'I have come to offer my apologies.'

'Apologies, you?' I stammered. 'Yes, I was rude earlier on, but your manners irritated me. I am not a piano teacher, *Eccellenza*, as I told you.' And when I said nothing, he went on: 'I shall give you what help I can, either here or at my place, every Tuesday. You will achieve nothing worthwhile by coming with the others.' I felt a terrible longing to say: 'Nor shall I achieve anything worthwhile on Tuesdays, whether here or at your place, if you explain nothing and if I am forbidden to ask questions.' But I dared not: it seemed to me that the Roman climate was already exerting a disastrous influence on my strength of character. . . .

As he was leaving, I suddenly seized his hand and kissed it with more ardour than the Italians I had found so degraded. Hardly had he taken a step outside when I gave myself some great punches on the head, crying out: 'What is happening to you here? *M'avvilisco*, I too!'

Part of the night I spent on the loggia, in rather an agitated state of mind, and only in the morning could I make a resolution to work hard. . . . I gave up my plan to visit churches and museums, deciding to devote my entire time to practice. At the next lesson, for which I had prepared very thoroughly, X to my surprise was not satisfied, finding my playing feeble and indecisive. In no way did I allow myself to be discouraged. Having a stout faith in my abilities, I simply increased my practice time.

Three months passed thus. I led a double life. I had a fever for art which, in my practice hours, absorbed me entirely, and a fever of the heart which caused a series of troubles and indescribable discomforts. I saw X once a week, and those were my bad days. In the mornings I would awaken with rapid and convulsive palpitations, and be unable to apply myself to anything at all for ten consecutive minutes. I would smoke cigar after cigar, which with me has always been a sign of agitation, and on my return from Santa Francesca Romana I would sit in a loggia and stay there for hours on end in a state of indefinable stupor, wondering what I was experiencing and not knowing the answer, listening, feeling within me something unknown and extraordinary that was welling up and taking possession of my heart. X busied himself conscientiously with me, but I sensed that he was not satisfied. 'That's only right,' I said to myself. 'I know nothing and must work harder.' And every week the number of hours I gave to practice increased.

One evening towards the end of July he said: 'Next month I am going to Germany for three weeks.' I turned very pale. 'Are you feeling unwell?' Calmly I replied: 'I have never felt so well in my life.'

He left me for a moment to give an instruction to his servant, and I walked hurriedly up and down the room. Certain bizarre notions came to me, like those vague and furtive flashes which tremble on the horizon at the approach of a storm. Suddenly I stopped: 'Why this agitation? He is returning in three weeks.' To my surprise I realized that I was speaking aloud.

X came in again. He was more affectionate and kept me longer than usual. When I was leaving, he took me in his arms; and with a savage movement I embraced him. My blood was on fire.

'*Eccellenza*, you have a fever.'

'The fever—the fever—is that I love you!!'

A great silence fell upon us. I was aghast, and as though frightened by the sound of my own voice, by the meaning of those words which had just revealed me fully to myself. I felt shattered. I invoked a thunderbolt from God. I could have wished for the earth to open up and swallow me. Had I been holding a pistol, I believe I would have blown my brains out. I was frightened neither by my avowal nor by my love. The only thing that made me tremble was the thought that his severe manner would return and that he would condemn me to exile.

He drew me into his arms, held me for a long time tightly against his chest, and then said very quietly: 'Never speak to me of love. I must not love.' At that I fled, forgetting both hat and gloves. His servant ran after me with my hat, bringing me a message from his master, who wished to see me at the station when the train left. . . . Incapable of speaking, I nodded agreement. Then I ran wherever my legs took me, saying to myself over and over again: 'The fever is that I love you.' Those words seemed to be written in the air in letters of fire. They danced before my eyes, came nearer, and I drew back quickly as though burnt by them. It was all too tiring and overwhelming for me. . . .

After having a score of times lost my way, I found myself at the foot of the Pincio. I climbed up. At the top, a wind coming from the sea blew on my burning brow and drove the vision away. I fell on to one of the seats set against the parapet surrounding the Pincio platform. All was silence and solitude, and in this solitude I let my heart brim over. For the first time in my life I was in love, and it was a love which was blossoming with a sombre magnificence. My heart, which had not wasted itself in life's little affections, had gathered treasures. I could love only with violence and frenzy. All my desires, all my energies, the blood in my veins, I placed at his feet; but I needed him—were it only for an hour and had I to die afterwards bearing with me into eternity no more than this hour of love! Suddenly, the words he had spoken to me rang ominously in my ears: 'Never speak to me of love; I must not love.' I rose menacingly. I remembered how all his life he was said to have lavished with full hands the best of his heart, to have scattered to the winds of every caprice all the tender affection of his soul, to have loved heedlessly wheresoever he had happened to be, to have followed like a menial the fastest and most commonplace women—and now he would resist one of those superb passions which, like the fabulous and magnificent plant of Brazil, flower scarcely once in a hundred years!

He would be mine or I would kill him!

I resumed my walk. On regaining my room I fell into a delirium lasting three days. By the time I had recovered, X had departed. . . .

X returns to Rome and they meet again.

He drew me into his arms, holding my head against his shoulder. I do not know how long we remained thus. Centuries could have passed. It was happiness in all its plenitude, an ineffable happiness which the intoxicating joys yet to come did not give me.

So he loved me!

He spoke: 'My reply to your letter is my return. I could not write. I must not love—but I *do* love and cannot suppress it. I beg you (and here his voice became so caressing that I shivered from head to foot) to have mercy on me now that you have extracted this confession from me. Let your love be sweet to me; let it not make me a perjurer.'

Chokingly I replied: 'Your wish will be sacred to me.'

'Call me Ferenc, *tutoie-moi*.' And he covered me with passionate kisses. Suddenly he pushed me back, took a few steps and opened the window. 'Your *infiorata* has made me dizzy. I have a confused head, *Eccellenza*.' And he began to banter sweetly.

Some people called to see him. He invited them to stay and we had a delightful evening. Never had I seen him so sparkling with verve and spirit. I was amazed at his warm, highly-coloured eloquence, and when I expressed my astonishment to one of those present I learnt that this gift of words had once earned him the nickname of Golden-Tongued. He seemed transfigured; his words were filled with adorable tenderness. Blossoming in this heart were benumbed flowers that the crushing rule of the ecclesiastical state wished to condemn to dryness; they were opening out under a ray of sunlight, the ray of the last love. But would not this sweet and invigorating warmth be banished on the morrow; would not narrow dogma pursue its work of sterility?

The next day I was brought this letter: 'The happiness of which one dreams is the forbidden fruit. Divine law prohibits us from gathering it, and mankind is merciless to those who attempt to do so. I beg you to grant my profoundly humble prayer: love me with pride and do not cause me to fail in my duty or to have to blush before anyone at all. Your noble heart will command you to grant me this mercy.'

My beautiful dream of the previous day had turned out as I had foreseen! I sprang up. The Church was taking him back. 'Right! I shall fight the Church for him!' From that moment this thought did not leave me. His mind took pleasure in the follies of Catholicism; the struggle would do no more than reinforce his objections and the feeling of what he called his duty. Remembrance of the remarks made the previous day in my room came to me. Yes, it was that; above all it was necessary to gratify the little vanities of this immense *amour-propre*. I no longer spoke to him of love, but acted. I took a handsome apartment in the Piazza Traiana which brought me nearer to him. . . .

At the beginning of winter X departed for Tivoli. The foreigners who invade Rome in November all knocked at the door of Santa Francesca Romana. They went to see X just as one goes to see the giraffe at the zoo; and they took advantage of the cordiality of his welcome to purloin everything possible from him, even the bits of paper on which he wiped his pens. Others asked for photographs with a personal dedication, and the boldest asked him to play the *Erlkönig* and the *Invitation to the Dance*. It was then that one had to see the English at work. While he was playing they queued up behind him, gravely removing hairs with tweezers, their preference being for those that had already turned silver. When one person had collected enough, he would put them in a paper bag and yield his place to the next. Absorbed in his music, X either felt nothing or was disinclined to make a fuss about so small a matter. His entire head of hair in all its abundance would have been taken, just as the kisses of the faithful have worn away the bronze foot of the statue of St Peter (which, incidentally, is a statue of Jupiter), had he not made a wise decision. It was not solely a matter of the depilation of his head, but of his time. He was no longer using it except to hand out photographs and to play the *Invitation to the Dance* and the *Erlkönig*. Cardinal H offered him hospitality at his beautiful Villa d'Este; he accepted and departed.

The first time that I went to see him at Tivoli he displayed a joy from which I could well see that solitude was weighing terribly on this passionate lover of the world and of homage. He made me visit his turret; nothing remarkable save a long terrace opening on to a vast horizon. The apartment itself was insignificant and not very comfortable, just like Italian apartments in general. The upper parts of the doors, bearing X's arms and monogram, looked well enough, but the chimneys did not work, the furniture was shabby and unmatching, and the rooms small and low.

I went to see him regularly twice a week, taking with me giant bouquets which I sent for from Alphonse Karr's garden at Nice. They were true love *selam*, songs blossoming and sweet-smelling. No one visited this god without a bouquet, but theirs were Roman bouquets, and I wanted mine to be different. They adorned and brightened the dismal little room in which he worked.

On arrival at the Villa d'Este I would run up the spiral staircase, burst through the doors like a hurricane, and fall into X's arms. And on each occasion his embrace would last a little longer than the one before.

On fine days we dined on the terrace; in the corner by the fireplace on rainy ones. He proved himself immensely thoughtful, showing me every kind of exquisite attention, for which I could have wept from gratitude, so little was I used to them. After the meal he would sit opposite the fireplace; I would curl up at his feet, and he would get me to give him news of Rome and of what his friends had been doing. And I, who had up to that time refused all invitations, now squandered my time in the salons, collecting all the gossip, tittle-tattle and little scandals which seemed to divert him.

At moments we fell silent. He would then place his hand on my head and look at me in such a strange manner that I would take fright, not divining the reason, and burst into tears. Then his features would grow darker and he would embrace me in silence. With the coming of night he took me to Tivoli's only *osteria*, where a phenomenally dirty room awaited me, but in which I used to fall asleep dreaming sweet dreams. At daybreak I would take the road for Rome, but on fine moonlit evenings returned that same day, as I had a pass for the gates.

We used, in those days, to walk as far as the olive grove, and there, protected by the night and emboldened by the pressure of his hand, I would relate to him the fatigues and sadnesses of my days spent far from him, the nervous irritation of the three-hour journey, the anxieties of my vague hopes, and the exasperations of the return; and when he interrupted me, speaking of his duties, reminding me of mine, I would knot my two hands around his neck, telling him that the glorious affirmation of passion was the absolute abandonment of all thoughts, all affections, all duties, and all virtues; that it was the joyous sacrifice of all esteem, security, even of honour, and of the holiest things one would like to invent if they did not exist, in order to provide lofty proofs of a limitless devotion, a royal love. And he would say: 'Go on speaking; don't stop!'—and his lips, seeking mine, would stifle me with kisses. Finally, he would press me against his heart one last time and I would climb into the carriage.

One day I was late. A steady downpour had broken up the roads; the horses could proceed only by slipping at every step. I was in torment. At the foot of the hill I left the carriage and took a short cut along a little rocky path; in a twinkling I was at the Villa d'Este. Down below they told me that X was worried about me, and that Ercole, his valet, had gone to meet me. The turret rooms were deserted. Opening the door of the terrace, I found myself face to face with X. He was quite changed, and looked like a man who had come to some violent decision. Shaking hands in silence, he indicated that I was to go in. Coming in after me, he turned the key in the lock, advanced with open arms and dilated eyes and said: 'I can resist you no longer!'

We did not dine that evening, and when the sun rose it found me leaning over X, who was asleep, and eagerly contemplating the grievous sadness that his features expressed. What was this sadness?

I kissed his dear lips, and in his sleep he returned my kiss. So he belonged to me! I was about to kiss him again when suddenly a frightful thought took hold of me. He was mine, but on awakening perhaps he would repulse me and, weeping, take refuge at the foot of the crucifix! And how would I regain possession of him? My recent efforts had wearied me; I had used up all the self-sacrifice, and all the extravagance, that was in me. To which new countries could I go to gather flowers? What feelings could I invent to lay at his feet? A terrible temptation came over me. Yes, I could lose him. On awakening, he would go in search of some priest, and, brow in the dust, would implore God's forgiveness for this crime of love, which at the tribunal of penitence he would stigmatize with names most odious. Absolution would be granted in return for forgetting me. They would promise him a much more beautiful place in Heaven; and the journey still before him on earth they would mark, as an advance, with ecclesiastical dignities, honours, and distinctions. He would accept, perhaps weeping—and in doing so he would assassinate me!

What if I were to kill him! My Circassian belt held a little dagger. Reaching for it at the foot of the bed where I had dropped it the previous evening, I drew out the weapon. The blade was poisoned: just a slight scratch and he would be mine for eternity, for they would cover us with the same shroud in the same tomb. . . He opened his eyes. I stopped breathing, holding the knife in the hollow of my hand and awaiting his first words. They were words of love. He was saved.

Slowly he raised himself; pensively but smilingly he regarded me. 'What is the matter?' he asked; 'you are as pale as a corpse and your eyes are mute and terrifying.' When I made no reply, he drew me towards him and saw the dagger. 'You wanted to kill me, child!' He clasped me deliriously, through his embrace softly murmuring promises of love, swearing to me that he wished to struggle and fight no longer—and ceaselessly I made him say it over and over again.[9]

To the publication (1874) of *Souvenirs d'une Cosaque,* Liszt responded with dignity. Writing to Augusz, he bracketed the author with 'the learned Nélida'. 'In days gone by both the one and the other wrote me numerous impassioned letters on the nobility of my character and the uprightness of my feelings. In this I shall not contradict them, and will continue to prize sincerely their remarkable and brilliant talents as artists, writers, and inventors, while regretting that they should turn them so vehemently against my poor self. . . . If I had to explain my conduct before a court of honour, even one composed of people prejudiced against me, I should find it not the least bit difficult to clear myself by correcting, in accordance with the truth, facts and dates repeatedly attested to by my adversary. . . . The real Robert Franz wrote to ask me to authorize him to protest in the newspapers against this abuse of his name by the pseudo-Franz. I replied by saying that the more estimable section of the public would certainly not confuse the composer of the beautiful *Lieder* and *Gesänge* with the croakings of *la cosaque*.'

'The mistake I made was to trust her,' he remarked later to Lina Ramann; 'I cannot guarantee that *passion* won't seize me once again.'

Souvenirs d'une Cosaque was followed by *Mémoires d'un pianiste*. Purporting to be Liszt's reply to the earlier volume, its real author was, again, Janina herself. From the same pen there came, in 1875, *Le Roman du Pianiste et de la Cosaque*, this time under the pseudonym Sylvia Zorelli.

Years later, when Olga Janina had settled in Geneva and was earning a living by teaching, Liszt did what he could to render assistance to her anonymously; and to Sophie Menter a few days before his death he remarked: 'The Janina was not wicked, just exalted.'

Liszt to Princess Carolyne. Rome, 27 November. Overbeck's death makes me think of my own. I expressly desire, request, and enjoin that my obsequies take place without any pomp whatsoever. I protest against such a burial as Rossini's, and even against any summoning of friends and acquaintances, as at Overbeck's funeral. Let there be no ostentation, no music, no procession, no unnecessary lighting, no eulogizing, nor speeches of any kind at all. Let my body be buried, not in a church, but in some cemetery*—and above all may care be taken to see that it is not removed from that grave to any other. I desire for my remains no other resting-place than the cemetery made available to them at the place where I die, nor any religious ceremony other than a low mass—not a requiem sung at the parish church. The inscription on my tomb could be: *Et habitabunt recti cum vulto suo*.† If I die at Rome, my wish is for my friend Don Antonio Solfanelli to officiate at this low mass. Lacking him, then perhaps some other priest who may retain an affectionate memory of me. My last blessing belongs to you, as do those of each day of my life.[10]

In 1869 Liszt began to plan two new oratorios: *The Legend of St Stanislas* (for his Polish Princess Carolyne) and *St Stephen, King of Hungary*. They would, he hoped, be completed in a year and a half. But at the time of his death, seventeen years later, the first (S688) was still unfinished and the second barely begun.

* In a letter to Cardinal Hohenlohe some years later, Liszt wrote: 'If I had the choice of my burial place, it would be the cemetery at Tivoli.' At other times he seems to have favoured the Franciscan monastery at Pest.

† Psalm 140: 'The upright shall dwell in His presence.'

In late 1869 *Edvard Grieg* (1843–1907) and his wife Nina (1845–1935) came to Italy from their native Norway. The government grant which made the journey possible was itself largely the result of Liszt's interest in the young composer, as is shown by a letter from Grieg to his biographer Aimar Grönvold.

It was indeed a distinction of great importance for me that one day in December 1868, just as the darkness seemed thickest in Christiania, I received a letter* from Liszt which brought sunlight into my universe. There was at that time no one at home who cared anything at all about me as a creative artist. I had expressed my despondent feelings in a letter to a Roman friend; he had spoken of it to Liszt, who he knew was warmly interested in me, and it shows a very noble trait in Liszt that he sat down immediately at his writing table, conscious of the good he could thereby accomplish. I had thought it worthwhile to apply for a travel grant but had little hope of getting one, since I was in the black books of our conservative musicians and the rest of the ruling music dilettanti. But Liszt's letter worked wonders.[1]

Writing to his parents from Rome on 17 February 1870, Grieg described his first meeting with Liszt, at Santa Francesca Romana.

That I had a little qualm in my stomach, I won't deny; but that I could have spared myself, for a more lovable man than Liszt it would hardly be possible to find.

He came smilingly towards me and said in the most genial way: 'We have corresponded a little, have we not?' I told him that I had his letter to thank for being where I was, which drew from him a roar of laughter like that of Ole Bull. All the while his eyes, with a certain ravenous expression in them, were fixed on the packet I had under my arm . . . and his long, spider-like fingers approached to such an alarming degree that I thought it wisest to set about opening the packet at once. He began now to turn over the leaves; that is to say, he read the first part of the sonata† through cursorily, and that there was no humbug about the reading was shown by the significant nod, 'Bravo' or 'Very fine!' with which he marked the best

* Liszt's letter, of 29 Dec. 1868, had run: 'I am glad to be able to tell you of the sincere pleasure it has given me to read your Sonata (Op. 8). It bears testimony to a vigorous, reflective, and inventive creative talent of excellent quality—which to achieve the heights has only to take its natural course. I am pleased to think that in your own country you are meeting with the success and encouragement you deserve. These will not be wanting elsewhere either; and if you come to Germany this winter I cordially invite you to stop for a while at Weimar, so that we may get to know one another.'

† Grieg's Violin Sonata in G, Op. 13.

bits. My spirits began to soar; but when he now asked me to play the sonata my courage altogether failed me. I had never before tried to put the whole thing together for the piano and I would gladly have escaped having to sit and make a mess of it before him. But there was no help for it.

So I began on his beautiful American grand piano. Right at the beginning, where the violin breaks in with a little baroque but national passage, he interrupted: 'Oh, how saucy! I like that. Once again, please!' And when the violin the second time slips into the Adagio, he played the violin part higher up on the piano in octaves, with such beautiful expression, so remarkably true and singing, that I smiled inwardly. These were the first notes I heard from Liszt. And now we went dashing into the Allegro, he the violin, I the piano. I got more and more into form; I was so happy over his applause, which in truth flowed so copiously that I felt the most singular thankfulness streaming through me. When the first part was over, I asked him if I might play something for the piano alone, and chose the Minuet from the Humoresques, which you no doubt remember.

When I had played the first eight bars and repeated them, he sang the melody with me, and did it with an air of heroic power in his bearing that I entirely understood. I saw very well that it was its national character that appealed to him. I had guessed it would be so, and had therefore taken things with me in which I had attempted to pluck the national string. When the Minuet was over I felt that if there was to be any question of getting Liszt to play, it must be now when he was obviously in great spirits. I asked him and he shrugged his shoulders slightly; but when I said that he couldn't surely intend to let me leave the South without having heard a note from him, he mumbled, with a little flourish: 'Well, I'll play what you like—I'm not like that!' and in a second he had out a score which he had just completed, a kind of ecclesiastical processional march to Tasso's grave,* a supplement to his famous symphonic poem for orchestra, *Tasso, Lamento e Trionfo*. Then down he sat and set the keys in motion. I assure you that he belched out, if I may use so unbeautiful an expression, one mass of fire and fervour and vivid thought after another. It sounded as if he were invoking Tasso's spirit. He paints in garish colours, but a subject like this is just for him; to portray tragic greatness is his strength. I did not know which to admire most, the composer or the pianist; for his playing was magnificent. He doesn't exactly play—one forgets that he is a musician, he becomes a prophet who announces the day of judgement so that all the spirits of the universe quiver under his fingers. He invades the most secret places of the soul and delves into one's innermost being with a demoniacal power.

When that was over, Liszt said quite casually: 'Now let's go on with your

* *Le Triomphe funèbre du Tasse* is the third of the *Trois Odes funèbres* for orchestra. The transcription for piano solo (S517) dates from 1866.

Sonata!' And I, naturally: 'No, thanks very much, after that I shouldn't like to.' But now comes the best. Says Liszt: 'Why not? Give it to me then, and I'll do it.' Now remember, first he didn't know the Sonata, had never heard or seen it before, and second, it was a violin sonata with a violin part that develops independently of the piano, now above, now below. And what did Liszt do? He played the whole affair, lock, stock and barrel, violin, piano, nay more, for he played with more fullness and breadth. The violin was given its due right in the middle of the piano part; he was literally all over the whole piano at once, without a note being missed. And how, then, did he play? With majesty, beauty, genius beyond compare in interpretation. I believe I laughed, laughed like an idiot. And when I stammered some words of admiration, he mumbled: 'You can surely expect an old hand like me to manage a bit of sight-reading.' Wasn't it all gracious and kind from first to last? No other great man I have met has been like him. Then finally I played the Funeral March, which was also to his taste, then I talked a little with him about all sorts of things—told him among other things that my father had heard him in London in 1824, which pleased him. ('Oh, yes, I have played a lot around the world, too much,' he said.) Then I took my leave and made my way home, wonderfully hot in the head but conscious that I had spent two of the most interesting hours of my life. And now I am asked to go to him again tomorrow, and naturally I am delighted.

The day after the visit I have just described for you, the Italians Sgambati and Pinelli played my 1st Violin Sonata at a *matinée* where the whole fashionable world was present. Liszt came in the middle of the concert, just before my sonata, and that was well. For I do not put down the applause the sonata received to my own credit . The thing is that when Liszt claps they all clap—each louder than the other.

To the same. Rome, 9 April. I must give you an account of my second visit to Liszt, which took place soon after I had sent my previous letter and was in no way behind the first in interest. Fortunately I had just received from Leipzig the manuscript of my Piano Concerto, and this I took with me. Besides me there were present Winding,* Sgambati, and a German Lisztian, unknown to me, who carries plagiarism so far as to wear the dress of an abbé; then there was a Chevalier de Concilium and a few young ladies of the kind that would like to eat Liszt up, with hair and hide. Their admiration is simply comic. They competed for the honour of standing by his side, of touching a corner of his long abbé's robe, making occasion to press his hand—even ignoring with complete want of consideration the space every player requires for the movements of his arms. These ladies crowded round him at the piano when he played later, their greedy eyes

* The Danish pianist and composer August Winding (1835–99).

fixed upon his fingers as though they might be expected to disappear at any moment into the already gaping mouths of the little beasts of prey.

Winding and I were very anxious to see if he would really play my concerto at sight. For my part I thought it an impossibility. Liszt, however, thought otherwise. 'Will you play?' he asked. I excused myself with a 'No —I cannot' (I have never so far practised it). So Liszt took the manuscript, went to the piano, and said with his own particular smile addressed to all present: 'In that case, I'll show you that I can't either.' Then he began. I admit that he took the first part of the concerto rather too quickly and the beginning lost a little by it, but later, when I made an opportunity to indicate the time myself, he played as only he and none other can play. It is characteristic that the cadenza, which is technically extremely difficult, he played perfectly. His dramatic gestures are beyond words. He does not rest content with playing only, no, he talks and criticizes at the same time. He flings brilliant remarks now to one, now to another in the company, deals out significant nods to right and left, most when something pleases him especially. In the Adagio, and even more in the finale, he reached his culminating point both in regard to execution and to the praise he gave. I must not forget a really divine episode. Towards the end of the finale the second theme is repeated, as you will remember, in a grand *fortissimo*. In the preceding bars, where the first note of the theme's first triplets, G sharp, changes to G in the orchestra, while the piano in a tremendous scale figure traverses all its range of the keys, he stopped suddenly, rose to his full height, left the piano and paced with stalwart, theatrical step and arm uplifted through the great hall of the monastery while he fairly bellowed the theme. At the G I have spoken of, he stretched out his arm commandingly like an emperor and shouted: 'G, G, not G sharp! Bravo, that is what I call real Swedish Banco!' and then, as if in parenthesis, almost *pianissimo*: 'Smetana recently sent me some of it.' Then he went back to the piano, repeated the whole strophe, and finished off.* At the end he said with a singularly cordial accent as he handed me the book: 'You carry on, my friend, you have the right stuff in you. And don't ever let them frighten you!' This last has infinite importance for me. There is something I shall call consecrated in it. Often, when disappointment and bitterness come, I shall think of his words, and that the remembrance of this moment will have a wonderful power to sustain me in days of adversity, I firmly believe.[2]

From Grieg's report to the Norwegian Government. The thing that has been for me personally of the greatest importance is my acquaintance and

* Oscar Meyer related another detail of this performance: 'In turning over a page in the midst of a *fortissimo* passage, where the notation was not quite clear Liszt changed the key from major to minor. Grieg ventured to call his attention to the mistake; Liszt gave him an indignant look, took a red pencil and with bold strokes made some changes and without a word proceeded. Grieg often imitated the whole scene to the great amusement of his friends.'

association with Franz Liszt. . . . I have learned to know in him not only the most talented of all pianists, but what is more—a phenomenon of spirit and greatness, with no limits in the domain of art. I brought him several of my compositions, he played them and it was of the greatest interest to me to observe how it was the national element in them that first startled—then roused him to enthusiasm. Such a triumph for my endeavours and my nationalist outlook is of itself worth the journey.[3]

Half a century or more later, the widowed Nina Grieg met Frederic Lamond, one of Liszt's last pupils. 'With tears in her eyes,' he recalled, 'she assured me that she and her husband owed their life's happiness to Liszt.'

In early April Liszt returned to Weimar. A new pupil here was *Laura Kahrer* (1853–1925).

I heard Liszt play daily, and often by the hour. To begin with, Bach and Scarlatti. The former he played remarkably slowly—such as is no longer heard!—and the piano seemed to become an organ. In Scarlatti on the other hand it became an eighteenth-century spinet; and yet it was the same Bechstein grand used by the rest of us. His touch changed so totally with each composer that we could have thought we were listening to an entirely different instrument. What struck me most of all was the way in which Liszt seemed as it were to *orchestrate* with his fingers, a phenomenon most noticeable in his performances of his own works, above all the Rhapsodies, in which he displayed an amazing and unprecedented range of colour. His playing was at once poetry and revelation! He differed from other great pianists, such as Rubinstein, in that his use of the fingers, and the resulting touch, was different for every composer; indeed, for every piece. Whereas with Rubinstein you always heard the same instrument—it was nevertheless wonderful playing—with Liszt you didn't hear the piano: you heard *him* and followed his tones, and were transported by the power of his imagination, which presented each work anew as though it were only then and there being brought into existence![4]

Having been away from Weimar since her mother's death the previous year, *Adelheid von Schorn* returned to the town at this time.

I had to leave the house and garden where I had spent the twenty-five best years of my life. As I left my old home, thinking that no walk had ever been so difficult for me, I ran into Liszt, whom I had not yet seen and who was on his way to me. Seeing him again, experiencing his warm-heartedness once more, and being accompanied by him to my new home in the Belvedere Allee, made this difficult hour so much easier for me. He was pleased that we were now such close neighbours. The next morning I was standing amidst all the chests and boxes when the door opened softly and through the narrow opening appeared a hand holding a beautiful red rose. It was Liszt's hand, and that was his welcome—for at such moments he could not find words.[5]

At Weimar in May the Allgemeine Deutsche Musikverein held a festival to commemorate the centenary (which fell in December) of the birth of Beethoven.

La Mara. On 30 April Liszt spent a few hours in Leipzig making the necessary arrangements with Riedel and the leader of the orchestra, David. In the afternoon there was a rehearsal at Riedel's with Mary Krebs, who was playing Liszt's Concerto in E flat. I had been invited too, and when I entered I found, in addition to the above-named and Adolf Stern, a lady who was introduced to me as Madame Janina, a pupil of Liszt's. Pale and slim, dressed in a lilac-coloured velvet suit with a swan motif, her close-cropped hair covered by a matching cap, she sat quietly observant in a corner, appearing to pay attention solely to Liszt. . . .

The festival began on Ascension Day, 26 May, and indeed as an authentic Ascension Day ceremony, for the Riedel Society performed the Missa Solemnis. (Earlier on, Nohl* had given a lecture on Beethoven's spiritual development.)

For the evening, Liszt had invited me to the Hofgärtnerei. There I met Pauline Viardot-Garcia and her husband, and the interesting and striking grey head of their writer friend Turgenev; the *Kladderadatsch* editor, Ernst Dohm, bubbling over with jokes; Liszt's cousin Eduard from Vienna; the Wagner champion Edouard Schuré;† Franz Servais; Ludwig Nohl; Count Dumoulin; Adolf Stern; Richard Pohl; Frau Merian-Genast; and many others. . . .

The second day of the festival was devoted to newer composers: the morning to chamber music, the evening to orchestral works. . . .

On the Sunday Liszt formed the central point of a matinée at Frau Emilie Merian's. With Hellmesberger he played Raff's fourth sonata for violin and piano. Frau Merian delighted us with songs by her brother-in-law, Raff, and Damrosch. Saint-Saëns played Beethoven variations and the March from the *Ruins of Athens.* To round off the proceedings, Liszt then joined him in a four-hand performance of *Festklänge* [S595]. Among those present, an illustrious company, were Anton Rubinstein, Tausig, Turgenev and the Viardots, and Madame Mouchanoff. And next to the last-named, two young and beautiful newcomers to the Liszt circle: Countess Schleinitz, wife of the Prussian Minister of the Interior and a supporter of Bayreuth, and Countess Dönhoff‡ (in Mme Mouchanoff's words, 'a little marvel of grace, goodness, naturalness, and intelligence').

* The musicologist and Beethoven biographer Ludwig Nohl (1831–85).

† French writer and music historian (1841–1929), author of the classic *Les Grands Initiés.*

‡ Maria Dönhoff (1848–1929). Born the Principessa di Camporeale, daughter of Donna Laura Minghetti (1829–1915), a member of Liszt's Rome circle, she was later the wife of Prince Bernhard von Bülow, the German Chancellor. In Liszt, she would say long afterwards, she admired 'not only his supreme art, but also his lofty spirit, his courage, his indifference to all questions of monetary gain. How greatly he surpassed his son-in-law, Richard Wagner, in nobility of mind, universality and mental grasp.'

Both outstandingly musical, the former was a pupil of Bülow, the latter of Tausig.

The evening brought us all together again at the Court Theatre for the final concert, 'dedicated to the memory of Ludwig van Beethoven'. Lassen conducted his new Beethoven Overture, put together from themes of the Master's out of *Fidelio, Egmont,* and other works. A prologue by Bodenstedt . . . preceded Liszt's [Second] Beethoven Cantata,* a setting of a poem by Adolf Stern with additions by Gregorovius. The great orchestral introduction includes, in all the dazzling colours of the orchestra, the whole of the Andante of Beethoven's Trio in B flat, Op. 97, whose theme returns in the choruses, the soli, and the intermezzi, as well as in a rhythmic and melodic transformation at the end.

From hundreds of throats came calls for the composer, making the house echo. As soon as he showed himself he was greeted by a fanfare, and flowers and laurels rained down upon him from all sides. Then Tausig gave a great and mighty performance of the Fifth Piano Concerto, and Liszt conducted the Ninth Symphony. The excellent solo quartet were Otto-Alvsleben, Krebs-Michalesi, Schild, and Milde. Among the first violins were the leaders of six different orchestras. Everyone was electrified. Liszt's interpretation of the gigantic work was for me a fresh revelation. . . . It was an ideal rendering of the world's sublimest work for orchestra, a performance beside which I can place none other of the many I have heard.[6]

Also present at the festival was *Berthold Kellermann* (1853–1926), a young pupil of Lina Ramann's. Not until 1873 did he begin his studies with Liszt, the championing and propagation of whose works he came in later years to regard as the principal duty of his life.

Like a spirit of light, radiating warmth and brilliance upon all about him, the Master moved amidst a crowd of musicians and music-lovers, an archetype of spiritual and physical strength. . . . His appearance alone cast a magic spell over me, one from which I was never to be released. . . .

It was the Ninth Symphony that was revealed to us by the master 'who could not conduct', as is impudently claimed to this day by certain people. Carrying his audience through all the depths and heights of this wonder-work, he aroused an endless storm of blazing enthusiasm. . . .

For those who had never before heard the mightiest master of the piano of all time, the peak of enthusiasm was to be reached by his rendering of the *Hammerklavier* Sonata. The performance, to be sure, was almost put in jeopardy by some high dignitary asking how Liszt could still be so vain as to play. Long accustomed to scorning all personal interests, he did indeed

* *Zur Säkularfeier Beethovens* (S68), composed 1869–70 and dedicated to the Grand Duchess Sophie.

strike the work from the programme—but, conscious of the disappointment this renunciation would cause, played it at the end of the public rehearsal. *How* he played, is beyond the power of words to describe. . . .[7]

On Sunday, 3 July, Liszt visited Leipzig.

La Mara. To attend the Riedel Society's performance at the St Nicholas Church of the first three parts of his *Missa choralis*, he brought with him Adelheid von Schorn, her cousin Octavie von Stein, and Olga Janina, plus a swarm of pupils. . . . When Mme Janina asked him ironically, during the fugue of a Bach motet: 'Est-ce que c'est beau, maître?' he replied with equal emphasis: 'Certainement, Madame, c'est très, très, très beau!' . . .

As arranged, at midday on 5 July I met him at Zschocher's. They were performing his *Ave Maria*. 'An old work,' he said; 'I conducted it once in Leipzig.'—'I was so fortunate as to hear it on that occasion,' I replied, 'and it made a great impression on me.'—'You could hardly say that today!' he said with a smile. Next came his *König in Thule*. He himself played the accompaniment, the song under his hands becoming a complete drama. The capable, vivacious singer he lifted far above her usual level. What he needed in abundance today was patience, for his *Consolations* were played 'inconsolably'. Mme Janina having appeared in the mean time, he invited her to play his *Cantique d'amour* for us. But she was not in the giving vein; at Leipzig, as latterly in Weimar, she was pleased to play the role of the spirit that always denies. To conclude, there came the Hungarian Storm March for eight hands. Its composer himself undertook the second bass, getting the amateurs' hands to move and their feelings to take fire. I stood beside him and found it priceless entertainment.

At the end, the guest of honour was asked to enter his name in the Institute's album. Mme Janina, too, was to perpetuate her memory therein. After doing so she came out of the adjoining room very merrily and whispered to me: 'Oh, I have written something good!' Her teacher, however, appeared not to share her opinion. In a serious tone of voice he called her back to the place of her misdeed, and only after some time had passed, and with a tearful face, did she reappear. She had given expression to her displeasure that the great master should have been expected to listen to such inferior performances; but at Liszt's demand had immediately had to erase the remark. And he was really angry with her. Even when we were sitting in the carriage taking us to Riedel's for lunch, she had to hear his reproaches. 'You don't know Goethe's fine saying, you don't know what is fitting!' When she began to speak French, he interrupted her: 'Here we do not speak French, which is not the fashion at Leipzig; here we speak German.' 'I do not understand what you are saying,' he replied again and again, until she finally spoke German.[8]

After attending performances of Wagner's *Das Rheingold* and *Die Walküre* at Munich (where his likeness was painted by the great German portraitist Franz

Lenbach) in mid-July, and before proceeding to Szekszárd, where, while the Franco-Prussian War was raging elsewhere in Europe, he spent several months with the Augusz family, Liszt made a pilgrimage (23 July), with Marie Mouchanoff and others, to the Bavarian village of Oberammergau to see the Passion Play. Admiring many aspects of the representation, he found the music, composed by Rochus Dedler, 'absolutely unbearable'. 'I advise musicians who visit Oberammergau to stuff a good deal of cotton wool in their ears.'

Staying in Szekszárd from 31 July until mid-November, he left the town only for a brief visit to Pest (21–3 August) and for excursions to Kalocsa and Nádasd.

On 25 August, at the Protestant church in Lucerne, Liszt's daughter Cosima (who had embraced the Protestant religion and whose marriage with Bülow had been annulled in July) was married to Richard Wagner, with whom she had been living since November 1868. His daughter not having written to him for a year, Liszt learnt of the marriage only through the newspapers.

Going to Nádasd on 21 September to visit the Bishop of Pécs, he was astonished when a fellow guest, Boldizsár Horvát (1822–98), the Hungarian Minister of Justice, recited in his honour, and from memory, Vörösmarty's great ode *Liszt Ferenchez*.

On the 25th of that month he attended a charity concert given at Szekszárd by Sophie Menter, Olga Janina, Mihalovich,* and Servais, all of whom had been lured to the town by Liszt's presence in it. Repeatedly called for by the audience, he contributed one of his Hungarian Rhapsodies.

On 18 October a dinner in his honour was given at the Szabó Hotel by Olga Janina; on the 21st there was a torchlight procession through the town to fête him, culminating in his playing to the crowd assembled outside the Augusz home; on Saturday the 22nd, his fifty-ninth birthday, a luncheon was given in his honour by Baron Augusz, and in the evening he gave a recital for his friends and admirers.

On 16 November Liszt arrived at Pest, where he stayed at the home of his friend Abbot Mihály Schwendtner (1820–85) in the Inner City Presbytery. Here, on the 27th, he instituted his Sunday musical matinées, at which he and various leading artists performed to small gatherings of musicians, writers, and other guests.

The most important event in which he took part during this visit to Pest was the Beethoven Festival held in December. It began on Wednesday the 14th with a performance at the National Theatre of Goethe's *Egmont*, to Beethoven's music. On the 15th Ferenc Erkel conducted *Fidelio* at the National Theatre. At the Vigadó the next day, the 100th anniversary of the birth of Beethoven, Liszt conducted the Ninth Symphony, the Violin Concerto (with Reményi), and his own Second Beethoven Cantata (its first performance in Hungary).

To seek advice about the interpretation of certain works of his, there came to him on 18 December *Pauline Fichtner* (1847–1916), a gifted German pianist who later undertook more regular studies with him at Weimar.

That we should 'think and behave with nobility and greatness' was a precept he impressed deeply upon the soul of each one of us. His own life

* The composer Ödön Mihalovich (1842–1929) became one of the closest of Liszt's younger Hungarian friends, and was also his successor as President of the Music Academy.

was based on this high principle, and in admiration and gratitude we looked up to him as a shining model and artistic ideal, striving to our utmost, both humanly and artistically speaking, to merit his goodwill and earn his approval. 'Unenvying recognition of the achievements of fellow pupils and colleagues' was one of the many dicta which had to be respected under his sceptre, non-observance of which sometimes brought severe consequences, a repetition of the offence being forbidden on pain of banishment. . . .

Study with Liszt was mostly concentrated on the spiritual and intellectual element of the music, on its shaping as a work of art. Mastery of technique was taken for granted. . . . He did no more than guide us fervently towards a freer, more natural position of the hands, elasticity of the wrist, and the practice of large-scale studies in passagework and octaves—plus the advice to practise anything difficult in all keys. Georg Leitert, Franz Servais, and I were once obliged to play the great C minor Etude of Chopin and his G major Prelude, as well as the last movement of Beethoven's Sonata in C sharp minor, in three different keys! . . . That our chief wish was to study the Master's complete works with him was understandable, but he always urged us to the study of other composers, and showed particular interest in anything new.[9]

It was at the beginning of the 1870s that Liszt entered upon the last phase of his life, the *vie trifurquée*, as he called it, in which his movements and activities were roughly divided between Pest, Weimar, and Rome. Naturally this did not rule out much travelling to other towns and countries as well.

Rome, which he liked least, he visited only with reluctance, making the long journey thither solely out of a sense of obligation to the Princess,* and in certain years (such as 1872 and the long period between January 1882 and December 1884) not troubling to go to at all. And even Weimar, where he felt much happier and more comfortable, particularly as his visits enabled him to keep in touch with musical life in Germany, he regarded as having no paramount or overriding claim upon him; and he did not find it necessary to travel to the town in 1874. Of omitting any of his annual sojourns—always lasting several months—in Hungary, however, there was never the least question. For Liszt the matter was one of simple duty: of putting his talents, knowledge, and experience at the disposal of his native country, to help promote and enrich its artistic and cultural evolution. As he wrote (7 May 1873) to his friend Augusz: 'From birth to death, and despite my lamentable ignorance of the Hungarian language, I remain heart and soul a Magyar, and therefore earnestly wish to foster the development and practice of Hungarian music.'

Fanny Lewald. Whether [Liszt's *vie trifurquée*] was altogether his free

* Malwida von Meysenbug: 'When he returned to Rome for the last time, and entered my home on a visit, I called out to him, "How nice it is that you remain loyal to Rome," to which he replied with the almost bitter resolution with which he spoke at times in contrast to his otherwise so gentle manner: "I come for one person alone—and but for that one person I would never set foot here again." '

choice, and in accordance with his inclination and (in his last years) needs, I rather doubt, judging by a remark he once made when we were talking about having both been born in the comet year of 1811. 'They talk about the influence of the stars on our destiny,' he said jocularly, 'but that doesn't hold good so far as you and I are concerned, even though we came into the light under the influence of the same heavenly body. Your life, despite your many travels, has become a stable one; you are spiritually rooted with your husband and materially in your homeland. *I* float about the world, and although I am a musician and no soldier I can sing with the *Wallensteiner* that I have no permanent abode on this earth!'[10]

1871

At the conclusion of a 'musical and aesthetic lecture' on Beethoven given by Ludwig Nohl on 2 January, Liszt played the Kreutzer Sonata with Reményi. The evening was a brilliant success.

Liszt to Princess Carolyne. Pest, 4 March. What a dreadful and heart-rending thought it is that eighteen centuries of Christianity, and a few more centuries of philosophy and of moral and intellectual culture, have not delivered Europe from the scourge of war! How much more time will be needed to cut one another's throats? When will the precepts of religion and the dreams of humanity succeed in achieving something positive? The decalogue commands us not to kill; Christian and other philosophers constantly preach goodness, gentleness, and love. Nevertheless, men kill one another ceaselessly, in fury and out of necessity! Suicides, duels, and battles stain the world with blood—even mankind's justice demands of the executioner the highest penalty! Oh! may God have pity on future generations, and may duels, wars, and the death penalty be abolished for ever! Statesmen ridicule these pastoral reveries, we know—but they have so often been mistaken in their fallacious wisdom that it is not utterly unreasonable to have aspirations that run counter to their pronouncements! Forgive me these humanitarian musings, which I shall abandon only with difficulty, while seeking to impose them on no one else.[1]

All through these years Princess Carolyne was continuing unflaggingly with her religious studies and writings; and on 9 March, the feast-day of St Frances of Rome (Santa Francesca Romana), she dedicated to Liszt her book *La matière dans la dogmatique chrétienne.*

That I have reflected passionately on this subject is thanks to you, whose great soul, great heart and great spirit have seized with such rare perspicacity the crux and vital nerve of the most delicate questions being debated today between Christianity and unbelief. Others will one day deal with it in more masterly fashion than I; but in the mean time it is right that I should offer you these pages, since you have not only taught me to ponder so many great matters, but have inspired in me a disinterested respect for and persevering love of work, as much by your words as by the shining example you have given me for four and twenty years. Your genius speaks the sublime and sympathetic language of art. However, loving goodness in speech no less than in action, your rich intelligence is a precious counsellor in all fields. Your candour, ever ambitious for me, has never been satisfied with my endeavours, whose defects it has shown me; while your unfailing indulgence has never wearied before my human frailties. Be thanked and a thousand times blessed, from the bottom of my heart![2]

In the morning of 23 April, Liszt arrived at the Schottenhof in Vienna.

Eduard Ritter von Liszt (1867–1961). To say hello to me, he hurried straight into the children's room. Frightened by his sudden lively appearance, I sought refuge under the Streicher grand pianoforte. Pursuing me, he caught hold of me and pulled me out, whereupon I burst into terrified shrieks. There then followed a scene in which the Master sat at a table, buried his face in his hands and said amid sobs: 'Does the boy consider me a stranger?' But in the end there was general merriment. My mother made him realize that as a small child I could only take him for a stranger after his many months of absence, and I was well behaved and trusting.[3]

The 2nd of May Liszt spent in Prague, where he visited Smetana, who first played to him excerpts from his opera *Dalibor* and then conducted a specially arranged performance of the overture to *The Bartered Bride*.* To dine, Liszt chose to sample the culinary delights of Schwertasek's gourmet restaurant in the former church of St Martin's in the Wall, situated near the Platýz Hall in which he had played during his first visit to the city more than thirty years earlier. Here he was joined by Ambros, to whose home they subsequently adjourned for coffee, and the critic Otakar Hostinský (1847–1910) among others. 'They spent two hours in one of the restaurant's cosy first-floor salons,' notes a Czech writer,† 'Liszt naturally being the focal point of attention, even if it was the ever-witty and intellectual Ambros who did most of the talking . . . and who brought the conversation back again and again to the admired guest and his art. Liszt listened with a gentle smile. The difference between his calm way of speaking and the explosive manner of Ambros was very noticeable. Liszt was then almost sixty years of age, but Hostinský remarked that he could now understand how on his first visit not only women but men too had been able to fall in love with him.'

Weimar, which he reached the next day, became Liszt's headquarters until his return to Rome in September.

During the 1860s he had made the acquaintance of the Russian diplomat

* It was their last meeting. Smetana died thirteen years later, carried off by syphilis, after it had first caused him to suffer deafness and madness. 'He was truly a genius!' wrote Liszt, deeply affected by the news.

† Jan Wenig, *Sie waren in Prag* (Prague, 1971), 158–9.

Baron Felix von Meyendorff and his wife Olga (1838–1926), *née* Gortchakova. First Secretary at the Russian Embassy in Rome, Meyendorff had later been appointed Ambassador to the Court of Weimar, and then, in 1870, transferred to Karlsruhe—but died suddenly in January 1871. His widow, a typical example of the masterful, intellectual type of woman to whom Liszt was attracted, seems then to have written the composer some kind of declaration. 'Your words penetrate the depths of my soul. . . . Will I be worthy of the sentiment, enigmatic but overflowing with conviction and loyalty, which you have vowed to me?' he wrote in reply.

Whatever the nature of their subsequent relationship, it was regarded by Princess Carolyne (whom Adelheid von Schorn kept well informed of Liszt's Weimar activities) as far less innocent than a mere *amitié amoureuse*. Be that as it may, the Baroness, who now returned to Weimar with her four young sons, became an important person in Liszt's life. She was his neighbour and frequently his hostess, and they maintained an animated correspondence during his absences from the town. As his letters reveal (hers to him have not survived, probably destroyed by Liszt himself), their friendship was founded above all on shared literary and intellectual interests. Olga was also musically knowledgeable and a proficient amateur pianist. It was to her that Liszt dedicated the very beautiful Impromptu in F sharp (S191), *Fünf kleine Klavierstücke* (S192), and transcription of Lassen's *Ich weil' in tiefer Einsamkeit*.

The impression formed (years later) by August Stradal was that the Baroness wished to dominate the great musician—'which was actually the case, for there was a certain subservience in his attitude to her'.

In Weimar this spring was the English writer *Matilda Betham-Edwards* (1836–1919).*

I was quartered in the then homely, friendly Erbprinz Hotel, and saw Liszt constantly at the midday *table d'hôte*. His strange impressive figure as he sat at the head of the table was a sight to remember; the brilliant eyes that flashed like diamonds, the long hair in those days only iron grey, the sensitive mouth, the extraordinary play of expression, once seen could never fade from memory. Everything indeed about Liszt was phenomenal —physiognomy, appearance, mental gifts; last, but not least, amiability of character, and an almost morbid terror of inflicting pain. . . . As I proposed to spend some months at Weimar, I engaged a music-mistress, one of Liszt's former pupils, whom I shall call Fräulein Marie. A very charming girl she was—half French, half German—graceful and pleasing rather than handsome, and a passionate admirer of her master.

I happened to say one day how sorry I was not to have so much as the gratification of shaking hands with him before his departure. 'I will myself introduce you to the Herr Doctor,' she said. 'To his pupils he refuses nothing.'

The poor girl, who was, as I soon found out, desperately in love with

* Whose *Reminiscences* (London, 1898) contain a slightly different account of her meetings with Liszt from that given here.

Liszt, got up a charming little *fête champêtre*—in his honour and my own. A carriage was ordered, picnic baskets packed, and one brilliant summer afternoon hostess and guests started for Tiefurt. The party consisted of Liszt, Fraülein Marie, a violinist of the other sex, a young lady pianist from a neighbouring town, and myself. Liszt's geniality and readiness to enter into the spirit of the occasion were delightful to witness. The places of honour were assigned to the English stranger and the violinist, Liszt insisting on sitting, a pupil on each side, on the opposite side of the carriage, not in the least disconcerted by such narrow accommodation. Thus, chatting and laughing, all of us in holiday mood, we reached the pretty park and château of Tiefurt. As the evening was cool we supped inside the little restaurant, and here a grievous disappointment awaited our hostess. Tiefurt is celebrated for its trout—indeed this delicacy is as much an attraction to many visitors as its literary and artistic associations. But although trout had been ordered by letter beforehand, none was forthcoming to fête the Master. Fräulein Marie was in tears. Liszt's gaiety and affectionateness, however, put everything right. He cut brown bread-and-butter for the two girls, and made them little sandwiches with the excellent cold *Wurst*. 'Oh, it tastes so nice,' they cried, as they thanked him adoringly. He told stories, and made the rest do the same. 'Give us news of Erfurt,' he said to the young lady guest. The moments passed all too rapidly. Then in the clear delicious twilight we drove back to Weimar, his pupils kissing his hands reverentially as he quitted us.

So far all had been bright, joyous, transparent; but I soon discovered that this charming girl, who possessed the vivacity of a Frenchwoman combined with the *Schwärmerei* or sentimentality of a Teutonic maiden, was rendered deeply unhappy by her love for Liszt. He was at that time enmeshed in the toils of another and far less guileless passion. Whilst to his gentle and innocent pupil he could accord only the affection of a loving and sympathetic friend and master, there were other women about him whose influence was of a different and fatal kind, whose infatuation led them into forgetfulness of womanly self-respect and duty, and into entanglements as damaging to his illustrious name as to their own of wife and mother.

Fräulein Marie's hapless sentiment could never discredit either herself or its object, but it occasioned a good deal of embarrassment and wretchedness, as we shall see.

A few days after this gay *al fresco* tea she came to me in great distress, begging me forthwith to deliver a little note into the Master's hands. I was reluctantly obliged to delegate the delicate mission to a hired messenger. Ill would it have become a stranger to interfere with these untoward imbroglios. Moreover, at that very time Liszt had, as I have hinted, a love affair on his hands—had, in fact, succumbed to the influence of one* of those women who were his evil genius. . . .

* The Baroness von Meyendorff, it may be surmised.

When the master suddenly absented himself from Weimar for a few days, Fräulein Marie followed him, vainly seeking an interview. On his return she was not informed of his movements. It was a lovers' quarrel, in which all the love was on one side. . . .

Just ten years later I revisited Weimar, and my first inquiry of common friends was after my sweet young music-mistress. 'Fräulein Marie! Alas!' replied my informant, 'the poor girl has long been in a *maison de santé*. Her love for Liszt ended in loss of reason.'

Quitting tragedy, let me now resume my reminiscences of Liszt at Weimar. . . . The first time I heard him play was on a very poor organ in a little church; and, seeing what his magical touches could do with such an instrument, I can better understand how great musicians of a former epoch made up for the want of an Erard or a Broadwood. He played, for some charitable purpose, his own exquisite *Ave maris stella*;* and if the sounds evolved from the grand piano constructed for his own use filled his listeners with awe and wonder, still more marvellous the strains that now issued from a poor little organ. The truth of the matter is this: Liszt's whole soul went into his playing. As with Milton, music to him was but another name for religion. Like all great geniuses, moreover, he put himself into every effort—stamped with individuality every outpouring. His playing naturally could resemble none other in the world, just because there lived no second Liszt.

We must also remember that there was a good deal of medieval mysticism in his temperament. In a certain romantic sense he may be said to have lived in the age of his own Saint Elisabeth of Hungary. . . .

Out of that little church we all poured, wending our way to his home in the park. I had already been invited to his 'At Home' that afternoon, but on the impulse of the moment he now invited almost the entire congregation! Some special service had just taken place in which he was much interested, and the greater number of those present consisted of his pupils and their own. We streamed gaily into the villa, crowding every part, nook and corner. Those who could not find room inside the house at all, listened from the garden.

I had a place of honour near the piano, and after some finely executed chamber music, the Master sat down to the piano. He touched the keys, not as one intending to throw out all his powers, but rather as one in a dream. There were many young girls present, and perhaps their youthfulness and the beauty of the rose-scented summer day inspired his improvisation. It was the soft music of Ariel's conjuring up—a strain so fairy-like, transporting, and ethereal, as to be wholly beyond description. That day Liszt summoned no awful spirits from the vasty deep. His music, the improvisation of the moment, was rather like the quelling of all evil,

* For chorus and organ (S34). It also exists in arrangements for piano solo (S506), organ solo (S669/2), voice and piano/harmonium (S680).

the magic lulling to sleep of all influences except those of a heavenly kind; the lifting of weary, earth-born souls into a region that pain, sorrow and mortality cannot reach.

Whilst he played, the same mood of ecstasy and transport that had overtaken his listeners was on himself. When the last note died away, he seemed to rouse himself by an effort, as if it were hard to realize what was passing around him. He was as one slowly awaking from a beautiful dream.

That evening I sent Liszt the following improvisation on his improvisation:

> Fain would I praise such poetry as thine,
> In fitting measures as a poet should,
> But ah! thy music brings a deeper mood;
> And tears alone acknowledge the divine.

'Vous me rendez tout fier,' wrote Liszt, 'd'avoir inspiré ce beau vers (And tears alone acknowledge the Divine).' Then he added, with his usual cordial affectionateness: 'Je reviendrai ici le printemps prochain et serai charmé que vous vouliez bien me compter parmi vous affectueux serviteurs.'

His farewell to me was of a piece with his geniality and thoughtfulness in little things. He was dining at a small side-table with some special friends at the Erbprinz, and I was occupying my usual place beside acquaintances at the *table d'hôte*. On a sudden, I saw a waiter coming towards me with a glass of champagne from Liszt's table. The tall figure of the Master rose, smiling and bowing, and we drank to each other across the room. Alike the deed and the action were very graceful. I shook hands with him later, and we never met again.[4]

On 13 June Liszt received from the King-Emperor Franz Joseph the title of Royal Hungarian Councillor and an annuity of 4,000 gulden.

On 17 July his great pupil Carl Tausig, one of the most stupendous pianistic talents of the century, died in a Leipzig hospital at the age of twenty-nine. 'Tausig was a person of vigour, intelligence, and consequence, who had the exceptional capacity, the temperament, the talent, and the patient industry of a great artist,' wrote Liszt to Carolyne. 'Further, he had much practical ability, was very well read, and thoroughly suited to occupying a dominant position in the world of music. He had been suffering for some six or eight months, and an affair of the heart had still further aggravated his physical troubles. . . . He was devoting himself to philosophical studies, and the systems of Kant, Schopenhauer, and Darwin had become familiar to him. He was also working out and perfecting with admirable care a number of musical works: piano studies, a concerto, and unpublished transcriptions of several of the Beethoven quartets and Bach chorales. In June he told me that he no longer knew what was to become of him, and that he felt inwardly broken. After a fortnight's illness he was carried off by typhoid fever.'

Via Eichstädt in Bavaria, where he attended the general assembly of the St

Cecilia Society, Liszt arrived on 9 September at Santa Francesca Romana. It seems to have been about this time that he was visited here by the French composer *Henri Maréchal* (1842–1924), winner in 1870 of the Prix de Rome.

Liszt's vision was at once lofty and great; he was full of vast ideas, declared insane in his day but now common currency. As a virtuoso he swept aside all doctrines and conventions. His enormous hands, which allowed him to play rapid sequences of tenths as easily as simple octaves or humble sixths, were the instruments of one of the most complex minds imaginable. . . .

An inordinate appetite for personal effect often masked the truth from what was nevertheless a first-rate intelligence. . . . He was a nomad, and everywhere he passed his habitual association with the finest intelligences had taught him, as it were, to think about a subject in three or four different ways. . . .

His bearing was proud but amiable, his gestures those of a kindly patron, and his gaze shielded rather than concealed by the thickness of several folded eyelids. These remained half closed for banalities, opened for generalities, and disappeared altogether for particularities, thus revealing a pair of magnificent light-blue eyes, which flashed at one before immediately closing again in keeping with his air of studied bonhomie. . . .

Taken as a whole, his clothes, words, and gestures gave an impression of valour. Before one there stood an imposing old man who would have had no need of El Cid to do his business for him; and under the velvet paw one still sensed the claw of a very self-assured lion. . . .

After a few remarks on this and that, our host evidently told himself that he could not allow these good people to leave without having heard Liszt, and he courteously offered to let us hear his Dante Symphony.

I was enchanted by the suggestion, for I had never heard Liszt and my admiration was entirely on trust!

Cigar still between his lips, and with those legendary hands whose familiar gestures were to deal slaps into the air, the *maître* first showed us the plan of his work, in a brief preamble interrupted by our respectful remarks which he endorsed by 'oui, oui', pronounced rapidly: 'Mouai, Mouai!'

Finally he went to the piano and played the whole score for us. I sat on his left and helped my friends turn the pages.

Nothing in my entire life has astonished me more, and I believe I am not greatly mistaken if I assert that anyone who has not heard Liszt can have no notion of what a piano can do!

An Iroquois watching a conjurer produce tomahawks from a pocket handkerchief could not be more of an Iroquois than was I that morning!

I could take my eyes neither from the keyboard nor from the hands whence came orchestral sonorities, sometimes light and misty like those produced by flutes and harps, sometimes terrifyingly thunderous like the trumpets we are promised in the valley of Jehosaphat!

And those constant slaps in the air! The ceaseless 'Mouai, Mouai!' coming from the chewed cigar! . . . And those terrifying eyes! . . . It was . . . it was . . . well, in a word it was the Dante Symphony, in which all the devils in Hell and all the angels in Paradise were rolling in spirals, just as on the day in which they posed for Michelangelo painting his *Last Judgement* in the Sistine Chapel!

What would this score have been, played by an ordinary first-magnitude virtuoso? What would it be, performed by an orchestra and voices? What would then remain of all those notes, when their creator's magic interpretation was no longer there to communicate his own fire to them, and perhaps also to give them their true meaning?

Since that occasion I have read the Dante Symphony, seeing in it at first only a good many incoherent, or even infantile, intentions in which, like fireflies, were hidden real treasures. Only later did I perceive in it the dawn of an art of which today we are seeing the twilight. . . .

'What did you think of that?' asked one of my friends as we came out.

'What a man!'

'Yes, but the score?'

'What fingers!'

Thus was Liszt always judged in his lifetime, and posterity has not yet been able to render to the master composer what the virtuoso of genius has demanded of it.[5]

Liszt left Rome in mid-November, spending a night *en route* at Lamporecchio near Pistoia (at the home* of his friends Prince and Princess Rospigliosi), and at Florence seeing Bülow (who lived in Italy from late 1869 until early 1872). At Pest a new home was waiting: a flat at No. 20 Nádor Street, found for him by Baron Augusz. It was into this residence that on Saturday, 25 November, armed with a revolver and several phials of poison, the self-styled 'Countess Janina' forced her way, threatening to kill Liszt and then herself. 'Spare me a recital of her violence and fury, and do me the kindness of speaking about her to no one,' he wrote to Carolyne a few days later. 'My guardian angel looked after me in this danger. After a further attempt at poisoning herself in my room, Mme Janina left for Paris, where she will probably remain. But, once again, I urge you not to talk about it—even to me— for as best I can I wish to forget this crisis, which, thanks to my good angel, turned into neither a catastrophe nor a public scandal.'

1872

At Vienna on Sunday, 31 December 1871, the Christmas Oratorio from *Christus* was conducted by Anton Rubinstein. The organist was Anton Bruckner.

* Described by Liszt as 'a superb palazzo built by Bernini for Pope Clement Rospigliosi'.

Liszt to Princess Carolyne. Vienna, 1 January. It produced a good impression on the majority of the performers and audience. My friends in both Vienna and Pest assure me it is a beautiful work—which will gain from being heard more often. Rubinstein conducted with great care. The *Stabat mater speciosa*, which was almost massacred at Ara Coeli,* caused a little difficulty at the rehearsals here too, so far as the intonation was concerned. However, they liked it, and the actual performance was almost entirely satisfying. . . . Tomorrow and the next day we shall read with what ears the critics listened.[1]

To the same, 6 January. In the articles that Eduard has sent you my little success of last Sunday is much contradicted and even invalidated. Hanslick,† Bernsdorf, and their cronies dominate the musical press—with the approval of the professors of aesthetics, superannuated composers, salon blabberers, and others, including many of my friends.‡ They indicate that as a person I am most amiable, very nearly respectable, whom one would be delighted to appreciate more. But unfortunately nature has not bestowed upon me the gifts necessary for a high-ranking musician—and as it is no longer possible to class me among the happy mediocrities, I must resign myself to finding 'no room at the inns' of the newspapers possessed by my antagonists. So be it! I shall remain in better company with the shepherds who listened to the voice of the Angel—announcing peace to men of good will! During their journey the Three Kings will admit me into their retinue. . . We shall thus proceed by the light of the Star of Bethlehem, and shall ascend the stations of Golgotha while blessing the God of Truth and Mercy![2]

Marie von Mouchanoff to Cosima Wagner, January. I do not know if Liszt found his public at Vienna—but he has found, in my opinion, his full and supreme expression in writing sacred music, in which he will never be surpassed, exhausting—without ever exhausting himself—all its riches of form and metaphysics. In his works he gives himself completely, just as he does in his playing. What creates the magic of this unique and fascinating playing, the captivating complexity of his character—is precisely what offends certain members of his audience when his religious works are performed. They find in them too much mystical piety and palpable lack of restraint, too many genuflexions, if I may put it thus; and they are also

* That is, the performance at the church of Ara Coeli (Rome) on 3 Jan. 1866.

† Eduard Hanslick (1825–1904), the most influential Austrian music critic of his day, was a champion of the music of Brahms and a diehard opponent of the works of Liszt (whom he admired as man and pianist) and Wagner. The last-named pilloried him as Beckmesser in *Die Meistersinger*.

‡ Writing to Anton Rubinstein the previous July, Liszt had quoted Voltaire, who 'used to put each of his friends in one of three classes: those who loved him, those who felt indifference for him, and those who detested him. Lacking his wit, one can still acquiesce in his experience.'

shocked at the theatrical pomp. The works contain decorative elements, no doubt—but we know why we understand these. Very few people have it in them to identify with the drama of a soul which bares itself to God, which cries out and weeps, which wants to take Heaven by storm, the struggle à la Pascal. That is what I adore in Liszt's music: it is the humanity of all times and periods, it is each one of us and above all style! Why did he accompany the Three Kings with a triumphal march? Out of respect for earthly greatness, which in his opinion must humble itself with grandeur! That he is right, is shown by the fact that St Thomas [Aquinas] has a chapter entitled: On Magnificence.[3]

On 9 January Liszt returned to Pest with Bülow, who gave two recitals there; and the 19th and 20th he spent in Pozsony for a Bülow recital in that city. 'The Viennese and Hungarian newspapers are unanimous in their praise of his immense talent,' he wrote to Carolyne, 'and accord only to Rubinstein the honour of sharing the palm of virtuosity with him. If Tausig were still alive, there would be three great pianists towering above all the others.'

Liszt to Princess Carolyne. Pest, 3 February. In obedience to your wishes, I shall add a few details to the account I sent you of the horrible incident with Mme Janina. In October she telegraphed from New York: 'Leaving this week, to pay you for your letter.' The letter to which she refers was couched in the most moderate terms, but intimating that since she heard from me fairly regularly I could hardly dispense with a certain degree of veracity. I understood at once what she meant by 'paying' me. In mid-November two letters—from Schuberth* in New York and Hébert† in Paris—warned me to be on my guard against the delirium of a provoked woman's vengeance. Apparently Mme Janina had openly notified her friends and acquaintances of her intention of coming to Pest, to kill first me and then herself. Indeed, she entered my room armed with a revolver and several bottles of poison—items she had already twice shown me last winter. I said calmly to her: 'What you intend doing is wicked, Madame. I advise you to give up such an idea—but am unable to prevent you.' After two hours, Augusz and Mihalovich found her with me; Mme Augusz came later. She told them categorically several times that nothing was left her in this world other than to assassinate me and then to kill herself. I was absolutely against fetching the police, which would in any case have been quite pointless—for Mme Janina is perfectly capable of firing a revolver before being seized. Enough, and too much, on this subject! The next day but one she left for Paris. For seven weeks I have had an arrangement with Mihalovich (who saw a good deal of her at Weimar, Szekszárd, and Pest) whereby I shall send to him sealed up any and every letter she may write

* Julius Schuberth (1804–75), founder of the Leipzig publishing firm.
† The French painter Ernest Hébert (1817–1908) was twice Director of the Villa Medici in Rome, where he was on friendly terms with Liszt and Carolyne.

me, without reading a single line. Mihalovich informed her of this. Once again, I beg you not to talk about Mme Janina with anybody. Don't write about her to Augusz—your silence will do me honour![4]

At a soirée in the home of his friend Count Imre Széchényi (1825–98) on 16 February, Liszt gave, with Reményi (for whose wedding celebrations it had been composed), the first performance of the *Epithalam* (S129) for violin and piano. On Monday, 18 March, on behalf of an orphanage and of a convent destroyed by fire, he played at the Vigadó before a brilliant audience which included the King-Emperor and other members of the imperial family.* His own contributions were Beethoven's Sonata Op. 27, No. 2; Chopin's Prelude in F sharp, Nocturne in B flat minor and Polonaise in A; and a Nocturne by Ábrányi. He also played Schubert's Wanderer Fantasy with Mihalovich, in the version for two pianos (S653), and accompanied Ilka Pauli in songs by Schumann and himself. On the 19th, at the Matthias Church in Buda, he conducted the Ofen Music Society in music by Hassler, Palestrina, and Bernabei.†

In January, Friedrich Nietzsche,‡ now Professor of Classical Philology at Basle University, had sent Liszt a copy of his recently published *The Birth of Tragedy*; and in a letter asking him to be favourably disposed towards the book, had written: 'When I look around me for the few people who have grasped with true instinct the phenomenon I have described, which I call Dionysian, it is to you above all that my eyes turn again and again: you in particular must be familiar with the most recondite mysteries of that phenomenon to such a degree that I consider you one of its most remarkable exemplifications, and have observed you time and again with the greatest theoretical interest.'

Liszt to Nietzsche. Pest, 29 February. Your enthralling book *The Birth of Tragedy* I have read twice. In its pages there glows and blazes a powerful spirit which stirred me profoundly. I have, it is true, to admit that I lack adequate preparation and knowledge for a complete appraisal of your work: with Hellenism, and the idolatry which is pursued hand in hand with it by the men of learning, I have remained somewhat unfamiliar; and the highest spiritual achievement of the Athenians I would extol as being their erection of the altar 'Deo ignoto'—on which the whole of Olympus was shattered so soon as Paul brought tidings of the *unknown God*. And my

* Including the heir to the Austro-Hungarian throne, the young Crown Prince Rudolf (1858–89), who, in the painting of the occasion by Schams and Lafitte, is shown sitting beside Liszt's piano. The bizarre death later met by Rudolf and his mistress Marie Vetsera has been depicted in *Mayerling*, a ballet using Liszt's music.

† For a comprehensive summary of the concerts and musical occasions at Budapest in which Liszt took part during these years, see D. Legány's *Liszt and His Country 1869–1873* (Budapest, 1983), 272–90.

‡ Liszt and Nietzsche had met, briefly, in 1869. Thus La Mara: 'On 26 February we welcomed Liszt to Leipzig . . . and at his side in the St Thomas Church heard Riedel's performance of Handel's *Israel in Egypt*. Later we fêted him at a festive supper in the Hôtel de Pologne, at which Friedrich Nietzsche, a pale young man, joined us at table and was introduced to him as a promising philologist and keen music-lover.'

eyes do not wander around Parnassus and Helicon; rather does my soul turn ever and anon to Tabor and Golgotha.

Forgive me, therefore, dear Sir, if the admiration I am able to express is rather deficient, but not, for all that, meagre or faint-hearted. . . . Nowhere have I found so beautiful a definition of Art—'the fulfilment and completion of existence leading to a further life'. . . .[5]

To Princess Carolyne, 20 March. I can prove that for years I have lived without any camaraderie at all. Neither at Weimar, nor in Rome and Pest, could I justly be reproached with having squandered my time and person. I am never seen in cafés or taverns, and the people with whom I associate all have some significance, whether through their talent, their character, or their position. My conversations are quite the opposite of flippant—never containing suggestive remarks, gossip, or aught unseemly. Certainly, none of those who know me can boast of camaraderie with me.*[6]

After spending his name day (2 April) with his cousin Eduard in Vienna, Liszt returned to Weimar, where in the early morning of the 9th he made a pilgrimage to the Altenburg. 'I do not know who is now living in the house, and did not go in,' he told Carolyne. 'After taking a few turns around the garden, I went down those steps without a handrail that lead to the bridge, and, thinking of the rosaries you used to recite through the park, I arrived at the church and took communion.' In the same letter, referring to a concert to be given that evening, he wrote: 'A new violin concerto by Raff will be played by Wilhelmj,† whom I consider the most abundantly talented and brilliant violinist of the new constellation of virtuosi. I took an interest in him in times gone by—and, strange to relate, he has remained grateful to me!'

Adelheid von Schorn. On 2 May I accompanied Liszt to Erfurt for a performance of his *St Elisabeth*. It was the day on which for the first time I became aware of the tiredness which later increased so much. 'Wake me at the right moment; I shall sleep through the performance,' he said even before we got there. Frankly, this work no longer interested him: he had heard it too often. On 8 May I went with him to Leipzig, where we heard Berlioz's *Requiem*. His attention this time was so active that he did not sleep at all. The Riedel Society's performance of the giant work pleased him greatly.[7]

This spring, Liszt's early love, Caroline d'Artigaux (*née* Saint-Cricq), died at Pau. 'Her long sufferings, endured with so much Christian sweetness and resignation, ripened her for Heaven,' he wrote (9 May) to the Princess. 'There, she is at last entering into the joy of the Lord— the world's did not touch her at all, and the Infinite alone was worthy of her celestial soul!'

* Such letters were Liszt's response to the many reproaches, of laziness, indecorous behaviour, and the like, heaped upon him by Carolyne from Rome.

† The German violinist and composer August Wilhelmj (1845–1908).

At Bayreuth on 22 May the foundation stone of Richard Wagner's festival theatre was laid. Longing for Liszt's presence at this event, Wagner wrote to him on the 18th.

Great and dear friend,
Cosima maintains you would not come, even if I invited you. That is something we should have to bear—just as we have had to bear so much! But to invite you is something I cannot omit. And what is it that I call to you when I say: come! You came into my life as the greatest man to whom I was ever able to use the familiar form of address. You broke off relations with me—perhaps because I had not grown so close to you as you to me. In your place there came to me your own reborn innermost being—which granted my desire for you to be wholly close to me. And thus you live in full beauty before and in me—and we are united as though beyond the grave! You were the first to ennoble me through your love. To a second, higher life am I now wedded in 'Her'—and can achieve what I could never have achieved alone. And so you were able to become everything to me—whereas I could remain so little to you. And how immensely is that to my advantage rather than yours! And so if I now say: come—then by doing so I am saying, come to yourself—for it is yourself that you will find here! Blessings and love whatever you decide!

Your old friend
Richard.[8]

Although still an enthusiastic admirer of Wagner's music, Liszt felt that the time had not yet come for a *rapprochement,* and he remained true to his promise to Carolyne (who was vehemently opposed to any reconciliation) in a letter of 21 April: 'On this point my mind is made up—I shall not go to Bayreuth just now.' But his conciliatory reply, of 20 May, to Wagner's letter, helped pave the way for the meeting that took place later in the year. 'God will forgive me for coming down on the side of mercy,' he told Carolyne.

Sublime, dear friend,
Profoundly moved by your letter, I am unable to thank you in words. But it is my ardent hope that all shadows and considerations which bind me at a distance will disappear—and that we shall soon see one another again. Then it will become clear to you, too, how inseparable my soul remains from both of you—living again in your 'second higher life, in which you can achieve what you could not have achieved alone'. Therein I see Heaven's amnesty! God's blessing be with both of you, as all my love!

F. L.[9]

Bearer of this note was the Baroness Meyendorff. 'The letter very nice,' thought Cosima, 'but the woman, unfortunately, very unpleasant. Her manner is cold and disapproving.'

Adelheid von Schorn was also at the ceremony, and, having herself been snubbed by Wagner, may have witnessed with a certain satisfaction his still rougher treatment of the Baroness, for whom she felt an intense, reciprocated, dislike.

The morning after my return to Weimar, a messenger from Liszt was knocking at my door even before I had opened my eyes—would I go to him at eleven and stay for lunch. . . . To my great surprise, Anton Rubinstein was there too, plus—coming straight from Bayreuth—Frau von Schleinitz, Countess Dönhoff, and Alexander Ritter.

That the events of Bayreuth were reported and discussed, can be imagined. But very soon music came into its own: Rubinstein and Liszt both played, first a duet and then each alone;* and a little incident occurred that I have never forgotten, so remarkable did I find it. Rubinstein was playing, with Liszt standing beside him and looking very attentively at his hands. When Rubinstein had come to an end, Liszt said: '*My dear Anton, please tell me how you did this*,' playing a few notes as he spoke. Whereupon Rubinstein stared at him in terror, then fell at his feet crying: '*Meister*! *You* ask *me* that?' He could not believe that there could be anything in piano-playing that was not known to the Master of masters. But Liszt, in his great honesty and simplicity, only said again and again: '*But I really don't know how you managed this fingering*.'

There was music until lunchtime, and after the meal we all went to the station, to keep the two ladies company until their departure. Liszt then took Rubinstein and me back to the Hofgärtnerei, to attend the lesson for which the pupils assembled at four o'clock. By six, Rubinstein was so tired that he could no longer listen; he was not as strong as Liszt, who could make music all day long without tiring. Coming with me to my home, he rested there for a while. Liszt had asked me to take Rubinstein to the theatre, and at nine o'clock to the Town Hall for a rehearsal of *Die Ideale*, which the Orchestral Society was studying. From there we went at ten to Frau von Meyendorff's, Liszt arriving shortly afterwards, where we had music until two in the morning. When I took my leave of Rubinstein, who was departing in the night, he said: 'I cannot come back to Weimar very soon, for *so much* music in one day makes me ill.'

When in Liszt's company, Rubinstein behaved charmingly towards him, just like a good son who loves and reveres his father and master; but in his musical thinking he had grown ever further away from him; and by this

* La Mara was present too, and reports that Rubinstein gave 'the finest performance of Schumann's Symphonic Studies that I have ever heard. It was a hot day, and he broke out into such a stream of perspiration that it rained down from his forehead on to the keys. Such violent natural outpourings I have seen with no other artist. . . . Liszt contented himself with preluding in his inimitable way and conjuring up for us his wonderful transcription of Lassen's song *Löse, Himmel, meine Seele*. How dematerialized, how ghostly it sounded! It was the playing of a god of music after that of a brilliant man exalted by the solemnity of the hour, the greatest master of the piano that the world possessed after Liszt.'

time he found Liszt's works unbearable.* Liszt knew this, for what he was not told he felt, and, with his great delicacy of perception, so long as Rubinstein was his guest he avoided anything that might create disharmony. On several occasions I heard the two masters playing duets together—it was the most perfect and most interesting experience of the kind that one could have. So different were they, in appearance (to their very fingertips), in expression, in everything; and yet such equals in the art of piano-playing. Alas, Rubinstein did not return to Weimar for another ten years, when much had changed—but not for the better.[10]

Liszt to Princess Carolyne. Weimar, 7 July. Unfortunately my time is dreadfully cut up and sectioned off—letters, manuscripts, and visits rain down upon me from all sides, and my difficulties with writing are increasing. If you were here to help me, my labours would be lightened considerably! In addition to my interminable correspondence, I have more than half a dozen pupils here, pianists and composers—Danes, Russians, Americans, Berliners, *et al.* I should reproach myself, were I to neglect them totally; consequently, I have to give them at least six hours a week. Add to that my work—too limited, alas, for lack of time—with different publishers, and you will see that I hardly have leisure for idling. . . . I beg you on my knees to believe firmly that any serious disagreement between us is impossible, and that I try with all my might to become entirely according to the wishes of your heart.[11]

Adelheid von Schorn. It is difficult to imagine with what masses of begging letters Liszt was inundated. They came from all over the world, from people who had not the least connection with him. The replies gave him great trouble and cost him much time. He was not a facile writer: every word was to be just the one to express what he meant. And then of course he had to bear in mind that his letters could go around the world as autographs. I used to go through a pile of them very quickly, and what I had done he considered right. And so with every year that passed I looked after these things more and more for him. Only in his very last years did he throw everything into the wastepaper basket, angered by the impudence with which people sought to take advantage of him. . . .

For certain practical things Liszt had no understanding at all; for example, payments by post he could for long not grasp and would not permit. He gladly availed himself of private opportunities to send money, books, music, etc., because he believed that to be safer. That one could have something registered in the post, and so have security, he could hardly credit.

* It was actually the forward-looking and progressive Liszt who had 'grown ever further away' from Rubinstein, one of the most conservative composers of the century. Nevertheless, in his famous Historical Concerts of the 1880s Rubinstein played a number of pieces by Liszt, original works as well as transcriptions.

One more peculiarity must be mentioned: he could not stand people knocking when visiting him. Strangers were of course announced by his servant; but acquaintances had to go in without either announcement or knocking. To begin with, I found it embarrassing, but I had to submit or be rebuked. If he was alone, I would almost always find him sitting at his desk. The kind of mood he was in I could tell from the tone of his voice, before I saw his face. If clouds sometimes disturbed the serene sky, I generally soon succeeded in dispelling them. But if nothing was bothering him, I could have wished for no kinder welcome; his hands would be stretched out towards me, the expression on his beautiful face would be radiant, and often he would embrace me like a father his daughter, in every way showing me that I was welcome, that he was fond of me.[12]

On Sunday, 1 September, Liszt received a letter from Wagner asking if he might visit him in Weimar. They had not met for five years. 'Since my reply to his invitation to the ceremony at Bayreuth, I had written neither to Wagner nor to my daughter,' Liszt later told Carolyne. 'In such circumstances I could not refuse him; it would have been quite out of character—which I do not separate from my conscience! And so I replied that he would always find in my home something worthier of him than a *friendly reception*.'

Liszt's daughter and son-in-law arrived in Weimar at 9.00 p.m. on the 2nd, and stayed at the Russischer Hof Hotel, where Liszt visited them that same evening. 'Wagner met me with a speech which lasted for about twenty minutes,' he told Alexander Siloti many years later. 'There was no one to hear it but his wife and myself. It was a speech I shall never forget. I was so touched by it that I forgot all except the good side in him.'

The Wagners stayed in Weimar until the 6th. 'I am terribly upset by my father's weariness of soul,' wrote Cosima in her diary. 'In the evening . . . I saw the tragedy of my father's life as in a vision— during the night I shed many tears!'

For his part, Liszt wrote to Carolyne: 'Cosima is indeed my formidable daughter, as I called her in earlier days, an exceptional woman of great merit, far above commonplace judgements, and altogether worthy of the feelings of admiration she inspires in those who know her—beginning with her first husband, Bülow! Her devotion to Wagner is absolute, like that of Senta to the Flying Dutchman—and she will be the saving of him, for he listens to and follows her clairvoyantly.'

Returning the visit, between 15 and 21 October Liszt spent a week in Bayreuth with the Wagners, at their rented house in the Dammallee. After a talk with her father, Cosima noted in her diary: 'Princess Wittgenstein is tormenting him on our account*—he should flee from Wagner's influence, artistic as well as moral, should not see me again, his self-respect demands this, we murdered Hans from a moral point of view, etc. I am very upset that my father should be tormented like this—he is so tired and is always being so torn about! Particularly this wretched woman in Rome has never done anything but goad him—but he does not intend to give me and us up.' On the 20th: 'In the evening, music: my father plays fugues

* In a letter to Liszt of 14 Sept., Carolyne had written that his visit to Bayreuth would 'be like Saint Peter going to Judas Iscariot!'

by Bach, the "A flat major" from *Tristan*, and several of his own works. A great, relaxed feeling that he belongs with us, that we should not let him part from us.'

Harmonious relations had now been established with Cosima and Wagner, but as a result Liszt had henceforth to endure many reproaches from Carolyne; further, from this time forward a resentful Bülow grew cooler in his attitude towards his formerly revered father-in-law.

Liszt left Bayreuth on 21 October so that he might be able to reassure Carolyne that he had not been there for his sixty-first birthday on the 22nd. Instead, he spent the day at Regensburg, where he stayed at the Golden Cross Hotel, birthplace of Don John of Austria, victor of the battle of Lepanto. 'The Cathedral is grandiose,' he wrote to Olga. 'In the past I dreamt there of a Music which I know not how to write.'

After a few days in Vienna with Eduard, he proceeded to Castle Horpács, in Hungary, to spend a fortnight as the guest of Count Imre Széchényi. On 4 November he made an excursion to nearby Raiding, his first visit to his native village for twenty-four years.

Liszt to Princess Carolyne. Horpács, 9 November. Today I wish to write you a pile of contestations—affectionate ones! I contest your right to forbid me to admire you in telegrams, in letters, and in any way I please! Admiration is one of the soul's noblest feelings, and the most lacking in selfishness, of which a few particles often mingle even with self-sacrifice. We admire the heroes, the saints, the geniuses, the wonders of nature and art—and so on to God in His works. Why not allow me to admire you very sincerely with all my heart and with complete conviction?[13]

On 11 November he arrived in Pest.

1873

At the Hotel Hungária on 12 January a soirée was given by the Rózsavölgyi publishing-house. Bach's Triple Concerto in D minor was played by Liszt, Mihalovich, and J. N. Dunkl; Liszt's two-piano *Concerto pathétique* was played by Alfred and Marie Jaëll; songs by Robert Franz were sung by Madame Dunkl; and Liszt's ballad *Lenore*, translated into Hungarian by Ábrányi, was recited to Liszt's accompaniment by the great actress Róza Laborfalvi (1817–86), wife of the novelist Mór Jókai. To end, Liszt played a solo: his transcription (S573) of Imre Széchényi's *Bevezetés és magyar induló* (Introduction and Hungarian March). 'The audience heard this lovely music with wonder, and when it ended it did all it could to have more,' wrote a reviewer. 'And Liszt yielded. For an encore he played one of Chopin's nocturnes, with the warmth and charm of poetry that the leading pianists of our time try to imitate. The enchanting power of this expressiveness can neither be learned from him nor described.'*

* Quoted by Legány, *Liszt and His Country*, 161.

Liszt to Princess Carolyne. Budapest, 6 March.* Yesterday evening I received your latest letter, and at once reply to your question about my will. I am expressing in it my desire to be clothed, in my coffin, in the habit of the tertiary order of St Francis. It is my last homage to the great saint who carried out his apostolate as a 'madman' of the Cross—and finished by obtaining from the Pope the *gran perdono*, solemnized by the Church. Those who may be with me at the moment of my death I shall enjoin to cover my sorry remains in this vestment of St Francis. I shall also ask that I may be spared the honours of an ostentatious funeral. If possible, let me be taken to my last resting-place in the obscurity of evening—two or three hired men will suffice to carry me. I should not like to trouble others to follow me to the cemetery—where I shall no longer be able to serve them![1]

In March Liszt took part in several concerts: a benefit for Robert Franz on the 2nd, at which Liszt's own contributions were works by Beethoven, Schubert-Liszt (Nos 4 and 6 of the *Soirées de Vienne*), and Schumann; a Hans Richter concert at the Vigadó on the 19th, at which Liszt conducted his orchestral transcription (S353) of Béni Egressy's *Szózat* and Ferenc Erkel's *Hymnus*; a charity concert on the 21st, at which he played works by Beethoven, Chopin, Mihalovich, and Ábrányi, as well as the piano version (S486) of the *Szózat and Hymnus*; and another charity concert on the 31st.

On 25 March he attended a concert in the great hall of the Hungarian Academy of Sciences. On the programme was a ballad by the young pianist and composer *Count Géza Zichy* (1849–1924), who, having lost his right arm in a hunting accident, had developed his left hand to formidable powers of pianistic virtuosity.

After the performance Franz Liszt came and spoke very kindly to me, at the same time inviting me to visit him. 'Then we can discuss your ballad in detail,' said this great and indulgent man. I had never previously visited him: Volkmann† had sympathy neither for the path he had taken in music nor for his person, which was too man-of-the-world for him; and, having full confidence in my teacher, I had avoided Liszt up to this time. But so kind an invitation I could not resist. Liszt seated himself at the piano and played my ballad; and oh, gracious Heavens, *how* he played it! Passages which struck him as too monotonous he changed on the spot; the main themes he transposed and broadened, enriching them with a wealth of passage-work; and he did not leave off saying again and again: 'I know! I know! *This* is how you imagined it, but not how it came out!' I tried to kiss his hand, but he embraced me and said: 'We shall get to know one another better, and I hope your master will forgive me if I concern myself somewhat with you.'

* In January 1873 Buda and Pest were united to form the new official name of the Hungarian capital.

† The Hungarian composer Robert Volkmann (1815–83).

As I left the great man I felt dizzy, and a new world opened before my eyes. . . .

My dear, dear master! The thick veils of time enshroud so many memories. Of many happenings we once found so important there remains no more than a hazy remembrance; and so much excitement and passion has melted and dissolved in our souls just as the sounds of music fade away and die. Persons once known to us are no more than blurred outlines, like bad cinematograph pictures, ghostly and phantom-like. Yet your figure stands before me, palpably alive in all its great humanity and undiminished totality. I see you now: your eyes, with their unusually small pupils, gazing at me keenly and yet so lovingly; your grey hair tumbling down in wavy abundance almost to your shoulders; your noble forehead traversed by single furrows making their way in roundish lines from one temple to the other, almost feminine in their softness; on your hips, your beautiful hands with their long stretched-out fingers; and your head held erect on your strong, manly neck. And I hear you call out proudly: 'I can wait, and my shoulders are strong.' . . .

If true nobility of heart forms the substance, the essence, of saintliness, then Franz Liszt was a saint—a worldly, lovable saint. Self-sacrificing, ever seeking to serve, unvindictive, unmindful of the wrongs done to him, he was one of the noblest and most humane men ever to have walked the earth. A strict believer, he was yet a man of tolerance not to be numbered with those Catholics who can at times be anything but Christian. His generosity and goodness of heart were still greater than his genius. He could refuse no request; he recommended everyone, and as a result his recommendations sometimes lost weight. Living always in the atmosphere of the eternal feminine, his matchless courtesy and kind-heartedness earned him the reputation of a Don Juan—which in reality he was far from being. He once said to me: 'If ladies are extremely complaisant, and men refuse to yield, then they must be brutal or ridiculous. One would choose to be neither.'

He loved splendour and flamboyance, and yet his own way of life could not have been more modest. I dined with him for months on end: the menu consisted of goulash, boiled vegetables, fruit, and cheese. At mealtimes he drank only sparingly. His favourite drink was light Hungarian wine and—unfortunately— brandy. During the day he would swallow mouthfuls at a time, but I can testify that I never saw him in a condition that deprived him of dignity. Strong wines he never drank. When I made him a present of some 1827 and 1834 Bakator wine, he said: 'My dear Géza, this is stronger than wine but weaker than brandy. I should have to drink very little to substitute table wine and very much to be able to dispense with brandy.'

He was an early riser: at six, seven at the latest, he went to church. In the coldest days of winter he wore his spring overcoat and a travelling rug which he pulled along the ground behind him. He smoked a great deal, mainly coal-black Italian cigars of which he would smoke the first half and then chew on the remainder for hours on end. He slept little at nights, but would walk up and down his room and from time to time sit at the piano or write. The sleep he lost thereby he would make up for with an afternoon nap lasting from one and a half to two hours. His temperament and disposition were cheerful, but he would occasionally fall into a state of severe depression. The misery of his fellows and the wretchedness of the human condition could make him very melancholy. . . . Of his son Daniel who had died young he could never speak without tears in his eyes. 'That was the greatest sorrow of my life', he told me.

He was often absent-minded. When a thought came suddenly to him he would look up at the ceiling and with one of his long fingers begin to beat time. One morning when his manservant was shaving him, Liszt raised his hand and put a finger straight into the razor, gashing it rather badly. . . .

One day as we were taking black coffee together, a man was announced who had behaved very badly towards Liszt and even caused him material damage. 'You will surely not receive him, *lieber Meister*!' I said. 'Certainly I shall—I forgave him long ago.' The man entered, and Liszt embraced him, saying with a smile: 'This is the greatest rascal in all Europe, but a dear fellow.'

Among the dead there are those who in the mind and consciousness of mankind become ever more alive—such a person was Franz Liszt.

When we were dining together one day I asked him why he kept no diary. 'To live one's life is hard enough. Why write down all the misery? It would resemble nothing more than the inventory of a torture chamber.' Only now do I understand those words.[2]

On his name day, 2 April, Liszt arrived in Vienna, where he stayed at the Schottenhof with Eduard von Liszt, who later accompanied him to Pozsony for a performance of the Gran Mass on Easter Sunday (13 April). On the 17th he returned to Weimar.

It was at this time that *Berthold Kellermann* became a pupil.

Liszt gave no instruction in the usual sense; elementary instruction, in particular, never. Rather, he would give splendid technical hints while, without saying much, conveying his feelings to the pupil by a glance from his glorious eyes and very characteristic movements of his soft but powerful hands. But one had to be born for Liszt, to understand him completely. . . . When he saw that someone had no musical vocation, he either told them so straight out or made them realize it by no longer concerning himself with them. If the people in question shut their eyes to it, Liszt would instruct me to tell them; but always stressing that I was to do so gently, without hurting them. If such people then continued to go to him in the afternoons with the general 'gang', he would not prevent, but simply ignore, them. . . .

He was a passionate smoker. When in 1873 I played to him again for the first time, he asked: 'Do you smoke?' When I replied in the negative, he said emphatically: 'A musician *must* smoke.'* He gave me a large Virginia, fetched a sixteen-part score and said: 'Now, let's to work!' Then he sat down beside me, struck away at the keys above and below my own fingers, and played everything that I left out. The severe mental concentration I found an antidote to the effect of the strong cigar, and from then on I could smoke. Thereafter he gave me cigars morning, noon, and night—Virginias and Havanas. . . .

Liszt was extremely grateful for any good turn done to him, even when it was merely of a quite trifling kind. He could then not find words enough to give expression to his gratitude. When he himself did someone a great kindness, however, he found it very embarrassing if the person in question came specifically to thank him. . . .

Anything smacking of gossip or slander he disliked greatly. He refused to listen when anybody spoke badly about someone else, even when the facts related were perfectly true. 'Even the righteous man stumbles seven times a day,' he would say on such occasions. He accordingly rejected everything that people tried to tell him about the behaviour of his pupils. In addition there was his inclination always to assume the best of everyone, and his broad tolerance of little moral weaknesses, particularly those of an erotic nature. 'Such transgressions are to be judged less severely than many others, as they always have the excuse of an overpowering passion,' he once remarked to me. . . .

Anything dishonourable was deeply repugnant to him, just as he was extremely sensitive to any kind of coarseness and indelicacy. About things he found disagreeable, about unpleasant incidents in daily life, just as about bad compositions submitted for his opinion, he spoke little. I never heard a spiteful word from him. If one of his pupils offended him, whether through bad playing, laziness, carelessness, or tactless behaviour, it was only rarely, and in the most serious cases, that he allowed himself to reprimand or speak severely to the miscreant in the presence of the other pupils. As a rule his features would give no hint of the inner hurt he felt; when the occasion arose, he would merely tell the person concerned to come to him at such and such a time as he had something to say to him. . . .

Liszt's goodness and gentleness knew no bounds. When he took a walk with me, his pocket was always full of thalers, and he would suddenly hurry across the street to press a coin into the hand of some needy person. He would then rejoin me and, without a word being said, we would continue on our way. He was delighted when he could render assistance to someone

* According to Jules Massenet, Liszt 'could not play unless he had a cigar in his mouth. But he did not light it nor smoke it; he used to eat it. He would sit down to the piano with a cigar in his mouth, and keep munching at it while he played. When the cigar was quite eaten up, he would rise from the instrument.'

without their realizing whence it came. I myself found that on the countless occasions when he did me some kindness great or small, he would again and again, and with really astonishing resourcefulness, so arrange it that I could almost have believed *I* had done *him* a favour. . . .

He rose at four every morning, even when he had been invited out the previous evening, had drunk a good deal of wine and not got to bed until very late. Soon after rising, and without breakfasting, he went to church. At five he took coffee with me, and with it a couple of dry rolls. Then work began: letters were written or read through, music tried out, and much else. At eight came the post, always bringing a huge pile of items. These were then looked through, personal letters read and answered, or music tried out. . . .

He worked uncommonly easily and quickly. Scores he wrote with rapid fluency from bottom to top, as speedily as other people write letters. It is only thus that it can be understood how this man, so immensely sought-after socially, was able to create such a multitude of works, the mere writing down of which would be a lifetime's work for an ordinary music-copyist. When in one of the last years of his life he was passing through Munich and stayed briefly at the Hotel Marienbad, I visited him with my young wife. The Master, who was working on a new composition, gave us a most hearty welcome; but then almost immediately sat down at his desk again, apologizing for having to go on with an urgent work. He would not let us depart, however, but chatted with us for some time most amiably, all the while uninterruptedly continuing his writing. . . .

At one o'clock, lunch was brought from the court kitchen when Liszt had not been invited out, which happened very frequently. I often ate with him. The meal was good and substantial, but simple. With it a glass of wine would be drunk, or water and brandy in the French manner, which he liked very much. Then he would smoke—indeed he smoked all the time when not eating or sleeping. Last of all there was the coffee machine. The coffee was burnt freshly every day, something on which Liszt placed great emphasis. . . .

His works are in places extremely demanding technically, but their chief difficulty lies in correctly understanding them, in empathy with Liszt's mind and spirit. This proved a stumbling block for the majority of even the better pupils; and so it can easily be understood how pleased he was when he found someone who was able to project himself into his world. When teaching, he always laid most stress on the interpretation—technique was something self-evident to him. To single technical shortcomings he attributed no special significance: they would easily be overcome, he said, in the course of time, and he would always find some friendly words of consolation: 'Don't get upset, you will easily repair matters.' Only bungling performances, devoid of musical understanding, were anathema to him. These he rejected roughly, and they could make him stern and angry. 'I am not here to wash your dirty linen,' I more than once heard him say in such cases. . . .

On one occasion he wished to explain to me how in his younger days he had been able to put audiences all over Europe into such ecstasies of enthusiasm. Saying 'now I'll show you how I played when travelling the world like a zany', he sat at the piano and played a lovely, sublime melody in the middle of the keyboard, while surrounding it with passages of extreme speed and complexity. Of his separate fingers there was often virtually nothing to be seen. . . .

At a music festival Raff's symphony *Im Walde* was to be performed; but part of the orchestra, coming from Berlin, had missed their train. 'My dear Raff, we must compensate the audience,' Liszt said; 'I shall play your symphony.' He then played the score at sight, while I turned the pages for him. With his eagle eyes he was always three of four bars ahead of what he was playing. At the same time he pointed out to me certain weaknesses or peculiarities in the scoring. Raff was deeply affected by this demonstration of unprecedented mastery.

An organist who lacked the third finger of his right hand once gave a recital in church, the chief item being Bach's great Fugue in G minor. Liszt, the greatest player and connoisseur of Bach, said to me when the church was empty: 'Kellermann, that missing-middle-finger trick I can do too. Look!' And before my eyes he played this difficult Fugue while in *both* hands stretching out and avoiding the use of the middle finger. I then practised it too, but found how extraordinarily difficult it was. In Vienna at a charity concert Liszt played the set programme, even though when getting into the train he had crushed the third finger of his right hand so badly in the slamming doors that he could not use it. Not a single member of the audience noticed. This was confirmed to me by the pupils who had accompanied him on the journey. The one-armed pianist Géza Zichy once brought him in my presence a volume of pieces for the left hand alone. Glancing through the volume fleetingly, Liszt then said: 'I can do that too.' And with the left hand alone he played the pieces at sight, but with the addition of many runs and difficult variations.

He could conjure out of the very worst piano a sound which one would scarcely have thought possible. His wonderful hands possessed unprecedented expressive power. When he passed from the stormy and tempestuous to the calm and peaceful, it was absolutely incomparable.

In Weimar, at the court festivities held on the occasion of the marriage of the Hereditary Grand Duke in 1873, I heard Liszt play for dancing. People of every possible nationality were present. He improvised the different national dances by letting his inspiration of the moment work up the relevant national anthem or other national melodies. It was a unique musical treat! And it showed so clearly Liszt's mastery of everything, the musical and technical alike.

During a passing visit of Liszt's to Nuremberg, the waltz king Johann Strauss and his orchestra happened to give a concert there. 'If you want to hear some really good music,' said Liszt, 'let's go to Strauss.' We were both delighted with the Viennese master's brilliant playing. This little incident shows how far Liszt was from being one-sided in his musical taste. True to his character, he everywhere sought out the good. The great masters of the past, Palestrina and Allegri, Bach, Gluck, and Handel, Mozart and Beethoven, he deeply revered, and his interpretation of them was classical; but modern masters he at all times championed likewise with the full weight of his personality and ability. His own works on the other hand he always completely neglected. He composed from inner compulsion; and what later happened to his works was quite indifferent to him, since, in contrast to Richard Wagner, he felt no urge to assert himself as a composer. 'The critics show me constant hostility,' he once remarked to me, 'but that doesn't help my opponents at all, as I don't change.'. . . Us, his pupils, he always urged not to become one-sided, but to cultivate all great masters. . . .

In his personal relations with his pupils, Liszt was always stimulating and instructive. Each of them took away with him helpful words and advice for his entire life. His all-embracing culture enabled him to explain his thoughts on the art of music in an uncommonly interesting way. He would often emphasize very strongly to us his view that the musician should be at home in all intellectual fields. Only then can he satisfy all the great demands that his profession makes upon him; and only on the basis of a thorough general education is he capable of thinking and feeling himself into the countless situations and moods which he has to render in the practice of his art.

Liszt's outstanding knowledge in every subject was all the more astounding since neither as a child nor subsequently had he gone to school. . . . But he more than made up later for what he had had to miss in early youth. His whole life long he worked at the broadening and deepening of his education—something which to be sure was very easy for one of his phenomenal ability. He was not only a musical genius but could probably have achieved the heights in another profession too. When a diplomat at the Berlin court once asked him, 'What would become of you if you suddenly lost your hands?' he replied composedly: 'I could still be the world's greatest diplomat.'

He had a special predilection for the sciences, and greatly appreciated the fact that it was precisely in this field that I was knowledgeable. How great was his love for all the wonders of nature is shown by the many infinitely sensitive descriptions of nature in his works. At the Hofgärtnerei he grew his own roses, of which he was very fond. Cut flowers on the other hand he did not like to see, as he felt sorry for them. All the more therefore did I cherish a rose he once presented to me, one which then kept its colour for many years. Along with roses, he loved lily of the valley in particular. To this day, when I smell lily of the valley, Liszt comes to life before my eyes.

Astonishing, too, was his knowledge of languages. . . . French especially he was always pleased to speak; and indeed he spoke it brilliantly, a consequence of his long sojourn in Paris. He could not bear it, however, when people whose command of French was bad, to say the least, addressed him in that language, expecting to flatter him thereby. On one such occasion he turned to me and said: 'Fromaaaschsch!'—which sounded quite dreadful. . . .

Remarkably, Liszt never of his own accord spoke of his countless interesting memories. Not that his memory let him down—on the contrary: when close friends now and again mentioned some particular incident which had taken place decades before, Liszt would relate the matter simply and smoothly, as though it had occurred only a few days earlier. This made it plain that he had at his disposal a really dazzling memory. But the view he took was this: 'The present makes such great demands on us that we can do it justice to a certain extent only if we devote our entire time and strength to it. We would be very wrong to squander part of them on such a futile exercise as memories of things which lie closed and finished behind us.' When a great publishing-house once approached him with the suggestion that he dictate his reminiscences to a stenographer, he declined categorically. Even when the publishers persisted, offering him an enormous fee, he stuck to his refusal—for such a pointless task he had no time at all. When his biographer Lina Ramann sent him a rather extensive questionnaire,* he did, it is true, answer all her questions with his usual conscientiousness, but said in reference to her book: 'I fear she cannot see the wood for the trees.'

In his relations with women, Liszt always behaved with the chivalry of a man of honour, one who did indeed set great store by physical beauty, but who had first and foremost sought and found the friendship of women who were on a high intellectual plane. . . .

His piety sprang from a deep inner conviction, and, accordingly, he was never blinded by dogma. He did not bother too much about the views and commands of the Church with regard to details, in contrast to the Princess Wittgenstein who was a downright bigot. When we once came to speak about papal infallibility, he exclaimed: 'What? Infallible? Fiddlesticks! Why, even *I* am not infallible.' Whereupon, taking his seat at the piano, he played a difficult passage, intentionally allowing himself to land on a few wrong notes. Then, calling out: 'But I, at least, can always at once put matters right again!' he played a passage of still greater complexity,

* Thirteen of the seventeen questionnaires sent to Liszt by Ramann were published, together with Liszt's replies, in her *Lisztiana*.

including a sequence of hair-raising skips, his fingers this time striking every note with flawless accuracy. . . .

Orthodox Catholic though he was, Liszt was always tolerant towards those of other beliefs. His relations with Jews and Protestants were friendly, and he never shared Wagner's hatred of the former. . . . In the Jews, as in all other human beings, it was only the good that he sought, and the religious fanaticism of many Catholics was something he always deplored.[3]

On 30 April, *Amy Fay* (1844–1928), an American pianist who had already spent four years in Germany studying with Theodor Kullak (1818–82) and with Tausig, arrived in Weimar hoping to become a pupil of Liszt's.

1 May. This evening I have been to the theatre, which is very cheap here, and the first person I saw, sitting in a box opposite, was Liszt. . . . He was making himself agreeable to three ladies, one of whom was very pretty. He sat with his back to the stage, not paying the least attention, apparently, to the play, for he kept talking all the while himself, and yet no point of it escaped him, as I could tell by his expression and gestures.

He is the most interesting and striking-looking man imaginable. Tall and slight, with deep-set eyes, shaggy eyebrows, and long iron-gray hair, which he wears parted in the middle. His mouth turns up at the corners, which gives him a most crafty and Mephistophelean expression when he smiles, and his whole appearance and manner have a sort of Jesuitical elegance and ease. His hands are very narrow, with long and slender fingers that look as if they had twice as many joints as other people's. They are so flexible and supple that it makes you nervous to look at them. Anything like the polish of his manner I never saw. . . .

Amy Fay, 7 May. I met Liszt two evenings ago at a little tea-party given by a friend and *protégée* of his to as many of his scholars as have arrived, I being asked with the rest. . . .

We were in the midst of supper, and having a merry time, when the door suddenly opened and Liszt appeared. We all rose to our feet, and he shook hands with everybody without waiting to be introduced. Liszt looks as if he had been through everything, and has a face *seamed* with experience. He is rather tall and narrow, and wears a long abbé's coat reaching nearly down to his feet. He made me think of an old-time magician more than anything, and I felt that with a touch of his wand he could transform us all. . . .

He is just like a monarch, and no one dares speak to him until he addresses one first, which I think no fun. . . . Someone asked him if he had heard R play that afternoon. R is a young organist from Leipzig, who telegraphed to Liszt to ask him if he might come over and play to him on the organ. Liszt, with his usual amiability, answered that he might. 'Oh,' said Liszt, with an indescribably comic look, 'he improvised for me a whole half-hour in this style,'—and then he got up and went to the piano, and without sitting down played some ridiculous chords in the middle of the keyboard, and then little trills and turns high up in the treble, which made us all burst out laughing. . . .

Amy Fay, 21 May. I practised tremendously for several days on Chopin's B minor Sonata. . . . When I thought I could play it, I went to Liszt, though with a trembling heart. I cannot tell you what it has cost me every time I have ascended his stairs. I can scarcely summon up courage to go there, and generally stand on the steps a while before I can make up my mind to open the door and go in! . . .

Well, on this day the artists Leitert and Urspruch,* and the young composer Metzdorff,† who is always hanging about Liszt, were in the room when I came. They had probably been playing. At first Liszt took no notice of me beyond a greeting, till Metzdorff said to him, 'Herr Doctor, Miss Fay has brought a sonata.' 'Ah, well, let us hear it,' said Liszt. Just then he left the room for a minute, and I told the three gentlemen that they ought to go away and let me play to Liszt alone, for I felt nervous about playing before them. They all laughed at me and said they would not budge an inch. When Liszt came back they said to him, 'Only think, Herr Doctor, Miss Fay proposes to send us all home.' I said I could not play before such great artists. 'Oh, that is healthy for you,' said Liszt, with a smile, and added, 'you have a very choice audience, now.' I don't know whether he appreciated how nervous I was, but instead of walking up and down the room as he often does, he sat down by me like any other teacher, and heard me play the first movement. It was frightfully hard, but I had studied it so much that I managed to get through with it pretty successfully. Nothing could exceed Liszt's amiability, or the trouble he gave himself, and instead of frightening me, he inspired me. Never was there such a delightful teacher! and he is the first sympathetic one I've had. You feel so *free* with him, and he develops the very spirit of music in you. He doesn't keep nagging at you all the time, but he leaves you your own conception. Now and then he will make a criticism, or play a passage, and with a few words give you enough to think of all the rest of your life. There is a delicate *point* to everything he says, as subtle as he is himself. He doesn't tell you anything about the technique. That you must work out for yourself. When I had finished the first movement of the sonata, Liszt, as he always does, said 'Bravo!' Taking my seat, he made some little criticisms, and then told me to go on and play the rest of it.

Now, I only knew half the other movements, for the first one was so extremely difficult that it cost me all the labour I could give to prepare that. But playing to Liszt reminds me of trying to feed the elephant in the Zoological Garden with lumps of sugar. He disposes of whole movements

* Anton Urspruch (1850–1907).
† Richard Metzdorff (1844–1919).

as if they were nothing, and stretches out gravely for more! One of my fingers fortunately began to bleed, for I had practised the skin off, and that gave me a good excuse for stopping. Whether he was pleased at this proof of industry, I know not; but after looking at my finger and saying 'Oh!' very compassionately, he sat down and played the whole three last movements himself. That was a great deal, and showed off all his powers. It was the first time I had heard him, and I don't know which was the most extraordinary—the Scherzo, with its wonderful lightness and swiftness, the Adagio with its depth and pathos, or the last movement, where the whole keyboard seemed to *donnern und blitzen* (thunder and lighten). There is such a vividness about everything he plays that it does not seem as if it were mere music you were listening to, but it is as if he had called up a real, living *form*, and you saw it breathing before your face and eyes. It gives *me* almost a ghostly feeling to hear him, and it seems as if the air were peopled with spirits. Oh, he is a perfect wizard! It is as interesting to see him as it is to hear him, for his face changes with every modulation of the piece, and he looks exactly as he is playing. He has one element that is most captivating, and that is a sort of delicate and fitful mirth that keeps peering out at you here and there! It is most peculiar, and when he plays that way, the most bewitching little expression comes over his face. It seems as if a little spirit of joy were playing hide and go seek with you.

Amy is invited to a matinée given by Liszt for Countess Mouchanoff.

After the company was assembled, it numbered eighteen persons, nearly all of whom were titled. I was the only unimportant one in it. Liszt was so sweet. He kept coming over to where I sat and talking to me, and promised me a ticket for a private concert where only his compositions were to be performed. He seemed determined to make me feel at home. He played five times, but no *great* work, which was a disappointment to me, particularly as the last three times he played duets with a leading Weimar artist named Lassen. He made me come and turn the leaves. Gracious! how he *does* read! It is very difficult to turn for him, for he reads ever so far ahead of what he is playing, and takes in fully five bars at a glance, so you have to guess about where you *think* he would like to have the page over. Once I turned it too late, and once too early, and he snatched it out of my hand and whirled it back. Not quite the situation for timorous me, was it?

Amy Fay, 29 May. I am having the most heavenly time in Weimar, studying with Liszt, and sometimes I can scarcely realize that I am at the summit of my ambition, to be *his* pupil! He is so overrun with people, that I think it is a wonder he is civil to anybody, but he is the most amiable man I ever knew, though he *can* be dreadful, too, when he chooses, and he understands how to put people outside his door in as short a space of time as it can be done. I go to him three times a week. At home Liszt doesn't wear his long abbé's coat, but a short one, in which he looks much more artistic. His figure is remarkably slight, but his head is most imposing. It is *so* delicious in that room of his! The walls are pale gray, with a gilded border running round the room, or rather two rooms, which are divided, but not separated, by crimson curtains. The furniture is crimson, and everything is so *comfortable*—such a contrast to German bareness and stiffness generally. A splendid grand piano stands in one window (he receives a new one every year). The other window is always wide open, and looks out on the park. There is a dove-cote just opposite the window, and the doves promenade up and down on the roof of it, and fly about, and sometimes whirr down on the sill itself. That pleases Liszt. His writing-table is beautifully fitted up with things that all match. Everything is in bronze—ink-stand, paper-weight, match-box, etc., and there is always a lighted candle standing on it by which he and the gentlemen can light their cigars. There is a carpet on the floor, a rarity in Germany, and Liszt generally walks about, and smokes, and mutters (he can never be said to *talk*), and calls upon one or other of us to play. From time to time he will sit down and play himself where a passage does not suit him, and when he is in good spirits he makes little jests all the time. His playing was a complete revelation to me, and has given me an entirely new insight into music. You cannot conceive, without hearing him, how poetic he is, or the thousand *nuances* that he can throw into the simplest thing, and he is equally great on all sides. From the zephyr to the tempest, the whole scale is equally at his command. . . .

Yesterday I had prepared for him his *Au bord d'une source*. I was nervous and played badly. He was not to be put out, however, but acted as if he thought I had played charmingly, and then he sat down and played the whole piece himself, oh, *so* exquisitely! It made me feel like a wood-chopper. The notes just seemed to ripple off his fingers' ends with scarce any perceptible motion. As he neared the close I remarked that that funny little expression came over his face which he always has when he means to surprise you, and he suddenly took an unexpected chord and extemporized a poetical little end, quite different from the written one. Do you wonder that people go distracted over him?[4]

La Mara. For Liszt's friends a great day now drew near: at Weimar's town church on 29 May his *Christus* was to be given its first complete performance, and the Master, who had taken over the rehearsals only shortly before, wished to conduct it himself. The soloists were the von Mildes, husband and wife, Fräulein Dotter, and Borchers; the Weimar choirs were augmented by those of Jena and Erfurt, and the Grand-Ducal Court orchestra by that of Sondershausen. At lunch in the Erbprinz I saw, in addition to the people from Leipzig, a number of whom had come with me, many visitors from further afield among the guests, at their head

Countess Mouchanoff, already visibly suffering; Liszt's Hungarian compatriots Count Albert Apponyi, Baron Végh,* Mihalovich, and Ábrányi; Gille and Naumann from Jena; Adolf Stern from Dresden; not forgetting the critics, Lessmann† from Berlin, Nohl, Zopff, and many others. Only one or two pupils were with Liszt, among them Georg Leitert, of whom he was very fond. Inside the church I found myself opposite Richard Wagner and his wife, who were with Countess Schleinitz. The performance began at six. It was not a flawless one. Yet profound and powerful was the effect of this mighty and thoroughly Catholic work, so incomparably original both in its formal structure—especially the interpolation of great orchestral movements—and its overall conception. . . .

To the celebration held later . . . Wagner and his wife came too. Arriving with them, Liszt had no sooner spotted me than he said: 'You must come to us!' 'You know my daughter?' he asked, and I had barely time to reply, 'I have not the honour of Frau Wagner's acquaintance,' when, taking me to the head of the table, where the Wagners were seated, he introduced me to them. Wagner greeted me in very friendly fashion. He was in splendid spirits, at one moment joking about opera texts with Lassen, and at the next reminiscing with Fräulein Hofmeister from Berlin.

Frau Wagner received me with the words: 'We saw each other only recently, at Leipzig.' Despite a certain reserve I felt towards her, which lasted not a quarter of an hour, this wonderful woman cast a spell over me, under which she still holds me fully forty years later. Of the magic of Liszt's mind and personality she inherited much. Her eyes, her smile, her conversation bring back to me the most beloved fatherly friend of my life. . . .[5]

According to Cosima, Wagner's reaction to *Christus* passed 'from ravishment to immense indignation in his attempt to do it both profound and loving justice'. Her own adverse opinion was that the work was 'thoroughly un-German'—a peculiarly fatuous comment on an oratorio in which a Latin text depicting episodes in the life of the Jewish founder of Christianity is set to music by a Hungarian composer.

Adelheid von Schorn, May. Critics were a sore point, and a subject that at the Hofgärtnerei one did well to avoid. They had given Liszt so much to endure that he spoke harshly about them, allowing them little that was good. By making imprudent remarks, people who did not know him well could be snubbed in a way they hardly deserved, because what they had said was often entirely harmless in itself and based only on ignorance of the situation. Indescribably kind though Liszt could be, there were neverthe-

* One of Liszt's closest Hungarian friends, the composer János Végh (1845–1918) was from 1881 Vice President of the Budapest Music Academy.

† Otto Lessmann (1844–1918), composer and critic, was a keen supporter and admirer of Liszt.

less moments when it was very difficult to deal with him, such as when he was physically or mentally out of sorts; a stranger then had a hard time of it. Initiates knew how to behave with him on such occasions, either by obtaining a rest for him, if he was overtired, or by dispelling his anger with a joke.[6]

In the spring the French composer *Vincent d'Indy* (1851–1931), a pupil of César Franck, visited Weimar and was taken to Liszt by Lassen.

It was 9.00 a.m. The Master, in his shirt sleeves, was eating the traditional *Frühstück*, and with a quick, severe gesture he motioned us through the half-open door of the salon. The thought that he would not receive me made me tremble, but I was soon reassured when I saw him draw back the door-curtain for us, feverishly buttoning up his long cassock as he did so. I was later to learn that he never received visitors without first putting on this semi-ecclesiastical costume.

Hardly had I recited, very imperfectly, the words I had spent no little time preparing the previous evening, when I felt a surge of confidence. It has been my lot to be introduced to a good many artistic celebrities, but none of them—Franck excepted—received me with such simplicity and kind-heartedness.

Running his eyes over the Saint-Saëns Cello Sonata, and then reading alone, at the piano, the four-hand arrangement of the Prelude to Franck's *Redemption*, he was not sparing in his praise of the two composers who had sent him copies of their works; then, questioning me about my own activities, and learning that I was working on a *Wallenstein*, he outlined for me the musical character of Schiller's work in a few words of wonderful logic and lucidity.

At the end of this first interview he invited me, in a manner that admitted of no reply, to spend an hour or so with him every morning and share his breakfast.

And that is how what I had envisaged as no more than a fleeting visit to Weimar turned into an unforgettable sojourn of several months.

I shall not attempt to describe our daily conversations, to which the Master himself, I must admit, contributed the lion's share and more, dealing with every topic equally thoroughly but showing a preference for philosophical subjects and those of a general aesthetic nature rather than purely musical ones. I for my part was more than happy to listen. But nothing that could be useful to my musical education was neglected. One evening, for example, on returning to my hotel I found a note worded thus: 'Hoping to see you at the theatre tomorrow morning, when two pieces of a lively and original nature will be tried out. Your Fr. Liszt.' And so it was my good fortune to witness the strangest of sights. The tiny Grand-Ducal orchestra—it had just two cellos—gathered in the semi-darkness of the Residence's small theatre was playing through some Russian symphonic poems which had recently been published, among them the second version of Rimsky-Korsakov's *Sadko*.* Liszt's manner of conducting this reading was still more *original* than the pieces being performed. Sure of his players, he contented himself with indicating the rhythm of the opening bars with his finger, then, folding his arms, letting the orchestra continue alone, making no more conducting gestures save at pauses or at changes of tempo. How delightful it was to hear this orchestra playing, as it were, 'chamber music', and to see the old master listening eagerly to these works whose conception and style of writing were then so new, and to whose pointless difficulties he occasionally drew attention with a significant grimace.

It was when we were leaving this session that the Master introduced me to several of his *official* pupils: Richard Metzdorff, a handsome Russian; John Orth, an American; Anton Urspruch, perhaps the only German musician who could appreciate the beauty and aesthetic purity of Gregorian chant; Berthold Kellermann, who later taught at the Munich Conservatoire; and Miss Amy Fay, a fair-haired and piquant American girl whom I was to meet again in New York thirty-two years later.† These likeable young people welcomed me with the greatest kindness, despite my status of rather *honorary* pupil. We enjoyed numerous musical sessions at the lodgings of one or other of us, and outings no less numerous into the surrounding countryside: snacks at Ober-Weimar, picnics in the Thuringian forest, village fêtes at Eringsdorf and elsewhere—joyous gatherings all of them, in which conversations on art and aesthetics were tempered by the coquettish gaiety of the two young American girls, Josie Bates and Amy Fay. . . .

It is difficult for those who were not present to imagine the interest offered by Liszt's master classes, when the Master, chewing the while on his long Hungarian cigars, would himself rectify some passage that the pupil had failed to understand, always giving his reasons for such correction and sometimes even playing through the entire piece. His rare and marvellous touch then ennobled the piano—which was just an ordinary one—to the point of creating an illusion of the most varied orchestral timbres.

But despite the natural goodness which formed the great charm of the man, what crushing severity towards those pupils who had not *understood* the work being interpreted, and were content to play 'with the fingers and not with the heart'! A piercing look from Liszt would tell them of their mistake, and no words of blame could have been more eloquent than that simple glance, which had the power of making the culprit creep away and of freezing with terror all the rest of the young audience. It was then that

* The symphonic poem on which Rimsky-Korsakov's later opera of the same name would be based.

† When Amy Fay visited his *Schola Cantorum* in Paris, D'Indy told a friend that she had been 'mon premier amour!'

the Master himself would go to the piano, in order, as he said, 'to make honourable amends to the work thus distorted'.

One morning I found him in joyful mood; he had just received the proofs of the score of his *Christus*, the oratorio he considered his most perfect work. . . . To me and a few other pupils he distributed the loose leaves of these proofs to read and correct, reserving for himself their final revision. Two days later, when I took back to him the corrected pages, he seemed satisfied with my remarks and, making me sit down, although it was not the time of our usual talks, gave me a kind of lecture on the role that he believed liturgical melodies would be called upon to play in the music of future ages, enlarging with satisfaction on the way in which he had treated the prose of the *Stabat mater dolorosa* in his oratorio. He also wanted me to read with him, at the piano, the proofs of the arrangement for four hands of the two symphonic pieces, the Shepherds and the Three Kings [S579]; and in spite of my very timid performance he seemed satisfied, making me a present of the first copy of this transcription to arrive in Weimar. A little later he invited me to play to him the sketch of my overture for Schiller's *Piccolomini*, and gave me some valuable advice about its orchestration. . . .

I made my way in easy stages back to Paris, still under the spell of the rare kindness shown by an established artist to a young one who had no claim to that kindness other than a deep and sincere love of Art.[7]

Amy Fay, 6 June. One day this week, when we were with Liszt, he was in such high spirits that it was as if he had suddenly become twenty years younger. A student . . . played a Liszt concerto. His name is V, and he is dreadfully nervous. Liszt kept up a little running fire of satire all the time he was playing, but in a good-natured way. I shouldn't have minded if it had been I. In fact, I think it would have inspired me; but poor V hardly knew whether he was on his head or on his feet. It was too funny. Everything that Liszt says is so striking. For instance, in one place where V was playing the melody rather feebly, Liszt suddenly took his seat at the piano and said, 'When *I* play, I always play for the people in the gallery, so that those persons who pay only five groschen for their seat also hear something.' Then he began, and I wish you could have heard him! The sound didn't seem to be very *loud*, but it was penetrating and far-reaching. When he had finished, he raised one hand in the air, and you seemed to see all the people in the gallery drinking in the sound. That is the way Liszt teaches you. He presents an *idea* to you, and it takes fast hold of your mind and sticks there. Music is such a real, visible thing to him, that he always has a symbol, instantly, in the material world to express his idea. One day, when I was playing, I made too much movement with my hand in a rotatory sort of a passage where it was difficult to avoid it. 'Keep your hand still, Fräulein,' said Liszt; '*don't make omelette*.' I couldn't help laughing, it hit me on the head so nicely. He is far too sparing of his playing, unfortunately, and, like Tausig, only sits down and plays a few bars at a time, generally. It is dreadful when he stops, just as you are at the height of your enjoyment, but he is so thoroughly *blasé* that he doesn't care to show off, and doesn't like to have anyone pay him a compliment. Even at the court it annoyed him so that the Grand Duchess told people to take no notice when he rose from the piano. . . .

How he can bear to hear *us* play, I cannot imagine. It must grate on his ear terribly, I think, because everything *must* sound expressionless to him in comparison with his own marvellous conception. I assure you, no matter how beautifully we play any piece, the minute Liszt plays it you would scarcely recognize it! His touch and his peculiar use of the pedal are two secrets of his playing, and then he seems to dive down in the most hidden thoughts of the composer, and fetch them up to the surface so that they gleam out at you one by one, like stars!

Amy Fay, 19 June. Anything so perfectly beautiful as he looks when he sits at the piano I never saw, and yet he is almost an old man now. I enjoy him as I would an exquisite work of art. His personal magnetism is immense, and I can scarcely bear it when he plays. He can make me cry all he chooses, and that is saying a good deal, because I've heard so much music, and *never* have been affected by it. Even Joachim, whom I think divine, never moved me. When Liszt plays anything pathetic, it sounds as if he had been through everything, and opens all one's wounds afresh. All that one has ever suffered comes before one again. . . .

But I doubt if he feels any particular emotion himself, when he is piercing you through with his rendering. He is simply hearing every tone, knowing exactly what effect he wishes to produce and how to do it. In fact, he is practically two persons in one—the listener and the performer. But what immense self-command that implies! No matter how fast he plays, you always feel that there is 'plenty of time'—no need to be anxious! You might as well try to move one of the pyramids as fluster *him*. Tausig possessed this repose in a technical way, and his touch was marvellous; but he never drew the tears to your eyes. He could not wind himself through all the subtle labyrinths of the heart as Liszt does.*. . .

I've never seen Liszt look angry but once, but then he was terrific. Like a lion! It was one day when a student from the Stuttgart Conservatorium attempted to play the Sonata Appassionata. He had a good deal of technique, and a moderately good conception of it, but still he was totally inadequate to the work—and indeed, only a *mighty* artist like Tausig or Bülow ought to attempt to play it. It was a hot afternoon, and the clouds had been gathering for a storm. As the Stuttgarter played the opening

* In his essay on Liszt, Franz Hueffer, music critic of *The Times*, singled out this paragraph of Fay's for special comment: 'Most people who have not heard Liszt will probably think this kind of encomium gushing, if not childish. To those who heard him, in his best days, it will appear only as a weak echo of what they felt themselves.'

notes, the tree-tops suddenly waved wildly, and a low growl of thunder was heard muttering in the distance. 'Ah,' said Liszt, who was standing at the window, with his delicate quickness of perception, 'a fitting accompaniment.' If Liszt had only played it himself, the whole thing would have been like a poem. But he walked up and down the room and forced himself to listen, though he could scarcely bear it, I could see. A few times he pushed the student aside and played a few bars himself, and we saw the passion leap up into his face like a glare of sheet lightning. Anything so magnificent as it was, the little that he *did* play, and the startling individuality of his conception, I never heard or imagined. I felt as if I did not know whether I were 'in the body or out of the body'. . . .

Liszt hasn't the nervous irritability common to artists, but on the contrary his disposition is the most exquisite and tranquil in the world. We have been there incessantly, and I've never seen him ruffled except two or three times, and then he was tired and not himself, and it was a most transient thing. When I think what a little savage Tausig often was, and how cuttingly sarcastic Kullak could be at times, I am astonished that Liszt so rarely loses his temper. He has the power of turning the best side of everyone outward, and also the most marvellous and instant appreciation of what that side is. If there is *anything* in you, you may be sure that Liszt will know it. Whether he chooses to let you think he does, may, however, be another matter.[8]

Liszt spent 23 to 26 June at Dornburg as guest of the Grand Duke Carl Alexander, whose birthday celebrations on the 24th included a performance of Goethe's short rococo opera *Erwin und Elmira*; and the rooms once occupied by the great poet were allocated to the great musician during his brief sojourn in the castle. On 6 July he went to Leipzig for the Riedel Society's performance of his *Missa choralis*.

La Mara. After the concert (which pleased him greatly) at the Nicholas Church, there followed—a rare event with Liszt, who was no walker—a stroll to the Valley of Roses, during which he answered all kinds of biographical questions that I put to him. . . . Over supper in the garden of the Thuringia station he told us many interesting things about Cherubini and Boïeldieu and their antiquated Beethoven judgements, and praised the merits of Habeneck, whose energy and enthusiasm had won Paris over to Beethoven's music. When, in reference to the forthcoming celebration at Budapest of his golden jubilee as an artist, I expressed amazement at its being dated from his second appearance, at Vienna's Redoute, instead of from his first, at the provincial hall, he talked about both of his first Vienna concerts and about the kiss of consecration given him by Beethoven, which Schindler had later sought to deny him. 'L'ami de Beethoven* wanted to rob me of my kiss—but I won't let it be taken from me.'[9]

* So proud was Anton Schindler of having been an associate of the great composer, that when residing in Paris he caused to be printed on his visiting-cards, 'Anton Schindler, Ami de Beethoven'.

Amy Fay, 15 July. Liszt gave a matinée the other day at which I played a *Soirée de Vienne* by Tausig. . . . I was just as frightened as I could be! Metzdorff and Urspruch sat down by me to give me courage, and to turn the leaves, but Liszt insisted upon turning them himself, and stood behind me and did it in his dexterous way. He says it is an art to turn the leaves properly! He was *so* kind, and whenever I did anything well he would call out '*charmant!*' to encourage me. It is considered a great compliment to be asked to play at a matinée, and I don't know why Liszt paid it to me at the expense of others there who play far better than I do. . . . With him 'nothing is to be presumed on or despaired of'—as the proverb says. He is so full of moods and phases that you have to have a very sharp perception even to begin to understand him, and he can cut you up all fine without your ever guessing it. He rarely mortifies anyone by an open snub, but what is perhaps worse, he manages to let the rest of the class know what he is thinking while the poor victim remains quite in darkness about it! Yes, he can do very cruel things.

After all, though, people generally have their own assurance to thank, or their own want of tact, when they do not get on with Liszt. If they go to him full of themselves, or expecting to make an impression on *him*, or merely for the sake of saying that they have been with him, instead of presenting themselves to sit at his feet in humility, as they ought, and learn whatever he is willing to impart—he soon finds out and treats them accordingly. . . . But the real *basis* of his nature is compassion. *The bruised reed he does not break, nor the humble and docile heart despise*!

Amy Fay, 24 July. Liszt's *Christus* is arranged for piano for four hands, and I wish I had it, and also Bülow's great edition of Beethoven's sonatas—Oh! you cannot *conceive* anything like Liszt's playing of Beethoven. When *he* plays a sonata it is as if the composition rose from the dead and stood transfigured before you. You ask yourself, 'Did *I* ever play that?'. . .

One evening I was there about twilight. . . . There was only a single lamp, and *that* rather a dim one, so that the room was all in shadow, and Liszt wore his Merlin-like aspect. I asked him to tell me how he produced a certain effect he makes in his arrangement [S441] of the ballad in Wagner's *Flying Dutchman*. He looked very *fin* as the French say, but did not reply. He never gives a direct answer to a direct question. 'Ah,' said I, 'you won't tell.' He smiled, and then immediately played the passage. It was a long arpeggio, and the effect he made was, as I had supposed, a pedal effect. He kept the pedal down throughout, and played the beginning of the passage in a grand *rolling* sort of manner, and then all the rest of it with a very pianissimo touch, and so lightly, that the continuity of the arpeggios was destroyed, and the notes seemed to be just *strewn* in, as if you broke a wreath of flowers and scattered them according to your fancy. It is a most striking and beautiful effect, and I told him I didn't see how he ever thought of it. 'Oh, I've invented a great many things,' said he, indifferently

—'*this*, for instance,'—and he began playing a double roll of octaves in chromatics in the bass of the piano. It was very grand and made the room reverberate. 'Magnificent,' said I. 'Did you ever hear me do a storm?' said he. 'No.' 'Ah, you ought to hear me do a storm! Storms are my *forte*!' Then to himself between his teeth, while a weird look came into his eyes as if he could indeed rule the blast, 'Then *crash* the trees!'. . .

Once again I saw Liszt in a similar mood, though his expression was this time *comfortably* rather than *wildly* destructive. It was when Fräulein Remmert* was playing his E flat concerto to him. There were two grand pianos in the room, and she was sitting at one, and he at the other, accompanying and interpolating as he felt disposed. Finally they came to a place where there were a series of passages beginning with both hands in the middle of the piano, and going in opposite directions to the ends of the keyboard, ending each time in a short, sharp chord. 'Pitch everything out of the window,' said he, in a cosy, easy sort of way, and he began playing these passages and giving every chord a whack as if he *were* splitting everything up and flinging it out, and that with such enjoyment, that you felt as if you'd like to lend a hand, too, in the work of general demolition! But I shall never forget Liszt's look as he so lazily proposed to 'pitch everything out of the window'. It reminded me of the expression of a big tabby-cat as it sits and purrs away, blinking its eyes and seemingly half asleep, when suddenly—!—! out it strikes with both its claws, and woe be to whatever is within its reach! Perhaps, after all, the secret of Liszt's fascination is this power of intense and wild emotion that you feel he possesses, together with the most perfect control over it.[10]

Princess Carolyne to Adelheid von Schorn, 27 July. His soul is too tender, too artistic, too full of feeling, to do without the company of women. He must have women around him; several even, just as in his orchestra he needs many instruments, several rich tone colours. Unfortunately there are so few women who are what they ought to be—clever and good—in harmony with his own mind, without laying mischievous hands on those strings which, if sounded, always echo painfully! I sometimes feel very sad when I think how he will eventually be misjudged. His triumphs will perhaps appear to later times like Bacchanalian processions, because a few Bacchantes intruded in them. But he never invited them. He was always quite content in the pure, spiritual domain, so long as he was not summoned out of it.[11]

Adelheid von Schorn. The topic 'Liszt and women' has been discussed so much that it might be thought that nothing remains to be said. But there are so many different aspects of Liszt on which light can be shed—almost as many as the number of women whose lives crossed his own. Towards

* Martha Remmert (1854–1928), a gifted German pianist who had joined the ranks of Liszt's pupils earlier this year.

every female Liszt behaved in a way that corresponded with what she demanded of him. That so many women wanted love from him, and came to him in passion, redounds little to the glory of our sex. Men grumbled dreadfully about him of course—but the reason for the most part, I fear, was sheer, naked envy. Liszt respected every decent woman, and once—in his later years—said to me in a very serious moment: '*I have never seduced an innocent girl.*' I know that to be the truth. Unfortunately, only too often did I see women forcing themselves upon him in a way that could have made me believe the roles had been reversed. I remember very well the day on which the Grand Duke had appointed Liszt a Chamberlain. My mother passed the news on to a cousin who also wore the Golden Key. Expressing great moral indignation, he said: 'This is the first time someone has received it for vice!'

'The rest of you didn't get it for your virtue!' my mother quickly replied.

The unexampled power of attraction that Liszt exercised over the female sex I have often witnessed almost with horror. And it did not end even when he grew old; it was really distressing that there could still be found those who regarded as desirable prey an old man in need of rest. But just as Liszt—despite everything—could see only the best side of every woman, so he did not allow himself to be confused when they pressed upon him. His chivalry was also one of the qualities which so attracted the female sex to him—and a sign of his noble character.[12]

Invited to Bayreuth for the roof-raising of the festival theatre under construction, Liszt arrived on 26 July, 'very tired out and worn out', according to his daughter. Some pleasant days were spent, enhanced by his playing, such as on 31 July when he performed the Adagio of the *Hammerklavier* Sonata—'unforgettably,' in the opinion of Cosima.* 'From time to time Richard contributes an explanatory word; our guests, completely unprepared, appear to be utterly overwhelmed.'

Leaving Bayreuth on 5 August, Liszt was accompanied as far as Bamberg by his daughter and son-in-law (who later visited upon Cosima a jealous outburst of the kind 'with which I am confronted after every reunion with my father') and their children. The rest of the day he spent at Nuremberg with Lina Ramann, whose diary account of her guest's playing concludes with the words: 'Now I know what music is—now I know what the word "genius" means. . . .'

After a few days with Cardinal Hohenlohe at Schillingsfürst, and a short visit to Langenburg, Liszt returned on the 17th to Weimar.

Amy Fay, 23 August. Yesterday he played us a study of Paganini's, arranged by himself, and also his *Campanella*. He gave it with a velvety softness, clearness, brilliancy and pearliness of touch that was inimitable. And oh, his grace! *Nobody* can compare with him! Everybody else sounds heavy beside him!

However, I have felt some comfort in knowing that it is not Liszt's genius

* 'Those who did not hear my father play Beethoven's Op. 106 can have no idea how it should sound,' she remarked long afterwards.

alone that makes him such a player. He has gone through such technical studies as no one else has except Tausig, perhaps. He plays everything under the sun in the way of *Etuden*—has played them, I mean. On Tuesday I got him talking about the composers who were the fashion when he was a young fellow in Paris—Kalkbrenner, Herz, etc.—and I asked him if he could not play us something by Kalkbrenner. 'Oh yes! I must have a few things of Kalkbrenner's in my head still,' and then he played part of a concerto. Afterwards he went on to speak of Herz, and said: 'I'll play you a little study of Herz's that is infamously hard. It is a stupid little theme,' and then he played the theme, 'but *now* pay attention.' Then he played the study itself. It was a most hazardous thing, where the hands kept crossing continually with great rapidity, and striking notes in the most difficult positions. It made us all laugh; and Liszt hit the notes every time, though it was disgustingly hard, and as he said himself, 'he used to get all in a heat over it'. He had evidently studied it so well that he could never forget it. He went on to speak of Moscheles and his compositions. He said that when between thirty and forty years of age, Moscheles played superbly, but as he grew older he became too old-womanish and set in his ways—and then he took off Moscheles and played his studies in his style. It was very funny. But it showed how Liszt has studied *everything*, and the universality of his knowledge, for he knows Tausig's and Rubinstein's studies as well as Kalkbrenner and Herz. There cannot be many persons in the world who keep up with the whole range of musical literature as he does.

Amy Fay, 9 September. This week has been one of great excitement in Weimar, on account of the wedding of the son of the Grand Duke. All sorts of things have been going on, and the Emperor and Empress* came from Berlin. There have been a great many rehearsals at the theatre of different things that were played, and of course Liszt took a prominent part in the arrangement of the music. He directed the Ninth Symphony, and played twice himself with orchestral accompaniments. One of the pieces he played was Weber's Polonaise in E major,† and the other was one of his own Hungarian Rhapsodies.‡ Of these I was at the rehearsal. When he came out on stage the applause was tremendous, and enough in itself to excite and electrify one. I was enchanted to have an opportunity to hear Liszt as a concert player. The director of the orchestra here [Lassen] is a beautiful pianist and composer himself, as well as a splendid conductor, but it was easy to see that he had to get all his wits together to follow Liszt, who gave full rein to his imagination, and let the tempo fluctuate as he felt inclined. As for Liszt, he scarcely *looked* at the keys, and it was astounding to see his hands go rushing up and down the piano and perform passages of

* Augusta, the Grand Duke's sister.
† That is, Liszt's own transcription.
‡ The Fantasia on Hungarian Folk Themes (S123), from the 14th Hungarian Rhapsody. It was dedicated to Bülow, who gave its first performance, under Erkel, at Pest on 1 June 1853.

the utmost rapidity and difficulty, while his head was turned all the while towards the orchestra, and he kept up a running fire of remarks with them continually. 'You violins, strike in *sharp* here.' 'You trumpets, not too loud there,' etc. He did everything with the most immense *aplomb*, and without seeming to pay any attention to his hands, which moved of themselves as if they were independent beings and had their own brain and everything! He never did the same thing twice alike. If it were a scale the first time, he would make it in double or broken thirds the second, and so on, constantly surprising you with some new turn. While you were admiring the long roll of the wave, a sudden spray would be dashed over you, and make you catch your breath! No, never was there such a player! The nervous intensity of his touch takes right hold of you. When he had finished, everybody shouted and clapped their hands like mad, and the orchestra kept up such a *fanfare* of applause, that the din was quite overpowering. Liszt smiled and bowed, and walked off the stage indifferently, not giving himself the trouble to come back, and presently he quietly sat down in the parquet, and the rehearsal proceeded. The concert itself took place* at the court, so that I did not hear it. Metzdorff was there, however, and he said that Liszt played fabulously, of course, but that he was not as inspired as in the morning, and did not make the same effect.

Amy Fay, 24 September. We had our last lesson from Liszt a few days ago, and he leaves Weimar next week. I played my Rubinstein concerto. . . . About seven Liszt came in, and the lamps were lit. He was in an awful humour, and I never saw him so out of spirits. 'How is it with our concerto?' said he to me, for he had told me the time before to send for the second piano accompaniment, and he would play it with me. I told him that unfortunately there existed no second piano part. 'Then, child, you've fallen on your head, if you don't know that at least you must have a second copy of the concerto!' I told him I knew it by heart. 'Oh!' said he, in a mollified tone. So he took my copy and played the orchestra part which is indicated above the piano part, and I played without notes. I felt inspired, for the piano I was at was a magnificent grand that Steinway presented to Liszt only the other day. Liszt was seated at another grand facing me, and the room was dimly illuminated by one or two lamps. A few artists were sitting about in the shadow. It was at the twilight hour, '*l'heure du mystère*'. . . I had studied the piece so much that I felt perfectly sure of it, and then with Liszt's splendid accompaniment and his beautiful face to look over to—it was enough to bring out everything there was in one. If he had only been himself I should have had nothing more to desire, but he was in one of his bitter, sarcastic moods. However, I went rushing on to the end

* On 7 Sept. For the wedding Liszt also composed his *Wartburg Lieder* (S345), settings for soloists, chorus, and orchestra of songs from J. V. Scheffel's festival play *The Bride's Welcome to the Wartburg*.

—like a torrent plunging down into darkness, I might say—for it was the end, too, of my lessons with Liszt! . . .

Amy Fay, Berlin, 8 October. Liszt was kindness itself when the time came to say goodbye, but I could scarcely get out a word, nor could I even thank him for all he had done for me. I did not wish to break down and make a scene, as I felt I should if I tried to say anything. So I fear he thought me rather ungrateful and matter-of-course, for he couldn't know that I was feeling an excess of emotion which kept me silent. I miss going to him inexpressibly, and although I heard my favourite Joachim last night, even *he* paled before Liszt. He is on the violin what Liszt is on the piano, and is the only artist worthy to be mentioned in the same breath with him. . . .

But Liszt, in addition to his marvellous playing, has this unique and imposing personality, whereas at first Joachim is not specially striking. Liszt's face is all a play of feature, a glow of fancy, a blaze of imagination, whereas Joachim is absorbed in his violin, and his face has only an expression of fine discrimination and of intense solicitude to produce his artistic effects. Liszt never looks at his instrument; Joachim never looks at anything else. Liszt is a complete actor who intends to carry away the public, who never forgets that he is before it, and who behaves accordingly. Joachim is totally oblivious of it. Liszt subdues the people to him by the very way he walks on to the stage. He gives his proud head a toss, throws an electric look out of his eagle eye, and seats himself with an air as much as to say, 'Now I am going to do just what I please with you, and you are nothing but puppets subject to my will.' He said to us in the class one day: 'When you come out on the stage, look as if you didn't care a rap for the audience, and as if you knew more than any of them. That's what I used to do. Didn't that provoke the critics though!' he added, with an ineffable look of malicious mischief. So you see his principle, and that was precisely what he did at the rehearsal in the theatre at Weimar. Joachim, on the contrary, is the quiet gentleman-artist. . . . In reality I admire Joachim's principle the most, but there is something indescribably fascinating and subduing about Liszt's wilfulness. You feel at once that he is a great genius, and that you *are* nothing but his puppet, and somehow you take a base delight in the humiliation![13]

With the departure of Liszt for Rome, Amy Fay returned to Berlin, where she became a pupil of Ludwig Deppe (1828–90), a teacher who specialized in a weight and relaxation system he had developed. In May 1875 she made a successful concert début. Later she returned to Liszt in Weimar, a move resented by Deppe but one that was fully consonant with words she wrote at the time: 'If I could begin my study over again, I should first stay three years with Deppe, in order to endow the spirit of music that I hope is within me, with the outward form and perfection of an artist. Next, I should study a year with Kullak, to give my playing a brilliant *concert dress*, and finally, I would spend two seasons with

Liszt, in order to add the last ineffable graces—(for never, *never* should an artist complete a musical course without going to LISZT, while he is on this earth!).'

Years later, she made further observations on Liszt *qua* teacher.

While Liszt resented being called a 'piano teacher', he nevertheless *was one*, in the higher sense of the term. It was the difference between the scientific college professor of genius and the ordinary school teacher which distinguished him from the rank and file of musical instructors.

Nobody could be more appreciative of talent than Liszt was—even of talent which was not of the first order—and I was often amazed to see the trouble he would give himself with some industrious young girl who had worked hard over big compositions like Schumann's *Carnaval* or Chopin's sonatas. At one of the musical gatherings at the Misses Stahr,* to whose simple home Liszt liked to come, I heard him accompany on a second piano Chopin's E minor Concerto, which was technically well played by a girl of nineteen from the Stuttgart Conservatorium.

It was a contrast to see this young girl, with her rosy cheeks, big brown eyes, and healthy, everyday sort of talent, at one piano, and Liszt, the colossal artist, at the other.

He was then sixty-two years old, but the fire of youth burned in him still. Like his successor, Paderewski, Liszt sat erect, and never bent his proud head over the 'stupid keys', as he called them, even deprecating his pupils' doing so. He was very picturesque, with his lofty and ideal forehead thrown back, and his magnificent iron-gray hair falling in thick masses upon his neck. The most divine expression came over his face when he began to play the opening bars of the accompaniment, and I shall never forget the concentration and intensity he put into them if I live to be a hundred! The nobility and absolute 'selflessness' of Liszt's playing had to be heard to be understood. There was something about his tone that made you weep; it was so apart from earth and so ethereal![14]

Early in October Liszt arrived in Rome, where he lodged at 43, Vicolo dei Greci. On the 13th he was granted a private audience with Pope Pius IX, with whom he conversed for more than a quarter of an hour.

Arriving at Budapest on 30 October, he took up residence at his new home in the Fish Market (Hal tér 4). 'I like my new lodging more than the one in which I spent the last two winters,' he wrote to Carolyne. 'It is quieter and very central, on the first floor and only a few steps from the Inner City Church, which is at once the city's main church and its best kept.'

* Anna and Helene, daughters of Adolf Stahr and his first wife. Having received much help and encouragement from Liszt, they had become piano teachers, and in their Weimar home gave musical matinées at which Liszt's pupils were welcomed and invited to play. The house was filled with souvenirs of their musical acquaintances, an entire room being set aside for photographs, busts, etc. of Liszt himself, whom they revered. After attending his funeral at Bayreuth, they wrote to Henriette von Liszt: 'Never again will the light come into our lives—for, with him, the sun of the universe has gone down into the history of art.'

The celebration of his jubilee as a public performer soon followed, it being fifty years since the Vienna concert (April 1823) at which his career had received consecration from Beethoven. Arranged by Liszt's friends, the celebrations took place at Budapest between 8 and 10 November. From abroad came Mesdames Mouchanoff, Dönhoff, and Meyendorff; and Hungarian representatives included Archbishop Haynald, Mihalovich, Counts Apponyi, Széchényi, and Karácsonyi. Among the hundred or so congratulatory telegrams (and almost as many letters) was one in verse from Richard and Cosima Wagner. Presented with a golden laurel wreath, Liszt also heard that he had been appointed an honorary member of the Imperial Academy of Music at St Petersburg.

The chief event of the celebrations took place at the Vigadó on Sunday the 9th: the first Budapest performance of *Christus*, conducted by Hans Richter. Earlier that same day, Henrik Gobbi's* *Liszt Cantata* had been performed, at the same venue, by the choir of the Liszt Society.

'Everything went off as well as possible,' Liszt was able to inform Carolyne. 'Our festival succeeded from A to Z.'

1874

On 8 January Liszt arrived at Vienna, where at a charity concert (in which among others Brahms took part) on the 11th he played two works with orchestra: his Hungarian Fantasia and transcription of the Wanderer Fantasy. His first public appearance in the Austrian capital, as a pianist, for nearly thirty years, it was, he assured Carolyne, 'successful in all points'. 'His playing is as perfect as ever, but calmer and gentler, not so dazzling and thrilling, but more coherent. . . than that of the young Liszt,' was the opinion of Eduard Hanslick. 'What a remarkable man! For the Liszt of today it was a great achievement—but one that he performed as though it were nothing and he still the Liszt of 1840. A darling of the gods indeed!'

Going on to Horpács, Liszt spent a month there with his friend Imre Széchényi. He was reading the third volume of Princess Carolyne's *Causes intérieures* at this time, and, in his letter of 22 January, ventured to differ with her on various matters: 'There is no point in my saying to you once again that several of your ideas strike me as unsound. . . . Despite all my efforts, I have not so far succeeded in seeing in contemporary events an essentially Christian, and specifically Catholic, movement!'

In a letter to her of 9 February, he returned to his own field: 'My sole musical ambition has been, and will be, to hurl my spear into the undefined void of the future. . . . So long as this spear be of good quality and fall not back to earth, the rest matters not in the least!'

At Budapest, where he stayed from mid-February to mid-April (with a week at Vienna in early April), Liszt's activities included a charity concert (for which 'I

* Hungarian composer and piano teacher (1842–1920) who received much support and encouragement from Liszt.

needed to spend several hours playing scales and brushing up old pieces') at the Vigadó on 4 March, another there on the 23rd, and a Literary and Artistic Club soirée on the 16th which saw the first performance of his *A holt költö szerelme* (The Blind Poet's Love) (S349), a setting of Mór Jókai's melodrama about the mysterious legend surrounding the death of Sándor Petőfi. With Liszt accompanying at the piano, the ballad was declaimed by Jókai's wife Róza Laborfalvi.

A young Hungarian who came more and more into Liszt's Budapest circle from this time forward was *Count Albert Apponyi* (1846–1933), who had been on friendly terms with the composer for some years. An outstanding orator, Apponyi was only at the beginning of his distinguished career as a statesman, but his maiden speech in the Hungarian Parliament had given powerful impetus to the movement calling for a national Academy of Music.

Supper at Liszt's always consisted of cold dishes, which he called 'cold treatment'. There were always stimulating and instructive conversations. In the course of them, Liszt would often take his seat at the piano, perhaps to illustrate his words, and the enviable members of that circle would hear fragments of Beethoven or Mozart sonatas played in the most spontaneous manner, untrammelled by any thought of a public. Those were real courses in musical history. It was understood that we should not ask Liszt to play. Whoever did so, fell from grace and spoilt the atmosphere of the whole evening: it had to be done at his own suggestion. I was a constant guest at these gatherings, where I felt, to a certain extent, like Saul among the prophets. Other famous artists used also to come there, musicians who had visited Budapest to pay their respects to Liszt, even if they were not giving a concert. These naturally took an active part in the musical performances, but they all sat as pupils at Liszt's feet, and listened to his every word as if it were the saying of an oracle. . . .

Now that I was able to observe Liszt almost daily in his own circle, there grew up, beside the admiration which I felt for the artist, genuine esteem and affection for the man. He was not without his faults. The seed of vanity which sprouts in every man could not be lacking in him, after an unparalleled career as a virtuoso such as he had enjoyed. This asserted itself sometimes in a way that detracted from his dignity. But he was a noble and good man, one of the best I have ever known. Jealousy and ill-will were unknown to him. How many musicians became known through Liszt, and owe any recognition they met with to the publicity he gave them! It was an immense satisfaction to him to discover talent, and anyone who wished to make serious progress in music always found him actively encouraging. I would stress this absence of jealousy in his character, because I have never met with it to such a degree in any man of importance having rivals in his own field.[1]

In mid-April, after a few days at Kalocsa with Haynald, Liszt went to Pozsony, where at a charity concert on the 19th both he and Sophie Menter played and his *Beatitudes* were performed.

After a further sojourn in Budapest, he returned to Rome, which he reached on 21 May.

Princess Carolyne to Adelheid von Schorn, 4 June. After so long an absence, and so long an interruption of his work, Liszt is at last back in *his Rome*. He has gone to his quarters at the Villa d'Este and begun to work. . . .

His genius is not yet understood—much less than Wagner's, because Wagner represents a reaction of the present; but Liszt has thrown his spear much further into the future. Several generations will pass before he is fully understood. But as it was given to me to understand his significance, then for Art I must do my utmost to demand of him what he can give so abundantly.[2]

Liszt to Princess Carolyne. Villa d'Este, 8 June. May I only finish my journey while fighting the good fight and serving the faith! For the moment, it suits me extremely well to stay here at the Villa d'Este. Everything pleases me here: landscape, atmosphere, trees, bells, rooms, memories—and there is nothing in any of them to bother or disturb me! This morning I enjoyed arranging my books and music on the shelves; soon I shall reread *St Stanislas* and set to work on composing the music for it. Before mass at the Franciscan church adjoining the Villa, I entered the sacristy (where I was at once cordially recognized) to consult the little book showing the feast-days. St Philip Neri's has been transferred this year from 26 May, Whit Tuesday, to today, 8 June. And so I began by invoking the patron saint of Rome, of the oratory, and of oratorios! He did not disdain music, and took a pious interest in musicians. And so I find it a good augury that here, where I propose to follow more profoundly his intentions relating to the oratorio, the first mass I heard was on his feast-day.[3]

To the same, 14 June. I have never expected or desired any position or title whatsoever at Rome. If the Holy Father had given me charge of the Sistine Chapel, I should have accepted from veneration for his kindnesses and out of obedience—and with the idea, perhaps erroneous, of rendering some service to religious art, but with no illusions about the fatigues and difficulties of such a task. Its lack imposes no cross on me; on the contrary, it lightens the one I bear. Accordingly, I have no self-denial to practise in this matter, and, my inner freedom long being fully assured, I am dispensed from the bother of seeking what I already possess![4]

To the same, 26 August. I was expecting a few words from you, and am uneasy at having received none. Are you perhaps unwell—or have I committed some new misdeed? If you do not send me a line, I shall not dare to come to Rome next Saturday as I was planning. The day before is the anniversary of the death of my father. On his deathbed, at Boulogne-sur-Mer, he told me that I had a kind heart and did not lack intelligence—but that he feared my life would be troubled, and I dominated, by women.

Such a prediction was remarkable, for at sixteen I knew nothing about women, and naïvely asked my confessor to explain God's sixth and ninth commandments to me, fearing that I had perhaps broken them unwittingly. Later, my *amours* began only too sadly—and I resign myself to seeing them finish in the same manner! Still, I shall never abjure Love, for all its profanations and false pretences![5]

Princess Carolyne having been seriously ill,* on 7 December *Adelheid von Schorn* arrived in Rome to undertake the role of companion for a few months. Liszt was waiting for her at the station.

He looked pale and tired, his hair was rather dishevelled, and his long coat covered in dust; but on his good, great face was that touchingly kind expression that can never be forgotten. My telegram had reached him at Tivoli, and for four hours he had put up with the jolting of the wretched omnibus so that he could be there to welcome me. There was still no railway between Rome and Tivoli at that time, and the sole cheap means of transport was the public coach, in which he sat among countryfolk, monks and models. He had newspapers and books in his pockets, and for the night a thick wax taper by whose light he read. No one in fashionable society would have used such a vehicle—but this pampered, idolized man, whose least whim his followers considered it a privilege to satisfy, was so unassuming in what concerned himself, so economical and undemanding, that he never gave in to the pleas of his friends, who thought that a comfortable carriage for his many journeys between Tivoli and Rome would be no great luxury for him. And now he had put up with this ordeal for me, in the cold and dark of winter. The warmth and cordiality with which he greeted me was like that of a father welcoming his daughter, just as though he owed me the greatest debt of gratitude. . . .

The Princess had not changed very much, having only become somewhat stouter; but the illness from which she had as yet scarcely recovered was still making her look pale and weak. She wore a dark-blue dress with red *passepoil*, and a white bonnet with ribbons that shimmered in every colour of the rainbow. The sitting-room still possessed the same furniture she had found in it. The chairs and armchairs were comfortable, but covered with ordinary flowered calico. On the walls hung some dreadful variegated engravings of dancing women, which she had left there so that people could see from them that everything belonged to the flat. On the sofa and several of the chairs lay pictures she had acquired over the years; but they had not been hung because they would not have gone with the furniture.

The Princess always sat in the middle of the room beside a large oblong table which contained both a mass of flowers and also the books she was

* So much so, that on 20 Sept., and without informing Carolyne, Liszt had undertaken the long journey from Rome (to which he returned on the 25th) to Duino, near Trieste, there to meet and seek advice from Marie Hohenlohe.

then using. Round about were chairs and armchairs. A grand piano, on which Liszt played her his latest works, was probably the only item she herself had added to the furnishings. They were completed by a large desk and some small cupboards and tables against the walls. Between this sitting-room and the Princess's bedroom there was a dining-room; but it was never used, and served merely as a passageway. It, too, was full of books. Meals were served to her on a low table in front of her armchair. . . .

That first evening was given entirely to conversation. To see those two outstanding and remarkable people together again I found still more moving than interesting, because of the great love and devoted friendship evident in every word uttered. They could often hold very differing opinions and even speak quite heatedly—I witnessed it often that winter; but these were surface disagreements which in no wise disturbed the depths of their hearts.

Liszt in every aspect of life possessed a penetrating insight. He understood human nature, and his judgement of the way in which matters would turn out was usually correct, even in politics. It was just the opposite with the Princess. This erudite woman, of whom men said that with each of them she could discuss his special subject, had no accurate understanding of the daily life of even the people closest to her; she was impractical in her judgement of persons and circumstances to a degree well-nigh unbelievable—and when she looked into the future she consequently saw as through a glass darkly. Later on, Liszt would sometimes say to me: '*The Princess is seeing that through her Roman glasses again.*' Her long sojourn in Rome may well have contributed to keeping her removed from real life and to making it more difficult for her to form accurate judgements. Be that as it may, she gradually came to realize that her advice helped no one. She would often complain bitterly to me that nobody heeded her; that neither Liszt nor her daughter, neither her friends nor her servants, acted according to her wishes. Unfortunately I too was soon numbered with those of whom she complained, for to live and behave among other people as she thought right was quite impossible. . . .

It was now a cause of sorrow to her that Liszt was frittering his life away and not working enough. If she could not have him entirely to herself, she at least wanted to keep him for Art; that is, to keep him *only to that* path which *she* believed to be the right one.

It was for this reason that she wanted the post of Director of the Papal Chapel for him; and the first necessary step towards that goal had been his admission into the clergy. That Liszt and his modern music would not have suited St Peter's, the Pope had realized long since. He had once visited him on Monte Mario and heard him play, but the matter had then come to nothing. That Liszt himself made no move in that direction, I am convinced. He knew better than anyone that despite being an abbé he had remained a man of the world. For the Princess, who wanted him to live permanently at Rome and Tivoli and create for the glory of God, that was dreadful. But Liszt *could* not compose at all times; he also needed stimulus from outside, needed the world. When he was in the mood to write serious things, he was very happy; but the mood was not always there. That that is how it *must* be, every *true* artist knows. When Liszt wanted only to *work*, he made transcriptions and paraphrases, and arranged pieces for piano duet or two pianos.

That with his earlier works, the symphonic poems and piano pieces, he had struck out on a new path and achieved great things, the Princess scarcely mentioned any longer; those had been works of his youth—a *fait accompli*. His prime and his old age should be dedicated solely to the Church. How much influence she had on Liszt, so long as they lived and worked together at the Altenburg, can be seen from his letters. The influence was a mutual one, of course, and Liszt always had an ally in Princess Marie. Between these two dearly loved persons, who understood one another so well, the Princess's life ran on a securer path than later, when she stood alone and could not adjust to the world outside.

From the day she left Weimar for Rome, to try to bring about the marriage, each of them had, without realizing it, set out on his and her own path. Thus it came about that their beneficial mutual influence could no longer be so effective. She wished to decide on the works he was to compose—but Liszt could create only according to his *own* inner voice, according to his *own* powers. All these matters occasioned constant conflicts, painful to both, whose mutual love and devotion was such that they could not do without one another. The Princess's entire life and thought revolved around Liszt, whether he was there with her or far away; she always worried *about* him, always cared *for* him. Liszt often said to me: 'The *only* person who has a claim on me is the Princess Wittgenstein. *All* the others I can dispense with from one moment to the next.' And then he would add with a very earnest expression: *'Et je me ferais hâcher pour elle!'*

That really was how he felt. All other relationships with women he regarded with such little seriousness that he generally spoke about them to the Princess. For him, they were transitory episodes which meant something quite different from the loyalty he felt towards her. That these confessions of his were often bitterly painful to her, will be understood by anyone who knows a woman's heart. But more than anything else she wished to be Liszt's *friend*; and, so that she might not lose his trust, was clever enough to conceal from him any feeling of jealousy. Liszt probably had no suspicion that she often grieved dreadfully, nor *how* bitterly she suffered from the knowledge that she was not the *only woman* in his life, after she had sacrificed everything for him, and when for her he had always been and for ever remained the *only man*. . . .

At Liszt's request, my first visit was to Frau von Keudell, wife of the

German Ambassador.* Liszt was on friendly terms with Herr von Keudell, and in any case the latter was such a good musician that Liszt held him in high regard in this respect too. He used to show his veneration for Liszt so charmingly that it did me good to witness it. Liszt often lunched at the Palazzo Caffarelli [the German Embassy], but never with more than a few other persons. Afterwards there would be music. . . . The gatherings were always most delightful, and a kinder host and hostess could not be imagined. Liszt was always in the best of spirits there. He would generally play duets with the master of the house, who from long experience was equal to the most fantastic inspirations dreamt up by Liszt in the upper keys. . . .

On 18 December Liszt returned to Rome [from Tivoli] for Christmas. He had a lodging in the Vicolo dei Greci. . . . On the same landing lived two of his pupils: Pinner,† a short, slight, swarthy American, and Zarembski,‡ a fair-haired Pole, an outstanding pianist. They were both very promising talents and both died young. Liszt used their rooms to give lessons, which were always attended by several pupils of both sexes. On the 18th Pinner gave a recital in the large hall of the Palazzo Caffarelli, for which Liszt fetched me. Although, unfortunately, it was half empty—the Italians have little feeling for serious music—there was an enthusiastic group in the front row: Liszt and the Keudells, Madame Helbig, Frau von Bernstorff and her daughter, Herr Renaud-Moritz from Szczecin, and I. . . .

Now that Liszt was back in Rome, almost no day passed without music somewhere or other. He generally took me with him, such as on 19 December when we went to the rehearsal of a Sgambati concert, thus enabling me to make the acquaintance of his favourite pupil, the representative in Rome of German music. A pale, soft, round, handsome face with rather long, curly black hair, a small moustache, and a soft gentle voice, did not indicate the energy with which Sgambati strove to gain acceptance for the New German school. His wife was one of the most beautiful Roman ladies I met. . . .

The Christmas Eve I spent in Rome was indeed quite different from those I was used to, but I did at least get to see a Christmas tree. In the morning Liszt and I brought the Princess flowers, and she gave me all kinds of Roman keepsakes as gifts. Neither of them wanted to see a Christmas tree or distribute presents—why they held such a genuine aversion, I do not know. After lunch, she and I took the carriage up on to the Pincio, where we drove slowly round and round and then stopped in the square in front of the band. . . . She knew many people, some by sight only. In earlier years she had associated solely with the Blacks; that is, adherents of

* Robert von Keudell (1824–1903).

† Max Pinner (1851–87).

‡ Juliusz Zarembski (1854–85), who was also a talented composer.

the Pope. But later with a number of Whites too. . . . For this reason she was distrusted by the Vatican. . . .

The evening I spent with Liszt and her. At one point their conversation fell on Schopenhauer. All philosophy was repugnant to Liszt, and he thoroughly disliked Schopenhauer's pessimistic teachings; but he nevertheless recognized that they contained much truth and a strange significance, to which he could not accommodate himself and therefore preferred to disregard. The Princess on the other hand damned Schopenhauer out of hand, and with the views she held nothing else was possible. She denied him, and believed him thus disposed of. But the evening did not end on this discordant note: Liszt sat at the piano and played from *Christus*. . . .

On the 27th he went back to Tivoli.[6]

1875

On 10 January Liszt returned to Rome for a few days as his manservant was ill. On the 16th, accompanied by Frau and Fräulein von Bernstorff, *Adelheid von Schorn* visited him at Tivoli.

I alighted in the outskirts . . . so that I could go straight to the Villa d'Este. . . . The turret room in which Liszt's desk stood overlooked the Campagna and the gardens; and his quarters were completed by a dining-room, bedroom, and music room. All four rooms gave on to the terrace. He at once made me feel at home by giving me some letters to write which had been set aside for me. Then we set out for the Hotel Regina to join the two ladies. Our walk took us through virtually the entire village, and I saw one bizarre sight after another. We had not even passed through the empty square in front of the Villa before some children gave the impression that they had been waiting for Liszt to appear so that they might attach themselves to him; and more and more joined us as we went on. He distributed coins among them, and people rushed from their houses to kiss his hands and coat. These scenes were re-enacted every time he went out—but that was only rarely: since the monastery church is hard by the Villa, there was no need for him to walk through the streets when he attended mass in the mornings. Besides, he had the wonderful gardens to enjoy—and to take a walk for its own sake was something Liszt never did.

As we strolled through the narrow alleyways, the picturesque Italian scenes passing on either side of us, my impression was that he belonged nowhere more than here. The hordes of beggars, who would have been an irritation to anyone else, merely amused him. He laughed with them, scolded them when they became too impudent, and gave them yet more. He looked like a patriarch whom all revere and from whom all want to receive. And so it was with a large retinue that we arrived at the hotel, where we collected the Bernstorff ladies and went with them to the Sibyl's Temple and the great waterfall. Liszt was our cicerone, something which amused me greatly, for I had hardly ever seen him face to face with nature before, he being little susceptible to its beauties. It could move him on occasion, but he did not need it, did not seek it out.

We stood at the top, by the great waterfall, where the broad, silver-green, clear surface of the water flows quietly out of the walled archway, only, a few paces further on, to come crashing down into the depths with a noise like thunder. That flowing water has a mesmerizing influence on anyone who regards it for long enough, probably everyone has felt; but such a power as it here possessed, I had never before experienced. Liszt seemed affected likewise, for he suddenly took my hand and said: 'Come away from here or the water will drag us into it.'

The evening was spent in Liszt's rooms. After the meal he played an Adagio by Mendelssohn; a melody which they play on trombones at St Peter's when the Pope gives his blessing; the *Pastorale* and *Tu es Petrus* from his *Christus*; and Isolde's 'Liebestod'.* Once again he proved the kindest of hosts and most enchanting of human beings; with each of us he knew what words would give the greatest pleasure and happiness. To me he said several times what I so loved to hear from him, and with which he so often made me feel at home: 'Faites comme vous voulez, vous êtes chez vous.'. . .

Liszt returned to Rome, where he stayed until his departure for Pest. On 27 January he took me to Monte Mario, and in its presbytery showed me the rooms he had long inhabited, in which he had been visited by Pius IX. Then we walked over to the Villa Mellini, whose garden offers a superb panorama of Rome and the Campagna. As Liszt knew its owner, we were allowed to go up on to the flat roof of the house, from which, since the sea can also be seen, a still more glorious view awaited us. . . .

On such outings Liszt was always in the most wonderful mood, reminiscing about old times and leaping from one subject to the other. Rarely can anyone have come to know Rome so pleasantly as I did. What the Princess had not yet told me I learnt from Liszt; and how kind and gentle he was at such times. The magic of his personality and his lofty character I felt and enjoyed more at Rome than anywhere else. He was more serene, pleased with the freedom for work that Tivoli provided him, and not harassed by too much music and socializing.

During these days I accompanied him to the Teatro Apollo to see Verdi's *Aida*, which was performed there that winter for the first time. We sat with the Sheremyetievs in their box. It was more a kind of social gathering, for serious listening to a work of art is out of the question in

* From Wagner's *Tristan und Isolde* in Liszt's piano transcription (S447).

Italy. The performance was glittering, but one which we found artistically inadequate, and Liszt was not satisfied with it. . . .

On the 9th he departed, accompanied by Pinner and Zarembski. I went to the station with him, and when the train pulled out I felt as though Rome had become a more dismal place, as though the sun itself now shone less brightly. He had made my stay so enjoyable, and wherever I had seen the kind, noble face of this beloved great man, the feeling had come over me of being at home.[1]

Liszt arrived in Budapest on the 11th. Shortly before, a theft had been committed at Carolyne's residence in Rome, and Liszt found that he was now victim of a similar crime. 'The cupboards were forced—silverware, linen, a gold ring, and several silver ones taken! Miska* is guilty only of excessive innocence—for the thief, now imprisoned, was frequently his table companion and obliging assistant, when Miska would favour him with confidential information about our possessions!'

At the Vigadó on Wednesday, 3 March, the Liszt Society of Budapest mounted a performance of the *Prometheus choruses*, the piano accompaniment being provided by Liszt and his former pupil Antal Siposs (1839–1923). Three days later, for a concert which offered local music-lovers the world première of Liszt's *Die Glocken des Strassburger Münsters*,† a performance of Beethoven's Fifth Piano Concerto, with Liszt as soloist, and excerpts from the *Ring des Nibelungen*, Richard and Cosima Wagner arrived in Budapest, finding Liszt (who was accompanied by Baroness Meyendorff), in Cosima's words, 'well, cheerful, and decidedly glad to see us'.

The concert was held at the Vigadó on 10 March; the rehearsal, on the 9th.

Count Albert Apponyi. As soon as the Wagner concert was announced in Budapest, opposition immediately arose. Voices were raised in the press, claiming that Budapest was not a German city, and that no defence could be put forward for the attempt to spend Hungarian money on the support of a German undertaking. Enthusiasm for Richard Wagner was not so general among the public of Budapest as it afterwards became. The protests caught on, and tickets for the concert were selling so badly that we began to fear a fiasco. . . . Liszt was informed of the state of things, and he at once said: 'I will play Beethoven's Concerto in E flat major at the same concert.'‡ On that day when this decision of the Master became known, all tickets were sold out; a material and artistic success which no other town could rival was assured. Wagner was deeply touched by this action on the

* Miska Sipka, a Hungarian, had been Liszt's servant since 1871. He died shortly afterwards in Rome and his place was taken by a Montenegrin, Spiridion Knezevics.

† 'The Bells of Strasburg Cathedral' (S6), a setting for baritone solo, chorus, and orchestra of the Prologue ('The Spire of Strasburg Cathedral') to the poem *The Golden Legend* by Longfellow, to whom Liszt's work, composed at Tivoli in 1874, is dedicated. It is preceded by a short prelude, *Excelsior* (after another Longfellow poem), whose theme was borrowed by Wagner for his *Parsifal*.

‡ He also offered to have his own work omitted—a sacrifice which Wagner did not accept.

part of his faithful friend, to whom, as I know from experience, he was warmly attached. . . .

I think I am safe in asserting that Liszt's playing of the E flat Concerto at the rehearsal marked his highest achievement as a pianist, perhaps the highest achievement of which artistic interpretation is capable. As if bewitched, Hans Richter and the orchestra followed the indications of the great Master whom they were privileged to accompany, and in no way did their playing disturb the perfection of the impression, or rather the impression of perfection, which one received from Liszt. It is now fifty-seven years since I had the experience of hearing Beethoven interpreted by Liszt for Wagner, yet it rings as freshly in my ears and in my mind as though it had been yesterday. One could feel how, at every important turn in that marvellous work, the two living masters, pianist and listener, were in spiritual communion with each other, happy in their common understanding of the dead genius. Invisible threads of suggestion passed from that source of profoundest feeling to us ordinary listeners, and found their way into our grateful and receptive souls. Words fail to describe what we experienced that day. It was simply music, an emotion evoked by sound more glorious than any expressible by thought or speech.

When the rehearsal was over, the few people who had been present went to luncheon together. Not a word was spoken, not a murmur of applause. Everyone felt instinctively that silence alone befitted the mood in which we were. Wagner had sought out Liszt, and they, too, were silent as they walked from the room. It was only when we were sitting at table that the spell was broken, and Wagner turned excitedly to Liszt with the words: 'My dear Franz, you have beaten me well and truly today! What can I do to compare with the playing we have just heard?' And so the talk went on, with exclamations of humble admiration for Beethoven's genius and of gratitude to Liszt, who could bring it so magically to life. We others had not the courage to intrude upon the conversation. What would have been the good of saying to Liszt: 'Master, you played beautifully today'? All commonplace praise would have been only a profanation of the heights to which we had climbed.*[2]

Georg von Schultz. By chance we arrived in Budapest at just the right time to attend the rehearsal of the Liszt-Wagner concert. . . . Liszt played the E flat concerto of Beethoven, the one with which at fifteen Ella[†] made her début at Petersburg. What a treat for the ears that was! When we returned to the Hotel Hungária for a meal, Liszt soon arrived too, with his daughter

* Cosima: 'My father absolutely overwhelms us with the way he plays the Beethoven Concerto—a tremendous impression! Magic without parallel—this is not playing, it is pure sound.'

† Schultz's daughter, the pianist and composer Ella von Adajewsky (1846–1926), who as a 12-year-old had studied with Liszt in Weimar. A few days later (14 March), Liszt played to a small but appreciative gathering excerpts from her opera *The Boyar's Daughter*.

Cosima, her husband Richard Wagner, and a whole train of counts bringing up the rear. Liszt now wears the dress of an *abbé*, similar to what our pastors once wore. His long, thick hair has turned grey, but he still plays as beautifully as in his prime. The long hair suits him: it gives dignity to his appearance. Why, I wonder, has man, to whom God has given long hair too, created another fashion and cut off this beautiful gift from above? Women are cleverer than us!

On Wednesday evening came the great concert itself. The only seats we could get were in the front—fifteen gulden each—right by Liszt's piano. There were 3,000 people in the hall, pure *beau monde*; sitting next to us was the Prince Primate of Hungary, Cardinal Simor,* wearing a crimson sash. The concert began with a choral piece by Liszt, *Die Glocken des Strassburger Münsters*. He conducted the performance himself—pretty singers, a good deal of noise, much ado about nothing. In my opinion this is one of his weakest works.† Then Beethoven and, to end, Wagner's infernal din. Beethoven between Liszt and Wagner made me think of Our Saviour at Golgotha between the thieves. What Wagner gave us from his *Ring* was not really music, just one long and terrible crashing, creaking, wheezing, whinnying, roaring and rattling. Weber wrote a Wolf's Glen too—but that is musical noise. . . . How curious that I, who believe in a more advanced mankind of the future, for whom music will be the highest goddess, cannot come to terms with this Music of the Future![3]

Neues Pester Journal (11 March). The most important event of the music season, which has been keeping the artistic circles of our capital in suspense for weeks, has come and gone. To any enquiry about the success of this monumental musical occasion, the answer, devoid of all prejudice and partisanship, must be that . . . it was a full and complete triumph for *Franz Liszt*, the unparalleled pianistic interpreter of Beethoven, but for Richard Wagner no more than a *succès d'estime*. . . . The concert was made possible only by Liszt's promise to contribute to it a performance of a major piano work. After today's success may it calmly be said that Liszt's piano-playing was the magnet which lured the public to the Wagner concert; all the rest—including the excerpts from the *Ring des Nibelungen* —was mere filling, standing far behind it in significance and artistic effect.

At a charity concert on the 15th, Liszt played Weber's Sonata in A flat, Chopin's Polonaise in C minor, the Eleventh Hungarian Rhapsody, and *Les Patineurs*. His reception by the audience packed into the small hall of the Vigadó was one of boundless enthusiasm. 'How did Liszt play?' asked the *Pester Lloyd*. 'To say, would be superfluous for those who heard him—and still more superfluous for those who did not! How to bring out poetic content with crystal clarity is

* János Simor (1813–91), Hungarian Prince Primate from 1867 until his death.

† The *Pester Lloyd* reviewer was of similar opinion, but added: 'Nevertheless, the impression created by certain passages . . . was great enough to make a further performance of this interesting work desirable.'

something he understands as does none other.' Of his playing of the Rhapsody, the *Neues Pester Journal* remarked: 'Who can describe the enthusiasm evoked by Liszt with his dazzling rendering of this masterpiece, when the well-known national melodies rang out in the magic sounds unique to him? The splendid Bösendorfer piano at which the Master sat seemed ever to be changing into a new and different instrument. At one moment came whirling cymbal clashes, at another the long-held notes of the violin, to which in its turn succeeded the sweet song of the flute—until the magic was dispelled by the thunderous applause of the audience.'

Liszt's sole fellow-performer, for whom he provided the accompaniments, was the American soprano Minnie Hauk (1851–1929). One of her contributions was Liszt's *Lasst mich ruhen*. 'Beside the great Comet,' reported the *Pester Lloyd*, 'she shone like a bright little star.'

Minnie Hauk. I have heard all the great pianists since the sixties, but none moved me as did the Abbé Liszt. Under his magic fingers the piano would become a whole orchestra, producing the most wonderful music imaginable. . . .

The élite of Hungarian society usually assembled on Saturdays,* and sometimes, after conversing with his friends, Liszt would rise, go to the Steinway grand piano, and play amidst silent awe. I was seated right in front of him, close to the piano, and could notice the wonderful change that would come over his face the moment his fingers touched the keys. When conversing in society he made grimaces, his lips would move incessantly and utter words one could understand only with close attention. When sitting at the piano he appeared like a god. He forgot everything around him, and played such sublime music that it seemed not to be of this earth; it was as though the entire heavenly chorus combined to shower it down on us hypnotized mortals, and when I closed my eyes all the graceful, angelic figures of Botticelli's paintings appeared before me with their instruments, and seemed to play. On several occasions this music moved me to tears, and on returning to my rooms I would cry like a baby.[4]

On Tuesday, 30 March, Ágoston Trefort (1817–88), the Minister of Education, presented Liszt with his appointment as President of the new Academy of Music, which was to be opened later in the year.

Via Vienna and Munich (where on 12 April he attended a performance of *Christus*) Liszt returned to Weimar, which he left again on 23 April to visit Hanover for a performance, on the 24th, of *St Elisabeth*. On 1 May, in response to an invitation from King William III (1817–90), brother of the Grand Duchess Sophie, he arrived at the Castle of Loo in Holland. Among fellow guests were Ambroise Thomas, Wieniawski, and Gevaert,† as well as several of the foremost Dutch and Belgian painters. The purpose of the gathering was for eminent artists

* At the Hotel Hungária overlooking the Danube.

† François Auguste Gevaert (1828–1908), Belgian composer and theorist and, from 1871, Director of the Brussels Conservatoire.

to judge the progress made in the different arts by students during the previous term. Liszt was decorated by the King, who also presented him with a 'magnificent writing-set in Egyptian alabaster and onyx'. On 12 May he returned to Weimar.

King William III of Holland to Liszt, 23 May. The remembrance of your presence at Loo is that of your indulgent, indeed I could say paternal, kindness. It is a memory which will remain indelibly engraved on my heart, as it will on the hearts of all those whose good fortune it was to associate with you at Loo and to enjoy your splendid musical inspirations. . . . When you are able to, return to us as soon as possible—to all of us, and first of all to me, *notre cher Grand Maître*![5]

Princess Carolyne to Eduard von Liszt. Rome, 30 May [1875?]. Although Liszt's imagination is very easily kindled by women (his father told him on his deathbed: beware of women; through them you will come to ruin)—he is not by nature a libertine. For ten years in succession he lived in continence. At Weimar as well as in Rome. He is merely weak, and when a woman *wants* to take possession of him, he cannot resist her. Mici [Mitzi] Genast tore him away from an intellectual life that had become almost habitual— and ten years later la Janina did exactly the same! And so by the time la Meyendorff arrived on the scene, the barriers of conscience had long since been brought tumbling down! But they can be set up again. So far as his *behaviour with women* is concerned, he is really prompted more by vanity than anything else, for the misfortune of his life consists in his having grown up in Paris, a city whose spiritual degeneration filled him with a *false ideal* difficult to eradicate: the so-called affinity of soul between man and woman. And in *this* respect he finds the slightest appearance of such a thing enough. For him it is like the scent of a flower that one breathes in and then forgets. . . . He must go through an inner process of repentance. I cannot assist him when *I* am the injured party. I would seem both judge and plaintiff—and my words would have no effect on him. That is why since 1860 I have adopted the method of relative silence: waiting for an occasion to present itself to entrust this serving of the truth to someone else. . . . Choose your moment well; both the *occasion and the manner* in which you speak to him, so that he may be unable to guess two things: (1) that for so long you suspected nothing—for your words would then strike him as an *arranged thing*, a *lecture on morals* to which he would pay little attention, instead of giving him the effect of a remonstrance *held in restraint* for many years, finally to come out in *given circumstances*. As you see, such a talk, if it is to have any effect, must be prepared long in advance. Don't speak to him from the point of view of the catechism. He is scrupulous about confessing. But his *de facto* sins being very few, he receives absolution without difficulty. What his confessor, not knowing it, is unable to tell him, is that the coarsening of feelings, the scandal created, the lost reputations, the appearance of one evil being produced by another (that of illicit connections), have all the moral disadvantages of forbidden relationships. . . . For it is enough for a man to have possessed a woman for her to make him commit all manner of follies, like Mici Genast at Weimar, Janina at Pest, and Meyendorff at present. . . . Tell him that some incident (no matter what) has made you realize the low esteem in which people hold him. That is what will strike home. Tell him that people are quite aware that Janina's booklet is full of inaccuracies, but that they say it is only the details which are untrue; the reality being worse, in the sense that my refusal to marry him, as soon as such a refusal was possible to me, is attributed to my knowledge of his liaison with Mici Genast. Stress the fact that people regard it as an act of *base ingratitude* on his part. Just as it is ingratitude to have *flaunted* his liaison with Mme Meyendorff by getting her to go to Weimar. Tell him that the world, which excuses the infidelities of a husband, does not excuse *such* doings. Stress *two* points above all: (1) Mici Gen. and la Meyend.—because of *Weimar*. (2) People's *opinion*, which does not find it worthy of a *gentleman* and man of honour.

Tell him that the world would have forgiven any secret infidelities, but protests against the publicity of this lack of consideration towards a woman from whom he has accepted *everything* and whose husband he should be. . . .

I am considering everything from the *abstract* viewpoint of good and bad—of the memory Liszt will leave behind him. It is my profound conviction that God will grant my prayer and that he will be cured. . . . Liszt is *indeed* a very *noble* person. But one of the things which has greatly contributed towards weakening his moral sense—that is to say, to making him lose proper understanding of good and bad—is the wrong opinion of the press about him. His works, which are truly his *good deeds*, as in them he reveals his *better self*, have had only derision and abuse heaped upon them in the newspapers, while his personality, which was never quite blameless, has been far too praised and admired. I have found out that he believes his luck with women supports this opinion of his personality and *makes a legendary man of him*! That is why he values only what gives a man the right to compromise a woman, since it furnishes the *prestige* of good luck. It is the only compensation that the *press* (by which he sets great store) gives him in return for its unjust treatment of his works. And so a radical cure would be for everything in this letter—*to be published*! That would cure him completely. But—*that is impossible*. I mention it to you so that you can make him fear a possible sudden change of attitude towards him in the newspapers, which could judge him very severely in his lifetime.[6]

At the Tempelherrenhaus in the Weimar park on 17 June a short concert was held in memory of Marie Mouchanoff, who had died the previous year. The works performed were all by Liszt: Requiem for Male Voices; *Ave Maria*;

Hymne de l'enfant à son réveil (S19); Legend of St Cecilia (S5); and Elegy (S130) for cello, piano, harp, and harmonium. The Legend (mezzo-soprano, chorus ad lib, and orchestra/piano) was performed on this occasion for the first time. According to *La Palestra Musicale* (26 October 1874), the Elegy, composed shortly after Marie Mouchanoff's death, had been performed in Rome on 23 October that year, at the home of Sofia Sarzana.

On 29 July, after visits to Sondershausen, Wilhelmsthal, and the Wartburg, Liszt arrived at Bayreuth, to stay with his daughter and son-in-law at Wahnfried, the new house into which they had moved the previous year, and to attend rehearsals of Wagner's *Ring* tetralogy, which in 1876 was to be performed in its entirety.

Emil Heckel (1831–1908), music publisher and Wagner enthusiast. Every evening from 8 to 10 there was a social gathering at Wahnfried, for Wagner felt at home in the midst of his friends and artists. If the weather was fine, we would stroll into the garden; but if *Liszt* sat down at the piano, we all rushed back indoors. Those who never heard him, even if they have known Bülow, Rubinstein or Tausig, can form no idea of the indescribable magic of his touch. He would often lend a work so personal a poetic charm, that one could feel in it that tenderness we know so well from his delightful correspondence with Wagner. And if fair ladies sat around him, his playing almost took on the character of a fascinating tête-à-tête. He no longer seemed to be reproducing a work, but immediately expressing, as it were, what once had found an utterance therein. His playing no longer seemed the rendering of a pianoforte piece, but artistic conversation: the conversation of a Liszt![7]

Leaving Bayreuth on 17 August, and journeying via Liebenstein, where he visited the Stahrs, as well as the theatre-loving Duke of Saxe-Meiningen, Liszt on the 19th arrived back in Weimar.

Here on 3 September he attended the ceremony (for which he had composed two festive songs*) of the unveiling of the equestrian statue of the Grand Duke Carl August, Goethe and Schiller's friend and patron. Also present were the German Emperor and Empress.

On 11 September he visited Leipzig, to hear excerpts from his *Missa choralis*. 'It seems,' he wrote to Carolyne, 'that many musicians are eager to fête me in this town, where for twenty years my opponents have done me all possible wrong, not only on the spot but elsewhere too, not excepting Paris, London, and even Vienna and Italy.'

The next day, Sunday, a private concert in his honour was mounted by Julius Blüthner (1824–1910) the piano manufacturer. Among the items on the all-Liszt programme were the *Prometheus choruses*, Psalm 13, and six of the *Lieder*, as well as the Elegy for piano, cello, harp, and harmonium, in which Liszt himself undertook the piano part. To the concert, 'armed with all possible appliances for investigating the great man's face and technique at a distance,' came the Irish composer *Charles Villiers Stanford* (1852–1924).

* *Der Herr bewahret die Seelen seiner Heiligen* (S48) and *Carl August weilt mit uns* (S92).

The moment his fingers touched the keys, I realized the immense gap between him and all other pianists. He was the very reverse of all my anticipations, which inclined me, perhaps from the caricatures familiar to me in my boyhood, to expect to see an inspired acrobat, with high-action arms, and wild locks falling on the keys. I saw instead a dignified composed figure, who sat like a rock, never indulging in a theatrical gesture, or helping out his amazingly full tone with the splashes and crashes of a charlatan, producing all his effects with the simplest means, and giving the impression of such ease that the most difficult passages sounded like child's play. It was the very reverse of the style of the young lady to whom Bülow, after hearing her performance, went up with a deep bow and said 'I congratulate you, Mademoiselle, upon playing the easiest possible passages with the greatest possible difficulty.' I and my companion, a very punctilious person, were so overwhelmed by the performance and the personality, that we could not but 'cap' him as he stalked out into the street. He had a magnetism and a charm which were all-compelling. We understood how he could meet Kings and Emperors on an equality, and fascinate with all the wiles of the serpent.[8]

Arriving in Rome on 19 September, Liszt stayed here (and at Tivoli) until the following February. Visiting the Eternal City again was *Adelheid von Schorn*.

I was able to celebrate Liszt's birthday with him. He came in from Tivoli to spend the day with the Princess, and took me for a drive, to show me all the houses he had lived in in Rome. . . . We also went into the church of Santa Maria degli Angeli, where a monk in a white habit received us and took us round. He was a German who had already spent many years of his life at the monastery and intended to die there. Liszt talked with him for a long time, and then remarked to me how enviable he found such a contemplative life. Even in his youth he had felt attracted towards the monastic life—but that in the long run he would have been unable to endure it, he himself doubtless realized. These contradictions in his character, which showed themselves again and again, I found very strange.[9]

Liszt to Princess Carolyne. Villa d'Este, 17/18 November. I shall need a few months of reflection to get used to the fact that the Budapest Music Academy exists.* Were it not for my antipathy to the writing down of bad jokes, I should have added, to vary the image of the millstone around the neck, that this Academy has been for me up to now only an appalling collection of swords of Damocles, in the form of pianos and bothersome compositions, suspended above my head! Fortunately, another Greek, Euripides, has given us this good advice: 'There is no point in getting angry with things, since that doesn't affect them.'[10]

* The Academy had been opened on 14 Nov. It was situated in the Fish Market, in the building which had been Liszt's Budapest residence since Oct. 1873.

To Olga von Meyendorff, 20 November. For the last couple of weeks I have been gloomily writing quantities of letters. I get nearly fifty a week, not counting . . . manuscripts, pamphlets, books, dedications, and all kinds of music. The time required to peruse them, even casually, deprives me of the time needed to answer them.[11]

1876

The German-born American pianist *Carl Lachmund* (1857–1928), who studied with Liszt in the 1880s, later came into possession of the diary kept by Liszt in 1876: the last, apparently, in which he made regular entries.

Reverently opening the book, one finds on the fly-leaf three aphorisms for the year ahead. The first is by a sculptor-painter-poet, the second by a great poet-thinker, the third by a celebrated naturalist; and they are written down in their original Italian, German, and French:

Michelangelo: Chi va dietro a altri, non li passa innanzi.
Goethe: Es gilt am Ende doch nur Vorwärts.
Humboldt: La vie est une équation des conditions.[1]

At the Villa d'Este in January Liszt worked at his *Weihnachtsbaum* (S186), a suite of twelve Christmas pieces for piano, written for and dedicated to his granddaughter Daniela.

Leaving Rome on 9 February, and stopping *en route* at Florence, Lamporecchio, and Venice, he arrived in Budapest on the 15th. At a Philharmonic Society concert on the 27th he was given an ovation after the first Budapest performance of *Hunnenschlacht*.

Liszt to Olga von Meyendorff, 1 March. All his life this poor FL has constantly been scolded, lectured, counselled, reprimanded, denounced. Sick persons have, on many occasions, proved to him that he was neglecting his health, though he was well; and people who were ruining themselves have triumphantly demonstrated to him that he understood nothing about his business interests, even though he has never owed a penny to anyone. He has, willy-nilly, had to learn that most of the time the best arguments are superfluous, and that of all faults, that of being right is the least excusable.[2]

To Princess Carolyne, 14 March. The newspapers tell me of the death of Daniel Stern.* Barring hypocrisy, I could not weep for her more after her death than during her life. La Rochefoucauld well said that hypocrisy is a

* Marie d'Agoult had died in Paris on 5 Mar. Like such acquaintances of hers as Chopin, Balzac, Delacroix, and Ingres, she was laid to rest in the cemetery of Père Lachaise.

homage rendered to virtue—but it is still permitted to prefer true homage to false. Mme d'Agoult possessed to a high degree a taste, and even a passion, for the false—except at certain moments of ecstasy, of which she could afterwards not bear to be reminded! At my age, moreover, condolences are no less embarrassing than congratulations. . . . The most desirable sacrament to receive, it seems to me, is that of extreme unction![3]

On 20 March Liszt took part in a concert at the Vigadó for the benefit of flood victims. His *Hymn to St Francis of Paola* (S28) for male voices was also performed. On the 26th was held the first concert of his pupils at the new Music Academy.

Liszt to Emile Ollivier, 27 March. The memory I retain of Mme d'Agoult is a painful secret, which I confide to God while praying that He may grant peace and light to the soul of the mother of my three dear children.[4]

In early April he returned to Weimar, which he left again on the 29th to go to Düsseldorf, where works of his were to be performed at a music festival. Hearing that the tickets were not selling well, he had offered not only to attend in person but also to play, and at once the financial success of the festival was assured.

The English composer and teacher Frederick Corder (1852–1932). I had the privilege of hearing excellent performances of the gigantic Gran Mass and the symphonic poem *Prometheus*, as well as the choruses to Herder's poem on the same subject. Between the parts of the concert Ferdinand Hiller good-naturedly introduced me to Liszt, with whom I had the unforgettable honour of a considerable conversation in several languages (we were all polygot then). The fascination of the great musician's manner and the benignity of his expression were things never to be forgotten, and render poignant my regret at not being able to be present on the following evening, when he improvised for a quarter of an hour on a couple of bars from a March by Schubert. The day after this, attending as usual at Hiller's house for a lesson, I found my teacher unable to do anything but rave over Liszt's playing (with which he had been familiar all his life). 'That old man,' he exclaimed, with tears in his eyes, 'he makes me feel like a schoolboy. I want to shut my piano and never open it again!' And he stamped his foot with a sort of comic vexation. The point of all this being that Hiller was himself a really wonderful extemporizer, at whom I had marvelled many and many a time.[5]

Clara Schumann had been passing through Düsseldorf; and her impressions were reported in a letter of 5 May to Johannes Brahms.

For the first time for many years I heard Liszt again, and was carried away by some of Schubert's things, which he played wonderfully, but not at all by his own works. . . . No one can rival him in his mastery of the instrument—but what a pity that so little *calm* enjoyment can be derived from it.* Instead, one is swept along as though driven by demons. Having a chance to observe him closely, I saw all his clever coquetry, his princely amiability, etc. The women were mad about him of course—it was disgusting.[6]

To Carolyne, Liszt reported: 'Hiller and Mme Schumann complimented me in public—on my indestructible youth!'

Between 15 and 25 May he was again the guest of King William III at the Castle of Loo. 'I am truly moved by His Majesty's kindnesses,' he wrote to Carolyne. 'Gérôme, Cabanel, and Gevaert talk very wittily; jests and anecdotes fly around incessantly, from morning till night, with the King sometimes adding his sovereign note! It would need a very subtle historiographer to relate the ephemerides of Loo.'

During the summer Liszt was visited at Weimar by *César Cui* (1835–1918), military engineer, propagandist for the national music of his native Russia, and member of the group of composers at St Petersburg led by Mili Balakirev and known as the *moguchaya kuchka* (mighty handful).

The evening of my first meeting with Liszt was spent with him at the home of his devoted friend Baroness Meyendorff. . . . Over tea I expressed my views on Wagner, the falseness of his system, the pitiful role assigned to the voice in his works, the poverty of melody resulting from his monotonous reiteration of themes, etc. The Baroness listened with horror, Liszt—with a slight smile. 'Il y a du vrai dans ce que vous dites là; mais, je vous en supplie, n'allez pas le répéter à Bayreuth!' he said when I had finished. Wagner was in general rather afraid of Liszt, and felt not quite at ease in his presence, just like an adolescent in the presence of a stern tutor. This comes as no surprise when one compares Liszt's gentle and forbearing nature with that of the harsh, arid, egotistical, and fanatically proud Wagner.[7]

Liszt to Princess Carolyne. Weimar, 18 June. The spontaneity of works of art is a very relative thing. Music, painting, and sculpture need much reflection, study, and preparation. Inspiration is spontaneous, without doubt, but not the recording of that inspiration. . . .

Thank you for sending me the article from *France* on the death of George Sand.† From long habit I pity the living more than the dead—and believe that this life is a blessing only for those who use it to reach Heaven![8]

'Not to be at Bayreuth in August is a moral and artistic inferiority!' Liszt declared; and he accordingly spent the whole of that month in the town, staying at Wahnfried with the Wagners and attending all three performances of the *Ring* cycle.

* Brahms's own opinion, expressed *c.*1890, was: 'Frankly, anyone who did not hear Liszt has no right to a say in the matter. He comes first, and then, at some considerable distance, no one else at all. His playing was something unique, incomparable, and inimitable.'

† Who had died at Nohant on 8 June.

Berthold Kellermann to his parents. Bayreuth, 20 August. Early on Friday morning [18 August] I was with Liszt. He invited me to take part in the great festival banquet beginning at eight that evening. It was filled with outstanding people, some five hundred in all. . . .

'For everything that I am and have attained,' said Wagner in his speech, 'I have one person to thank, without whom not a single note of my music would have been known; a dear friend who, when I was outlawed from Germany, was the first to recognize me and, with matchless devotion and self-denial, to draw me into the light. To this dear friend the highest honour is due. It is my sublime friend and master, Franz Liszt!'

The two embraced and wept. A hushed silence reigned in the large hall, all of us held spellbound by the solemnity of that moment in which we saw our two greatest masters clasped in each other's arms.

An endless storm of cheering finally burst out, however. So great and holy was the moment that it all but made me sink to my knees. Everyone felt that Wagner's human failings were now forgotten, and the cheers became positive shouts of joy when Liszt spoke a few words. Pale from excitement, he said: 'For those words of appreciation I offer thanks to my friend, to whom I remain most profoundly and humbly devoted.'[9]

Also present at this first Bayreuth festival was *Count Albert Apponyi.*

One of the evenings we spent at the Wahnfried villa led to the only musical experience which I can set beside the rehearsal at which Liszt played Beethoven's E flat Concerto. A few of us were together at Wahnfried after dinner. Wagner, being tired, had left the company, and Liszt took the lead in a conversation which turned on Beethoven's last sonatas. He was very interesting on the subject. He spoke especially of the famous Hammer-klavier Sonata, and more particularly of the fine Adagio in F sharp minor which it contains. In the midst of a sentence he stood up and exclaimed: 'I will prove it to you!' We retired to the music-room, which at Wahnfried reached from ground level, past the first floor and up to the glass roof. On the first floor there is an open gallery, on which the bedroom doors open, and from which a spiral staircase leads down to the ground floor. In the middle of the hall stood the huge piano, at which Liszt sat down, and filled our souls with the mysticism of Beethoven's last works. The atmosphere in which we listened was essentially that of the rehearsal in Budapest, but the absence of any accompaniment, or of any visible *mise en scène*, and the thought that we were in Richard Wagner's house, gave it a character of its own. As on that other occasion, Liszt seemed once more to have surpassed himself, to have established an inexplicable, direct contact with the dead genius whose interpretation was for him a religious task. When the last bars of that mysterious work had died away, we stood silent and motionless. Suddenly, from the gallery on the first floor, there came a tremendous uproar, and Richard Wagner in his nightshirt came thunder-ing, rather than running, down the stairs. He flung his arms round Liszt's neck and, sobbing with emotion, thanked him in broken phrases for the wonderful gift he had received. His bedroom led on to the inner gallery, and he had apparently crept out in silence on hearing the first notes and remained there without giving a sign of his presence. Once more, I witnessed the meeting of those three—Beethoven, the great deceased master, and the two best qualified of all living men to guard his tradition. This experience still lives within me as vividly as the other, and has confirmed and deepened my innermost conviction that those three great men belonged to one another.[10]

Another visitor to Bayreuth was Piotr Ilyich Tchaikovsky (1840–93). 'I have met many new people; visited Liszt, who was most kind; and Wagner, who at the moment does not receive anyone,' he wrote to his brother Modest. Liszt's fine transcription (S429) of the Polonaise from Tchaikovsky's *Eugene Onegin* dates from three years later.

Steeped in the music of Liszt, Berlioz, and Wagner, whom he admiringly called the Thunderers Three, was the English poet and linguist John Payne (1842–1916), much of whose verse was inspired by their works;* and he, too, probably made Liszt's acquaintance at Bayreuth. In his autobiography, after paying tribute to Wagner and Berlioz, Payne continues: 'But Liszt above all is my composer. With his transcendent purity of aspiration (the nostalgia of another and a nobler world), his mystic spirit harmonies and his interstellar splendour of expression, he appeals to my personality more than any other master.'

Liszt to Princess Carolyne. Weimar, 6 September. In all humility, I believe I do not deserve the letter I received from you today. With the most sorrowful sincerity I maintain what I told you in Rome: you are gravely mistaken about your daughter, about my daughter, and about me. God knows that to alleviate your sufferings has been my sole task for many years! I have had little success, it seems! For my part, I wish to remember only the hours in which we have wept and prayed together, as one! After your letter of today, I am giving up any thought of returning to Rome.[11]

To the same, 16 September. Your latest letter is full of kindness and indulgence. I thank you for it with all my heart, which is still bleeding from recent wounds. Allow me to cure myself alone, without further discussion of my faults and wrongdoings![12]

After a week or two at Hanover with Bülow, who was suffering from depression, three days at Nuremberg with Lina Ramann, and a brief visit to Regensburg, Liszt proceeded via Vienna and Budapest to Szekszárd for a ten-day stay (late October) with the Augusz family. In early November, by way of Kalocsa and a couple of days with Haynald, he returned to Budapest.

Janka Wohl. Liszt was very fond of a well-turned phrase, of 'painting with

* Payne's sonnets on Liszt's Piano Concertos in E flat and A, *Glanes de Woronince* No. 3, Dante Symphony, and other works, have been reprinted in *The Liszt Society Journal*, v (1980), 46–7.

the pen'. His musician's ear enjoyed the harmony of language just as it did a sweet melody; and we often spent hours searching for the exact word which without changing the meaning of a sentence would round it off with the right rhythm. To spur me on and to ensure that I would keep to such a course, he often quoted his favourite saying: 'Writings live only on account of their style.' . . .

The rich collection of little notes written by Liszt which I possess shows how keen he was to make his sentences complete and concise, and also as full of meaning as possible. These miniature masterpieces would furnish an original instruction manual of the thousand ways in which a few words can be cleverly put. He never lost an opportunity, however trivial, to put into action the marvellous mechanism of his mind. He never used the same phrase twice, and on every occasion some happy thought can be found in those little notes of ten or twenty lines.

The master had got into the habit of sending me in the morning one of these notes to say that he would call on us in the evening, and asking if we were free. He would then come *sans cérémonie*, just to have a few hours' chat, and would always bring me the latest publications which were sent to him from every country, a newspaper article which had struck him, or a volume of music. The Secretary of the Hungarian Academy, the distinguished historian Monseigneur Fraknói, Cardinal Haynald,* who was a close friend of the master's, Count Zichy, or one or two jolly ladies, would sometimes be of the company too; and, while playing whist, would enjoy with us the fireworks with which this inexhaustible mind of a thousand facets loved to dazzle us.

We talked of everything at these friendly meetings. There is nothing in art or science, not to mention abstract questions, upon which we did not touch; and I was often flabbergasted at his colossal memory, embellished as it was by boundless learning, which he was constantly adding to. But despite all this mass of knowledge, Liszt was always regretting that he had not gone through regular and consecutive studies. He maintained that he always felt the want of that rudimentary teaching which they had neglected to give him. 'I scribbled music before having written a letter of the alphabet, and plunged into mystical and philosophical books before being quite certain about my grammar. Oh! that confounded grammar has given me lots of trouble at times.' Nevertheless, Liszt was possessed of wonderful erudition, which was all the more remarkable in that it comprised several literatures.

For several winters in succession, M. Rogeard,† author of the *Propos de Labiénus*, a pamphlet which under the Second Empire had brought about his expulsion from France, gave very interesting lectures at Budapest in the

* At this time still Archbishop Haynald.

† The French writer and publicist Louis Auguste Rogeard (1820–96). Liszt is known to have attended lectures given by Rogeard in Dec. 1876.

salon of Mme [Antonina] de Gerando, *née* Countess Teleki, the great friend of Michelet and Reclus. . . . An élite public would assemble at these delightful soirées, which were seasoned with conversation. When the master was in Budapest he never failed to be present, following with the keenest interest the propounding of all those things which he himself knew so well. There was no set programme. Sitting at a little table, Rogeard would begin to talk to his audience, announcing there and then what he intended to lecture on: 'The philosophers and writers of the seventeenth century'; 'The eighteenth-century salons'; 'Sixteenth-century patrons of literature'; etc. It was on a number of occasions my pleasure to sit next to Liszt, and then he used to whisper to me in advance the names, facts, dates, etc. of which Rogeard was going to speak.

It was equally curious and amusing, for often he would find fault with the lecturer—not aloud, of course, but loud enough for him to hear if his hearing was acute enough. Nor had German philosophy any secrets for Liszt; and I could never understand how the same brain could be on such good terms with all the great atheists, and enjoy their arguments as if he were a judge and gourmet in such matters, and, at the same time, have a faith so lively, so simple and profound, as to be like that of some illiterate village girl.

The idea of God had been present in his mind from his childhood. His soul seemed like a diamond which the rust of doubt could not tarnish. The sacred fire which animated him brought him so near to his divine origin, that no philosophy could lead astray the deep-rooted intuition which was drawing him towards the Eternal. . . .

On one occasion he said to me: 'The moment I am alone I pick up the thread of my thoughts, of my interrupted work. One should never "muse". It is an enervating habit, wastes a great deal of time, and never leads to anything.'

What excellent teaching! Those words also explain how Liszt was able to complete the immense work represented by his life. And he was aware of it, moreover. 'Have you written the story of your life?' I asked him one day. 'It is enough to have lived such a life as mine,' he replied in a grave voice.

As I have said, we talked of everything; still, there were subjects which, as a rule, he preferred to avoid. But if one could once start him on them he was inexhaustible. One evening I read to him a witty little thing my sister Stefánia* had written.

'And what is it called?' asked Liszt. '*Eve*, dear Master, a subject you must know thoroughly.' 'Not at all, not at all,' he replied, shaking his head. 'I have not sufficiently eaten of the apple!'. . .

Having lived all his life in contact with the world, and having seen society

* Like Janka, Stefánia Wohl (1848–89) was a writer by profession.

in every form, he had contracted the habit of exhibiting a certain surface amiability which differed appreciably from his manner amongst tried friends. The courtier, the artist *grand seigneur*, would then disappear, and we would be astounded by a captivating simplicity which, for all that, was not wanting in grandeur. His conversation would then become less ironical but more profound, and brilliant remarks would follow one another so rapidly that, when I was alone and tried to make a note of them, I found to my dismay that I did not remember one half of what Liszt had said.[13]

From the diary of Count Géza Zichy, 10 December. Liszt and Mihalovich dined with us; we were in the merriest of moods. After the meal I mentioned that my dearest wish was a performance of *The Legend of St Elisabeth*—but Liszt advised me against it most firmly. 'You would experience only unpleasantness, not to speak of the financial deficit. Believe me, dear Géza!' I replied that I had already begun preparations and had held two sessions at the Conservatoire. 'I regret that sincerely,' Liszt rejoined, 'for here in Pest people come together only immediately to part company again.' However, my plan to found a music journal he supported most warmly. Then he seated himself at the piano and played—utterly incomparably—the Third Leonora Overture. When I went into the next room, I found my corn-chandler kneeling at the door. 'Count Zichy,' he said, 'what have I heard? It was worth fifty gulden; no, a hundred and one gulden.'—'Why the one gulden?' I asked. 'Because through the crack I could see his fingers and hair flying!'

Zichy, 21 December. Home again after a hunting trip, I found Liszt very poorly and in bed. Slipping and falling when leaving his carriage, he had struck his right arm and chest against a corner-stone. He greeted me most cheerfully, but I was concerned to see that he was having difficulty in breathing. 'It's nothing,' he said with a smile; 'just a small bruise on my right arm. I should be ashamed to complain in the presence of the classic of the one arm.'—'Take care of yourself, *lieber Meister*, I cannot see you suffer.'—'I am not suffering,' he replied, but biting his lips from pain as he did so. . . .

Zichy, 22 December. When with a heavy heart I went to Liszt this morning, I found him already up and in good spirits: in the space of one night his strong constitution had prevailed over his indisposition. We spoke about art and artists, Liszt saying among other things that it was by no means an advantage for an artist to be born an aristocrat. 'No one believes that he is serious about art, and he is taunted with dilettantism. . . . An aristocrat who composes decent works can, it is true, use his connections to obtain a performance. He can come *to* it more easily, but will come *through* it only with more difficulty.' . . .

Later we spoke about Russian music. 'The Russians are in several respects superior to us Hungarians,' said Liszt. 'Their national airs haven't the rhythmic strength and versatility of the Hungarian folk song, but in art forms they are more advanced. There is still no school in Russia, but they have a very promising group of talents. Music culture in Hungary is in process of development; we have a great deal of talent, but not nearly so much diligence and perseverance. Erkel is a very great talent, but unfortunately in his operas he has shown no consistent style.'

When his servant reported the death of an acquaintance, the Master became serious. 'Yes, that is the ultimate problem, the Promethean riddle that only faith can solve. The final scene in life's tragedy I find so *very* revolting. Decomposition is disgusting. I hardly dare say it since I should be condemned by my ecclesiastical superiors, but *I should like my own body to be cremated*. We owe that both to ourselves and to our fellows. If we have lived decently, then we should be annihilated decently too!'

Zichy, 26 December. Liszt and Baron Augusz dined with us. During the meal Liszt mentioned that as a boy he too had been hunting; and, indeed, that even Beethoven had been a hunter, but an extremely dangerous one as he had wanted to shoot all the time and at anything and everything, becoming as a result the terror of the entire hunting party. 'When I dined at Prince Esterházy's,' continued Liszt, 'he told me some anecdotes about Beethoven the hunter and then turned with a laugh to one of his old huntsmen, asking him in the most serious tone of voice: "Did you have the honour to be shot by Herr van Beethoven?"—"Yes indeed, Your Highness! To this day I carry his pellet in my body as a most sacred memento." The Prince, solemnly: "Where?"—"By your leave, Your Highness, below the back, at the rear!" was the reply.'

Our talk jumped to the ballet, and I remarked that I had yet to experience a ballerina who could make an artistic and aesthetic impression on me. . . . With a smile, Liszt replied: 'Perhaps we both lack the requisite sense for it. I have known so many excellent men who were enthusiastic about the art of the dance, that my own indifference I must attribute to myself. As for the rest, it is always a pretty sight when a beautiful woman appears before us in a dress which begins too late above and finishes too early below!'

Zichy, 30 December. When I visited Liszt, he was holding Arnold Ruge's book *Religion de l'incroyant* in his hands. 'This is an interesting book you have sent me, my dear Géza,' he said, 'but the author's views are opposed to those of my ecclesiastical authorities, and, as you know, every authority is always right.' He smiled, and gave me a book by De Maistre, one rationally written and very calming. Then the great man went to the window and for a long time gazed out. It was a dark afternoon and a few snowflakes were wafting along the street. All at once he came over to me, took me by the hand and spoke very softly: 'The year is coming to an end, and we must be prepared for anything. Who knows whether I shall live another one? I should like to ask you something: on the short path I have still before me—remain my friend!' Impetuously I embraced the great man, and could only nod 'yes'. He understood, and believed me. The room grew darker and darker. I sat beside him, and he spoke about art, human misery, politics, religion, history, about every aspect of life; and I felt as though I were standing on a lofty mountain top from which I could see the whole world spread out below me. Liszt is a totality, a microcosm in the full sense of the word.[14]

1877

Liszt to Princess Carolyne. Budapest, 14 January. You have a passion for the Great—and you reproach Hegel and Cardinal Antonelli with having not been great enough! I listen to what you say—and fail to understand! Baptism gave me for a patron saint, Francis of Paola, of obscure origins and founder of the Order of Minims. He fasted, mortified the flesh, did not write down his sermons, and concerned himself very little with literature. Your patron, St Charles Borromeo, scion of an illustrious family, early became a cardinal and so took part in the government of the Church. He even took an interest in music, and supported the reform of the Sistine Chapel which was allowed at that time, as desired by Palestrina. While fasting and mortifying the flesh, just like St Francis of Paola, and taking 'Humilitas' as his motto—he remained Archbishop of Milan and *Porporato*.* Our differences of opinion are best explained by our respective patron saints.[1]

To Olga von Meyendorff, 28 January. So long as there is work to be done, I still feel relaxed and in fairly good form. For the rest, I am overcome by indescribable depression and have reached the point where Carthusians and Trappists often seem garrulous to me.

From Rome† I receive nothing but superb admonitions in the finest style. I answer these by an increasing devotion to the penitent thief; his cross was close to that of Our Lord Jesus—may all hearts bless him!—and the penitent thief administered justice to himself with the words: 'I deserved my punishment.' This confession earned him the divine promise, in which I have complete faith.[2]

Géza Zichy. In the evening of 30 January I found Liszt in the merriest of moods in the company of Martha Remmert. All at once the door flew open

* 'One clothed in purple', hence a cardinal.
† That is, from Princess Carolyne.

and a short, plump girl rushed in. It was Vera Timanova,* who was so pleased to see the Master again that she could not utter a word but only give vent to ejaculations and bursts of laughter. . . . A few days later her concert took place; she played with great success. A young female violin virtuoso† took part too. After the concert there was supper at the Master's. On his right sat Frau von Vörös, a highly intelligent old lady who delighted Liszt with her caustic wit. His nickname for her was Baby—something she most certainly was not. On his left was Fräulein H, who had played at the concert. In her conversation she sought to appear still younger and more inexperienced than she was, telling us that her favourite reading consisted of children's stories and fairy tales, that she still took her favourite doll to bed with her, and that whenever she played well her father gave her a bag of sweets. Liszt had sincere doubts about all this. When a gentleman began to talk of love, and the young lady asked most affectedly, 'What is that then?'—the old Olympian burst out laughing: '*Liebes Fräulein*, this evening you played the violin rather well; why do you now wish to play the *ingénue* rather badly?' Whereupon he rose and turned to cards. For his sake I had learnt whist, and, I admit, often cheated. Liszt was very indignant when he lost, and to make sure that he usually won Frau von Vörös and I valiantly exchanged cards under the table. In this dubious art we achieved an admirable dexterity, and, which was the main thing, Liszt never noticed. . . .

At the twenty-sixth meeting held to discuss the performance of *St Elisabeth* [5 March, at the Vigadó] there was general consternation: music dealers, orchestra, and choir all made unbelievable pecuniary demands, the total costs coming to about 3,000 gulden. The secretary of the committee informed the Master, who was furious, and no one dared approach him. Thrusting an old pistol into my pocket, I hurried to him. On entering, I offered him the pistol with the words: 'You have no weapons. I have brought you one in case you wish to shoot me!' Liszt embraced me and said: 'These conditions are quite unacceptable, this haggling over money thoroughly unpleasant.' I spoke consolingly and begged him not to excite himself. 'You have only to conduct. Should there be a financial deficit, I shall cover it!'—'What are you thinking of? *I* shall see to it!' said Liszt in the greatest excitement. 'What a business! We are going to the dogs with our music. I came to Budapest to be useful. I want to raise Hungarian music culture to a higher level and train competent pupils—and all they can do is hinder me. My noble-minded King has provided for me; I shall show myself grateful! Charity I cannot, wish not to, and shall not

* The Russian pianist Vera Victorovna Timanova (1855–1942), one of the most talented of Liszt's women pupils. In a letter at this time he referred to her 'fingers of steel and seductive Slav personality'.

† Undoubtedly the 17-year-old violinist Bertha Haft, who was on a concert tour with Timanova and the soprano Anna Maria d'Orgeny.

accept! No charity, Géza, no charity!' These last words Liszt shrieked, and tears started to his eyes. 'But *lieber Meister*,' I sought to calm him, 'how can you take these trifles so seriously! You have lived *for* Art; these poor people on the other hand must live *on* Art. That they wish to make as much out of it as possible is quite understandable. I try to get the highest price I can for my wheat and pigs, but that does not make me a bad man. Believe me, every musician, good and bad alike, reveres you; but many sincerely regret that you have written such long and difficult works—for the taste of most musicians of the kind is for easy works which are soon over!' Liszt had to smile at that. Then he calmed down and we discussed the musical evenings which were to be held at my home. Later we drove to the fortress for a meal. On the way we took a look at the old church, and I pointed to the glorious old portals, which were partly walled up. Vexed to see it, Liszt remarked: 'It was not the Turks who perpetrated this. You wouldn't believe how silly our Princes of the Church are in matters of Art.'[3]

Liszt to Princess Carolyne, 7 March. I am greatly distressed to find you accusing me of ingratitude. If I thought I deserved this reproach, nothing would be left to me but to die at the very earliest. Having to bear the shame of ingratitude seems to me to be a fate worse than the forced labour of a galley slave! You also take me to task for not writing about what I am doing. Alas! I am hardly interested in my existence any more, and do not find that its details make an agreeable communication! During these last four months my time has been spent in reading about a thousand letters and notes—and in replying as well as I can to the most urgent of them. My best hours are those spent teaching at the new Academy of Music. Four times a week, from 4.00 to 6.00 p.m., I teach about fifteen artists of both sexes—some of whom are already eminent talents—to play the piano and to understand music. In addition, I have been to about twenty concerts and a dozen opera performances.[4]

On 11 March Liszt left for Vienna, where on Friday the 16th, at a concert for that city's Beethoven monument, he was soloist* in the Fifth Piano Concerto and the Choral Fantasy, and also accompanied Caroline Gomperz-Bettelheim in the Scottish songs. 'His touch superb as ever, the quiet passages enchanting,' was Eduard von Bauernfeld's opinion. 'In the trill and the powerful passages, no longer his old strength. On the other hand, he was calmer, played the fool less than he used to. His accompaniment of the Scottish songs was matchless, as was his playing of the Choral Fantasy.'

* Despite an injured finger, as he remarked to August Göllerich some years later: 'I played the E flat Concerto without using the fourth finger of my right hand, which had been cut that morning when I was being shaved.' This handicap, and lack of 'his old strength', doubtless contributed to the disappointment felt by the 11-year-old Ferruccio Busoni (1866–1924), who apparently found the performance cold and uninspiring. Later an outstanding Liszt player and editor, Busoni was also taken to the Schottenhof to play to the great man—but unfortunately no account of the meeting has survived.

The Austrian composer Wilhelm Kienzl (1857–1941). It can readily be understood what a sensation was caused by this pianistic reappearance of the venerable, world-famed artist, already a legendary figure. Everyone wanted to have seen and heard him. And so the rehearsals, to which the public were admitted on payment, took on the look of sold-out concerts. . . . If to many he seemed a man risen from the dead, he was now indeed a transfigured and purified spirit, far removed from mere virtuosity, one for whom the outer expression of his inner interpretation was facilitated by sovereign mastery of technique. The impression I received from his performance of the E flat Concerto of Beethoven remains ineffaceable. It was an absolutely personal interpretation, yet without any violation, wholly in the spirit of Beethoven. Liszt played the work in such a free, improvisatory manner, that it was as though he were composing it under the very eyes of his listeners. I remember as if it were yesterday how he rendered the main theme of the last movement, storming titanically up the keyboard in the eight-bar ascent, slowing down slightly and languishing humorously in the falling octaves, only to storm up anew in the two bars following.[5]

Later that evening a banquet in Liszt's honour, arranged by the President of the Beethoven Monument Committee, was held at the Hotel Imperial. Among the guests was Brahms. The next day Liszt was presented by the Mayor of Vienna, in expression of the city's gratitude, with the gold Redeemer Medal. He also paid a courtesy call on the Emperor and Empress of Brazil and attended the Artists' Evening at the Musikverein.

Via Nuremberg and a day with Lina Ramann, hard at work on his biography, he arrived on 24 March at Bayreuth, where he stayed with the Wagners until 3 April. The eve of his departure for Weimar Cosima described as: 'A lovely, cherished day, on which I can thank Heaven for the comforting feeling that nothing . . . could ever separate us three.'

Princess Carolyne to Baron Augusz. Rome, 29 March. Since '70, what has been happening? What is Liszt doing, far away from me, since the time when his letters started resembling a correspondence that one would be ready to drop? He is no longer writing anything. He is sterilizing his genius prematurely, for I do not believe that his powers failed him before he left off making the most of the talent God gave him. Yes indeed, had I been able, I would have followed him when he left Rome; but as Monsignor Haynald knows, I could not. Besides, could I foresee . . . that things would turn out so badly for him, at Pest and elsewhere? Could I foresee that Rome would be implacable in its harshness and injustice towards him. That the Pontiff who *led him into temptation* by according him the unparalleled honour of a personal visit and of a thousand little accessory favours, would abandon him without scruple, after having caused him to take so conclusive a step as that of donning clerical garb? While he and I were dreaming of the reform of *Christian art*, of the *language of the Church*, whether at Rome or at Pest, the College of Cardinals and the entire priesthood could only treat him shamefully!!!

Among my hurts and bitternesses, one of the most intense is the thought that my letters upset and agitate him, that he would rather not receive them. But I have not promised God to be nice to him—I have promised to be useful to him, and not to abandon him, to support him *by word and deed*! The deed is always welcome, not always the word! This I know, but it will not make me change my ways until he changes his.

And may God take pity on me and make him give up this vagabond life he is leading![6]

Living in Weimar at this time was the explorer *Gerhard Rohlfs* (1831–96), who had made Liszt's acquaintance some years earlier. 'Liszt fascinated me at once. He could not really be called handsome, but in his eyes there was a Something which it was impossible to resist. Later, when I got to know him better, I was able to test this power often, in increasing measure. When, in particular, he sat at the piano, surrounded by a large crowd of pupils and followers, and turned his gaze on one, the effect could be utterly bewitching. It was not I alone, a mere male, who found this to be so; it was exactly the same with everyone, young and old, male and female.'

One day I had invited the Grand Duke to be my guest; and punctually, as was his wont, he arrived at five. All the other guests had of course got there beforehand—only Liszt was lacking. After ten minutes I gave my wife a sign and she offered the Grand Duke her arm to take him into the dining-room, saying: 'We were actually waiting for Liszt, but he seems not to be coming.'—'Oh, then let us wait further, dear lady; Liszt does not always arrive punctually, but that matters not at all.' And so now we had to wait, until after about half an hour I saw Liszt coming quite slowly up the narrow lane to our house. . . . At last he had arrived, but he in no way apologized for his lateness, behaving indeed as though nothing had happened. He must have experienced some vexation, for he was—which happened very rarely—in the worst possible mood. We went to table, and my wife sat next to the Grand Duke and a venerable old gentleman to whom I had assigned the place in the mean time, believing that Liszt was not coming—but about which he was now most indignant. 'Who is that old gentleman?' he asked me rather loudly. When I gave him my explanation, it by no means softened his wrath; on the contrary, his mood *remained* exceptionally bad.

In the course of conversation the Grand Duke expressed his enthusiasm for the violin virtuoso Sarasate, who had come to Weimar for the first time* and the previous day played at court. 'Sarasate is not a great artist,

* The Spanish violin virtuoso and composer Pablo de Sarasate (1844–1908) first played at Weimar on 31 Dec. 1876, but Liszt did not hear him until the violinist's appearance in Budapest two months later. Although it was still being discussed in the newspapers long afterwards, the Bremerhaven disaster had actually occurred in Dec. 1875, when Liszt was in Rome. The juxtaposition by Rohlfs of these meetings and conversations with Liszt is bound therefore to be chronologically inexact, but not for that reason inaccurate in substance.

merely puffed up,' said Liszt. 'But, *lieber Meister*, permit me to say that he played quite excellently and pleased me exceedingly.'—'Your Royal Highness,' retorted Liszt so loudly that the whole table could hear him, 'certainly understands very well the art of ruling, but as far as the art of music is concerned I believe my judgement to be the better, and in my opinion he is not a great artist.'—'Speaking generally you may indeed be right, *lieber Meister*, but I stick to my opinion.' Liszt's all but rude attack on the Grand Duke had on their friendly relationship not the slightest effect whatsoever.

Soon after this dinner I had a very serious conversation with the Master. The frightful disaster at Bremerhaven* had just occurred, in which hundreds of innocent people had become the victims of an American. Visiting Liszt, I found him reading the report. 'It is enough to drive one to despair,' said the Master; 'one could begin to doubt God's justice.'—'Do you then believe in a personal God?' I asked him. The Master looked at me and said: 'If you mean a personal God such as has been portrayed by Raphael—no, I cannot believe in a God like that. But I do believe in a personified, or, if you like, personless justice which compensates for all that happens here on earth.'—'If you believe that,' I replied, 'then who will bring back to life those innocent people—for I assume that the majority of those involved had committed no great sin—and who will do justice to the thousands who are killed daily, the number rising to hundreds of thousands in time of war?' The Master became cross and merely said: 'We must leave that to the inscrutable will of God.'—'That is an easy answer, and it means that you do believe in a personal God, for your reasoning is that of a Protestant theologian.' Liszt pensively repeated what he had said, adding: 'It is indeed an immense, unfathomable mystery.' . . .

Liszt was a zealous Catholic, and he put into practice his fellowship of the faith by attending early mass every morning. This marked a strange dichotomy in his character, since he was an eager reader of and subscriber to the *Revue scientifique*, and someone who always kept himself up to date with the latest theories and developments. And so I had to lend him several of the more recent scientific books: Darwin's *The Descent of Man*, Wallace's *Contributions to the Theory of Natural Selection*, and so on. He was thoroughly modern in outlook, seeking to keep abreast of everything.[7]

On 15 May Liszt went to Hanover to attend a meeting of the Allgemeine Deutsche Musikverein held between the 19th and 24th. Several of his works were

* A German ship, the *Mosel*, had been about to leave Bremerhaven harbour at the start of a voyage to New York, when a case of dynamite among the passengers' luggage had exploded. The quay was thronged with people, and the carnage was accordingly terrific, the whole ship being covered with blood, pieces of flesh, and other human remains. An American named Thomson had planted the dynamite, intending that it should explode and sink the ship in mid ocean (after he himself had disembarked at Southampton), enabling him to collect a large sum for goods he had insured. After the premature explosion he committed suicide. It is thought that he may have accounted in similar fashion for another ship, the *City of Boston*, which had disappeared on a voyage to America five years earlier.

performed, including the *Concerto pathétique*, the Dante Symphony, and *St Elisabeth* (the last part of which Liszt was himself obliged to conduct after the drunken conductor had fallen off the podium). To these official items were added the Concerto in A—'brilliantly played by Pinner'—and the Legend of St Cecilia. Cornelius's *Barber of Bagdad*, so ill received at its première in 1858, was also performed, and heard by the composer's widow. (Cornelius had died in 1874.) 'This time there was much applause,' wrote Liszt, 'especially from the musically knowledgeable.' On the 31st he returned to Weimar.

Liszt to Princess Carolyne. Weimar, 15 June. Without complaining, I often feel pain in continuing to live; health of the body remains to me, that of the soul is lacking. *Tristis est anima mea*! However, to my numerous real and alleged faults will never be added that of ingratitude, the very worst of all! From the bottom of my heart I bless you for persevering for thirty years in actively wishing for me the Good, the Beautiful, and the True. In this, you are heroic and sublime—and I feel unworthy to unlace your shoes.[8]

From the time of his visits to Russia in the 1840s and his first acquaintance with the music of Glinka, Liszt had been greatly interested in Russian music, and his opinion of the younger generation of composers at St Petersburg was very high.* To Carolyne he would write (30 July 1879), after naming Rimsky-Korsakov, Balakirev, Borodin, Cui, and Lyadov: 'I am attracted to their works, which deserve serious consideration. Fashionable society in Petersburg as yet scarcely knows the names of these gentlemen . . . but it is my belief that the five musicians I have named are ploughing a more fruitful furrow than the belated imitators of Mendelssohn and Schumann.'

On Sunday, 1 July, he made the acquaintance of Alexander Borodin (1833–87), whose First Symphony he already knew and admired. A chemist by profession, Borodin was in Germany on a scientific expedition, but made a special excursion to Weimar to see Liszt.

Borodin to his wife Catherine (née Protopopova), 3 July. Scarcely had I sent in my card when there arose before me, as though out of the ground, a tall figure with a long nose, a long black frock-coat and long white hair.

'You have written a fine symphony,' growled the tall figure, in a resonant voice and in excellent French; and he stretched out a long hand and a long arm. 'Welcome, I am delighted to see you. Only two days ago I played your symphony to the Grand Duke, who was charmed with it. The first movement is perfect. Your Andante is a *chef d'œuvre*. The Scherzo is enchanting . . . and then this passage is so ingenious.'

And then his long fingers began to peck (*picorer*), to use a picturesque

* He was in his turn one of the Western composers most admired by the Balakirev circle; and among the congratulatory messages sent to him at his jubilee in 1873 had been a telegram from Balakirev, Bessel, Borodin, Cui, Mussorgsky, Rimsky-Korsakov, Sherbachov, and Stasov. It ran: 'A group of Russians, devoted to art, believing in its everlasting progress and aspiring to participate in this progress, warmly greet you on the day of your jubilee. As a composer and performer of genius who has broadened the boundaries of art, as a great leader in the struggle against the old and routine, as an indefatigable artist before whose immense and lasting achievements we bow.'

expression which Mussorgsky* made use of to describe the progression of distant intervals, *pizzicato*, in the Scherzo and Finale of my first symphony. He ran on incessantly; his strong hand caught my own and held me down to a sofa where there was nothing left for me to do but nod approval and lose myself in thanks.

The fine face of the old man, with its energetic, vivacious features, was uplifted before me, while he talked incessantly, overwhelming me with questions, passing from French to German and vice versa. When I told him I was only a Sunday musician, he answered me with ready wit, 'But Sunday is always a feast day, and you have every right to officiate.'

He complimented me upon my piano arrangement, adding that my *pianisme* revealed an experienced musician and a complete command of modern technical science. He made but one criticism, relative to a passage which could be made easier for the left hand, just where the fingers peck like birds and the performer's hands cross, as they do in Madame Rimsky-Korsakov's† arrangements. I modified this passage in accordance with his advice.

When he questioned me on the success of my symphony, on its reception, etc., I told him that I saw many faults in it myself, that I was often criticised for my want of experience, for excessive modulation, for going beyond bounds, etc. Liszt constantly interrupted me: 'Heaven forbid! Do not touch it; alter nothing. Your modulations are neither extravagant nor faulty. You have gone far, indeed, and this is precisely your special merit; but you have never made any mistakes. Do not listen to those who would hold you back; believe me, I entreat you, you are on the right road. Your artistic instinct is such that you need not fear to be original. Remember that the same advice was given to Beethoven and Mozart in their day. If they had followed it, they would never have become masters.' I could do nothing but thank him confusedly in French and German.

He asked me about Korsakov, whom he esteems very highly, and told

* Music by Modest Mussorgsky (1839–81) was likewise known to and esteemed by Liszt. In May 1873, the St Petersburg music-publisher V. V. Bessel (1842–1907) had visited Weimar and supplied Liszt with recent publications by the leading Russian composers, leaving with him *inter alia* Mussorgsky's *Nursery* song cycle, which Liszt had greeted with delight. On learning of this, Mussorgsky had been almost incredulous. 'If the event is to be believed, how happy Russian music should be, to find such recognition from an ace like Liszt. . . . How many worlds might be revealed to me in conversations with him!' Nevertheless, when invited by Stasov on a visit to Germany and Liszt, Mussorgsky had declined with regret, pleading above all the necessity for starting work on his *Khovanshchina*. But Stasov later offered another explanation: 'He couldn't quite trust Liszt's sympathy and was surprised by it. Not he alone, but we also, many of his comrades and friends. Why were we all surprised? Because we were still unfamiliar with that great sun-like beneficence and profound mother-like loving nature of Liszt . . . none of us comprehended what life-giving and loving strength resided in that man, how he understood and valued many of those to whom the rest of Europe was deaf and blind.'

† Nadezhda Nikolayevna Rimskaya-Korsakova (*née* Purgold) (1848–1919), an excellent pianist and musician whom Rimsky-Korsakov had married in 1872.

me of the horrible failure of *Sadko* at Vienna. Rubinstein, who conducted, said when he brought him the score: 'Here, this work proved a fiasco, but I am sure it will be to your taste.' In truth it pleased him much, and he thinks a great deal of it.

He asked also about Balakirev and Cui, and wanted news about the performance of *Christus* at the concert of the Free School.* When I told him that the choruses went well, but that the *Stabat mater* [*speciosa*] could be given only with harmonium accompaniment instead of organ, he said: 'That is a great difficulty. I shall make some alterations; the organ must come in with the voices and accompany them throughout.' I told him Korsakov had had recourse to another method. 'I can guess,' Liszt broke in; 'he made the harmonium enter a little before the voices. I know what conducting means. He took a very intelligent course.'

Then, changing the subject: 'It is a pity,' he said, showing me *Islamey*,† 'that you did not hear this played by your countrywoman, Mademoiselle Vera Timanova. Today I have had a musical matinée, and she just happened to play this piece.' Afterwards I was told that when he asked her to play this composition, Liszt had said: 'Mademoiselle Vera, would you kindly decide the Eastern question in your own way?' She played *Islamey* at the last audience of the Grand Duke. 'Do you know,' continued Liszt, 'that the Grand Duke is well acquainted with Russian music and appreciates it highly. Nevertheless, here in Germany it is evidently not liked. You know Germany; it is full of composers. I am lost in a sea of music which threatens to submerge me entirely; but Heavens, how insipid it all is, not one living idea! With you there exists a vitalising stream. Sooner or later, though probably later, this stream will make a way for itself in Germany.'

Then he scolded me like a father for not having published my scores; this, he said, was indispensable, not only on my own account, but in order that they might be circulated, they must be performed, etc. He also said: 'Judging from your card you seem to be an authority in chemistry, but how, when and where did you succeed in acquiring so much musical knowledge? Where have you studied? Certainly not in Germany.'

When I told him I had never been to any Academy, he began to laugh.

* At St Petersburg on 20 Mar. (NS) this year, when excerpts from the oratorio had been conducted by Rimsky-Korsakov.

† Balakirev's brilliant 'Oriental fantasy' for piano, dedicated to and first performed by Nikolai Rubinstein, but, according to Balakirev himself, 'made known in the musical world thanks to Liszt'. Leader of the 'mighty handful', Mili Balakirev (1837–1910) greatly admired Liszt, and in 1884 dedicated to him his symphonic poem *Tamara*. Twenty years after Liszt's death he wrote: 'I cannot imagine that after Liszt it is possible for the art of the piano to be taken any further—unless this instrument be *considerably improved*, enabling some future genius, on the scale of a Liszt, to advance "pianistic instrumentation" still more. Of such geniuses, however, only one a century is born!' Balakirev's veneration for the Hungarian master was shared by his great pupil Sergei Lyapunov (1859–1924), whose *Etudes d'exécution transcendante* complete the key sequence begun by Liszt in his own. The twelfth and last of the set is entitled 'Elegy in memory of Franz Liszt'.

'There you are lucky, dear master,' he said, adding: 'Work, always continue to work. Even if your compositions are not performed, not published, even if they have no success, believe me they will make themselves an honourable way. You have an original talent; listen to no man and work on in your own fashion.'

I thanked him for his kindness. 'But I am not paying you compliments,' he broke in, with a shade of annoyance. 'I am too old to say anything but what I mean. That is why I am not altogether loved here. But can I say that they turn out good music when I find it insipid, and lacking in inspiration and vitality?' . . .

It would be impossible to reproduce literally, or even to recall, everything that Liszt said in this comparatively short time. He speaks both French and German very fluently, rather loudly, with vivacity, animation and volubility. He might be taken for a Frenchman. He never sits still for a moment, but walks about and gesticulates; there is nothing of the priest about him.

Among other things he told me that Napravnik's* trio had given him much pleasure. At a first reading it struck him as long and wearisome, but after repeated playing he found it excellently written and highly effective. He asked me who had played this trio in Russia. I mentioned Goldstein. 'Don't know him,' Liszt interrupted abruptly. 'He is a pianist from the Leipzig Conservatorium.'—'That is no recommendation. They have turned out a number of mediocrities.' . . .

The next day we went to the cathedral at Jena. . . . We had, by good fortune, hit upon the hour of rehearsal for the concert which was to take place at four; it was now a little past ten. You can imagine with what pleasure we listened. . . .

About twelve o'clock there was a great commotion near the door. 'The Master is coming, the Master is here!' The organisers of the concert, in their black coats, hastened forward. The great door was thrown open, displaying the dark and characteristic figure of Liszt in the dress of an abbé. On his arm was the Baroness Meyendorff. . . . She is still young and very attractive in appearance, though far from being a beauty. A widow, she has made her home in Weimar, and Liszt lives in her house like one of the family. He was followed by a train of pupils, chiefly feminine; the masculine element was represented only by Zarembski, a highly-gifted Polish pianist. This galaxy made their inroad into church without any regard for the sanctity of the place, chattering in every language, with a noise resembling a steam saw-mill. There were German, Dutch and Polish women, without counting our compatriot, Mademoiselle Vera Timanova. . . .

* E. F. Napravnik (1839–1916), a composer and conductor of Czech origin who lived in Russia. His Fantasy on Russian Folk Melodies was dedicated to Liszt.

Liszt conducts with his hand, without a baton, quietly, with precision and certainty, and makes his remarks with great gentleness, calm and conciseness.

When it came to the numbers for pianoforte, he descended into the choir and soon his grey head appeared behind the instrument. The powerful sustained tones of the piano rolled like waves through the Gothic vaults of the old temple. It was divine! What sonority, power, fulness! What a *pianissimo*, what a *morendo*! We were transported. When it came to Chopin's 'Funeral March' it was evident that the piece was not arranged. Liszt improvised at the piano, while the organ and 'cello were played from written parts. With each entrance of the theme it was something different; but it is difficult to imagine what he made of it.

The organ lingered *pianissimo* on the harmonies in the bars in thirds. The piano, with pedal, gave out the full harmonies, but also *pianissimo*. The 'cello sang the theme. The effect was prodigious. It was like the distant sound of a funeral knell, that rings out again before the first vibration has quite died away. I have never heard anything like it. And what a *crescendo*! We were in the seventh Heaven! . . .

Later, at the hotel.

Zarembski came up to me and said many pleasant things about my symphony, speaking Russian with a strong Polish accent. He was there with his *fiancée*,* a very pretty, but coquettish, young lady from Berlin. . . .

Two o'clock struck and we moved towards the dining-room. The table was laid and decked with flowers.

Liszt made his entrance with the organisers of the concert, the inevitable Baroness Meyendorff, Lassen, and several others. 'Ah, welcome!' he exclaimed on catching sight of me.

He then introduced me to the Baroness, to Lassen, and to his friend Gille, the chief promoter of the concert. My place was kept on the left hand of Liszt, who took the head of the table; the Baroness sat on his right hand, opposite me. She immediately took the lead in the conversation, related a number of things, and told me that it was she herself who, with Liszt, had played my symphony to the Grand Duke two years ago. Like Lassen she knew every detail of it. Liszt was most agreeable and talked a great deal. He poured out wine for his neighbours and joked with them. He asked many particulars about Russian music, about which the Baroness seemed well-informed . . . and what success my second symphony had won.

* Johanna Wenzel, also a pupil of Liszt, from whom some years earlier she had received this wise exhortation: 'I beg of you earnestly no longer to think of having the barbarous operation performed upon your fingers; rather all your life long play every octave and chord wrong than commit such a mad attack upon your hands.'

'Will you be staying long in Jena?' he inquired. 'I am going to buttonhole you. Come and see me again in Weimar; we will play your symphony.' I assured him I was incapable of playing with him.

'Well, then, the Baroness will kindly play it with Herr Lassen,' he said. 'Have you a good publisher? I will introduce you to Herr Kahnt,* my publisher in Leipzig; he might be of use to you.' And he called Kahnt to introduce him to me. . . .

In the Cathedral I had no occasion to trouble about the place I had kept for myself. I remained in Liszt's company. As his name was not upon the bills with those of the other performers, I asked him who would be at the piano. He muttered something under his breath, and said it would be Naumann, an organist who had just come. Why? I have not the least idea. For afterwards we could perfectly well distinguish Liszt's grey head behind the piano, and his rendering of Chopin's 'Funeral March' was totally different from what we had heard at the rehearsal. It was evidently an improvisation. 'He always tells his little fibs,' said Mademoiselle Timanova. 'He will never admit that he is going to play. He is a curious old man.'

At the end of the concert, when the Grand Duke had withdrawn, after having exchanged a few words with Liszt, the public unceremoniously surrounded the Master and stared at him unblushingly. Our young friends followed their example. Gille then came up and invited me to go to his house with Liszt's party. In fact, the whole procession set off for his house, which was some distance from the Cathedral. Liszt led the way with the Baroness, we followed with Gille, and the Master's pupils brought up the rear. In spite of the rain we were accompanied by a compact crowd. Passers-by, soldiers, students, merchants, officers, citizens, all respectfully saluted Liszt. Our young scamps were not ashamed to march by his side and stare at him without restraint. . . .[9]

A few days later Liszt went to Berlin, where he stayed at the Ministry with the Schleinitzes. He also saw his old friend Kurd von Schlözer once again, and, at Potsdam on 7 July, waited upon the German Crown Prince and Princess† (subsequently the Emperor and Empress Frederick), as he reported to Carolyne in his letter of the 14th, from Weimar.

I stayed with them for about two hours, a few piano pieces being played without effort. The Crown Prince possesses a lofty, correct, and kindly simplicity, very becoming for great sovereigns. Nor will his wife let him down. She showed me an album containing the autographs of Pius IX, Cardinal Antonelli, and others. I shall speak to you further about this interview, very flattering for me. The Prince and Princess openly admire Wagner, which straightaway put me at ease in their presence. I remember

* C. F. Kahnt (1823–97), editor for many years of the *Neue Zeitschrift für Musik* and publisher of a number of Liszt's works.

† Victoria, eldest child of Queen Victoria and Prince Albert.

that, at the Villa d'Este, Queen Olga of Würtemberg told me that no sensible person thought anything of the *Ring des Nibelungen*, an absurd work and impossible to perform, according to the most learned professors of aesthetics. I permitted myself to observe very humbly to Her Majesty that infallibility was not the attribute of professors![10]

Alexander Borodin to his wife. Jena, 12 July. At half-past four [Monday, 9 July, at Weimar] I went to Liszt's, and on the advice of the Baroness I announced myself as somebody come specially from Vienna to take part in the lesson. Otherwise, she assured me, the servant would absolutely refuse me admittance.

I went in. A Dutch pianist was performing a piece by Tausig. Liszt was standing by the piano, surrounded by fifteen pupils. 'Ah! there you are,' exclaimed the Master, giving me his hand; 'but why did you not come yesterday? I would have shown you that I still have it in me to play Chopin's violoncello sonata.'

He then introduced me to his pupils. 'They are all celebrated pianists,' he said; 'or if they are not yet, they will become such.' The young folk all began to laugh. . . . 'We have put off our lesson until today,' said Liszt, 'and do you know who is the cause? Little Mademoiselle Vera. She does as she pleases with me. She wished the lesson to be today; there was nothing to be done but to put it off.' These words were received with a general burst of laughter.

The lesson went on. From time to time Liszt would interrupt his pupils, play himself, or make remarks, generally characterised by humour, wit and kindliness, which drew a smile from the young students, and even from the one to whom the observation was addressed. He did not get ruffled, or lose his temper, and avoided everything that might hurt the feelings of the pupil. 'Try to play it *à la* Vera,' he said, when he wanted a pupil to try one of those tricks of fingering to which Mademoiselle Vera was obliged to have recourse when her hands were too small to master a difficulty.

He laughed at their want of success. If one of the pupils said that he could not manage to execute a certain passage, Liszt would make him sit down to the piano, saying: 'Well, now, show us how you can *not* play it.' In all his familiar observations he used the greatest delicacy, an extreme gentleness, and invariably endeavoured to spare the pupils' dignity.

When it came to Mademoiselle Timanova's turn, he made her play his Rhapsody in B minor [S244/5], which she was studying for her concert at Kissingen. After a few little remarks he sat down to the piano and played a few passages from the piece with his iron fingers. 'This must be as solemn as a triumphal march,' he cried. Springing up from his chair and putting his arm through Mademoiselle Timanova's, he paced solemnly up and down the room, humming the theme of the Rhapsody. The young people began to laugh.

Timanova resumed the piece, paying attention to his remarks. Liszt leaned towards me and said: 'She is a splendid fellow, that little Vera.' Then addressing himself to her: 'If you play like that at the concert, you will see what ovations! But they will not be more than you deserve.' Tears of joy ran down her blushing cheeks. Tapping her kindly on the cheek, Liszt kissed her on the forehead while she kissed his hand; this is the custom between Liszt and his pupils. He has a way of tapping them sharply on the shoulder to attract their attention. All his relations with his pupils are simple and familiar. There is nothing of the professor about him; he is a father, or rather a grandfather among his grandchildren.

Occasionally, however, a malicious irony lurks in his remarks, especially when he speaks of the Leipzig school. 'Do not play like that,' he said to a pupil; 'one would think you came from Leipzig. There, they would tell you that this passage is written in augmented sixths, and would imagine that was sufficient; but they would never show you how it ought to be played.'

Liszt never sets pieces for study; he allows his pupils full liberty of selection. At the same time, they generally ask his advice, to avoid being interrupted, after the first few notes, by an observation of this kind: 'What a strange taste to play such stuff!'

He does not give much attention to technique or fingering, but occupies himself especially with the rendering and expression. With rare exceptions, however, his pupils possess a great deal of execution, but belong, in this repect, to very different schools.

Liszt impressed me above all by his personality.

The lesson lasted two hours and a half. Mademoiselle Timanova begged Liszt to put off the next lesson from Friday to Saturday, on account of her concert. 'This is the way she always gets over me,' said Liszt. 'How can I refuse? She is always right, and makes me go her way. Well,' he asked the pupils, 'are you willing to postpone till Saturday?' 'Yes, yes,' was the unanimous reply. 'Well, then, be it so! Till Saturday.'

He appeared particularly prepossessed in favour of Mademoiselle Timanova. When she played really well he exclaimed: 'Bravo, not one of you can play like this!'

He escorted his pupils to the hall and helped them to dress. The ladies kissed his hand as they took their leave, and he saluted them on the forehead. It is evident that he has a weakness for the fair sex. 'What excellent creatures,' he said when we were alone. 'If you only knew what life there is in them!' 'If they have life in them, dear Master, it is you who have created it,' I replied. . . .

I was invited to tea by the Baroness for half-past eight. Having secured a room at the Thuringerhof, I started for her house; Liszt was already there. A servant announced that tea was served. Liszt gave the Baroness his arm and we went into the dining-room. The mistress of the house presented me to her son, aged sixteen, and we sat down to a richly-appointed table, I on the right, Liszt on the left hand, of the Baroness; there were no other guests. The Baroness made tea herself with a kettle and spirit lamp, English fashion. We had all manner of *zakouski*,* wine and beer, just as we have at home. But the service was much better than in Russia. Liszt talked a great deal. We discussed music.

After tea our hostess led the way to the piano in the drawing-room and gave Liszt one of his own Rhapsodies, asking him to show us how such and such passages should be played. It was a feminine ruse, but an innocent deception; Liszt began to laugh. 'You want me to play it,' he said; 'very well, but first I want to play Monsieur Borodin's symphony with the composer. Do you play treble or bass?' he asked me. I refused absolutely, and eventually persuaded the Baroness to sit down to the piano. She consented to play the Andante only. Liszt played the bass. How interesting to me was this performance to which I was the sole listener! But Liszt was not satisfied. 'The Baroness is very kind,' he said, 'but I want to play with you. It is impossible that you cannot play your own symphony. You have arranged it so perfectly that I cannot believe that. Sit down there.' And without another word he took me by the hand and made me sit down to the bass, he himself taking the treble. I wished to protest. 'Play,' said the Baroness, 'or Liszt will be annoyed with you. I know him.'

I wanted to recommence the Andante that was open before me, but Liszt turned over the pages and we attacked the finale, then the Scherzo and the first movement. Thus we played the whole symphony with all the repeats. Liszt would not let me rest; after every movement he turned the pages, saying, 'Let us go on.' When I made mistakes, or omitted anything, he would say, 'Why did you not do that; it is so fine?'

When we had finished he repeated several passages, growing enthusiastic over their novelty and the freshness of the ideas. He subjected my symphony to a most discriminating criticism; according to him, the Andante is a perfect masterpiece. 'As to form,' he said, 'there is nothing superfluous; all is fine.'

He told me that he had given my modulations as models to his pupils. Referring to one or two specimens, he remarked that nothing like them was to be found in Beethoven or Bach, and that with all its novelty and originality the work defied criticism; it was so complete, so definite and of such a natural beauty. He particularly values the first movement and is very much delighted with its pedal-points, and especially the one on C. He said nothing particular about the other two movements, but gave me a few practical hints in case I should prepare a second edition; for instance, to write certain passages an octave lower, or *octava*, in order to facilitate the reading.

I recognised in this the results of an exhaustive study of my symphony, in

* Cold dishes, generally served in Russia before a meal.

which he had made pencil notes and corrected the printer's errors.

Finally, he told me that I wrote for the piano like a master, and that he was surprised to find I was not a pianist. 'This is not like the symphonies of our composers,' he said. 'I know whom you refer to,' interrupted the Baroness. 'We know, generally speaking, very little of your music,' he added, 'but at any rate you see that we have studied it thoroughly.'

Liszt and the Baroness then begged me to sing my romances, or to let them hear something from *Prince Igor*.* 'Glinka had no voice,' persisted the Baroness, 'yet he sang his own compositions.'

To put an end to their entreaties, I went through a short chorus from *Prince Igor*, which seemed to give them pleasure, and then in my turn I begged Liszt to play something. He played some of his Rhapsodies and a few other pieces. He did not play much, because it was getting late; but what a wonderful execution! What expression! What astonishing light and shade—*pianissimo*, *piano*, *forte*, *fortissimo*! What a *crescendo* and *diminuendo*, and what fire!

He made me promise to return to Weimar and let them hear my second symphony, and asked me if I had no manuscript to show him. It was arranged that I should return the following Saturday, that I should attend the lesson at his house and afterwards go to the Baroness; I was to stay in Weimar and be at his matinée on Sunday morning.

At midnight we took our leave, and I escorted Liszt, whose sight is not good, as far as his door. Nevertheless, he returned with me to the end of the street to show me the nearest way to my hotel.

I had heard Liszt under unhoped-for conditions! I was under a spell and could not sleep. The next morning I telegraphed to Bessel to send my second symphony and my songs to Liszt. . . .

Just fancy, in Weimar many people bow to me who do not know me, because they have seen me with Liszt; and the same in Jena. . . .

To the same, 18 July (reporting a visit to Weimar on the 14th). We began to discuss Rubinstein's scores, which were lying on the piano. Liszt sat down to play a few passages from them; among others, the overture, the dances, and a few fragments from *Nero*. I told him that the dances in *The Demon* were superior. 'Pass me the score of *The Demon*,' he said; 'I do not know those dances.' He played them all, and even repeated some passages. It reminded me so much of Balakirev's *soirées*. I was on Liszt's right hand turning the pages for him; Mademoiselle Timanova was on his left. What a delight to hear Liszt thus, in such a homely way!

He improvised new arrangements like Balakirev, sometimes altering the bass, sometimes the treble notes. By degrees there flowed from this improvisation one of those marvellous transcriptions in which the

* Borodin's unfinished opera, which after his death was completed and scored by Rimsky-Korsakov and Glazunov.

arrangement for piano surpasses the composition itself. Liszt extemporised for a long time. When we took our leave he detained me. 'We shall meet tonight at the Baroness's,' he said. 'Come and call for me, will you? We shall go together; you will find Zarembski here with me. I wish to go through your symphony with him in your presence. . . .'

By eight o'clock I was at Liszt's, where I found Zarembski in a black coat and white tie. I went through my symphony, Liszt playing bass and Zarembski treble. They played marvellously, especially in the Scherzo, where a quantity of details that are generally lost were given due prominence. Liszt, however, made a few slips owing to his failing sight. . . .

At Baroness Meyendorff's.

The Grand Duke made his entrance. He is a tall, middle-aged man. He wore a black frock-coat, a star on his breast, a white waistcoat and pearl-grey gloves. The introductions over, he offered me his hand and gave vent to a string of pleasant phrases which he had been keeping ready for use. He had a profound esteem for our School of Music, was very fond of our music, and was interested in its vitality; but, so far, he had only had occasion to make the acquaintance of Cui (whom he called Monsieur Coui), and that only very slightly, at Bayreuth; he was charmed to make mine, etc. I took refuge in thanks, and everybody moved towards the drawing-room, where stood the piano.

The Grand Duke was accompanied by a certain *Excellenz*, equally bedizened with decorations, and a lady-in-waiting, who kept on her gloves and bonnet the whole evening, even during tea and supper. Was it a rule of etiquette? I have no idea. We began with my symphony. I stood by the piano and turned over the pages. The Grand Duke, at a little distance, listened with earnest attention, exchanging glances at the most original and *piquant* passages with Liszt, who was aglow with delight, and in his turn smiled and shot triumphant glances towards me.

When it was over the Grand Duke was profuse in his compliments, and analysed various details of the symphony. 'The highest compliment I can pay you, Monsieur Borodin, is to say that your music, beautiful as it is, does not resemble anything we have heard before. Monsieur Borodin's symphony must certainly be given by the orchestra this year,' he added, addressing Liszt, who replied that there was nothing to prevent it, if they had the score. . . .

To the same. Marburg, 22 July. As my road lay through Weimar, I stopped once more at my Venusburg to see for the last time my elderly Venus—Liszt. First I went to bid the Baroness Meyendorff goodbye.

Last Thursday they had received from Bessel all my songs and my second symphony. The Baroness had read the latter with Liszt the evening before, and seemed very delighted. Liszt intended to have it performed the following day at his matinée, when the Grand Duke was to be present. The Baroness invited me to tea in the evening, when Liszt and I were to be the only guests, in order to run through my songs.

From her house I went on to the lesson at Liszt's, who was very pleased to see me again. 'Welcome, dear Borodin,' he said. 'Yesterday we played your second symphony. Suberb!' he exclaimed, kissing the tips of his long fingers. The lesson was over, but he detained me. He was expecting Zarembski, with whom he wanted to look through my symphony before the matinée next day. As soon as Zarembski had arrived, the indefatigable old man sat down to the piano. 'You shall play the Andante,' he said, 'then I shall take your place. I shall render the finale better than you,' he added, laughing. And indeed he played the finale with wild and unearthly spirit. I asked him to criticise, to give me his candid opinion and advice; I did not want compliments, I sought only real benefit from his criticism. 'Do not alter anything,' he said to me. 'Leave it just as it is. Its construction is perfectly logical. Generally speaking, the only advice I can give you is to follow your inclinations and listen to nobody. You are always lucid, intelligent and perfectly original. Recollect that Beethoven would never have become what he was, if he had listened to everybody. Remember Lafontaine's fable—"The Miller, his Son and his Donkey." Work in your own way and pay no attention to anyone, that is my advice, since you ask for it.' Then, analysing my symphony in detail, he said that the critics might find fault with me, for instance, for not presenting the second theme of the first movement *amoroso*, or something of that sort, but that they could not pretend in any case that my symphony was badly constructed, having regard to the elements upon which it was based. 'It is perfectly logical in construction, ' he repeated, passing from one movement to another. 'It is vain to say there is nothing new under the sun; this is quite new. You would not find this in any other composer,' continued the great master, instancing such and such a passage. 'Yesterday, a German came to call upon me and brought his third symphony. Showing him your work, I said, "We Germans are still a long way from this".' He suggested, however, a few little technical criticisms, for a second edition, on the method of adapting it for the piano.

At the Baroness Meyendorff's, in the evening, we three read through nearly all my songs. Liszt accompanied most of the time, while I sang and explained the words. The Baroness preferred *La Reine des Mers*, but Liszt thought it too highly spiced. 'It is Paprika,' I said. 'No, it is Cayenne pepper,' he answered conclusively.

There was a crowd of pianists at his matinée; the violinist, Sauret, had just arrived, so that they played only the Scherzo from my symphony and not nearly so well as on the previous day. Liszt's sight was bad and he played wrong notes. Besides, he was absent-minded. He was impatiently expecting his daughter, who was to arrive the same day. . . .

Liszt has many talented pupils, but what gave me most pleasure, what really touched me, was that their style of playing the piano reminded me of yours.* It has neither the continual restlessness of Goldstein's, nor the affectation of feminine pearliness. Their movements are, as a rule, moderate. Simplicity, breadth and nobility are the qualities personified in Liszt. How I regret that you were unable to hear him![11]

In between these meetings with Borodin, Liszt had received a letter from *Wilhelm Kienzl*, who wondered whether to expect a reply.

Are the Immortals in the habit of writing to the young and unknown? Round and round my head went such thoughts. My timid hopes were quickly followed by their fulfilment: Liszt actually sent me a reply. For a long time I could not bring myself to open the letter with its Weimar postmark and the handwriting I knew so well from facsimiles. I danced blissfully around the room, kissing the letter—and uneasily putting it aside, until at last I opened it. . . .

A manservant admitted me [15 July], and a few moments later I was standing in Liszt's music and workroom, a room of modest dimensions which contained both a mighty Steinway concert grand and an upright piano. Some reliefs hung on the walls, and on the small desk stood liqueurs and wines.

The door leading from the bedroom opened, and in his abbé's cassock out came the Master, asking me with a friendly smile how he could be 'of service' to me, and offering me a cigar which—half smoked—I preserve as a relic to this day. After a brief, stimulating conversation he invited me to the piano, to show him my pieces. I sat there—and could only stare at him in embarrassment: was I to play the piano to a Liszt? My misgivings he quickly dispelled, however, and I began to introduce to him the—as I thought—best of the sins of my youth: piano works, songs, and a melodrama. And how kindly and comprehensively he expressed himself, with what earnestness and goodwill, discussing every detail, giving precious advice, inviting me to play certain pieces a second time, praising and criticizing, even playing some of my works to me himself, so that I felt as though I were in a dream. He, the great interpreter who had no equal in his ability to project himself into the individuality of others, did, to be sure, not play everything exactly as I had felt it; but it was an experience that I shall never forget. With an incomparable rendering of his own piano-poem *Ricordanza*, he gave me yet another special present. When I thanked him, he said, with a strange mixture of the charming coquetry of the spoilt and

* Borodin's wife was herself a professional pianist.

of sincerely meant self-criticism: 'Oh, I am already quite a disabled old piano-player!'—to which I involuntarily had to splutter that even such a joke as that seemed a kind of crime, coming from him, since he could not possibly be speaking in earnest! He was not angry with me, but smiled almost as though embarrassed. But when he delivered himself of an opinion the truth of which he thought he had not convinced me, he added self-confidently: 'You can believe me, for I flatter myself that I have had something to do with this instrument from time to time.' His observation had been about pedal-markings in piano music, always given very conscientiously by Chopin, but neglected by Schumann. There followed a number of important remarks about both my playing and my works, his masterly counsel being worth more than dozens of lessons from average teachers. The morning not sufficing, he generously invited me to continue the session in the afternoon. The intensive interest which he seemed to take in my modest talents made me very happy, and reinforced my decision to devote myself wholly to composition. The kind-hearted dedication which this great man brought to my youthful efforts should be extolled and emphasized, because it was eminently characteristic of Liszt, and distinguishes him from the many great artists who remain inaccessible, shunning contact with the young generation needing their advice.

Liszt's noble-mindedness is widely known; all who came into contact with him were able to confirm it. He really did forget himself for others; and when he was neglected as a composer he always had his part-proud, part-modest reply: 'I can wait!' His *noblesse* was unique. He gave to others like a prince. . . . His conversation was always replete with wit, but never of a hurtful kind. At all times sincerely modest, like every great man, he was nevertheless conscious of the strength and abundance of his own exceptional gifts. If, however, he stumbled on narrow-minded contradiction, then more likely than not, maintaining his point of view he would counter the speaker with impressive self-confidence: 'That is what *I* say!'[12]

In the last week of July the Wagner family came to Weimar, a visit which in mid-August Liszt returned, spending three days (12th to 15th) at Bayreuth. On the 19th he arrived at Rome, whence he withdrew a week later to Tivoli. Here, in September, as he described in a letter to Carolyne of the 23rd, he composed the threnodies *Aux cyprès de la Villa d'Este*, two of the finest of his late piano works.

These three days I have spent entirely under the cypresses! It was an obsession, impossible to think of anything else, even of church. Their old trunks were haunting me, and I heard their branches singing and weeping, bearing the burden of their unchanging foliage! At last they are brought to bed on music paper; and after having greatly corrected, scratched out, copied and recopied them, I resign myself to touching them no more. They differ from the cypresses of Michelangelo by an almost loving melody.[13]

The two pieces were included in the *Années de pèlerinage, troisième année* (S163, published in 1883), placed between two other works composed this same year: *Angelus! Prière aux anges gardiens*, and the magnificent quasi-impressionistic *Les jeux d'eau à la Villa d'Este*. The set was completed by *Sunt lacrymae rerum, en mode hongrois* (dating from 1872), *Marche funèbre* (1867, in memory of the Emperor Maximilian of Mexico), and *Sursum corda* (1877).

At about this time the German writer *Richard Voss* (1851–1918) came to Rome.

Although I am no connoisseur of music, I was quite captivated by the genius of Liszt, who was also a great man; great, too, in his goodness. At that time I always saw him with the Princess, who made a disquieting—indeed, disturbing—impression on me, so that I did not understand how it could be *she* who was the Master's muse. To see those two outstanding people together was like watching a play. . . . The Princess possessed in a high degree the gift of talking, but far less that of listening. She talked ceaselessly: always intelligently and ingeniously, always stimulatingly, and always with a disquieting effect on persons like myself. Even when Liszt was with her, she was the talker and he the listener. His manner of listening remains vividly in my memory. The expression of gentle, very gentle, resignation which shone from his luminous, gold-bronze features gave him a classical serenity and repose which by those who witnessed it can never be forgotten.

It was extraordinary how the Princess could divide her life into different compartments; and great was the effect of her personality on the most different people, groups and individuals alike. Her visitors, all of whom were under the spell of her personality, would mostly be received one at a time so that she could work on them without the distraction of a third person. If I was to see her at four, then my wife would be allowed to come at five. But whom did she not receive? All sorts and conditions: princes and statesmen, the aristocrats of every nation, distinguished strangers, scholars, artists, musicians, poets. It was astonishing, admirable!

She was not only a convinced Catholic but also a convinced Spiritualist; and she always felt that she was surrounded by ghostly visitants, with whom she not only conversed as with living persons but whose presence she intimated to her earthly visitors, introducing to the latter their invisible counterparts. When with ecstatic cheerfulness she would announce the names of the departed who were present, it gave one no very comfortable feeling. Unlike the living, whom she received only one at a time, the dead were allowed to come to her *in corpore*. . . .[14]

On 22 October, Liszt's sixty-sixth birthday, Nadine Helbig brought a young American, *Margaret Chanler* (1862–?), to him.

I had not met him before and felt as though I were being taken into a supernatural presence. Pictures of him as an old man are familiar to all, but

I never saw one that was not something of a caricature, a portrait of his warts; none gave the exalted distinction of his personality, the look of penetrating intelligence combined with kindly gaiety. . . .

When we left he whispered to Madame Helbig that he was going to give lessons to a group of young pianists and that she was to be sure to come and bring the 'little one', meaning me. I was not particularly little, but under Madame Helbig's huge protecting wing I seemed a very small chicken. . . . To be admitted even as a listener to those famous classes was an unhoped-for privilege. Liszt in those days occupied with infinitely more prestige the position later held by Leschetizky. . . .

On the appointed day we found our way to the Sala Dante. . . .

It was interesting to notice the varied degrees of tension that he brought to the different composers. When Chopin was being played, only the most delicate precision would satisfy him. The *rubatos* had to be done with exquisite restraint and only when Chopin had marked them, never *ad libitum*. Nothing was quite good enough to interpret such perfection. A student played one of Liszt's own Rhapsodies; it had been practised conscientiously, but did not satisfy the master. There were splashy arpeggios and rockets of rapidly ascending chromatic diminished sevenths. 'Why don't you play it this way?' asked Liszt, sitting at the second piano and playing the passage with more careless bravura. 'It was not written so in my copy,' objected the youth. 'Oh, you need not take that so literally,' answered the composer. He intended his Rhapsodies to be played rhapsodically, with a certain character of improvisation.

One of these lessons, the most memorable, was given to a young man who had prepared Beethoven's Hammerklavier Sonata, an arduous work alike for listeners and performer. The boy had worked hard and played all the notes in all their harshness. Liszt was not happy about the performance. He corrected and discussed; the boy had in no wise reached the soul of the matter. When it came to the divine Adagio, Liszt took the pupil by the shoulders, gently shoved him out of his seat, and sat down to play it himself, pouring out his soul to us in the dusk of that room, turning it into a space between stars, with the distant splash of the Fontana di Trevi as bourdon to the heavenly melody. I do not think that movement can ever have been played better or have moved any group of people so deeply before or since. It was the end of the lesson. Donna Laura and Madame Helbig had tears streaming down their faces. We had been in the Great Presence.[15]

Liszt left Rome on 17 November, spending the next day at Florence with Jessie Laussot and the 19th at Lamporecchio. 'Prince Rospigliosi', he told Carolyne, 'reproached me charmingly for so limiting the length of my stay, which according to him was just like a doctor's visit!' In the evening of the 21st he arrived in Budapest.

Princess Carolyne to Adelheid von Schorn, 19 November. Liszt's health worries me greatly—the Pest climate is too cold. This gypsy-like existence is quite unsuitable for a man of his age; he is undermining his strength; his digestive organs are much weakened; his diet is fatal; every evening he has a temperature. I got the doctor to come—but as he laughed in his face it was extremely difficult to do anything. His constitution is strong, but the years are approaching seventy! I have gone through some very troubled days, and put everything in God's hands! Yet I had one great and sublime joy: his genius, which in Germany seems to wither, comes to new life in Italy. The song* he composed for you was the happy beginning of a long series of wonderful works, so magnificent in their noble, heavenly feeling! Never has he composed like this; one could believe that he had left earth's highest peak to swim in the blue ether. Pray for him, dear child. Ask God to allow him to live so that he may give to the world many many more new creations![16]

Géza Zichy. More and more did I fall under Liszt's spell. His inexhaustible goodness of heart, his chivalry, his incomparable conversation, which in the most agreeable way revealed a rich storehouse of knowledge and experience, were unique. . . .

As a rule cheerful and good-humoured, he could sometimes be very melancholy. One evening in particular comes to mind. We had arranged to spend it at Madame von B's.† But this lady was suddenly taken ill, and when I arrived I found Liszt standing on the steps, lost in thought. 'You see, Géza, this is the fate of an old artist living alone, to be on the steps, in the street. . . . I gave my servant the evening off, and so now there is no one at my place, the stove is cold, everything dark. Oh yes, we have banquets and brightly-lit salons, but never a home. The music fades away and dies, the joyful hearts slow down and stop, and "the rest is silence".' He took me by the arm—and a hot tear fell on my hand. How that tear scalded me! I had never seen Liszt weep before, nor ever did again. Marshalling all my youthful energy, I accompanied him to his home, lit the lamps, and then knelt down and got the stove going. All of a sudden I felt a kiss on my then fair curls. 'Master,' I said laughingly, 'someone who has friends to heat the stove for him is not entirely forsaken.' With a smile, Liszt nodded agreement. I ordered a good supper, and in an hour saw my beloved master blossoming into his usual cheerful self.[17]

Liszt to Olga von Meyendorff. Budapest, 28 November. It seems that several newspapers say that I am sick. This is not at all the case, but . . . I feel I am reaching the end and even succumbing—and no longer want an extension. . . .

* *Sei still* (S330), a setting of a poem (written under the pen-name Nordheim) by Adelheid's mother, Henriette von Schorn.

† Probably Marianne von Blaskovics, a neighbour and close friend of Liszt's in Budapest.

Let me tell you once again that I am extremely tired of living; but as I believe that God's Fifth Commandment, 'Thou shalt not kill,' also applies to suicide, I go on existing with deepest repentance and contrition for having formerly ostentatiously violated the Ninth Commandment.[18]

Liszt to Princess Carolyne. Budapest, 1 December. Alas, I am only too well aware of the excessive part played by human weaknesses in my life! My sole excuse is that my faults have generally been due to stupidity rather than to wickedness! To tell the truth, I do not recall having committed even a single bad act intentionally. After having for thirty years, from 1830 to 60, grievously denied myself the sacrament of penitence—it was with complete conviction that when I turned to it once more I was able to say to my confessor, Hohmann, our priest at Weimar: 'My life has been only a long deviation on to the wrong path of the feeling of love.' I add: conspicuously led by music, the art which is at once divine and diabolical—more than all others does it lead us into temptation! Today I concede that the Utopian Comte de Selon was entirely right when, in 1835, he implored me not to contribute to corrupting the morals of Geneva by facilitating the foundation of a conservatoire in the city of Calvin and St Francis of Sales. . . .[19]

At Weimar on 2 December, thanks to Liszt's support and untiring efforts, Saint-Saëns' opera *Samson and Delilah* was given its world première, being very well received. Liszt was not present, having settled in Budapest for the winter, but he was delighted with the composer's telegram informing him of the successful performance.

A lifelong student of the literature of mysticism, he was at this time giving particular attention to the writings of the fourteenth-century Flemish mystic Jan van Ruysbroeck, as he told Princess Rospigliosi. 'His mysticism does not go on all fours; it has wings and shafts of celestial light. At a musical tangent, I sometimes "half-hear" the harmonies of the mystical region in which Beethoven and other lofty geniuses soar during their great moments of inspiration. "Who loves, understands." '

1878

On 3 January, accompanied by Zichy, Liszt attended a performance of the ballet *Coppélia*, with music by Léo Delibes (1836–91). The conductor was Delibes himself, in whose honour Liszt the next evening gave a soirée at his home in the Fish Market.

Early in the year the veteran Norwegian violinist Ole Bull came to Budapest and visited Liszt. Present at the meeting was *Ilka Horovitz-Barnay*, a pupil of Liszt's at the Budapest Academy between 1876 and 78.

Ole Bull wanted to play a few things to the Master; and, to conclude, I was to accompany him in Beethoven's Kreutzer Sonata. But in his quick, chivalrous way Liszt forestalled me by himself taking a seat at the piano, and I accordingly turned the pages for him. . . .

After no more than a few bars, however, things went wrong. Liszt glanced up in some surprise, smiled, nodded, and with easy flexibility indulged the old Arion. A second attempt failed likewise. The old Scandinavian, who had ever been a self-taught virtuoso, was unable to keep strict time, and notwithstanding Liszt's extraordinary patience and courtesy, the first movement of the sonata was a series of derailments.*

Ole Bull grew ever more flustered and fidgety. Liszt's unimpaired affability seemed only to add to his uncertainty; he groaned and sweated, muttered inarticulately to himself, and with his bow scratched on the music to show Liszt where to begin again. The whole thing was immensely comic, and Liszt laughed like a street urchin—but went on patiently starting afresh.

Then, all of a sudden, Ole Bull, his face as red as a beetroot, shrieked: 'It's quite impossible to play with you; you can't keep time and you are always playing wrong notes!'

At this, something terrifying happened. Just as a serene sky gives way to a sudden storm, so did Liszt's smiling features change. His whole face altered, lightning flashed from his eyes, his long white hair literally bristled and stood out around his distorted countenance like some fearsome mane. The words came bubbling over his lips like a cataract: 'You dare say that to me, you old humbug—to me, Franz Liszt!'

Instead of placating him, Ole Bull hurled insults back, provoking Liszt quite needlessly. I shall not repeat here all the violent and unvarnished expressions that were exchanged, but merely say that at the end, as Bull was feverishly packing his violin, the Master shouted: 'Your name will already be forgotten while the world is still kneeling before my memory!' With these words he seized a chair, and in his blind fury, and with the strength of a far younger man, smashed it to the floor. Ole Bull fled.

I had difficulty in calming Liszt, and feared that the outburst of rage could be harmful to him. It took a long time for his anger and indignation to simmer down. But the next evening, at Ole Bull's recital in the hall of the Music Club, Liszt sat smiling and cheerful in the front row. Most of the audience, who were hearing Ole Bull for the first time, looked astonished —for the old virtuoso played woefully badly; and in that one recital buried the reputation he had enjoyed for so long. Liszt applauded conspicuously after every number, and, in thanks, Ole Bull bowed specially to him.

'He wanted to give me piano lessons, the old scraper—*me!*' Liszt remarked

* According to Bull's biographer, Mortimer Smith, the violinist 'was not very fond of Beethoven and was unused to playing him, and besides his ear was no longer as keen as it had been'.

to me with a smile. The total fiasco of the recital had given him his revenge and completely restored his good humour.[1]

Happily, the two old warriors were not bad friends for long. On 19 February, the eve of the Norseman's departure, Liszt wrote, *amicalement*, to invite him and Mrs Bull to spend the evening with his 'old colleague and devoted friend'; adding in a postscript the assurance that 'there will be no "violin" or even piano'.

'At midnight, however,' recalled Sara Bull, 'the violin was sent for at Liszt's request, and not till after two in the morning did the company disperse. The walk to the hotel along the fine river embankment in the brilliant starlight, with the wonderful tones still sounding in one's brain, cannot be forgotten. After a brilliant improvisation on the same motives which Ole Bull had chosen for the violin, Liszt had closed with a dreamy, tender nocturne.'

'The courage to thank you *de vive voix* for your princely hospitality quite fails me,' wrote Bull later in the morning. 'Your precious counsels, inseparable companions of your soul, inseparable and illuminating souvenirs of our reunion after so many years of tests and trials, are a sincere token of friendship—at once a token and a promise! Still wholly under the moving influence of your so gracious genius, my dear wife asks me to express her gratitude; and I beg you to permit me to wish that the Supreme Being grant you all possible happiness. This is what is ardently desired by your devoted admirer and friend, Ole Bull.'

On 17 April Liszt arrived back in Weimar, having spent some days *en route* at Vienna, and a week at Bayreuth, where Wagner complained of the shortness of the visit. 'His old idea that we should live in the same town has remained with him,' remarked Liszt to Carolyne. 'Fate has decreed otherwise.'

Having been asked by the Hungarian Government to represent Hungary at the Paris International Exhibition that June, Liszt reached the French capital on the 9th, staying at the home of Mme Camille Erard (widow of Pierre Erard) in the rue du Mail. Representing Austria on the musical adjudication committee was *Eduard Hanslick*.

At the first session of the adjudicating committee, and warmly welcomed by all its members, appeared—*Liszt*. I seized the moment to move that the committee elect him its honorary president by acclamation. This was at once done, and seemed to please him. The actual president was Gevaert, the learned and witty Director of the Brussels Conservatoire. . . . That for its few musical instruments a country like Hungary should have sent its own adjudicator to Paris, and no less a figure than Liszt into the bargain, seemed rather strange, but turned out well enough. No other country had so great a man to play. It was rather as though the Emperor of Austria (as actually happened in some rural communities) had been elected a town councillor. Any more practical advantage was frankly not to be gained from it.

Since he had to hurry off to the music festival at Erfurt, Liszt could only attend the first session of the committee and join us in two fleeting promenades through the ranks of the instruments on display. But even had he been able to stay longer, this celebrated musician would hardly have been the most suitable adjudicator—precisely because of his celebrity. Any remark he might have made on the merits or shortcomings of a particular instrument would have had a powerful and undesirable influence on the entire committee. And being fully sensible of this, he diplomatically refrained from expressing any opinion. He knew that, disseminated hither and thither by a hundred lips, any judgement of his would have brought both rain and sunshine, and that the sunshine of his praise could at the same time have turned into the most damaging downpour for the competitors of the commended one. So far as the piano manufacturers were concerned, Liszt found himself in the delicate position of a monarch. And as one of the most benevolent of monarchs he avoided saying anything that might have brought consequences. So he walked along with us and, without trying any of the instruments himself, bestowed an encouraging word here, a friendly smile there. We had not gone far before our party showed a considerable increase in numbers. More and more people tagged on to us, and barely a moment passed in which I did not have to answer some stranger's polite question: 'De grâce, Monsieur, n'est-ce pas Litz?' For it is 'Litz', and nothing else, that the name is pronounced by all Frenchmen, none of whom know what to make of its Hungarian *sz*. If only from portraits, everyone knew the lean figure in priestly dress and broad-rimmed hat, and the Jupiter head with its finely-chiselled features so characteristically framed by that long white mane. In his time Liszt was without question the best-known personality in Europe.

About midday, rather fatigued he came to a stop and admitted that he would now regard a knife and fork as the most praiseworthy instruments. We gladly accepted his invitation to a meal at the Hungarian *csárda* in the Exhibition Park. The suntanned landlord gave a delighted laugh under the pointed spires of his moustache, the cook put himself out to please, as did the gypsy band, and we were soon enjoying ourselves most cosily. Seldom have I seen Liszt in such expansive high spirits—I would say so amiable, had I ever seen him anything else. After years of estrangement I was experiencing once more, just as of old, the fascinating power of his personality. He recalled an informal supper to which some musicians had invited him at Vienna in 1858, and how he had taken Schubert's *Divertissement à la hongroise* for piano duet off the piano and placed it on the music rack with the words: 'Well, gentlemen, who is going to play it with me?' We had all modestly stepped back, no one wanting to deprive his neighbour of the honour. When the self-deprecation continued, I felt it a great pity that I was going to miss the one chance of a lifetime to play a duet with Liszt, and since no one else would do so—I stepped forward. 'Bravo,' cried Liszt, 'but criticism plays second fiddle, does it not, to production? So you play *secondo*!' That he did not make it easy for me, I can truly say. Whether it was artistic exuberance, or just an imp of mischief, which took hold of him, he not only played with rhythmic abandon but also improvised, in the gypsy manner and quite wonderfully, long embellishments, passages, chains of trills, cadenzas, as and where the fancy took him. Luckily I knew the piece so well that I needed to give my attention to his playing only, and not to the score. And so there came my way an experience never to be forgotten, plus a friendly word of praise from Liszt for not letting myself be 'thrown from the saddle'.* In the *csárda* he recalled many another Viennese interlude while pouring us generous libations from a bottle of red Hungarian wine. One could spend hours in his company without any fear that he would touch dissonant chords or let differences of opinion cause him either to give or take offence. He had the gift and the merit of winning the sincere affection even of those who were openly antagonistic to his works. . . .

On the activities of the World Exhibition, Liszt had absolutely no influence at all. He came and went like a dazzling showpiece. But for me the three days under his honorary presidency were the gayest and most tranquil of the entire time I spent in Paris on the adjudicating committee; and from that city I took home with me the most delightful memories of this rare man, who, unbowed by the burden of either years or fame, even played the adjudicator for a change, and played it as only *Liszt* could. On the last day he arranged to meet me at the exhibition of French paintings which he wished to see, and asked me to take my wife along too. Towards ladies his charm was positively bewitching in its mingling of worldly gallantry and clerical dignity. It came as a surprise when he promised to visit us in Vienna the next winter. Months went by, and I would not for a moment have expected him to remember his promise. But he did indeed call upon us, chatted for a while and then invited my wife to sing. She chose the simplest, and for that reason the best, of his songs, *Es muss ein Wunderbares sein*, and sang it so as to please him. That is how my wife shares with me the beautiful memory of having made music with Liszt.[2]

While in Paris Liszt met Victor Hugo once again, renewing to him personally 'the constant homage of my cult for genius—homage to which he responded in friendly fashion, just as some thirty years ago'. (Among fellow guests at Hugo's was Ernest Renan.) He also played at the home of Princess Caraman-Chimay, last of the mistresses of Napoleon III, waited upon Prince Napoleon, and attended a performance of Gounod's *Faust*.

Returning to Weimar on 19 June, he spent the 22nd to the 27th at Erfurt, where his Psalm 13, Two Episodes from Lenau's Faust, *Hungaria*, and Hungarian Fantasia were performed at the Allgemeine Deutsche Musikverein festival.

Adelheid von Schorn, 1 July. This morning I was at Liszt's. He was writing,

* Liszt to Princess Marie Wittgenstein (20 Apr. 1858): 'Hanslick . . . played his part wonderfully. If only this little incident could later become a *symbol* and *omen* for the happy alliance of Art and Criticism.'

was very gentle and kind, and spoke charmingly about Bülow, whom he loves very much. His character he regards very highly, and asks of others that they accept his weaknesses calmly, as he does himself. A bust of Liszt having just arrived, the work of the sculptor Silbernagl, he asked my opinion of it. I found mouth and lower jaw too strong, too material. His delight at my absolving him of materialism moved him to tears.

At Erfurt he arranged everything, conciliated everyone; he is gentle and good. May God keep our dear Master thus for us for a long time yet. When called for by the audience, and what with all the throwing of flowers and the endless ovation, the impression he made in his venerable beauty was an unforgettable, melancholy one.[3]

Between 9 and 12 July Liszt took part in the celebrations held at Weimar to mark the 25th anniversary of the accession of Carl Alexander, with whom in mid-August he spent a week at the Wartburg. After a brief visit to the Duke of Meiningen at Liebenstein, he arrived on 20 August at Bayreuth, 'looking better than I have seen him for years,' thought Cosima, 'a delight both for Richard and me'. And on the 21st: 'Richard enlarges on my father's unique aristocratic personality. Everything about him refined, princely, grand, yet at the same time full of artistic genius.'

Another guest of the Wagners, from the 27th onwards, was *Malwida von Meysenbug*, who described her visit in letters to Alexander Herzen's daughter, Olga Monod.

28 August. Cosima was waiting for me at the station with the children, and could hardly have given me a warmer welcome. She at once told me that her father was still here, which delighted me, even if they could not now accommodate me so 'munificently', as Wagner puts it. In the house he came to meet me with his old heartiness, and for the time being I have been put in Daniela's room, upstairs next to the children, until Liszt leaves, when I shall come downstairs to the guest room. Liszt was likewise very cordial, and after light-hearted talk over supper Wagner asked him to play his Dante Symphony, which I had already heard in Rome; the Francesca da Rimini episode, which you know, is portrayed in music just as Scheffer has done it in painting. And so once again I heard this wonderful playing, which truly has its equal nowhere in this world. . . . Cosima looks very well, and between Wagner and her father, who now get on very well together, she is very happy; and it is true that with these two men and the lovely children a more perfect life than hers is scarcely to be imagined.

I hope Liszt will continue to play a good deal while he is here—it really is a heavenly joy.

30 August. I cannot rejoice sufficiently at having found Liszt here, for to hear him playing, in the most intimate circle like this, *con amore*, is something truly unique. Yesterday afternoon he played us the beginning of

Parsifal; at first only to Cosima, Wolzogen,* and me; but then Wagner came too and began to sing. Yes, I could not have heard it better for the first time. . . . Yesterday evening, to please Liszt, the three of them played whist, and I looked on, having quite forgotten the game. But during it we nearly died of laughter at Wagner's bubbling merriment and jokes. High spirits exude from his every pore; and in contrast Liszt's gentle smile, he being always kind and yet deep down rather sad—it was very interesting to observe them in their difference.

2 September. Liszt departed on Saturday [31 August], straight to Rome. He has promised me that we shall see one another there often, which pleases me very much as he is such a glorious personality when one gets to know him better: so kind, so gentle, so noble— and what an artist! On the last day he again played a great deal to us: it was truly divine. Such playing simply cannot be heard anywhere else in this world. The children were very sorry that he was going: they are extremely fond of him, and he too is very affectionate towards them. One can see that it does him good to be among this cheerful, youthful element.[4]

Arriving in Rome on 3 September, Liszt returned on the 12th to Tivoli, where, apart from the occasional trip into Rome, he stayed until the end of the year. It was here that news reached him of the death, on 9 September, of Baron Augusz, his longstanding, loyal, and devoted Hungarian friend and host, himself a talented pianist and singer. He was the dedicatee of the Eighth Hungarian Rhapsody; and it was he who, thirty-eight years earlier, had translated into Hungarian the speech pronounced by Liszt when presented with the sword of honour. 'We were *one* in heart,' wrote Liszt.

Two years previously, after playing to Liszt at the Schottenhof in Vienna, *Moriz Rosenthal* (1862–1946), one of the greatest pianists of his generation, had been accepted as a pupil.

To me his encouraging words about my talent and future sounded like an incantation calculated to throw the portals of the future and of art wide open for me; and I followed the great magician to Weimar, Rome, and Tivoli. . . . When I saw him he was nearly always surrounded by a retinue of loyal pupils and admirers, in whose midst he moved with the amiability and grandeur of a reigning prince. His urbanely brilliant manner always exerted a fascinating effect, whether he was being captivatingly kind or, as occasionally, indulging in witty sallies.

At Tivoli, where in the autumn of 1878 it was my good fortune to be his sole pupil, I found him essentially different; he appeared to me then in a warmer and highly artistic light. Going to the Villa d'Este every afternoon, I would find the Master composing in his study; sometimes on the terrace, gazing pensively into the blue distance. The sparkling Roman autumn, the

* A close associate of the Wagner family, Hans von Wolzogen (1848–1938) was the editor of the *Bayreuther Blätter*, a periodical founded by Wagner.

picturesque beauty of the place, the Master's lofty teaching—everything merged within me into a bliss which I can still feel today.

What made his instruction so specially interesting, was his elucidation of the musical structure, his emphasis on hidden subtleties and his explanation of the historical relationship of any one particular work to musical progress in general. This was because he saw everything with the eyes of a creative artist. When I once played to him the first of Chopin's Etudes Op. 10, he said: 'Gounod composed a "Meditation" to fit the first Prelude of Bach's *Well-Tempered Clavier*. One day I should like to write a counter melody to this Etude; it would have to be no "Meditation", however, but a "Jubilate".' For Chopin his admiration was limitless, and on one occasion when we were talking about the Dioscuri of the Romantic movement, he said in his cogent way: 'Schumann is broader-shouldered, but Chopin goes higher.'

Among present-day music the new Russian school interested him because of its modern approach to harmony and orchestration; and he greatly appreciated Saint-Saëns, of whose organ-playing he also related marvels. Rubinstein, for all his powers of invention, he found too perfunctory, too superficial. '*We* are not geniuses, *we* must work,' he often said humorously when works by the Russian master were played to him. Brahms he described as 'unexciting and very hygienic'. But when, not long afterwards, I brought him the Paganini Variations, he praised their polyrhythmic content highly and said: 'They are better than my Paganini Etudes—but they were written much later, and after he had become acquainted with mine.'

A few months later, shortly before I left to give concerts in Paris and Petersburg, he made me play Rafael Joseffy's* second *Danse arabesque*, which he liked very much on account of its harmonic subtleties. He then improvised brilliantly on the main theme, as well as playing some pieces by Schubert, the C minor Etude, Op. 25, and several Preludes by Chopin—and all with such tenderness, such boldness of feeling and expression, that even six years later I felt compelled to tell the Master of the indelible impression his playing had made upon me. With a modesty that only a Liszt could allow himself, he said with a smile: 'People have always exaggerated my playing a little.'[5]

Elsewhere, Rosenthal returned to the subject of how Liszt played.

As no one before him, and as no one probably ever will again. I remember when I went to him as a boy, he used to play for me in the evening by the hour, nocturnes by Chopin, études of his own, all of a soft, dreamy nature that caused me to open my eyes in wonder at the marvellous delicacy and

* Eminent Hungarian (later American) pianist and teacher (1852–1915), a pupil of both Liszt (at Weimar in the summers of 1870 and 1871) and Tausig. Now best known for his edition of the works of Chopin.

finish of his touch. The embellishments were like a cobweb—so fine—or like the texture of costliest lace. I thought, after what I had heard in Vienna, that nothing further would astonish me in the direction of digital dexterity, having studied with Joseffy, the greatest master of that art. But Liszt was more wonderful than anybody I have ever known, and he had further surprises in store for me. . . .[6]

On 1 November, All Saints' Day, Liszt was granted an audience with Pope Leo XIII (1810–1903), who as Cardinal Pecci had been elected to the papal throne earlier in the year after the death of Pius IX.

Princess Carolyne to Adelheid von Schorn, 17 December. This year he has once again composed sublime things, ones more beautiful, much more beautiful—and that is saying a lot—than those of last year. Especially a *Via crucis** and the *Septem Sacramenta*,† among which the Matrimonium will—I hope—become popular, even at Weimar. It is very short, requires few performers, and is so *weihevoll*! It must be sung with organ at the moment preceding the sacred ceremony. Get married, dear Adelheid, and I promise to have this short motet sung at the church for you—as the expression of my far-off blessing![7]

Liszt to Princess Carolyne. Villa d'Este, 23 December. Your Roman habits have given you a measure of absolutism which brooks no argument. The most discreet and respectful observations you regard as slights, and even as outrages! You take no account of the logical honour of my life. It is by no means the salons which cause the divergence in our points of view, but your daughter, and to some extent mine too! When I am dead you will realize that my soul always was and remained deeply devoted to yours![8]

To the same, Christmas Day. When having my little supper yesterday evening, I found your very dear and consoling letter, surrounded by an admirable assortment of flowers. It made me almost ashamed of the lines I sent you the day before.[9]

1879

After a private audience with the Pope on Sunday, 12 January, Liszt returned to Budapest. Here, a few weeks later, he was deeply grieved to learn of the death,

* S53. The 14 Stations of the Cross, for chorus and soloists with organ accompaniment. The text—biblical passages, hymns, and chorales—was prepared for Liszt by Princess Carolyne.

† S52. The Seven Sacraments. Responsoria cum organo vel harmonio concinente, for soloists, mixed chorus and organ.

on 8 February, of his uncle-cousin Eduard*—'my steadfast and supportive friend who showed me the same unshakeable confidence as did my mother', he wrote sadly to Carolyne.

In mid-March, accompanied by Zichy and Bösendorfer† among others, he spent a few days in Kolozsvár, a town he had not visited since 1846. 'Our reception was a moving one,' Zichy recalled. 'Choral societies had streamed in from far and near to see and honour the great master. As he stepped out of the train a forest of flags dipped in front of him and tumultuous shouts of "Éljen" made the very air tremble. We stayed at the home of Countess Max Teleki, where another guest was Count Sándor Teleki, an old friend and travelling companion of Liszt's.'

During their visit they heard, in *Zichy's* words, 'the shocking news that the large and prosperous city of Szeged had been engulfed by water'.

'We shan't achieve anything by lamenting; we must do something to help,' said Liszt. 'Come to the piano!' We sat down and played his Rákóczy March, which I had arranged for three hands. Then we drew up a programme. Before many hours had passed posters announcing the concert could be seen at every street corner, and by the evening it was sold out. When, after thirty-three years, Liszt once again took his place at a piano in Kolozsvár, he was greeted by an ovation that baffles description. The entire platform resembled a flower garden. When he stepped out on to it, the audience as one man rose to their feet as though before a king. With deep emotion he sat at the piano . . . and, in moving, mournful Hungarian phrases such as had never yet been heard or played by mortal being, played the Szeged disaster, the passing of his youth, and the transitoriness of all things. . . . To end the concert we played the Rákóczy March, and I strove to add audible basses to the orchestral might of his ten fingers. The enthusiasm was elemental. Students rushed to the stage and lifted the great master on to their shoulders.[1]

At a concert in which extracts from *St Elisabeth* were performed, the nine-year-old *Franz Lehár* (1870–1948) was present. 'Look at that man very carefully, so that you never forget his face,' his father, a violinist in the orchestra, told him, indicating Liszt; 'he is one of the very, very great.'

In my young soul there awakened for the first time the awareness that music, 'basic form of all the arts', is more than mere entertainment or earning a living; that God has given it for the lifting up of hearts, for the

* Who was buried in Vienna's Pötzleinsdorf cemetery. When he next visited that city, two months later, Liszt drove with Eduard's widow, Henriette, and two sons, Franz and young Eduard, to see the grave. 'There he prayed fervently,' recalled the last-named, 'and, weeping bitterly, expressed the wish to be buried here beside "his Eduard".'

† Head of the Viennese pianoforte firm after the death of his father in 1859, Ludwig Bösendorfer (1835–1919) was one of the leading figures in the musical life of Vienna, and a devoted admirer and supporter of Liszt. In 1872 he turned the Liechtenstein riding-school in the Herrengasse into a concert hall, the much-loved Bösendorfer-Saal.

bringing of comfort and consolation; and that the musician's profession is service to mankind's affirmation of life and joy in life.[2]

On 16 March, Liszt arrived back in Budapest.

Polyxena Pulszky, daughter of Ferenc Pulszky (1814–97), Director of the National Museum.

The Master's knowledge of everything that happened often astonished us, as did his keen interest in matters both great and small. Amongst other things I possess a letter from him which well illustrates this. In it he talks about a great speech made by Tisza* in Parliament, and about a bazaar held at the Károlyi Palace on behalf of the Szeged flood victims, inquires how far Ödön Mihalovich had progressed with his opera, and concludes by prophesying a brilliant political career for the charming and highly cultured Count Albert Apponyi. Even so short a letter as this reveals the old gentleman's concern with everything, and how informed he was about everything happening around him.

We were never allowed to invite the Master to play; but when his opponents played badly at whist, and Liszt won, we would be given a royal recompense. The Master would sit at the piano and begin to improvise, or play Beethoven and Chopin for us. The latest works of the most modern composers were gone through one by one, Mihalovich and Végh were put through the mill, and Wagner was played as a duet or at two pianos.

The sight of a closed piano was something Liszt could not bear; so we used to lock the instrument secretly and then hide the key. Engrossed in some interesting conversation, chewing on his long Havana (he was a passionate smoker of the very strongest cigars), the Master would glance sideways at the piano and become restless. Eventually he would stand up and try the lid. Then the key would have to be fetched, the lid would fly open, Liszt would seat himself and begin to play—a potpourri of any pieces that took his fancy. He would sometimes improvise for hours on end, and under his hands the strings of the piano would be transformed into a human voice or an entire orchestra. The tones would exult and weep, while we, quiet as mice, would be listening rapt, with the feeling that through this music we had become better and nobler.

Times past—but unforgettable! Memories of a man who was in every respect outstanding; who was not only a genius with vast knowledge at his command, but who had a great and noble heart, one which beat warmly for his fellow-beings, for all that was great, true and sublime in art, and for the land of his birth.[3]

Writing to Carolyne from Budapest on 18 March, Liszt referred once again to the will he had made at Weimar in 1860.

* Kálmán Tisza (1830–1902), the Hungarian statesman who between 1875 and 1890 was Prime Minister and virtual dictator.

I have never thought of withdrawing or changing this will—when death comes to me, I shall add to it my last blessing for you! If I die before you, I beg you to favour my beloved daughter Cosima when distributing the objects in my possession. With regard to the Budapest Museum, I stick to the determination I wrote to you about and then repeated orally. No ostentation, even in generosity—let us remain simple and true, and restrict our gifts to the Museum to those items designated in 1873. The sword presented to me in public, at the Pest Theatre, in 1840. The golden goblet, a gift from Hungarian ladies and inscribed with their names: likewise given to me in 1840. The piano given to Beethoven by the Broadwood firm—it remained in Beethoven's room until his death and was then bought by Herr Spina, who in the most friendly manner chose to make me a present of it. I had no thought of appropriating such a relic for myself, and accepted it only when he insisted. The magnificent silver music-rack, the result of a subscription on my behalf at Vienna in 1846. . . . Your wonderful baton, in solid gold, adorned with precious stones. Your still more wonderful platinum ink-stand, designed so poetically. More, would be too much! You know that I wanted to offer these objects to the Museum immediately after the fifty years of my artistic career had been celebrated at Budapest in November 1873. Your objections were respected—but I cannot change my opinion in this matter. To ask for a special place at the Museum for my gifts is repugnant to me; I even find it *nicht vornehm*! If after my death they were put in a place apart, that would be different.*[4]

On 26 March Liszt took part in another concert for the benefit of the Szeged victims; and between 2 and 10 April he stayed in Vienna, where on the 4th he played at a soirée given at the Bösendorfer-Saal in his honour by the Wagner Society.

Friedrich Eckstein (1861–1939).† It was my good fortune to see and hear the Master at the piano for the first time as, quite lost to the world, he long improvised on some of his own works.

So far as tenderness of expression and the immense power of his *forte* are concerned, Liszt's playing was quite different from that of anyone else I have ever heard. Certain runs in the bass, which like the claw strokes of a furious tiger seemed to tear shreds out of the piano, I can remember clearly; and then again the soothing peace radiated by an incomparably sweet *cantilena*; and how finally, as it were 'behind' this song-like melody,

* The two had already been at odds over this matter in 1873. Carolyne not only wanted other items to be given, but also wished for a separate room to be set aside at the Museum. Beethoven's Broadwood and the other objects were eventually presented to the Hungarian National Museum after her death in 1887.

† A chemist and parchment manufacturer whose encyclopaedic knowledge of, *inter alia*, philosophy, literature, music, history, science, and esoteric lore, made him a notable personality in Viennese intellectual circles. A pupil of Anton Bruckner, he was also a friend of such outstanding men as Hugo Wolf, Sigmund Freud, and Hugo von Hofmannsthal.

there greeted us from the far distance the same *pianissimo* theme transposed into the key of the major third! On that same evening the Master also played his *Au lac de Wallenstadt** and some *Chants polonais*† by Chopin.

The news that Franz Liszt would appear at the Wagner Society had spread only too quickly; and so it came about that the Bösendorfer-Saal was packed with people who had somehow or other been able to obtain admission. In front of the first row of seats, gilt velvet armchairs had been placed, on which the most distinguished members of Viennese society took their places: Excellencies, ministers, and high-ranking officers bedecked with orders and ribbons, and princesses, each cocooned in her network of glittering jewels. Before Liszt took his seat at the piano he came out below the platform, in front of the rows of honorary guests, and there held court.

I shall never forget how, on being addressed by the Master, some of the ladies rose from their seats, dropped a deep curtsey and kissed his—the priest's—hand; how with calm dignity, smiling, he submitted to all these acts of homage; how, crowned by the snow-white head of hair which formed so vivid a contrast with the black cassock, his tall figure visibly stood out even at a distance from the throng around him; and how the eyes of the ladies sparkled while he chatted with them.

And how afterwards, still quite dazed and lost in reverie, I came out into the street, the then sparsely illuminated Herrengasse, where everything was dominated by the jumble of carriages, with liveried footmen on the running-boards and coachmen in three-cornered hats, and the muffled clatter of the horses, so that it was only with difficulty that one could somehow manage to scramble through it all.[5]

On 7 April, at the home of Count Gyula Andrássy, the Minister for Foreign Affairs, and before an audience which included the Emperor Franz Joseph, Liszt again participated in a concert for the Szeged victims. The next morning parts of his *Septem Sacramenta* were performed in the Hofburg Chapel; and in the evening, as part of the celebrations preceding the silver wedding anniversary of the Emperor and Empress, he conducted a performance of the Gran Mass at the Musikverein. Present was *Eduard Hanslick*.

At Hellmesberger's last quartet soirée [3 April], Franz Liszt happened to enter the hall unobserved while Schubert's Trio in E flat was being played. Staying unobtrusively in the background until the end of the work, he then passed along the rows of the audience to seek his place in the Circle. General attention, which had already begun to flag during the finale of the Trio, now turned so exclusively, and in such high spirits, towards the

* Writing in the *Abendblatt des Pester Lloyds* (7 Apr.), Theodor Helm opined that Liszt's playing of this work was 'more ethereal, more transfigured, more ideal than two years ago . . . like a divine improvisation'.

† Liszt's transcriptions (S480) of six Polish songs by Chopin. The *Wiener Zeitung* described those played on this occasion as 'a glorious improvisation on themes of Chopin, which was received with jubilation'.

celebrated newcomer, that as though at a signal the whole assembly began to applaud, and would not leave off until he stepped forward and bowed in acknowledgement of the reception given him. It was a charming and unforgettable moment. We know of no other instance when, on entering a concert hall, not as composer or performer but simply as a member of the audience, an artist has found himself acclaimed with such noisy unanimity by the entire gathering. Were Bismarck and Gambetta, Wagner and Verdi, the youngest and loveliest prima donna and the oldest virtuoso to appear at a concert or theatre today, they would be able to boast of no such scene. Liszt alone, in all Europe. The instinctive feeling that flashed upon the greater part of the audience—to give *Liszt* greeting—spread like a chain reaction, until it burst out in thunderous expression almost simultaneously all over the hall. . . . This universal affection, shown as much to the human being as to the artist, is manifested wherever Liszt appears. What an aura of magic still surrounds this ageing man!

When he himself conducts one of his own works, not only are the well-known sounds of disapproval of his opponents silenced . . . but the opposition itself, the inner antagonism felt by so many towards Liszt's creations, is mollified and muted when, sparkling with intellect and benevolence, the old firebrand's gaze falls upon them and his music speaks to us as it were through his own mouth. . . .

Despite the interest of its numerous dazzling qualities, its penetrating musical exegesis, and the impressive earnestness and greatness of its intentions; and although any such creation of a phenomenally talented, brilliant man cannot but be remarkable, the Gran Mass, we maintain, is . . . a thoroughly unedifying, unhealthy, and artificial work, in which a striving for religious expression and an invincible addiction to theatrical effect ceaselessly contend for supremacy. Like Mahomet's coffin, Liszt's Mass hovers homelessly between Heaven and Earth. . . .

He conducted the performance himself—if 'conducted' is the right word to describe a few gently suggestive movements of the hands. 'The conductor should be a helmsman not an oarsman,' runs a well-known remark of Liszt's. When one is so fortunate as to have two excellent 'oarsmen' working at one's side, then frankly it matters little if the helmsman now and then moves not a finger. Herr Kremser, who had most conscientiously prepared the entire performance, conducted with a baton; Herr Hellmesberger did the same with a violin bow. Hovering above the two of them, like the Holy Ghost, was Franz Liszt. When he occasionally stretched out a hand over singers and players, he seemed more to be blessing than conducting them. But, be it what it may, everything he does is done with elegance and distinction, while on young and old alike he continues to exert the magical fascination he has now been exercising for half a century. Nor did the soloists fail to succumb: their difficult parts they sang with truly apostolic devotion.[6]

Writing to Carolyne, Liszt commented: 'Yesterday evening my Gran Mass came into the full light for the first time—thanks as much to the splendid performance as to the very friendly reception given to it by the audience.'

During Liszt's stay in Vienna, the young Austrian conductor and composer Felix Mottl (1856–1911) was brought to him by the music-publisher *Albert Gutmann*.

Liszt received us with captivating kindness. After a few words of greeting had been said, Mottl opened the songs he had brought with him, to play them to Liszt. But Liszt had already taken them out of his hand, given a fleeting glance at the rows of music, then placed the book on the rack the wrong way round, so that the music was upside down, and begun to play Mottl's songs fluently—a trick, incidentally, which I had seen him do on several occasions, even with orchestral scores. He praised Mottl's melodic invention, but thought the accompaniments much too complex. 'Songs,' he said, 'should have a simple accompaniment and avoid any unnecessary modulation. Wagner has modulated only when compelled to do so by poetic or musical necessity. And as far as my own modest songs are concerned,' he added, 'they have very simple accompaniments; *Es muss ein Wunderbares sein*, for example. That, my dear young friend, is something you should mark well!'*[7]

After attending a music festival at Hanover, Liszt went on to Frankfurt† for a performance of *Christus* (21 April) and then returned to Weimar. In June, after a visit to Wiesbaden for the Tonkünstler-Versammlung of the Allgemeine Deutsche Musikverein (at which Bülow conducted a 'wonderful' performance of the Faust Symphony), he returned to Frankfurt, where at the Conservatorium was held a matinée at which pupils‡ and teachers performed only his works.

He spent 6 and 7 July in Sondershausen, where *Mazeppa* and *Ce qu'on entend sur la montagne* were performed. 'They reminded me', he wrote to Carolyne, 'of the good old days at the Altenburg—"when we were so unhappy!" Many happy people would have been envious of what we had then!'

On the 10th he conducted his *Septem Sacramenta* at Weimar's town church.

Liszt to Princess Carolyne. Weimar, 18 July. You better than anyone know of my utter lack of ambition in regard to an ecclesiastical career. When I

* At Weimar the following year Mottl's opera *Agnes Bernauer* received its extremely successful première after being recommended by Liszt.

† Principal of the Hoch Conservatorium at Frankfurt since 1877 had been Liszt's old friend and associate Joachim Raff. According to his daughter Helene: 'Liszt and my father had once been very close, but many things had occurred to divide them. During Liszt's visit to Frankfurt, I was astonished to see how completely my father fell under the spell of this powerful early love once again. Liszt had to promise to come back.'

‡ Among them the American composer and pianist Edward Macdowell (1860–1908), who with another student played the 2-piano version of *Tasso, Lamento e Trionfo*. At Weimar in June 1882 he played his 1st Piano Concerto to Liszt (to whom it was dedicated) and received much friendly encouragement. Liszt also recommended the young American's First Modern Suite (piano solo) for performance in July 1882 at a meeting of the Allgemeine Deutsche Musikverein in Zurich.

took the minor orders at the Vatican in 1865, in my fifty-fourth year, the idea of any outer advancement could not have been further from my thoughts. In simplicity and uprightness of heart I was merely following the old Catholic leaning of my youth. Had it not been thwarted in its first ardour by my dear mother and by my confessor, the Abbé Bardin, it might well have led me to the seminary in 1830, and later to the priesthood. My mother had no other support than myself, her only child; and the Abbé Bardin, something of a music-lover, took perhaps too much notice of my bit of precocious celebrity when advising me to serve God and the church as an artist, without aspiring unrestrainedly towards the sublime virtues of the ministry. Thus randomly does one ratiocinate about the Ideal! I know of none as lofty as that of the priest practising, teaching, and meditating on the three theological virtues: Faith, Hope, and Charity—to the point of the voluntary sacrifice of his life, crowned by martyrdom, when God gives it! Would I have been worthy of such a calling? Divine grace alone could accomplish it! The fact remains that my mother's loving tenderness, and the Abbé Bardin's prudence, left me at grips with temptations that I have been able to overcome no more than inadequately! Poetry and music, not forgetting a few particles of innate rebellion, have subjugated me for too long! *Miserere mei, Domine!*[8]

In early August, for a Tennyson Album to be published in London, Liszt wrote his only English song: a setting of *Go not, happy day* (S335). The last ten days of the month (in which he had also visited the music festival at Arnstadt and been Carl Alexander's guest at Wilhelmsthal) he spent in Bayreuth with the Wagners.

Wilhelm Kienzl, writing of 28 August. When, during a party with close friends which was held at Wahnfried on Goethe's birthday, Liszt went to the piano and, playing from the score, gave an unforgettable rendering of his Faust Symphony, filling with the most profound emotion the little circle of listeners gathered around him as he sat there bathed in the moonlight pouring in through the open doors, the unbelievable happened: Wagner, who initially sat there without uttering a word, manifestly under the spell of what he had just experienced, suddenly got to his feet, rushed over to the piano, and, saying self-importantly, 'Look, I can play the piano too!'—struck out senselessly at the patient keyboard with both hands, just like a child. It was an incident which all us found both vexing and brutal, and involuntarily I found myself wondering what could have taken place in Wagner's mind to induce him to behave with such extreme bad taste. Or was it one of those cases of emotion which seems to be ashamed of itself, and which, proudly veiling itself in front of non-intimates, hides behind the mask of insensitivity?

At the beginning of the Faust Symphony there had been another little incident. The brooding main theme of the first movement is note for note identical with a theme which appears at the close of the Second Act of

Wagner's *Die Walküre*. Wagner had studied the score of his friend's symphonic work in the solitude of Mornex,* when taking the cure at that resort, and the theme had obviously impressed him to the point that, intentionally or not, he had used it in his own work. Be that as it may, when the theme rang out, Wagner hurried to the piano and said laughingly to Liszt: '*That*, Papa, is something I stole from you!' Liszt, who was above envy, even though his works, in contrast to those of Wagner, had been irresponsibly neglected and attacked, replied with ready repartee: 'That's all right—at least it will now be heard!'[9]

By early September Liszt was back in Rome and Tivoli. In July, Cardinal Hohenlohe had written, as Bishop of Albano, to inform him that the Chapter of the Cathedral of Albano had unanimously elected him an Honorary Canon of the Cathedral. In October he accordingly spent several days in the town, entering into possession of his honorary canon's stall during a solemn service at the Cathedral on Sunday the 12th.

In Rome this same month was *Adelheid von Schorn*, who visited Liszt at Tivoli on the 20th.

His pupil R and his mother came as well. We arrived in the afternoon, and I at once went to the Villa d'Este by myself, to write various things for Liszt. Frau Thon, with Frau R and her son, followed in the evening, for Liszt had invited us to supper. Everything went very pleasantly until the time when Liszt seated himself at the piano, thereby giving great delight to the two ladies, who had never heard him. But then something very strange happened, and for the first and last time I was to see Liszt in a royal fury. That he could be very violent I already knew from both the Princess and Liszt himself; indeed, he had told me that once when he was young he had in a fit of anger broken a windowpane with his fist.

What he played that evening in Tivoli, I no longer remember—I can only recall him sitting at the piano, his pupil standing beside him turning the pages. All at once the young man seemed to grow bored with his task—or considered it no longer necessary—for, hands in pockets, he suddenly strolled down to the lower end of the piano and leant over a volume of music which he began to read. I saw Liszt's face darken—and in that same instant he broke off his playing, sprang to his feet, and with one step was beside the youngster, whom he seized by the shoulders. It was a Liszt I had never seen before: his eyes blazed, his hair literally bristled, and he shook the transgressor to such effect that the latter could scarcely stand, showering him the while with a torrent of reproaches about his bad

* During his sojourn at Mornex, in the summer of 1856, Wagner had actually spent his time studying Liszt's symphonic poems. Although the Faust Symphony was not set down on paper until 1854 (the year of the composition of *Die Walküre*), Liszt had first begun to sketch it in the 1840s, and it is probable that he played it—albeit fragmentarily—to Wagner during his visit to the latter at Zurich in 1853. Wagner later wrote to Liszt: 'I regard you as the creator of my present position. When I compose and orchestrate, I always think only of you.'

manners and inattention when he, his teacher, was playing to him. The whole thing was over more quickly than it takes to tell of it. Releasing the youngster, he then quickly left the room. We were all more dead than alive; the ladies were trembling, the youth howling and protesting—but that did him no good as the three of us now set about him. Leaving this chastisement to his mother, I followed Liszt. Bare-headed, his white hair tossed by the wind, he was pacing rapidly up and down. Shining through the racing clouds, the moon made his face appear still paler than it was already. I went up to him; without a word he gave me his arm, and for some ten minutes we walked to and fro until he had calmed down somewhat. Then we stood at the end of the terrace and looked out over the moonlit Campagna. He spoke about the ill-mannered boy, saying that he could not bring himself to send away someone of such great talent. He was annoyed with himself for having lost his temper, but at length his mood mellowed and he returned to the stricken company. But naturally the harmonious atmosphere was now quite spoilt, just as the music had been; and before long, at my suggestion, my fellow guests and I took our leave of him.

The next day, Liszt returned to Rome with us. On the 22nd I accompanied him on a visit to Gobineau,* of whom he was very fond and whose acquaintance he wished me to make too. This brilliant Frenchman, diplomat, writer, and sculptor, had settled in Rome, and was on very friendly terms with Liszt and the Princess, as well as being a close friend of the Wagners. I found him a most likeable old man; very tall and slim, grey-haired and with a slight stoop, he came towards Liszt with great heartiness, and soon I too felt as though I were with an acquaintance of long standing. He showed us various busts he had done, which revealed considerable talent.[10]

The youth referred to as R in the foregoing was *Alfred Reisenauer* (1863–1907), one of the most gifted pupils of Liszt's last years. Long afterwards he remembered the composer thus:

When I had reached a certain grade of advancement it was my great fortune to become associated with the immortal Franz Liszt. I consider Liszt the greatest man I have ever met. By this I mean that I have never met, in any other walk of life, a man with his mental grasp, splendid disposition and glorious genius. This may seem a somewhat extravagant statement. I have met many, many great men, rulers, jurists, authors, scientists, teachers, merchants and warriors, but never have I met a man in any position whom I have not thought would have proved the inferior of Franz Liszt, had Liszt chosen to follow the career of the man in question. Liszt's personality can be expressed by only one word: *colossal*.[11]

* Joseph Arthur, Comte de Gobineau (1816–82), author of *L'Inégalité des races humaines*.

Liszt to Princess Carolyne. Villa d'Este, November. To thank you as I should like, I should need to have the blessings of all 259 Popes at my disposal! Lacking them, rest content with knowing that I love you more than words can say![12]

In late November, *Bettina Walker* (?–1893), an Irish student, came to Liszt with a letter of introduction from Sgambati.

I went by myself to the Villa d'Este, and . . . was shown into a room in which there was a grand pianoforte and handsome antique furniture; but if I noticed anything here it was the glorious view of the Campagna on which one looked out through the quaint windows.

After about five minutes Liszt came in. He impressed me both then and since as one of the largest and most widely sympathetic natures I have ever come across. I had heard some things against him 'as a man', and I heard more later on, and all I heard was what would prejudice one who never could quite lose the strong impressions of her early Puritan training. But Liszt's individuality was a thing apart; and in spite of the awe I had for his great genius, and the discomposing sensation of being in the presence of one who was 'a demon'—in Goethe's sense of the word—I was at home at once with him. He seated me on the sofa beside him, asked me about Sterndale Bennett, and then about Sgambati, and whether I liked Bülow's or Sgambati's playing best. I replied that, though I did greatly admire Bülow, yet I found more charm in Sgambati; and I even ventured to say to Liszt, 'Has not Sgambati *un poing doux*?' (my way of describing Sgambati's wrist-playing). Liszt replied, '*Vous avez parfaitement raison, mademoiselle.*' He then said he would like to hear me play . . . and though I confess that when I was leaving my sister, and while I was coming up to the Villa d'Este, I had felt much as if I were about to 'undergo an operation', yet I . . . played the piece from beginning to end very respectably, and with much go and swing. Liszt was kind enough to suggest that I should play another piece to him; but by not doing so, but simply saying, 'You are too good; you have heard enough of my attempt' (for I had a keen perception of whose presence I was in), I got something which Sgambati told me afterwards did not always fall to the lot of those who were admitted to Liszt on a letter of introduction. He sat down himself to the pianoforte, and played a long piece—a concert-study of his own. He thrilled even more than he astonished me by his sweet penetrative tone, and the tender pathetic ring which pervaded the whole. The winter afternoon sunlight streamed in, and lighted up the silvery hair that reached down to his shoulders, and I felt as I listened and looked, and realized that he was *aged*, and therefore could not be with us very long, that I would gladly give up my life just to add it to *his* precious existence.[13]

In December *Gerhard Rohlfs* and his wife came to Rome, where they saw Liszt and with him called upon Princess Carolyne.

I must admit that the Princess was one of the most brilliant women I have ever encountered. On our way home the Master told me that in recent years she had become entirely addicted to mysticism, and had written fat volumes on the nature of angels. 'In that case,' I replied, 'she will be trespassing on Stanley's preserves.' 'Really? I didn't know he had published anything on angels,' remarked Liszt. 'Yes, indeed. In his conversations with King Mtesa of Uganda he tried to explain the nature of angels to him.' 'Then he knows more than I do,' said Liszt.[14]

The year ended with a charity concert on Tuesday, 30 December, at the Villa d'Este.

Nadine Helbig. The harvests had been bad throughout the Sabine mountains, and as a result the local people were suffering a famine. Cardinal Hohenlohe accordingly suggested that the Master might arrange a concert for their benefit in the great hall of the Villa. With his usual kindness of heart, Liszt agreed at once. . . . Professional pianists would not willingly play the piano either before or after Liszt, and so the honour of participation fell upon Alfred Reisenauer, a young prodigy then studying with Liszt, and me. The news that Liszt would once again play in public spread through Rome like wildfire, and Americans, Britons, and other foreigners frenziedly sought tickets. The trains were quadrupled and ran up and down unceasingly. Next to the railway line, the country road, covered with carriages, looked like a black line running through the Campagna. Not for centuries had Tivoli so swarmed with people.

I have in front of me this last programme* on which Liszt's name appeared as one of the performers: a scruffy, badly-printed little leaflet, the bungled production of a Tiburtini printing-house, hardly a word without a printing error. For me it is a precious treasure, a diploma of honour of which I am proud.[15]

1880

Leaving Rome on 11 January, and stopping *en route* at Florence to see Jessie Hillebrand (formerly Laussot), and also in Venice, Liszt reached Budapest on the 15th, where he resumed his classes at the Music Academy. Since the suite of rooms being prepared for him there was not yet ready, the Ministry of Education had reserved him an apartment at the Hotel Hungária, which enjoyed a superb view over the Danube to Buda and the hills. 'In my class of at least fifteen pianists, four or five stand out,' he wrote to Gille; 'in particular a Polish girl, Mlle Majewska. She plays the most difficult things excellently.'

* Liszt opened the concert by playing a Schubert duet with Reisenauer, and concluded it with his own *Ave maris stella*.

From Venice he had written to Carolyne: 'Joachim is giving a concert here this evening. Although I am not in the least embarrassed to find myself confronting anyone at all, I prefer to have no sudden encounter with Joachim, who has behaved more than singularly towards me.' But it chanced that the violinist also came to Budapest at this time—and the two met after an estrangement lasting a quarter of a century.

Géza Zichy. At the beginning of the 1880s, Joseph Joachim entered my room early one morning [23 January 1880]. 'Please help me, I am in a very difficult situation,' he said, seeming rather agitated. 'You probably know that I was very close to Liszt, but later we served different gods. And then there were the many tale-bearers. And so I left him.'

'I know!' I replied dryly.

Passing his hand through his curly brown hair, Joachim asked me hesitatingly: 'Will he receive me? Here I am in Budapest, running around his home and not daring to go in. I should like to see him—great, kind, and outstanding man that he is!' Joachim spoke softly, warm sincerity in his voice.

'He will certainly receive you, and tomorrow you must both dine at my place. But in order to set your mind entirely at rest, come with me here and now. I shall call on Liszt to ask him if he will receive you. No, not *if*, but *when* he will receive you. Liszt understands and forgives everything!'

We went to Liszt's flat. Joachim stayed in the anteroom. When I entered, my dear master was sitting at his desk writing. Going slowly up to him, I placed a hand on his shoulder. Turning round, he pushed his glasses up on to his forehead and said: 'What brings you here so early, Géza? Is anything the matter?'

'I bring a penitent whom you alone can absolve!'

'Done!' exclaimed this angelically good man. 'Who is it?'

'He dare not enter, because he once sinned against you!'

Liszt smiled. 'If we wished to associate only with those friends and acquaintances who have not sinned against us, we should have to become hermits. So, who is it?'

'Joseph Joachim!'

'Joachim!' exclaimed Liszt in joyous excitement. 'Joachim! Where is he?'

'Here,' I said, opening the door. Flying into one another's arms, they long embraced. 'Forgive me, Franz!' said Joachim.

'Say not a word!' was Liszt's reply.[1]

Attending Joachim's rehearsal in the morning of 30 January, and the concert itself that evening, Liszt the next day invited the violinist to dinner, together with Zichy and Bonawitz (Joachim's accompanist). 'Zichy told me later that Joachim had confided to him that he felt at fault in regard to me,' he told Carolyne. 'That gives me a tacit satisfaction!'

On 21 March he arrived in Vienna, where as usual he stayed at the

Schottenhof. In a concert at the Gesellschaft der Musikfreunde on the 23rd he conducted *Die Ideale*, *Die Glocken des Strassburger Münsters*, and the Mass for male voices and organ (S8/2). 'The large audience was very kind and applauded me warmly,' he reported to Carolyne, 'but Dame Criticism took care to add her rather muddy waters to my wine.'

'The newspaper critics are jibbing at my public success, which they had neither foreseen nor desired,' he remarked in his next letter. 'They deign to mention it this time, however, while ascribing it to my *likeable personality*! Let us leave our adversaries to grouse, growl and grimace as much as they find fitting—and ourselves quietly follow the motto: "Do what must be done, come what may." '

As he had done the previous year, Liszt attended, and played at, a soirée given by the Wagner Society (24 March). 'He seemed completely rejuvenated, and we have never heard him play more perfectly or more ideally,' reported Theodor Helm in the *Abendblatt des Pester Lloyd*.

On the 25th the *Missa choralis* was performed under Josef Böhm; on Easter Sunday, the 28th, Hans Richter included *Les Préludes* in a Philharmonic Society concert; and on Easter Monday the Hungarian Coronation Mass was performed at the Hofburg Chapel.

Weimar, which he reached on 3 April, was Liszt's base until his return to Rome in August. His main excursion during this time was to the Tonkünstler-Versammlung of the Allgemeine Deutsche Musikverein at Baden-Baden (20–3 May). At a concert on the 22nd, two of the pieces from *Christus* (*Beatitudes* and *The Foundation of the Church*) had to be repeated by command of the German Empress, who granted Liszt a friendly audience. The concert, which also included his *Jeanne d'Arc au bûcher*,* sung and declaimed 'with wonderful pathos' by Marianne Brandt,† was a complete success.

Adelheid von Schorn. Hans von Bülow came to Weimar that June. Attending the matinées and Liszt's lessons, he was appalled to find a crowd of pupils who deserved this privilege neither as persons nor as artists. Alas! it was only too true, and for the Master's genuine friends had long been a cause of deep distress. Basically, Liszt always remained the same: that could be felt during the moments when he spoke earnestly and wistfully to old friends; but human weakness—which increases in old age—and innate kindness made him tolerate many who in earlier times would have had to keep their distance. . . . The female sex in particular sent representatives to the Hofgärtnerei who should never have been allowed to set foot in those rooms, later to ease their path through the world with the title of Liszt pupil, or even that of *favourite pupil*. While he was here on this occasion, Bülow gave a lesson in Liszt's place when the Master felt unwell. Immediately afterwards he came to me to say that he had just shown a number of these *unworthy ones* to the door. Liszt had voiced no objection, he added, and he hoped he had cleared the gang out for good. '*I have done*

* Liszt's arrangement (S373) for voice and orchestra of his song (S293/2) for mezzo-soprano and piano of that title, a setting of a 'dramatic romance' by Alexandre Dumas *père*.

† Austrian singer (1842–1921), famous for vocal and dramatic gifts alike. For many years she was attached to the Berlin Court Opera, sang at Bayreuth, etc.

for Liszt just what I would do for my poodle when ridding him of his fleas.' Racing around my room as he spoke, Bülow rubbed his hands in glee—but I prophesied to him that it would not last long. And so it proved: at the next lesson the whole pack was there again. Liszt had become so accustomed to such company that it was not disagreeable to him.[2]

'This last fortnight, Bülow has been exercising a kind of terrorism here, on some twenty pianists of both sexes,' Liszt remarked in a letter of 3 July to Princess Carolyne. 'He told them categorically that . . . with the exception of about three or four, they were unworthy to receive my lessons, and too badly trained to profit from them. Almost all have already played in public concerts at Berlin, Hamburg, Frankfurt, Naples, and London, and claim the celebrity of a Rubinstein or a Mme Schumann! Judge of their discomfiture at being thus harangued by Bülow!'

A visitor on 30 June was *Theodore Thomas* (1835–1905), the German-born American conductor under whose baton were given the premières in the United States of no fewer than thirteen of Liszt's works, including the First Piano Concerto, *Mazeppa*, *Die Ideale*, *Prometheus*, *Orpheus*, and *Héroïde funèbre*.

A memorable day. Liszt received me in his private rooms, and alone. At first I instinctively looked *up* to meet his eye, and could hardly believe my own when I found myself as tall as he—perhaps a half an inch difference! His geniality was beyond all expression, and this meeting with him was, in itself, worth the journey from New York. . . .

After my call, he accompanied me not only downstairs but even through the garden, by a private way, to my hotel. I smoked a light German cigar which he gave me, remarking, 'Bechstein always sends me cigars; I do not smoke Havana cigars because they are too expensive.' As we walked to the hotel it began to rain and I expected to see Liszt turn back, but he continued to walk with me, unconscious of the storm. 'You do not seem to mind the weather,' I exclaimed. Liszt laughed and replied, 'I never take notice of that which takes no notice of me!'

Now I am very glad to have seen the giant, for the world looks so much the smaller to me.[3]

Also to Weimar this summer came a visitor from the Russia of whose new and original music Liszt was so keen an admirer: the Hungarian-born violinist and teacher *Leopold Auer* (1845–1930).

When I was first confronted by this amiable old man, with his long gray hair hanging down upon his shoulders, with his piercing glance and encouraging smile, I was for a moment overcome by emotion. He engaged me in a conversation regarding music in Russia, seeming to be especially eager for details touching on the younger school of composers, whose works he knew and esteemed.

He honoured me with an invitation to dinner for the following day, and asked me to play for him before we sat down to table. The dinner was fixed for one o'clock in the afternoon, Before it I played first some Bach compositions for solo violin and then—to his own accompaniment at the piano—a *Fantaisie russe* by Napravnik, which that composer had dedicated to me and with which Liszt was much pleased. . . . The dinner was a very merry one. Liszt at his best was one of the wittiest and most amiable of hosts, and he put the entire company at ease by the unpretentious heartiness with which he presided at the table. It is true that he had no need for striving to impress anyone; his greatness was so evident and beyond any question.[4]

Liszt to Princess Marie Hohenlohe. Weimar, 30 July. Supreme serenity still remains the Ideal of great Art. The shapes and transitory forms of Life are but stages towards this Ideal, which Christ's religion illuminates with His divine light.[5]

By the end of August Liszt was once again in Rome, whence he returned to Tivoli. In mid-September he journeyed to Tuscany, for a holiday with the Wagners at the Villa Torre Fiorentina, a palazzo near Siena which they were renting. About his grandchildren, he wrote to Carolyne: 'Siegfried is showing an extraordinary aptitude for architecture—and is sketching vaults, frontispieces, and towers. He has one of the most charming and lively natures of any child I have known; and his sisters could not be better brought up or more gifted. All the young members of the family show me marked fondness and regret my early departure.' On the 25th, by way of Orvieto which he visited to see the Cathedral, he returned to Rome.

Liszt to Princess Carolyne. Villa d'Este, 29 October. I am jotting down a few observations on Lina Ramann's volume;* consequently I am reading slowly, and not without sadness, despite my sincere gratitude for the too favourable sentiments of my biographer in my regard. No one will believe me if I say that I am becoming more and more impersonal! Yet it is the simple truth—to the point that to hear myself spoken of, even to be praised, often pains me. May God temper the wind to the shorn lamb![6]

Princess Carolyne to Adelheid von Schorn, 9 November. Liszt, thank Heaven, is really well at Tivoli, where he is working quite hard—something now becoming difficult for him! Not because of old age: Humboldt, Thiers, and many others continued working until about their ninetieth year, with the same freshness and with the greater facility brought by long experience. But they kept themselves in constant practice. Since Liszt has taken to running around so much, he has entirely lost his concentration. But I don't want to be always complaining needlessly! If God helps him bring to a beautiful conclusion the work with which he is now occupied, I shall require no more of him. If he then creates some other

* The first volume of Lina Ramann's biography of Liszt (*Franz Liszt als Künstler und Mensch*) had been published earlier that month.

trifle, it will be a gift from God! *Un surplus à la mesure désirée*! And yet—he could still have created so much, so very much![7]

Liszt to Princess Carolyne. Villa d'Este, 10 November. In an article in the latest number of the *Gazette de Hongrie* it is stated, quite correctly, that I did not carry off Mme d'Agoult inside a grand piano—as was said wittily in Paris at the time! The end of the article is accurate when it says that not a word escaped Comte d'Agoult, of honoured memory, in his own defence—nor a word against the Comtesse. 'It's all right, I shall bear it,' he contented himself with saying. It is also true that he said of me: 'Liszt is a man of honour.' I applied the same epithet to Mme d'Agoult's brother, Comte de Flavigny. I carried his sister arm in arm with him from one room to another at the time of her serious illness in 1840. My conscience often pains me—but not always according to what other people like to say! That is why I have become absolutely impersonal!

In my letter to la Ramann I am asking her to correct, in the second edition, the very erroneous passage about my insistence on marrying Mme d'Agoult—in advising her, to that end, to be converted to Protestantism. Whoever knows me, even minimally, would never attribute such a thing to me![8]

On 17 November Liszt was visited at the Villa d'Este by the *Revd Hugh Reginald Haweis* (1838–1901), English writer and celebrated preacher who was for long the incumbent of St James's, Marylebone.

After a walk around the gardens, they return to Liszt's 'little inner sitting-room'.

Here stood his grand Erard piano. 'As we were talking of bells,' he said, 'I should like to show you an *Angelus* I have just written;' and, opening the piano, he sat down. This was the moment I had so often and so vainly longed for.

When I left England, it seemed to me as impossible that I should ever hear Liszt play, as that I should ever see Mendelssohn, who has been in his grave for thirty-three years. How few of the present generation have had this privilege! . . . A favourite pupil, Pohlig,* who was then with him at the Villa d'Este, told me he rarely touched the piano, and that he himself had seldom heard him—'but,' he added with enthusiasm, 'when the Master touches the keys, it is always with the same incomparable effect, unlike anyone else, always perfect.'

'You know,' said Liszt, turning to me, 'they ring the "Angelus" in Italy carelessly; the bells swing irregularly, and leave off, and the cadences are often broken up thus:' and he began a little swaying passage in the treble—like bells tossing high up in the evening air: it ceased, but so softly that the half-bar of silence made itself felt, and the listening ear still carried the

* Karl Pohlig (1858–1928).

broken rhythm through the pause. The Abbé himself seemed to fall into a dream; his fingers fell again lightly on the keys, and the bells went on, leaving off in the middle of a phrase. Then rose from the bass the song of the Angelus, or rather, it seemed like the vague emotion of one who, as he passes, hears in the ruins of some wayside cloister the ghosts of old monks humming their drowsy melodies, as the sun goes down rapidly, and the purple shadows of Italy steal over the land, out of the orange west!

We sat motionless—the disciple on one side, I on the other. Liszt was almost as motionless: his fingers seemed quite independent, chance ministers of his soul. The dream was broken by a pause; then came back the little swaying passage of bells, tossing high up in the evening air, the half-bar of silence, the broken rhythm—and the Angelus was rung. . . .

I had conceived, ever since I had studied the life and works of Chopin, the greatest desire to hear him played by Liszt. . . . I ventured to say, 'Chopin always maintained that you were the most perfect exponent of his works. I cannot say how grateful I should be to hear, were it only a fugitive passage of Chopin's, touched by your hand.'

'With all the pleasure in the world,' replied the immortal pianist; and again I sat down by the grand piano, and humming to him a phrase of Op. 37, I begged that it might be that.

'I will play that, and another after it.' (The second was Op. 48.)

It is useless for me to attempt a description of a performance every phrase of which will be implanted in my memory, and on my heart, as long as I live. . . .

There was a strange concentrated anticipation about Liszt's playing, unlike anything I had ever heard—not for a moment could the ear cease listening; each note seemed prophetic of the next: one felt that in the soul of the player the whole nocturne existed from the beginning—as one and indivisible, like a poem in the heart of a poet. The playing of the bars had to be gone through seriatim; but there were glimpses of a higher state of intuition, in which one could read thoughts without words, and possess the soul of music, without the intervention of bars and keys and strings; all the mere elements seemed to fade, nothing but perception remained. Sense of time vanished; all was as it were realized in a moment, that moment the Present—the eternal Present—no Past, no Future. . . .

When Liszt passed silently to Op. 48, he arrived at some stiff bravura passages, which called forth his old vigour. Yet here all was perfect; not a note slurred over or missed; the old thunder woke beneath his outstretched hands; the spirits of the vasty deep were as obedient as ever to their master's call. With the last chord he rose abruptly; abruptly we came out of the dim, enchanted land of dreams; the common light of day was once more around me. . . .

Great heart, great brain, daring originality, electric organization, iron nerve, and a soul vibrating to sound like an Aeolian harp to the wind; there you have the personality, phenomenal and unique, of Franz Liszt.[9]

Liszt to Olga von Meyendorff. Villa d'Este, 25 December. Zola's study of Flaubert is most remarkable. What interested me most is Flaubert's lengthy method of work in eager search of the *mot juste*, suitable, expressive, simple, and unique. I know similar torments in music. This or that chord, or even pause, have cost me hours and numerous erasures. Those who know the meaning of *style* are a prey to these strange torments.[10]

1881

Fanny Lewald. From the last winter I spent in Rome, one in which I saw Liszt far more rarely as he stayed at Tivoli a great deal, a long quiet talk I had with him I have never forgotten. Having visited someone living close to us, he had then come round to see me. He had recently done an American sculptor* a kindness by sitting to him for a life-size bust, and the sculptor, otherwise a man of taste and talent, had been led so far astray by the so-called realism in art which had become the fashion, that he had produced a portrait of Liszt which could really pass for caricature. True, Liszt's face had grown puffier, and his head was no longer held up so proudly; but as soon as he did raise it, begin to look about him and to speak, his eyes flashed and the power of his spirit radiated forth. The change which time had wrought even in him was no longer to be seen; what had perished was forgotten, because the imperishable was still there in all its might.

As I knew the sculptor, esteemed him as a person, took an interest in his work and yet had been vexed by this example of it, I asked Liszt what he thought, not concealing from him my own opinion. 'It is not alluring, this bust,' he said with a smile, 'but I believe it is useful! Let us accept it, like many severe judgements on us from which we can derive instruction for our lives.'

I asked what he meant by that. 'We,' he said, 'who long preserve in ourselves something of our youth, are very easily led into deluding ourselves, and the friend who could enlighten us, our good friend the mirror, is not a trustworthy friend. We are used to it; the friends who have

* Moses Ezekiel (1844–1917), whose studio was at the Baths of Diocletian. His bust of Liszt was made at Tivoli in late 1880 and early 1881, and he records Liszt's opinion as being: 'I have been made so many times as I am not, that I am glad to find an artist who does make me as I am and as God made me!' The bronze bust (head and torso) is now at the Skirball Museum, Los Angeles; the marble bust (head only) is in the museum of the Virginia Military Institute.

grown old with us are likewise used to us; and so we remain for one another the same young friends. That deceives and seduces us; and so that is why it is perhaps really useful when such a youngster comes along and sees us with eyes that have not grown used to us, and cries out: "Look, my friend! This is how I see you, and this is how you are!" '

'The first time I saw you,' I argued, 'I heard you say: we are always young so long as we can please!'

'For the others! Not for ourselves! For we know more about ourselves than they. But, anyway, a work of art such as the bust is in the end a favourable background for the original to look better against; and that is also worth something! It is here, and so it is good!'

Again I had to admire the indulgence with which he tolerated this total failure of a work, one which had certainly cost him a good deal of time; and as one remark led to another I said that in all art, in poetry as much as in the plastic arts, a dry, abrupt rendering of nature was for me something imperfect, indeed negligible, and that it seemed to me nowhere more out of place than in the portrait. It was my opinion, I said, that the artist has to keep to those qualities in his sitter which are both beautiful and lasting. Whether the pair of warts Liszt had on his face were reproduced—as the American had done, giving them particular prominence—was of no consequence; the defect lay in his failure to bring out the indestructible nobility of profile, the spirituality of expression. . . .

'One could,' said Liszt, and his words linger in my mind to this day, 'speak not only of secular and religious art. One should always and only speak of divine art; and if people are taught from their early years onwards that God has given them reason, free will and conscience, one should always add: and Art—for Art is the truly divine!'

I quoted: 'Art, O Man, is thine alone!'*

'Certainly,' he continued. 'He who has been given feeling for Art, and totally he who has been given talent to practise it, has received consecration for his life's path which he must respect. He who develops to the utmost the talent he has, and achieves with it what he can, is participating in the uplifting of the human race and securing both the individuality which Providence has created in him and the little piece of earthly immortality to which we all cling—some more, others less.'

I remarked how beautiful and elevating it was that throughout the entire generation since we had first met he had remained true to his belief in the perfectibility of the human race. 'We are all missionaries! Each of us in his own way!' he rejoined, and when, thinking of his words on earthly immortality, I then observed that the Jews, who have not been taught of the immortality of the soul, strove to ensure their immortality by early marriage and a numerous progeny, he replied:

* From Schiller's *Die Künstler*.

'In that, too, lies something just and true. We live on in our children, and it is hard to see one's children die; it has a damaging effect on our own lives. I have had the proof of it myself.'

He paused for a moment and then said: 'But part of us lives on in our works, and another good part in our pupils; that is something I have always felt. In what we sow, cultivate, and bring to ripeness in them, we keep alive a piece of ourselves; and so,' he added with a smile, 'in our love for our pupils, in our pleasure in their progress and successes, there is perhaps—as in all love—both self-seeking and egoism. We satisfy ourselves and allow ourselves to be loved for it, and the one is as pleasant as the other.'

He was not the man to brag about his merits; he depreciated his achievements, joking about them, and it was no empty expression that once, when his royal patron and friend [the Grand Duke Carl Alexander] asked him what motto he would choose for himself, after pondering for a moment, as His Royal Highness tells me, he replied: 'Faire sans dire.'[1]

Liszt to Princess Carolyne. Villa d'Este, 6 January. How should I not be mortally sad? Your immense and strenuous intellectual toil for some thirty years, superimposed on your almost continuous physical and mental suffering, has caused you to contract habits of arrogance of mind, and even of violent harshness towards your fellows.[2]

Leaving Rome on 15 January, Liszt reached Budapest on the 20th. He was met by Zichy and Ábrányi, who escorted him to the rooms which had been made ready for him at the Music Academy's new building.* 'You know from the newspapers,' he wrote to Carolyne, 'that some ten or twelve ladies have been so kind as to decorate the armchairs and sofas with their embroidery. They are magnificent, worthy of a royal palace—Balzac would have taken pleasure in describing them with their monograms, crowns, and emblems. . . . The most precious and dear tapestry-talisman that you embroidered at Weimar is attached to the wall close to my bed, on which is spread, during the day, the beautiful efflorescent cover given by Cardinal Hohenlohe. . . .'

In February he attended two recitals given at the Vigadó (14th and 18th) by Hans von Bülow, the first of which was devoted to works by Liszt, the second to Beethoven. 'Bülow', he declared, 'is no longer only the marvellous and almost fabulous artist that we know—but he is becoming the fashion, and this time fashion is right!'

Liszt to Princess Carolyne. Budapest, 8 March. In the perpetual movement of my life, there is a good deal of monotony; even music offers some variety only at rare intervals. Without being *blasé*, I feel an extreme weariness in going on living! No effective remedy for that, here below—the best relief is resigned prayer![3]

Accompanied by Zichy, Liszt went on 3 April to Pozsony, to take part in a concert on behalf of that city's Hummel monument. 'When Liszt appeared in his

* In the Sugár-út, today's Népköztársaság útja.

flower-wreathed box,' recalled Zichy, 'the fanfare of the Crusaders' March* rang out from the orchestra, the audience rose from their seats, and an indescribable jubilation broke out.' To conclude the concert, Liszt and Zichy gave a three-hand performance of the Rákóczy March.

After a brief visit to Vienna, Liszt set out for Sopron, where he stayed at the home of Prince Paul Esterházy. His travelling companions were his nephew and godson Franz von Liszt (1851–1919), the composer Adalbert von Goldschmidt (1848–1906), Bösendorfer, and Zichy; and with the last-named he played on Wednesday, 6 April, in a concert at the Casino. The next day he journeyed to Raiding, where a plaque was to be unveiled on the house of his birth. His resistance to the plan—'to make me illustrious before my death seems to me most inopportune'—had proved of no avail.

Géza Zichy. The long line of coaches set off. In front, the four-in-hand with the president of the Sopron Artists' Society; and behind our own carriage came about twenty others. . . . At the boundary post of the village of Raiding, Liszt was welcomed by a troop of horsemen who formed his escort. Our entry into the village was a moving one. The whole place looked resplendent with bunting, and the arch of a large triumphal gate soared over the festivally dressed countryfolk as they enthusiastically greeted the village's greatest son. . . .

In front of the house József Hannibal, Chief Notary of the county, made a nice speech, after which the memorial plaque donated by the Sopron Artists' Society was unveiled. Golden letters on grey marble announce that in this house, on 22 October 1811, Franz Liszt was born.

When he crossed the threshold of his birthplace, Liszt was very moved. He stopped still in every room, looking earnestly about him. After a few minutes he went into the little village church and long knelt in deep devotion on the altar steps. Whoever saw Liszt at prayer felt how sincere his belief was; to see him thus was altogether uplifting. Then we went to the tables bearing refreshments, and Liszt became cheerful once again. One toast followed another, and our mood became ever jollier. An elderly presbyter, J. Berlakovics, related a nice little anecdote about Liszt's childhood. It had been at Whitsun, in 1820, when Liszt's mother had visited the fair at Nyék, little Franzl to his delight being allowed to accompany her. They had stayed with the local schoolteacher, a man named Haller. An old piano stood in the room, and the master of the house and his guests asked the little virtuoso to play one or two pieces for them. Franzl, however, showed himself quite disinclined to do so, replying to every entreaty: 'I don't want to!' For this he had his reasons. He was playing with a very pretty little girl, and thoroughly enjoying himself. His companion had a beautiful red egg which the two of them were rolling around together. When the schoolmaster again and again urged the little artist to go to the piano, the latter eventually said: 'Well, I'll play the piano

* From *The Legend of St Elisabeth*.

if I can have the red egg.' This is a very remarkable occurrence: the first and last time that Liszt was selfish. But the little girl would not be parted from her egg; and the schoolmaster had to buy it from her with a piece of cake, ten cherries, and a copper kreutzer. Whereupon little Franzl played the whole evening, to everyone's astonished admiration.

When the presbyter had finished his tale, I asked Liszt if he still remembered the incident. 'Certainly,' he said with a laugh, 'it was all exactly as he said, except for one thing: I didn't get the egg. The little minx hoodwinked me even then!'

After the meal we went on another tour of the house. Suddenly Liszt stopped before a large green-tiled stove, a rather dilapidated one which clearly revealed old and extensive repairs. Laughing, he said: 'This stove was once a sacrifice to my mischief and a witness of my humiliation. I liked going hunting with my father, and enjoyed hearing the bang of the gun. I had noticed that when loading the gun my father poured powder into the barrel. This powder was kept in little tubes in his hunting bag. On one occasion when we returned home from a hunt, I thought: if the gun bangs so beautifully with a little powder, what a bang there would be if all this powder were ignited at once! Obviously I already possessed a feeling for mass effects. In the stove a fine fire was burning, and so I took up the hunting bag and threw it in. There came a tremendous explosion. Part of the stove burst and fell into the room, I myself being hurled to the floor by the blast. There was a glorious banging effect, but unfortunately it was at once followed by a striking effect that was far less attractive, as my father gave me a good thrashing.'[4]

Writing to the *Vizegespan* (Deputy Chief) of the county of Sopron the next day, to express his thanks for the reception given him, Liszt enclosed 200 gulden for Raiding's church and school, 'to give the inhabitants of my native village a small token of my sincere devotion'.

At Vienna on 9 April he took part in a concert in aid of the Red Cross and of a school in Lemberg.

Neue Freie Presse (10 April). The cream of Viennese high society were assembled. . . . Princess Marcelline Czartoryska, a pupil of Chopin, played a number of her master's works,* and Frau Gomperz-Bettelheim gave an admirable rendering of several songs. The remainder of the evening belonged almost exclusively to Liszt. To great applause he performed with Hellmesberger senior and Sulzer a Beethoven Trio [D major, Op. 70, No. 1]. His song, *Es war ein König in Thule*, sung by Frau Gomperz-Bettelheim, evoked a real storm of applause, which was surpassed only by the ovation accorded to Liszt's playing of the final item.† The audience would not leave off applauding until he gave an encore.

* Including the Larghetto of the Piano Concerto in F minor, in which she was accompanied by Liszt.

† One of the Schubert-Liszt *Mélodies hongroises*.

Via Nuremberg, where he visited his biographer Lina Ramann, Liszt arrived on Easter Saturday, 16 April, at Weimar.

Adelheid von Schorn. He had already been rather unwell in Budapest, and when he reached Weimar his feet were swollen and it was evident that some initial dropsy was present. There were days when he could eat very little, and it got worse until he became really ill and had to stay in bed for a few days. I would spend almost the whole day at the Hofgärtnerei; he was so touchingly sweet and gentle that I count such hours among the most beautiful I spent with him. So long as Liszt felt wretched he followed the doctor's orders, one of the first of which was always the banning of brandy. Here I must touch upon a dark side of his life—his love of strong drink. In describing Liszt's life and character, no one need be afraid of mentioning his faults; of the good there still remains more than enough.

During his concert tours up to 1848 he had got into the habit of often drinking more than he could take. The lively company which everywhere gathered around the likeable, generous artist was partly to blame; and partly, too, the great fatigues to which he subjected himself. Today, when the railway and the telegraph make life so much easier, people no longer have any idea of the time and strength required for travel in those days. Liszt gave a concert almost every evening and travelled both day and night. His secretary, Belloni, was always ahead of him, seeing to and arranging everything. . . . After almost every one of these concerts the journey would be resumed. That such over-exertions sometimes induced him to resort to apparently strengthening drinks, is understandable. In the Altenburg years matters improved considerably; having doubtless seen how such an existence was harming him, the Princess kept him away from it by an orderly family life. . . . He *needed* wine and cognac only to a certain extent as a pick-me-up; without their stimulating effect he felt weak. He never consumed large amounts, but if any kind of excitement came along, vexation for example, he would gulp down a glassful very quickly, and, since he could stand very little, it would go to his head. And so it came about that sometimes when I went over to him he would already be excited in the morning. When I asked his manservant what had happened, it was *always* either that someone had been there or that a letter had come which had angered him; it was *never* the wine alone. . . . He could no longer eat enough: his stomach had been ruined by cognac and strong Virginia cigars. The weaker he felt, the more he drank red wine with cognac. This was a vicious circle from which he escaped only when it had made him really ill and on doctor's orders he was allowed nothing but wine and water. While he was ill he was never irritable, but gentle and communicative—his better self rose to the surface in all its splendour. 'I know that cognac is my worst enemy, but I can no longer do without it,' he remarked to me on one occasion.[5]

Spending a few days in Berlin to attend various concerts, including a performance of *Christus* (25 April), Liszt stayed with Count and Countess Schleinitz. His granddaughter Daniela von Bülow had been living with them for some time, and Liszt seized the opportunity to arrange for her to meet her father, whom she had not seen since 1868 (when, taking the children with her, Cosima had abandoned Bülow and gone to Switzerland to live with Wagner). 'Seeing them together again was the best part of my five days in Berlin,' he told Carolyne.

Christus was a great success. The performance was attended by the Empress Augusta, who the next day received Liszt in audience; and to an 'extremely brilliant soirée' given by his hosts in his honour came the 'cream of Berlin'. A concert of his works, followed by a banquet, was also mounted by the Berlin Wagner Society.

Concerts followed at Freiburg im Breisgau, Baden-Baden, Antwerp, and Brussels. Everywhere his works were received with immense enthusiasm. At Baden-Baden the *Totentanz*, with Liszt's pupil Eduard Reuss (1851–1911) as soloist, was performed (6 May)—the first time that Liszt had heard the work with orchestra.* The second and third hearings followed soon afterwards: a 'masterly' rendering by Zarembski at Antwerp (26 May), and another by Martha Remmert at Magdeburg.

This last occasion formed part of the Allgemeine Deutsche Musikverein festival held in that city between 9 and 12 June, when the Hungarian Coronation Mass and *Ce qu'on entend sur la montagne* were also performed. The orchestra, conducted by the later celebrated Arthur Nikisch (1855–1922), was that of the Leipzig Gewandhaus; and the exceptional abilities of his young compatriot did not escape Liszt, who concluded a toast to Nikisch with the words: 'To the elect among the elect!'

Alexander Borodin to César Cui. Magdeburg, 12 June. I arrived at Magdeburg at 10.50 in the morning. One of my travelling companions had advised me to stay at the Kaiserhof, as being the best hotel, and the nearest to the church of St John, where the first concert of the Festival was to take place, so I hired a porter to carry my bag, and started on foot with him. We had hardly left the station when he said to me: 'There was a festival here yesterday.' 'What festival?' 'What? You don't know? We welcomed a celebrated guest, the old Abbé Liszt. You have not heard of it? There was quite a crowd—the whole town was at the station. When the old Master arrived he was received with as much enthusiasm as a king; the men waved their hats and the ladies their handkerchiefs, and even their skirts.'

Such was the graphic description of my porter. I learnt, in fact, from Gille, that the previous evening an immense crowd had welcomed Liszt at the station with indescribable enthusiasm, and that the ovations had continued until he reached the hotel, where the bands of the local troops had serenaded him. On his alighting at the hotel where the officers usually

* The première had been given by Bülow at The Hague on 15 Apr. 1865, when Liszt was in Rome.

mess, and where they occupy the best quarters, they unanimously offered to dine in the public room in order to place their dining-room at his disposal.

Having learnt from my porter of Liszt's arrival, I inquired at which hotel he was staying. 'Hôtel Koch,' he replied. 'Then take my baggage quickly to the Hôtel Koch,' I said.

It was opposite the station. Liszt occupied No. 1 on the first floor. No. 34 on the second floor was at liberty. There I flung down my travelling-bag, found a visiting-card, and went downstairs. Suddenly I came face to face with Spiridion, Liszt's servant. He recognised me at once, overwhelmed me with salutations in Italian, and flung the double doors wide open before me; unannounced, I entered a large room, in the midst of which stood a Blüthner grand, and on the piano I at once caught sight of the arrangement of *Antar** for four hands, and the well-known second edition of the *Paraphrases*. Liszt, near the window, was thanking three ladies who had just brought him some flowers. There were already several vases of flowers on the table, and Liszt was arranging fresh bouquets. He asked the youngest of the ladies to place one of these nosegays in a vase, and offered her one in his turn.

As soon as he saw me he held out both hands to me, exclaiming: 'Ah! dear Monsieur Borodin, welcome indeed. How glad I am to see you, when did you come? You will dine with me today? Where are you staying? etc.' And my hands were clasped in his iron fingers as in a vice. . . .

Spiridion . . . urged him to shave and get dressed. But the indefatigable old man would not give in, and continued to overwhelm me with questions. I tried once more to steal away, but Liszt detained me. 'Come now, you must stay! I am charmed to see you at Magdeburg; I regret not having met you at Baden-Baden. Your symphony [E flat] had an enormous success there [May 1880]. You should have heard it; you would have been pleased. It is good for us to do these kind of things in Germany; wakes us up, eh? Now, stay with me; sit down here,' he added, observing that I made a move to depart. 'You have not yet seen this programme. Read it!'

After numerous reminders on the part of Spiridion, Liszt passed into his bedroom, which adjoined, where the Montenegrin seated him in an armchair and set to work to shave him. Liszt continued to question me in spite of the door between us. 'Come in here; I am not going to act the coy damsel. You will kindly allow me to finish my toilet in your presence, Monsieur Borodin; it will not take long.'

I went into his room; Liszt was seated in the armchair; the valet was tying a napkin under his chin, as one does to children lest they should soil their frocks. To the left of the door stood a little table, littered with music that had evidently been thrown off in a moment of inspiration. Involuntarily I bent over it, and saw a score, and beside it a transcription for

* The symphonic suite by Rimsky-Korsakov.

pianoforte, both in Liszt's autograph, with blots, erasures and cancelled passages. 'Do you know what that is?' said Liszt, without waiting for me to ask. 'It will amuse you. I am writing a second Mephisto Waltz.* The desire came upon me suddenly; it is quite new. I am busy with the piano arrangement. If you care to see it, take the score. No, not that one,' he exclaimed, 'it is a bad copy; take this one,' And before I had time, the venerable grey-headed master escaped from his armchair and the razor of the Montenegrin, his cheeks lathered with soap, and turned over the music until he found another score. 'Here! Look through this.' But that was impossible, for Liszt talked ceaselessly, asking me if I had brought any manuscript with me, when my symphonies would be published, and if any new works of mine were being performed in Russia. When I thanked him for his kind collaboration in our *Paraphrases*,† he laughed, and said: 'I am exceedingly fond of them. It is such an ingenious idea! They never lie on the shelf with me.'

I mentioned how agreeable and flattering it was to me that he should have written a kind of introduction to my Polka. 'It is only to be regretted,' I added, 'that Rahter published it without my knowledge, for my own bars of introduction ought to have been left out.'

'Oh, no,' he said, 'do not do that; they are necessary, and must be preserved at any cost, for I wrote the close of my introduction on purpose to dovetail with your few bars. I beg of you not to cut them out.'

Hearing me mention the *Steppes*‡ and my quartet, he asked me where they would be published; on learning that I intended them for Rahter, he exclaimed vivaciously: 'Ah, he is not bad, that Monsieur Rahter; he sent me the *Paraphrases*, and at the same time deigned to send me Bach's *Chaconne*, arranged by my friend Count Zichy; no doubt you have it too. It was charming of him to have published this edition without even asking permission, eh?'

When I told him that I should like to hear his *Totentanz*, which I considered the most powerful of all works for piano and orchestra for its originality of idea and form, for the beauty, depth and power of its theme, the novelty of its instrumentation, its profoundly religious and mystical sentiment, its Gothic and liturgic character, Liszt became more and more excited. 'Yes,' he exclaimed, 'look at that now! It pleases you Russians,

* Which exists in three forms: the original work for orchestra (S111), the transcription for piano solo (S515), and that for piano duet (S600).

† Variations on a 'chopsticks' theme by Borodin, Cui, Lyadov, and Rimsky-Korsakov. Displaying much invention and ingenuity, they had delighted Liszt, who considered them 'a work of serious value in the form of a jest' and 'an admirable compendium of the science of harmony, of counterpoint, of rhythms, of figuration, and of what in Germany is called *Formenlehre*!' His own variation, written as a prelude to Borodin's Polka, he had given to Cui in July 1880 for the second edition of the '*marvellous* work'. He had also played the *Paraphrases* in their entirety to Cui, who wrote afterwards: 'I do not think I shall ever again hear them played so elegantly, so transparently.'

‡ Borodin's 'orchestral picture' *In the Steppes of Central Asia*, composed in 1880.

but here it is not liked. It has been given five or six times in Germany, and despite excellent performances it turned out a complete *fiasco*. How many times have I asked Riedel to put it in the Society's programmes! He was afraid and could not make up his mind. This time the orchestra seemed much surprised at the first rehearsal, and only became accustomed to it by degrees. If you care for it, you will be completely satisfied. Do you know Martha Remmert? No? She is a remarkable young pianist who plays it admirably; you will judge for yourself, and will find that I speak the truth.'. . .

At the church of St John, where the rehearsal was to take place, rows of chairs were arranged opposite the organ with their backs turned to the altar, for distinguished guests, the managers and the concert committee. The audience, who faced the altar with their backs to the organ, were fairly numerous, although the rehearsals were not, properly speaking, open to the public. On our entrance there was a general movement and the whole audience rose to do honour to Liszt. . . . The first number on the programme, a symphony for organ and orchestra, was over, and the rehearsal of the Coronation Mass had begun. Liszt listened with lowered head, closing his eyes from time to time. Now and then his lips moved and he murmered his remarks to himself, or communicated them to us, commenting upon various passages of the work itself, or upon its execution. On reaching the Gradual, Liszt bent towards me to explain that this portion, which is often left out in other Masses, is obligatory in the 'Coronation Mass', and that the use of fourths constitutes a characteristic feature of Hungarian music. Most of his observations were distinguished by his habitual bonhomie and humour. . . .

At the concert in the evening he sat in the front row, between Gille and Major Klein, and afterwards near his pupil, Martha Remmert, a blonde and good-looking German, whose lips were faintly shaded with down. She was tall and graceful, slightly affected, and with a touch of coquetry. Opposite to Liszt was a row of ladies seated on the church benches. On the chairs were seated, besides Liszt and the members of the committee, the performers, composers, reporters, authorities, etc. Although I was not a member of the committee, I was invited to take my place in the front row, near to Major Klein and Liszt.

The public in the front row stared at Liszt and his neighbours, made remarks, followed Liszt's slightest movements, and even tried to overhear his conversation. When, on seeing Mademoiselle Remmert bow to him as she moved towards her place, Liszt stopped her and made room for her to sit down by him, with that sweet and caressing smile which is so characteristic of him, the ladies nearby flushed with spite, and glared shamelessly at the fortunate Remmert, and never ceased, during the whole concert, to smile and cackle, while they devoured her with envious glances. Liszt chatted to her good-naturedly, thereby only increasing the anger of these dames. Mademoiselle Remmert gave me at first an impression of affectation, but, as soon as I knew her better, I was convinced that it was merely external. As a pianist she is of the first rank, as regards energy, vigour, expression and rhythm. . . .

After the concert, all Liszt's intimate friends assembled in the hotel dining-room, round the Master, who presided at the supper and had become once more the gayest, wittiest and most amiable company, eating and drinking with good appetite, chatting, joking incessantly, and saying the most brilliant things. The supper went off gaily and noisily. Naturally there were toasts in honour of the hero of the day. The naughty old man, a great admirer of the fair sex, had placed on either side of himself the pianist, Martha Remmert, and the singer, Fraülein Breidenstein* of Erfurt; he paid them assiduous court, as usual. He remained until midnight, and most of the guests left with him.

To his wife. Weimar, 19 June. Liszt is a real Balakirev. What a true-hearted man! There, as you would say, are 'really friendly friends'. Fancy, on my arrival at Weimar he inquired where I was staying. 'Probably at the Russischer Hof?' he said. I had hardly had time to tell him that I did not like that hotel, and that Lutter, the pianist from Hanover, had advised me to take a room in a private house, when the friendly old man hastened to say: 'But Lutter has not come yet. Wait a little, I will find you a lodging.' Then, calling his servant: 'Pauline! Pauline! We must find an apartment in a private house for Herr Borodin. Go and inquire at No. So-and-So and So-and-So,' and he began to enumerate a series of addresses. 'Ten years ago I would not have let you go at any cost and you would have been my guest; but nowadays, you see, I am lodged like an old maid; where could I find room for you?'

I endeavoured to thank him and to excuse myself in every way for troubling him, but I was obliged to await the return of Pauline, who had found me a small room, very clean and *freundlich* as the Germans say. Under my windows is the garden of Goethe's house; on the other side is a garden through which I can get to Liszt's; about twenty yards away is the Grand Duke's park, and everywhere one's ear is filled with the song of the nightingale. Close at hand I have Liszt and the Baroness Meyendorff, who is always charming to me.

In taking leave of me, Liszt said: 'Tomorrow, at eight in the morning, I shall pay you my formal call, as I wish to see if you are comfortably housed.'

He was much pleased with my *Steppes*, and urged me to arrange it for four hands by the following day. 'Wait, I will get you some paper. Spiridion, bring me the music-paper I have there.' But without waiting for

* Marie Breidenstein (d. 1892), a gifted interpreter of Liszt's *Lieder* and oratorios to whom he had also given piano tuition.

his order to be carried out, my Balakirev stumped off with heavy steps to search the cupboard, and produced a sheet of paper upon which he himself inscribed *primo* and *secondo* with a bit of pencil. What will you think of me? I forgot this piece of paper and was not able to go back for it.

The following morning, between eight and nine, just as I had gone out to get my early coffee, the dear old fellow brought it himself and left it with his card. I found both on my return and went off to his house at once to thank him for his thoughtfulness and attention. 'Well!' replied my Venus of the white locks, 'it is because I want you to set to work upon the pianoforte arrangement.'

Under various pretexts he was always enticing me to him and the Baroness. The following day he told me that Prince Wittgenstein had sent me a pressing invitation to go to his house with Liszt and the Baroness, and that the Grand Duke, who desired to see me, would be there, and also his daughters. . . .

It was a case of putting on evening dress, white tie, black coat and opera hat. But chance alone had brought me to Weimar, and I had not the necessary equipment; however, no sooner had Liszt's pupils heard of the case than one lent me his hat, another helped to tie my evening bow, and even came to my rooms with his wife, an English lady, to inspect me from head to foot. At last my Balakirev arrived. Catching sight of my transcription of the *Steppes*, which was half finished, he exclaimed: 'Here they are at last, your famous camels! Come, we'll take this with us and play it at the Wittgensteins',' and the old man folded the music and slipped it into his pocket. I entreated him to abandon the project, saying that the transcription was not finished, and that we could not possibly play it without looking through it first; but he became irritable. 'Do not vex me,' he said, 'you shall thump the bass and I will bang the treble, and it will go splendidly; the latter part you must thump by yourself.' And the obstinate old gentleman actually did as he threatened. At the Wittgensteins' we played the first portion as a duet, and I had to finish it alone.

When shortly afterwards I showed him the complete transcription, I asked his opinion upon a passage that was somewhat difficult for me. 'Leave it as it is,' he answered. 'If Monsieur Borodin cannot manage it, Madame Borodin will do so with ease. Give her my compliments and tell her what I said.' I should mention that in the course of conversation I had told him you were a good pianist.

I dedicated the *Steppes* to Liszt. He embraced me and thanked me warmly.[6]

Adelheid von Schorn. It was at this time that Bülow came to Weimar [24 June] for a stay of several weeks, as did his daughter Daniela. Since the separation from his wife, Bülow had scarcely seen his children, whom he had handed over to Cosima and Wagner, fully confident that with them they would have the best upbringing. Father and daughter were now to be together for some time, to get to know one another properly—and it was for this purpose that Weimar had been chosen.

During their stay we had a great fright when Liszt slipped on the stairs and tumbled down several steps [2 July].

It seemed that no harm had been caused, but the doctor was sent for and found a graze on the right thigh. Liszt of course made nothing of it; but he soon felt that his whole body was bruised, and submitted to staying in bed. For the first few days Bülow and his daughter kept him company. Daniela tended her grandfather until after a few days she departed with her father. I then took over the task, spending nearly the whole day with the patient. I read to him, either wrote for or took dictation from him . . . and tried to make things cosy and comfortable, to keep him in bed for as long as possible. During those days his gentle, noble nature came to the fore once again; he patiently followed all the doctor's orders, drank no cognac, and tried to work as soon as he felt a little better. After only a few days he got up and gave lessons; although, to be sure, he had to lie in a comfortable armchair to do so. The fall left no bad consequences in the short term, but from that time forward a complete change came over him. Whether the shock caused his illness to make quicker progress, or his irregular life was no longer suitable for his weakened body—in short, he became both physically and mentally a different person. His figure grew stouter and stouter, his face was often bloated, his feet constantly swollen, and his beautiful, delicate hands got to look quite different. Mentally, too, he became another person, for he often had so little control over himself that every word irritated him, and he would speak roughly to people not known to him, even though they might be completely innocent of any offence and quite unaware that they had said the wrong thing. His eyes also began to weaken at this time, so that working and reading became difficult for him. As he was used to being constantly occupied, he took to cards, and with pupils or friends would play whist by the hour—naturally not for money—and so kill time this way. All these signs of ageing began in the summer of 1881 and intensified from year to year. Writing to the Princess immediately after the accident, I received two letters from her in reply. After she had posted the first she received my news about the fall and at once wrote the second (8 July): 'You know, Liszt is not one of those who say much in letters; in fact they are a disaster for him! And as soon as he is in Rome the past no longer interests him—he has survived it!'[7]

After Bülow's departure on the 9th, Liszt wrote to Carolyne: 'Bülow's health is now tolerable—but he is not given to conciliation, nor to indulgence! He suffers from an excess of brain, wit, study, work, travel, and continual fatigues. His horror of the Jews has not diminished—at every turn he heaps abuse upon them; witty abuse, moreover, and his signature appears beneath the anti-Semitic petition. If one is drawn up against the Freemasons, he will sign that too, for his hatred of their methods and dealings goes hand in hand with his loathing of the Israelites. Despite that, his successes as an artist, and a strange kind of personal popularity, are increasing. . . . You know the excellent joke he has had printed and nailed to his door: "Mornings not available; afternoons not at home." It is an example I wish I could follow!'

Adelheid von Schorn. One day when Liszt had already been up and about again for some time, and I was taking a meal with him, we suddenly heard a lively exchange of voices outside—Liszt's servant was giving someone a delighted greeting—and a voice unknown to me replied in Hungarian, while in the doorway there appeared a tall, slim young man with only one arm. I realized that it must be Count Géza Zichy, Liszt's friend and pupil, about whom he had already often spoken to me in terms of the warmest affection. Their joy at this reunion was as great as if they had been father and son. Count Zichy was deeply attached to his beloved master; and to have this handsome, gifted, cheerful young man there, with his fund of witty anecdotes, really gave Liszt new life. What Zichy was able to do at the piano with a single hand borders on the miraculous; had one not seen it for oneself one would scarcely have noticed that what others need ten fingers to accomplish he could do with five.[8]

Another visitor at this time was *La Mara.*

About his fall, still in evidence in a small injury to his face, our kindly host spoke as of something unimportant: he had merely bruised a rib, which made breathing difficult for him, and so he had stayed in bed for a few days. . . .

On taking my leave I had to promise to return soon. 'Don't wait too long!' he called after me. That struck me like a warning. In the autumn it would be his seventieth birthday, and yet today he had been so particularly kind and gentle. I had never thought that I could lose him. Today, I found that all of a sudden he had become older, and Pauline Apel confided to me that he really felt not at all well, but would not admit it and had been kept in bed only with difficulty. He simply *would* not recognize illness. And yet swollen feet, which compelled him to wear light, low-cut shoes, and growing heaviness of the face and of the once so slim figure, announced the first symptoms of dropsy. The beginning of the end had come. Sadly I left the beloved house.

Before I could keep a promise I had made him, I heard from the Master: 'Were you so kind as to order Buckle's *History of Civilization*?* If the book is already on its way to me, please do not trouble to reply. . . .'[9]

* In his *History of Civilization in England*, Henry Thomas Buckle (1821–62) adopted a scientific approach which took into account such matters as climate. Interestingly, his biographer remarks that Buckle, a brilliant linguist and chess player, was quite indifferent to music, which he enjoyed on only one occasion in his life—'when Franz Liszt played'.

Liszt to Princess Carolyne, 4 August. You know my aversion to advice and condolences about my health. These last few weeks I have been overwhelmed with both. I am touched by it, but very tired. More than fifty letters and telegrams are on my table. How to cope with the replies!? I should find it more expedient to quit this earthly existence! All the same, I shall never be guilty of ingratitude.[10]

To the same, 6 September. I have to say that my recovery is not complete. There has been no relapse, nor pain—but it is dragging on, and an unpleasant sensation has remained in my right side. Furthermore, for about a year I have been suffering violent nausea when getting up each morning—not during the rest of the day. I know the cause: an irregular diet, too many and too strong cigars, too much brandy, but not to the point that people say. I never drink it without a good portion of water, and I abstain from other drinks and strong wines. . . . My trouble is a simple contusion, without serious injury to any organ. I must be patient for a while, take a dozen hot baths and perspire afterwards. To this end, I have been sent a bath tub from the palace. . . .

This last fortnight I have been working enthusiastically at my *Cantico di San Francesco** . . . which I consider one of my best works. I shall have it performed at some music festival next year—despite the antipathy of the critics, and of the public influenced by them, to religious works outside the conventional forms. . . . At Bayreuth I shall finish scoring the symphonic poem *From the Cradle to the Coffin*.†. . . Just imagine, Monseigneur [the Grand Duke], to whom I played my Second Mephisto Waltz, sketched at the Villa d'Este and finished here, finds it a masterpiece, filled with spirit, originality and youthful vigour! I am dedicating it to my friend Saint-Saëns.[11]

Between 22 September and 10 October Liszt stayed at Bayreuth, again declining Wagner's pressing invitation to live there permanently. Accompanied by his granddaughter Daniela, he then set out for Rome, spending a night at Verona *en route* and also stopping in Venice.

Visiting Rome once again was *Adelheid von Schorn*.

They arrived in mid-October. I was shocked when I first saw him. He looked pale and bloated, his hands and feet were swollen, and he had become very stout. His mood varied greatly, probably according to how he felt physically, and he was almost always tired. On the 22nd we celebrated his seventieth birthday together. He did not want a proper party, but all his

* The *Cantico del sol di San Francesco d'Assisi* (S4), for baritone solo, male chorus, orchestra, and organ. Revised by Liszt at this time, its original version dates from 1862.

† The title of this last of Liszt's symphonic poems was later, at Princess Carolyne's suggestion, changed to *From the Cradle to the Grave* (S107). Its inspiration was a drawing by the Hungarian painter Mihály Zichy (1827–1906).

acquaintances came, as did a mass of letters and telegrams; and at Weimar Lassen gave the first stage performance of *St Elisabeth*.

At the end of October I moved into the Hotel Aliberti. Liszt had two rooms with a terrace—giving him a view over the Pincio—and his granddaughter and manservant were both lodged nearby. The Princess was entirely confined to her room; it was not that she was really unwell at the time, but she would not allow herself to go out into the fresh air. We took turns to visit her, and she directed our lives from her armchair, something that at times we found not a little inconvenient.[12]

Cosima Wagner to Daniela von Bülow. Bayreuth, October. How sad, how very sad, what you tell me. . . . Carolyne Wittgenstein is simply disgusting, seeing that he is there *only* for her sake, and—Marie Hohenlohe is right! Absolutely no feeling at all! Oh, how everything is avenged! Just think, that for this relationship we children, who worshipped him, were constantly and sternly rejected by him! And how I should like there to have been no such revenge! . . . Oh! how painful what you are seeing and what I saw! And Grandpapa's sorrow is ours.

To the same. Palermo, 12 November. Rome personifies for him the failure of everything—that of his principal relationship, that of his artistic career in Germany, that of his relationship to the Church. It weighs heavily on him, I believe, as does his association with the Princess, whose judgement he no longer trusts, after following it blindly for decades! Malwida wrote that she had never seen him so cheerful—which I don't quite understand. The Princess's words made me shudder. That is not the voice of love, which always sees beauty, even when it has disappeared for others; and when it no longer sees it, remains silent.[13]

Adelheid von Schorn. Liszt went out very little. Most of the time he sat working at his desk, often even falling asleep over it. The evenings were generally given to cards, but on occasion he would delight us by going to the piano. . . . Daniela's presence was a great comfort, both for Liszt, who was very fond of her, and for me, who took a great liking to her. It was also a good thing that there were two of us, as one or other had always to be at hand. Only very seldom could we allow ourselves to go out together. That we found it necessary to have daily air and exercise, Liszt could never regard as anything but a seeking after pleasure. He had long had no need of them himself, and could not understand those who did. There were sometimes difficult days for us, when Liszt obviously felt utterly wretched—but would not hear a word on the subject. Then, as he always felt very cold, he had the fire built up until the temperature in his room was 24 degrees Réaumur. We were not allowed to send for a doctor, which would have angered him dreadfully—he positively *refused* to be ill. When we were at our wits' end, we asked [Jakob] Moleschott to visit us. I had made the famous physiologist's acquaintance at the Princess's. He came as requested, and found Liszt sitting in the over-heated room. In a friendly way he told him how harmful that was, and gave him some other advice too; and advised Daniela and me to have a fake thermometer prepared which would show a higher temperature than was actually the case, enabling us to bring it down a few degrees. But with Liszt such things helped little or not at all. I have never known anyone so indifferent to his health as he. The subject was not even allowed to be mentioned. He simply took no notice of it—until the moment when he felt too unwell to go on, and then he would capitulate without a murmur. That moment, praise Heaven, did not arrive. On the contrary, he gradually got better, just as his mood, early on very difficult, became more and more cheerful. . . .

Now we had to see that he went out into the fresh air occasionally. But to induce him to do so was difficult. One day, in very fine weather, he drove to the Villa Doria Pamphili with us. Since he was to take some exercise, we got out and went for a walk in the park. Liszt soon tired, however, and, sitting down on a pile of wood, he took a newspaper out of his pocket, telling us to continue our walk and return for him later. When we went back after a while, there he was, busy reading, his hat removed and his long white hair fluttering in the warm, gentle breeze. But he was no longer alone, for all around him sheep and horses were grazing, having come right up to him without his noticing; and behind, having a good sniff at him, was a little lamb. It was a picture I shall never forget!

Another time we lured him out on the pretext of visiting Pradilla's* studio. He too wished to see the painting which had just been finished: 'Mulei Hassan Surrendering the Keys of the City of Granada to Queen Isabella of Castile.' When we arrived, he chatted for a long time with the artist—but hardly looked at the beautiful picture. His interest in it had passed, and he was glad when he was once again sitting quietly at his desk.

And so in this way we spent November, December, and January. But the fact that, illness and difficult moments notwithstanding, we had much delight in the company of our beloved *Meister*, and that many interesting people joined our little circle, makes this time attractive to look back upon. The loyal Sgambati often came of an evening to keep his dear master company at the piano or at the card table. And Liszt's pupil Friedheim†

* The Spanish painter Francisco Pradilla y Ortiz (1846–1921) was at this time Director of the Spanish Academy in Rome.

† The Russian pianist and composer Arthur Friedheim (1859–1932) had first attempted to become a pupil of Liszt's in the summer of 1878: 'When I stood with exalted spirits in the presence of that august and legendary figure, Franz Liszt, my greatest hour had struck. . . . He found my playing chaotic and his laconic verdict was that "at seventeen one has not cut one's wisdom teeth." ' Brought back early in 1880 by Carl Gille, however, Friedheim was more fortunate. 'I played a piano concerto I had written, and Liszt, at a second piano, played the accompaniment at sight. . . . I was so excited, so exalted, that I could not hide my

was living in the hotel, doing various things for him and so brought into contact with us. Various acquaintances of Liszt's and Daniela's, as well as my own friends, visited us. Comte Gobineau came several times, which was the greatest pleasure for all of us, as he had an indescribably fascinating personality, and his conversation was always most interesting and engaging. . . .[14]

Nadine Helbig. Shortly before Christmas 1881 Liszt entrusted me with the manuscript of his *Weihnachtslied** for tenor and female voices. Hastily copying out the parts, I found six willing ladies and a passable tenor, and got them to rehearse the beautiful work. Early on the morning of Christmas Day we met at the Hotel Aliberti, in front of Liszt's bedroom, and waited until he rang for his servant, Spiridion.† Only then did we begin the beautiful, sweet, simple, moving song, which we performed quite nicely. Our dear, revered old *Meister* had tears in his eyes when he came out of his room before we had time to disappear as we had arranged among ourselves. How heartily he thanked us. As I wished to go to mass, I left the score and parts with him. The next day he brought them back to me himself, and said he had found it necessary to add another five bars to the end of the piece. And he had done it with his own hand, quite painstakingly, on each of the parts as well as on the score itself; and on the latter in his already shaky handwriting he had added the dedication: *A Madame Helbig, en bon souvenir de la belle production de ce chant, 25 décembre 81 à Rome, son très affectionné serviteur, F. Liszt.*[15]

1882

Adelheid von Schorn. Liszt had fixed his departure for the end of January. Fearing for his health, the Princess did everything she could to prevent this winter journey, even going so far as to write to friends in Budapest to say that Liszt was too unwell to travel. This caused a report to appear in the newspapers that Liszt was seriously ill, and we received countless letters and telegrams of inquiry, something that at first we were at a loss to explain. Count Géza Zichy was one of those who wrote to ask me how Liszt was. My reply reported the true state of affairs: that Liszt's health was not good, but much better than it had been in the autumn. . . . When I told

emotion, and at last Liszt was favourably impressed. From this joyous day in 1880 until the black moment of his death more than six years later, I was to be away from him only when I was out on concert tours.'

* S49, from the second piece (*O heilige Nacht*) of the *Weihnachtsbaum* for piano solo.

† Spiridion Knezevics, whom Liszt described as a 'conceited scoundrel', had actually left Liszt's service in August this year, to get married. His successor was Achille Colonello.

the Princess that a false report of a serious illness of Liszt's had been published in the press, but that we had denied this in response to all direct enquiries, she became quite angry, telling me that she had herself spread this rumour, to prevent Liszt's departure. But such machinations had absolutely no influence on Liszt, at most annoying him. . . . He had arranged to be in Budapest at the end of January—and that was how it remained.[1]

Spending the weekend of 28–9 January in Florence, Liszt dined at the home of Count Zsigmond Pallavicini, where a fellow guest was the Italian orientalist *Count Angelo de Gubernatis* (1840–1913).

After the meal Liszt went over to the piano unprompted. It had been locked. Baron Augusz* had told us that he would not play if he found the piano open, for he disliked being *asked* to perform; but if people seemed indifferent as to whether or not they heard him, he himself would have the piano opened. And that is what happened. Having asked for the key, the great master began to play—like an inspired demon to begin with, but then, in conclusion, like an angel. On behalf of my wife I asked him if he would play Arcadelt's *Ave Maria*,† which he had unearthed and made more brilliant [S183/2]. '*Ave Marias*?' he replied; 'my pockets are full of them'—and he soon began to play one, but it was not the Arcadelt.

As Augusz had told me that Liszt would be calling on us the next day, and since my wife was extremely keen for the great master to bestow his blessing on her piano, I advised her to begin to play Arcadelt's *Ave Maria*, in Liszt's own transcription, at the moment when he arrived and was announced. Entering, and at once seeing through our little plot, he was obviously very amused. I went towards him, but, shaking my hand as we met, he continued to walk forward on tiptoe, whistling the *Ave Maria*. Not budging from the piano until he was right beside her, my wife then withdrew, yielding up the stool to him; and Liszt, who enjoyed anything original, went on with that wonderful *Ave Maria* from the point where she had left off, playing it right to the end—and then began again from the beginning, his marvellous fingers producing a shower of pearly notes which quite intoxicated us.[2]

Via Venice and Vienna, Liszt reached Budapest on 4 February.

Liszt to Princess Carolyne. Budapest, 5 April. These threefold annual moves, Budapest, Weimar, and Rome—not to mention the supplementaries—are causing me extreme weariness. To get out of them is hardly possible. And so I have to put up with various chronic discomforts, and to

* Imre Augusz (1859–86), son of Liszt's late friend Antal Augusz.

† Research has shown that this *Ave Maria* was actually an arrangement by the French musician P. L. P. Dietsch (1808–65)—conductor of the notorious Paris première of *Tannhäuser*—of Arcadelt's 3-voice song *Nous voyons que les hommes*.

treat them like 'itinerant' rheumatism. The doctors have no prescriptions for certain ills.[3]

En route to Weimar, Liszt spent 15 to 18 April in Vienna, where he dropped in on the celebrated Polish piano pedagogue Theodor Leschetizky (1830–1915), who had moved to the Austrian capital from St Petersburg a few years earlier. Leschetizky had been on the point of leaving to attend the first Mannheim performance (19 April) of his opera *Die erste Falte*, but, overjoyed to see Liszt again,* he detained him with one pretext and another until the train-time was long past. 'Surely, *lieber Meister*,' he remarked reassuringly, 'you will believe that talking with you is a greater pleasure for me than being present at the Mannheim première of my opera!'

'Notwithstanding the gigantic proportions of his intellect,' recalled Leschetizky in later years, 'Liszt had a charm of manner, a certain gracious cordiality without a tinge of condescension; he seemed to see into everyone's mind and feel with him.'

On 22 April the Weimar classes were attended for the first time by *Carl Lachmund*.

Above all it was the *spirit* of the work being studied that Liszt strove to bring out. But no more than with religion can ordinary words make music better understood. And so, like Christ, Liszt sometimes taught by using images and parables—which enormously enhanced the effect of his influence on his pupils. Those who were already advanced enough to be able to understand the great master properly, obtained knowledge thereby which they could have obtained from no one else in this world. The player's technique, as such, he considered little or not at all. Indeed, he regarded it as outside his own province, for those who wished to play to him were supposed already fully to have mastered the technical demands of the work they were studying. . . .

In the Largo of Chopin's Sonata in B minor, van Zeyl† did not play with sufficient repose, and so the Master exchanged places with him and played the movement himself. . . . What wonderful repose and spiritual exaltation! An invisible Something seemed to be floating majestically in the air; we could not see it but only feel it. It was as though something holy were wafting around us. . . . We sat spellbound, as though he had summoned down an angel from Heaven! I am reminded of a later occasion when he performed a slow movement from a Beethoven sonata, and we all turned pale at the unearthly beauty of his rendering. . . .

During the Scherzo of the Chopin Sonata, he stood beside the piano. His grey eyes flashing as he looked at the pianist, he snapped his fingers and waved his hands to and fro; and although not a word was uttered, his meaning was quickly grasped by van Zeyl, who played the movement much more vividly, with a quite magical effect!

* They had met on several occasions over the years, the first being in the 1840s when the boy Leschetizky was studying with Czerny.

† Henri van Zeyl, a Dutch pupil.

In such ways did our beloved master exert an influence over his pupils; but no one would be able to describe his method accurately or expound it correctly. With a word or gesture, or occasionally even a grimace, he knew how to convey instant comprehension of what was necessary. And when he had obtained the desired effect, then with a pleased smile and uplifted hand he would turn towards the rest of us, as though saying: 'Note the difference!'. . .

Extremely kind and friendly though he was as a rule, we had the occasional feeling that we were sitting on the edge of a volcano. If anything happened to set his nerves on edge, or to offend his sense of justice or propriety, his anger and vexation could break out like lightning—only, happily, for the most part to die down again equally quickly. After such an outburst he was always scrupulously keen to show through word and deed that he retained no trace of ill feeling over what had occurred.[4]

On 30 April Liszt went to Brussels for a 'fairly tolerable' performance (the first in French) of *St Elisabeth*. One of the friends sharing his box was Saint-Saëns, who had travelled from Paris for the occasion; and among those who came during the interval, to offer their congratulations, were Jules Massenet and Francis Planté. At a private dinner in his honour, 'several Hungarian pieces and a Strauss waltz were well played by a dozen costumed gypsies who were passing through Brussels. Later, Zarembski and Planté went to the piano and played my *Tasso* and the Concerto in A [S651]. The audience were delighted. The mistress of the house, Mme Bérardi, was so delicately tactful as not to ask me to go to the piano —and I did not deem it fitting to do so. But this resulted in no cooling of the atmosphere!'

Carl Lachmund, 27 May. Fräulein [Emma] Grosskurth played Schumann's great Fantasy in C excellently. In suspense we awaited that passage at the end of the second movement where there is a sequence of hazardous skips —which are all the more difficult because the hands are moving in opposite directions. The pianist came through with flying colours. With a pleased smile, the Master said he wished to change places with her. Saying no more than, 'Yes, yes, it is a dangerous passage,' he then played it himself—without missing a note and without visible effort. I have heard many great pianists play the Fantasy, but all of them, even Rubinstein, displayed physical exertion in this passage. Not Liszt, however, whose hands glided over the keys with such ease that one was no longer conscious of difficulty. He seemed not to notice the keyboard, but had his head turned towards us with the engaging smile which captivated everyone. And thereby he hammered into us afresh his principle of not keeping the eyes glued to the keys, so that more freedom is gained for the expression.[5]

On this same day, 27 May, Liszt's pupils were joined by *Eugen d'Albert* (1864–1932). Hearing the young pianist in Vienna the previous month, Liszt had embraced him, saying: 'Not since Tausig have I heard such playing!' D'Albert, who spent two years with Liszt (whose nickname for him was 'Albertus Magnus'), developed into one of the greatest pianists of the late nineteenth and early twentieth centuries; and also a gifted composer, whose opera *Tiefland* still delights audiences. Often after hearing d'Albert play, Liszt would embrace him and say: 'In my younger days I should have enjoyed competing with you—nowadays I can no longer do so!' For his part, d'Albert would maintain in later life that Liszt's rendering of the Adagio of the *Hammerklavier* Sonata was 'the sublimest playing ever achieved on the pianoforte'; and that Liszt's performance of the *Emperor* Concerto had reminded him of Beethoven's remark: 'Music is a higher revelation than all wisdom and philosophy.'

No one knew as did Liszt how to shape a performance of a Beethoven work and renew its spiritual content as though it had been composed for him. His playing of the E flat Concerto I shall never forget. Generally speaking, everything I know and have learnt about the higher piano-playing, I owe to Liszt![6]

Carl Lachmund, 1 June. Once again we heard Liszt play. Not an entire piece, which he did only rarely, but part of his difficult, albeit wonderful, *Feux follets*, which Fräulein Grosskurth, one of the best of his women pupils, had brought. She did not succeed in bringing out the peculiar charm of the part marked *scherzando*, where the right hand passes over the left to play the little *staccato* bass, which is then answered by the sparkling *leggero* passages in the treble. To show us how he wished it played, the Master then sat down at the piano himself. The extraordinary charm which he put into the bass, and into the answering shimmering and flickering passages in the treble, it is impossible to describe, even approximately. He did it without visible exertion, merely a slight shaking of the head as the right hand flew back and forth from treble to bass, and bass to treble. The expression on his face changed constantly with the contrasting passages in the music, and he seemed totally to have forgotten his surroundings.[7]

In early June Liszt was visited by *Walter Damrosch* (1862–1950), son of Leopold Damrosch, who had in 1871 emigrated to America. Although he had at this time barely begun his career, the younger Damrosch himself later became a well-known conductor, and it was he who at New York in March 1887 conducted the first performance in the United States of *Christus*.

I was naturally overwhelmed at the idea of seeing the great Liszt face to face. His name had been, ever since I could remember, a household word in our family. My father and mother had told me so much of his friendship for them, his genius and his triumphs as a piano virtuoso, and of his voluntary relinquishment of all this to devote himself exclusively to creative work and to helping the entire modern school of young composers. My father had kept up a desultory correspondence with Liszt during the years he had spent in America, and as soon as I arrived in Weimar I went . . . to pay my respects to the old master. I entered his room in great trepidation, and when I managed to stutter a few words to tell him that I was the son of Dr. Leopold Damrosch, I was amazed at the kindness of his reception. He immediately spoke of my father and mother with such love that I forgot some of my timidity. . . . He then asked me how long I expected to stay in Weimar. I said two days and that I was then going to Ems for a cure and to Bayreuth to hear the first *Parsifal* performances.

A curious change came over Liszt as I spoke. He repeated several times, 'Two days, ha, yes, *Parsifal*, of course, Bayreuth. *Parsifal*, of course,' and then he picked up a box of cigars. 'Well, at least you'll take a cigar before you leave Weimar?' I said: 'No, *Meister*, thank you very much, I do not smoke.'

'You should then go tonight to the theatre to hear the first performance of Calderón's play *Above all Magic is Love*, for which your father's old friend Lassen has written the music and which he will conduct.'

I assured the Master that I would certainly go, but sensing a certain frigidity in the air, and feeling that so unimportant a person as myself must not take any more time of the great Liszt, I withdrew.

That evening I went to the historic little theatre doubly hallowed by the productions and ministrations of Goethe, as well as the memorable times in the '50s when Liszt officiated there and conducted the first performances of Wagner's *Lohengrin*. . . . The theatre was so small that you could almost see every person in it as in a drawing-rooom, and, to my astonishment, in the first interval one of the servants of the theatre came and asked me if I were Herr Damrosch, saying that Kapellmeister Lassen wished to see me. I followed him to the stage and was immediately accosted thus by Lassen: 'What did you do to the Master this morning? I came in just after you left and found him in tears. He said, "a young son of Damrosch called on me this morning. I thought of course he would stay here and study with me, but instead of that he told me he was going to stay for only two days. The young generation have forgotten me completely. They think nothing of me, and have no respect for us older men of bygone days. Am I an hotel in which one takes a room for a night, then to pass on elsewhere?" '

Needless to say, I was overcome at such a dreadful development of a perfectly innocent remark of mine. I could not conceive it possible that so small a person as myself should have unwittingly brought about so tragic a result, and I implored Lassen to tell me how I could efface it. Lassen, seeing my unhappy state, advised me to go the next morning at 8 o'clock to see Liszt again and to explain everything to him. I sat through the rest of the play, but actually did not hear a word of it or a note of Lassen's music; I was too occupied with my own misery. I did not sleep all night, but tossed about restlessly and at six arose and wandered about dismally until seven when a frowsy waiter in the dining-room of my hotel gave me a cup of coffee.

Punctually at 8 o'clock I knocked at Liszt's door, and as I entered I saw this wonderful-looking old man with his splendid white hair and deep-set eyes, already at his work-table. As he saw me his eyebrows arched and said: 'What, still in Weimar?'

I came forward and tried to speak, suddenly burst into tears and then managed to stammer out my great admiration for him, how my father had always held him up as the ideal musician of our times, and how he must have misunderstood my words of yesterday if he thought that I intended any lack of respect or reverence for such a man as he. As I re-read this it seems quite articulate, but as I told it to Liszt it must have sounded very ridiculous, but nevertheless I suddenly felt his arms about me and a very gentle furtive kiss placed upon my forehead. He led me to a chair, sat down by me and began again to talk and reminisce about my father and mother. He then invited me to come that afternoon to his piano class, and I left very much relieved at the outcome of my visit.

I then called on another old friend of my parents and also of Liszt's, Fräulein von Schorn. I found at her house a friend of hers, Baron von Joukovsky,* a Russian painter of distinction and a highly interesting man, who had become very friendly with the Wagner family and had designed the Hall of the Holy Grail for the *Parsifal* production at Bayreuth. When I told them of my experience with Liszt they explained to me that Liszt had grown very old, that he felt the modern musical world was forgetting him and that in choosing a sacred text like *Parsifal*, Wagner had been, so to speak, encroaching somewhat on his domain. . . .They also told me that Liszt was now surrounded by a band of cormorants in the shape of ostensible piano students, many of whom had no real talent or ambition, but who virtually lived on the Master's incredible kindness, abusing it in every way and altogether making the Weimar of that day a travesty of former times. . . .

I attended the audition in Liszt's rooms that afternoon and found that there was indeed a pitiful crowd of sycophants and incompetents assembled; but there were a few exceptions, notably Eugen d'Albert who . . . played wonderfully and to Liszt's great satisfaction. . . . But another one, who shall be nameless, sat down to play the Beethoven sonata in E flat and botched the introduction so horribly that Liszt gently pushed her off the chair and sat down himself saying, 'This is the way it should be played,' and then the music seemed to just drop from his fingers on to the piano keys, and such a heavenly succession of sounds ravished my ear that I did not think it possible human hands could evoke it. He then said to her: 'Now, try it again.' And she did, and, if anything, played even worse than before. Again Liszt played the opening phrases, and then, somewhat

* Paul von Joukovsky (Zhukovsky) (1845–1912), son of the Russian poet and translator who had been private tutor to Tsar Alexander II when young. Later this year he painted a portrait of Liszt for the Canadian piano manufacturers Rich & Mason.

irritated, he said: 'Now, make a fool of yourself again.' But by that time to our relief she felt that both she and we had had enough.

After this I met Liszt several times and he always treated me with uniform cordiality, but every once in a while the memory of our first meeting would come to him and he would make some gently malicious remark, such as 'Oh, here comes our young American; like lightning he flashes through the world!'[8]

Adelheid von Schorn. In June I went to Nordheim to visit relatives. Passing through Meiningen I happened to run into Bülow* at the station, and as we were so near his home he invited me there. That suited me very well as there was something I wished to speak to him about. He had recently stopped coming to see Liszt; both inwardly and outwardly he was turning away from him. Knowing that this greatly hurt Liszt, I intended to appeal to Bülow, for which reason his invitation was most welcome, and the three hours at my disposal I spent entirely with him.

A short time previously, he had got engaged to Fräulein Schanzer,† an actress appearing in Meiningen; and he told me that after the wedding his bride would return to her old lodgings, at the other end of the town from his own. Such a course was, he believed, the only right way to a perfect marriage. Assuming that he was joking, I was just about to laugh out loud when he seized my hand and said quickly: 'Don't laugh; I am completely serious.'

We had a long conversation about Liszt, and at first he was so inflexible in his sudden aversion to him that I very nearly got up and went away in anger. But realizing that I would achieve nothing by so doing, I restrained myself and talked both of us into a calmer state. He had never forgiven Liszt for not having stood by him more vigorously during the difficult times that had passed. Further, he had gradually become estranged from his music. The more he had—with the utmost sorrow—turned away from Wagner and towards Brahms, the more he had grown to dislike Liszt's works too. And in latter years Liszt's entourage, which he was compelled to endure every time he visited the Hofgärtnerei, had become such anathema to him that merely talking about it made him fall into a rage. It was the sum of all these things that made it difficult for him to associate with Liszt.

Talking as persuasively as I could, I succeeded in mellowing him somewhat by reminding him how fond of him Liszt always had been and still was; how difficult it was for such a man as Liszt to become old and frail and, because of a deterioration in sight and hearing, almost to be prevented from working or music-making; and how distressing he was bound to find it to be abandoned by his nearest and dearest and

* Hans von Bülow was conductor of the Meiningen Court Orchestra from 1880 to 1885.

† Marie Schanzer (1857–1941).

surrendered to the inferior company which would then cling to him all the more. In the end he had to admit that I was right, and when I took my leave of him he promised an early visit to Weimar. He kept his word, giving Liszt great pleasure thereby.

Years later, when I too was vexed at all the disagreeable things going on around Liszt, and was on the point of withdrawing from the Hofgärtnerei, it was Bülow who came and reminded me of my words. Just as I had kept *him* from disloyalty to his old master, so he kept *me*—and I thanked him warmly for preventing me from committing such an injustice. . . .

In September, passing through Meiningen on my way from Nuremberg to Weimar, I visited Bülow again, to make the acquaintance of his wife. Everything was different from what I had expected. He had been seriously ill on return from the honeymoon, and, soon realizing that she could not look after him properly if she was not living with him, his bride had moved in one day with bag and baggage. I was unable to see him, but got to know his attractive and likeable young wife, who had to begin her marriage in such difficult circumstances. Its continuation will most likely have been difficult too, for Bülow had 'no talent as a husband', as Liszt once remarked to me.[9]

Towards the middle of June, *Felix Weingartner* (1863–1942), Austrian conductor (in 1908, Mahler's successor at the Vienna Court Opera), composer and writer, met Liszt for the first time.

My fellow-student Conrad Ansorge* mentioned to me one day that he had just returned from Weimar, where he had played to Liszt. 'How did you manage to get to him?' I asked in astonishment. 'You can write to him at any time and he will receive you on certain days,' Ansorge replied. 'If you like, you can come with me next time. If you have been with him just once, it is something you will remember for the rest of your life.'

In my imagination I thought of Liszt as a king, living in a palace and holding court for a small select circle. Nevertheless, I plucked up courage and wrote to ask whether I might visit him and show him some of my compositions. Would I receive a reply? I doubted it. But the unassuming little letter which came by return of post, in an envelope bearing the old Imperial stamp and a Weimar postmark, I have to this day. It runs: 'Dear Sir! Until 22 June, on any afternoon between 3 and 7, you will receive a friendly welcome from F. Liszt. 8 June '82, Weimar.'

A few days later Ansorge and I set off for Weimar. . . . At about 3 o'clock we went along the Marienstrasse, at the end of which stood a small, one-storey house with a carelessly kept garden: the Hofgärtnerei. This was the 'palace' in which dwelt the musician I had imagined to be so inaccessible. There was not the least sign of a sentinel at the door, but

* German pianist and composer (1862-1930).

through the open window came the sound of piano-playing; and with a peculiar nervousness I climbed the narrow, winding staircase. . . .

The door opened. Liszt was standing with his back to it, beside the piano, scolding a youngster who had evidently been playing badly. He was not so tall as I had imagined, being even somewhat shorter than I myself, though his bent back and stoutened figure doubtless contributed to this impression. What had he looked like as a young man when, slim as a darling of the gods, he had been the magnet around which a charmed circle had gathered?

The youth slunk away like a condemned criminal. Growling something about 'dirty linen', Liszt angrily threw the music on to the piano. Never again did I see him in such an ill humour as in that first moment. Then he turned around and his eyes fell on the newcomer. For the first time I saw his face: the features just as I had long known them from pictures, but broadened. The brilliant eyes, which looked straight at me, were light in colour. Some large warts were immediately noticeable; but his face was altogether too imposing to be disfigured by such minor blemishes. One large wart in the middle of his forehead was nearly a quarter of an inch long; as he was short-sighted and could not read without glasses, he used it to hold them when not needed. I gave my name and referred to his kind letter. 'Quite right,' he said very affably, extending his hand. Soft and warm to the touch, it was delicately fashioned, with slim, exceptionally long fingers.

The company I met at Liszt's in no way resembled a school. Some twenty to thirty people moved unceremoniously around a plainly furnished, rather large room in which stood both a huge concert grand and an upright piano. Near the window were a plain writing-desk and a few chairs. A portrait of Beethoven on the wall caught my eye at once.

Liszt corrected the performers, interjected witty, often sarcastic, comments, and occasionally played a few bars himself. I watched greedily when those long thin fingers glided apparently aimlessly over the keys, overcoming without effort difficulties which would have brought the sweat to the brow of any other player. Eventually he came over to me and gently but firmly propelled me towards the piano. I had brought with me the sketches of my *Phantasiebilder*. To the first piece he gave high praise, and was particularly appreciative of an unexpected change in the harmony. The others he seemed to like too, for he spoke very encouragingly about them. Once I bungled a passage—and, indeed, I was feeling rather nervous at having to exhibit my far from virtuoso technique in front of no less a person than Franz Liszt. But by reminding myself that I had come to him as a composer rather than as a pianist, I was able to retain my composure. 'No muddling!' he called out; 'that is what they do at the Conservatorium.' I played the passage again, this time successfully. He then gave me a friendly invitation to visit him often and to take more of my things with me. I thanked him, bowing in silence. The next week I went there again, but only as a listener. At the time I had not the least inkling that in the last years of his life the great man would become a fatherly friend to me.

One of the performances I heard during my first or second visit to Weimar has remained permanently in my memory. An inconspicuous, long-haired youth, rather reminiscent of portraits of the prematurely-deceased Carl Tausig, went to the piano and played Chopin's great Etude in A minor so wonderfully that we were all struck dumb with astonishment. Beside himself with joy, Liszt took hold of the little man, virtually lifting him from the floor, and kissed him repeatedly. Not long afterwards the world resounded with the name of a new genius on the piano: Eugen d'Albert.

Fleeting though it was, my first meeting with Franz Liszt had a permanent effect upon me. It was my first encounter with a great man, a prince in the realm of music. A childhood dream which, like so many others, later proved prophetic, comes back to my mind. It had been several years earlier when I was still at school in Graz. In front of me I had seen a gently-rising hill, shining brightly in the sunlight pouring down upon it from a radiant blue sky. Towering high above me on the summit of the hill stood a venerable figure in a black robe, his silver-white hair glistening in the sun: Franz Liszt, as I knew him at that time from his portraits. He had beckoned to me, but I had been unable to reach him. Now, however, we had actually met. He had, it is true, been less sparkling and towering than in the dream, had even looked rather portly—but a heavenly, occasionally even a demoniacal, fire still flashed from his eyes, giving one a notion of the power they must once have emitted. I still stood far away from the Master, could only gaze upon him and remember him with mingled awe and astonishment. But even this was enough to restore my spirits and fill me with gratitude for my lot.[10]

After brief visits to Jena and Freiburg im Breisgau, on each occasion for a performance of *Die Glocken des Strassburger Münsters* (and at Freiburg also of the Gran Mass), and to a Liszt Concert at Baden-Baden, Liszt in early July spent several days in Zurich, where from the 8th to the 12th the annual Tonkünstler-Versammlung of the Allgemeine Deutsche Musikverein was held. His companions included Saint-Saëns, Sophie Menter, and Marie Jaëll, recently widowed. Also present, a cellist in the orchestra, was the young Victor Herbert (1859–1924). After Liszt had accompanied performances of *Die Loreley* and the dramatic monologue *Lenore*, he and Saint-Saëns played the duet version of the Second Mephisto Waltz. 'You should have heard that playing,' recalled Herbert. 'We were afraid every moment that the piano would go to smash under Liszt's gigantic hands that came down like very sledge hammers. He played *primo* and Saint-Saëns *secondo*, and though Saint-Saëns had the more powerful end of the piano, Liszt soon overpowered his bass notes completely. . . . The great pianist was fairly worshipped by all present. I see his kindly beaming face yet, his white locks, as sitting in a box listening to the orchestra and choruses, he would fall into a short doze, then suddenly wake up again.'

Saint-Saëns had been accompanied to Zurich by Gabriel Fauré (1845–1924). It was the latter's first meeting with Liszt. 'Saint-Saëns claims I was green about the gills when he introduced me to his famous friend, and I cannot tell you how gracious he was towards me,' he wrote. The description of his son Philippe Fauré-Fremiet was blunter: 'When he found himself in front of the marvellous old man, Fauré turned pale and began to tremble.'

Liszt played to the two French composers the piano solo version (S499) of his *Cantico del sol*. 'He was like a humble child showing you a piece of homework!' was Fauré's comment. 'Tomorrow it's my turn to show what I can do! Please put a shoulder to my burden of emotion, otherwise it will bring me to my knees!'

The next day, Fauré brought his Ballade to Liszt, who sat down and began to play the difficult work at sight. But after five or six pages, saying 'I've no longer any fingers', he broke off and asked the composer to take over and play the piece to the end. When, afraid that the Ballade was too long, Fauré made a remark to this effect, he received from Liszt the splendid reply: 'Too long, young man? Makes no sense. One writes as one thinks.'

Of *St Elisabeth*, performed on 9 July, Fauré's opinion was—'magnificent'.

On the 15th, Liszt arrived at Bayreuth, where preparations were afoot for the first performance (26 July) of Wagner's music drama *Parsifal*.

The Austrian pianist August Göllerich (1859–1923). In the new park the people were making their way towards the attractive hill crowned by the festival theatre. And then suddenly—it was an uplifting sight—they all bared their heads: driving past us in an open carriage were Wagner and his wife, with, in the back seat, Liszt and young Siegfried.

Wagner, who in the evenings at Wahnfried was always bubbling over with high spirits, looked at that moment remarkably angelic in expression, as though gazing into another world.

Liszt's head seemed that of a god enthroned above the clouds, gently smiling down on bustling humanity. In the second long interval I sat opposite him at table. Never shall I forget how his voice excited me. Uttering a few friendly sounds, with which he expressed more than many another does in well-chosen words, its tone was deep, as though springing up from the source of all things.

Only one other have I heard talk in so gentle and courteous a manner: Pope Leo XIII shortly before his death.[11]

Returning to Weimar on 5 August, Liszt then travelled back to Bayreuth on the 24th for the civil marriage ceremony on the 25th of his granddaughter Blandine to Count Biagio Gravina (1850–97), and the church ceremony on the 26th. From 30 August until mid-November he remained in Weimar (apart from a day trip to Arnstadt in September).

At one of the classes in September he played the Scherzo and Adagio from the *Hammerklavier* Sonata to the pupils.

Carl Lachmund. When he came to the Adagio—it is marked *Appassionato e con molto sentimento*—his eyes began to water and he seemed to breathe with more difficulty, so ardently did he love the Beethoven slow movements. . . .

When he had ended, we felt as though we had experienced a vision, as though we had heard angels singing! No one moved, only a slight sigh could be heard from more than one mouth.

At the last chord, which is repeated slowly four times, I watched his hands, which, in complete disregard of the usual rules, he held in a manner all his own; and I noticed that he could barely reach the tenth note in each chord easily enough to be able to play the chords quietly and without breaking them. I believe he thought the same thing at that moment, for as he slowly began to rise he fell back again and said after a short hesitation: 'People generally believe that I am endowed with very large hands, but they are mistaken. As you see, I can just reach the tenth to play it quietly as it should be played.'

His hands were slender and of a poetic-spiritual kind, quite unlike the typical pianist's hand of a Rubinstein, a d'Albert, or a Rosenthal. His knuckles were virtually concealed, and not broad or chubby; his thumbs did not stretch away from the palm of the hand but clung to it; and the palm itself was neither fleshy nor muscular.

When Liszt was at the piano, his hearers gave no thought to the technical, material, modern aspects of the performance; in his wonderful playing there was only, and to a unique extent, a fervid and passionate outpouring of soul and spirit. Not only was he the *greatest* pianist the world has ever known, he was the *only perfect one*.[12]

Princess Carolyne to Adelheid von Schorn, 9 November. You have hit the nail on the head. That is how I looked after him for twelve years. Always doing my own work in the same room, otherwise he would never have composed all the things that mark the Weimar period! It is not genius he has lacked, but *Sitzfleisch* (an ugly word but a great virtue), diligence and perseverance. If no one helps him with it, he is powerless; and when he feels that he is powerless, he resorts to stimuli. And so it gets worse and the vicious circle begins. . . .

I see the shadows drawing slowly near; yet the hope sometimes remains within me that he may even now do some more great work! I have so prayed! But he needs some external spur, and to have you at his side. . . . One has to sit with him over a work for as long as one wishes him to keep at it. Without such a calm, but constant, gentle, mild, and devoted female companionship, he *can* do nothing great, merely polish.[13]

In mid-November, by way of Nuremberg, Zurich, and Milan (where he visited Ricordi's and readmired the Cathedral), Liszt journeyed to Venice, having been invited to spend Christmas and the New Year with the Wagners at their rented palazzo overlooking the Grand Canal. At Zurich he was gratified when the proprietor of his hotel refused all payment for 'a charming room, with dinners, suppers, and excellent wines'—but at the customs in Milan less pleased to be fined for having brought 50 cigars with him. Venice was reached on the 19th.

Liszt to the Grand Duke Carl Alexander. Venice, 24 November. Coming through the magnificent St Gotthard tunnel, I felt as did the ultra-French idler who cried out in the Place Vendôme: 'Oh, when one looks at the column, how proud one is to be French!' Yes, one is proud to belong to the human race when the enormous intellectual and material achievements of our century are considered. Each of us should contribute to them as much and as well as he can. Above all, Terence's famous line, *Homo sum, et humani nihil a me alienum puto*, must be practised as loftily as it was by Your ancestors, and by Goethe, Humboldt, and their colleagues, including my most illustrious friend R. Wagner. I am his guest at the Palazzo Vendramin, where I shall stay, enjoying princely accommodation, until the New Year. He neither makes nor receives visits, and goes out solely to take the air. For thinkers and labourers alike that is a good example, and I regret that I can follow it only rarely. The pincers of daily life hold me in a kind of wordly grip, one which often runs counter to the Ideal I dream of and sometimes strive to express in music.[14]

To Princess Carolyne. Venice, December. You know what a sad feeling children inspire in me*—their future is exposed to so many contrary chances! Human life is so full of bitterness and disappointments, that I no longer feel able to rejoice very much at the coming into the world of a little creature subject to all our frailties, follies, and misfortunes. On the other hand, I do not grieve excessively at the deaths of those I have known. I even find their fate enviable, for they no longer have to bear the heavy yoke of life, and the responsibility it implies. The sole active and very keen feeling I retain is that of compassion—for the intense vibrations of human sorrows. Sometimes, for brief moments, I feel those of the sick in the hospitals, of the wounded at war, and even those of people condemned to torture or to death. It is something analogous to the stigmata of St Francis—without the ecstasy, which is for the Saints alone! This strange hypertrophy of the feeling of compassion came to me at the age of sixteen, when I wanted to let myself slowly die of hunger in the cemetery of Montmartre.[15]

The painter Alexander Wolkov-Mouromtzov (1844-1928). Italian society understood very little of the immense reputation which men like Liszt and Wagner enjoyed in Germany and Austria, and one often saw odd little scenes. Thus, for example, at one of the evening parties Princess Metternich was giving in honour of Liszt, while she and I were looking at and criticising a family portrait, painted by Kirchmayer, in the next room, a young lady, well known in Venetian society, came into the room, and going straight up to Liszt, said to him, 'Sir, they have asked me to sing something. Will you accompany me?'

* These reflections were prompted by news of a child born to Emile Ollivier and Marie-Thérèse Gravier, the woman who had in 1869 become his second wife.

The cheek with which she asked this favour gave the measure of her ignorance as to the exceptional position which Liszt occupied in the world, and the impossibility of suggesting such a thing to him. Princess Metternich and I could only smile, but Liszt, without even turning to the lady in question, said dryly, 'No, madam.'

After two or three minutes he went back to the drawing-room, which was full of people, and said rather loudly, 'Hohenlohe,* come and sing Schumann's *The Two Grenadiers*. I'll accompany you.'

The face of Liszt as an old man was amazingly interesting, because of the way the expression, and even the very shape, changed according to his moods. Ladies would get up at six in the morning to go and contemplate his praying in church and to admire his look of beatitude. It was especially his thick and almost black eyebrows which accentuated his various expressions to an extraordinary degree. One day when he was making Frontali† read one of his violin compositions, the latter stopped suddenly at a passage he could not play, saying, 'But it can't be done.' At this phrase the face of Liszt, seated at the piano, darkened. He drew his great brows together, his lips tightened and the corners went down, his closed eyes disappeared under his eyebrows, but he continued to play the chord on which Frontali had stopped.

The latter, seeing this, put all his efforts into trying to play the phrase, first a little better, then still better, at last quite well. I watched Liszt all the time—his face was far more interesting than the piece of music. Every improvement in Frontali's playing was reflected in his features. His lips untightened, his eyebrows lifted, and his eyes opened. It would be impossible to represent more graphically the change from a stormy day to beautiful sunny weather. But directly afterwards, probably remembering the remark just made to him that a passage of his composition could not be played, his features assumed once more their severe expression, and he dryly repeated Frontali's phrase in a belated reply: 'It can't be done. Yes, it *can*, when people aren't asleep.'

Liszt's face changed completely when, as he composed, some musical phrase absorbed him and he let the muscles of his face drop, forgetting that he no longer had any teeth. His mouth went up towards his ears, the point of his nose went down, becoming more aquiline, and the chin protruded forward—all this framed by his beautiful white hair coming almost to the middle of his cheek. When I saw this transformation, I asked myself each time what that face reminded me of. . . . Very clearly of a lion—less clearly of the Sphinx—and sometimes of Dante.[16]

Siegfried Wagner (1869–1930). We children were devoted to our grandfather. Sigius—his name for me—was always allowed to visit him in his

* Philip Hohenlohe (son of Prince Chlodwig). According to Liszt, he possessed 'a very agreeable baritone voice'.

† Raffaele Frontali (1849–1916), Italian violinist and teacher.

room. I then enjoyed scrabbling around in his wastepaper basket, where music paper and rare stamps became my booty. In Venice one day he took me to church with him. We sat in the beautiful old choir stalls of the Frari. High Mass began, and from the organ there rang out the most commonplace galops and polkas, as was then the fashion in Italy. During the consecration we could hear the song 'I want to kiss your pretty black eyes'. In a word, from the less than perfect organ there came a right consecration! I noticed my grandfather becoming restless, and he gave me a prayerbook which he told me to read. The ceremony was no sooner over than he grasped me firmly by the hand and hurried out with me. Just before we got to the doorway the ingenuous organist rushed up and asked him—goodness knows why—how he had liked the music. 'Pour vous dire la vérité, c'était une saleté, une cochonnerie,' replied Liszt. Visibly surprised, the polka player ran off over the nearest bridge. During our ride home by gondola my grandfather must have repeated a dozen times: 'Saleté, cochonnerie.' It was painful to him that I could have received such a cheap impression in church. . . .

In Venice he and my parents came upon me sitting at the piano playing the accompaniment to the slumber aria from *La Muette de Portici* while whistling the melody. In this same manner I also rendered the sextet from Donizetti's *Lucia*, which I had heard and enjoyed several times in the market place. My reward, perhaps also my shame, was that Liszt afterwards sat down and reproduced in his own way what he had just heard —with, of course, a rather more sumptuous accompaniment than that which I, or even Auber and Donizetti, had provided. Of all the pianists I heard later, frankly, with the exception of Sophie Menter, no one but Mottl made such an impression on me; and, indeed, not on account of technique—Mottl had no pretensions to being a pianist—but rather because of some magnetic, magical, demoniacal quality transmitted to the brittle piano keys by way of the finger tips. It is only by some such magic that the electrifying effect on his audiences can be explained. Technique alone will arouse the Philistines, but not those innocent listeners desirous of something more profound.

From the space I am giving to my grandfather in these brief memoirs, readers will be aware of the love and affection I feel for him. . . .[17]

The weeks in Venice passed agreeably enough, marred to some extent only by Wagner's increasing intolerance. Accustomed to being surrounded by a reverential family, and by younger friends and hangers-on for whom his least wish was law, his every word holy writ, he found it difficult to accept the presence —even as his own invited and wanted guest—of another great and famous man who could, and often did, choose to spend the evenings and leisure hours with his own friends and admirers.

Paul von Joukovsky. Less and less with the coming of old age did these two great men and unique friends have the capacity to understand the other's way of life. Liszt enjoyed having many people about him; Wagner could endure the company of only a few intimate friends. And when they talked together, neither paid attention to what the other was saying: they would both speak at the same time, which often led to the most comical quid pro quos. Each of them was so accustomed to being the sole centre of attention that there was always a certain awkwardness when they were together.[18]

Nor were Wagner's musical sympathies broad enough to enable him to divine the new musical world into which the works being created by Liszt in these years were leading; and for those works he could find—when Liszt was not present—only words of harsh criticism and incomprehension.

1883

'This time we've both got in each other's way,' remarked Wagner cheerfully when Liszt took his departure on 13 January—a reference, presumably, to the strains imposed on both by the coming into contact, or collision, of their very different habits and life-styles. As always, however, he urged 'his Franz', and very sincerely, to make his home with the family once and for all. As on earlier occasions, Liszt wisely declined the well-meant offer.

The next day he reached Budapest; and here, a month later, he received news of Wagner's sudden death (13 February). Telegraphing at once to Cosima, to ask if she wished him to come to Venice to accompany her on the journey home to Bayreuth, he received a reply in the negative. 'At Bayreuth there will be a hullabaloo of very legitimate enthusiasm and glorification,' he wrote to Carolyne. 'I associate myself with it in thought at a distance. . . . You know my sad feeling about life: dying seems to me to be much simpler than living! Death, even when preceded by the long and frightening pains of "dying", is our deliverance from an involuntary yoke.'

At Venice a few weeks earlier he had composed the hauntingly beautiful piano elegy *La lugubre gondola* (S200/1), almost a presentiment of Wagner's death shortly afterwards in the same building and the bearing of his corpse, by gondola, along the Grand Canal.* 'I doubt whether it will obtain any success at concerts,' said Liszt, 'seeing its sad and sombre character, scarcely mitigated by a few dreaming shadows. The public demand other things—and if they were wrong, that would not worry them!'

Some time after his return to Budapest he was visited by *Géza Zichy*.

It was the first time I had seen Liszt since Wagner's death. I knew that he had been profoundly shaken by this catastrophe, and must admit that I

* In 1885 Liszt composed a kindred piece for cello (or violin) and piano (S134), of which he made another very beautiful arrangement for piano solo (S200/2). Wagner's death he commemorated in two other piano works: *R. W.—Venezia* (S201) and *Am Grabe Richard Wagners* (S202), both dating from 1883. Of this last work, there exist versions for string quartet and harp (S135) and for organ (S267).

entered his room somewhat nervously. Embracing me, he held me in his clasp for some time. At last, and with emotion, he said: 'We have suffered a heavy loss. Wagner is dead—relatively dead, for such men never quite die. He enjoyed a splendid, glorious sunset. His last work was a prayer. In his heart he had dedicated *Parsifal* to the everlasting God. Wagner could not pray liturgically, and so in this way he created his own prayer. What a beautiful life, and what a magnificent death! Fully lived out, fully expressed, fully recognized: we have no right to complain! Besides, I have no time left to do so, as for me too the second departure bell has already rung.' These words of Liszt's, with their foreboding of death, are most beautifully characteristic of the great man, and are deeply engraved on my memory.[1]

Returning to Weimar in early April, Liszt stopped *en route* at Vienna. Here, on Friday the 6th, he granted an interview to one of his most fervent, and most gifted, admirers: the young Hugo Wolf (1860–1903). After hearing with great interest the songs which the fledgling composer played as examples of his work, and rewarding him with a kiss on the brow, Liszt expressed the hope that he might soon hear a larger-scale composition from Wolf—who shortly afterwards began work on his *Penthesilea*, a symphonic poem employing the Lisztian device of thematic metamorphosis. A year later, sending Liszt a copy of *Die Spinnerin*, one of the songs performed at their meeting, Wolf was delighted to receive it back with a letter of kindly encouragement, and to find that in the margin of the manuscript Liszt had also taken the trouble to mark a necessary correction.

Liszt to Princess Carolyne, 26 April. When I write music, there is no possibility of writing letters the same day, in view of visits and local obligations. In the evenings I am overcome by fatigue, and no longer feel capable of anything other than playing whist—an amusement which will not ruin me as my partners consent to play for nothing. The knaves, queens, and kings of cards are acquaintances more inoffensive than the humans corresponding to the same titles! Without any misanthropy, my age allows me a certain lassitude![2]

Princess Carolyne to Adelheid von Schorn, 28 April. From Venice I was informed that *St Stanislas* would be completely finished by Christmas. But it is very natural to create slowly. Thank Heavens the brandy has disappeared! His new works are full of manly life! No sign of ageing there. . . .

I have just been told that asparagus is a sovereign remedy for dropsy. Speak about it to the doctor, and get Liszt to eat some. . . .[3]

It was in April that the brilliant Marie Jaëll came to Weimar, where she stayed for several months (as again in 1884 and 1885). When, in allusion to the fact that Liszt was now in his declining years, a friend asked her what she was doing there, she replied, finely: 'Don't you know what the very fragments of Greek art can teach us?'

It was while Marie was in Weimar that Liszt composed the Third Mephisto Waltz (S216), which he dedicated to her. A few days later she played the work to a small gathering, including Liszt. Seeming unusually excited, he exclaimed over and over again: 'That's it! Repeat that passage! Begin again!' Since, when making her repeat the piece, Liszt evinced a pleasure that was unusual for him in connection with his own works, Marie believed him to be delighted. What, therefore, was her astonishment the next day to find that he had rewritten the piece so completely as to make it almost unrecognizable. 'It was your playing of it yesterday that showed me how it ought to be,' he remarked. In her own old age many years later, Marie recorded in her memorandum book one day: 'This evening I played the Third Mephisto Waltz, which seemed prodigiously intense and frenzied. . . . If only I had been able to play it thus to Liszt! What joy he would have had in hearing this music which is his and mine.'

At Marburg, where, on a three-day visit at the end of April for a performance of *St Elisabeth* (1 May), he was the guest of his cousin Franz von Liszt, a professor at Marburg University, Liszt enjoyed the company not only of Marie Jaëll but also of Lina Schmalhausen (1863–1928). The latter was a young pianist who had come to him in the summer of 1879 with a recommendation from the Empress Augusta. Although she was by virtually all accounts one of his least gifted pupils (her playing being marred by extreme rhythmic instability), Liszt soon grew very fond of this gentle and attractive girl, who joined him on occasion at Budapest (1881 and 1885) and in Rome (winters of 1879 and 1885), besides attending his Weimar masterclasses for several successive summers; and it was to her that he dedicated the Mephisto Polka (S217) for piano, composed this year.

Lina's companionship he cherished above all in the Hungarian capital, where, with the severe Baroness Meyendorff far away in Weimar, and the redoubtable Princess Wittgenstein still further away in Rome, she was able to make a comfortable home for him 'by cooking, looking after his wardrobe, and reading to him in the evenings'.*

Naturally enough, these years of study and friendship with so great a figure as Liszt made upon the young woman an impression that no later experiences could ever efface: 'He was the light of my being; he raised and ennobled my thoughts and feelings; he was my creator, yes, my entire world.'

Adelheid von Schorn. Early in May, Liszt went to Leipzig to attend the Tonkünstler-Versammlung of the Allgemeine Deutsche Musikverein. He had earlier told me that he would be going on from there to Bayreuth. I went to Leipzig for one day only, to hear Liszt's *Prometheus*, and found him in a dreadfully excited state: he had received a letter from Wahnfried asking him to postpone his visit as Frau Wagner could see *no one*. That his daughter was shutting herself away from *everyone*, Liszt knew, but that *he* was to be no exception, hurt him bitterly.[4]

During this visit of Liszt's to Leipzig a young Russian pianist, *Alexander Siloti* (1863–1945), was introduced to him, at La Mara's home. A cousin of Sergei

* Geraldine Keeling, 'Liszt and Lina Schmalhausen', *Journal of the American Liszt Society*, v (June 1979), 48.

Rachmaninov, Siloti had already studied with Nikolai* and Anton Rubinstein, Zverev, and Tchaikovsky.

Having been accepted by Liszt as a pupil, Siloti finds accommodation in Weimar, but, overcome by homesickness, decides to return home.

Taking with me Chopin's Ballade in A flat, I went to Liszt for my lesson, as to a final ordeal before starting back for Russia. Somebody played something—I do not remember what it was—and then came my turn. I sat down and began the Ballade, but I had played only two bars when Liszt stopped me, saying, 'No, don't take a sitz-bath on the first note.' He then showed me what an accent I had made on the E flat. I was quite taken by surprise. '*Si signore, si signore*,' said Liszt in Italian, smiling a trifle maliciously. I continued playing, but he stopped me several times and played over certain passages to me. When I got up from the piano I felt bewitched. I looked at Liszt and was conscious of a gradual change in myself. My whole being became suffused by a glow of warmth and goodness, and by the end of my lesson I could not believe that, only two hours before, I had packed my things and wanted to run away. I left Liszt's house a different being, and was convinced that I should, after all, stay and study with him. I had become all at once a man who knew his own mind; I realized that there was a sun to whose rays I could turn for warmth and comfort.

To describe Liszt's lessons in such a way as to give an idea of his personality would be impossible. It is necessary to see certain things and certain people if one would have a clear impression of them. There were thirty or forty of us young fellows, and I remember that, gay and irresponsible as we were, we looked small and feeble beside this old man, shrunken with age. He was literally like a sun in our midst; when we were with him we felt the rest of the world to be in shadow, and when we left his presence our hearts were so filled with gladness that our faces were, all unconsciously, wreathed in rapturous smiles.

Liszt's lessons were of a totally different order from the common run. As a rule he sat beside, or stood opposite to, the pupil who was playing, and indicated by the expression of his face the nuances he wished to have brought out in the music. It was only for the first two months that he taught me in front of all the other pupils; after that I went to him in the morning when I was working at any specially big thing, and he taught me by myself. I always knew so thoroughly what I wanted to express in each piece of music that I was able to look at Liszt's face all the time I was playing. No one else in the world could show musical phrasing as he did, merely by the expression of his face. If a pupil understood these fine shades, so much the better for him; if not, so much the worse! Liszt told me that he could

* Nikolai Grigorevich Rubinstein (1835–81), younger brother of the more famous Anton, to whom, according to Tchaikovsky and others, he was the equal as a pianist and the superior as a teacher. He was the founder and first Principal of the Moscow Conservatoire, and it was his early and much lamented death that inspired Tchaikovsky's Piano Trio in A minor, dedicated 'to the memory of a great artist'.

explain nothing to pupils who did not understand him from the first. He never told us what to work at; each pupil could prepare what he liked. All we had to do when we came to the lesson was to lay our music on the piano; Liszt then picked out the things he wished to hear. There were only two things we were not allowed to bring: Liszt's Second Rhapsody (because it was too often played) and Beethoven's *Sonata quasi una fantasia* (Op. 27, No. 2) which Liszt in his time had played incomparably, as was afterwards proved to me. Nor did he like anyone to prepare Chopin's Scherzo in B flat minor, which he nicknamed the 'Governess' Scherzo, saying that it ought to be reserved for those people who were qualifying for the post of governess. Everything else of Chopin's, particularly his Preludes, he delighted in hearing. He insisted on a poetical interpretation, not a 'salon' performance, and it irritated him when the groups of small notes were played too quickly, 'conservatorium-fashion' as he called it. . . .

Liszt hardly ever scolded anyone. He had a favourite expression, the one word: 'good!' But he sometimes said it in such a tone that no word could have been more offensive. This manner of his gave some people the mistaken expression that Liszt was not genuine, as he did nothing but pay compliments. But it was the people who had seen him for a few moments only who said this. When he was irritated by anyone's playing, he always said: 'I know half a dozen pianists who play this as well as you, and half a dozen more who play it better.' Sometimes he worked himself into quite a frantic state of mind, but I only saw him in this condition about four times during the three years I was with him. On these occasions he strode to and fro in a way that reminded me of Salvini* as Othello, where he paces up and down Desdemona's room like a tiger in the last act. In moments such as these Liszt was simply terrifying; his face was Mephistophelian, and he would literally scream at the unlucky pupil: 'I take no payment from you, but, if I did, there is *no* money which could give you the right to come and wash your dirty linen here. I am not a washerwoman. Go to the Conservatorium, that is the place for you.' This state of mind would last some time—about ten minutes. Afterwards, when we were more intimate, I always began talking to him at these times to divert his thoughts. . . .

As a rule, he got up at four o'clock in the morning; two hours later he went back to bed, rising for the day at eight o'clock. He dined at one, and then slept for about an hour and a half. He went to bed at about ten o'clock in the evening. The early morning was his favourite time for composing. In former years, his housekeeper told me, this was his time for reading the 'crrritiques'—as he always called them—on his compositions. It always made him angry if anyone boasted of having had a good critique.

'If you have a good "crrritique",' he would say, 'you probably have a good certificate from the Conservatorium too.'

* Tommaso Salvini (1829–1915), celebrated Milanese dramatic actor.

Liszt once wittily defined a critic. There were three of us with him—Friedheim, a lady whose name I do not remember, and myself. Liszt wanted a game of whist, but Friedheim objected that he did not know how to play and understood absolutely nothing about it. 'Then,' said Liszt, 'you must be a critic.'

During my summer at Weimar I began to make rather frequent journeys to Leipzig, where I was paying attentions to the sister of one of Liszt's pupils. I was only nineteen, and this courtship so absorbed me that I stopped writing to my mother. The result was that my mother wrote to Liszt to ask what I was doing. One day at a lesson, Liszt came up to me and said: 'Come here, I want to speak to you.'

We went into an adjoining room—his bedroom. (I can recall distinctly the severe way in which it was furnished: there was a bed, near it—on the wall—a crucifix, a metal washstand, and two chairs.) Liszt suddenly became serious as he asked me gravely: 'Tell me, please, when did you last write to your mother?' It dawned on me at once that I had not written for a long time, but I lied coolly, saying that I had written the day before—having decided in my own mind, of course, to write that very evening. Liszt looked at me penetratingly as if he knew that I had lied to him, and said in a strange voice, severe and yet paternal (which I had never heard before): 'Now my dear boy, don't do this again, because your mother has written to tell me that she is anxious about you. You are young, and there is one thing you should remember. I am 72 years old, and have lived my life happily enough, but it is entirely owing to the fact that I have always been a good son to my mother. Remember what I say.'

His words had a tremendous effect upon me. The intimacy of the scene—there was no one in the room but our two selves—his words, and the strange note in his voice, which I heard only once more shortly before he died, all combined to make an impression which will never lose its freshness for me as long as I live.

In the course of my life I have come across many charming personalities among musicians, but never—either before or since—have I seen anyone as impressive as Liszt. You had only to say good morning to him to know, instantly and instinctively, that there was something majestic, god-like, in him—to feel that he was a great all-embracing spirit. . . .

It is impossible to describe Liszt's playing. A pianist myself, I am yet unable to show how he played, or to give an idea of his playing in words. I cannot say that he had a 'big' tone; it was rather that when he played there was no sound of the instrument. He sat at the very piano which we young fellows used to break with our playing, an entirely unreliable, unequal instrument; but he would produce from it, discordant as it was, music such as no one could form any idea of without hearing it. I am a tremendous admirer of Anton Rubinstein's playing, and consider that all we living pianists are mere pygmies compared with him. He used to say, however, as

I was told, that he was worth nothing as a pianist compared with Liszt. . . .

But I had always wanted to compare the two pianists for myself. It was not long before an opportunity occurred. Anton Rubinstein was giving one of his Historical Concerts one morning at the Gewandhaus for the musicians of Leipzig, and I went to hear him, acting on the advice of Liszt. I was to go back to Weimar after the concert, and tell him all about it. It was a recital of Beethoven sonatas. Rubinstein was at his best, and played each one better than the last. I was particularly struck with his rendering of the 'Moonlight' Sonata, which seemed to me simply marvellous. Two hours later I was back at Liszt's house, arriving just at the beginning of a lesson. I could hardly wait to say good afternoon to Liszt before plunging into a breathless description of this amazing music, the glamour of which was still over me. Speaking with all the fervour and enthusiasm of youth, I told him how wonderful Rubinstein's performance had been, and that I had never heard such a fine rendering of the 'Moonlight' Sonata. All at once it seemed to me that Liszt winced, and the thought flashed across my brain that I was saying this to a man who was acknowledged to be a specialist in the interpretation of this very sonata. He listened to my glowing account, and then said composedly: 'Very good, very satisfactory.' I began to feel uneasy. Liszt walked away and began to examine the music which the pupils had brought to play. Seeing a copy of the 'Moonlight' Sonata amongst the pieces, he asked who was playing it. It turned out to be a young American lady. 'My dear child,' said Liszt, looking at her, 'this piece must not be brought to the lessons; I allow no one to play it because, when I was young, it was my *spécialité*. But as "we" are in a good humour today, I shall play it to you.' Saying which, he turned his head, and, as I thought, gave me a look which meant: 'Now listen, you will hear something.'

He began to play, and I held my breath as I listened. Rubinstein had played on a beautiful Bechstein in a hall with very good acoustic properties; Liszt was playing in a little carpeted room, in which small space 35 to 40 people were sitting, and the piano was worn out, unequal and discordant. He had only played the opening triplets, however, when I felt as if the room no longer held me, and when, after the first four bars, the G sharp came in in the right hand, I was completely carried away. Not that he accentuated this G sharp; it was simply that he gave it an entirely new sound which even now, after 27 years, I can hear distinctly. He played the whole of the first movement, then the second; the third he only commenced, saying that he was too old and had not the physical strength for it. I then realized that I had completely forgotten having listened to Rubinstein two hours before. *As a pianist he no longer existed*. I make this statement deliberately, with a full knowledge of what I am saying—and as my readers know my opinion of Rubinstein they may thus gain some faint idea of what Liszt was like as a pianist. When he had finished playing, Liszt got up and came across to me. I had tears in my eyes, and was quite unstrung. I could only say: '*Meister*, I am quite dazed. I never heard anything like it.' Upon which he smiled kindly, and said: 'We know how to play after all, eh?'

I now understand what Anton Rubinstein meant by calling himself a common soldier and Liszt a General, and how true this estimate was. In my opinion Liszt was as far removed from Rubinstein as Rubinstein from the rest of us. I have never played this sonata in public; in fact I never heard it again, for if I happened to be at a concert where it was to be played, I always left the hall. It seemed to me that by listening to it I should be soiling the impression I had received, insulting Liszt's memory, not to speak of the martyrdom it implied to myself.[5]

Siloti was at one time courting a Jewish girl, Fanny Kahn. 'I brought her to Weimar to introduce to Liszt. When I next saw him, and asked his opinion, he said that she was very attractive, but he seemed rather cold. A year later, when I told him I was breaking with Fanny, he could not conceal his joy, and called to his servant: "Miska, bring champagne!" I drank to the health of the "Old Man", who told me that if ever I took it into my head to marry, it would be better to marry a girl who shared my religion, since this was the first prerequisite for mutual understanding.'

Princess Carolyne to Adelheid von Schorn, 14 May. Any company is better for Liszt than that of persons whose empty minds, being powerless to offer anything more than the futile and childish, have brought about the gradual apathy of a mind once so luminous and so vigorously steadfast! You can imagine how heart-breaking it is for me, who knew him in all his strength and ardour!! Do not fail to tell me about him. My sole consolation is to have news of him from others, since what he himself tells me has come to signify less and less! A doctor tells me that it is now impossible to find a substitute for the card-playing, since everything would fatigue his brain and reduce more and more the musical faculties remaining to him. You do well to keep him at Weimar. May he remain there and work at *St Stanislas*—if still possible![6]

Liszt was visited at this time by *Siegfried Ochs* (1858–1929), German composer and chorus-master.

While awaiting the great man, I walked for a while up and down the room used as a waiting-room, and was just by a small door when it suddenly opened and Liszt came in, so that I almost collided with him. But it was not this which made a quite unexpected—I could almost say a fearful—impression on me. It was rather the indescribably majestic and solemn impression created by the appearance of the famous man. As he stood before me like a giant, his long white hair falling down over his shoulders and his features expressing earnestness and goodness combined, I was reminded of antique statues or of paintings by old masters. As I gazed at him I was quite speechless and could not even manage to thank him for having received me. The delicacy of feeling which everyone had to praise who came into close contact with Liszt, and which is also found in his letters, was shown on this occasion too. He had certainly noticed my embarrassment, but at once helped me over the painful moment by apologizing for having entered so suddenly. He added that he was in a hurry because a pupil was waiting for him, and he invited me to attend the lesson, adding that as long as I was in Weimar I was welcome to come at any time and listen to the lessons he gave.

I need hardly say that I made full use of this permission during my stay. In doing so I learnt much which left a curious impression upon me, such as for example the indescribably tactless behaviour of certain of his pupils, especially the women. The kissing of hands, the making of sheep's eyes, and striving to outdo one another in the laying on of every kind of flattery, was all irritatingly distasteful to those not involved in it. But Liszt was by this time quite accustomed to it, and it seemed not to confuse him when teaching; indeed, I witnessed an incident which demonstrated this quite clearly. An English lady had brought some piece or other with her that displeased him greatly. Hardly had she begun to play when he interrupted her and, brushing her hands from the keys, said: 'My dear child, why are you bringing me stuff like this once again?' The lady kissed his hands, saying that the piece was not at all a bad one. But Liszt dispatched her, not losing his temper for a moment however, but merely smiling and saying: 'No, my child, it is not bad music; it is not music at all.' Whereupon the crushed pianist began to weep, and disappeared into the adjoining room for a long time until she had to some extent composed herself. In the mean time it had become the turn of another pupil. He had brought Beethoven's *Hammerklavier* Sonata—but Liszt was not satisfied. He stressed that he had asked countless times for expression marks in Beethoven to be followed not merely to a certain extent but with considerable vigour; that Beethoven made an enormous difference between *piano* and *pianissimo*, and that the distance from *piano* to *forte* was to be regarded as greater in Beethoven than that between North and South poles. Finally, to put matters in a nutshell, he sat at the piano and played the whole of the first part of the sonata himself. Thus I too came to hear Liszt. Undoubtedly as a pianist he was no longer what he had been in his earlier years; old age showed itself unmistakably in his hard touch. Perhaps, too, the relatively small room may have played an unfavourable part; for, after I had become more accustomed to the sound, I realized that so far as the playing of classical works was concerned, a new world was being revealed to me, similar to the one I had experienced during Bülow's rendering of the symphonies. This piece, which had been for me hitherto no more than an object of dutiful admiration, suddenly blossomed into life, and seemed so simple, so natural, and filled with such warmth, that I could not understand or explain to myself what I had ever found cold in it.

The next day I heard Liszt again, when he played to Emma Koch his Fantasy on themes from Auber's *La Muette de Portici*. His way of doing so, and his poetic illumination of individual passages, belonged among those rare artistic performances which make one forget all axioms. Notwithstanding my prejudice to this very day against anything in the nature of an operatic transcription or paraphrase, I should count myself fortunate if I could ever again hear that piece played as Liszt played it.[7]

It was during this summer that *Bettina Walker* came to Weimar, where she lodged with J. N. Hummel's granddaughters. Liszt remembered her, received her graciously, and invited her to attend the masterclasses—which for health reasons she was able to do as a listener only. Her first musical experience with the Liszt pupils, however, was at one of the Sunday matinées given by the Stahr sisters.

When Liszt . . . entered the room, everyone stood up, and all the younger people went towards him and kissed his hand. He looked as if he enjoyed all this homage, and his face lighted up as he glanced kindly at the eager faces which, from the moment he appeared, seemed to have no eyes but for him. Indeed, from the moment he came in, we were all listening to try and catch whatever he might please to say to those nearest to him. He did not play; but his expressive face showed the most cordial interest in all that was going on. Siloti played a Tausig–Berlioz piece with great bravura; Reisenauer and Emma Koch played some duets at sight; there was some singing, some violin-playing by a very clever little boy of eleven, and then a small slight girl sat down and charmed me by the ease and beautiful clearness with which she played one of Liszt's Hungarian Rhapsodies. . . .

I cannot remember all that was played that afternoon, for, like those around me, I was far more occupied in watching the Meister's movements and trying to catch his words, than in either listening to the music or getting into talk with my neighbours. After about two hours and a half—during which time there had been one or two short pauses, when cake and wine and lemonade were handed round—Liszt rose to depart, and, as was the case when he came in, all the guests present rose, and remained standing until he had left the room. When he was gone I was conscious of a sensation which I am quite sure was shared by pretty nearly everyone in the room, whether they were quite aware of the feeling or not. Everything seemed to have become all at once flat and dull and uninteresting; conversation languished; it was as if a shadow had fallen on a landscape, and that which a moment before, when illumined by the sun, was a mass of warm and glowing colours, was now all grey, monotonous, and chill. . . .

Being only a listener at Liszt's classes, I was all the better able to give my whole attention to everything that went on; and out of a number of smaller and larger details which came under my notice during those weeks, I arrived (without ever consciously trying to do so) at certain general conclusions, which, be they right or wrong, have at least the merit of being unbiased by any spirit of either clique or school. Liszt was unvaryingly just in appreciating and encouraging all those who had really any 'talent'; but towards one or two who really had neither school nor talent he would, if their personality pleased him, be so indulgent as to let the very worst faults, the greatest shortcomings, pass without any adverse criticism. On the other hand, woe betide either an incorrect or badly drilled player, or one who merely played the notes, and gave no musical reading of the piece, if his or her personality had made an unfavourable impression on the Meister! In the case of a badly drilled player, he would show his anger without disguise, and send the performer from the piano in a most summary manner; while in the latter case he would either get up from his seat, and walk up and down the entire length of the room, looking the very picture of an individual who is profoundly bored, but who has made up his mind to go through with it to the end, or else he would stand a minute or two beside the player, seeming to listen to the performance, and then, quietly observing, 'That is very nice, but I think we shall turn to something else,' he would take the piece off the music-desk, move away from the piano, and call on another pianist to come forward.

The following may serve as an example of how he treated a bungling and badly trained player. A young man began to play one of the Meister's own compositions—a difficult Polonaise—and in a few bars from the start came down with a jumble of wrong notes on a difficult chord, and when Liszt said in a loud voice, 'Begin again!' the luckless player, trying the piece a second time, made the same blunder over again. 'Shame, shame!' said Liszt, in a still louder voice; 'begin once more!' The unfortunate individual started off once again, came to the passage and, for the third time, played the chord all wrong. Then, indeed, there was a scene which I cannot easily forget. Liszt's voice trembled with anger and scorn, as, flinging the music from the desk, and saying more than once in a voice which was calculated to terrify us all, 'Do you know to whom you have been playing? You have no business here. Go to the Conservatoire; that is the place for such as you.'

To my surprise the young man did not leave the room, but merely moved back among the others; and if he was at all sensitive, he must have been conscious that he had spoilt that afternoon for the young girl [Lina Grosskurth] who played next after him. She was a mere child, not yet sixteen, and was favoured by Liszt not only because of her youth, but for the sake of her sister, Fräulein [Emma] Grosskurth, a most refined and charming pianist, who played Chopin's Nocturnes exquisitely. On this day, however, Liszt absolutely clawed this poor little girl, to whom he was usually so gentle, that when there was any want of clearness in a passage played by her, he would stop her with the gentle reprimand, 'We don't want any neighbours here, my dear; play it again.' But the young man's performance had stirred up Liszt's bile, and after saying in an angry tone two or three times, 'We don't wash dirty linen here,' he pushed the piece into her hands and sent her away from the piano, and she got into a far corner behind the others, to hide the tears which she could not restrain. . . .

Mademoiselle Ranuschewitz seemed to have an endless repertoire, and a wonderful faculty of being always ready to play everyone else's pieces besides her own. Once, in playing the *Patineurs*, she broke her nail in doing the *glissando*, which Liszt told her to do three times instead of twice as it is printed. She made a wry face, and Liszt asked her what was the matter. She replied that she had broken her nail. He seemed highly amused, and said, as if he really enjoyed the notion of making us all see that a broken nail ought never to be an excuse for pausing in a performance, 'Well, what of that? Go on, my child.' Liszt was very fond of Katy Ranuschewitz, and was constantly laying his hand on her head, as if in affectionate paternal approval.

And Liszt himself, though he only played fragments of the pieces brought to him by the young pianists, and usually but a few bars of those fragments, was indeed a dazzling sun, that shone with a radiance before which all the younger talents, like so many stars, paled into insignificance. He gave one the impression of possessing an almost terrible mastery over every imaginable variety of passage—especially in leaping intervals so wide apart, that to play them with ease is as nearly as possible like being in two different places at the same time. I have listened to him twice in the *Patineurs*, and a cold shiver has passed through me, not so much at what he actually bestowed on us, as at what he suggested as having still in reserve. To his interpretation of Chopin—three of whose Ballades, many of the Preludes, several Etudes, three Polonaises, and one Concerto, I heard him play in Weimar—I have listened with delight mingled with awe. His sight-reading of difficult manuscript compositions, which were brought to him on different occasions, was simply marvellous. He would listen to the player for a minute or two with a smile which betrayed a sort of scornful sense of absolute mastery, and then he would sit down and execute the most intricate passages with as much ease as if they were the ABC of a language every syllable, every word of which was familiar to him. What astonished and impressed me most was, not so much that his fingers were responsive to every motion of his mind; I wondered at the *mind*, which one felt instinctively was gifted with the power of taking in at one rapid glance every possible variety of passage which has ever been written for the pianoforte. His glance seemed to be at once penetrative and all-embracing. He thought it out at once with clearness and rapidity; and instead of being any longer surprised at the almost adoring attitude of his followers, I was, though he knew it not, one of those who paid him homage with every single nerve and fibre of my nature. I think it is Lenz who, in the little book called *Beethoven et ses trois styles*, has called Liszt 'the apotheosis of the pianoforte'; and let me say that no words from any pen, were they ever so forcible, ever so suggestive, could give the most imaginative reader any adequate idea of what Liszt was all round. One felt as if one were standing at the foot of a great mountain, whose summit was veiled in luminous clouds. Whichever way you viewed him, there was immense variety. He was grand and colossal. He was a large nature, and yet full of grace and sweetness. His rendering of the middle part in Chopin's B minor Scherzo (which Siloti brought him) will linger in my memory as 'a joy for ever'. On another occasion he played, 'with pauses' (in showing a young American lady his reading of the piece), the greater part of Chopin's fourth Ballade, and on that afternoon, being in an especially genial mood, he spoke of the composition, and bade her observe how the composer, having wandered away from the opening thought, seemed afterwards to be as it were groping for it; and this groping, this seeking, Liszt pictured to us most wonderfully in his playing—when, without losing that which is the very life of a composition, its rhythmic beat, he seemed to waver and sway, as if uncertain whether to go on in that rhythm or not. During this wavering and swaying, he turned at intervals to the young lady and observed, 'He has not found it yet, but it is coming'. 'It is very near now,' he finally said, just before he struck a note of triumph, and came in with a full sweep on the opening theme.

When I had been about three weeks in Weimar, Liszt sent round one Sunday morning to say that he would pay me a visit after he came from hearing morning service. At nine o'clock he came in, and I remember most of what he then said, as well as if it had happened but yesterday. He told me that no pianofortes lasted anything like so well as those of Broadwood—that the firm had been very generous to him, both on the occasion of his first visits to England, which took place when he was a boy, and his second, many years later on, when he had grown up to manhood. On the first of these occasions, the Messrs. Broadwood sent a very fine instrument to his father, and when, on leaving London, his father asked what they were indebted for the use of the instrument, Messrs. Broadwood replied that the instrument was a gift which they felt pleased in offering for his acceptance. 'We left the instrument behind us,' said Liszt; 'and I am sorry to confess that having, as youngsters will do, got into debt a little while after, I sold it. Later on the Broadwoods gave me another instrument, and this I still possess. It is in the keeping of the Princess Wittgenstein.'

He admired the charming rooms of the von Hummels; and, casting a glance around at the different objects of interest which were there, went finally over to Hummel's grand pianoforte, and, opening it, sat down and played the whole of Hummel's Fantasia from beginning to end. When he had concluded, he stood up, saying, 'This is one of the pieces which will never die; and I am going to have Hummel's A minor Concerto—also a favourite of mine—played at one of my *réunions des jeunes pianistes*.' When he went away I stood at the door, and looked after him as he crossed the street. He raised his hat to me, and smiled—a smile I still seem to see! —that smile of genial, kindly benevolence which has charmed and spell-bound so many, and won them to be his devoted and lifelong followers.[8]

Carl Lachmund. The Master often lapsed into a dejected musing and meditating. G. Schirmer,* founder of the great New York publishing-house, reported that he had once found Liszt in a very melancholy mood—and the Master had admitted that he was brooding and pondering about the end of his earthly life, an event which he believed to be drawing near. Asked if his religion were not of help to him at such moments, he replied that his anxiety was purely personal:

'Here on earth I have been given the opportunity, and also the ability, to undertake a leading role in the service of Art, of artists, and of mankind itself. I now wonder again and again whether, after the great transition, I shall be able to continue to do so.'[9]

Liszt to Paul von Joukovsky. Weimar, 10 September. My morbid aversion to letters is reaching a paroxysm. It is an idiosyncrasy like that of being unable to bear the sight of cats or dogs. When, in Rome, the illustrious Ingres used to honour me with his visits, I took great care to shut my black greyhound in the attic.[10]

To Princess Carolyne, 29 September. For me, writing letters is becoming not so much tedious as torturous! The kind of celebrity I possess leads to cretinism—and so I told a friend that I was thinking of settling in the Valais canton, classic ground of cretins![11]

In mid-October Edvard Grieg gave a concert in Weimar at which his Piano Concerto, *Spring* and *Heart's Wound* for string orchestra were performed. 'It was a brilliant beginning, and for that I must thank Liszt first and foremost. Ah, how wonderful he was to me. Besides the applause of the audience, I heard Liszt's grunt—the well-known sound that is elicited only by something he thinks highly of. . . . He has become unbelievably old since I saw him in Rome. It was sad to see him again.'

A visitor that same month, to attend Liszt's birthday celebrations on Monday, 22 October, was *Géza Zichy*.

He welcomed me with the greatest joy and affection, and I spent some very happy days at the Hofgärtnerei. Adelheid von Schorn was looking after him most touchingly, discharging her duties with calm dignity. And that was necessary, for Liszt was overrun by a mass of the most varied people:

* Gustav Schirmer (1829–93).

those who wished to become pupils, or were already; those who sought his patronage for one scheme or another; inquisitive outsiders and autograph hunters; and a host of beggars, of both the well and the badly dressed variety. Not one did he turn away. To every adventurer, male and female, he was kind, courteous and, to the great dismay of the good Adelheid, unfailingly generous with his money. The Hofgärtnerei was no Buen Retiro for old men in need of rest, but an arena of every kind of ambition, justified or otherwise. And in all this bustle, he, the great and good old man, had just one wish: to be allowed to take a nap for an hour or two after lunch. His birthday was celebrated sincerely by everyone from the Grand-Ducal court down to the last and least musician; and the Court Theatre presented [21 October] a quite excellent stage performance of *St Elisabeth*.[12]

Eschewing, once again, the winter visit to Rome, Liszt remained in Germany for the rest of the year. To the Princess he wrote, on 6 November: 'It was a heavy cross for me not to be able to kiss your dear and adored hands on your name day [4 November]. I often grieve at our separation and have to make an effort to bear it! . . . Alas! the *Index* has objected to your immense work*—I would have had my two hands cut off to prevent that!'

Liszt to Princess Carolyne. Meiningen, 16 December. The ancients thought that to die young was a signal favour of the gods! As Christians we say with the voice heard by St John: 'Blessed are the dead which die in the Lord!' I hope that it will soon be the case with me—until the last moment I shall bless your great and holy soul, superabundant in sublimities!

Without leaving the thought of death, I shall mention that my daughter Cosima is doing her utmost not to survive Wagner. From what I am told—for I neither receive nor request direct news—she spends hours every day at Wagner's tomb, ignoring all entreaties to the contrary. A decisive vocation![13]

1884

Leaving Weimar on 31 January, and travelling via Nuremberg (where word reached him of the death on 1 February of his servant Achille†), Liszt arrived in Budapest on 4 February.

Vilmos von Csapó. When, after a visit to us, Liszt was on the point of

* Even before its completion, the Princess's magnum opus, the 24-volume *Des causes intérieures de la faiblesse extérieure de l'Eglise*, had been placed on the Vatican's *Index librorum prohibitorum*.

† The last of Liszt's manservants, a Hungarian named Mihály (Michael) Kreiner, entered his service on 1 Mar.

leaving, he heard piano-playing coming from an adjoining room. It was my son Daniel having his lesson, and to the fright of teacher and pupil alike the Master went in without more ado and had the little sonata repeated while he beat time with his long thin index finger. 'For without rhythm,' he said, 'there is no music.' Then he sat down and played through the piece. 'That is how it must be played—more or less!'

He asked my son his name. 'Daniel,' he repeated sadly, doubtless thinking of his deceased only son of the same name. . . . Taking his leave of us, for he would soon be setting off on his travels again, he said: 'Espérons au revoir—par conséquent, pas de longs adieux!' We never saw him again.[1]

From 24 to 26 February Liszt stayed at Pozsony, where his Coronation Mass was performed as part of the Bishop's jubilee celebrations; and in early March he was the guest at Gran of Cardinal Simor. Easter he spent at Kalocsa with Cardinal Haynald.

In Rome meanwhile, *La Mara* was visiting Princess Carolyne.

Our conversations were mainly about Liszt. . . . Talking about him was something of which the Princess could never tire. Near or far, he remained the sun of her life.

Once she spoke in detail of his relations with the opposite sex, the Comtesse d'Agoult in particular. 'The misfortune of his life is his taste for women,' she said with emphasis. His partiality to brandy she likewise considered his undoing; it poisoned his health, she declared, and would sap his strong constitution. . . .

She asked me if I felt like writing a biography of Liszt, one which would not only complete the unfinished Ramann work,* but also broaden and deepen it. Lina Ramann, she said, was 'too unworldly, too bourgeois', to get to the root of a phenomenon as complex and many-sided as Liszt. 'A mind rich in gifts of the intellect which let itself be saturated by secret Slavic, French, and Hungarian sweetnesses and bitternesses,' was, she declared, difficult for 'a simple German soul' to fathom. And so it was 'a kind of old Brendel'—who had been her ideal†—that Liszt's 'rather narrow' biographer was making of him. She would give her no more material, she said, but would on the other hand gladly place it at my disposal. I could only reply that were I to make such an intervention I would regard myself as wronging Fräulein Ramann.[2]

From Kalocsa Liszt returned to Weimar. At the Vienna Schottenhof, where he stopped *en route* for a few days, he was visited by *August Göllerich*.

* Part One of Lina Ramann's *Franz Liszt als Künstler und Mensch* had appeared in 1880. Part Two, dealing with Liszt's life and work from 1839/40 to his death in 1886, eventually appeared in two volumes (1887 and 1894).

† Lina Ramann had been a pupil of Franz Brendel.

'Don't torment the poor child too much,' he was calling through the door after the mother of a fashionable infant prodigy who had been playing to him. It was April 1884. . . . Toni Raab,* his 'petite Retzoise', one of the most brilliant personalities and performers of the Liszt circle of that time, had brought me to him. . . .

Just as the dentist asks where the pain is, so he, used to alleviating the pains of budding pianists, asked me kindly: 'Well, what have you brought with you?' Profoundly moved, I stammered something about the importance of the long-desired moment which I did not wish to profane with my playing; and never shall I forget his utter amazement at for once meeting a pianist not avid to play to him. . . .

He then asked 'Madame de Retz' for further information about this strange fellow, and learnt that the latter's favourite pieces were the two threnodies *Aux cyprès de la Villa d'Este*. . . .

'But, I ask you, how can you play such bad stuff?' were the words he greeted me with next day, alluding to the works in question. 'They will blackball you in all the clubs!' . . .

At further meetings I was favoured by the Master's invitation to go to him at Weimar. My acceptance was to prove a decisive turning-point in my life.

'There you must play me the *cypresses*,' he said at the station when leaving Vienna after his Easter visit.

On a stormy evening in early spring I had accompanied him to the departure point. The train had almost started to move when his friend Bösendorfer hastily helped him into the carriage. Quickly Liszt let down the window, beckoned to me and called down merrily: 'Do you know that Bösendorfer made a good joke today? He said that what the elephant is among animals, Beethoven is among musicians!'

At that moment a gust of wind ruffled the Master's long white hair, and a lantern past which the train was moving glaringly illuminated his Titan's head—an unforgettable sight![3]

On 17 May Liszt arrived in Leipzig to attend a performance of *Christus* on the 18th. ('Riedel is keen to do my *Christus* a second time,' he had written to Carolyne on 27 April. 'I have in vain tried to dissuade him—after they have been written, corrected, and printed, my poor works preoccupy me not in the least. I generally even advise against their performance.') Here he was approached in his quarters at the Hôtel de Prusse by *Emil Sauer* (1862–1942), a young pianist who had been recommended to him by no less a person than the Princess herself, to whom Sauer had played in Rome.

I was very conscious of the solemnity of the moment, for my heart was

* Antonia Raab (1846–1902) of Retz had been one of Liszt's most gifted pupils at the Budapest Music Academy in the mid-1870s. It was a poem of hers which in 1883 inspired him to compose the nocturne *Schlaflos, Frage und Antwort* (S203).

pounding mightily as we crossed the threshold; but this initial anxiety quickly changed to confidence. How effective our recommendation had been was at once shown by the cordial reception given us. Yes, that was exactly how I had often pictured the Master to myself, according to what I had read or heard about him, as he now came towards me with both hands outstretched, just like a father—the same venerable, chivalrous figure, with his sharply marked profile and his head and features sparkling with character and intelligence. I felt the gigantic power of this man even before he opened his mouth. He was wearing a black cassock-like overcoat, trousers of the same material, an unstarched, badly-ironed stand-up collar, and leather morning shoes, with which he glided over the floor towards us. His voice was both sweet and melodious, and he spoke with short, disjointed sentences, mingled with an habitual 'hm', a kind of clearing of the throat as though to confirm what had been said. With the gesture of a man of the world he invited us to sit down. To begin with, the conversation turned on our impressions of Spain, our experiences in Rome, and the Princess's state of health. Then he said: 'My expectations are truly pitched very high—hm—the Princess writes to tell me that she is quite delighted with your playing—hm—(here he addressed my patron* in French) and also the selflessness with which you, my dear Sir, have interested yourself in this talent. That is noble and high-minded—hm—disinterested behaviour is today becoming ever rarer.' Brabazon beamed! It had always been his dream to see the great Liszt face to face—now he even heard him singing his praises. The Master regretted, too, that the programme of the music festival† was so overloaded with novelties that it was impossible to fit me in at such a late hour. He then invited us to accompany him that afternoon to the general rehearsal of his *Christus*, which was to be performed the next day. 'Tomorrow, too, we must improvise a brief session at Blüthner's,' he said in conclusion, 'for I am really curious to hear you.' His servant had meanwhile announced other visitors, and so we took our leave. A consecrational kiss on the brow accompanied me, and we went happily down the stairs. In front of the porter's lodge I bumped into my colleague of earlier days, Siloti, who after the death of our teacher [Nikolai Rubinstein] had spent some time with Anton Rubinstein and then a summer with Liszt. He was in the company of Rosenthal and Friedheim, two other in the best sense of the word feared Lisztians, to whom he at once introduced me. This three-leafed clover, incidentally, appeared to stand very high in the 'Old Man's' favour, as without further ceremony it skipped unannounced upstairs to an audience.

When we returned that afternoon the first shower fell on my rosy mood. The salon was filled with people who were obviously quite out of place

* The English painter H. B. Brabazon (1821–1906).

† The Tonkünstler-Versammlung of the Allgemeine Deutsche Musikverein, held at Weimar from 23 to 26 May.

there; indeed, who did not even really know why they had come. Petty jealousy was far removed from my thinking; not an atom of Liszt's halo did I begrudge any worthy person. But what I observed, both here and in the days that followed, was sufficient to make me aware that a great part of this entourage consisted of shameless wretches who would flatter you to your face one minute and run you down behind your back the next, or creatures devoid of talent who abused Liszt's proverbial kindness by becoming hangers-on and then later besmirching his reputation by calling themselves 'favourite pupils'—even if they had never played a note to him. After the performance, both in and outside the church, as also at supper in the evening, there began those objectionable scenes which were subsequently to be repeated still more drastically in Weimar. Men of ability, of true devotion to Liszt, were obliged modestly to take a back seat or were shoved aside by toadies and sycophants, who even begrudged their prey a little respite during his frugal meal. The very tips of one's fingers itched; how one would have liked to intervene! What pained me most of all was that the old gentleman seemed blind or accessible to the very worst of these flatterers, and the 'dear Master here, dear Master there' which was all they bandied about; that he should be weak enough to take any pleasure at all in such offensively fulsome flattery.

At the little private matinée which took place at Blüthner's, only a few listeners were present: Madame Jaëll, Krause,* Friedheim, Rosenthal, and one or two others. I played some pieces by Chopin and Grieg, Rubinstein's Staccato Etude, and Liszt's Twelfth Rhapsody. Although because of continual travelling around I was not in practice, and my performances revealed more technical defects than I would have wished on such an important occasion, the Master was tolerant enough to show warm appreciation, especially in his Rhapsody. From time to time he called out such encouraging words as 'bravo', 'bravissimo', 'pretty . . .', 'hm,' 'very pretty . . . ,' 'hm!' When I had come to an end he confirmed his pleasure with a kiss on the forehead, and also seemed delighted to grant my request to enrol me among his pupils for the summer. Friedheim, on whom Liszt had bestowed the nickname 'Friedheimus', and who at about this time had set Leipzig in a regular uproar with his bravura, then took my place at the piano and thundered out the Fantasy on *Lucrezia Borgia* [S400], and indeed with such stupendous verve and infallibility that I felt rather bankrupt with what I had just offered, and privately resolved to put my time in Weimar to good use by filing and polishing my rather dilapidated technique. So much was certain: if Liszt's crack troops contained many such 'Friedheimusses', at Weimar there would be a very high standard indeed!

* Martin Krause (1853–1918), a Liszt pupil who himself became a notable teacher, of, among others, Edwin Fischer and Claudio Arrau.

In the evening we accompanied the Master *in corpore* to the Thuringia Station, naturally not without a number of the parasites worming their way in again. I admired the patience of this man, who, modestly taking a second-class compartment, still had a friendly word for everyone and generously dispensed handshakes in all directions, like a Member of Parliament after a great oratorical victory. 'Proofs of the affection of such a great man should really be an object of worth, of which not every groveller should be able to boast,' I thought to myself on the way home. The next day we returned to Weimar. . . .

The town now looked completely different. It seemed as though with Liszt it had taken on new life. A ceaseless coming and going began, which, steadily increasing until the turn of the summer, came to an end only with Liszt's departure for Budapest. It was not only that a complete locust swarm of Lisztians roused the peaceful little town out of its slumbers; a heavy influx of strangers who in a trice filled all the hotels to overflowing was also noticeable. Visitors came and went: members of the old aristocratic families who regarded the Master as one of themselves; famous contemporaries of his, or pupils from earlier years paying their tribute of homage and gratitude; budding composers and busy publishers—down to the unavoidable gapers and gadflies drawn out of mere curiosity. The Athens on the Ilm exhibited its 'season', just like popular watering places and summer resorts.

Turning to Liszt's teaching itself, it should not be imagined that this consisted of lessons in the usual sense; rather were they like university lectures, which anyone could attend or cut at pleasure. Although they were interesting for laymen and duffers, just as is any *aperçu* from the mouth of a brilliant man, such persons *learnt* as little as does anyone who attends a university without prior grammar-school education. He who did not have as it were the *examen abeundi* behind him—that is, had not already been prepared to a considerable level of competence, would have done better first to provide himself with the necessary pianistic equipment, either through private tuition or by attending a conservatoire and diligently practising finger exercises at home. Now, the Master certainly had a dreadful dislike of conservatoires. In *that* sense, that very many of them nowadays breed a ghastly proletariate, I frankly admit that I share Liszt's opposition to many of these institutions. It cannot be gainsaid, however, that his aversion and wholesale condemnation went too far, since it was to many of the music schools of which he made fun that he owed the material he was able to work on and obtain results with; even Leipzig, about which he spoke particularly harshly. And so ignorance and megalomania had taken root in even such a rationalist as Liszt. Those who because of lack of talent or industry had been shown the door by their previous teachers, or had spent time futilely breathing the air of the conservatoires, sought compensation for their unrecognized genius by seeking shelter in the

Master's camp and settling cosily under his wing. This category formed an alarming majority in comparison with the handful who, furnished with the necessary preliminary experience, were equal to the situation. The real corps of pianists could therefore be counted on one's fingers: Friedheim, Rosenthal, Reisenauer, Stavenhagen, Siloti, Dayas*, van der Sandt, S. Liebling, Stradal, Göllerich, and a few others, all of whom had previously undertaken exhaustive studies with such teachers as Rubinstein, Joseffy, Pruckner, Köhler, Kullak, and others, and were consequently in good condition when coming to the last polisher of all. The rest were unnecessary trimming, mere rigging which was not only itself out of place but—what was worse—sometimes hindered the really gifted from coming forward. This gang of flaneurs could be divided into two groups: females, who relied more on their pretty little faces than on smooth scales, and youths who had recourse to the most refined arts of flattery to make themselves the 'Old Man's' favourites. Both camps went to work systematically; they went for the old gentleman's weakest side, and with their incessant intriguing also pulled the rug from under the feet of others when necessary. Liszt, incidentally, did not seem to feel comfortable without these clinging plants; and it is only by a regrettable need of incense—increasing as he got older—that one can explain his failure to extirpate these weeds root and branch. . . .

Such little characteristics can strikingly highlight the weaknesses of a great man, but not detract from his immense merits. Liszt's unrivalled art, which opened new paths for us, and to which for half a century friend and foe alike paid homage, belongs to history and needs no eulogy from me. . . . The reforms he made have been equalled in this century only by his great contemporary Wagner, the eventual victorious outcome of whose struggles is hardly to be thought of without the support of Liszt. To thousands of musicians whose good fortune it was to be allowed to come into contact with him, he seemed a messenger from Heaven, a kind-hearted, humane, and charitable emissary who scattered his treasures abundantly and undiscriminatingly over all. In this sense Liszt founded a school as did no one before him. About his entire life is entwined like ivy the motto: 'Come unto me all ye that labour and are heavy laden, and I will give you rest!'[4]

Also present at the Leipzig performance of *Christus* was *August Göllerich*; and he, too, soon afterwards joined the pupils at Weimar.

The first and last never-to-be-forgotten impressions which I received from the Master's works in his presence are associated with one of the most sacred emanations of the human mind: his life's work, *Christus*. . . . 'When and where it is given a hearing,' he wrote on its completion, 'bothers me not at all. To write my things is an artistic necessity for me; and

* William Dayas (1863–1903), American pianist and teacher.

to have written them is quite sufficient for me,'—and Princess Wittgenstein saw rightly when she called *Christus* a work 'which will grow with the centuries'. . . .

Often he played Preludes and Fugues from *The Well-Tempered Clavier* off the cuff to us . . . and loved giving us single pieces from it to transpose rapidly, as well as studies from the Gradus ad Parnassum or Etudes by Chopin.

'Clementi,' he said, 'was a mere mechanic.'

'Bach never gave a tempo indication; he who understands it will find it. The openings of several of his Preludes remind me of Chopin, but you may take no pinch of snuff with them nor play them as unevenly as the Weimar pavement. Bach has at most two or three Preludes as beautiful as the one for the Fugue in G minor. I prefer it even to the Fugue, in itself very beautiful. Every day after lunch my father got me to play and transpose six Bach Fugues.'

'The cultivation of rhythm I consider one of the best educative measures. It was *entirely* wanting in Moscheles' playing. I like his first Concerto. So far as the virtuoso passages are concerned, it is very good; he also writes very purely.'

'Octave sequences—that's quite a problem! When Chopin writes them they are always ingenious. His Etudes are a unique compound of poetry and utility. He was quite incomparable—at his most captivating in the salon, when he dreamt up his little musical stories, for he played with the most delicate tenderness and had little strength. His Etude in C minor he never played.'

'We both loved Kessler's Etudes, and even now they are very much to be recommended.'

Whoever heard Liszt *play* and still doubted his *creative* genius, never understood his playing. It was the *expression of love*. Its beauty flowed out of harmony of the will. When one partook of this food for the soul, the piano disappeared—as Heine described—and music revealed itself. . . . His inimitable magic sprang from complete mastery of the whole field of musical art; it gushed forth from the destined composer of *all*—alike the *largest* and the most *intimate*—forms of that art. . . . Often though one heard him, one could still claim never to have heard him *thus*.

When he proceeded to the practice of his art, it was as though a prince were ascending the throne. Around his brow would be the aura of majesty, and his eyes would see into another world. . . .

Thus the 'lessons' were consecrated moments in which one of the supremely great raised up lesser talents by his counsel, offering them 'steps to ascend to God'.

Striving after effect he loathed as much in musical performance as in composing and in life; and, equally, playing of the sickly-sentimental variety on the one hand or the mechanical and pedantic on the other.

His remarks in this regard ran thus: 'Don't rock back and forth like that, child! That is only outer intensification! Feeling does not lie in the nose! Since you are no Ophelia, I advise you to go not to a *nunnery* but to a *conservatorium*—I am no professor!'

'No trills for investing in the savings bank! I love very long, rich trills!'

At the 'lessons', players had to appear before an audience of concert-artists, an ordeal which intimidated many; and one had to have one's wits about one, for, to the horror of those who could play only their repertoire, you could be called upon to play new things at sight, and not only piano pieces but orchestral scores too.

Ever and again it was *human beings* that Liszt wanted to hear, not academic *pedants*. Those lacking ability he would leave in no doubt about the hopelessness of their plans. He would disabuse them gently, to be sure, but very firmly. 'For,' he declared, 'art and sympathy should never be mixed; that produces nothing at all.'

That concert fashions allow only a *small* number of works to be given a hearing, Liszt constantly deplored, and he would always say that celebrated pianists were like 'sheep': 'If one of them jumps forward—that is, if a famous name finally manages to give a *rarely*-played piece—all the rest jump after him.'

In giving practical *technical* advice he was not at all sparing; nor did he fail to spice the lessons with *historical* retrospects. . . .

'I fell in love with Weber's poetical piano works at the age of seventeen. He was the first to write *dialogues*, of which I am very fond. Those of Beethoven are less developed. Weber's D minor Sonata contains the first example of a cantilena in the *left* hand; before him no one had written such a thing. The opening theme of the first movement of that sonata you must play like a tiger. The *Allegro feroce* indication is fully apt; it had not been used before that time, and was not used again until I wrote it in my own works.'

'Weber also made appearances as a pianist; but unfortunately I never heard him. Him, Schubert, and Goethe I did not know personally.'

'Weber's famous *Concertstück* I also liked very much, and soon made fashionable. But the additions I allowed myself were the primary reason why my fidelity as an interpreter was brought into disrepute.'

'Mendelssohn was another who played the *Concertstück* very nicely; he had much more warmth than Thalberg, but less technique.'

'My *first* Paganini Etudes were enormously difficult.'

'In Paris, Thalberg was much more popular than I at that time. I was the superior, to be sure, but with him everything seemed smooth and polished; with me, wild and chaotic—a tohu bohu of feelings.'

'On the day of one of my Vienna concerts a gentleman came into a barber's shop in the Graben and in the course of conversation gave vent to the opinion that I was jealous of Thalberg. I could not refrain from interjecting: Liszt is perhaps bizarre—I know him a little—but he is a stranger to jealousy. After the concert the same man came up to me in enthusiasm and apologized.'[5]

A May visitor to Weimar, to hear his First Symphony at the music festival, was the young Alexander Glazunov (1865–1936), who, as a talented representative of the musical Russia so keenly admired by Liszt, was given a warm welcome by the old master.

Another arrival was *Felix Weingartner*, whose opera *Sakuntala* was performed, thanks to Liszt's support, at the end of the Tonkünstler-Versammlung.

The festival opened with a stage performance of Liszt's *St Elisabeth*. He is said to have been reluctant to give permission for such a representation of his oratorio, and yet the effect was genuine and beautiful; in many places even dramatic, as though it had been written for the stage. . . .

Of the rest of the programme, I recall only one outstanding moment: *for the last time in his life Liszt mounted the conductor's podium*—to conduct Bülow's *Nirvana* and his own *Salve Polonia*.* What an unforgettable impression he created when he came on in his priest's robe. Greeted by thunderous applause and a fanfare from the orchestra, he appeared on the platform and with slow, dignified bows made his salutations first to the Grand-Ducal box and then to the public. The pieces themselves were weak and the performance rather timid; Liszt was no longer used to conducting an orchestra. In the *Salve Polonia* things even went positively awry, and the music would have come to a halt had not the principal cellist, Professor Grützmacher, begun to play an easily recognizable passage and been followed by the rest of the orchestra. Liszt made a royal gesture of thanks towards Grützmacher and one of reassurance to the Grand Duke, and without mishap the remainder of the work was played to an end. Once again a roar of applause. . . . And yet the whole scene was pervaded by a wintry aura of leave-taking; no one could fail to see that before us there stood a tired old man whose clock was running down.[6]

Some of Liszt's friends arranged a surprise repeat performance of the *Salve Polonia* at the next day's concert. To Carolyne he wrote (29 May): 'I feel rather tired . . . but as the valiant Arnauld† said, "Do we not have eternity to rest?" '

Felix Weingartner. My opera went well, and I received much praise and applause from the visitors. In the box beside Liszt was Saint-Saëns, who had attended all the festival performances. He came to one of Liszt's 'lessons', and Liszt introduced the best pupils to him. Going to the piano himself, he played a transcription of his new opera, *Henry VIII*, and afterwards—incomparably beautifully—Mozart's Rondo in A minor.

* Liszt composed the *Salve Polonia* (S113) in 1863, as a separate piece, but later decided to insert it, as an interlude, in his *Legend of St Stanislas*.

† Antoine Arnauld (1612–94), French theologian and controversialist who wrote against the Jesuits and in defence of the Jansenists.

Again that glorious light* in Liszt's eyes. 'That is real piano-playing,' he called out repeatedly and embraced his French friend.[7]

Adelheid von Schorn. That Liszt had been working on *St Stanislas*, I know for sure. After his death the Leipzig publisher Kahnt laid claim to what existed of the work, because he had paid Liszt an advance on it. If anything had been finished he would certainly have tried to turn it to account—but there was *nothing* that could be used. Could Liszt have left only such beginnings? Absolutely no rough sketches which could have been worked out? Such corruption had spread around him that not only with a change of servant did things go missing—they also disappeared from his immediate proximity without anyone being able to *prove* who had taken them. Under the pretext of having a memento of the Master, it began with such trifles as pencils and then proceeded to gloves, silk handkerchiefs, and so on.

Liszt had very few needs, and he cared nothing for useless things. Gifts he had received lay around unused, and he readily gave them away if he saw that someone liked them. So it may have begun with someone appropriating his belongings under his very eyes. But with manuscripts it was another matter altogether; only what he threw into the waste-paper basket was free for the taking. . . . His many moves made it all the easier: his possessions were in three different places, and nobody could tell whether something had merely been left behind or had disappeared, and by the time he returned it had been forgotten.[8]

To attend performances of Wagner's *Parsifal*, Liszt spent the period from 12 July to 8 August at Bayreuth. Here, until the arrival of Baroness Meyendorff, he was able to enjoy the agreeable company of Lina Schmalhausen. About Cosima, who a year and a half after her husband's death was still refusing to see anyone but her children, he wrote to Carolyne: 'My daughter remains engulfed by her mourning. I have not seen her again.' Shortly afterwards, however, he caught a brief glimpse of her in the darkness of the theatre.

Among those who came into contact with him at Bayreuth was *Franz Hueffer* (1843–89), German-born music critic of *The Times* and translator into English of the Liszt–Wagner correspondence.

One did not care much to trouble the Master with a visit, but being told by Hans Richter that he wished particularly to see me, I called on him at the house where he used to take up his quarters. . . . He received me with the profusion of politeness, 'gratitude for what I had done for his music in England,' and the like, which belonged to his courtly manner and always reminded one of his own saying, that if he had not been a musician he would have been the first diplomatist in Europe. He did not play at that

* When writing of an 'almost frightening fire' he had seen in Liszt's eyes a short time previously during a performance of Berlioz's *Carnaval romain* overture, Weingartner added: 'If I could rediscover the same fire in the eyes of a young musician, I should be more hopeful of the future of our art than I am able to be as things are.'

time, and I did not expect to see him again; but the next morning, at a little after seven, I heard a loud knock at my bedroom door, and when, with the disregard of the imperfections of attire which one acquires abroad, I asked the supposed waiter or chambermaid to enter, in came Liszt with many excuses for his early call. He always rose, he said, at four in the morning, and his time for visits was from six to eight a.m. Having shown the Master into a more fitting apartment and finished my toilet in great haste, I had another long and interesting conversation, and as I accompanied him back across the fine old square in which that dirtiest and most malodorous of hostelries, the Reichsadler, is situated, he asked me to come to his house that afternoon to hear some of his pupils perform. No sooner had the ladies of our party heard of this invitation than they insisted upon being included in it, and when this had been accomplished they demanded, with the urgency peculiar to their sex, that I should make the Master play to them. This I knew from experience to be by no means an easy task, for Liszt never played when directly asked to do so. . . . Diplomacy, therefore, would be necessary, and this in the presence of the great *diplomate manqué*! We arrived, however, in due season, at the house of Liszt, whom we found surrounded by a number of pupils and by a miscellaneous company, including a nun* and a Russian princess,† one of the most portly and amiable ladies I have ever met. The conversation turned upon general and subsequently upon musical topics, but what was in everyone's mind—the wish that the Master should play—no one dared to utter. At last, despair brought me sudden inspiration. Happening to talk of Italian literature, in which Liszt, as in every other literature, was perfectly at home, I referred to the difficulty which the sonnet, with its rhythmical division into double quartet and final sestet, offered for musical setting, and added with perfect sincerity that the only composer who had completely overcome that difficulty was Liszt himself in his three Petrarch Sonnets. Citing the opening lines of the first of these sonnets:

Benedetto sia 'l giorno, e 'l mese, e l'anno,
E la stagione, e 'l tempo, e l'ora, e 'l punto,

I pretended to have forgotten for the moment the tune to which those lines are wedded. This was enough for Liszt. Bounding up from his corner of the sofa, he went to the piano and played the beautiful melody from beginning to end. This naturally led to the two other sonnets of the collection, and the ice once being broken, one piece followed the other in uninterrupted and delightful succession. I shall not attempt any description of how Liszt played; I may, however, say the following. Our party consisted of a hard-worked and weary critic, a much-admired and therefore much-employed prima donna, a distinguished amateur, and one of our leading conductors,

* Probably Adelheid von Schorn, who had become a canoness.
† Nadine Helbig.

all case-hardened, one would say, against ordinary musical impressions. When Liszt had finished we did not feel inclined, like the young ladies of Berlin, to fight over fragments of his furniture; we did not even applaud; but when we left the house we felt that we had been in the presence of something supremely great, something unique of its kind, something, as one of the party expressed it, 'as unlike any other man's playing, as Wagner's music is unlike any other man's music'.[9]

Returning to Weimar on 9 August, Liszt went at the end of the month to Munich for a performance of Wagner's *Ring*. He then proceeded to Schloss Itter, the 'fairy-tale' home near Wörgl (Austrian Tyrol) of his friend Sophie Menter, where he spent a few days before journeying back to Weimar.

Visiting Eisenach on 28 September for the unveiling of a statue of J. S. Bach (to the cost of which he had contributed 3,000 thalers),* he also attended, that same evening, a performance of the B minor Mass, and on the 29th a Bach concert. The conductor on both occasions was Joachim.

Via Nuremberg, Vienna, and Pozsony, Liszt returned to Budapest at the end of October, but left on 1 November to stay with his friend *Géza Zichy* at the latter's home in Tetétlen, near Debrecen.

At last we received the telegram announcing Liszt's imminent arrival. What a red-letter day that was for my family and me. To make him as comfortable as possible, and at the same time to ensure his complete independence, I had a little house in the park made ready for him. Four of its rooms were placed at his disposal, and in the salon stood the accustomed Bösendorfer.

'Liszt is coming! Liszt is coming!'—the whole village, the whole neighbourhood, could talk of nothing else. In the early morning of the day he was to arrive, the village girls were already plundering my flower beds. It was one of those lovely Novembers not uncommon in Lower Hungary, and as the autumn flowers were in their full splendour, bouquets and garlands were prepared, and in all hearts reigned a mood of festive gaiety. And yet these poor country girls, who early each morning milked the cows and scrubbed the floors, were actually quite ignorant of who Franz Liszt was. At most they knew that he was a famous man, the pride of Hungary; and that was quite enough for them to welcome him with all love and enthusiasm.

At midday my four-in-hand drove into the village with our guest. When Liszt caught sight of the festive crowd, he bared his noble head and placed his hat on his knees; my pleas to him to put it on again were unavailing. Shaking his head, he said with visible emotion: 'My politeness is a way of

* Liszt had always greatly revered Bach, whom he designated 'the St Thomas Aquinas of music'. In a letter to Carl Gille of Sept. 1863, in which he mentioned both Bach and Handel and expressed his preference for the former, he continued: 'And when I have edified myself sufficiently with Handel's common chords, I long for the precious dissonances of the Passion, the B minor Mass, and other of Bach's polyphonic wares.'

thanking them!' When we reached the Protestant church, a frenzy of enthusiasm broke out. Hundreds of girls pressed against the carriage, showering the guest with flowers and garlands. The Protestant pastor greeted the Catholic abbé with a lively speech, partly in German and partly in Hungarian—but which was understood by none of us, by the speaker himself probably least of all, He ended his address, or rather he *wanted* to end it, for he got stuck and repeated several times over: 'How delighted we are to be able to gr- gr- . . .'

Lowering his eyes, Liszt whispered the words to him: 'Greet you!'

Immediately after this reception we sat down to a meal, at which a thoroughly bad gypsy band appeared uninvited and set about providing music for us. When Liszt saw that I was about to send them on their way, he quietly asked me to leave them be, saying that people could offer only what lay within their powers.

A tranquil and idyllic life now began. At 6.30 each morning the Master went to the little chapel for mass, served by the old Franciscan. To my shame I must admit that I was seldom up and about at such an early hour, and contented myself with watching Liszt from his window as he made his way there pulling his brown rug along the ground behind him. To the old sexton who officiated he gave a gulden every day in payment of his services.

I knew the Master's habits pretty well. At night he slept very little, and would breakfast before daybreak. On the table in his room there always stood coffee, tea, and red wine. Brandy, I deliberately refrained from providing, as my Budapest doctor had made a special point of asking me to withhold this drink from him. The mornings he spent writing letters, reading, and praying; his breviary he was scrupulous about reading every morning and evening. After lunch he would have a good sleep of two hours or more. Towards evening he would usually come over to us in the salon and with great enthusiasm play whist until supper. . . .

One morning I was surprised to receive a note he sent me with my servant. It ran: 'Franz Liszt asks for some brandy. A very experienced doctor has prescribed me this risky beverage. With spirits, one has only to remember to take them in moderation. If wine is old men's milk, then brandy is their cream!'

I shook with laughter when reading the Master's request, and of course at once took him the desired drink. To be on the safe side, I had already obtained in advance a cognac that was particularly good without being too strong. When I entered, the bottle under my arm, he laughed heartily. 'Master!' I said, 'my doctor's opinion of brandy is very different.' 'I know——; he is a stupid bungler,' replied Liszt.

A few days after his arrival, this great and good man said to me: 'Géza, the welcome given me by these good people moved me sincerely, and I should like to show my gratitude by playing to them. Even if it gives them no pleasure to hear me, they may be pleased to have heard me; especially if a buffet is provided too. So invite *tutti quanti*, as many as the room can hold. You and your children must help too when the great concert takes place!' And that is what happened: this great, immortal master, whom many crowned heads could no longer hear, who a few months earlier had declined an invitation from Queen Victoria of England, played to an audience consisting for the most part of simple countryfolk.

The programme was as follows:

Tetétlen, 10 November 1884.

Prelude	Franz Liszt
Hungarian Overture	Géza Zichy
Impromptu	Franz Liszt
F. Liszt: 2nd Hungarian Rhapsody	Margareta Zichy*
Rákóczy March	Franz Liszt and Géza Zichy

Be it said to the honour of the Hungarian peasant that he was fully capable of appreciating the distinction conferred upon him. After the concert the great master excelled himself in kindness, waiting upon his unsophisticated guests, offering them food and filling their glasses with wine. The Hungarian peasant is half aristocrat, calm, reserved, and *sympathique*. After Liszt had captivated everyone, despite his inability to speak Hungarian fluently, a snow-white old man went up to him at the end of the meal and, glass in hand, said: 'What you are *called*, the Count has told us; what you can *do*, you have shown us; but what you *are*, we have seen for ourselves—and for that, may the great God of the Hungarians bless you!'[10]

A description of the event which was published in *Fővárosi Lapok* (Leaves of the Metropolis) on 14 November reports that as an encore after the Impromptu Liszt played a piece by Chopin. Margareta Zichy, whose teacher, Miska Müller, also took part in the concert, was rewarded by a Lisztian kiss on the brow; and the occasion was brought to an end by a brilliant fireworks display organized by Count Ernő Zichy. 'Thunderous mortar shots carried the joy of this day far out into the countryside.'

On 17 November Liszt returned to Budapest, leaving the capital again on 8 December to journey to Rome. At Florence, where he spent a night at the home of Jessie Hillebrand, he renewed acquaintance with the Swiss painter Arnold Böcklin (1827–1901) and made that of the Scottish composer and conductor *Alexander Mackenzie* (1847–1935), later the Principal of the Royal Academy of Music in London.

Our first meeting was not a fortunate one for me, and . . . may serve to illustrate at least one side of his much-discussed and oft-maligned character. Seated opposite him, I happened to tell a musical anecdote to my table-neighbour in which Tausig's name was mentioned among others,

* One of Zichy's daughters, then aged nine.

when Liszt rather snappily said: 'No! Tausig would never have said that.' Our host, Hillebrand,* intervened with the explanation that I had never suggested any such thing. Whereupon the master, leaning across to me, remarked: 'Pardon me, I am a little deaf.'

But afterwards in the drawing-room, where he played to us, he seemed upset and cross. I must confess that I committed a mistake in conveying a request from my friend Niecks† for the favour of an interview with reference to certain points in Chopin's life. I ought to have waited for a more propitious moment, as my tactlessness only drew the brusque refusal, 'I've heard enough about that,' and an unmistakable indication that the whole subject was distasteful to him. The rebuff was deserved.

Having been invited to supper, I felt obliged to tell Mde. Hillebrand that I could hardly count myself a *persona grata* and therefore begged to be excused. My surprise was great when, later in the evening, an urgent message was sent to the effect that Liszt wished me to come up at once. Immediately on arrival he had inquired for '*der Schotte*', and desired to see some of my work.

'Yes, certainly, *Meister*; but after supper.'

But the postponement did not suit him, and, a fourhand edition of my *Burns* having been produced, he sat down to play it with Buonamici‡ (or Hatton) before being dragged off to table. I was then sent for, and, the meal over, the reading of the piece was resumed. All his amiability returning, he declared himself extremely pleased. Pointing to a passage of exceptionally Scottish flavour, he said, 'I've done much of this sort of thing, but not that.' He asked for an orchestral score, and his promise to send it to Budapest was kept. . . .

Between dinner and supper he had taken himself to task—as I knew later to be his habit—for loss of temper; some cases came under my own ken. Thinking that he had been quick-tempered with a somewhat eccentric violinist then living in Florence, the old man mounted many flights of stairs to appease his conscience by making reparation. And again (at Westwood House, Sydenham§), when a talkative pianist had ruffled him, he abruptly left us. I silently followed him to ascertain whether he had gone to his room and saw him gazing out of a window half-way up the staircase. After a few minutes' reflection he slowly descended and joined us as if nothing had happened to upset him.

My own lapse proved a blessing in disguise, for not only did he grant a prolonged and profitable meeting to Niecks at Leipzig, but when his devoted pupil Bache—who had met with a previous refusal to visit London—invited him to hear *St Elisabeth* at the Novello Oratorio

* Mackenzie's memory has failed him here, for Hillebrand had died in October.
† The German-born musician and writer Frederick Niecks (1845–1924).
‡ The Italian pianist and composer Giuseppe Buonamici (1846–1914).
§ During Liszt's visit to England in April 1886.

Concerts, he wrote: 'Mackenzie: I owe him something,' and came, after a forty-five years' absence from England.

Surely penance for a momentary show of irritation could no farther go!

One late afternoon I slipped noiselessly into the room just when he had begun to play one of the later sonatas of Beethoven from memory in the twilight when only Mde. Hillebrand was present; after which I had reluctantly to take the left-hand part in a piece with which he wished to become acquainted.

Much interesting information was given about the newer Russian composers, then almost unknown in Western Europe, of whom he had a high opinion: of the pioneers Balakirev, Rimsky Korsakov, Borodin, Cui and some others he explained that they were army officers and chemists by profession. Liszt was not only keenly interested in national musical idioms of every country, but persistently urged their use in composition. Accompanying him to an early train to Rome, I was glad to inform him of a performance of his Psalm XIII in the North of England (by an enthusiast, the late Nicholas Kilburn). With a cynical smile he quoted its opening line: 'O Lord, how long?'—referring to the tardy acceptance of his compositions in this country.

For consumption on these journeys certain special sandwiches were made by Miss Rosa Williams. Following her to the kitchen, he would ask, with a chuckle, for them to be given to himself and not to his manservant. The service of a valet was, he told me, the only luxury he could afford. These trivial touches exhibit the contrast between the natures and habits of Liszt and Wagner. In old age the former travelled modestly, his food in his pocket; while the latter disdained the accommodation of a first-class carriage. To Buonamici, Wagner once exclaimed: 'Help me to faint! They can't give me a saloon carriage,' and preferred to postpone his departure until the following day.[11]

1885

Lillie de Hegermann-Lindencrone, January*. Just now we are revelling in Liszt. Rome is wild over him, and one leaves no stone unturned in order to meet him. Fortunate are those who have even a glimpse of him, and thrice blessed are those who *know* and hear him. He is the prince of musicians—in fact, he is treated like a prince. He always has the precedence over everyone; even Ambassadors—so tenacious of their rights—give them up without hesitation. Everyone is happy to pay this homage to genius. . . .

* The former Lillie Moulton, now wife of the Danish Ambassador in Rome.

I received a very queer letter the day Liszt dined here, from the Princess Wittgenstein:

I hear that you are going to have the Master to dine at your house. I beg of you to see that he does not sit in a draught of air, or that the cigars he will smoke will not be too strong, and that the coffee he drinks will be weak, for he cannot sleep afterwards, and please see that he is brought safely to his apartment.

Yours, etc., etc.

All these instructions were carried out to the letter. . . .

There was a large dinner given by the German Ambassador, Herr von Keudell, for the Princess Frederick Carl. Liszt and many others, including ourselves, were present. The Ambassador allowed the gentlemen only a short time to smoke; he gave them good but small cigars. I do not know how the great Master liked this, for he is a fervent smoker. However, as *le charbonnier est maître chez lui*, our host had his way and the music commenced, as he wished, very soon after dinner. . . . Liszt begged the Princess to whistle, and opened his book of *Lieder* at *Es muss ein Wunderbares sein* (a lovely song) and said, 'Can you whistle that?' Yes, she could; and did it very carefully and in a *wunderbares* manner. Liszt was astonished and delighted.

Then Liszt played. Each time I hear him I say, 'Never has he played like this.' How can a person surpass himself? Liszt does. He had the music of *Comment, disaient-ils** in the same book and begged me to sing it. 'Do you think,' he said 'you could add this little cadenza at the end?' And he played it for me. . . .

Liszt is not always as amiable as this. He resents people counting on his playing. When Baroness K. inveigled him into promising to take tea with her because he knew her father, she, on his accepting, invited a lot of friends, holding out hopes that Liszt would play. She pushed the piano into the middle of the room—no one could possibly have failed to see it. Everyone was on the *qui vive* when Liszt arrived, and breathless with anticipation. Liszt, who has had many surprises of this sort, I imagine, saw the situation at a glance. After several people had been presented to him, with his most captivating smile he said to the hostess:

'*Où est votre piano, chère madame?*' and looked all about for the piano, though it was within an inch of his nose.

'Oh, Monseigneur! Would you, really . . .?' advancing towards the piano triumphantly. 'You are too kind. I never should have dared to ask you.' And, waving her hand towards it: '*Here* is the piano!'

'Ah,' said Liszt, who loves a joke, '*c'est vrai. Je voulais y poser mon chapeau.*' Very crestfallen, but undaunted, the Baroness cried, 'But,

* A setting for voice and piano (S276) of a poem by Hugo. Two versions exist, the first dating from 1842, the second from 1859.

Monseigneur, you will not refuse, if only to play a scale—merely to *touch* the piano!'

But Liszt, as unkind as she was tactless, answered, coldly, 'Madame, I never play my scales in the afternoon,' and turned his back on her and talked with Madame Helbig.

As they stood there together, he and Madame Helbig, one could not see very much difference between them. She is as tall as Liszt, wears her hair short, and is attired in a long waterproof which looks like a soutane; and he wears his hair long, and is attired in a long soutane which looks like a waterproof. As regards their clothes, the only noticeable difference was that her gown was buttoned down the front and his was not. Both have the same broad and urbane smile. . . .

Liszt honoured me by coming to my reception, brought by Herr von Keudell—Liszt is always brought. Imagine the delight of my friends who came thus unexpectedly on the great Master. They made a circle around him, trying to edge near enough to get a word with him. He was extremely amiable and seemed pleased to create this manifestation of admiration. (Can one ever have enough?) There are two young musical geniuses here at the Villa Medici, both *premier prix de Rome*. One is Gabriel Pierné, nicknamed 'Le Bébé' because he is so small and looks so boyish—he really does not seem over fourteen years of age—and another, Paul Vidal, who is as good a pianist as Pierné, but not such a promising composer.

I asked Liszt if he would allow these two young artists to play some of their compositions for him. He kindly consented, and the appointed day found them all in the salon. Liszt was enchanted (so he said); but how many times has he said, clapping the delighted artist on the shoulder, '*Mon cher, vous avez un très grand talent . . . Vous irez loin*; *vous arriverez*,' a great phrase! And then he would sit down at the piano, saying with a smile, 'Do you play this?' and play it and crush him to atoms, and they would depart, having *la mort dans l'âme* and overwhelmed with their imperfections. Instead of encouraging them, he *dis*couraged them, poor fellows! Speaking of young artists in general, he said once, '*Il n'y a personne qui apprécie comme moi les bonnes intentions, mais je n'en aime pas toujours les résultats*.'[1]

When recalling* their time in Rome, neither Gabriel Pierné (1863–1937), who wrote of 'the great master whom I admired then and venerate now', nor Paul Vidal (1863–1931) omitted to pay tribute to Liszt's counsel and kindness. Vidal, in particular, stressed 'the inestimable encouragement he gave me'.

It was Vidal, too, who recorded a memorable Lisztian aphorism. 'When I asked Liszt which of Wagner's works was his favourite, he replied with this striking assertion that I have never forgotten: "Wagner's *œuvre* is a sculpture in bas-relief; one admires it while walking round it." '

* See *Les Grands Prix de Rome de Musique*, ed. H. Rebois (Paris, 1932).

The novelist Thomas Adolphus Trollope (1810–92). I was one of a very gay and pleasant dinner-party, given by an American lady, at which Liszt and Senator Mamiani,* then octogenarian and a good bit more, were among the guests. After dinner, which had been a somewhat long and very merry one, an attempt was made to induce Liszt to go to the piano, which had been carefully introduced into the room, and disguised by cloths into the innocent semblance of a sideboard. We all knew that the enterprise in hand was likely to be a difficult one, for the great musician was apt to be somewhat chary in responding to such impromptu calls upon him; and in fact he showed manifest signs of not being minded to comply with the entreaties of those around him, till Mamiani said: 'Maestro, will you go to the instrument if I beg you to do so *on my knees*?'

'I cannot answer for what might happen in such circumstances,' said the old musician, shaking his flowing white locks, 'for I never had a senator on his knees before me.'

No sooner were the words out of his lips, than Mamiani, not only a senator, but one of the most illustrious of the Senate, and with his eighty-four or eighty-five years still as playful as a boy of *le bon vieux temps*, jumped up, ran round the table, and with napkin in hand—I can see the two venerable white heads now, laughing into each other's eyes—plumped down before him. Liszt, placing his hands on the kneeling senator's shoulders to help him in rising from his chair, went to the instrument without another word; and once there, was not niggardly in the treat he gave us.[2]

Princess Carolyne to Adelheid von Schorn, late January. When he arrived [in Rome], he was physically and morally so tired, benumbed, and sad to behold, that for two days I could only weep to myself. But gradually, as the climate began to exert its beneficial effect, his amiability of mind returned in full. I could only see how much his mental state depends on his health. He eats very little—but cannot go for more than four hours without nourishment—and must have a *déjeuner à la fourchette* at 9.30, as he is awake at four in the morning. If he does not, then he is in a wretched state and can neither swallow anything nor sleep at night. Nevertheless, he could still live if he would look after himself! If people would only take pity on him and not always treat him as though he were a young man, inviting him hither and thither, at all hours and on all floors. . . . His life is hanging by a thread! People don't realize it, and yet the thread can quickly snap. Happily, his constitution is a very strong one, or he would long since have departed this world.[3]

On Sunday, 25 January, Liszt left Rome to return to Budapest, which he reached on the 29th. One of his pupils here was the Bohemian pianist *August Stradal*

* Terenzio Mamiani della Rovere (1799–1885), Italian statesman and philosopher.

(1860–1930), who had first come to the masterclasses at Weimar the previous September.

Liszt was then working on among other things the last of his Hungarian Rhapsodies [S244/19]. I often had the opportunity of observing the Master during the composition of this work. Like all great masters, he composed in his mind, without calling upon the services of the piano. In lengthy passages he would from time to time play upon the desk with his fingers, perhaps to set down the fingering. The themes of this Rhapsody, which Liszt began in Rome at the end of 1884, and which, with interruptions, he worked at for a long time, he took from the *Csárdás nobles* of his friend Kornél Ábrányi, who taught composition at the Budapest Music Academy. They are, of course, gypsy themes, which Ábrányi published in a *csárdás* collection. . . .

Whereas in the two Rhapsodies which preceded the Nineteenth he had turned, so far as technical demands are concerned, more towards the simpler piano technique of his last period, in the Nineteenth he again used the daring technical combinations of earlier times, but simultaneously raised this technique into the magic realm of expression of his last works.

When I entered the Master's room one morning, he had just finished this Rhapsody. . . . 'Copy it out for the publisher straightaway, and play it from memory at the music teachers' concert next week,' he said. In that first moment, because of the near date of the concert, I felt slightly alarmed, but did not allow it to show, and merely asked the Master if he would do me the great kindness of playing the Rhapsody to me. He stood up, we went through his dining-room and salon into the adjoining concert hall of the Music Academy. And there, to me alone, the Master now played the Rhapsody, which he had probably never tried out on the keyboard, altogether matchlessly, overcoming at the age of seventy-three, and with unbelievable ease and accuracy, all its very great technical difficulties. What a singing and resounding in the *Lassan*! It was of all life's sorrows, of memories of blissful times that were past, that he sang. And then came the *Friska*. It was as though a whole army of gypsies on fiery steeds were raging over the puszta. Exhausted, the Master finished. . . . I had experienced a rendition such as I would never hear again. . . .

I could at first find no words to describe the profound impression which the work and Liszt's playing had made upon me. It was a revelation. The piano had lost everything material; from the strings there cried out a voice of yearning; it was the artistic outpouring of a great and lonely soul, of the singer of sorrow who is taking leave of life and, after all its bitter experiences, seeking to glide gently into realms of eternal rest and heavenly peace. . . .

In Budapest I was shocked to notice that the Master's cuffs had been fastened by his servant with thread!—and that he therefore possessed no cuff-links. When I then made him a present of a pair of beautiful gold links, he seemed very pleased and wore them for a week or so—but soon afterwards I saw the thread again! . . .

Everything connected with money was repellent to him. . . . Every Saturday his servant had to show him his calculation of expenses for the week, but only in gulden, without kreutzer. When I once happened to see one of these calculations, I remarked to the Master in astonishment that it was surprising that in Pest everything cost only gulden and no kreutzer. His reply was that he had told his servant to round everything off to the nearest gulden, so that when examining it he would 'not have to bother with too much mathematics'! 'For,' he continued, 'so far as money is concerned, I am consumed with neither envy nor anxiety.' And so Liszt was the greatest anti-capitalist of the century.

The principal feature of his character was an immense goodness and love of his fellow beings, to whom he could refuse no request, so that he often possessed nothing himself. This goodness sometimes bordered on weakness; thus, in my opinion at least, he should have shown many of the female pupils the door, especially as he never accepted any remuneration for his teaching. . . . Added to his goodness was also the gift of mastering himself in every situation, of behaving according to etiquette, and of always being socially up to the mark. He was the clever courtier who never committed a *faux pas*. The following incident is comical. When, in evening dress, I accompanied the Master to a concert for the first time, I handed my top hat in at the cloakroom—which he at once noticed and criticized. Improper behaviour by young people was something he disliked intensely, and he generally rebuked them severely. This applied to table manners as well, and woe to the miscreant who cut up a potato with his knife instead of his fork, or took a melon apart in the same way. If in his presence anyone had taken a fish to pieces with his knife, Liszt might well have dismissed him from the table. His old friend Gille, who so often dined with Liszt in Weimar, had the habit, when eating, of 'smacking' his lips when anything tasted good. And so he often received a little ticking off from Liszt, at which Gille and I would laugh heartily. . . .

Two souls dwelt within his breast, the religious and the liberal. They were not divided, however, but fused together in *one* personality, the 'good man'. Although he had always been a believer, it was by way of different philosophical theories that he returned to true religion, in which he saw the salvation of both the individual and the state. His social outlook had undergone great changes too. Whereas as a young man he had been a passionate friend of the people, as an old man he stood, like Goethe, on a lofty philosophical plane, looking down with Olympian calm on to the bustle of humanity and speaking with sarcasm about slogans concerning social democracy. Nevertheless, he retained his love of mankind, but without regarding the people as capable of governing themselves. And so, virtually foreseeing our own time, he said: 'In republics it is always the least capable who are at the head of the country, but those who rule should be aristocrats in the Greek sense of the word—that is, the best and most capable. Only the monarchy, led by a wise and just ruler whose ministers are specialists of distinction in their own fields, has ethical justification.' . . .

All violence, dirt, and coarseness in the people he found repellent. He felt at his ease in aristocratic circles where the cream of the beautiful world of women inspired him. In their palaces he felt at home, and because of his brilliant conversation, and despite all the celebrities and members of the nobility who came and went, he was always the real centre of attraction, especially when he was induced to set the keys of the piano in motion.

What was his playing like in old age? First of all, a marvel of technique! Liszt, who had ended his virtuoso career at the age of thirty-six and since that time played only occasionally in public for charitable purposes, was when I knew him still the possessor of an immense technique, which was inborn and not acquired. Added to this, there was a supernatural, transcendental gift of presentation, which moved his listeners to their depths. His cantilena was pure song; the stringed instrument lost its material qualities. It was a spiritualized performance of a kind achieved neither before nor after him. His touch was spell-binding, his *fortissimo* mighty in its power, but without ever passing the bounds of the beautiful. Of modern pianists who employ an ugly and excessive *fortissimo* he used to say: 'Nowadays they do not *play*, but beat and thrash the piano!' What the Periclean age was for Greece, Liszt was for the culture of the piano. . . .

That Liszt never fought for his own works and often said 'I can wait', can be explained by his Christianity, which made it his duty to help others and to show nobility of soul. When one bears in mind that as a virtuoso and writer, and apart from his own artistic achievements, he promoted the works of Bach, Beethoven (the *Hammerklavier* Sonata!!), Schubert, Weber, championed Chopin, Schumann, Berlioz, Wagner, Franz, Raff, Saint-Saëns, Smetana, Joachim, Bülow, and many others, and in return for his selflessness was mostly rewarded with base ingratitude, then his destiny must be considered a tragic one. . . .

I sometimes spoke with the Master about this ingratitude which he earned from so many sides, but on each occasion he had words of forgiveness and excuse, stressing that it was a Christian duty to do good, irrespective of whether one were thanked for it.

When in Budapest, Liszt used to subscribe to the local newspaper and to the Munich *Allgemeine Zeitung*, remarking jocularly that he shared his liking for the latter with Beethoven. I often read to him from these two papers, but never from the political sections, which interested him not at all. I also had to read from various religio-philosophical works. . . .

Once I took along Schopenhauer's *Parerga und Paralipomena* and read out the paragraphs dealing with writers. The one in which Schopenhauer divides them into 'meteors', 'planets' and 'fixed stars' met with his warmest approval, and at the sentence, 'But because of the height of the fixed stars their light takes many years to reach earth-dwellers,' the Master interrupted me and pensively repeated those words! And the passage in which Schopenhauer speaks of a pyrotechnician who has let off his fireworks in a meadow and then seen that the spectators are merely members of an institute for the blind, Liszt found beautifully expressed; and he remarked that he had already long been such a pyrotechnician and that perhaps the blind would one day regain their sight. . . .

I also played him his *Der nächtliche Zug* after Lenau's *Faust*, a work which is certainly to be placed among Liszt's most important. After he had related a number of things about the unfortunate Lenau,* he said that when travelling he always took Goethe's *Faust* and the *Divina Commedia* with him, and that without these two masterworks, which he read again and again, he could not live. . . . No work, he said, had caused such a revolution in his views as Goethe's *Faust*. The *Divina Commedia* he had read for the first time, he told me, at Bellagio on Lake Como, under Comolli's statue of Dante and Beatrice.[4]

In early March Liszt again spent a day in Gran at the invitation of Cardinal Simor, the Prince Primate, who urged him to 'come more often and stay longer'. At Easter (2–6 April) he was Cardinal Haynald's guest at Kalocsa. Then, via Pozsony, where on 13 April he attended Anton Rubinstein's recital in aid of the Hummel monument, he reached Vienna.

August Stradal. One morning, when Dr Standhartner, the longstanding friend of Wagner, Schoenaich, the well-known writer on music, and I were at the Master's, Anton Bruckner appeared. He was wearing an old-fashioned tailcoat, and in his hand held an opera hat. His clothes were not quite up to date, for with the coat he wore short grey leggings out of which peeped a pair of enormous boots. A smile came over all faces, especially when Bruckner addressed Liszt humbly with the words, 'Your Grace, Herr Canon'. He had come to ask Liszt to recommend a performance of his Seventh Symphony at the Karlsruhe Tonkünstler-Versammlung (under Mottl). Liszt apparently found Bruckner's request difficult to refuse. It was no longer possible to include the whole work, however, as the programme had already been drawn up. Otherwise amenable to all requests, he seemed to find Bruckner's reiterated entreaties disagreeable. At this short meeting between the two masters I felt that Liszt had no great liking for Bruckner as a composer. To be sure, I remember that on saying farewell he showed Bruckner great friendliness, promising that if it were still possible he would comply with his request. But at the Tonkünstler-Versammlung only the Adagio of the symphony was played. After the return from

* The German poet Nikolaus Lenau (1802–50) was insane for the last six years of his life and died in an asylum.

Karlsruhe to Weimar, Liszt did indeed express a favourable opinion of the Adagio, but, all the same, one had the impression that the work did not impress him particularly. . . .

Before leaving Vienna he visited the Musicians' Society. Rubinstein, who was in the Austrian capital to attend rehearsals of his opera *Nero*, also turned up that evening, as did Brahms, the Society's honorary president.[5]

Moriz Rosenthal. Seldom has a small salon brought together a triumvirate of such musical significance. Brahms, Liszt, and Rubinstein at one table, and seated so close to one another that a stimulating and interesting conversation could easily have got going between the three great masters, but which for reasons unknown to me did not do so. When in the course of the evening the lady sitting next to Rubinstein asked him for an autograph, the piano titan took out of his pocket and gave her a visiting card. This strange 'autograph' made its way over to Liszt, who below the printed name of Rubinstein wrote: 'and his admirer F. Liszt'. But this was merely a curtain raiser. For a very pretty and very celebrated Russian pianist,* whose ambition went higher and who wished to retain a souvenir of the evening in the form of a lock of hair from each of the masters, approached Rubinstein with clicking scissors, putting her request to him with all the power of persuasion and in the sweetest words of their common homeland. Rubinstein, who in his opera *Nero* had already shown both his dislike of cruelty and the true kind-heartedness of his character, resignedly offered his head to the fair petitioner. The sails of hope fanned by a fresh wind, she then turned to Liszt, who, with a bow of consent and a sardonic smile, said: 'Samson and Delilah! But have no fear, Madame—I shall not pull down the pillars of your conjugal happiness.' Slightly flustered, perhaps bowed, but still unbroken, Delilah now fiercely attacked Brahms, who however, averse to homages so trite and out of date, refused with both word and gesture, cutting a finger on the scissors in the process. An awkward silence followed, and the atmosphere became distinctly chilly. Then the music-publisher Albert Gutmann hurried over with a glass of water, caught a few drops of blood in it and said solemnly: 'Whosoever drinks of this blood will understand the language of Hanslick.' The situation was saved.[6]

It was probably on this same occasion that someone pointed a finger at the three celebrated musicians and called out: 'The Triumvirate!' After a moment's silence, Rubinstein, pointing at Liszt, said loudly: 'Caesar!' Then, at himself: 'Brutus!' And at Brahms—'Lepidus!'

On 18 April Liszt left Vienna to return to Weimar.

Princess Carolyne to Adelheid von Schorn, 28 April. Liszt's frequent dozing off is really sad. He could spare himself such things if he would only

* Anna (or Annette) Essipova (1851–1914), second of the four wives of Theodor Leschetizky. From 1893 she was engaged as a piano teacher at the St Petersburg Conservatoire, where Prokofiev was among her pupils.

allow himself more sleep at night and in the morning hours. Please remind Pauline and Michael [Mihály] that at half past nine Liszt must have not only eggs, but also meat and warm vegetables, or perhaps some porridge or rice. But tastefully cooked. . . .

When he is hungry his stomach and throat become as tight as a pouch, nervous irritability takes hold of him, he begins to tremble, cannot sleep at night, and the entire twenty-four hours are disturbed for him.[7]

August Stradal, May. One day Liszt invited me to join him in a box at the Court Theatre for a performance of Nessler's *Trompeter von Säckingen*, which was capturing the hearts of all the women just then. To my astonishment, his servant put a small travelling lamp and the score of the work into the box; Liszt then followed the opera with the score, his merriment increasing from one scene to the next. After the first act he told me to fetch his servant and the carriage, as he could listen to no more of it —then came his favourite expression: 'Mundus vult Schundus.'* On the return journey he took delight in the sentimentality of his dear Weimarians, and added: 'Something as shallow as that is being performed everywhere after *Tristan* and *Die Meistersinger*. The stone which with untold difficulty Sisyphus rolled up the hill, has come crashing down again! Effort without purpose. Great music is written for aristocrats of the spirit. For the masses, the only nourishment is rubbish. A masterpiece like the *Barber of Bagdad* was booed; the *Trompeter* is a sensation!'

When I went to the Master early one beautiful May morning, I found him already sitting at his desk. He had just finished a little nocturne, *En rêve* [S207], on which he wrote the words: 'This manuscript, badly written, belongs to my young friend Stradalus.' Together with the usual Virginia cigar he then presented me with the manuscript, at which I was deeply moved and with tears in my eyes thanked him again and again for so great an honour and distinction—whereupon he took his seat at the piano and played me the piece. Never shall I forget the manner in which, as though utterly detached from the material world, he breathed out on the keyboard the transcendent little masterpiece. Of supernatural beauty, *En rêve* is genuinely late Liszt; soft and dreamy, it sounds like a gentle floating over into a sunny Beyond, a radiant farewell from life![8]

'As well as music paper and trouble with my eyes, I have had several other bothers these last weeks,' Liszt reported to Carolyne on 24 May. 'A quantity of letters regarding the Karlsruhe Music Festival, to which I have been able to reply to barely half. . . . An excursion to Sondershausen for Reisenauer's concert took two days [30 April/1 May]—and I am now feeling extreme fatigue. I suffer fairly often from bad nerves, so that I have to lie down.'

At Mannheim in the last week of May he collected his granddaughters Isolde and Eva, who accompanied him to the festival of the Allgemeine Deutsche

* 'The world wants trash!'

Musikverein at Karlsruhe (28–31 May), where several of his works were performed. After attending further concerts of his music at Strasbourg, Antwerp, and Aachen, he returned on 15 June to Weimar.

Later that month *Frederic Lamond* (1868–1948), a young Scottish pianist, was brought to him by Arthur Friedheim.

The meeting took place in the music room of Liszt's house. I remember it as a pleasant room with tall windows looking on to the park. . . . It breathed an atmosphere of infinite peace and culture; something of the spirit of Goethe and Schiller hovered over the house. In the room were two pianos: a Bechstein grand and an Ibach upright. . . .

Suddenly the door of the bedroom opened, and there before me stood the man who as a child had received the kiss of consecration from the mighty Beethoven himself: who had been the friend of Chopin: the pioneer for Berlioz and Wagner: the inventor of a new form in orchestral music, namely the symphonic poem: the teacher, the preceptor of Carl Tausig and Hans von Bülow, and all the great pianists from the 1840s down to that day in 1885. Here was the outstanding personality who had exercised such an incredible influence on music, not only in France and Germany, but in Russia. It would have been a moving experience to meet such a man today. To the boy I then was, it was simply overwhelming.

He read the letter of introduction, turned to me with his commanding, yet kindly eye, and said: '[Max] Schwarz writes that you play among other things the Fugue from Op. 106.' Here he hummed the theme, which sounded from his lips like the growl of a lion, and said, giving me a friendly slap on the shoulder: 'Tomorrow you play the Fugue from Op. 106'—and the interview was at an end. I rushed from that room in an indescribable state of mind. . . .

We who were studying with Liszt met together every second day at the Hofgärtnerei. Sometimes there were only a few of us. He could be very strict, even severe, in his remarks. The mere mechanical attainments of pianoforte technique meant very little to him. Speed, pure and simple, of which so much is made by so many pianists of the present day, he held in contempt. I remember a pianist who was performing Chopin's Polonaise in A flat, and playing it with great gusto. When he came to the celebrated octave passage in the left hand, Liszt interrupted him by saying: 'I don't want to listen to how fast you can play octaves. What I wish to hear is the canter of the horses of the Polish cavalry before they gather force and destroy the enemy.'

These few words were characteristic of Liszt. The poetical vision always rose before his mental eye, whether it was a Beethoven sonata, a Chopin nocturne, or a work of his own; it was not merely interpreting a work, but real reproduction. Take the C sharp minor variation from Schumann's *Etudes symphoniques*. No other pianist—and I have heard them all—ever got that sighing, wailing, murmuring sound of the accompaniment in the left, and certainly no other pianist played the noble melody in the right hand with such indescribable pathos as Liszt did. . . .

At one of the lessons, a Hungarian pianist played the Concerto in A major, with my good friend Friedheim playing the orchestral accompaniment on a second piano from memory. The orchestral part is rather complex. Liszt said to Friedheim: 'What! You play the orchestral part from memory?' And Friedheim answered: 'Yes, and I love every note of it.' I shall never forget the solemn look on Liszt's face, as he raised his hand and with eyes uplifted said quietly: 'I can wait.'[9]

August Stradal. That summer an American concert agent came to Liszt and offered him two million marks to go to America the next season, saying that he would appear with other performers and would have to play only a single piece at each concert. It was a proposal that Liszt found very amusing, and he replied: 'What am I, in my seventy-fourth year, supposed to do with two million? Am I to tour America giving 300 performances of the *Erlkönig*? An old poodle doesn't do its tricks any more!' . . .

At one of the classes a lady gave a very bad rendering of Liszt's *Les jeux d'eau à la Villa d'Este*. When she had come to an end, the Master said: 'Madam, that was not the fountains in the gardens of the Villa d'Este, but the water being flushed in the Villa's smallest room; it is something I don't wish to hear, and you may wash your dirty linen at home.'

The impudence of many of the women pianists sometimes went beyond all endurance, and so I was glad that the Master had for once spoken out firmly against it.[10]

On 18 July Liszt went to Halle to visit Robert Franz, who, afflicted by deafness and a nervous disease, had virtually ceased to compose in 1868. His companion on the journey was *August Göllerich*.

In comparison with Franz, Liszt at that time seemed the more vigorous. Greater contrasts than the two of them could not be imagined. Even in their outer appearance. One would have taken Franz for either a clergyman or a bourgeois schoolmaster, but never for the poetic creator of such tender, heartfelt songs.

Conversation was fatiguing, as every word had to be written down for him.

When the meal was over and Liszt had gone to take a rest, Franz remarked solemnly to me as we took coffee together: 'To *him*, I owe everything!'* And with great emotion he described how untiringly Liszt had provided for him from the moment when his ailments had forced him to cease work.

* In March 1872 Franz had written to Liszt: 'When I look back objectively on my past life, I find you running through it like a golden thread—you, who at critical moments have always stood protectively beside me. . . . Accept a thousand thanks for so much love and kindness.'

He mentioned the Christmas gift given him in 1871 by Liszt and the Grand Duchess of Weimar, the security provided by the Franz Fund, and the honorarium awarded to him by the Beethoven Foundation—all of these things having been arranged on his behalf by Liszt.

'Without him,' he said in tears, 'I could have starved!'

A soulful little *Albumblatt* of his had just been published. 'Believe it or not,' he said, 'I *dreamt* the whole thing, got out of bed and wrote it down there and then in the middle of the night.'

As by this time it had become painful for Franz to listen to music, the two masters took their leave of one another at the church door, never to meet again. Embracing Liszt with emotion, Franz said: 'Thank you for everything—everything!'[11]

Arthur Friedheim. It had been an ardent wish of mine for years that I might hear Beethoven's Kreutzer Sonata with the Master at the piano. This wish was finally gratified in a very unexpected manner. Liszt told me that he intended to give a matinée [20 July] which the Grand Duke and perhaps some foreign princes would attend. 'How about the music?' he asked. I suggested that it might be pleasant for a change to have some chamber music. 'Excellent!' he exclaimed, well pleased with the idea. 'Why not? You will play the Kreutzer Sonata with Miss Senkrah.' Now this young American violinist* disliked me exceedingly and took no pains to disguise her feelings, nor were my feelings for her any more cordial; and Liszt, wizard that he was, knew all about the aversion between us. I temporized as diplomatically as I could, Liszt meanwhile making no sign until the very moment when I was supposed to perform the Kreutzer. At the very last second he leaned over to me and said, in a curt undertone: 'I find it advisable to take your place at the piano.'

His incredible rendition of the remarkable work produced the usual sensation of breathless awe. Emil Sauer was so transported that he turned somersaults afterwards in the adjoining room, shouting with exuberance: 'Where the devil does he get even the technique let alone all the rest?' As for me, I was conscious of nothing but a blinding revelation of the true majesty of a performance; and I have always treasured that hour as the last colossal 'lesson' I received from Franz Liszt.[12]

The work which occupied Liszt during July and August was his *Historische ungarische Bildnisse—Magyar történelmi arcképek* (S205), musical portraits of

* Arma Senkrah (1864–1900), who had obtained her surname by reversing the letters of her family name of Harkness, was actually a Canadian. 'She had a splendid talent,' writes Adelheid von Schorn, 'and Liszt was so delighted with her playing that he often made music with her. People prophesied a brilliant career for the gifted and attractive girl, but fate decided differently. She gave up music to get married, and then, the marriage proving very unhappy, in despair took her own life—here in Weimar! Who would have suspected such a thing when she played the Kreutzer Sonata with Liszt, without rehearsal but so beautifully that the old master embraced her with deep emotion.'

six eminent deceased compatriots, István Széchenyi, Ferenc Deák, László Teleki, József Eötvös, Mihály Vörösmarty, and Sándor Petőfi, plus the funeral music for his friend Mihály Mosonyi.

A. W. Gottschalg, 3 August. Liszt asked Dr Gille for information about the cremation facilities at Gotha. In earlier days he once said to me: 'Gottschalg, don't let too much grass grow on my grave!'[13]

August Göllerich. The afternoon of 25 August brought a visit from the Russian cello virtuoso [Carl] Davidov and his wife. With inimitable aplomb Liszt played the whole of Anton Rubinstein's Cello Sonata with him.

For the latter, Liszt retained friendly feelings to the end, and, despite Rubinstein's great peculiarities, always showed him just recognition—in beautiful contrast to the petty and malevolent opinions on Liszt's works and playing expressed to me by Rubinstein shortly before his death in a regular outburst of envy and resentment.*[14]

Accompanied by Friedheim, Stavenhagen, and Thomán,† Liszt left Weimar on Thursday, 15 October, and journeyed first to Munich and then to Schloss Itter, where he was the overnight guest (18/19 October) of Sophie Menter. At Innsbruck, where they spent several days and celebrated Liszt's seventy-fourth birthday on the 22nd, the little party was joined by Lina Schmalhausen, who then travelled with them to Rome, which was reached on the 25th. 'My fatigue in living is extreme,' Liszt told the Princess; 'I no longer feel good for anything.'

Felix Semon (1849–1921), doctor and laryngologist. During our stay in Rome we visited Franz Liszt. Though he had left the concert stage and become a priest, he was still as much surrounded by ladies as in the days of his phenomenal career. Tadema,‡ who knew him of old, had paid him a visit during the last days of our stay and had told him of us. The result was an invitation to call on him. We found the old gentleman very imposing. His stately figure in simple black abbé's attire, with a fine sharp-cut face, an artist's high forehead, eyes full of spirit, long white smoothly-combed hair, was most fascinating. A large circle of enthusiastic admirers, mostly ladies, surrounded him. He received us most kindly. The general conversation was carried on in many languages. After a while Liszt addressed my wife [Augusta Raedeker], and said he had heard so much about her beautiful singing from our friend Tadema, would she allow him to hear her voice?

* Nevertheless, in an interview given towards the end of his life, Rubinstein observed of Liszt: 'His piano-playing, words are far too poor to describe—incomparable in every way; culmination of everything that pianoforte rendering could require. What a grievous pity that the gramophone did not exist in the years 1840 to 1850, to receive his playing and hold it for the future generations who can have no idea of real virtuosity. One must have heard Chopin, Liszt, Thalberg, and Henselt to know what genuine piano-playing means.'

† The Hungarian pianist and teacher István Thomán (1862–1940) studied with Liszt from 1882 onwards, mainly at the Academy of Music in Budapest. Between 1888 and 1906 he was himself a professor of piano at the Academy, where Bartók and Dohnányi were among his pupils.

‡ Lawrence Alma-Tadema (1836–1912), the Anglo-Dutch painter.

Gustchen readily consented, and when further asked what she would sing, selected Liszt's own composition of Mignon's song, *Kennst du das Land, wo die Citronen blüh'n?* Apparently very pleased, Liszt said 'Oh, that is kind of you,' and then requested a Russian princess [?Nadine Helbig] to accompany her. How the lady dared to comply with his wish is incomprehensible to me. She possessed neither the technique nor the understanding to play the very difficult accompaniment. The impression was painful and I was furious. Liszt, however, with rare tact, saved the situation. 'That was beautiful,' he exclaimed, when the torture had come to an end, '*so* beautiful, that you must give us an encore to my accompaniment.' Gustchen, rising to the occasion, and inspired by the composer's wonderful personality, sang divinely! Liszt's poetic accompaniment was above all praise. The whole company held their breath. I still see Tadema before me, leaning against the wall, his hands folded, his head on his breast, and big tears rolling down his cheeks. When the song had ended, and during the stormy applause, Liszt took my wife's hand in his, and kissed her forehead, thanking her again and again.[15]

August Stradal. One day the Master invited me to drive with him to the monastery of Sant' Onofrio (at the foot of the Janiculum). After viewing the cell in which Tasso had died on 25 April 1595, he sat down under the Tasso oak in the monastery garden (the tree was shattered by lightning in 1842; only a few remains still exist, against which a bench has been placed) and spoke at length about the hostility which Tasso had to endure. We then drove along the streets through which Tasso's corpse had been taken to the Capitol to be crowned with the poet's laurels. . . .

For me it was unforgettable to see the creator of the symphonic poem *Tasso* at the place where the immortal poet from Ferrara* had spent his last days. Of all Liszt's remarks to me on that occasion, one in particular has remained in my memory: 'I shall not, it is true, be borne in triumph to the Capitol, but the time will indeed come when my works will be appreciated. For me, however, it will be too late—for I shall no longer be amongst you.'[16]

It seems to have been in November that Liszt was heard by the young Claude Debussy (1862–1918), a Prix de Rome winner living at the Villa Medici. 'I have heard only two fine pianists,' Debussy remarked in later life, 'my old piano teacher [Antoinette-Flore Mauté], and Liszt. . . .'

What the aged musical revolutionary played to the young one is not known,† but it is interesting to speculate that Debussy may have been among the very first to hear some of such forward-looking works as *Nuages gris* (S199), the *Csárdás*

* Torquato Tasso was born (1544) at Sorrento, but for much of his adult life was attached to the court of the Duke of Ferrara. It was here, too, that he was confined for seven years.

† The report of an occasion in which Debussy heard Liszt and Sgambati playing Saint-Saëns' 2-piano Variations and Fugue on a Theme of Beethoven, is now known to be one of the inventions of André de Ternant.

macabre (S224) and *Csárdás obstiné* (S225/2), *Unstern* (S208), the four *Valses oubliées* (S215), and the *Bagatelle sans tonalité* (S216a)—all of which were composed in the last half-dozen years of Liszt's life.*

On at least one occasion the roles of pianist and listener were exchanged. Thus Paul Vidal: 'Debussy and I played to Liszt one day Chabrier's two-piano waltzes [*Valses romantiques*].'

August Göllerich. Among the pieces played to the Master at the last lessons in Rome, he was particularly interested, so far as his own works were concerned, in the *Triomphe funèbre du Tasse*, the *Bénédiction et serment*† from Berlioz's *Benvenuto Cellini*, the *Robert* and *Huguenots* fantasies, the Paganini Etudes, and *Vallée d'Obermann*.

He had repeatedly declined to hear the last-mentioned work. But after we had returned home one evening from a performance of Spontini's *Olympia* at the Sala Dante (12 December), he asked me to play it to him there and then. While listening, he burst into tears.

On New Year's Eve he gave to a select circle a transfigured performance of Mozart's *Ave verum corpus* from his *A la Chapelle Sixtine*. Together with the *Dies Irae* and *Lacrymosa* from the *Requiem*, this heaven-soaring work was among his special favourites.

'The sequences of the *Ave verum* are among the most beautiful things that Mozart wrote,' he remarked. Then he added: 'I don't think he would have had anything against my development of them.'

The old year was brought to an end with a cosy whist session. During the game, a clock in the Master's study, otherwise ticking away merrily, suddenly stopped so abruptly that we could not help looking up in surprise. 'A bad omen,' said Liszt; 'that one of us will die in the coming year is quite *certain*!'[17]

1886

August Göllerich. On the morning of New Year's Day the Master greeted me with the words: 'You will see, this will be a disastrous year for me, for it begins with a *Friday*.'

On 13 January he invited me to a solemn farewell breakfast before my trip to Naples. He knew it had been my secret wish to see that city, and he felt that I would not let him down so far as the journey to Budapest was concerned.

'I have thrice been to the station to go to Naples, but something always

* Worthy of note, too, is this remark of Busoni's (letter to his wife, 24 Sept. 1919): '[Isidor] Philipp told me he had been present when Debussy heard Liszt's *Les jeux d'eau* for the first time, and how dumbfounded Debussy was by it! Yes, Liszt in his last period was prophetic. . .'

† Liszt's transcription for piano solo (S396).

prevented my going. *You*, however, shall see it,' he said cheerfully; and it was touching how he finally brought about the fulfilment of my heart's desire under the pretext of asking me to go to Naples on a private errand for him.

The last words I heard him utter in Rome were in reply to a lady present at the breakfast who made a disparaging remark about someone who was not present: 'Mark what I say, one should *never* be hard-hearted!'[1]

On Wednesday, 20 January, Liszt left Rome to return to Budapest, which he reached on the 30th. As was now his habit, he journeyed via Florence (where he saw his friends Jessie Hillebrand and Princess Fanny Rospigliosi and attended mass at Santa Croce) and Venice (where he was the guest of Princess Hatzfeldt at the Palazzo Malipiero). At Gorizia he spent two days with his cousin Marie von Saar (1853–1919), the surviving daughter of Eduard Liszt's first marriage.

August Stradal. Whereas in 1885 I was the only pupil who had travelled to Pest from abroad, Stavenhagen and Ansorge now came too; and, later, Göllerich as well. The Master did not teach us with the Academy pupils, but separately in his salon.

Shortly after Liszt's arrival in Budapest there appeared a pianist (from Hanover, if I am not mistaken) who wished to become a pupil, and who played him his *St François de Paole marchant sur les flots*. The Master . . . expressed a very unfavourable opinion of the young man, who did not play well. When the pianist went away quite shattered, I consoled him, saying that he should come back, that I too had fared no better the first time I had played to the Master. The next day we heard that the young man had shot himself. With great difficulty we managed to conceal this news from the Master, who, had he learnt of it, would certainly have given way to despair. . . .

Liszt's eyes now began to give him trouble, so that his letters often became quite illegible, and only with the greatest difficulty could he write music. The last piece on which he worked was the orchestration of the accompaniment to his setting* of Uhland's ballad *Die Vätergruft*. Knowing him to be engaged on such a work had a most melancholy effect upon me: the feeling came to me that he himself would now be 'descending to the coffins of his forefathers'.

A concert was arranged at the Academy [10 March], and the Master invited me to take part and to play his *Funérailles*. When my turn came, Liszt climbed on to the platform with me, stood by the piano, turned his face to the audience and looked down solemnly and sadly. 'Liszt feels that he is soon going to die, and is taking leave of Budapest,' was the sudden vision which came to me. And that was why I was to play *Funérailles*! An unspeakable sadness came over me. . . .[2]

* S281, dating from 1844. As Stradal indicates, the version with orchestra (S371) was Liszt's last completed work.

In the late evening of 11 March, and accompanied by Göllerich and Stradal, Liszt took the train from Budapest for the last time, setting out on what he mockingly called his 'last tour', the highlights of which were visits to Paris and London. First he spent a weekend at Vienna, where on Sunday the 14th *Friedrich Eckstein* once again came into contact with him.

It was my good fortune to be a fellow guest of his at a private house and to hear him playing to a small circle. This was in the home of my friend Adalbert von Goldschmidt, a close associate of Liszt's of whose works the Master thought highly. For several consecutive winters musical gatherings took place on Sunday afternoons at his residence in the Opera Ring, where a select number of distinguished and intellectually prominent people met together over tea and sandwiches.

During his visit to Vienna that March Liszt was pleased to accept Goldschmidt's invitation to attend one of these gatherings. Not long beforehand he had written a magnificent transcription of themes from Goldschmidt's oratorio *Die sieben Todsünden*,* which at the Schottenhof the previous evening had been rendered in true virtuoso style by his pupil August Göllerich, to the delight of all present.

The next afternoon Liszt came to Goldschmidt's home. Earnestly entreated by the mistress of the house and led by her to the piano, the Master preluded briefly and then played—with an expression altogether beyond compare—one of his favourite pieces by Franz Schubert, the *Divertissement à la hongroise*.† When, standing right beside the piano, I saw his figure there before me, and observed his devotion to the work and the tender love with which he brought its most hidden beauties into the light, there flashed upon me the realization that it was this same man who, as a small boy long before, had been tempestuously hugged and kissed by Beethoven. . . . And when I was introduced to Liszt later that afternoon, and he looked at me with a gentle smile as he offered me his hand, there came over me, as I bowed low before him, the happy feeling that I too was now receiving a little of the benedictory kiss of Beethoven.[3]

The Swiss composer Friedrich Klose (1862–1942). The power of Liszt's personality was indescribable. Ladies and gentlemen alike, and whatever their rank in society, rose from their seats, all conversations died away, the gaze of everyone in the room was held, as though spellbound, by the awe-compelling figure of this God-gifted king of men. And when his brilliant eyes looked around the gathering, not one of those upon whom they briefly rested can but have been aware that he was experiencing one of the greatest moments of his life.

* 'The Seven Deadly Sins'. Goldschmidt revered Liszt, regarding him 'as creator, artist, and man the earthly embodiment of my ideal', and this secular oratorio represents Liszt, to whom it is dedicated, as the 'Singer' who liberates mankind from the Powers of Darkness. Its first performance was at Berlin in May 1876. Liszt's transcription (S490), of 1880, is of the *Liebesszene und Fortunas Kugel*.

† As Klose relates, Liszt probably played his Fantasy (S425/3) on Schubert's work.

Several people were introduced to him. Whether or not Hugo Wolf, a fanatical admirer of the Master, was among these, I no longer recall. What *is* still a vivid memory, however, is the way in which we youngsters, including Wolf, who were sitting modestly in the adjacent room, all without exception leapt to our feet when Liszt entered it for a moment.

As usual at the Goldschmidt Sunday afternoons, we had music. And last of all, amidst a breathless silence, Liszt himself went to the piano and played the third part of his *Mélodies hongroises* (after Schubert). . . . What a tremendous experience that was for me, who had never before heard this unparalleled master of the piano. And so to me too there came the great good fortune of being able to admire *that Liszt* as well, who with the magic sounds he was able to entice from even the least perfect of musical instruments had in days gone by brought the whole world to his feet, and as an inconceivable and legendary wonder will live on for generations to come.

It was my last meeting with the Master. I can still see him as, accompanied by Göllerich and Stradal, he took his departure, leaving me with the hope of perhaps still having, on some future occasion, an opportunity of telling him what a devoted disciple he always had had, and always would have, in me. My wish was not to be granted, for a few months later the radiant, visionary eyes of this great and noble man closed for ever.[4]

In the afternoon of the 15th Liszt left Vienna to travel to Liège, where he attended an extremely successful concert of his works (17 March) and was the guest, at nearby Argenteau, of the Comtesse Louise Mercy-Argenteau (1837–1900), champion of the new Russian composers.

Between 20 March and 3 April he was in Paris, where he stayed at the Hôtel de Calais, rue des Capucines. Several of his works were performed during this fortnight, including *Orpheus*, *Les Préludes*, and the Gran Mass. Their success was considerable. On the 23rd he contributed the piano 'epilogue' at a great musical soirée given in his honour by the Hungarian painter Mihály von Munkácsy (1844–1900) and his wife Cécile (1845–1915), a native of Luxembourg (and, according to Rudolf Lehmann, a 'very loquacious, masterful lady'). 'Liszt is just now the centre of excitement here,' wrote the novelist George Gissing (1857–1903) to his sister on 29 March; 'he and Pasteur divide attention.' Among acquaintances seen during the visit was the eighty-year-old Ferdinand de Lesseps, recently made a father for the eleventh time.

Some months earlier, Liszt had accepted Walter Bache's invitation to come to London in April, the 'accented point' of the visit being to attend a performance of *St Elisabeth*. 'Without Walter Bache and his long years of self-sacrificing efforts in the propaganda of my works,' he had written, 'my visit to London were indeed not to be thought of.'

His advent was heralded in the newspapers, and many periodicals published extensive biographies, most of which were concerned with Liszt the pianist, notwithstanding that nearly four decades had elapsed since the ending of his professional career. As the *Spectator* remarked: 'It does not fall to our lot every day to see a man who made Schumann "shiver with ecstasy" and drew tears from Clara Wieck . . . who has been the object of more legitimate admiration, of more extravagant idolatry, than any other figure in the annals of his art.'

The seal on such tributes was set by *Frederick Buffen* when, in a brief memoir published shortly before Liszt's arrival, he hailed the celebrated musician as one who 'must always claim a foremost place amongst the natural kings of men', and went on to link his name with some of the sublimest artists in world history.

I confess to an enthusiasm for art, and I recognise in Shakespeare the secretary of the world. In Byron and Goethe I see the poets for all time; that Raphael, Rubens, and Turner are representative men; that Michael Angelo is the sculptor; and Beethoven and Mozart the musicians for all future generations; and, for my own part, I hesitate not to affirm that Liszt is the greatest pianoforte player who ever lived, and I reverence him as such, and regard him as one who represents the embodiment of art in its highest possible form of cultivated expression.[5]

Leaving Paris at 11.00 a.m. on Saturday, 3 April, Liszt arrived some nine hours later in the south London suburb of Sydenham, where he was to be the guest, at Westwood House, of Henry Littleton (1823–88), head of the Novello music-publishing firm. Accompanied from Paris by Cécile Munkácsy, Miss Beatty-Kingston, and his pupil Bernhard Stavenhagen, among others, he had been joined at Calais by Alfred Littleton (son of Henry) and Alexander Mackenzie; and at Dover by Walter Bache and another former pupil, the Prussian pianist Emil Bach (1849–1902). At Penge station the train had made a special stop to allow the party to alight; and here, according to the *Sydenham, Forest Hill & Penge Gazette* (10 April)), some of Liszt's compatriots had assembled 'and bade him welcome in a few words, to which an equally brief and graceful reply was made'. 'A basket of flowers was handed to him and more flowers were strewn on the ground as he walked to the carriage outside.' Not surprisingly, *The Times* (5 April) was to predict, with complete accuracy: 'That the world-famed musician will be distinguished to the verge of surfeit by every demonstration of hero-worship, is a prophecy upon which one may safely venture even before the event.'

Shortly before 8 o'clock Liszt entered Westwood House. 'He had hardly arrived,' reported the *Observer*, 'when a long line of carriages began to set down the guests invited to meet him.' In addition to such socially prominent persons as the German Ambassador, Count Esterházy, Count Metternich, and Lady Walter Scott, and such representatives of the plastic and pictorial arts as Sir James Linton, Sir Frederick Leighton, W. Q. Orchardson, and Edgar Boehm, they included many of the best-known names in contemporary British musical life: Grove, Sullivan, Hallé, Mackenzie, Carl Rosa, John Stainer, Edward Dannreuther, Otto Goldschmidt (husband of Jenny Lind), August Manns, Oscar Beringer, Georg Henschel, Ebenezer Prout, the pianist Agnes Zimmermann, and the singer Annie Wheelwright (who had participated in Liszt's Pest concert of 4 March 1874).

The music critic Hermann Klein (1856–1934). An hour after his arrival Liszt entered the vast oak-panelled apartment which had just been added as a music-room to Westwood House. . . . Dressed in his semi-priestly garb, the venerable abbé walked slowly down the steps leading to the floor of the room, and smiled graciously upon the groups that saluted him as he passed. He looked somewhat tired, and it was remarked by those who knew him that he had aged considerably during the last few years. But his still bright eye, his still brilliant powers of conversation, his still industrious habits, all precluded the smallest suspicion that the end was so near. His attention that evening was largely monopolized by old friends; still, many new ones were brought to his notice, and I had the pleasure of being introduced with a kind word or two by the loyal and indefatigable Walter Bache, who, with others, took part in a programme of his compositions.*[6]

The next day, Sunday, Liszt spent quietly at Westwood House, in the evening giving a lesson to Stavenhagen on the E flat Concerto, which the young pianist was soon to play in public.

From London society a flood of invitations now began to pour in upon the world celebrity at Sydenham. On Monday, 5 April, the *Pall Mall Gazette* reported that 'among others the Archbishop of Canterbury† and the Bishop of London have invited him to visit Lambeth and Fulham Palaces, and Mr. Henry Irving has placed a special box at his disposal'.

It was on the Monday that the travels and fatigues of the London fortnight began, with the 'full grand rehearsal' of *St Elisabeth* at St James's Hall‡ in central London. Emma Albani and Charles Santley were the principal soloists; the orchestra and Novello Choir were conducted by Alexander Mackenzie. 'There were more than 1,500 people present,' Liszt informed Carolyne. 'I am overwhelmed with attentions and testimonies of goodwill—it's more than a success!' According to Mackenzie, Liszt made but one suggestion at the end of the rehearsal; the *Daily Telegraph*, however, reported that he tended 'very decided and persistent advice'.

That evening a private practice for members of the chorus was held at the Neumayer Hall, Bloomsbury. To show his appreciation of their efforts, Liszt went to the piano at the *Tu pro nobis* and improvised upon the theme 'in the most masterly way conceivable', following this with a 'matchless' performance of his own *Ave Maria* for piano solo. His listeners, reported the *Musical Times*, 'applauded until the roof rang'.

In the afternoon of Tuesday the 6th he visited the Royal Academy of Music (Tenterden Street, Hanover Square), 'to become the practical donor of the endowment of a Liszt scholarship for young composers and pianists,' in the words of the *Musical Times*, 'the funds for which, amounting to about £1,100, had been subscribed in a very brief period, thanks to the activity of Mr. Walter Bache, Mr. C. A. Barry, and other ardent partisans of the master'.

* A *Tarantella*, played by Frederic Lamond, the transcription (S181) of the Sarabande and Chaconne from Handel's *Almira*, played by Walter Bache (its dedicatee), and several vocal items.

† Who was at this time Edward White Benson (1829–96), father of A. C. Benson (writer of, *inter alia*, the words of 'Land of Hope and Glory') and the novelists E. F. and R. H. Benson.

‡ Which stood on the site now occupied by the Piccadilly Hotel, Regent Street.

Accompanied by the Principal, the blind Sir George Macfarren (1813–87), and others, Liszt entered the Academy's densely packed concert hall shortly after 3.00 p.m.

Revd H. R. Haweis. The moment his noble head, with its thick white hair, was seen a roar of applause rose on every side. He looked like a figure out of one of the old engravings of Sebastian Bach or Mozart, truly a man who belongs to another age than ours—an age of art creators, painters, poets, and musicians since passed away, himself among the mightiest of them. No sooner had he taken his seat than a little girl with an enormous flower wreath in the form of a lyre advanced towards him. The wreath was placed on a table in front of him. Liszt bent down tenderly and kissed the child—who, I am told, is the infant phenomenon of the Academy—on her forehead. A kiss to be remembered. . . .

I could describe the excellent and interesting programme* patiently enough had Liszt not been there, but in the minds of everyone, expressed or unuttered, there was but one thought—'*Will he play?*'

'If he does,' I whispered to Mr. Burnett, the violinist, 'mark me, it will be after young Webbe'. . .

But the applause which greeted Webbe continued long after Webbe had gone and the Master had resumed his seat. He rose twice, bowed all round, and sat down twice. Then something like an agony of despair and suspense seized upon the audience. . . . I have seen transports of enthusiasm at Bayreuth when Wagner appeared in front of the curtain on the last great day of *Götterdämmerung*; I have seen the people at St. James's Hall *rise at* Rubinstein; but I never saw anything comparable to what took place at the Royal Academy of Music—when Liszt rose for the *third time* and instead of sitting down moved towards the platform. When he reached the piano, people were standing on their seats beside themselves. The ladies tore the daffodils and lilies from their bosoms and flung them at him. . . . Then a stillness as of death fell on the excited assembly. Liszt looked into the air in front of him. He was grave, dreamy, and like one who saw before him the forms and visions of long ago. Inexpressibly tender, the music stole softly from the keys. . . . It was not piano-playing; it was the whisper, the plaint, the meditation of a soul—all the *technique*, though absolutely perfect, and the touch beyond compare, was entirely forgotten. . . . The multitudes of little subsidiary notes slipped in like the spray of a fountain broken in the wind. Liszt seemed scarcely to heed them; they fell about him, those wondrous passages, like magic; the noble face still looked into the air—seemed to have nothing to do with the keyboard: the soul was far away in

* According to Mackenzie, it consisted of: Liszt's Goethe Festival March; Sterndale Bennett's Caprice in E, played by Dora Bright; Mackenzie's Violin Concerto, played by Winifred Robinson; Liszt's Etude in D flat, played by Septimus Webbe; and Macfarren's Overture *John the Baptist*. The conductor was William Shakespeare.

another world. . . . At the close there went up the piano a something wholly indescribable—from the bass to the treble—a soft, melting flow of sound, not notes, but a mingling of notes. . . . A hardened critic—middle-aged and not easily pleased—turned to me and echoed my own thoughts. 'I should like to have cried outright,' he said, 'if I hadn't been ashamed!' As for myself, for at least two hours afterwards I had a peculiar choking sensation and perceptible quickening of the pulse as bits of it came floating into my head. The excitement of the students was unexampled.[7]

Hermann Klein. Even at seventy-five, Liszt was a pianist whose powers lay beyond the pale to which sober language or calm criticism could reach or be applied. Enough that his greatest charm seemed to me to lie in a perfectly divine touch, and in a tone more remarkable for its exquisitely musical quality than for its volume or dynamic force, aided by a technique still incomparably brilliant and superb.[8]

The composer Orsmond Anderton (1861–1934). We had most of us felt some reserve beforehand, but no sooner did he appear than the whole gathering rose in a sort of frenzy of enthusiasm. Such was his peculiar hypnotic influence. He was persuaded to play; nothing big, merely an extemporisation upon a song;* but no piano has ever sounded the same to me, before or since.[9]

That evening came the performance of *St Elisabeth*† at St James's Hall. Earlier, Liszt was the dinner guest of Walter Bache and his sister.

Constance Bache. We sat down eight. When dinner was announced, Walter, smiling sweetly on us three ladies, said, 'Well, I will take the Master down,' and offered his arm to Liszt. Liszt smilingly put him aside, and came and gave his arm to me! Of course he was quite right, and everything he does is so gracefully and beautifully done. We had a charming couple of hours—the happiest, I think, of the whole week. We all went at the appointed time to the concert—I with an enormous basket of roses (in allusion to the 'Rose-Miracle'), really magnificent, tied with the Hungarian colours, and with my verses pinned on; these I presented to the Master when he came in. . . .

Well—the performance was splendid; Albani is simply perfect as St Elisabeth, I never heard anything more refined and beautiful than her whole rendering of it. Liszt had to go into the orchestra both after the first part and at the end of the work, and the audience literally rose at him. *Such a reception*, such cheers and clappings. . . .[10]

* Mackenzie writes that Liszt played one of the *Chants polonais* and *Cantique d'amour*.

† This was not the first hearing of the work in Britain. It had already been given, in a performance conducted by Bache, at St James's Hall in Feb. 1876, and by 'London amateurs', under Henry Wylde, in 1870. St Elisabeth's story would already have been familiar to many of the audience from Charles Kingsley's drama *The Saint's Tragedy*.

The Athenaeum (10 April). Not only is he, by the unanimous testimony of those who have heard him, the greatest pianist that the world has ever seen, but he has throughout his long life shown a single-hearted devotion to what he believes to be the true interests of the art of which he is so bright an ornament. It was, therefore, only natural that St James's Hall should be crowded to its utmost capacity. . . . He was recalled to the platform again and again after the first part and at the close of the work. The concert was attended by the Prince and Princess of Wales, the Duchess of Edinburgh, and the Princess Louise; and the Prince paid the composer the compliment of fetching him to introduce him to the Princess.

At the invitation of Queen Victoria, Liszt proceeded on Wednesday, 7 April, to Windsor, being accompanied from Paddington Station by W. G. Cusins (1833–93), the Queen's Master of Music (and conductor of the British premières of *Tasso* and *Hungaria*). 'By the time he got to Windsor,' reported the *Pall Mall Gazette*, 'the streets were crowded as for a Royal progress, and on his appearance everyone took off his hat. The Queen sent a royal carriage to meet him—a compliment seldom bestowed upon anyone under a Minister of State. At the Castle, the whole of the Royal household and servants turned out to meet him.'

Liszt and Queen Victoria met in the Red Drawing Room. After an improvisation, he played to her the Miracle of the Roses from *St Elisabeth* (at the Queen's request), a Hungarian Rhapsody, and Chopin's Nocturne in B flat minor. The last time their paths had crossed had been at the Beethoven Festival in Bonn, and at Brühl, forty-one years earlier, when the young Queen had irritated not a few people, Liszt included. But after this Windsor meeting he was able to write to Carolyne: 'The Queen was most gracious this time and conversed in good German.' For her part, Victoria noted in her diary: 'From having been a wild, phantastic-looking man, he was now a quiet, benevolent-looking old priest, with long white hair and scarcely any teeth.' To her daughter, the Crown Princess of Prussia, she wrote that same day: 'We have just heard Liszt, who is such a fine old man. He came down here and played four pieces beautifully. What an exquisite touch. . . .'

Present at the meeting was *Princess Marie of Battenberg* (1852–1923).

He was entertained at the table of the Master of the Household, and the Queen did not see him until later. As he was to play, he had brought his own grand piano* with him from London, and when we came into the drawing-room the famous artist, in his clerical costume, was standing beside his instrument. The Queen greeted him very kindly, and I much appreciated the sight of the two figures as they stood facing one another. Both little, both white-haired, both in black, both dignified and amiable, both a little embarrassed. She the ruler of the great British Empire, he ruler in the realm of music. Franz Liszt played for about half an hour, the

* According to the *Illustrated London News* (10 Apr.), 'Messrs. Erard were commanded by the Queen to send a pianoforte to Windsor for his use.'

notes falling from his fingers like pearls, while sounds as from another world floated through the room. The intellectual head and the soutane would have suited an organ well, although, with the Abbé Franz Liszt, the man of the world showed everywhere through the priestly garment. The Princess and I had armed ourselves with our birthday-books in order to obtain Liszt's autograph, but when he was about to take leave of the Queen none of us could make up our minds to proffer our request; we all felt too bashful. In the end I was pushed forward, crossed the room, and boldly laid my book on the piano before the great man. He bowed smilingly and wrote his name in it, and also in those of the shy princesses, who were hanging back, and finally in that of Her Majesty herself. The Queen sent me later, as a remembrance, a little bust of Franz Liszt by the sculptor Boehm, and often teased me about the bold attack I had made on the great man.[11]

The *Court Journal* recorded that the Queen, while complimenting Liszt on his artistry, 'had also much to speak with him about the past'. 'He is a courtier,' it continued, 'and speaks as well as he plays.'

In the evening of Thursday the 8th a private dinner was given for Liszt at the Langham Hotel, Portland Place. 'The management had taken quite a personal interest in it,' Constance Bache was pleased to find, 'and begged to be allowed to decorate the place a little; so there was red carpet down the steps for us, just as if we were royalty, and a crowd on each side to see him pass.'

Liszt and his party then proceeded to the Grosvenor Gallery, Bond Street, where Walter Bache had arranged a brilliant reception and musical soirée. Among the guests were Sullivan, Grove, Hallé, Mackenzie, Joachim, Stanford, Hubert Parry, Edward Dannreuther, August Manns, Vladimir de Pachmann, Carl Rosa, Emma Albani, Fanny Davies, Antoinette Sterling, Leighton, Alma-Tadema, Lord and Lady Walter Scott, the Baroness Burdett-Coutts, and the Austrian Ambassador. A literary luminary who did not appear, for all his passionate love of music, was the septuagenarian Robert Browning. But his failure to turn up was apparently regretted by the eminent poet as early as the next day, when he remarked, presumably after seeing the morning papers: 'The Listz [*sic*] affair would seem to have been worth assisting at!'

The music consisted exclusively of works by Liszt: his *Angelus* for string quartet (S378/2); *Chor der Engel* from Goethe's *Faust* (S85), sung by students of the Royal Academy of Music, conducted by William Shakespeare; *Bénédiction de Dieu dans la solitude*, played by Bache; and Three Songs* from Schiller's *William Tell* (S292), sung by William Winch.

'At the conclusion of this short programme,' in the words of Constance Bache, 'came *the* event of the evening, that for which everyone had been silently hoping and waiting.'

Alfred Hollins (1865–1942). I shall never forget the sudden hush in the animated conversation and the sigh of expectant delight when Liszt walked

* *Der Fischerknabe, Der Hirt, Der Alpenjäger.*

over to the piano. His first piece was one I did not know. I was told afterwards that it was a *Divertissement* by Schubert transcribed by Liszt himself. Next he played the Allegro from his 13th Hungarian Rhapsody. Although his touch had lost some of its vigour, it was very beautiful and clear. He was still a great pianist. During the evening several of the guests, including myself, were presented to him. Hartvigson, speaking in German, said: 'Master, may I present a talented blind pupil, Mr. Hollins?' Liszt shook hands with me and said: '*Ich habe von ihm gehört.*' He had a deep voice and spoke quietly. His hand felt rather large, and its grasp was cordial.[12]

George Grove. I went to Liszt's reception and was delighted (1) by his playing, so calm, clear, correct, refined—so entirely unlike the style of the so-called 'Liszt School'—(2) by his face. Directly he sat down he dismissed that very artificial smile, which he always wears, and his face assumed the most beautiful serene look with enormous power and repose in it. It was quite a wonderful sight.[13]

The critic J. A. Fuller-Maitland (1856–1936). His playing was a thing never to be forgotten, or approached by later artists. The peculiar quiet brilliance of his rapid passages, the noble proportion kept between the parts, and the meaning and effect which he put into the music, were the most striking points.[14]

Wilhelm Kuhe. To those who had heard him at his zenith, and received an impression never to be effaced, it was, of course, most interesting to listen to him again in his sere and yellow leaf. But, for my part, I cannot look back upon that last visit of the lamented genius, for whom I entertained so profound an admiration, without a feeling of regret that he should have been led to display once again his rare gifts. For, in great measure, the old *feu sacré*, which had taken so many countless thousands out of themselves into a new world of music, had left him; and those who then, for the first time, heard the Abbé, can have formed no adequate idea of his unexampled powers in the years that were past.[15]

The Athenaeum (17 April). His performance will certainly never be forgotten by those who were fortunate enough to hear it. Though he no longer possesses the physical power of earlier years, there is still that indescribable beauty of touch, that unrivalled mastery of the gradations of tone, and, more than all, that wonderful depth of expression which have placed him absolutely alone among pianists . . . and there were occasional glimpses of the stupendous execution for which he was formerly renowned, to enable his hearers to form a conception of what he must have been in his prime. . . . The chief characteristic of his performance on this occasion was its exquisite delicacy and finish. . . . Such playing is an absolute revelation, unapproached, and in all probability unapproachable hereafter, by anyone else.

On Friday, 9 April, there was an 'entirely successful' Liszt concert at St James's Hall. Emil Bach 'played Liszt's E flat Concerto and other pieces in a manner indicating earnest and careful study of that difficult music,' commented *The Times*. 'Herr Bach was evidently inspired by the occasion and his performance showed considerable improvement upon previous efforts.' The March of the Three Holy Kings from *Christus* and the symphonic poem *Orpheus* were also performed. Georg Henschel sang the ballad *Die Vätergruft* (with the new orchestral accompaniment), and other Liszt songs were rendered by Mrs Henschel and Liza Lehmann. Later that evening the composer sat next to the Prince of Wales at a Royal Amateur Orchestral Society concert (Prince's Hall, Piccadilly) to which he was taken by Arthur Sullivan.

Near his host's home at Sydenham stood the famous Crystal Palace; and it was here, on the 10th, that Stavenhagen made his English début (playing Liszt's First Concerto and some solos), at a concert in which August Manns conducted *Les Préludes*, *Mazeppa*, and the Fourth Hungarian Rhapsody (the orchestral version of the Second for piano)—doing so, reported *The Times*, in a manner that evoked 'the warmest applause of the audience, in which the composer joined'. 'I did not know till today that I had written such beautiful music,' Liszt remarked appreciatively to Manns. According to the *Sydenham, Forest Hill & Penge Gazette*, the gathering* at the concert 'exceeded anything previously known'.

In the evening Liszt once again undertook the long journey into London, where he was the guest of the German Athenaeum (Mortimer Street), a literary and artistic club. Going to the piano after a short programme of his music had been given, he played his transcription (S558/7) of Schubert's *Frühlingsglaube* and Weber's *Momento capriccioso*.

Sunday the 11th he began by hearing a Palestrina Mass at Brompton Oratory, South Kensington. For the afternoon he had been invited to the home of William Beatty-Kingston in St John's Wood, where, on his host's 'favourite Bechstein',† he extemporized for several minutes, 'taking for his theme the melody of my daughter's song, which he had committed to memory while glancing over it with seeming inattention or, at the very least, indifference'. By the *Musical Times* the improvisation was described as 'simply unapproachable'.

The later visits of the day are described in Liszt's letter of 16 April to Princess Carolyne.

The Duchess of Cambridge‡ had asked for me for 7 o'clock. In '40 she showed me great kindness. She is now over eighty, but still mentally alert and most gracious. Since her ear was causing her some suffering, I played her two short pieces, with the soft pedal, on an upright piano.

At 8.00 dinner at the Prince of Wales's, Marlborough House. About twenty guests,§ among whom the celebrated beauty of Lady Herbert's

* Which included the 28-year-old Edward Elgar.

† This instrument, later owned by the Duke of Norfolk, is now the possession of Mrs Margaret Ellaway of Cheltenham.

‡ An aunt, by marriage, of Queen Victoria, the German-born Duchess (1797–1889) was the last surviving daughter-in-law of George III. She lived in Ambassador's Court, St James's Palace.

§ They included the Duchess of Teck, her daughter Princess Mary of Teck (the later Queen Mary), the Duke of Connaught, Lord and Lady de Grey, Lady Cadogan, Baron F. Rothschild, and Edgar Boehm the sculptor.

daughter shone out. The Russian and Italian ambassadors, Staal and Corti, who were both present, were not unknown to me. Corti reminded me of an evening at Ettersburg, after the Congress of Berlin. As *chasse-café* my little piano pieces were received most favourably.[16]

On 12 April *The Times*, reviewing the concerts of the 9th and 10th, discussed the Liszt fever which was now gripping London.

The presence of the master was on each occasion sufficient to fill the hall to the last seat and to rouse the audience to an absolutely frantic pitch of enthusiasm. Ovations such as those offered to Liszt have never before been witnessed in musical England, and for the psychological student it was an interesting phenomenon to see quiet and decorous persons mounting on seats, waving hats and handkerchiefs, and clamouring with unrestrained lung power. Even outside the hall the composer's arrival was always waited for by crowds, who raised their hats to him as if he were a king, and the very cabmen on Saturday were fain to raise a cheer for the 'Habby Liszt'. These humble admirers have never heard a note of his music, and would probably not be very much the wiser were they to have that privilege. What impresses them, as with electric force, is the noble face and form and the bearing worthy of a leader of men, and denoting an overpowering personality. . . .

In the afternoon of Monday the 12th, Liszt visited Dr Theodore Duka, President of the Hungarian Association of London, at 55 Nevern Square, Earl's Court. Later he attended the Beethoven recital given by Joachim, Hallé, and Piatti in the series of 'Monday Pops' at St James's Hall, where he was received 'with Royal honours'. The next day he lunched with Baroness Burdett-Coutts, the banking heiress and philanthropist, at her home on the corner of Stratton Street and Piccadilly.

On the 14th he went to the Lyceum Theatre, Wellington Street, to see Henry Irving play Mephistopheles in W. G. Wills's spectacular stage version of *Faust*. The great actor's business manager was *Bram Stoker* (1847–1912), future author of *Dracula*, who took care to see that Liszt, in his box at the Lyceum, was protected from all who might intrude upon him, 'enthusiasts, interviewers, cranks, autograph-fiends and notoriety seekers'. However, the composer was recognized and given an ovation by the audience, and the orchestra played his Hungarian Storm March (S119). In his reminiscences of Irving, Stoker recalled the supper given afterwards in the Beefsteak Room.

Liszt sat on the right hand of Ellen Terry* who faced Irving. From where I sat at the end of the table I could not but notice the quite extraordinary resemblance in the profiles of the two men. After supper Irving went round

* Constance Bache: 'Liszt sat between Ellen Terry and Mme Munkácsy. E. Terry is so naive and so fascinating that I think she would have had the best of it, only that unfortunately she does not talk anything but English, consequently Mme Munkácsy took the wind out of her sails.'

and sat next to him and the likeness became a theme of comment from all present. Irving was then forty-eight years of age; but he looked still a young man, with raven black hair and face without a line. Liszt, on the other hand, looked older than his age. His stooping shoulders and long white hair made him seem of patriarchal age. Nevertheless, the likeness of the two men was remarkable.

Stavenhagen played, but as it was thought by all that Liszt must be too tired after a long day, no opening was made for him, much as all longed to hear him. The party did not break up till four o'clock in the morning. The note in my diary runs:

'Liszt fine face—leonine—several large pimples—prominent chin of old man—long white hair down on shoulders—all call him "Master"—must have had great strength in youth. Very sweet and simple in manner. Irving and he very much alike—seemed old friends as they talked animatedly though knowing but a few words of each other's language—but using much expression and gesticulation. It was most interesting.'[17]

Also at the supper was Max Müller (1823–1900), the eminent German-born philologist and orientalist, who had first heard Liszt at Leipzig more than forty years earlier. 'I saw him last,' he wrote afterwards to Irving, 'as a beautiful young man with black hair in a flowing velvet coat with open sleeves—and now—an extinct volcano—with ever so many tourists dancing attendance around him.'

On Thursday the 15th, after attending a recital by Frederic Lamond at St James's Hall, Liszt returned to Westwood House for dinner. Constance Bache: 'Liszt played*—*at his very best*—one of the *Soirées de Vienne* and Chopin's Studies in A flat major and F minor (Op. 25 Nos. 1 and 2) and other pieces.'

On the 16th he attended a recital of his works given by Stavenhagen at the Prince's Hall. It was either on this occasion, or that of his later visit to the Hall, that he was handed a telegram, despatched elsewhere in London, which bore the words: *Etes-vous prêt à mourir? La mort vient vite!* A companion, whom he asked to open the telegram, then withheld the contents from him.

The next day brought another performance of *St Elisabeth*, this time at the Crystal Palace.

It was also on the 17th that the Catholic weekly, *Universe*, gave its readers a long and detailed description of the Westwood House quarters of 'the greatest virtuoso of all time', making particular mention of the characteristic 'prevailing confusion' and the litter caused by 'newspapers, music, miscellaneous correspondence, a pair of deep German pipes, a bundle of the long and strong Vevey cigars he is accustomed to smoke, and a small army of dictionaries.'

Sunday the 18th began with the drive into London again and mass at

* On a Broadwood provided for him by A. J. Hipkins, an authority on keyboard instruments who was for many years the Broadwood firm's principal technician. In a letter of thanks to Hipkins, Walter Bache wrote: 'Before leaving, Liszt spoke in detail of the Broadwood which he played upon on Thursday evening. . . . He said he liked playing on it because it lent itself so well to different shades and nuances, on which he professes to be now entirely dependent for producing musical effect, for he says he has no longer any fingers for difficulties.'

Brompton Oratory. Lunch was taken at Baron Orczy's* in Wimpole Street, where Liszt played part of the Dante Symphony and a Hungarian Rhapsody. With Walter and Constance Bache he then went to the studio of the sculptor Edgar Boehm (1834–90), to whom he had promised a sitting.

Constance Bache. It was a most delightful hour, and you can fancy how interesting it was to watch Mr. Boehm at his work. Boehm also is a Hungarian, but has lived in England since he was quite a young fellow, and has been naturalized.

After the sitting came the long drive back to Westwood House, and then another big dinner, about twenty-six of us as before, being a return compliment to Irving and Miss Terry. That evening was, as it were, the climax of all. Liszt played again *most divinely*—not more beautifully than on the Thursday, but if anything more powerfully. He played two of the *Soirées de Vienne*, including the one that Bülow calls 'Liebst du mich?' because those words seem to go to the opening, questioning, phrase. Also a Polonaise of Weber's, and his *Momento capriccioso*. Also (a little joke, in answer to an anecdote I had told him in the course of the day), one of Cramer's Studies. Then a Bach Fugue [Book One, No. 5 in D major]. Of this he forgot nearly half, but do you suppose he made a mistake? Not a bit of it! He simply joined on the end of the fugue to the beginning most beautifully, and this second time played it all through complete. It is delicious to watch him when he gets into what, to other people, would be a fog—he just smiles, and you watch, wondering breathlessly how he is going to get out of it; by some judicious turn he puts himself just where he intended to be, and you follow the rest of the course of the piece undisturbed. I forgot to say that he opened with the lovely Beethoven Variations [in F].[18]

Alexander Mackenzie. Much more than mere flashes of his former supremacy were exhibited that night. All this in return for an invitation to *Faust* and supper at the Lyceum Theatre, when the lateness of the hour prevented him from playing. I preserved a scrap of paper on which the intensely impressed actor hastily pencilled these words for my interpretation:

To Dr. Franz Liszt (the Master)
Will you let me send you a trifling souvenir in
remembrance of the glimpse you have given me of Olympus?

Your devoted servant
H. Irving.

18 April, 1886.
God bless you, Master![19]

* Whose daughter Emmuska, creator of the 'Scarlet Pimpernel', recalled the occasion in her autobiographical *Links in the Chain of Life*.

Also of the company was the art historian Dr G. C. Williamson (1858–1942), who found Liszt's playing 'the most perfect that I ever heard'.

The next day, Monday the 19th, Liszt attended at the Prince's Hall a private concert given by Countess Sadowska (a singer) and others. Here a 'Farewell to Liszt' was read out, whose author, William Beatty-Kingston, later recalled 'the exhaustion which was only too manifest in Liszt's appearance on the eve of his departure, when I pressed my lips upon his wonder-working hands for the last time'.

On Tuesday, 20 April, Liszt left Herne-hill station at 10.30 a.m. on the Continental express. At Dover a reception committee was waiting, headed by the Mayor, W. J. Adcock, the Town Clerk, E. W. Knocker, and the Borough Surveyor, M. Curry. A 'congratulatory address' was read out by Mr Adcock, whose daughter then presented Liszt with a bouquet. Shortly afterwards the composer embarked on the *Foam* for the Channel crossing.

The Musical Times (1 May). Surely never before did any composer or executant enjoy such a succession of triumphs as have waited on the Abbé Liszt during his sixteen days' sojourn in London. The record is a dazzling array of festivals, receptions, Royal favours, organised greetings, both public and private—in short, a never-ending array of ceremonials, in which the Hungarian virtuoso stood as the central figure. The ordinary round of musical entertainments has been pursued, notwithstanding the attraction of the lion of the day; but . . . it must be felt that, so far as the heart of the nation was stirred, nothing quickened its beat but the all-absorbing and dominating presence of the famous musician. . . . The visit has been something more than a nine days' wonder, and is indeed so momentous an occurrence in the annals of the musical history of this country that it cannot be permitted to pass by with only such cursory remark as might have been elicited by the sudden appearance of a less brilliant luminary in the artistic firmament. For the sake of those who come after, more than for the behoof of contemporaneous readers, we propose to give a full record of the proceedings. . . . As a manifestation of feeling, it probably is unique. . . . Never before has such a thing been known as for any individual, save a Royal personage, to be received by the audience uprising. Yet this was one of the invariable forms of public etiquette adopted when Liszt entered any public place of entertainment. . . . The year 1886 will long be remembered by the lustre thrown upon it by the presence of a truly great man, the most imposing figure in the musical world, not only of today, but for a generation past. And now that he has tested the warmth of English feeling, we can only express the hope—wherein we but re-echo the wish of thousands—that he may be long spared to put our friendliness again and again to the proof. . . .

From Antwerp, where he spent a week (20 to 27 April) with his friends the Lynens,* Liszt returned to Paris, this time as guest of the Munkácsys. A

* Victor Raymond Lynen (1834–94) was head of the firm of W. Lynen & Co.

companion at a performance of *St Elisabeth* in the Trocadéro on 8 May was Gounod, who observed after the final chorus: 'The bricks with which it is built are holy ones.'

Forgetting his overcoat on one occasion, however, Liszt caught a heavy cold, and his last four days in Paris he was obliged to spend in bed. 'How can I describe my dismay when I saw him again!' writes August Stradal of the return, on Monday, 17 May, to Weimar. 'We had virtually to lift him out of the train and carry him to the carriage, so weak had he become.'

The next evening saw the advent of Cosima, who, having for three years entirely excluded her father from her life, was now determined that various events of importance to her should be graced by his presence. Stradal, who concealed himself at the station to witness the meeting, reports that Liszt, as he embraced his daughter, was 'weeping and sobbing'. The visit was of short duration. Having secured her father's promise to attend Daniela's wedding at Bayreuth in early July, as also the festival performances—which it had earlier been his intention to avoid—later that month, Richard Wagner's grim widow the next afternoon returned whence she had come.

Princess Carolyne to Adelheid von Schorn, 20 May. Please give me news of my poor great man, who would not have reached the point of falling asleep at his hosts' table for half an hour, even at his age, if he took things more easily. Now Sondershausen is coming—and then Bayreuth! It would be enough to kill an ox! And you know how violent his illnesses are. What I fear greatly is water, which can come and rise to the heart so quickly. . . . How are his eyes?[20]

In response to the entreaties of Baroness Meyendorff, Liszt accompanied her on 1 June to Halle, to consult Professor Volkmann and Gräfe the oculist. The diagnoses of the two doctors were, respectively, dropsy and cataract; and their recommendation was that he take the waters at Kissingen and then undergo an eye operation.

August Stradal. Liszt, who got up at 4.00 a.m., so that until 8.00 he could compose undisturbed, kept a cigar in his mouth from morning till night; and when playing whist with him we pupils had, at his behest, to smoke too. The Master used accordingly to spend the whole day sitting in a smoke-filled room, which was of course very bad for his eyes. Baroness Meyendorff then charged me with seeing that at least we pupils did not smoke in the Master's presence. And so at the next game of whist none of us smoked the cigars offered by Liszt, despite his invitation to do so. 'What is the matter? Why is no one smoking?' he asked indignantly. Whereupon I apprehensively told him of the Baroness's instructions. 'Who is the Baroness to give orders here, and who is Stradalus to interfere!? Now, smoke!' said Liszt very angrily. When we were in the middle of our whist session, and the room was so filled with smoke that we could hardly breathe, the door opened and in walked the severe Baroness. And now, lo and behold!—the Master became very nervous and apologized for the smoke in a manner that was all but timorous, while the Baroness looked at me scornfully, uttering not a word. 'Poor Stradalus, as a diplomat he has no talent at all!' said the Master in high good humour when I went to him the next morning. Presenting me with a box of his best Havanas, he laughed heartily over the incident.[21]

Between 2 and 6 June Liszt was at Sondershausen for the Tonkünstler-Versammlung of the Allgemeine Deutsche Musikverein (3–6 June). *Christus*, *Ce qu'on entend sur la montagne*, *Hamlet*, *Die Ideale*, *Hunnenschlacht*, the *Totentanz* (with Siloti), and some of the *Historische ungarische Bildnisse* (orchestrated by Friedheim) were performed.

August Göllerich. We stayed at the *Tanne*. No sooner had we got there than I had to read him Grimm's description of the destruction of Rome. 'I have nothing against it,' he said, referring to the protests which had been voiced against modernization of the Eternal City, 'if it means fewer dunghills.'

In contrast to the southern casualness, he was pleased to recall the *English* comfort he had recently enjoyed, emphasizing with a priceless gesture: 'English houses are constructed with the same harmony of style as a sonata.'

'So far as real *comfort* is concerned, in England they are far in advance of other nations. The houses are not very tall, and the kitchens are restricted to the ground floor or basement—unlike Paris and Vienna, where you get the stench of cooking on every floor.'. . .

On 5 June came the final rehearsal and excellent performance of *Christus* at the town church. At the end of the first part of the March of the Three Kings, Liszt remarked softly: 'Your friend Bruckner would have insisted on a repetition here!'

'The Hungarian part of the March greatly shocked Müller-Hartung at one time. However, Rubens drew Flemings in his picture, so *I* can give one of my Magi a waxed moustache. That bothers me not *at all*!'

He particularly wished to stress the realistic quality of the tempest; the despairing shriek of the disciples could not be too exaggerated for him. When the singer of Christ came out with 'O ye of little faith!' as though indulging in a soft *bel canto* aria, Liszt flew at him almost fiercely, saying: 'You must reproach them bitterly, as though you wanted to say—"What cowardly fellows you are!" '[22]

Walter Damrosch. Together with Baron Joukovsky and Fräulein von Schorn, I accompanied him back to Weimar. During the trip Liszt was in a very gay mood and kept us in gales of laughter with a number of outrageous puns and amusing comments on certain phases of the festival, especially on a long debate between Dr Riemann,* an eminent musical

* Hugo Riemann (1849–1919).

theorist, and another man whose name I have forgotten, on certain theories regarding the science of harmony. This debate, which was wholly technical and very 'gründlich', lasted for two hours, during which poor Liszt had to sit in the front row in a room crowded to suffocation and with not a door or window open. I can still see the venerable head of Liszt drooping and dropping every now and then from sheer fatigue, and then the *Meister* raising it again with that ineffable smile on his face in order to show an interest in the discussion.

When we arrived in Weimar, Joukovsky invited us all, together with Lassen, to dinner. . . . It was a jolly affair. Champagne was served immediately after the soup, and Liszt reminisced so brilliantly and beautifully of the old Weimar days of which Fraülein von Schorn and Lassen had been a part, and with which I, too, could claim some connection through my parents, that we all sat spellbound.

It was not until midnight that we accompanied Liszt through the park and the lovely Goethe Garden back to his house. It was a gentle summer night with a hazy moon giving an indescribable glamour to the trees and bushes, and suddenly Liszt laid his hand on my shoulder and said 'Listen!'

From the bushes came the song of a nightingale. I had never heard one before and stood spellbound. It seemed incredible that such ecstatic sweetness, such songs of joy and sorrow, could come from the throat of a little bird, and to hear it all at twenty-four years of age and standing at the side of Liszt! Today, thirty-five years later, I still thrill at the memory of it.[23]

August Göllerich. On his way to church through the sweet-smelling park, Liszt would enjoy the fragrant morning freshness with childlike pleasure, stopping to admire every fine tree, for to him *all* life was something sacred to be cherished; the power of God's expression he felt everywhere.

'Yes,' he often remarked, 'the trees, the birds, the garden and the good air are the best things at my home.'. . .

At noon on Whit Monday, 14 June,* he paid a call on the Grand Duke at Schloss Belvedere. On his return he was so silent and depressed when he appeared at table that I felt most apprehensive.

Suddenly he blurted out: 'Something dreadful has happened! The Grand Duke has just told me that the King† has come to an end in Lake Starnberg!'

Not another word was spoken until the lesson at 4.00. When, during this, a special edition of the paper arrived, reporting the tragic end of the sovereign whom the Master had described as being 'in receptivity what Wagner was in productivity'—Liszt forbade all the usual expressions.[24]

* Göllerich erroneously wrote '13 June'.

† Ludwig II of Bavaria. His habitual state of exaltation having apparently deteriorated into insanity, he had been put under restraint; and his attendant physician and keeper, Dr Gudden, was drowned with him. The exact circumstances of their last moments, in the afternoon of Sunday, 13 June, are still a matter of conjecture.

23 to 25 June Liszt spent at Dornburg with the Grand Duke and his family. In his company here was *August Göllerich*.

Our conversation fell on Wagner, and Liszt said: 'The first time that Wagner heard music of mine was in the building of the St Gallen Library, at a concert under the aegis of the conductor Sczadrowsky. I conducted *Orpheus* and *Les Préludes*, Wagner the Eroica Symphony. *Orpheus* he particularly liked. He later bought all my scores for his library. The Faust Symphony, of which he was very fond, he studied in great detail; the Dante Symphony I had to play to him twice in succession.'. . .

'King Ludwig II had not only a special performance of *Christus* put on for himself, but also one of *St Elisabeth*, which I dedicated to him. If I were a king, or had the necessary fortune, I too should hold private performances.'

'After I had received the Order of St Michael [1866] I had an unforgettable audience of the King.'[25]

Gerhard Rohlfs. We attended one of the very last matinées. Several of his pupils had already played, when Liszt stood up, took his seat at the piano, and to all our joy and amazement played a Beethoven sonata; but so wondrously beautiful was his rendering that it became a kind of spiritual experience, beyond anything that any of us is ever likely to hear again. We were all profoundly moved; but the Grand Duke, who was also present, rose when Liszt had finished and with tears in his eyes said: '*Lieber Meister*, let that suffice: we do not wish this music to be profaned by the playing of others. This is what we shall take home with us.' Extremely moved, we all went quietly away. That was to some extent the Master's swansong. He was a great and noble man, and his equal as an artist is yet to appear.[26]

La Mara. The 27th of June was the last Sunday Liszt spent in Weimar. He had invited me for lunch, and, going early, I took with me copies of a number of his letters to various persons, which with his permission I wished to include in my *Musicians' Letters*,* and asked him to inspect them. Without so much as a glance at my sheaf of papers, he quickly interrupted me. 'My dear child, for me to look through the letters, I would not have to be *me*, you would not have to be *you*. *Anything* of mine that you wish to print, you may.' I felt that he was making me a bequest, which both moved and exalted me, and which, when in gratitude for his trust I held out my hand to him, he sealed with a kiss on my forehead. At that moment there came to me the thought that by collecting and publishing his letters I could erect a monument to him. . . .

Marie Breidenstein, Gille, Bruno Schrader, and Göllerich had also been invited and now appeared. . . . I do not know who brought the conversation to Madame Janina and asked where she was. 'Under the name of Olga Cezano, *la fameuse Cosaque* is now living in Geneva, where she teaches. I have tried, unbeknown to her of course, to be helpful to her

* *Musikerbriefe aus fünf Jahrhunderten* (2 vols., 1886).

in her present activity, and on my behalf Bülow has done what he can, with some success too.'

'You are an angel, *Meister*!' I cried.

'Not at all,' he replied with a smile. 'I am merely trying to be a Christian.'

The fiancé* of his granddaughter Daniela had recently been to see him, he remarked, and had made as excellent an impression on him as had his book on Francis of Assisi. 'I hope he is the right man for Daniela, who was not born for everyone, and has in addition too much of the uncomfortable mixture of her father.'

After the meal, Baroness Meyendorff, Miss Senkrah, Lassen, Siloti, Friedheim, and Martin Krause, the founder and director of the Leipzig 'Liszt Society' (originally planned by Siloti for Weimar), which he had made dazzlingly successful, arrived for music. Siloti performed Balakirev's *Islamey* and Liszt's Fourteenth Hungarian Rhapsody. The Master did not himself play, preferring a few rubbers of whist, in which Lassen came secretly to the aid of my clumsy playing. When I left, Liszt accompanied me outside. I had no suspicion that it was our final farewell. '*Auf Wiedersehen* in Bayreuth, Leipzig, Weimar, Vienna—we run into one another everywhere!' he called after me on the steps; and again a last: 'God be with you!'

With those words the gates of my musical Paradise closed behind me. *My* Weimar was no more![27]

On Thursday, 1 July, leaving Weimar for the last time, Liszt travelled to Bayreuth for Daniela's wedding on the 3rd. Accompanying him was *August Göllerich*.

Liszt was in the most captivating mood. While reminiscing, he related *inter alia*:

'After the first performance of the Faust Symphony all my friends advised me to strike out the final chorus.'

'Madame Pleyel once wanted a piece from me with brilliant passages à la Thalberg. So I dedicated the *Norma* fantasy to her, writing her into the bargain a nice, witty letter. When I met Thalberg later, I said: "I copied it all from you." To which he replied: "Yes, there are Thalberg passages in it which are positively *indecent*." '

'Verdi complimented me highly on the codas I allowed myself in the *Ernani* and *Trovatore* [S433] fantasies. Those pieces, which must be played as stupidly as possible, full of tenor fervour, I wrote for Bülow's "Court Concerts" at Berlin. Since he was complaining that people were always asking for something from those operas, I said: "Very well, in ten days I shall send you something, as this is not your own field." '

* Henry Thode (1857–1920), a distinguished art historian; and, later, author of the booklet *Franz Liszt* (Heidelberg, 1911).

'The *Agnus Dei* of Verdi's *Requiem* is very similar to my incense motif in the *March of the Three Kings*; it's a kind of cousinship.'

As we were nearing Bayreuth, the Master said: 'I have always been very keen on cremation. It is the only right way. But for a probable *brouillerie* with the clergy, I should even stipulate it in my will.'[28]

From Bayreuth Liszt journeyed to the Grand Duchy of Luxembourg, having been invited to Castle Colpach, home of his friends the Munkácsys. Arriving in the city of Luxembourg at 7.30 p.m. on 5 July, he was welcomed by Charles Papier (1811–97), father of Cécile Munkácsy, and by Stavenhagen, who had come on an earlier train with Cardinal Haynald, a fellow guest at Colpach for the first two days of Liszt's visit.

'A crowd of onlookers had gathered to see the illustrious visitor,' reported the *Luxemburger Wort* (7 July). 'The great artist . . . has grown old and frail, so that he needs assistance merely to get from one place to another. His head is bowed, his long hair snow-white; yet his eyes are still bright, his voice still powerful, and taken all in all he gives a pleasing impression of an otherwise really healthy man, who will, we hope, survive for Art and its admirers for many years yet.'

Via Arlon, Liszt reached Castle Colpach at 2 o'clock in the morning of the 6th. The fortnight he spent here with the Munkácsys was a tranquil, restful one—but his health declined still further during this time. 'To my physical condition, already so pleasant, has now been added these five days a most violent cough which plagues me day and night,' he wrote on the 17th to Olga von Meyendorff. 'To comfort me, the doctor says that this type of cough is very tenacious. So far, neither cough medicine nor infusions, nor mustard plasters, nor foot-baths have rid me of it.'

Journal de Luxembourg (18/19 July). Liszt's society, we learn from Colpach, is extremely agreeable. The contact he has always maintained with celebrated contemporaries enables him to dip into his memory for numerous fascinating anecdotes with which to sprinkle his conversation. His erudition is unbelievable, his memory prodigious. Very lively in his disposition, he is very simple in his tastes; he knows how to put those around him at their ease and how to create an atmosphere of life and spirit.[29]

Having accepted an invitation to attend a Luxembourg Music Society concert, which, planned for the 21st, was then at his request brought forward to the 19th, Liszt returned to the capital on that day, and—having consented to play a few pieces at the concert—in the afternoon selected a piano* at the music shop run by Guillaume Stomps (1855–1927).

Held at the Casino, and consisting of the Overture to *Der Freischütz*, a work by Svendsen, Haydn's Drum Roll symphony, Hamm's Polonaise for clarinet and orchestra, and a Grand Fantasy on *Lohengrin*, the concert was scheduled to begin at 8.30 p.m.

* A Steinway, of which several photographs are reproduced in the *Liszt Society Journal*, ix (1984), 51–2.

Journal de Luxembourg (20 July). The orchestra was complete, the conductor ready, everywhere an expectant hush. At 8.40 there was a stir, and the entire audience rose and bowed: the illustrious Master made his entrance, accompanied by his peer, Munkácsy, prince of painting, Mme Munkácsy, and a few close friends. The board of directors had received their illustrious guests at the foot of the staircase, and had presented Liszt with the magnificent bouquet the Master was holding. He is a fine-looking old man, with long silver hair and distinctive features, slightly stooping; his eyes are bright, a kindly smile plays around his lips, his long, delicate hands seem to be caressing something. . . .

The Grand Fantasy on *Lohengrin* concluded the concert, but not the evening. Mme Munkácsy . . . speaks a few words to the Master, who smiles—and we know that the King of the Piano is going to play.

It is 9.55 p.m., and he is at the piano. How can I speak of Liszt's playing? I dare not, because words fail me to describe worthily what made our hearts beat while the illustrious musician made his instrument by turns speak, sing, weep and thunder. . . .[30]

There has been speculation about the pieces played by Liszt on this occasion, the last time he touched a piano in public, or even at all. The Luxembourg journalists report a *Soirée de Vienne*, but seem confused about the other items. Fortunately, Stavenhagen was present too, and it is likely to have been to him that such contemporaries as Göllerich and La Mara turned for their information.

'With the first of his *Liebesträume*,' writes the last-named, 'the *Chant polonais* from the *Glanes de Woronince*, and the sixth of his *Soirées de Vienne*, Liszt's magic playing fell silent for ever.'*

Because his health was rapidly deteriorating, Liszt was urged by his host and hostess, and by their doctor, to postpone his departure; but having promised his daughter that he would go to Bayreuth, he was not to be dissuaded. On 20 July, the day after the concert, he left Luxembourg by train, spending that night in Frankfurt and arriving at Bayreuth in the afternoon of Wednesday the 21st.

Cosima Wagner. He was in a condition that gave rise to anxiety. Without complaining, he mentioned that in the late evening fellow-travellers had not wished the compartment window to be closed.[31]

Adelheid von Schorn. He lodged near Wahnfried at the home† of Herr Fröhlich, a head forester. He occupied the ground floor, and Joukovsky a few rooms on the first. When I arrived, and saw Liszt, I was appalled at the change in his condition. He was being given morphine for his dreadful

* In her *Lisztiana*, Lina Ramann mentions a Steingräber piano at Liszt's lodgings in Bayreuth 'on which he is said to have played for a short time on two occasions, the last time approximately ten days before he was taken ill'. Ten days before being taken (seriously) ill, however, Liszt was still in Luxembourg.

† On the corner of the Siegfriedstrasse, today's Lisztstrasse. Had Richard Wagner been alive, Liszt would have stayed at Wahnfried—but he now firmly declined Cosima's invitation to do so.

coughing and was in a virtual stupor; his eyes were watering and his body more swollen than ever. He was still able to attend performances of *Parsifal* [23 July] and *Tristan* [25 July], but sat in the Wagner family's box more asleep than awake.[32]

Felix Weingartner. At the immensely successful performance of *Tristan*, I sat beside him in a box in the so-called Princes' Gallery. 'How is your cough, Master?' I ventured to ask after an alarmingly long pause in his otherwise constant coughing and gasping. 'It is civilized,' he replied with a faint smile; 'during the music it leaves me in peace. In the interval it will begin again.' But it was precisely this long period of respite which was the beginning of the end. The mucous which accumulated he was able to expectorate still less adequately than before, and as a result developed inflammation of the lungs.

When I asked him if he were satisfied with the performance, he looked at me meaningly and said slowly, with the special emphasis he was wont to give to important pronouncements: 'It is my opinion that—in the circumstances now obtaining—it could not be better.'

Those words, imbued with the gentle irony so typical of Liszt, were the last I heard from him. He did not speak again after the third Act. I took him to his carriage, which soon disappeared into the darkness. It reminded me of how, four years earlier, I had seen Wagner, exuding health and vigour, climb into *his* carriage in front of the festival theatre and disappear into the darkness; and I felt that Liszt was now separated from his great friend by only a very short span of time.[33]

Adelheid von Schorn. One morning Joukovsky and I went to his sitting-room. He was seated on the sofa, cards in hand, and around him some pupils with whom he was playing whist. Beside him was his former pupil Sophie Menter,* whom I here saw for the first time. He was coughing, nodding off for a moment or two and then resuming play, scarcely aware of who was there and hardly able to hold himself upright. Deeply distressed we went away again, for there was nothing we could do for the poor, beloved Master. That was my last meeting with him; the next day he was confined to bed with inflammation of the lungs.

Going to Frau Daniela Thode, I offered to undertake the necessary nursing duties, adding that I would withdraw whenever Frau Wagner wished to come to the sickbed. For it seemed obvious to me that in view of the festival performances and everything connected with them, she and her daughters would have insufficient time to attend to all the nursing

* Others present on this occasion, Saturday, 24 July, were Siloti, Lassen, and Lessmann. The pupils most in Liszt's company, until banned by Cosima, seem to have been August Göllerich and Lina Schmalhausen, who took it in turns to read to him as he lay, half asleep, on the sofa. Until being confined to bed, he went for lunch each day to his friend Princess Hatzfeldt and for dinner to Wahnfried.

themselves. Frau Thode and Fraülein Eva Wagner accepted my offer joyfully, and the latter went to the sickroom to tell her mother. Returning after a few minutes, she thanked me but said that her mother 'wished her father to be tended by herself and her daughters alone'. Liszt's manservant later told me that he had received strict orders to admit no one.

There was no point in my staying at Bayreuth any longer. To know that my old friend, whom I had so often cared for, was so ill, and not to be allowed to go to him—that was too much for me. I later regretted my hasty departure; perhaps my help could still have been used. Before leaving . . . I asked Joukovsky to telegraph me if there were any change for the worse. I also wrote to tell Princess Wittgenstein how matters stood, receiving in reply a telegram asking me to remain at Bayreuth. But when it arrived I had returned there in any case, for the end had come more quickly than any of us could have imagined.[34]

From Monday, 26 July, Liszt was entirely confined to bed. Lina Schmalhausen stayed with him that evening until midnight—but, returning in the morning, was soon shown the door by Cosima, who then instructed Liszt's servant, Mihály, to admit 'family only'. (Lina did, however, see Liszt again—for the last time—on Thursday the 29th.)

Wednesday the 28th saw the arrival of August Stradal, whom Liszt had earlier asked to accompany him to Kissingen. He, too, was excluded from the sickroom, but after pleading with Mihály was allowed to stand at the threshold and gaze upon his slumbering master. 'His dreams must have been pleasant ones,' he wrote later to Lina Ramann, 'for he was smiling and the expression on his features was a happy, ecstatic one.' In the night of Friday the 30th, however, the dreadful pain of his heart spasms caused Liszt to utter shrieks loud enough to be heard at a considerable distance.

Cosima Wagner. Asked how he felt, he replied in that enigmatic tone of voice characteristic of him when implying something other than what he was apparently saying: 'Well—until I shall be still better.' . . .

Since the doctor summoned from Erlangen could offer only a slight hope of recovery, I asked my father if there were anyone he wished to have with him. Pulling himself up with what strength he could muster, he all but roared out the single word: '*No-one!*' That was the last clear word he uttered.[35]

August Stradal. In the afternoon of the 31st the doctor said the end was approaching; but Liszt's strong constitution was still resisting death, which finally came only late that evening, not long before midnight. We pupils [Göllerich, Stavenhagen, Stradal] were waiting in the front garden, which was bathed in the wonderful light of the full moon,* when suddenly, from some neighbouring house, there rang out Isolde's 'Liebestod' from *Tristan*

* The night of 31 July was actually the first of a new moon.

in Liszt's piano transcription.* Every window was in darkness, not one of them showed a light, and we could not tell whence the sounds were coming. But about that music there was something mystical, transcendental! . . . And then, shortly before midnight, Liszt's manservant came to the door, weeping: our great and beloved Master had passed away. . . .

Profoundly shaken, I returned to my room feeling as though I had been orphaned, filled with the single agonizing thought: 'You have lost your master for ever!'[36]

Felix Weingartner. 'Dr Liszt died in the night,' were the words with which our Swabian maid awakened Reisenauer and myself on the morning of 1 August.

The catastrophe had happened. Reisenauer wept like a child. I stared up through the window at the grey skies. Wagner, King Ludwig, Liszt—around all three death had now entwined its mystic fetters. A great artistic epoch had passed.

We dressed and went to the house of mourning. The Master had already been laid on his bier. His face had fallen in and his hair was still damp from the washing of the body. . . . He looked a little old man, one that it was difficult to reconcile with him who had filled the mortal frame only a short while before, the creator of the Faust and Dante symphonies. His long, delicate hands, which had once enchanted the whole world with their wonderful playing, were folded and held a crucifix.†. . .

Because of the summer heat the process of decay began quickly; after a few hours the lid of the coffin had to be closed. From earthly eyes the beloved figure disappeared for ever. . . .

Farewell to what was mortal in thee, thou noble, great and good Franz Liszt—henceforth we can meet thy spirit only.[37]

August Stradal. I had brought the score of the Faust Symphony with me, so that at Kissingen, when the opportunity arose, I could consult the Master about certain passages. . . . The score was lying on top of the piano in my room, and when I awoke, and all the pain and sorrow of my loss came back to me, lo!—pouring through the open window and converging in radiant splendour on the score of the symphony, came the rays of the rising sun. Gazing for a long time upon this wonder of the light . . . I then sprang up with a sudden rush of happiness. 'Liszt is not dead,' I thought. 'He lives on in his works, and in them he will be with us always!'[38]

* It seems to have penetrated the dying man's consciousness, for shortly before his death he is said to have whispered, barely audibly, the one word 'Tristan'.

† And also some forget-me-nots. Finding Lina Schmalhausen praying in front of Liszt's bier, Cosima had taken the weeping girl in her arms, allowed her to put the flowers in the dead man's hands, and to cut off and keep a lock of his hair. The diary kept by Lina during these days in Bayreuth is held at Weimar's Goethe-und-Schiller Archiv and has not yet been published.

Hugo Wolf writing in the Wiener Salonblatt *(8 August).* Once more a great power has been called to his eternal rest. A star has fallen, whose overwhelming light blinded untruth and dishonesty but shone with a friendly, a wondrous radiance upon the way of the distressed, guiding him to where, although opposition and disfavour may await him, yet also fulfilment and victory: a star of holy fire, sending forth lightnings to destroy the altars of the false gods, flaming high to ignite the blaze of inspiration, to encourage and to defend true greatness. The eye of this brilliant phenomenon is for ever closed; but it was the eye of an immortal.

Legendary tales will surely weave themselves around the wonderful achievements of this greatest of virtuosi; yet, that we may keep his remembrance vivid for future generations, not only in the visions of memory or in biography, but as a living verity, the Great Departed leaves us a priceless heritage: his works.

A determined nature, ever planning something new, ever pressing forward, the Master inspired a reformation in every realm of vocal and instrumental music. Soul, depth of thought and emotion, a unique feeling for beauty in musical form, are the characteristic marks of his creations. . . .

Throned on a solitary height, he remained incomprehensible to the multitude. As he himself said in his famous preface to his symphonic poems, he 'wanted no everyday popularity'. Yet, to anyone who could submerge himself in this radiant individuality, a world of ideal splendour, only to be dreamed of by a poet, has been revealed.

He who never rested is now at rest. The all-vitalizing spark is extinguished; the hand that summoned new worlds into existence, only to destroy them again, lies stark in death. Death claims the man who like a second Orpheus shed life, new blossoming life, over our sphere. . . .

Let us faithfully cherish his revered memory, let us throng around the banner victoriously borne by the Master against paltry doubt, and, above all, let us treasure the legacy of his genius, let us defend this priceless hoard; and may his soul hover in benediction over our lives.[39]

Constance Bache writing in the Monthly Musical Record *(1 September).* In Liszt we have lost not only the greatest musician of our time, but also the most generous of masters, the truest of friends. How, in all the petty strife and warfare, all the jealousy, all the envy, that we know goes on behind the scenes of artistic life—how Liszt's grand character has ever towered above all this smallness, as a giant above pygmies! His was the last living link that bound us to Beethoven; his the strongest link in the chain that binds us to many another—Chopin, Berlioz, Schubert, Schumann, Cornelius, Wagner. Our first knowledge of Schubert we owe to him; he it was who generously refused ever to have his own interpretation of the Rákóczy March played as long as Berlioz lived, because he found that Berlioz had also adopted it, and he did not wish his own to interfere with his friend's; to him we owe a first hearing of Cornelius's masterpiece, the *Barber of Bagdad*, some twenty-seven years ago, which lost Liszt his own place at the time! Liszt was just twenty-seven years before his time, for this same opera has now been at length again brought to the light of day in Munich, and with the most brilliant results. What Liszt has done for Wagner is more within the history of today and now, but we may also recall how he brought *Lohengrin* to a hearing, when Wagner was still an exile in Switzerland, and unknown. A noble enemy (if, indeed, he can be said to have had any, since he never made them himself), and a staunch and noble friend!

The day after his death numbers of people flocked to the house where he had been living, which was only a stone's throw from Wahnfried, Wagner's house, to look for the last time upon those powerful and grand features, now silent in the last sleep of death. And a veritable sleep it seemed to be, so peaceful did those features look, in which Time had placed many a deep furrow, and the experiences of a long and eventful life had left their mark. From the very first morning after his death floral offerings began to pour in —wreaths, palm-leaves, simple bunches of flowers; everyone had some token of homage to lay at the Master's feet.

The funeral was fixed for Tuesday, 3 August, and was a most solemn and impressive sight to those who were privileged to be present. The gathering was an immense one, filling all the large drive of Wahnfried, in the hall of which the coffin had been placed previous to its last journey to the cemetery. But the numbers would assuredly have been doubled had not the funeral been fixed for such an untimely date. As it was, many, very many, who would have wished to show the last honours to the memory of the great Master, were precluded from doing so by the impossibility of arriving in time, and many actually came only just in time to join the funeral *cortège* as it emerged from Wagner's house into the road. The streets were hung with black flags, and the lighted lamps were veiled in crape. Both sides of the road were lined with spectators, as the long procession wended its slow way to the sound of the distant cemetery bell.

The religious service over, the mayor of Bayreuth spoke a few words over the lowered coffin, and alluded in touching language to the great loss they, we, all the world, has sustained. One or two other speeches followed, including a few broken words from an old and beloved friend of the Master's, Herr Hofrat Gille, from Jena, but his words were almost incoherent from the sobs that broke from him, and everyone must have deeply sympathized with the grief of the poor old man, who had just lost his old and dear friend—and *such* a friend!

The next morning a requiem service was held in the Catholic church in Bayreuth, at which all the eminent people who were present at the funeral attended. The musical part of the service was in the highest degree unsatisfactory, and the feeling of many must have been that if nothing better than that could be done, it would have been far better to have no service at all. When the composer of the Symphonic Poems, the Gran Mass, the *St Elisabeth*, had just passed away, in the very town where the air is rife with Wagner and music, where two of the most renowned conductors and numbers of Germany's most gifted song-birds were on the spot, it does seem strange that no better memorial service could have been arranged than the nasal chanting of two or three harsh-voiced priests, in response to the very inharmonious and discordant singing and playing of an inefficient choir and organist!* However, enough of this; happily, his memory does not hang upon a funeral service!

The Master's grave lies quite near another celebrated monument—the tomb of Jean Paul Richter, Bayreuth's own child, a large ivy-covered rock in its natural shape. The last time we looked upon the Master's grave it had been all covered with branches of cypress, and wreaths and palm-leaves lay strewn about—two from the royal house of Saxe-Weimar, one from Joachim, a palm from Servais, etc., etc. But the greater number were to be seen in the cemetery chapel hard by. The Queen of England sent a wreath; the Liszt Verein; the Wagner Verein, both of Bayreuth and London; the orchestra of the Richard Wagner theatre; the artists of the same; the Bayreuth Liederkranz; the theatres of Vienna, Leipzig, and Weimar; the town of Weimar; the town of Jena; the Allgemeine Deutsche Musikverein, of which Liszt was president. There were wreaths also from Robert Franz; Sophie Menter; Frau Materna; a faithful and loving disciple of the Master's in London; and many others . . . and even for many days afterwards floral homage continued to be paid to the Great Dead.

Yes, he is gone, and the magic of those wondrous hands we shall never never hear again; but, though dead, he yet speaketh in his works—that undying part of himself which he leaves behind, and which is our inheritance.

The 'faithful and loving disciple' referred to is undoubtedly Constance's brother, the admirable Walter Bache, who writing a few weeks later to Jessie Hillebrand remarked that if Liszt's life had been spared he would have had to support the affliction of blindness, partial or total. 'What has been our loss has been his gain: *his courage was marvellous*: of this last, Buonamici wrote me a most touching account. The calmness with which he looked forward to blindness, or death, or whatever might happen, was really majestic.'

At her home in Rome Princess Carolyne continued to work at *Des causes intérieures de la faiblesse extérieure de l'Eglise*, and completed the last of the twenty-four volumes—a task which had occupied her for sixteen and a half years —on Ash Wednesday, 23 February 1887. The two final volumes had been written, as the reader is informed on the last page of all, 'in the anguish of profound grief'.

A fortnight later she died peacefully in her sleep.

* The organist was Anton Bruckner.

One of the regular visitors to this remarkable woman during her final months was *Malwida von Meysenbug*.

In the autumn of 1886 it was with a certain apprehension, so far as seeing the Princess was concerned, that I returned to Rome. . . . I found her quieter than hitherto, looking older, and confined more than ever to her armchair and her fusty room, from which all fresh air was excluded. I saw at once that . . . life had lost its value for her. Liszt had spoken with true prescience when he had once expressed his conviction that she would not survive him. After a few weeks she was entirely confined to bed and saw few people. I was among those admitted to her, and I continued to spend many hours at her bedside. She now spoke to me a great deal about her departed friend, and I saw that she derived comfort from the hope of a speedy reunion. It had always been her habit to write me many and lengthy letters, even when I was living in the same city; and even now from her sickbed I received them frequently, such as the one in which she spoke only of him and of her hope of finding him again, closing with the words: '*He lives—yes, he lives*, for he loved Jesus Christ.' And once, when I had been sitting a long time with her, she suddenly asked: 'Oh, my dear, why won't you believe in Christ's divinity?' I saw that it was still her heart's desire to bring about this last work of conversion, and it truly grieved me to have to give her the same bitter disappointment once again in these hours of farewell. . . .

I was unable to go to her for some days, and also heard that her daughter had come and that she was therefore not alone. I had planned to go to see her on 10 March 1887, when in the evening of the 9th I received from an acquaintance a note telling me of the Princess's death. . . .

The funeral service took place [Saturday, 12 March] at the attractive church of Santa Maria del Popolo.* Cardinal Hohenlohe read the Mass, and a Requiem of Liszt's was performed.† I attended with Madame Minghetti, and when the Cardinal blessed the coffin containing the Princess's mortal remains, I sent her a silent, tender farewell, As we left the church, Monsieur Hébert, who was at that time still Director of the French Academy at the Villa Medici, and who had been a friend of the Princess's, came to greet us, saying: 'Oui, c'était quelqu'un!' They were the right words: Princess Carolyne Wittgenstein *was* someone, and of how few persons can that be said.[40]

On learning of the Princess's death, *Lina Ramann*, in far-away Nuremberg, brought her long series of 'Lisztiana' to a fitting close.

With her, pass away the last remnants of a tragedy of the heart and of destiny, full of human error and yet of the rarest greatness and sublimity . . . *Peace and rest to them both!*[41]

* The Princess was buried in the German cemetery at the Vatican.
† Conducted by Sgambati.

ENDNOTES

LIST OF ABBREVIATIONS USED

AM	Agoult, Comtesse d', *Mémoires 1833–1854*, ed. D. Ollivier (Paris, 1927).
BLB	La Mara (ed.), *Briefwechsel zwischen Franz Liszt und Hans von Bülow* (Leipzig, 1898).
BLCA	La Mara (ed.), *Briefwechsel zwischen Franz Liszt und Carl Alexander, Grossherzog von Sachsen* (Leipzig, 1909).
CAB	P. Cornelius, *Ausgewählte Briefe*, 2 vols. (Leipzig, 1905).
CLA	D. Ollivier (ed.), *Correspondance de Liszt et de la Comtesse d'Agoult*, 2 vols. (Paris, 1933–4).
CLMO	D. Ollivier (ed.), *Correspondance de Liszt et de sa fille Madame Emile Ollivier 1842–1862* (Paris, 1936).
CLPR	J. Chantavoine (ed.), *Franz Liszt: Pages romantiques* (Paris, 1912).
FLB	La Mara (ed.), *Franz Liszt's Briefe*, 8 vols. (Leipzig, 1893–1905).
JALS	*Journal of the American Liszt Society* (Louisville, K., 1977–87).
LAG	La Mara (ed.), *Aus der Glanzzeit der Weimarer Altenburg* (Leipzig, 1906).
LBM	La Mara (ed.), *Franz Liszt's Briefe an seine Mutter* (Leipzig, 1918).
LCRT	La Mara (ed.), 'Franz Liszt auf seinem ersten Weltflug: Briefe seines Vaters, Adam Liszt, an Carl Czerny', *Classisches und Romantisches aus der Tonwelt* (Leipzig, 1892).
LCS	B. Litzmann, *Clara Schumann: Ein Künstlerleben*, 3 vols. (Leipzig, 1902–8).
LLM	*The Letters of Franz Liszt to Olga von Meyendorff 1871–1886.* Trans. W. R. Tyler; ed. E. N. Waters. (Dumbarton Oaks, 1979).
LSJ	*The Liszt Society Journal* (London, 1976–87).
LZB	F. Lewald, *Zwölf Bilder nach dem Leben* (Berlin, 1888).
R*LKM*	L. Ramann, *Franz Liszt als Künstler und Mensch*, 3 vols. (Leipzig, 1880–94).
SJ	G. Sand, *Journal intime* (Paris, 1926).
S*RB*	K. von Schlözer, *Römische Briefe 1864–1869* (Berlin, 1924).
SZM	A. von Schorn, *Zwei Menschenalter: Erinnerungen und Briefe* (Berlin, 1901).
ZAL	Graf G. Zichy, *Aus meinem Leben*, 3 vols. (Stuttgart, 1911–20).

1811–1828

1. The diary is now lost. This extract was quoted by J. d'Ortigue in his 'Franz Liszt: Etude biographique', *Gazette musicale*, 14 June 1835, 198.

2. A. Göllerich, *Franz Liszt* (Berlin, 1908), 158–60. The remarks are here reproduced in a different sequence.
3. J. Kapp, *Franz Liszt* (Berlin, 1911), 12.
4. F. Liszt, *Des Bohémiens et de leur musique en Hongrie* (Leipzig, 1881), 471–3.
5. C. Czerny, *Erinnerungen aus meinem Leben* (Strasbourg, 1968), 27–9.
6. LCRT 234–8.
7. 'De la situation des artistes et de leur condition dans la société', published in instalments in the *Gazette musicale*, 1835. Reprinted in *CLPR*, 1–84. This extract 38–40.
8. LCRT 240–3.
9. La Mara (ed.), 'Aus Franz Liszts erster Jugend: Ein Brief seines Vaters mit Briefen Czernys an Ihn', *Die Musik*, V. Jahr 1905/6, xiii (Berlin, 1905/6), 16–20. Ludwig Hofer's identity has recently been established by G. J. Winkler, 'Franz Liszts Kindheit: Versuch eines biographischen Grundrisses', *Die Musikforschung* (39. Jahrgang 1986, iv, Kassel), 339.
10. LCRT 244–50.
11. Ibid. 251–4.
12. Ibid. 254–61.
13. Quoted by M. Eckhardt, 'Liszt à Marseille', *Studia Musicologica Academiae Scientiarum Hungaricae*, xxiv (1982), 165.
14. Ibid. 168–9.
15. Comte de Montbel, *Souvenirs* (Paris, 1913), 182.
16. Lady M. Leconfield (ed.), *Three Howard Sisters* (London, 1955), 64.
17. 'Lettre d'un bachelier ès musique à un poète voyageur', *Revue et gazette musicale*, 12 Feb. 1837. Reprinted in *CLPR* 97–110. This extract 101–2.
18. C. Salaman, 'Pianists of the Past', *Blackwood's Edinburgh Magazine*, clxx (Sept. 1901), 314.
19. W. von Lenz, *Die grossen Pianoforte-Virtuosen unserer Zeit* (Berlin, 1872), 8–17.

1829–1832

1. J. d'Ortigue, 'Etude biographique', 202.
2. Quoted in the *Norfolk Chronicle*, 26 Sept. 1840. Reprinted in *LSJ*, ix (1984), 12.
3. F. Hiller, *Felix Mendelssohn-Bartholdy: Briefe und Erinnerungen* (Cologne, 1874), 23–4.
4. E. Legouvé, *Soixante Ans de Souvenirs*, i (Paris, 1886), 297–8.
5. C. Barbey-Boissier, *La Comtesse Agénor de Gasparin et sa famille: Correspondance et Souvenirs 1813–1894,* i (Paris, 1902), 136–7, 142–3, 150–1, 156–8, 165–6, 167–8, 171–80, 185–7.
6. A. Fontaney, *Journal intime* (Paris, 1925), 117.
7. Barbey-Boissier, *La Comtesse Agénor*, 194–5.
8. Ibid. 199.
9. Fontaney, *Journal intime*, 132–3.
10. *Vingt-Cinq Ans à Paris (1826–1850): Journal du Comte Rodolphe Apponyi, Attaché de l'Ambassade d'Autriche à Paris*, ii (Paris, 1913), 179.
11. *FLB* i. 7–8.

1833

1. AM 19–27.
2. Ibid. 29–33.

1834

1. *CLA* i. 82–4.
2. Ibid. 88–9.
3. *LBM* 16.
4. *CLA* i. 120.
5. Ibid. 123.
6. M. Pincherle (ed.), *Musiciens peints par eux-mêmes: Lettres de compositeurs écrites en français, 1771–1910* (Paris, 1939), 103.
7. *SJ* 8.
8. AM 37.

1835

1. J. K. Laughton, *Memoirs of the Life and Correspondence of Henry Reeve, C. B., D. C. L.*, i (London, 1898), 48–9.
2. AM 43–5.
3. R. Bory, *Une Retraite romantique en Suisse* (Lausanne, 1930), 31–3.
4. AM 51–6.
5. Bory, *Une Retraite*, 55.
6. AM 63–5.
7. *LBM* 25–6.

1836

1. *LBM* 30–1.
2. H. de Balzac, *Correspondance*, iii (Paris, 1964), 65.
3. *Vingt-Cinq Ans à Paris*, iii (Paris, 1914), 264–6.
4. Bory, *Une Retraite*, 35–8.
5. G. Sand, *Lettres d'un voyageur* (Paris, 1869), 289–90.
6. A. Pictet, *Une Course à Chamounix: Conte Fantastique* (Geneva, 1930), 15–29.
7. F. Denis, *Journal: 1829–1848* (Fribourg and Paris, 1932), 60.
8. C. E. and M. Hallé (eds.), *Life and Letters of Sir Charles Hallé* (London, 1896), 226–7.
9. Ibid. 37–8.

1837

1. The complete review is reprinted, in the original French, in *LSJ* (1986), 36–8.
2. J. G. Huneker, *Franz Liszt* (New York, 1911), 285–7.
3. E. A. Sharp (ed. and trans.), *Heine in Art and Letters* (London, 1895), 23–4.
4. 'Lettre d'un bachelier ès musique à M. Adolphe Pictet', *Revue et gazette musicale*, 11 Feb. 1838. Reprinted in *CLPR*, 128–46. This extract 129–36.
5. *SJ* 45–7.
6. AM 92.
7. Ibid. 105–6.
8. Ibid. 107–8.
9. Ibid. 112.

10. 'Lettre d'un bachelier ès musique à M. Louis de Ronchaud', *Revue et gazette musicale*, 25 Mar. 1838. Reprinted in *CLPR* 147–63. This extract 159–63.
11. 'Le Lac de Como: Lettre d'un bachelier ès musique à M. Louis de Ronchaud', *Revue et gazette musicale*, 22 July 1838. Reprinted in *CLPR* 164–76. This extract 164–8.
12. J. Vier, *Franz Liszt—L'Artiste, le clerc: Documents inédits* (Paris, 1950), 36.
13. *AM* 118–9.
14. Ibid. 119–20.
15. 'Lettre d'un bachelier ès musique à M. Lambert Massart', *Revue et gazette musicale*, 2 Sept. 1838. Reprinted in *CLPR* 207–40. This extract 212–14.

1838

1. *CLA* i. 209–10.
2. Vier, *Franz Liszt*, 39.
3. *CLPR* 215–17.
4. *AM* 138.
5. Ibid. 139.
6. *CLPR* 232–3.
7. *CLA* i. 214.
8. *LCS* i. 199.
9. Ibid.
10. P. von Neumann, *Diary: 1819–1850*, ii (London, 1928), 77.
11. F. Wieck, *Briefe aus den Jahren 1830–1838* (Cologne, 1968), 93.
12. *LCS* i. 199–200.
13. Neumann, *Diary*, 77.
14. Wieck, *Briefe*, 94.
15. *LCS* i. 198
16. Ibid. 200.
17. Neumann, *Diary*, 78.
18. Quoted by D. Legány, *Franz Liszt: Unbekannte Presse und Briefe aus Wien 1822–1886* (Budapest, 1984), 34–5.
19. Ibid. 39–40.
20. *CLA* i. 230–1.
21. W. Kuhe, *My Musical Recollections* (London, 1896), 130–2.
22. H. Ehrlich, *Dreissig Jahre Künstlerleben* (Berlin, 1893), 119–21.
23. Legány, *Unbekannte Presse*, 32–3.
24. *L'Artiste* (Paris, 1839), 2e Série, iv. 156.
25. Ibid. 157.

1839

1. *FLB* i. 25.
2. Ibid. 26.
3. *AM* 167.
4. 'Lettre d'un bachelier ès musique à M. Hector Berlioz', *Revue et gazette musicale*, 24 Oct. 1839. Reprinted in *CLPR*, 257–67. This extract 261–3.
5. Ibid. 265.
6. Legány, *Unbekannte Presse*, 61–2.
7. Ibid. 65.
8. Ibid. 70–1.

1840

1. J. Pardoe, *The City of the Magyar, or Hungary and her Institutions in 1839–40, iii (London, 1840), 343–55.*
2. *CLA* i. 357.
3. W. von Csapó (ed.), *Franz Liszt's Briefe an Baron Anton Augusz 1846–1878* (Budapest, 1911), 3–4.
4. *CLA* i. 391–2.
5. Ibid. 411–12.
6. R. Schumann, *Music and Musicians: Essays and Criticisms* (London, 1877), 144–6.
7. L*CS* i. 413.
8. Ibid. 414.
9. Ibid.
10. Schumann, *Music and Musicians*, 147–9.
11. L*CS* i. 416.
12. Ibid. 417.
13. Schumann, *Music and Musicians*, 150–4.
14. F. Mendelssohn, *Letters*, ed. G. Selden-Goth (London, 1946), 289–90.
15. F. Niecks, *Frederick Chopin as a Man and Musician*, ii (London, 1890), 342.
16. Barbey-Boissier, *La Comtesse Agénor*, 332–3.
17. *CLA* i. 444.
18. C. K. Rogers, *Memories of a Musical Career* (Plimpton Press, 1932), 54.
19. F.F. Buffen, *Franz Liszt: A Memoir* (London and New York, 1886), 36–7.
20. *CLA* i. 450.
21. Numerous press reviews of Liszt's British concerts have been reprinted in *LSJ* (1983–7).
22. *CLA* ii. 14–15.
23. Ibid. 17–18.
24. Ibid. 25.
25. Ibid. 26–7.
26. Ibid. 29.
27. Ibid. 30.
28. C. Reinecke, *'Und manche liebe Schatten steigen auf': Gedenkblätter an berühmte Musiker* (Leipzig, 1910), 11–13.
29. H. C. Andersen, *A Poet's Bazaar*, trans. C. Beckwith, i (London, 1846), 48–54.
30. *Revue des Deux Mondes*, xxiv (Paris, 1840), 612.
31. The full texts of the diaries kept by Parry on this and the earlier tour have been published in *LSJ* vi (1981), 2–16, and vii (1982), 16–26.

1841

1. Neumann, *Diary*, 168.
2. C. Moscheles, *Aus Moscheles' Leben, nach Briefen und Tagebüchern*, ii (Leipzig, 1873), 76.
3. 'Lettre d'un bachelier ès musique à M. Léon Kreutzer', *Revue et gazette musicale*, 19 Sept. 1841, 418–19.
4. M. Herwegh, *Au Banquet des Dieux: Franz Liszt, Richard Wagner et leurs amis* (Paris, 1931), 24.

5. E. Jacobs, 'Franz Liszt und die Gräfin d'Agoult in Nonnenwerth 1841–1842', *Die Musik* (Oct. 1911), 35–8, 40–2.
6. Ibid. 94, 95, 98–9, 102.
7. K. von Schlözer, *Briefe eines Diplomaten*, ed. H. Flügel (Stuttgart, 1957), 9–10.
8. E. Genast, *Aus Weimars klassischer und nachklassischer Zeit: Erinnerungen eines alten Schauspielers* (Stuttgart, 1905), 308–10.
9. E. Schumann, *Robert Schumann: Ein Lebensbild meines Vaters* (Leipzig, 1931), 313.
10. Ibid. 313–15.
11. *CLA* ii. 184.
12. E. Schumann, *Robert Schumann*, 315–16.
13. K. A. Varnhagen von Ense, *Tagebücher*, i (Leipzig, 1861), 385–6.
14. L. Rellstab, *Franz Liszt: Beurtheilungen, Berichte, Lebensskizze* (Berlin, 1842), 2–5.

1842

1. E. Devrient, *Aus seinen Tagebüchern: Berlin-Dresden 1836–1852*, ed. R. Kabel (Weimar, 1964), 136–7.
2. *CLA* ii. 191.
3. Ibid. 194–5.
4. Ibid. 197–200.
5. Varnhagen, *Tagebücher*, ii. 16.
6. *CLA* ii. 262–5.
7. Rellstab, *Franz Liszt*, 74–5.
8. Jacobs, 'Franz Liszt und die Gräfin d'Agoult', 105–6.
9. Devrient, *Aus seinen Tagebüchern*, 140.
10. Rellstab, *Franz Liszt*, 37–9, 46.
11. Devrient, *Aus seinen Tagebüchern*, 140.
12. R*LKM* ii (i), 183.
13. *LZB* 332–3.
14. V. V. Stasov, *Liszt, Schumann and Berlioz in Russia* (St Petersburg, 1896), 10–12.
15. Ibid. 21–2.
16. *CLA* ii. 218–19.
17. G. Vinant, *Malwida de Meysenbug: Sa Vie et Ses Amis* (Paris, 1932), 46.
18. *CLA* ii. 242.
19. R. Wagner, *My Life*, i (London, 1911), 289–92. (A few minor alterations have been made to this and later quotations from the same source to make them a more faithful rendering of the original German.)

1843

1. E. Hanska, 'Journal', *L'Année Balzacienne* (Paris, 1962), 20–3.
2. Stasov, *Liszt, Schumann and Berlioz*, 33.
3. Hanska, 'Journal', 23.
4. A. Herzen, *My Past and Thoughts*, trans. C. Garnett, i (London, 1924), 143–4.
5. Hanska, 'Journal', 24–8.
6. J. Werner, *Maxe von Arnim: Ein Lebens- und Zeitbild* (Leipzig, 1937), 123–4.

1844

1. Quoted in R*LKM* ii (i), 225.
2. J. Janin, *Correspondance* (Paris, 1877), 72.
3. M. Carrières, *Franz Liszt en Provence et en Languedoc en 1844* (Béziers, 1981), 13–14.
4. *LBM* 61–2.

1845

1. D. Ollivier (ed.), *Autour de Mme d'Agoult et de Liszt (Alfred de Vigny, Emile Ollivier, Princesse de Belgiojoso): Lettres publiées avec introduction et notes* (Paris, 1941), 186–7.
2. S. I. M. *Revue musicale mensuelle*, xii (1911), 78–9.
3. Quoted by R. Stevenson, 'Liszt on the East Coast of Spain', *JALS* iv (Dec. 1978), 15.
4. Vier, *Franz Liszt*, 77–8.
5. K. Schorn, *Lebenserinnerungen: Ein Beitrag zur Geschichte des Rheinlands im neunzehnten Jahrhundert*, i (Bonn, 1898), 193–200.
6. Moscheles, *Aus Moscheles' Leben*, 140–1.
7. Schorn, *Lebenserinnerungen*, 201–5.
8. Moscheles, *Aus Moscheles' Leben*, 142.
9. Schorn, *Lebenserinnerungen*, 205–11.
10. Quoted by J. Penning, 'Liszt in Luxembourg', *LSJ* ix (1984), 46.

1846

1. *CLA* ii. 345.
2. Ibid. 350–3.
3. J. Schondorff (ed.), *Europäische Zeitenwende* (Munich, 1960), 143.
4. A. Rubinstein, *Autobiography*, trans. A. Delano (Boston, 1890), 20–32.
5. J. N. Dunkl, *Aus den Erinnerungen eines Musikers* (Vienna, 1876), 6–9.
6. H. Berlioz, *Mémoires*, ii (Paris, 1887), 254–6.
7. A. Buchner, *Franz Liszt in Bohemia*, trans. R. F. Samsour (London, 1962), 146–7.
8. *CLA* ii. 363–4.
9. Dunkl, *Aus den Erinnerungen*, 9–12.
10. C. Glossy (ed.), 'Aus Bauernfelds Tagebüchern', i (1819–1848), 126, in *Jahrbuch der Grillparzer-Gesellschaft* (Vienna, 1895).
11. Dunkl, *Aus den Erinnerungen*, 12–18.
12. *LBM* 72–5.

1847

1. *CLA* ii. 370–2.
2. *FLB* viii. 50–1.

1848

1. *FLB* iv. 30.
2. Ibid i. 72.
3. Dunkl, *Aus den Erinnerungen*, 19–22.
4. *LZB* 334–51.
5. H. Rollett, *Begegnungen: Erinnerungsblätter (1819–1899)* (Vienna, 1903), 167–9.

6. Reinecke, *Gedenkblätter*, 13–19.

1849

1. Wagner, *My Life*, i. 500–1.
2. H. von Bülow, *The Early Correspondence*. Edited by His Widow; selected and trans. C. Bache (London, 1896), 32–3.
3. Ibid. 34–6.
4. *BLCA* 26.
5. L*ZB*, 352–60.
6. R. Göhler (ed.), *Grossherzog Carl Alexander und Fanny Lewald-Stahr in ihren Briefen 1848–1889*, i (Berlin, 1932), 33.

1850

1. Vier, *Franz Liszt*, 99.
2. L. Meinardus, *Ein Jugendleben*, ii (Gotha, 1874), 155–61, 169–71.
3. Ibid. 188–9.
4. M. Marchesi, *Aus meinem Leben* (Düsseldorf, 1889), 50–2.
5. *CLMO*, 48–50.
6. Ibid. 55–6.
7. Reinecke, *Gedenkblätter*, 20–2.

1851

1. *FLB* iv. 43.
2. E. Kloss (ed.), *Briefwechsel zwischen Wagner und Liszt* (3rd rev. edn.; Leipzig, 1910), i (1841–53), 114–15.
3. *FLB* iv. 96–8.
4. L*ZB*, 360–70.
5. Bülow, *Correspondence*, 81–2.
6. Meinardus, *Ein Jugendleben*, 298–9.
7. Bülow, *Correspondence*, 85–6.
8. Meinardus, *Ein Jugendleben*, 300–1.
9. L*CS* ii. 263–4.
10. Bülow, *Correspondence*, 91.
11. T. von Bernhardi, *Aus dem Leben*, ii (Leipzig, 1893): 'Briefe und Tagebuchblätter aus den Jahren 1834–1857', 98–9, 101–5.
12. Bülow, *Correspondence*, 95–6.
13. Bernhardi, *Leben*, 107–8.

1852

1. Kloss, *Wagner–Liszt Briefwechsel*, 337.
2. Bülow, *Correspondence*, 106.
3. Ibid. 111–13.
4. Ibid. 116.
5. H. C. Andersen, *Dagbøger 1851–1860* (Copenhagen, 1974), 88–91.
6. Bülow, *Correspondence*, 118.
7. Ibid. 121.
8. C. Wagner, *Franz Liszt: Ein Gedenkblatt von seiner Tochter* (2nd edn., Munich, 1911), 74–5.

9. *SZM* 48.
10. A. Moser, *Joseph Joachim* (London, 1901), 94.

1853

1. *CAB* i. 140–1.
2. W. Mason, *Memories of a Musical Life* (New York, 1901), 90–144.
3. R. Wagner, *My Life*, ii. 598–9.
4. Meinardus, *Ein Jugendleben*, 315–17.
5. *FLB* iv. 156–7.
6. Buchner, *Liszt in Bohemia*, 157–61.
7. Ibid. 166–7.
8. R. Wagner, *My Life*, ii. 605–9.
9. J. Janin, *735 Lettres à sa femme*, ii (Paris, 1975), 379–80.
10. F. Soret, *Un Genevois à la Cour de Weimar* (Paris, 1932), 72, 94, 121.
11. *FLB* i. 144–5.
12. *CAB* i. 146–7.
13. Ibid. 150.

1854

1. E. Ritter von Liszt, *Franz Liszt: Abstammung, Familie, Begebenheiten* (Vienna and Leipzig, 1937), 82–3.
2. C. Wagner, *Franz Liszt*, 76–7.
3. *FLB* iv. 195.
4. J. W. Cross (ed.), *George Eliot's Life as Related in Her Letters and Journals*, i (Edinburgh and London, 1885), 344–9. (Some short omissions from the text, as edited by Cross, have been added from the full version of certain paragraphs given in the following source.)
5. G. S. Haight, *George Eliot: A Biography* (Oxford, 1968), 168.
6. *Fraser's Magazine* (July 1855), 48–9.
7. *CLMO* 106.
8. R. Pohl, *Franz Liszt: Studien und Erinnerungen* (Leipzig, 1883), 58–64.
9. *CAB* i. 174.
10. Ibid. 175–7.
11. Ibid. 181.
12. F. von Milde, *Ein ideales Künstlerpaar*, i (Leipzig, 1918), 35.

1855

1. Milde, *Ein ideales Künstlerpaar*, 35–6.
2. Kloss, *Wagner–Liszt Briefwechsel*, ii (1854–82), 65.
3. La Mara, *Durch Musik und Leben im Dienste des Ideals* (Leipzig, 1917), i. 24.
4. *LCS* ii. 378.
5. Soret, *Un Genevois*, 137–41.
6. *FLB* iv. 222–3.
7. Ibid. iii. 33.
8. Ibid. iv. 235.
9. Ibid. iii. 39.
10. Lady W. Paget, *Scenes and Memories* (London, 1912), 40–1.
11. R. Bory, *Liszt et ses enfants* (Paris, 1936), 105–9.

12. O. Roquette, *Siebzig Jahre: Geschichte meines Lebens* (Darmstadt, 1894), ii. 74–5.
13. *BLB* 152–3.

1856

1. *BLB* 173–4.
2. *SZM* 81–2.
3. La Mara, *Musik und Leben*, i. 26–32.
4. Andersen, *Dagbøger 1851–1860*, 215–16.
5. Kloss, *Wagner–Liszt Briefwechsel*, ii. 124–6.
6. *FLB* iv. 316.
7. Ibid. 328.
8. Csapó, *Liszt's Briefe*, 4.
9. *FLB* iii. 80–1.
10. M. Prahács (ed.), *Franz Liszt: Briefe aus ungarischen Sammlungen, 1835–1886* (Kassel, 1966), 93.
11. R. Wagner, *My Life*, ii. 648–55.
12. *SZM* 87–9.
13. A. W. Gottschalg, *Franz Liszt in Weimar und seine letzten Lebensjahre* (Berlin, 1910), 50.

1857

1. *FLB* i. 263.
2. La Mara, *Musik und Leben*, i. 35–6.
3. *FLB* i. 269.
4. Ibid. 271.
5. G. von Schultz, *Briefe eines baltischen Idealisten* (Leipzig, 1934), 144–7.
6. *LBM* 111–12.
7. *SZM*, 92–3.
8. Quoted by F. Bartos, *Smetana in Briefen und Erinnerungen* (Prague, 1954). Reprinted by W. Reich, *Gespräche mit Komponisten* (Zurich, 1965), 131–4.
9. M. Herwegh, *Au Printemps des Dieux* (Paris, 1929), 215.

1858

1. W. Weissheimer, *Erlebnisse mit Richard Wagner, Franz Liszt und vielen anderen Zeitgenossen* (Stuttgart, 1898), 16–20.
2. *FLB* iv. 423–4.
3. *CAB* i. 275–6.
4. F. Hebbel, *Werke*, v (Munich, 1967), 796–7.
5. *FLB* iii. 111.
6. Roquette, *Siebzig Jahre*, 110–13.
7. O. von Riesemann, 'Alexander Serov and his Relations to Wagner and Liszt', *The Musical Quarterly*, ix (New York, 1923), 465–6.
8. Varnhagen, *Tagebücher*, xiv. 333–4.
9. *LAG*, 343–4.
10. Legány, *Unbekannte Presse*, 157.
11. 'Pauline Viardot-Garcia to Julius Rietz: Letters of Friendship', *The Musical Quarterly*, i (New York, 1915), 357–8, 361–3.

12. *CAB* i. 301–2.
13. Ibid. 302–3.
14. Ibid. 304.
15. Viardot-Garcia, 'Letters', 365–7.

1859

1. *LAG*, 352–3.
2. Weissheimer, *Erlebnisse*, 37–43.
3. Moscheles, *Aus Moscheles' Leben*, 292.
4. Herwegh, *Au Printemps*, 228.
5. *FLB* iv. 490.
6. Ibid. i. 329–31.
7. Ibid. iv. 492–3.
8. Ibid. 495.
9. Ibid. 500–4, 506–7.

1860

1. Csapó, *Liszt's Briefe*, 93–5.
2. Weissheimer, *Erlebnisse*, 51–3, 57.
3. *CLMO* 242.
4. *CAB* i. 450.
5. Ibid. 461.
6. *FLB* v. 25–6.
7. Kloss, *Wagner–Liszt Briefwechsel*, ii. 296.
8. *FLB* v. 52–3, 55–6, 63.
9. *CAB* i. 521.
10. Ibid. 522.
11. *FLB* iii. 135–6.
12. *SZM* 103.
13. Ibid.

1861

1. *FLB* v. 128–9.
2. Weissheimer, *Erlebnisse*, 62–3.
3. Herwegh, *Au Printemps*, 238.
4. *FLB* v. 168–9.
5. R. Wagner, *My Life*, ii. 779–80.
6. Quoted in E. Ollivier, *Journal 1846–1869*, ii (Paris, 1961), 454–6.
7. Ibid. 21–3.
8. *CLMO* 274.
9. Ibid. 278.
10. *CAB* i. 605.
11. Milde, *Ein ideales Künstlerpaar*, i. 164–5.
12. Weissheimer, *Erlebnisse*, 68–72.
13. R. Wagner, *My Life*, ii. 787–8.
14. E. Ollivier, *Journal 1846–1869*, ii. 28.
15. R. Wagner, *My Life*, ii. 788–9.
16. Gottschalg, *Liszt in Weimar*, 46–7.
17. R. Wagner, *My Life*, ii. 789–90.

18. *SZM* 106–7.
19. M. P. Eckhardt and C. Knotik, *Franz Liszt und sein Kreis in Briefen und Dokumenten aus den Beständen des Burgenländischen Landesmuseums* (Eisenstadt, 1983), 35–6.
20. *CLMO* 297–8.

1862

1. *CLMO* 313–14.
2. C. Bache, *Brother Musicians: Reminiscences of Edward and Walter Bache* (London, 1901), 151–2.
3. Ibid. 157.
4. E. Ollivier, *Journal*, 56–7.
5. *BLCA* 115–16.
6. *FLB* ii. 32–3.
7. *LBM* 145–6.

1863

1. *FLB* ii. 41.
2. Ibid. 46.
3. Ibid. viii. 161.

1864

1. F. Gregorovius, *Roman Journals 1852–1874* (London, 1911), 202.
2. Ehrlich, *Künstlerleben*, 114–19.
3. *SRB* 71–4.
4. Ibid. 105–6.
5. Riesemann, 'Alexander Serov', 467–8.
6. *LZB* 375–7.
7. *SRB* 168–70.

1865

1. *SRB* 181–2.
2. E. M. Oakeley, *The Life of Sir Herbert Oakeley* (London, 1904), 94–6.
3. *FLB* ii. 78–9.
4. Ibid. vi. 72–3.
5. *SRB* 211.
6. Gregorovius, *Roman Journals*, 230.
7. E. Ollivier, *Journal*, 188–9.
8. *FLB* vi. 78.
9. *SRB*, 214–15.
10. Gregorovius, *Roman Journals*, 231.
11. *FLB* ii. 81.
12. Ibid. viii. 170–1.
13. *SRB* 217–18.
14. The diary of Anna Augusz is reproduced, in the original French, in: A. Hadnagy and M. Prahács, 'Liszt szekszárdi kapcsolatairol', *Tanulmanyok Tolna* megyetörténetéből ii (Szekszárd, 1969). These excerpts, 230–2, 233–5, 239, 241–2, 243.
15. *SZM* 113–14.

1866

1. Gregorovius, *Roman Journals*, 245.
2. Ibid. 247–8.
3. E. Ollivier, *Journal*, 238.
4. J. Harding, *Saint-Saëns and His Circle* (London, 1965), 48–9.
5. Bache, *Brother Musicians*, 192–3.
6. *FLB* vi. 100–2.
7. L. de Hegermann-Lindencrone, *In the Courts of Memory* (New York and London, 1912), 161–5.
8. *FLB* vi. 110–11.
9. Ibid. 113.
10. Csapó, *Liszt's Briefe*, 117.
11. E. Ollivier, *Journal*, 243.
12. Ibid. 246–7.
13. *FLB* iii. 188–90.
14. *LZB* 379–81.

1867

1. A. Stahr and F. Lewald, *Ein Winter in Rom* (Berlin, 1871), 155.
2. *FLB* iii. 191–2.
3. *SRB* 321.
4. J. Wohl, *François Liszt: Souvenirs d'une compatriote* (Paris, 1887), 20–4.
5. *SRB* 336–7.
6. *LAG* 429–30.
7. *SZM* 117–18.
8. *CAB* ii. 535.
9. D. Halévy, *The Life of Friedrich Nietzsche* (London, 1911), 57.
10. *SZM*, 122–3.
11. E. Ollivier, *Journal*, 299.
12. Weissheimer, *Erlebnisse*, 371–2.
13. La Mara, *Musik und Leben*, i. 79–84.
14. R. Pohl, 'Liszts Besuch in Triebschen', *Richard Wagner-Jahrbuch* (Stuttgart, 1886), i. 80–4.

1868

1. *SRB* 354–5.
2. Ibid. 358.
3. C. L. Graves, *The Life and Letters of Sir George Grove, C. B.* (London, 1903), 162–4.
4. H. Kiener, *Marie Jaëll* (Paris, 1952), 64.
5. M. Jaëll, *La Musique et la psychophysiologie* (Paris, 1896), 103–5.
6. E. Ollivier, *Journal*, 325–6.
7. *FLB* vi. 174–5, 179, 183–4, 186.
8. N. Helbig, 'Franz Liszt in Rom', *Deutsche Revue* (1907), i. 175–6.
9. *SZM* 141–2.
10. G. P. A. Healy, *Reminiscences of a Portrait Painter* (Chicago, 1894), 219–21.

1869

1. *SZM* 148–9.
2. Ibid. 152.

3. Ibid. 155.
4. W. Beatty-Kingston, *Men, Cities and Events* (London, 1895), 120–1, 123–4; *Music and Manners*, i (London, 1887), 41–2, 227–30.
5. Princess M. von Thurn und Taxis, *Memoirs of a Princess* (London, 1959), 71–2.
6. *SZM* 165.
7. J. Gautier, *Le Troisième Rang du collier* (Paris, 1909), 146–57.
8. V. V. Stasov, *Selected Essays on Music,* trans. F. Jonas (London, 1968), 49.
9. R. Franz, *Souvenirs d'une cosaque* (Paris, 1874), 98–101, 110–21, 138–42, 161–5, 169–71, 173–6.
10. *FLB* vi. 228–9.

1870

1. D. Monrad-Johansen, *Edvard Grieg* (New York, 1938), 115.
2. Ibid. 123–5, 126–7.
3. Ibid. 127.
4. Kapp, *Franz Liszt*, 112–13.
5. *SZM* 175–6.
6. La Mara, *Musik und Leben*, i. 111–16.
7. B. Kellermann, *Erinnerungen: Ein Künstlerleben* (Zurich, 1932), 15–16.
8. La Mara, *Musik und Leben*, i. 118–21.
9. A. von Schorn, *Das nachklassische Weimar*, ii (Weimar, 1912). 244–5. (A reprint from the *Münchner Neueste Nachrichten*, 22 Oct. 1911.)
10. *LZB* 382.

1871

1. *FLB* vi. 290.
2. Ibid. 293.
3. E. Ritter von Liszt, *Franz Liszt*, 67–8.
4. B. E., 'Reminiscences of Liszt', *Temple Bar*, lxxviii (London, 1886), 55–60.
5. H. Maréchal, *Rome: Souvenirs d'un musicien* (Paris, 1904), 110–19.

1872

1. *FLB* vi. 321.
2. Ibid. 322.
3. Ibid. 334–5.
4. Ibid. 330.
5. G. Colli and M. Montinari (eds.), *Briefe an Friedrich Nietzsche* (Berlin, 1977), ii (ii), 557–8.
6. P. Raabe, *Liszts Leben* (Tutzing, 1968), 217.
7. *SZM* 211–12.
8. *FLB* vi. 349–50.
9. Ibid. 350.
10. *SZM* 219–20.
11. *FLB* vi. 351–2.
12. *SZM* 222–4.
13. *FLB* vi. 369–70.

1873

1. *FLB* vii. 10.
2. *ZAL* i. 159–60; ii. 12, 20–2.

3. Kellermann, *Erinnerungen*, 19–26, 31–4, 43–53.
4. A. Fay, *Music Study in Germany* (London, 1886), 187–8, 189–92, 193–6, 197, 199–201.
5. La Mara, *Musik und Leben*, i. 171–2.
6. *SZM* 234.
7. V. d' Indy, 'Franz Liszt en 1873', S. I. M. *Revue musicale mensuelle* (Sept. 1911), 6–10.
8. Fay, *Music Study*, 203–5, 207–11.
9. La Mara, *Musik und Leben*, i. 173–4.
10. Fay, *Music Study*, 212–13, 217–22.
11. *SZM* 236.
12. Ibid. 237–8.
13. Fay, *Music Study*, 228–30, 231–2, 242–9.
14. Huneker, *Franz Liszt*, 396–7.

1874

1. Count A. Apponyi, *Memoirs* (London, 1935), 69–75.
2. *SZM* 242.
3. *FLB* vii. 72.
4. Ibid. 73.
5. Ibid. 81–2.
6. *SZM* 250–1, 256–7, 260–2, 265–7, 269–71, 273.

1875

1 *SZM* 278–80, 281–3, 286.
2. Apponyi, *Memoirs*, 82–8.
3. Schultz, *Briefe* 280–2.
4. M. Hauk, *Memoirs of a Singer* (London, 1925), 104–6.
5. *Briefe hervorragender Zeitgenossen an Franz Liszt* (ed. La Mara), iii (Leipzig, 1904), 191–2.
6. Eckhardt and Knotik, *Franz Liszt*, 66–9.
7. *Letters of Richard Wagner to Emil Heckel* (London, 1899), 87–8.
8. Sir C. V. Stanford, *Pages From An Unwritten Diary* (London, 1914), 148–9.
9. *SZM* 309–10.
10. *FLB* vii. 118.
11. *LLM* 213.

1876

1. C. V. Lachmund, *Mein Leben mit Franz Liszt* (Eschwege, 1970), 140.
2. *LLM* 235
3. *FLB* vii. 131.
4. Ibid. viii. 309.
5. F. Corder, *Ferencz Liszt* (London, 1925), 109–10.
6. B. Litzmann (ed.), *Clara Schumann–Johannes Brahms. Briefe aus den Jahren 1853–1896*, ii (Leipzig, 1927), 68.
7. Stasov, *Liszt, Schumann and Berlioz*, 166.
8. *FLB* vii. 144–5.
9. Kellermann, *Erinnerungen*, 193–5.
10. Apponyi, *Memoirs*, 100–1.
11. *FLB* vii. 155.

12. Ibid.
13. Wohl, *François Liszt*, 91–111.
14. *ZAL* ii. 23–30.

1877

1. *FLB* vii. 172.
2. *LLM* 266–7.
3. *ZAL* ii. 32–3, 37–8.
4. *FLB* vii. 177.
5. W. Kienzl, *Meine Lebenswanderung* (Stuttgart, 1926), 44–5.
6. From an unpublished letter held at the Dept. of Music, National Széchényi Library, Budapest.
7. K. Guenther, *Gerhard Rohlfs: Lebensbild eines Afrikaforschers* (Freiburg im Breisgau, 1912), 304–7.
8. *FLB* vii. 193.
9. A. Habets, *Borodin and Liszt* (London, 1895), 111–27.
10. *FLB* vii. 197.
11. Habets, *Borodin and Liszt*, 131–41, 143–8, 154–8.
12. Kienzl, *Lebenswanderung*, 57–60.
13. *FLB*, vii. 202.
14. R. Voss, *Aus einem phantastischen Leben* (Stuttgart, 1920), 95–7.
15. Mrs W. Chanler, *Roman Spring* (Boston, 1934), 83–6.
16. *SZM* 339–40.
17. G. Zichy, 'Franz Liszt: Erinnerungen', *Deutsche Revue*, Apr/June 1904 (Stuttgart, 1904), 163–4.
18. *LLM* 299.
19. *FLB* vii. 207.

1878

1. I. Horovitz-Barnay, 'Im Hause Franz Liszts: Erlebnisse und Gespräche mit dem Meister', *Deutsche Revue*, July/Sept. 1898 (Stuttgart, 1898), 82–3.
2. E. Hanslick, *Aus meinem Leben*, ii (Berlin, 1894), 184–9.
3. *SZM* 348.
4. M. von Meysenbug, *Im Anfang war die Liebe: Briefe an ihre Pflegetochter* (Munich, 1926), 92–6.
5. M. Rosenthal, 'Franz Liszt: Erinnerungen und Betrachtungen', *Die Musik* xli (Berlin and Leipzig, 1911–12), 46–7.
6. Huneker, *Franz Liszt*, 367.
7. *SZM* 352.
8. *FLB* vii. 237.
9. Ibid. 237–8.

1879

1. *ZAL* ii. 57–8.
2. S. Czech, *Schön ist die Welt: Franz Lehár's Leben und Werk* (Berlin, 1957), 42.
3. Quoted by Prahács, *Franz Liszt*, 381.
4. *FLB* vii. 245–6.
5. F. Eckstein, *'Alte unnennbare Tage!'* (Vienna, 1936), 241–2.

6. E. Hanslick, *Concerte, Componisten und Virtuosen der letzen fünfzehn Jahre: 1870–1885* (Berlin, 1886), 241–4.
7. A. Gutmann, *Aus dem Wiener Musikleben: Künstler-Erinnerungen 1873–1908*, i (Vienna, 1914), 51.
8. *FLB* vii. 258–9.
9. Kienzl, *Lebenswanderung*, 85–6.
10. *SZM* 364–6.
11. J. F. Cooke, *Great Pianists on Piano Playing* (Philadelphia, 1913), 226–7.
12. *FLB* vii. 267.
13. B. Walker, *My Musical Experiences* (London, 1890), 80–4.
14. Guenther, *Gerhard Rohlfs*, 308–9.
15. Helbig, 'Franz Liszt in Rom', 176.

1880

1. *ZAL* ii. 8–9.
2. *SZM* 373–4.
3. R.F. Thomas, *Memoirs of Theodore Thomas* (New York, 1911), 184.
4. L. Auer, *My Long Life in Music* (London, 1924), 239–41.
5. H. E. Hugo (ed.), *The Letters of Franz Liszt to Marie zu Sayn-Wittgenstein* (New York, 1953), 246.
6. *FLB* vii. 302.
7. *SZM* 379.
8. *FLB* vii. 303.
9. Revd H. R. Haweis, *My Musical Life* (London, 1884), 653–4, 663–6, 608.
10. *LLM* 391–2.

1881

1. *LZB* 391–5.
2. *FLB* vii. 306.
3. Ibid. 311–12.
4. *ZAL* ii. 101–4.
5. *SZM* 383–5.
6. Habets, *Borodin and Liszt*, 160–78, 188–92.
7. *SZM* 390–1.
8. Ibid. 394.
9. La Mara, *Musik und Leben*, i. 355–6.
10. *FLB* vii. 324.
11. Ibid. 325–7.
12. *SZM* 398.
13. M. Freiherr von Waldberg (ed.), *Cosima Wagners Briefe an Ihre Tochter Daniela von Bülow 1866–1885* (Stuttgart and Berlin, 1933), 235, 240.
14. *SZM* 398–403.
15. Helbig, 'Franz Liszt in Rom', 177–8.

1882

1. *SZM* 413–14.
2. A. de Gubernatis, *Fibra: Pagine di Ricordi* (Rome, 1900), 344–5.
3. *FLB* vii. 337–8.
4. Lachmund, *Mein Leben*, 31–6, 53.

5. Ibid. 67–8.
6. W. Raupp, *Eugen d'Albert: Ein Künstler- und Menschenschicksal* (Leipzig, 1930), 42.
7. Lachmund, *Mein Leben*, 82–3.
8. W. Damrosch, *My Musical Life* (London, 1924), 36–40.
9. *SZM* 423–5.
10. F. Weingartner, *Lebenserinnerungen* (Vienna, 1923), 151–6.
11. Göllerich, *Franz Liszt*, 1.
12. Lachmund, *Mein Leben*, 163–5.
13. *SZM* 432.
14. *BLCA* 192–3.
15. *FLB* vii. 368–9.
16. A. Wolkoff-Mouromtzoff, *Memoirs* (London, 1928), 205–10.
17. S. Wagner, *Erinnerungen* (Stuttgart, 1923), 20–2.
18. C. F. Glasenapp, *Das Leben Richard Wagners*, vi (Leipzig, 1911), 735.

1883

1. *ZAL* iii. 39–40.
2. *FLB* vii. 379.
3. *SZM* 441.
4. Ibid.
5. A. Siloti, *My Memories of Liszt* (Edinburgh, 1913), 14–18, 20–1, 24–32, 35–40.
6. *SZM* 442.
7. S. Ochs, *Geschehenes, Gesehenes* (Leipzig, 1922), 205–8.
8. Walker, *Musical Experiences*, 104–7, 118–21, 125–30.
9. Lachmund, *Mein Leben*, 247–8.
10. *FLB* viii. 408.
11. Ibid. vii. 388.
12. *ZAL* iii. 43.
13. *FLB* vii. 395.

1884

1. Csapó, *Liszt's Briefe*, 36–7.
2. La Mara, *Musik und Leben*, ii. 61–2.
3. Göllerich, *Franz Liszt*, 2–4.
4. E. Sauer, *Meine Welt* (Stuttgart, 1901), 163–76.
5. Göllerich, *Franz Liszt*, 5, 16–21.
6. Weingartner, *Lebenserinnerungen*, 241–2.
7. Ibid. 243.
8. *SZM* 452–3.
9. F. Hueffer, *Half a Century of Music in England, 1837–1887* (London, 1889), 111–14.
10. *ZAL* iii. 56–61.
11. Sir A. C. Mackenzie, *A Musician's Narrative* (London, 1927), 125–8.

1885

1. L. de Hegermann-Lindencrone, *The Sunny Side of Diplomatic Life* (New York and London, 1914), 151–61.
2. T. A. Trollope, *What I Remember*, iii (London, 1889), 240–1.

3. *SZM* 456–7.
4. A. Stradal, *Erinnerungen an Franz Liszt* (Berne, 1929), 52–4, 62–4, 64–6, 68–9, 70–2.
5. Ibid. 90–2.
6. Rosenthal, 'Franz Liszt', 50–1.
7. *SZM* 457–8.
8. Stradal, *Erinnerungen*, 94–5.
9. F. Lamond, *Memoirs* (Glasgow, 1949), 66–70.
10. Stradal, *Erinnerungen*, 99–100.
11. Göllerich, *Franz Liszt*, 111–12.
12. A. Friedheim, *Life and Liszt: The Recollections of a Concert Pianist* (New York, 1961), 146–7.
13. Gottschalg, *Liszt in Weimar*, 153–4.
14. Göllerich, *Franz Liszt*, 114–15.
15. F. Semon, *Autobiography* (London, 1926), 126–7.
16. Stradal, *Erinnerungen*, 125–6.
17. Göllerich, *Franz Liszt*, 119–22.

1886–1887

1. Göllerich, *Franz Liszt*, 122–3.
2. Stradal, *Erinnerungen*, 136–7.
3. Eckstein, '*Alte unnennbare Tage!*', 89–90.
4. F. Klose, *Meine Lehrjahre bei Bruckner: Erinnerungen und Betrachtungen* (Regensburg, 1927), 405–6.
5. Buffen, *Franz Liszt*, 38–9.
6. H. Klein, *Thirty Years of Musical Life in London 1870–1900* (London, 1903), 178–9.
7. *Pall Mall Gazette*, 7 Apr. 1886, 4–5.
8. Klein, *Thirty Years*, 180.
9. Quoted by H. Westerby, *Liszt, Composer, and His Piano Works* (London, 1936), 87.
10. Bache, *Brother Musicians*, 289–90.
11. Princess Marie zu Erbach-Schönberg, *Reminiscences* (London, 1925), 233–4.
12. A. Hollins, *A Blind Musician Looks Back* (Edinburgh and London, 1936), 160–1.
13. Graves, *Letters of Sir George Grove*, 311–12.
14. *Grove's Dictionary of Music and Musicians*, ii (London, 1906), 749.
15. Kuhe, *Recollections*, 145.
16. *FLB* vii. 436–7.
17. B. Stoker, *Personal Reminiscences of Henry Irving*, ii (London, 1906), 145–7.
18. Bache, *Brother Musicians, 293–5.*
19. Mackenzie, *Narrative*, 149.
20. *SZM* 464.
21. Stradal, *Erinnerungen*, 140–1.
22. Göllerich, *Franz Liszt*, 149–57.
23. Damrosch, *Life*, 47–9.
24. Göllerich, *Franz Liszt*, 164, 176.
25. Ibid. 170–2.

26. Guenther, *Gerhard Rohlfs*, 309–10.
27. La Mara, *Musik und Leben*, ii. 127–9.
28. Göllerich, *Franz Liszt*, 183–5.
29. Quoted by G. May, *Franz Liszt und Luxemburg* (Luxemburg, 1986), 104.
30. Quoted by Penning, 'Liszt in Luxembourg', 49.
31. C. Wagner, *Franz Liszt*, 70.
32. *SZM* 466.
33. Weingartner, *Lebenserinnerungen*, 341.
34. *SZM* 466–7.
35. C. Wagner, *Franz Liszt*, loc. cit.
36. Stradal, *Erinnerungen*, 144.
37. Weingartner, *Lebenserinnerungen*, 341–3.
38. Stradal, *Erinnerungen*, 144–5.
39. Translation by M. Boileau, *Monthly Musical Record* (London), Jan. 1929.
40. M. von Meyensbug, *Der Lebensabend einer Idealistin* (Berlin and Leipzig, 1898), 103–5.
41. L. Ramann, *Lisztiana: Erinnerungen an Franz Liszt in Tagebuchblättern, Briefen und Dokumenten aus den Jahren 1873–1886/87* (Mainz, 1983), 383.

BIBLIOGRAPHY

AGOULT, Comtesse d', *Mémoires 1833–1854*, ed. D. Ollivier (Paris, 1927).
ANDERSEN, H. C., *A Poet's Bazaar*, trans. C. Beckwith, i (London, 1846).
—— *Dagbøger 1851–1860* (Copenhagen, 1974).
ANDREWS, C. B. (ed.), *Victorian Swansdown: Extracts from the early travel diaries of John Orlando Parry* (London, 1935).
The Annual Register: A Review of Public Events at Home and Abroad, for the Year 1875 (London, 1876).
APPONYI, Comte R., *Vingt-Cinq Ans à Paris (1826–1850)* (3 vols., Paris, 1913–14).
APPONYI, Count A., *Memoirs* (London, 1935).
L'Artiste (Paris, 1839).
ASHBROOK, W., *Donizetti* (London, 1965).
AUER, L., *My Long Life in Music* (London, 1924).
AUGUSZ, A., *Diary*. In: Hadnagy, A., and Prahács, M., 'Liszt szekszárdi kapcsolatairol', *Tanulmanyok Tolna megyetörténetéből 11* (Szekszárd, 1969).
AUTEXIER, P. A., *Mozart & Liszt sub Rosa* (Poitiers, 1984).
BACHE, C., *Brother Musicians: Reminiscences of Edward and Walter Bache* (London, 1901).
Baker's Biographical Dictionary of Musicians, 7th edn., rev. N. Slonimsky (Oxford, 1984).
BALZAC, H. DE, *Béatrix*, trans. R. and S. Harcourt-Smith (London, 1957).
—— *Correspondance*, iii (Paris, 1964).
BARBEY-BOISSIER, C., *La Comtesse Agénor de Gasparin et sa famille: Correspondance et Souvenirs 1813–1894*, i (Paris, 1902).
BARBIERA, R., *Il Salotto della Contessa Maffei* (Milan, 1903).
BARTOS, F., *Smetana in Briefen und Erinnerungen* (Prague, 1954).
BARZUN, J., *Berlioz and the Romantic Century* (2 vols., New York and London, 1969).
BAUDELAIRE, C., *Petits Poëmes en Prose—Les Paradis Artificiels* (Paris, 1869).
B. E., 'Reminiscences of Liszt', *Temple Bar*, lxxviii (London, 1886).
BEALE, W., *The Light of Other Days* (2 vols., London, 1890).
BEATTY-KINGSTON, W., *Men, Cities and Events* (London, 1895).
—— *Music and Manners*, i (London, 1887).
BECCHETTI, P., *Fotografi e fotografia in Italia 1839–1880* (Rome, 1978).
BEDBROOK, G. S., 'Liszt in Lisbon', *The Liszt Society Journal*, vi (London, 1981).
—— 'Liszt in London' (unpublished manuscript).
BÉKEfi, E., *Liszt Ferenc: Származása és Családja* (Budapest, 1973).
BELLAIGUE, C., 'Un Evêque Musicien', *Revue des Deux Mondes*, 15 Sept. 1922.
BELLAS, J., 'Un Virtuoso en tournée . . . Franz Liszt dans le Sud-Ouest en 1844', *Littératures VIII* (*Annales* of the Faculté des lettres of Toulouse, 1960).
—— 'Du Fantastique au Merveilleux: Liszt, Fils d'Hoffmann, chez M. de Pontmartin', *Missions et Démarches de la Critique: Mélanges offerts au Professeur J. A. Vier* (Université de Haute-Bretagne, 1973).
BERLIOZ, H., *Mémoires*, ii (Paris, 1887).
—— *Memoirs*, trans. D. Cairns (London, 1970).

BERNHARDI, T. VON, *Aus dem Leben*, ii (Leipzig, 1893): 'Briefe und Tagebuchblätter aus den Jahren 1834–1857'.
BLAKE, Mrs W. (ed.), *Memoirs of a Vanished Generation 1813–1855* (London, 1909).
BLUME, F. (ed.), *Die Musik in Geschichte und Gegenwart* (14 vols., Kassel and Basel, 1949–68).
BORY, R., 'Diverses Lettres inédites de Liszt', *Schweizerisches Jahrbuch für Musikwissenschaft*, iii (Aarau, 1928).
—— *La Vie de Franz Liszt par l'Image* (Geneva, 1936).
—— *Liszt et ses enfants* (Paris, 1936).
—— 'Quatre Lettres inédites de F. Liszt à Pierre Erard', *Mitteilungsblatt der schweiz. musikforschenden Gesellschaft* (Zurich, Jan. 1934).
—— *Une Retraite romantique en Suisse* (Lausanne, 1930).
BOTTING, D., *Humboldt and the Cosmos* (London, 1973).
BOWEN, C. D., *'Free Artist'—The Story of Anton and Nicholas Rubinstein* (New York, 1939).
BROMBERT, B. A., *Cristina: Portraits of a Princess* (London, 1978).
BUCHNER, A., *Franz Liszt in Bohemia*, trans. R. F. Samsour (London, 1962).
BUFFEN, F. F., *Franz Liszt: A Memoir* (London and New York, 1886).
BÜLOW, H. VON, *Briefe* (7 vols., Leipzig, 1899–1908).
—— *The Early Correspondence*. Edited by His Widow; selected and trans. C. Bache (London, 1896).
BURCKHARDT, J., *Letters*, ed. A. Dru (London, 1955).
BURGER, E., *Franz Liszt: Eine Lebenschronik in Bildern und Dokumenten* (Munich, 1986).
BUSONI, F., *Letters to His Wife*, trans. R. Ley (London, 1938).
CARRIERES, M., *Franz Liszt en Provence et en Languedoc en 1844* (Béziers, 1981).
Chambers Biographical Dictionary (2 vols., Edinburgh, 1975).
CHANLER, Mrs W., *Roman Spring* (Boston, 1934).
CHANTAVOINE, J. (ed.), *Franz Liszt: Pages romantiques* (Paris, 1912).
CHIESA, M. T., 'Franz Liszt in Italia (con pagine e lettere inedite di F. Liszt e di G. Sgambati)', *Nuova Antologia*, lxxi (Rome, July 1936).
CHORLEY, H. F., *Modern German Music* (London, 1854).
CLARK, F. H., *Liszts Offenbarung: Schlüssel zur Freiheit des Individuums* (Berlin, 1907).
CLARY, Prince E., *A European Past*, trans. E. Osers (London, 1978).
COLLI, G., and MONTINARI, M. (eds.), *Briefe an Friedrich Nietzsche* (Berlin, 1977).
CONNELY, W., *Count D'Orsay—the Dandy of Dandies* (London, 1952).
COOKE, J. F., *Great Pianists on Piano Playing* (Philadelphia, 1913).
CORDER, F., *Ferencz Liszt* (London, 1925).
CORNELIUS, P., *Ausgewählte Briefe* (2 vols., Leipzig, 1905).
CROSS, J. W. (ed.), *George Eliot's Life as Related in Her Letters and Journals*, i (Edinburgh and London, 1885).
CSAPÓ, W. VON (ed.), *Franz Liszt's Briefe an Baron Anton Augusz 1846–1878* (Budapest, 1911).
CURTISS, M., *Bizet and His World* (London, 1959).
CZECH, S., *Schön ist die Welt: Franz Lehár's Leben und Werk* (Berlin, 1957).
CZERNY, C., *Erinnerungen aus meinem Leben* (Strasbourg, 1968).
DAMROSCH, W., *My Musical Life* (London, 1924).

DASH, Comtesse, *Mémoires des autres* (4 vols., Paris, 1898).
DENIS, F., *Journal: 1829–1848* (Fribourg and Paris, 1932).
DENT, E. J., *Ferruccio Busoni* (London, 1933).
DEUTSCH, O. E., *Schubert: Memoirs by His Friends* (London, 1958).
DEVRIENT, E., *Aus seinen Tagebüchern: Berlin-Dresden 1836–1852*, ed. R. Kabel (Weimar, 1964).
DONATH, A., 'Franz Liszt und Polen', *Liszt Studien*, i. *Kongress-Bericht, Eisenstadt 1975* (Graz, 1977).
DUNKL, J. N., *Aus den Erinnerungen eines Musikers* (Vienna, 1876).
DUNNINGTON, G. W., *Carl Friedrich Gauss: Titan of Science* (New York, 1955).
ECKHARDT, M., 'Diary of a Wayfarer: The Wanderings of Franz Liszt and Marie d'Agoult in Switzerland, June–July 1835', *Journal of the American Liszt Society*, xi (June 1982).
—— 'Liszt à Marseille', *Studia Musicologica Academiae Scientiarum Hungaricae*, xxiv (1982).
—— 'Liszt in His Formative Years: Unpublished Letters 1824–1827', *The New Hungarian Quarterly*, ciii (Autumn 1986).
ECKHARDT, M. P., and KNOTIK, C., *Franz Liszt und sein Kreis in Briefen und Dokumenten aus den Beständen des Burgenländischen Landesmuseums* (Eisenstadt, 1983).
ECKSTEIN, F., *'Alte unnennbare Tage!'* (Vienna, 1936).
EHRLICH, H., *Dreissig Jahre Künstlerleben* (Berlin, 1893).
ELIOT, G., *Letters*, ed. G. S. Haight (12 vols., New Haven, 1954).
ELKIN, R., *The Old Concert Rooms of London* (London, 1955).
ENGEL, C., 'Truth Shall Prevail', *The Liszt Society Journal*, x (London, 1985). Reprinted from *The Musical Quarterly* (New York), July 1936.
EŐSZE, L., *119 Római Liszt-Dokumentum* (Budapest, 1980).
ERBACH-SCHÖNBERG, Princess MARIE ZU, *Reminiscences* (London, 1925).
EZEKIEL, M. J., *Memoirs from the Baths of Diocletian* (Detroit, 1975).
FAY, A., *Music Study in Germany* (London, 1886).
FETIS, F. J., *Biographie universelle des Musiciens* (8 vols., Paris, 1860–5).
FITZLYON, A., *The Price of Genius: A Life of Pauline Viardot* (London, 1964).
FONTANEY, A., *Journal intime* (Paris, 1925).
FOSTER, M. B., *History of the Philharmonic Society of London: 1813–1912* (London, 1912).
FRANZ, R., *Souvenirs d'une cosaque* (Paris, 1874).
Fraser's Magazine (July 1855).
FRIEDHEIM, A., *Life and Liszt: The Recollections of a Concert Pianist* (New York, 1961).
GARDINER, W., *Music and Friends* (London, 1838).
GAUTIER, J., *Le Troisième Rang du collier* (Paris, 1909).
GENAST, E., *Aus Weimars klassischer und nachklassischer Zeit: Erinnerungen eines alten Schauspielers* (Stuttgart, 1905).
GLASENAPP, C. F., *Das Leben Richard Wagners*, vi (Leipzig, 1911).
GLOSSY, C. (ed.), 'Aus Bauernfelds Tagebüchern', i (1819–1848), *Jahrbuch der Grillparzer-Gesellschaft* (Vienna, 1895).
GÖHLER, R. (ed.), *Grossherzog Carl Alexander und Fanny Lewald-Stahr in ihren Briefen 1848–1889*, i (Berlin, 1932).
GÖLLERICH, A., *Franz Liszt* (Berlin, 1908).

GOTTSCHALG, A. W., *Franz Liszt in Weimar und seine letzten Lebensjahre* (Berlin, 1910).
GRAF, M., *Composer and Critic: Two Hundred Years of Musical Criticism* (New York, 1946).
GRAVES, C. L., *The Life and Letters of Sir George Grove, C. B.* (London, 1903).
GRAVINA, M. (ed.), 'Une Correspondance inédite de Liszt', *La Revue hebdomadaire*, Mar. 1927.
GREGOROVIUS, F., *Roman Journals 1852–1874* (London, 1911).
Grove's Dictionary of Music and Musicians, ii (London, 1906).
GUBERNATIS, A. DE, *Fibra: Pagine di Ricordi* (Rome, 1900).
GUENTHER, K., *Gerhard Rohlfs: Lebensbild eines Afrikaforschers* (Freiburg im Breisgau, 1912).
GUTMAN, R. W., *Richard Wagner: The Man, His Mind and His Music* (London, 1968).
GUTMANN, A., *Aus dem Wiener Musikleben: Künstler-Erinnerungen 1873–1908*, i (Vienna, 1914).
HABETS, A., *Borodin and Liszt* (London, 1895).
HAIGHT, G. S., *George Eliot: A Biography* (Oxford, 1968).
HALEVY, D., *The Life of Friedrich Nietzsche* (London, 1911).
HALLÉ, C. E. and M. (eds.), *Life and Letters of Sir Charles Hallé* (London, 1896).
HAMBURGER, K., *Franz Liszt* (Budapest, 1973).
—— 'Madame Liszt', *Studia Musicologica*, xxvii (Budapest, 1985).
HANSKA, E., 'Journal', *L'Année Balzacienne* (Paris, 1962).
HANSLICK, E., *Aus meinem Leben*, ii (Berlin, 1894).
—— *Concerte, Componisten und Virtuosen der letzten fünfzehn Jahre: 1870–1885* (Berlin, 1886).
HARDING, J., *Massenet* (London, 1970).
—— *Saint-Saëns and His Circle* (London, 1965).
HARASZTI, E., *Franz Liszt* (Paris, 1967).
—— 'Liszt à Paris', *La Revue Musicale*, Apr. and July 1936.
HATTINGBERG, M.VON, *Rilke and Benvenuta*, trans. C. Brooks (London, 1949).
HAUK, M., *Memories of a Singer* (London, 1925).
HAWEIS, Revd H. R., *My Musical Life* (London, 1884).
HEALY, G. P. A., *Reminiscences of a Portrait Painter* (Chicago, 1894).
HEBBEL, F., *Werke*, v (Munich, 1967).
HEDLEY, A., *Chopin* (London, 1953).
HEGERMANN-LINDENCRONE, L. de, *In the Courts of Memory* (New York and London, 1912).
—— *The Sunny Side of Diplomatic Life* (New York and London, 1914).
HEINE, M. E., *Ricordi della vita intima di Enrico Heine* (Florence, 1880).
HELBIG, N., 'Franz Liszt in Rom', *Deutsche Revue* (1907), vol. i.
HERWEGH, M., *Au Banquet des Dieux: Franz Liszt, Richard Wagner et leurs amis* (Paris, 1931).
—— *Au Printemps des Dieux* (Paris, 1929).
HERZEN, A., *My Past and Thoughts*, trans. C. Garnett, i (London, 1924).
HILL, R., *Liszt* (London, 1936).
HILLER, F., *Felix Mendelssohn-Bartholdy: Briefe und Erinnerungen* (Cologne, 1874).
—— *Künstlerleben* (Cologne, 1880).

HOFFMAN, A., and MISSIR, N., *Sur la tournée de concerts de Ferenc Liszt en 1846–47 dans le Banat, la Transylvanie et les Pays Roumains*. Report of the second Liszt-Bartók musicological conference, Budapest, 1961.

HOFFMANN VON FALLERSLEBEN, A. H., *Mein Leben: Aufzeichnungen und Erinnerungen* (Hanover, 1868).

HOLLINS, A., *A Blind Musician Looks Back* (Edinburgh and London, 1936).

HOROVITZ-BARNAY, I., 'Im Hause Franz Liszts: Erlebnisse und Gespräche mit dem Meister', *Deutsche Revue*, July/Sept. 1898 (Stuttgart, 1898).

HORVATH, E. K., *Franz Liszt: Kindheit 1811–1827* (Eisenstadt, 1978).

HUEFFER, F., *Half a Century of Music in England, 1837–1887* (London, 1889).

HUGO, H. E. (ed.), *The Letters of Franz Liszt to Marie zu Sayn-Wittgenstein* (New York, 1953).

HUNEKER, J. G., *Franz Liszt* (New York, 1911).

HUSCHKE, W., *Musik im klassischen und nachklassischen Weimar* (Weimar, 1982).

HUTH, A. H., *The Life and Writings of Henry Thomas Buckle* (London, 1880).

INDY, V. D', *César Franck*, trans. R. Newmarch (London, 1910).

—— 'Franz Liszt en 1873', S. I. M. *Revue musicale mensuelle* (Sept. 1911).

International Liszt Centre for 19th Century Music Ltd., *Liszt Saecula*, ed. L. Rabes.

JACOBS, E., 'Franz Liszt und die Gräfin d'Agoult in Nonnenwerth 1841–1842', *Die Musik* (Oct. 1911).

JAËLL, M., *La Musique et la psychophysiologie* (Paris, 1896).

JANIN, J., *Correspondance* (Paris, 1877).

—— *735 Lettres à sa femme*, ii (Paris, 1973).

JOACHIM, J., *Letters*, trans. N. Bickley (London, 1914).

JOHNS, K. T., 'A Concert in Jena', *The Liszt Society Journal*, xiii (London, 1988).

JONES, B., 'Liszt and Eugene Onegin: Some Reflections on a Transcription', *Liszt Society Journal Centenary Issue* (London, 1986).

Journal of the American Liszt Society (Louisville, Kentucky, 1977–87).

JUNG, H. R., *Franz Liszt in seinen Briefen* (Berlin, 1987).

KAPP, J., *Franz Liszt* (Berlin, 1911).

KARENINE, W., *George Sand: Sa Vie et Ses Œuvres* (4 vols., Paris, 1899–1926).

KEELING, G., 'Liszt and Lina Schmalhausen', *Journal of the American Liszt Society*, v (June 1979).

—— 'Liszt and the Legion of Honour', *The Liszt Society Journal*, x (London, 1985).

—— 'Liszt Pianos—Année de Pèlerinage', loc. cit.

—— 'Liszt's Appearances in Parisian Concerts, 1824–1844', Part 1: '1824–1833', *Liszt Society Journal Centenary Issue* (London, 1986); Part 2: '1834–1844', *The Liszt Society Journal*, xii (London, 1987).

—— 'The Liszt Pianos—Some Aspects of Preference and Technology', *The New Hungarian Quarterly*, civ (Winter 1986).

KELLERMANN, B., *Erinnerungen: Ein Künstlerleben* (Zurich, 1932).

KEMBLE, F. A., *Records of Later Life*, ii (London, 1882).

KIENER, H., *Marie Jaëll* (Paris, 1952).

KIENZL, W., *Meine Lebenswanderung* (Stuttgart, 1926).

KLEIN, H., *Thirty Years of Musical Life in London 1870–1900* (London, 1903).

KLOSE, F., *Meine Lehrjahre bei Bruckner: Erinnerungen und Betrachtungen* (Regensburg, 1927).

KLOSS, E. (ed.), *Briefwechsel zwischen Wagner und Liszt* (3rd rev. edn., Leipzig, 1910).
KOCH, L., *Liszt Ferenc. Bibliográfiai Kísérlet : Franz Liszt, ein bibliographischer Versuch* (Budapest, 1936).
KOPF, J. VON, *Lebenserinnerungen eines Bildhauers* (Stuttgart and Leipzig, 1899).
KROLL, E., 'Franz Liszt: Ehrendoktor der Albertina', *Musikstadt Königsberg: Geschichte und Erinnerung* (Freiburg im Breisgau and Zurich, 1966).
KUHE, W., *My Musical Recollections* (London, 1896).
LACHMUND, C. V., *Mein Leben mit Franz Liszt* (Eschwege, 1970).
LA MARA, *An der Schwelle des Jenseits: Letzte Erinnerungen an die Fürstin Carolyne Sayn-Wittgenstein, die Freundin Liszts* (Leipzig, 1925).
—— (ed.), *Aus der Glanzzeit der Weimarer Altenburg* (Leipzig, 1906).
—— (ed.),'Aus Franz Liszts erster Jugend: Ein Brief seines Vaters mit Briefen Czernys an Ihn', *Die Musik*, V. Jahr 1905/6, xiii (Berlin, 1905/6).
—— (ed.), *Briefe hervorragender Zeitgenossen an Franz Liszt*, iii (Leipzig, 1904).
—— (ed.), *Briefwechsel zwischen Franz Liszt und Carl Alexander, Grossherzog von Sachsen* (Leipzig, 1909).
—— (ed.), *Briefwechsel zwischen Franz Liszt und Hans von Bülow* (Leipzig, 1898).
—— *Durch Musik und Leben im Dienste des Ideals* (2 vols., Leipzig, 1917).
—— (ed.), 'Franz Liszt auf seinem ersten Weltflug: Briefe seines Vaters, Adam Liszt, an Carl Czerny', *Classisches und Romantisches aus der Tonwelt* (Leipzig, 1892).
—— (ed.), *Franz Liszt's Briefe* (8 vols., Leipzig, 1893–1905).
—— (ed.), *Franz Liszt's Briefe an seine Mutter* (Leipzig, 1918).
—— *Liszt und die Frauen* (Leipzig, 1911).
LAMENNAIS, F. DE, *Correspondance Générale*, ed. L. Le Guillou (7 vols., Paris, 1971–8).
LAMOND, F., *Memoirs* (Glasgow, 1949).
LARGE, B., *Smetana* (London, 1970).
LAUGHTON, J. K., *Memoirs of the Life and Correspondence of Henry Reeve, C. B., D. C. L.*, i (London, 1898).
LAWRENCE, A., *Sir Arthur Sullivan* (New York, 1907).
LAYTON, R., *Franz Berwald* (London, 1959).
LECONFIELD, M., Lady (ed.), *Three Howard Sisters* (London, 1955).
LEGÁNY, D., *Ferenc Liszt and His Country 1869–1873*, trans. G. Gulyás (Budapest, 1983).
—— (ed.), *Franz Liszt: Unbekannte Presse und Briefe aus Wien 1822–1886* (Budapest, 1984).
—— 'Liszt and the Budapest Musical Scene: Influences and Contacts 1869–1886', *The New Hungarian Quarterly*, ciii (Autumn 1986).
—— *Liszt Ferenc Magyarországon 1874–1886* (Budapest, 1986).
—— *Liszt in Rom—nach der Presse* (Budapest, 1977).
—— 'Liszt's and Erkel's Relations and Students', *Studia Musicologica* (Budapest, 1976).
—— 'Liszt's Homes in Budapest', *The New Hungarian Quarterly*, xciii (Spring 1984).
LEGOUVE, E., *Soixante Ans de Souvenirs*, i (Paris, 1886).
LEHMANN, J., *Ancestors and Friends* (London, 1962).
LEHMANN, R., *Erinnerungen eines Künstlers* (Berlin, 1896).

LENZ, W. VON, *Die grossen Pianoforte-Virtuosen unserer Zeit* (Berlin, 1872).
LEON-BERARD, M., 'Une Elève de Liszt', *Revue des Deux Mondes*, 15 Apr. 1960.
LEWALD, F., *Zwölf Bilder nach dem Leben* (Berlin, 1888).
LEYDA, J., and BERTENSSON, S., *The Musorgsky Reader: A Life of Modeste Petrovich Musorgsky in Letters and Documents* (New York, 1947).
LISZT, E. RITTER VON, *Franz Liszt: Abstammung, Familie, Begebenheiten* (Vienna and Leipzig, 1937).
LISZT, F., *Des Bohémiens et de leur musique en Hongrie* (Leipzig, 1881).
—— *Frederick Chopin*, trans. J. Broadhouse (London, 1879).
—— *Gesammelte Schriften*, ed. L. Ramann (6 vols., Leipzig, 1880–3).
—— *Tagebuch 1827*, ed. D. Altenburg and R. Kleinertz (2 vols., Vienna, 1986).
Liszt Society Journal, The (London, 1976–87).
LITZMANN, B., *Clara Schumann: Ein Künstlerleben* (3 vols., Leipzig, 1902–8).
—— (ed.), *Clara Schumann–Johannes Brahms. Briefe aus den Jahren 1853–1896*, ii (Leipzig, 1927).
LOCKSPEISER, E., *Debussy: His Life and Mind* (2 vols., Cambridge, 1962–5).
MACKENZIE, Sir A. C., *A Musician's Narrative* (London, 1927).
MALVEZZI, A., *La Principessa Cristina di Belgiojoso* (3 vols., Milan, 1936–7).
MARCHESI, M., *Aus meinem Leben* (Düsseldorf, 1889).
MARECHAL, H., *Rome: Souvenirs d'un musicien* (Paris, 1904).
MARIX-SPIRE, T., *Les Romantiques et La Musique: Le Cas George Sand 1804–1838* (Paris, 1954).
MARLOW, J., *Mr and Mrs Gladstone* (London, 1977).
MASON, W., *Memories of a Musical Life* (New York, 1901).
MAUROIS, A., *Lélia ou La Vie de George Sand* (Paris, 1952).
—— *Prométhée ou La Vie de Balzac* (Paris, 1965).
MAY, G., *Franz Liszt und Luxemburg* (Luxembourg, 1986).
MEINARDUS, L., *Ein Jugendleben*, ii (Gotha, 1874).
MENDELSSOHN, F., *Letters*, ed. G. Selden-Goth (London, 1946).
METTERNICH, Princess P., *The Days That Are No More* (London, 1921).
MEYSENBUG, M. VON, *Der Lebensabend einer Idealistin* (Berlin and Leipzig, 1898).
—— *Im Anfang war die Liebe: Briefe an ihre Pflegetochter* (Munich, 1926).
—— *Rebel in a Crinoline*, ed. M. Adams (London, 1937).
—— *Stimmungsbilder* (Berlin and Leipzig, 1905).
MILDE, F. VON, *Ein ideales Künstlerpaar*, i (Leipzig, 1918).
MONRAD-JOHANSEN, D., *Edvard Grieg* (New York, 1938).
MONTANDON, M., 'Liszt en Roumanie', S. I. M. *Revue musicale mensuelle* (Nov. 1911).
MONTBEL, Comte de, *Souvenirs* (Paris, 1913).
MOSCHELES, C., *Aus Moscheles' Leben, nach Briefen und Tagebüchern*, ii (Leipzig, 1873).
MOSER, A., *Joseph Joachim* (London, 1901).
MOUCHANOFF-KALERGIS, M. VON, *Briefe an ihre Tochter* (Leipzig, 1911).
MÜNZ, S., *Prince Bülow: The Statesman and the Man*, trans. A. Chambers (London, 1935).
Musical Quarterly, The, i (New York, 1915), 'Pauline Viardot-Garcia to Julius Rietz: Letters of Friendship'.
NECTOUX, J., *Gabriel Fauré: His Life Through His Letters*, trans. J. A. Underwood (London and New York, 1984).

NEUMANN, P. VON, *Diary: 1819–1850*, ii (London, 1928).
New Grove Dictionary of Music and Musicians, The (20 vols., London, 1980).
NEWMAN, E., *The Life of Richard Wagner* (4 vols., London, 1933–47).
—— *The Man Liszt* (London, 1934).
NIECKS, F., *Frederick Chopin as a Man and Musician*, ii (London, 1890).
NIGGLI, A., 'Franz Liszt in der Schweiz', *Schweizerische Musikzeitung und Sängerblatt*, 1911.
NOHL, L., *Beethoven, Liszt, Wagner* (Vienna, 1874).
NORRIS, G., *A Musical Gazetteer of Great Britain & Ireland* (Newton Abbot, 1981).
OAKELEY, E. M., *The Life of Sir Herbert Oakeley* (London, 1904).
OCHS, S., *Geschehenes, Gesehenes* (Leipzig, 1922).
OLLIVIER, D. (ed.), *Autour de Mme d'Agoult et de Liszt (Alfred de Vigny, Emile Ollivier, Princesse de Belgiojoso): Lettres publiées avec introduction et notes* (Paris, 1941).
—— (ed.), *Correspondance de Liszt et de la Comtesse d'Agoult* (2 vols., Paris, 1933–4).
—— (ed.), *Correspondance de Liszt et de sa fille Madame Emile Ollivier 1842–1862* (Paris, 1936).
OLLIVIER, E., *Journal 1846–1869*, ii (Paris, 1961).
ORTIGUE, J. D.', 'Franz Liszt: Etude biographique', *Gazette musicale,* 14 June 1835.
PAGET, W., Lady, *Scenes and Memories* (London, 1912).
Pall Mall Gazette (London, 7 Apr. 1886).
PARDOE, J., *The City of the Magyar*, iii (London, 1840).
PAVIE, A., *Médaillons romantiques* (Paris, 1909).
PAYNE, J., *Autobiography* (Olney, 1926).
—— *Vigil and Vision: New Sonnets* (London, 1903).
PENNING, J., 'Liszt in Luxembourg', *Liszt Society Journal*, ix (1984).
PFOHL, F. (ed.), *Arthur Nikisch* (Berlin, 1922).
PICTET, A., *Une Course à Chamounix: Conte Fantastique* (Geneva, 1930).
PIGGOTT, P., *The Life and Music of John Field 1782–1837* (London, 1973).
PINCHERLE, M. (ed.), *Musiciens peints par eux-mêmes: Lettres de compositeurs écrites en français, 1771–1910* (Paris, 1939).
POHL, R., *Franz Liszt : Studien und Erinnerungen* (Leipzig, 1883).
—— 'Liszts Besuch in Triebschen', *Richard Wagner-Jahrbuch* (Stuttgart, 1886).
POTOCKA, Countess A., *Theodor Leschetizky* (London, 1903).
PRAHÁCS, M. (ed.), *Franz Liszt: Briefe aus ungarischen Sammlungen, 1835–1886* (Budapest, 1966).
PRETZSCH, P. (ed.), *Cosima Wagner und Houston Stewart Chamberlain im Briefwechsel, 1888–1908* (Leipzig, 1934).
PROD'HOMME, J. G., *Paganini* (Paris, 1908).
RAABE, P., *Franz Liszt: Leben und Schaffen* (2 vols., 2nd rev. edn., Tutzing, 1968).
RAFF, H., *Blätter vom Lebensbaum* (Munich, 1938).
—— 'Franz Liszt und Joachim Raff im Spiegel ihrer Briefe', *Die Musik*, i (Berlin and Leipzig, 1901–2).
RAGG, L. M., *The Lamartine Ladies* (London, 1954).
RAMANN, L., *Franz Liszt als Künstler und Mensch* (3 vols., Leipzig, 1880–94).
—— *Lisztiana: Erinnerungen an Franz Liszt in Tagebuchblättern, Briefen und Dokumenten aus den Jahren 1873–1886/87* (Mainz, 1983).
RAPPOLDI-KAHRER, L., *Memoiren* (Dresden, 1929).

RAUPP, W., *Eugen d'Albert: Ein Künstler- und Menschenschicksal* (Leipzig, 1930).
REBOIS, H. (ed.), *Les Grands Prix de Rome de Musique* (Paris, 1932).
REHBERG, P., *Franz Liszt: Die Geschichte seines Lebens, Schaffens und Wirkens* (Zurich, 1961).
REICH, W. (ed.), *Gespräche mit Komponisten* (Zurich, 1965).
REINECKE, C., *'Und manche liebe Schatten steigen auf': Gedenkblätter an berühmte Musiker* (Leipzig, 1910).
REIS, P. B., *Liszt na sua passagem por Lisboa em 1845* (Lisbon, 1945).
RELLSTAB, L., *Franz Liszt: Beurtheilungen, Berichte, Lebensskizze* (Berlin, 1842).
RHODES, S. A., *Gérard de Nerval 1808–1855* (New York, 1951).
RIESEMANN, O. VON, 'Alexander Serov and his Relations to Wagner and Liszt', *The Musical Quarterly*, ix (New York, 1923).
ROGERS, C. K., *Memories of a Musical Career* (Plimpton Press, 1932).
ROLLETT, H., *Begegnungen: Erinnerungsblätter (1819–1899)* (Vienna, 1903).
ROQUETTE, O., *Siebzig Jahre: Geschichte meines Lebens* (Darmstadt, 1894).
ROSENTHAL, M., 'Franz Liszt: Erinnerungen und Betrachtungen', *Die Musik*, xli (Berlin and Leipzig, 1911–12).
RUBINSTEIN, A., *Autobiography*, trans. A. Delano (Boston, 1890).
—— *A Conversation on Music* (New York, 1892).
SAINTE-BEUVE, *Correspondance Générale*, ed. J. Bonnerot, iii (Paris, 1938).
SALA, G. A., *Things I Have Seen and People I Have Known* (2 vols., London, 1894).
SALAMAN, C., 'Pianists of the Past', *Blackwood's Edinburgh Magazine*, clxx (Sept. 1901).
SALLES, A., *Liszt à Lyon* (Paris, 1911).
SAND, G., *Journal intime* (Paris, 1926).
—— *Lettres d'un voyageur* (Paris, 1869).
SARTORIS, A., *A Week in a French Country-House* (London, 1902).
SAUER, E., *Meine Welt* (Stuttgart, 1901).
SAUNDERS, E., *The Prodigal Father* (London, 1951).
SCHLÖZER, K. VON, *Briefe eines Diplomaten*, ed. H. Flügel (Stuttgart, 1957).
—— *Römische Briefe 1864–1869* (Berlin, 1924).
SCHONBERG, H. C., *The Great Pianists* (London, 1964).
SCHONDORFF, J. (ed.), *Europäische Zeitenwende* (Munich, 1960).
SCHORN, A. VON, *Das nachklassische Weimar*, ii (Weimar, 1912).
—— *Zwei Menschenalter: Erinnerungen und Briefe* (Berlin, 1901).
SCHORN, K., *Lebenserinnerungen: Ein Beitrag zur Geschichte des Rheinlands im neunzehnten Jahrhundert*, i (Bonn, 1898).
SCHRADER, B., *Franz Liszt* (Berlin, 1917).
SCHULTZ, G. VON, *Briefe eines baltischen Idealisten* (Leipzig, 1934).
SCHUMANN, E., *Robert Schumann: Ein Lebensbild meines Vaters* (Leipzig, 1931).
SCHUMANN, R., *Music and Musicians: Essays and Criticisms* (London, 1877).
SCHWEITZER, A., *My Life and Thought* (London, 1954).
SEARLE, H., *The Music of Liszt* (New York, 1966).
—— and Winklhofer, S., 'Liszt', *The New Grove: Early Romantic Masters 1* (London, 1985).
SELLARDS, J., *Dans le sillage du romantisme: Charles Didier (1805–1864)* (Paris, 1933).
SEMON, F., *Autobiography* (London, 1926).
SHARP, E. A. (ed.), *Heine in Art and Letters* (London, 1895).

SHERARD, R. H., *Twenty Years in Paris* (London, 1905).
SIETZ, R., 'Das 35. Niederrheinische Musikfest 1857 unter dem Dirigenten Franz Liszt', *Zeitschrift des Aachener Geschichtvereins*, lxix (Aachen, 1957).
SILOTI, A., *My Memories of Liszt* (Edinburgh, 1913).
SIMONI, D., *Un soggiorno di Francesco Liszt a San Rossore* (Pisa, 1936).
SITWELL, S., *Liszt* (New York, 1967).
SMITH, M., *The Life of Ole Bull* (New York, 1943).
SMITH, R., *Alkan, Volume One: The Enigma* (London, 1976).
SORET, F., *Un Genevois à la Cour de Weimar* (Paris, 1932).
STAHR, A., and LEWALD, F., *Ein Winter in Rom* (Berlin, 1871).
STANFORD, Sir C. V., *Pages From An Unwritten Diary* (London, 1914).
STASOV, V. V., *Liszt, Schumann and Berlioz in Russia* (St Petersburg, 1896).
—— *Selected Essays on Music*, trans. F. Jonas (London, 1968).
STERN, A. (ed.), *Franz Liszts Briefe an Carl Gille* (Leipzig, 1903).
STERN, D., *Mes Souvenirs 1806–1833* (Paris, 1877).
—— *Nélida* (Brussels, 1846).
STEVENSON, R., 'Liszt at Barcelona', *Journal of the American Liszt Society*, xii (Dec. 1982).
—— 'Liszt at Madrid and Lisbon: 1844–45', *The Musical Quarterly*, lxv (Oct. 1979).
——'Liszt on the East Coast of Spain', *Journal of the American Liszt Society*, iv (Dec. 1978).
STOKER, B., *Personal Reminiscences of Henry Irving*, ii (London, 1906).
STRADAL, A., *Erinnerungen an Franz Liszt* (Berne, 1929).
Studia Musicologica, xxviii (Budapest, 1986).
SUTTONI, C., 'Franz Liszt's Published Correspondence: An Annotated Bibliography', *Fontes Artis Musicae*, xxvi, 3 (Kassel, 1979).
SYDOW, B. E., *Correspondance de Frédéric Chopin* (3 vols., Paris, 1953–60).
SYLVAIN, Abbé C., *Life of the Reverend Father Hermann*, trans. Mrs F. Raymond-Barker (London, 1882).
SZABOLCSI, B., *The Twilight of Ferenc Liszt* (Budapest, 1959).
THOMAS, R. F., *Memoirs of Theodore Thomas* (New York, 1911).
THURN UND TAXIS, Princess M. VON, *Memoirs of a Princess* (London, 1959).
TOYNBEE, W. (ed.), *The Diaries of William Charles Macready 1833–1851*, ii (London, 1912).
TROLLOPE, T. A., *What I Remember*, iii (London, 1889).
VALLAS, L., *Vincent d'Indy* (2 vols., Paris, 1946–50).
VARNHAGEN VON ENSE, K. A., *Tagebücher* (14 vols., Leipzig, 1861–70).
VIARDOT-GARCIA, P., 'Letters of Friendship [to Julius Rietz]', *The Musical Quarterly*, i (New York, 1915).
VIER, J., *Franz Liszt—L'Artiste, le clerc: Documents inédits* (Paris, 1950).
—— *La Comtesse d'Agoult et son temps* (6 vols., Paris, 1955–63).
VINANT, G., *Malwida de Meysenbug: Sa Vie et Ses Amis* (Paris, 1932).
VOSS, R., *Aus einem phantastischen Leben* (Stuttgart, 1920).
WAGNER, C., *Diaries*, trans. G. Skelton (2 vols., London, 1978–80).
—— *Franz Liszt: Ein Gedenkblatt von seiner Tochter* (2nd edn., Munich, 1911).
WAGNER, R., *Letters to Emil Heckel* (London, 1899).
—— *My Life* (2 vols., London, 1911).

WAGNER, S., *Erinnerungen* (Stuttgart, 1923).
WALDBERG, M. FREIHERR VON (ed.), *Cosima Wagners Briefe an Ihre Tochter Daniela von Bülow 1866–1885* (Stuttgart and Berlin, 1933).
WALKER, A., 'A Boy Named Daniel', *The New Hungarian Quarterly*, ci (Spring 1986).
—— (ed.), *Franz Liszt: The Man and His Music* (London, 1970).
—— *Franz Liszt: The Virtuoso Years: 1811–1847* (New York, 1983).
WALKER, B., *My Musical Experiences* (London, 1890).
WALKER, F., *Hugo Wolf* (London, 1951).
WALLACE, W., *Liszt, Wagner and the Princess* (London, 1927).
WATERS, E. N., 'Liszt and Longfellow', *The Musical Quarterly*, xli, 1 (Jan. 1955).
—— 'Presenting Mrs Liszt', *Journal of the American Liszt Society*, vii (June 1980).
—— (ed.), *The Letters of Franz Liszt to Olga von Meyendorff 1871–1886*, trans, W. R. Tyler (Dumbarton Oaks, 1979).
—— *Victor Herbert: A Life in Music* (New York, 1955).
WATSON, D., *Liszt* (London, 1989).
WEINGARTNER, F., *Lebenserinnerungen* (Vienna, 1923).
WEISSHEIMER, W., *Erlebnisse mit Richard Wagner, Franz Liszt und vielen anderen Zeitgenossen* (Stuttgart, 1898).
WENIG, J., *Sie waren in Prag* (Prague, 1971).
WERNER, J., *Maxe von Arnim: Ein Lebens- und Zeitbild* (Leipzig, 1937).
WESTERBY, H., *Liszt, Composer, and His Piano Works* (London, 1936).
WIECK, F., *Briefe aus den Jahren 1830–1838* (Cologne, 1968).
WILLIAMSON, G. C., *Memoirs in Miniature* (London, 1933).
WINKLER, G. J., 'Franz Liszts Kindheit: Versuch eines biographischen Grundrisses', *Die Musikforschung* (1986), vol. iv.
WINKLHOFER, S., 'Editorial Censorship in Liszt's Letters to Agnes Street-Klindworth', *Journal of the American Liszt Society*, ix (June 1981).
—— 'Liszt, Marie d'Agoult and the "Dante" Sonata', *19th Century Music* (July 1977).
—— *Liszt's Sonata in B minor: A Study of Autograph Sources and Documents* (University of Michigan, Ann Arbor, 1980).
WOHL, J., *François Liszt: Souvenirs d'une compatriote* (Paris, 1887).
WOLKOFF-MOUROMTZOFF, A., *Memoirs* (London, 1928).
ZEZSCHWITZ-STUMPF, H. VON, 'Berthold Kellermann: Pupil of Liszt', *The Liszt Society Journal*, xii (London, 1987).
ZICHY, Graf G., *Aus meinem Leben* (3 vols., Stuttgart, 1911–20).
—— *'Franz Liszt: Erinnerungen', Deutsche Revue*, Apr./June 1904 (Stuttgart, 1904).
ZILOTI, V. P., *In Tretyakov's House* (New York, 1954).

INDEX OF LISZT'S WORKS

PROSE WRITINGS

GENERAL INDEX

Page numbers in italic type refer to main-text quotations